Future value of an (ordinary) annuity:

$$FV_n = PMT\left[\frac{(1+k)^n - 1}{k}\right] = PMT\sum_{t=0}^{n-1}(1+k)^t$$

Net present value, NPV:

$$NPV = \sum_{t=1}^{n}\frac{CF_t}{(1+k)^t} - CF_0$$

where CF = cash flow after tax
CF_0 = initial cash outlay
t = time period

Internal rate of return, IRR:

$$\sum_{t=1}^{n}\frac{CF_t}{(1+IRR)^t} = CF_0$$

Present value with more-frequent-than-annual discounting:

$$PV_0 = \frac{FV_n}{[1+(k/m)]^{nm}}$$

where m = number of compounding periods per year

Effective annual interest rate:

$$k_{\text{effective}} = \left(1 + \frac{k_{\text{nominal}}}{m}\right)^m - 1$$

where $k_{\text{effective annual}}$ = actual annual interest rate based on compounding frequency
k_{nominal} = stated, or nominal, interest rate

VALUATION (4)

Value of a bond:

$$B_0 = \sum_{t=1}^{n}\frac{I_t}{(1+k_b)^t} + \frac{M}{(1+k_b)^n}$$

where I = interest on a bond (in dollars or rate)
M = maturity (par) value of a bond
k_b = percentage of return on a bond

Value of common stock:

$$P_0 = \sum_{t=1}^{n}\frac{D_t}{(1+k_s)^t} + \frac{P_n}{(1+k_s)^n}$$

where k_s = percentage of return on a stock

Value of nongrowing stock:

$$P_0 = D/k_s$$

Value of constant-growth common stock:

$$P_0 = D_1/(k_s - g)$$

RISK AND RETURN (5)

Expected return (or mean), $\bar{k}$:

$$\bar{k} = \sum_{i=1}^{n}k_iP_i$$

where $\bar{k}_i$ = probability of incident or state occurring
P_i = return per incident or state

(*continued on back endpapers*)

Essentials of Financial Management

Essentials of Financial Management

Fifth Edition

George E. Pinches
University of Kansas

HarperCollins*CollegePublishers*

To Carole, Susan, Katherine, and Bill

Acquisitions Editor: Joan Cannon
Developmental Editor: Ann Torbert
Project Editorial Manager: Melonie Salvati
Senior Designer: John Callahan
Text Design: Interactive Composition Corporation
Cover design: John Callahan
Cover Photo: © 1995 PhotoDisc, Inc.
Art Studio: Vantage Art, Inc.
Electronic Production Manager: Su Levine
Senior Manufacturing Manager: Willie Lane
Electronic Page Makeup: Interactive Composition Corporation
Printer and Binder: R. R. Donnelley & Sons Company
Cover Printer: New England Book Components

Photo credits: Unless otherwise acknowledged, all photographs are the property of Scott, Foresman and Company.

16: Ralph Mercer/Tony Stone Images. **64:** Santi Visalli/The Image Bank. **122:** Dean Abramson/Stock Boston. **170:** Jean Kugler/FPG. **188:** Mark Wagner/Tony Stone Images. **300:** Peter Russell Clemens/International Stock Photo. **321:** Donovan Reese/Tony Stone Images. **393:** Johnny Stockshooter/International Stock Photo. **409:** Mugshots/The Stock Market. **457:** Tom Carroll/FPG. **474:** Dennis O'Clair/Tony Stone Images. **533:** John Henley/The Stock Market.

Essentials of Financial Management, Fifth Edition

Library of Congress Cataloging-in-Publication Data

Pinches, George E.
    Essentials of financial management / George E. Pinches. — 5th ed.
      p. cm.
    Includes index.
    ISBN 0–673–99029–X
    1. Business enterprises—Finance.   2. Corporations—Finance.
  I. Title.
  HG4026.P57   1995
  658.15—dc20   95–20267
                                     CIP

95 96 97 98 9 8 7 6 5 4 3 2 1

Brief Contents

Detailed Contents

Preface

The world of business in the 1990s presents financial managers with tremendous challenges, as they attempt to deal with the major changes in the field of financial management begun in the 1980s. Numerous mergers, acquisitions—(friendly and hostile) bankruptcies, and recapitalizations have occurred, as firms have devised strategies for maximizing shareholder value and providing managerial independence for public firms that are being privatized. The market for options and other synthetic securities (derivatives) has matured and provided financial managers with new tools for managing risk. Global financial markets have become a fact of life, and computers have fundamentally changed how financial managers do their jobs. Access to technology through the Internet is changing the way that firms and individuals function. Given these changes, I felt that a fresh, new approach was needed to provide students a basis for understanding the financial management of corporations.

The instructor teaching a class in financial management accepts a daunting task. He or she faces a class of students intending to major in accounting, management, marketing, MIS, or finance. For many, this course may be their only exposure to finance. Accounting majors will appreciate exposure to the depreciation and taxation issues financial managers face; management students may want to delve into the ethical issues involved in insider trading; marketing majors may want to understand the basics of capital budgeting decisions that will affect new-product introductions; MIS majors will want to understand how financial concepts and decisions affect a firm's management information system. Finance majors will undoubtedly want to receive a sound grounding in the foundations of time value, risk and return, market theories, valuation, and the role of financial intermediation in finance. Given these divergent interests, I have tried to present a modern view of the key ideas and make them come to life through the use of contemporary examples. To this end, I have refocused and shortened the fifth edition of *Essentials of Financial Management*, streamlined and updated it, and built it around seven key ideas that affect financial decision making.

Distinguishing Features

Students who use this book should realize that there is more to know about finance than what appears between these covers. It is my hope that finance majors extract an understanding of the core ideas of finance that they can apply in future courses and throughout their careers, and that non-majors will leave with an understanding of the key ideas of finance and an appreciation of the role of finance in business. With this in mind, the fifth edition of *Essentials of Financial Management* contains a number of distinguishing features.

Fundamental Concepts

The text links financial decisions to seven key ideas:

1. *The goal of the firm is to maximize its value.* By market value, we mean the price that someone is willing to pay for the firm. For publicly traded firms this translates to the total market value of the firm's stock plus the total market value of its debt.
2. *Financial markets are efficient.* In efficient markets the current prices reflect all publicly available information. Students can understand financial management

and the implications of their decisions only if they understand the financial environment and markets, and how they operate.

3. *Individuals act in their own self-interest.* This concept focuses on what is referred to as "agency theory." As a follow-up to how financial market efficiency works, agency theory is examined extensively so that students can appreciate the human issues involved in finance.

4. *Firms focus on cash flows and their incremental effects.* By emphasizing the incremental inflow and outflow of cash we focus on the financial lifeblood of the firm. This would not be the case if we incorrectly focused our attention on the firm's accounting earnings.

5. *A dollar today is worth more than a dollar tomorrow.* The timing of the cash flows is important; in finance we employ time value of money concepts and net present value to deal with cash flows that occur at different points in time. This organizing principle underlies all of financial management, and it is stressed throughout the book so that students accept it as a paradigm, rather than an equation to be memorized and applied.

6. *Risk and return go hand-in-hand.* By focusing on risk and return we emphasize that in all financial decisions risk and return go hand-in-hand. In order for any firm or individual to increase its return, more risk must be incurred.

7. *Options are valuable.* An option provides the right, but not the necessity, of acting. Because options appear in many financial activities, the ideas behind them are introduced. Although the details are left to other courses, a basic understanding of options is important in financial management.

The emphasis on these key ideas has three major advantages. First, it provides a logical and consistent structure that ties together all of the firm's decisions. Second, it provides students a framework to which they can relate; put simply, it enables students to see the forest and not get lost in the trees. Finally, this approach is theoretically correct; therefore, without any special effort we develop an appreciation for the subject that can be applied to further study in finance.

A Balanced, Modular Approach

The book contains balanced coverage of all of the primary facets of financial management, including four chapters on short-term financial management, where coverage is sometimes skimpy. A modular approach allows greater flexibility in terms of sequencing of chapters.

This textbook has been designed to provide instructors with flexibility in course design, allowing them to include or exclude certain material. To facilitate flexibility an end-of-book Appendix D, "If the Last Is First," is provided for instructors who cover short-term financial management (Chapters 15–18) before covering Chapter 3, "Time Value of Money."

Additionally, a systematic effort has been made to shorten the fifth edition of *Essentials of Financial Management*, and to substantially reduce the number of appendices that contained higher-level topics. In that line, the number of appendices has been cut to four, down from thirteen in the previous edition.

Examples

Step-by-step examples illustrate the calculation so that students can understand the tools used in the decision-making process. Students should not be left guessing how the calculation was made.

International Topics

Because of its growing importance, international financial management is fully integrated into the appropriate chapters. In the past many texts left international finance to the last chapter, where it rarely got covered. By integrating it into selected chapters, we help students understand some of the international aspects of finance without taking attention away from topics at hand.

Up-to-Date Coverage

The text has been completely updated, to include the latest changes in the tax code, requirements in interest calculations, financial ethics, completely integrated coverage of agency issues, the presence of options in many of the financial activities that firms undertake, and coverage of derivatives and their impact on financial management.

Flexibility in the Classroom

Essentials of Financial Management, Fifth Edition, is designed to have a strong unifying theme, to be completely up-to-date, and to provide flexibility in sequencing course topics. Many instructors will cover the first five chapters in order, and then move to long-term investment decisions in Chapters 6 through 9. Some instructors have suggested two basic alternatives to this course sequence:

1. Instructors who want more coverage of stocks and bonds before or immediately after Chapter 4, "Valuation of Bonds and Stocks," will want to include Chapters 10 and/or 11 either before or after Chapter 4.
2. Chapter 6, "The Opportunity Cost of Capital," can be held until later, by moving directly from the first five chapters to Chapters 7 and 8. Chapter 6 can then be covered either immediately after Chapter 9, "Risk, Capital Budgeting, and Value Creation," or as part of the section on long-term financing decisions (Chapters 10 through 14).

Another course design favored by many instructors is to cover accounting statements, financial planning, and/or short-term financial management early in the course. In such a case, the fifth edition of *Essentials of Financial Management* provides a strong and consistent framework. There are a number of possible approaches when covering accounting statements, financial planning, and/or short-term financial management early in the course, including the following:

1. Cover Chapter 19, "Analyzing Accounting Statements," immediately after Chapter 2, "The Financial System, Interest Rates, and Foreign Exchange." Chapter 20, "Financial Planning and Forecasting," can then follow Chapter 19, if desired.
2. Short-term financial management, Chapters 15 through 18, can then be covered directly after Chapters 19 and/or 20, if desired. For instructors who want to cover Chapters 15–18 before Chapter 3, a unique, new end-of-book Appendix D, "If the Last Is First," provides the time value material needed for students to master Chapters 17–18 before covering Chapter 3.
3. A third alternative, one I have used increasingly in recent years, is to omit any lecture or testing on Chapter 19, "Analyzing Accounting Statements," but to require students to complete a major project that incorporates common-size statements, financial ratios, an analysis of the footnotes (or discussion) accompanying the firm's annual report, an analysis of the statement of cash flows, a major

expansion in financing for the firm, and pro forma accounting statements. This project is described in more detail in the *Instructor's Manual*. I have found that skipping Chapter 19, and including Chapter 20 between Chapters 15 and 16, provides a very solid and integrated treatment of accounting issues, short-term financial management, and financial planning and forecasting.

Many other chapter sequences have been successfully employed by instructors using previous editions of *Essentials of Financial Management*. The ability to sequence material in the desired manner has been further strengthened in the fifth edition.

Changes in the Fifth Edition

In many respects the fifth edition of *Essentials of Financial Management* is almost a completely new text. Major changes incorporated in this new edition are (1) the continual focus on seven key ideas that underlie finance; (2) the systematic approach taken to substantially shorten, update, and enliven the text based on the rapidly changing developments both in finance and the world in which we live; and (3) the substantial increase in pedagogical features.

The major changes in the fifth edition include:

1. *A shorter book*—now 20, rather than 23, chapters.
2. *Continuous coverage of international topics* as a main part of selected chapters where appropriate, so students gain an international perspective as they proceed through the course.
3. *Real-world executive interviews*, used as part openers and in-chapter interviews, which demonstrate how executives employ the ideas and concepts of finance in their daily corporate lives.
4. *Currency*—all material has been updated, and many chapters have been substantially rewritten, as detailed below. Special emphasis is given to financial ethics, agency issues, options and their occurrence in the day-to-day activities of firms, and derivatives.
5. Several *completely new features*, described in more detail later in the preface: learning objectives; marginal notes, which highlight the seven key ideas in financial management presented in Chapter 1 or provide additional explanatory material; concept review questions at the end of each section of text; and concept review problems at the end of each chapter, with solutions at the end of the book.

As was true in the first four editions of *Essentials of Financial Management*, there continues to be an emphasis on the role that cash inflows and outflows play in financial management. With the increased emphasis on seven key ideas in finance, this emphasis is reinforced throughout the text.

Chapter-by-Chapter Changes

The specific major chapter-by-chapter changes made in the fifth edition are as follows:

Chapter 1 expands from four to seven the key ideas in finance, which are then employed throughout the text; introduces net present value, in simple form; and includes a section on ethics and finance.

Chapter 2 includes a modified and streamlined discussion on interest rates, and uses data directly from *The Wall Street Journal* to construct a term structure of interest rates. Chapter 2 also discusses the returns from common stock demanded by investors, which parallels the discussion on the returns from bonds demanded by investors, and actual rates of inflation and yields on risk-free U.S. Treasury bills. This chapter contains an in-depth discussion of foreign exchange rates, since their impact must be understood before really dealing with international financial management issues.

Chapter 3 presents an extensively modified, rearranged, and streamlined discussion of present and future values. It introduces growing annuities and calculates their present value, and discusses how to make financial calculations. In the discussion of determining interest rates, the chapter explains that finding an interest rate is a specific application of the internal rate of return, and discusses internal rates of return. Finally, Chapter 3 provides an extensive, completely up-to-date discussion on effective interest rates, including why the annual percentage rate, *APR*, required under the Truth-in-Lending Act *is not* an effective annual rate, and why the annual percentage yield, *APY*, required under the Truth-in-Savings act *is* an affective annual interest rate.

Chapter 4 now has a completely new section on price/earnings ratios, the present value of growth opportunities, and how accepting positive net present value projects leads to increases in the value of the firm.

Chapter 5 has been streamlined, simplified, and shortened. It illustrates how information obtained from *Value Line Investment Survey* can be employed in determining information needed to estimate the expected return on the market portfolio. Also, Chapter 5 provides data and discussion on the use of, and pitfalls of using, historical data to estimate the expected return on the market portfolio.

Chapter 6 has been moved forward in the chapter sequence, to be the first in the long-term investment part. It now estimates the opportunity cost of capital for PepsiCo (as of the end of 1994) and shows the use of *Value Line Investment Survey* data in the analysis. Chapter 6 also includes a completely new section on using historical information to estimate the return on the market portfolio and risk premiums. Finally, this chapter covers new material on finding the cost of capital for multinational firms.

Chapters 7 and 8 have been rearranged to provide a clearer, more coherent presentation. For simplicity all of the calculations involving depreciation both in these chapters and throughout the text employ straight-line depreciation and ignore the half-year convention required by the Internal Revenue Service. A completely new section in Chapter 8, "Those Hard-to-Estimate Costs and Benefits," discusses how to proceed with difficult estimations, and also incorporates some ethical issues by reference to specific examples. Appendix 8A discusses the modified accelerated recovery, MACRS, system of depreciation.

Chapter 9 substantially changed and streamlined, contains new sections on factors to consider when estimating risk, what leads to positive *NPVs*, and the results of relying on market values. The revamped section on break-even analysis begins with a complete discussion of the accounting approach to break-even analysis. This thorough coverage of capital investment decision making ends with some guidelines for structuring and evaluating capital investment, including ten items required for effective capital investment decision-making systems.

Chapter 10 includes a new discussion and table on the sources of financing—external versus internal—for firms and an expanded discussion on the role played by investment banking firms in helping firms raise capital. Further, Chapter 10 addresses the topic of financial ethics in investment banking. This chapter also includes a new section on venture capital.

Chapter 11 discusses term loans and amortization schedules. It has an expanded coverage of junk (high-yield) bonds, and a new section on hybrids, asset-backed securities, and other innovations.

Chapter 12 has been substantially rewritten. It continues to focus on the Modigliani-Miller capital structure propositions, but in less detail. Chapter 12 contains an additional discussion of the many and varied approaches to capital structure theory that have led to the current thinking about the impact of capital structure on the value of the firm.

Chapter 13 rewritten and streamlined, contains a new section on the Modigliani-Miller dividend irrelevance argument, plus a section on why firms pay cash dividends.

Chapter 14 includes an abbreviated treatment on leasing, and discusses the underlying ideas about options and what influences their value. This chapter also discusses why stock is "just a call option," and covers new material on warrants and convertible securities.

Chapter 15 provides more discussion on the managerial implications of the cash conversion cycle. The chapter differentiates between aggressive (action oriented) and conservative (passive) asset or liability management policies and discusses financial slack, its tie to a firm's capital structure, and the role of liquidity. A new section on the changing nature of risk management highlights the tremendous changes occurring in how firms deal with short-term financial management issues and how they hedge some of their risk exposure.

Chapter 16 includes a new section on paper-based (e.g., check-driven) versus electronic payment systems. The chapter discusses the Expedited Funds Availability Act of 1987 and its rules on fund availability, as well as electronic funds transfer (EFT), electronic data interchange (EDI), and how firms are changing their ordering and payment systems.

Chapter 17 explains the use of an aging schedule for monitoring the collection of accounts receivable. The chapter now provides more material on collecting international receivables.

Chapter 18 provides extensive discussion of the role that nominal interest rates play in determining effective annual interest rates.

Chapter 19 provides a step-by-step analysis of the accounting statements of General Mills, and financial implications of the analysis. It also discusses the quality of earnings. Chapter 19 includes a short section on derivatives and the problems created by their lack of disclosure in the accounting process. This chapter also contains material on the financial effects of differing accounting standards in other countries.

Chapter 20 contains a new discussion of the statement of cash flows, using General Mills as an example. Discussion of forecasting sales has been streamlined in Chapter 20 as well.

Pedagogical Features

The fifth edition of *Essentials of Financial Management* has been designed with the student in mind. To that end, there are substantially more pedagogical features than in previous editions. The primary pedagogical features are:

1. Complete *step-by-step discussions and illustrations* of how to proceed in making decisions and conducting financial analysis. Instead of backing off and downplaying any discussion of the details, a hallmark of *Essentials of Financial Management* has always been that it provides complete step-by-step examples. This emphasis has been heightened in the fifth edition, and includes many more examples of where to obtain the necessary information, how to proceed with the analysis, and what the conclusions are from the analysis. This format focuses

student learning on how to use the concepts and techniques of financial management in real-world situations.

2. The use of *timelines* to represent cash inflows and outflows remains in the fifth edition of *Essentials of Financial Management*, to help students visualize the firm's cash flows.

3. Highly interesting and informative *Executive Interviews* have been added at the beginning of each of the six parts of the text, and in selected chapters. In these interviews, highly qualified executives have been encouraged to provide their thoughts, in their own words, to link the material in the text to its application in the business world.

4. *Learning objectives* have been added at the start of each chapter, and then repeated where the material is covered in the chapter, to help students organize their study progress and to provide an organizational *roadmap* for instructors.

5. A *marginal glossary*, with simplified definitions, provides a quick review of important vocabulary.

6. *Marginal notes* refer back to the seven key ideas in finance presented in Chapter 1. The continuous reinforcement of underlying themes provides students with a means of focusing on the concepts that are crucial throughout finance. Other marginal notes clarify or elaborate on various important points in the text, to provide additional reinforcement and learning.

7. *Concept review questions* at the end of each section in a chapter encourage students to focus on the key points to be obtained from each section before they move on to the next.

8. Boxed *Financial Management Today* items, in selected chapters, make real-world connections for students. These boxes provide additional illustrations of how finance operates at selected firms, or emphasize how to employ the concepts discussed in the text.

9. A discussion of *financial calculators* in Chapter 3, followed by detailed, "how-to" instructions in a booklet accompanying the textbook, shows how financial calculators can be used to solve the calculations needed to master financial management.

10. All *financial calculations* are shown in step-by-step fashion throughout the text. That is, there are no leaps of faith that cause students and instructors difficulty in determining how the author got from the data to the answer. Where financial calculation requires present or future value concepts, the answers are provided using a financial calculator solution and, in a footnote, the same calculation and answers are provided using a financial table. The same dual presentation using financial calculators and financial tables is carried throughout the Concept Review Problems and their solutions (provided in Appendix A), the Answers to Selected Problems (provided in Appendix C), and all problems in the *Instructor's Manual*. Therefore, students and instructors can have complete confidence that the appropriate answers are provided, whether a financial calculator or a financial table is employed.

11. A *bulleted summary* at the end of each chapter provides a focused synopsis of the key points to be learned in the chapter.

12. Completely new *Concept Review Problems* are included at the end of each chapter. These problems, with solutions provided in Appendix A, give students a valuable opportunity to apply chapter material before they undertake assigned problem material.

13. End of chapter *Problems* have been reworked and many new cues added, to make assignments more user-friendly. All problems and solutions are now

based on calculator answers, with financial table answers also provided where appropriate.

14. *A Mini Case* at the end of each chapter pulls together important strands of chapter coverage for comprehensive review.

15. *Selected references* are provided to topics covered in *Financial Management,* my upper level textbook, that are outside the desired introductory-level coverage of the fifth edition of *Essentials of Financial Management.*

16. The book's *endpapers* provide an annotated listing of all relevant equations employed in the text.

A Complete Teaching Support Package

Essentials of Financial Management, Fifth Edition, offers a complete support package designed to enhance the teaching of the text and maximize student understanding and mastery of financial management. The entire teaching support package has been extensively reviewed for accuracy. The following supplementary items are available:

Instructor's Manual. I have personally prepared the *Instructor's Manual* to accompany the book. It contains the answers to all of the chapter questions and complete step-by-step solutions to all of the problems in the text.

Test Bank. A separate *Test Bank*, prepared by Kathryn M. Kelm of Emporia State University and me, contains multiple-choice items as well as longer problem-type test items. The multiple-choice items are available in a computerized format as well as in a printed form.

Lecture Outlines and Transparencies (LOTS). An extensive set of lecture notes and transparencies, prepared by Kathryn M. Kelm, is available to adopters. Some of the transparencies are available in acetate form, and all of the transparencies are available as masters or on diskette for use with a projector pad and an IBM-compatible PC.

Study Guide. An extensive *Study Guide*, authored by Michael B. Madaris, University of Southern Mississippi, is available to provide students with explanations and extensions of the material in the text. The *Study Guide* contains an outline for each chapter, summaries of key equations, and over 200 problems with detailed worked-out solutions that illustrate the key concepts presented in each chapter.

Using Financial and Business Calculators

Shrinkwrapped free with every new copy of the text is a 36 page booklet on "Using Financial and Business Calculators." It includes extensive coverage of how students can most effectively use any of three popular financial calculators: HP10B, HP12C, and the TIBAII+. For all of the calculations in the book and in the *Instructor's Manual,* solutions using both financial tables and a financial calculator are provided. In addition, for the different types of homework problems that can be solved by a financial calculator, step-by-step calculations are shown for all three calculators.

ACKNOWLEDGMENTS

A book like *Essentials of Financial Management* cannot be created in isolation. Teachers, colleagues, manuscript reviewers, and former students have all affected how I approach the field of finance and how I teach the subject. All are owed a debt of gratitude. Individuals who have commented on the first four editions of *Essentials of Financial Management* and *Financial Management* have helped in clarifying my thoughts and presentation. These individuals are: J. Amanda Adkisson, Raj Aggarwal, Nasser Arhadi, Ashish Arora, Bruce D. Bagamery, Sheldon Balbirer, Earl S. Beecher, Tom Berry, Carol J. Billingham, Robert J. Boldin, Helen M. Bowers, Mary Helen Blakeslee, Harry Blythe, John Boquist, Kevin Bracker, Dallas Brozik, Mary Ellen Butcher, Ka-Kung C. Chan, George M. Coggins, Phil Cooley, Larry W. Courtney, Thomas J. Coyne, Maryanne P. Cunningham, Charles J. Cuny, Wilfred L. Dellva, Benoit Deschamps, Art DeThomas, Peter DeVito, Norman S. Souglas, Gene Drzycimski, David Dubofsky, Ed Dyl, John W. Ellis, Marjorie K. Evert, Dave Ewert, Thomas H. Eyssell, Al Frankle, E. Bruce Fredrickson, Stephen Gardner, Larry Gitman, George L. Granger, Anita Ground, Manak C. Gupta, Pranav Gupta, Lance Hart, R. Stevenson Hawkey, Hal Heaton, Ronald Hennigar, Larry Hexter, Kendall P. Hill, Laura Hoisington, Ghassem Homaifar, Jerry G. Hunt, Christine Hsu, Pearson Hunt, James F. Jackson, Stanley Jacobs, William P. Jennings, Mike Joehnk, Eldon C. Johnson, O. Maurice Joy, Jarl G. Kalberg, Ravindra R. Kamath, David C. Ketcham, Narendra Khilnani, Robert T. Kleiman, Shirley A. Kleiner, Christopher G. Lamoureux, David B. Lawrence, Rick LeCompte, Chan H. Lee, Hyong J. Lee, John Legler, Dean R. Longmore, David A. Louton, Laurian C. Lytle, Gerald A. McIntire, Ginette M. McManus, Judy E. Maese, Leo P. Mahoney, Paul Malatesta, Herman Manakyan, Terry S. Maness, Mary Kay Mans, Stephen G. Marks, Stanley A. Martin, Edward M. Miller, Lalatendu Misra, Eric Moon, Steven P. Mooney, Scott Morre, Fraser Montgomery, Saeed Mortazavi, Tarun Mukherjee, Prafulla G. Nabar, Gary Noreiko, Robert A. Olsen, Larry G. Perry, Robert W. Phillips, Gary E. Powell, K. Ramakrishnan, Verlyn Richards, Lawrnce C. Rose, Gary C. Sanger, Emmanual S. Santiago, Bill Sartoris, Carl Schwendiman, David L. Scott, Jaye Smith, Carl Stern, George S. Swales, Gary Tallman, Martin Thomas, A. Frank Thompson, John Traynor, Gary Trennepohl, Keith Van Horn, Mridu Vashist, James A. Verbrugge, Jerry Viscione, David A. Volkman, Daniel G. Weaver, John B. White, Nancy Wiebe, Stephen E. Wilcox, Jimmy B. Williams, Bob Wood, B. J. Yang, Mike York, Kent Zumwalt, and Edward J. Zychowicz.

The reviewers for the fifth edition of *Essentials of Financial Management* provided substantial guidance and many fine suggestions to enhance the clarity and user-friendliness of the text. They are: V. T. Alaganar, Hofstra University; Nat Baker, University of San Francisco; F. Thomas Bear, Stetson University; Jeffrey A. Born, Northeastern University; Robert A. Clark, University of Vermont; David B. Cox, University of Denver; Anand S. Desai, Kansas State University; Thomas H. Eyssell, University of Missouri—St. Louis; Peggy Fletcher, Northeastern University; Stephen D. Hogan, Eastern Illinois University; Christine Hsu, California State University—Chico; Ravi R. Kamath, Cleveland State University; Robert T. Kleiman, Oakland University; Laurian C. Lytle, University of Wisconsin—Whitewater; Robert B. McElreath, Jr., Clemson University; Michael J. McNamara, University of Memphis; S. K. Mansinghka, San Francisco State University; Timothy A. Manuel, University of Montana; Joseph Messina, San Francisco State University; K. G. Viswanathan, Hofstra University; Shee Q. Wong, University of Minnesota; Steve Wyatt, University of Cincinnati; Donald R. Yarzebinski, Western Michigan University.

In addition, a number of other individuals made important contributions to the book. Alfie Davis, of Queen's University, my co-author for *Canadian Financial Management*, contributed to my thinking on numerous topics. Marlene Bellamy secured the Executive Interviews for each part and the selected in-chapter interviews. Jim Gentry, Mike McNamara, Tim Manuel, and Joe Messina contributed ideas for marginal notes. Mridu Vashist worked long and hard on the calculator booklet that accompanies the book; Gennady Zalko provided the original thoughts for learning objectives; Laurian C. Lytle, University of Wisconsin—Whitewater, provided helpful comments on ethics in finance; and David A. Volkman of the University of Nebraska—Omaha provided the new Concept Review Problems. Ann Torbert, the development editor for the fifth edition of *Essentials of Financial Management* did a truly outstanding job. Without Ann's talents, organizational skills, and constant good humor and enthusiasm, this project would have not been completed. I owe Ann a true vote of thanks. The staff at HarperCollins deserves a special thanks for their efforts on this book. They include Lisa Pinto, Arlene Bessenoff, Mary McGeary, and Ed Yarnell. Melonie Salvati pulled, pushed, and persuaded to get the material through the production process. Thanks, too, to Kate Steinbacher, marketing manager, whose enthusiasm and ideas help support this book both before and long after publication. Special thanks to Kirsten Sandberg and Joan Cannon, finance acquisitions editors, who labored long and hard to make the fifth edition of *Essentials of Financial Management* a reality and a success.

Finally, I must acknowledge the continued love and support of my wife, Carole. Without her understanding, neither previous editions of *Essentials of Financial Management* and *Financial Management*, nor the fifth edition of *Essentials of Financial Management*, could have been completed. Thank you, Carole!

To the extent I have written an up-to-date, clear statement of the fundamental concepts, theoretical developments, and practical aspects of financial management, I owe a large debt of thanks to the help and criticism I have received from others. I encourage all users to provide me with comments, suggestions, and criticism. All are most welcome in my attempt to provide an ever improving means of learning financial management.

George E. Pinches
School of Business
University of Kansas
Lawrence, KS 66045
(913) 864–7533

Essentials of Financial Management

George E. Pinches
University of Kansas

Fifth Edition
ISBN 0-673-99029-X

Reflecting the dramatic changes and challenges of today's business world, the

fifth edition of *Essentials of Financial Management* provides students with a modern view of the fundamental concepts in finance. Pinches builds the text around the seven key ideas that affect financial decision making: (1) the goal of the firm is to maximize its value; (2) financial markets are efficient; (3) individuals act in their own self-interest (agency theory); (4) firms focus on cash flows and their incremental effects; (5) a dollar today is worth more than a dollar tomorrow (time value and net present value); (6) risk and return go hand-in-hand (portfolio theory and capital asset pricing model); and (7) options are valuable. The text stresses applications by providing step-by-step illustrations for both long- and short-term financial management. Including the most recent international developments, tax codes, interest calculations, and ethical concerns, *Essentials* illustrates the role of finance in today's business world. Refocused and redesigned, this fifth edition also offers more real-world examples, interviews with practicing finance professionals, an enriched learning system, and cases to help students understand financial concepts.

PART 1

THE FINANCIAL MANAGEMENT ENVIRONMENT

Chapter 1   Why Financial Management Matters
Chapter 2   The Financial System, Interest Rates, and Foreign Exchange

EXECUTIVE INTERVIEW WITH DONALD M. MUIR

Treasurer
Stratus Computer, Inc.,
Marlborough,
Massachusetts

Stratus®

Donald Muir received a B.B.A in accounting from the University of Massachusetts, Amherst, and a M.B.A. in finance from Boston University. From 1978 to 1987, he held various accounting, financial, and operations management positions at Wallace Murray Corporation and at Prime Computer, Inc. He joined Stratus Computer, Inc. in 1987, where he served as controller of two business units and director of finance and administration before being promoted to treasurer in 1993. We asked Mr. Muir to discuss the financial management environment.

As business students and as business professionals you will be continuously exposed to a wide variety of financial data and information. How well you understand, interpret, test, and use it will greatly influence your ability to make sound business decisions. Every aspect of business requires managers to analyze and report financial results. This is true for activities ranging from developing new-product sales projections to choosing insurance coverage or buying capital equipment. Both operations managers and financial managers must understand how the numbers are derived in order to explain their ideas and justify their proposals.

In the computer industry today financial management plays a key role in helping firms survive difficult economic and technological times. The proliferation of low-cost desktop computers and improved microprocessor technology have increased competition and eroded gross margins for hardware manufacturers.

Stratus Computer's ability to grow is largely the result of its financial strength. The company was formed in 1980 to provide continuously available computer systems that virtually eliminate the risk of computer downtime. Our systems are used by industries for whom continuous availability is critical, such as telecommunications companies, banks, stock exchanges and brokerage

EXECUTIVE INTERVIEW

At the beginning of each part of the book, *Executive Interviews* show students how what they learn in the classroom is applied in the real world by highlighting the key content issues used by a real-world practitioner.

SEVEN KEY IDEAS

Seven key ideas of finance, introduced and discussed in chapter 1 and then integrated throughout the text, reinforce how the firm's decisions are tied together while providing students with a view of the role of finance in today's business world.

FINANCIAL MARKETS
Markets outside the firm in which financial transactions take place.

PROPRIETORSHIP
An unincorporated business owned by one individual.

PARTNERSHIP
A business owned by two or more individuals.

CORPORATION
A legal entity with the power to act as an individual and with limited liability.

LIMITED LIABILITY
By law, a restriction on the amount owners of a corporation can lose in the case of bankruptcy.

COMMON STOCK
An ownership share of a corporation.

BONDS
Long-term debt instruments (IOUs) issued by firms and governments.

vacuum. Performance is affected by a variety of external factors: the health of the economy, taxes, interest rates, international tensions, and the prevailing political and regulatory moods. In fact, the performance of the firm is ultimately judged by the external **financial markets,** where stocks and bonds are traded.

The ideas, tools, and techniques of financial management apply to all kinds of firms as well as to individuals. Our focus in this book will be on corporations, rather than on proprietorships or partnerships. A **proprietorship** is an unincorporated business owned by one individual. A **partnership** is a business owned by two or more individuals. Proprietorships or partnerships often are used in the early stages of a business, but most successful ones are eventually converted into corporations. A **corporation** is a legal entity given the power to act as an individual, and it has limited liability. **Limited liability** is a major advantage of a corporation; it means that if the firm goes bankrupt, the owners can lose no more than the money they have invested in the firm.

Corporations can raise funds by issuing and selling shares of their **common stock.** In return for investing in the firm the common stockholders become the owners of the firm. Corporations can also obtain funds by selling **bonds,** which are long-term debt instruments. Bonds are nothing more than IOUs that firms use to obtain financing. The bondholders have a fixed, but limited, claim on the firm. In addition, firms obtain needed funds, and incur financial obligations, through bank loans and credit extended to the firm.

CONCEPT REVIEW QUESTIONS

■ What are the three main elements in the definition of financial management?

■ Describe the three forms of business organization.

KEY IDEAS IN FINANCIAL MANAGEMENT

■ **LEARNING GOAL 2**

List and discuss the seven key ideas underlying financial management.

In this course, you'll learn to speak the language of finance. In the business world, a command of the finance "lingo" is critical.

Throughout this book you will encounter new terms, ideas, and relationships. Although they are all important in one way or another, certain key ideas underlie the theory and practice of financial management. Since these will come up over and over again, it makes sense to understand them from the start. The seven key ideas that guide our discussions are:

1. The goal of the firm is to maximize its market value.
2. Financial markets are efficient.
3. Individuals act in their own self-interest.
4. Firms focus on cash flows and their incremental effects.
5. A dollar today is worth more than a dollar tomorrow.
6. Risk and return go hand-in-hand.
7. Options are valuable.

Before we begin to use these ideas in making financial decisions, let's briefly explore them one by one.

---

sensitive to changes in domestic demand. In commenting on the Fed's 1994 efforts, one European banker noted: "Even if the one pair of brakes the Fed hasn't seemed to be working that effectively, it's still the only pair of brakes they have. And they'll have to use them."

International Financial Markets

In addition to the domestic financial market, the financial marketplace is now worldwide. Large U.S. firms routinely issue bonds or secure short-term financing overseas. Some even list their stock on foreign stock exchanges. While many of the same forces are at work worldwide, there are two fundamental differences. First, the role of a single government, or governmental unit such as the Federal Reserve, is diminished since funds tend to flow fairly freely between many countries. Second, the value of a foreign currency relative to other currencies—called *exchange rates*—can and do change. As discussed later in this chapter, understanding exchange rates is important for financial managers who deal in almost any financial management transaction. The internationalization of the money and capital markets is a fundamental development affecting financial management.

Why Is the Financial System Important?

You may already see the need to know about financial institutions and markets. Here are some of the reasons:

Remember Key Idea 2—in developed countries, like the United States, financial markets are efficient.

1. The financial system provides an effective means of bringing together suppliers and demanders of funds. It enables firms that have excess funds, or firms that need funds, to make transactions quickly and cheaply.
2. The financial system includes the crucial secondary market. By facilitating the buying and selling of outstanding securities, an organized secondary market makes it easier for a firm to raise external debt or equity capital. This occurs because potential investors would be reluctant to buy securities if they thought they might be stuck with them forever. Only in industrialized countries with well-developed secondary markets are the financial markets efficient. Thus, only in countries where an extensive array of financial institutions and markets does the value of a firm's outstanding securities provide a good estimate of the value, or economic worth, of the firm.
3. The financial system changes rapidly, affording new opportunities. New institutions, securities, and markets appear every year. These allow astute firms to use new sources or securities for raising capital.
4. The value of the firm is determined in the financial markets. That value depends on the interaction of supply and demand in the financial marketplace—given the external business environment and management's strategies and policy decisions. The welfare of the firm and all of its stakeholders—its owners, creditors, employees, managers, and the community at large—rests directly on the value of the firm as determined in the financial markets.

CONCEPT REVIEW QUESTIONS

■ How do financial institutions aid the transfer of funds between suppliers and demanders?

■ How do primary and secondary markets differ?

■ Why are financial markets important to financial managers?

CHAPTER 2

The Financial System, Interest Rates, and Foreign Exchange

Sections in this chapter:

- **The Financial System**
  The major players in finance and where the action takes place.
- **Interest Rates and the Required Rate of Return**
  Two sides of the same coin—the cost to the borrower equals the return to the lender.
- **Returns and Risk**
  The steadiest couple in finance.
- **Foreign Exchange Rates**
  "I'll give you 2 pesos for 1 guilder."

In finance, the 1980s were the decade of junk bonds and high leverage. In the 1990s the emphasis has switched to globalization, the information superhighway, interest in health care reform, and attempts to shrink the role of the federal government. Freer trade, through NAFTA (the North American Free Trade Agreement), GATT (General Agreement on Tariffs and Trade), expansion of the European Community, and other bilateral or regional agreements, is becoming

...globalization, American Exp... joined a number of ... such as McDonald's, Philip Morris, 3M, and Walt Disney—in having its common stock listed on the Tokyo Stock Exchange. "We think," the company explained, "it broadens the market for American Express stock with investors around the world and will enhance our reputation in Japan because there will be a lot of publicity surrounding the listing." Likewise, multinational firms are increasingly raising capital in the United States, in the form of both debt and equity financing.

Learning Goals

After studying this chapter, you should be able to:

1. Explain the role of financial institutions and distinguish between the primary and secondary markets.
2. Determine the required returns for bonds and for stock, and explain how interest rates affect these returns.
3. Know how returns are measured, and understand the relationship between risk and return of financial assets.
4. Understand the relationship between current (as of today) and forward exchange rates of two currencies.

27

CHAPTER 9

Risk, Capital Budgeting, Value Creation

Sections in this chapter:

- **Risk and Strategic Decisions**
  When and why more risk can be beneficial.
- **Opportunity Cost of Capital for Capital Budgeting Decisions**
  Which opportunity cost is important?
- **Information About the Riskiness of Projects**
  We can't ignore risk.
- **What Leads to Positive *NPVs*?**
  What to watch for in the capital budgeting process.
- **Other Capital Investment Decisions**
  We aren't finished yet!

Intel is the world's largest manufacturer of microprocessor chips—the silicon "brains" that make a computer work. The vast majority of personal computers sold contain Intel chips. Intel dominated the market with its 486 processor, and its successor, the Pentium. Yet, others are attempting to seize part of Intel's market share: Advanced Micro Devices (AMD) and Cyrix, both much smaller firms, make Intel-compatible chips. In addition, IBM and Apple Computer have joined up to develop an alternative microprocessor, the PowerPC. While the combination of IBM and Apple Computer seems formidable, the PowerPC is handicapped in a couple of ways. First, it will not run many of the current software packages, and software makers are reluctant to redesign their programs to run on the PowerPC. Second, Microsoft, the developer of the DOS and Windows operating software, says its new Windows version will not be compatible with the PowerPC.

To maintain its lead in supplying microprocessors to the computer industry, Intel must keep spending larger and larger sums to develop the next generation of chips. While the 486 is still here the Pentium chip is the dominate chip in personal computers. And the successor to the Pentium, the P6, is already far along in development at Intel. To keep ahead of the competition, Intel continues with a high level of capital expenditures every year.

Investment decisions can have unforeseen consequences, and it is not easy to conduct a capital budgeting analysis in the face of a continuing stream of future investment opportunities. As an executive of a major firm recently stated, "You simply can't put a dollar sign on a technological future that may have a tremendous payoff." He noted that quantitative analysis is complicated by uncertainty. Which opportunities

247

FINANCIAL MANAGEMENT TODAY BOXES AND IN-CHAPTER EXECUTIVE INTERVIEWS

In selected chapters, *Financial Management Today* boxes provide an additional illustration of how finance operates in some firms, and emphasize how to employ concepts discussed in the text. In other chapters, shorter *Executive Interviews*— similar to those at each part opening—show more real-world applications.

EXECUTIVE INTERVIEW WITH KATHERINE GREENBERG

*Chief Financial Officer
Ace Medical Company, Los Angeles, California*

Katherine Greenberg joined Ace Medical Company as vice president and chief financial officer in 1987. Her prior work experience included 3 years as a CPA at Deloitte & Touche, New York, and 7 years in sales and corporate communications at Norton Company, Worcester, Massachusetts. She received her B.A. from Mount Holyoke College and an M.B.A. from Columbia University School of Business. We asked Ms. Greenberg to discuss the importance of accounts receivable and inventory in the medical equipment industry.

Accounts receivable and inventory comprise 90 percent of total assets for Ace Medical Company, a privately held manufacturer of titanium orthopedic implants for fracture repair. When two assets account for such a large portion of the balance sheet, managing them efficiently is critical to the company's financial health. Also, bankers and other financial analysts evaluate how well the company manages its working capital and cash flow by comparing the firm's results (in terms of asset management ratios) to industry benchmarks.

Ace and its competitors set accounts receivable terms in line with practices in the health care industry. Hospital buying groups, health care conglomerates, and government health institutions contract for products at set terms. Typically we have little room to negotiate. Most hospital revenues come from third-party payers (insurance companies, Medicare, Medicaid), who pay very slowly. Until the hospitals collect their receivables, they can't pay us. Our industry uses several strategies to improve receivables collection: cash discounts for early payment, interest charges on customers' accounts, and different pricing strategies. Cash discounts are not very effective for us and are time-consuming to manage; interest charges seem to work better in our industry.

Our receivables terms for international customers (about 50 percent of sales) must be in line with practices in the countries to which we sell. For example, some European and Latin American countries have receivables terms of up to 180 days. We can't sell to distributors on net 30-day terms if they won't collect from their customers for 180 days or more. Also, we set terms in line with the company's goals. Building export sales requires more flexible receivables terms. It's a tradeoff: Increasing market share calls for aggressive credit and pricing terms, but it also carries greater risk.

Setting receivables policies requires cooperation between marketing and sales and finance. These departments can be at cross purposes—although everyone should have the same end goal, to make money and increase the firm's value. We promote good interdepartmental communication and work together to understand the other's viewpoint—for example, there may be a cost in order to gain market share—and we develop a practical compromise.

Inventory management in the medical equipment industry is rather unique. We hold higher levels of inventory than we would by choice, and it moves slowly. There is little tolerance of stockouts in the industry; if we don't have the product when the doctor needs it, we lose the customer. With the rising cost of health care, hospitals now require manufacturers to carry their inventory and deliver it when needed; they don't pay until they use it. This helps the hospital's cash flow but is a two-edged sword for them: We hold the inventory for them, but they pay a higher price for the privilege. We really don't have an option if we want to compete in this market.

3. *Banks*. Most banks maintain credit departments and may provide credit information about firms for their customers who are considering extending credit to the firms.

4. *Trade Associations*. Many trade associations provide reliable means of obtaining credit information about their business members.

5. *Company's Own Experiences*. Past experience may have led the firm to establish some formal guidelines for gathering credit information and "sizing up" the

---

FINANCIAL MANAGEMENT TODAY

Diversifying Internationally

Portfolios can also be generated when two groups of assets, like two stock indices, are employed. Say one asset is the Standard & Poor's 500 Index of U.S. stocks, and the other is Morgan Stanley's Europe, Australia, and Far East (EAFE) Index. For a recent ten-year period, the means of the yearly returns were 16.7 and 19.1 percent, respectively; the standard deviations were 12.4 and 28.2 percent, respectively. Security returns in different countries do not move exactly together; that is, the returns are less than perfectly positively correlated. The corre-

lation between these two indices (or markets) was +0.50 over the time period. Graphically, the possible combinations for these two sets of securities is shown below.

Both the returns and risks for foreign stocks were higher than for U.S. stocks. Investors who wanted to increase their expected return from that available with U.S. stocks, and to take advantage of the less than perfectly positive correlation between the returns in different countries, needed to diversify internationally. The minimum-risk portfolio for this period would have had about 20 percent of its assets in foreign stocks and the other 80 percent in U.S. stocks. If more than 20 percent had been invested in foreign securities, both the expected return and the total risk would increase.

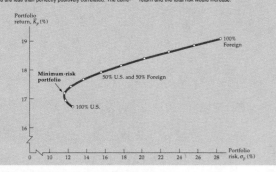

Diversifiable and Nondiversifiable Risk

Results of studies indicate that on average 45% to 55% of a stock's total risk can be diversified away. The figures are larger when you consider diversifying internationally.

We've seen that risk can be reduced by forming portfolios. But just *how much* risk reduction can we achieve? The answer has been provided by a number of studies, as shown in Figure 5.4. The total portfolio risk, measured by its standard deviation, declines as more stocks are added to the portfolio. Adding more stocks to the portfolio can eliminate some of the risk, but it cannot eliminate all of it. The total risk can thus be divided into two parts: diversifiable risk (sometimes called *company-specific* or *unsystematic* risk) and nondiversifiable (sometimes called *systematic* or *market*) risk, so that

$$\text{total risk} = \text{diversifiable risk} + \text{nondiversifiable risk} \qquad (5.5)$$

The fees earned by investment bankers represent the cost to the issuing firm or government for the underwriting and marketing assistance received. New offerings of stock by firms that had not publicly issued stock before (called *initial public offerings, IPOs*) generated for investment banking firms fees of about 7.2 percent of the proceeds raised in 1993. Secondary offerings of common stock, where stock was already outstanding but a firm or individual wanted to sell a large block of stock, generated investment banking fees of about 5.5 percent. Preferred stock offerings resulted in investment banking fees of 2 percent in 1993. Turning to long-term debt financing, investment-grade debt (as discussed in Chapter 11, this is debt in the top four bond ratings) resulted in fees of about 0.05 percent of the total proceeds. More risky bonds provided investment bankers with fees of about 2.4 percent of the issue, and convertible bonds (i.e., bonds that can be converted into common stock) provided investment banking firms with fees about 2.9 percent of the proceeds raised in 1993. The differences in fees are a function of competition, the risk incurred by the investment banking firm, and how difficult it was to market the issue.

Investment Bankers and Financial Ethics

Rarely are investment bankers accused of unethical or illegal activities. The reason is obvious—their continued business and profitability are tied directly to their reputation. Any word of unethical or illegal activity can have serious short- and long-run consequences. However, exceptions do occur.

When auctioning Treasury bonds, the U.S. Treasury awards them first to the highest bidder and then moves to the next highest bidder. If the Treasury receives more than one bid at the price that exhausts the issue, it allocates the remaining bonds in proportion to the size of the bid. In 1990 Paul Mozer, the head of Salomon Brothers government-bond trading desk, submitted bids for more than 100 percent of the 4-year notes to be auctioned. He later followed this up with other similar bids, including a bid

TABLE 10.3

Top Underwriting Investment Banking Firms, 1993 (in millions)

Though many firms, both in the United States and in other countries, provide investment banking services, U.S.-based firms dominate the global market.

Top Underwriters of U.S. Debt and Equity			Top Underwriters of Non-U.S. Debt and Equity		
Firm	Amount	Market Share	Firm	Amount	Market Share
Merrill Lynch	$173,784	16.4%	Goldman Sachs	$23,875	5.9%
Goldman Sachs	127,265	12.0	Deutsche Bank	23,526	5.8
Lehman Brothers	115,996	10.9	Morgan Stanley	21,217	5.2
Kidder Peabody	94,471	8.9	First Boston CS	20,152	5.0
Salomon Brothers	91,177	8.6	Merrill Lynch	19,000	4.7
First Boston	90,374	8.5	Nomura Securities	16,687	4.1
Morgan Stanley	67,717	6.4	Lehman Brothers	14,115	3.5
Bear Stearns	56,237	5.3	Banque Paribas	14,040	3.5
Donaldson Lufkin	36,911	3.5	Salomon Brothers	13,658	3.4
Paine Webber	29,890	2.8	J. P. Morgan	13,064	3.2
	$883,822	83.2%		$179,334	44.3%
1,062,871		100.0%	$404,925		100.0%

anuary 3, 1994), p. 32.

ETHICS

Ethical issues, integrated throughout the text, introduce students to questions and issues about the responsibilities that firms have to the conflicting interests of stakeholders.

International Capital Structure Issues

At the foreign subsidiary level there are a number of important points that go into determining its capital structure. First and foremost, it is important to recognize that unless the parent is willing to let the subsidiary fail and default on its debt, there is *no independent risk for the subsidiary's debt*. Rather, its debt is explicitly or implicitly guaranteed by the multinational parent. Given this, it is really the parent's overall capital structure, not the subsidiary's, that is of primary concern.

Once this point is understood, then the objective is to acquire funds in the most cost effective manner at the subsidiary level. For example, a subsidiary that has low debt financing costs might have a capital structure of almost 100 percent debt. Yet another subsidiary, where the cost of debt was much higher, could have a capital structure with much less debt. The objective of the multinational parent is to raise capital as cheaply as possible on a worldwide basis and make suitable adjustments at the overall firm level to achieve its target worldwide capital structure.

Finally, multinational firms often call (and structure) their investment in a subsidiary as debt, rather than equity. They do so because of exchange controls and tax effects. From the standpoint of repatriating funds to the parent, a firm typically has wider latitude with interest and loan payments than with cash dividends or other reductions in equity. Also, by structuring the investment as debt, taxes are generally reduced.

Although some latitude exists, multinationals do not have complete freedom in choosing debt/equity ratios for foreign subsidiaries. If they have too little equity, they may run into restrictions placed on them by the host countries. But to the extent possible, the goal is to structure the foreign subsidiaries' capital structure to minimize costs subject to the requirement that the multinational parent be viewed as responsible by the host country. Then the multinational manages its capital structure on a global basis to maximize the value of the firm.

CONCEPT REVIEW QUESTIONS

■ Briefly describe some methods used to determine a firm's debt capacity.
■ What are three key variables that affect a firm's capital structure?
■ What factors impact the capital structure decision of a foreign subsidiary of a domestic firm?

Summary

■ In the absence of taxes and other financial market imperfections, the choice of a capital structure is "a mere detail." The value of the firm is a function of the investment decisions it makes, not its financing decisions.
■ There are three places to look when examining the possible impact of capital structure decisions on the value of the firm: taxes, transactions costs, and interrelationships between the firm's financing decisions and its capital investment decisions.
■ Once corporate taxes are introduced, the firm can increase its total value and reduce its opportunity cost of capital by replacing equity financing with debt financing.
■ If the effective personal tax rate on stock income is less than the effective personal tax rate on bond income, there is less advantage to the firm from using debt financing than implied by the MM tax case.
■ Because of taxes, transactions costs, and interactions between financing and investment decisions, firms choose capital structures that have more than zero debt and less than 100 percent debt.

INTERNATIONAL TOPICS

International issues are integrated fully throughout the fifth edition to help focus students' attention on the global nature of finance and increase their understanding of financial issues.

CONCEPT REVIEW QUESTIONS

Concept Review Questions appear at the end of each section to reinforce comprehension of chapter material as it is covered.

Key Idea 1—the goal of the firm is to maximize its market value.

$325,000, or you could invest the $250,000 in your next best alternative, which was a "market basket" to common stocks with an expected return of 12 percent. We concluded that you should make the investment. Now let's revisit that decision and formally discuss two of the primary decision criteria in finance—net present value and internal rate of return.

In financial management we deal with investment decisions by determining the net present value, *NPV*, of the proposed investment. The net present value tells us how much a proposed investment contributes to increasing or decreasing the value of the firm. The procedure is to discount the future cash inflows at a rate that reflects the opportunities bypassed and the risks involved, and then subtract the initial investment. As discussed in Chapter 1, the net present value when there is only one future cash inflow from a proposed investment is:

$$\text{net present value} = \frac{\text{future value of cash inflows}}{1 + \text{discount rate based on forgone opportunities}}$$

$$- \text{initial investment} = \frac{\$325,000}{1.12} - \$250,000 = \$40,179$$

Thus, you should invest in the office complex because it makes a net contribution to value of $40,179 after considering the timing of the expected cash flows and the alternative use of the funds. If the net present value had turned out to be negative, it indicates you would have lost money on the investment. In that case, you would choose not to invest in the office complex. The ~~general rule~~ for determining the ~~value of any proposed i~~

---

question the decision, the individual is making what to him or her is a rational decision, one based on self-interest. Say the individual's alternative is to spend those 4 days working for $150 per day (to keep things simple, let's ignore taxes). By going to the beach instead, the individual has placed a value on going to the beach of more than the $150 per day that could have been earned. Economists call the value associated with choosing one course of action instead of another the **opportunity cost**. It represents the cost of the best forgone alternative. In this example, the opportunity cost is the $150 per day salary bypassed by choosing to go to the beach.

The idea of self-interest comes up in many ways in finance. Considered together, these examples of self-interest are referred to as "agency problems" or "agency relationships." Narrowly defined, an **agency relationship** is a contract in which one party (the *principal*) engages another (the *agent*) to perform a service and delegates some decision-making authority to the agent. In the context of firms, the owners (the principals) engage the managers as their agents to operate the firm on their behalf.

In a slightly broader perspective, the idea of agency relationships emphasizes that managers, stockholders, bondholders, and other interested parties act in their own self-interest and that costly conflicts may arise due to these self-interests. For example, think of a small business where you are both owner and manager of the firm. As the owner-manager, you will maximize your wealth by balancing the combination of wages, perks (such as a company car and luxurious offices), and so on against the market value of the firm's common stock. Because you are both management and stockholder, actions taken in the stockholders' best interests also serve the self-interests of the manager. As long as a firm is owned and operated by a single owner-manager, no complications arise with the objective of maximizing stockholders' wealth.

In larger firms, however, management often owns only a small percentage of the firm's outstanding common stock. In this case, managers may be "satisfiers" rather than maximizers. That is, their goal may be performance that ensures their own career security and advancement, rather than the goal of maximizing the value of the firm. Why? Because only a small percentage of a manager's wealth comes from changes in

OPPORTUNITY COST
The cost of the best forgone alternative.

AGENCY RELATIONSHIP
Contract in which the principal engages an agent to perform a service and delegates some decision-making authority to the agent.

Agency problems occur elsewhere: A lawyer hired by the hour has an incentive to "book" hours. A better deal is to pay the lawyer only if you win the case to help align the self-interests of the principal (you) with those of the agent (the lawyer).

Depreciation will be straight-line over 5 years, the appropriate tax rate is 30 percent, and the discount rate is 15 percent.

1. What is the base-case *NPV*?
2. What is the *NPV* if each of the following occurs?
   (a) Cash inflows in time periods *t* = 1 through *t* = 8 decrease by 20 percent per year.
   (b) Cash outflows in time periods *t* = 1 through *t* = 8 increase by 20 percent per year.
   (c) The tax rate increases by 20 percent.
   (d) The initial investment increases by 20 percent.
   (e) The discount rate increases by 20 percent.
   (f) The life of the project decreases to 6 years.
   To which variable is the *NPV* most sensitive?
d. How is break-even analysis just another form of sensitivity analysis?

Note: In (2) each part is separate and distinct from the other parts.

Note: In (2d) this also changes the per year depreciation.

MARGINAL ANNOTATIONS

Three kinds of marginal annotations appear. Key concepts listed frequently throughout each chapter provide additional insights or refer students to the *seven key ideas in finance* presented in the first chapter, providing continuous reinforcement of the underlying themes and helping students focus on crucial underlying concepts. Helpful hints clarify difficult material. A marginal glossary provides additional reinforcement of key terms.

END-OF-CHAPTER MATERIALS: CONCEPT REVIEW PROBLEMS AND PROBLEMS

End of chapter materials such as summaries, questions, *Concept Review Problems,* problems, and mini cases allow the student to review, apply, and integrate the concepts presented in the chapter.

Questions

9.1 The divisional opportunity cost of capital approach to capital budgeting, employing categories of projects with different risks, might be graphed as follows:

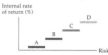

Explain how divisional opportunity costs capture many of the risk and return ideas of the capital asset pricing model. In what significant ways do the two differ?

9.2 Explain the importance of the stand-alone principle. Why are opportunity costs (or the forgone returns from bypassed investments) so important in making wealth-maximizing capital budgeting decisions?

9.3 Adam believes that sensitivity analysis is a viable way to deal with risk. Do you agree with him? Why or why not?

9.4 Why does break-even analysis, when conducted employing GAAP accounting numbers, result in understating the financial break-even point? Can you see any redeeming features of an accounting-based break-even analysis?

9.5 How are positive *NPV*s, the unique attributes of firms and projects, and good data related?

Concept Review Problems

See Appendix A for solutions.

CR9.1 Rodrigo Inc. is considering purchasing a coal mine in Wyoming. Cost of the coal mine is $8 million, and the opportunity cost is capital of 15 percent. Rodrigo's engineers believe (with 50 percent probability) there is enough coal to produce $2 million in after-tax cash flows for the next 5 years. On the other hand, there may be (with 50 percent probability) enough coal to produce $2 million in after-tax cash flows for 10 years. What is the expected net present value of the project?

CR9.2 Suzanne, owner of Belles Fleurs, is considering expanding into the silk floral market. She estimates the expansion will cost $60,000 and that she will sell approximately 600 different silk floral arrangements per year over the next 4 years, at an average price of $100 per arrangement. Her operating costs are estimated to be approximately 50 percent of revenue.

Note: For simplicity in (a), assume no depreciation will be taken on the $60,000 expenditure.

a. If Belles Fleurs' tax rate is 28 percent and the opportunity cost of capital is 10 percent, what is the net present value of this project?

b. Suzanne is concerned about the risk of the silk floral arrangement project. She is concerned that sales may not be 600 floral arrangements per year. Perform a sensitivity analysis on the number of silk floral arrangements sold per year in which the floral arrangements drop by 10 percent, 20 percent, or 30 percent, or increase by 10 percent, 20 percent, or 30 percent.

CR9.3 Using the information for Belles Fleurs given in CR9.2, what is the (accounting) break-even for the number of units of floral arrangements sold per year?

CR9.4 Suzanne is concerned about the effects of a fluctuating economy on the profitability of the silk flower expansion in CR9.3. If a downturn in the economy occurs,

Essentials of Financial Management

THE FINANCIAL MANAGEMENT ENVIRONMENT

EXECUTIVE INTERVIEW WITH DONALD M. MUIR

Treasurer
Stratus Computer, Inc.,
Marlborough,
Massachusetts

Stratus®

Donald Muir received a B.B.A in accounting from the University of Massachusetts, Amherst, and a M.B.A. in finance from Boston University. From 1978 to 1987, he held various accounting, financial, and operations management positions at Wallace Murray Corporation and at Prime Computer, Inc. He joined Stratus Computer, Inc. in 1987, where he served as controller of two business units and director of finance and administration before being promoted to treasurer in 1993. We asked Mr. Muir to discuss the financial management environment.

As business students and as business professionals you will be continuously exposed to a wide variety of financial data and information. How well you understand, interpret, test, and use it will greatly influence your ability to make sound business decisions. Every aspect of business requires managers to analyze and report financial results. This is true for activities ranging from developing new-product sales projections to choosing insurance coverage or buying capital equipment. Both operations managers and financial managers must understand how the numbers are derived in order to explain their ideas and justify their proposals.

In the computer industry today financial management plays a key role in helping firms survive difficult economic and technological times. The proliferation of low-cost desktop computers and improved microprocessor technology have increased competition and eroded gross margins for hardware manufacturers.

Stratus Computer's ability to grow is largely the result of its financial strength. The company was formed in 1980 to provide continuously available computer systems that virtually eliminate the risk of computer downtime. Our systems are used by industries for whom continuous availability is critical, such as telecommunications companies, banks, stock exchanges and brokerage firms, retailers, and health care providers and insurers. Our current business strategy is to expand our core business beyond hardware; to achieve that goal we offer products that extend continuous availability to application software and networks. This requires financial resources for research and development, market expansion, and acquisitions of companies with complementary products.

Because Stratus followed conservative financial management practices—retaining earnings and building up cash—it has the financial resources to make these broad strategic changes. This gives Stratus a tremendous competitive advantage, allowing us to seek new products, solutions, and business partners through mergers and acquisitions at a time when many other companies cannot.

Financial managers at Stratus focus on both profitability and maximizing the firm's value. Profitability alone should not be a firm's ultimate objective. It is important from a competitive and long-term viability standpoint, but the primary goal of the financial manager should be to maximize the firm's value for the long term. That means we must allocate financial resources to those areas and projects that offer the greatest potential for future growth and return. Doing so often involves making trade-offs. For example, Stratus has to allocate appropriate amounts to research and development, but not at the expense of other areas such as service or sales.

Understanding the economic, regulatory, tax, and political environment in which the firm operates is also essential to making financial decisions that increase value. The finance staff closely monitors federal, state, local, and international developments so we can respond quickly to new situations. Our focus on regulated industries like telecommunications, financial services, casinos, and health care makes this monitoring critical for Stratus.

As a multinational corporation with subsidiaries in 17 countries and customers in over 50 countries, Stratus is affected by international economic and political issues. These include changes in foreign currencies and interest rates, and laws affecting foreign investments and cross-border fund transfers. Our managers must be familiar with business, legal, political, demographic, labor market, and financial issues in countries where we do business. Financial managers must also comply with myriad U.S. and international tax regulations. Taxes represent a very large expense and must be managed to lower the company's tax liability. They are also a factor in many business decisions, from building a new plant to opening an overseas subsidiary.

The financial marketplace is another key component of the firm's operating environment. Although a company may start with private funding, as it grows it will require additional funding. Financial managers must know which financial institutions—banks, investment bankers, insurance companies—and which capital markets, either domestic or international, to use to raise debt and equity financing at the lowest possible cost.

The financial markets react to interest rate movements, ultimately affecting the firm's value. Interest rates have a far-reaching impact, from world economies to specific businesses and industries. Many business decisions—borrowing or making capital investments, for example—are based on interest rate levels. So managers must understand how changing interest rates affect capital markets and, therefore, bond and stock prices. In today's volatile markets, historical patterns are no longer very helpful in predicting the future. You can't make assumptions about market and economy performance; you have to stay current and be flexible enough to support any outcome.

The globalization of the financial markets has worked to our advantage. Stratus's initial success was in the financial services area, so the internationalization of financial markets has helped us to grow worldwide. Today, we are working with the Shanghai Metal Exchange and the Wuhan Stock Exchange in the People's Republic of China, as that country establishes a financial infrastructure.

This is an exciting time to be a financial manager. As the world begins to embrace capitalism, opening up new markets, the scope of the global finance manager has never been broader.

Dramatic advancements in information technology place more financial data into the hands of decision makers more rapidly than ever. Today's successful financial managers must harness these data inputs and quickly translate them into useful management information. Managing this communication process effectively has a tremendous impact on the ultimate success of the firm.

Financial management provides the rationale and tools for firms to make effective decisions. These decisions fall into three main categories: (1) the investments the firm makes in both long- and short-term assets, (2) how the firm is financed, and (3) how the firm makes its day-to-day operating decisions.

We begin our journey by examining seven key ideas that underlie financial decision making in Chapter 1. An understanding of these key ideas is needed before we explore other topics in financial management. Next, Chapter 2 examines financial institutions and markets, interest rates, and foreign currency exchange.

Why Financial Management Matters

Sections in this chapter:

■ **What Is Financial Management?**
What this course is about and why it matters.
■ **Key Ideas in Financial Management**
Seven ideas you'll encounter over and over again.
■ **Finance, Business, and Ethics**
Can you "do good" and do well in business?
■ **The Financial Manager**
Who makes the money decisions?
■ **The Internationalization of Business and Financial Management**
The world is getting smaller all the time.

The age of the information superhighway is upon us; firms are returning to South Africa after leaving during the 1980s; and there is a rush to privatize many government-owned companies around the world. At the same time, firms are investing in the People's Republic of China and other countries in Asia as well as in Eastern Europe, and they are facing new competition as foreign-owned firms enter their traditional markets. In the United States productivity is increasing. Despite the dire predictions of some, the North American Free Trade Agreement (NAFTA) appears to be benefiting industry more than hurting it. Women now own about one-third of all U.S. firms that employ fewer than 500 people, while changing demographics signify expanding markets that firms catering to the needs of senior citizens or teenagers are scrambling to capture. The health care industry is becoming more competitive, with or without major new legislation.

The rapid changes occurring both domestically and internationally are having profound effects on the financing needs and patterns of firms, their investment decisions regarding new plant and equipment, and how they structure themselves to compete in this environment. For example, Fiat, the Italian auto maker, purchased a Polish firm for $640 million; it plans to invest an additional $450 million in the venture. General Electric, after a slow start, is now beginning to reap the benefits of its $550 million investment in the Hungarian lightbulb-maker Tungsram. On the other side of the world, Japan continues to export increasing amounts to the Far East and Pacific Rim countries, and is steadily widening its export margin over the United States in that fast-growing region. To meet the demands of the increasingly globalized economy, Ford Motor has merged its manufacturing, sales, and product development operations in North America and Europe, and eventually will do so in Latin America and Asia. In a related move Ford is setting up five program centers with worldwide responsibility to develop new cars and trucks.

Businesses continually face decisions like these—decisions with important financial implications. Every day firms choose to move into new lines of business, replace equipment, change suppliers, reorganize operating structures, start new advertising campaigns, or raise funds either domestically or internationally. The financial consequences of these and many other actions may be direct or indirect, but they cannot be ignored. In this book, we examine the financial aspects of a firm's ongoing business decisions. We see how and why firms plan investments, financing, and operations. As we move along, you will become familiar with terms, concepts, and ideas that are constantly in the news. More importantly, you will gain the tools and theory, along with the rationale, goals, and strategies, that will enable you to be an effective decision maker in your own business activities.

LEARNING GOALS

After studying this chapter, you should be able to:

1. Define and explain financial management.
2. List and discuss the seven key ideas underlying financial management.
3. Discuss ethical issues in business and finance.
4. Explain the role of the financial manager in the firm.
5. Discuss why financial managers need an international perspective.

WHAT IS FINANCIAL MANAGEMENT?

■ LEARNING GOAL 1

Define and explain financial management.

FINANCE
Money resources of firms, governments, or individuals and the management of those resources.

Finance is the word that describes both the money resources available to governments, firms, or individuals, and the management of those resources. Our focus is on the second aspect, management. For our purposes, **financial management** is the acquisition, management, and financing of resources for firms by means of money, with due regard for prices in external economic markets. Let's look at this definition, part by part.

FINANCIAL MANAGEMENT
The acquisition, management, and financing of resources for firms by means of money, with regard for prices in external economic markets.

First, let's focus on the *acquisition, management, and financing of resources needed by firms*. Resources are generally physical, such as cash, inventory, equipment and machinery, or distribution facilities. But resources also include people—the managers and employees of the firm. The money for acquiring these resources comes from a variety of sources: It comes from both the internal cash flow generated by the firm's activities and from external cash flows such as borrowing, leasing, and new stock issues. The firm's goal is to provide and manage all of its resources as efficiently as possible, that is, to balance the need for resources against the risks and the returns expected from their use.

It is actually cash flow that matters to both creditors and stockholders. Hence, financial management focuses on the firm's cash flows.

Second, firms keep track of resources in terms of *money*. They could use production runs, tons, boxcar loads, or any other unit. But it is far simpler if all firms use a single standard. That standard is money, and the unit is dollars. The results of almost any activity of a firm can be expressed in dollars. For example, one firm might con-

FINANCIAL MARKETS
Markets outside the firm in which financial transactions take place.

PROPRIETORSHIP
An unincorporated business owned by one individual.

PARTNERSHIP
A business owned by two or more individuals.

CORPORATION
A legal entity with the power to act as an individual and with limited liability.

LIMITED LIABILITY
By law, a restriction on the amount owners of a corporation can lose in the case of bankruptcy.

COMMON STOCK
An ownership share of a corporation.

BONDS
Long-term debt instruments (IOUs) issued by firms and governments.

sider using its stock to purchase another firm. The value of the transaction can be expressed in dollars, even though stock is used to finance the deal.

The third part of the definition expands our focus to include the firm's *external environment*. Our primary concern is the firm and its operations, but no firm exists in a vacuum. Performance is affected by a variety of external factors: the health of the economy, taxes, interest rates, international tensions, and the prevailing political and regulatory moods. In fact, the performance of the firm is ultimately judged by the external **financial markets,** where stocks and bonds are traded.

The ideas, tools, and techniques of financial management apply to all kinds of firms as well as to individuals. Our focus in this book will be on corporations, rather than on proprietorships or partnerships. A **proprietorship** is an unincorporated business owned by one individual. A **partnership** is a business owned by two or more individuals. Proprietorships or partnerships often are used in the early stages of a business, but most successful ones are eventually converted into corporations. A **corporation** is a legal entity given the power to act as an individual, and it has limited liability. **Limited liability** is a major advantage of a corporation; it means that if the firm goes bankrupt, the owners can lose no more than the money they have invested in the firm.

Corporations can raise funds by issuing and selling shares of their **common stock.** In return for investing in the firm the common stockholders become the owners of the firm. Corporations can also obtain funds by selling **bonds,** which are long-term debt instruments. Bonds are nothing more than IOUs that firms use to obtain financing. The bondholders have a fixed, but limited, claim on the firm. In addition, firms obtain needed funds, and incur financial obligations, through bank loans and credit extended to the firm.

CONCEPT REVIEW QUESTIONS

- What are the three main elements in the definition of financial management?   *ACQUISITION, MANAGEMENT & FINANCING OF RESOURCES*
- Describe the three forms of business organization.   *PROPRIETOR PARTNER CORP.*

KEY IDEAS IN FINANCIAL MANAGEMENT

■ LEARNING GOAL 2

List and discuss the seven key ideas underlying financial management.

In this course, you'll learn to speak the language of finance. In the business world, a command of the finance "lingo" is critical.

Throughout this book you will encounter new terms, ideas, and relationships. Although they are all important in one way or another, certain key ideas underlie the theory and practice of financial management. Since these will come up over and over again, it makes sense to understand them from the start. The seven key ideas that guide our discussions are:

1. The goal of the firm is to maximize its market value.
2. Financial markets are efficient.
3. Individuals act in their own self-interest.
4. Firms focus on cash flows and their incremental effects.
5. A dollar today is worth more than a dollar tomorrow.

As we proceed, we'll highlight in the margin where these seven key ideas occur throughout the book.

6. Risk and return go hand-in-hand.
7. Options are valuable.

Before we begin to use these ideas in making financial decisions, let's briefly explore them one by one.

Key Idea 1: The Goal of the Firm Is to Maximize Its Market Value

To achieve the goal of acquiring, managing, and financing resources efficiently, the firm must have an objective—a purpose. The fundamental objective of the firm is to maximize—or at least to increase significantly—its market value. To understand this objective, think of the firm as a pie, as shown in Figure 1.1. The ingredients that go into the pie include the basic factors that financial management stresses: the acquisition of resources for the firm, and the financing and management of these resources. How effectively these resources are used, however, is determined by *how much someone else is willing to pay for a claim on them.* That is, if firm B believes it can use firm A's resources more efficiently, it will offer to buy those resources. Market forces will operate in the negotiations between the two firms so that the firm that places the higher value on the resources will obtain them. For publicly owned firms, the value of the firm itself is determined by the trading of stocks and bonds in the financial markets.

Though you may hear of other goals, such as maximizing sales, revenue, or net income, these are only means to an end—and the end is maximizing the market value of the firm.

Thus the financial markets come into play. Decisions that maximize the usefulness of a firm's assets create value for the firm. Firms that make value-maximizing decisions will be rewarded: The financial markets will recognize the results of the value-maximizing decisions, and the market value of the firm will increase. Conversely, the financial markets will also respond when the firm makes poor decisions: The market value of the firm will decrease. The point to remember is this: You can't fool the financial markets very long—they will recognize both good decisions and poor decisions within the firm and determine the value of the firm accordingly.

We can express the value-maximization goal mathematically. The total value of the firm, V, or size of the pie, is a function of the claims of both stockholders and bondholders on the firm, so that:

$$\text{market value of firm, } V = S + B$$

FIGURE 1.1

The Firm as a Pie

Depending on how the investment community assesses a firm's decisions (via the financial markets), the size of the pie—the firm—can be enlarged or shrunk, often dramatically.

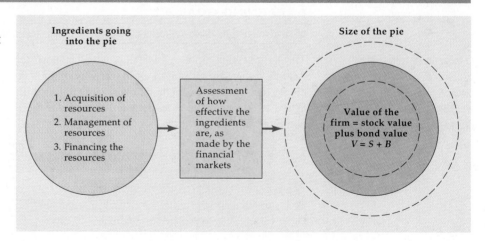

STOCKHOLDER WEALTH MAXIMIZATION
A key objective of the firm—to maximize the value of stockholder claims by maximizing the market value of the firm.

Though there are many classes of creditors, for simplicity we'll ignore many of their differences and use the generic term "bond-holders" to represent the firm's creditors.

where S is the market value of the firm's stock, and B is the market value of the firm's bonds (and other debt). The objective is to maximize V, the market value of the firm. For simplicity, we sometimes assume that this can be accomplished by maximizing S, the market value of stockholders' claims. This objective of **stockholder wealth maximization,** which typically does help to maximize the total value of the firm, underlies most financial decisions.

The way to achieve the objective of maximizing the firm's market value is to maximize the value of stockholders' and bondholders' (or creditors') claims on the firm. An alternative way to think about these claims is to recognize the difference between the claims on the firm held by stockholders and those held by bondholders. First, let's consider stockholders. The value of the stockholders' claims is a function of the total value of the firm. Thus, the potential payoff for stockholders can be depicted as follows:

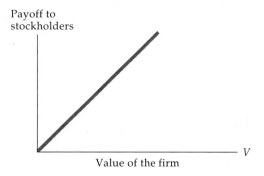

The angled 45 degree line allows us to move from the total value of the firm on the horizontal axis, to the value of stockholders (and bond-holders) on the vertical axis.

Next, consider the claims of bondholders (without considering the stockholders' claims). Suppose bondholders loan $100 to a firm, with the loan to be repaid in 1 year. Ignoring interest (for simplicity), we can depict this claim as follows:

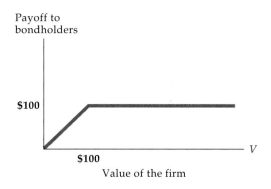

The straight horizontal line says that as the value of the firm increases above $100, the bondholders' value remains at $100.

As long as the firm is healthy and the total value of the firm exceeds the claims of the bondholders, then everything is fine. What happens, however, if the firm is not doing well? Stockholders, by law, have limited liability. Therefore (with a few exceptions) stockholders *are not personally responsible* for seeing that the firm's debts are paid if the value of the firm is not sufficient to pay the bondholders' claims.

If in 1 year the market value of the firm, V, is at least $100, the loan will be repaid and the bondholders will get their $100. Even if the firm is worth a lot more than $100, the bondholders still receive only $100 (as depicted by the horizontal line above). As creditors, they have agreed to a fixed claim of $100, no matter how well the firm does.

If in 1 year the firm is not worth at least $100, the stockholders receive nothing, and the bondholders take over the firm. But if the firm is worth more than $100, the bondholders receive their $100, and the stockholders claim the rest of the value of the firm. Putting both stockholder and bondholder claims together, we have:

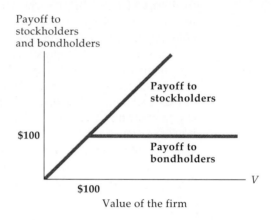

where the total claims are shown as a function of the total firm value, V. Viewed in this context, the bondholders have a fixed, but limited, claim on the value of the firm. The stockholders may receive nothing (if the firm is worth less than $100 in 1 year) or they may receive a lot (everything beyond the $100 claimed by the bondholders). Whether viewed in this manner or in terms of a "pie," the goal of the firm remains the same—to maximize market value.

The objective of maximizing the market value does not mean that stockholders are more deserving than the firm's **stakeholders** (other parties who have an interest in the firm, such as creditors, employees, customers, suppliers, or the community in which the firm is located). Rather, value maximization means that *all* corporate resources should be allocated to the point where marginal costs equal marginal benefits among all parties having an interest in the firm. Decision making that maximizes value allocates resources to each important party to improve the terms on which they deal with the firm.

We should consider one final point in discussing market value and its maximization. Theoretically, maximizing the market value results in maximizing the value of the firm both in the short-term and in the long-term. However, if there is ever any conflict, *it is the long-term market value in which we are interested.*

STAKEHOLDERS
Parties, other than stockholders, management, and creditors, who have an interest in a firm.

Key Idea 2: Financial Markets Are Efficient

In developed countries—such as the United States, Great Britain, and Germany—the financial markets, where stocks and bonds trade, have been found to be "efficient." Let's see what that means. Think about what you already know about financial markets. Choose a firm (for example Coca-Cola, McDonald's, Toyota, or Wal-Mart) and ask yourself these questions: Is the firm well known? Is there plenty of information available about the firm? Is new information made readily and quickly available (in newspapers, on television, and the like) to anyone who is interested in the firm? Do many investors rush to place buy or sell orders for common stock in these firms when they receive important new information about the firm or the economic setting in which it operates? The answer to all these questions is "yes."

For example, brokerage firms and investment advisory services, such as Value Line Investment Service, regularly publish current financial information and provide forecasts of various firms' prospects.

EFFICIENT MARKET
Market in which prices quickly reflect all available information.

The preceding questions describe the characteristics of an efficient market. An **efficient market** is one in which market prices quickly reflect all available information about the firm. If the information about the economy, the firm, or the firm's prospects for the future is favorable, the price of the firm and its common stock will go up over time. Likewise, if the information about the firm indicates hard times, increased competition that will drive down profit margins, or the like, the market price of the firm and its common stock will reflect that information by going down. Hence, *in an efficient market, the best indication of what a firm is worth is to look at what someone is willing to pay for a claim on the firm.*

This simple idea may seem a little strange at first, but apply it to yourself. Let's say you are going to buy a used car. What is that car worth? One way to attempt to determine its worth is to calculate the value of the steel, plastic, aluminum, glass, and rubber that make up the car. A second way is to see what the separate parts of the car— such as the tires, engine, transmission, and so forth—would sell for if you dismantled the car. But neither of these ways of valuing the car is very direct, and both suffer from a variety of problems. What, then, is the most direct way to determine the worth of the car? Simply to determine what you are willing to pay and what someone else is willing to sell the car for. If you are willing to pay $5,000, but the seller wants $8,000, and neither of you will budge, we don't know what the car is worth. Either you are a tightwad or the seller overly estimated the car's value. But, if after negotiation, you jointly arrive at a price of $6,700, then we know what the car is worth. It is worth the price that you, a purchaser with other options (or cars) available, and the seller, with other individuals interested in the car, agree to.

When there is plenty of information and many informed and active investors, markets tend to be efficient. The financial markets in developed countries have been found to be highly efficient. One of the key lessons from knowing that markets are efficient is the following: *If the market is efficient, trust market prices.* That is, if you want to know what an asset is worth, and it trades in an efficient market where there are many informed buyers and sellers, then look to the market price—the price at which knowledgeable parties to the transaction (buyers and sellers) are "willing to deal." A second key lesson from knowing markets are efficient is this: *Start from the market price, and then look for factors that, if changed, could make the asset worth more or less.* For example, if your firm decides to purchase another publicly traded firm, the market value of that firm's assets is already known—it is given by the market value of the firm. If you are going to pay a premium (an amount over and above its current market value) to purchase the firm, you should ask yourself, "Why are the assets worth more to me than their current market value?"

Although financial markets are efficient, or nearly so, the markets for real assets (e.g., plant and equipment) are not. Thus, a firm's choice of real assets is more likely to add value than its choice of financial assets.

The idea of market efficiency is both simple and important and is very well supported by the facts. You will see it underlying many of the financial decisions we consider. At the same time, there are some financial markets that are not efficient. These are most likely to occur in places where the government or other forces interfere with the markets, where information is not freely or readily available, where there are few informed buyers and sellers, or in developing countries. In such situations, market values do not necessarily reflect the economic value of the assets.

Key Idea 3: Individuals Act in Their Own Self-Interest

Underlying much of what you will study in this book is the idea that individuals usually act in their own self-interest. As a simple example, assume an individual chooses to go to the beach 4 days a week to relax in the sun. Although you and I might

OPPORTUNITY COST
The cost of the best forgone alternative.

AGENCY RELATIONSHIP
Contract in which the principal engages an agent to perform a service and delegates some decision-making authority to the agent.

Agency problems occur elsewhere: A lawyer hired by the hour has an incentive to "book" hours. A better deal is to pay the lawyer only if you win the case to help align the self-interests of the principal (you) with those of the agent (the lawyer).

AGENCY COSTS
The costs associated with minimizing agency problems.

An investor we know makes it a rule not to vote for any potential director of a firm who owns fewer shares in the company than he does. Why? "I want the directors to take a financial hit if the company is not well run."

question the decision, the individual is making what to him or her is a rational decision, one based on self-interest. Say the individual's alternative is to spend those 4 days working for $150 per day (to keep things simple, let's ignore taxes). By going to the beach instead, the individual has placed a value on going to the beach of more than the $150 per day that could have been earned. Economists call the value associated with choosing one course of action instead of another the **opportunity cost.** It represents the cost of the best forgone alternative. In this example, the opportunity cost is the $150 per day salary bypassed by choosing to go to the beach.

The idea of self-interest comes up in many ways in finance. Considered together, these examples of self-interest are referred to as "agency problems" or "agency relationships." Narrowly defined, an **agency relationship** is a contract in which one party (the *principal)* engages another (the *agent)* to perform a service and delegates some decision-making authority to the agent. In the context of firms, the owners (the principals) engage the managers as their agents to operate the firm on their behalf.

In a slightly broader perspective, the idea of agency relationships emphasizes that managers, stockholders, bondholders, and other interested parties act in their own self-interest and that costly conflicts may arise due to these self-interests. For example, think of a small business where you are both owner and manager of the firm. As the owner-manager, you will maximize your wealth by balancing the combination of wages, perks (such as a company car and luxurious offices), and so on against the market value of the firm's common stock. Because you are both management and stockholder, actions taken in the stockholders' best interests also serve the self-interests of the manager. As long as a firm is owned and operated by a single owner-manager, no complications arise with the objective of maximizing stockholders' wealth.

In larger firms, however, management often owns only a small percentage of the firm's outstanding common stock. In this case, managers may be "satisfiers" rather than maximizers. That is, their goal may be performance that ensures their own career security and advancement, rather than the goal of maximizing the value of the firm. Why? Because only a small percentage of a manager's wealth comes from changes in the value of the firm's common stock. This conflict in goals might cause managers to bypass a risky but potentially beneficial new investment. They may prefer a safe project to a risky one that, if it fails, might cause the loss of their jobs.

Firms take certain actions to minimize these types of agency problems. The costs associated with these actions are called **agency costs.** These costs can be classified as follows:[1]

1. *Financial Contracting Costs:* the costs of structuring formal or informal contracts, the opportunity costs that arise when firms make decisions or bypass opportunities that lower the value of the firm, and the costs of incentive plans designed to encourage the agent to act in the principals' best interests.
2. *Costs of Monitoring:* the expenses incurred to check the performance of the agents, such as auditing the firm's accounting statements and performance.
3. *Loss of Wealth When Agents Pursue Their Own Interests:* the costs of excessive expense accounts or other perks.

All organizations in which there are divergent interests suffer some loss in value due to agency costs. *Agency costs are borne by the principals*—in this case the stockholders. To minimize these costs, firms such as Eastman Kodak and Chrysler now require

---

[1] *The examples of agency costs relate to those between managers and owners.*

top managers to purchase an amount of stock equal to at least 1 year's salary. These firms believe this requirement is the simplest and most effective way to align the interests of managers and stockholders.

Firms also face a second source of agency costs; these are related to the creditors from whom they obtain funds. **Creditors** are parties that hold fixed-type financial claims against the firm: long-term debt (bonds, mortgages, leases), short-term debt (such as bank loans), accounts payable, wages and salaries, pension liabilities, and so forth. The creditors' claims against the firm create agency costs. For example, creditors may require limits on which assets the firm should hold, have restrictive provisions written into bonds or loan agreements, and impose restrictions on the payment of cash dividends. The purpose of such restrictions is to help ensure repayment of the creditors' funds. To the extent that the restrictions keep the firm from maximizing its value, the firm faces agency issues and incurs agency costs.

Finally, in addition to stockholders, management, and creditors, agency costs may be borne by a variety of stakeholders. Employees of the firm can bear agency costs if they earn less than they could due to managerial inefficiency or if they lose their jobs in plant closings or firm bankruptcies. Customers may face higher prices, and even the U.S. economy as a whole may bear the agency costs, if foreign competitors can operate more efficiently because of a lower level of agency costs. (For example, researchers have postulated that Japan's corporate structure may reduce agency costs for Japanese firms by establishing close working relationships between creditors, stockholders, and managers.) Thus, constraints exist because of the possibility of conflicts of interest between the goal of maximizing the value of the firm and the self-interests of other parties. These constraints are reflected in the form of agency costs, and requirements imposed by the government, if stockholders attempt to expropriate wealth from the firm's stakeholders.

Agency problems arise when not all parties have the same information—that is, when there is **asymmetric information.** Throughout the book, we will explore a number of agency problems that involve parties having differing amounts of information. The important point to remember is that the self-interests of various groups must be taken into account as financial decisions are made. Also, because of differing self-interests and amounts of information, virtually all organizations incur agency costs. Firms seek to minimize total agency costs as they make financial decisions.

Key Idea 4: Firms Focus on Cash Flows and Their Incremental Effects

You know by now that firms seek to maximize their value. The next question we need to ask is how they go about doing that. First, note that in finance we measure the value of the firm as its value *in the financial marketplace.* Other measures of value, such as **book value** (assets minus liabilities in an accounting sense) or replacement value, are not our focus. So, as managers or investors we are interested in the highest *market value* of the firm.

How then do we go about valuing a firm? Theoretically, *the value of the firm is determined by the magnitude of the future cash flows to be received, the timing of these cash flows, and the risks involved.* By **cash flows** we mean *actual cash* to be received or paid. This amount is not the same as earnings or net income in an accrual-based accounting sense. There is a fundamental difference between accounting and financial management: *The accountant looks at earnings; financial managers use cash flows.* Earnings are only a clue to the ability of the firm to generate cash flows. Earnings, in fact, are often misleading, because they are calculated by matching

---

CREDITORS
Parties that hold fixed-type financial claims against a firm.

Agency problems also occur in government. Contributions by special-interest groups increase the potential for the public's agent (the politician) not to act in the best interest of the principals (the public).

ASYMMETRIC INFORMATION
Unequal information available to interested parties.

As discussed later in the book, one of the main reasons many firms pay regular quarterly cash dividends is to help alleviate the information asymmetry problem.

BOOK VALUE
Assets minus liabilities, or stockholders' equity

CASH FLOW
The actual movement of cash into or out of a firm; not earnings.

INCREMENTAL CASH FLOW
The difference between new and existing cash flow.

TAXES
A fee levied on individuals or firms by a federal, state, or local government.

Cash flow, and not earnings, matter for a simple reason: A firm cannot pay its employees, its suppliers, or its providers of funds unless the cash is available. Accounting earnings are a bookkeeping entry—not something you can take to the bank.

Taxes are an important consideration when determining a firm's cash flow. They will be considered throughout this book, especially in Appendix 8A.

BALANCE SHEET
Accounting statement that records assets, liabilities, and owners' equity as of a specific point in time.

INCOME STATEMENT
Accounting statement that records revenues, expenses, and net income over some period of time.

EARNINGS BEFORE INTEREST AND TAXES, *EBIT*
Earnings prior to deducting interest on debt and income taxes.

EARNINGS BEFORE TAX, *EBT*
Earnings before income taxes are deducted.

EARNINGS AFTER TAX, *EAT*
Net income; earnings after all costs, interest, and income taxes are deducted.

CASH DIVIDENDS
Distribution of cash to a firm's stockholders.

revenues and expenses in the proper time period based on historical costs. *The accounting system is not designed to report the inflows and outflows of cash.* Although some exceptions exist, accounting's primary focus is on recording what has happened in the past, and matching income and expense in the appropriate time period. In finance, our concern is preparing for the future and tracking cash inflows and outflows.

While we are interested in cash flows, our primary focus is on **incremental cash flows**, that is, new minus existing cash flows. For example, assume you currently take home $9,000 a year from a part-time job, and due to a promotion, you will take home a total of $11,000 in the future. The incremental amount by which you are better off is $2,000. However, there is one other factor that has to be taken into consideration—**taxes**. If you have to pay an additional $200 in taxes because of the additional $2,000 in earnings, your net incremental benefit after taxes is only $1,800. Financial management is always concerned with these incremental after-tax cash flows.

Why are cash flows so important? Because *cash flow is unambiguous and essential to the well-being of the firm.* The firm can spend cash; it cannot spend net income. Financial theory has its roots in economics. Based on economic considerations, the value of the firm at any point in time is equal to the present value of the expected cash flows. Only by calculating cash flows will the firm and investors be able to determine if actions taken are consistent with the goal of maximizing the value of the firm.

By emphasizing cash flow, we have an unambiguous measure of the returns coming to the firm. This would not be true if we used net income as determined by *generally accepted accounting principles* (GAAP). Under GAAP, different inventory, depreciation, or other generally accepted alternatives can result in differences in reported net income for two firms that are otherwise the same. Alternatively, two firms can report the same net income but have vast differences in actual cash flows for the period. Firms also employ different depreciation amounts for tax purposes (based on the Internal Revenue Service code) than they incorporate in their GAAP accounting statements. The use of cash flow instead of net income removes all of these accounting-induced ambiguities.

Finally, the flow of cash is essential to the well-being of the firm. Firms may have high profits but inadequate cash flow, or low profits but high cash flow. Let's consider the example in Table 1.1. The **balance sheet** for a firm reports the accounting-based value of the firm's assets, and the claims against those assets in the form of liabilities (held by creditors) and owners' (stockholders') equity. In addition to the balance sheet, firms also provide **income statements,** which show sales, cash and non-cash expenses, and other adjustments. Because interest on borrowing is important in financial management, **earnings before interest and taxes, *EBIT,*** is determined. Then, when interest is deducted we arrive at **earnings before tax, *EBT*.** Subtracting taxes, we are left with **earnings after tax, *EAT,*** or net income. Table 1.1 also shows that the firm is paying **cash dividends.** These are a distribution of some of the firm's cash to the firm's stockholders. Cash dividends are a direct cash outflow.

At the bottom of Table 1.1 is the firm's projection of its cash flows (inflows and outflows) for the next 3 months. Looking closely, we realize that only half of the firm's sales of $2,000 will be for cash, and that $1,480 in cash expenses must be paid, along with $20 in interest, taxes of $120, a cash dividend of $60, and repayment of a $200 short-term loan. Even after drawing its cash account down to zero, the firm has projected cash outflows that exceed projected inflows by $680. Over time, as the credit sales are collected, the firm's cash flow problem will probably be corrected. But the firm will suffer from a shortage of cash during the next quarter. If we had looked only at the $280 net income figure as reported in the income statement, we would not know of the firm's financial problems until the crunch was on.

TABLE 1.1

Difference Between Net Income and Cash Flow

Cash flow and net income are never the same. In some situations, cash flows far exceed net income; in others, they fall short. For this reason, the emphasis in financial management must be on cash flow.

Balance Sheet

Assets		Liabilities and Stockholders' Equity	
Cash	$ 200	Short-term debt*	$ 200
Other assets	800	Long-term debt	300
Total	$1,000	Equity	500
		Total	$1,000

Projected Income Statement for Next 3 Months

Sales (50% cash)	$2,000
Cash expenses except interest	1,480
Depreciation	100
Earnings before interest and taxes, *EBIT*	420
Interest	20
Earnings before tax, *EBT*	400
Taxes (30%)	120
Earnings after tax, *EAT* (or net income)	$ 280
Cash dividend to be paid in 2 months	$ 60

Cash Flows

For the next 3-month period, the projected cash inflows and outflows are as follows:

Cash Inflows		Cash Outflows	
Sales for cash	$1,000	Cash expenses	$1,480
Cash on hand	200	Interest	20
Total	$1,200	Taxes	120
		Cash dividend	60
		Repay short-term debt	200
		Total	$1,880

Resulting cash shortage = $1,880 − $1,200 = $680

* Due in 2 months

Firms may use accounting gimmicks to try to fool markets about financial results. But poor cash flow can't be hidden for long. In an efficient market, the firm's market price will quickly reflect any cash flow problems.

One additional point needs to be emphasized. Even though cash flow is the proper focus for financial decision making, in practice many firms concentrate on growth in sales, market share, or earnings. Too much attention is often given to these numbers and not enough to how they relate to cash flows. By focusing on cash flow, financial decision makers can most directly serve the interests of owners, creditors, and stakeholders of the firm. If cash flows are maximized, the accounting numbers (over time) will reflect this success, and the value of the firm will be maximized. Inadequate cash flows also will be reflected eventually in the firm's accounting statements and its market price. The firm pays a price if it ignores, or pays too little attention to, cash flows. That price is an opportunity cost equal to the attainable maximum market value of the firm minus the actual value of the firm.

FINANCIAL MANAGEMENT TODAY

Go with the Flow

When chief financial officers, CFOs, of major firms, such as Ashland Oil, Philip Morris, Tenneco, and E-Systems, talk about "going with the flow," they mean cash flow. Although many people look at profit as a key indicator of a firm's financial health, net profit is essentially an accounting mechanism, and it can be manipulated by changes in accounting assumptions. Both CFOs and Wall Street recognize that it is cash flow that drives business decisions and leads to healthy, value-maximizing firms. As one analyst noted, "Companies with good cash flow don't go out of business, even though companies with good profits and bad cash flow do."

Many different definitions of cash flow exist. The simplest definition is:

$$\text{cash flow} = \text{net income} + \text{depreciation} + \text{depletion} + \text{amortization}$$

By adding back depreciation, depletion, and amortization, which are non-cash charges, we get a rough estimate of the cash generated by the firm. This cash flow number—called *simple cash flow*—however, isn't a particularly useful figure. It's just a way station.

Instead most firms and analysts prefer *free cash flow*, which is:

$$\text{free cash flow} = \text{cash flow} - \text{capital expenditures} - \text{dividends}$$

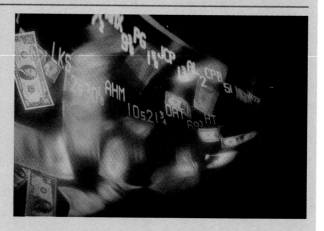

By focusing on the discretionary cash left after maintaining the firm's capital plant and paying stockholders, we get a useful indicator of funds available to boost dividends, buy back shares, or pay down debt. Thus, cash flow has moved to the forefront—and sophisticated managers and investors go with the flow.

Key Idea 5: A Dollar Today Is Worth More than a Dollar Tomorrow

The next key idea in finance is easy. Simply put, a dollar today is worth more than a dollar tomorrow. That is, if I offer you $100 today, or the same $100 one year from now, you will be better off if you take the $100 today. In finance, we formalize this idea by using present value and future value techniques. But without even knowing about those, *your basic instincts are correct: when in doubt, take the cash sooner rather than later.*

When dealing with timing problems, finance uses a standardized methodology to determine whether the cash flows associated with making an investment are worthwhile. Say you are offered an investment that promises a return of $150 in 1 year by investing $100 today. (To keep things simple, let's assume there's no risk—that is, the investment is a sure thing.) The question is, should you make the proposed investment? By investing $100 today you will receive $150 in 1 year. What should you do? If you are rational and act in your own self-interest, you would make the investment *unless* you had another opportunity that provided a better return. Let's say your next best opportunity would provide a return of $120 in 1 year for the same $100 investment. Faced with these alternatives, you would make the investment that provides the return of $150 in 1 year. By doing so, you are making a value-maximizing decision.

NET PRESENT VALUE, NPV
The present value of the future cash flows, discounted at the opportunity cost of capital, or required rate of return, minus the initial investment.

In financial management we deal with similar problems by determining the **net present value, *NPV,*** of the proposed investment. The procedure is to **discount** the future cash inflows at a rate that reflects the opportunities bypassed and risks involved, and then subtract the initial investment. Thus, the net present value of any proposed investment is:

$$\text{net present value} = \frac{\text{future value of cash inflows}}{1 + \text{discount rate based on forgone opportunities}}$$
$$- \text{ initial investment} \tag{1.1}$$

DISCOUNT
To determine the value today of an amount to be received in the future.

In this case the discount rate (or forgone return) on the next best investment is $120/$100 − 1 = 1.20 − 1 = 0.20. The net present value of the proposed investment is then $150/(1 + 0.20) − $100 = $125 − $100 = $25. Because the net present value of $25 is positive, you would make the investment. This approach is employed in financial management to ensure that value-maximizing decisions are made.

Key Idea 6: Risk and Return Go Hand-in-Hand

RISK
The uncertainty of something happening or the possibility of a less-than-desirable outcome.

The next important idea is the relationship of risk and return. By **risk,** we mean the uncertainty of something happening, or the possibility of a less-than-desirable outcome. *Other things being equal, rational individuals require a higher return for exposing themselves to higher risk.* Thus, if you believe investment B has more risk than investment A, investment B would have to offer you a higher return potential before you would invest in it.

The other side of this idea is that in order to increase the return expected from any kind of investment, we must increase our exposure to risk. Put more directly, we could say "there is no free lunch!" The key ideas are captured in the following diagram:

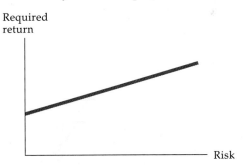

REQUIRED RETURN
The return necessary in order for a firm or investor to accept a certain level of risk.

where, other things being equal, the **required return** demanded by investors increases as they take on more risk. *If firms or individuals desire higher returns, then they must bear more risk.*

Likewise, if firms or individuals are exposed to more risk, they have two basic choices. *The first choice is to price the risk*—that is, to see if the expected returns are high enough to justify undertaking that much risk. *The second choice is to do something to eliminate part or all of the risk*—in financial terms, to *hedge.* In what follows we discuss "pricing the risk" by demanding a high enough return to compensate for the risk involved.[2] In a practical sense, if someone promises you a

---

[2] *In Chapters 23 and 28 of my upper-level textbook,* Financial Management *(published in 1994 by HarperCollins Publishers), the topic of how firms can hedge specific kinds of risk—arising from fluctuations in market prices, interest rates, or foreign exchange rates—is examined. Occasional footnotes in this book will refer readers to the more advanced material in* Financial Management *that is outside the scope of the first finance course.*

"guaranteed" 25 percent return with no risk, my advice is simple—be extremely skeptical! Firms and individuals have lost billions by not understanding that risk and return go hand-in-hand.

Key Idea 7: Options Are Valuable

OPTION
Investment that allows, but does not require, one to undertake some financial opportunity on or before a specified date.

The final key idea relates to **options**, investments that provide the opportunity, but not the requirement, to undertake some financial activity. Let's go back to the example where you could put $100 into an investment that would return $150. Let's assume the investment opportunity was available to you, and to you alone, for 10 days. During those 10 days you hold an option to make the investment, *but you are not required to make the investment*. If something better comes along during that time period, you can elect to bypass this opportunity. If that happens, you have decided not to "exercise the option." If at the end of the 10 days you make the $100 investment, you have exercised the option. The flexibility provided by options, to either exercise them or let them expire, is what makes options so valuable.

During the last 30 years we have found that options exist in many different and unusual ways in financial management. And, we have also developed the ability to value both simple and very complex options. Any time a firm or individual has the opportunity, but not the requirement, to undertake some financial opportunity, an option exists. Options in financial management include the managerial flexibility associated with making capital investment decisions; they are present in various securities employed by firms; and they are part of any guarantee, loan, or insurance contract. Without the ability to incorporate and value options, we cannot properly evaluate the various courses of action available to firms and the costs or benefits associated with these alternatives. Financial management cannot be fully understood without understanding options.[3]

We have encountered seven key ideas that underlie financial management. To recap, they are:

1. The goal of the firm is to maximize its market value.
2. Financial markets are efficient.
3. Individuals act in their own self-interest.
4. Firms focus on cash flows and their incremental effects.
5. A dollar today is worth more than a dollar tomorrow.
6. Risk and return go hand-in-hand.
7. Options are valuable.

In studying these ideas, we have come across some of the main subjects and topic areas in the study of finance: wealth maximization, stakeholders, market efficiency, opportunity costs, agency problems and costs, cash flows, net present value, risk, required return, and options. These topics form the foundation of this book.

CONCEPT REVIEW QUESTIONS

■ What is the fundamental objective of any firm?
■ Define an efficient market and how it affects the worth of a firm.

---

[3]*Options in financial management are covered in detail in* Financial Management; *we will deal with the underlying ideas and implications in this book but will omit detailed treatment on valuing options.*

■ Define an agency relationship and describe how it affects financial decision making.
■ Explain why firms focus on incremental cash flows instead of accounting figures.
■ Why is a dollar today worth more than a dollar tomorrow?
■ How are risk and return related?
■ Explain what an option is and why options are valuable.

FINANCE, BUSINESS, AND ETHICS

■ LEARNING GOAL 3

Discuss ethical issues in business and finance.

During the 1980s and 1990s the field of finance, and business in general, witnessed a greater focus on ethics. The source of the problem, some assert, is the loss in value, lost jobs, and lack of caring for employees and other stakeholders of a firm due to the unleashing of market forces as firms and industries are deregulated, or privatized. At the same time, we heard of the tremendous problems in South Africa due to apartheid, the lack of human rights in countries like Burma and the People's Republic of China, and the potential loss of jobs in the United States as firms take advantage of the North American Free Trade Agreement (NAFTA) and move production to Mexico or to other low-cost countries in the Pacific Rim or Eastern Europe.

In analyzing the issue of ethics, it is helpful to distinguish between two types of ethical concerns. The first involves firms taking action to prevent conduct that either violates the law or that walks the line of illegality by instituting policies and procedures. The second deals with much broader stakeholder and societal considerations, such as human rights, environmental concerns, and balancing the value-maximization interests of the shareholders against those of stakeholders in general.

Most would agree that, in general, larger firms in a free market society practice responsible ethical behavior. Most firms do not violate the law, and they generally avoid questionable business practices. Although there may be short-run adverse financial consequences to ethical behavior, in the long run only firms that act ethically will be in a position to maximize their value. This is true because in a free market society, grossly unethical behavior will affect the long-run ability of the firm to maximize its value.

There is much less agreement, in terms of the firm's responsibilities and value-maximizing consequences, on whether firms should be proactive in dealing with the broader societal and stakeholder aspects of ethical behavior. At one end of this issue is Levi Strauss & Co., the world's biggest supplier of brand-name apparel. What Levi's aspires to be in the area of ethics includes the following:

New Behaviors: Management must exemplify "directness, openness to influence, commitment to the success of others, and willingness to acknowledge our own contributions to problems."

Diversity: Levi's "values a diverse workforce (age, sex, ethnic group, etc.) at all levels of the organization. . . . Differing points of view will be sought; diversity will be valued and honesty rewarded, not suppressed."

Recognition: Levi's will "provide greater recognition—both financial and psychic—for individuals and teams that contribute to our success . . . those who create and innovate and those who continually support day-to-day business requirements."

Ethical Management Practices: Management should epitomize "the stated standards of ethical behavior. We must provide clarity about our expectations and must enforce these standards throughout the corporation."

Communications: Management must be "clear about company, unit, and individual goals and performance. People must know what is expected of them and receive timely, honest feedback. . . . "

Empowerment: Management must "increase the authority and responsibility of those closest to our products and customers. By actively pushing that responsibility, trust, and recognition into the organization, we can harness and release the capabilities of all our people."[4]

Levi's' commitment to an ethical business approach stems from the beliefs of Chairman and Chief Executive Officer, Robert Haas, the great-great-grandnephew of founder Levi Strauss. (It doesn't hurt that Levi Strauss is a private company, with almost all of the stock held by members of the Haas family.) The company believes that the interests of their employees, suppliers, and other stakeholders are directly related to financial success. Toward that end, since Haas became CEO in 1984, Levi's has doubled the percentage of minority managers to 36 percent, and increased the percentage of women managers from 32 percent to 54 percent. Also, Levi eliminated suppliers in the People's Republic of China because of human rights concerns, and company inspectors monitor its roughly 700 contract factories throughout the world.[5] On the other hand, Levi Strauss is still a business, as decisions like the one to close a plant in San Antonio—idling 1,110 workers—and move its operations to Costa Rica to take advantage of lower wages demonstrate. Levi's reply when asked about this type of action is that guaranteed employment is not part of the Levi value system.

Levi's is at one end of the spectrum; most firms have a much more low-key approach to the issue of ethics in finance and business. Sometimes firms find themselves in unanticipated situations because of actions they have taken. For example, a few years ago Sears faced consumer indignation and legal sanctions due to reports of unnecessary expensive auto repairs. The reason for the unnecessary repairs was not that Sears did not believe in an ethical approach to business, but because of a faulty compensation system that encouraged managers and employees in their auto service business to maximize sales—at almost any cost. Thus, its faulty compensation system had a direct, and unanticipated, impact on Sears. One lesson from this example is that firms should spend more time considering potential conflicts of interests among the firm's management, employees, customers, suppliers, creditors, communities, and shareholders than they typically do. By examining these conflicts, firms will—by necessity—adopt a broader view. Their actions will encourage and support broad-based ethical behavior that is consistent with, and supportive of, value maximization.

CONCEPT REVIEW QUESTIONS

- What are the two types of ethical issues faced by firms?
- What are the key elements of Levi Strauss's approach to ethics? What, in part, enables them to take this approach?
- Describe how conflicts of interest can lead to unanticipated consequences.

[4] *"Managing by Values,"* Business Week, *August 1, 1994, p. 47.*
[5] *"Levi Tries to Make Sure Contract Plants in Asia Treat Workers Well,"* The Wall Street Journal, *July 28, 1994, pp. 1 and 6.*

THE FINANCIAL MANAGER

■ LEARNING GOAL 4

Explain the role of the financial manager in the firm.

FINANCIAL MANAGER
Anyone directly engaged in making or implementing financial decisions.

**CHIEF FINANCIAL OFFI-
CER, CFO**
The person who is ultimately responsible for a firm's financial activities.

TREASURER
Financial officer responsible for day-to-day financial activities of the firm.

CONTROLLER
Financial officer responsible for accounting and tax activities of the firm.

In this book, we use the term **financial manager** to refer to anyone directly engaged in making or implementing financial decisions. Except in the smallest firms, many individuals are responsible for financial activities. In most large firms, the person ultimately responsible is the financial vice-president, who is the **chief financial officer, CFO**, of the firm. The CFO is deeply involved in financial policy making, as well as in corporate or strategic planning.

Typically, at least two individuals report directly to the CFO. The **treasurer** is usually the person responsible for ensuring that the firm obtains funds as needed, that cash is collected and invested, that relations are maintained with banks and other financial institutions, and that bills are paid on time. In some organizations, the treasurer also oversees capital budgeting decisions and credit management. The **controller** (or comptroller) oversees the preparation of accounting statements, cost accounting procedures, internal auditing measures, budgets, and the firm's tax department.

Because of the importance of financial decisions to the long-run success of the firm, major decisions are often made by the board of directors or the executive committee. For example, major capital expenditures, proposed financing changes, and the firm's dividend policy are decided at the highest level of the firm. However, authority for less important decisions, such as small- or medium-sized investments, credit policies, and cash management changes, is often delegated to division managers or others at lower levels in the firm. Financial managers are all those individuals whose decision-making responsibility affects the financial health of the firm.

CONCEPT REVIEW QUESTIONS

■ Who is a financial manager in a firm?
■ What two individuals within a firm report directly to the chief financial officer?

THE INTERNATIONALIZATION OF BUSINESS AND FINANCIAL MANAGEMENT

■ LEARNING GOAL 5

Discuss why financial managers need an international perspective.

Roughly 25 percent of the assets of U.S.-based manufacturing firms are located outside the United States. Moreover, the growth rate of international investment exceeds the growth rate of U.S. domestic investment. At the same time, major changes are taking place all over the world. The Japanese, after making rapid industrial progress for the last four decades, have experienced an economic slowdown. To spur growth on our own continent, Canada, Mexico, and the United States entered into the North American Free Trade Agreement (NAFTA) on January 1, 1994, which removed tariffs on over 50 percent of all goods flowing between these countries. In the future, additional tariffs covered by NAFTA will also be reduced. One result is the increasing cross-border integration of the economies of Canada, Mexico, and the United States, linking states and provinces with an increased north-south flow of products. Other regional trade agreements exist, both in Europe and in the Pacific Rim. At the same time, the recent agreement among the 117 member nations of the General Agreement on Tariffs and Trade (GATT) removed or lowered many tariffs throughout the world.

As cross-border trade and investment flows reach new heights, global firms are increasingly making decisions with little regard for national boundaries. Though they are still tied to their home countries, the trend toward becoming a stateless firm is unmistakable. Increasingly, European, Japanese, and U.S. firms are learning how to juggle multiple identities and loyalties. To combat the increasing emergence of regional trading blocks in Europe, North America, and the Pacific Rim, global firms are developing the ability to resemble insiders no matter where they operate. At the same time they may move factories and labs around the world with little reference to national borders.

Some of these stateless firms include the following:

Percent of Sales Outside Home Country	Firm	Home Country
Over 90%	Nestle	Switzerland
	SKF	Sweden
	Philips	The Netherlands
Over 75%	SmithKline Beecham	Great Britain
	Reuters	Great Britain
	Volvo	Sweden
	Michelin	France
	Hoechst	Germany
Over 50%	Canon	Japan
	Northern Telecom	Canada
	Sony	United States
	Bayer	Germany
	Colgate	United States
	IBM	United States
	Dow Chemical	United States

These developments have profound implications for financial management. More than ever we live and work in a worldwide economy. Business, and financial management, is increasingly conducted on a global basis. The fundamental ideas discussed in this chapter and the remainder of the book generally apply equally well in any country in the world. However, two important differences exist. First, some of the specifics assumed—such as efficient financial markets, details of the tax code, the primacy of shareholder wealth maximization, and so forth—often differ. Second, any time cash flows move between two countries, the impact of *exchange rates*—that is, how much one currency is worth in terms of another currency—must be considered. Important aspects of international financial management will be discussed throughout the book.

CONCEPT REVIEW QUESTIONS

■ What is the impact of NAFTA, other regional trade agreements, and GATT?
■ How are many firms dealing with the increasingly global economy?

Summary

- Financial management focuses on the acquisition, management, and financing of resources. While the ideas are universal, we focus on applying them to firms organized as corporations.
- The first key idea of financial management is that firms strive to maximize their long-run market value, as reflected by the market value of the owners' claims (through stock) and by the creditors' claims.
- The second key idea is that financial markets in developed countries are efficient. Thus, the best indication of value is what someone else is willing to pay for an asset. When valuing assets in efficient markets, look first to market prices.
- The third key idea is that individuals operate in their own self-interest. When differences in interests exist, agency costs are incurred in an attempt to ensure that joint interests are pursued. Differences in interests and information may exist between owners (stockholders) and management, between owners and creditors, and between any of them and other stakeholders (e.g., employees, customers, and suppliers).
- The fourth key idea is to focus on cash flows and their incremental effects. Do not be misled by accounting-induced influences; you can't spend net income.
- The fifth key idea is that a dollar today is worth more than a dollar tomorrow.
- The sixth key idea is that risk and return go hand-in-hand. The only way for individuals or firms to increase their expected return is to increase their risk exposure.
- The seventh key idea is that options, which provide the right but not the requirement to undertake some financial opportunity, are valuable.
- By focusing on maximizing the long-run market value of the firm, financial management in a free enterprise economy leads to the most efficient allocation of all resources—financial, real, and human.
- All firms face ethical issues; some are much more active than others in terms of how proactively they approach the issue of finance, business, and ethics.
- Financial managers are all the individuals in a firm who make decisions that have financial consequences. The chief financial officer, CFO, is ultimately responsible for the financial operations of a firm.
- The business world and financial management is increasingly becoming internationalized.

Questions

1.1 Explain what is meant by the statement, "Financial management is the acquisition, management, and financing of resources for firms by means of money, with due regard for prices in external economic markets."

1.2 The fixed nature of the bondholders' claims and the limited liability associated with common stock are important when considering the potential payoffs to bondholders and stockholders. Explain the potential payoffs as a function of the total value of the firm.

1.3 Explain why cash flow and net income are not, and cannot be, equal for firms.

1.4 Comment on the following statement made by Chris in the firm's executive suite: "I'm on the spot because I'm going to be judged by the common stockholders on the basis of market price, over which I have absolutely no control. In fact, I can't even control sales or earnings per share as well as I'd like, and they are the primary determinants of the market price."

1.5 What are the key ideas you should understand after reading this book?

Concept Review Problems

See Appendix A for solutions.

CR1.1 Prepare a projected income statement for Shapleigh & Associates from the following information: sales, $700,000; cost of goods sold, $100,000; administrative expenses, $300,000; depreciation, $50,000; interest paid, $60,000; and a tax rate of 40 percent.

CR1.2 Wheeler Inc. has the following balance sheet and projected income statement:

<table>
<tr><td colspan="4" align="center">Balance Sheet</td></tr>
<tr><td>Assets</td><td></td><td colspan="2" align="center">Liabilities and Stockholders' Equity</td></tr>
<tr><td>Cash</td><td>$ 500</td><td>Short-term debt</td><td>$ 1,500</td></tr>
<tr><td>Other assets</td><td>80,000</td><td>Long-term debt</td><td>59,000</td></tr>
<tr><td align="center">Total</td><td>$80,500</td><td>Stockholders' equity</td><td>20,000</td></tr>
<tr><td></td><td></td><td>Total</td><td>$80,500</td></tr>
</table>

<table>
<tr><td colspan="2" align="center">Projected Income Statement for 6 Months</td></tr>
<tr><td>Sales (70% cash)</td><td>$30,000</td></tr>
<tr><td>Expenses</td><td>15,000</td></tr>
<tr><td>Depreciation</td><td>1,000</td></tr>
<tr><td>Earnings before interest and taxes, EBIT</td><td>14,000</td></tr>
<tr><td>Interest</td><td>6,000</td></tr>
<tr><td>Earnings before tax, EBT</td><td>8,000</td></tr>
<tr><td>Taxes (40%)</td><td>3,200</td></tr>
<tr><td>Earnings after tax, EAT (or net income)</td><td>$ 4,800</td></tr>
<tr><td>Cash dividend to be paid in 5 months</td><td>$ 500</td></tr>
</table>

The following information also pertains to Wheeler Inc.:

a. All of the short-term debt of $1,500 will become due within 6 months.

b. Wheeler will receive $5,000 in cash from sales made previously.

c. Eighty percent of the estimated expenses will be paid in the next 6 months. The remaining 20 percent will be paid after 6 months.

d. Taxes will be paid in full during the next 6 months.

What are Wheeler's expected cash inflows and outflows for the next 6 months? Is there a cash shortage or a cash excess?

CR1.3 Barbara and Ross were discussing a problem assigned to them in their financial management course. They were to find the net cash flow for XYZ firm. The firm had sales of $80,000, expenses of $60,000, depreciation of $15,000, and interest expense of $10,000. The firm collected 80 percent of its sales in cash and paid 80 percent of its expenses in cash. In addition, the firm's marginal tax rate was 40 percent, and no dividends were paid. Barbara and Ross calculated the firm had a negative net income of $5,000, but they were confused when they found net cash flow was a positive $6,000.

Did Barbara and Ross correctly calculate net income and net cash flow? Is it possible to have a negative net income and a positive net cash flow?

Problems

See Appendix C for answers to selected problems.

Cash Shortage

1.1   Korchun Transit has run into some cash flow problems due to rapid expansion. Tom, the chief financial officer, is making plans for the next 6 months. The balance sheet for the year just completed and the firm's projected income statement (for both accounting and tax purposes) for the next 6 months are as follows:

Balance Sheet		Projected Income Statement for Next 6 Months	
Assets	$300	Sales	$500
		Expenses	360
Liabilities and Stockholders' Equity		Depreciation	30
Current debt	$100	*EBIT*	110
Long-term debt	50	Interest	25
Stockholders' equity	150	*EBT*	85
Total	$300	Taxes (40%)	34
		Net income	$ 51

In addition, Tom notes the following:

a. Eighty dollars of the $100 in current debt comes due in the next 6 months, and the bank has indicated it will not renew the loan.
b. A long-term debt issue of $50 is planned during the next 6 months.
c. Seventy percent of the sales projected for the next 6 months will be received in cash; the remainder will not be collected until after 6 months.
d. Forty dollars in cash will be received during the next 6 months from sales made in the last 6 months. (Thus, this is an account receivable that will be collected.)
e. Ninety percent of the estimated expenses for the next 6 months will be paid in cash during the period; the remainder can be paid after the next 6 months.
f. Taxes and interest must be paid in full during the next 6 months. Also, cash dividends of $16 are payable during this same time period.
g. The cash account cannot be reduced from its present level.

Prepare an estimate of Korchun's expected cash inflows and outflows for the next 6 months. Do you foresee any problems? What actions might Tom take to secure the additional cash needed?

Depreciation, Taxes, and Cash Flows

1.2   Riverview Hotel has the following income statement for reporting purposes:

Income Statement	
Revenues	$180,000
All operating expenses except depreciation	142,000
Depreciation	15,000
EBIT	23,000
Interest	11,000
EBT	12,000
Taxes (30%)	3,600
Net income	$ 8,400

A firm does not operate in a vacuum. Its financial performance, cash flows, and ability to raise and invest funds are determined by its actions within the financial environment of markets, institutions, and interest rates. Understanding the financial environment is important for effective financial decision making.

LEARNING GOALS

After studying this chapter, you should be able to:

1. Explain the role of financial institutions and distinguish between the primary and secondary markets.
2. Determine the required returns for bonds and for stock, and explain how interest rates affect these returns.
3. Know how returns are measured, and understand the relationship between risk and return of financial assets.
4. Understand the relationship between current (as of today) and forward exchange rates of two currencies.

THE FINANCIAL SYSTEM

■ LEARNING GOAL 1

Explain the role of financial institutions and distinguish between the primary and secondary markets.

A key idea of both economics and finance is that by consuming less now—thereby saving more—individuals can consume more in the future. If more is consumed now, individuals will have less for consumption in the future. The fundamental goal of financial markets is to allow individuals, firms, or governments to channel funds between consumption (or uses) today and consumption (or uses) in the future. The financial system that has developed to support the financial markets has the same purpose. An extensive financial system, such as that in developed countries like the United States, Great Britain, Germany, and Japan, provides an effective means of bringing together suppliers and demanders of capital. The basic relationships are shown in Figure 2.1. Note that not only are suppliers, demanders, and the financial markets part of the system, but so are the financial institutions that have evolved to increase the efficiency and smoothness of the system.

Financial Institutions

FINANCIAL INTERMEDIARIES
Financial institutions that assist in the transfer of funds from suppliers to demanders of funds.

Financial institutions exist to facilitate bringing together suppliers and demanders of funds. These institutions, often referred to as **financial intermediaries**, accept savings; in return, the suppliers of funds acquire claims against the intermediaries. Then the intermediaries make loans or investments to the demanders of funds. As a reward for entrusting savings to a financial intermediary, the supplier of funds expects some return in the form of interest or cash dividends.

The major institutions in the U.S. financial system include:

1. Commercial banks, the traditional department stores of finance.
2. Insurance companies and pension funds, including life insurance companies, fire and casualty companies, and private and government retirement plans.

FIGURE 2.1

Relationship Among Suppliers and Demanders of Funds, Financial Institutions, and Financial Markets

Funds are supplied through the financial markets directly or by going through financial institutions. A well-developed network of financial institutions and financial markets is important for financial decision making.

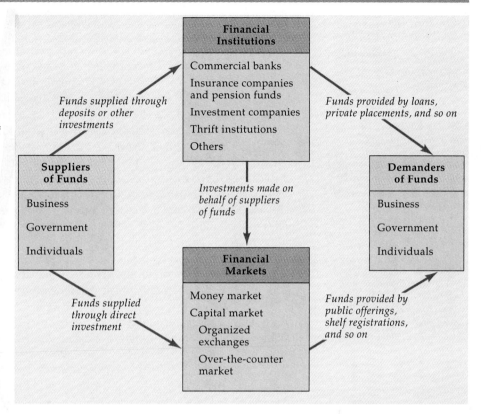

3. Investment companies, including various mutual funds in which investors pool their funds into a large fund managed by an investment advisor.
4. Thrift institutions, including savings and loan associations, mutual savings banks, and credit unions.
5. Other financial organizations, including both "full-service" institutions as well as finance companies, mortgage companies, and real estate investment trusts.

PRIVATE PLACEMENT
Financing that occurs directly between a demander of funds and a supplier of funds, bypassing the public.

INVESTMENT BANKING FIRM
A firm that serves as a middleperson between the financial markets and the demanders of capital; specializes in underwriting and selling new securities.

Financial institutions provide a substantial portion of the funds available to corporations and other demanders of funds. Commercial banks have been the largest supplier of funds in recent years. Other financial institutions, such as insurance companies and pension funds, also supply funds to firms through the purchase of stocks and bonds in the financial markets. Firms may also approach a financial institution to make a **private placement**. If Bristol-Myers Squibb, for example, needs to raise additional funds, it might approach the New York State retirement system directly for private placement of a new issue of bonds. **Investment banking firms**, such as First Boston, Klienwort Benson, Morgan Stanley, Nomura Securities, and Paine Webber, also assist in bringing together suppliers and demanders of funds. The investment banking firm may purchase a new stock or bond issue from the firm and then immediately resell it to investors—the suppliers of funds. Investment banking firms provide financial expertise and marketing capabilities to firms needing funds. Without investment banking firms, the worldwide financial system would not operate as smoothly as it does.[1]

[1]Investment banking firms, and the raising of long-term funds, are discussed in Chapter 10.

Financial Markets

MONEY MARKET

Financial market in which funds are borrowed or lent for short periods of time (up to 1 year).

CAPITAL MARKET

Financial market in which long-term (longer than 1 year) financial assets such as bonds and stock are bought or sold.

PRIMARY MARKET

Market in which financial assets are originally sold, with the proceeds going to the issuing firm or governmental unit.

SECONDARY MARKET

Market for financial assets that have already been issued, including both the organized exchanges and the over-the-counter market.

ORGANIZED SECURITY EXCHANGES

Formal organizations that have a physical location and exist to bring together buyers and sellers of securities in the secondary market.

OVER-THE-COUNTER (OTC) MARKET

A market for securities in which buyers and sellers are brought together through computer and/or telecommunications facilities.

A financial market exists whenever a financial transaction takes place. There are two general types of financial markets: the money market and the capital market. The **money market** is the market for short-term (1 year or less) debt. Money market securities, as discussed in Chapter 16, include U.S. Treasury bills and certificates of deposit (that mature in 1 year or less). In contrast, the **capital market** is the market for long-term bonds or stocks. Included in the capital markets are (1) long-term government notes or bonds, (2) municipal bonds, (3) various forms of debt issued by firms, and (4) common and preferred stock issued by firms. The primary distinguishing feature of capital market securities is their life—they all have an anticipated life of longer than 1 year. They may range from a 5-year note, issued by the government or some business, to common stock, which has no maturity date.

All securities, when they are originally offered for sale—that is, when the proceeds of the sale go to the issuer of the securities—are issued in the **primary market.** (This applies to both money market and capital market securities.) By primary, we mean that the proceeds go to the issuer, which is typically a corporation or some government unit. After securities begin to trade between individuals and/or institutional investors, they become part of the **secondary market.** In the primary market the firm and its lead investment banking firm generally work together to set the price at which securities are issued. However, in the secondary market the original issuer has no part in the transaction. The secondary market exists to facilitate investor trading.

Transactions in the secondary market occur on both **organized security exchanges** and in the over-the-counter market. Among organized exchanges, the New York Stock Exchange, NYSE, is the largest secondary market for stocks in the world (in total dollar volume). (A few years ago the market value of stocks listed on the Tokyo Stock Exchange surpassed the market value of stocks listed on the NYSE. However, with the substantial decline in the value of Japanese stocks, the NYSE is again the largest stock exchange.) Approximately 1,500 common stocks and numerous preferred stocks are listed on the NYSE. It accounts for over 60 percent of the total dollar value of all stock outstanding in the United States. The next largest U.S. exchange is the American Stock Exchange, AMEX, which has more than 1,300 stocks listed. Information on the relative size of the secondary markets in the United States is provided in Table 2.1.

Other stocks are traded on various regional stock exchanges, or they may be unlisted on an organized exchange, in which case they trade in the **over-the-counter, OTC, market.** OTC is the term used to describe all buying and selling activity that does not take place on an organized exchange. The OTC market is made up of security dealers or brokers who, using an on-line computer network, interact to create a market for various securities. The total number of firms traded in the OTC market in the United States is around 10,000; however, many of those are not actively traded. In addition to the common stock of many smaller companies, most bonds are also traded in the OTC market. The one exception is that corporate bonds issued by large firms are sometimes traded on the New York exchange. In addition, large institutional investors often trade among themselves in what is called the "fourth market."[2]

The U.S. government regulates or supports many activities of the domestic financial system. The issuance of securities in the primary market, unless they are privately placed, is regulated by the Securities and Exchange Commission (see Chapter 10). The Comptroller of the Currency regulates certain aspects of banking, and the

---

[2] There is also a "third market"; it involves OTC trading of exchange-listed securities.

> ## TABLE 2.1
>
> ### Secondary Equity Markets in the United States
>
> NASDAQ, which stands for the National Association of Security Dealers Automated Quotation System, is used for trading in the over-the-counter, OTC, market. Trading on the New York Stock Exchange has been diminishing; although it is still the largest equity market in the United States, both the share and dollar volume in the over-the-counter market (NASDAQ) has gained substantial ground in recent years.
>
> | | Share Volume | | Dollar Volume | |
> |---|---|---|---|---|
> | | (in millions) | Percent | (in millions) | Percent |
> | New York Stock Exchange | 73,420 | 44.0% | $454,242 | 55.6% |
> | American Stock Exchange | 4,523 | 2.7 | 58,511 | 1.3 |
> | Regional Stock Exchanges | 7,859 | 4.7 | 225,806 | 5.1 |
> | NASDAQ | 74,353 | 44.5 | 1,449,301 | 32.8 |
> | NASDAQ/OTC trading in listed securities | 6,891 | 4.1 | 230,364 | 5.2 |
> | | 167,046 | 100.0% | $4,418,224 | 100.0% |

Source: *NASDAQ 1993 Fact Book,* NASDAQ, New York.

FEDERAL RESERVE SYSTEM
The central banking system in the United States.

Federal Reserve System (the Fed) plays a major role in shaping monetary policy. The Fed has at its disposal an array of tools that can influence the operations of commercial banks and, therefore, the entire financial system. A powerful Fed tool, and the one used least, is the power to change the reserve requirement (the percentage of deposits member banks must keep on reserve at the Fed).

Two other important Fed tools are the authority to change (1) its pattern of open-market operations and (2) the discount rate. Open-market operations are the purchases or sales of U.S. government bonds.[3] Through buying and selling these securities, the Fed can expand or shrink the amount of money in the public's hands. Likewise, by raising or lowering the discount rate (that is, the rate charged to commercial banks when they borrow at Federal Reserve banks), the Fed can affect the cost of funds and signal its intentions as economic conditions change. Use of all three of these tools can affect the availability and cost of funds provided through the financial system.

Options and futures markets also exist. These securities are sometimes called "derivatives" because they derive their value from some underlying security (like common stock) or other asset.

An example of monetary action occurred in 1994 when the Fed, in a series of steps, increased interest rates by almost 3 percent in an effort to control inflation. Increasingly, structural changes are making the Fed's job more difficult. The three primary structural changes conspiring against the Fed's efforts are: (1) the shrinking role of bank deposits as a percent of private nonfinancial debt, which reduces the impact of changing bank interest rates; (2) the growing role played by service industries, which are relatively insulated from changes in interest rates; and (3) the growing role played by global financial markets, and the role of U.S. exports, which are less

[3]Note that the U.S. Department of the Treasury is responsible for raising funds for the government by selling U.S. government bonds, notes, and bills. On the other hand, as part of its monetary policy the Fed often buys or sells outstanding government bonds.

sensitive to changes in domestic demand. In commenting on the Fed's 1994 efforts, one European banker noted: "Even if the one pair of brakes the Fed has hasn't seemed to be working that effectively, it's still the only pair of brakes they have. And they'll have to use them."

International Financial Markets

In addition to the domestic financial market, the financial marketplace is now worldwide. Large U.S. firms routinely issue bonds or secure short-term financing overseas. Some even list their stock on foreign stock exchanges. While many of the same forces are at work worldwide, there are two fundamental differences. First, the role of a single government, or governmental unit such as the Federal Reserve, is diminished since funds tend to flow fairly freely between many countries. Second, the value of a foreign currency relative to other currencies—called *exchange rates*—can and do change. As discussed later in this chapter, understanding exchange rates is important for financial managers who deal in almost any financial management transaction. The internationalization of the money and capital markets is a fundamental development affecting financial management.

Why Is the Financial System Important?

You may already see the need to know about financial institutions and markets. Here are some of the reasons:

1. The financial system provides an effective means of bringing together suppliers and demanders of funds. It enables firms that have excess funds, or firms that need funds, to make transactions quickly and cheaply.
2. The financial system includes the crucial secondary market. By facilitating the buying and selling of outstanding securities, an organized secondary market makes it easier for a firm to raise external debt or equity capital. This occurs because potential investors would be reluctant to buy securities if they thought they might be stuck with them forever. Only in industrialized countries with well-developed secondary markets are the financial markets efficient. Thus, only in countries where an extensive array of financial institutions and markets does the value of a firm's outstanding securities provide a good estimate of the value, or economic worth, of the firm.

Remember Key Idea 2—in developed countries, like the United States, financial markets are efficient.

3. The financial system changes rapidly, affording new opportunities. New institutions, securities, and markets appear every year. These allow astute firms to use new sources or securities for raising capital.
4. The value of the firm is determined in the financial markets. That value depends on the interaction of supply and demand in the financial marketplace—given the external business environment and management's strategies and policy decisions. The welfare of the firm and all of its stakeholders—its owners, creditors, employees, managers, and the community at large—rests directly on the value of the firm as determined in the financial markets.

CONCEPT REVIEW QUESTIONS

■ How do financial institutions aid the transfer of funds between suppliers and demanders?
■ How do primary and secondary markets differ?
■ Why are financial markets important to financial managers?

INTEREST RATES AND THE REQUIRED RATE OF RETURN

■ **LEARNING GOAL 2**

Determine the required returns for bonds and for stock, and explain how interest rates affect these returns.

In a market economy, funds or capital are allocated by means of the price system—that is, through the interaction of supply and demand. The cost of borrowing, or debt capital, is reflected in the interest rate paid by the firm; the cost of equity capital is a function of both cash dividends and the price of the stock. In this section, we seek to understand how interest rates, inflation, and risk interact.

Interest Rates

INTEREST
The rate paid on money that is borrowed or the rate received on money that is lent; usually stated as a percentage per year.

PRINCIPAL
The amount of money that must be repaid by a borrower or that is lent by a lender; the basis on which interest is figured.

The higher interest rates for longer periods of time indicates investors were expecting higher inflation in the future; a maturity premium—discussed subsequently—also accounts for some of the higher long-term rates.

COUPON INTEREST RATE
The stated rate a bond will pay.

BID PRICE
The amount security dealers would pay to buy a security issue.

ASKED PRICE
The amount for which security dealers would sell a security.

YIELD
The before-tax return for a lender or the cost of borrowing for a borrower.

Interest rates are the prices paid when an individual, firm, or government unit borrows funds. **Interest** is the cost incurred by demanders of funds when they use debt financing. From the supplier's standpoint, interest is the reward for loaning money. So, interest is both a cost and a revenue—depending on whether you are a demander or a supplier of funds.

Interest is generally stated on a percentage per year basis. If you borrow $1,000 (the **principal**) and agree to repay $1,070 (principal plus interest) in 1 year, you are paying 7 percent interest for the use of the funds ($1,000 × 1.07 = $1,070). Even if you borrow or lend for periods longer or shorter than 1 year, the interest is almost always stated on an annual basis.

To understand interest rates, let's begin by looking at Table 2.2 which indicates what it would cost the U.S. government to borrow—the interest rate—for different lengths of time as of July 15, 1994. *U.S. Treasury bonds* had a maturity of 10 years or more at the time of issue, *Treasury notes* had a maturity of less than 10 years when issued, and *Treasury bills* had a maturity of less than 1 year at the time of issue. For the bonds and notes the **coupon interest rate** (or stated rate the bond will pay) is given in the first column, followed by the maturity date. Then the bid and asked prices, along with the change from the previous day's quote, are given. For securities that trade in the over-the-counter market, the **bid price** represents what security dealers would pay to buy the issue; the **asked price** is what they would sell it for. From the standpoint of an investor, the asked price is what he or she would pay to acquire the issue, while the bid price is what they could sell it for. Finally, the yield, Ask.Yld., is given in the far right column in Table 2.2; the **yield**, or return, is the before-tax return for an investor in U.S. government securities, or the cost of borrowing for the U.S. government. For 6 months (to January 1995) the yield on Treasury bills was about 3.66 percent. Going out 1 year (to July

TABLE 2.2

Selected Prices and Yields for U.S. Treasury Securities as of July 15, 1994

U.S. Treasury bonds and notes pay interest every 6 months. Notes are indicated by the "n" after the maturity. Because bonds and notes are traded in 1/32s, a bid of 100:02 means the bid was 100 2/32 percent of par, or for a $1,000 par value note, the bid price was $1,000.625. Treasury bills do not pay interest directly; rather, they are issued at a discount from par and then are worth par at maturity.

(Continued)

TABLE 2.2

Selected Prices and Yields for U.S. Treasury Securities as of July 15, 1994 *(Continued)*

TREASURY BONDS, NOTES & BILLS

Friday, July 15, 1994

Representative Over-the-Counter quotations based on transactions of $1 million or more.

Treasury bond, note and bill quotes are as of mid-afternoon. Colons in bid-and-asked quotes represent 32nds; 101:01 means 101 1/32. Net changes in 32nds. n-Treasury note. Treasury bill quotes in hundredths, quoted on terms of a rate of discount. Days to maturity calculated from settlement date. All yields are to maturity and based on the asked quote. Latest 13-week and 26-week bills are boldfaced. For bonds callable prior to maturity, yields are computed to the earliest call date for issues quoted above par and to the maturity date for issues below par. *-When issued.

Source: Federal Reserve Bank of New York.

U.S. Treasury strips as of 3 p.m. Eastern time, also based on transactions of $1 million or more. Colons in bid-and-asked quotes represent 32nds; 101:01 means 101 1/32. Net changes in 32nds. Yields calculated on the asked quotation. ci-stripped coupon interest. bp-Treasury bond, stripped principal. np-Treasury note, stripped principal. For bonds callable prior to maturity, yields are computed to the earliest call date for issues quoted above par and to the maturity date for issues below par.

Source: Bear, Stearns & Co. via Street Software Technology Inc.

GOVT. BONDS & NOTES

Rate	Maturity Mo/Yr	Bid	Asked	Chg.	Ask Yld.
4 1/4	Jul 94n	99:31	100:01	....	3.24
6 7/8	Aug 94n	100:06	100:08	− 1	3.41
8 5/8	Aug 94n	100:10	100:12	− 2	3.46
8 3/4	Aug 94	100:10	100:12	− 1	3.58
12 5/8	Aug 94n	100:20	100:22	− 2	3.21
4 1/4	Aug 94n	100:00	100:02	....	3.65
4	Sep 94n	99:29	99:31	....	4.11
8 1/2	Sep 94n	100:26	100:28	− 1	3.98
9 1/2	Oct 94n	101:05	101:07	− 1	4.27
4 1/4	Oct 94n	99:29	99:31	+ 1	4.32
6	Nov 94n	100:12	100:14	....	4.58
8 1/4	Nov 94n	101:03	101:05	− 1	4.56
10 1/8	Nov 94	101:23	101:25	− 1	4.46
11 5/8	Nov 94n	102:06	102:08	− 1	4.47
4 5/8	Nov 94n	99:31	100:01	....	4.51
4 5/8	Dec 94n	99:28	99:30	+ 1	4.76
7 5/8	Dec 94n	101:05	101:07	− 1	4.83
8 5/8	Jan 95n	101:23	101:25	....	4.89
4 1/4	Jan 95n	99:20	99:22	....	4.85
3	Feb 95	97:21	98:21	− 10	5.40
5 1/2	Feb 95n	100:07	100:09	....	5.00
7 3/4	Feb 95n	101:16	101:18	....	4.96
10 1/2	Feb 95	103:03	103:05	− 1	4.87
11 1/4	Feb 95n	103:14	103:16	− 1	5.00
3 7/8	Feb 95n	99:08	99:10	+ 1	5.02
3 7/8	Mar 95n	99:03	99:05	....	5.12
8 3/8	Apr 95n	102:07	102:09	....	5.20
3 7/8	Apr 95n	98:29	98:31	....	5.23
5 7/8	May 95n	100:13	100:15	+ 1	5.29
8 1/2	May 95n	102:16	102:18	....	5.28
10 3/8	May 95	104:03	104:05	− 1	5.16
11 1/4	May 95n	104:24	104:26	− 1	5.21
12 5/8	May 95	106:02	106:06	....	4.88
4 1/8	May 95n	98:31	99:01	....	5.28
4 1/8	Jun 95n	98:27	98:29	+ 1	5.32
8 7/8	Jul 95n	103:09	103:11	− 1	5.36
4 1/4	Jul 95n	98:25	98:27	....	5.42
4 5/8	Aug 95n	99:03	99:05	....	5.44
8 1/2	Aug 95n	103:03	103:05	....	5.44
10 1/2	Aug 95n	105:07	105:09	− 1	5.38
3 7/8	Aug 95n	98:08	98:10	+ 1	5.45
3 7/8	Sep 95n	98:02	98:04	+ 1	5.51
8 5/8	Oct 95n	103:18	103:20	....	5.56
3 7/8	Oct 95n	97:27	97:29	+ 1	5.59
5 1/8	Nov 95n	99:10	99:12	+ 1	5.62
8 1/2	Nov 95n	103:17	103:19	....	5.65
9 1/2	Nov 95n	104:27	104:29	− 1	5.61
11 1/2	Nov 95	107:13	107:17	− 1	5.53
4 1/4	Nov 95n	98:04	98:06	+ 1	5.65
4 1/4	Dec 95n	97:29	97:31	+ 1	5.73
9 1/4	Jan 96n	104:29	104:31	+ 1	5.72
4	Jan 96n	97:13	97:15	....	5.75
7 1/2	Jan 96n	102:15	102:17	+ 1	5.75
4 5/8	Feb 96n	98:05	98:07	....	5.82
7 7/8	Feb 96n	103:00	103:02	+ 3	5.81
8 7/8	Feb 96n	104:16	104:18	....	5.80
4 5/8	Feb 96n	98:04	98:06	+ 1	5.81
7 1/2	Feb 96n	102:15	102:17	....	5.84
5 1/8	Mar 96n	98:23	98:25	+ 1	5.89
7 3/4	Mar 96n	102:29	102:31	+ 1	5.89
9 3/8	Apr 96n	105:19	105:21	+ 1	5.91
5 1/2	Apr 96n	99:07	99:09	+ 1	5.93
7 5/8	Apr 96n	102:26	102:28	+ 3	5.90
4 1/4	May 96n	97:02	97:04	+ 2	5.94
7 3/8	May 96n	102:12	102:14	....	5.95
5 7/8	May 96n	99:24	99:26	....	5.98
7 5/8	May 96n	102:27	102:29	+ 2	5.96
6	Jun 96n	99:31	100:01	+ 1	5.98
7 7/8	Jun 96n	103:13	103:15	+ 1	5.96
7 7/8	Jul 96n	103:12	103:14	+ 1	6.02
7 7/8	Jul 96n	103:14	103:16	+ 2	6.02
4 3/8	Aug 96n	96:24	96:26	+ 2	6.03
7 1/4	Aug 96n	102:07	102:09	+ 2	6.09
7	Sep 96n	101:25	101:27	+ 2	6.09
8	Oct 96n	103:25	103:27	+ 1	6.14
6 7/8	Oct 96n	101:14	101:16	+ 1	6.16
4 3/8	Nov 96n	96:04	96:06	+ 2	6.16
7 1/4	Nov 96n	102:07	102:09	+ 1	6.18
6 1/2	Nov 96n	100:20	100:22	+ 2	6.18
6 1/8	Dec 96n	99:28	99:30	+ 1	6.15
8	Jan 97n	103:30	104:00	....	6.24
6 1/4	Jan 97n	100:00	100:02	+ 2	6.22
4 3/4	Feb 97n	96:13	96:15	+ 1	6.26
6 3/4	Feb 97n	101:02	101:04	+ 1	6.28
6 7/8	Mar 97n	101:11	101:13	+ 1	6.30
8 1/2	Apr 97n	105:10	105:12	+ 1	6.33
6 7/8	Apr 97n	101:10	101:12	+ 1	6.33
6 1/2	May 97n	100:11	100:13	+ 1	6.34
8 1/2	May 97n	105:13	105:15	+ 1	6.35
6 3/4	May 97n	100:31	101:01	+ 1	6.35
6 3/8	Jun 97n	100:03	100:05	+ 1	6.32
8 1/2	Jul 97n	105:20	105:22	+ 1	6.38
5 1/2	Jul 97n	97:17	97:19	+ 1	6.39
8 5/8	Aug 97n	105:31	106:01	....	6.43
5 5/8	Aug 97n	97:22	97:24	+ 2	6.43
5 1/2	Sep 97n	97:08	97:10	+ 1	6.44
8 3/4	Oct 97n	106:17	106:19	+ 2	6.46
5 3/4	Oct 97n	97:26	97:28	+ 1	6.48
8 7/8	Nov 97n	106:31	107:01	+ 1	6.49
6	Nov 97n	98:15	98:17	+ 2	6.49
6	Dec 97n	98:12	98:14	+ 1	6.51
7 7/8	Jan 98n	104:02	104:04	+ 1	6.53
5 5/8	Jan 98n	97:02	97:04	....	6.55
8 1/8	Feb 98n	104:28	104:30	....	6.55
5 1/8	Feb 98n	95:12	95:14	+ 1	6.56
5 1/8	Mar 98n	95:07	95:09	+ 1	6.58
7 7/8	Apr 98n	104:05	104:07	+ 1	6.58
5 1/8	Apr 98n	95:02	95:04	+ 1	6.60
9	May 98n	107:28	107:30	+ 1	6.62
5 3/8	May 98n	95:23	95:25	+ 1	6.63
5 1/8	Jun 98n	94:23	94:25	+ 1	6.65
8 1/4	Jul 98n	105:14	105:16	....	6.66
5 1/4	Jul 98n	95:00	95:02	+ 1	6.67
9 1/4	Aug 98n	109:00	109:02	....	6.67
4 3/4	Aug 98n	93:03	93:05	+ 1	6.68
4 3/4	Sep 98n	92:30	93:00	+ 1	6.69
7 1/8	Oct 98n	101:15	101:17	+ 1	6.70
4 3/4	Oct 98n	92:23	92:25	....	6.72
3 1/2	Nov 98	91:22	92:22	+ 1	5.42
8 7/8	Nov 98n	107:29	107:31	+ 1	6.72
5 1/8	Nov 98n	93:29	93:31	....	6.74
5 1/8	Dec 98n	93:25	93:27	....	6.75
6 3/8	Jan 99n	98:17	98:19	+ 2	6.74
5	Jan 99n	93:05	93:07	....	6.76
8 7/8	Feb 99n	108:05	108:07	+ 2	6.76
5 1/2	Feb 99n	95:02	95:04	+ 1	6.75
5 7/8	Mar 99n	96:11	96:13	+ 1	6.78
7	Apr 99n	100:25	100:27	+ 1	6.79
6 1/2	Apr 99n	98:24	98:26	+ 1	6.79
9 1/8	May 99n	109:13	109:15	+ 1	6.79
6 3/4	May 99n	99:21	99:23	+ 1	6.82
6 3/4	Jun 99n	99:21	99:23	+ 1	6.82
6 3/8	Jul 99n	98:02	98:04	....	6.82
8	Aug 99n	104:30	105:00	....	6.82
6	Oct 99n	96:07	96:09	....	6.86
7 7/8	Nov 99n	104:13	104:15	....	6.86
6 3/8	Jan 00n	97:21	97:23	+ 1	6.88
7 7/8	Feb 95-00	101:10	101:14	+ 3	5.31
8 1/2	Feb 00n	107:11	107:13	+ 2	6.88
5 1/2	Apr 00n	93:17	93:19	+ 1	6.87
8 7/8	May 00n	109:10	109:12	− 3	6.89
8 3/8	Aug 95-00	102:18	102:22	− 6	5.76
8 3/4	Aug 00n	108:24	108:26	− 1	6.95
8 1/2	Nov 00n	107:20	107:22	− 2	6.98
7 3/4	Feb 01n	103:27	103:29	− 1	7.00
11 3/4	Feb 01	124:29	125:01	+ 1	6.94
8	May 01n	105:05	105:07	− 2	7.02
13 1/8	May 01	132:29	133:01	+ 2	6.96
7 7/8	Aug 01n	104:14	104:16	....	7.06
8	Aug 96-01	102:25	102:29	+ 7	6.48
13 3/8	Aug 01	135:00	135:04	+ 2	7.00
7 1/2	Nov 01n	102:08	102:10	− 1	7.09
15 3/4	Nov 01	149:12	149:16	+ 4	7.00
14 1/4	Feb 02	141:24	141:28	− 4	7.03
7 1/2	May 02n	102:06	102:08	....	7.12
6 3/8	Aug 02n	95:05	95:07	+ 1	7.17
11 5/8	Nov 02	127:20	127:24	....	7.15
6 1/4	Feb 03n	93:29	93:31	+ 1	7.21
10 3/4	Feb 03	122:13	122:17	....	7.19
10 3/4	May 03	122:22	122:26	....	7.21
5 3/4	Aug 03n	90:04	90:06	+ 1	7.24
11 1/8	Aug 03	125:15	125:19	....	7.23
11 7/8	Nov 03	130:27	130:31	....	7.25
5 7/8	Feb 04n	90:19	90:21	....	7.24
7 1/4	May 04n	100:02	100:04	....	7.23
12 3/8	May 04	135:08	135:12	− 2	7.27
13 3/4	Aug 04	145:15	145:19	+ 1	7.28
11 5/8	Nov 04	130:26	130:30	....	7.31
8 1/4	May 00-05	104:21	104:25	+ 6	7.23
12	May 05	134:08	134:12	+ 3	7.34
10 3/4	Aug 05	125:12	125:16	+ 1	7.35
9 3/8	Feb 06	115:17	115:21	+ 2	7.34
7 5/8	Feb 02-07	100:18	100:22	+ 2	7.50
7 7/8	Nov 02-07	102:03	102:07	+ 2	7.51
8 3/8	Aug 03-08	105:19	105:23	....	7.50
8 3/4	Nov 03-08	108:08	108:12	− 2	7.49
9 1/8	May 04-09	111:10	111:14	+ 2	7.46
10 3/8	Nov 04-09	120:25	120:29	− 1	7.44
11 3/4	Feb 05-10	131:03	131:07	− 1	7.44
10	May 05-10	118:21	118:25	+ 1	7.44
12 3/4	Nov 05-10	139:30	140:02	+ 2	7.45
13 7/8	May 06-11	149:27	149:31	+ 2	7.45
14	Nov 06-11	151:29	152:01	− 1	7.47
10 3/8	Nov 07-12	123:11	123:15	+ 1	7.55
12	Aug 08-13	138:02	138:06	+ 1	7.55
13 1/4	May 09-14	150:04	150:08	− 1	7.56
12 1/2	Aug 09-14	143:24	143:28	− 1	7.57
11 3/4	Nov 09-14	137:17	137:21	− 3	7.56
11 1/4	Feb 15	137:03	137:05	− 5	7.64
10 5/8	Aug 15	130:28	130:30	+ 28	7.65
9 7/8	Nov 15	123:05	123:07	− 2	7.65
9 1/4	Feb 16	116:21	116:23	− 4	7.65
7 1/4	May 16	95:24	95:26	− 3	7.65
7 1/2	Nov 16	98:09	98:11	− 2	7.66
8 3/4	May 17	111:17	111:19	− 3	7.67
8 7/8	Aug 17	112:29	112:31	− 4	7.67
9 1/8	May 18	115:25	115:27	− 2	7.67
9	Nov 18	114:17	114:19	− 1	7.67
8 7/8	Feb 19	113:07	113:09	....	7.67
8 1/8	Aug 19	105:01	105:03	− 1	7.66
8 1/2	Feb 20	109:10	109:12	− 2	7.66
8 3/4	May 20	112:05	112:07	− 2	7.66
8 3/4	Aug 20	112:07	112:09	− 2	7.66
7 7/8	Feb 21	102:15	102:17	− 3	7.65
8 1/8	May 21	105:14	105:16	− 2	7.64
8 1/8	Aug 21	105:19	105:21	− 2	7.63
8	Nov 21	104:09	104:11	− 4	7.62
7 1/4	Aug 22	95:29	95:31	− 3	7.60
7 5/8	Nov 22	100:10	100:12	− 2	7.59
7 1/8	Feb 23	94:20	94:22	− 1	7.58
6 1/4	Aug 23	84:26	84:28	− 2	7.54

TREASURY BILLS

Maturity	Days to Mat.	Bid	Asked	Chg.	Ask Yld.
Jul 21 '94	2	3.61	3.51	+0.26	3.56
Jul 28 '94	9	3.85	3.75	+0.07	3.81
Aug 04 '94	16	3.87	3.77	+0.01	3.83
Aug 11 '94	23	3.87	3.77	−0.01	3.83
Aug 18 '94	30	3.84	3.80	+0.01	3.87
Aug 25 '94	37	3.99	3.95	....	4.02
Sep 01 '94	44	4.00	3.96	−0.02	4.03
Sep 08 '94	51	4.02	3.98	−0.03	4.06
Sep 15 '94	58	4.03	3.99	−0.02	4.07
Sep 22 '94	65	4.18	4.16	−0.05	4.25
Sep 29 '94	72	4.07	4.05	−0.02	4.14
Oct 06 '94	79	4.22	4.20	−0.02	4.30
Oct 13 '94	**86**	**4.26**	**4.24**	**−0.04**	**4.34**
Oct 20 '94	93	4.32	4.30	−0.05	4.41
Oct 27 '94	100	4.34	4.32	−0.03	4.43
Nov 03 '94	107	4.41	4.39	−0.03	4.51
Nov 10 '94	114	4.45	4.43	−0.03	4.56
Nov 17 '94	121	4.47	4.45	−0.03	4.58
Nov 25 '94	129	4.49	4.47	−0.04	4.61
Dec 01 '94	135	4.52	4.50	−0.03	4.64
Dec 08 '94	142	4.54	4.52	−0.02	4.67
Dec 15 '94	149	4.53	4.51	−0.04	4.66
Dec 22 '94	156	4.57	4.55	−0.03	4.71
Dec 29 '94	163	4.56	4.54	−0.02	4.70
Jan 05 '95	170	4.62	4.60	−0.03	4.77
Jan 12 '95	**177**	**4.68**	**4.66**	**−0.01**	**4.84**
Feb 09 '95	205	4.78	4.76	−0.01	4.95
Mar 09 '95	233	4.85	4.83	−0.01	5.03
Apr 06 '95	261	4.93	4.91	−0.01	5.12
May 04 '95	289	5.02	5.00	−0.02	5.23
Jun 01 '95	317	5.05	5.03	−0.02	5.28
Jun 29 '95	345	5.07	5.05	−0.01	5.31

Source: Table, "Selection from Quotes of Treasury Bonds, Notes & Bills," *The Wall Street Journal* July 18, 1994, p. C18. Reprinted by permission of The Wall Street Journal, ©1994 Dow Jones & Company, Inc. All Rights Reserved Worldwide.

1995), 2 years (to July 1996), and so on, we see that the yields, or interest rates, are as follows:

Time Period	Maturity Date	Approximate Interest Rate
6 months	January 1995	3.66%
1 year	July 1995	5.39
2 years	July 1996	6.02
3 years	July 1997	6.38
4 years	July 1998	6.66
5 years	July 1999	6.82
7 years	August 2001	7.03
10 years	August 2004	7.28
20.5 years	February 2015	7.64

YIELD CURVE

A plot of the relationship between yield to maturity and length to maturity for equally risky bonds.

TERM STRUCTURE

The relationship between the yield to maturity and the length to maturity for bonds that are equally risky.

The interest rates for U.S. Treasury securities as of July 1994 are plotted in Figure 2.2. The line is called a **yield curve,** and the graph depicts the **term structure** of interest rates *for a given risk class of securities*. Thus, a yield curve shows the relationship between the term (or length to maturity) and the yield (return or cost). The risk class we are examining is Treasury securities; a similar but higher-yield curve exists for various classes of corporate debt, which have more risk than debt instruments issued by the U.S. government. An *upward-sloping* yield curve, like that in July 1994, indicates higher inflation expected in the future. Alternatively, if inflation was expected to be lower in the future, the term structure of interest rates would be *downward-sloping*. Here are some observations concerning yield curves:

1. They fluctuate depending on the general supply and demand for funds.
2. Their shape changes from downward-sloping, to being flat, to upward-sloping, *depending on the future rate of inflation expected by investors.*
3. The yield curve tends to be upward-sloping during economic expansions and either flat or downward-sloping during economic recessions.
4. Yield curves for firms will be above those of the government. *The more risky the firm is perceived to be, the higher the yield curve.*
5. Yield curves are for a given point in time, and they may change tomorrow, next week, or next month as interest rates throughout the economy change.

FIGURE 2.2

The Term Structure of Interest Rates as of July 1994

An upward-sloping yield curve occurs when inflation is expected to increase. Alternatively, if inflation is expected to decrease in the future, the yield curve would be downward-sloping.

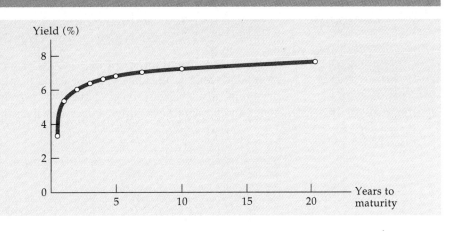

RISK-FREE RATE, k_{RF}
The interest rate on assets that are viewed as being free of any risk premium; equals the real rate of interest plus an inflation premium.

INFLATION
A condition in which the price level increases rapidly.

TREASURY BILLS
Short-term securities issued by the U.S. government; often used as a proxy for the risk-free rate.

Remember Key Idea 6—risk and return go hand-in-hand.

RISK PREMIUM
Extra amount of return required in the face of risk or uncertainty.

MATURITY PREMIUM
Additional return required on longer-term bonds to compensate investors for the greater price fluctuation as market interest rates change.

DEFAULT PREMIUM
Additional return required to compensate investors for the risk that the bond issuer will not make interest payments or repay the principal on schedule, or that the firm issuing stock will fail.

We have just seen that the federal government's cost of borrowing in July 1994 was higher if it borrowed for longer periods of time. But what factors determine the cost that the government, or any borrower, pays? Or, looked at from the other side of the transaction, what determines the return earned by investors when they lend money? To answer those questions, we need to think about the idea of risk—the uncertainty of a particular outcome. As we saw in Chapter 1, the greater the risk of an investment or loan, the greater the return that is required to compensate the investor or lender. *In the absence of risk, the interest or discount rate required to satisfy borrowers and lenders is the* **risk-free rate, k_{RF}.** The nominal (or observed) risk-free rate is equal to the real risk-free rate, plus the expected inflation.[4] As a "rough" approximation, we can think of the risk-free rate as compensating investors for expected changes in inflation, where **inflation** refers to a change in purchasing power as reflected by changes in the price level. That is, the risk-free rate compensates suppliers of funds for expected inflation, but not for the risk of any other loss such as failure to repay the loaned funds. The best proxy we have for the risk-free rate, k_{RF}, is short-term government borrowings called **Treasury bills,** which typically mature in 90 or 180 days. The following data show the actual return from investing in U.S. Treasury bills, along with changes in the rate of inflation, for different time periods:[5]

Time Period	Treasury Bills	Inflation
1926–1994	3.7%	3.2%
1960–1994	6.1	4.8
1970–1994	7.0	5.7
1980–1994	7.5	4.6

The data show that investing in Treasury bills has provided returns that have been greater than inflation. They also support an important point: *On average, the return on short-term Treasury securities compensates investors slightly better than changes in the rate of inflation.* Although short-term Treasury securities are safe, investors won't get rich investing in them. The returns on Treasury bills, on average, have kept slightly ahead of changes in the rate of inflation.

When the world is uncertain, a greater return is required. For example, the return required on a bond, k_b, is equal to the risk-free rate, k_{RF}, plus a **risk premium** to compensate for additional risk, so that:

$$\text{required return on a bond, } k_b = k_{RF} + \text{risk premium} \tag{2.1}$$

We may think of the risk premium demanded by investors in bonds issued by firms as being composed of:

$$\text{bond risk premium} = \frac{\text{maturity}}{\text{premium}} + \frac{\text{default}}{\text{premium}} + \frac{\text{liquidity}}{\text{premium}} + \frac{\text{other}}{\text{premiums}} \tag{2.2}$$

The **maturity premium** arises because, as general interest rates change, longer-term bonds tend to fluctuate more in value than shorter-term bonds. The **default premium** arises because bonds issued by firms are more risky than government bonds and because firms differ in terms of their financial condition and likelihood

---

[4] *The* Fisher effect *says that the nominal, or observed, risk-free interest rate ≈ the real rate of interest, plus the expected inflation. The real rate of interest, which is unobservable, is the rate in the absence of inflation. This rate is estimated to be in the neighborhood of 2 to 3 percent. In recent years, the data indicate that the real rate has been in that vicinity.*

[5] *Adapted from* Stocks, Bonds, Bills, and Inflation 1995 Yearbook™, *Ibbotson Associates, Chicago.*

LIQUIDITY PREMIUM
Additional return required to compensate investors for investing in less-liquid bonds or stocks.

of failing. The **liquidity premium** arises because investors in securities that are harder to sell, or less liquid, incur more transactions costs; they therefore demand additional compensation. Finally, individual bonds may contain many other features. Some are more or less attractive to investors; hence, different features result in other premiums.[6]

Putting this all together, the return required by bond investors—which is the same as the cost to the bond issuers—is a function of the risk-free rate and premiums related to maturity, default, liquidity, and other characteristics of the bond.

Bonds Issued by the Government

For the moment, let's go back and reconsider the long-term bonds issued by the U.S. government from Table 2.2. In this case we can ignore the last three types of premiums and say that:

$$k_{\text{long-term Treasury securities}} = k_{RF} + \text{maturity premium} \qquad (2.3)$$

Let's consider the two primary determinants of the return demanded by investors from long-term Treasury securities—expected inflation and the maturity premium.

Expected Inflation

U.S. Treasury bonds are backed by the government's power to create money. Thus they have virtually no default risk, and they carry lower interest rates than equivalent-maturity corporate bonds. However, like all bonds, they do have substantial inflation risk. In July 1994 the yield on long-term government bonds was about 7.5 percent, while the yield on long-term corporate bonds ranged from 8 to 11 percent, depending on the riskiness of the bonds.

MARKET RATE OF INTEREST
Current interest rate generally demanded by the market for securities of similar quality and maturity.

Assume the government issues a 25-year bond that will pay interest of $70 per $1,000 bond per year; that is, they will pay 7 percent per year for the privilege of borrowing your money. At the time the bond is issued, all investors hold expectations as to future inflation. Suppose that after the bond is issued, due to changes in either worldwide or domestic economic conditions, expected inflation suddenly and unexpectedly jumps by 4 percent. Other things being equal, this jump will cause the **market rate of interest**, that is, the current rate for bonds of similar risk and maturity, to increase from 7 to 11 percent. This change in market interest rates will also cause the required rate of return demanded by investors on *all outstanding bonds of similar quality and maturity* to increase—again, to 11 percent. This occurs because investors considering the 7 percent coupon rate bond will not be willing to settle for less than they can receive in newly issued securities of comparable quality but with a higher coupon rate. The only way to receive an 11 percent return when the stated coupon interest rate is 7 percent is for the bond to sell at a substantial discount from its par, or stated, value of $1,000.

Remember, for bonds, as yield goes up price goes down, and vice versa.

A fundamental point to remember about the pricing of bonds (as discussed further in Chapter 4) is this: *The price of a bond and general market interest rates move inversely.* If the general market interest rate is more than a bond's coupon rate, the bond will sell *at a discount*; that is, it will be worth less than its $1,000 par value. If general market interest rates are less than the coupon rate on a bond, the bond will sell *at a premium*; that is, it will be worth more than its $1,000 par value. A second point

---

[6]*Bond valuation and other features of bonds are discussed in Chapters 4 and 11.*

to remember, as discussed previously, is: *The primary determinant of market interest rates is expected inflation.*

Interest Rate Risk and the Maturity Premium

INTEREST RATE RISK
Change in market price of a bond as general interest rates change.

Bond prices are influenced not only by the general market interest rates (influenced by inflation) but also by the term (or length) to maturity of the bonds. This is exactly what we saw when we examined the relationship between the interest rate on U.S. Treasury bonds of different lengths to maturity in Figure 2.2. When general interest rates change, the prices on short-term bonds fluctuate less in response to market interest rate changes than do the prices on long-term bonds; this is called **interest rate risk**. It is because of interest rate risk that the return on long-term bonds typically incorporates a maturity premium (or requires a higher interest rate) over comparable short-term bonds.[7]

Bonds Issued by Firms

Up to now, we have discussed the relationship between the prices on U.S. Treasury bonds, the returns required by investors, expected inflation, bond maturity, and bond prices. Corporate bonds are subject to additional risks arising from the possibility of default, liquidity, or "other" features. One impact of these other risks is to increase the whole structure of interest rates for corporate bonds versus U.S. Treasury bonds. That is, investors demand a higher return to compensate them for the additional risks of investing in corporate bonds. Because investors demand more return, the cost to the firm for issuing bonds is higher than the cost to the government.

How might various factors affect the value of a firm's bonds? Consider what happens if Warehouse SuperStores is close to bankruptcy and files for protection under the federal bankruptcy laws. What will happen to Warehouse SuperStores's outstanding bonds? Because the risk of loss due to default is high, the required rate of return demanded by investors increases, leading to lower market prices for the outstanding bonds. The same effect occurs if the bond is not very liquid (i.e., if there is a "thin market" with few potential buyers). Similarly, if the bond differs in terms of some of its features, it may be seen as either more risky or less desirable than other bonds of comparable maturity. The result is higher returns demanded by investors, which translates into higher costs when firms issue new bonds with these features.

REINVESTMENT RATE RISK
Risk that arises when a bond is called or matures and investors have to reinvest at a lower coupon interest rate.

Two other sources of risk exist for corporate bonds. One is **reinvestment rate risk**, which is the risk that an investor's income may fall if there is a need to reinvest in another bond issue. Suppose you purchased a bond a few years ago that had a 13 percent coupon rate. Due the changes in economic conditions, bonds of comparable maturity and risk now provide a 9 percent return. If your bond matures, or is called by the issuing firm, and you reinvest in a new 9 percent bond, you will now receive only $90 per year; in other words, you have lost $130 − $90 = $40 in interest per year.

EVENT RISK
Risk caused by a drastic, unexpected increase in a firm's debt that causes the market price of its outstanding bonds to fall.

Another source of risk is **event risk**, where a drastic change in circumstances turns a "safe" bond into a "risky" one. This type of risk can be illustrated by looking at the leveraged buyout of RJR Nabisco that occurred in 1989. Before the buyout, RJR Nabisco had about $5 billion in bonds outstanding. To fund the leveraged buyout, another $16 billion in borrowing took place. Overnight, the possibility of default went up, and investors demanded a higher return to compensate for the increased risk. The

---

[7] *Various theories of the term structure of interest rates are discussed in Appendix 3A of* Financial Management.

FIGURE 2.3

The Price of an RJR Nabisco Bond Around the Time the Firm Was Privatized

The prices are as of the end of the month for the 8⅝ percent coupon rate subordinated debenture that matures in 2017. Prices on bonds are quoted as a percent of their par value, which is usually $1,000.

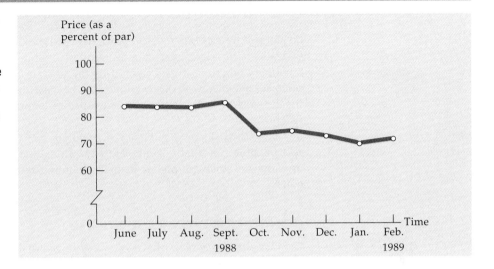

market value of already-outstanding RJR Nabisco bonds dropped about 15 percent almost overnight. In Figure 2.3 the month-end market price for one specific RJR Nabisco bond is shown. If you owned $100,000 of this RJR bond, it was worth $85,250 [i.e., ($100,000)(0.8525)] at the end of September 1988, but only $69,750 [($100,000)(0.6975)] by the end of January 1989. This is an example of a completely new kind of risk that most bondholders are not protected against. It also involves *risk shifting*, where part of the potential value created by the leveraged buyout was, in fact, due to the shift in risk from owners to bondholders.

Many factors can affect bond prices. The key point to remember is that as risk increases, market price decreases, and vice versa. Higher risk leads to higher returns demanded by investors and higher costs to the firm.

Common Stock Issued by Firms

The same general ideas from our discussion of bond prices and returns also apply for stock prices. If financial markets are efficient, then the actual market price of a share of common stock is a direct function of the cash flows expected, the time value of money, the risks involved, and the returns required by investors. Like investors in bonds, the return demanded by common stock investors, k_s, is equal to the risk-free rate plus a risk premium, or:

$$\text{required return on a stock, } k_s = k_{RF} + \text{risk premium} \qquad (2.4)$$

We can think of the risk premium demanded by common stock investors as being composed of

$$\text{stock risk premium} = \frac{\text{default}}{\text{premium}} + \frac{\text{liquidity}}{\text{premium}} + \frac{\text{other}}{\text{premiums}} \qquad (2.5)$$

How do the various premiums that apply to bonds affect the required return for stocks? The maturity premium that bond investors demand is not relevant when considering common stock because common stock has an infinite life. Common stock investors have a residual (or the last) claim on the firm; that is, the government and creditors have a prior claim that must be met before anything can be distributed to common stockholders. Therefore, the size of the default premium demanded by common stock investors will be larger than that demanded by investors in the same firm's bonds. Similarly, common stock investors will demand a liquidity premium if they cannot sell the stock or if when they do sell, the market price has a tendency to drop significantly because there is a small, or "thin," market for the stock. Finally, other characteristics of common stock may also affect their risk.[8]

Due to the risks involved, the risk premium on stocks is typically higher than the risk premium on bonds. With rare exceptions, the required return demanded for investing in stocks is higher than the required return demanded for investing in bonds.

CONCEPT REVIEW QUESTIONS

■ In the absence of risk, what determines the return demanded on a bond? How about when risk is considered?
■ How do risk factors for common stock differ from risk factors for bonds?

RETURNS AND RISK

■ **LEARNING GOAL 3**

Know how returns are measured, and understand the relationship between risk and return of financial assets.

Now that we understand something about what determines the returns demanded by investors (and, hence, the costs to the firm of raising capital by borrowing or issuing stock), let's take a look at returns and risk. We'll define how returns are measured and then examine returns and risk from investing in various financial market securities.

Expected Versus Realized Returns

RETURN
The sum of cash dividends and interest plus any capital appreciation or loss in the value of the financial asset.

The **return** from investing in any financial asset comes from one of two sources: (1) income from interest, dividends, and so forth; and (2) capital gains or losses—that is, the difference between the asset's beginning and ending market values. For common stocks these returns are cash dividends received during the period, and capital appreciation or loss. For any period (e.g., month, year) we can define the return, k, on a stock as

$$\text{return, } k = \frac{D_1 + (P_1 - P_0)}{P_0} \qquad (2.6)$$

where

D_1 = cash dividends at time 1

P_1 = the market price at time 1

P_0 = the market price today, at time 0

[8]*Some other features, such as different classes of stock, are discussed in Chapter 10.*

If a firm expects to pay cash dividends of $3.50 per share one year from now at time $t = 1$, the market price today is $40, and the expected price at time $t = 1$ is $42, then the return is

$$k = \frac{\$3.50 + (\$42 - \$40)}{\$40} = \frac{\$5.50}{\$40} = 0.1375 = 13.75\%$$

In the example, this is an *ex ante* (expected or required) rate of return; it is what investors anticipate receiving *before* the fact. Their *ex post* (realized) rate of return over the period (calculated using Equation 2.6, but with historical data) may differ from the expected return if cash dividends are more or less than the expected $3.50, or if the ending market price is different from the $42 projected. While the *ex ante* (expected) return is always positive, the *ex post* (realized) return is not. Suppose we expect a 13.75 percent return, but the actual market price of the stock at the end of the year was only $35. The *ex post* (realized) return was only

$$k = \frac{\$3.50 + (\$35 - \$40)}{\$40} = \frac{-\$1.50}{\$40} = -0.0375 = -3.75\%$$

In this case, although we expected a positive return before the fact (otherwise we never would have made the investment), we ended up losing money.

You don't have to sell a stock (or other asset) to have a positive or negative return.

Returns from bonds or from any other financial asset can be computed in exactly the same way, using appropriately specified values in Equation 2.6. In practice, we can measure returns over any time period, but a year is typical. Also, note that we can calculate realized returns *whether or not we actually sell the financial asset*. To illustrate this, suppose an investor purchased a stock and plans to hold it for 3 years. If the actual cash dividend received at the end of the first year was $3.50 and the actual ending market price was $42, then the return over the first year was 13.75 percent—whether or not the investor actually sold the security. For the second year $42 represents the initial price; any capital gain or loss for the year is measured against the $42 figure. This process is repeated over and over again, and a series of realized, or *ex post*, returns exists as long as the stock is owned by the investor.

Returns and Risk for Financial Assets

Key Idea 6 again—risk and return go hand-in-hand.

We will explore the topic of returns and risk in detail in Chapter 5; here, it is important to establish the fundamental relationship. The relationship between returns and risk is also the relationship between risk and cost to the issuer. Looking at it from the investor's viewpoint, if you expose yourself to more risk, you require a higher return. *Higher returns demanded by investors have to come from somewhere: They come from the higher costs of raising capital borne by the firm.*

To understand more about returns and risk, let's examine realized returns for the 1960–1994 period. Figure 2.4 shows the growth of a dollar invested in common stocks in general, small-company common stocks, and long-term corporate bonds. All results assume reinvestment of dividends or interest, and no taxes. Each of the indexes is initiated at $1.00 at the beginning of 1960. Figure 2.4 shows that the return from small-company stocks over this time period was far greater than from the other securities shown. If $1.00 had been invested in small-company stocks at the beginning of 1960, it would have grown to $95.38 by the end of 1994. Likewise, for common stocks, $1.00 would have grown to $28.62, while a dollar invested in long-term corporate bonds would have

FIGURE 2.4

Return Indices, 1960–1994

The vertical scale is logarithmic; equal distances represent equal percentage changes any place along the scale. Small-company stocks were the big winners over this time period.

Source: *Stocks, Bonds, Bills, and Inflation 1995 Yearbook™*, Ibbotson Associates, Chicago (annually updated work by Roger G. Ibbotson and Rex A. Sinquefield). Used with permission. All rights reserved.

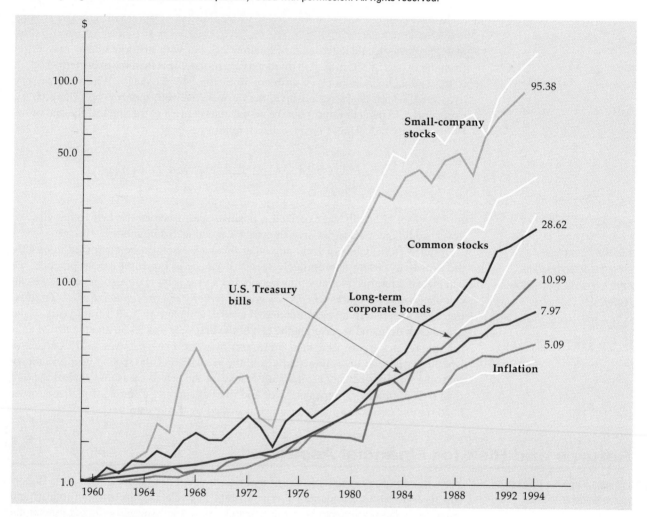

grown to only $10.99. Finally, $1.00 invested in risk-free U.S. Treasury bills would have grown to only $7.67. For comparison, inflation is also graphed. What we purchased for $1.00 at the beginning of 1960 required an expenditure of $5.09 by the end of 1994. While all three long-term securities outperformed inflation, small-company common stocks were the big winner over this time period.

This return is not without substantial risk, however. In Figure 2.5, the annual percentage realized returns for common stocks, small-company stocks, and corporate bonds are presented. Note that the variability of returns for small-company stocks is much greater than for common stocks in general. Likewise, the variability of returns for long-term corporate bonds is less than for common stocks. Finally, though not

FIGURE 2.5

Histograms of Annual Percentage Returns, 1960–1994

Common stocks, especially small-company stocks, exhibit much more volatility in their returns than do bonds.

Source: *Stocks, Bonds, Bills, and Inflation 1995 Yearbook*™, Ibbotson Associates, Chicago (annually updated work by Roger G. Ibbotson and Rex A. Sinquefield). Used with permission. All rights reserved.

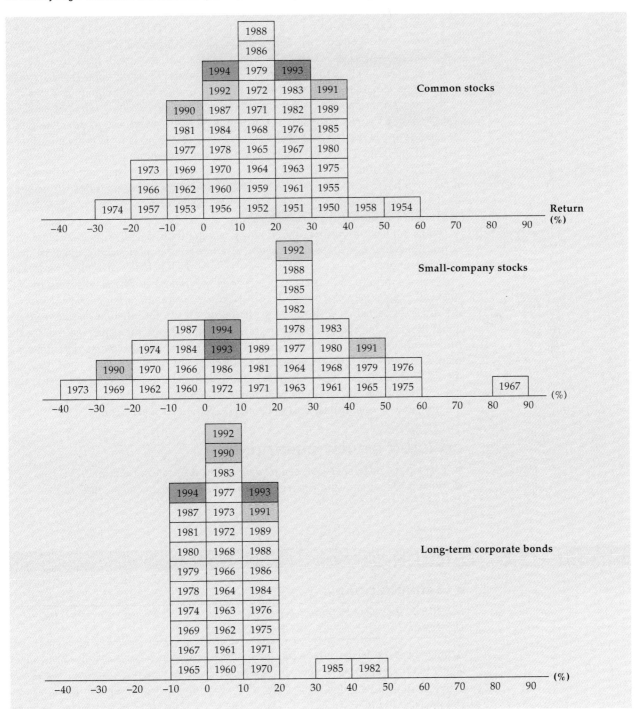

The message for those planning for retirement is clear: To maximize your retirement income, devote a good portion of your retirement funds to common stock.

shown directly in Figure 2.5, note that the direction and magnitude of the returns are not consistent across the three securities, or over time. For example, in 1968 the returns for common stocks was 11.06 percent, for small-company stocks it was 35.97 percent, and for corporate bonds it was 2.57 percent. In 1994 the returns on the three securities were 1.31 percent, 3.11 percent, and −5.76 percent, respectively.

An investor's realized return may differ from his or her expected return. In theory, expected (or required) returns are always positive, because investors will not expose themselves to risk without the prospect of appropriate returns over and above the risk-free rate. But an examination of Figure 2.6 shows that realized common stock returns have not always been positive. While the dividend component is relatively stable, the capital (or price) appreciation (or loss) is not. Over the 1960–1994 time period, between 35 and 40 percent of the total return on common stocks came from dividend income; the remainder was due to changes in the market price of common stocks.

Figures 2.4 through 2.6 visually demonstrate that higher return and higher risk go hand-in-hand. As risk increases for different types of securities, so does the return demanded by investors, and therefore the cost to the issuer. This relationship is depicted in Figure 2.7 (p. 46). The relationship between return (or the cost to the firm) and risk is one of the key ideas of finance; it will be pursued throughout the book. For now, all you need to remember is this: If a firm increases its risk exposure, it increases the return demanded by investors, and hence its costs. *There is no free lunch; increases in risk cause increases in costs.*

While we have been focusing on understanding the risk and costs associated with various financial assets, this information also has great importance for financial management. Figure 2.8 (p. 46) illustrates the relationship between return, risk, bond prices, stock prices, and managerial decisions. Beginning at the top left, we start with financial management decisions. These affect the magnitude, timing, and riskiness of the firm's expected cash flows. Next, based on all the information coming to them about the firm, the economy, and so forth, investors assess the perceived risk for the firm—which directly affects the returns they demand. These actions determine the market value of the firm. Based on the performance of the firm's stock and bonds and the firm's opportunity cost of capital, additional financial management decisions are made: The relationship between financial management decisions, the market value of the firm, and its opportunity cost of capital is continuous and ongoing.

CONCEPT REVIEW QUESTIONS

- Explain the difference between *ex ante* and *ex post* rates of return.
- What is the relationship between return and risk for financial assets?

FOREIGN EXCHANGE RATES

■ LEARNING GOAL 4

Understand the relationship between current (as of today) and forward exchange rates of two currencies.

A fundamental difference between international and domestic financial management is that international transactions are conducted in more than one currency. The dollar is used in the United States, the franc in France, the rupee in India, the yen in Japan, and the peso in Mexico.

FIGURE 2.6

Total Returns, Dividend Income, and Capital Appreciation for Common Stocks, 1960–1994

Returns from dividends are much more dependable than those attributed to price appreciation or loss.

Source: *Stocks, Bonds, Bills, and Inflation 1995 Yearbook*™, Ibbotson Associates, Chicago (annually updated work by Roger G. Ibbotson and Rex A. Sinquefield). Used with permission. All rights reserved.

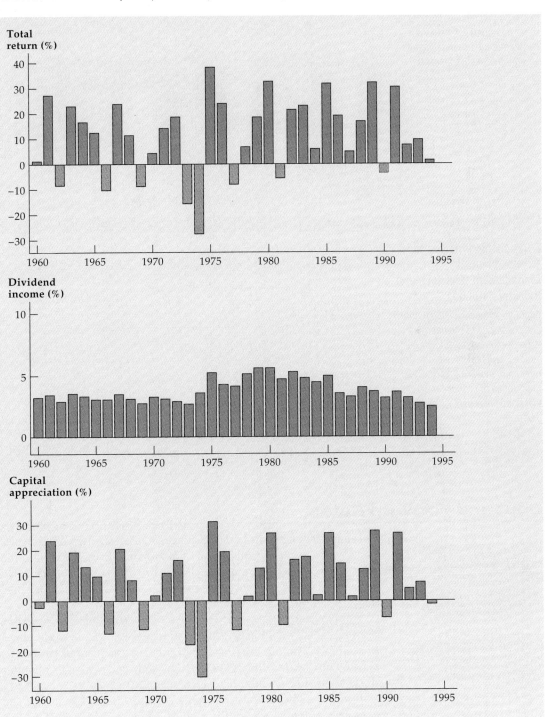

FIGURE 2.7

Relationship Between Required Return (or Cost to the Issuer) and Risk

U.S. Treasury bills provide a risk-free return. As risk increases (as evidenced by default, liquidity, or other premiums), the returns demanded by investors increase; so do the costs to the issuer.

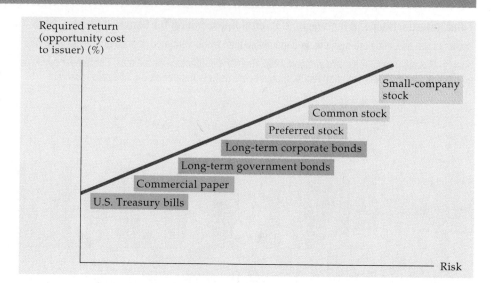

FIGURE 2.8

Relationship Between the Firm's Financial Management Decisions and Investors' Actions

Because of the interrelated and circular nature of the decision-making process, investors' actions, and the value of the firm, managers must understand the importance of financial markets and financial assets in the decision-making process.

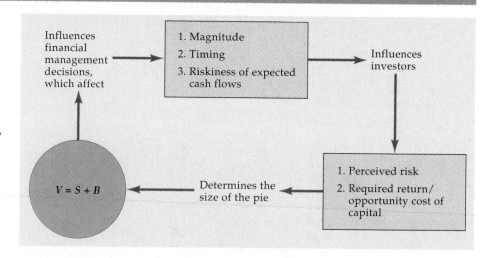

Spot and Forward Rates

Foreign exchange rates are the conversion rates between currencies. They depend on the relative supply and demand for two currencies, inflation in the countries, and other factors. The **spot rate of exchange** between the U.S. dollar and other currencies on July 15, 1994, is shown in Table 2.3. The spot rate shows the exchange rate between two currencies for immediate delivery.

Until the early 1970s, the world was on a fixed exchange rate system. Since 1973, it has operated on a "managed" floating system. Major world currencies move, or float, freely with market forces. Nevertheless, the central banks of countries intervene by buying or selling in the foreign exchange market to smooth out some of the fluctuations. Each central bank also attempts to keep its exchange rates within prescribed government limits to help the country's export or import situation. Floating exchange rates are a fact of life with which all managers must be prepared to cope.

TABLE 2.3

Foreign Exchange Rates Between the U.S. Dollar and Foreign Currencies as of July 15, 1994

Exchange rates can be stated in terms of the number of U.S. dollars per unit of the foreign currency, or in terms of the number of units of the foreign currency per U.S. dollar. Conversion from one to another is straightforward; thus, for the Australian dollar as of Friday, July 15, the number of U.S. dollars per Australian dollar of 1.3633 equals 1/0.7335.

CURRENCY TRADING

EXCHANGE RATES

Friday, July 15, 1994

The New York foreign exchange selling rates below apply to trading among banks in amounts of $1 million and more, as quoted at 3 p.m. Eastern time by Bankers Trust Co., Dow Jones Telerate Inc. and other sources. Retail transactions provide fewer units of foreign currency per dollar.

Country	U.S. $ equiv. Fri.	U.S. $ equiv. Thurs.	Currency per U.S. $ Fri.	Currency per U.S. $ Thurs.
Argentina (Peso)	1.01	1.01	.99	.99
Australia (Dollar)	.7335	.7365	1.3633	1.3578
Austria (Schilling)	.09146	.09141	10.93	10.94
Bahrain (Dinar)	2.6522	2.6522	.3771	.3771
Belgium (Franc)	.03122	.03121	32.03	32.05
Brazil (Real)	1.0729614	1.0799136	.93	.93
Britain (Pound)	1.5607	1.5590	.6407	.6414
30-Day Forward	1.5601	1.5584	.6410	.6417
90-Day Forward	1.5597	1.5580	.6411	.6418
180-Day Forward	1.5595	1.5578	.6412	.6419
Canada (Dollar)	.7260	.7241	1.3775	1.3810
30-Day Forward	.7251	.7232	1.3792	1.3827
90-Day Forward	.7231	.7212	1.3830	1.3865
180-Day Forward	.7191	.7173	1.3906	1.3941
Czech. Rep. (Koruna)				
Commercial rate	.0357577	.0358680	27.9660	27.8800
Chile (Peso)	.002430	.002430	411.56	411.56
China (Renminbi)	.115221	.115221	8.6790	8.6790
Colombia (Peso)	.001217	.001217	821.90	821.90
Denmark (Krone)	.1637	.1637	6.1084	6.1104
Ecuador (Sucre)				
Floating rate	.000462	.000462	2164.03	2164.03
Finland (Markka)	.19373	.19329	5.1617	5.1737
France (Franc)	.18758	.18739	5.3310	5.3365
30-Day Forward	.18739	.18720	5.3365	5.3420
90-Day Forward	.18719	.18700	5.3422	5.3477
180-Day Forward	.18706	.18686	5.3460	5.3515
Germany (Mark)	.6433	.6427	1.5545	1.5560
30-Day Forward	.6416	.6410	1.5585	1.5600
90-Day Forward	.6434	.6428	1.5542	1.5557
180-Day Forward	.6447	.6441	1.5511	1.5526
Greece (Drachma)	.004234	.004253	236.20	235.15
Hong Kong (Dollar)	.12945	.12944	7.7250	7.7255
Hungary (Forint)	.0099840	.0100291	100.1600	99.7100
India (Rupee)	.03212	.03212	31.13	31.13
Indonesia (Rupiah)	.0004610	.0004610	2169.01	2169.01
Ireland (Punt)	1.5372	1.5344	.6505	.6517
Israel (Shekel)	.3298	.3298	3.0320	3.0320
Italy (Lira)	.0006452	.0006459	1549.86	1548.23

Country	U.S. $ equiv. Fri.	U.S. $ equiv. Thurs.	Currency per U.S. $ Fri.	Currency per U.S. $ Thurs.
Japan (Yen)	.010220	.010145	97.85	98.57
30-Day Forward	.010243	.010168	97.63	98.35
90-Day Forward	.010292	.010217	97.16	97.88
180-Day Forward	.010386	.010309	96.28	97.00
Jordan (Dinar)	1.4832	1.4832	.6742	.6742
Kuwait (Dinar)	3.3841	3.3841	.2955	.2955
Lebanon (Pound)	.000596	.000596	1679.00	1679.00
Malaysia (Ringgit)	.3854	.3861	2.5945	2.5900
Malta (Lira)	2.7285	2.7285	.3665	.3665
Mexico (Peso)				
Floating rate	.2942475	.2942475	3.3985	3.3985
Netherland (Guilder)	.5737	.5733	1.7431	1.7443
New Zealand (Dollar)	.5890	.5978	1.6978	1.6728
Norway (Krone)	.1470	.1467	6.8033	6.8168
Pakistan (Rupee)	.0328	.0328	30.52	30.52
Peru (New Sol)	.4683	.4683	2.14	2.14
Philippines (Peso)	.03861	.03861	25.90	25.90
Poland (Zloty)	.00004471	.00004495	22364.00	22248.00
Portugal (Escudo)	.006249	.006250	160.04	160.00
Saudi Arabia (Riyal)	.26665	.26665	3.7503	3.7503
Singapore (Dollar)	.6609	.6605	1.5132	1.5140
Slovak Rep. (Koruna)	.0319285	.0319285	31.3200	31.3200
South Africa (Rand)				
Commercial rate	.2730	.2736	3.6635	3.6555
Financial rate	.2247	.2215	4.4502	4.5150
South Korea (Won)	.0012408	.0012408	805.90	805.90
Spain (Peseta)	.007783	.007793	128.48	128.32
Sweden (Krona)	.1292	.1285	7.7414	7.7800
Switzerland (Franc)	.7642	.7630	1.3085	1.3107
30-Day Forward	.7645	.7632	1.3080	1.3102
90-Day Forward	.7655	.7642	1.3064	1.3086
180-Day Forward	.7678	.7665	1.3025	1.3047
Taiwan (Dollar)	.037509	.037509	26.66	26.66
Thailand (Baht)	.04005	.04005	24.97	24.97
Turkey (Lira)	.0000325	.0000325	30755.22	30809.17
United Arab (Dirham)	.2723	.2723	3.6725	3.6725
Uruguay (New Peso)				
Financial	.199521	.199521	5.01	5.01
Venezuela (Bolivar)	.00588	.00588	170.00	170.00
SDR	1.46321	1.46604	.68343	.68211
ECU	1.22950	1.22890	....	....

Special Drawing Rights (SDR) are based on exchange rates for the U.S., German, British, French and Japanese currencies. Source: International Monetary Fund.

European Currency Unit (ECU) is based on a basket of community currencies.

In The Wall Street Journal, exchange rates are quoted both ways—the number of units of the foreign currency per U.S. dollar and the number of units of a U.S. dollar per unit of the foreign currency.

Source: Table, "Selection from Exchange Rate Quotes," *The Wall Street Journal,* July 18, 1994, p. C6. Reprinted by permission of The Wall Street Journal, © 1994 Dow Jones & Company, Inc. All Rights Reserved Worldwide.

In practice, foreign currencies are generally quoted as the number of units of the foreign currency per dollar. An exception to this is the pound sterling, which is generally quoted in dollars per pound sterling. We will begin by concentrating on understanding foreign exchange rates as units of foreign currency per dollar. Thus, if the current, or spot, rate of exchange between Germany (whose currency is the deutsche mark, M) and the United States is 1.500, that means M/$1 = 1.500, which indicates that 1.500 marks equal $1, or that the dollar price of a single mark is $0.667 (i.e., 1/1.500).

In addition to a spot rate of exchange there are also **forward rates of exchange** that, quoted as of today, indicate the future rate of exchange for some period, such as the 30-day forward rate, the 60-day forward rate, and the 180-day forward rate.

FORWARD RATE OF EXCHANGE
The rate of exchange between two currencies as set today but for delivery at some specified future date.

In Table 2.3, the spot rate of exchange are given between the U. S. dollar and many currencies, along with forward rates of exchange between the U.S. dollar and the British pound, the Canadian dollar, the French franc, the German mark, the Japanese yen, and the Swiss franc. Looking at Table 2.3, the 180-day forward rate of exchange between the German mark and the U.S. dollar was 1.5511. This simply says that the current rate of exchange for delivery 180 days from July 15, 1994, was 1.5511 M/$.

To generalize, country 1 is the domestic currency, and country 2 is the foreign currency.[9] Then, at any time the relationship between spot and forward rates of exchange of the number of units of country 2's currency per country 1's currency unit is given by:

$$F_{2/1} = \frac{S_{2/1}(1 + k_{RF2})}{1 + k_{RF1}} \qquad (2.7)$$

where

$F_{2/1}$ = forward rate in units of country 2's currency to one unit of country 1's currency

$S_{2/1}$ = spot rate in units of country 2's currency to one unit of country 1's currency

k_{RF2} = risk-free interest rate in country 2 for the appropriate forward period

k_{RF1} = risk-free interest rate in country 1 for the appropriate forward period

To see this relationship for the 180-day forward rate of German marks per U.S. dollar of 1.5511 M/$ mentioned previously, we have:

$$F_{M/\$} = \frac{S_{M/\$}(1 + k_{RFM})}{1 + k_{RF\$}}$$

where

$F_{M/\$}$ = the current 180-day forward exchange rate in marks per dollar

$S_{M/\$}$ = the current spot exchange rate in marks per dollar

k_{RFM} = risk-free interest rate on 180-day German securities, expressed in terms of a 180-day return

$k_{RF\$}$ = risk-free interest rate on 180-day U.S. securities, expressed in terms of a 180-day return

Assume that the risk-free rate in Germany is 4.52 percent and that the risk-free rate in the United States (as approximated by the 180-day U.S. Treasury bill rate) is 4.96 percent. Then, assuming (for simplicity) a 360-day year, the 180-day rates are 2.26 percent (i.e., 4.52%/2) and 2.48 percent (i.e., 4.96%/2), respectively. With a current spot rate of 1.5545 M/$ given in Table 2.3, the forward rate of exchange is:

$$F_{M/\$} = \frac{1.5545(1.0226)}{1.0248} \approx 1.5511$$

If we contract today, in 180 days we would deliver (receive) 1.5511 marks per dollar.

---

[9]*More detail on the relationships among spot rates, forward rates, inflation, and interest rates is provided in Chapter 27 of* Financial Management.

Interest Rate Parity

INTEREST RATE PARITY
Theory that the interest rate differential between two countries equals the difference between the spot and forward exchange rates.

The relationship specified by Equation 2.7 can be written in a form often called **interest rate parity,** where:

$$\frac{1 + k_{RF2}}{1 + k_{RF1}} = \frac{F_{2/1}}{S_{2/1}} \tag{2.8}$$

That is, the ratio of the forward rate to the spot rate is a reflection of the risk-free interest rates in the two countries. Because we know from our earlier discussion that the risk-free interest rate is affected by expected inflation, we see that the forward rate of exchange is primarily affected by differences in expected rates of inflation between the two countries.

Let us summarize and clarify this example by spelling out what the relationship means. If k_{RF2} is *less than* k_{RF1}, then

If a firm, such as Exxon, borrows in German marks, it must consider not only the difference in interest rates in various countries, but also how the value of the dollar might change against marks over the term of the loan.

1. The forward rate, $F_{2/1}$, is less than the spot rate, $S_{2/1}$.
2. Country 2's currency is selling at a premium.
3. Country 2's currency is strengthening relative to country 1's currency.

This was exactly what was occurring with the German mark on July 15, 1994; it was strengthening relative to the U.S. dollar. Alternatively, if k_{RF2} is *greater than* k_{RF1}, then:

1. The forward rate, $F_{2/1}$, is greater than the spot rate, $S_{2/1}$.
2. Country 2's currency is selling at a discount.
3. Country 2's currency is weakening relative to country 1's currency.

If Germany is country 2 and the United States is country 1, then the situation on July 15, 1994, was:

$$\text{if the M strengthens} \rightarrow \text{price of M}\uparrow \text{ so } \begin{cases} \text{M/\$} \downarrow \text{, you get fewer M/\$,} \\ \text{\$/M} \uparrow \text{, it takes more \$ to buy a M} \end{cases}$$

This result implies that future interest rates and inflation in Germany are expected to be *lower* than in the United States.

Alternatively, if the opposite situation occurs:

$$\text{if the M weakens} \rightarrow \text{price of M}\downarrow \text{ so } \begin{cases} \text{M/\$} \uparrow \text{, you get more M/\$,} \\ \text{\$/M} \downarrow \text{, it takes fewer \$ to buy a M} \end{cases}$$

By the year 2020, the People's Republic of China, India, and Indonesia, along with the United States and Japan, are projected to be the largest countries in the world in terms of gross domestic product, GDP.

This result implies that future interest rates and inflation in Germany are expected to be *higher* than in the United States.

Why is it important in financial management to know about exchange rates and how they change? And why do we need to consider them this early in the book? The reason is simple—competition is now global in nature for most major industries, and almost all firms are affected one way or another by changing foreign exchange rates. Consider, for example, the experience of Eastman Kodak. During the early 1980s, the economic performance of Eastman's photography sector was coming under increasing pressure from competitors. In particular, Fuji Photo of Japan had become a major worldwide competitor of Eastman Kodak. Fuji was benefiting from the quality of its product and from its marketing efforts. In addition, Fuji was benefiting from the weak yen/dollar exchange rate. With a weak yen, Fuji's largely yen-denominated cost of production was lower than Kodak's dollar-denominated cost of production. The effect was to make Kodak film less price-competitive with Fuji film both in Japan and in other parts of the world, and to make Fuji more price-competitive in Kodak's domestic

EXECUTIVE INTERVIEW WITH GEORGE SETTON

Assistant Treasurer
Schneider North
America/Square D Company
Palatine, Illinois

SQUARE D
GROUPE SCHNEIDER

George Setton received his B.A. and M.A. in English from the University of Wisconsin, Madison, and an M.B.A. from the Columbia University School of Business. After four years in international banking with Bankers Trust, he joined Square D Company in 1977 as International Treasury Manager. Mr. Setton was promoted to Assistant Treasurer in 1984. From 1991 to 1993 he worked at Groupe Schneider's Paris headquarters developing a groupwide currency exposure management system. We asked Mr. Setton to discuss international finance and exchange risk.

Today international considerations affect more businesses than ever before. Companies no longer limit themselves to one market or geographical area. A New Jersey-based company would probably want to sell its products in other states as well. It's the same with the world economy. To survive, companies must look beyond national borders, both for customers and for financing.

Square D Company is a major supplier of products, systems, and services for electrical distribution, automation, and industrial controls. Its international operations began in 1945 in Latin America and spread to Europe in the 1950s. In 1991, Groupe Schneider, a French firm, acquired and reorganized Square D, consolidating its North America operations with Square D's and merging Square D's European operations with other Groupe operations there.

One of the most important considerations in doing business internationally—whether for a major multinational corporation with overseas plants or a small business that just exports parts—is managing foreign currency exposure. A U.S. company could eliminate foreign exchange risk by selling only in dollars, but it would lose sales because customers generally prefer to use their local currency. Dealing with foreign exchange is therefore a critical part of the financial manager's job. Currency values can fluctuate 10 to 20 percent in a short time period. You may sell your product today for the French franc equivalent of $100 but find that upon collection the $100 on your books is worth only $75 because the exchange rate has changed. Clearly, good foreign currency management practices can mean significant savings to a company.

Centralizing foreign currency operations allows a multinational company to minimize its exposure and, therefore, its risk. If one subsidiary has large Swiss francs (Sf) payables and another has high Sf receivables, netting out the two reduces the company's total Sf exposure. Groupe Schneider has two centers for currency management: Paris and Palatine, Illinois. We deal with France in dollars, so Paris manages the Franc-dollar exposure. We deal with other European countries in their currency, and Square D manages those exposures.

It's not easy to predict exchange rate movements and trends, which are partly a function of the differential between interest rates in the U.S. and other countries, as well as political and trade factors. Managers have to actively monitor and manage foreign exchange rates and positions. Although forward contracts lock in a guaranteed exchange rate at a future date, providing certainty, covering all exposure with forwards is not always the best strategy. If the exchange rate moves against you, locking in the rate could put you at a competitive disadvantage. You might have to raise your price because you paid more dollars for imported items—solely due to exchange rate differences.

market—the United States. The currency exposure, which arose from the denomination of Kodak's costs primarily in dollars and the denomination of Fuji's costs primarily in yen, was having a direct bearing on Kodak's sales and bottom line cash flows.

Another example of the impact of changing exchange rates comes every time a firm buys goods from abroad. Assume a domestic firm orders some new equipment from a Swiss tool maker. The equipment will be shipped in 6 months, and the cost is 900,000 Swiss francs (Sf), due when the machinery is shipped. If the spot rate of exchange is 1.50 Sf per dollar, the outlay if paid today would be 900,000/1.50 = $600,000. What will it be if in 6 months the spot rate of exchange is only 1.25 Sf/$? The outlay will be 900,000/1.25 = $720,000. Due to the change in exchange rates, the outlay will end up being $120,000 more than if payment had occurred immediately or if exchange rates had not changed. Firms dealing with buying and selling in the global economy face such situations all the time. If the risk appears to be small, the firm may do nothing; on the other hand, many firms hedge some, but generally not all, of their foreign exchange risk.[10]

In practice things are not quite so simple. Various complications crop up: Trade barriers exist between countries; government actions through their central banks have an impact on interest rates and foreign exchange rates; and other imperfections exist. Even with these imperfections, the relationships provide a means of estimating the relationship between spot and future exchange rates, using data supplied by the financial markets. While all of this may seem complex at first, understanding these ideas and terms is important for financial managers in today's increasingly internationalized environment.

CONCEPT REVIEW QUESTIONS

■ What are the spot rate of exchange and the forward rate of exchange?
■ Briefly describe the relationship between the spot and forward rates of exchange based on interest rate parity.

Summary

■ The role of the financial system is to provide an effective and efficient way to bring together suppliers and demanders of capital.
■ Secondary markets allow investors to buy and sell financial securities, such as bonds and stocks, after they have been issued.
■ On average, the return from risk-free Treasury bills have provided returns slightly in excess of changes in inflation.
■ The return required, or demanded, by an investor is equal to the risk-free rate of interest plus a risk premium. For a bond the risk premium may include a maturity premium, a default premium, a liquidity premium, and other premiums. For a stock the risk premium may include a default premium, a liquidity premium, and other premiums. Due to greater risk, the risk premium for stocks is generally higher than the risk premium for bonds. Consequently, the return demanded by investors in stocks is generally higher than the return demanded by investors in bonds.
■ As general market interest rates increase, the market price of a bond decreases. Alternatively, as general market interest rates decrease, the market price of a bond increases.
■ *Ex post* (or realized) returns will not necessarily equal *ex ante* (expected) returns.

[10] *Hedging foreign exchange risk is discussed in Chapter 28 in* Financial Management.

- The *ex post* returns on common stocks, especially small-company stocks, has exceeded the returns on long-term corporate bonds, Treasury bills, and inflation.
- Higher returns demanded by investors lead to higher costs of debt and equity financing for the firm.
- Return and risk go hand-in-hand. To increase expected returns, it is necessary to increase the exposure to risk.
- The spot rate of exchange is for settlement today, whereas the forward rate of exchange is determined today but with settlement set for some specified time in the future.
- The expected relationship between the rate of interest, and spot and forward exchange rates can be specified using interest rate parity. In practice, government intervention, transactions costs, and other imperfections cause these relationships to hold more in the long run than in the short run.

Questions

2.1 How do financial institutions and financial markets interact to bring together suppliers and demanders of funds? Why are financial institutions so important in this process?

2.2 Distinguish between primary and secondary markets. Why is a well-developed secondary market important even though the firm does not actively participate in it?

2.3 How is a yield curve constructed? Can both U.S. government and corporate securities be used to determine a single yield curve? How does expected inflation and the risk premium affect the yield curve?

2.4 Explain the relationship between risk and return for both bonds and stocks. What kinds of risk premium are required for each? Why? If you purchase a common stock today for $20, with an expected cash dividend of $1.50 and an expected price in one year of $22, what return are you expecting? Will your *ex post* return necessarily equal your *ex ante* return? Why or why not?

2.5 Explain the difference between spot and forward exchange rates. How are expected inflation, interest rates, and spot and forward rates of exchange related?

Concept Review Problems

See Appendix A for solutions.

CR2.1 Assume the following yields, or interest rates, are currently shown in *The Wall Street Journal* for government securities:

Maturity	Yield
6 months	5.8%
1 year	6.9
3 years	6.6
5 years	6.2
7 years	5.9

a. Plot the term structure on interest rates for government securities. What can we say about the term structure, and expected inflation?

b. Now assume that Lander Computers wants to estimate its term structure. The default premium is estimated to be 2 percent for 6 months, and to increase by 0.1 percent every 6 months. Also, due to the small size of the bond, there is a liquidity premium of 0.5 percent and due to some unusual features of the bond, the "other premium" is 0.3 percent. Calculate and plot the term structure for Lander Computers. What can we say about it relative to the yield curve for government securities?

CR2.2 Use Table 2.3 to answer the following questions:
   a. If a Honda Accord costs $20,000 in the United States, what will it cost in yen in Japan?
   b. If a BMW costs 47,356 marks in Germany, what will that BMW cost in dollars in the United States?
   c. If a British MG costs $15,000 in the United States, how many pounds will it cost in Britain?

CR2.3 Assume the risk-free rate of interest *for the next 6 months* is expected to be 3 percent in the United States and 6 percent in France. Using Table 2.3, what is the 6-month forward rate of exchange between the franc and the dollar?

Problems

See Appendix C for answers to selected problems.

Term Structure

2.1 The following data exist on U.S. Treasury securities at three different points in time:

Maturity	4 Years Ago	2 Years Ago	Today
3 months	6%	10%	17%
1 year	7	11	16
5 years	8	11	15
10 years	9	11	14
20 years	9	11	14

   a. Plot the three yield curves on the same graph.
   b. Describe the shape of each yield curve, and, then, assuming that the unobservable real rate of interest (that is, the rate of interest with no inflation) at each point in time was 2 percent, discuss what has happened to inflationary expectations over the last 4 years.

Yield Curves

2.2 Assume that the rate of interest with no inflation (or, the real rate of interest) is 1 percent and that investors expect inflation to be 6 percent in 1 year, 8 percent in 5 years, and 9 percent in 10 years and thereafter. A maturity premium on Treasury securities exists as follows: 0 percent in 1 year, 0.25 percent in 5 years, and increasing by 0.25 percent every 5 years.
   a. Determine the nominal risk-free interest rate for years 1, 5, 10, 15, and 20 for these Treasury securities.
   b. Plot these to form a yield curve.
   c. Suppose now that Shell Oil (a AAA firm) and Flyer's Hot Air Balloons (a very risky firm) are both attempting to estimate their yield curves. Plot each in relation to the Treasury yield curve and explain how each is similar to or different from your original yield curve.

Risk Premiums and Required Rates of Return

2.3 The following information exists for four securities:

	Treasury Bills	Long-Term Treasury Bonds	Listed Corporate Bonds	Risky OTC Common Stocks
Real, or inflation-free, interest	2.5%	2.5%	2.5%	2.5%
Expected inflation	6.5	6.5	6.5	6.5
Maturity premium	—	1.0	1.0	—
Default premium	—	—	3.0	2.0
Liquidity premium	—	—	—	1.0
Issue-specific premium	—	—	—	5.0

a. Calculate the risk-free rate, k_{RF}, and then calculate the risk premiums and required returns for Treasury bonds, corporate bonds, and risky common stocks.

b. If you were to plot the data, what general relationship would exist between risk and required return? Why?

Spot and Forward Rates

2.4 Spot and forward rates for Canada and France relative to the U.S. dollar are:

	Units of Foreign Currency per U.S. Dollar	
Rate	Canadian Dollar	French Franc
Spot	1.192	6.253
30-day forward	1.198	6.247
90-day forward	1.205	6.241
180-day forward	1.213	6.232

a. What can we say about the expected rate of inflation in both countries relative to the expected rate of inflation in the United States?

b. How about the expected rate of inflation in Canada relative to the expected rate of inflation in France?

Different Currencies

2.5 If the British pound has a spot rate of 1.771 U.S. dollars per pound while the German mark has a spot rate of 0.544 dollars per German mark, what is the spot rate of exchange between the pound and the mark?

Expected Spot Rate

2.6 The current spot rate for the Israel shekel is 1.817 shekels to the U.S. dollar, while it is 7.15 Chinese renmenbi to the U.S. dollar. What is the spot rate of exchange between the shekel and the renmenbi?

Implied Forward Rate

Note: For simplicity, in 2.7 assume a 360-day year and 30-day months.

2.7 Assume that the current rate of exchange is 1,250 Italian lire per dollar. If the current yearly nominal risk-free interest rate in Italy is 14 percent per year, while it is 6 percent in the United States, what is the implied 6-month forward rate between the lira and dollar?

Interest Rates, Returns, and Foreign Exchange

2.8 **Mini Case** Wallingford Associates has hired you to conduct a seminar on interest rates, the returns required by investors, and foreign exchange rates. In preparing for this seminar you decide there are a number of important points that must be explained.

a. What is the risk-free rate of interest, and what does it compensate investors for?

b. Once maturity premiums are considered, for bonds of equal default risk (like U.S. Treasury securities) a term structure of interest rates exists. Explain what the term structure is and what it indicates when it is upward-sloping versus downward-sloping.

c. Looking at a recent edition of *The Wall Street Journal*, you note the following yields:

ATT		RJR Nabisco	
Issue/Maturity	Yield	Issue/Maturity	Yield
4 3/4 98	5.1%	8.3s 99	8.7%
6s 00	6.3	7 5/8 03	9.3
6 3/4 04	7.2	8 3/4 05	10.0
8 1/8 22	8.2	9 1/4 13	10.8

What are the coupon interest rates and maturities for each of the bonds issued by ATT and RJR Nabisco? What can we say about the term structure of interest rates as of this point in time? What can we say about the relative riskiness of ATT versus RJR Nabisco?

d. What other risks exist that investors require compensation for? What is the required rate of return equal to? In explaining this remember to discuss common stocks and their risks as well as bonds. Also, explain how the data in Figures 2.4 and 2.5 relate to risk and return.

e. You decide to relate the idea of returns required by investors to the costs of financing incurred by firms. How are these two related? What is the important message for management to understand?

Note: Assume a 360-day year.

f. If the spot rate of exchange is 3 francs per dollar, and the risk-free rate in the United States is 9 percent while it is 6 percent in Switzerland, what are the implied 180-day and 360-day forward rates of exchange? Is Switzerland's currency strengthening or weakening relative to the U.S. dollar?

g Finally, what is interest rate parity? What does it imply about forward rates and inflation?

PART 2

FOUNDATIONS OF FINANCIAL MANAGEMENT

EXECUTIVE INTERVIEW WITH LINDA CARTER

*Senior Investment
Analyst
John Hancock Advisers,
Boston, Massachusetts*

A chartered financial analyst (CFA) specializing in fixed-income securities, Linda Carter began her career at United Business Service in 1983. She joined Allmerica Financial, Worcester, Massachusetts, in 1987 and held several investment officer positions before her promotion to vice-president. In 1994 Ms. Carter joined John Hancock Advisers as senior research officer, Fixed Income. Ms. Carter has a B.S. degree in management from the University of Massachusetts and an M.S. in finance from Boston College. We asked her to discuss how some fundamental concepts of finance are applied.

Time value of money, valuation, and risk and return are major financial concepts managers use when deciding how to invest corporate resources. Corporate treasurers use them to analyze the best way to raise funds in the capital markets or to invest in financial instruments and capital projects. Mutual fund managers use time value and valuation techniques daily to value possible investments for their portfolios. Most financial decisions require analyzing whether an investment's return is adequate for the risk, or uncertainty, involved. Therefore financial managers must understand how to evaluate and measure the various types of risk.

Time value is the foundation for other key financial management concepts such as valuation and risk and return. Time value is also important for personal financial decisions. For example, time value helps you calculate whether it is better to finance a car by leasing or by borrowing, and how much you need to save to reach a desired goal. Understanding time value principles is one of the first steps to becoming a successful financial manager.

Time value calculations are essential in many areas of financial management. Both financial and operations managers who make capital investment decisions apply present value calculations to a project's cash flows to see if it earns a return above the firm's required rate. Time value helps treasury managers get the best returns when investing temporary cash surpluses. Human resource managers analyze employee benefits costs and pension plans using time value. When I choose bond investments for our mutual funds, I use present value to determine a bond's price, or value. Suppose I can buy a $10,000, 15-year, 6 percent coupon bond with 10 years left to maturity and the market rate on similar bonds today is 7 percent. The bond's current value—the price I am willing to pay—is $9,297.64.

Valuation concepts are also important for understanding how the financial markets value debt and equity. Many factors affect security prices, which in turn affect a company's overall value. Today's financial markets are quite volatile. Without an awareness of the changing costs of debt and equity, managers may make financial decisions that are not in the firm's best interests.

The securities valuation process is very challenging. Equity valuation models—whether based on dividends, price/earnings ratios or some other approach—are only as good as the information that goes into them. Determining the dividend growth rate for equity valuation models is an art and depends on the analyst's assumptions about a company's sales, costs, growth, profitability, and similar factors.

Most strategic decisions affect the company's value and will be reflected in the cost to raise financing in the capital markets. Corporate actions send messages to the public that ultimately affect value. Raising the dividend paid to stockholders, for example, is a strong positive message; cutting it sends a negative message. If a company raises its common stock dividend, the price of its publicly traded bonds will probably increase due to the favorable market perception of the firm. Likewise, if analysts assume that an announced merger will create synergy between two companies, they will assume a higher earnings growth rate than if they are pessimistic about the outcome.

Risk is also a key component of many financial decisions. It's not enough to assume that a new plant will earn a 12 percent return. You must also consider the types of risk that affect the project and the company—general economic risk, business risk, financial risk—and the probability that they will occur and result in a lower return. The higher the risk, the higher the required return.

Measuring risk can be difficult. When choosing investments for our mutual funds, we have to achieve a balance between risk and return for our investors. Not all factors can be easily quantified, so we look at qualitative as well as quantitative factors. When analyzing securities we must assess the effect of more subjective factors—competition, trends in national and international economic conditions, stability of materials suppliers and customer base—on a company's performance. The rate of return must be sufficiently high to reflect the investment's risk.

Capital investment decisions also require the application of risk-return concepts. For example, the required return for building a high-technology factory would obviously be higher than that company would get by investing in a U.S. Treasury bill, a risk-free alternative. Will the technology enhance productivity? Is the technology proven? These and other factors affect the risk-return analysis, and there is considerable subjectivity involved. To account for project risk, the analyst can adjust either the discount rate or the expected cash flows.

Almost every decision a manager makes affects the firm's market value, as determined by its stock price. To maximize the firm's value, managers must use time value of money concepts combined with good business judgment to find the right balance of risk and return for the company.

In order to make effective financial decisions, managers need to understand the concepts employed throughout the study and practice of financial management. Chapter 3 discusses the timing of cash inflows and outflows, and the time value of money. Next, Chapter 4 focuses on two primary vehicles employed by firms to raise funds—bonds and common stock—and their valuation. Finally, Chapter 5 examines risk and return in detail. These chapters provide the foundation for making decisions that assist in maximizing the long-run market value of the firm.

Time Value of Money

Sections in this chapter:

■ **Present and Future Values**
"Neither a borrower nor a lender be" does not apply in finance.
■ **Determining Internal Rates of Return**
Being able to calculate IRRs makes this course a lot simpler.
■ **Applications**
Knowing time value without understanding how to apply it is like knowing how to drive but not having a car.

During a recent 10-year period, the price of Boeing's common stock increased at a 19 percent annual compound growth rate. In the same period, Marriott increased at 21 percent, Shoney's at 23 percent, Wal-Mart at 38 percent, and Digital Equipment at 25 percent. To compare the performance of these companies, investors and managers must understand compounding and be able to calculate compound growth rates. From the stock market to your savings account, knowing the performance of your investment over time is essential to effective financial decision making.

Parker Hannifin, headquartered in Cleveland, just approached a group of banks—First Wachovia, Chase Manhattan, First Chicago, and Wells Fargo—for a $20 million loan. After discussion, the parties agreed on the length of the loan, the rate of interest, and the frequency of repayments. The question remained: How much would the payments be? Part of each payment would go to pay back the original $20 million, part to pay interest on the loan—but just how much? This is basically the same question you face when you obtain a car or home loan. You are borrowing money, and you must determine how much interest you will pay over time. You can answer this question with present value techniques.

Finally, United Airlines is planning its future fleet of planes. The capital budgeting group proposes that United spend $7.5 billion over the next 5 years to replace a portion of its current fleet with newer, more fuel-efficient planes. The savings are expected to be $900 million per year for the 20-year average life of the new planes. Should United make the investment? What additional information is needed to make an intelligent, informed decision?

All of these topics, and many more, require an understanding of the time value of money. Time value is important whenever cash flows occur at various times. In this chapter we learn how to account for time differences in the inflow or outflow of cash.

LEARNING GOALS

After studying this chapter, you should be able to:

1. Determine present and future values of cash flows one period apart.
2. Determine present and future values of cash flows more than one period apart.
3. Determine the present value of multiple cash flows: perpetuities, annuities, and uneven cash flow series.
4. Calculate the internal rate of return for various types of cash flows.
5. Distinguish between net present value and the internal rate of return.
6. Calculate compounding and discounting rates for cash flow intervals of less than a year.

PRESENT AND FUTURE VALUES

This entire chapter focuses on Key Idea 5—a dollar today is worth more than a dollar tomorrow.

In order to maximize the value of the firm—or the size of the pie, as we put it in Chapter 1—it is important to understand how the decisions the firm makes and the cash flows generated by these decisions impact the value of the firm. In this part of the book we concentrate on how three basic ideas affect the size of the pie: (1) the timing of the cash flows—the ingredients going into the pie; (2) the valuation of bonds and stocks—the size of the pie; and (3) risk—the baking conditions. To maximize the value of the firm we must understand the impact that the timing, magnitude, and riskiness of the firm's cash flows has on its value. Holding other things constant, we can visualize this as follows:

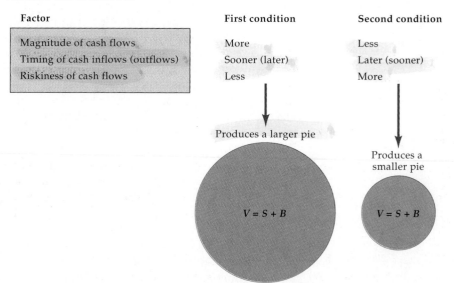

Factor	First condition	Second condition
Magnitude of cash flows	More	Less
Timing of cash inflows (outflows)	Sooner (later)	Later (sooner)
Riskiness of cash flows	Less	More

Produces a larger pie

$V = S + B$

Produces a smaller pie

$V = S + B$

When Cash Flows Are One Period Apart

Key Idea 4—firms focus on cash flows and their incremental effects—is important when firms and individuals make decisions.

■ **LEARNING GOAL 1**

Determine present and future values of cash flows one period apart.

Suppose you were left with a tax-free gift of $250,000, and your current job brings in enough to take care of all of your (and your loved ones') current and anticipated future desires. The question, then, would be what to do with the $250,000. You could bury it in the ground, give it away, or invest it. Let's rule out the first two possibilities and focus on investing the $250,000. Your financial advisor proposes that you invest the money in a small, new office complex. The total cash outflow required to purchase the office complex is $250,000. Your financial advisor believes that due to the shortage of office space in that part of town, the office complex could be sold for a cash inflow of $325,000 in 1 year. The decision you face is simple—do you proceed with the office complex?

To answer that question we have to compare the cash inflow of $325,000 to be received in 1 year with the $250,000 cash outflow to be made today. That comparison rests on understanding how to determine the **present value** of a set of future cash flows. The present value of a cash flow that will occur in 1 year is found by discounting as follows:

PRESENT VALUE
The value today of a given future series of cash flows, when discounted at a given discount rate.

$$\text{present value, } PV_0 = \frac{FV_1}{1 + k} \tag{3.1}$$

where

The present value is the most you would pay today to receive a given amount(s) in the future.

PV_0 = the present value today, at time $t = 0$, of a future cash flow

FV_1 = the cash flow occurring at time period 1

k = the return demanded for accepting the delayed receipt of the funds

If we assume the investment is as safe as investing in the stock market, what kind of return, k, would you demand on the investment? An alternative is to invest in a "market basket" of common stocks, as measured by the Standard & Poor's 500 stock index. Suppose your investment advisor believes common stocks will return 12 percent for the next year; that is, for every $1 invested today, you can expect to receive back $1.12 in 1 year. What is the present value *today* of $325,000 to be received in 1 year? It's simply:

$$PV_0 = \frac{FV_1}{1 + k} = \frac{\$325,000}{1 + 0.12} = \$290,179$$

DISCOUNT RATE
The rate used to calculate the present value of future cash flows.

where k is the **discount rate**.

Should you make the investment? That's easy to answer: By making an investment of $250,000, you are acquiring something that is worth (in present value terms) $290,179. Because $290,179 is greater than $250,000, you are better off; make the investment in the office complex!

FUTURE VALUE
The amount to which a series of cash flows will grow by a given future date when compounded at a given interest rate.

Alternatively, we can determine whether to make the investment by determining how much you would earn by investing the $250,000 at your next best alternative (in this case, common stocks with an expected return of 12 percent) and comparing it with the $325,000 you could earn by investing in the office complex. We can find the **future value** in one period of a given amount today, by rearranging Equation 3.1 as follows:

$$FV_1 = PV_0(1 + k) \tag{3.2}$$

$$FV_1 = \$250,000(1 + 0.12) = \$280,000$$

COMPOUND RATE
The rate applicable when interest is earned on both the initial principal and the accumulated interest from previous periods.

where k is now the **compound rate**, which includes the full amount (principal) plus the interest. (In this case, interest is compounded for only one period. If the investment continued for several years, year 1's compounded amount, $280,000, would be the basis for year 2's compounding, year 2's compounded amount would be the basis for year 3's compounding, and so on.) The amount of $325,000 that you would obtain

The term "compound interest" means that interest is earned on not only the original principal but also on the prior interest.

in 1 year from investing in the office complex is greater than the $280,000 that you would receive by investing in your next best alternative. Therefore you would make the same decision—invest in the office complex.

Understanding present and future value is critical to making value-maximizing financial decisions. So far, we have discussed present and future values in situations where there are only two time periods—today and one period (or year) from now. We also need to learn how to deal with cash flows that are more than one period apart and cash flows that occur over multiple time periods.

Making Financial Calculations

When solving time value of money problems, you will find that while there is only one correct answer, there may be several ways of determining it.

Before proceeding, let's stop and address another issue that crops up at this time for many students: how to make the financial calculations required in this chapter and throughout the book most effectively. This chapter assumes that all students have a basic calculator. If that is what you have and plan to use throughout the book, you can do just fine (providing your instructor does not have other ideas). Later in the chapter we provide formulas for use with your basic calculator to determine the present or future value of various amounts. Or, you (and your instructor) may decide to use the financial tables provided in Appendix B at the end of the book.

However, many students find that *financial* calculators are inexpensive and that they make financial calculations extremely simple. While using a financial calculator is *in no way* a prerequisite to getting a good grade in this course, it does simplify many of the calculations and allows you to focus on learning finance—providing you don't wait until a couple of days before the first exam to determine how to use your financial calculator! The most important thing is to become comfortable with some method of making the calculations accurately and efficiently.

Detailed instructions on how to use three different popular financial calculators to solve problems in this course are available as a free supplement with new copies of this book.

We make all calculations in this book using a financial calculator. However, in this chapter we also provide information in the footnotes about how to use a basic calculator to make the calculations. In this and following chapters, we also provide (in footnotes) solutions using the financial tables in Appendix B for all present and future value calculations. Finally, both financial calculator and financial table solutions are provided for Concept Review Problems and the end-of-chapter problems.

When Cash Flows Are More Than One Period Apart

■ LEARNING GOAL 2

Determine present and future values of cash flows more than one period apart.

Let's continue by considering cases where there are cash flows at two time periods, when these periods are not necessarily right next to each other. For example, the cash flows might occur today ($t = 0$) and 3 years from now ($t = 3$).

Present Value

To understand present values better, consider the following situation: What if you need $665.50 in 3 years to pay off a loan? How much would you have to put aside today, if you can earn a 10 percent annual compound interest rate on that amount, to end up with the $665.50? We can use a timeline to show this graphically:[1]

---

[1] *By convention, the present value is usually shown as an outflow (with the arrow going down), while the future value is shown as an inflow (with the arrow going up).*

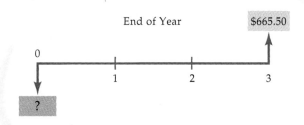

The general equation for the present value of a single amount to be received n periods in the future, discounted at k percent, is:

$$\text{present value, } PV_0 = \frac{FV_n}{(1 + k)^n} \tag{3.3}$$

With a calculator it is easy to compute the present value of any amount for any period of time. To determine the amount to put aside today (i.e., the present value), we have:[2]

$$PV_0 = \frac{\$665.50}{(1.10)^3} \approx \$500$$

Equation 3.3 may also be written as follows:

$$PV_0 = FV_n\left[\frac{1}{(1 + k)^n}\right] \tag{3.3a}$$

PRESENT VALUE FACTOR, $PV_{k,n}$
Set of factors that for different rates, k, and periods, n, converts a future value into a smaller present value.

The term in brackets is called the **present value factor, $PV_{k,n}$.** Table B.1, found at the end of the book, provides present value factors. Using PV factors, the basic present value equation (Equation 3.3) is:[3]

$$PV_0 = FV_n(PV_{k,n}) \tag{3.4}$$

Thus:

$$PV_0 = FV_3(PV_{10\%,\,3yr}) = \$665.50(0.751) \approx \$500$$

While either Equation 3.3 or 3.4 can be used, we employ Equation 3.3 (or a financial calculator) throughout the book.

Future Value

As we saw previously, finding the future value involves taking a cash flow today and determining what it will be worth sometime in the future if it earns a return of k percent per period. If you purchase a security worth $1,000 today that pays 8 percent

[2] Using a basic calculator, you divide $665.50 by $(1.10)^3$. With a financial calculator the answer is also $500.
[3] While we get the same answer in this example of $500 using either the end-of-book tables or a calculator, often there are minor differences between the two due to rounding in the tables. Do not be concerned about minor differences of this type.

interest compounded annually, how much will it be worth in 4 years? Graphically, this is

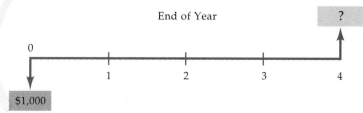

In general, the future value at the end of n periods is

$$\text{future value, } FV_n = PV_0(1 + k)^n \tag{3.5}$$

so:[4]

$$FV_4 = \$1,000(1.08)^4 = \$1,360.49$$

FUTURE VALUE FACTOR,
$FV_{k,n}$
Set of factors that for different rates, k, and periods, n, converts a present value into a larger future value.

Tables are also available that provide **future value factors, $FV_{k,n}$,** for the quantity $(1 + k)^n$ in Equation 3.5. Table B.3, given at the end of the book, provides future value factors for single amounts. In terms of future value factors, Equation 3.5 can be rewritten as:

$$FV_n = PV_0(FV_{k,n}) \tag{3.6}$$

FINANCIAL MANAGEMENT TODAY

The Value of Manhattan

According to popular legend, Manhattan Island was purchased from the Canarsee Indians in 1626 for a price of 60 guilders, or about $24. Who won and who lost on this transaction? It's really a question of the time value of money. The purchase occurred 369 years ago (1995 − 1626), so we can use Equation 3.5 to find the value of the original $24 under different interest rate assumptions. The equation is:

$$1995 \text{ value} = \$24(1 + k)^{369}$$

The value of the $24 in 1995 is as follows:

If k is	$\$24(1 + k)^{369}$
0.02	$35,783
0.04	46,292,799
0.06	52,248,700,000
0.08	51,710,290,000,000

It's hard to know the rate of interest that the Canarsee Indians could have received, or the value of Manhattan today, but some comparisons can be made. If they received a rate of 6 percent, the value in 1995 will be more than $52 billion; at 8

percent it will be in excess of $51 trillion. For comparison, the population of the United States is approximately 260 million. At a 6 percent compound rate, the present value in 1995 of the original $24 would allow about $200 to be given to everyone in the country. At 8 percent it would be worth almost $200,000 to each person in the United States. Now that's compounding.

---

[4] To solve for the value $(1.08)^4$ using a basic calculator, it is necessary to use the exponential function, y^x. In this problem, $y = 1.08$, $n = x = 4$, $y^x = 1.360...$, and $FV_4 = \$1,000(1.360...) = \$1,360.49$. With a financial calculator the answer is the same.

Using this equation, we find the future value is:

$$FV_4 = PV_0(FV_{8\%, 4yr}) = \$1,000(1.360) = \$1,360$$

Except for a rounding difference of 49 cents, the answer is the same as before. We employ Equation 3.5 (or a financial calculator) throughout the book, but we also provide solutions using the future value table.

When There Are Multiple Cash Flows

■ **LEARNING GOAL 3**

Determine the values of multiple cash flows: perpetuities, annuities, and uneven cash flow series.

Up to now we have considered situations that involve only two cash flows and time periods. However, real life is more complicated, so it is also necessary to deal with a series of cash flows. Let's begin by discussing the present value of a *perpetuity*, which is simply a series of cash flows of the same amount that continues indefinitely. We will then consider the special case of an *annuity*, where the constant cash flows continue for only a finite period of time. Finally, we will examine the case of an uneven series of cash flows.

Perpetuities

PERPETUITY
A stream of equal cash flows expected to continue forever; an infinite annuity.

Instead of single cash flows, let's go to the other extreme and consider how to value a series of cash flows of a constant amount that goes on indefinitely—a **perpetuity**. Suppose your wealthy great-aunt Sophie is going to provide you with an allowance that goes on forever. (*Note*: When she dies, a trust has been set up to make the payments; also, for simplicity, we will assume you will live forever, or at least for a long time.) Great-aunt Sophie needs to know now how much money to set aside today, the present value, so she can provide for you—her favorite relative. The present value of a perpetuity, with the first payment starting one period from now, is equal to the constant cash flow stream, often called *PMT* (for payment), divided by the discount rate k, as follows:

$$\text{present value of a perpetuity, } PV_0 = \frac{\text{cash flow}}{\text{discount rate}} = \frac{PMT}{k} \qquad (3.7)$$

Thus, if great-aunt Sophie wants to provide a perpetuity of \$25,000 per year *beginning 1 period (or year) from now,* and the discount rate is 8 percent,

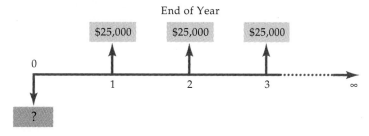

its present value is:

$$PV_0 = \frac{PMT}{k} = \frac{\$25,000}{0.08} = \$312,500$$

So, great-aunt Sophie needs to set aside \$312,500 today in an account that earns 8 percent per year to provide for your perpetuity.

Growing Perpetuities

Suppose that instead of a constant amount per year, the size of the allowance provided by your great-aunt Sophie is growing at a constant (percentage) rate of 3 percent per year (to cover expected changes in inflation). In this case the cash flow stream is:

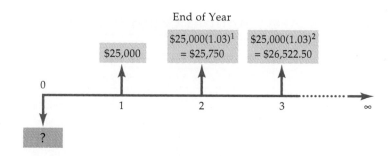

GROWTH RATE, *g*
The compound percentage rate at which an amount increases in size.

Given the **growth rate, *g*,** the present value of this stream of growing cash flows is:

$$PV_0 = \frac{PMT}{(1 + k)^1} + \frac{PMT\,(1 + g)^1}{(1 + k)^2} + \frac{PMT(1 + g)^2}{(1 + k)^3} + \cdots$$

As long as the discount rate, k, is greater than the growth rate, g, this complicated-looking equation simplifies to:

$$\text{present value of a growing perpetuity, } PV_0 = \frac{PMT}{k - g} \tag{3.8}$$

With the size of the cash flow increasing by 3 percent per year, the present value of the growing perpetuity provided by great-aunt Sophie is

$$PV_0 = \frac{\$25,000}{0.08 - 0.03} = \frac{\$25,000}{0.05} = \$500,000$$

As common sense tells us, the value of a growing perpetuity must be substantially greater than the value of a level perpetuity. Hence, great-aunt Sophie needs to put more money aside to fund your growing perpetuity.

Present Value of an Ordinary Annuity

ANNUITY
A series of equal cash flows for a specified number of periods. *You will often encounter annuities in life: A car or home loan or rental payments are annuities.*

Once we understand how to value perpetuities, it is easy to value an **annuity,** which is just a limited-life perpetuity. That is, an annuity is a series of cash flows of the same amount that continues for a limited period of time, say, 4 years. In this case assume your great-aunt Sophie has promised you an allowance of $25,000 per year for the time you are in college (through the remainder of your undergraduate program and for a 2-year masters degree). With the payments of $25,000 made to you at the *end* of each of the 4 years we have:

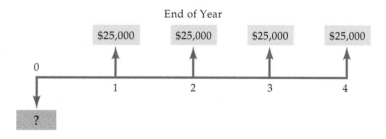

End of Year

When the cash flows occur at the end of each period, this is an **ordinary annuity.** If the discount rate is 9 percent, instead of the 8 percent used previously, what is the present value of this annuity?

Figure 3.1 indicates that there is an easy way to determine the present value of an annuity. For a typical perpetuity with the first cash flow starting 1 year from now, its value (as given by Equation 3.7) is:

$$PV_0 = \frac{PMT}{k}$$

Now consider a second perpetuity that does not begin its cash flows until time period $n + 1$. That is, the second perpetuity is a *delayed perpetuity* whose constant cash flows start $n + 1$ periods in the future. The present value of this delayed perpetuity *at time n* is PMT/k, so its present value *today* (at $t = 0$) is:

$$\text{present value of a delayed perpetuity, } PV_0 = \left(\frac{PMT}{k}\right)\frac{1}{(1 + k)^n} \tag{3.9}$$

Both perpetuities provide payments from time period $n + 1$ onward. The first perpetuity also provides cash flows from period 1 to period n. Therefore, as shown in Figure 3.1, by taking the difference between the present value of the typical perpetuity,

ORDINARY ANNUITY
A series of equal cash flows for a specified number of periods, with each cash flow occurring at the end of the period.

FIGURE 3.1

The Present Value of an Annuity Equals the Difference in the Present Value of Two Perpetuities

An ordinary, or typical, perpetuity has constant cash flows that begin at time $t = 1$ and continue to infinity. A delayed perpetuity has constant cash flows that begin at time $n + 1$ and continue to infinity. By determining the present value at time $t = 0$ of the delayed perpetuity and subtracting it from the present value of the ordinary perpetuity, we determine the present value of an annuity that has constant cash flows from time $t = 1$ to time $t = n$.

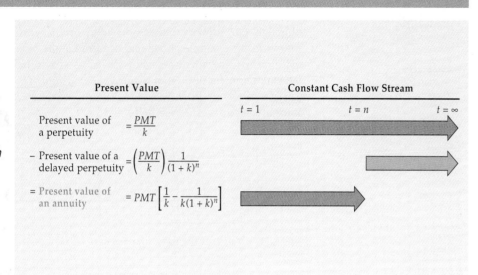

and the present value of the delayed perpetuity, we have the *present value of an annuity of amount PMT for n periods* or years. This is:

$$\text{present value of an (ordinary) annuity, } PV_0 = PMT \left[\frac{1}{k} - \frac{1}{k(1 + k)^n} \right] \quad (3.10)$$

Although financial tables may be useful, one cannot rely solely on them. Assume you purchase a $15,000 car with 4.9% financing and a 42-month payment plan. Either a financial calculator or Equation 3.10 is required to determine the exact monthly loan payment.

The present value of an annuity of $25,000 to be received at the end of each of the next 4 years discounted at 9 percent is:

$$PV_0 = \$25,000 \left[\frac{1}{0.09} - \frac{1}{0.09(1.09)^4} \right] = \$25,000(3.2397\ldots) \approx \$80,993$$

An alternative to Equation 3.10 for the present value of an annuity, using a summation sign, is:

$$\text{present value of an (ordinary) annuity, } PV_0 = PMT \sum_{t=1}^{n} \frac{1}{(1 + k)^t} \quad (3.10a)$$

We employ Equation 3.10a throughout when signifying the present value of an (ordinary) annuity.

Instead of using complicated-looking Equation 3.10, we can use a financial calculator that deals with annuities.[5] Or financial tables are available for the bracketed portion in the equation; these are called **present value factors for an annuity, $PVA_{k,n}$.** Using the value from Table B.2, the present value of this annuity is:

PRESENT VALUE FACTOR FOR AN ANNUITY, $PVA_{k,n}$
Set of factors that for different rates, k, and periods, n, converts an annuity into its present value.

$$PV_0 = PMT(PVA_{k,n}) \quad (3.11)$$

$$PV_0 = \$25,000(PVA_{9\%,4yr}) = \$25,000(3.240) = \$81,000$$

We use a financial calculator throughout when valuing annuities, which gives answers equivalent to using Equation 3.10.

Present Value of an Annuity Due

Although our primary concern is with ordinary annuities, what if the four cash inflows in the example above had occurred at the *beginning* of each period, not at the end? In this case, great-aunt Sophie wants you to have the money to use for pizzas and entertainment throughout your year at school. This is the case of an **annuity due.** Each of the payments is shifted back one period, or year, on the timeline, so they now occur at $t = 0$, $t = 1$, $t = 2$, and $t = 3$:

ANNUITY DUE
A series of equal cash flows for a specified number of periods, with each cash flow occurring at the beginning of the period.

End of Year

| $25,000 | $25,000 | $25,000 | $25,000 |

0   1   2   3

?

[5]Using a financial calculator the answer is $80,993.

To calculate the present value of an annuity due, we multiply the present values determined before by the term $(1 + k)$. Equations 3.10a and 3.11 become:

$$PV_0 \text{ (annuity due)} = PMT \sum_{t=1}^{n} \left(\frac{1}{(1 + k)^t} \right) (1 + k) \tag{3.12}$$

and

$$PV_0 \text{ (annuity due)} = PMT(PVA_{k,n})(1 + k) \tag{3.13}$$

For our example, the present value in the case of an annuity due using a financial calculator is approximately \$88,282. Using Equation 3.13 and the end-of-book Table B.2, we have:

$$PV_0(\text{annuity due}) = \$25,000(PVA_{9\%,4yr})(1.09)$$
$$= \$25,000(3.240)(1.09) = \$88,290$$

Since the payments are made in advance, the present value of an annuity due is more valuable than if it is an ordinary annuity. Talk to your great-aunt Sophie and convince her to provide the money at the beginning of the school year—not the end!

Future Value of an Ordinary Annuity

What if instead of finding the present value of an annuity, we need to find its future value? That is, you decide not to spend your great-aunt's payments, but to invest them so as to have a "nest egg" upon graduation. If you receive \$25,000 at the end of each year and immediately invest it at 9 percent, how much will you have at the end of the 4 years? Graphically this is:

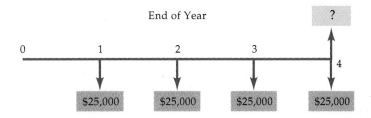

To find the future value of an annuity, we can make use of the knowledge developed previously. We know that the present value (at time $t = 0$) of an annuity, as given by Equation 3.10, is:

$$PV_0 = PMT \left[\frac{1}{k} - \frac{1}{k(1 + k)^n} \right]$$

And we also know that we can move any single (or lump-sum) present value to the future, using Equation 3.5 as follows:

$$FV_n = PV_0(1 + k)^n$$

Therefore, the future value of an annuity is equal to its present value at time $t = 0$, multiplied by the appropriate future value factor, so:

$$FV_n = PMT \left[\frac{1}{k} - \frac{1}{k(1 + k)^n} \right](1 + k)^n$$

This simplifies to:

future value of an (ordinary) annuity, $FV_n = PMT \left[\dfrac{(1 + k)^n - 1}{k} \right]$ (3.14)

Using a financial calculator (instead of Equation 3.14), the future value of an annuity of $25,000 to be received at the end of each of the next 4 years at 9 percent is approximately $114,328. Another equation for the future value of an annuity, using a summation sign, is:

future value of an (ordinary) annuity, $FV_n = PMT \displaystyle\sum_{t=1}^{n-1} (1 + k)^t$ (3.14a)

We employ Equation 3.14a throughout when signifying the future value of an annuity.

FUTURE VALUE FACTOR FOR AN ANNUITY, $FVA_{k,n}$
Set of factors that for different rates, k, and periods, n, converts an annuity into a single future value.

An alternative way to make this calculation is to use financial tables. **Future value factors for an annuity, $FVA_{k,n}$,** have been calculated for the bracketed portion of Equation 3.14. These are presented in Table B.4 at the end of the book. In terms of the table values, the future value of an ordinary annuity is:

$$FV_n = PMT(FVA_{k,n}) \tag{3.15}$$

$$FV_4 = \$25,000(FVA_{9\%,4yr}) = \$25,000(4.573) = \$114,325$$

We employ a financial calculator throughout when valuing annuities, and also provide answers using Equation 3.15.

Future Value of an Annuity Due

How much larger will your nest egg be if great-aunt Sophie provides your allowance at the beginning of the year and you continue to invest it at 9 percent? With the cash flows occurring at the beginning of the year, they are compounded forward an extra year to determine the future value of an annuity due, so that:

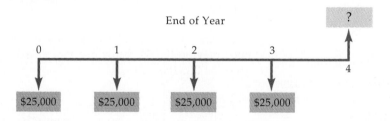

Because each cash flow is compounded for an extra year, Equations 3.14 and 3.15 are modified as follows:

$$FV_n \text{ (annuity due)} = \left(PMT \sum_{t=1}^{n-1} (1 + k)^t \right)(1 + k) \tag{3.16}$$

and

$$FV_n(\text{annuity due}) = PMT(FVA_{k,n})(1 + k) \tag{3.17}$$

Solving the earlier example as an annuity due, using a financial calculator, our answer is approximately $124,618. Using Equation 3.17 the answer is:

$$FV_4 = \$25{,}000(FVA_{9\%,4\text{yr}})(1.09) = \$25{,}000(4.573)(1.09) = \$124{,}614$$

where the $4 difference is again due to rounding. Notice that the future value of an annuity due is larger than the future value of an ordinary annuity because of the extra year's compounding. Other things being equal, an annuity due is more valuable than an ordinary annuity.

Present Value of an Uneven Cash Flow Series

It is also important to understand how to determine the present value when an uneven series of cash flows occurs. First, consider cash flows of $100 at year 1, $150 at year 2, $325 at year 3, and a discount rate of 12 percent. Graphically, this is:

The general equation to find the present value of any series of cash flows is:

$$\text{present value of any cash flow series, } PV_0 = \sum_{t=1}^{n} \frac{FV_t}{(1 + k)^t} \tag{3.18}$$

FIGURE 3.2

Present Value of an 8-Year Uneven Series Incorporating an Annuity, Discounted at 12 Percent

Instead of six separate steps, it is easier and faster to value the annuity at time $t = 2$ and then discount it to time $t = 0$. This step is unnecessary when using a financial calculator.

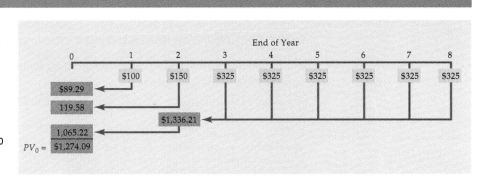

Using Equation 3.18, we see that:[6]

$$PV_0 = \frac{\$100}{(1.12)^1} + \frac{\$150}{(1.12)^2} + \frac{\$325}{(1.12)^3}$$

$$= \$89.29 + \$119.58 + \$231.33 = \$440.20$$

Now consider another example in which the cash flows are $100 at year 1, $150 at year 2, and then $325 for *each* of years 3 through 8, so that:

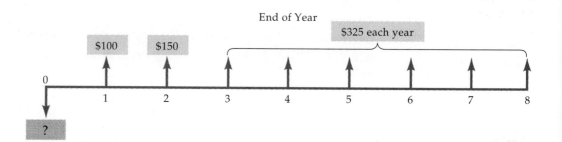

The discount rate remains 12 percent. This problem can be solved in 8 separate steps using Equation 3.18, but time can be saved by using the techniques we have learned for annuities. To solve, proceed as follows:

STEP 1: Determine the present value at $t = 2$ of the annuity of $325 to be received in years 3 through 8. Because this annuity is for 6 years (years 3, 4, 5, 6, 7, and 8), its present value at $t = 2$ is $1,336.21 using a financial calculator. Or, using Equation 3.11, it is:

$$PV_2 = \$325(PVA_{12\%,6yr}) = \$325(4.111) = \$1,336.075 \approx \$1,336.08$$

STEP 2: Using the more precise figure of $1,336.21, this lump sum is then discounted back to time $t = 0$, which is $1,065.22 [i.e., ($1,336.21)/(1 + 0.12)^2], as shown in Figure 3.2.

STEP 3: Discount the $100 to be received at the end of year 1 and the $150 to be received at the end of year 2 back to time $t = 0$. The amounts are $89.29 and $119.58, respectively.

STEP 4: Sum the values from Steps 2 and 3. Thus, $89.29 + $119.58 + $1,065.22 = $1,274.09. This is the present value of the entire cash flow series discounted at 12 percent.[7]

CONCEPT REVIEW QUESTIONS

■ Explain how you would find the present and future values of a single cash flow and of multiple cash flows.

■ What is the difference between an ordinary annuity and an annuity due?

---

[6] With a financial calculator, you enter the three cash inflows, and $i = k = 12$. Selecting present value (typically called NPV, for net present value) produces the answer of $440.19. The 1 cent difference results from rounding.
[7] Using a financial calculator, the present value is $1,274.08. The 1 cent difference results from rounding.

■ How do you modify the equations for the present value and future value of an ordinary annuity to determine the present and future value of an annuity due?

DETERMINING INTERNAL RATES OF RETURN

■ LEARNING GOAL 4

Calculate the internal rate of return for various types of cash flows.

INTERNAL RATE OF RETURN, *IRR*

The interest rate that equates a given amount in the future with its present value.

In many cases both the present value (or cash outflow) at time $t = 0$ and the future cash flows and timing are known, but the interest or discount rate is not. For that information, we need to determine the **internal rate of return, *IRR***, that equates a given amount in the future (a future value) with some amount today (the present value). Assume you invest $100 today and the investment promises to provide $113 at the end of 1 year. What is your return on this investment? To find out, we compare the cash inflow in 1 year with the initial cash outflow. The return is divided by the original investment, so ($113 − $100)/$100 = $13/$100 = 0.13 = 13 percent. The internal rate of return of this 1-year investment is 13 percent.

To determine the interest or discount rate, which is simply an internal rate of return, we begin by examining individual cash flows. We then consider annuities and the case of a series of uneven cash flows.

Individual Cash Flows

Most managers think in terms of annual rates of return, so it is common to quote interest rates on a per-year basis, whether the length of the investment period is 5 years or 5 days.

Suppose you borrowed $1,000 today and agreed to pay the principal (of $1,000) and interest back in a lump sum in 5 years. The payment you agree to make at that time is $2,011.36. What compound annual rate of interest are you paying on the loan? To determine the compound rate of interest, we need to solve for the unknown discount rate k, which is an internal rate of return, where:

$$PV_0 = \frac{FV_n}{(1 + k)^n} \tag{3.19}$$

$$\$1,000 = \frac{\$2,011.36}{(1 + k)^5}$$

$$PV_0 = FV_n \left(PVF_{k,n} \right)$$
$$1000 = 2011.31 \left(PIF_{k,n} \right)$$

You can approximate the correct answer using the present or future value tables (Tables B.1 or B.3).[8] A far easier way involves using a financial calculator, which indicates that the interest rate, or internal rate of return, is 15 percent.[9]

Annuities

Precisely the same approach can be used when an (ordinary) annuity is being considered. Suppose you borrow $2,300 today and agree to repay $900 at the end of each of

---

[8]*Using the present value table (Table B.1), divide the present value of $1,000 by the future value of $2,011.36, which produces a factor of 0.4972. Now go to Table B.1 and look across the 5-period (or 5-year) row until you find the tabled factor closest to the calculated value of 0.4972. The tabled factor for 5 periods and 15 percent is 0.497, so the internal rate of return is approximately 15 percent.*

If we use the future value table (Table B.3), we divide the future value of $2,011.36 by the present value of $1,000, which results in a factor of 2.0114. Looking across the 5-period row in Table B.3, the tabled factor for 5 periods and 15 percent is 2.011; the internal rate of return is about 15 percent.

[9]*With a financial calculator the exact rate is 15.00003 percent.*

the next 3 years. What is the annual rate of interest you are paying on the loan? To determine this, we need to determine k, where:

$$PV_0 = PMT \sum_{t=1}^{n} \frac{1}{(1 + k)^t}$$

$$\$2,300 = \$900 \sum_{t=1}^{3} \frac{1}{(1 + k)^t}$$

$PV_0 = PMT \, (PVAFk_N)$

$2300, = 900 \cdot (PVAFk_N)$

We can solve this equation (at least approximately) using Table B.2, but again the simpler way is to use a financial calculator.[10] The compound interest rate, or internal rate of return, is about 8.5 percent.[11]

Uneven Cash Flow Series

The internal rate of return can also be determined if the cash flow series is uneven. Suppose you invest $350 today and the series of payments promised is $80 at $t = 1$, $125 at $t = 2$, and $225 at $t = 3$. What is your expected annual compound percentage return? The problem becomes determining k in the following equation:

$$\$350 = \frac{\$80}{(1 + k)^1} + \frac{\$125}{(1 + k)^2} + \frac{\$225}{(1 + k)^3}$$

We need to determine what specific (single) rate *causes the present value of the cash inflows to exactly equal the initial present value,* which in this example is $350. This is a harder problem to solve using the tables in the back of the book; however, it can be done.[12] Using a financial calculator is far easier; with it, we find the interest rate, k, is about 9.3 percent.[13]

CONCEPT REVIEW QUESTION

■ What is an internal rate of return? How is it determined for lump sums? For annuities? For uneven cash flows?

---

[10] To solve this employing Table B.2 we divide the present value of $2,300 by the annuity of $900, which produces a factor of 2.5556. Going to Table B.2, and looking across the 3-period (or 3-year) row, the tabled factor closest to the calculated factor of 2.5556. The tabled factor for 3 periods and 8 percent is 2.577, whereas it is 2.531 for 3 periods and 9 percent. The internal rate of return is between 8 and 9 percent; since it is about equidistant between the two rates, let's call it about 8.5 percent.

[11] The exact rate is 8.46654... ≈ 8.5 percent.

[12] Using the end-of-book tables, this is a trial-and-error approach. The question often asked is, "What interest rate should I start with?" One approach is to calculate a "simulated" annuity by summing the inflows and then dividing by the number of periods. Thus, ($80 + $125 + $225)/3 = $430/3 = $143.33. Dividing the present value of $350 by the simulated annuity of $143.33 gives a PVA factor of 2.442, which indicates what the rate would be if the series were in fact an annuity. Looking across the row for period 3 in Table B.2 indicates the simulated annuity interest rate is about 11 percent.

However, note that the cash flows increase each year, with those in year 2 being higher than in year 1, and those in year 3 being higher than in year 2. In such a case the simulated annuity approach produces a high estimate of the actual rate. Using a lower rate of 10 percent as our initial guess, then we proceed by trial-and-error from scratch. To proceed we have to find the rate that makes the present value of the series of future cash flows exactly equal to the present value of $350. At 10 percent we have $80/(1.10)¹ + $125/(1.10)² + $225/(1.10)³ = $72.727 + $103.306 + $169.046 = $345.079. Since our calculated value of $345.079 is lower than the present value of $350, we are using too high a rate. (If the first guess produced a higher value than the present value, it would indicate that our first guess was too low.)

Let's drop the rate to 9 percent, where $80/(1.09)¹ + $125/(1.09)² + $225/(1.09)³ = $73.394 + $105.210 + $173.741 = $352.345. Since this rate is larger than the present value of $350, the interest rate, or internal rate of return, is between 9 and 10 percent, but a little closer to 9 percent. The advantage of the simulated annuity approach is that it provides a reasonable first guess.

[13] The exact rate is 9.31927... ≈ 9.3 percent.

APPLICATIONS

We now have the necessary time value tools to make most of the investment decisions encountered in financial management. In this book most of the time when we employ present values, future values, and internal rates of return, we will assume that the cash flows occur on a yearly basis. However, in practice other discounting and compounding periods (such as monthly, daily, etc.) occur; later in this section we will explain how to proceed when the cash flows (and discounting or compounding) occur more frequently than yearly.

Net Present Value and Internal Rate of Return

■ LEARNING GOAL 5

Distinguish between net present value and the internal rate of return.

At the beginning of this chapter we presented an example where you were left with a tax-free gift of $250,000. You could invest it for 1 year and secure a return of $325,000, or you could invest the $250,000 in your next best alternative, which was a "market basket" to common stocks with an expected return of 12 percent. We concluded that you should make the investment. Now let's revisit that decision and formally discuss two of the primary decision criteria in finance—net present value and internal rate of return.

Key Idea 1—the goal of the firm is to maximize its market value.

In financial management we deal with investment decisions by determining the net present value, *NPV*, of the proposed investment. The net present value tells us how much a proposed investment contributes to increasing or decreasing the value of the firm. The procedure is to discount the future cash inflows at a rate that reflects the opportunities bypassed and the risks involved, and then subtract the initial investment. As discussed in Chapter 1, the net present value when there is only one future cash inflow from a proposed investment is:

$$\text{net present value} = \frac{\text{future value of cash inflows}}{1 + \text{discount rate based on forgone opportunities}} - \text{initial investment}$$

$$= \frac{\$325,000}{1.12} - \$250,000 = \$40,179$$

Thus, you should invest in the office complex because it makes a net contribution to value of $40,179 after considering the timing of the expected cash flows and the alternative use of the funds. If the net present value had turned out to be negative, it indicates you would have lost money on the investment. In that case, you would choose not to invest in the office complex. The general equation for determining the net present value of any proposed investment project is:

$$\text{net present value, } NPV = \sum_{t=1}^{n} \frac{CF_t}{(1 + k)^t} - CF_0 \qquad (3.20)$$

where CF_t are the expected future cash flows, k is the return on forgone opportunities, and CF_0 is the initial investment today.

Instead of calculating the net present value of the proposed office complex, we can make the same decision another way. This approach involves finding the *internal rate of return* on the project. The internal rate of return calculation will give us the compound return we can expect from the investment in the office complex, and we can then compare that return to the return offered by the next best investment. For the office complex, where there are only two time periods—today and one year from today—the internal rate of return is determined as follows:

$$\frac{FV_1}{1 + IRR} = PV_0 \tag{3.21}$$

$$\frac{\$325,000}{1 + IRR} = \$250,000$$

$$\$325,000 = \$250,000 + \$250,000(IRR)$$

$$IRR = (\$325,000 - \$250,000)/\$250,000 = 30\%$$

By investing in the project you achieve a return of 30 percent. Because this return is greater than the 12 percent you could earn by investing in an equally risky alternative, you would accept the project. On the other hand, if the internal rate of return was less than 12 percent, you would reject the office complex and invest in your next best alternative.

When there are more cash flows, or they are more than one period apart, the internal rate of return is determined by solving for the unknown discount rate, where:

$$\sum_{t=1}^{n} \frac{CF_t}{(1 + IRR)^t} - CF_0 = 0 \quad \text{or} \quad \sum_{t=1}^{n} \frac{CF_t}{(1 + IRR)^t} = CF_0 \tag{3.22}$$

We will encounter both net present value and internal rate of return throughout the book.

Thus, we have two ways to determine whether to make the investment or not:

1. *Net Present Value:* Accept the proposed opportunity if the *NPV* is positive. The net present value is equal to the present value of the future cash flow minus the initial investment required.
2. *Internal Rate of Return:* Accept the proposed opportunity if the return is greater than the discount rate, *k*. The return is the compound return earned based on the initial investment and the future cash inflows.

OPPORTUNITY COST OF CAPITAL

The rate, *k*, that is forgone in order investment in a capital project; also called the *discount rate*.

The rate *k* is an *opportunity cost;* it is the return on the forgone opportunity that was bypassed in order to make the investment. This rate *k* is often referred to as the **opportunity cost of capital.** We use the terms "discount rate," "*k*," and "opportunity cost of capital" interchangeably. Because there are a few instances where net present value and internal rate of return do not lead to the same decision, we primarily employ the net present value decision criteria throughout.[14]

More Frequent Cash Flows

■ LEARNING GOAL 6

Calculate compounding and discounting rates for cash flow intervals of less than a year.

So far we have assumed that the compounding and discounting is done annually. That is, the period has been specified as "years." However, compounding or discounting

---

[14]*When there are more than two cash flows, the two decision criteria may not produce the same decision. This topic is explored in Chapter 7. At that time we will discuss why net present value provides a better basis for decision making than internal rate of return.*

NOMINAL INTEREST RATE
The quoted rate of interest per year.

EFFECTIVE INTEREST RATE
The true rate of interest *per time period,* based on both the frequency of compounding and the nominal rate.

intervals of *less than a year* are employed, and in such cases there are two different rates that apply. The **nominal interest rate** is the quoted rate per year. The **effective interest rate** is the true rate *per time period,* and it depends both on the frequency of compounding and the nominal rate. Thus:

$$\text{effective rate per period} = \frac{\text{nominal interest rate, } k}{\text{number of compounding periods per year, } m} \qquad (3.23)$$

For example, if the nominal rate of interest is 8 percent per year, the effective *semiannual* rate is 8%/2 = 4%, and the effective *monthly* rate is 8%/12 = 0.66667%.

Discounting and Compounding

To illustrate more frequent periods, let's determine the present value of $10,000 to be received at the end of 2 years when the nominal interest rate is 8 percent, using different discounting intervals. Equation 3.3 becomes:

$$\text{present value with more frequent discounting, } PV_0 = \frac{FV_n}{[1 + (k/m)]^{nm}} \qquad (3.24)$$

where

$$k = \text{the annual nominal rate}$$
$$m = \text{the number of discounting intervals per year}$$
$$k/m = \text{the effective rate per period}$$
$$n = \text{the number of years}$$

A recent ploy to entice consumers to buy big-ticket items is to offer 0% financing. No firm can afford to give a 0% loan; they offset the financing costs by increasing the price of the item sold.

The present value, employing different discounting intervals, is:

$$PV_0 \text{ (annual)} = \frac{\$10,000}{[1 + (0.08/1)]^{2(1)}} = \$8,573.39$$

$$PV_0 \text{ (semi-annual)} = \frac{\$10,000}{[1 + (0.08/2)]^{2(2)}} = \$8,548.04$$

$$PV_0 \text{ (quarterly)} = \frac{\$10,000}{[1 + (0.08/4)]^{2(4)}} = \$8,534.90$$

$$PV_0 \text{ (monthly)} = \frac{\$10,000}{[1 + (0.08/12)]^{2(12)}} = \$8,525.96$$

Likewise, when continuous discounting is employed, Equation 3.3 becomes:[15]

$$\text{present value with continuous discounting, } PV_0 = FV_n/e^{kn} = FV_n e^{-kn} \qquad (3.25)$$

where e is the value 2.71828. The present value of $10,000 to be received 2 years from now if the nominal discount rate is 8 percent, employing continuous discounting, is:[16]

$$PV_0 = \$10,000e^{-0.08(2)} = \$8,521.44$$

---

[15] Note that dividing FV_n by e^{kn} is the same mathematically as multiplying FV_n by e^{-kn}. The minus sign in the exponent simply indicates the inverse.
[16] On a calculator, enter -0.16 [i.e., $(0.08)(2) = 0.16$] followed by the e^x key. Then multiply by 10000 to get $8,521.4379 \approx \$8,521.44$.

To determine future values instead of present values, Equation 3.5 is modified to:

$$\text{future value with more frequent compounding, } FV_n = PV_0 \left(1 + \frac{k}{m}\right)^{nm} \quad (3.26)$$

To illustrate, the future value in 4 years of $3,000 today, with a nominal interest rate of 9.5 percent, using daily compounding, is:

$$FV_4 = \$3,000 \left(1 + \frac{0.095}{365}\right)^{4(365)} = \$4,386.64$$

Alternatively, continuous compounding could be employed instead of daily compounding. The future value equation using continuous compounding is:

$$\text{future value with continuous compounding, } FV_n = PV_0 e^{kn} \quad (3.27)$$

The future value at $t = 4$ of $3,000 today, when the nominal interest rate is 9.5 percent and continuous compounding is used, is:[17]

$$FV_4 = \$3,000 e^{0.095(4)} = \$4,386.85$$

While daily or even hourly compounding will provide a result that approaches that provided by continuous compounding, continuous compounding always provides the highest future value. Thus, if you have to choose between an investment that employs daily compounding or continuous compounding, always choose continuous compounding—since it always provides the highest future value.

Effective Annual Interest Rates

There is one other item to cover—how to determine an **effective annual interest rate,** which is the "true" rate of interest per year, based on the nominal rate and the frequency of compounding. The effective annual interest rate is:

$$\text{effective annual interest rate, } k_{\text{effective annual}} = \left(\frac{1 + k_{\text{nominal}}}{m}\right)^m - 1 \quad (3.28)$$

Note that dividing k_{nominal} by m provides the effective rate per period as indicated by Equation 3.23. Then, Equation 3.28 converts this effective rate *per period* to an effective *annual* rate. For example, if the nominal rate is 12 percent per year, and the compounding period is quarterly, the effective annual rate is:

$$k_{\text{effective annual}} = \left(1 + \frac{0.12}{4}\right)^4 - 1 = 0.1255 = 12.55\%$$

Being able to understand effective interest rates comes into play any time you borrow from or deposit money into a financial institution. Unfortunately, two different rates are mandated—one if you are borrowing money and a second if you are depositing money! As part of the Consumer Protection Act passed in 1968, Regulation Z (the

---

[17] *On a calculator enter (0.09)(4) = 0.38 followed by the e^x key. Then multiply by 3,000 to get $4,386.85.*

ANNUAL PERCENTAGE RATE, *APR*
The interest rate calculated by multiplying the rate per period by the number of periods in a year.

You might ask your bank or financial institution how many days it uses to calculate interest on loans and deposits. The procedure can vary from one institution to another and between types of accounts.

Truth-in-Lending Act) requires that consumers be told the **annual percentage rate, *APR,*** for any loan taken out.[18] The annual percentage rate is calculated by multiplying the rate per period by the number of periods in a year. Hence, it is:

$$\text{annual percentage rate, }APR = \left(\frac{\text{effective rate}}{\text{per period}}\right)\left(\frac{\text{number of compounding periods}}{\text{per year, }m}\right) \quad (3.29)$$

Because the *APR* is determined by *multiplying* the rate per period by the number of periods in a year, *it is a nominal rate*, not an effective annual rate. For example, say you are quoted an *APR* of 12 percent per year, with 12 (monthly) payments per year on a loan. While the *APR* is 12 percent, the effective annual rate is higher than 12 percent. To determine the effective annual rate using Equation 3.28, you first find the effective rate per period, which is 12 percent/12 payments, and then compound it as follows:

$$k_{\text{effective annual}} = \left(1 + \frac{0.12}{12}\right)^{12} - 1 = 0.1268 = 12.68\%$$

The effective annual rate, which is the "true" compound rate paid, is 12.68 percent, not the 12 percent specified by the *APR*.

When it comes to depositing money at a financial institution, all depository institutions (such as banks and savings and loan associations) must comply with Regulation DD of the Truth-in-Savings Act, which was part of the FDIC Improvement Act of 1991. Under that act, institutions must calculate and report the **annual percentage yield, *APY,*** on all deposit accounts. The annual percentage yield is the compound annual return earned on the investment. Thus, if you have a savings account or purchase a certificate of deposit, the institution is required to report the annual percentage yield, which is calculated as follows:

ANNUAL PERCENTAGE YIELD, *APY*
The compound annual return earned on an investment.

$$\text{annual percentage yield, }APY = 100\left[\left(1 + \frac{\text{interest}}{\text{principal}}\right)^{(365/\text{days in term})} - 1\right] \quad (3.30)$$

To understand the *APY*, assume $1,000 is deposited for 1 year, with the interest to be paid at a nominal rate of 8 percent, compounded quarterly. The interest earned the first quarter is ($1,000)(0.08/4) = $20. For the second quarter the total principal on deposit is the original $1,000 *plus* the $20 interest earned for the first quarter, for a total of $1,020. The interest earned for the second quarter is ($1,020)(0.08/4) = $20.40. Proceeding in the same manner, the interest earned in the third quarter (on the new principal of $1,040.40) is $20.808, and for the fourth quarter it is $21.224. The total interest earned for the year is $82.432 (i.e., $20 + $20.40 + $20.808 + $21.224). The annual percentage yield, given by Equation 3.30, is:

$$\text{annual percentage yield} = 100\left[\left(1 + \frac{\$82.432}{\$1,000}\right)^{(365/365)} - 1\right] = 8.243\% \approx 8.24\%$$

Instead of employing Equation 3.30, we can use the equation for the effective annual rate given by Equation 3.28, as follows:

$$k_{\text{effective annual}} = \left(1 + \frac{k_{\text{nominal}}}{m}\right)^{m} - 1$$

---

[18]*The original Truth-in-Lending Act was modified by the Truth-in-Lending Simplification and Reform Act of 1980.*

$$= \left(1 + \frac{0.08}{4}\right)^4 - 1 = 0.08243 \approx 8.24\%$$

The rate is 8.24 percent, whether one uses Equation 3.30 or 3.28. Thus, we see that *the annual percentage yield required under the Truth-in-Savings Act is, in fact, an effective annual rate.* The advantage of Equation 3.30 is that it can be employed in more complex situations sometimes encountered by financial institutions.[19]

CONCEPT REVIEW QUESTIONS

- Briefly describe the net present value and internal rate of return methods. What role does the return on forgone opportunities play in each method?
- What changes would you make to the future value and present value equations if the interest rate were compounded for less than a year?
- What is an effective annual interest rate? What factors have to be taken into consideration when calculating an effective annual interest rate?

Summary

- A dollar today is worth more than a dollar tomorrow. To determine the present value of tomorrow's dollars, you discount the future cash flows by the opportunity cost of capital.
- The present value of some future cash flow is $PV_0 = FV_n/(1 + k)^n$. The future value is $FV_n = PV_0(1 + k)^n$.
- The present value of a perpetuity is $PV_0 = PMT/k$. The present value of a perpetuity growing by a constant percentage rate per period is $PV_0 = PMT/(k - g)$.
- The present value of an annuity is:

$$PV_0 = PMT\left[\frac{1}{k} - \frac{1}{k(1 + k)^n}\right] = PMT \sum_{t=1}^{n} \frac{1}{k(1 + k)^t}$$

while the future value of an annuity is:

$$FV_n = PMT\left[\frac{(1 + k)^n - 1}{k}\right] = PMT \sum_{t=0}^{n-1} (1 + k)^t$$

- The net present value is the present value of the expected cash inflows minus the initial cash outflow on an investment. The internal rate of return is the compound rate that equates the present value of future cash inflows and the initial cash outlay. Typically, either procedure produces the same accept-reject decision.
- With more frequent than annual discounting, the present value is:

$$FV_0 = \frac{FV_n}{[1 + (k/m)]^{nm}}$$

- In order to determine the effective annual interest rate, the yearly nominal rate is converted to an effective per period interest rate and then annualized, so that:

$$k_{\text{effective annual}} = \left(1 + \frac{k_{\text{nominal}}}{m}\right)^m - 1$$

[19]*Some financial institutions use simple interest. In this situation the interest is received on the initial principal amount only; the interest is not compounded.*

■ While the annual percentage rate, *APR*, on loans is not an effective annual interest rate, the annual percentage yield, *APY*, required for depository institutions is an effective annual interest rate.

Questions

3.1 Present value and future value are the inverse, or mirror images, of each other. Explain why this is true. Then demonstrate how present value and future value relate to each other.

3.2 The following series of cash flows exists:

Time Period	Amount
$t = 1$	$300
$t = 2$	200
$t = 3$	100
$t = 4$	100

Show at least four different ways you could set up the cash flow stream to solve for the present value of this stream of cash inflows.

3.3 A firm's earnings are expected to increase by 50 percent, from $200,000 at the end of $t = 3$, to $300,000 at the end of $t = 8$. Show why the compound (or annual) growth rate is less than 10 percent per year.

3.4 Explain the relationship between net present value and internal rate of return. Is it true that the net present value can be positive only if the internal rate of return is greater than the forgone return that could have been earned, k?

3.5 Explain why you are not indifferent to having your money invested in a bank that may, at its discretion, compound annually, semiannually, quarterly, monthly, daily, or continuously. (*Note:* Assume everything else stays the same.)

Concept Review Problems

See Appendix A for solutions.

CR3.1 What will the following investments accumulate to?
  a. $6,000 invested for 10 years at 10 percent compounded annually.
  b. $8,000 invested for 5 years at 5 percent compounded annually.
  c. $500 invested for 7 years at 8 percent compounded annually.
  d. $10,000 invested for 3 years at 6 percent compounded annually.

CR3.2 What is the present value of the following investments?
  a. $6,000 due in 10 years discounted at 10 percent annual rate.
  b. $8,000 due in 5 years discounted at 5 percent annual rate.
  c. $500 due in 7 years discounted at 8 percent annual rate.
  d. $10,000 due in 3 years discounted at 6 percent annual rate.

CR3.3 What is the present value of the following perpetuities?
  a. A perpetuity with an $80 payment discounted back to time $t = 0$, at 10 percent.
  b. A perpetuity with an $80 payment growing at 4 percent per year, discounted back to the present at 10 percent.
  c. A perpetuity with an $80 payment starting in 4 years, discounted back to the present at 10 percent.

CR3.4 You recently sold your Jaguar for $25,000. With this nest egg, you place your funds in a savings account paying 8 percent compounded annually for 3 years and then move it into another savings account paying 10 percent interest compounded semiannually. How large will your nest egg be at the end of 7 years?

CR3.5 Kathryn is trying to save $5,000 for a vacation.
   a. How much will she need to place in her account today if the rate of interest is 10 percent compounded monthly and she expects to make the trip in 3 years?
   b. What is the effective annual interest rate paid on her savings account?

CR3.6 You recently won $1,000,000 from a national magazine firm. Upon announcing the winner, the entry officials notified you that you will be receiving the $1 million in equal payments over the next 20 years.
   a. If you receive the first payment after 1 year and all other payments at the end of subsequent years, and the appropriate discount rate is 8 percent, what is the present value of your winnings?
   b. If you receive the first payment immediately and then all other payments at the beginning of subsequent years, given the appropriate discount rate of 8 percent, what is the true present value of your winnings?

CR3.7 What is the future value of $500 deposited each year if:
   a. The interest rate is 10 percent, deposits are at the end of each year for 5 years, and interest is compounded annually?
   b. If the deposits are at the beginning of each year for 5 years?
   c. If the interest rate is 8 percent compounded quarterly and the deposit is at the end of the year?

CR3.8 M. Eliot Enterprises is considering an investment with the following cash flows:

Year	Cash Flow
0	−$500,000
1	140,000
2	200,000
3.	250,000

   a. If the opportunity cost of capital is 12 percent, what is the project's net present value?
   b. What is the project's internal rate of return?

CR3.9 Mary is considering purchasing a new car costing $20,000. The dealership is offering its customers one of two financing packages. Mary can receive either a $2,000 rebate or 2.9 percent financing with monthly financing for 2 years (24 payments). If she can obtain financing at her bank for 8 percent with monthly payments for 2 years, should she take the rebate or the 2.9 percent financing?

Problems

See Appendix C for answers to selected problems.

Present Values

3.1 Determine the present values (at $t = 0$) of the following:
   a. A single cash flow of $1,142 at time $t = 6$ discounted at 8 percent.
   b. An annuity of $300 per year to be received for each of 7 years discounted at 15 percent.
   c. An annuity of $400 per year to be received for each of 5 years, followed by a single cash flow of $1,000 at the end of year 6, discounted at 20 percent.
   d. An annuity of $200 for each of 6 years followed by an annuity of $800 for years 7 through 10, all discounted at 12 percent.

Future Values

3.2 Determine the future value of each of the following amounts:

a. An initial $325 compounded at 12 percent for 4 years.
b. An initial $650 compounded at 6 percent for 9 years.
c. An annuity of $150 per year for each of 6 years compounded at 10 percent.
d. An annuity of $480 per year for each of 3 years compounded at 17 percent.

Ordinary Annuity Versus Annuity Due

3.3 Sam Mart, M.D., is establishing a fund to pay off a $200,000 lump-sum loan when it matures in 10 years. The funds will earn 8 percent interest per year. What is the size of the yearly payment in each case below?
a. The payment is made at the end of the year.
b. The payment is made at the beginning of the year.

Perpetuity

3.4 After graduating from college you make it big—all because of your success in financial management. You decide to endow a scholarship for needy finance students that will provide $3,000 per year indefinitely, beginning *1 year* from now. How much must be deposited *today* to fund the scholarship under the following conditions?
a. The interest rate is 10 percent.
b. The interest rate is 8 percent.
c. For both 10 and 8 percent, if everything stays the same except that the first disbursement will not be made until *3 years* from now.

$30,000 \left(\text{DISCOUNT IT FOR} \atop 2 \text{ YRS.} \right)$

Future Value of an Annuity

3.5 You plan to deposit $250 in a savings account for each of 5 years, starting 1 year from now. The interest rate is 9 percent compounded annually. What is the future value in each of the following cases?
a. At the end of 5 years?
b. At the end of 6 years if *no additional deposits* are made?
c. At the end of 5 years, as in (a), if an *additional* $250 is deposited today (i.e., at $t = 0$), so there are six deposits of $250 each?

Future Value

Note: Ignore any tax considerations.

3.6 Your firm has a retirement plan that matches all contributions on a one-to-two basis. That is, if you contribute $2,000 per year, the company will add $1,000 to make it $3,000. The firm guarantees an 8 percent return on the funds. Alternatively, you can "do it yourself"; you think you can earn 11 percent on your money this way. The first contribution will be made 1 year from today. At that time, and every year thereafter, you will put $2,000 into the retirement account. If you want to retire in 25 years, which way are you better off?

Future Values

Note: Ignore any tax implications.

3.7 Davis is planning for retirement. He plans to work for 25 more years. For the next 10 years, he can save $3,000 per year (with the first deposit being made 1 year from now), and at that time he wants to buy a weekend vacation home he estimates will cost $40,000. How much will he need to save in years 11 through 25 so that he has saved up exactly $300,000 when he retires? Assume he can earn 10 percent compounded annually for each of the next 25 years.

Present Value

3.8 Olympia Electric has a line of small motors that no longer fits its corporate image. It is attempting to determine the minimum selling price for the small-motors line. Olympia presently receives $250,000 per year after taxes in cash flows from the line. If the opportunity cost of capital is 16 percent, how much should Olympia ask if it thinks the life expectancy of the line is as follows?
a. 10 years.
b. 20 years.
c. infinity.

Present Value and Future Value

Note: In series B, simply retain the negative sign associated with the cash flow for year 3, and then proceed as usual.

3.9 Calculate the present value (at $t = 0$) and then the future value at the end of year 4 for the following series. The appropriate rate is 14 percent.

| | Series | | |
Year	A	B	C
1	$100	$300	$400
2	300	100	0
3	200	−100	50
4	50	200	100

Return

3.10 If the present value is $150 and the future value in 1 year is $180, what is the discount rate?

Interest Rates

3.11 Find the interest rates or internal rates of return implied by the following:

a. You lend $500 today and receive a promise for repayment 3 years from now of $595.

b. You invest $500 today and have a promise of receiving $200 for each of the next 3 years.

c. You invest $1,400 today and will receive $2,590 back at the end of 8 years.

d. You lend $1,400 today and the repayments will be $282 for each of the next 8 years.

Internal Rate of Return

3.12 Barnaby & Associates has decided to automate to increase efficiency. By purchasing word processing equipment costing $6,625, it can save $1,800 per year for each of 10 years in labor costs. What is the internal rate of return on the word processing equipment?

Internal Rate of Return

3.13 You are a lucky winner in the Down South Lottery. As a result, you have a choice between three alternative payment plans.

Plan I: A lifetime annuity of $60,425 annually, with the first payment 1 year from now.

Plan II: A $70,000 annual annuity for 20 years, with the first payment 1 year from now.

Plan III: $800,000 today.

Your life expectancy is 45 more years. Ignoring any tax effects, determine the following:

a. At what interest rate would you be indifferent between Plans I and III?

b. At what interest rate would you be indifferent between Plans II and III?

Note: It is easier to solve (c) by trial-and-error than algebraically.

c. At what interest rate (to the nearest whole number) would you be indifferent between Plans I and II?

d. What if (c) is now changed so you know the interest rate for both Plans I and II is 12 percent for the first 20 years? What rate would you have to earn on the remaining 25 years of the $60,425 annuity to be indifferent between Plans I and II?

Uneven Cash Flows

3.14 Determine the internal rate of return for the following series of cash flows:

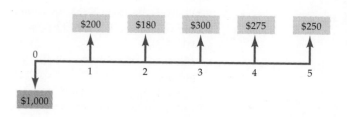

Present Value and *IRR*

3.15 Consider the following set of annual cash flows: $t_1 = \$200$, $t_2 = \$200$, $t_3 = \$200$, $t_4 = \$500$, and $t_5 = \$500$.

a. Find the present value of this series if the discount rate is 12 percent.

b. If you could acquire the right to receive this series of cash inflows by paying $1,000 today, what would the compound percentage return (or internal rate of return) be on your investment?

Cost of Alternative Loans

3.16 Hacienda Winery needs $500,000 for expansion of its warehouse. The company plans to finance $100,000 with internally generated funds but wants to secure a loan for the remainder. The contracting firm's finance subsidiary has offered to provide the loan based on six annual payments of $97,300 each. Alternatively, Hacienda's bankers will lend the firm $400,000, to be repaid in six equal annual installments (covering both principal and interest) at a 15 percent interest rate. Finally, an insurance firm would also loan the money; it requires a lump sum payment of $750,000 at the end of 6 years.

a. Based on the respective annual percentage costs of the three loans, which one should Hacienda select?

b. What other considerations might be important in addition to cost?

Compounding Periods

3.17 If $1,000 is invested today, how much will it be worth in (a) 5 years or (b) 10 years, if interest at a 12 percent nominal rate is compounded annually, semiannually, or quarterly?

Future Value and Compounding

3.18 How much would you have in the future in each of the following cases?

a. $2,500, invested today, if continuous compounding is employed, the nominal rate is 9 percent, and the period is 2 1/2 years.

b. $4.80, invested today, if the nominal rate is 12.6 percent continuously compounded, and the period is 15 years.

c. $100 invested today, if the nominal rate is 14 percent compounded annually, and the period is 10 years.

d. Same as in (c), except interest is compounded continuously.

Present Value and Compounding

3.19 Find the present value of each of the following:

a. $1,500 to be received in 8 years at a nominal rate of 6 percent discounted continuously.

b. $10 to be received in 4 years, and $50 to be received in 5 years, at a nominal rate of 15 percent discounted continuously.

Effective Annual Interest Rate

3.20 What is the effective annual interest rate if the nominal rate is 9 percent per year, a 365-day year is used, and the compounding period is (a) yearly, (b) quarterly, (c) daily, or (d) hourly?

APR and APY

Note: Use a 365-day year for the daily compounding.

3.21 If the nominal yearly rate is 10 percent, what is the (a) annual percentage rate and the (b) annual percentage yield if interest is compounded (1) semiannually, (2) quarterly, (3) monthly, and (4) daily.

Time Value of Money

3.22 **Mini Case** Your best friend does not understand much about financial decision making and time value. To help your friend, you have found the following questions from some old financial management books. However, you don't have any answers to determine if your friend's answers are correct. Thus, you need to answer the following, so that the two of you can compare answers:

a. What is the future value of $300 at the end of 4 years if the interest rate is 9 percent compounded annually? What would be the future value at the end of 6 years if for the last 2 years the interest rate decreased from 9 to 7 percent?

b. What is the present value today (at $t = 0$) of $600 to be received at $t = 6$ if the discount rate is 8.6 percent per year?

c. An annuity of $300 per year for 7 years exists. If the discount rate is 10 percent, what is the present value if it is an ordinary annuity? An annuity due? Explain the difference in values between the annuity and the annuity due.

d. You just won the Big Payoff. The payments are $350,000 for each of 13 years, with the first payment to be made at $t = 2$ and the last at $t = 14$. If the discount rate is 12 percent, what is the present value of your winnings?

e. What is the present value of a perpetuity of $200 per year if the discount rate is 16 percent? What if the first payment on the perpetuity does not occur until $t = 4$? Calculate the new present value of the perpetuity.

f. A cash flow stream exists as follows:

Year	Cash Flows
1	$100
2	300
3	−200
4	500

   (1)   What is the future value at $t = 4$ if the interest rate is 11 percent?
   (2)   What is the future value at $t = 6$ if the interest rate remains 11 percent?
   (3)   What is the present value of the stream if the annual interest rate is 8 percent?

g. If an investment requires an outlay of $400 today, and promises to pay $50 at $t = 1$, $350 at $t = 2$, and $150 at $t = 3$, what compound percentage return would you earn if you made the investment?

h. What is the present value of $20,000 to be received 4 years from now if the discount rate is 10 percent and discounting is done:
   (1)   annually?
   (2)   quarterly?
   (3)   monthly?
   (4)   daily? (Assume all years have 365 days.)
   (5)   continuously?

i. Explain the difference between the nominal interest rate, the effective annual interest rate, the annual percentage rate, *APR*, and the annual percentage yield, *APY*.

Valuation of Bonds and Stocks

Sections in this chapter:

■ **Determining Bond Values and Yields**
Why bond values seem contrary to the market.

■ **Determining Common Stock Values**
Just how much is ownership in a firm worth?

■ **The Present Value of Growth Opportunities**
What increases the value of a firm.

■ **Appendix 4A: Reading the Financial Pages**
Finding your way around stock and bond quotes.

What's a security really worth? When there are many buyers and sellers, the ultimate answer is simple. The value of the security is the price at which the security changes hands. But even for widely traded securities, it's important to understand what drives the worth of securities, in order to determine if the relationship between what the security trades for and what determines its value have any resemblance.

For bonds, the value of the bond is a function of three items: the risk of the firm or government issuing the bond, the cash flows expected from the bond, and what's happening to inflation, the business climate, and the macro economic climate. In practice U.S. Treasury bonds, which are widely traded, are priced at the last sale, whereas corporate bonds are priced by comparing them with similar bonds and with U.S. Treasury securities. With more complicated bonds, such as mortgage-backed securities—often called CMOs, for collateralized mortgage obligations—determining their value is much more difficult.

What determines the value of a share of common stock? The return that an investor anticipates receiving from investing in common stock has to come from one of two sources—cash dividends and/or the change in the price of the stock, leading to capital appreciation (gain) or capital loss. Although projections on both dividends and the change in price can be made, determining the value of common stock is much more difficult than determining the value of many bonds. The reason is that with a bond there is a prior legal claim, whereas common stock has only a residual claim after the claims of creditors and bondholders. That is, the common stock can be worth a lot if the firm prospers, but its value can be dissipated to nothing if the firm falls on hard times.

Though it's easy to see why investors must understand the basics of valuing bonds and stocks, it's also of vital importance that managers understand what determines the value of bonds and stocks. Many of the firm's investments and financing decisions are directly influenced by current and anticipated bond and stock prices and by investors' required returns. So managers must understand how risk, required return, and market prices interact.

LEARNING GOALS

After studying this chapter, you should be able to:

1. Determine the value of a bond and its yield to maturity.
2. Determine the value of consols and preferred stock.
3. Determine the value of common stock for no-growth, constant growth, and non-constant growth conditions.
5. Explain the impact of a firm's growth opportunities on its value.

DETERMINING BOND VALUES AND YIELDS

PAR (MATURITY) VALUE
The stated or face value of a bond, typically $1,000.

The interest rate is called the coupon because in the past, investors had to clip a coupon and send it in to receive their interest payments.

As we learned in Chapter 1, a *bond* is a specific form of borrowing by a firm or government. Bonds carry a stated **par** (or **maturity**) **value,** typically $1,000. Thus, the firm has borrowed $1,000 from investors with a promise to repay the principal of $1,000 in the future. The firm also pays interest on the borrowing as determined by the coupon interest rate stated in the bond.[1] For example, on a borrowing of $1,000 and assuming a coupon interest rate of 9 percent, interest of ($1,000)(0.09) = $90 is paid by the firm to the owners of the bond each year. Although some bonds are relatively short-lived, most have an initial maturity of 10 to 30 years. Recently, Disney issued a 100-year bond. At the maturity of the bond the firm pays to the bondholder the principal of $1,000.

The bond is initially sold in the primary market, with the proceeds going to the issuer. When bonds are sold initially, they are typically priced so they sell close to their par value. On the other hand, the prices of *outstanding bonds*, all bonds that have previously been issued and are still held by investors, vary tremendously. When outstanding bonds are bought or sold in the secondary market, their price may be close to or far from par value.

Bond Valuation

Bond valuation, as well as stock valuation, is based on Key Ideas 4 and 5—firms (and individuals) focus on cash flows, and a dollar today is worth more than a dollar tomorrow.

■ LEARNING GOAL 1

Determine the value of a bond and its yield to maturity.

How is the price of a bond valued in the secondary market? The market price of a bond is equal to the present value of the series of interest payments to be received over the bond's life, plus the present value of the maturity value of $1,000, all discounted at the investor's required rate of return for the bond. Thus, a bond's price is equal to

$$\text{price, } B_0 = \sum_{t=1}^{n} \frac{I_t}{(1 + k_b)^t} + \frac{M}{(1 + k_b)^n} \tag{4.1}$$

[1]*Another type of bond, the zero-coupon bond, does not have a stated coupon interest rate. These bonds are discussed in Chapter 11.*

where

B_0 = the current market price of the bond

I = the dollar amount of interest expected to be received each year
(or par value × coupon interest rate)

n = the number of years to **maturity** for the bond

k_b = the required rate of return for the bond

M = the par or maturity value of the bond

MATURITY
A bond's length (or term),
expressed in years; at
maturity the issuer must
redeem the bond at its
par value.

As discussed in Chapter 2, the return demanded on bonds equals the risk-free rate, plus a risk premium. The risk premium may include a maturity premium (for longer maturity bonds), a default premium (for corporate bonds), a liquidity premium (for bonds that trade only infrequently), and other premiums. Thus k_b, the return demanded by bond investors, may change depending on the bond being considered.

Consider a $1,000 par bond that has a 10 percent coupon rate and a 25-year maturity. If investors require a return of 10 percent on this bond and it pays interest annually, its value is

$$B_0 = \frac{\$100}{(1.10)^1} + \frac{\$100}{(1.10)^2} + \cdots + \frac{\$100}{(1.10)^{25}} + \frac{\$1,000}{(1.10)^{25}}$$

$$B_0 = \sum_{t=1}^{25} \frac{\$100}{(1.10)^t} + \frac{\$1,000}{(1.10)^{25}} = \$1,000$$

In this example, the bond has a current market value of $1,000, which is exactly equal to its par value.[2] Thus, *if the required rate of return demanded by investors is equal to the bond's coupon rate, the current market value of a bond is equal to its par value.*[3]

Expected Inflation

*Interest rate volatility
increased dramatically in the
1980s and 1990s. Increased
volatility creates more risk
for financial managers when
deciding when to borrow
and for how long.*

Assume the 25-year bond discussed above is a U.S. Treasury bond. At the time it is issued, investors hold expectations as to future inflation, and those expectations influence the rate of return they will require. Suppose that after the bond is issued, due to changes in either international or domestic economic conditions, expected inflation suddenly and unexpectedly jumps by 4 percent. Other things being equal, this jump will cause the market rate of interest demanded by investors for new bonds of similar quality and maturity to increase from 10 to 14 percent. This change in market interest rates will also cause the required rate of return demanded by investors on *all outstanding bonds of similar quality and maturity* to increase—again, to 14 percent. This occurs because investors considering the 10 percent coupon rate bond will not be willing to settle for less than they can receive in newly issued securities of comparable quality but with a higher coupon rate.

What would be the market value of these U.S. Treasury bonds? To determine this new market price, the interest payments and principal (or maturity value) are

[2]*As indicated in Chapter 3, all financial calculations in this book are made with a financial calculator. If present value tables are employed, $B_0 = \$100(PVA_{10\%,25}) + \$1,000(PV_{10\%,25}) = \$100(9.077) + \$1,000(0.092) = \$907.70 + \$92.00 = \$999.70 \approx \$1,000$.*

[3]*Bonds actually sell at their current market price plus accrued interest. For a new issue there is typically little or no accrued interest. However, if the bond were purchased one-fourth of the way through the year, then its actual purchase price would be $\$1,000 + \frac{1}{4}(\$100)$, or $1,025.*

discounted at the new market rate of interest (or required rate of return) of 14 percent, so that:[4]

$$B_0 = \sum_{t=1}^{25} \frac{\$100}{(1.14)^t} + \frac{\$1,000}{(1.14)^{25}} = \$725.08$$

An investor purchasing this 10 percent coupon rate bond for $725.08 and holding it for 25 years expects to receive a compound return of 14 percent. This return is composed of two parts—the 10 percent coupon, which is expected to provide $100 per year, plus the expected capital appreciation of $274.92 (i.e., $1,000 − 725.08) that occurs over the life of the bond. The difference between the $1,000 par value and the current market price of $725.08 is called the **discount** on the bond.

Bonds may also sell at a **premium.** To continue our example, what if economic conditions suddenly change, causing general market interest rates to drop unexpectedly to 6 percent on bonds of comparable quality and maturity? The current market price of the 25-year, 10 percent coupon rate Treasury bond becomes:[5]

$$B_0 = \sum_{t=1}^{25} \frac{\$100}{(1.06)^t} + \frac{\$1,000}{(1.06)^{25}} = \$1,511.33$$

Because the coupon rate of 10 percent is greater than the new market interest rate of 6 percent, investors pay a premium of $511.33 (i.e., $1,511.33 − $1,000) for the bond. The relationship between the current market yield and the market price is graphed in Figure 4.1. The fundamental point to remember is this: *The price of a bond and general market interest rates move inversely.* If the market interest rate is less than a bond's coupon rate, the bond will sell at a premium. If market interest rates are greater than the coupon rate on a bond, the bond will sell at a discount. A second point to remember, as discussed previously, is: *The primary determinant of changes in market interest rates is expected inflation.*

DISCOUNT (ON A BOND)
Difference between the par value of a bond and its current market price selling below its par value.

PREMIUM (ON A BOND)
Difference between a bond's par value and its current market price selling above its par value.

FIGURE 4.1

Relationship Among a Bond's Market Price and the Current Market Rate of Interest

As market interest rates fall, the bond price rises. Similarly, a rise in the market interest rates causes bond prices to decline.

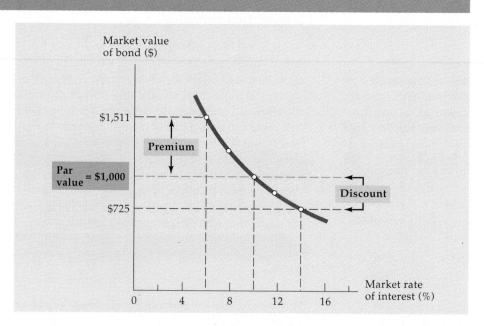

[4]*With present value tables, $B_0 = \$100(PVA_{14\%,25}) + \$1,000(PV_{14\%,25}) = \$100(6.873) + \$1,000(0.038) = \$687.30 + \$38.00 = \$725.30.$*

[5]*With present value tables, $B_0 = \$100(PVA_{6\%,25}) + \$1,000(PV_{6\%,25}) = \$100(12.783) + \$1,000(0.233) = \$1,278.30 + \$233.00 = \$1,511.30.$*

FIGURE 4.2

Relationship Among a Bond's Market Price, the Current Market Rate of Interest, and Bond Maturity

The market price of shorter-maturity bonds fluctuates substantially less than for longer-maturity bonds as market interest rates change.

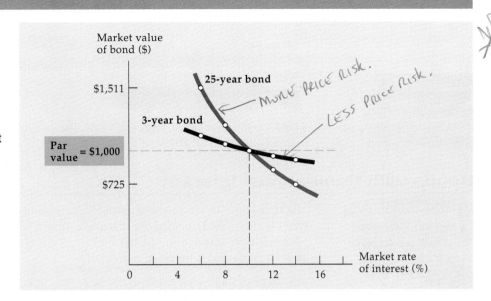

Interest Rate Risk and the Maturity Premium

Bond prices are influenced not only by market interest rates but also by the term (or length) to maturity of the bonds. To see this relationship, consider what happens to the current market price of the 10 percent U.S. Treasury bonds as they get closer to maturity. Assume they have only 3 years left until maturity, instead of 25. As Figure 4.2 shows, the market prices of the 3-year bonds adjust substantially less to changes in market interest rates than do the prices of 25-year bonds. The change in the market price of a bond as general interest rates change is called *interest rate risk*. The tendency is for prices on short-term bonds to fluctuate less in response to interest rate changes than the prices on longer-term bonds. The reason is fairly obvious: Because they are relatively close to maturity, short-term bonds face less interest rate risk. It is because of interest rate risk that the return on long-term bonds typically incorporates a maturity premium (or requires a higher interest rate) over comparable short-term bonds.

Determining the Yield to Maturity

The promised yield to maturity assumes that you reinvest each coupon payment at the promised yield to maturity for the remaining time to maturity.

YIELD TO MATURITY, *YTM*
The compound return earned on a bond if it is purchased at a given price and held to maturity.

Instead of being given the required rate of return on a bond, suppose you are told that a 15-year maturity, $1,000 par bond with a 7 percent coupon rate sells for $915. What is the compound rate of return, called the **yield to maturity, *YTM***, you would earn if you purchased the bond and held it for the entire 15 years? Answering this question involves finding the unknown discount rate, k_b, as follows:

$$\$915 = \sum_{t=1}^{25} \frac{\$70}{(1 + k_b)^t} + \frac{\$1,000}{(1 + k_b)^{15}}$$

Before starting this calculation, note two points: First, the yield to maturity is simply an internal rate of return, as discussed in Chapter 3. Hence, we already know how to determine the unknown rate, k_b, which is the bond's yield to maturity. Second, because the market price of $915 is *less* than the par value of $1,000, the yield to maturity will be *greater* than the coupon interest rate of 7 percent. Using a financial calculator, we find that k_b is 7.78 percent. Thus, the yield to maturity, which represents the investor's expected compound return by buying the bond at $915 and holding it to maturity, is 7.78 percent.

If the bonds can be called by the firm and retired prior to maturity, it is often helpful to compute the **yield to call, YTC,** which is the unknown k_b such that:

YIELD TO CALL, YTC
The compound return earned on a bond purchased at a given price and held until called.

$$B_0 = \sum_{t=1}^{n} \frac{I_t}{(1 + k_b)^t} + \frac{\text{call price}}{(1 + k_b)^n}$$

where n is the number of years until call. The call price is typically greater than (or occasionally equal to) the bond's par value.

Bonds with Semi-annual Interest

The promised yield to maturity for a bond that makes semi-annual interest payments is what we defined as an annual percentage rate, APR, in Chapter 3.

Most bonds pay interest semi-annually. Valuing bonds with semi-annual interest payments is easy *if* we remember the discussion from Chapter 3 on discounting and compounding when it is done more frequently than yearly. Our basic bond valuation equation (Equation 4.1) is modified as follows:

$$\text{price with semi-annual interest, } B_0 = \sum_{t=1}^{2n} \frac{I_t/2}{(1 + k_b/2)^t} + \frac{M}{(1 + k_b/2)^{2n}} \tag{4.2}$$

Note that the yearly interest, I, is divided by 2 in order to determine the *semi-annual* interest payments. Also, the number of periods, n, is doubled to $2n$, and the required return is halved to $k_b/2$.[6]

To illustrate bond valuation with semi-annual interest payments, consider the earlier example of a 25-year, 10 percent coupon rate bond. With semi-annual interest and a rate of 14 percent per year or 7 percent per semi-annual period, the value of the bond is[7]

$$B_0 = \sum_{t=1}^{50} \frac{\$50}{(1.07)^t} + \frac{\$1,000}{(1.07)^{50}} = \$723.99$$

What if we want to determine the yield to maturity when interest is paid semi-annually? Assume the current market value of a bond, B_0, is $1,060, the coupon interest rate is 11 percent per year, interest is paid semi-annually, and the bond has a maturity of 8 years. We divide the coupon interest rate in half, so it becomes 5.5 percent per 6 months, and double the maturity to 16 periods. The yield to maturity is found by solving for the unknown discount rate, where

$$\$1,060 = \sum_{t=1}^{16} \frac{\$55}{(1 + k_b)^t} + \frac{\$1,000}{(1 + k_b)^{16}}$$

Using a financial calculator, the yield is 4.95 per semi-annual period, so the *YTM* on an annual basis is (4.95 percent)(2) = 9.90 percent. At a purchase price of $1,060 for the bond, with interest paid semi-annually, the bond's expected yield to maturity is 9.90 percent per year.

---

[6] *By halving k_b, we are assuming it is a nominal interest rate, as discussed in Chapter 3. An alternative assumption is that k_b is an effective annual interest rate. In that case, k (if k_b is an effective annual annual rate) = $(1 + k_b)^{0.5} - 1$. For example, if k_b is 10 percent, then assuming it is a nominal rate produces a rate k of $^{10}/_2 = 5$ percent; assuming it is an effective annual rate means that k is $(1.10)^{0.5} - 1 = 4.881$ percent. We follow the convention and assume k_b is a nominal rate.*
[7] *Using present value tables, $B_0 = \$50(13.801) + \$1,000(0.034) = \$690.05 + \$34.00 = \$724.05$.*

Consols and Preferred Stock

■ LEARNING GOAL 2

Determine the value of consols and preferred stock.

CONSOL
Perpetual coupon rate bond.

A **consol** is a perpetual coupon rate bond. In Chapter 3 we determinded how to find the present value of a perpetuity. Using that same idea, the market price of a perpetual bond is:

Perpetuities were used to help "consol"-idate the British war debt after the Napoleonic wars and were thus nicknamed consols.

$$\text{price of perpetual bond (or perferred stock), } B_0 = \frac{I}{k_b} \qquad (4.3)$$

where I is the interest to be received at time $t = 1$ and every subsequent t, and k_b is the required return demanded by investors. If the return demanded by investors is 9 percent, and the coupon interest rate is 4 percent, then a $1,000 par value perpetual bond would be worth $40/0.09 = $444.44.

PREFERRED STOCK
Stock that has a prior but limited claim on assets and income before common stock, but after debt.

In addition to common stock, firms occasionally employ **preferred stock** which has a prior, but limited, claim on the firm. This claim takes precedence over the claim of the firm's common stockholders. The valuation of preferred stock that is not expected to be retired (either ever, or at least not for a long time) is similar to consols. As such, the same approach can be employed using dividends, instead of interest, in Equation 4.3. If the preferred stock has an $80 par value,[8] and the dividend is 12 percent per year, the yearly dividend is ($80)(0.12) = $9.60. If the required rate of return is 10 percent, the value of noncallable preferred stock is $9.60/0.10 = $96.

The ability of the firm to call a bond or preferred stock is an option held by the firm; remember Key Idea 7— options are valuable. Virtually all corporate bonds are callable.

What happens, however, if the preferred stock is callable (i.e., the firm can retire it)? In that case the preferred stock is valued like any bond, so that with cash dividends of D per year, the price is

$$\text{price of callable perferred stock, } P_0 = \sum_{t=1}^{n} \frac{D_t}{(1 + k_{ps})^t} + \frac{\text{call price}}{(1 + k_{ps})^n} \qquad (4.4)$$

where k_{ps} is the required return on the preferred stock. In the case of the above preferred stock, if it is callable in 7 years, its price is[9]

$$P_0 = \sum_{t=1}^{7} \frac{\$9.60}{(1.10)^t} + \frac{\$80}{(1.10)^7} = \$87.79$$

Thus, if the preferred stock is callable it is only worth $87.79, while it is worth $96.00 if it is valued as a perpetuity.

Bonds trade every day in the financial markets based on their discounted present value. Thus, the actual market price and yield to maturity for bonds are a direct function of the cash flows expected, the time value of money, and the returns demanded by investors.

---

[8] *While most bonds have a par value of $1,000, the par value on preferred stock can be almost anything; often it is $100 or less.*
[9] *With present value tables, $P_0 = $9.60(4.868) + $80(0.513) = $46.73 + $41.04 = $87.77.*

CONCEPT REVIEW QUESTIONS

■ What series of payments determines a bond's market price?
■ What are the different risk premiums that compose the bond risk premium required by investors?
■ Explain what happens to the price of a bond if (1) interest rates increase or (2) decrease.
■ How are consols, perpetual preferred stocks, and callable preferred stocks priced?

DETERMINING COMMON STOCK VALUES

■ **LEARNING GOAL 3**

Determine the value of common stock for no-growth, constant growth, and nonconstant growth conditions.

Cash dividends provide a return to owners of the firm; the owners also benefit by growth in dividends and share price.

The valuation of common stocks, although conceptually similar to bond valuation, has some additional complications because neither the cash dividends nor the ending values are constant (as are the interest and maturity value for bonds). Also, with bonds the interest and maturity value are a legal liability of the firm; they have to be paid or the firm can be forced into bankruptcy. With common stock, the cash dividends and any anticipated future price of the stock can be predicted only with a great deal of uncertainty. And, there is no legal requirement that forces firms to pay cash dividends.

Remember Key Idea 2— financial markets are efficient. For example, immediately after the 1994 earthquake, stocks of California construction firms rallied while property insurer stocks dipped.

If financial markets are efficient, then the actual market price of a share of common stock is a direct function of the cash flow expected, the time value of money, the risks involved, and the returns required by investors. As discussed in Chapter 2, the return required by common stock investors, k_s, is equal to the risk-free rate plus a risk premium. The risk premium may include a default premium (with a bigger default premium required for more risky firms), a liquidity premium (for smaller, or less frequently traded issues), and other premiums, depending on the firm in question. Due to the risks involved, *the risk premium on stocks is typically higher than the risk premium on bonds*. With rare exceptions, the required return demanded for investing in stocks is higher than the required return demanded for investing in bonds. Likewise, the cost of common stock to the firm is higher than the cost of debt.

Dividend Valuation

To start, think of common stock valuation as being exactly like bond valuation. The current market price of a share of common stock is theoretically equal to the present value of the expected cash dividends and future market price, where

$$\text{price, } P_0 = \sum_{t=1}^{n} \frac{D_t}{(1 + k_s)^t} + \frac{P_n}{(1 + k_s)^n} \tag{4.5}$$

where

D_t = the amount of cash dividends expected to be received at the end of the tth period (or year)

k_s = the rate of return required by investors on the stock

n = the number of time periods, or years

P_t = the expected market price of the stock at the end of period t

The current market price of a stock that is expected to pay cash dividends of $1.00 at $t = 1$, $1.50 at $t = 2$, and $2.00 at $t = 3$, and have an expected market value of $40.00 at $t = 3$, can be determined in a straightforward manner. If the return demanded by investors is 14 percent, the price of this stock is[10]

$$P_0 = \frac{D_1}{(1 + k_s)^1} + \frac{D_2}{(1 + k_s)^2} + \frac{D_3 + P_3}{(1 + k_s)^3}$$

$$= \frac{\$1.00}{(1.14)^1} + \frac{\$1.50}{(1.14)^2} + \frac{\$42.00}{(1.14)^3} = \$30.38$$

If an investor pays $30.38 for the stock, and the stream of dividends and ending market price occurs as projected, the compound rate of return realized on the stock will be 14 percent.

What if we keep adding more years of dividends to Equation 4.5, so that we can think of the cash dividends going on forever? In that case, we have the fundamental common stock model—the **dividend valuation model**—which states that the market price of a share of common stock is equal to the present value of all future dividends:

DIVIDEND VALUATION MODEL
Valuation model which says that the market price of a share of common stock equals the present value of all future dividends discounted at the investor's required rate of return.

$$\text{price, } P_0 = \sum_{t = 1}^{\infty} \frac{D_t}{(1 + k_s)^t} = \frac{D_1}{(1 + k_s)^1} + \frac{D_2}{(1 + k_s)^2} + \cdots + \frac{D_\infty}{(1 + k_s)^\infty} \qquad (4.6)$$

D_1 and D_2 in Equation 4.6 refer to cash dividends at time $t = 1$ and $t = 2$, respectively. In Equation 4.5, the second term is $P_n/(1 + k_s)^n$, where P_n represents the market price at time $t = n$. But what determines the market price at time n? It is simply the present value of all cash dividends expected to be received *from period $n + 1$ to infinity*, discounted at the investor's required rate of return of k_s. Equation 4.5 is simply a special case of the more general Equation 4.6. This relationship will prove useful when we consider valuing stocks that are expected to have nonconstant growth in future cash dividends. However, before doing that, we want to consider the simpler cases of no growth in cash dividends and constant growth in cash dividends.

No Growth in Cash Dividends

In the special case of no future expected growth in cash dividends, assume that the stock will pay a constant dividend of, say, $2 per year from now until infinity. Although the **no-growth model** is often unrealistic, it provides a convenient benchmark. In such a case, the dividend valuation equation (Equation 4.6) is simply a perpetuity. For a common stock with a constant expected cash dividend from $t = 1$ to infinity, its current market price is given by:

NO-GROWTH MODEL
Form of the dividend valuation model in which no growth in future cash dividends is expected.

$$\text{price with no growth, } P_0 = \frac{D}{k_s} \qquad (4.7)$$

---

[10]*With present value tables,* P_0 = $1.00(0.877) + $1.50(0.769) + $42.00(0.675) = $0.877 + $1.154 + $28.350 = $30.381 ≈ $30.38.

If we have a no-growth stock that is expected to pay a cash dividend of $2 per year from time $t = 1$ until infinity, and the investor's required rate of return is 16 percent (or 0.16), then its current price, P_0, is $2/0.16 = 12.50. A rational investor would pay no more than $12.50 for this stock if his or her required rate of return is 16 percent.

Constant Growth in Cash Dividends

CONSTANT-GROWTH MODEL
Form of the dividend valuation model in which cash dividends are expected to grow at a constant rate until infinity.

In another special case, consider what happens if cash dividends are expected to increase at a constant (percentage) rate each year. This situation is just a growing perpetuity, so we can use our knowledge from Chapter 3 (Equation 3.8) to value this stream of constantly growing dividends. The **constant-growth model** (which is often called the Gordon growth model) is:

$$\text{price with constant growth, } P_0 = \frac{D_1}{k_s - g} \tag{4.8}$$

where g is the constant percentage growth rate in cash dividends. In valuing a stock with constantly growing cash dividends, we must use *the cash dividends expected 1 year hence,* or D_1. If we have a stock whose current cash dividend, D_0, (at time $t = 0$) is $2, the constant compound growth rate in dividends is 10 percent per year, and the return demanded by investors is 16 percent, the value of this stock is

Be careful using the constant growth model; if a high growth rate is assumed (until infinity), you are likely to overvalue the stock.

$$P_0 = \frac{D_1}{k_s - g} = \frac{D_0(1 + g)}{k_s - g} = \frac{\$2(1.10)}{0.16 - 0.10} = \frac{\$2.20}{0.06} = \$36.67$$

Note that this price of $36.67 is substantially higher than the $12.50 computed using the no-growth model. This makes common sense because, other things being equal, an investor would value a growing cash flow stream at a higher rate than a nongrowing stream.

Nonconstant Growth in Cash Dividends

The assumption that dividends grow at a constant annual rate is a simplification. Younger, smaller firms often have a period of high growth in profitability and dividends, followed by a period of slower growth as they mature.

The next situation we consider is when a firm grows at a fast rate for a few years and then reverts to a constant- or no-growth situation. This might occur because a firm made previous positive net present value investments that produced high cash flows and increases in value but faces increasing competition that is expected to reduce the future growth rate. For example, if the required rate of return demanded by investors remains at 16 percent, consider how we would value this stock: (1) Dividends at time $t = 0$ are $2; (2) followed by 10 percent growth in dividends for each of years 1, 2, and 3; (3) followed by 3 percent compound growth thereafter until infinity. This set of cash flows is graphed in Figure 4.3.

We would use the following four-step procedure to solve this problem:

STEP 1: Determine the cash dividends until the series reverts to either constant growth to infinity or no growth. Thus,

$D_1 = \$2.00(1.10)^1 = \$2.20$
$D_2 = \$2.00(1.10)^2 = \$2.42$
$D_3 = \$2.00(1.10)^3 = \$2.66$

STEP 2: Determine the first year's dividend *after* the growth rate changes to either constant growth to infinity or no growth.

$D_4 = D_3(1.03) = \$2.66(1.03) = \$2.74$

FIGURE 4.3

Cash Dividend Series Growing at 10 Percent for 3 Years Followed by 3 Percent Growth to Infinity

Due to the compounding effect, the lines between years 0 and 3 and between years 3 and 6 are not quite straight.

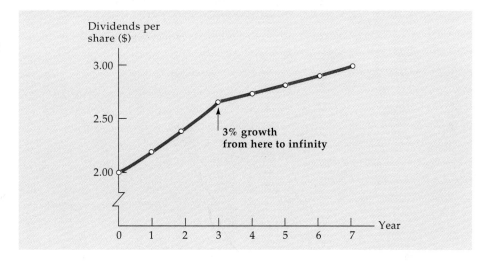

Because the growth rate changed to 3 percent (from 10 percent), the new growth rate of 3 percent must be used in this step.

STEP 3: Determine the market price of the stock as of time $t = 3$ for the constant-growth period. Thus

$$P_3 = \frac{D_4}{k_s - g} = \frac{\$2.74}{0.16 - 0.03} = \frac{\$2.74}{0.13} = \$21.08$$

Note that (1) the growth rate used is the constant one expected from time $t = 3$ until infinity, and (2) the market price is as of time $t = 3$.

STEP 4: Using Equation 4.5 and the required rate of return of 16 percent, discount both the expected cash dividends from Step 1 and the expected market price from Step 3 back to the present. As shown in Figure 4.4, the present value of this stream of expected cash flows is $18.91.[11] Thus, the current market value of the stock should be $18.91.

FIGURE 4.4

Timeline and Solution for Nonconstant Dividend Series

The dividend in year 4 equals $2.66(1.03)[1]. The market price determined using D_4 is the price at time $t = 3$. This market price must be brought back to time $t = 0$, as are the cash dividends for years 1, 2, and 3, by discounting at 16 percent.

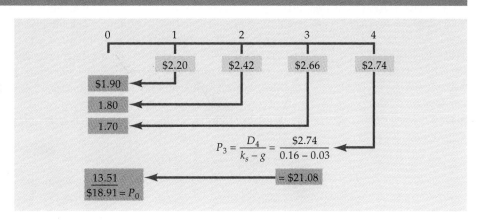

[11] *Using present value tables,* $P_0 = \$2.20(0.862) + \$2.42(0.743) + \$2.66(0.641) + \$21.08(0.641) = \$1.896 + \$1.798 + \$1.705 + \$13.512 = \$18.911 \approx \$18.91$

TABLE 4.1	

Relationship Between Expected Growth and Market Price

There is a direct relationship between the amount and length of expected growth in cash dividends and a stock's market price.

Condition*	Resulting Market Price (P_0)
No future growth in expected cash dividends	$12.50
10 percent compound growth in expected cash dividends for times $t = 1$, $t = 2$, and $t = 3$, followed by no future growth†	16.05
10 percent compound growth in expected cash dividends for times $t = 1$, $t = 2$, and $t = 3$, followed by 3 percent compound growth to infinity	18.91
10 percent compound growth in expected cash dividends to infinity	36.67

* $D_0 = \$2$ and $k_s = 16$ percent for all conditions.
† From footnote 12.

When investors require a higher rate of return on common stock, the result is a lower stock price today. A lower stock price means a higher cost of raising equity funds if the firm sells additional common stock.

To see the relationship between growth opportunities, the growth rate in expected cash dividends, and the current market price of a stock, consider Table 4.1, which summarizes our calculations. In the case of no future growth, the market price is $12.50, whereas it is $36.67 at a 10 percent compound rate to infinity. Finally, growth at 10 percent for 3 years followed by low or no growth[12] thereafter produces market prices of $18.91 and $16.05, respectively. Clearly, *the rate and duration of expected growth opportunities leading to growth in cash dividends have a major impact on the market price of a common stock.* Accurate estimation of growth opportunities and expected growth rates is the most important aspect of common stock valuation using the dividend valuation approach. It is also one of the most difficult.

Non-Dividend-Paying Stocks

Since the mid–1920s stocks have averaged a return (cash dividends and capital gain or loss) of about 12% per year. Over the same time the return on long-term government bonds was about 4.9%. For short time periods, however, the returns of stocks may be substantially above or below 12%.

We have discussed stock valuation when the firm pays cash dividends, but not all firms pay dividends. How, then, should we value non-dividend-paying stocks? There are three ways. The first is to estimate *when* the firm will start paying dividends, their size, growth rate, and so forth; then simply proceed as we have discussed. The second is a variation of the first, except you must estimate some future market price and then discount it back to the present, as we have done previously. The final approach employs earnings and multiplies (or capitalizes) them by some factor (based on perceived growth, risk, and/or estimates derived by looking at "similar" firms) to arrive at an estimated value. Often this approach relies on price/earnings (P/E) ratios discussed later in the chapter.

Most investors, amateur or professional, do not employ the dividend valuation model exactly as we have described it. However, their decision making does have characteristics in common with the model: (1) They focus on cash flows and dividends, (2) they consider the returns needed to compensate them for the risks

[12]*If there was no growth in cash dividends expected after year 3, $P_3 = D_4/k_s = \$2.66/0.16 = \$16.625$. Discounting this back to time zero at 16 percent and adding it to the discounted value of the cash dividends to be received for periods 1, 2, and 3 produces a market price of $16.05*

incurred (given their alternatives and economic conditions), and (3) they look for growth opportunities. Thus, the intuition behind the dividend valuation model underlies much of what drives decisions made by investors.

Finally, what about the value of stocks and bonds that are issued by firms in developing countries, or where there is a less-developed market for buying and selling securities? For example, what determines the value of a bond issued by a firm in India, or the value of a common stock issued by an Armenian firm? Theoretically, their value is determined in exactly the same way as bonds and stocks issued by firms in developed countries. However, in practice the process of determining their value becomes even more difficult. Laws and practices differ between countries, and inflation may have important implications for valuing securities in some countries. Also, the theoretical value, based on ideas similar to those discussed in this chapter, and what a buyer is actually willing to pay for a security may differ significantly. Hence, though the underlying ideas are similar throughout the world, the lack of developed and efficient financial markets, different business practices and legal traditions, different ideas about the role of free enterprise, and widely different rates of inflation all affect the valuation of bonds, and stocks in developing countries.

CONCEPT REVIEW QUESTIONS

- What are the risk premiums that affect a stock's price?
- What are the cash flows that determine a stock's price?
- Describe how you would price a stock with nonconstant growth and cash dividends.

EXECUTIVE INTERVIEW WITH MARY J. REILLY

Vice President
BancBoston Capital,
Boston, Massachusetts

Joining the Bank of Boston's Loan Review staff in 1978, Mary J. Reilly taught the bank's lending officer trainees for a couple of years and then served as lending officer for key corporate accounts. In 1983 she moved into her current position in venture capital financing of mature companies. Ms. Reilly holds a B.A. degree in history from Connecticut College and an M.B.A. from Virginia Commonwealth University. We asked Ms. Reilly to describe how BancBoston values the firms it considers as investment candidates.

Our investment targets are mostly private companies or subsidiaries of public firms, with track records of profitable operations. We make different types of investments depending on the situation. In some cases, we provide equity financing. In others, we provide mezzanine capital, which is the layer of financing between equity and debt, with features of both.

We make one basic investment decision: Should we invest $x to receive $y dollars and z% return? Our return comes from interest payments on debt and from capital gains on equity. So, our ability to value the equity of these companies is critical. Our valuation is based on our judgment about the appropriate return for the company's risk, as well as the perceived risk of the security. For example, preferred stock is a riskier—and therefore more expensive—investment than subordinated debt, so a company pays more if it needs preferred stock on its balance sheet.

It's a challenge to value a privately held company. Public companies have an earnings record, maybe a dividend stream, and comparable public companies to point you to a range of equity values. Valuing private companies requires all the same judgments as valuing public companies, but we don't have as much published information. Also, we can't sell our investment easily if we make a mistake; there's not much liquidity.

(continued)

Therefore, we must perform a very rigorous analysis, including valuation. We look at the facilities, operations, products, and markets; study the industry research for competition and technological change; and talk to company suppliers and customers. Our objective is to predict what the firm will be worth in 5 years when we harvest our capital gains. We use a multiple of *current* cash flow to value companies. We talk in terms of the value of the company—not simply the value of the equity—because our transactions are buyouts of the whole company. Using current cash flow focuses our analysis on current operations, not on expectations of future improvements which may or may not be realized.

Calculating cash flow for valuation purposes isn't straightforward. As a start, it can be earnings before interest, taxes, depreciation, and amortization. We adjust up or down for such factors as capital expenditures, working capital, nonrecurring items, or excess expenses by previous management. Then we apply a multiple to that cash flow and come up with the firm's value. Most of our companies trade at five or six times cash flow. For example, if the cash flow after adjustments is $25 million and similar companies sell for six times cash flow, the company is worth $150 million. We'll use a higher multiple if there are favorable circumstances, such as a hot new product or a valuable brand or franchise, or a lower multiple if negative factors exist. While we're deciding what we think the company is worth, we're negotiating with the seller to see if we have a deal. It's a dynamic process.

THE PRESENT VALUE OF GROWTH OPPORTUNITIES

■ LEARNING GOAL 4

Explain the impact of a firm's growth opportunities on its value.

Based on what we have just learned, a number of important observations can be made about stocks and the creation of value for the firm. First, let's go back to determining the stock price when the firm and its cash dividends are expected to grow at a constant compound rate g until infinity. As given by Equation 4.8, the stock price is

$$P_0 = \frac{D_1}{k_s - g}$$

Assume you are looking at two firms, Growth and Nongrowth. For simplicity, assume both will pay dividends of $1 at time $t = 1$ and the required rate of return is (for illustration purposes) the same in each case—15 percent. What should their market prices be if g is 10 percent for Growth and 0 percent for Nongrowth? The prices are:

$$P_0 \text{ (Growth)} = \frac{\$1}{0.15 - 0.10} = \$20$$

$$P_0 \text{ (Nongrowth)} = \frac{\$1}{0.15 - 0} = \$6.67$$

Other things being equal, we see that the market price of a firm that is expected to grow is higher than the market price of a firm that is not expected to grow. Although firms do not grow at a constant percentage compound rate forever, and the return required by investors might not be the same for both Growth and Nongrowth, the basic conclusion from this example holds: *Expected growth is valuable.*

Price/Earnings Ratios

PRICE/EARNING, *P/E*, RATIO
Market price per share of common stock divided by earnings per share.

EARNINGS PER SHARE, *EPS*
Total earnings available for common stockholders divided by the number of shares of common stock outstanding.

DIVIDEND PAYOUT RATIO
Cash dividends paid per share of common stock divided by earnings per share.

The **price/earnings, *P/E*, ratio** is often used when common stocks are analyzed. Indeed, high *P/E* ratios are sometimes touted as proof that a stock is valuable. To know whether this is true, we need to understand how this figure relates to the valuation of common stock. The price/earnings ratio is simply the market price per share of common stock divided by the **earnings per share, *EPS***, where earnings per share equal the total earnings available for common stockholders, divided by the number of shares of common stock outstanding. Likewise, the **dividend payout ratio** is simply cash dividends paid per share of common stock, divided by earnings per share of common stock. For example, if a firm has earnings of $5 per share and pays a cash dividend of $2 per share, the dividend payout ratio is $2/$5 = 40 percent. Let's go back to the constant-growth model given by Equation 4.8 and define the dividend next year, D_1, as being equal to the earnings per share, EPS_1, times the dividend payout ratio. Thus, $D_1 = (EPS_1)$(dividend payout ratio). Therefore, Equation 4.8 becomes:

$$P_0 = \frac{EPS_1(\text{dividend payout ratio})}{k_s - g} \tag{4.9}$$

Rearranging Equation 4.9, we find the price/earnings ratio is:

$$\frac{P_0}{EPS_1} = \frac{\text{dividend payout ratio}}{k_s - g}$$

Looked at in this manner, *the price/earnings ratio is a function of the firm's dividend payout ratio, the return demanded by investors, k_s, and the expected future growth, g, for the firm.*

Should a firm and investors be happy if a stock has a "high" price/earnings ratio? That all depends! One way a firm can have a high *P/E* ratio is if it has little or no earnings. For example, if the market price for a stock is $15 and the firm had a very bad year and expects earnings will be only $0.20, its *P/E* would be 75 times (i.e., $15/$0.20 = 75). In this instance, the high price/earnings ratio is due to the depressed level of earnings.

But, another possibility that leads to high *P/E* ratios is for the expected growth, g, to be high. As we saw in the previous example of Growth and Nongrowth, other things being equal, higher expected growth and higher stock prices go hand-in-hand. Thus, a second and more favorable meaning of a high *P/E* ratio is that the expected growth for the firm is "high." The message is simple and straightforward: High *P/E* ratios may be "good news" or "bad news." Don't automatically assume a high *P/E* ratio signals good news in the form of high expected growth.

Growth Opportunities and Value Creation

Remember Key Idea 1—the goal of the firm is to maximize its market value.

Now let's consider growth opportunities and how firms create value. Assume Everyday Supply is not growing at all. The earnings are $100 per year and the required return demanded by Everyday's investors is 10 percent. Because the firm is not growing, all of the earnings can be distributed to the common stockholders; thus, the dividend payout ratio is 100 percent, or 1.0. The market value of Everyday, using Equation 4.9, is:

$$P_0 = \frac{EPS_1(\text{dividend payout ratio})}{k_s - g} = \frac{\$100(1.00)}{0.10 - 0} = \$1,000$$

and the firm pays all of the earnings of $100 out in cash dividends each year.

What if Everyday has the opportunity to make a $100 investment next year in a project that promises to return $10 forever? In order to make the capital investment, Everyday will forgo paying cash dividends at time $t = 1$, but from $t = 2$ on the dividends will be $110. This project is as risky as the firm, so the required return on it is 10 percent. What is the net present value of the proposed project? With the returns going on forever, this investment is a perpetuity. The net present value is equal to the present value of the future cash flows minus the initial investment, so:

$$\text{net present value}_1 = \frac{\$10}{0.10} - \$100 = 0$$

What about the market price of Everyday after it makes this investment? Earnings (i.e., dividends) will not be paid out to investors at time $t = 1$, but from time $t = 2$ until infinity they will be $110. What is the new market price of Everyday? Because the cash inflow stream is still a perpetuity, the price at $t = 1$ is EPS_2/k_s, so its price at $t = 0$ is

$$P_0 = \frac{P_1}{1 + k_s} = \frac{EPS_2/k_s}{1 + k_s} = \frac{\$110.00/0.10}{1.10} = \frac{\$1,100}{1.10} = \$1,000$$

This example indicates a simple and important fact: *The value of a firm does not increase or decrease when it accepts zero net present value projects.*

Opportunities to make future investments are another form of an option—and from Key Idea 7—we know that options are valuable.

What if there is another project to consider? Suppose this project requires Everyday to invest $100 at $t = 1$, promises a return of $20 from $t = 2$ on, and the investor's required return remains 10 percent? The net present value at $t = 1$ is $100, where

$$\text{net present value}_1 = \frac{\$20}{0.10} - \$100 = \$100$$

and the new market price of Everyday at $t = 0$, after making this positive net present value investment, is $1,091, or

$$\text{new } P_0 = \frac{\$120/0.10}{1.10} = \frac{\$1,200}{1.10} = \$1,091$$

By investing in a positive net present value project, Everyday has increased its market value.[13]

What if Everyday could invest the $100 in another project that promised a return of $30 forever, or alternatively one that promised a return of only $5 forever? The figures for these alternative investments, along with the two already considered are as follows:

Return from $t = 2$ on	Investment at $t = 1$	Net Present Value	Market Price
$30	$100	$200	$1,182
20	100	100	1,091
10	100	0	1,000
5	100	− 50	955

In looking at these figures, the message is clear: *To increase the value of the firm, positive net present value projects—which promise to return above average returns—are*

---

[13] *An alternative calculation is: new P_0 = original P_0 + NPV of the new project. With the NPV of $100 being at time* $t = 1$, *the new P_0 = $1,000 + $100/1.1 = $1,091.*

necessary. Simply investing in projects that provide the return demanded by investors, which is also the firm's opportunity cost of capital, does not create value. Likewise, *when firms accept projects that have a negative net present value, the firm and its investors suffer a loss in value.*

The above discussion can be summarized as follows: The stock price can be thought of as being composed of the capitalized value of the assets in place under a no-growth policy plus the **present value of growth opportunities, *PVGO*,** where *PVGO* represents the opportunities available in the future based on new investments that the firm makes,

PRESENT VALUE OF GROWTH OPPORTUNITIES, *PVGO*
Value created by the presence of profitable future investment opportunities that are expected to return more than the required rate of return.

$$\text{stock price, } P_0 = \frac{EPS_1}{k_s} + PVGO \qquad (4.10)$$

$$= \begin{array}{c}\text{present value of} \\ \text{assets in place}\end{array} + \begin{array}{c}\text{present value of} \\ \text{growth opportunities}\end{array}$$

For a firm to prosper, it must find and exploit investment opportunities that allow it to grow.[14] Investing in a project that provides an average rate of return is not growth! Likewise, investing in projects that can be easily replicated by others invites immediate competition and price cutting, and therefore limits the opportunity of the firm to increase its value. The message is simple and direct: The way for firms to create value is to find and exploit investment projects that have positive net present values. *Positive net present value projects and value creation are synonymous with one another.* This finding is one of the central ideas of finance. We examine net present value, and how to make wealth-maximizing capital investment decisions, in Chapters 7 through 9.

CONCEPT REVIEW QUESTIONS

■ Is it true that investors prefer a high *P/E* ratio stock? Explain.
■ How does the growth rate affect a firm's value?
■ How does the net present value of growth opportunities affect a firm's market value?

Summary

■ Based on cash flows, their timing, and their riskiness, the market price of any financial asset, like a bond or stock, is equal to the expected cash flows coming from the asset, discounted at the investor's required rate of return.
■ The return required, or demanded, by an investor is equal to the risk-free rate of interest, plus a risk premium. For a bond the risk premium may include a maturity premium, a default premium, a liquidity premium, and other premiums. For a

---

[14]*An alternative approach has been employed by the investment banking firm of Goldman Sachs. They value the perpetual dividend stream and then estimate the value of future growth that will arise from the retention and reinvestment of future cash flows as follows:*

$$P_0 = \frac{dividends}{k} + \frac{(ROE/k)[(earnings)(b)]}{k/(1 + g)}$$

where, k *is the discount rate,* ROE *is the firm's return on equity,* b *is the percentage of the cash flows (approximated by earnings) that are retained, and* g *is the growth rate.*

stock the risk premium may include a default premium, a liquidity premium, and other premiums.

■ Due to greater risk, the risk premium for stocks is generally higher than the risk premium for bonds. Consequently, the return demanded by investors in stocks is generally higher than the return demanded by investors in bonds; and the cost of stock to firms is higher than the cost of debt.

■ As general market interest rates increase, the market price of a bond decreases. Alternatively, as general market interest rates decrease, the market price of a bond increases.

■ The yield to maturity is the compound rate of return expected to be earned by purchasing a bond at the current market price and holding it to maturity.

■ The rate and duration of the expected growth in cash dividends have a major impact on the market price of common stock. Other things being equal, higher expected growth and higher stock prices go hand-in-hand.

■ The firm's stock price is composed of the present value of the assets in place, plus the present value of growth opportunities. The firm can create value, as shown by increases in the market price, only by accepting positive net present value projects.

Questions

4.1 Using both stocks and bonds, explain why their current market price is equal to the present value of the future cash flows expected by investors, discounted at their required rate of return.

4.2 Why is it that bonds do not typically sell at face value? How do fluctuations in market interest rates and the length of time to maturity influence bond price fluctuations?

Note: In answering 4.3, ignore any reinvestment problem associated with the future interest to be received.

4.3 The rate of return you will receive on a bond if you buy it today and hold it until maturity is its yield to maturity, *YTM*.
   a. What happens to the *YTM* as market interest rates change?
   b. Will you receive any more, or any less, if interest rates change as long as you hold the bond to maturity? Why?
   c. Will you receive any more, or any less, as interest rates change if you are forced to sell before maturity? Why?

4.4 The following formula is used when dividends have been estimated for a few years, at which time the estimated future market price is then employed:

$$P_0 = \sum_{t=1}^{n} \frac{D_t}{(1 + k_s)^t} + \frac{P_n}{(1 + k_s)^n}$$

Explain where the term P_n comes from.

4.5 Does a high price/earnings ratio mean a firm is a "growth firm?" Explain.

Concept Review Problems

See Appendix A for solutions.

CR4.1 Colorado Conglomerate has a bond with a 10 percent coupon rate and a $1,000 face value. Interest is paid semi-annually, and the bond has 15 years to maturity.
   a. If investors require an 8 percent yield, what is the bond's value?
   b. If the bond is expected to be called in 5 years at $1,100, what is the bond's value?

CR4.2 Burnett bonds are selling for $945. These 20-year $1,000 par value bonds pay 6 percent interest semi-annually. If they are purchased at the market price, what is the yield to maturity?

CR4.3 You are thinking of buying 300 shares of MainStreet preferred stock which currently sells for $70 per share and pays annual dividends of $6.50 per share.
a. What is the expected return?
b. If you required a 10 percent return, what would you pay for MainStreet's preferred stock?

CR4.4 Ewing Systems's common stock paid $1.65 in dividends last year (at time $t = 0$) and is expected to grow indefinitely at an annual rate of 6 percent. What is the value of the stock if you require a 14 percent return?

Note: In CR4.5, the required return remains the same.

CR4.5 In the previous problem (CR4.4), what would the stock sell for today if the dividend is expected to grow at 20 percent for the next 4 years and grow at 6 percent per year thereafter?

CR4.6 Pima Inc. recently paid a dividend of $2.00 per share and is expected to have a growth rate of -15 percent infinitely. If you require a 20 percent return, what is the current value of Pima?

Problems

See Appendix C for answers to selected problems.

Bond Prices

4.1 New Century Computer bonds pay $80 annual interest, mature in 10 years, and pay $1,000 at maturity. What will their price be if the market rate of interest is (**a**) 6 percent, or (**b**) 10 percent, and interest is paid (**1**) annually, (**2**) semi-annually?

Bond Price Change and Time to Maturity

4.2 Find the current market price of a 20-year, 9 percent coupon rate bond with a par value of $1,000, if interest is paid annually and if current market rates are (**a**) 11 percent, or (**b**) 7 percent. What are the current market prices if everything is the same except the bond has only (**1**) 10 years to maturity, or (**2**) 2 years to maturity? What can we say about the relative influence of changing market interest rates on the market prices of short-term versus long-term bonds? Can you speculate on why this is so?

Yield to Maturity

4.3 Sandberg Engineering has some 15-year, $1,000 par bonds outstanding, which have a coupon interest rate of 9 percent and pay interest annually. What is the yield to maturity on the bonds if their current market price is
a. $1,180?
b. $800?
c. Would you be willing to pay $800 if your minimum required rate of return was 11 percent? Why or why not?

Yield to Maturity

4.4 Greenman Resources has some 12-year, $1,000 par bonds outstanding. The bonds have a coupon interest rate of 10.4 percent and pay interest semi-annually. What is the yield to maturity on the bonds if their current market price is
a. $960?
c. $1,125?

YTM and YTC

4.5 A $1,000 par value bond has a 12 percent coupon rate, pays interest annually, and has 15 years remaining until it matures.
a. If $B_0 = \$1,160$, what is its yield to maturity, *YTM*?
b. If the bond can be called in 6 years at $1,030, what is the bond's yield to call, *YTC*? Why is the *YTC* in this problem lower than the *YTM*? Would this always be true?

Preferred Stock

4.6 You are interested in buying 100 shares of a $60 par value preferred stock that has an $8\frac{1}{2}$ percent dividend rate.

a. If your required return is 11 percent, how much would you be willing to pay to acquire the 100 shares?

b. Assume no dividends will be paid until $t = 3$. At the same required return, how much would you now be willing to pay?

Implied Growth Rate

4.7 Reilly Supermarkets' common stock is selling at $54, the cash dividend expected next year (at time $t = 1$) is $3.78 per share, and the required rate of return is 15 percent. What is the implied compound growth rate (to infinity) in cash dividends?

Different Growth Rates

4.8 A stock currently pays cash dividends of $4 per share ($D_0 = \$4$), and the required rate of return is 12 percent. What is its market price in the following cases?

a. There is no future growth in dividends.

b. Dividends grow at 8 percent per year to infinity.

c. Dividends grow at 5 percent for each of 2 years, and there is no growth expected after D_2.

Declining Growth Rate

4.9 Minos Mines' ore reserves are depleted. Hence, the expected future rate of growth in the firm's cash dividends is −5 percent (i.e., the cash dividends will decline 5 percent per year). The cash dividend at time $t = 0$ is $4.40, and the required rate of return is 11 percent. What is the current market price of the stock if we assume dividends decline at 5 percent per year until infinity?

Constant Versus Nonconstant Growth

4.10 Brett is contemplating the purchase of a small, one-island service station. After-tax cash flows are presently $20,000 per year, and his required rate of return is 14 percent.

a. What is the maximum price Brett should pay for the service station if he expects cash flows to grow at 4 percent per year to infinity? Look @ Pg 96

b. If Brett decides he needs a 15 percent return, and there will be no growth in after-tax cash flows for 3 years, followed by 10 percent per year for years 4 and 5, followed by 3 percent growth to infinity, what is the maximum amount he should pay?

Nonconstant Growth: Delayed Start

4.11 Yee Energy is a new enterprise that is not expected to pay any cash dividends for the next 5 years. Its first dividend (D_6) is expected to be $2, and the cash dividends are expected to grow for the next 4 years (through $t = 10$) at 25 percent per year. After that, cash dividends are expected to grow at a more normal 5 percent per year to infinity. If $k_s = 18$ percent, what is P_0?

Length of Holding Period

4.12 Sandy is considering purchasing stock and holding it for 3 years. The projected dividends (at a 5 percent growth rate) and market price are: $D_1 = \$4.20$; $D_2 = \$4.41$; $D_3 = \$4.63$; and $P_3 = \$97.23$. Her required rate of return, given the risk involved, is 10 percent.

a. What is the maximum price Sandy should pay for the stock?

b. If the dividends for years 1 and 2 remain at $4.20 and $4.41, respectively, and are expected to grow at 5 percent per year to infinity, what would the market price have to be at the end of the second year if Sandy sold the stock but still demanded a 10 percent return?

c. What is the current price, which is composed of the dividends from years 1 and 2, and the market price you determined in (b) above?

d. Why are your answers the same for (a) and (c), aside from any rounding errors?

e. Does the price of the stock today depend on how long Sandy plans to hold it? That is, does its price today depend on whether she plans to hold the stock for 2 years, 3 years, or any other period of time?

No Cash Dividends

Forgoing Cash Dividends

Note: Calculate the current price, P_0.

Growth Opportunities and NPV

PVGO

Change in Value

4.13 Suppose you believe that Pinto Products common stock will be worth $144 per share 2 years from now. What is the maximum you would be willing to pay per share if it pays no cash dividends and your required rate of return is 16 percent?

4.14 Downing Enterprises is a no-growth firm that pays cash dividends of $8 per year. Its current required rate of return is 12 percent.

a. What is Downing's current market price?

b. Management is considering an investment that will convert the firm into a constant-growth firm, but it requires stockholders to forgo cash dividends for the next 6 years. When cash dividends are resumed in year 7, they will be $8 *plus* the expected constant growth of 11 percent [i.e, ($8)(1.11)]from year 6 to year infinity. If its new required return is 16 percent, will the stockholders be better off?

c. What happens if everything is the same as in (b), except that the growth rate is only 10 percent?

4.15 McGeary's is able to generate an *EPS* of $4 on its existing assets. If the firm does not invest except to maintain the existing assets, its *EPS* is expected to remain at $4 per year. A new investment opportunity has come up which requires an investment of $4 per share at time $t = 1$. The return required by investors is 10 percent.

a. What is the net present value of the project, and the market price of McGeary's if:

(1) The project provides a return of $1 per year forever?

(2) The project provides a return of $1 per year for only 10 years (that is, for $t = 2$ through $t = 11$)?

b. How much did the market price increase in each case in (a) from what the market price was before the investment?

4.16 Consider three firms with market prices, earnings per share, and returns required (or expected) by investors, as follows:

Firm	Market Price, P_0	Earnings per Share, *EPS*	Required Return, k_s
A	$40	$2.00	0.18
B	90	8.50	0.10
C	76	7.00	0.17

a. Determine the price/earnings ratio, the implied present value of growth opportunities, *PVGO*, and the ratio of *PVGO* to P_0 for each of the firms.

b. Do each of the firms look as if they are valued properly by investors?

4.17 Mini Case As a junior analyst for Yarnell and Sons, your boss just gave you the following group of securities to analyze:

Security	Today's Market Value
7% coupon rate, $1,000 par, 20-year bond, paying interest annually	$ 900
10 shares of $7\frac{1}{2}$ percent, $100 par, preferred stock	900
18 shares of a low-growth common stock	900
30 shares of a high-growth common stock	900
Total value	$3,600

a. What is the yield to maturity on the 20-year bond?

b. What is the required return on the preferred stock?

c. Your boss is afraid that due to international economic and political problems, expected inflation will increase. If that happens, she predicts the required rates of return demanded for all securities will increase. Her specific projections for the securities are as follows:

Security	New Required Return
Bond	11%
Preferred stock	$11\frac{1}{2}$
Low-growth common stock	17
High-growth common stock	20

The details for the two common stocks are as follows:

Low-growth: D_0 = $4.00, growth at 6 percent per year for 3 years, followed by a decline from 6 percent *to* 4 percent forever.

High-growth: D_0 = $1.00, growth for the next 4 years at 40 percent per year, followed by a decline from 40 percent *to* 5 percent forever.

(1) Do you agree that required rates of return would increase if expected inflation increases? Why or why not? Explain.

(2) What would be the new market price for the bond, the preferred stock, and the two common stocks if your boss is correct?

(3) What is the new total market value of the group of securities?

(4) How much, in terms of percentage, does the value of the group of securities fall? Which security suffers the most loss in value? The least loss in value? Why does this occur?

d. Explain, in terms of the low-growth and high-growth stocks, the present value of growth opportunities. Other things being equal, does a high price/earnings ratio mean the stock is a high-growth stock and a low price/earnings ratio mean the stock is low-growth? Explain.

Reading the Financial Pages

■ LEARNING GOAL

After studying this appendix, you should be able to: understand stock and bond quotes.

Detailed information on a firm's stock can be found in Value Line Investment Survey and Standard & Poor's Stock Reports. Also, individual brokerage firms often prepare special reports on selected stocks.

Being able to read and understand the financial pages is one of the first things students of finance want to learn to do. This appendix presents a brief overview of stock and bond quotations. Many sources of financial quotations exist, and local newspapers also provide varying coverage of the financial markets. The most comprehensive daily listing is provided in *The Wall Street Journal (WSJ)*. The *WSJ* provides information on all listed stocks that are traded on any given day, plus a variety of other financial information on other stocks, bonds, money market instruments, foreign exchange rates, options, and the like.

A partial listing of quotation information for stocks traded on the New York Stock Exchange from the *WSJ* is provided in Table 4A.1. First, let's look at the information provided for a common stock, such as the very first stock listed, AAR Corp. The first two columns indicate the high and low stock prices for the last 52 weeks. Note that stocks are typically traded in 1/8's, so 17 3/8 means $17.375. "Stock" indicates the firm and stock, while "Sym" stands for the ticker symbol for the stock. The "Div" column indicates the yearly cash dividend. For example, we see that AAR pays

TABLE 4A.1

Common Stock Quotations from *The Wall Street Journal*

Over 1,500 stocks are listed on the New York Stock Exchange. Obviously, this is only a small sample of what appears in *The Wall Street Journal* every business day.

NYSE COMPOSITE TRANSACTIONS

Quotations as of 5 p.m. Eastern Time
Friday, July 15, 1994

-A-A-A-

	52 Weeks Hi	Lo	Stock	Sym	Div	Yld %	PE	Vol 100s	Hi	Lo	Close	Net Chg
	17⅜	12⅝	AAR	AIR	.48	3.5	23	49	13⅞	13¾	13⅞	...
	23⅝	14⅝	ABM Indus	ABM	.52	2.7	13	21	19¼	19⅛	19¼	+ ⅛
	12⅝	10⅛	ACM Gvt Fd	ACG	1.10a	10.1	...	1339	11	10⅞	10⅞	...
	10¼	7⅞	ACM OppFd	AOF	.80	9.6	...	123	8⅜	8⅛	8⅜	+ ⅛
	12¼	9⅛	ACM SecFd	GSF	1.10	11.6	...	875	9⅝	9½	9½	− ⅛
	10⅝	8	ACM SpctmFd	SI	.96	11.8	...	231	8¼	8	8⅛	...
n	15⅛	10⅝	ACM MgmdInc	ADF	1.46	13.3	...	517	11⅛	10⅞	11	...
	12⅜	8⅝	ACM MgdIncFd	AMF	1.08a	11.8	...	628	9¼	9	9⅛	− ⅛
	9⅜	7⅞	ACM MgdMultFd	MMF	.72	8.7	...	44	8¼	8⅛	8¼	+ ⅛
	14½	11⅜	ACM MuniSec	AMU	.90a	7.7	...	21	11⅞	11¾	11¾	− ⅛
	11⅛	8⅛	ADT	ADT		...	13	9060	10¼	10	10¼	+ ⅛
	35	24¾	AFLAC	AFL	.46f	1.3	14	2745	35	34⅜	34⅞	+ ½
	46¼	16¾	AGCO Cp	AG	.04	.1	8	914	42⅜	41¾	42	+ ⅛
	60⅜	27½	AGCO pf		1.63	2.9	...	186	56¼	55½	56¼	+1
	26	12¾	AL Labs A	BMD	.18	1.3	40	36	13⅝	13⅜	13½	...
n	23¼	19¾	AMLI Resdntl	AML	.21p	...	...	128	21¾	21½	21¾	+ ⅛
	73	57	AMP	AMP	1.68	2.3	25	1891	71⅞	71⅝	71¾	− ¼
	72¾	52⅛	AMR	AMR		...	dd	3424	63	62	62¼	− ⅛
	50½	39⅞	ARCO Chm	RCM	2.50	5.5	21	474	45⅞	45½	45⅝	+ ¼
	5	2¼	ARX	ARX		...	10	37	3¾	3⅝	3¾	...
	56⅛	38½	ASA	ASA	2.00	4.4	...	384	45⅛	44⅞	45	...
n	30⅜	21½	ATT Cap	TCC	.27e	1.2	...	76	22¾	22½	22¾	+ ⅛
	65	49½	AT&T Cp	T	1.32	2.4	18	22930	54⅞	54¼	54⅜	− ⅛
	31⅜	22¾	AbbotLab	ABT	.76	2.7	16	10401	27⅞	27½	27¾	...
	8⅛	2⅞	Abex	ABE		...	dd	40	7¼	7⅛	7¼	+ ⅛
	13¾	8¼	Abitibi g	ABY		...	...	752	12¾	12½	12¾	+ ½
	15⅝	11⅛	AcceptIns	AIF		...	16	7	13⅜	13¼	13⅜	...
	36	22¾	ACE Ltd	ACL	.44f	1.9	5	41	23⅝	23⅝	23⅝	...
	15½	8½	AcmeCleve	AMT	.44	3.8	19	122	11⅞	11¼	11⅝	+ ¼
	11⅜	6⅜	AcmeElec	ACE		...	dd	21	8⅛	8	8⅛	+ ⅛
	28¾	21	Acordia	ACO	.60	2.2	13	30	26⅞	26⅝	26¾	...

	52 Weeks Hi	Lo	Stock	Sym	Div	Yld %	PE	Vol 100s	Hi	Lo	Close	Net Chg
	9⅜	5¾	ActavaGp	ACT	.09	1.0	dd	200	8⅞	8⅝	8¾	...
	15⅝	11	Acuson	ACN		...	68	177	13	12¾	12⅞	− ¼
	21	16½	AdamsExp	ADX	1.63e	9.4	...	142	17¼	17⅛	17¼	...
	32⅝	16¾	AdvMicro	AMD		...	9	8412	26⅜	25	25⅜	− ⅝
	66¼	46½	AdvMicro pf		3.00	5.6	...	508	55⅛	53⅛	53⅜	−1¾
	8⅛	5	Advest	ADV		...	9	35	5⅛	5⅛	5⅛	− ⅛
	20	14¼	Advo	AD	.10	.6	92	167	17½	17⅛	17½	+ ⅜
n	9⅞	8¼	Advocat	AVC		...	...	203	9⅛	8⅞	9	...
	58½	43½	AEGON	AEG	2.09e	3.8	10	37	54¾	54⅝	54⅝	−1
	66¼	49¾	AetnaLife	AET	2.76	4.8	dd	2747	58	57	57½	+ ½
n	19⅝	17⅛	AgreeRlty	ADC	.35p	...	...	27	18⅛	17⅞	18	− ¼
	31	23⅝	AgriMinl	AMC	2.64	9.0	11	163	29½	28¾	29¼	+ ⅜
	20⅜	16⅜	Ahmanson	AHM	.88	4.4	dd	2049	20⅛	19¾	20	+ ⅛
	27¼	23⅜	Ahmanson pfC		2.10	8.6	...	136	24⅝	24⅜	24½	...
n	51¾	45	Ahmanson pfD		3.00	6.3	...	3	47½	47½	47½	+ ¼
	28½	25⅜	Ahmanson pf		2.40	9.1	...	6	26½	26⅜	26⅜	...
s	27¾	22	Ahold	AHO	.41e	1.6	...	22	25⅞	25⅝	25⅞	+ ⅛
	6⅛	1⅜	vjAileen	AEE		...	...	40	2	2	2	...
	50	37½	AirProduct	APD	.98f	2.3	34	3977	43⅜	42½	42⅝	− ¾
	39⅞	19⅛	AirbornFrght	ABF	.30	1.0	16	1379	29½	28⅝	28⅝	− ⅞
s	28¼	15⅞	Airgas	ARG		...	44	225	28	27½	27¾	...
	17	13½	Airlease	FLY	1.84	11.5	12	25	16⅛	15¾	16	+ ⅛
n	27¼	19⅞	AirTouch	ATI		...	...	7619	24⅞	24½	24⅝	− ¼
	27	23⅝	AlaPwr pfA		1.90	7.8	...	76	24⅜	24¼	24¼	+ ¼
	27½	23	AlaPwr pfH		1.90	8.0	...	54	24¼	23⅝	23⅝	− ⅜
n	25½	20½	AlaPwr pfB		1.70	8.1	...	7	21½	20⅞	20⅞	− ⅝
	18⅞	12¼	AlaskaAir	ALK	.05j	...	dd	2641	15½	14¾	15¼	+ ½
	21¼	16½	AlbanyInt	AIN	.35	1.8	28	33	19⅜	19⅛	19⅜	...
n	17¼	12½	Albemarle	ALB	.10e	.6	...	394	16⅛	15⅞	16⅛	...
	26¾	19⅜	AlbertoCl	ACV	.28	1.2	16	204	22½	22	22½	+ ⅛
	21⅞	17	AlbertoCl A	ACVA	.28	1.4	15	83	20⅝	20¼	20⅝	+ ⅛
s	30⅞	23⅜	Albertsons	ABS	.44	1.6	20	2216	27¾	27⅛	27⅜	+ ⅛
	25⅛	18¼	Alcan	AL	.30	1.2	dd	3263	24⅝	24¼	24⅜	...
	30¾	20	AlcatelAsthom	ALA	.53e	2.3	...	1236	23⅛	23	23	− ⅛
	60⅜	42⅜	AlcoStd	ASN	1.00	1.7	dd	1916	59⅛	58¾	59	− ⅛
	30½	22½	AlexBrown	AB	.60	2.3	5	120	26½	26	26⅛	...

Source: Table, "Selection from NYSE Composite Transactions," *The Wall Street Journal,* July 18, 1994. Reprinted by permission of The Wall Street Journal, © 1994 Dow Jones & Company, Inc. All Rights Reserved Worldwide.

$0.48 in dividends. The "Yld" (or dividend yield) column is calculated by dividing the cash dividend by the stock price and is expressed as a percentage. The "P/E" (price/earnings) ratio is calculated by dividing the market price by the earnings available for common stockholders (after any preferred dividends are paid). The "Vol" column indicates that 4,900 shares [i.e., (49)(100)] of AAR traded on this day. The next three columns indicate the high, low, and closing (or last) price for the day. "Net Chg" indicates the difference between today's quoted closing price and the closing price on the preceding day. In this case, the closing price of AAR did not change from its closing price the day before.

In addition to common stock, preferred stock is also listed on the New York Stock Exchange. Going to the second column, and down to the second AdvMicro (Advanced Micro Devices, Inc.), we see the letters "pf" right after AdvMicro, which indicate that it is preferred stock. The rest of the data is the same for preferred stock as for common stock, except the *P/E* (price/earnings) ratio is not calculated for preferred stocks. If you look down to Alabama Power (AlaPwr) you will see that it has three series of preferred stock outstanding—series A, series H, and series B.

TABLE 4A.2

Listed Corporate Bond Quotations from *The Wall Street Journal*

Most bonds trade in the over-the-counter, OTC, market. Hence, although many corporate and municipal bonds trade every business day, very few are reported in *The Wall Street Journal.*

NEW YORK EXCHANGE BONDS

CORPORATION BONDS
Volume, $24,034,000

Bonds	Cur Yld	Vol	Close	Net Chg
AMR 9s16	9.7	10	93⅛	− ⅜
AMR 8.10s98	8.0	28	100⅝	+ 1⅛
ATT 7½06	7.6	32	98⅞	+ ½
ATT 4¾99	4.9	29	89½	+ ⅛
ATT 6s00	6.4	66	94	− ¼
ATT 5⅛01	5.8	15	88¾	+ ⅝
ATT 8⅝31	8.5	61	102	+ ¼
ATT 7⅛02	7.2	821	98½	...
ATT 8⅛22	8.2	469	99⅝	+ ¼
ATT 8⅛24	8.1	28	99¾	+ ⅝
ATT 6¾04	7.1	121	94½	− ⅛
AirbF 6¾01	cv	40	101½	− 1
AlskAr 6⅞14	cv	35	80	...
AlskAr zr06	...	1	40	+ ½
AlbnyInt 5s02	cv	14	90	...
AlldC zr96	...	62	91	+ ½
AlldC zr09	...	25	28¾	− ⅜
AlegCp 6½14	cv	5	94	...
AlgLud 02	cv	5	108	...
Allwst 7¼14	cv	38	89	− 1
Alza zr14	...	20	36⅝	+ 1
AMAX 14½94	14.0	50	103⅜	+ ⅜
ACyan 8⅜06	8.3	33	100⅜	...
Ametek 9¾04	9.7	45	100¼	− ½
ConNG 7¼15	cv	28	102¼	...
CnPw 6⅞98	7.1	5	96⅝	− ½
CnPw 7½01	7.8	3	96½	+ 1⅛
Coopr 10⅝05f	...	10	72¾	+ 3¾
Corni 7¾98	7.7	1	101	− ¾
Datpnt 8⅞06	cv	30	52½	− ½
Deere 8½22	8.4	25	100⅝	− 2⅞
DetEd 6.4s98	6.6	95	97	− 1
duPnt dc6s01	6.5	482	91¾	− ⅜
EMC 4¼01	cv	68	99½	− 2½
Eckerd 9¼04	9.7	241	94⅞	+ ⅜
EmbSult 11s99	10.6	5	104	− 1½
EBP 6¾06	cv	10	74½	+ ¾
Enron 10¾98	10.3	13	104½	− ⅞
EthAln 8¾01	8.8	165	99⅝	+ ⅛
F&M 11½03	17.3	133	66½	− 1⅜
FabrCtr 6¼02	cv	14	76	...
FairCp 13⅛06	13.5	7	96⅞	+ ⅛
FairCp 13s07	13.8	10	94	− ⅞
Fldcst 6s12	cv	56	81¼	+ 1¼
Frpt dc6.55s01	cv	62	90	− ½
FreptM zr06	...	11	34⅛	− ⅛
GMA dc6s11	7.6	33	78¾	+ ¼
GMA zr12	...	99	216½	+ ⅞
GMA zr15	...	148	174⅝	+ 1⅞
GMA 8¼16	8.7	444	95¼	− ¼
GMA 8s94	7.9	50	100¾	+ 3/16

Quotations as of 4 p.m. Eastern Time
Friday, July 15, 1994

Volume $24,441,000

SALES SINCE JANUARY 1
(000 omitted)

1994	1993	1992
$4,243,581	$5,789,625	$6,708,625

	Domestic Fri.	Domestic Thu.	All Issues Fri.	All Issues Thu.
Issues traded	341	352	346	358
Advances	173	201	177	204
Declines	99	90	100	92
Unchanged	69	61	69	62
New highs	7	4	8	4
New lows	10	17	10	17

Dow Jones Bond Averages

–1993– High	–1993– Low	–1994– High	–1994– Low		–1994– Close	–1994– Chg.	–1994– %Yld	–1993– Close	–1993– Chg.
109.77	103.49	105.61	96.43	20 Bonds	97.32	+0.27	7.55	107.41	....
105.59	102.30	103.43	92.85	10 Utilities	93.23	+0.37	8.08	104.31	− 0.08
114.51	104.58	107.93	98.76	10 Industrials	101.41	+0.17	7.02	110.51	+ 0.07

Source: Table, "Selection from New York Exchange Bonds," *The Wall Street Journal,* July 18, 1994, p.C18. Reprinted by permission of The Wall Street Journal, © 1994 Dow Jones & Company, Inc. All Rights Reserved Worldwide.

Looking closely at Table 4A.1, you will see the letter "n" to the left of some of the entries; this indicates that stock was newly issued in the last 52 weeks. Also, the information for three stocks—ADT, Abitibi, and AlaskaAir—is underlined; this indicates those stock had a large change in volume for that day, compared with the stock's average trading volume. In addition, a careful examination of Table 4A.1, indicates the other following symbols:

Symbol	*Meaning*
a	Extra dividend or in addition to regular dividend.
dd	Loss in the most recent four quarters.
e	Indicates a dividend was declared in the preceding 12 months, but that there isn't a regular dividend rate.
f	Annual rate, increased on last declaration.
g	Indicates the dividends are expressed in Canadian money. The stock trades in U.S. dollars. No yield or *P*/*E* ratio are shown.
j	Indicates a dividend was paid this year, and that at the last dividend meeting a dividend was omitted or deferred.
p	Initial dividend; no yield calculated.

In addition to these symbols, others are also employed by *The Wall Street Journal*; for these see the "Explanatory Notes" section that is incorporated as part of the NYSE transaction data.

In addition to the NYSE, similar information is also included in the *WSJ* about stocks traded on the American Stock Exchange and the NASDAQ (National Association of Securities Dealers Automated Quotation system) National Market issues. Less complete information is provided about NASDAQ Small-Cap Issues (that is, smaller capitalization, or smaller size, stocks); ADRS (American Depository Receipts of foreign-domiciled firms); Emerging Companies (that is, very small firms); and numerous foreign firms.

Additional information about specific bond issues can be found in either Moody's Manuals *or* Standard & Poor's publica- *tions. The issuance and maturity dates, interest payment dates, and call features may be found in either source.*

Some corporate bonds are also listed on the New York Exchange; data on them is shown in Table 4A.2. Let's examine the first bond on Table 4A.2, which is issued by AMR, which is the holding company for American Airlines. This first bond says that it is "AMR 9s 16." The vast majority of bonds have a face (and maturity) value of $1,000. The coupon rate signifies how much interest will be paid per bond per year. Someone holding one AMR bond will receive $90.00 [i.e., (0.09)($1,000)] in interest each year. This interest is typically paid semi-annually. The "16" after the coupon rate for the AMR bond indicates it matures in 2016. The "Cur Yld" (i.e., current yield) is simply the coupon rate divided by the closing price. Since each bond has a maturity value of $1,000, we see that $10,000 [i.e., (10)($1,000)] face value in AMR bonds changed hands. The "Close" column indicates the price of the bond expressed as a percentage of the $1,000 face or maturity value. Thus, the closing price for the AMR bond was $931.250 [i.e., (93 1/8%)($1,000)]. The "Net Chg" column shows that the AMR bond closed off 3/8th of a point (or $3.75) from the close on the previous day.

Next let's go to AlskAr (Alaska Air Group) and look at two different types of bonds. The AlskAr 6 7/8 14 bond has a coupon interest rate of 6 7/8 percent, and it matures in 2014. What is different about it is indicated by the "cv"—which indicates it is a *convertible bond*. That is, as discussed in Chapter 14, the bond can be converted into common stock of Alaska Air at the option of the stockholder. The second Alaska Air bond is the AlskAr zr06. It is a zero-coupon bond (as discussed in Chapter 11) that matures in 2006.

Problems

Listed Stock Quotations

4A.1 On one day *The Wall Street Journal* reported the following information for Burlington Northern, Federal Express, and Illinois Power:

30¼	23	BurlgtnNthn	BNI	1.64	5.7	—	669	28⅞	27⅞	28¾	+1⅛
52¼	31¼	FedlExp	FDX		—	31	1160	50½	49¾	50⅛	+⅛
20	13¾	IllPow	pf	2.04	11	—	80	18¾	18⅝	18⅝	−⅛

   a. Which firm had the widest stock price range in the previous 52 weeks?
   b. Which stock is a preferred stock?
   c. What is a dividend yield? Why doesn't one of the stocks listed above have a dividend yield?
   d. Which firm is operating at a loss?
   e. What does the price/earnings ratio signify?
   f. What were the total number of shares of each stock traded?
   g. Which stock fluctuated most in price during the day?
   h. What was the closing price of each stock on the *previous* day?

Listed Bond Quotations

4A.2 Information on two separate IBM bonds from *The Wall Street Journal* on one day were as follows:

IBM9¾04	9.4	88	99⅜	. . .
IBM7⅞04	cv	289	101½	+ ¼

   a. What are the coupon rates and the year each bond matures? How many dollars in interest would you receive each year from owning *one* of each of the bonds?

Hint: In (b), does it have something to do with the convertible feature?

b. Which bond is convertible into IBM common stock?

c. What is the difference between the current yield and the coupon rate?

d. What bond sold more during the day?

e. How many dollars did the price of each bond increase or decrease from the previous day's close?

f. Why does the lower coupon rate bond trade at a higher price than the higher coupon rate bond?

Risk and Return

Sections in this chapter:

A few years ago, Phillips Petroleum was faced with a problem. Two different groups wanted to take over the company and then sell out to someone else or dismantle the firm. To repel the takeover, Phillips needed cash quickly. It soon more than tripled its debt to a peak of $8.9 billion. At the same time, oil prices, already in their worst slump in 50 years, were falling. As a Phillips executive commented: "Prices are a major topic of conversation around here. . . . The price of our principal commodity is going southward, and the debt tends to magnify that risk." However, within a few years Phillips reduced its debt by over two-thirds and remained a viable, but smaller, firm.

Phillips was experiencing risk from two primary sources: declining oil prices—which affected it very directly—and substantially increased use of debt financing. But all firms face risks. For Caterpillar and Westinghouse Electric, both of which do significant overseas business, a major source of risk has been fluctuating exchange rates between different currencies. Extremely volatile exchange rates can be dangerous; they increase risk and make planning, controlling, and monitoring operations more difficult and expensive.

Risk cannot be avoided in financial decision making; along with cash flows and time value, risk affects the value of any asset. Thus, financial managers must understand what causes risk and how it should be measured. They can then study its impact on required returns. Without understanding risk, managers cannot make effective decisions.

In order to understand risk and return, we will first examine portfolio theory, for which Harry Markowitz was a co-recipient of the 1990 Nobel Prize for economics.

We will then examine the capital asset pricing model developed by William Sharpe, who was also a co-recipient of the 1990 Nobel Prize for economics.

LEARNING GOALS

After studying this chapter you should be able to:

1. Understand probability distributions and the expected value and standard deviation measures.
2. Discuss portfolio risk and return, and the effect of diversification on portfolio risk.
3. Explain what beta measures and how the capital asset pricing model is used to estimate required return.
4. Discuss changes in risk and prices, and the equilibrium nature of the CAPM.

MEASURING RISK

UNCERTAINTY
A situation in which the outcome is unknown. In finance, used interchangeably with the term *risk*.

One of the fundamental financial decisions for firms and individuals is where to invest money. Risk is simply the chance that the future outcome of the investment will not turn out as expected.

PORTFOLIO
A combination of various securities.

■ LEARNING GOAL 1

Understand probability distributions and the expected value and standard deviation measures.

Whenever you are in a situation in which the outcome is unknown, you are exposed to risk, or **uncertainty.** We use these terms interchangeably to mean two things: (1) that the outcome is subject to chance and not definitely known or (2) that a situation exists in which there is exposure to possible loss. If you gamble in the casinos in Nevada or elsewhere, you bear risk. Investing in stocks, bonds, real estate, or gold bullion also exposes you to risk. Most of the decisions a business makes—to raise prices, to expand production, or to bring out a new product—expose the firm, its owners, its creditors, and other stakeholders to risk. Risk arises from many different sources and has a number of different meanings in practice. The important point to remember is this: *As firms face risk, so do their owners, creditors, and other interested parties.*

To understand risk, we focus on it from an investor's standpoint. The ideas developed, however, enable us to understand the risks that financial managers must consider in order to make wealth-maximizing decisions. To measure risk, we begin with individual assets and then move to **portfolios,** which are just groups of assets. To start, suppose we are interested in measuring the risk associated with two common stocks—Houston International and American Chemical. Although we employ common stock throughout this chapter, the concepts and ideas apply to all financial assets.

Probability Distributions

PROBABILITY
The chance of a single event's occurrence.

The **probability** associated with an event is the chance the event will occur. Because we are interested in future financial events, we focus on the expected states of the economy and returns. In column 1 of Table 5.1 the possible states of the economy are given,[1] followed by the estimated probabilities associated with the various states in column 2. The probability of a boom during the next period is 0.30, the probability of a normal state of the economy is 0.40, and the probability of a recession is 0.30. Note that the probabilities sum to 1.00. Column 3 shows the estimated returns associated

[1] *In this example we deal with only three states of the economy—boom, normal, and recession—although more could be used if desired.*

TABLE 5.1

Probability Distributions for Houston International and American Chemical

The rates of return are those expected to occur under various states of the economy. These rates could be given in decimal form, but we employ percentages throughout.

State of the Economy (1)	Probability of State Occurring (2)	×	Associated Rate of Return (3)	=	Mean or Expected Rate of Return (4)
Houston International					
Boom	0.30		60%		18.0%
Normal	0.40		20		8.0
Recession	0.30		−20		−6.0
	1.00		Expected rate of return, $\bar{k} = 20.0\%$		
American Chemical					
Boom	0.30		25%		7.5%
Normal	0.40		15		6.0
Recession	0.30		5		1.5
	1.00		Expected rate of return, $\bar{k} = 15.0\%$		

with the three states of the economy. One point should be stressed: *Finance is future-oriented; our interest is in the expected rate of return.* Because the future is uncertain, there is risk associated with owning either Houston International or American Chemical common stock.

The probability distributions presented in Table 5.1 and graphed in Figure 5.1 are called *discrete* probability distributions. By discrete, we simply mean that the probabilities are assigned to specific outcomes. In this book we emphasize discrete distributions.

FIGURE 5.1

Discrete Probability Distributions for Houston International and American Chemical

A discrete probability distribution means that a spike occurs at each specific outcome. A continuous probability distribution would show a smooth curve.

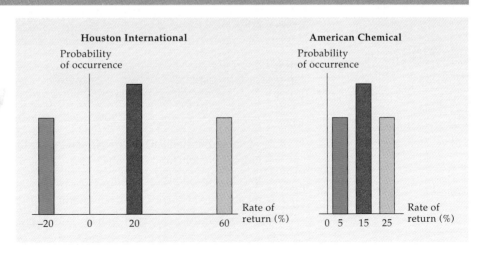

The Mean or Expected Rate of Return

MEAN (EXPECTED VALUE)
The weighted average of all possible outcomes, where the weights are the probabilities assigned to the expected outcomes.

Two measures are typically employed to summarize information contained in probability distributions. The first is the **mean** or **expected value.** It is the weighted average of all possible outcomes, where the weights are the probabilities assigned to the expected outcomes. This is calculated by multiplying the probabilities of occurrence by their associated outcome values, so that

$$\text{expected value, } \bar{k} = \sum_{i=1}^{n} k_i P_i \tag{5.1}$$

where

$\bar{k}$ = the expected value or expected return

n = the number of possible states

k_i = the rate of return associated with the ith possible state

P_i = the probability of the ith state occurring

Thus, the expected value (or expected return) is the weighted average of the possible outcomes (k_i values), with the weights being determined by the probability of occurrence (P_i values).

The expected returns for both firms are presented in Table 5.1. Houston International's expected return is 20 percent; American Chemical's is 15 percent. As noted in Chapter 2, these expected rates of return will generally not be equal to the actual rates of return. The actual rate of return depends on which specific state of the economy occurs.

Standard Deviation

STANDARD DEVIATION, σ
A statistical measure of the spread of a distribution from its mean or expected value.

TOTAL RISK
For a security or portfolio, the risk measured by the standard deviation.

Looking back at Figure 5.1, we can easily see that American Chemical's possible rates of return are more tightly bunched together than those of Houston International. However, it is hard to say much else about the riskiness of the two stocks without some measure that allows us to determine the spread of the distribution. The **standard deviation, σ,** is such a measure. This second summary measure arising from probability distributions is a measure of risk or variability in the possible outcomes. Standard deviation measures the **total risk** of a security or portfolio. It indicates how "tightly" the probability distribution is centered around the expected value. Thus,

$$\text{standard deviation, } \sigma = \left[\sum_{i=1}^{n} (k_i - \bar{k})^2 P_i \right]^{0.5} \tag{5.2}$$

where

σ = sigma or the standard deviation (the bigger the spread of the distribution, the larger the standard deviation)

k_i = the outcome associated with the ith state

$\bar{k}$ = the expected value or expected return

P_i = the probability associated with the ith outcome

The standard deviation gives an idea of how large the difference between the actual outcome and the expected outcome is likely to be, regardless of whether the outcome is caused by factors unique to the firm or factors common to all firms.

To calculate the standard deviation, we use the steps shown in Table 5.2.[2] We see that the standard deviation is 30.98 percent for Houston International, and 7.75 percent for American Chemical. These results confirm our observation from Figure 5.1: There is more total risk associated with Houston International because it has a larger standard deviation.

Two additional points should be made concerning standard deviations. First, the scale of measurement for the standard deviation is exactly the same as the original data and the expected value. In our example, the original unit of measure was the percentage rate of return per unit of time. Both the expected value and the standard deviation are expressed in exactly the same unit of measure. Thus, we can summarize the information contained in a probability distribution simply by reporting its expected value and standard deviation.[3]

The second point is that as long as we are talking about single assets, the standard deviation, which measures total risk, *is the appropriate measure of risk.* However, let's suppose that the asset is part of a portfolio of two assets, with 95 percent represented by one asset and only 5 percent by the second. (Such a portfolio is called *nondiversified.* We'll discuss the concept of diversification in the next section.) The risk of the asset that makes up 95 percent of the portfolio will affect the portfolio much

---

TABLE 5.2

Calculation of Variances and Standard Deviations for Houston International and American Chemical

Calculating standard deviations based on discrete returns is easy following this procedure, as long as there are not too many possible outcomes.

$(k_i - \bar{k})$	$(k_i - \bar{k})^2$	$\times$	P_i	$=$	$(k_i - \bar{k})^2 P_i$
Houston International					
(60 − 20)	1,600		0.30		480
(20 − 20)	0		0.40		0
(−20 − 20)	1,600		0.30		480
					Variance, $\sigma^2 = 960$

Standard deviation, $\sigma = (\sigma^2)^{0.5} = (960)^{0.5} = 30.98\%$

American Chemical					
(25 − 15)	100		0.30		30
(15 − 15)	0		0.40		0
(5 − 15)	100		0.30		30
					Variance, $\sigma^2 = 60$

Standard deviation, $\sigma = (\sigma^2)^{0.5} = (60)^{0.5} = 7.75\%$

COEFFICIENT OF VARIATION, CV

A measure of relative risk; the standard deviation divided by the mean.

[2] *Sometimes it is useful to calculate the **coefficient of variation, CV,** which is the standard deviation divided by the mean. This is a measure of risk relative to the mean and is useful for examining the relative variability when two or more means are not the same.*

[3] *This statement assumes that the probability distributions are relatively normal. This assumption, although not strictly true for securities, allows considerable simplification. Also, for groups of securities in a portfolio, the portfolio returns tend to be approximately normal.*

more than the risk of the other asset. As long as this is so (that is, for a security that dominates a nondiversified portfolio), then the standard deviation is still a valid measure of risk. However, *when we consider an asset in a portfolio with a number of other assets (a diversified portfolio), the standard deviation is not the most appropriate measure*. Before developing this idea further, let's focus first on understanding more about portfolios of securities.

CONCEPT REVIEW QUESTIONS

■ What two measures are typically employed to summarize information contained in probability distributions?
■ What is a standard deviation?
■ What type of risk does the standard deviation measure?

PORTFOLIO RISK AND DIVERSIFICATION

■ LEARNING GOAL 2

Discuss portfolio risk and return, and the effect of diversification on portfolio risk.

Up to now, we have been examining risk for single assets. However, most individuals do not hold just one asset; rather, they hold a portfolio of assets. If you hold only one asset, you will suffer a loss if the return on that asset turns out to be very low. If you hold two assets, the chance of suffering a loss is reduced: Returns on both assets must be low for you to suffer a loss. By **diversifying,** or investing in multiple assets that do not move proportionally in the same direction at the same time, you reduce your risk: *It is the total portfolio risk and return that is important*. Thus, the risk and return of individual assets should not be analyzed in isolation; rather, they should be analyzed in terms of how they affect the risk and return of the portfolio in which they are included. Much of what is known as "portfolio theory" is based on the work of Harry Markowitz, a recent Nobel Laureate in economics.

DIVERSIFYING
Investing in more than one asset, where the assets do not move proportionally in the same direction at the same time.

Portfolio Returns

EXPECTED RETURN ON A PORTFOLIO, $\overline{K}_p$
The average of the expected returns for a group of securities weighted by the proportion of the portfolio devoted to each security.

Measures of risk and return for a portfolio are exactly the same as for individual assets—the expected return and the total risk as measured by the standard deviation. The **expected return on a portfolio, $\overline{K}_p$,** is simply the average of the returns for the assets, weighted by the proportion of the portfolio devoted to each asset. We can write this as

$$\text{expected return on a portfolio, } \overline{K}_p = W_A\overline{k}_A + W_B\overline{k}_B + \cdots + W_Z\overline{k}_Z \qquad (5.3)$$

where

$\overline{K}_p$ = the expected rate of return on a portfolio

W_A, W_Z = the proportion of the portfolio devoted to asset A through asset Z (the sum of the W's = 1.00, or 100%)

$\overline{k}_A, \overline{k}_Z$ = the expected rates of return on assets A through Z

To illustrate, consider a portfolio of three stocks, A, B, and C, with expected returns of 16 percent, 12 percent, and 20 percent, respectively. The portfolio consists of 50 percent stock A, 25 percent stock B, and 25 percent stock C. The expected return on this portfolio is

$$\overline{K}_p = W_A\overline{k}_A + W_B\overline{k}_B + W_C\overline{k}_C$$
$$= 0.50(16\%) + 0.25(12\%) + 0.25(20\%) = 8\% + 3\% + 5\% = 16\%$$

Risk

CORRELATION

A statistical measure of the degree of linear relationship between two random variables, which can vary from +1.0 to −1.0.

Unlike the expected return, the portfolio risk, as measured by its standard deviation, is *not* a weighted average of the standard deviations of the assets making up the portfolio.[4] To understand why, we must consider the concept of **correlation.** Correlation (*Corr*) measures the degree of linear relationship to which two variables, such as the returns on two assets, move together. *Corr* takes on numerical values that range from +1.0 to −1.0. The sign (either + or −) indicates whether the returns move together or inversely. If the sign is *positive*, the returns on the two assets tend to move up and down together. If it is *negative*, the assets move inversely. That is, when the return for one asset (or stock, in our example) decreases, the return on the other increases. Further, the *magnitude* of the correlation coefficient indicates the strength (or degree) of relationship between the returns on the two assets. If the correlation is +1.0, the returns on the two assets move up and down together at *exactly the same rate*. If *Corr* is between 0.0 and +1.0, the returns usually move up and down together, but not all the time. The closer the *Corr* is to 0.0, the less the two sets of returns move together. When the correlation is exactly 0.0, there is no relationship between the returns. Similarly, when the *Corr* is negative, the closer it is to −1.0, the more the returns on the two assets tend to move *exactly opposite* to each other. These general relationships are shown in Figure 5.2. Returns on most securities are positively correlated (but not perfectly positively correlated). This occurs because the returns on most assets tend to move, to a greater or lesser degree, with the general movements in the economy. For stocks issued by U.S.-based firms, the correlation tends to be between about +0.30 and +0.75.

Two-Security Portfolios

To see how risk and return interact in a portfolio, let's look at the simplest type of portfolio—one with two securities. When you understand the workings of a two-security portfolio, it becomes easier to think about a portfolio of many securities.[5]

A portfolio's standard deviation depends on two things: the risk of the individual securities *and* the correlations between their returns. We calculate portfolio risk, σ_p, for a two-security portfolio as follows:

$$\text{standard deviation, } \sigma_p = (W_A^2\sigma_A^2 + W_B^2\sigma_B^2 + 2W_AW_B\sigma_A\sigma_B Corr_{AB})^{0.5} \qquad (5.4)$$

where

W_A, W_B = the proportion of the total portfolio devoted to asset A and to asset B, respectively

σ_A^2, σ_B^2 = the variances for securities A and B, respectively

---

[4] *There is one exception to this statement, which is discussed in Chapter 4 of* Financial Management, *page 119.*
[5] *More advanced aspects of portfolio theory are discussed in* Financial Management, *or covered in investment courses.*

FIGURE 5.2

Correlation Coefficient Under Three Different Conditions

If the correlation were perfectly positive (+1.0), all the points in (a) would lie on a straight line with an upward (to the right) slant. Likewise, perfectly negative correlation (−1.0) would result if all points in (b) plotted on a straight line with a downward slant.

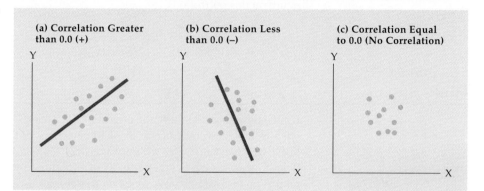

(a) Correlation Greater than 0.0 (+)

(b) Correlation Less than 0.0 (−)

(c) Correlation Equal to 0.0 (No Correlation)

$Corr_{AB}$ = the degree of correlation between the returns on assets A and B

σ_A, σ_B = the standard deviations for assets A and B, respectively

$\sigma_A \sigma_B Corr_{AB}$ = the co-movement, or *covariance*, between assets A and B

To understand why portfolio theory is important, let's go back to our two stocks and consider two different portfolios made up of Houston International and American Chemical. Assume, for simplicity, that the returns of Houston International and American Chemical are not correlated at all; that is, any movement of the returns for Houston have no bearing on the movement of the returns for American. In statistical terms, they are uncorrelated and have a correlation coefficient of 0.0. First, let's consider the portfolio return and risk if 75 percent of the portfolio is invested in Houston International, with the other 25 percent in American. Then we will consider a second portfolio—one that is 40 percent invested in Houston International and 60 percent in American Chemical.

With 75 percent of the portfolio invested in Houston International, the expected portfolio return found by using Equation 5.3 is

$$\overline{K}_p = W_{HI}\overline{k}_{HI} + W_{AC}\overline{k}_{AC}$$
$$= 0.75(20\%) + 0.25(15\%) = 15\% + 3.75\% = 18.75\%$$

while the standard deviation of the portfolio, using Equation 5.4, is

$$\sigma_p = (W_{HI}^2\sigma_{HI}^2 + W_{AC}^2\sigma_{AC}^2 + 2W_{HI}W_{AC}\sigma_{HI}\sigma_{AC}Corr_{HI:AC})^{0.5}$$
$$= [(0.75)^2(30.98\%)^2 + (0.25)^2(7.75\%)^2 + 2(0.75)(0.25)(30.98\%)(7.75\%)(0.0)]^{0.5}$$
$$= (539.87\% + 3.75\% + 0\%)^{0.5} = (543.62\%)^{0.5} \approx 23.32\%$$

Thus, with 75 percent of the portfolio invested in Houston International and the rest in American Chemical, the expected return on the portfolio is 18.75 percent. With a correlation of 0.0, the total risk, as given by the standard deviation of the portfolio, is 23.32 percent.

Let's see what happens to the expected return and standard deviation as we re-allocate the portfolio by now investing 40 percent of the portfolio in Houston International and 60 percent in American Chemical. The new expected return for the portfolio is

$$\overline{K}_p = 0.40(20\%) + 0.60(15\%) = 8\% + 9\% = 17\%$$

while the new standard deviation of the portfolio is

$$\sigma_p = [(0.40)^2(30.98\%)^2 + (0.60)^2(7.75\%)^2 + 2(0.40)(0.60)(30.98\%)(7.75\%)(0.0)]^{0.5}$$
$$= (153.56\% + 21.62\% + 0\%)^{0.5} = (175.18\%)^{0.5} \approx 13.24\%$$

With less of the total portfolio invested in Houston International, the expected portfolio return has decreased to 17 percent. And, because of the lower risk of American Chemical, the portfolio standard deviation has also fallen— to 13.24 percent. Hence, both the expected return and the expected risk have decreased.

If we were to keep changing the amount invested in Houston International and American Chemical, we would come up with a whole series of portfolio expected returns and standard deviations—one for each different portfolio weight. The plot of all of these different portfolios—each with the same two securities, with the same security expected returns and standard deviations, and a correlation between their expected returns of 0.0—is shown in Figure 5.3. This curved line is the **feasible set;** that is, the set of all possible portfolios that can be formed from two securities for a given correlation. A rational investor will choose the portfolio from the feasible set that best suits his or her personal risk-return preferences. More about correlation and risk reduction is contained in Appendix 5A.

What would happen if we were to consider two other securities—with different expected returns, standard deviations, and correlation between the securities? We would get a different curve, or feasible set, that could be plotted like Figure 5.3. As we move to more securities, and different stocks and other assets, the shape of the curve for the feasible set will change. And, other things being equal, we would find that the less the returns on two or more securities move together, the more diversification benefits are realized. Thus, if you want to diversify your personal portfolio of two stocks, it's better to invest in stocks that are in very different industries (such as in the retail industry and the public utility industry) than to invest in two stocks in the same industry (like two public utility stocks). By doing so, you gain the benefits of diversification. An alternative way to think about the benefits of diversification is captured by the old saying, "Don't put all of your eggs in one basket." That is the fundamental message of portfolio theory.

FEASIBLE SET

The set of all possible portfolios.

The closest thing to a free lunch you are ever likely to find is diversification: By diversifying, you can hope to earn a higher return without taking on more risk.

FIGURE 5.3

Feasible Set of Portfolios

When the correlation between the returns of Houston International and American Chemical is 0.0 (i.e., there is no relationship), the feasible set of possible portfolios is a curved line.

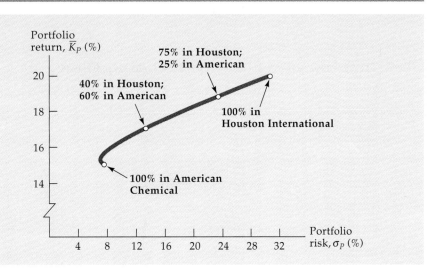

FINANCIAL MANAGEMENT TODAY

Diversifying Internationally

Portfolios can also be generated when two groups of assets, like two stock indices, are employed. Say one asset is the Standard & Poor's 500 Index of U.S. stocks, and the other is Morgan Stanley's Europe, Australia, and Far East (EAFE) Index. For a recent ten-year period, the means of the yearly returns were 16.7 and 19.1 percent, respectively; the standard deviations were 12.4 and 28.2 percent, respectively. Security returns in different countries do not move exactly together; that is, the returns are less than perfectly positively correlated. The corre-lation between these two indices (or markets) was +0.50 over the time period. Graphically, the possible combinations for these two sets of securities is shown below.

Both the returns and risks for foreign stocks were higher than for U.S. stocks. Investors who wanted to increase their expected return from that available with U.S. stocks, and to take advantage of the less than perfectly positive correlation between the returns in different countries, needed to diversify internationally. The minimum-risk portfolio for this period would have had about 20 percent of its assets in foreign stocks and the other 80 percent in U.S. stocks. If more than 20 per-cent had been invested in foreign securities, both the expected return and the total risk would increase.

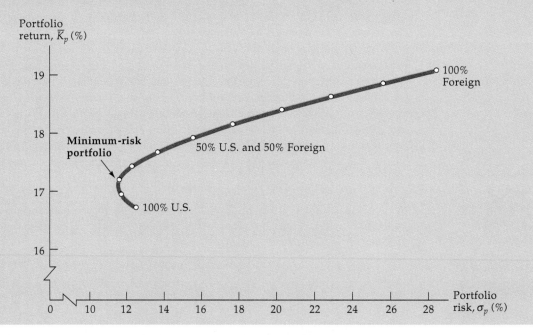

Diversifiable and Nondiversifiable Risk

Results of studies indicate that on average 45% to 55% of a stock's total risk can be diversified away. The figures are larger when you consider diversifying internationally.

We've seen that risk can be reduced by forming portfolios. But just *how much* risk reduction can we achieve? The answer has been provided by a number of studies, as shown in Figure 5.4. The total portfolio risk, measured by its standard deviation, declines as more stocks are added to the portfolio. Adding more stocks to the portfolio can eliminate some of the risk, but it cannot eliminate all of it. The total risk can thus be divided into two parts: diversifiable risk (sometimes called *company-specific* or *unsys-tematic* risk) and nondiversifiable (sometimes called *systematic* or *market*) risk, so that

$$\text{total risk} = \text{diversifiable risk} + \text{nondiversifiable risk} \qquad (5.5)$$

FIGURE 5.4

The Impact of the Number of Securities on Portfolio Risk

By the time 20–30 securities are in a portfolio, most of the diversifiable risk has been eliminated, leaving only nondiversifiable (i.e., systematic or market) risk. The benefits of diversification arise from reducing the exposure to diversifiable risk.

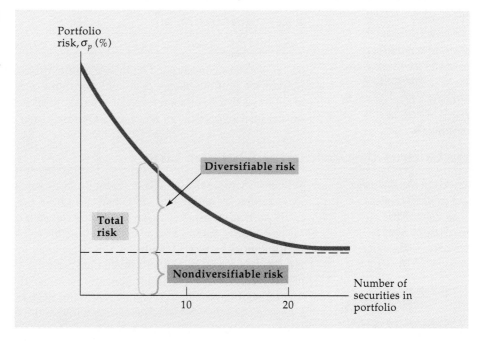

DIVERSIFIABLE RISK
That part of a security's total risk that can be eliminated in a diversified portfolio.

NONDIVERSIFIABLE RISK
That part of a security's total risk that cannot be eliminated in a diversified portfolio; measured by beta.

Diversifiable risk relates to events that affect individual companies. Examples of such events would be strikes, product development, new patents, and other activities unique to an individual firm. Because these events occur somewhat independently, they can be largely diversified away, so that negative events affecting one firm can be offset by positive events for other firms. The second type, **nondiversifiable risk,** includes general economic conditions, the impact of monetary and fiscal policies, inflation, and other events that affect all firms (to a greater or lesser extent) simultaneously. These risks remain, whether or not a portfolio is formed.

Since diversifiable risk can be largely or totally eliminated in a portfolio, the only relevant risk to the investor is the nondiversifiable risk:

relevant risk = nondiversifiable risk

The only risk a well-diversified portfolio has is the nondiversifiable or systematic portion. Therefore, the *contribution of any one asset to the riskiness of a portfolio is its nondiversifiable or systematic risk.*

CONCEPT REVIEW QUESTIONS

- Describe how diversifying your assets will help lower the risk of your portfolio.
- If the expected return on portfolio, $\overline{K}_p$, is simply the average of the returns for the assets weighted by the proportion of the portfolio devoted to each asset, then is the portfolio standard deviation of the portfolio, σ_P, simply a weighted average of the standard deviations of the assets making up the portfolio? Explain.
- Describe the two types of risks comprising an individual stock's total risk.

THE CAPITAL ASSET PRICING MODEL

For investors who hold diversified portfolios the standard deviation over-estimates the riskiness of the stock. Risk factors unique to the firm do not matter to a diversified investor.

■ **LEARNING GOAL 3**

Explain what beta measures and how the capital asset pricing model is used to estimate required return.

So far, we have concentrated on the ideas of portfolio theory. As articulated by Harry Markowitz, portfolio theory deals with portfolios of risky assets. By "risky assets" we mean those that have some exposure to risk, as measured by a standard deviation of greater than zero, but offer an expected return greater than zero.

Beta and the Security Market Line

Key Idea 6 was that risk and return go hand-in-hand. The CAPM is employed by many in finance to formalize this concept.

MARKET PORTFOLIO
A broad-based collection of securities, such as represented by a stock index like the New York Stock Exchange Index or the Standard & Poor's 500 Stock Index.

BETA, β_j

A statistical measure of an asset's nondiversifiable risk.

CAPITAL ASSET PRICING MODEL, CAPM
A model of required rates of return for financial assets, which uses the asset's nondiversifiable risk as measured by beta.

SECURITY MARKET LINE, SML
The graphic presentation of the capital asset pricing model for the expected return on any asset held in a diversified portfolio or for a portfolio.

William Sharpe, who is also a recent Nobel Laureate in economics, carried these ideas further by noting that individuals also have the ability to invest in (or, alternatively, to lend) a risk-free asset. By *adding the idea of risk-free borrowing and lending to portfolio theory,* Sharpe makes it possible to examine investment not only in a portfolio of risky assets but also in a risk-free asset (e.g., Treasury bills). His findings indicate that for assets held in a diversified portfolio, the contribution of any one asset to the riskiness of a particular portfolio is its nondiversifiable, or systematic, risk. Therefore, for assets in a diversified portfolio, risk can best be measured by how their returns move (are correlated) with the returns of the portfolio as a whole. If the portfolio is reasonably well diversified, we can, for simplicity, talk about the returns for assets in general as measured by the **market portfolio,** not just for the portfolio in question. This market portfolio is often measured by some broad-based stock index, like the New York Stock Exchange Index or the Standard & Poor's 500 Stock Index.

The important point about the market portfolio is that *for individuals holding diversified portfolios of assets, the appropriate measure of risk is how the return on an individual asset moves relative to the returns for the market portfolio.* This nondiversifiable risk is measured by **beta, β_j,** where the subscript j refers to the jth asset. Thus, beta reflects the nondiversifiable risk remaining for asset j after a portion of its total risk has been diversified away by forming a portfolio. The beta coefficient, β_j, is the measure of the asset's volatility in relation to the riskiness of the market portfolio as a whole. In other words, it measures what the returns on the asset are expected to be, relative to the returns on the market.

These ideas have been formalized in the **capital asset pricing model, CAPM**. The capital asset pricing model assumes that rational investors diversify, as discussed when we considered portfolio theory. Once they diversify, they can then allocate funds between risky assets (like stocks) and a risk-free asset (like Treasury bills). The expected return on any single asset, held in a diversified portfolio, can be graphed as in Figure 5.5, where higher expected returns and higher risk go hand-in-hand. The line shown in Figure 5.5 is called the **security market line, SML;** its simply a graphic representation of the capital asset pricing model. It shows the risk-return trade-off for individual assets, securities, and portfolios.

The SML relationship depicted in Figure 5.5 is specified as:

security market line, $k_j = k_{RF} + \beta_j(k_M - k_{RF})$ (5.6)

where

k_j = the required (or expected) rate of return on any risky asset j held in a diversified portfolio

FIGURE 5.5

The Security Market Line, SML

The security market line is a graphic representation of the capital asset pricing model, CAPM.

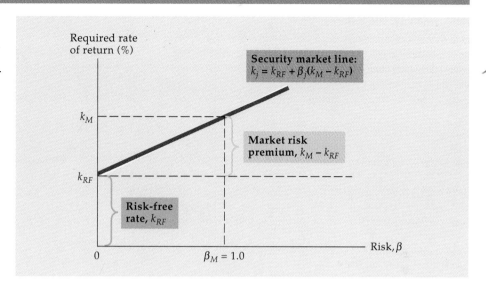

k_{RF} = the risk-free rate of return, which is often measured by the return on Treasury bills[6]

β_j = the beta coefficient for the asset

k_M = the expected rate of return on the market portfolio

$(k_M - k_{RF})$ = the market risk premium required to encourage investment in the market portfolio as opposed to investing in some risk-free asset

$\beta_j(k_M - k_{RF})$ = the risk premium for the asset or security in question. This premium is greater than or less than the market risk premium depending on the size of β_j, which measures how the returns on asset j move in relation to the returns for the market portfolio.

The security market line, Equation 5.6, when graphed as in Figure 5.5, shows that the rate of return required, or demanded, by an investor is equal to the return on a risk-free asset, k_{RF}, plus a risk premium $\beta_j(k_M - k_{RF})$. In a risk-free world, only the risk-free rate would be relevant. However, because the world is not risk-free, the risk premium is added to the risk-free rate to determine the required return an investor demands for investing in a risky asset.

Generally the stock market as a whole is our frame of reference; it has a beta of 1.0. The beta for an individual stock indicates the expected volatility of that stock in relation to the volatility of the market portfolio. Any stock whose returns fluctuate over time exactly as the market does has average systematic risk and thus a beta of 1.0. Risky stocks, such as airlines and high-technology firms, whose returns are more volatile and tend to move up and down faster than the general market's returns, have betas greater than 1.0 (see Figure 5.6).

We can be even more specific: The returns on a stock with a beta of 1.40 will, on average, increase 40 percent faster than the market in up markets; likewise, they will

[6]*If the term structure of interest rates is essentially flat, then the use of Treasury bills as the risk-free rate is justified. However, if the term structure is upward-sloping, so that the interest rate on long-term government bonds is substantially higher than the rate on Treasury bills, then the long-term government bond rate is a better proxy for the risk-free rate.*

FIGURE 5.6

Beta, Volatility, and Returns

High-beta stocks have much greater volatility in their returns relative to market portfolio returns than do low-beta stocks.

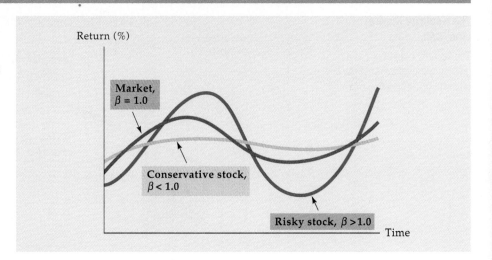

decrease 40 percent faster in down markets. Lastly, as also shown in Figure 5.6, conservative firms with very stable cash flows and returns, such as public utilities, fluctuate less than the market and therefore have betas of less than 1.0.

Both Standard & Poor's and Value Line publish estimates of beta. Estimates from different sources can vary substantially. Moreover, the betas of individual stocks are not necessarily stable over time.

Betas for a select group of stocks are listed in Table 5.3. The range of beta values in the table, from 0.60 to 1.90, indicates the general range of betas in practice. Examining this table we see that IBM, Kellogg, and McDonald's had betas close to 1.00, which means that their returns were of average volatility. On the other hand, Biogen, with a beta of 1.90, and Paine Webber Group, with a beta of 1.80, had very volatile returns. Returns for Consumers Water, Exxon, and Texas Utilities, with betas of 0.60, were very stable.

Determining Beta

Beta is generally determined by calculating a least squares regression line.[7] However, beta can also be determined if we know the standard deviation of the asset's returns, the standard deviation of the market's returns, and the correlation between the two returns. Employing this approach, we find that beta equals the covariance (the co-movement) between the asset's and market's returns divided by the variance of the market's returns, or:

$$\text{beta, } \beta_j = \frac{\text{covariance}_{jM}}{\text{variance}_M} = \frac{Cov_{jM}}{\sigma^2_M} \tag{5.7}$$

The covariance of the returns between asset j and the market is equal to the standard deviation of asset j, σ_j, times the standard deviation of the market, σ_M, times the correlation between asset j and the market M, $Corr_{jM}$, so:

$$Cov_{jM} = \sigma_j \sigma_M Corr_{jM} \tag{5.8}$$

---

[7] *Calculation of beta is discussed in Chapter 4 of* Financial Management.

TABLE 5.3

Beta Coefficients for Selected Firms

Beta is a measure of the volatility of the firm's returns versus the market's returns. It measures risk for individual stocks, or assets, in well-diversified portfolios.

Amdahl	1.25	Kellogg	1.05
American Express	1.45	Limited	1.45
Biogen	1.90	McDonald's	1.05
Consumers Water	0.60	Monsanto	1.10
Exxon	0.60	Paine Webber Group	1.80
General Motors	1.10	Telefones de Mexico	1.20
Glaxo Holdings	1.10	Texas Utilities	0.60
IBM	0.95	Xerox	1.20

Source: *Value Line Investment Survey* (July 15, 1994).

Inserting Equation 5.8 into Equation 5.7 and simplifying, we have

$$\beta_j = \frac{Cov_{jM}}{\sigma^2_M} = \frac{\sigma_j \sigma_M Corr_{jM}}{\sigma^2_M} = \frac{\sigma_j Corr_{jM}}{\sigma_M} \tag{5.9}$$

Note that the standard deviation of the market returns, σ_M, appeared in the numerator of Equation 5.9 before simplifying, while the variance of the market returns, σ^2_M, appeared in the denominator. By dividing through, we are left with the result that beta is equal to the standard deviation of the asset's returns, times the correlation between the returns on the asset and the market's returns, divided by the standard deviation of the market's returns.

If the standard deviation of stock j is 14.68, the standard deviation of the market portfolio is 8.94, and the correlation between the return on stock j and the market is +0.85, then

$$\beta_j = \frac{\sigma_j Corr_{jM}}{\sigma_M} = \frac{(14.68)(0.85)}{8.94} = \frac{12.478}{8.94} \approx 1.40$$

With a beta of 1.40, the returns on stock j are expected to increase and decrease 40 percent faster than the market. If the market decreases by 20 percent, we would expect the returns on stock j to decrease by 1.40(20%) = 28 percent.

Portfolio Betas

PORTFOLIO BETA
A weighted average of the betas for the securities in a portfolio, where the weights are determined by the proportions of each security in the portfolio.

We have been discussing the capital asset pricing model and examining betas for individual assets. As you might expect, a *portfolio* of assets also has a beta. This **portfolio beta** is a weighted average of the betas of individual assets:

$$\text{portfolio beta, } \beta_p = \sum_{j=1}^{n} W_j \beta_j \tag{5.10}$$

where

β_p = the portfolio beta or volatility of the entire portfolio relative to the market

n = the number of assets in the portfolio

W_j = the percent of the total value of the portfolio in asset j

β_j = the beta for asset j

Depending on the composition of the portfolio, the beta can be more than 1.0, equal to 1.0, or less than 1.0.

Suppose you have $10,000 invested in each of 10 stocks, so that your total investment is $100,000; the amount invested in each stock is 10 percent, or 0.10. If all the stocks have a beta of 1.20, then the portfolio beta is also 1.20. What happens if you sell one of the stocks and reinvest in another stock with a different beta? If the new stock has a beta of 0.60, then the new portfolio beta will be:

$$\text{new portfolio beta} = \beta_P = \sum_{j=1}^{n} W_j \beta_j = 0.90(1.20) + 0.10(0.60) = 1.14$$

Similarly, if the new stock has a beta of 2.00, then the portfolio's new beta will be 1.28 [i.e., 0.90(1.20) + 0.10(2.00)]. The required return on the portfolio of stocks can be estimated using the CAPM, based on the portfolio beta, and the expected returns on risk-free assets and on the market portfolio.

Let's summarize what we've learned about diversification, portfolios, and required returns.

- The standard deviation of portfolio returns, σ_p, represents the total risk of a portfolio.
- The best measure of an asset's relevant or nondiversifiable risk is its beta.
- Betas are distributed around 1.0, the beta of the market.
- Investors want to be compensated for the time value of money (i.e., the risk-free rate) plus the relevant, or nondiversifiable, risk.

Using the Capital Asset Pricing Model

Both firms and individual investors use the capital asset pricing model. In order to use the model to estimate the rate of return required, it is necessary to have three elements: the expected risk-free rate, k_{RF}; the expected return on the market portfolio, k_M, and the asset's (in this instance, the stock's) beta, β_j. At any point in time, these might be estimated as follows:

1. *Risk-Free Rate, k_{RF}*

The risk-free rate is primarily a function of expected inflation and economic conditions. Often the rate on Treasury bills is employed as a proxy for k_{RF}. By looking at *The Wall Street Journal*, or some other source of current financial market information, we can determine the return on 1-year Treasury bills. Let's assume it is 7 percent.[8]

2. *Expected Return on the Market Portfolio, k_M*

The expected return on the market portfolio can be obtained from various brokerage firms or forecasting services. Alternatively, we can view the expected return on the market as a function of three items: expected inflation, real growth in the economy, and the risk premium of stocks over bonds:

$$k_M = \frac{\text{expected}}{\text{inflation}} + \frac{\text{real growth in}}{\text{the economy}} + \frac{\text{risk premium of}}{\text{stocks over bonds}} \tag{5.11}$$

---

[8] *This assumes, in line with the discussion in footnote 6, that the term structure is essentially flat.*

TABLE 5.4

Forecasted Economic Data from *Value Line Investment Survey*

These forecasts were as of September 16, 1994. Note that *Value Line* forecasts for 1994 and 1995, and then for the 1997–1999 time period.

THESE ARE THE NATIONAL INCOME SERIES TO WHICH VALUE LINE SALES, EARNINGS AND DIVIDEND ESTIMATES ARE CORRELATED

ANNUAL STATISTICS	1983	1984	1985	1986	1987	1988	1989	1990	1991	1992	1993	1994	1995	1997-99
Gross Domestic Product ($Bill.)	3405	3777	4039	4269	4540	4900	5251	5547	5722	6035	6378	6750	7100	8200
Real GDP ($Bill. 1987)	3907	4149	4280	4404	4540	4719	4838	4897	4861	4986	5136	5316	5438	5983
Consumer Spending ($Bill.)	2258	2460	2667	2851	3052	3296	3523	3761	3906	4140	4391	4650	4930	5710
Capital Spending ($Bill.)	400	469	504	492	498	545	568	587	556	566	623	680	740	825
Industrial Production (% Change, Annualized)	3.7	9.3	1.7	9.5	4.9	4.5	1.5	0.0	-1.8	1.1	2.5	3.1	-0.8	1.5
Housing Starts (Mill. Units)	1.71	1.77	1.74	1.81	1.63	1.49	1.38	1.20	1.01	1.21	1.29	1.40	1.42	1.50
Total Car Sales (Mill. Units)	9.2	10.4	11.0	11.5	10.2	10.6	9.9	9.5	8.4	8.4	8.7	9.4	9.0	9.0
Personal Savings Rate (%)	6.8	8.1	6.5	6.0	4.3	4.4	4.1	4.2	4.8	5.3	4.0	3.7	4.1	5.6
National Unemployment Rate (%)	9.6	7.5	7.2	7.0	6.2	5.5	5.3	5.5	6.7	7.6	7.4	6.4	6.2	6.0
AAA Corp. Bond Rate (%)	12.0	12.7	11.4	9.0	9.4	9.6	9.3	9.3	8.7	8.0	7.1	8.2	8.0	7.8
30-Year Treasury Bond Rate (%)	11.2	12.4	10.8	7.8	8.6	9.0	8.4	8.6	8.1	7.7	6.6	7.4	7.3	7.0
3-Month Treasury Bill Rate (%)	8.6	9.5	7.5	6.0	5.8	6.7	8.1	7.5	5.4	3.4	3.0	4.2	5.1	4.2
ANNUAL RATES OF CHANGE														
Real GDP	3.9	6.2	3.2	2.9	3.1	3.9	2.5	1.2	-0.7	2.6	2.9	3.4	2.4	3.4
GDP Price Deflator	3.9	4.5	3.7	2.6	3.2	3.9	4.6	4.3	3.9	2.9	2.6	2.5	2.6	2.8
Consumer Price Index	3.2	4.3	3.5	1.9	3.7	4.1	4.8	5.4	4.2	3.0	2.9	3.1	3.2	3.5

QUARTERLY ANNUALIZED RATES	1st	2nd	3rd	4th		1st	2nd*	3rd*	4th*		1st*	2nd*	3rd*	4th.*
		1993					**1994***					**1995***		
Gross Domestic Product ($Bill.)	6262	6328	6396	6526		6623	6725	6815	6905		7010	7075	7170	7265
Real GDP: ($Bill. 1987)	5078	5102	5138	5226		5261	5317	5354	5388		5422	5453	5484	5514
Consumer Spending ($Bill.)	4296	4360	4419	4492		4564	4600	4675	4760		4800	4850	4920	5000
Capital Spending ($Bill.)	595	619	625	656		668	690	700	715		735	750	755	760
Industrial Production (%Change,Annualized).	5.7	2.2	2.6	6.7		8.3	3.5	4.4	2.0		1.3	1.1	1.0	1.0
Housing Starts (Mill. Units)	1.16	1.23	1.31	1.48		1.37	1.43	1.35	1.40		1.37	1.35	1.40	1.40
Total Car Sales (Mill. Units)	8.4	9.0	8.6	9.0		9.4	9.3	9.5	9.4		9.2	9.1	9.1	8.9

*Estimated

Thus, if the expected (not historical) rate of inflation is 6.5 percent, real growth (in constant dollars) in gross domestic product (GDP) is expected to be 2.5 percent, and the risk premium (or return) of stocks over bonds is 4 percent, then we would estimate k_M equal to 13 percent. Forecasts of some of these items can be obtained in various publications. For example, as shown in Table 5.4, *Value Line Investment Survey* provides forecasts of numerous economic figures, including expected inflation (as measured by the Consumer Price Index), and real growth in GDP.

3. *Beta, β_j*

We could estimate a stock's riskiness by relying on published betas by *Value Line,* Merrill Lynch, or other investment advisory services. For now, let's assume we estimate beta to be 1.40.

To find the required (or expected) return on the asset, we use Equation 5.6 as follows:

$$k_j = k_{RF} + \beta_j(k_M - k_{RF})$$
$$= 7\% + 1.40(13\% - 7\%) = 7\% + 8.4\% = 15.4\%$$

This approach can be used to find the required rate of return for any asset, or a portfolio of assets.

Historical Risk Premiums

An alternative approach to estimating the returns on the market portfolio, k_M, is to use the **market risk premium.** The market risk premium is simply the difference

MARKET RISK PREMIUM
The difference between the returns on the market portfolio, k_M, and the risk-free rate, k_{RF}.

between the returns on the market portfolio, k_M, and the risk-free rate, k_{RF}. Thus, this alternative way of estimating the return on the market portfolio is:

$$k_M \text{ (based on market risk premium)} = k_{RF} + \text{market risk premium} \qquad (5.12)$$

Data for three different time periods, all ending with 1994, for historical returns on common stocks and Treasury bills are as follows:[9]

	1960–1994	1970–1994	1980–1994
Common stock returns	11.1%	12.1%	15.2%
− Treasury bill returns	6.1	7.0	7.5
Market risk premium	5.0%	5.1%	7.7%

An examination of these data indicates that historical market risk premiums have fluctuated over time. Hence, *the use of historical market risk premiums to estimate the expected return on the market portfolio using Equation 5.12 invites trouble.* Remember, the returns on the market portfolio when using the capital asset pricing model *must be the expected returns, not historical returns.*

The same problem of using historical data exists with the premium that common stocks have earned relative to long-term corporate bonds, as required in Equation 5.11. The historical risk premium of stocks over bonds is:[10]

	1960–1994	1970–1994	1980–1994
Common stock returns	11.1%	12.1%	15.2%
− Corporate bond returns	7.6	9.9	12.1
Risk premium of stocks over bonds	3.5%	2.2%	3.1%

Just like the market risk premium, the risk premium of stocks over bonds has fluctuated over time, although not as widely. The message from looking at all of these historical returns is simple: No matter what method is used to estimate the expected return on the market portfolio, *it is the future returns in Equation 5.6 that are important.* Any past returns provide, at best, only a rough guideline to the expected returns in the future.

CONCEPT REVIEW QUESTIONS

■ What type of risk does beta measure?
■ Verbally describe the capital asset pricing model and how it is used to determine a stock's required rate of return.
■ What three elements are necessary to employ the capital asset pricing model when estimating an investment's required rate of return?

---

[9]*Adapted from* Stocks, Bonds, Bills, and Inflation 1995 Yearbook™, *Ibbotson Associates, Chicago.*
[10]*Adapted from* Stocks, Bonds, Bills, and Inflation 1995 Yearbook™, *Ibbotson Associates, Chicago.*

MORE ON THE CAPITAL ASSET PRICING MODEL

■ **LEARNING GOAL 4**

Discuss changes in risk and prices, and the equilibrium nature of the CAPM.

There are three other points related to the capital asset pricing model that we need to discuss: changes in risk and prices, the equilibrium nature of the capital asset pricing model, and some cautions about applying the CAPM.

Changes in Risk and Prices

The CAPM can help firms and individuals see what happens to the required rate of return and to the market price of a firm's stock as risk changes. To illustrate the price impact, let's suppose that a firm is expecting a constant growth in dividends of 8 percent per year, the current cash dividend (at $t = 0$) is $3, and the required rate of return (which is the return demanded by investors) is 16 percent. Employing the constant growth formula (Equation 4.8) for valuing stocks, we find that the current market price of the stock is

$$P_0 = \frac{D_0(1 + g)}{k_s - g} = \frac{\$3.00(1 + 0.08)}{0.16 - 0.08} = \frac{\$3.24}{0.08} = \$40.50$$

What happens if, because of changes in risk, the investors' required rate of return increases to 18 percent, while everything else remains unchanged? With an increase in risk and required return, the new market value falls to $P_0 = \$3.24/(0.18 - 0.08) = \$32.40$. Or, what happens if, because of changes in risk, the investors' required rate of return decreases to 13 percent, while everything else remains unchanged? A

EQUILIBRIUM
Point at which the expected return equals the required rate of return and assets are neither overpriced nor underpriced.

decrease in risk and required return results in an increase in market value to $P_0 = \$3.24/(0.13 - 0.08) = \$64.80$. Other things being equal, *increased risk lowers the market value of the firm's stock, and reduced risk increases its value.* This result shows that risk, as perceived by investors, has a major impact on the value of the firm. Managers must always be aware of the impact of their actions on the *perceived* riskiness of the firm, for this is how they influence the firm's market value.

The Equilibrium Nature of the CAPM

UNDERPRICED
Situation wherein an asset's expected return is greater than the required rate of return.

The capital asset pricing model specifies what the required rate of return on any asset should be. In **equilibrium,** the required rate of return, as specified by the CAPM, equals its expected return. What happens if this is not the case? Consider Figure 5.7, which shows a security market line based on investor beliefs about the relationship between required rates of return and nondiversifiable risk. Suppose that for some reason the two stocks from earlier in the chapter, Houston International and American Chemical, are improperly priced: Houston is underpriced and American Chemical is overpriced. This mispricing occurs because Houston International's expected rate of return is greater than its required rate of return (as specified by the SML); therefore, the stock is **underpriced.** Likewise, American Chemical's expected rate of return is less than the required return; consequently, it is **overpriced.**

OVERPRICED
Situation wherein an asset's expected return is less than the required rate of return.

FIGURE 5.7

Process When Securities Are Not in Equilibrium

Houston International is underpriced and therefore is providing an excess (risk-adjusted) return; the opposite is true for American Chemical. The price of Houston will increase and that of American Chemical will decrease until their expected and required returns are equal.

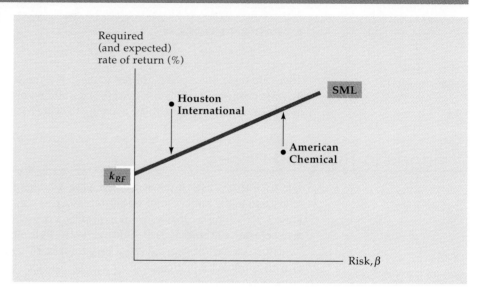

To solidify our understanding, let's use an example. Assume Houston does not pay cash dividends, its current market price, P_0, is $20, and its expected market price, P_1, is $28. Using Equation 2.6 to calculate the expected return, we have

$$k = \frac{D_1 + (P_1 - P_0)}{P_0} = \frac{0 + (\$28 - \$20)}{\$20} = \frac{\$8}{\$20} = 0.40 = 40\%$$

The fundamental approach to investment analysis focuses on finding companies whose expected returns are above and below the line.

If Houston's required return, as given by the security market line, is 25 percent, what will happen to the current market price? It will increase as investors see that Houston is undervalued and begin to buy it, and the rate of return will be driven down. To what level will the price rise? We can determine that by setting k equal to 25 percent and solving for the equilibrium price as follows:

$$k = \frac{P_1 - P_0}{P_0}$$

$$0.25 = \frac{\$28 - P_0}{P_0}$$

$$1.25(P_0) = \$28$$

$$P_0 = \frac{\$28}{1.25} = \$22.40$$

We see that if the price increases from $20 to $22.40, the expected and required rates of return for Houston will be equal, at 25 percent.

Exactly the opposite will happen to American Chemical. Because its expected return is below its required return, investors will sell American Chemical, driving the market price down. This will continue until the expected and required rates of return are equal—that is, until they are in equilibrium.

Some Words of Caution

Much can be said in favor of the capital asset pricing model: It is simple and logical, its assumptions (which are many!) can be relaxed without invalidating the model, and it describes in a formal manner how nondiversifiable risk and return are related. Even so, caution needs to be employed when using it, for the following reasons:

1. The model is based on expected conditions, yet we have only realized data. To use historical data without adjustment for future expectations invites trouble. Future, not past, risk and return are the items of concern.
2. The capital asset pricing model explains, on average, only about 30 percent of the fluctuations in firms' returns as a function of the fluctuations in the returns on the market portfolio. Thus, many other factors also affect the returns on common stocks.
3. Evidence exists that certain stocks provide realized returns *greater than could be expected* based on the CAPM. Three of these "anomalies" are stocks of smaller firms, stocks with low price/earnings ratios, and certain seasonal effects. The seasonal, or January, effect refers to the fact that a large part of the total returns for stocks historically has occurred in January.
4. Recently, Fama and French showed that the size of the firm and the book to market equity ratio were as important as beta in explaining past returns for 1963–1990.[11] In effect, they said that beta doesn't matter. Given the Fama and French results, we can confidently say that the next few years will produce much more empirical and theoretical work on risk and return.

Despite these cautions, the capital asset pricing model is the simplest model available at present that depicts the relationship between risk and return. Although other models are available, the CAPM is still the general frame of reference. Firms employ it, as we will see in Chapter 6 and elsewhere in the book.

CONCEPT REVIEW QUESTIONS

■ Explain why past data must be employed with care when using the capital asset pricing model.
■ Describe what will happen to the security market line, SML, if investors become more risk averse and require higher market risk premiums.

Summary

■ Financial management deals with the future; hence, it is future returns and actions that are important.
■ The mean, or expected value, and the standard deviation are used to capture the information contained in probability distributions.
■ When the correlation between the returns on two or more assets is less than $+1.0$, there are benefits to be gained by diversifying in terms of lower risk, as shown by a lower portfolio standard deviation.
■ Because part of the total risk can be diversified away, the relevant risk for assets in a diversified portfolio is the nondiversifiable, or systematic, risk measured by beta, β_j.
■ The capital asset pricing model, CAPM, describes the return required, or demanded, on an asset as a function of the return on a risk-free asset plus a risk premium that incorporates beta. Thus, increases in expected returns require increases in risk.
■ In estimating the capital asset pricing model, it is the future risk-free rate, the future return on the market portfolio, and the future beta that are relevant.

[11] *Eugene F. Fama and Kenneth R. French, "The Cross-Section of Expected Stock Returns,"* Journal of Finance *47 (June 1992), pp. 427–65.*

- Other things being equal, increases in risk lead to decreases in the prices of financial assets.
- The expected returns and required return for financial assets are generally equal; that is, they are in equilibrium.

Questions

5.1 Security A has a mean of 25 and a standard deviation of 15; security B has a mean of 40 and a standard deviation of 10.

   a. Which security is riskier? Why?

   b. What if the standard deviation on security B was 15? 20?

Note: In answering 5.1(b), you must consider whether it is absolute risk, or relative risk, CV, that is important.

5.2 Explain how forming a portfolio may reduce risk. What is the necessary condition for this risk reduction to happen?

5.3 The primary outcome of the capital asset pricing model, CAPM, is the security market line, SML, which is $k_j = k_{RF} + \beta_j(k_M - k_{RF})$. What do all these terms mean? How can they be estimated?

5.4 Security J has a beta of 0.90, the risk-free rate is 8 percent, and the expected return on the market portfolio is 16 percent. What will happen to the required rate of return on security J under the following conditions? (Assume each part is independent.)

   a. Inflation is expected to increase by 3 percent over the next number of years.

   b. Due to stringent monetary and fiscal controls, the government is shrinking its deficits and encouraging additional optimism for industry, consumers, and investors.

   c. The company just won an unexpected victory in a major lawsuit concerning patent infringement.

   d. International competition is increasing rapidly in the firm's market areas, leading to increased risk.

   e. The government has decided to place an excess profits tax, amounting to 50 percent, on all corporate profits.

5.5 Two securities exist as follows: security A has an expected return of 10 percent and a standard deviation of 15 percent, while security B has an expected return of 8 percent and a standard deviation of 20 percent. Explain in detail whether this information supports or refutes the notion that risk and return are related.

Concept Review Problems

See Appendix A for solutions.

CR5.1 Peter is considering investing in one of two stocks, IBM or Bargain Computers (BC). Given the following probability distribution of returns, what is the expected rate of return for each stock? What is the expected rate of return for the market?

State	Probability	IBM	BC	Market
1	0.2	−15%	42%	−8%
2	0.6	10	12	10
3	0.2	35	−30	25

CR5.2 Given the probability distributions in CR5.1, what is the standard deviation for each of the investments?

CR5.3 Assume that Peter is holding a well-diversified portfolio in which the expected returns on his portfolio resemble the expected market returns as in CR5.1. If Peter adds IBM to his investment portfolio, in which the new portfolio is comprised of

20 percent of IBM and 80 percent of the old portfolio, what is the new portfolio's expected return? If Peter added Bargain Computers instead of IBM to his new portfolio in the same proportion, what would be the expected return on his new portfolio?

CR5.4 Jon has been asked to estimate the required rate of return for two different investment opportunities, Abraham Inc. and Stoker Labs. A local brokerage firm estimates that beta for Abraham is 0.55, beta for Stoker is 1.19, the expected risk-free rate of return is 6 percent, and that investors require a return from the market of 11 percent. What is the required rate of return for both Abraham and Stoker?

Note: Other things being equal, does k_M stay at 11 percent or change in CR5.5?

CR5.5 After estimating the required rate of return for both Abraham Inc. and Stoker Labs in CR5.4, Jon was interested in what would happen to the required rates of return of both firms if inflation expectations increased the risk-free rate to 8 percent. What are the required returns?

CR5.6 Abraham Inc. recently paid a dividend of $2.00 per share and is expected to grow at 3 percent indefinitely. Stoker Labs just paid a dividend of $4.00 per share and has an anticipated growth rate of 6 percent.

a. Using the required rates of returns estimated in CR5.4, what is the stock price for each of the firms?

b. Now assume that inflation increased by 2 percent as stated in CR5.5. What is the stock price for both Abraham and Stoker after the increase in inflation?

Problems

See Appendix C for answers to selected problems.

Expected Value and Standard Deviation

5.1 A firm is considering investing in one of two projects, which have the following returns and probabilities of occurrence:

Probability	Project A	Project B
0.10	40%	50%
0.20	20	20
0.40	10	5
0.20	0	−20
0.10	−20	−40

a. Calculate the expected return for each project. Which is more profitable?

b. Calculate the standard deviation for each project. Which is more risky?

c. Which project is preferable?

Portfolio Risk

Note: In (a), convert the individual security returns for A and B to a single series of returns via 0.50(60) + 0.50(50) = 55, which has a 0.30 probability of occurrence. Do the same for A and B for the other two probabilities, and then for A and C. Once you have the probability distributions in (a), then in (b) you can treat the returns like that of a single security.

5.2 Securities A, B, and C have rates of return and probabilities of occurrence as follows:

	Security Return (%)		
Probability	A	B	C
0.30	60	50	10
0.40	40	30	50
0.30	20	10	90

a. Calculate the probability distribution of expected rates of return for a portfolio composed 50 percent of security A and 50 percent of security B. Now do the same for a portfolio composed of 50 percent security A and 50 percent security C.

b. Calculate the expected value (or mean) and standard deviation for portfolios AB and AC from (a).

c. Which portfolio has the highest expected return? The lowest risk? Which portfolio is preferable?

d. Assume that the standard deviation calculated for portfolio AC is 21 percent, but that everything else remains the same. Which portfolio would now be preferable? Why?

Correlation and Standard Deviation

5.3 Consider two stocks, A and B, with their expected returns and standard deviations, as follows:

	A	B
Expected return, $\bar{k}$	15%	10%
Standard deviation, σ	10	8

a. What is the expected return if the portfolio contains equal amounts (0.50) of each security?

b. What is the standard deviation for the equally weighted portfolio in (a) if the correlation between the security returns is (1) $Corr_{AB} = +1.00$, (2) $Corr_{AB} = +0.50$, and (3) $Corr_{AB} = -0.50$?

c. How does the decrease in the portfolio standard deviation (as the correlation between the security returns drops) relate to diversifiable and nondiversifiable risk?

CAPM

5.4 The risk-free rate is 8 percent, and the expected return on the market portfolio is 14 percent. What are the required rates of return for the four stocks listed below?

Stock	R	S	T	U
Beta	2.0	0.6	1.0	−0.2

What can we say about the volatility of each stock relative to the market's volatility?

Required Rate of Return

5.5 Susan is attempting to estimate the required rate of return for Brown Metals. The risk-free rate is 7 percent. Based on the analysis provided by a number of investment advisory firms, Susan estimates the expected return on the market portfolio is 15 percent and the beta for Brown Metals is 1.25.

a. What is the required rate of return for Brown Metals?

b. Susan decides to estimate the expected return on the market herself. She believes expected inflation is 6 percent, the real rate of growth in the economy is 3 percent, and the risk premium of stocks over bonds is 4 percent. The risk-free rate remains at 7 percent, and beta is still 1.25. What impact does this have on Susan's estimate of Brown's required rate of return?

Calculation of Beta

5.6 The returns and probabilities for a stock and the market are as follows:

Probability of Occurrence	Stock Returns	Market Returns
0.20	45%	50%
0.30	0	20
0.30	−5	10
0.20	−10	−10

a. What is the expected rate of return for each?

b. What is the standard deviation of each?

c. If the correlation between the stock's and the market's returns is +0.95, what is the beta for the stock?

CAPM, Beta, and Variance

5.7 If a security's required rate of return is 18 percent, the return on the market portfolio is 15 percent, the risk-free rate is 9 percent, the correlation between the security's and the market's returns is +0.50, and the standard deviation of the security's return is 16 percent, what is the variance about the expected market return?

Risk, Return, and Correlation

5.8 Assume that you hold the following two securities, Y and Z:

	Security Y		Security Z	
Probability, P_i	Return, k_i		Probability, P_i	Return, k_i
0.40	40%		0.30	65%
0.40	10		0.40	15
0.20	−10		0.30	−15

Note: You are not given the standard deviation of the market, σ_M, in (b), but it is the same for each security and therefore does not affect your answer.

The correlation between security Y and the market M is +0.50.

a. Calculate the expected return and standard deviation for each security.

b. What must the value of $Corr_{ZM}$ be to make the two securities equally risky in terms of their beta coefficients?

Portfolio Required Return

5.9 Excalibur Fund has a total investment in five stocks as follows:

Stock	Investment (market value)	Beta
1	$3.0 million	0.50
2	2.5 million	1.00
3	1.5 million	2.00
4	2.0 million	1.25
5	1.0 million	1.50

The risk-free rate, k_{RF}, is 7 percent, and the returns on the market portfolio are given by the following probability distribution:

Probability	k_M
0.10	8%
0.20	10
0.30	13
0.30	15
0.10	17

What is Excalibur Fund's required rate of return?

Portfolio Betas

5.10 Hoisin Resources has the following portfolio:

Stock	Investment	Beta
A	$20 million	0.90
B	40 million	1.40
C	10 million	2.00
D	30 million	1.20

a. What is the portfolio's beta coefficient?

b. If the risk-free rate is 8 percent and the return on the market portfolio is 15 percent: (1) What is the SML? (2) What is the (percentage) return Hoisin should be earning on the portfolio if its risk-return pattern puts it right on the SML?

c. Hoisin has just received $25 million in additional funds and is considering investing it in security E, which has a beta of 1.80 and an expected return of 19 percent. (1) Should stock E be purchased? (2) If not, at what rate of return would it be suitable for purchase (if its beta remains at 1.80)?

Required Return and Common Stock Valuation

5.11 Danford Products has dividends today, D_0, of $2 per share, an expected growth rate of 9 percent per year to infinity, a beta of 1.40, $k_M = 13\%$, and $k_{RF} = 8\%$.

a. What is the required rate of return?

b. What is the current market price of Danford's common stock?

c. Danford is contemplating the divestiture of an unprofitable but stable revenue-pro-ducing division. The effect will be to increase the growth rate in cash dividends to 11 percent, and also increase beta to 1.60. What will be the new market value?

d. Instead of (c), Danford could merge with another firm that is a steady cash producer but is less risky. The effect would be to lower beta to 1.20 and reduce the growth rate in dividends to 8 percent. What would be the market value in that case?

e. Instead of either (c) or (d), a new, aggressive management could be brought in. Beta would go to 2.00, and the growth rate in dividends would be 13 percent. Now what would be the stock price?

f. Is Danford better off staying where it is, or moving to one of the plans outlined in (c), (d), or (e)? Which plan should the firm choose? Why is this the best plan?

Risk and Stock Price

5.12 El Paso Electronics' common stock is expected to pay a dividend of $3.15 next year, D_1; the growth rate is 5 percent, its beta is 1.50, $k_M = 15$ percent, and $k_{RF} = 7$ percent.

a. What is the current market value of El Paso Electronics' common stock?

Note: In (b), at every beta, the SML is 2 percent less than before.

b. The combined actions of the Federal Reserve and the Treasury cause the risk-free rate to drop to 5 percent. What is the new market price?

c. *In addition to the change in (b),* risk aversion has decreased, so the return on the market is now 11 percent. What is the current market price?

d. Finally, *in addition to the changes in (b) and (c),* the firm closes some of its marginal operations. Beta decreases to 0.80, while D_1 is $3.12 and g decreases to 2 percent. What is the current market value for El Paso Electronics?

Risk, Correlation, and Stock Price

5.13 O'Meara Instruments is in the process of evaluating the effect of different factors on its market value. O'Meara expects to pay dividends of $3 a year from now ($D_1 = 3), and the growth rate in its dividends is 4 percent per year until infinity. O'Meara estimates the following: $k_{RF} = 6\%$, $k_M = 11\%$, $\sigma_j = 16\%$, $\sigma_M = 10\%$, and $Corr_{jM} = 0.50$.

a. What is the required rate of return for O'Meara and the current market value of its stock?

Note: $\beta_j = (\sigma_j)(Corr_{jM})/\sigma_M$.

b. What is O'Meara's required rate of return and stock market value if everything stays the same, except that its correlation with the market increases to 0.75?

c. If all the conditions are as in (a) except that σ_j increases to 64 percent and σ_M increases to 20 percent, what is the required rate of return and market price for O'Meara?

d. If all the conditions are as in (a) except that σ_j decreases to 8 percent, what is the required rate of return and market price for O'Meara?

Disequilibrium and Stock Price

5.14 The stock of Ross Furniture is currently selling for $25. You have evaluated the future prospects of both the firm and the market and made the following esti-mates. Ross is expected to pay a dividend of $2.00 at $t = 1$, and this dividend is expected to grow indefinitely at 6 percent a year. The standard deviation for Ross and the market are 10 percent and 6.25 percent, respectively. The correlation between the returns for Ross and for the market is +0.80. If the return on the market is 14 percent and the risk-free rate is 8 percent, is Ross a good buy?

Disequilibrium and CAPM

5.15 The risk-free rate is 5 percent, and the expected return on the market portfolio, k_M, is 10 percent. The expected returns and betas for four stocks are listed below:

Stock	Expected Return	Beta
Meade Copper	12.0%	1.3
Steel Printing	9.5	0.8

| Krishnan Electronics | 10.5 | 1.1 |
| Topper Entertainment | 13.0 | 1.7 |

a. Which stocks are over- or undervalued?
b. In an efficient market, what occurs to bring expected and required rates of return back into equilibrium?
c. Which stocks are over- or undervalued if the risk-free rate increases to 7 percent and the expected return on the market portfolio goes to 11 percent?

Risk and Return

5.16 **Mini Case** Answer the following questions that deal with portfolios and the capital asset pricing model.

a. Total risk for a stock is measured by its standard deviation. What do we mean by total risk?
b. Two stocks, Cyclical and Stable, exist with probability distributions and associated possible rates of return as follows:

State of the Economy	Probability of State Occurring	Rate of Return	
		Cyclical	Stable
Boom	0.30	50%	25%
Normal	0.50	15	10
Recession	0.20	-20	5

Calculate the mean, or expected value, for each stock, and its standard deviation.

c. The correlation between the returns on Cyclical and Stable is estimated to be $+0.20$. What are the expected portfolio return and standard deviation for a portfolio of these two securities if the following portfolio weights are employed?

Weight	
Cyclical	Stable
0.00	1.00
0.25	0.75
0.50	0.50
0.75	0.25
1.00	0.00

Plot the results. What does the feasible set tell us?

d. What is the primary lesson to be learned from portfolio theory?
e. Distinguish between diversifiable and nondiversifiable risk. Why is nondiversifiable risk, as measured by beta, the relevant measure of risk?
f. Assume the two stocks in (b) have prices and betas as follows: $P_{Cyclical} = \$50$ while $\beta_{Cyclical} = 1.58$, and $P_{Stable} = \$25$ while $\beta_{Stable} = 0.75$. A portfolio with 20 percent invested in Cyclical and 80 percent invested in Stable has been formed. What is the beta of the portfolio? If the stock market as a whole increases by 30 percent, by approximately what percent should the value of the portfolio increase? What should be the new market price of the two stocks after the 30 percent increase in the stock market?
g. Independent of (f) assume the risk-free rate is 9 percent and the expected return on the market, k_M, is 15 percent. What is the required return on the two stocks, Cyclical and Stable? What do we know about the two stocks?
h. Assume the risk-free rate increases to 10 percent while the expected return on the market portfolio increases to 18 percent. What are the new required returns for Cyclical and Stable?

APPENDIX 5A

Correlation and Risk Reduction

■ LEARNING GOAL

After studying Appendix 5A, you should be able to explain the relationship between correlation and risk, and define the efficient frontier.

To see the impact of different degrees of correlation on portfolio standard deviation, consider a portfolio made up of 20 percent Houston International and 80 percent American Chemical. *Any portfolio's expected rate of return, no matter what the correlation is between the two assets, will always be determined by Equation 5.3.* Recalling that Houston International had an expected return of 20 percent and American Chemical had an expected return of 15 percent, our portfolio's expected return would be

$$\overline{K}_p = W_{HI}\overline{k}_{HI} + W_{AC}\overline{k}_{AC}$$
$$= 0.20(20\%) + 0.80(15\%) = 4\% + 12\% = 16\%$$

Now let's see what effect the correlation between the assets will have. (*Note:* Here we are holding the proportions invested in the two securities constant and changing the correlation coefficient; in the example in Chapter 5, we held the correlation constant and changed the proportions invested in each security.) Assume for the moment that the correlation between the returns for the two stocks is perfectly positive, or +1.0 (i.e., $Corr_{HI:AC} = +1.0$). Also, recall that Houston had a standard deviation, σ_{HI}, of 30.98 percent, while American's standard deviation, σ_{AC}, was 7.75 percent. With this information, we can use Equation 5.4 to calculate the portfolio's standard deviation, as follows:

$$\sigma_p = (W_{HI}^2\sigma_{HI}^2 + W_{AC}^2\sigma_{AC}^2 + 2W_{HI}W_{AC}\sigma_{HI}\sigma_{AC}Corr_{HI:AC})^{0.5}$$
$$= [(0.20)^2(30.98\%)^2 + (0.80)^2(7.75\%)^2 + 2(0.20)(0.80)(30.98\%)(7.75\%)(1.00)]^{0.5}$$
$$= (38.39\% + 38.44\% + 76.83\%)^{0.5} = (153.66\%)^{0.5} \approx 12.40\%$$

Now consider the other extreme case—the returns on the two assets have a perfect negative correlation, $Corr_{HI:AC} = -1.0$. What happens to the portfolio standard deviation in this case? Using Equation 5.4, we find that the standard deviation in this example is now zero:

$$\sigma_p = [(0.20)^2(30.98\%)^2 + (0.80)^2(7.75\%)^2$$
$$+ 2(0.20)(0.80)(30.98\%)(7.75\%)(-1.00)]^{0.5}$$

$$= (38.39\% + 38.44\% - 76.83\%)^{0.5} = 0.00\%$$

Because the returns for these two assets move exactly opposite to one another in both sign and magnitude, when one goes up the other goes down. *The result is that the portfolio standard deviation is zero.* Obviously, this is the best of all worlds: We have maintained our 16 percent portfolio expected return but eliminated the risk. Why? Because the correlation between the two assets was perfectly negative. (*Note that the total elimination of risk in this example is a direct result of how it was constructed.* More generally, when the returns on two assets are perfectly negatively correlated, the standard deviation is reduced, but not all the way to zero.)

In practice, combining stocks with correlations as high as +0.60 to +0.70 still provides diversification benefits.

What about correlations between the extremes? What happens to the portfolio risk, for example, when we have positive, but less than perfectly positive, correlation between the returns? To answer this, let's calculate the portfolio standard deviation when the correlation between the returns for the two assets is +0.50:

$$\sigma_p = [(0.20)^2(30.98\%)^2 + (0.80)^2(7.75\%)^2$$
$$+ 2(0.20)(0.80)(30.98\%)(7.75\%)(+0.50)]^{0.5}$$
$$= (38.39\% + 38.44\% + 38.42\%)^{0.5} = (115.25\%)^{0.5} \approx 10.74\%$$

Remember that when we had perfectly positive correlation, the portfolio standard deviation was 12.40 percent. We see that with positive but less than perfectly positive correlation in the returns, some risk reduction has occurred. *The primary finding is that, because the portfolio standard deviation is less than the weighted average of the individual asset standard deviations, portfolio diversification led to a reduction in total portfolio risk.* We conclude that investors can reduce, or diversify away, part of an asset's total risk. Table 5A.1 presents the portfolio standard deviation for various correlations; the weighting of the two stocks remains the same—20 percent of the portfolio is invested in Houston International and 80 percent is invested in American Chemical. We see that the portfolio standard deviation declines as the degree of correlation goes from $+1.0$ to -1.0.

In addition, it is important to recognize that in a two-security case with perfect negative correlation, *some* set of weights will cause the portfolio standard deviation to be zero. For our two stocks the weights are 20 percent and 80 percent, respectively. *However,* the weights that drive a portfolio's standard deviation to zero may be anything; they depend on the specific standard deviation of returns for the two assets in question. Therefore, *do not* assume that a 20:80 weighting always results in a portfolio standard deviation of zero.

The foregoing section shows that, given any particular pair of asset weights, *the standard deviation of a portfolio's returns decreases as the correlation between the assets' returns decreases.* An investor is not restricted, however, to investing only one fixed amount in each asset. Table 5A.2 shows a sample of the many portfolios of

---

TABLE 5A.1

Standard Deviation for a Two-Security Portfolio Composed of 20 Percent Houston International and 80 Percent American Chemical as the Degree of Correlation Changes

With perfect positive correlation, the portfolio standard deviation is a weighted average of the two assets' standard deviations. In all other cases, the portfolio standard deviation is less.

Data

Houston International:	$W_{HI} = 20\%$	$\bar{k}_{HI} = 20\%$	$\sigma_{HI} = 30.98\%$
American Chemical:	$W_{AC} = 80\%$	$\bar{k}_{AC} = 15\%$	$\sigma_{AC} = 7.75\%$

$$\bar{K}_p = W_{HI}\bar{k}_{HI} + W_{AC}\bar{k}_{AC} = 0.20(20\%) + 0.80(15\%) = 16\%$$
$$\sigma_p = (W_{HI}^2\sigma_{HI}^2 + W_{AC}^2\sigma_{AC}^2 + 2W_{HI}W_{AC}\sigma_{HI}\sigma_{AC}Corr_{HI:AC})^{0.5}$$

$Corr_{HI:AC}$	Portfolio Return, $\bar{K}_p$	Portfolio Standard Deviation, σ_p
$+1.00$	16.00%	12.40%
$+0.50$	16.00	10.74
$+0.00$	16.00	8.77
-0.50	16.00	6.20
-1.00	16.00	0

Portfolio Expected Returns and Standard Deviations for Various Correlations and Weights

With perfect positive correlation there is no benefit to diversification, because the portfolio standard deviation is a weighted average of the two assets' standard deviations. With perfect negative correlation there is one portfolio that has a standard deviation of zero. Most assets, or securities, are positively, but not perfectly positively, correlated; therefore, forming portfolios of these assets can reduce, but not eliminate, risk.

Weight		Portfolio Expected Return, $\overline{K}_p$	Portfolio Standard Deviation, σ_p Given $Corr_{HI:AC}$				
HI	AC		1.00	0.50	0.00	−0.50	−1.00
0.00	1.00	15.0%	7.75%	7.75%	7.75%	7.75%	7.75%
0.10	0.90	15.5	10.07	8.93	7.63	6.05	3.87
0.20	0.80	16.0	12.40	10.74	8.77	6.20	0.00
0.30	0.70	16.5	14.72	12.89	10.76	8.09	3.87
0.40	0.60	17.0	17.04	15.26	13.24	10.84	7.75
0.50	0.50	17.5	19.36	17.75	15.97	13.96	11.62
0.60	0.40	18.0	21.69	20.32	18.85	17.25	15.49
0.70	0.30	18.5	24.01	22.94	21.81	20.62	19.36
0.80	0.20	19.0	26.34	25.60	24.84	24.05	23.24
0.90	0.10	19.5	28.66	28.28	27.90	27.51	27.11
1.00	0.00	20.0	30.98	30.98	30.98	30.98	30.98

Houston International and American Chemical that could be formed and their expected return and standard deviation for various correlations. Figure 5A.1 graphs the set of all possible portfolios that could be formed from these two stocks when the correlation between their returns is +1.0, 0.0, and −1.0, respectively.

We see that if the correlation is either of the extremes (+1.0 or −1.0) the feasible set is a straight line. For example, if the correlation is +1.0, the feasible set is a straight line from AC, where 100 percent of the portfolio is invested in American, to HI, where 100 percent is invested in Houston. If the correlation is −1.0, the feasible

The Feasible Sets of Portfolios That Can Be Formed from Houston International and American Chemical if the Correlation Between Them Is −1.0, 0.0, or +1.0

The feasible set for a two-security portfolio is a straight or a curved line.

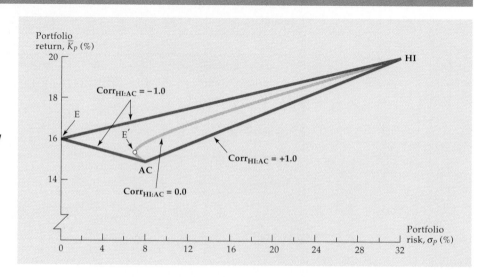

set is made up of two straight line segments, and there is one portfolio in the set (in this case, portfolio E) for which the risk of the portfolio is zero.

If the correlation is anything other than +1.0 or –1.0, we have a feasible set that is a curve. This situation is representative of most portfolios, because risk can be reduced but not eliminated. Not all portions of the feasible sets in the figure represent reasonable portfolios. If the correlation between Houston and American is –1.0, then the portion of the set from E to HI dominates the portion from AC to E because it offers a higher return for risk levels between 0.0 and 7.75 percent. Thus, E to HI represents the upper limit of reasonable portfolios when the correlation is –1.0. This general limit—the part of the feasible set that contains only reasonable portfolios—has been named the **efficient frontier**. Similarly, E' to HI is the efficient frontier of portfolios when the correlation is 0.0. Rational investors choose their portfolio from those on the efficient frontier.

EFFICIENT FRONTIER
Set of portfolios that have the highest expected return at each level of risk, and the lowest risk at each level of expected return.

Problems

See Appendix C for answers to selected problems.

Portfolio Risk, Return, and Efficient Frontier

5A.1 You have estimated the following probability distribution of returns for two stocks:

Alpha		Omega	
Probability	Return	Probability	Return
0.20	8%	0.20	26%
0.30	4	0.30	12
0.30	0	0.30	0
0.20	−4	0.20	−4

a. Calculate the expected rate of return and standard deviation for each stock.
b. If the correlation between the returns on the two stocks is −0.40, calculate the portfolio return and the standard deviation for portfolios containing 100 percent, 75 percent, 50 percent, 25 percent, and 0 percent of Alpha, respectively.
c. Plot the results from (b). Which portfolios lie on the efficient frontier?
d. Which portfolio would *you* prefer? Why? Would other individuals necessarily choose the same portfolio?

Efficient Frontier

5A.2 The following portfolios are available for selection:

Portfolio	Return, K_p	Risk, σ_p
1	16%	16%
2	14	10
3	8	4
4	12	14
5	9	8
6	10	12
7	7	11
8	5	7
9	11	6
10	3	3

a. By plotting the data, determine which portfolios lie on the efficient frontier.
b. Which portfolio would *you* prefer? Why? Would other individuals necessarily choose the same portfolio?

PART **3**

LONG-TERM INVESTMENT DECISIONS

Chapter 6 The Opportunity Cost of Capital

Chapter 7 Capital Budgeting Techniques

Chapter 8 Capital Budgeting Applications

Chapter 9 Risk, Capital Budgeting, and Value Creation

EXECUTIVE INTERVIEW WITH JAMES M. CORNELIUS

Vice-President, Chief Financial Officer, and Treasurer
Eli Lilly and Company, Indianapolis, Indiana

Eli Lilly is a research-based pharmaceutical and health care products corporation. James Cornelius has served as vice-president of finance and chief financial officer of the firm since 1983. He was elected to the firm's board of directors and executive committee in 1986. Mr. Cornelius earned an undergraduate degree in accounting and an M.B.A. degree from Michigan State University, after which he spent two years with the U.S. Army Finance Corps before beginning his 25-year career with Lilly. We asked Mr. Cornelius to discuss the long-term investment practices used at Eli Lilly.

I have seen major changes both in our industry and at this firm over the past decade. Nowhere are these changes more evident—or more important—than in the long-term investment area. To remain competitive, we must commit ever-larger amounts of capital, placing a high premium on making good investment decisions.

At Eli Lilly, our largest long-term investment category is research and development (R&D). Although R&D finds its way into the expense side of the income statement, it is indeed a long-term investment. We analyze R&D cash outflows just as we do plant and capital, using the same cost of capital and discounted cash flow tools.

Calculating the Cost of Capital

To evaluate long-term investment projects, Lilly uses a firmwide cost of capital as the hurdle rate. Although we make other medical products, we consider ourselves primarily a pharmaceutical firm, and so we calculate one cost of capital for the whole company. Currently it's 15 percent—and has been for about 20 years. This relatively high rate reflects our industry's high risk.

We are now facing a very different business climate. The political issues surrounding health care costs require that we take a hard look at our calculations and the assumptions on which they are based. I predict that we'll probably lower the cost of capital to reflect the next—rather than the past—decade's investment opportunities.

A major change at Eli Lilly is the addition of more debt to our capital structure. Our longstanding philosophy was that the pharmaceutical business has enough operating risk that we shouldn't add financial risk to it. Like most major pharmaceutical firms, we borrowed very little. In late March 1993, we issued $200 million of 10-year bonds with a before-tax interest rate of 6.35 percent, which is relatively inexpensive capital. We're rated AAA, so we can borrow at favorable rates. With more lower-cost debt in our financing mix, I expect our revised cost of capital will drop below 15 percent.

In terms of actually calculating cost of capital, the easiest part is the after-tax cost of debt. When it comes to valuing our common stock, we use the capital asset pricing model (CAPM). The difficult part is the required premium for equity capital. Data for the past 10 to 15 years suggest equity premiums of 4 to 6 percent. Our beta has been about 1. It will probably become more volatile. I expect new calculations will give us a beta of 1.05 to 1.1.

The lower equity premium and the addition of more debt will obviously lower our weighted average cost of capital. I don't know whether the new cost of capital will be closer to 13 or to 10 percent. But that new rate is probably more realistic; it will reflect possible government price constraints and lower profitability levels.

Capital Budgeting at Eli Lilly

Our capital budgeting process works from the top down. First, we make companywide estimates of the coming year's sales, income, and cash flow. We then divide the company into seven or eight strategic business units (SBUs). We look at each SBU as if it were an independent company. We pull together sales, unit costs, R&D expenses, and allocation of common manufacturing costs, to get the SBU income and profit contribution. Usually the SBU capital budgets total more than the corporate allocation. So the SBUs rank projects, defer some, speed up others. It's a process that results in an acceptable operating plan for the next year.

In our capital budgeting, we use both net present value, *NPV*, and internal rates of return, *IRR*, complementing that with a graphic analysis of the payback. Of two projects with similar *NPVs* or *IRRs*, the one that pays back more quickly would be ranked higher. We graph the cash flows to see how deep the curve is. You may have a project that requires $300 million and pays back in 3 years, compared to another that may cost $30 million and also pays back in 3 years. The depth of the investment obviously makes the $300 million project riskier than the $30 million one. And even though the $300 million project might have a terrific return, we can do only so many big-risk projects. We need to balance risk across the whole portfolio each year, with one large project, a few at $100 million, and several smaller ones in the $20 to $50 million range.

We use scenario analysis to adjust for risk. We keep the 15 percent cost of capital but run sensitivity analyses changing cash flow assumptions: What if we can charge only 50 cents rather than a dollar per day for the new therapy? What if the product launch is delayed 6 months, costs are different, or competitive entry is sooner/later?

The international factor is another dimension we incorporate into our capital budgeting analysis. We may prepare domestic versus international cost and revenue forecasts, but they are combined in the total analysis to make a global decision. Every country in the world right now wants jobs, and that presents a strategic dilemma. Pricing negotiations are quasi-political; elements like job creation, employment, and balance of trade enter into those discussions. So Lilly manufacturing facilities are distributed around the world, even though we'd probably prefer fewer plants and larger economies of scale.

Historically, we relied almost exclusively on products developed in-house. Now there is an explosion in life sciences research in academic settings and the biotechnology industry. We have opportunities for new product acquisitions and strategic alliances but typically don't have as much data on them as on in-house projects. This obviously makes the analysis more difficult, and sometimes we invest in a product that fails. You can have a good analysis on the front end, but the marketplace or science can turn it into a bad decision. That's the nature of doing business in an industry with a high rate of innovation and risk.

In Chapter 6 we examine how firms determine firmwide, divisional, and project-specific opportunity costs of capital. Chapter 7 discusses capital budgeting techniques, and Chapter 8 examines the issues that arise when these techniques are applied. In Chapter 9 we consider how risk is handled and how firms make value-creating capital investment decisions.

The Opportunity Cost of Capital

Sections in this chapter:

■ **What Is the Firm's Opportunity Cost of Capital?**
A weighty—and weighted—issue.

■ **Calculating Costs and Financing Proportions**
Mixing the financing ingredients.

■ **Calculating the Opportunity Cost of Capital**
The recipe and some instructions.

■ **Calculating PepsiCo's Opportunity Cost of Capital**
The "real thing."

■ **Other Issues When Calculating a Firm's Opportunity Cost of Capital**
Not all projects are equal.

The *Wall Street Journal* reported that Philadelphia Electric was applying for an increase in the electric rates it is allowed to charge its customers. Philadelphia Electric, like other public utilities, is a regulated firm. It is permitted to charge rates designed to allow it to recover its operating costs and provide reasonable compensation for its providers of capital. Investors in stocks and bonds weigh their risk preferences and returns: The more the risk, the higher the required return. But a higher return to investors means higher costs to the firm. It's not surprising, then, that a major area of testimony—and controversy—in hearings before utility commissions is the cost to the firm of various sources of capital. Company witnesses argue that the firm's costs of capital are high, so higher rates are needed to compensate the providers of capital. Opponents, on the other hand, argue that the firm's capital costs are lower, and hence lower rate increases (or even rate decreases) are desirable; otherwise the firm's providers of capital will be overcompensated for the risks taken. Ultimately the regulatory authorities, by setting the allowable rates, determine the amount of revenue public utilities will have for operating expenses and returns to the providers of capital.

A nonregulated firm is not subject to the rate hearing process, but it too needs sufficient cash flows to cover the costs of operations and ensure a suitable return to investors. This is true for both domestic and foreign firms. Recently Daimler-Benz, a German conglomerate, has begun to rethink its approach to determining the returns needed on capital invested. This rethinking came about in part because Daimler-Benz became the first German firm to be listed on the New York Stock Exchange. As a result Daimler-Benz has determined that its cost of capital is above 12 percent, which is much higher than the 8 percent that is average for German companies. Daimler-Benz is now employing its cost of capital to assess new investment projects, as well as in strategic planning as it evaluates its existing businesses.

Knowing the cost of capital enables successful firms to make capital investments that provide adequate returns. If too low a cost estimate is employed, firms will make capital investments that provide inadequate returns, and the value of the firm will decrease because the costs exceed the returns.

LEARNING GOALS

After studying this chapter, you should be able to:

1. Understand the concept of the opportunity cost of capital and its underlying assumptions.
2. Determine the costs of debt and preferred stock.
3. Determine the cost of common equity under three different approaches: dividend valuation, CAPM, and bond yield plus expected risk premium.
4. Determine the opportunity cost of capital, and discuss when firms should make this calculation.
5. Explain the rationale for a divisional opportunity cost of capital and how it is determined.
6. Discuss the issues involved in determining the opportunity cost of capital for a multinational firm.

WHAT IS THE FIRM'S OPPORTUNITY COST OF CAPITAL?

■ LEARNING GOAL 1

Understand the concept of the opportunity cost of capital and its underlying assumptions.

The most important element in determining the value of the firm is its investment decisions. A thorough understanding of capital budgeting techniques is required in order to maximize the market value of the firm, V. An important part of the decision involves using the proper opportunity cost as the discount rate for net present value decisions.

To keep things simple, we begin by looking at projects that can be viewed as being equal in risk to the firm as a whole. The proper rate to use can be viewed in one of two ways:

1. *The Opportunity Cost of Capital* When viewed as the **opportunity cost of capital,** the discount rate is what the funds could earn in an alternative investment of similar risk. If a firm has a million dollars that could be invested externally to yield 15 percent, then an internal (i.e., capital investment) project with equal risk should return more that 15 percent. Otherwise, the value of the firm will not be maximized.

2. *The Weighted Average Cost of Capital* The **weighted average cost of capital** is simply the *average* after-tax cost of new funds available for investment by the firm. For example, if the firm's average after-tax cost of the last dollar of new funds is 15 percent, then it must earn more than 15 percent (after taxes) on new investments in order to maximize the value of the firm. The rationale behind the weighted average cost of capital is that unless a firm earns more than the average cost of the last dollar invested, it is losing money on the investment.

We use the terms "opportunity cost of capital," "required rate of return," or "weighted average cost of capital" interchangeably. To understand why we do so, it is

---

OPPORTUNITY COST OF CAPITAL

Required return that is forgone by choosing one investment over an alternative investment of similar risk.

WEIGHTED AVERAGE COST OF CAPITAL

The cost of the last dollar of additional funds secured; the firm's opportunity cost of capital.

Remember Key Ideas 1 and 4, which directly relate to estimating and using the opportunity cost of capital—the goal of the firm is to maximize its market value, and firms focus on cash flows and their incremental effects (and use net present value to do so).

important to recognize that the feasibility of a project depends on how much it will cost the firm to raise new funds to finance the project. Therefore, the opportunity cost of capital represents the cost of *new funds* needed to finance the project—which is the weighted average cost of capital. Whatever the appropriate discount rate is called, it is the minimum rate the firm must earn to ensure that the value of the firm does not fall.

Accurate estimation of the firm's opportunity cost of capital is important. We begin by determining how to calculate the firm's opportunity cost of capital—first for a hypothetical example and then for an actual company, PepsiCo. Remember, if a project returns less than it costs, then the net present value, *NPV*, will be negative and the value of the firm will decrease if the project is accepted. So, *the opportunity cost of capital represents the minimum return a firm must earn.* Accepting projects whose expected returns are higher than their costs, as evidenced by positive *NPV*s, assists in maximizing the value of the firm. Later in the chapter we briefly discuss the approach to employ when the risk of proposed capital budgeting projects differs from the firm's average risk, and how multinational firms deal with the opportunity cost of capital.

Definitions and Calculations

Before calculating the firm's opportunity cost of capital, we begin by defining some terms we will use throughout:

opportunity cost of capital = the weighted average of the cost of the last dollar of capital expected to be raised by the firm.

k_b = the before-tax cost of new debt issued by the firm. Ignoring flotation costs, this is equal to the yield to maturity, *YTM*, expected by investors, as defined in Chapter 4.

k_i = $k_b(1 - T)$, the after-tax cost of new debt issued by the firm, where T equals the firm's effective marginal corporate tax rate.

k_{ps} = the after-tax cost of new preferred stock issued by the firm.

k_s = the after-tax cost of equity capital. This k_s is identical to the k_s defined in Chapter 4, where it was called the investor's required return on common stock.

W_i = the weights that indicate the future financing proportions to be employed by the firm.

The firm's opportunity cost of capital is a weighted average of the various sources of new capital. Note that the costs are expressed on an after-tax basis. This is to *ensure consistency for decision-making purposes with the cash flows that are also calculated on an after-tax basis.* If a firm raises capital with debt, preferred stock, and internally generated common equity, the opportunity cost of capital would be

$$\text{opportunity cost of capital} = k_i W_{\text{debt}} + k_{ps} W_{\text{preferred stock}} + k_s W_{\text{common equity}} \quad (6.1)$$

where the W's indicate the proportions of future funding to be raised from each specific source.

Basic Assumptions

In order to determine a firm's opportunity cost of capital, we begin by going back to the notion that financial markets in developed countries are efficient. As informed investors in efficient financial markets process all available information and make decisions to invest in various financial assets (like stocks and bonds), their actions reflect all that is known about the firm, the economy, and the future. Hence, to determine what a financial asset is worth, we "look to market values." In determining the firm's opportunity cost of capital, we also "look to market values." Today's investors expect future returns at least equal to today's returns and so they expect future investments will provide returns at least that high. Efficient financial markets play an important role in many of the firm's decisions; one of them is determining the firm's opportunity cost of capital.

The returns demanded by the firm's investors, and the possible returns that could be earned on comparable risky investments, can best be determined by examining the firm's existing financial assets. As returns demanded by investors increase or decrease, the costs to the firm must also increase or decrease. In addition, the best estimate of the amount of debt financing relative to the amount of equity financing the firm plans to use in the future is also estimated by looking at today's use of debt and equity.

To use the firmwide opportunity cost of capital for decision-making purposes, two basic conditions must be met. First, the risk of the project under examination must be approximately equal to the risk of all new projects being undertaken by the firm. Although, as we discuss in Chapter 9, the precise estimation of project risk is not easy, our concern is that the risk not be substantially above or below that of the other projects being undertaken. When risk differs significantly, a divisional opportunity cost of capital (as briefly discussed later in the chapter) should be employed. Second, it is important that the firm not materially change its financing policies as a result of the investments it undertakes. Because these proportions directly affect the opportunity cost, the cost of capital will change as changes occur in the financing mix and the firm's **capital structure,** that is, its mix of debt and equity.

CAPITAL STRUCTURE
A firm's mix of debt and equity financing.

At this point, we are assuming that the firm's **target capital structure** (or desired ratio of debt/market value of equity) will be constant. The reason for making this assumption is that different capital structures may influence the firm's cost of capital.[1] Our concern here is with determining the opportunity cost of capital, assuming a firm is at the appropriate target capital structure. In Chapter 12 we examine the impact the firm's capital structure may have on the value of the firm.

TARGET CAPITAL STRUCTURE
The desired ratio of debt to equity employed by a firm.

Before proceeding, it is important to emphasize that *the opportunity cost of capital is a marginal cost.* What is meant by the term "marginal"? We use "marginal" in the economic sense—as the cost of raising the last dollar of funds. For each of the components—debt, preferred stock, and common equity—we are interested in the cost of the last dollar of additional funds. If the cost of the last dollar of additional funds increases, so does the firm's required return. *Calculation of the firm's cost of capital has a future orientation.* The opportunity cost of capital is a weighted average of the after-tax costs of various future sources of capital; *any past or historical costs are irrelevant.* The only reason to consider historical costs when calculating an opportunity cost is to obtain some idea of the future-oriented estimates that must be made. But, in general, it is best to ignore historical costs; considering historical costs or proportions often leads to incorrect conclusions.

The opportunity cost of capital is the minimum that must be earned in order that the value of the firm does not fall.

---

[1] *In addition, we are assuming that risk does not change and that the firm's cash dividend policy is constant. If one of these changes, some of the costs might change, affecting the whole decision-making process.*

CONCEPT REVIEW QUESTIONS

■ What does a firm's opportunity cost of capital measure?
■ What two basic conditions must be met to use the firmwide opportunity cost of capital for decision-making purposes?
■ What is meant by the term "marginal cost of capital" when describing the opportunity cost of capital?

CALCULATING COSTS AND FINANCING PROPORTIONS

First we will consider the explicit costs of three types of financing—debt, preferred stock, and common equity—and then we will look at the specific financing proportions.

Cost of Debt

■ LEARNING GOAL 2

Determine the costs of debt and preferred stock.

The cost of debt to be used for cost of capital purposes is the before-tax cost, k_b, adjusted for the tax "subsidy" provided by the government to profitable firms ("subsidy" because interest is a tax-deductible expense). This provides the after-tax cost of debt, k_i, which is

$$\text{after-tax cost of debt, } k_i = k_b(1 - T) \tag{6.2}$$

where

k_b = the before-tax cost of debt

T = the firm's marginal corporate tax rate

To solve this equation, we need to know the before-tax cost of debt. To calculate the before-tax cost for long-term debt, we must find the expected yield to maturity, *YTM*. Thus, the before-tax cost to the firm, k_b, is found by solving for the unknown discount rate:

$$B_0 = \sum_{t=1}^{n} \frac{I}{(1 + k_b)^t} + \frac{M}{(1 + k_b)^n} \tag{6.3}$$

where

B_0 = the net proceeds from the bond

I = the dollar amount of interest paid on a bond each year

M = the par or maturity value of the bond (typically $1,000)

n = the number of years to maturity for the bond

k_b = the before-tax cost to the firm

This is no different from solving for the yield to maturity as discussed in Chapter 3.[2]

[2] *In reality there are often flotation (or issuance) costs associated with issuing new debt and equity. While flotation costs for small or more risky firms may become important, for larger firms they typically do not materially impact the firm's cost of capital. For simplicity, we ignore the impact of flotation costs when determining a firm's opportunity cost of capital.*

Let's consider an example: Ambassador Corporation plans to issue a new 20-year bond that has a $1,000 par value, carries a 12.75 percent coupon rate, and pays interest annually. The firm expects to receive $980. The before-tax cost to Ambassador is

$$\$980 = \sum_{t=1}^{20} \frac{\$127.50}{(1 + k_b)^t} + \frac{\$1,000}{(1 + k_b)^{20}}$$

so, $k_b = 0.13035 \approx 13\%$.[3]

The before-tax cost is 13 percent. The after-tax cost, calculated using Equation 6.2 and assuming a marginal tax rate of 40 percent, is

$$k_i = k_b(1 - T) = 13\%(1 - 0.40) = 7.8\%$$

The after-tax cost of debt is used because it is, in fact, the cost to the firm. Although the firm pays out a before-tax cost of 13 percent, as long as the firm is profitable, interest is a deductible expense for tax purposes. So, the after-tax cost with a 40 percent effective marginal tax rate is only 7.8 percent.

Remember Key Idea 6— risk and return (or cost to the firm) go hand-in-hand.

Remember that we are interested in the cost of *new debt financing*. The coupon rate on existing debt is not relevant, nor are any costs connected with existing debt. The explicit cost of debt tends to be the *least expensive* of the three sources we consider (debt, preferred stock, and common equity) for two reasons: First, from the investor's standpoint, it is a fixed legal claim; bondholders have greater security than preferred or common stockholders. On a risk-return basis, we would expect bond investors to demand less return than stockholders—which they do. Second, the tax status of interest also makes debt cheaper than other sources, as long as the firm is profitable.[4]

Determining the cost of debt financing for a firm becomes more complicated in practice than in our example, because most firms employ many different kinds of debt. Some of these include short-term debt, zero-coupon bonds, convertible securities, and leases. The cost of some of these alternative sources of debt financing may differ from the cost of debt financing given by Equation 6.3.[5]

Cost of Preferred Stock

The cost of preferred stock is calculated in much the same manner as the cost of debt, except for one basic difference: Because dividends on preferred stock are paid out of after-tax earnings, no tax adjustment is required. Thus, the cost of preferred stock, k_{ps}, is:[6]

$$\text{cost of preferred stock, } k_{ps} = \frac{D_{ps}}{P_0} \tag{6.4}$$

where

D_{ps} = the cash dividends paid on the preferred stock each year

P_0 = the proceeds from the sale of the preferred stock

[3] Using a financial calculator, k_b is 13.035 percent.
[4] Occasionally, a firm may use so much debt that the cost of debt becomes as or more expensive than the cost of equity. Also, if a firm is operating at a loss, its marginal tax rate is zero. For a firm that does not expect to pay taxes for a long time, there is no tax subsidy for using debt, and $k_i = k_b$.
[5] The cost of other types of capital, such as leases and convertible securities, is discussed in Financial Management.
[6] Equation 6.4 assumes the preferred stock is a perpetuity. If it is expected to be called or retired in a specific number of years, the cost of preferred stock should be obtained by solving for k_{ps} using Equation 4.4.

If Ambassador is planning to issue a $50 par preferred stock that pays $6 in dividends per year and the firm expects to realize $48 per share, the after-tax cost of the preferred stock is:

$$k_{ps} = \frac{D_{ps}}{P_0} = \frac{\$6}{\$48} = 0.125 = 12.5\%$$

Compared with the 7.8 percent cost of debt calculated above, the cost of preferred stock is higher. This occurs primarily because the dividends on preferred stock are not tax-deductible.

Cost of Common Equity

■ LEARNING GOAL 3

Determine the cost of common equity under three different approaches.

INTERNALLY GENERATED FUNDS

Cash flows generated by operations, which, after the costs of operation are met, can be paid out to stockholders or reinvested in the business.

The final cost to be considered is that of common equity. Actually, there are two possible costs here—one if the firm uses internally generated funds, and the other if it expects to issue additional shares of common stock. **Internally generated funds** are those cash flows that arise as a function of the firm's ongoing activities and that can be reinvested in the business. Because internally generated funds typically supply most of the common equity, we focus primarily on their cost.

Like the cost of debt and preferred stock, the cost of equity capital is also a function of the returns expected by investors. To estimate the cost of equity, k_s, it is necessary to estimate the returns demanded by investors. As with preferred stock, there is no need to adjust for taxes, because cash dividends on common stock are paid out of after-tax earnings. The difficulty in estimating the cost of equity capital arises because, unlike debt or preferred stock, there is no stated interest or dividend rate. In addition, due to the ability to share in both the good and bad fortunes of the firm, common stock may experience substantial price changes. So, estimating the cost of equity capital is more difficult than estimating the cost of debt or preferred stock. We examine three approaches for estimating the cost of common equity: the dividend valuation approach, the capital asset pricing model, CAPM, and an ad hoc method using bond yield plus a risk premium.

Don't be fooled into thinking that internally generated funds are costless! When a firm reinvests funds in the business, it makes a preemptive investment decision for its stockholders.

The logic behind assigning a cost to internally generated funds involves the opportunity cost concept. Management faces a choice with the funds generated by the firm: It can distribute them to the firm's owners (its common stockholders) in the form of cash dividends, or it can reinvest them in the firm on behalf of the same common stockholders. The decision to reinvest funds instead of paying them out involves an opportunity cost. Stockholders could have taken the funds and reinvested them in something else. Therefore, *the firm must earn a return on the reinvested funds equal to what common stockholders could have earned in alternative investments of comparable risk.* What return is this? It's simply k_s, which is the return investors require on investments with comparable risk. If the firm cannot earn a return of at least k_s on the reinvested internally generated funds, it should distribute the funds to investors so they can invest them in other assets that provide an expected return equal to k_s.

Dividend Valuation Approach

In Chapter 4, we saw that one way to determine the value of a share of stock was the dividend valuation model. This model states that the market value, P_0, is equal to the

Remember Key Ideas 4 and 5—firms (and individuals) focus on cash flows, and a dollar today is worth more than a dollar tomorrow.

present value of the future dividends, $D_1, \ldots, D_\infty$, where the discount rate, k_s, is the investor's required rate of return. Thus,

$$P_0 = \frac{D_1}{(1 + k_s)} + \frac{D_2}{(1 + k_s)^2} + \cdots + \frac{D_\infty}{(1 + k_s)^\infty} \tag{6.5}$$

If the growth rate in dividends, g, is expected to be constant and less than k_s, Equation 6.5 reduces to

$$P_0 = \frac{D_1}{k_s - g} \tag{6.6}$$

where D_1 is the cash dividend expected 1 year from now, k_s is the investor's required rate of return, and g is the constant percentage growth rate in cash dividends. Solving Equation 6.6 for k_s, we have one way of estimating the investor's required rate of return (which is the firm's cost of common equity). Thus,

dividend valuation approach, k_s = expected dividend yield + expected growth

$$= \frac{D_1}{P_0} + g \tag{6.7}$$

DIVIDEND YIELD
Dividend per share divided by market price per share.

Investors expect to receive a **dividend yield,** D_1/P_0, plus growth of g, for a total return of k_s.

To illustrate, assume the present market price on Ambassador's common stock is $25, dividends to be paid in 1 year, D_1, are $1.75, and the expected growth in dividends is 9 percent per year. The dividend valuation approach to estimating the cost of equity capital yields[7]

$$k_s = \frac{D_1}{P_0} + g = \frac{\$1.75}{\$25} + 9\% = 0.07 + 9\% = 7\% + 9\% = 16\%$$

Estimating the expected growth rate in cash dividends is the most difficult aspect of applying the dividend valuation approach. We could start by analyzing past growth rates. That information is generally supplemented, however, by projections made by the firm itself or by security analysts. And, remember, it is the future growth rate that is important.

Capital Asset Pricing Model Approach

The second approach to estimating the cost of common equity employs the capital asset pricing model, CAPM. As described in Chapter 5, the CAPM states that the investors' required rate of return is equal to the risk-free rate plus a risk premium, so that

CAPM approach, k_s = risk-free rate + expected risk premium

$$= k_{RF} + \beta_j(k_M - k_{RF}) \tag{6.8}$$

---

[7] If the expected growth rate in cash dividends is not constant, the nonconstant growth valuation approach discussed in Chapter 4 will have to be employed. Also, be careful if the expected growth rate in cash dividends is "high." In such a case, blind usage of the constant dividend valuation approach often leads to a "high" estimate of the cost of equity capital.

where

k_{RF} = the risk-free rate of return

β_j = the beta of security j

k_M = the expected rate of return on the market portfolio

The risk-free rate is generally measured by the yield on Treasury securities. Betas can be obtained by referring to *Value Line Investment Survey,* Merrill Lynch, or many other investment advisory services. Although the expected rate of return on the market cannot be measured directly, it can be approximated. One approach to estimating the expected return on the market, k_M, involves focusing on three components: (1) expected inflation, (2) expected real growth in the economy, and (3) an expected risk premium commanded by stocks relative to bonds.[8]

To illustrate the CAPM approach, assume Ambassador's beta is 0.95, the yield on Treasury securities is 11 percent, expected growth in the economy (as measured by projected GDP growth in constant dollars) is 2 percent, and the expected risk premium of stocks over bonds is 5 percent. Adding the last three components together provides an estimate of the future returns on the market of 11 + 2 + 5 = 18 percent. The investor's required rate of return, which is the cost of common equity, is

$$k_s = 11\% + 0.95(18\% - 11\%) = 11\% + 6.65\% = 17.65\%$$

This second approach to estimating the cost of common equity provides a figure of 17.65 percent, versus the earlier figure of 16 percent estimated by the dividend valuation approach. The dividend valuation and CAPM approaches should provide approximately the same answer, unless some drastic differences in assumptions are made. Our difference is not too large and should give us some confidence in the reliability of the estimates.

Bond Yield Plus Expected Risk Premium Approach

The third approach to estimating the cost of common equity is an ad hoc method that states the investor's required rate of return is equal to what he or she could get on the bonds of the firm, plus a premium for risk, so that

$$\text{bond yield} + \begin{matrix}\text{expected}\\ \text{risk premium}\\ \text{approach, } k_s\end{matrix} = \begin{matrix}\text{bond}\\ \text{yield}\end{matrix} + \begin{matrix}\text{expected risk premium}\\ \text{of common stock}\\ \text{over corporate bonds}\end{matrix} \qquad (6.9)$$

This method is especially useful when the firm does not pay any cash dividends (in which case the dividend valuation approach is not applicable) or when the common stock is not traded (so that neither the dividend valuation nor CAPM approaches can be employed). To continue our earlier example, the before-tax bond yield of Ambassador was 13 percent, and the risk premium of stocks over corporate bonds was expected to be 5 percent.[9] The required rate of return is then

$$k_s = \text{bond yield} + \text{expected risk premium} = 13\% + 5\% = 18\%$$

Again, the estimate is close to those obtained from the other approaches.

[8] *Another way would be to add the expected market-risk premium (k_M - k_{RF}) to the risk-free rate. Research indicates that risk premiums are not constant over time. See "Estimating the Expected Return on the Market Portfolio and Risk Premiums Using Historical Data" later in this chapter.*

[9] *This risk premium is firm-specific and may be more or less than the market-risk premium employed in estimating k_M. For simplicity, we assume the two risk premiums are equal.*

Putting It All Together

For Ambassador, we have three estimates of its cost of common equity:

Approach	Estimated k_s
Dividend valuation	16%
CAPM	17.65
Bond yield plus expected risk premium	18

All differ slightly, but they are close. Taking everything into account, we would estimate Ambassador's cost of common equity is between 16 and 18 percent. A simple average of these estimates is 17.22 percent [i.e., (16% + 17.65% + 18%)/3]. We will round this to 17.25 percent for use below when calculating Ambassador's opportunity cost of capital.

Although the use of three different approaches may seem unduly complicated, it is very useful in practice. By using several alternative approaches to estimating the cost of common equity, managers are forced to consider which estimates are most useful. Estimating the cost of equity capital requires both judgment and an understanding of what the firm's common stockholders expect.

Notice that the cost of common equity is higher than the cost of debt or preferred stock. This occurs because, from the investor's standpoint, there is more risk with common stock than with debt or preferred stock. Investors therefore have a higher required rate of return for common stock. But because the investor's required rate of return is the firm's cost, we see that the cost of common equity is the *most expensive* form of financing to the firm. Even though it is the most expensive source of financing, firms routinely use extensive common equity financing (generally through the reinvestment of funds in the firm instead of paying them out to shareholders in the form of cash dividends). They do so to retain ownership of the firm (especially for smaller firms) and to balance the benefits of debt financing versus the increased risks that go along with it (as we will discuss in Chapter 12).

The Financing Proportions

FINANCIAL LEVERAGE
The use of securities bearing a fixed charge (such as bonds or preferred stock) to finance a portion of the firm's capital needs.

Now that we know how to calculate the specific after-tax costs of debt, preferred stock, and common equity, we are almost ready to calculate the firm's after-tax opportunity cost of capital. Before doing that, however, we need to determine the financing proportions, or amount of **financial leverage,** to be employed by the firm. These proportions are a function of the firm's target capital structure (its desired mix of debt to total market value). The target capital structure should be the long-run desired mix of financing the firm intends to employ for meeting all of its financing needs, *measured in market value terms*. To calculate the financing mix, we again employ current market value information, assuming that financial markets are efficient and incorporate all that is known about the firm.

Thus, if the firm intends to finance with 50 percent debt and 50 percent equity, the target capital structure should reflect that mix. Although many things influence a firm's target capital structure, it can be approximated by determining the current market value of the firm's outstanding securities. *These current market values provide the best estimate of the firm's future financing mix.*[10] However, temporary deviations from the target capital structure should be taken into account if the firm knows its current

---

[10]*An alternative would be to employ a cash budget that provides an estimate of the expected sources of funds over the next 3 to 5 years.*

Remember Key Idea 1—the goal of the firm is to maximize its market value. Therefore, it is the market value proportions of the expected financing that are important, not the book value proportions.

market-value-based capital structure does not provide a valid indication of the future target capital structure. Proper estimation of the future financing proportions is essential when estimating the firm's opportunity cost of capital.

CONCEPT REVIEW QUESTIONS

- What are the three primary component costs used when estimating the opportunity cost of capital?
- Is a tax adjustment required when estimating the cost of either preferred or common stock? Why?
- Describe three methods used to estimate the cost of common equity.

CALCULATING THE OPPORTUNITY COST OF CAPITAL

■ LEARNING GOAL 4

Determine the opportunity cost of capital, and discuss when firms should make this calculation.

Once we have the specific market costs and proportions, calculating the firm's opportunity cost of capital is straightforward. Let's return to the Ambassador example, and then we'll briefly discuss what happens if Ambassador decides to increase its capital substantially. Finally, before proceeding to an extended real-world example, we'll consider the question of how often a firm should calculate its cost of capital.

The Opportunity Cost for Ambassador

Earlier we calculated the specific costs of debt, preferred stock, and common equity for Ambassador Corporation. In addition to these after-tax costs, let's assume the market value proportions of financing to be employed are 30 percent debt, 10 percent preferred stock, and 60 percent common equity. Given these market value costs and proportions, Ambassador's opportunity cost of capital is 13.94 percent, as shown below:

Component	After-Tax Cost	×	Market Value Weight	=	Opportunity Cost of Capital
Debt	7.8%		0.30		2.34%
Preferred stock	12.5		0.10		1.25
Common equity	17.25		0.60		10.35
				Opportunity cost of capital =	13.94%

By using about 14 percent as the minimum discount rate for net present value calculations, Ambassador can make investment decisions for projects of average risk that assist in maximizing the long-run market value of the firm.[11]

What If the Amount of Required Financing Increases?

So far we have considered a firm raising a specific dollar amount of financing at a specific period in time. However, what if *additional* investment opportunities come along that require financing? Not only are there new investment opportunities, but *the total amount of capital to be raised increases*. In such a case, the risks involved—and therefore the costs of financing—may increase substantially. If that

---

[11] *We are assuming Ambassador is at its target (or optimal) capital structure.*

happens, the firm's opportunity cost of capital should be recalculated, and the new higher discount rate should be used in making all investment decisions faced by the firm.

How Often Should the Cost of Capital Be Calculated?

How often does the firm's cost of capital need to be recalculated? There is no hard-and-fast rule—we know firms that do it yearly and others that estimated their opportunity cost 5 years ago and have not really looked at it since. The best guide is to re-examine it periodically, especially when the financing proportions have changed (or are expected to change); when economic conditions, such as interest rates, have changed substantially; or when very large projects are under consideration. In these rapidly changing economic times, firms would be wise to review their cost of capital at least every year. Given the rapid rise in actual and expected inflation in the late 1970s and early 1980s, firms that did not reestimate their cost of capital ended up underestimating their real cost of funds. Likewise, when inflation decreased, as it did in the early 1990s, a downward revision was necessary.

CONCEPT REVIEW QUESTIONS

■ What goes into computing a firm's opportunity cost of capital?
■ Comment on why a firm should recalculate its opportunity cost of capital when considering a number of new investment opportunities requiring substantial amounts of financing.

CALCULATING PEPSICO'S OPPORTUNITY COST OF CAPITAL

In practice, calculating a firm's opportunity cost of capital follows the same process we have described. We will use PepsiCo, Inc.; *our calculations are made as of December 1994.* This is an example of how to make the calculations, but obviously they would have to be reestimated to calculate today's opportunity cost of capital, or required return, for PepsiCo.

Market Value Proportions

The book value balance sheet for PepsiCo as of December 31, 1994, in millions, was as follows:

Assets		Liabilities and Stockholders' Equity	
Current	$ 5,072	Payables, accruals, and other	$ 4,591
Long-term	19,720	Deferred taxes	1,973
Total	$24,792	Interest-bearing debt and lease	
		obligations	11,371
		Stockholders' equity	6,857
		Total	$24,792

Note that we have grouped the liabilities in a somewhat different manner than is used by accountants. All accounts payable, accruals (for taxes, cash dividends, and so forth), and other are lumped together. *These are typically ignored for cost of capital purposes.* The reason is that for capital budgeting purposes, we will net out increases in current liabilities against increases in the current assets and will deal only with incremental net working capital needs. Because of this netting-out process (and assuming the firm pays these on time so their direct cost is zero), accounts payable and accruals are typically ignored. Deferred taxes are also excluded, because this is an accounting phenomenon that arises from using different depreciation methods for tax and accounting purposes. However, *short-term debt is typically included* when firms calculate their cost of capital. We will also follow this procedure. Also, lease obligations are included, because they represent a form of long-term financing.

PepsiCo's interest-bearing debt and lease obligations are listed in Table 6.1. Its commercial paper and other short-term notes payable are not listed on any exchange, but we'll assume their current market value is approximately equal to their book value of $679 million. Then the notes and bonds are listed along with their market prices. Market prices were not available for a number of PepsiCo's long-term debt securities, so we used book values. Looking again at Table 6.1, we see that although the par value of PepsiCo's debt is $11,371 million, its estimated market value as of December 1994 was $11,304 million.[12]

Looking farther down Table 6.1, we see that the book value (the sum of the common stock, additional paid-in capital, retained earnings, and any other common equity accounts on the balance sheet) of PepsiCo's common equity is $6,857 million, whereas the market value of the firm's common stock is $28,960 million. (As is typical of most firms, the book value and market value for PepsiCo's common equity are not very similar.) Using these market value proportions, we estimate that PepsiCo will raise approximately 28.1 percent of its new financing with debt; the other 71.9 percent will be raised through common equity financing. This common equity financing for most firms is largely funded through the retention of cash in the firm, instead of paying it out to the shareholders in the form of cash dividends.

These are the proportions to use in calculating PepsiCo's opportunity cost of capital. Obviously, PepsiCo plans to rely on its internal cash-generation capability to finance about three-quarters of its financing needs.

Cost of Debt

The before-tax cost of debt for PepsiCo is the amount the firm has to pay to raise additional debt. PepsiCo had a number of intermediate term notes outstanding, and all had an A rating according to Moody's Investment Service. We can assume that any new long-term debt will have a 10-year or longer maturity.

What rate of return would the market require on a new issue with this risk? One approach is to calculate the yield to maturity on PepsiCo's existing long-term debt. However, a more straightforward approach is to determine what the market rate of return (or interest) was on comparable debt in December 1994. At that point in time, the yield to maturity on bonds rated A was about 8.8 percent. In our judgment, if PepsiCo had decided to issue new intermediate- to long-term debt in December 1994, the firm would have had to pay approximately 8.8 percent. This is their before-tax cost, k_b. We estimate that PepsiCo's effective marginal tax rate is 34 percent.[13] Therefore, our estimate of the after-tax cost of debt is

$$k_i = k_b(1 - T) = 8.80\%(1 - 0.34) = 5.81\%$$

[12] *As is fairly typical, the book value and market value of debt are close. This is especially true when current market interest rates are close to the coupon interest rates on the firm's debt.*

[13] *Be careful in estimating a firm's effective marginal tax rate. From its income statement, PepsiCo's tax rate is about 34.5 percent for 1993 and 33.4 percent for 1994. For some firms the actual taxes paid (per the statement of case flows) may indicate a far different effective tax rate. This is not the case for PepsiCo, so we averaged the two rates and employ an effective tax rate of 34 percent.*

TABLE 6.1

Calculation of Market Value Weights for PepsiCo, as of December 31, 1994

Where market prices are not available, judgment has to be employed to determine the estimated market value. For both short-term and other debt and lease obligations, the par (or book) value was employed.

Interest-Bearing Debt and Lease Obligations	Par (or Book) Value (in millions)	Market Price	Market Value (in millions)
Short-term debt	$679	—	679†
5 7/8% notes of '95	200	99 1/2	199
5.45% notes of '95	250	—	250†
7 7/8% notes of '96	250	99 3/4	249
7% notes of '96	200	98 1/4	197
6 7/8% notes of '97	250	97 1/4	243
5% notes of '97	250	93 7/8	235
6 7/8% notes of '98	300	94 3/4	284
7 3/4% notes of '98	250	98 5/8	247
7 5/8% notes of '98	300	98 1/4	295
7 5/8% notes of '98	164	99 1/4	163
6 1/4% notes of '99	200	92 1/2	185
Zero-coupon notes of 2012	859	—	859†
Swiss franc perpetual foreign interest payment bonds	400	—	400†
Eurobonds	354	—	354†
Other long-term debt and lease obligations	6,465	—	6,465†
Total debt	$11,371		$11,304
Common equity	$6,857	36 1/4	$28,960††

Market Value	Dollars	Proportions
Short-term debt	$ 679	0.017
Long-term debt and lease obligations	10,625	0.264
Common equity	28,960	0.719
Total	$40,264	1.000

* Bond price as a percent of par.
† Book value employed because market information was not available.
†† 798,900,000 shares($36 1/4) = $28,960,120,000.

PepsiCo also had short-term debt and lease obligations in its capital structure. What should we do about them? The term structure of interest rates was upward-sloping in December 1994, so short-term debt was cheaper than intermediate- or long-term debt. We will use 6.70 percent for the approximate before-tax cost of short-term debt, or 4.42 percent on an after-tax basis. Finally, the cost of both debt and lease financing should be the same for the firm. We will use 8.80 percent for the before-tax cost of leasing for PepsiCo.

TABLE 6.2

Growth Rates of Earnings per Share and Dividends per Share for PepsiCo

The historical growth rates are useful only as guides for the future. In this case there are some differences between historical and expected growth rates for both earnings and cash dividends.

Year	Dividends per Share	Earnings per Share
1984	$0.19	$0.24
1985	0.20	0.50
1986	0.21	0.58
1987	0.22	0.77
1988	0.27	0.97
1989	0.32	1.13
1990	0.38	1.37
1991	0.46	1.35
1992	0.51	1.61
1993	0.61	1.96
1994	0.68	2.22

10-year growth rate $\$0.19(1 + g)^{10} = \$0.68$ $\quad\quad$ $\$0.24(1 + g)^{10} = \$2.22$
$$g \approx 14\% \quad\quad\quad\quad\quad\quad g \approx 25\%$$

5-year growth rate $\quad\$0.32(1 + g)^5 = \$0.68$ $\quad\quad$ $\$1.13(1 + g)^5 = \$2.22$
$$g \approx 16\% \quad\quad\quad\quad\quad\quad g \approx 14\%$$

Projected by *Value Line* for
1997–1999 $\quad\quad\quad\quad\quad\quad$ 14.5% $\quad\quad\quad\quad\quad\quad\quad\quad$ 14.5%

Cost of Common Equity

In recent years PepsiCo has financed almost all its common equity needs through internally generated funds, so our approach is to ignore any possible sale of common stock. The first step is to estimate the growth rate in future dividends, as required by the dividend valuation approach. As Table 6.2 shows, the 10-year and 5-year historical growth rates in dividends per share are 14 and 16 percent, respectively. In 1994, as indicated in Table 6.3, *Value Line* was projecting a 14.5 percent expected growth rate in dividends over the next 2 to 4 years. Note also that the historical and projected growth rates in earnings are 25 to 14 percent and 14.5 percent, respectively. We raised the *Value Line* estimates slightly to a 15 percent compound growth rate as of December 1994.

All three approaches discussed earlier were employed to estimate the cost of equity capital for PepsiCo. First, using the dividend valuation approach (shown in Table 6.4), the cost of equity capital is estimated to be 17.15 percent. Then, employing PepsiCo's beta of 1.10 (from *Value Line* in Table 6.3), a risk-free rate of 7.50 percent,[14] and an expected return on the market portfolio of 13.50 percent, the CAPM approach produces an estimated cost of common equity of 14.10 percent. Finally, the bond yield plus expected risk premium approach produces an estimated

[14]As noted in Table 6.3, the term structure of interest rates was upward-sloping as of December 1994. The yield to maturity on short-term Treasury bills was about 4.70 percent, the yield on intermediate Treasury securities was 7.70 percent, and the yield on longer-term Treasury securities was about 8.00 percent. In such a situation we recommend employing the intermediate- or long-term bond rate, or some average of them. We employed 7.50 percent.

TABLE 6.3

Information on PepsiCo as of November 1994

While *Value Line Investment Survey* can provide some of the information, other sources are required for data not included in *Value Line*. Also, note that the proportion of debt and equity given under the "Capital Structure" information is based on book values, not market values. Hence, the 50 percent debt and 50 percent equity is the capital structure as recorded from the firm's accounting-recorded balance sheet.

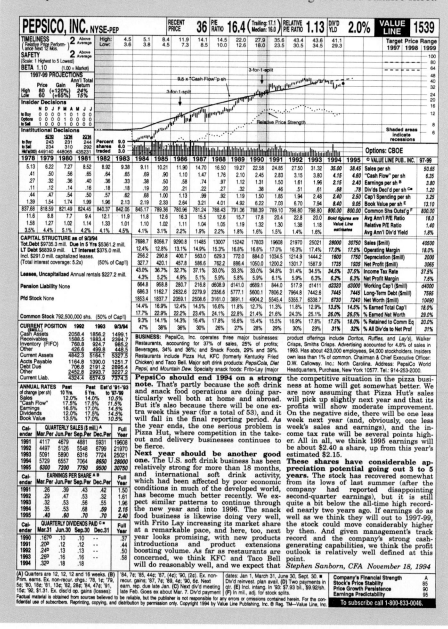

TABLE 6.4

Calculation of PepsiCo's Cost of Equity Capital as of December 1994

These three estimates provide some measures of the "reasonableness" of the final k_s figure.

Assumptions

Current market price, $P_0 = \$36\frac{1}{4}$
Expected growth rate in dividends, $g = 15\%$
Next year's cash dividends, $D_1 = \$0.68(1.15) = \$0.78$
Risk-free rate,* $k_{RF} = 7.50\%$
Market risk for PepsiCo, $\beta_j = 1.10$
Expected return on market portfolio, k_M = expected inflation + expected
   real growth in economy + expected risk premium = $7.50\% + 3\% + 3\%$
   $= 13.50\%$
Expected bond yield = 8.80%
Expected long-term risk premium of stocks over bonds = 3%

Dividend Valuation Approach

$$k_s = \frac{D_1}{P_0} + g = \frac{\$0.78}{\$36.25} + 15\% = 0.0215\% + 15\% = 17.15\%$$

CAPM Approach

$$k_s = k_{RF} + \beta_j(k_M - k_{RF}) = 7.50\% + 1.10(13.50\% - 7.50\%)$$
$$= 7.50\% + 6.60\% = 14.10\%$$

Bond Yield Plus Expected Risk Premium

$$k_s = \text{bond yield plus expected risk premium} = 8.80\% + 3\% = 11.80\%$$

---

*As of December 1994 the term structure of interest rates was fairly steeply upward-sloping. The yield on Treasury bills was about 4.70 percent, the yield on intermediate-term Treasury securities was about 7.70 percent, and the yield on longer-term Treasury securities was about 8.00 percent. When the yield curve is upward-sloping, as it was then, we recommend employing the intermediate- or long-term Treasury security rate (or some average of these rates) for the risk-free rate when estimating the opportunity cost of capital.

cost of 11.80 percent. The three approaches produce somewhat different estimates of PepsiCo's cost of equity capital. For simplicity, we averaged the three estimates to provide an estimate of PepsiCo's cost of equity capital of 14.35 percent [i.e., $(17.15\% + 14.10\% + 11.80\%) / 3$].[15]

PepsiCo's Opportunity Cost of Capital

Now that we have estimates of PepsiCo's after-tax cost of short-term debt of 4.42 percent, long-term debt of 5.81 percent, and an estimated cost of equity of 14.35 percent,

[15]*With the three approaches producing different estimates of the cost of equity capital, we could have tried to reconcile the differences in the estimates. To do so, we would have gone back and investigated the assumptions going into the various calculations.*

we can calculate the opportunity cost of capital as of December 1994. As shown below, we estimate that PepsiCo's opportunity cost of capital is 11.93 percent.

Component	After-Tax Cost	× Market Value Weight	= Opportunity Cost of Capital
Short-term debt	4.42%	0.017	0.08%
Long-term debt	5.81	0.264	1.53
Common equity	14.35	0.719	10.32
		Opportunity cost of capital =	11.93%

Given all the estimates that go into calculating an opportunity cost of capital, we would round this up to 12.50 percent. This is the minimum discount rate PepsiCo should use as of December 1994 for projects of average risk; accepting projects with less than a 12.50 percent expected return is not consistent with the goal of maximizing the long-run market value of the firm.[16]

This opportunity cost of capital can be used for making capital budgeting decisions (for projects of average risk) *as long as PepsiCo does not attempt to increase its level of financing substantially*. If it seeks to secure a large increase in financing, then the cost of some or all of its capital sources would increase. Consequently, PepsiCo's opportunity cost of capital would also increase. Also, PepsiCo has three primary divisions: soft drinks (featuring Pepsi, Mountain Dew, 7-Up, etc.), snack foods (Doritos, Lays, Ruffles, Tostitos, etc.), and restaurants (Pizza Hut, Taco Bell, and KFC). Due to differences in risk between divisions, it may not be reasonable to use 12.50 percent as the opportunity cost of capital for each of the three divisions. As we'll see later, individual divisional opportunity costs can be calculated.

Estimating a firm's opportunity cost of capital is part science and part art. The important things are to make sure (1) it is forward-looking and (2) that you are asking the right questions. If in doubt, change some of your assumptions and check the effect on the opportunity cost of capital.

Estimating the Expected Return on the Market Portfolio and Risk Premiums Using Historical Data

In order to estimate a firm's opportunity cost of equity capital, certain assumptions have to be made. These assumptions depend on the approach that is employed. If the capital asset pricing model is used, assumptions must be made about the expected return on the market portfolio, k_M. If the ad hoc bond yield plus expected risk premium approach is employed, assumptions must be made about the expected risk premium commanded by stocks over corporate bonds. For PepsiCo, we employed 13.50 percent as the expected return on the market portfolio, k_M, and 3 percent for the risk premium commanded by common stocks over corporate bonds. As discussed in Chapter 5, care must be taken in estimating these amounts, especially if historical data is employed. The annual compound rates of return on common stocks, corporate bonds, long-term U.S. government bonds, and U.S. Treasury bills for various periods are as follows:[17]

	1960–1994	1970–1994	1980–1994
Common stocks	11.1%	12.1%	15.2%
Corporate bonds	7.6	9.9	12.1
Long-term government bonds	7.2	9.4	11.9
Treasury bills	6.1	7.0	7.5

[16] *In their annual report PepsiCo indicated their cost of capital was about 10 percent. Our calculations indicate Pepsico's opportunity cost of capital appears to be higher than 10 percent. Based on our calculations, accepting projects that return only 10 percent will, in fact, lead to a decrease in the value of PepsiCo.*

[17] *Adapted from* Stocks, Bonds, Bills, and Inflation 1995 Yearbook™, *Ibbotson Associates, Chicago.*

In looking at all of these figures, remember that interest rates were very high in the early 1980s and have fallen a good deal since then. Consequently, the rates on government bonds, long-term corporate bonds and Treasury bills are higher for these more recent time periods (relative to stock returns) than longer term data would indicate.

Let's see what happens if we use this historical data to estimate the expected return on the market portfolio, k_M, for use with PepsiCo as of December 1994. One way to estimate k_M would be to take the historical return on common stocks as our expected return on the market portfolio. If we use the 1960–1994 data, the expected return on the market is 11.1 percent; however, if we decide to use the more recent 1980–1994 period, the expected return on the market is 15.2 percent. It's easy to see that the choice of the specific prior time period can have varying effects on the expected return on the market portfolio.

To alleviate some of this problem, we could estimate the expected return on the market portfolio to be:

$$\text{expected return on } k_M = \text{risk-free rate} + \text{expected risk premium}$$

As of December 1994, the yield to maturity on Treasury bills was about 4.7 percent, and the yield to maturity on long-term government bonds was about 8.0 percent. First, we might estimate the return on the market portfolio using the Treasury bill rate. The historical difference in the return on common stocks and Treasury bills for the three time periods is:

1960–1994	$11.1\% - 6.1\% = 5.0\%$
1970–1994	$12.1\% - 7.0\% = 5.1\%$
1980–1994	$15.2\% - 7.5\% = 7.7\%$

Therefore, the expected return on the market portfolio, k_M, using the 4.7 percent return on Treasury bills and the historical risk premiums, could be anything from 9.7 to 12.4 percent as follows:

$4.7\% + 5.0\% = 9.7\%$ (using 1960–1994 data)
$4.7\% + 5.1\% = 9.8\%$ (using 1970–1994 data)
$4.7\% + 7.7\% = 12.4\%$ (using 1980–1994 data)

An alternative approach is to employ a longer-term government bond rate as the risk-free rate. (This is more in line with what we did by using 7.5 percent as the expected risk-free rate when estimating the expected return on the market portfolio for PepsiCo. We chose this rate due to the upward-sloping term structure of interest rates at that point in time.) If the long-term bond rate of 8.0 percent is employed, along with the historical risk premium of stocks over long-term government bonds, then the expected return on the market portfolio would be anything from 11.9 to 10.7 percent:

$8.0\% + (11.1\% - 7.2\%) = 11.9\%$ (using 1960–1994 data)
$8.0\% + (12.1\% - 9.4\%) = 10.7\%$ (using 1970–1994 data)
$8.0\% + (15.2\% - 11.9\%) = 11.3\%$ (using 1980–1994 data)

As can be seen, these estimates of the expected returns on the market portfolio differ somewhat from the earlier ones. The moral of this discussion is straightforward: Although it may be tempting to use historical data, estimation of the expected return on the market portfolio requires judgment based on an understanding of what has gone on in the past, current economic conditions, and expected economic and financial market conditions.

There is one other topic that we need to mention: the ad hoc bond yield plus risk premium of stocks over corporate bonds approach. What is the appropriate expected risk premium to employ is this case? Using historical data, the risk premium of common stocks over corporate bonds could be anything from 3.5 to 2.2 percent:

1960–1994	11.1% − 7.6% = 3.5%
1970–1994	12.1% − 9.9% = 2.2%
1975–1994	15.2% − 12.1% = 3.1%

Again, we see the differences in historical risk premiums, this time between the returns on common stocks and those on corporate bonds. *When estimating the opportunity cost of capital, don't be lulled into an easy (and often incorrect) decision by using historical information on returns without questioning the wisdom of that approach.*

CONCEPT REVIEW QUESTIONS

- When estimating PepsiCo's opportunity cost of capital, accounts payable, accruals, and deferred taxes were excluded. Why?
- Describe the steps used to estimate PepsiCo's opportunity cost of capital.
- Describe some of the complications that may arise when using historical data to estimate the cost of capital.

OTHER ISSUES WHEN CALCULATING A FIRM'S OPPORTUNITY COST OF CAPITAL

Up to now we have determined how to calculate the *firm's* opportunity cost of capital, which can be employed if new projects have a risk approximately equal to the firm's overall risk. However, each project must stand on its own legs if the firm is going to maximize its value. Firms must expect to receive a return sufficient to compensate them for the risk involved—that is, what they could get by investing in an equally risky project outside the firm. The realities of the business world are that different projects will offer different levels of risk and return. To deal with differences in risk, many medium- and large-size firms employ an approach that calculates the divisional cost of capital. In addition, there are other complications when firms operate internationally that have to be taken into consideration.

Divisional Opportunity Costs of Capital

■ LEARNING GOAL 5

Explain the rationale for a divisional opportunity cost of capital and how it is determined.

Remember Key Idea 6—risk and return go hand-in-hand. Therefore, changes in risk will lead to changes in a firm's cost of capital.

The essence of using divisional costs of capital is shown in Figure 6.1, where different discount rates are employed depending on the riskiness of the division. If a firm employs a *firmwide* opportunity cost of capital when differences in risk exist, it makes the mistake of setting too high a required return for low-risk projects and too low a return for high-risk projects. The result is to underallocate capital to low-risk divisions and to overallocate funds to high-risk divisions.

FIGURE 6.1

Relating Risk to Divisional Opportunity Costs of Capital for Capital Budgeting Purposes

Use of a firmwide opportunity cost of capital when risk differs results in underallocation of resources to low-risk divisions and overallocation to high-risk divisions.

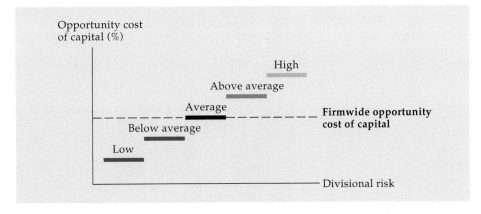

In practice, the most widely used method to implement risk adjustment is based on the assumption that project risks within divisions are somewhat similar, but that risk between divisions differs. To estimate **divisional opportunity costs of capital,** we proceed as follows:

DIVISIONAL OPPORTUNITY COSTS OF CAPITAL
The required return for a specific business unit, used when risk for that unit differs from firmwide risk.

STEP 1: Determine the firm's after-tax cost of debt, k_i, and use this as the cost of debt for each division. (Slightly more precision can be obtained by using separate after-tax costs for each division, but our approach is simpler and generally provides approximately the same answer.)

STEP 2: Because we don't have any market-based estimate of the risk of the division and its cost of equity capital, identify one or more firms to use for comparison. Called **pure-play firms,** these should be publicly traded firms that are engaged solely in the same line of business and that have the same operating risks as the division.

PURE-PLAY FIRMS
Firm in the same line of business and with the same operating risk as a division of a firm.

STEP 3: Employing the beta of the pure-play firm, calculate each division's cost of equity capital as if each were a separate firm.[18] Thus, each division's estimated cost of common equity is:

$$\text{divisional cost of equity} = k_{RF} + \beta_{\text{division}}(k_M - k_{RF}) \qquad (6.10)$$

STEP 4: Estimate the division's target or appropriate capital structure as if it were a freestanding firm. Due to differences in the basic risk and business conditions between divisions, some may be able to employ substantially more debt than others.

STEP 5: Calculate the division's opportunity cost of capital using the costs and financing proportions estimated in Steps 1, 3, and 4 above.

To illustrate the calculation of divisional opportunity costs of capital, consider the example of Wagner Industries. As shown in Table 6.5, with a beta of 1.25, k_{RF} of 10 percent, $k_M = 18$ percent, $k_i = 8$ percent, and using 40 percent debt and 60 percent common equity, we would estimate Wagner's firmwide opportunity cost of capital to be 15.20 percent. This would be the appropriate rate for capital budgeting purposes if all of Wagner's divisions were equally risky.

---

[18]*In practice some adjustments may have to be made before employing the beta of the pure-play firms; this issue is discussed in* Financial Management.

> ### TABLE 6.5
>
> **Calculation of Opportunity Cost of Capital for Wagner Industries**
>
> This firmwide opportunity cost is appropriate for divisions or projects whose risk is approximately equal to the average risk of new projects undertaken by the firm.
>
> ---
> Assumptions
> ---
>
> After-tax cost of debt, $k_i = 8\%$
> Market risk, $\beta_j = 1.25$
> Risk-free rate, $k_{RF} = 10\%$
> Expected return on the market portfolio, $k_M = 18\%$
>
> ---
> Cost of Common Equity
> ---
>
> $$k_s = k_{RF} + \beta_j(k_M - k_{RF})$$
> $$= 10\% + 1.25(18\% - 10\%) = 10\% + 10\% = 20\%$$
>
> ---
> Opportunity Cost of Capital
> ---
>
> | Component | After-Tax Cost | $\times$ Market Value Weight $=$ | Opportunity Cost of Capital |
> |---|---|---|---|
> | Debt | 8% | 0.40 | 3.20% |
> | Common equity | 20 | 0.60 | 12.00 |
> | | | Opportunity cost of capital $=$ | 15.20% |

But what if Wagner has three very different divisions? The furniture division is in a very mature industry with low risk; the paper division has a risk that is close to the average risk of the firm; the data services division is very risky. Due to the differences in risk, the divisions have different betas, which range from 0.75 for furniture, to 1.25 for paper, to 2.0 for data services (as determined by examining publicly traded pure-play firms with similar product lines). The financing proportions also differ, with the more risky divisions being less able to employ as much debt financing. As shown in Table 6.6, these differences produce very different divisional opportunity costs of capital. The furniture division's opportunity cost is 12 percent, and 15.20 percent is appropriate for the paper division. The data services division's opportunity cost of capital is 22.40 percent, indicating that projects originating from that division must have a substantially higher expected return to compensate for the increased risk.

Estimating divisional opportunity costs of capital in practice requires a thorough understanding of the firm's divisions and identification of appropriate publicly traded firms that are similar to the divisions. The most difficult part of the process is finding "good" pure-play firms.

The Opportunity Cost of Capital for Multinationals

■ **LEARNING GOAL 6**

Discuss the issues involved in determining the opportunity cost of capital for a multinational firm.

When discussing capital budgeting decisions for domestic firms we indicated that the project should stand alone in terms of cash flows and that the opportunity cost of capital

TABLE 6.6

Calculation of Divisional Opportunity Costs of Capital for Wagner Industries

Using divisional opportunity costs improves resource allocation decisions if risk differs substantially between a firm's divisions.

Furniture Division

$$\beta_{furniture} = 0.75$$
$$k_{furniture} = k_{RF} + \beta_{furniture}(k_M - k_{RF})$$
$$= 10\% + 0.75(18\% - 10\%) = 10\% + 6\% = 16\%$$

Divisional Opportunity Cost of Capital

Component	After-Tax Cost	× Division's Financing Proportions	= Opportunity Cost of Capital
Debt	8%	0.50	4.00%
Common equity	16	0.50	8.00
Furniture Division's opportunity cost of capital =			12.00%

Paper Division

$$\beta_{paper} = 1.25$$
$$k_{paper} = 10\% + 1.25(18\% - 10\%) = 10\% + 10\% = 20\%$$

Debt	8%	0.40	3.20%
Common equity	20	0.60	12.00
Paper Division's opportunity cost of capital =			15.20%

Data Services Division

$$\beta_{data\ services} = 2.00$$
$$k_{data\ services} = 10\% + 2.00(18\% - 10\%) = 10\% + 16\% = 26\%$$

Debt	8%	0.20	1.60%
Common equity	26	0.80	20.80
Data Services Division's opportunity cost of capital =			22.40%

used to apply to those cash flows should signify the amount of risk related to the cash flows. An important question for multinational firms is whether the opportunity cost of capital for foreign projects should be different from that for similar-risk domestic projects. The answer to that question depends on two items: First, what is the systematic risk for multinational firms? Second, what are the expropriation and creditor risks?

Systematic Risk and Portfolio Concerns

Based on the capital asset pricing model, we know it is the nondiversifiable risk (measured by beta, β_j) that is important in determining the opportunity cost of equity capital. By operating in a number of countries, multinational firms expose themselves to economic cycles that are not perfectly in phase with one another. That is, while the world economy generally moves somewhat together, there are often important differences in demand among countries. For example, demand in the United States will differ from demand in either Japan or Egypt. By having a significant portion of their operations and cash flows diversified over a number of countries, multinational firms

FINANCIAL MANAGEMENT TODAY

Was the Cost of Capital Lower in Japan?

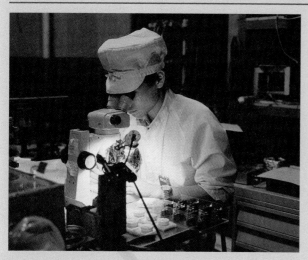

During much of the 1970s and 1980s Japanese firms became world leaders in industries such as automobiles and electronics. One point often raised, in addition to productivity differences and the Japanese emphasis on quality, is that the cost of capital was cheaper in Japan than in the United States and other developed countries. A lower cost of capital would provide more positive net present value projects. Equally important, it would allow and encourage Japanese firms to invest in projects that had much longer lives while still providing positive returns to the firm.

The opportunity cost of capital (ignoring preferred stock) is

$$\text{opportunity cost of capital} = k_b(1 - T)W_{\text{debt}} + k_s W_{\text{common equity}}$$

where

k_b = the before-tax cost of debt
T = the marginal tax rate
k_s = the cost of equity
$W\text{'s}$ = the financing proportions

For the cost of capital to be lower in Japan than in the United States, one of four explanations, or some combination of the four, had to apply: (1) the before-tax cost of debt was lower, (2) the cost of equity was lower, (3) the Japanese used more debt, or (4) the marginal tax rate was higher in Japan (thereby driving down the after-tax cost of debt).

Many studies have examined this question. Although some disagreements exist, the primary findings suggest that (1) the before-tax cost of debt was lower in Japan; (2) the cost of equity, particularly in the mid- and late-1980s, was lower in Japan; (3) the use of debt financing may have been more pervasive in Japan; and (4) the tax rate was not significantly higher in Japan.

One of the most interesting aspects of this question relates to the different structural arrangement of firms in Japan, where firms are often members of an industrial grouping known as *keiretsu*. There are indications that both the cost of financing and the risk of bankruptcy may have been less for firms that were members of a *keiretsu* than for those that were not. Most of the borrowing during this period of time was done from the firms' main banks (during the 1970s and 1980s corporate bond markets were very small in Japan), and all loans were backed by collateral. Studies suggest that banks and other members of the *keiretsu* went out of their way to buffer firms from financial distress and/or bankruptcy. Accordingly, Japanese firms may have been able to use more debt than firms in the United States and other developed countries.

In the 1990s any advantage Japanese firms might have received due to a lower cost of capital appears to have disappeared. This is due to an increase in the cost of debt, the over 50 percent decline in Japanese stock prices, and a move to more of a market-based financing system, in which the former benefits of the *keiretsu* are less important. Thus, while differences in the cost of capital may have existed in the past, that does not appear to be the case in the 1990s.

may lessen the variability of their cash flows. This is true whether the nations they have diversified into are industrialized (such as the European Common Market and Japan), newly industrializing (such as Korea or Taiwan), or less developed (such as Honduras, Pakistan, or Zaire).

The important implication is that the nondiversifiable risk for a multinational firm may be less than if the firm had not diversified geographically. This means that the opportunity cost of equity capital will be lower and, other things being equal, the returns demanded will be lower.

Expropriation and Creditor Risks

The potential advantage from geographic diversification may be offset because of the increased possibility of expropriation of part or all of the firm's investment in a foreign subsidiary. We view expropriation broadly, to include not only pure nationalization, but also lesser forms such as increased ownership by the host country.[19] In either case, the multinational loses part or all of its investment or claim on cash flows from its subsidiary. Expropriation may be gradual, with an increase in demand for participation by locals or by the host government in the ownership of the business. Initially, it may take the form of a high tax or the right to buy the equity of the firm at some price. Often this price is extremely low relative to the market-determined worth of the subsidiary. A more dramatic form of expropriation was that suffered a number of years ago by some multinational firms whose investments in Iran were expropriated by that country's government.

Multinational firms can use various strategies in attempting to minimize the risk of expropriation. Generally, these fall into two categories. The first involves positive approaches, such as joint ventures, local participation, prior agreements for sale, and the like. All are designed to foster a positive, long-term relationship. The second involves limiting the investment of the parent, or controlling the raw material, production, or sales process so the subsidiaries' success is fully dependent on the parent.

Note, too, that default risk is often more serious in lesser developed countries. Because bankruptcy laws similar to those in developed countries often do not exist, creditors have little recourse to recoup losses. This factor must also be considered when multinational firms make capital budgeting and marketing decisions.

If increased expropriation or creditor risk is present, it would offset, in part or total, any reduced opportunity cost from investing overseas. The net result is that the opportunity cost of capital may be the same, lower, or higher for an international capital budgeting project. It all depends on the project itself and the country where the investment is made.

CONCEPT REVIEW QUESTIONS

- Why is it important to use divisional opportunity costs of capital rather than a firmwide opportunity cost of capital?
- Describe the steps used to estimate a divisional opportunity cost of capital.
- What are some major concerns when estimating the opportunity cost of capital for a multinational firm?

Summary

- The opportunity cost of capital is a future-oriented marginal cost which is used as the discount rate in net present value calculations when average-risk projects are being evaluated. It is the forgone return that could have been earned by investing in a similar-risk project.
- In order to determine the firm's opportunity cost of capital, we employ the knowledge that financial markets are efficient and, therefore, fully reflect the returns demanded by the firm's providers of capital and the risks faced by the firm.

---

[19]Instances of "pure" expropriation by countries has decreased significantly over the last 15 to 20 years.

■ By accepting all investment projects with positive net present values, in which the returns are more than the costs involved, the firm is making wealth-maximizing decisions that assist in maximizing the long-run market value of the firm.

■ Debt is typically the least expensive source of financing, whereas common equity capital is the most expensive. This is because of tax considerations and the risk and return requirements of investors.

■ The opportunity cost of capital is a weighted average of the expected future costs of funds. The weights are given by the market value proportions of the firm's capital structure.

■ The use of historical data to estimate the expected returns on the market portfolio, or the risk premium of stocks over corporate bonds, without considering current conditions, can lead to estimation errors.

■ When risk differs substantially across various divisions of the firm, the use of a firmwide opportunity cost of capital overallocates capital to safer divisions and underallocates capital to more risky divisions. The misallocation serves to reduce the value of the firm.

■ The opportunity cost of capital may be the same, lower, or higher for multinationals; it all depends on the circumstances.

Questions

6.1 "Internally generated funds are costless. Accordingly, the cost of new common stock is the only relevant cost of common equity for cost of capital purposes." Evaluate this statement.

6.2 Compare and contrast the dividend valuation, CAPM, and bond yield plus expected risk premium approaches to estimating the cost of common equity. Which do you believe is theoretically the best? Which is best in a practical sense?

6.3 Discuss the practical aspects of estimating a firm's opportunity cost of capital. Under what circumstances can you ignore payables and accruals? What about leases?

6.4 What problems exist when employing historical data to provide any of the estimates needed for determining a firm's cost of capital?

6.5 How would each of the following affect the firm's after-tax cost of debt, k_i; cost of equity, k_s; and opportunity cost of capital? Use a plus sign ($+$) to indicate an increase, a minus sign ($-$) to indicate a decrease, and a zero to indicate either no effect or an indeterminate effect. (*Note:* Treat only the direct effect, not any secondary effects.)

	k_i	k_s	Opportunity Cost of Capital
a. The corporate tax rate is decreased	—	—	—
b. The firm begins to make substantial new investments in assets that are less risky than its present assets.	—	—	—
c. The firm is selling more bonds. Because Standard & Poor's decides the firm is more risky, it lowers the bond rating.	—	—	—
d. The firm decides to triple its financing.	—	—	—
e. Investors become less risk-averse.	—	—	—

Concept Review Problems

See Appendix A for solutions.

CR6.1 Bravo Inc. is planning to issue new debt; to estimate its cost historical data will be used. Bravo's outstanding debt has an annual coupon interest rate of 10 percent, pays interest semi-annually, has 20 years to maturity, and is currently trading at $1,198 per bond. If Bravo's tax rate is 35 percent, what is the after-tax cost of debt?

CR6.2 In addition, Bravo Inc. is planning to issue $100 par value preferred stock with an $8.50 dividend payment. The firm expects to receive $93 per share. What is the cost of preferred stock?

Note: Use all three methods and then average them.

CR6.3 Bravo's stock is currently selling at $40 per share, has an expected *EPS* at $t = 1$ of $7.20, a dividend payout ratio of 50 percent, and an expected growth rate of 4 percent. *Value Line* has estimated Bravo's beta at 1.5. If the risk-free rate of return is 6 percent, the return on the market is 12 percent, and the average return on corporate bonds is 9 percent, what is Bravo's cost of equity?

CR6.4 If Bravo's target capital structure is 20 percent debt, 10 percent preferred stock, and 70 percent equity, what is Bravo's opportunity cost of capital?

The following facts given for Los Amigos Products are needed for CR6.5–CR6.9.

Los Amigos Products (in millions)			
Assets		**Liabilities and Stockholders' Equity**	
Cash	$ 5	Accounts payable	$ 5
Accounts receivable	5	Short-term debt	10
Inventories	10	Long-term debt	30
Long-term assets	55	Preferred stock	10
Total assets	$75	Common stock	
		(2 million shares	
		outstanding)	5
		Retained earnings	15
		Total liabilities and	
		stockholders' equity	$75

1. Short-term debt consists of bank loans that currently cost 6 percent.
2. Long-term debt consists of 20-year semi-annual payment bonds with a coupon rate of 12 percent. Currently these bonds provide a yield to investors of 9 percent.
3. Los Amigos Products' perpetual preferred stock has a $100 par value, pays a dividend of $12, and has a yield to investors of 10 percent.
4. The current stock price is $37.50. The firm expects to pay a dividend of $4.00 next year, the growth rate is 6 percent, beta is 1.2, the required return on the market is 15 percent, the marginal tax rate is 35 percent, and the risk-free rate is 6 percent.

Note: In CR6.5, carry to 3 decimal places.

Note: In CR6.6, calculate all 3 costs of common equity and then average them.

CR6.5 What are the market value proportions of debt, preferred stock, and common equity for Los Amigos?

CR6.6 What is the cost of short-term debt, long-term debt, preferred stock, and common equity for Los Amigos Products?

CR6.7 What is Los Amigos' opportunity cost of capital?

Note: In CR6.8, use only the dividend valuation approach to determine the cost of common equity.

CR6.8 Now assume all equity financing for Los Amigos Products will have to be obtained from external sources. If the underpricing is $3.50 per share of common stock, what is the firm's new opportunity cost of capital?

CR6.9 The CEO of Los Amigos wants to expand. The new division is expected to be riskier than the firm as a whole. Therefore, the capital structure of the division will contain no short-term financing, no preferred stock financing, 20 percent long-term debt, and 80 percent common equity financing. The estimated beta for the division is 1.34, while its tax rate is 40 percent. What is the opportunity cost of capital for the division?

Problems

See Appendix C for answers to selected problems.

After-Tax Cost of Debt

6.1 Calculate the after-tax cost of debt under the following conditions if the maturity value of the debt is $1,000, interest is paid annually, and the corporate tax rate is 35 percent.

a. Coupon interest rate is 8 percent, proceeds are $900, and the life is 20 years.

b. Bond pays $100 per year in interest, proceeds are $960, and the life is 10 years.

c. Coupon interest rate is 14 percent, proceeds are $1,120, and the bond has a 30-year life.

d. Proceeds are $1,000, coupon interest rate is 12 percent, and the life is 5 years.

Cost of Preferred Stock

6.2 What is the after-tax cost of preferred stock under the following circumstances?

a. Par is $80, dividend is $8 per year, and the proceeds are $76.

b. Proceeds are $46, and dividends are $7.

c. Par is $60, dividend is 9 percent (of par), and proceeds are $55.

d. Par is $40, dividend is 11 percent (of par), and proceeds are $40.

Cost of Common: Dividend Valuation Approach

6.3 Given the following information, calculate the cost of common equity, k_s, under each of the following conditions.

a. $P_0 = \$80$, $g = 8$ percent, and $D_1 = \$5$.

b. It is now January 1, 19X7; cash dividends in 19X2 were $2.05; they were $3 in 19X6. $P_0 = \$47$.

c. Historical growth in dividends is 4 percent, expected growth is 7 percent, $D_0 = \$4$, and $P_0 = \$73$.

d. $P_0 = \$50$, and the past dividends have been

Year	Dividends per Share
−5	$2.50
−4	2.80
−3	2.80
−2	3.10
−1	3.67
0	3.67

Cost of Common: All Three Approaches

Note: For (b) remember that $\beta_s = \sigma_s Corr_{sM}/\sigma_M$.

6.4 Calculate the cost of common equity, k_s, under the following conditions:

a. Expected return on the market portfolio is 16 percent, risk-free rate is 6 percent, and beta is 1.50.

b. $k_M = 18$ percent, $k_{RF} = 12$ percent, σ_M (standard deviation of the market) = 14 percent, σ_s (standard deviation of stock s) = 35 percent, and $Corr_{sM}$ (correlation between returns on stock s and returns on the market) = +0.80.

c. The current market interest rate on comparable long-term debt is 9 percent, and the expected risk premium differential of stocks over bonds is 4 percent.

d. The coupon rate on the firm's existing debt is 9 percent, current market yield on short-term debt is 10 percent, current market yield on long-term debt is 12 percent, and the expected risk premium differential of stocks over bonds is 5 percent.

Cost of Common: All Three Approaches

6.5 Luxury Suites has hired you as a consultant to estimate its cost of common equity. After talking with its CFO and an econometric forecasting firm, you have come up with the following facts and estimates:

Estimates	Year	Dividends per Share
$P_0 = \$85$	−5	$1.21
$\beta_{\text{Luxury Suites}} = 1.50$	−4	1.21
Treasury security rate = 10%	−3	1.30
Market yield on comparable	−2	1.40
quality long-term debt = 13%	−1	1.71
Expected return on the market	0	1.86
portfolio = 16%		
Expected risk premium of stocks		
over bonds = 4%		
Current earnings per share, $EPS = \$5.75$		

Luxury Suites plans to use 30 percent debt and 70 percent equity for its incremental financing. Also, the firm's marginal tax rate is 33 percent.

a. What do you estimate the past growth rate in cash dividends per share has been? Employ this as your estimate of g (round to the nearest whole number).

b. What is the estimated cost of common equity employing the following approaches: (1) dividend valuation, (2) CAPM, and (3) bond yield plus expected risk premium?

c. Explain why one of the estimates from (b) is substantially lower than the other two.

d. Take an average of all three answers from (b) for your estimate of Luxury's cost of common equity.

e. What is your estimate of Luxury's opportunity cost of capital? How confident of it are you?

OCC: Debt, Internally Generated, and New Common Stock

6.6 Giant Electronics plans to raise $20 million this year for expansion. The firm's current market value capital structure, shown below, is considered to be optimal.

Debt	$ 40,000,000
Common equity	_60,000,000_
	$100,000,000

Note: Remember in (b) it is the cost of the last dollar of each feasible source that is important. Firms tend to use internally generated funds before they issue additional common stock.

New debt will have a market interest rate of 10 percent. Common stock is currently selling at $40 per share, expected growth in dividends is 7 percent, and $D_1 = \$3.60$. If new common stock is sold, the proceeds are expected to be $36 per share. Internally generated funds available for capital budgeting purposes are expected to be $6 million, and Giant's marginal tax rate is 30 percent.

a. Calculate the market value proportions of debt and common equity.

b. Calculate the cost of the two relevant sources of capital.

c. What is Giant's opportunity cost of capital?

OCC: Debt, Preferred Stock, and Common Equity

6.7 The chief financial officer of Soldier Tire has given you the assignment of determining the firm's cost of capital. The present capital structure, which is considered optimal, is as follows:

	Book Value	Market Value
Debt	$50 million	$ 40 million
Preferred stock	10 million	5 million
Common equity	30 million	55 million
	$90 million	$100 million

The anticipated financing opportunities are these: Debt can be issued with a 15 percent before-tax cost. Preferred stock will be $100 par, carry a dividend of 13 percent, and can be sold to net the firm $96 per share. Common equity has a beta of 1.20, $k_M = 17$ percent, and $k_{RF} = 12$ percent.

a. If the firm's tax rate is 40 percent, what is its opportunity cost of capital?

b. What happens to its opportunity cost of capital if Soldier's marginal tax rate is zero?

Opportunity Cost of Capital

6.8 The management of Taft Communications is considering further expansion. To evaluate the various alternatives, management needs to estimate Taft's cost of capital. Various financial data are given, as follows:

Balance Sheet (in millions)	
Total assets $500	
Accounts payable and accruals	$ 50
Short-term debt	100
Bonds ($1,000 par)	100
Common stock (50 million shares)	50
Retained earnings	200
Total liabilities and stockholders' equity	$500

Estimates	Year	Dividends per Share
$P_0 = \$15.50$	−7	$1.00
Expected return on the market portfolio = 12%	−6	1.00
Risk-free rate (Treasury securities) = 7%	−5	1.05
Market interest rate on comparable bonds = 9%	−4	1.05
Beta for Taft Communications = 0.80	−3	1.10
	−2	1.10
	−1	1.18
	0	1.23

a. Calculate the historical growth rate in cash dividends per share. Estimate the dividends to be paid in year +1.

b. Estimate the cost of common equity using both the dividend valuation and CAPM approaches. Average the two estimates and then round to the nearest whole number.

c. Calculate Taft's after-tax cost of long-term debt if the firm's marginal tax rate is 35 percent.

d. The short-term debt will carry a different cost. Using the Treasury security rate and adding 1 percent to estimate Taft's before-tax cost of short-term debt, calculate the after-tax cost of Taft's short-term debt.

e. Determine the market value proportions if all of the following hold simultaneously:

1. Accounts payable and accruals are ignored.
2. Short-term debt is taken at face value.
3. The current market value of long-term debt is $125 million.
4. Common equity is determined by multiplying the number of shares times the stock price.

f. What is Taft's opportunity cost of capital?

Opportunity Cost of Capital

6.9 Bach Batteries is in the process of estimating its cost of capital. Financial data for the firm are as follows:

Balance Sheet

Total assets $100,000	Accounts payables and accruals	$ 15,000
	Short-term debt	15,000
	Bonds ($1,000 par)	25,000
	Common stock (12,000 shares)	20,000
	Retained earnings	25,000
	Total liabilities and stockholders' equity	$100,000

Estimates	Year	Dividends per Share
$P_0 = \$8.00$	-5	$0.25
Expected return on the market portfolio = 17%	-4	0.25
Risk-free rate (Treasury securities) = 10%	-3	0.28
Market interest rate on comparable bonds = 13%	-2	0.28
Beta for Bach = 1.30	-1	0.36
	0	0.40

Note: In (a) round the growth rate to the nearest whole number.

a. Calculate the historical growth rate in cash dividends per share. Estimate the dividends to be paid in year + 1.
b. Estimate the cost of equity capital using the dividend valuation, CAPM, and bond yield plus expected risk premium approaches. Assume the expected risk premium is 6 percent. Average the three estimates and then round to the nearest whole number.
c. Calculate Bach's after-tax cost of long-term debt if the firm's marginal tax rate is 40 percent.
d. For short-term debt, the before-tax cost is the Treasury security rate plus 1 percent. Calculate Bach's after-tax cost of short-term debt.
e. Determine the market value proportions if all of the following hold simultaneously:

1. Accounts payable and accruals are ignored.
2. Short-term debt is taken at face value.
3. The current market value of long-term debt is $21,000.
4. Common equity is determined by multiplying the number of shares times the stock price.

f. What is Bach's opportunity cost of capital?

Increase in Opportunity Cost of Capital

6.10 Thomas Inc. requires $15 million to fund its current year's capital projects. Thomas will finance part of its needs with $9 million in internally generated funds. The firm's common stock market price is $120 per share. Dividends of $5 per share at $t = 0$ are expected to grow at a rate of 11 percent per year for the foreseeable future. Another part will be funded with the proceeds (at $96 per share) from an issue of 9,375 shares of 12 percent $100 par preferred stock that will be privately placed. The remainder will be financed with debt. Five thousand 10-year $1,000 par bonds with a coupon rate of 15 percent will be issued to net the firm $1,020 each. Interest is paid annually on the bonds. The firm's tax rate is 30 percent.

a. What is Thomas's opportunity cost of capital?

b. Thomas has now decided to double its funding requirements. The financing proportions will remain as in (a). No additional internally generated funds are available. New common stock can be sold at $100 per share. Additional preferred stock and debt can be sold with all of the same conditions as in (a) *except* the dividend rate on preferred stock is 13.5 percent and the coupon interest rate on bonds will be 17 percent. What is Thomas's opportunity cost of capital for this second increment of financing?

Increase in Opportunity Cost of Capital

6.11 Markley Markets is calculating its opportunity cost of capital. The following has been determined:

Debt. $1,000 par value, 20-year, 9 percent coupon-rate bond can be sold at a discount of $50 per bond. Interest is paid annually, and the marginal corporate tax rate is 40 percent.

Preferred Stock. $100 par value, 8.5 percent preferred stock can be sold at a discount of $9 per share.

Common Equity. The present market price is $75 per share. The cash dividend next year is expected to be $5, and the growth rate is expected to be 7 percent for the foreseeable future.

Internally Generated Financing. All the common equity needs will be funded by internally generated funds.

Markley's current market value capital structure is as follows:

Debt	30%
Preferred stock	20
Common equity	50
	100%

a. What is Markley's opportunity cost of capital?

b. Assume now that instead of (a), Markley decides to increase its financing substantially. Everything is the same as in (a) except:

Debt. 11 percent coupon interest rate.

Preferred Stock. 10 percent dividend rate.

Common Stock. Underpricing is $12 per share.

Internally Generated Financing. All used up, so none available.

c. What is Markley's new opportunity cost of capital?

Divisional Cost of Capital

6.12 Turquoise Products has three different divisions—A, B, and C. In estimating divisional opportunity costs of capital, management has determined that $\beta_A = 1.20$, $\beta_B = 0.60$, and $\beta_C = 2.00$. Also, $k_{RF} = 8$ percent and $k_M = 13$ percent. If the after-tax cost of debt is 5 percent and the appropriate capital structures for the divisions are given below, what are the three divisional opportunity costs of capital?

	Target Financing Proportions		
	Division A	Division B	Division C
Debt	0.50	0.20	0.60
Common equity	0.50	0.80	0.40

Firmwide Versus Divisional Cost of Capital

6.13 Schaeffer Equipment has traditionally employed a firmwide opportunity cost of capital for capital budgeting purposes. However, its two divisions—machinery and farm implements—have different degrees of risk. Data on the firm and the divisions are as follows:

	Schaeffer Equipment	Machinery Division	Farm Implement Division
Beta	1.4	1.0	2.0
Appropriate percentage of debt	40%	50%	20%
Appropriate percentage of common equity	60	50	80

The following estimates have been made: $k_i = 7$ percent, $k_{RF} = 10$ percent, and $k_M = 15$ percent. The firm is considering the following capital expenditures:

	Proposed Capital Projects	Initial Investment (in millions)	IRR
Machinery	M−1	$1	15%
	M−2	3	12
	M−3	2	9
Farm implements	F−1	4	16
	F−2	6	20
	F−3	5	12

a. Calculate Schaeffer Equipment's firmwide opportunity cost of capital.
b. Based on your answer in (a), which projects should Schaeffer select? What is the size of the capital budget?
c. Calculate the opportunity costs of capital for the two divisions.
d. Which projects should now be selected? What is the size of the resulting capital budget?
e. What happens if a firm uses a firmwide opportunity cost for capital budgeting purposes when it should be using divisional opportunity costs?

Opportunity Cost of Capital

6.14 Mini Case Major Consolidated's new CFO is undertaking a thorough review of how the firm makes its capital investment decisions. A major component of this review is to examine how the firm determines its opportunity cost of capital.

a. What is meant by "opportunity cost of capital"? What assumptions are employed in arriving at a firm's opportunity cost of capital? What role do efficient financial markets play?
b. What sources are the least expensive? The most expensive? Why? What role do corporate taxes play?
c. Debt can be issued at par and will carry a 13.5 percent coupon interest rate. Preferred stock can also be issued at par and will carry a 13 percent dividend. Information on common stock is as follows:

Estimates	Year	Dividends per share
$P_0 = \$40$	−4	$2.00
$\beta = 1.25$	−3	2.00
$k_{RF} = 11\%$	−2	2.40
Expected return on the market portfolio = 16%	−1	2.75
Expected risk premium of stocks over bonds = 5%	0	2.93

The market value capital structure for Major is 40 percent debt, 50 percent common equity, and 10 percent preferred stock. The firm's marginal tax rate is 35 percent.

Note: In (1) for the dividend valuation approach, round g to the nearest whole percent.

(1) Determine the cost of common equity using the three different approaches. Take an average of the three estimates for Major's cost of equity.

(2) What is Major's opportunity cost of capital?

d. After further investigation it is determined that Major's three divisions have vastly different risks. Hence, divisional opportunity costs of capital are required. What occurs if a firmwide opportunity cost is employed when risk differs significantly among divisions?

e. For Major Consolidated the betas for the three divisions are division A, 1.75; division B, 1.20; and division C, 0.75. What are the appropriate opportunity costs of capital for the three divisions if $k_{RF} = 11\%$, $k_M = 16\%$, $T = 0.35$, and the following are the appropriate percentages of debt and stock for the three divisions?

	Division A	Division B	Division C
Debt	0.167	0.412	0.524
Equity	0.833	0.588	0.476

CHAPTER 7

Capital Budgeting Techniques

Sections in this chapter:

■ **Capital Budgeting and the Value of the Firm**
How to enlarge the size of the pie.

■ **The Capital Budgeting Process**
A general outline of how capital budgeting works.

■ **Selecting Capital Budgeting Projects**
Several capital budgeting methods, one of which is always a winner.

■ **Some Complications**
Some curves—the first of many—that the real world puts in the capital budgeting road.

apital investment in the United States began to expand again in 1994 after declining over 25 percent from mid-1990 through mid-1993. Why the upsurge? According to one analyst, "Spending for new facilities is long-term investment that reflects confidence in the durability of the expansion and the competitiveness of U.S. industry in world markets." In fact, lower U.S. manufacturing wages and land cost are key factors leading Japanese firms to increase their level of investment in the United States. Recently, Toyota decided to spend $900 million to add to its Kentucky auto assembly plant; Mitsubishi Materials is spending $240 million to build a new silicon wafer plant in Oregon; and Ricoh is spending $30 million to double the size of its Georgia thermal paper plant. As an example of the differences in costs, Ricoh estimates it will cost the firm 30 percent less to expand its factory in the United States than to expand in Japan.

While some of the increased capital spending is for typical plant and equipment, a large part of the current spending boom is directed toward computers, electronics, and office equipment. Also, firms such as heavy-duty truck manufacturer Freightliner are investing in machinery to increase the productivity of their existing plant and personnel, in order to lower the cost of labor. Likewise, firms such as Pacific Bell, the San Francisco-based regional phone company, recently announced plans to spend $16 billion over the next seven years on a powerful system to allow homes and businesses to process voice, data, and video communications. Firms like MCI, Bell Atlantic, and AT&T are also making significant investments in line with the developments in the information superhighway.

All successful firms, whether large or small, invest in new long-term, or capital, assets. The profitability of these investment decisions directly affects the value of the firm. Effective capital budgeting procedures for making long-term investment decisions

This whole chapter builds on three of the Key Ideas from Chapter 1: the goal of the firm is to maximize its market value, firms focus on cash flows and their incremental effects, and a dollar today is worth more than a dollar tomorrow.

are therefore a key ingredient for success. Successful firms, as evidenced by increases in market value, make good capital budgeting decisions. Let's see how they do it.

LEARNING GOALS

After studying this chapter, you should be able to:

1. Explain how net present value affects the value of a firm.
2. Discuss the steps in the capital budgeting process.
3. Compare three methods for selecting capital budgeting projects: payback period, net present value, and internal rate of return.
4. Explain why net present value is the preferred capital budgeting method.
5. Explain how firms evaluate capital budgeting projects with unequal lives.
6. Discuss how firms rank projects in cases of capital rationing.

CAPITAL BUDGETING AND THE VALUE OF THE FIRM

CAPITAL BUDGET
A statement of the firm's planned long-term investment projects.

CAPITAL BUDGETING
The process by which long-term investments are generated, analyzed, and placed on the capital budget.

EXPANSION PROJECT
Project designed to improve the firm's ability to produce or market its goods by expanding its scale of operations.

REPLACEMENT PROJECT
Project that replaces existing assets.

■ LEARNING GOAL 1

Explain how net present value affects the value of a firm.

The primary goal of the firm is to maximize its long-run market value, or, in the analogy of Chapter 1, to maximize the size of the pie. Although many things contribute to maximizing the value of the firm, the most important single factor is the investments the firm makes. These investments determine the direction of the firm; over time, how the firm has positioned itself (in terms of its products or services, its position in its industries, and so forth) is a direct function of its past, present, and future investment decisions. Good investment decisions build on the firm's growth opportunities and take advantage of the unique aspects and advantages a firm has vis-a-vis its competitors.

Financial managers use capital budgeting techniques to evaluate proposed investments in long-term assets. *Long-term* is taken to mean any investment for which returns are expected to extend beyond 1 year. An investment can be as small as the purchase of some office furniture or as large as a complete new plant. The **capital budget** contains estimates of cash flows for long-term projects. **Capital budgeting** is the process by which long-term investments are generated, analyzed, and placed in the capital budget.

Project Classification

REGULATORY PROJECT
Required project for which no measurable cash inflows are expected to occur.

MUTUALLY EXCLUSIVE PROJECTS
Capital budgeting alternatives, of which only one will be selected.

INDEPENDENT PROJECTS
Projects whose cash flows are unrelated.

Capital budgeting projects can be classified into three broad categories: expansion, replacement, and regulatory. **Expansion projects** improve the firm's ability to produce or market its products. If a firm decides to add a new line of machine tools, the plant necessary to produce the tools is an expansion project. **Replacement projects** take the place of existing assets that have become physically or economically obsolete. Finally, **regulatory projects** provide no direct cash benefits to the firm but must be completed for the firm's operations to continue. For example, the federal Occupational Safety and Health Administration (OSHA) and the Environmental Protection Agency (EPA) can require firms to spend billions of dollars to improve the health and safety of the workplace or to prevent harm to the environment.

Another method of classifying projects is to view them either as **mutually exclusive projects** or as **independent projects.** When two projects are mutually exclusive, the acceptance of one precludes the acceptance of the other. For example, a company would choose only one of two proposals to purchase a computer network system, if only one system is needed. The two proposals are mutually exclusive. However, a proposal to acquire a computer network system and another proposal to build a new warehouse are independent. The cash flows are unrelated, and the firm may choose one, both, or neither.

Value Maximization

In capital budgeting, we calculate the net present value, *NPV*, a concept we first encountered in Chapter 1 and discussed further in Chapter 3. Net present value is equal to the present value of the expected after-tax cash inflows, discounted at the opportunity cost of capital (the minimum required rate of return), minus the initial cash investment required.

Accepting positive *NPV* projects directly impacts the value of the firm. Consider an all-equity firm that has a current market value of $6 million. That amount includes $2 million in cash that can be invested in new long-term investment projects. As financial manager, you have to decide whether to invest the $2 million in a proposed capital investment or to keep it in cash. The choice is as follows:

Examining a project's NPV is a cost-benefit analysis. We find the time and risk-adjusted present value, PV, of future cash inflows; if the PV of the future benefits is greater than the cost, the project is accepted.

	Market Value (in millions)	
Asset	Reject New Project	Accept New Project
Cash	$2	$0
Other	4	4
New project	$\underline{0}$	$\underline{PV}$
	$6	$4 + PV

Clearly, the new project is worthwhile if its present value, *PV*, is greater than the $2 million required investment. The *PV* will be greater than the required investment only if the *NPV* is greater than zero. Why? Recall from the definition of *NPV* that the initial investment is subtracted from the present value of the discounted cash flows expected from the project. Therefore, when the *NPV* is zero, the discounted cash inflows from the project would *just equal* the initial investment of $2 million.

What happens, for example, if the proposed project has a net present value of $3.5 million? The firm will receive back its $2 million investment plus an additional $1.5 million (both after discounting). What will happen to the value of the firm? It will increase by $1.5 million as investors recognize the impact of the capital investment decision. *Only by accepting positive* NPV *projects can a firm increase its long-run market value; accepting projects with negative* NPV *leads to a decrease in the value of the firm.*

CONCEPT REVIEW QUESTIONS

- Describe three different types of capital budgeting projects.
- How is the long-run market value of a firm related to a project's net present value?

THE CAPITAL BUDGETING PROCESS

■ LEARNING GOAL 2

Discuss the steps in the capital budgeting process.

While the ideas behind capital budgeting using net present value are simple and straightforward, complications develop when we put our knowledge to work. To see why, it is important to understand that capital budgeting is a process involving a

Projects originate as ideas, and most ideas never make it past the first phase. Many potential projects are evaluated and discarded at the idea stage on strategic grounds, with only a rough cost benefit analysis.

number of somewhat separate but interrelated activities. The *capital budgeting process* can be broken down into four steps:

1. Search for and identify growth opportunities.
2. Estimate the magnitude, timing, and riskiness of cash flows.
3. Select or reject projects.
4. Evaluate performance through control procedures and postcompletion audit.

The relationships among these steps are shown in Figure 7.1.

Identifying Growth Opportunities

The search and identification stage involves actively searching for new growth opportunities within the firm's expertise *or* identifying problems that need attention. It is a triggering process: The thrust of this phase is not to analyze and solve well-defined problems, but *to identify growth opportunities* for possible capital investment.

FIGURE 7.1

The Capital Budgeting Process

Capital budgeting is an ongoing process in which effective feedback should assist in improving decision making for subsequent capital investments.

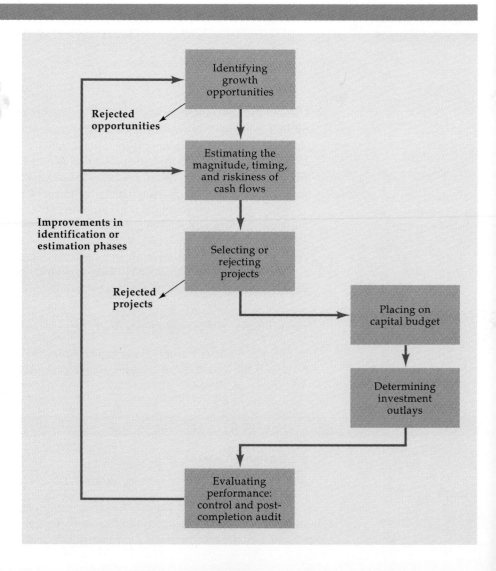

In the broadest sense, the search and identification stage connects directly to the firm's overall strategic objectives. The relationship between long-term strategic objectives and the capital budgeting process must be fully integrated and consistent. Too often in practice, this is not the case. The decision to enter a new market or adopt a new production technology is often just the first in a long series of investment decisions. Then either additional investments are made because they "are necessary" given the previous decision, or the capital budgeting decision-making process is employed only *within* the previously defined strategic plan. Either way, the firm has the cart before the horse. It should be the firm's capital budgeting techniques that determine the firm's long-run strategic decisions—not the other way around!

Estimating the Magnitude, Timing, and Riskiness of Cash Flows

The most serious capital budgeting errors arise from misestimating cash flows. Playing the "what if?" game is crucial: What if sales grow less than expected? What if there is a recession? What if the competition cuts prices?

Once growth opportunities have been identified, the next step is to develop alternative courses of action and to estimate the magnitude, timing, and riskiness of the cash flows associated with each one. This is often the most difficult part of the capital budgeting process. It requires extensive knowledge, hard work, and an understanding of how possible competitor actions will affect cash flow projections. The estimation phase tends to become narrower in focus than the search and identification phase. The reason is that the desired outcome is detailed and specific: a set of alternative capital budgeting projects and associated cash flows, with risk estimates and specification of the key assumptions incorporated into the forecasts. This topic is examined in detail in Chapter 8.

Selecting or Rejecting Projects

In presenting the analysis to senior management many firms follow the procedure of providing worst-case, best-case and most-likely scenarios, and the assumptions underlying each.

After the estimates have been made, the firm will select the most promising projects. The important points to remember about this phase are these:

1. The methods used to select or reject projects must be consistent with the objective of maximizing the value of the firm.
2. The key underlying assumptions concerning the techniques employed and the data used must be understood by the firm's capital budgeting experts as well as by senior management.
3. The firm must consider alternative courses of action (including the possibility of delaying a project and the follow-on nature of many capital investment growth opportunities), changes in risk, and possible actions of competitors.

Evaluating Performance: Control and Postcompletion Audit

Obviously, managers can manipulate the numbers in capital budgeting—such as cash inflows or outflows or project life— to make a project look better. That makes the auditing procedure important.

The final phase is that of control and postcompletion audit. Control can be thought of as the process by which the actual cash flows are compared with the projections. In addition, this phase should involve the subsequent reevaluation of the economic merits of ongoing projects—in order to determine whether to continue them. Evaluating the performance of ongoing capital investments is important for any complete capital budgeting process. A successful feedback program suggests needed revisions in the identification procedure, provides information to improve future estimates of cash flows and risk, and indicates projects that should be abandoned. Effective control and postcompletion audits are vital to maximizing the long-run market value of the firm.

All four steps are important. In our study of financial management, we will focus on the second and third—estimation of the magnitude, timing, and riskiness of cash flows, and project selection. *Throughout this chapter and the next, we assume that all projects being considered are equally risky.* That is, their risk is equal to the firm's overall level of risk. Although this assumption is obviously unrealistic, it allows us to focus on the essential elements of the capital budgeting process. Assuming all projects are equally risky means we can use a single hurdle (or discount) rate throughout. This rate is the firm's opportunity cost of capital. In Chapter 9 we will consider situations in which the risk of the project is not equal to the firm's overall risk level.

CONCEPT REVIEW QUESTIONS

- Describe the four steps of the capital budgeting process.
- Why is estimating the magnitude, timing, and riskiness of cash flows important in capital budgeting decisions?

SELECTING CAPITAL BUDGETING PROJECTS

■ LEARNING GOAL 3

Compare three methods for selecting capital budgeting projects.

Firms use a variety of techniques to determine whether to accept proposed projects: the payback period, net present value, and internal rate of return are three of the most popular.[1] The payback period is a simple but unsophisticated technique that does not employ discounting. The net present value, *NPV*, and internal rate of return, *IRR*, techniques both employ discounting to deal with the magnitude, timing, and riskiness of the cash flow stream. The relevant cash flow stream for capital budgeting purposes is the *incremental after-tax* cash flow stream related to the project. By incremental, we mean the difference in the "new" cash flow stream minus any "existing" (or "old") cash flow stream. This stream is referred to as cash flow, *CF*.

Payback Period

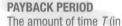

PAYBACK PERIOD
The amount of time T (in years) for the expected cash inflows from a capital budgeting project to just equal the initial investment.

The **payback period** is the number of years it takes for the firm to recover its initial investment in a project. Payback occurs when the cumulative net cash inflows minus the initial investment equals zero, or

$$\text{payback is the time, } T, \text{ such that } \sum_{t=1}^{T} CF_t = CF_0 \qquad (7.1)$$

The decision rule for the payback period is as follows:

1. If T is less than the maximum T, accept.
2. If T is greater than the maximum T, reject.
3. If T is equal to the maximum T, you are indifferent.

Consider the two projects in Table 7.1. Project A has an initial investment of $442 and cash inflows of $200 for each of 3 years. Project B requires an initial investment of $718, followed by cash inflows of $250, $575, and $100, respectively, for the 3 years. For project A (which is an annuity) the payback period can be found simply by dividing the initial investment by the annual CF. Thus, $442 divided by $200 yields a payback period, T, of 2.21 years. For project B, the payback is found by determining how many years are needed to recoup the initial investment of $718. In the first year,

[1] *The other techniques are the average (or accounting) rate of return and the profitablity index. Given the deficiencies of accounting data for effective decision making, we should be wary of any attempt to make capital investment decisions with the average rate of return. The profitability index is discussed in footnote 10.*

TABLE 7.1

Calculation of the Payback Period for Projects A and B

When the cash inflows are unequal, as in project B, interpolation can be employed to determine the exact payback period.

Cash Flow Streams

Project A (an annuity)

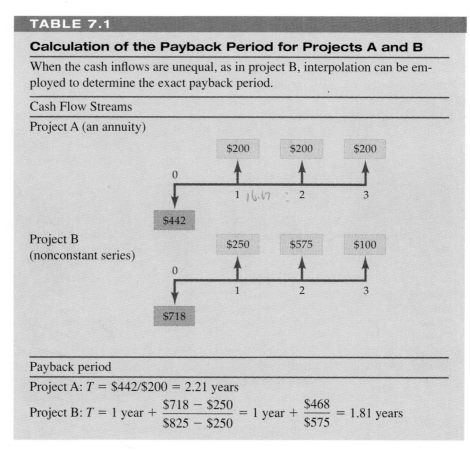

Payback period

Project A: $T = \$442/\$200 = 2.21$ years

Project B: $T = 1 \text{ year} + \dfrac{\$718 - \$250}{\$825 - \$250} = 1 \text{ year} + \dfrac{\$468}{\$575} = 1.81 \text{ years}$

$250 is recovered; by the end of the second year, a total of $825 is recovered. So, the payback period is between 1 and 2 years. Table 7.1 shows that the payback period is 1.81 years. Thus, project B has the shorter payback period. If a firm's maximum acceptable payback period is 2 years, it would accept project B and reject project A.

The payback period has some advantages. First, it is simple to calculate. Second, it is easy to understand and simple to explain. Third, it provides a rough indicator of the riskiness of the project, because projects that pay back sooner are often viewed as being more liquid and hence less risky than those with longer payback periods.

At the same time, the payback period has three significant disadvantages. The first is that the maximum acceptable payback period is arbitrary; that is, it is set without any economic justification. Second, it does not account for the timing of the cash flows, because discounting is not employed. Third, it does not deal with any cash flows that occur beyond the payback period. To illustrate, suppose that we had two projects with cash flows as follows:

Recently I visited a firm where the payback for a particular type of investment had to be 1 year or less. In such cases, the payback method is strongly biased toward short-term projects.

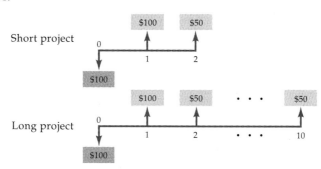

FINANCIAL MANAGEMENT TODAY

Capital Budgeting at Boeing

Boeing, with more than a 60 percent share of the market, dominates the world's commercial aircraft business. One source who worked at Boeing years ago when the company was making the capital budgeting decision on its highly successful 747 plane, has shed some light on Boeing's decision making. In determining the cash flows for the 747, Boeing did not consider any side benefits or costs about how the 747 would interact with any of their present or planned planes. That is, the firm considered the 747 to be independent of any other projects; by introducing the 747 it assumed the 747 would neither increase nor decrease the sales (or costs) of other planes manufactured by Boeing. Such an approach is unique, and it is unusual to think that such an endeavor would not affect any of the other activities of the firm!

Launched in 1969, the 747 ran into a devastating market downturn in 1971, forcing Boeing to lay off 95,000 of its 148,000 employees. But the 747 turned out to be one of the best investment decisions Boeing ever made. Now Boeing has launched its new wide-body, the 777. But Airbus Industries got the jump on Boeing with its A330 and A340 models. Boeing is focusing even more on cutting costs and outsourcing production on many of the large parts for its 737, 767, and 777 planes to the People's Republic of China and Japan. Not only is Boeing interested in cutting costs, but the Chinese and Japanese plane markets are projected to become the biggest in the world. Having a business presence in that part of the world may pay off big for Boeing in the future.

The development costs for Boeing are enormous—it spent over $4 billion to develop the 777, making it the firm's biggest project since the 747 was launched over 25 years ago. And, if Boeing develops the talked about superjumbo, the development costs are projected to be at least $10 billion. To develop such a huge project, Boeing will have to work with others. However, rolling the dice in the aerospace industry is a way of life. As a Boeing executive stated: "You can't be in this business and not take risks. But we need to be reflective before we take risks." Boeing's past and future successes rest on risk-taking and developing strategic alliances with firms in many parts of the world.

It is obvious that the longer project is better than the shorter one. However, both projects have the same payback of 1 year. Because of these disadvantages, the payback period is not normally considered an appropriate decision-making criterion.[2]

Remember Key Idea 3—individuals act in their own self-interest. This applies to managers as well as to other individuals.

Although the payback period does not appear to be a viable decision criterion, it is widely employed in practice. Why? One possible explanation is due to agency-related issues that exist between the firm's managers (the agents) and the firm's stockholders (the principals). *Moral hazard* is said to exist when the information available to the firm's managers is superior to that available to outside investors (a case of asymmetric information). In such a case the agent (or managers) can take unobserved self-interested actions that are detrimental to the principals. For risk-averse managers, three important areas in which they can take self-interested actions relate to (1) the amount of effort they expend, (2) the amount of risk (or total variability in firm value) they expose the firm to, and (3) the time horizon adopted for decision making (e.g., will they be with the firm for 6 months, 5 years, or 20 years?). Because of self-interest, managers may prefer short-payback capital investment projects, especially when the risk (or total possible variability) in a project's cash flows is high.

Net Present Value

The appropriate selection technique is our familiar net present value, *NPV*. The *NPV* is determined by discounting the cash inflows back to the present ($t = 0$) at the opportunity cost, k, and then subtracting the initial investment, so that

---

[2]*Some firms calculate a discounted payback period to overcome the timing disadvantage, but the other problems remain.*

$$\text{net present value, } NPV = \sum_{t=1}^{n} \frac{CF_t}{(1+k)^t} - CF_0 \qquad (7.2)$$

The decision rule for net present value is as follows:

1. If NPV is greater than zero, accept.
2. If NPV is less than zero, reject.
3. If NPV is equal to zero, you are indifferent.

When the NPV is greater than zero, the firm is generating funds above and beyond those necessary to (1) repay the initial investment and (2) provide it with a return of k percent on its investment. This incremental return represents the funds generated by the project that can be used for other purposes by the firm.

Let's see how NPV works for our example of projects A and B. Their net present values are calculated in Table 7.2, using an assumed opportunity cost of 12 percent.

TABLE 7.2

Calculation of the Net Present Value for Projects A and B

The opportunity cost employed was 12 percent. Because both $NPVs$ are positive, both projects assist in maximizing the value of the firm.

Cash Flows Streams

Project A (an annuity)

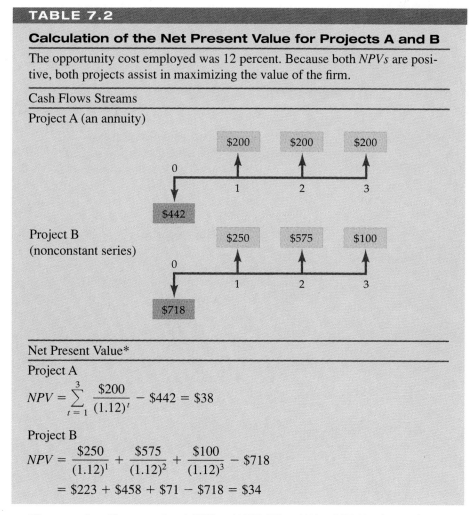

Project B (nonconstant series)

Net Present Value*

Project A

$$NPV = \sum_{t=1}^{3} \frac{\$200}{(1.12)^t} - \$442 = \$38$$

Project B

$$NPV = \frac{\$250}{(1.12)^1} + \frac{\$575}{(1.12)^2} + \frac{\$100}{(1.12)^3} - \$718$$
$$= \$223 + \$458 + \$71 - \$718 = \$34$$

*If present value tables are employed, $NPV_A = \$200(2.402) - \$442 = \$480.40 - \$442 = \$38.40$, while $NPV_B = \$250(0.893) + \$575(0.797) + \$100(0.693) - \$718 = \$223.25 + \$458.28 + \$69.30 - \$718 = \$750.83 - \$718 = \$32.83$.

Because both projects have positive *NPVs*, both should be accepted. Notice that the net present value criterion says project A is preferable (because it has a larger *NPV*), whereas the payback criterion (from Table 7.1) indicates project B is preferred. If we were choosing between the two projects, the net present value would lead us to make the correct decision; the payback period would lead to an erroneous decision.

We can also graphically depict the capital budgeting decision using *NPV*. When a variety of rates are used to discount a project's cash flows, a present value profile can be constructed. For project A, employing various discount rates results in the following net present values:

Discount Rate	Net Present Value
0%	$158
5	103
10	55
15	15
20	−21
25	−52

Plotting these values produces the present value profile shown in Figure 7.2. The present value profile provides a pictorial representation of the sensitivity of *NPV* to the discount rate employed. The steeper the slope of the present value profile, the more sensitive the *NPV* is to the opportunity cost of capital employed.

Internal Rate of Return

A third decision criterion is the internal rate of return, *IRR*. It is the discount rate that equates the present value of the cash inflows with the initial investment. Stated differently, the *IRR* is *the rate that causes the net present value to equal zero*. The internal rate of return is found by solving for the unknown *IRR* in Equation 7.3:

FIGURE 7.2

Present Value Profile for Project A

A present value profile shows what happens to the *NPV* as the discount rate changes. The internal rate of return is the point at which the present value profile line intersects the horizontal axis (or discount rate).

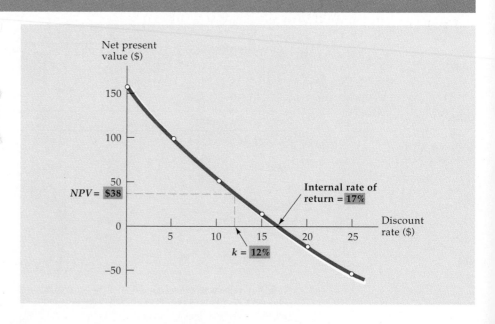

$$\sum_{t=1}^{n} \frac{CF_t}{(1 + IRR)^t} - CF_0 = 0, \text{ or } \sum_{t=1}^{n} \frac{CF_t}{(1 + IRR)^t} = CF_0 \qquad (7.3)$$

This internal rate of return for a project is then compared with the hurdle rate, k, which is the opportunity cost of capital. The internal rate of return decision rule is as follows:

1. If *IRR* is greater than k, accept.
2. If *IRR* is less than k, reject.
3. If *IRR* is equal to k, you are indifferent.

We discussed determining the internal rate of return in Chapter 3. As shown in Table 7.3, the calculated *IRR* for project A is 17 percent, whereas for project B it is 15 percent.[3] Because the hurdle rate is 12 percent, both projects would be accepted by this criterion.

Another way to think about the *IRR* can be seen by going back to the present value profile in Figure 7.2. The point where the present value profile intersects the horizontal axis is the internal rate of return on a project. As shown in Figure 7.2, the profile line intersects the horizontal axis at 17 percent.

Why *NPV* Is Preferred

■ **LEARNING GOAL 4**

Explain why net present value is the preferred capital budgeting method.

MULTIPLE INTERNAL RATES OF RETURN
Condition that may arise if there are nonsimple cash flows when calculating the internal rate of return.

SIMPLE CASH FLOW
A sequence of cash flows where there is only one change in sign and therefore a maximum of one (real) internal rate of return.

NONSIMPLE CASH FLOWS
A set of cash flows whose sign changes more than once and for which there may be an internal rate of return for every change in sign.

Surveys and discussions with firms indicate that the internal rate of return tends to be widely employed in practice, presumably because it is easier to understand than the *NPV* technique. For example, an *NPV* of $25 may not have the same intuitive appeal as an *IRR* of 18 percent. However, there are circumstances when employing the internal rate of return may lead to incorrect decisions that do not maximize the value of the firm. For this reason, net present value is the preferred capital investment decision criterion. To understand why this is so, it is necessary to consider two additional topics—multiple internal rates of return and ranking problems.

Multiple Internal Rates of Return

One problem that occasionally occurs when the *IRR* is calculated is that there may be more than one return. **Multiple internal rates of return** may occur when a nonsimple cash flow series occurs. A **simple cash flow** sequence occurs when there is an initial investment (which is negative) followed by a series of positive cash inflows:

Because there is only one change of sign, from negative to positive, there can be only one *IRR*.[4] A **nonsimple cash flow** series, however, has more than one change in the cash flow sign:

[3] *The* IRR *can be determined using a financial calculator, by trial-and-error, or using the graphical approach discussed in the next paragraph.*
[4] *Mathematically this is a result of Descartes' rule of signs, which implies that every time the sign of the cash flows change, there will be a maximum of one new real root.*

TABLE 7.3

Calculation of the Internal Rate of Return for Projects A and B

Because both projects have internal rates of return that exceed the hurdle rate, or opportunity cost of capital, of 12 percent, both would be selected.

Cash Flow Streams

Project A (an annuity)

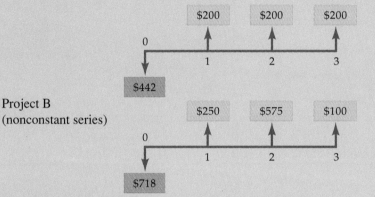

Project B
(nonconstant series)

Internal Rate of Return

Project A

$$\sum_{t=1}^{n} \frac{CF_t}{(1 + IRR)^t} - CF_0 = 0$$

$$\sum_{t=1}^{3} \frac{\$200}{(1 + IRR)^t} - \$442 = 0$$

The *IRR* is 16.988 ≈ 17 percent.

Project B

$$\frac{\$250}{(1 + IRR)^1} + \frac{\$575}{(1 + IRR)^2} + \frac{\$100}{(1 + IRR)^3} - \$718 = 0$$

The *IRR* is 14.993 ≈ 15 percent.

In this case, there are three changes in sign, and there may be three internal rates of return. *None is meaningful for decision making.* When there is more than one *IRR*, all of them are mathematically correct, but none of them make any financial sense. Graphically, a present value profile of this multiple-*IRR* problem with three sign changes might appear as follows:[5]

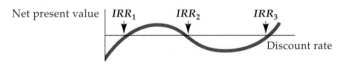

[5]The present value profile could have other shapes and still be consistent with three sign changes. For example, the profile could be just the opposite and still have three intersections with the discount rate line. Alternatively, it could also be tangent to (just touch) the discount rate line and then go back up (or down). Finally, it could turn back up (or down) before reaching the discount rate line, in which case the roots are imaginary.

Under these circumstances the *IRR* criterion is inappropriate for decision making, and the net present value approach should be used. Examples of projects producing non-simple cash flows are strip mining or forest harvesting, where after a section of land has been mined or harvested, an after-tax cash outlay is required to return the land to its original condition.

Ranking Problems

The net present value and internal rate of return always make the same accept-reject decision *for independent projects*.[6] However, when two (or more) mutually exclusive projects are considered, the firm can select only one. The project selected should contribute most to the value of the firm. Unfortunately, *IRR* and *NPV* do not always rank projects in the same order in terms of their economic desirability. Consider two projects, F and G, with cash flows as follows:

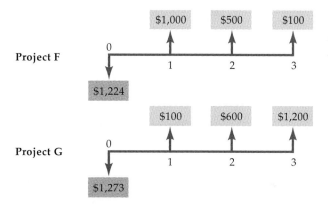

The net present values for these two projects at 11 percent are $156 for project F and $181 for project G. According to the *NPV* criterion, we should select project G. This is easy to see with *NPV* because if we select project F, we give up the opportunity to take project G. The opportunity cost associated with taking F instead of G is

$$NPV_{F-G} = \$156 - \$181 = -\$25$$

The internal rate of return for project F is 21 percent, whereas it is 17 percent for project G. According to the *IRR* criterion, we should select project F. Obviously, a conflict exists. We can calculate the net present values at various discount rates, as follows:

Discount Rate	Project F	Project G
0%	$376	$627
5	268	403
10	173	215
15	89	57
20	14	−79
25	−53	−195

We now have the data necessary to plot the projects' present value profiles in Figure 7.3. As shown in the figure, up to the crossover discount rate of 12.67 percent, the net present value of project G will be higher than the *NPV* of project F. Above 12.67 percent, however, the net present value of project F is greater than that of project G.

---

[6] *Excluding the possibility of multiple internal rates of return.*

FIGURE 7.3

Conflicting Rankings Between Net Present Value and Internal Rate of Return

Using *NPV,* the firm would select project G: however, project F has a higher *IRR.*

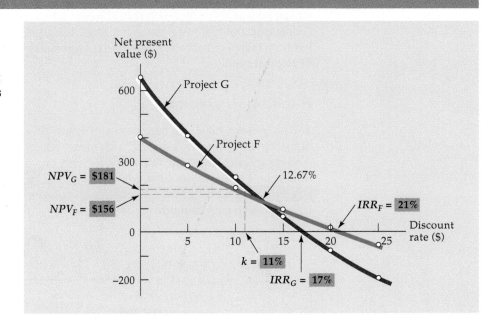

Conflicting rankings can occur with mutually exclusive projects under two conditions: (1) when the *size of the initial investment* for one project is considerably different than the initial investment for the other, and (2) when the *timing of the two projects' cash inflows* differs significantly. Looking at the cash flow streams for projects F and G, we see that the timing of their cash inflows does differ significantly.

The ultimate factor that causes the difference in rankings is the *implicit reinvestment* rate assumptions incorporated into the *NPV* and *IRR* formulas. The *NPV* method assumes that intermediate cash flows (those from years 1 and 2 for projects F and G) are reinvested at a rate equal to the discount rate employed. In our example the *implicit reinvestment* rate for the *NPV* method is the opportunity cost of capital of 11 percent for both projects. The *IRR* method assumes that these same intermediate cash flows can be reinvested at the project's internal rate of return. Under the *IRR* method, the implicit reinvestment rate assumption is 21 percent for project F and 17 percent for project G.

Which reinvestment rate assumption is better—the opportunity cost of capital in the *NPV* approach or the project's *IRR* in the internal rate of return method? The answer is the opportunity cost of capital because (1) it is a market-based rate that is the same across all projects of similar risk, (2) any project that returns more than it costs is contributing to the maximization of the long-run market value of the firm, and (3) it allows us to maximize dollars, not percentages.[7]

MODIFIED INTERNAL RATE OF RETURN, *MIRR*
The discount rate that equates the initial investment with a project's terminal value, where the terminal value is the compounded future value of the cash inflows.

Modified Internal Rate of Return

An attempt to "save" the internal rate of return has been proposed. This method computes an *IRR* with an *explicit* reinvestment rate assumption. It assumes that the intermediate cash inflows are reinvested at the opportunity cost of capital, *k,* not at the project's internal rate of return. This **modified internal rate of return, *MIRR,*** calls for the project's cash inflows to be compounded out to the end of the project's useful life

[7]*It is possible to reconcile the* NPV *and* IRR *approaches to capital budgeting decision making; see Chapter 7 in* Financial Management.

at k to obtain their future value, FV. Then the discount rate that equates this *future value* to the initial investment is determined. The modified internal rate of return is found by solving for the unknown $MIRR$ in Equation 7.4:

$$\frac{\sum_{t=1}^{n} CF_t(1+k)^{n-t}}{(1+MIRR)^n} - CF_0 = 0, \text{ or } \frac{\sum_{t=1}^{n} CF_t(1+k)^{n-t}}{(1+MIRR)^n} = CF_0 \qquad (7.4)$$

The calculations of $MIRR$ for projects F and G are shown in Table 7.4. With the required rate of return of 11 percent used as the explicit reinvestment rate, we see that project F has an $MIRR$ of 15.52 percent, whereas for project G it is 16.04 percent. Because these projects are mutually exclusive, we would choose the project with the higher $MIRR$—project G. This is the same choice made when these projects are evaluated by the NPV criterion.

Does this mean the $MIRR$ will *always* give the same result as NPV? The answer is "no." The $MIRR$ will select the same project as NPV *if the initial investments are of equal size*. In addition, $MIRR$ also overcomes the problem of multiple rates of return.[8] If the initial investments differ significantly in size, however, $MIRR$ may not rank the projects in the same order as NPV. For example, assume we are considering the following two mutually exclusive projects, D and E:

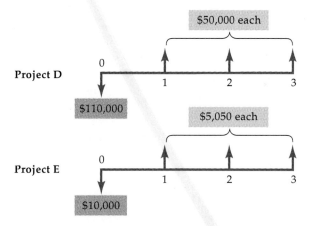

If the minimum opportunity cost of capital, k, is 14 percent, then

	Project	
	D	E
NPV (at 14%)	$6,082	$1,724
IRR	17.27%	24.04%

Using the net present value, we would select project D. Using the internal rate of return criterion, we would select project E. If a modified internal rate of return is calculated using 14 percent as the reinvestment rate, then we have

	Project D	Project E
Future value at $t = 3$	$171,980	$17,370
MIRR	16.06%	20.21%

[8] *This is accomplished because the* MIRR *approach allows any negative cash flow that occurs after* $t = 0$ *to retain its negative value when calculating the future value of the flows. If the sum of the individual future values is greater than zero, there will be only one* MIRR *for the project; however, if the future sum is less than zero, there is no real* MIRR *for the project.*

TABLE 7.4

Calculation of the Modified Internal Rate of Return for Projects F and G

With an opportunity cost of 11 percent, project G is chosen. For these two projects, this is the same project that was selected using *NPV*.

Project F

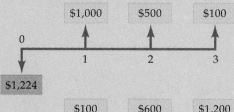

Project G

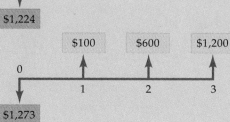

Modified Internal Rate of Return*

Project F

Future value of inflows:

$$FV_3 = \$1,000(1.11)^2 + \$500(1.11)^1 + \$100(1.11)^0$$
$$= \$1,232 + \$555 + \$100 = \$1,887$$

Calculation of MIRR:

$$\frac{\$1,887}{(1 + MIRR)^3} - \$1,224 = 0$$

The *MIRR* is 15.52 percent.

Project G

Future value of inflows:

$$FV_3 = \$100(1.11)^2 + \$600(1.11)^1 + \$1,200(1.11)^0$$
$$= \$123 + \$666 + \$1,200 = \$1,989$$

Calculation of MIRR:

$$\frac{\$1,989}{(1 + MIRR)^3} - \$1,273 = 0$$

The *MIRR* is 16.04 percent.

*If future value tables are employed FV_3 for project F is $1,000(1.232) + $500(1.110) + $100(1.000) = $1,232 + $555 + $100 = $1,887, while for project G, FV_3 = $100(1.232) + $600(1.110) + $1,200(1.000) = $123.20 + $666 + $1,200 = $1,989.20.

Based on *MIRR*, project E is still preferred to project D—the same conclusion reached with the *IRR* criterion and exactly opposite to the ranking provided by the *NPV* criterion. Thus, incorporation of an explicit reinvestment rate assumption for the *IRR* criterion *does not overcome the ranking problem associated with significant size disparities between projects*. Hence, the *MIRR* criterion only partially solves the ranking problem and may not lead a firm to select those projects with the highest net present value. The message is clear: Attempts to "save" the internal rate of return by modifying it do not erase the problems associated with *IRR*. Why not simply stick with net present value? It is easy to calculate and always provides the correct wealth-maximizing investment decision.

Are There Redeeming Qualities of Internal Rate of Return?

As indicated before, the internal rate of return is widely used. The primary redeeming quality of the internal rate of return is that the expected return on a project, such as a new plant, can be communicated to executives and the board of directors *in percentage terms*, such as "it provides an expected return of greater than 30 percent."

In practice, firms often require that the initial investment be negative and that all subsequent inflows be positive. Therefore, any possibility of multiple internal rates of return is avoided. Hence, firms act as if they understand some of the problems with internal rate of return. Over time there appears to have been some movement away from internal rate of return in practice. Our best guess is that its demise will be slow but continual, as the problems with internal rate of return are more widely known.

CONCEPT REVIEW QUESTIONS

- What are some of the advantages and disadvantages of using the payback period?
- Describe how you would use a project's internal rate of return when evaluating whether to accept or reject a project.
- What are some problems with the internal rate of return?
- Describe the steps performed when calculating the modified internal rate of return.

SOME COMPLICATIONS

A number of complications exist when making wealth-maximizing capital budgeting decisions. Two of these are how to deal with unequal lives and how to proceed when capital rationing exists.

Unequal Lives

■ **LEARNING GOAL 5**

Explain how firms evaluate capital budgeting projects with unequal lives.

Firms must often make a decision between two or more mutually exclusive projects that have unequal lives, where the projects (often machines) will continue to be replaced in the future. Consider the choice between purchasing two different sanding machines. Model A-3 is semi-automated, requires an initial investment of $320,000, and produces after-tax cash flows of $160,000 for each of 3 years, at which time it will have to be replaced. Model B-6 is an automated machine with a 6-year life, requires an initial investment of $420,000, and produces annual after-tax cash flows of $120,000. As Table 7.5 shows, at a 10 percent discount rate the net present value of the automated machine is greater. With an *NPV* of $102,631, it appears that Model B-6 should be chosen.

But the net present value is a function of the life of the project. Although this does not matter when projects are independent, it does matter when they are mutually exclusive and future replacement is expected (i.e., when it is *not* a one-shot investment). To make a valid comparison, it is necessary *to equalize the lives of the two projects.* There are a number of ways to do this. One is the **replacement chain** approach in which the lives are physically equalized. Under this procedure, the life of Model A-3 would have to be extended to equal that of Model B-6 as follows:

NPV for Model A-3 over 6 years = original 3-year *NPV* + second 3-year *NPV*

$$= \$77,896 + \$77,896/(1.10)^3 = \$136,420$$

Comparing this 6-year *NPV* for Model A-3 of $136,420 with the *NPV* of $102,631 for Model B-6, we see that the wealth-maximizing decision is to invest in Model A-3 and then reinvest in another Model A-3 in 3 more years. The replacement chain procedure works fine in this case, but what happens if the lives of the two projects are 7 years and 9 years? Then the analysis has to be taken out to 63 years, because that is the least common denominator of the lives of the two projects.

Due to potential problems of this type, we use the equivalent annual *NPV* method. The **equivalent annual *NPV*** approach to the unequal-life problem converts the original *NPVs* to yearly net present value figures. The effect is to assume the existing projects will be replicated over and over, with the result that the *NPV* can be stated as a yearly figure. The equivalent annual *NPV* is:

$$\text{equivalent annual } NPV = \frac{NPV_n}{\left[\dfrac{1}{k} - \dfrac{1}{k(1 + k)^n}\right]} \tag{7.5}$$

where

$$NPV_n = \text{the project's net present value over its original life}$$

$$\left[\frac{1}{k} - \frac{1}{k(1 + k)^n}\right] = \begin{array}{l}\text{the present value of an annuity based on the opportunity cost}\\\text{of capital and original life of the project}\end{array}$$

The equivalent annual *NPVs* for the two models are[9]

$$\text{Model A-3: } \frac{\$77,896}{\left[\dfrac{1}{0.10} - \dfrac{1}{0.10(1.10)^3}\right]} = \$31,323$$

$$\text{Model B-6: } \frac{\$102,631}{\left[\dfrac{1}{0.10} - \dfrac{1}{0.10(1.10)^6}\right]} = \$23,565$$

[9]*If present value tables are employed, the equivalent annual* NPV *for Model A-3 is $77,896/2.487 = $31,321, while for Model B-6 it is $102,631/4.355 = $23,566.*

REPLACEMENT CHAIN
Capital budgeting method for dealing with projects of unequal lives, in which the lives are physically equalized.

EQUIVALENT ANNUAL *NPV*
Capital budgeting method for dealing with projects of unequal lives, in which a yearly equivalent *NPV* is calculated.

TABLE 7.5

Net Present Value for Two Mutually Exclusive Projects, Ignoring Their Unequal Lives

Other things being equal, Model B-6 would be chosen because it has the higher *NPV*. However, because *NPV* is a function of the life of the project, it is necessary in mutually exclusive cases to adjust for differences in lives.

Cash Flow Streams

Model A-3

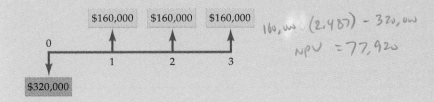

$160,000 (2.487) − 320,000
NPV = 77,920

Model B-6

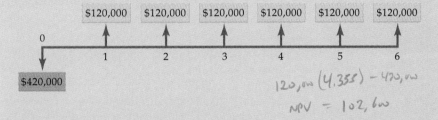

$120,000 (4.355) − 420,000
NPV = 102,600

Net Present Value*

Model A-3

$$NPV = \sum_{t=1}^{3} \frac{\$160,000}{(1.10)^t} - \$320,000$$

$$= \$397,896 - \$320,000 = \$77,896$$

Model B-6

$$NPV = \sum_{t=1}^{6} \frac{\$120,000}{(1.10)^t} - \$420,000$$

$$= \$522,631 - \$420,000 = \$102,631$$

*If present value tables are employed, $NPV_{A-3} = \$160,000(2.487) - \$320,000 = \$397,920 - \$320,000 = \$77,920$, while $NPV_{B-6} = \$120,000(4.355) - \$420,000 = \$522,600 - \$420,000 = \$102,600$.

Because Model A-3 has the higher equivalent annual *NPV, it contributes more to the firm's goal of maximizing the value of the firm per year.* Therefore, Model A-3 is preferable.

Two points should be stressed. First, managers and students sometimes get the impression that different lives have to be taken into account for *all* projects. This is not true: Unequal lives must be dealt with *only for mutually exclusive projects*. For all independent projects, the *NPV* criterion already takes into account timing differences. By selecting independent projects with the largest *NPV*, we are making the correct decision without having to adjust for unequal lives.

Second, neither the replacement chain nor the equivalent annual *NPV* approaches allows for differing rates of inflation or other changes (such as new technology). The best way to handle complications such as these is to build the effects of expected inflation, new technology, and so forth, into the cash flow estimates. Then the lives of the two projects will have to be equalized—perhaps by assuming some common termination point and considering the resale value at that point in time for each project. The *NPVs* for the two projects can then be calculated and compared.

Capital Rationing

■ **LEARNING GOAL 6**

Discuss how firms rank projects in cases of capital rationing.

CAPITAL RATIONING
A situation in which a constraint is placed on the funds available such that some wealth-maximizing projects cannot be accepted.

SOFT CAPITAL RATIONING
Capital rationing limits imposed by management as a financial control aid.

HARD CAPITAL RATIONING
Capital rationing limits caused by the inability to raise funds in the capital markets.

Unfortunately, all acceptable projects cannot always be undertaken. This is the case of **capital rationing**: a limit is placed on the size of the capital budget. It generally arises because of *internally imposed constraints* on the amount of external funds a firm will raise or because of dollar limits imposed on the capital expenditures that various divisions of firms can undertake. These can be thought of as **soft capital rationing** constraints; they are limits adopted by management. There exists another type of capital rationing—**hard capital rationing**—in which the firm cannot raise any more funds in the capital markets. Theoretically, hard capital rationing rarely, if ever, exists if the proposed project has a positive *NPV* because additional funds should be available (at some cost) to finance the project.

To see the effect of capital rationing, consider the following information on four independent proposed projects:

Project	CF_0	NPV
L	$10	$5
M	20	5
N	30	8
P	30	4

Without any capital rationing constraint, the value-maximizing decision is to accept all four projects. The initial cash outlay is $90, and the total *NPV* is $22. But, what occurs if a capital rationing constraint exists and only $30 is available? The objective is to maximize the total *NPV* up to the constraint. This can be accomplished by accepting projects L and M; the outlay is $30, and the total *NPV* is $10.

Capital rationing leads to suboptimal decisions because it does not allow the firm to attain its maximum value. It is another opportunity cost that reduces the value of the firm if positive *NPV* projects are bypassed. In the face of capital rationing, the goal is to *maximize the total net present value over all projects accepted*. If there are not too many projects, this can be accomplished by listing all feasible combinations (within the budget constraint) and then determining which combination has the largest total NPV.[10]

Remember Key Idea 3 again—individuals act in their own self-interest.

If capital rationing, especially soft capital rationing, is an opportunity cost and tends to reduce the value of the firm, why does it exist? One possibility is that in large firms the use of fixed (or relatively fixed) divisional allocations of capital is simply a means of imposing control on the activities of subordinates. One of the key ideas in finance is that individuals act in their own self-interest. Subordinates have a vested interest in proposing capital expenditure projects and having them accepted. Employees look good by doing so, and being a self-starter who produces results is one of the keys to promotion and financial well-being in many firms. Imposing capital limits on divisions may simply be one means of dealing with the tendency of employees to be overly optimistic or aggressive in proposing capital projects for inclusion on the firm's capital budget.

A second possibility is that soft capital rationing simply reflects that managers have large amounts of firm-specific human capital. That is, managers have both their reputation and their chances for advancement, as well as their financial livelihood, invested in the firm. With a great deal of their own wealth tied up in the firm, managers have incentives to manage the firm "conservatively" and, therefore, to reduce the firm's riskiness and any possibility of financial distress. Risk reduction can be accomplished by practicing *asset substitution*—that is, by accepting projects that have less total risk (or variability in their cash flows) than might be desirable. Managers may also have incentives to retain more cash in the firm and to employ less debt than might be optimal. These actions are simply another form of agency costs that arise due to differential interests between the firm's managers and its owners. Whatever the reasons, capital rationing tends to be practiced by many firms. As such, we need to be aware of possible reasons for and the consequences of capital rationing.

CONCEPT REVIEW QUESTIONS

■ What are two methods used to evaluate capital budgeting projects with unequal lives?
■ When using either the replacement chain or the equivalent annual NPV to compare projects of unequal lives, what assumptions are being made?
■ Define the terms "soft capital rationing" and "hard capital rationing."
■ Why does capital rationing exist?

Summary

■ Only by accepting positive net present value investment projects can the firm maximize its long-run market value.
■ Expansion projects result in the net addition of assets as the firm makes decisions that expand the scope of its activities; replacement decisions involve the consideration

PROFITABILITY INDEX, *PI*
A relative measure based on the present value of the future cash flows, discounted at the required rate of return, divided by the initial investment of the project.

[10]*An alternative selection criterion, the **profitability index,** is often recommended when a 1-period capital rationing constraint is considered. The profitability index is*

$$\text{profitability index} = \frac{\sum\limits_{t=1}^{n} \dfrac{CF_t}{(1+k)^t}}{CF_0}$$

Because the discounted after-tax operating and terminal cash flows are divided by the initial investment, CF_0, the profitability index is a relative measure of economic desirability. Projects are ranked from highest to lowest, and all those with PIs greater than 1.0 are selected up to the dollar limit. With a 1 period capital rationing constraint, this approach selects the best set of projects only if all the funds available for investment (up to the capital constraint) are expended. Because the total NPV approach is not affected by this problem, it is a more appropriate selection criterion.

of retaining existing assets or replacing them with other assets. When projects are independent of one another, all positive *NPV* projects should be taken in order to maximize the market value of the firm. However, when projects are mutually exclusive, accepting one automatically leads to the rejection of the other project(s).

■ In practice, the capital budgeting process has four phases: search for and identify growth opportunities; estimate the magnitude, timing, and riskiness of cash flows; select or reject projects; and evaluate performance through control procedures and post-completion audits. While all are important, we focus on the second and third steps.

■ Although the payback period is widely employed in practice, it is not economically justifiable; it does not account for the timing of the cash flows, and it does not account for expected cash flows that occur beyond the payback period.

■ Net present value, *NPV,* is the only decision criterion that always produces decisions consistent with the goal of maximizing the value of the firm. Despite its widespread use, the internal rate of return suffers from possible multiple internal rates of return and ranking problems.

■ The modified internal rate of return may provide an incorrect ranking of which mutually exclusive project to accept when projects require different initial investments.

■ When the lives of mutually exclusive projects are unequal, they must be equalized. The easiest way to accomplish this is by employing equivalent annual *NPVs.*

■ Under capital rationing, the firm should select the set of positive *NPV* projects that maximizes total *NPV* and stays within the budget constraint.

Questions

7.1 Trace the important relationships among the four phases of the capital budgeting process. Irrespective of Figure 7.1, indicate how all four phases could be related to one another.

7.2 Three decision criteria examined in this chapter were payback period, net present value, and internal rate of return. Why is the *NPV* an appropriate technique, whereas the payback period and *IRR* are not?

7.3 What does it mean when the *NPV* is zero? What decision should be made? What is the *IRR* when the *NPV* is zero?

7.4 Under what conditions do the *NPV* and *IRR* methods provide different rankings? Explain the cause of the difference.

7.5 Many firms calculate the equivalent annual *NPV* of mutually exclusive projects when making capital budgeting decisions. In what circumstances does or doesn't this approach lead to sensible investment decisions?

Concept Review Problems

See Appendix A for solutions.

CR7.1 M & O Railroad is considering purchasing one of two different types of locomotives. Both cost $500,000 and are expected to last for 3 years. Cash inflows from each of the locomotives are as follows:

Locomotive	CF_1	CF_2	CF_3
A	$350,000	$250,000	$ 80,000
B	0	0	800,000

What is the internal rate of return for each of the locomotives?

CR7.2 If M & O Railroad's opportunity cost of capital is 10 percent, what is the net present value of the two projects considered in CR7.1?

CR7.3 M & O Railroad is also considering a third project, project C, with the following cash flows:

CF_0	CF_1	CF_2	CF_3
−$500,000	$8,000,000	$8,000,000	−$20,000,000

What is the internal rate of return and the net present value of project C? Should the project be accepted?

CR7.4 Calculate the modified internal rate of return for projects A and B being considered by M & O Railroad in CR7.1.

CR7.5 Farmer Brown is planning to plant one of two types of alfalfa seed. The more expensive of the two will produce higher yields over a 3-year period. The projects are mutually exclusive, and the opportunity cost of capital is 12 percent. He has calculated the following after-tax net cash flows:

Year	Select Seed	Cheap Seed
0	−$4,000	−$840
1	3,000	630
2	2,000	630
3	1,000	420

Calculate each project's net present value, internal rate of return, and modified internal rate of return. Which type of alfalfa seed should Farmer Brown plant?

CR7.6 GreenCorp is considering two mutually exclusive pieces of machinery. One piece of machinery, A, has a 3-year life, and the other piece of machinery, B, has a 9-year life. The two alternatives provide the following after-tax cash flows:

Year	Machine A	Machine B
0	−$40,000	−$40,000
1	25,000	13,200
2	25,000	13,200
3	25,000	13,200
4		13,200
5		13,200
6		13,200
7		13,200
8		13,200
9		13,200

Using the replacement chain approach, which project should be accepted? Assume GreenCorp's opportunity cost of capital is 15 percent.

CR7.7 Using the equivalent annual net present value approach, evaluate both of the machines considered by GreenCorp in CR7.6.

CR7.8 Jankowski is considering 6 capital investment proposals, as follows:

Project	CF_0	CF_n	Years
A	$500	$175	4
B	1,000	350	4
C	200	50	6
D	150	40	7
E	200	100	3
F	150	42	6

Under a capital rationing constraint of $1,200, and assuming an opportunity cost of capital of 13 percent, in which projects should Jankowski invest?

Problems

See Appendix C for answers to selected problems.

Payback Versus NPV

7.1 Cash flow streams for two mutually exclusive projects are given below.

	After-Tax Cash Inflows	
Year	Project A	Project B
1	$300	$600
2	400	200
3	50	100
4	50	700

Project A requires an initial investment of $600, and project B requires an initial investment of $1,000.
a. Use the payback period to determine which project should be selected.
b. If the opportunity cost is 8 percent, determine the net present value for both projects.
c. Which project should be chosen? What are the drawbacks of the payback period method?

Present Value Profile

7.2 HH Productions is contemplating the acquisition of a new multiperson word processing system for $90,000. The system is expected to produce after-tax cash inflows of $25,800 for each of 5 years.
a. What is the net present value of the system if the discount rate is 0, 5, 10, 15, or 20 percent?
b. Graph the project's present value profile. What is the project's approximate *IRR*?

Internal Rate of Return

7.3 The initial cash outlay for a machine is $300,000. The expected after-tax cash inflows from the machine are $90,000, $104,400, $88,800, $84,000 and $82,800 in years 1 through 5, respectively. The machine has no anticipated resale value in 5 years. What is the project's internal rate of return, *IRR*?

NPV and *IRR*

7.4 Each of two mutually exclusive projects involves an investment of $120,000. The estimated *CF*s are as follows:

Year	X	Y
1	$70,000	$10,000
2	40,000	20,000
3	30,000	30,000
4	10,000	50,000
5	10,000	90,000

The opportunity cost is 11 percent. Calculate the *NPV* and *IRR* for both projects. Which project should be chosen? Why?

NPV and *IRR*

7.5 The projected cash flows from a project are as follows:

Year	After-Tax Cash Inflows
1	$1,000
2	1,300
3	2,000
4	2,500
5	1,400

a. If the opportunity cost is 16 percent, what is the maximum the firm can afford to invest in the project?
b. If the firm can actually implement the project by making an initial investment of $4,200, what is the project's internal rate of return?

NPV and IRR

7.6 Projects A and B both require a $20,000 initial investment and have projected cash inflows as follows:

	After-Tax Cash Inflows	
Year	Project A	Project B
1	$10,000	$7,000
2	8,000	7,000
3	6,000	7,000
4	4,000	7,000

a. Calculate each project's net present value if the opportunity cost is 12 percent.
b. Calculate the internal rate of return for each project.
c. Should either project be rejected if they are independent?
d. Which project should be selected if they are mutually exclusive?

Multiple Internal Rates of Return

7.7 A mining company can open a new strip mine for an initial investment of $24 million (at $t = 0$). In year 1, the mine produces a net cash inflow of $78 million. In year 2, the land must be returned to its original state, which requires an outflow of $60 million.

a. Find the net present values not calculated below.

Rate (%)	NPV (in millions)
0	$_____
25	_____
50	_____
75	0.980
100	0
125	−1.185

b. Construct a present value profile with the data from (a).
c. Should the mine be built if the hurdle rate is 20 percent?

Conflicting Rankings

7.8 Michael's Costumes is analyzing two mutually exclusive projects. Both require an initial investment of $65,000 and provide cash inflows as follows:

	After-Tax Cash Inflows	
Year	Project C	Project D
1	$40,000	0
2	30,000	0
3	20,000	$104,200

a. If the opportunity cost is 10 percent, which project would Michael's choose if NPV is employed?
b. Calculate the internal rate of return for both projects. Which project should be selected according to IRR? Why does the difference in rankings occur?

IRR, Indifferent Discount Rate, and MIRR

7.9 Sacks Industries is considering two mutually exclusive projects, each with a 5-year life. Project P requires an initial investment, CF_0, of $20,000 and has CFs of $6,541.00 for each of 5 years. Project Q has an initial investment of $100,000 and CFs of $29,831.56 for each of 5 years.

a. Calculate the IRR for each project, and select the preferred project.
b. Assuming the projects are of equal risk and the opportunity cost is 13 percent, which project is preferable? Defend your answer.
c. At what specific discount rate would the firm be indifferent between the two projects?
d. Calculate the MIRR for each project, and select the preferred project. Has the use of MIRR given the same choice as NPV? Explain.

Unequal Lives

7.10 Consider a firm in need of a stamping machine. It can buy a one-speed machine that requires an initial investment of $350 and produces after-tax cash inflows of $300 for each of 2 years, or it can purchase a three-speed machine that costs $1,200 and produces cash inflows of $500 for each of 4 years. Neither machine has any resale value, and the opportunity cost is 16 percent. Which machine should be purchased?

Unequal Lives

7.11 Either of two new molding machines that makes drinking glasses requires an initial investment of $2,000. Model 3SR produces short glasses and has a 5-year life. Model 3TR produces tall glasses and has a 9-year life. *CFs* expected from the purchase of model 3SR and model 3TR are $700 and $500 per year, respectively. If the opportunity cost is 13 percent and there is no resale value, which model should be purchased?

Mutually Exclusive: *IRR* and *NPV*

7.12 Arrowhead Associates is contemplating replacing its existing boiler, which is worn out and has no resale value. One of two boilers will be chosen; both offer increased operating efficiency. The after-tax cash flows are as follows:

Year	Short-Life Boiler	Long-Life Boiler
Initial investment	$5,000	$8,000
1	2,500	2,750
2	2,500	2,750
3	2,500	2,750
4		2,750
5		2,750

a. Calculate the internal rate of return and net present value for both boilers over their original lives. The appropriate opportunity cost is 18 percent.
b. Which boiler should be chosen? Why?

Capital Rationing

7.13 Terra Products has the following independent investments under examination:

Project	Initial Investment	After-Tax Cash Flow per Year	Life of the Project (in years)
A	$100,000	$39,000	4
B	50,000	12,000	6
C	80,000	39,000	3
D	60,000	15,000	7
E	75,000	25,000	5
F	90,000	25,000	6

Terra Products' opportunity cost of capital is 14 percent.
a. In the absence of capital rationing, which projects should be selected? What is the size (in total dollars) of the capital budget? The total *NPV* of all of the projects selected?
b. Now suppose that a limit of $250,000 (maximum) is placed on new capital projects. Which projects should be selected?
c. What is the total *NPV* determined in (b)? What is the loss to Terra Products due to the capital rationing constraint?

Capital Budgeting and Selection Criteria

7.14 **Mini Case** Harris Manufacturing is expanding into producing see-through bottle caps. The relevant data has been estimated as follows: The initial cash outlay is $44,000, and the after-tax cash inflows are $14,800, $16,480, $14,660, $14,100 and $25,960 in years 1 through 5, respectively.
a. What is the purpose of capital budgeting? How does it relate to the firm's objective?

b. Assuming the opportunity cost of capital is 15 percent, calculate the payback period, net present value, and internal rate of return. Should the project be accepted?

c. Instead of the machine outlined above, a second machine that requires substantially less investment but has higher operating cash outflows could be employed to produce the see-through bottle caps. The estimated after-tax cash flows for the second machine are as follows: CF_0, −$11,000; CF_1, $7,000; CF_{2-5}, $5,000 each. Calculate the payback period, net present value, and internal rate of return for this second alternative. Which machine—the first or second—should be selected? Does a ranking problem exist?

d. Why is the net present value the preferred decision criterion for making capital investment decisions while the internal rate of return is not?

e. One of the firm's managers has heard of the modified *IRR* criterion, but does not understand it completely. Explain it to the manager. Then calculate modified *IRR*s for the two alternatives. Does the modified *IRR* lead to the correct decision in this case? In all cases?

f. Your boss is continually lamenting that many profitable capital budgeting projects have to be turned down because funds are not available. How would you make your boss understand that from a financial standpoint funds are not limited and can always be secured for good projects? What causes your boss, and many managers, to argue that funds are limited?

CHAPTER 8

Capital Budgeting Applications

Sections in this chapter:

- **Estimating Cash Flows**
  Getting the cash right.
- **Expansion Projects**
  Deciding whether to expand.
- **Replacement Decisions**
  The importance of increments.
- **More on Cash Flow Estimation**
  Trouble spots in capital budgeting.

Firms make all kinds of capital investments. For instance, Pulsaski Furniture recently poured $10 million into a new computerized manufacturing facility. They expect the plant to use 35 percent less labor and boost sales by $40 million. Likewise, Timken invested $500 million to build a superclean steel mill. Timken needed better-quality steel for its tapered roller bearings—the antifriction devices it invented—to ward off Japanese competitors. Timken made that investment while experiencing one of its worst periods ever, but the alternative was to lose an increasingly large portion of its business to the Japanese.

There are other ways to make capital investments. Research and development (R&D), while not capitalized on a firm's balance sheet, is like any other capital investment. And with shrinking budget increases, firms are adjusting in new ways: ditching marginal projects, decentralizing R&D efforts, creating teams to rush project ideas from lab to market, and collaborating with outside experts (e.g., other firms, consortiums, universities, or government labs). Another type of capital investment decision involves the purchase, in whole or part, of another firm. When all of the hype and emotion is put aside, a merger is simply one way, but often not the most effective way, of moving into a new area. Unfortunately, what often looks before the fact to be a promising merger turns out to cost far more and have far fewer benefits than expected.

In Chapter 7 we ignored how to estimate the expected costs and benefits from proposed capital investments. However, this *step* is actually one of the most important in the capital budgeting process. At the same time, dealing with unforeseen contingencies, anticipating changes in demand, and dealing with competitor actions and reactions are also vitally important. An important fact of life that must be considered when making capital investment decisions is inflation or disinflation. When prices can be raised to pass increased costs on to consumers, many capital expenditures look desirable; but when prices cannot be raised, other strategies often come into play. As one CEO observed, "Increased productivity and new products are the key ways to keep profits up in times of disinflation. New products help market penetration. And new products generally have a higher profit margin, at least in the early growth stages before pricing becomes competitive."

LEARNING GOALS

After studying this chapter you should be able to:

1. Explain the impact of taxes on capital budgeting, and describe the three relevant cash flow segments.
2. Determine relevant cash flows for expansion projects.
3. Determine relevant cash flows for replacement projects.
4. Discuss hard-to-handle costs and benefits, and how firms should proceed.
5. Explain how inflation affects cash flow estimates.
6. Explain why financial costs are not considered in the capital budgeting decision.
7. Determine relevant cash flows for interrelated projects.

ESTIMATING CASH FLOWS

■ LEARNING GOAL 1

Explain the impact of taxes on capital budgeting, and describe the three relevant cash flow segments.

DEPRECIATION
The writing off of the original cost of an asset over the normal recovery period for tax purposes.

To estimate the relevant cash flows for making capital budgeting decisions, you must understand how corporations treat **depreciation** and taxes under the Internal Revenue Service Code. In accounting, depreciation is employed in order to better match revenue with its associated expense; however, *in finance you are not concerned with depreciation as typically used by accountants.* Rather, the depreciation you are concerned with is the depreciation, or charge, for using equipment as allowed by the Internal Revenue Service, IRS, when a firm determines its taxable income. Do not be led astray by what is used for generally accepted accounting principle, GAAP, purposes. Only what firms do as required by the IRS is important when making capital budgeting decisions—because it directly affects the taxes paid and hence the cash flows of the firm.

Depreciation and Tax Assumptions

In this chapter we focus primarily on Key Idea 4— firms focus on cash flows and their incremental effects.

Numerous complications are introduced by the government due both to the way depreciation is determined for tax purposes and the complications of the tax system. Some of the complexities are covered in Appendix 8A. The major depreciation and tax assumptions employed in this text for capital budgeting purposes are summarized in Table 8.1. *The major simplifications that are made in this book (both in the discussion that follows and in all of the problems) are fourfold.* First, accelerated depreciation is ignored; only straight-line depreciation is employed throughout. Second, the half-year convention employed by the IRS in determining depreciation is ignored. As discussed in Appendix 8A, the half-year convention means that all real assets, except

TABLE 8.1

Major Depreciation and Tax Assumptions

Although there are many more complexities, these are the basic ideas used in this book for capital budgeting.

Category	Item	Assumption
Depreciation	Method	Straight-line over the normal recovery period, ignoring the half-year convention
	Life	3, 5, 7, 10, 15, or 20 years
	Resale value	Not relevant under tax code when calculating depreciation
	Real estate	Not dealt with
Corporate taxes	Marginal corporate tax rate	30 to 40%
	Tax loss	Direct reduction in tax liability (assumes firm as a whole is profitable)
	Firm in loss position	No taxes paid
	Carryback or carry-forward of losses	Ignored
	Tax payment date	Tax paid or credit received immediately; at time t_0

real estate, are assumed to be purchased halfway through the year. Third, all assets will be depreciated over 3, 5, 7, 10, 15, or 20 years as required by the Internal Revenue Service. (Note that other depreciation periods are not allowed for tax purposes, and we are only concerned with depreciation as specified by the IRS for tax purposes.) Finally, the progressive nature of the corporate tax code (as discussed in Appendix 8A) is also ignored. The intent of these simplifications, and others contained in Table 8.1, is to allow us to focus on financial management, not on taxes.

There is one other point that needs to be emphasized when making the transition from what you have been exposed to in accounting to what is needed in financial management. This relates to what is typically referred to as "salvage value" in accounting. If you purchase a piece of equipment that costs $10,000, will be depreciated using straight-line depreciation, has a 5-year useful life, and has an estimated salvage value of $2,000, in your financial accounting class you would subtract the salvage value from the original purchase price and determine the per year depreciation to be ($10,000 − $2,000)/5 = $1,600. However (as discussed in Appendix 8A), for income tax purposes, *the IRS assumes that all assets are depreciated to zero over their "normal recovery period."* If the asset in question has a 5-year normal recovery period, then the IRS assumes the asset is depreciated to zero over this period. The relevant amount of depreciation per year for financial management purposes is $10,000/5 = $2,000.[1] Keeping this in mind is important as you proceed.

[1] *As discussed earlier, we are ignoring the half-year convention employed by the IRS, and using straight-line depreciation.*

The Relevant Cash Flows

The appropriate cash flows are the incremental cash flows, including opportunity costs, that occur only as a result of accepting the project. Any cash flows that occur whether or not the project is accepted are irrelevant.

Three points should be mentioned in connection with estimating cash flows: First, we are interested in cash flows (both inflows and outflows) as stated on an *after-tax basis*. Because taxes are an important determinant of cash flows, we are interested in looking at cash flows after all taxes have been taken into account. These are called cash flows after tax, *CF*, to distinguish them from cash flows before tax, *CFBT*. Second, we must guard against carelessly counting costs or benefits that should not be considered. A classic example is the treatment by accountants of certain overhead costs. If these overhead costs are fixed and their total amount does not change as a result of implementing a project, they do not affect the cash flows and are irrelevant for decision-making purposes. Finally, it is helpful to divide the cash flow stream into three segments:

1. The *initial investment* is the net after-tax cash outflow that typically occurs at the start of the project under consideration (i.e., at time $t = 0$).
2. The *operating cash flows* are the relevant net after-tax cash flows expected over the economic life of the project.
3. The *terminal cash flow* is the net after-tax inflow or outflow that occurs when the project is terminated.

CONCEPT REVIEW QUESTIONS

■ Why is it important to focus on depreciation as required by the Internal Revenue Service when estimating the cash flows for capital budgeting decision making?
■ What three major segments should be considered when estimating a firm's cash flows?

EXPANSION PROJECTS

■ **LEARNING GOAL 2**

Determine relevant cash flows for expansion projects.

First we will consider the cash flow stream for a simple decision in which the firm is expanding, not replacing, existing assets. Then we will consider the relevant incremental cash flows for replacement decisions.

The Initial Investment

INITIAL INVESTMENT, CF_0
The net after-tax outflow associated with a capital budgeting project to get it started.

NET WORKING CAPITAL
Current assets minus current liabilities.

The **initial investment, CF_0,** is the initial cash cost to start the project. More specifically, it is the net after-tax cash flow that occurs at time zero. For an expansion project, it is calculated as follows:

1. Cost of equipment, facilities, and land purchased.
2. All other costs related to the investment (transportation, installation, additional personnel, training expenses, and so forth, net of taxes).
3. Additional **net working capital** required.[2]

[2]*Often a project requires an increase in accounts receivable or inventory, say by $300,000, while at the same time causing a spontaneous increase in accounts payable of, perhaps, $100,000. The additional net working capital attributable to the project would be $200,000. At the end of the project the additional capital may no longer be needed; accordingly the cash tied up in net working capital is then freed.*

4. Opportunity costs, net of taxes (e.g., land used for this project that could have been sold).

Although the initial investment in many complex projects is spread over a number of years, for simplicity we treat it as occurring at the present ($t = 0$). When after-tax cash outflows occur beyond $t = 0$, they are treated like other CFs, except that a negative sign is used to indicate that the amount is flowing out (and not in).

Operating Cash Flows

OPERATING CASH FLOWS, *CFs*
Cash flows, after taxes, that are expected to occur over the economic life of a capital budgeting project.

The second part of the cash flow stream, **operating cash flows, *CFs*,** are the net cash flows that occur while the asset is in operation. They begin in year 1 and continue throughout the project's useful life. These operating cash flows are typically positive, although there may be occasional years when the outflows are greater than the inflows. Operating cash flows are calculated by taking the difference in the cash inflows minus the cash outflows; the result is the cash flow before tax, *CFBT*, attributable to the proposed project. IRS depreciation then enters into the picture, because it is a deductible expense for tax purposes and serves to reduce taxes.

When we are considering cash flows, only cash expenses are subtracted directly. However, when we calculate the tax liability, depreciation must be considered because of its impact on taxes paid.

To illustrate the calculation of operating cash flows for an expansion project, consider Warner Manufacturing, a firm that is in the process of evaluating a new $1,800,000 project. The firm estimates the project's annual before-tax cash inflows and outflows will be $5,000,000 and $4,000,000, respectively, for each of 3 years. Furthermore, assume that the firm employs straight-line depreciation and that the equipment falls into the 3-year class. Ignoring the half-year convention employed by the IRS, the depreciation is $600,000 in each of years 1, 2, and 3. The firm's marginal tax rate is 40 percent. Consequently, the firm will incur $160,000 [i.e., ($5,000,000 − $4,000,000 − $600,000)(0.40)] in taxes in each of years 1, 2 and 3. One method of calculating the annual after-tax operating cash flows for the project is:

$$\text{operating } CF_t = (\text{cash inflows}_t - \text{cash outflows}_t) - \text{taxes}_t$$
$$= CFBT_t - \text{taxes}_t \tag{8.1}$$

CASH FLOW BEFORE TAX, *CFBT*
Cash inflows minus cash outflows.

where $CFBT_t$ is the **cash flow before tax, *CFBT*.** Applying this to Warner we have

$$\text{operating } CF_t = (\$5,000,000 - \$4,000,000) - \$160,000 = \$840,000$$

An alternative way of stating Equation 8.1 highlights the **tax shield** that depreciation provides. By tax shield, we mean that the presence of depreciation reduces (or shields) profitable firms from paying as much tax as they would without depreciation. This alternative presentation recognizes that:

TAX SHIELD
The reduction in income taxes paid by a firm because the IRS allows depreciation (a noncash expense) to be written off as an expense.

$$\text{taxes}_t = (CFBT_t - Dep_t)T \tag{8.2}$$

where T is the firm's marginal tax rate. Substituting Equation 8.2 into Equation 8.1 we get:

$$\text{operating } CF_t = CFBT_t - (CFBT_t - Dep_t)T$$
$$= CFBT_t - CFBT_t(T) + Dep_t(T)$$
$$= CFBT_t(1 - T) + Dep_t(T) \tag{8.3}$$

1,000,000 (.60) + 600,000 (.40)
600,000   + 240,000   = 840,000

The second part of Equation 8.3—that is, $Dep_t(T)$—is the depreciation tax shield. Because depreciation is a tax-deductible expense, even though no cash outflow occurs at the time of the depreciation charge, the presence of depreciation allows firms to reduce their income taxes. That is, they receive a "tax shield" due to depreciation. Equation 8.3 can be employed directly to calculate the **cash flows after tax, CF**. Applying it to Warner we have

$$\text{operating } CF_t = (\$5,000,000 - \$4,000,000)(1 - 0.40) + \$600,000(0.40)$$
$$= \$1,000,000(0.60) + \$600,000(0.40)$$
$$= \$600,000 + \$240,000 = \$840,000$$

We employ Equation 8.3 throughout.

In calculating depreciation, remember that land cannot be depreciated and that all other assets are depreciated to zero for tax purposes under the Internal Revenue Service Code. Finally, sometimes there are opportunity costs that have to be considered as part of the operating cash flows.

Depreciable Life Versus Economic Life

Under the tax code, the **depreciable lives,** as specified by the IRS normal recovery periods, have been shortened for virtually all assets. The result is that the normal recovery period is generally less than the asset's **economic life,** the amount of time it will be economically useful. In such a case, cash inflows and outflows may occur every year, whereas the effects on the operating CF from depreciation will occur only in the early years of the project's life.

Consider the example of Sunbelt Industries, which is contemplating the purchase of a new machine with a 5-year tax life, or normal recovery period, but with a 10-year economic life. If the machine costs $200,000; cash flow before tax, $CFBT$, is $50,000 for each of 10 years; and the tax rate is 35 percent, then the straight-line depreciation and operating cash flow stream are as shown in Table 8.2. Notice that because depreciation occurs only in the first 5 years, the cash flows in the early years are greater than in the later ones.

Opportunity Costs

Opportunity costs also have to be considered. For example, suppose a firm is analyzing a project that would employ warehouse space currently being rented out for $4,800 a year. If the company decides to expand, it loses the benefit of $4,800 per year in rental income. If the firm has a marginal tax rate of 40 percent, the loss in after-tax cash inflows of $2,880 [i.e., $4,800(1 − 0.40)] is an opportunity cost, and it must be deducted from each year's operating cash flows. Similarly, if an auto maker decides to market a new model, sales of the firm's other models may decline. The decline in after-tax cash inflows due to reduced sales of the other models is an opportunity cost of the new model.

Sunk Costs

Equally important is the notion of **sunk costs,** that is, cash outflows that have already been incurred and therefore do not affect the decision. For example, suppose a firm spent $200,000 2 years ago for a detailed feasibility study by some consultants about

CASH FLOW AFTER TAX, CF
Cash flow before tax minus tax ($CFBT$ − tax); or cash flow before tax times 1 minus the marginal tax rate, plus depreciation for tax purposes times the marginal tax rate [$CFBT(1 − T) + Dep(T)$].

DEPRECIABLE LIFE
An asset's normal recovery period specified by the IRS for tax purposes.

ECONOMIC LIFE
The length of time an asset will be economically useful.

SUNK COSTS
Cash outflows that have already been incurred and therefore do not affect the capital budgeting decision.

TABLE 8.2

Depreciation and Operating Cash Flows for Sunbelt Industries

The approach used to calculate the operating cash flows highlights the importance of the depreciation tax shield.

Depreciation

Year	Original Cost	×	Straight-Line Depreciation Factor	=	Depreciation
1	$200,000		0.20		$40,000
2	200,000		0.20		40,000
3	200,000		0.20		40,000
4	200,000		0.20		40,000
5	200,000		0.20		40,000

Operating Cash Flows

Year	CFBT	CFBT(1 − T)*	+	Dep(T)*	=	CF
1–5	$50,000	$32,500		$14,000		$46,500
6–10	50,000	32,500		0		32,500

* The tax rate equals 35 percent.

In making capital budgeting decisions we ignore allocated overhead (money that would be spent anyway) and sunk costs (money already spent).

the possibility of doubling the size of the firm's present physical plant. No action was taken then, but now the firm is reassessing the project. Should the $200,000 be included as a cash outflow of the project for capital budgeting purposes? The answer is "no." *Sunk costs should be ignored*; they are not incremental cash flows that are relevant for decision making.

Terminal Cash Flow

TERMINAL CASH FLOW
The net after-tax cash inflow or outflow that occurs when a capital budgeting project is terminated.

Terminal cash flows are the net after-tax cash flows other than the operating cash flows that occur in the last year of the project's life. For an expansion project, they are calculated as:

1. Funds realized from the sale of the asset plus a tax benefit if it is expected to be sold at a loss, or minus a tax liability if it is expected to be sold at a gain.[3]
2. Release of net working capital
         minus
3. Disposal costs (net of taxes).

The terminal cash flow is typically positive, but it may be negative.

An Expansion Project Example

To refine our understanding of the capital budgeting process, consider an expansion project. Ideal Industries is contemplating the purchase of special equipment with a total

[3]*Assuming the firm is profitable.*

cost of $120,000 to increase the efficiency of its production force. The equipment will be depreciated via straight-line to zero over its 3-year normal recovery period; at that time Ideal estimates the equipment will have a resale value of $15,000. The cash inflows and cash outflows are $70,000 and $20,000 per year, respectively. The firm's marginal tax rate is 30 percent, and the opportunity cost of capital is 14 percent.

The initial cash outflow is $120,000 while the operating cash flows for each of years 1 through 3 are $47,000, as shown in Table 8.3. Because all equipment is depreciated to zero for tax purposes and the estimated resale value in 3 years is $15,000, Ideal must pay taxes on the $15,000. At a rate of 30 percent the taxes are $4,500, resulting in a net terminal cash inflow of $10,500.

When projecting future cash flows, one of the most common errors is to forget what other firms will be doing. If positive NPV projects exist, more and more competitors will enter the industry until the positive NPVs are eliminated.

Finally, the net present value is calculated. As shown in Table 8.3 it is −$3,796. Because the net present value is negative, Ideal Industries should not proceed with the acquisition of the special equipment. If they proceed, the value of Ideal Industries would decrease. Think of a firm as a portfolio of projects: The value of the firm is equal to the sum of the project *NPV*s. Acceptance of positive *NPV* projects increases the value of the firm, while acceptance of negative projects decreases the value of the firm. Ideal is contributing to the maximization of its value by rejecting the project. Expansion projects can be either simple or very complex. The analysis of a merger from the standpoint of the potential acquiring firm is another expansion-type capital budgeting decision. This topic is considered in Appendix 8B.

TABLE 8.3

Calculation of the After-Tax Cash Flow Stream and Net Present Value for an Expansion Project

This approach emphasizes the operating cash flows as being equal to $CFBT(1 - T) + Dep(T)$.

Initial Investment

Cost of equipment, $CF_0 = \$120,000$

Operating Cash Flows

Year	Cash Inflows	−	Cash Outflows	=	CFBT	$CFBT \times (1 - T)^*$	+	$Dep\ (T)^*$	=	CF
1	$70,000		$20,000		$50,000	$35,000		($40,000)(0.30) = $12,000		$47,000
2	70,000		20,000		50,000	35,000		(40,000)(0.30) = 12,000		47,000
3	70,000		20,000		50,000	35,000		(40,000)(0.30) = 12,000		47,000

Terminal Cash Flow

Estimated resale value	$15,000
Less: Tax on sale	4,500
Net terminal cash inflow	$10,500

Net Present Value†

$$NPV = \frac{\$47,000}{(1.14)^1} + \frac{\$47,000}{(1.14)^2} + \frac{\$47,000 + \$10,500}{(1.14)^3} - \$120,000$$

$$= \$41,228 + \$36,165 + \$38,811 - \$120,000 = -\$3,796$$

* The tax rate is 30 percent.
† If present value tables are employed the *NPV* is $47,000(0.877) + $47,000(0.769) + $57,500(0.675) − $120,000 = $41,219 + $36,143 + $38,812 − $120,000 = −$3,826.

CONCEPT REVIEW QUESTIONS

- ■ Briefly describe how to calculate a project's initial investment.
- ■ How are operating cash flows calculated?
- ■ How do opportunity costs and sunk costs affect a firm's cash flows?

REPLACEMENT DECISIONS

■ LEARNING GOAL 3

Determine relevant cash flows for replacement projects.

Replacing assets is often necessary. Determining the cash flows for a replacement project can be complicated. These are *incremental cash flows*—that is, the cash flows related to the new equipment less the cash flows for the old equipment. Although the idea seems straightforward, it is fundamental to effective capital investment decision making.

Incremental Cash Flows

Consider Bits & Bytes, a computer software firm that produces a popular computer game called Spacelords. The firm estimated after-tax operating cash flows, *CFs*, over a 3-year period as follows:

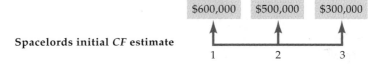

Spacelords initial *CF* estimate

The estimated cash flows decline due to an anticipated increase in competition and the development of more complicated and challenging games. Bits & Bytes planned, therefore, to withdraw Spacelords from the market after 3 years.

Recently, Bits & Bytes came up with a new computer game called Rampagers. Although similar to Spacelords, Rampagers has many features that make it more challenging. The estimated initial investment and subsequent cash inflows were estimated as follows:

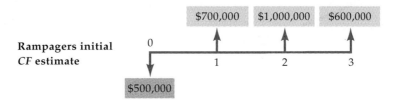

Rampagers initial
CF estimate

Given the favorable cash flow estimates, Bits & Bytes developed and is now marketing Rampagers. All indications are that the projected *CFs* appear accurate, but a strange thing is happening—Spacelords' sales have fallen off dramatically. What did Bits & Bytes forget to consider when it developed the after-tax *CF* estimates for Rampagers?

The answer should not surprise you. The two games have overlapping markets, with the result that the products are viewed as being partial *substitutes* for each other. Instead of buying Spacelords, many would-be purchasers are now acquiring

Rampagers. As a result, the cash flows from Spacelords have declined sharply. The newly revised cash flows for Spacelords are

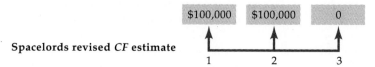

Spacelords revised *CF* estimate

Some projects can "cannibalize" existing projects. For example, the introduction of "improved" or "large size" products will likely reduce the cash flows from existing products. Reduction in cash flows from existing products must be considered in the decision process.

The problem arose because in making the initial estimate of the *CFs* attributed to Rampagers, Bits & Bytes did not properly evaluate the incremental cash flows. *It is the incremental (denoted by a delta, Δ) cash flows that are important.* The relevant incremental operating cash flow stream, ΔCF, that Bits & Bytes should have considered before introducing Rampagers is calculated as follows:

	Year		
	1	2	3
Original *CFs*, Rampagers	$700,000	$1,000,000	$600,000
Less: Decrease in *CFs*, Spacelords	500,000	400,000	300,000
Incremental (Δ) operating *CFs*	$200,000	$600,000	$300,000

Based on this more complete analysis, the incremental cash flow stream for the new product should have been estimated as follows:

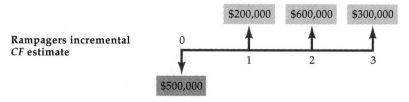

Rampagers incremental *CF* estimate

Even with this revised set of after-tax *CFs*, the *NPV* (at any reasonable discount rate) is positive, so Bits & Bytes should still come out ahead on its investment. But the message is clear: *To make effective investment decisions, managers must focus on the incremental cash flow stream.* This involves an analysis of the cash inflows and outflows related to the new investment, minus the anticipated inflows and outflows associated with an existing investment.

Often it is important to ask, "What will happen to the existing (or anticipated) cash flows if we do not make the investment?" In today's highly competitive and rapidly changing environment, managers cannot simply assume that existing cash flows will continue. Price cutting, product or marketing innovations, and the like can undermine a profitable investment. For this reason, managers need to know what to look for when calculating incremental cash flows.

As Lee Iacocca, former CEO of Chrysler, stated in a television ad, "You either lead, follow, or get out of the way." In today's business world if you stand still, the competition will surely run you over.

Estimating Incremental Cash Flows for Replacement Decisions

To calculate incremental after-tax cash flows, we proceed by breaking them into three parts, as we did for expansion decisions—initial investment, operating cash flow, and terminal cash flow. We make our capital budgeting decision by *focusing on the difference between the new and the existing cash flows.* Any other cash flow stream is erroneous and may lead to incorrect replacement decisions.

The Initial Investment

The incremental initial investment, ΔCF_0, is calculated as follows:[4]

1. Cost of new equipment, facilities, and land purchased.
2. All other costs related to the investment (transportation, installation, additional personnel, and so forth, ~~net of taxes~~).
3. Additional net working capital required.
4. Opportunity costs, net of taxes

             minus

5. Funds realized from the sale of replaced assets plus tax benefit if it is expected to be sold at a loss, or minus tax liability if it is expected to be sold at a gain.

Be careful in estimating the after-cash proceeds from selling the old equipment; tax consequences are normally present and cannot be ignored.

As with expansion projects, we assume the initial investment occurs at time $t = 0$; in practice, however, it may be spread out over a number of time periods.

Operating Cash Flows

The incremental operating after-tax cash flow, ΔCF, must take into consideration the difference in the cash flows before tax, $CFBT$, for both the new and the old projects, as well as the depreciation for tax purposes on both the new and the old assets. To calculate the incremental operating cash flows, we have the following:

$$\text{incremental operating } CF = (CFBT_{t\,new} - CFBT_{t\,old})(1 - T)$$
$$+ (Dep_{t\,new} - Dep_{t\,old})(T)$$
$$\Delta CF_t = \Delta CFBT_t(1 - T) + \Delta Dep_t(T) \qquad (8.4)$$

The first term, $\Delta CFBT(1 - T)$, is the change in the cash flows expected, ignoring the tax shield due to depreciation. The net effect on the tax shield is captured in the second term, $\Delta Dep(T)$. As we saw in the Bits & Bytes example, it is especially important to consider the exact nature of the cash flow before tax, $CFBT$, stream expected from the old (or existing) asset. Often a good deal of interchange between the marketing department, the production department, and the capital budgeting group will be required to arrive at reasonable estimates of both the new and the old $CFBT$ streams. In addition, opportunity costs must also be considered.

Terminal Cash Flow

Finally, we need to estimate the incremental after-tax terminal cash flow that occurs in the last year of the replacement project's life. The incremental terminal after-tax cash flow, ΔCF_n, is calculated as follows:

1. Funds realized from the sale of the new asset plus tax benefit if it is expected to be sold at a loss, or minus tax liability if it is expected to be sold at a gain.
2. Release of net working capital (assuming the project will be terminated at time period n)

             minus

3. Disposal costs for the new asset (less any disposal costs on the old asset, if any, net of taxes).

[4] *In calculating the initial, operating, and terminal incremental cash flows, we assume that the firm is profitable and, therefore, taxes are relevant.*

4. Funds realized from the sale of the replaced asset plus tax benefit if it is expected to be sold at a loss, or minus tax liability if it is expected to be sold at a gain.

A Replacement Project Example

Consider Phoenix Industries, which is investigating replacing an existing assembly line with a new, automated one. The existing assembly line was installed 3 years ago at a cost of $500,000. It is being depreciated for tax purposes via straight-line to a zero value over its normal recovery period of 5 years. The straight-line depreciation is $100,000 per year. Because 3 years have already elapsed, $300,000 has already been depreciated; therefore the remaining undepreciated value is $200,000. Depreciation will continue for 2 more years at $100,000 per year. The old equipment will last 5 more years, at which time its resale value will be $10,000, but it could be sold now for $40,000.

The main benefit of the project would be to reduce yearly expenses from $600,000 on the existing line to $200,000 for the newer, automated line. However, the new line would require a $20,000 increase in inventory, cost $1 million, and be depreciated via straight-line over its 5-year normal recovery period.[5] The estimated resale value of the new assembly line in 5 years is $80,000. Phoenix's tax rate is 40 percent, and the opportunity cost of capital for this project is 16 percent.

In solving this replacement problem, it is useful to begin by calculating the depreciation on the new assembly line equipment, less the depreciation on the old assembly line, as follows:

Year	Original Cost	× Straight-Line Depreciation Factor	= New Depreciation	− Depreciation on Old Assembly Line	= Incremental Depreciation
1	$1,000,000	0.20	$200,000	$100,000	$100,000
2	1,000,000	0.20	200,000	100,000	100,000
3	1,000,000	0.20	200,000	0	200,000
4	1,000,000	0.20	200,000	0	200,000
5	1,000,000	0.20	200,000	0	200,000

Now we can proceed to calculate the incremental initial investment, operating cash flows, and terminal cash flows. As shown in Table 8.4, the incremental initial investment is the $1 million for the new assembly line, less $40,000 to be received from selling the old assembly line, less $64,000 due to the tax consequences of selling the existing equipment at a loss. This last item arises because the old assembly line has an undepreciated value of $200,000, but it could be sold for only $40,000, producing a $160,000 tax loss. Because the equipment was underdepreciated, we can write off the full $160,000 in the year of replacement and reduce taxes by $64,000 [i.e., ($160,000)(0.40)], provided that the firm is profitable. Finally, the cost of the additional net working capital (due to the increase in inventory required) must be treated as part of the initial investment. So, the net incremental investment needed to replace the existing assembly line is $916,000.

Next, we calculate the incremental operating cash flows. The old assembly line had cash outflows of $600,000 a year, whereas the new one has cash outflows of $200,000 per year. The incremental savings (or $\Delta CFBT$) from the replacement is $400,000 per year. Taking this and the incremental depreciation, we can calculate the

[5]For simplicity, the lives of the old and new assembly lines are both 5 years. If the lives were unequal, then the techniques discussed in Chapter 7 for unequal-lived projects would have to be employed.

TABLE 8.4

Calculation of Incremental After-Tax Cash Flow Stream and Net Present Value for Replacement Project

For replacement projects the incremental cash flow must be calculated for all portions of the cash flow stream. The comparison is between keeping the existing equipment, versus selling the existing equipment at time $t = 0$ and purchasing the replacement equipment.

Initial Investment

Cost of new assembly line	$1,000,000
Plus: Additional net working capital	20,000
Less: Sale of old assembly line	−40,000
Tax savings on sale of old assembly line*	−64,000
Incremental initial investment, $\Delta CF_0 =$	$ 916,000

Operating Cash Flows

Year	Cash Outflows (Old)	−	Cash Outflows (New)	× Incremental CFBT	Incremental $CFBT \times (1 - T)$†	+	Incremental $Dep\ (T)$†	=	Incremental CF
1	$600,000		$200,000	$400,000	$240,000		$40,000		$280,000
2	600,000		200,000	400,000	240,000		40,000		280,000
3	600,000		200,000	400,000	240,000		80,000		320,000
4	600,000		200,000	400,000	240,000		80,000		320,000
5	600,000		200,000	400,000	240,000		80,000		320,000

Terminal Cash Flow

After-tax proceeds from sale of new assembly line, $80,000(1 − 0.40)	$48,000
Less: After-tax proceeds from sale of old assembly line, $10,000(1 − 0.40)	−6,000
Incremental after-tax proceeds	$42,000
Release of net working capital	20,000
Incremental terminal cash flow	$62,000

Incremental Cash Flow Stream

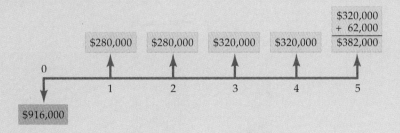

Net Present Value‡

$$NPV = \frac{\$280,000}{(1.16)^1} + \frac{\$280,000}{(1.16)^2} + \frac{\$320,000}{(1.16)^3} + \frac{\$320,000}{(1.16)^4} + \frac{\$382,000}{(1.16)^5} - \$916,000$$

$$= \$241,379 + \$208,086 + \$205,010 + \$176,733 + \$181,875 - \$916,000 = \$97,083$$

---

* (IRS depreciated value of old asset − selling price)(tax rate), or ($200,000 − $40,000)(0.40) = $64,000.

† The tax rate is 40 percent.

‡ If present value tables are employed the *NPV* is $280,000(0.862) + $280,000(0.743) + $320,000(0.641) + $320,000(0.552) + $382,000(0.476) − $916,000 = $241,360 + $208,040 + $205,120 + $176,640 + $181,832 − $916,000 = $96,992.

incremental operating cash flows, as shown in Table 8.4. Finally, the difference in the after-tax expected resale values in 5 years and the release of the $20,000 of additional net working capital are treated as terminal cash inflows in year 5.[6] Given the incremental after-tax *CF* stream shown in Table 8.4 and the 16 percent opportunity cost of capital, the *NPV* is $97,083. The decision is to replace the old assembly line with the new line; doing so contributes to maximizing the value of the firm.

Replacement decisions are an important part of the capital budgeting process. Following the steps outlined, and making sure we understand incremental cash flows, we can make the proper decisions needed to maintain the firm's competitive advantage and maximize its value.[7]

CONCEPT REVIEW QUESTIONS

- What are the incremental cash flows in a replacement decision?
- What are the differences in the cash flows for an expansion project compared to a replacement project?

MORE ON CASH FLOW ESTIMATION

So far in Chapters 7 and 8 we have focused on three primary topics—the capital budgeting process, gaining a fuller understanding of net present value and internal rate of return, and estimating the incremental cash flows. Now we need to consider hard-to-estimate costs and benefits, inflation, why financing costs are excluded, and how to proceed when cash flows between projects are interrelated.

Those Hard-to-Estimate Costs and Benefits

■ LEARNING GOAL 4

Discuss hard-to-handle costs and benefits, and how firms should proceed.

Some costs and benefits are inherently more difficult to estimate than others. For example, how do you estimate the benefits (and the costs, for that matter) from implementing a total quality management, TQM, system? Or, if your firm is taking advantage of new developments in information technology, how do you estimate the costs and benefits likely to be gained by such an investment? If you introduce a totally new technology-driven information system, it will be thoroughly intertwined with the firm's total operations. In addition to the direct costs associated with computers and software, the firm may need to consider its business strategy, faster product cycles, potential reorganization of operations and divisions, changes in the number and types of employees, improved job training, and many other factors.

Alternatively, there are other possible items such as potential legal costs and loss in value of the firm arising from product liability lawsuits, manufacturing pollution, and the impact of closing a plant on the welfare of both its employees and the

---

[6] *This assumes that the project terminates at this point in time. In reality, net working capital may be an ongoing commitment that cannot be assumed to be released.*
[7] *Some additional tax complications arise if presently owned equipment is traded in on new equipment. For simplicity, these complications are ignored.*

neighborhood in which the plant is located. For firms operating multinationally, what are the costs associated with the mountains of toxic waste that the burgeoning industrialization is creating in developing countries? Are these costs that firms need to consider directly in determining the relevant cash flows for capital budgeting, or should these costs be ignored until governments force firms to pay for maintaining the environment?

None of these issues are easy to address. Because of the uncertainties involved, and the non-firm-specific nature of some of the issues, the quantification of the costs and benefits increases in complexity, while the confidence in the estimates decreases. In such cases, firms have two general approaches that can be considered. First, they can ignore quantifying the costs and benefits and simply make seat-of-the-pants decisions. Second, they can quantify the costs and benefits—even if with a great deal of uncertainty—and then make sure that the decision makers are fully aware of the level of uncertainty in the estimates. We strongly recommend the second approach; quantify what you can, communicate all of the assumptions and uncertainties to the decision makers, and then deal with the nonquantifiable factors. By doing so, the capital budgeting process can provide the best possible basis for making informed, value maximizing, decisions.

Inflation

■ **LEARNING GOAL 5**

Explain how inflation affects cash flow estimates.

Often cash flows are estimated on the basis that they are not expected to change much over the life of the project. If inflation is low, the cash flows may not change significantly. But if inflation is high or if it changes during the life of the project, then we have to consider the specific impact of inflation on the estimated cash flows. In only one special case do the effects of inflation not affect the decision—when both the cash flows and the opportunity cost of capital properly anticipate and adjust for the same percentage rate of inflation. *If this special case occurs, then the effects of inflation cancel each other out and inflation does not have to be considered as a separate issue.*

Projects that are more likely to be able to sustain their cash flows in light of inflation are those that produce necessities and/or have highly differentiated products.

A more likely occurrence, however, is for the opportunity cost of capital to reflect expected inflation while the cash flows do not. Investors incorporate expectations of inflation into their required rates of return. Because this is the case, the firm's opportunity cost of capital also reflects expected inflation. But what about the estimated cash flows? If inflation is taken into account in the discount rate but not in the after-tax *CFs*, then the calculated *NPV* will be biased downward. Alternatively, if low expected inflation is reflected in the discount rate used but a higher inflation estimate is built into the *CFs*, then the *NPV* will be biased upward.

To see the importance of adjusting for inflation, consider Sullivan Paper. Table 8.5 shows that the firm calculated the net present value of a proposed capital expenditure to be $2,974 at its opportunity cost of capital of 15 percent. On that basis, the project should be selected, because it returns more than the 15 percent required. But what happens if expected inflation was ignored in estimating the cash outflows in Table 8.5? Once inflation is taken into account the cash outflows are projected to increase by $1,000 per year. As Table 8.6 shows, the project's *NPV* is now −$74, which changes Sullivan's decision. Now the firm should reject the project.

TABLE 8.5

Cash Flows and Net Present Value for Sullivan Paper Project, Without Adjusting for Inflation

The $21,000 investment was depreciated to zero over 3 years by straight-line depreciation ignoring the half-year convention.

Initial Investment

$21,000

Operating Cash Flows

Year	Cash Inflows	−	Cash Outflows	=	CFBT	CFBT × (1 − T)*	+	Dep(T)*	=	CF
1	$20,000		$8,000		$12,000	$8,400		$2,100		$10,500
2	20,000		8,000		12,000	8,400		2,100		10,500
3	20,000		8,000		12,000	8,400		2,100		10,500

Terminal Cash Flow

None

Net Present Value†

$$NPV = \frac{\$10,500}{(1.15)^1} + \frac{\$10,500}{(1.15)^2} + \frac{\$10,500}{(1.15)^3} - \$21,000$$

$$= \$9,130 + \$7,940 + \$6,904 - \$21,000 = \$2,974$$

* The tax rate is 30 percent.
† If present value tables are employed the NPV is $10,500(0.870) + $10,500(0.756) + $10,500(0.658) − $21,000 = $9,135 + $7,938 + $6,909 − $21,000 = $2,982.

In the early 1980s the United States had lower inflation and stronger growth. With a strong dollar, foreign goods are cheaper for U.S. buyers. For example, ski resorts in Colorado lost revenue because the strong dollar made ski trips to Europe cheaper than trips to Colorado.

Anticipating inflation is not easy, but it is important if the proper capital budgeting decisions are to be made. Managers should remember the following:

1. Be consistent—make sure the inflation consequences are built into the cash flows, because they are already incorporated in the discount rate (unless a real instead of a nominal discount rate is employed).
2. Even if cash inflows and regular cash outflows change in line with the general rate of inflation, *CF*s generally do not change, due to the tax structure. Taxes tend to increase more than proportionately as cash inflows rise. Also, inflation often requires an increased working capital investment above and beyond that required with little or no inflation.
3. Inflation is not constant across different sections of the economy. Therefore, it may *not* be reasonable to use a general price index to incorporate the effects of changing rates of inflation on expected *CF*s for a project.
4. Differential price changes may occur due to supply and demand considerations. These effects, which are due to factors other than the rate of inflation, can also significantly impact the *CF*s and must be taken into account.

It should be mentioned that in some countries, where inflation is very high, many other factors have to be considered. Thus in 1994, the projected rate of inflation was 15 percent in the People's Republic of China, 91 percent in Turkey, 40 percent in Kenya, and 58 percent in Venezuela. The whole capital budgeting process is affected in countries where the rate of inflation is very high, and investing in assets that are expected to keep ahead of inflation become paramount.

TABLE 8.6

Cash Flows and Net Present Value for Sullivan Paper Project, Taking Account of Inflation

With the substantial increase in the estimated cash outflows once inflation is taken into account, the project should be rejected.

Initial Investment

$21,000

Operating Cash Flows

Year	Cash Inflows	− Cash Outflows	= CFBT	CFBT × (1 − T)*	+ Dep(T)*	= CF
1	$20,000	$9,000	$11,000	$7,700	$2,100	$9,800
2	20,000	10,000	10,000	7,000	2,100	9,100
3	20,000	11,000	9,000	6,300	2,100	8,400

Terminal Cash Flow

None

Net Present Value[†]

$$NPV = \frac{\$9,800}{(1.15)^1} + \frac{\$9,100}{(1.15)^2} + \frac{\$8,400}{(1.15)^3} - \$21,000$$

$$= \$8,522 + \$6,881 + \$5,523 - \$21,000 = -\$74$$

* The tax rate is 30 percent.
[†] If present value tables are employed the *NPV* is $9,800(0.870) + $9,100(0.756) + $8,400(0.658) − $21,000 = $8,526 + $6,880 + $5,527 − $21,000 = −$67.

Why Are Financing Costs Excluded?

■ **LEARNING GOAL 6**

Explain why financial costs are not considered in the capital budgeting decision.

We have ignored one cash flow that a firm incurs when undertaking a capital budgeting project—the financing costs. Suppose that a firm is evaluating whether to build a new plant. If the firm decides to use debt financing, should we recognize the after-tax interest and principal repayments as ongoing cash outflows? Similarly, if equity is employed, should any costs related to it be treated as part of the ongoing cash outflow stream? *In both cases, the answer is "no"!* The investment, or capital budgeting, decision should be separated from the financing decision. The investment decision is based on the economic desirability of the project, irrespective of how it is financed; the financing costs are built into the opportunity cost of capital. If financing costs were to be deducted from the after-tax cash flows, they would be double-counted (once in the numerator of the *NPV* and again in the denominator, as part of the opportunity cost of capital), and the project's net present value would be underestimated. *However*, there are some decisions in which the investment and financing cash flows are interrelated. These are beyond the scope of this book.[8]

---

[8]*Interrelated investment and financing decisions are covered in Chapter 14 of* Financial Management.

EXECUTIVE INTERVIEW WITH DAVID B. ELLIS

Assistant Treasurer
Sara Lee Corporation
Chicago, Illinois

David B. Ellis joined Sara Lee Corporation in 1984 and moved through positions in financial planning and treasury. For 7 years before he arrived at Sara Lee, Mr. Ellis was an environmental consultant, having earned an A.B. degree in earth sciences from the University of California at San Diego and a M.S. degree in oceanography from Oregon State University. Mr. Ellis then switched course and earned his M.B.A. degree from the University of Chicago.

Best known for frozen baked goods, Sara Lee Corporation also markets brand-name apparel. We asked Mr. Ellis to explain Sara Lee's strategies for analyzing expansion projects.

Our mission at Sara Lee is to be a premier consumer packaged goods company with globally recognized brands. To achieve our mission, we emphasize two major corporate strategies: margin improvement through profitable growth, and global expansion.

Sara Lee has had an international presence since about 1962, when we acquired Jonker Fris (a Dutch food processor), and we continue to expand our global operations, primarily through acquisitions. Europe is our first priority because of the market size. We are also expanding our presence in Asia and Latin America, two markets with excellent growth potential. Our goal is to move into newly developing markets, where consumers are eager to buy the brand-name products we sell. For example, we were among the first companies to move into Central Europe.

We build our presence in a country by acquiring leading local brands that consumers already like and then expanding them. We find that works better than trying to bring in a new brand. Our strategy is to maintain the acquired brand's identity and increase the manufacturing, distribution, and marketing resources available to it.

Our acquisition analysis is similar for international and U.S. companies. After we complete the basic financial analysis of an overseas acquisition, we also consider funds remitted to the United States. Each country has different laws governing how funds may be taken out of the country. However, for decision-making purposes, we assume that we will bring the cash back into the United States. We also take into account the various taxes that might have to be paid on those dividends.

We look at cash flow in local currencies, using local inflation rates. Then we convert the cash flow into dollars, based on a differential between the countries' inflation rates. We compare the resulting return in U.S. dollars to a U.S. hurdle rate based on a current cost of capital; both figures include estimates of U.S. inflation. We use the same cost of capital for both domestic and international acquisitions; if we did not, we would have methodological problems in determining hurdle rates for different countries.

Because of the scope of our international operations, we pay close attention to the assets and liabilities—and to the accounting practices—in different countries. We must convert all our financial statements to conform to generally accepted accounting principles in the United States, and we make decisions based on the numbers after this conversion.

Other areas of financial management are affected by operating multinationally. Just as with international acquisitions, we evaluate capital expenditures based on strategic fit and the discounted cash flow of the remitted funds. When we're dealing with international capital investment, there are also concerns that are difficult to quantify, such as political risk. However, we have to estimate these risks and adjust the expected cash flows for them. Most everything involved in international operations has to be done on a case-by-case basis, which makes the decisions particularly challenging.

Interrelated Projects

COMPLEMENTARY PROJECTS
Two or more capital budgeting projects that interact positively so that the total cash flows are more than the simple sum of their individual cash flows.

■ LEARNING GOAL 7

Determine relevant cash flows for interrelated projects.

In Chapter 7 we classified projects as either mutually exclusive or independent. A more accurate picture would show a continuum of relationships among projects, as in Figure 8.1. At one end stand **complementary projects.** If one of several complemen-

FIGURE 8.1

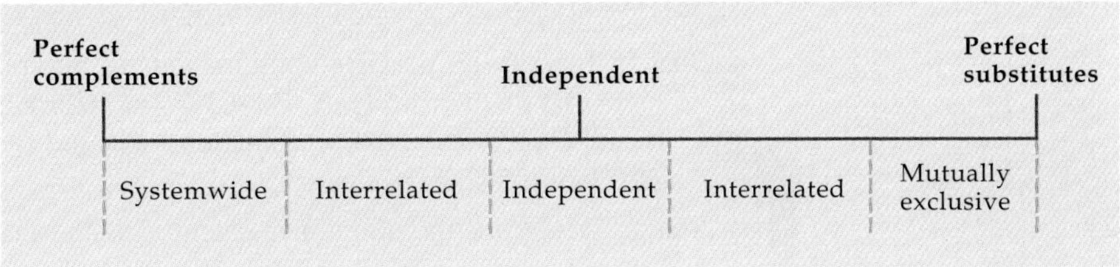

Degree of Dependence Among Captial Budgeting Projects

A continuum of projects exists from those that are perfect complements to those that are perfect substitutes. Knowing the degree of dependence is necessary for effective decision making.

SYSTEMWIDE PROJECT
Capital budgeting projects that must be accepted or rejected as a package, because they are 100% complementary projects.

SUBSTITUTE PROJECTS
Capital budgeting projects the acceptance of which results in total cash flows less than the sum of their individual cash flows.

INTERRELATED PROJECTS
Capital budgeting projects in which the cash flows are intertwined and cannot be examined separately.

tary projects is undertaken, the cash flows of all related projects also increase. An example is a combination self-service gasoline station and convenience store; combining both in one operation generally produces incremental business beyond the simple sum of what each would generate separately. In the extreme case, the cash flows and success or failure of the projects are so closely related that a decision has to be made to accept or reject a **systemwide project.** The entire system must be evaluated, because accepting only part of it produces nothing of value.

At the other end of the continuum are **substitute projects.** In this case acceptance of one project reduces the cash flows from another. If the effect is pronounced enough, the projects are said to be *mutually exclusive*; that is, accepting one precludes accepting others. A special case, lying between systemwide and mutually exclusive projects, is that of *independent projects.* In this case acceptance of one has no appreciable impact on the cash flows of other independent projects.

Finally, as shown in Figure 8.1, we have a broad spectrum of **interrelated projects,** where the acceptance of one project can partially affect—either positively or negatively—the cash flows of other possible projects. *The joint cash flows for two (or more) interrelated projects must be analyzed together.* For example, suppose that Wilson Paint, which as part of its activities manufactures paint sprayers, is evaluating the desirability of producing two new models—the Quik Painter and the Quik Painter II. The firm has the choice of producing and selling either or both paint sprayers. The initial investment, cash inflows, and *NPVs* for both are as follows:

	Producing and Selling Only Quik Painter	Producing and Selling Only Quik Painter II	Producing and Selling Both
Initial investment	$200,000	$250,000	$400,000
After-tax cash flows for each of 10 years	50,000	60,000	70,000
Net present value at 13%	71,312	75,575	−20,163

At the opportunity cost of capital of 13 percent, both projects considered independently have positive net present values and should be selected.

But look what happens if Wilson decides to introduce both sprayers. Wilson's combined initial investment is slightly less than the sum of the two separate outlays, so there are some economies from producing both. The total after-tax cash flows, however, increase only slightly when both sprayers are introduced. Why? Because the two paint sprayers are really substitutes. A customer needs only one of the sprayers, and two different models provide very little in the way of incremental sales. The cash inflows are interrelated, so the total *NPV* from producing both paint sprayers is negative. Obviously, Wilson shouldn't introduce both sprayers—and because the Quik Painter II has the higher *NPV*, it should be produced and sold.

This example suggests a basic procedure to be followed when interrelated projects exist:

STEP 1: Identify all possible combinations of interrelated projects. For instance, assume that three projects, A, B, and C, are interrelated. In addition to analyzing A, B, and C separately, the combinations of A and B, A and C, B and C, and A and B and C must also be evaluated.

STEP 2: Determine the initial investment and after-tax cash flow stream for each project and combination, along with the total *NPV* of each project and combination.

STEP 3: Choose the individual project or combination of projects that has the highest total *NPV*.

In reality, few projects are completely independent. However, if the interrelationships are small, the projects should be treated as if they are independent.

One could argue that all projects within a firm are somewhat related. If this is the case, then the analysis of any project is a tremendous chore, because all possible combinations have to be considered. In fact, however, many projects are mutually exclusive, independent, or systemwide. The key is to make sure that proper analysis has been done to determine the appropriate relationship, if any, between proposed capital budgeting projects. When the analysis has been done correctly, the proper projects are considered, the proper cash flows are identified, and the proper decisions will result.

CONCEPT REVIEW QUESTIONS

- What are some hard-to-handle costs and benefits? What choices do firms have in dealing with them, and what is the recommended procedure?
- Why is it important to adjust a firm's cash flows for inflation?
- Comment on the statement: "A firm's cash flows will be biased downward if financing costs are included."
- What are complementary projects and substitute projects?

Summary

- For effective capital budgeting to occur, the relevant incremental after-tax cash must be determined. This determination requires an understanding of depreciation as specified by the Internal Revenue Service and certain other aspects of the tax code.
- Opportunity costs are an important component of the costs; they must be considered. Sunk costs are just that; they should be ignored in determining the proper cash flows, which are the incremental (new minus old) *CFs*.
- The cash flows must be determined at three times: at the initiation of the project; over the expected economic life of the project, using the operating cash flows (including incremental depreciation tax shields); and at the termination of the project.
- For replacement-type decisions, the focus is on the incremental cash flows.
- Proper decision making requires that all quantifiable costs and benefits, including inflation, but not financing costs, be considered in the after-tax cash flow stream.
- When projects are interrelated, the net after-tax cash flow stream over the projects must be employed in order to make wealth-maximizing decisions.

Questions

8.1 Explain the idea of opportunity costs. How do they relate to the notion of the operating *CF* stream?

8.2 Which of the following should be considered when calculating the incremental *CFs* associated with a new warehouse? Assume the firm owns the land but that existing buildings would have to be demolished.

   a. Demolition costs and site clearance.

   b. The cost of an access road built a year ago.

   c. New forklifts and conveyer equipment for the warehouse.

   d. The market value of the land and existing buildings.

   e. A portion of the firm's overhead.

   f. Lost earnings on other products due to managerial time spent during the construction and stocking of the new warehouse.

   g. Future IRS depreciation on the old buildings and equipment.

   h. Landscaping for the warehouse.

   i. Financing costs related to the bonds issued to build the new warehouse.

   j. The effects of inflation on future labor costs.

8.3 By comparing the calculations necessary for determining ΔCFs of replacement decisions with the calculations for determining *CFs* for expansion decisions, identify the *specific* differences that exist for the initial, operating, and terminal cash flows.

8.4 Explain the difference between complementary and substitute projects. How are they related to (**a**) systemwide projects, (**b**) interrelated projects, (**c**) independent projects, and (**d**) mutually exclusive projects?

8.5 Differentiate between financing and investment decisions. Why are financing costs excluded when calculating the *CFs* necessary for capital investment decision making?

Concept Review Problems

See Appendix A for solutions.

CR8.1 Paymore Rent-a-Car just purchased a new fleet of cars with an average cost of $18,000 per car.

   a. The normal recovery period for automobiles is 5 years. Using straight-line depreciation, what is the depreciation per year, and the remaining undepreciated value each year?

   b. The firm plans to sell the cars after 3 years at 50 percent of the purchase price. Determine Paymore's tax liability and net cash proceeds, after paying taxes, from the sale of the cars. Paymore's tax rate is 30 percent.

   c. What is the tax liability and net cash proceeds if the cars are sold at only 25 percent of the purchase price?

The following information is used in CR8.2 through CR8.6.

Simmonds Products has spent $500,000 on research to develop lowfat imitation wine. The firm is planning to spend $200,000 on a machine to produce the new wine. Shipping and installation costs of the machine will be capitalized and depreciated; they are $100,000. The machine has an expected life of 5 years, a $10,000 estimated resale value, and straight-line depreciation will be employed. Revenue from the lowfat wine is expected to be $650,000 per year, with costs of $400,000 per year. The firm has a tax rate of 35 percent, an opportunity cost of capital of 14 percent, and it expects net working capital to increase by $40,000.

CR8.2 What is the initial investment, CF_0, for the imitation lowfat wine project?

CR8.3 What are the operating cash flows for years 1 through 6?

CR8.4 What are the terminal cash flows of the project?

CR8.5 What is the net present value of the project? Should Simmonds expand into the lowfat wine market?

CR8.6 John, who is in charge of Simmonds' regular wine division, estimates that the lowfat wine would lower regular wine sales by approximately $125,000 per year. Now what is the *NPV*?

CR8.7 Sal's Pizzeria is considering replacing its old pizza ovens with new ovens. The old ovens have a current resale value of $100,000, a book value of $60,000, and are being depreciated at $20,000 per year. It is estimated that if the machines are held for 3 years, the old machines will have a resale value of $20,000.

The new pizza ovens will cost $300,000 and be depreciated using straight-line over their 3-year normal recovery period. Sales using the old pizza ovens were 75,000 pizzas at $t = 0$, with an average selling price of $10 per pizza. Sales have been growing at a rate of 1 percent per year. The selling price with the new pizza ovens remains at $10 per pizza; the units sold at $t = 1$ are 81,600 and are expected to grow at 2 percent per year.

Operating costs using the old pizza ovens are 80 percent of total revenue, while operating costs using the new pizza ovens are expected to be 75 percent of total revenue. Management estimates the new pizza ovens will have a resale value of $50,000 in 3 years. The corporate tax rate is 40 percent, and the opportunity cost of capital is 12 percent. Should Sal's replace the ovens?

Problems

See Appendix C for answers to selected problems.

Overhead and Opportunity Costs

8.1 Windsor Stores is considering opening a new store in Portland. Gross cash inflows are expected to be $1,000,000 per year, and cash outflows are predicted to be $800,000 per year. In addition, Windsor's cost accounting department estimates that overhead costs of $75,000 per year should be charged to the new store. These costs include the store's share of the firm's management salaries, general administrative expenses, and so forth. Finally, the new store is expected to reduce *CFBTs* by $50,000 per year from one of the firm's existing stores. Windsor's marginal tax rate is 30 percent.

Note: For simplicity in 8.1, ignore any impact of depreciation.

   a. If all the overhead consists of fixed costs that will be incurred whether or not the new store is opened, what is the relevant operating *CF?*
   b. What if $50,000 of the overhead consists of variable costs related to the new store, and $25,000 consists of fixed overhead costs? What is the relevant operating *CF* now?

Relevant Cash Flows

8.2 A firm is considering an investment requiring the purchase of a machine that will cost $800,000 and be depreciated via straight-line depreciation over its 5-year normal recovery period. The firm's marginal tax rate is 35 percent. The cash inflows expected over the 5-year life of the project are $240,000 per year, cash expenses are $80,000 per year, and the reduction in the before-tax cash inflows from other machines currently owned will be $20,000 per year if this new machine is purchased. Finally, the new machine will require a one-time increase both in accounts receivable of $15,000 and in inventory of $25,000. At the end of 5 years the machine will be worthless, and the firm will not replace it because it will be emphasizing other products by then. What is the relevant *CF* stream?

Incremental Initial Investment on Replaced Asset

8.3 A $32,000 machine with a 5-year normal recovery period was purchased 2 years ago. The machine will now be sold for $24,000 and replaced with a new machine costing $40,000, with a 5-year normal recovery period. Straight-line depreciation is employed for both machines, and the marginal corporate tax rate is 30 percent.
a. What is the depreciated value for tax purposes on the old machine?
b. What is the tax liability from selling the old machine and the net proceeds, considering both the selling price and the tax?
c. What is the gross outlay for the new machine by itself?
d. What is the incremental initial investment that is determined by subtracting the net proceeds on the old machine (calculated in b), from the gross outlay on the new machine (calculated in c)?

Unequal Depreciable and Economic Life

8.4 Pasteur Hospital is a private hospital that has an opportunity to purchase a generator. The generator costs $98,000 and will be depreciated to zero under straight-line depreciation over its 7-year normal recovery period. The tax rate is 30 percent, and the cash flows before taxes over its 9-year economic life follow:

	Years				
	1	2	3	4–5	6–9
CFBT	$10,000	$12,000	$16,000	$20,000 each	$30,000 each

If the opportunity cost of capital is 17 percent, should the generator be purchased?

Opportunity Costs

8.5 Rosen Fashions is contemplating bringing out a new line of sweaters to add to its existing lines. The projected initial investment is $100,000, CF is expected to be $40,000 per year for each of 5 years, and the cost of capital is 15 percent.
a. Should the new line of sweaters be produced?
b. What happens if you discover that introducing the new line of sweaters will reduce CFs from existing sweater lines by $12,000 per year?
c. Why must the possibility of opportunity costs always be considered when the cash flow stream is being estimated?

Expansion

Note: Take the tax on the $8,000, because the dismantling costs are tax-deductible.

8.6 New equipment costs $40,000, freight is $1,000, and site preparation costs are $5,000. Both the freight and site preparation costs occur at $t = 0$, but they are tax-deductible. Cash inflows are $21,000 per year for each of 5 years, and cash outflows are $6,000 per year. Straight-line depreciation (based on the cost of $40,000) to a value of zero at the end of its normal recovery period of 5 years will be employed. In 5 years it is estimated that the equipment can be sold for $10,000, less $2,000 in dismantling costs. The firm's tax rate is 30 percent, and the opportunity cost of capital is 15 percent. Should the equipment be acquired?

CFs and NPV

8.7 Preston Products manufactures electronic devices. Sales have recently been lost because of the inability to store sufficient finished goods inventory, even though Preston has the capability of increasing production. The solution under discussion is to increase production to create a larger finished goods inventory so that lost sales will not occur in the future. To increase the inventory, Preston estimates the following will be required:

1. The finished goods inventory needs to be expanded by $150,000.
2. Existing vacant warehouse space is available for storing the additional inventory. However, new equipment costing $80,000 with a 5-year normal recovery period is required. Straight-line depreciation will be employed, and Preston's marginal tax rate is 40 percent. Additional wages will be $40,000 per year.

3. The sales and production people estimate that the increased sales will result in a net cash inflow to the firm (after all production costs, but before considering the additional warehouse expense and taxes) of $100,000 per year.

4. In 5 years the equipment will have a resale value of zero. The $150,000 buildup in inventory is no longer required.

a. If the opportunity cost of capital is 13 percent, should the expansion take place?

b. What decision should be made if everything remains the same as in (a), except that the warehouse space is currently rented out for $50,000 (before taxes) per year?

Expansion

8.8 Yukon Industries has a proposed project for $210,000 of research and development equipment that falls under the 3-year category. Straight-line depreciation will be employed, and a $40,000 addition to net working capital will be required. The estimated benefits, *CFBT,* are $95,000 per year for each of 3 years; the equipment has an estimated resale value of $50,000 in 3 years; the firm's tax rate is 35 percent; and Yukon estimates that a 20 percent return is required for this project. Should the new equipment be acquired?

Expansion

8.9 A firm is considering a major expansion of its operations. If it expands, the firm anticipates an initial investment in equipment of $500,000 that will be depreciated via straight-line depreciation over 5 years. The projected cash inflows are $200,000, $250,000, $200,000, $200,000, and $150,000, respectively, over the 5 years. At that time the resale value of the equipment is estimated to be $125,000. The marginal tax rate is 35 percent, and the opportunity cost of capital is 15 percent.

a. Should the investment be made?

b. After running the analysis in (a) you remember that if the investment is made the firm will have to use a building that is presently rented out for $70,000 per year (before taxes) *payable in advance* (i.e., at $t = 0, t = 1, \ldots, t = 4$). Does this new information affect the decision you reached in (a)?

Replacement

8.10 W. Woods Inc. has moved into new quarters and wants to replace its office equipment. The existing equipment is fully depreciated, but it can be sold today for $40,000. In another 5 years it will have a resale value of zero. The new equipment costs $250,000, has a 5-year life, and has zero resale value in 5 years. Straight-line depreciation will be employed, the tax rate is 35 percent, and the opportunity cost of capital is 12 percent. Due to increased worker productivity and morale, the estimated benefits before tax, $\Delta CFBT,$ are $65,000 per year.

a. Determine the relevant cash flows.

b. Should the equipment be replaced?

Replacement

8.11 Hinkle Manufacturing bought a $140,000 piece of equipment 2 years ago; its present depreciated value is $101,500. Because of substantial increases in the demand for used equipment, it can be sold today for $140,000 (before taxes). If kept, however, it will last 5 more years and produce expected cash flows, *CFBTs,* of $13,000 for each of 5 years. A replacement machine costs $180,000, and it is expected to produce *CFBTs* of $28,000 for each of 5 years. Assume neither machine has any resale value in 5 years. If the marginal tax rate is 40 percent and the discount rate is 10 percent, should the equipment be replaced, assuming straight-line depreciation is employed for both pieces of equipment?

Replacement

8.12 Duncan Design is considering replacing its two delivery trucks. The models being used have been fully depreciated to zero, but can be sold today for $3,000 *each*. In 5 years these two trucks can be sold for $500 *each*. The two new trucks will cost $20,000 *each* and have a 5-year normal recovery period. Straight-line depreciation will be employed, the firm's marginal tax rate is 35 percent, and the trucks are expected to have a resale value of $3,500 *each* (before taxes) 5 years from now. Because of the efficiency of the new trucks, the total benefit will be a reduction in after-tax operating costs of $9,000 [i.e., *(CFBT)*(0.65)] per year. Should these new trucks be purchased if the opportunity cost of capital is 12 percent?

Replacement

8.13 Villa Inc. is contemplating the replacement of one of its machines. The new machine costs $1,400,000, has a 10-year economic life, and is expected to save $250,000 (before taxes) in operating expenses each year. It will be depreciated under straight-line over its 7-year normal recovery period. The old machine cost $980,000, has a 10-year economic life remaining, but is being depreciated for tax purposes with the 7-year straight-line method. It was purchased 2 years ago, so there are still 5 years of depreciation remaining on the existing machine. The incremental initial investment, Δ*CF,* is $1,100,000, but the incremental operating cash inflows have yet to be calculated. At the end of 10 years, neither machine will have any resale value. The discount rate is 14 percent, and the marginal tax rate is 40 percent. Should the old machine be replaced?

Interrelated Projects

8.14 SouthWest Developers has designed an apartment building that will cost $7 million and produce after-tax cash inflows of $1.5 million for each year of its 10-year life. The firm also has plans for a recreation center that would cost $3.2 million and produce after-tax cash flows of $600,000 per year for 10 years. The firm owns land near Los Angeles and must decide which project to build. The land is large enough to accommodate both projects. SouthWest believes that if both projects are built next to each other, the residents of the apartment building will use the recreation center and increase its expected cash inflows to $700,000 per year. If the opportunity cost of capital is 14 percent, what should the company do?

Interrelated Projects

8.15 Tipton Products is considering two possible capital projects. Project I has the following *CFs*:

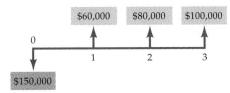

Project II can be undertaken only if the $150,000 initial investment for project I has been made. The *additional CFs* for project II are as follows:

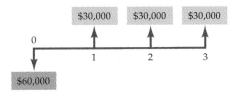

However, because projects I and II are partial substitutes, the *CFs* from project I will decrease by $10,000 in each of years 1, 2, and 3 if project II is also undertaken. If the discount rate is 14 percent, what should the company do?

Inflation

8.16 A project has an initial investment of $30,000, *CFBT* of $16,000 for each of 3 years, and an opportunity cost of capital of 13 percent. Straight-line depreciation will be employed, and the firm's marginal tax rate is 40 percent.

a. What is the project's *NPV*? Should it be accepted?

b. Due to inflation, the *CFBT* in years 2 and 3 was overstated. It should be $14,000 in year 2 and $12,000 in year 3. Does this information cause you to change the decision made in (a)?

Profitability and Taxes

8.17 A project requires an initial investment of $300,000 and is expected to produce *CFBTs* of $95,000 for each of 5 years. Straight-line depreciation will be used over the 5-year normal recovery period. No-Tax Company has substantial tax losses and does not expect to pay any taxes in the foreseeable future. Tax Company has a marginal tax rate of 35 percent.

Note: In 8.17, no carryback or carryforward of the tax credit is feasible.

a. If both companies have an opportunity cost of capital of 14 percent, to which company is the investment worth more?

b. Is it reasonable to use the same cost of capital for both companies? Why or why not?

More Capital Budgeting

8.18 Mini Case Enterprise Services is considering the replacement of a piece of equipment that was purchased 3 years ago for $60,000 and is generating *CFBT* of $15,000 per year. The equipment is being depreciated by the straight-line method over its 5-year tax life. If sold today it would bring $18,000; its estimated resale value if kept for 5 more years is $10,000. The new piece of equipment costs $75,000 and will require installation-related expenses of $8,000, which will be expensed. The *CFBT* for the new equipment is $30,000 per year, and straight-line depreciation over 5 years is being used. At the end of 5 years the new equipment's estimated resale value is $20,000. The marginal tax rate is 40 percent, and the opportunity cost of capital is 14 percent.

a. You, as chief financial analyst for the firm, have been assigned the responsibility of deciding whether Enterprise Services should keep or replace the existing system. What is your recommendation?

b. In presenting your recommendation, you mention that a replacement capital budgeting decision can be broken down into two separate components: (1) whether or not to accept the new project, and (2) to keep or abandon the existing project. Thus,

$$NPV_{\text{replacement}} = NPV_{\text{new}} - NPV_{\text{keep or abandon}}$$

Your boss does not believe you and challenges you to prove it. In order to do so, proceed as follows: First, take *only those cash flows* that would exist for the new equipment in (a). This is simply an expansion project. Calculate the *NPV* for the new equipment. Then take the remaining cash flows that involve keeping the old equipment for 5 more years versus abandoning it today. Calculate the *NPV* for the keep-versus-abandon decision. Now, use these figures to prove the point to your boss.

c. In further conversation with your boss you mention that the two projects considered in (a) and (b) are mutually exclusive. What is meant by the term "mutually exclusive"? How would you have to proceed if the two projects were either partial complements or partial substitutes, not mutually exclusive?

d. Two other projects exist with after-tax cash flows as follows, where the required return is now 16 percent:

Year	Project A	Project B
0	−$20,000	−$30,000
1	5,000	18,000
2	7,000	15,000
3	9,000	13,000
4	9,000	10,000
5	9,000	
6	16,000	

(1) Calculate the internal rate of return for each project.

(2) If the projects are independent, what decision should be made? Why?

(3) If the projects are mutually exclusive, what decision should be made? Why? What assumptions are you making in this decision? How comfortable are you with the assumptions?

Note: In (e), the cash flow for project A in year 1 will be $5,000 (1 − 0.06). For year 2 it will be $7,000(1 − 0.06)^2, etc.

e. In estimating the *CFs* for the two projects in (d), you inadvertently ignored the effects of inflation on the operating cash flows. The net after-tax cash flows for project A will decline at 6 percent each year, and those for project B will decline at 8 percent each year. If the projects are independent, does this new information change the decisions made in (d2)?

Probability, Cost of Capital, and Capital Budgeting

8.19 Mini Case Wadsworth Associates is a diversified firm that raises capital in the following proportions: debt, 30 percent; preferred stock, 15 percent; and common equity, 55 percent. Wadsworth estimates that new debt financing can be secured at 12 percent and additional preferred stock financing at 11.5 percent. It has come up with the following estimates of the expected returns on its common stock and the market portfolio:

	Probability of	Return	
State	State Occurring	Wadsworth Resources	Market Portfolio
Boom	0.30	50%	35%
Average	0.50	20	15
Recession	0.20	−20	−10

The risk-free rate is 10 percent, Wadsworth's marginal tax rate is 40 percent, and the correlation between Wadsworth's returns and the market returns is +0.70.

Note: In (a), remember that $\beta_s = \sigma_s Corr_{sM}/\sigma_M$. In (b), round to the nearest whole number.

a. What is beta for Wadsworth's stock? Its required return on equity?

b. What is the opportunity cost of capital for Wadsworth Resources?

c. Two sizable investments Wadsworth is considering have after-tax cash flows as follows:

Time Periods	Project A	Project B
0	−$20,000,000	−$20,000,000
1	−3,000,000	6,000,000
2	−1,000,000	6,000,000
3	2,000,000	6,000,000
4–10	5,000,000	2,700,000
11–15	10,000,000	

(1) Calculate the internal rates of return for the projects. If the two projects are independent, what decision should be made?

(2) What decision should be made if the two projects are mutually exclusive?

Important Depreciation and Tax Ideas

■ LEARNING GOAL

After studying this appendix you should be able to discuss the impact of depreciation and corporate taxes on relevant cash flows.

To calculate the relevant cash flows for capital budgeting decision making, the financial manager must understand both depreciation and corporate taxes.

DEPRECIATION

Under generally accepted accounting principles, GAAP, the purpose of depreciation is to match revenues and associated expenses in the same time periods. This is not the meaning of depreciation for tax purposes, especially since the enactment of the Economic Recovery Tax Act of 1981, as modified by the Tax Reform Act of 1986. The major impact of these laws was to simplify the treatment of depreciation for tax purposes and shorten the period over which depreciation is charged.

Personal Property

MODIFIED ACCELERATED COST RECOVERY SYSTEM, MACRS
Depreciation system for tax purposes set up by the Economic Recovery Act of 1981 and modified by the Tax Reform Act of 1986.

The Tax Reform Act of 1986 introduced the **modified accelerated cost recovery system, MACRS,** of depreciation. The essence of MACRS was to divide all assets (excluding real estate) into six classes, as shown in Table 8A.1. Firms and individuals have no choice in determining the asset class. Thus, all assets of a certain type have a

TABLE 8A.1

Normal Recovery Period and Property Classes

Instead of MACRS, straight-line depreciation may be used over the normal recovery period.

Normal Recovery Period (Years)	Property
3	Certain short-lived property and special-purpose tools
5	Automobiles, light trucks, buses, technological equipment, information systems, construction equipment, electronic and semiconductor manufacturing equipment
7	Most manufacturing equipment, office furniture and equipment, railroad cars and locomotives, amusement parks
10	Some manufacturing equipment, cement plants, petroleum refineries, barges and tugs
15	Industrial steam and electric-generation equipment, sewage treatment plants, telephone distribution plants, pipelines
20	Most public utility property, railroad structures

specified class life. For example, all light trucks have a class life of 5 years for tax purposes. Firms must depreciate all assets within a class over the **normal recovery period** for that class of assets.

One complication is that the Internal Revenue Service, IRS, assumes all assets (excluding real estate) are purchased halfway through the year; hence, the first year's depreciation is one-half of the "normal" rate. Likewise, all assets are assumed to have a useful tax life of one-half year *longer* then their class life. For example, light trucks and other 5-year class-life assets have a tax life of 5 1/2 years. Firms can employ accelerated percentages, as specified in Table 8A.2, or they can employ straight-line depreciation over the class life.[1] For 5-year class-life assets, the relevant depreciation percentages per year are:

Year	MACRS	Straight-Line
1	20.00%	10.00%
2	32.00	20.00
3	19.20	20.00
4	11.52	20.00
5	11.52	20.00
6	5.76	10.00

Thus, even though the assets are in a 5-year class, they are depreciated over 6 years. The same procedure is required by the IRS for all other asset classes.

TABLE 8A.2

MACRS Depreciation Factors by Normal Recovery Period and Year

The first year's factors are lower because a half-year convention is employed—that is, all assets are assumed to be purchased halfway through the fiscal year. Likewise, all assets are depreciated for one-half year longer then their normal recovery period.

Year	Normal Recovery Period					
	3-year	5-Year	7-Year	10-Year	15-Year	20-Year
1	0.3333	0.2000	0.1429	0.1000	0.0500	0.0375
2	0.4445	0.3200	0.2449	0.1800	0.0950	0.0722
3	0.1481	0.1920	0.1749	0.1440	0.0855	0.0668
4	0.0741	0.1152	0.1249	0.1152	0.0770	0.0618
5		0.1152	0.0893	0.0922	0.0693	0.0571
6		0.0576	0.0893	0.0737	0.0623	0.0528
7			0.0893	0.0655	0.0590	0.0489
8			0.0445	0.0655	0.0590	0.0452
9				0.0655	0.0590	0.0446
10				0.0655	0.0590	0.0446
11				0.0329	0.0590	0.0446
12–15					0.0590	0.0446
16					0.0299	0.0446
17–20						0.0446
21						0.0225

[1] For 3-, 5-, 7-, and 10-year assets, the 200 percent (or double) declining balance method is used, whereas the 150 percent declining balance method is used for 15- and 20-year assets. Switching to straight-line depreciation is incorporated in the MACRS percentages.

In addition, there is another difference between depreciation for tax purposes and GAAP accounting depreciation. In accounting, the firm often takes the original cost of the equipment and then subtracts the estimated salvage value before determining the per year depreciation. But, *under the tax code any estimated salvage value is irrelevant when determining depreciation; the original value of any asset is not reduced by the estimated salvage value, and all assets are depreciated to zero*. Thus, for a light truck that costs $15,000, the relevant depreciation for tax purposes—and the only depreciation that is relevant—is as follows:

Year	MACRS	Straight-Line
1	(0.2000)($15,000) = $ 3,000	(0.10)($15,000) = $ 1,500
2	(0.3200)(15,000) = 4,800	(0.20)(15,000) = 3,000
3	(0.1920)(15,000) = 2,880	(0.20)(15,000) = 3,000
4	(0.1152)(15,000) = 1,728	(0.20)(15,000) = 3,000
5	(0.1152)(15,000) = 1,728	(0.20)(15,000) = 3,000
6	(0.0576)(15,000) = 864	(0.10)(15,000) = 1,500
Total	$15,000	$15,000

As you can see, either MACRS or straight-line depreciation results in the same total amount of depreciation being allowed for tax purposes. The difference is that the firm actually pays less taxes in the early years, due to the greater depreciation charged off in the early years, under MACRS. The firm thereby reduces the present value of the cash outflows for taxes. Other things being equal, profitable firms would prefer to pay the taxes later rather than sooner; hence, firms have a strong incentive to use MACRS rather than straight-line depreciation for income tax purposes.[2] While MACRS makes sense for profitable firms, for simplicity throughout we (1) employ straight-line depreciation and (2) ignore the half-year convention.

Real Estate

Real estate is covered by two special depreciation classes: The 27 ½-year class includes residential rental property, defined as buildings or structures with 80 percent or more of their rental income from dwelling units. The 31 ½-year class includes nonresidential real estate. For both classes the straight-line method of depreciation is required. We ignore real estate throughout the text.

CORPORATE TAXES

Aside from a progressive feature at very low levels of taxable income, the top marginal corporate tax rate, as specified by the Budget Reconciliation Act of 1993, is 35 percent; the alternative minimum tax is 20 percent. In addition, earlier tax law changes did away with different tax rates for ordinary income versus capital gains for firms, as well as the investment tax credit. The investment tax credit is a provision that has been in and out of the tax code over the years; its purpose is to spur capital investment by allowing firms a credit against their income tax for making capital investments.

---

[2] *It is simpler to employ tables when dealing with depreciation as specified by the Internal Revenue Service. These tables, which are available for both straight-line and MACRS depreciation, are discussed at length in* Financial Management.

Sale of Assets

Depreciable assets acquired by the firm are generally subject to taxes when they are sold. No matter how long the asset is held, any gain is treated as an ordinary, or operating, gain; likewise, any loss on the sale of assets is treated as an ordinary loss.

To illustrate, suppose Metroplex Distributors acquired some equipment 4 years ago for $20,000 that has now been depreciated down to $6,000 for tax purposes. It plans to sell the equipment and wants to determine its tax liability and net cash proceeds from the sale (after paying taxes). First, consider the simplest case: Metroplex sells the equipment for its IRS-depreciated value of $6,000. In this case there is no tax liability: the net cash proceeds are simply the $6,000 received from the sale.

Next, consider the sale of the equipment for more or for less than its depreciated tax value. Those two different situations are shown below.

One disadvantage of corporations is that their earnings are taxed twice—once when the firm pays its corporate taxes, and a second time when individuals pay personal taxes on earnings distributed as cash dividends.

	Sold at a Gain	Sold at a Loss
	(1)	(2)
Selling price	$11,000	$ 2,000
Depreciated value	6,000	6,000
Gain (loss) on sale	$ 5,000	($4,000)
Tax at 35%	$ 1,750	($1,400)
Net proceeds	$11,000 − 1,750 = $9,250	$2,000 + $1,400 = $3,400

In column (1), the equipment is sold for $11,000. Because the selling price is greater than the depreciated value, the IRS says Metroplex overdepreciated the asset—and thus it underreported its taxable income and underpaid its taxes. The difference between the $11,000 selling price and the depreciated value of $6,000 is subject to recapture. At a 35 percent marginal corporate tax rate, Metroplex's additional tax is $1,750, resulting in net proceeds from the sale of $9,250.

Now consider column (2), when the asset is sold for $2,000 while its value for tax purposes is $6,000. In this case, the firm underdepreciated the asset, with the result that it realizes a tax savings *if the firm as a whole is profitable*. At a 35 percent marginal tax rate, the tax loss of $4,000 results in a $1,400 reduction in the firm's tax liability. The net cash flow due to selling the asset is the $2,000 plus the $1,400 reduction in cash outflow for taxes, for a total of $3,400.

Operating Losses

An operating loss refers to the situation in which the firm has a negative taxable income. In this case, the firm has no income tax liability. These losses will first be carried back for a maximum of 3 years and then are carried forward for up to 15 years.[3] For simplicity, in this book we ignore carryback and carryforward.

Problem

Tax on Asset Sold

Note: Assume the firm is profitable.

8A.1 An asset has a remaining depreciable value for tax purposes of $48,000. The marginal tax rate is 34 percent. Find the tax liability (or credit) if the asset is sold for **(a)** $60,000, or **(b)** $20,000.

---

[3] *Firms can "irrevocably" give up the carryback option and elect to use the carryforward provision.*

DECIDING WHETHER TO MERGE

■ **LEARNING GOAL**

After studying this appendix you should be able to discuss how capital budgeting techniques are used to evaluate mergers.

So far we have discussed the steps in the capital budgeting process for evaluating expansion and replacement decisions. The process for assessing whether to purchase assets via a merger is similar, but it has some additional considerations.[1] For simplicity, we look at the merger only from the viewpoint of the potential purchasing firm. We will refer to the potential purchaser as the *bidder,* or the bidding firm. The firm it seeks to acquire is the *target firm.*

Mergers and corporate restructuring are complex, large transactions that involve the tendency to fluctuate in number over time. Table 8B.1 shows the level of corporate restructuring activity for the 1986–1994 period. During this period, activity rose until 1990, after which it declined until 1993 and 1994. The data indicate that foreign firms were active in acquiring U.S. firms or assets (13.9% of all transactions) and that U.S.-based firms also were acquiring foreign firms or assets (10.6% of all transactions). The data also indicate that about 44 percent of the transactions involved one firm divesting some of its assets while another firm acquired the divested assets. Thus, although one often hears the term "merger" employed, it is important to recognize that entire firms are not always acquired; often it is only parts of firms. Table 8B.1 also indicates that 6.1 percent of the corporate restructuring during this time period involved firms going private through a leveraged buyout.

TABLE 8B.1

Number of Mergers Involving U.S. Firms, 1986–1994

All acquisitions of at least $5 million in size, including the acquisition of 40 percent or more of a firm if the value was at least $100 million, are shown. A divestiture is when a firm sells a division or part of its assets. A leveraged buyout occurs which a firm or division is bought by another group, with little equity and a lot of debt being employed.

Year	U.S Firm Acquiring Another U.S. Firm	Non-U.S Firm Acquiring U.S. Firm	U.S. Firm Acquiring Non-U.S. Firm	Total	Number (of Total) That Are Divestitures	Number (of Total) That Are Leveraged Buyouts
1986	2,042	352	127	2,521	1,078	240
1987	1,956	375	182	2,513	996	215
1988	2,224	547	237	3,008	1,257	305
1989	2,724	703	371	3,798	1,601	306
1990	3,086	791	410	4,287	1,891	185
1991	2,576	513	424	3,513	1,760	175
1992	2,807	373	498	3,678	1,651	214
1993	3,096	355	519	3,970	1,840	159
1994	3,570	423	632	4,625	1,884	145
Total	24,081	4,432	3,400	31,913	13,958	1,944
% of Total	75.5%	13.9%	10.6%	100%	43.7%	6.1%

Source: Mergers & Acquisitions, various issues.

[1] *Mergers are considered in substantially more detail in Chapter 26 of* Financial Management.

Another *NPV* Problem

From the bidding firm's standpoint, a merger is another capital budgeting problem. To decide whether to merge, the bidding firm needs to estimate three items: (1) the benefits in terms of the firm acquired and the incremental cash flows resulting from the acquisition, (2) the costs in terms of the cash or securities to be offered, and (3) the opportunity cost of capital that reflects the risk and forgone opportunities. Thus, the basic framework is:

$$NPV = \text{benefits} - \text{costs} \qquad (8B.1)$$

where

$$\text{benefits} = \Delta \text{value} + \text{value}_T$$
$$\text{costs} = \text{the price paid, in cash or stock}$$

The Δvalue represents the present value of the incremental economic and/or tax benefits expected to arise due to the merger. Value$_T$ is the current (or pre-offer) market value of the target firm. Note that in an efficient market and with no incremental benefits, the *NPV* would be zero because the bidding firm would not be willing to pay more than the current market value for the target firm. *For a positive* NPV *to exist, the bidding firm must be able to realize economic or tax benefits not available to the target firm.*

BENEFITS

A number of Key Ideas come into play when evaluating mergers: 1—firms maximize their market value; 2—financial markets are efficient; 4—firms focus on cash flows and their incremental effects; 5—a dollar today is worth more than a dollar tomorrow; and 6—risk and return go hand-in-hand.

The current value, value$_T$, of a publicly traded target firm is simply the market price of its outstanding securities. The incremental benefits, Δvalue, can be determined via:

$$\Delta \text{value} = \sum_{t=1}^{n} \frac{\Delta CF_t}{(1 + k)^t} \qquad (8B.2)$$

where ΔCF_t is the incremental after-tax cash flows resulting from the acquisition of the target by the bidder, and k is the opportunity cost of capital appropriate for the incremental cash flows.

The incremental after-tax cash flows, ΔCF_t, are made up of the following items:

1. Incremental cash operating inflows, incremental operating cash outflows, and the incremental depreciation. Therefore (as for a replacement capital budgeting decision), we have

$$\Delta \text{after-tax cash flows, } \Delta CF_t = \Delta CFBT_t(1 - T) + \Delta Dep_t(T)$$

where

$$\Delta CFBT_t = \text{the incremental cash inflows in time period } t$$
$$T = \text{the firm's marginal tax rate}$$
$$\Delta Dep_t = \text{the incremental depreciation in time period } t$$

2. Any additional outlays for new equipment (including required increases in net working capital).

3. Finally, the amount to be realized from the sale of any of the target firm's assets, when the after-tax proceeds of the sale are anticipated to be greater or less than their going-concern value (which is already reflected in the market value of the target firm).

The total ΔCF_t from the merger is the net incremental benefits, where for any year t:

$$\Delta CF_t = \Delta CFBT_t\,(1 - T) + \Delta Dep_t(T) - \begin{array}{c}\Delta \text{ investment in} \\ \text{long-term assets} \\ \text{and net working} \\ \text{capital}\end{array} \pm \begin{array}{c}\text{after-tax gain or loss on the disposition} \\ \text{of some of the target firm's assets} \\ \text{(when above or below their going-} \\ \text{concern value)}\end{array} \qquad (8B.3)$$

Most firms project incremental cash flows for 5 to 10 years and assume they revert to a no-growth situation thereafter.

COSTS

The cost of the acquisition to the bidder is the value of the cash or securities (i.e., the offer price) the bidder will give to stockholders of the target firm. Cash is easier to consider than stock, so we will start by examining how cost is determined when the bidder uses cash to effect the acquisition.

Cash

If cash is employed, then the cost of the acquisition is simply the amount of cash itself. For example, assume that the bidder and target are both publicly traded all-equity firms that have market values of $250,000 and $150,000, respectively. To determine the incremental value, Δvalue, the bidder has estimated the incremental cash flows before tax, incremental depreciation, and incremental investment (some of which occurs in the future) as shown in Table 8B.2. (For simplicity, no incremental benefits are estimated beyond 5 years in this example.) Using the bidder's tax rate of 40 percent and a discount rate of 15 percent, we find the incremental value of the target to be $60,990. The total benefits of the merger are the incremental value plus the present going-concern value of the target, or:

> benefits $= \Delta$value $+$ value$_T$ $= \$60,990 + \$150,000 = \$210,990$

Studies indicate that tar-gets firms "win" from mergers while bidders don't. Targets win because a premium—often up to 50 percent above the pre-merger market price—is paid. From the bidders' standpoint, most mergers look like zero NPV projects.

The bidder has to offer more than the current market value of the target, which is $150,000. At the current market value, the owners of the target firm have no incentive to merge. With 10,000 shares of stock outstanding, the market price per share of the target before the merger is $15 (i.e., $150,000/10,000). Suppose that the bidder decides to offer $18.50 per share, or a total of $185,000, to the stockholders of the target firm. The net present value if the offer is financed with cash is:

> $NPV = $ benefits $-$ costs $= \$210,990 - \$185,000 = \$25,990$

It's easy to overestimate the potential benefits and un-derestimate the costs. One of the most difficult aspects of mergers is the post-merger integration neces-sary to achieve the antici-pated benefits.

The postmerger value *of the combined firm* will be the sum of the premerger value of the bidder of $250,000 plus the $25,990 *NPV* from the merger, or $275,990. Note that the bidder suffers an outflow of cash of $185,000 in order to effect the merger.

Suppose that there are 5,000 shares of stock of the bidding firm. Before the merger the stock was worth $50.00 per share (i.e., $250,000/5,000). After the merger the per share value is approximately $55.20 (i.e., $275,990/5,000). Because cash was used

TABLE 8B.2

Estimated Incremental Value of Proposed Acquisition

In order to achieve all the benefits, the bidder estimates that it will have to invest an additional $30,000 in year 1 and $40,000 more in year 2.

Incremental Benefits and Investments

Year	$\Delta CFBT$	ΔDep*	ΔInvestment
1	$30,000	$10,000	$30,000
2	60,000	20,000	40,000
3	70,000	15,000	0
4	50,000	10,000	0
5	40,000	10,000	0

Calculation of Δvalue

Year	$\Delta CFBT(1-T)$	$+$ $\Delta Dep(T)$	$-$ ΔInvestment	$=$ ΔCF	$\div$ $(1+k)^n$	$=$ Present Value†
1	$18,000	$4,000	30,000	$-$8,000	$(1.15)^1$	$-$6,957
2	36,000	8,000	40,000	4,000	$(1.15)^2$	3,025
3	42,000	6,000	0	48,000	$(1.15)^3$	31,561
4	30,000	4,000	0	34,000	$(1.15)^4$	19,440
5	24,000	4,000	0	28,000	$(1.15)^5$	13,921

Δvalue = $60,990

* ΔDep is for the ΔInvestment in the column immediately to the right.

† If present value tables are employed, the present value is $(-\$8,000)(0.870) + \$4,000(0.756) + \$48,000(0.658) + \$34,000(0.572) + \$28,000(0.497) = -\$6,960 + \$3,024 + \$31,584 + \$19,448 + \$13,916 = \$61,012$.

and the target's former stockholders sold their stock to the bidder for cash, all of the net benefits (i.e., the *NPV*) from the merger go to the bidder's stockholders.

Stock

What if common stock is used to finance the merger? In this case, the benefits of the merger are shared, because the target firm's stockholders end up owning part of the combined firm. Let's see what happens to the cost and the *NPV* when stock is employed.

Suppose that the same offer of $185,000 is made to the target's stockholders, but this time stock is used. The premerger price of the bidding firm's stock is $50, so 3,700 shares [i.e., ($185,000/$50)] will be issued to acquire the target. With stock being employed, the stockholders of the target share in the fortunes (and costs) of the combined firm. The portion of the combined firm owned by the target's stockholders, as represented by W, is determined as follows:

$$W = \frac{\text{shares held by the target firm's former stockholders}}{\text{total shares outstanding after the merger}} \qquad (8B.4)$$

$$W = \frac{3,700}{5,000 + 3,700} = 0.425$$

In the combined firm, the target's former stockholders own 42.5 percent of the total firm.

To determine the cost of the merger when stock is employed, we use a slightly different procedure than before. The total value of the combined firm is given by:

$$\text{total value of combined firm when stock is employed, value}_{BT} = \text{value}_B + \text{benefit} \qquad (8B.5)$$

$$\text{value}_{BT} = \$250,000 + \$210,990 = \$460,990$$

The cost when stock is employed is a function of the percent of the total value of the combined firm given up by the bidder's original stockholders, so:

$$\text{cost with stock} = W(\text{value}_{BT}) \qquad (8B.6)$$

$$\text{cost with stock} = 0.425(\$460,990) = \$195,921$$

Note that this cost is higher than when cash was employed. The *NPV*, using Equation 8B.1, is:

$$NPV = \$210,990 - \$195,921 = \$15,069$$

Although the merger is still beneficial, the *NPV* is lower when stock is employed than when cash was used. *This is always true if the same dollar value of cash or stock is employed to finance the merger.*

The use of cash or stock to finance the acquisition can be summarized as follows:

	Before Acquisition		After Acquisition	
	Bidder	Target	Cash	Stock
Market value	$250,000	$150,000	$275,990	$460,990
Number of shares	5,000	10,000	5,000	8,700
Price per share, P_0	$50	$15	$55.20	$52.99

When the same offer price is used for either cash or stock, we see that the total value of the combined firm is greater for the stock-financed acquisition. Due to sharing of the costs between the stockholders of the bidder and the target, the market value per share is $55.20 when cash is used, versus $52.99 when stock is used. If all else is equal (i.e., if the offer price is the same in either case), then the bidder's existing stockholders are better off with a cash-financed acquisition.

While mergers may seem very complicated, and they can be, the financial evaluation of the desirability of any merger from the bidder's standpoint is just a big (and more complicated) capital budgeting problem. As such, many of the concerns are the same.

CONCEPT REVIEW QUESTIONS

■ What are the basic steps for evaluating a proposed merger?
■ For a positive *NPV* to exist, what must the bidding firm be able to realize?

Problems

See Appendix C for answers to selected problems.

Basic Merger Analysis

8B.1 DeLuca Equipment is analyzing the possible acquisition of Borgia Products. DeLuca's market value is $3,000,000, and its market price per share is $40.

Borgia's market value is $800,000; DeLuca estimates the incremental value, Δvalue, is $250,000, and the total purchase price would be $1,000,000.

a. If cash is used, what is the *NPV* of the proposed acquisition?
b. What is the *NPV* if stock is employed?
c. Why is the *NPV* for a cash-financed merger greater than if stock is employed? How much more cash could be offered if the *NPV* for a cash-financed deal just equaled the *NPV* for the stock-financed deal?

Cash-Financed Merger

8B.2 Virginia Resources is investigating a possible acquisition financed with cash. It estimates the incremental benefits and investment as follows:

Year	$\Delta CFBT$	ΔDep^*	ΔInvestment
0	$ 0	$ 0	$300,000
1	40,000	60,000	—
2	50,000	96,000	—
3	60,000	57,000	—
4	100,000	45,000	—
5	100,000	42,000	—
6	70,000	0	—
7	20,000	0	—

*ΔDep is for the ΔInvestment in the column immediately to the right.

Without the incremental investment, Virginia estimates there will be very few benefits from the acquisition. Should it proceed with plans for the acquisition if the marginal tax rate is 35 percent and the appropriate opportunity cost of capital is 18 percent?

Stock-Financed Merger

8B.3 The estimated incremental benefits and investments for a proposed acquisition are:

Year	$\Delta CFBT$	ΔDep^*	ΔInvestment
0	$ 0	$ 0	$ 100,000
1	200,000	400,000	1,200,000
2	400,000	500,000	300,000
3	500,000	200,000	200,000
4 – ∞	800,000	50,000	200,000

*ΔDep is for the ΔInvestment in the column immediately to the right.

The tax rate is 0.35, and the opportunity cost of capital is 20 percent. The present market value of the target is $1,000,000, and the bidder's market value is $4,500,000. What is the *NPV* if the target firm's shareholders will control 25 percent of the combined firm's shares after the acquisition? Should the proposed acquisition be completed?

Incremental Cash Flows and Merger Analysis

8B.4 Lawrence Inc. is examining the possible acquisition of Berry Manufacturing. Lawrence has estimated the following anticipated incremental benefits and investments:

Year	$\Delta CFBT$	ΔDep^*	ΔInvestment
0	$ 0	$ 0	$ 50,000
1	80,000	30,000	100,000
2	150,000	60,000	25,000
3	150,000	60,000	—
4	150,000	25,000	—
5	60,000	—	—

* ΔDep is for the ΔInvestment in the column immediately to the right.

a. If Lawrence's tax rate is 0.30, calculate the incremental after-tax cash flows, ΔCF, expected from Berry.

b. The market value of Lawrence before the merger is $900,000, and Berry's pre-merger market value is $400,000. The market price per share of Lawrence's stock is $100, and the appropriate opportunity rate is 12 percent. Calculate the *NPV* for both a cash-financed and a stock-financed merger if Lawrence pays a premium of 25 percent above Berry's current market value.

Risk, Capital Budgeting, and Value Creation

Sections in this chapter:

■ **Risk and Strategic Decisions**
When and why more risk can be beneficial.

■ **Opportunity Cost of Capital for Capital Budgeting Decisions**
Which opportunity cost is important?

■ **Information About the Riskiness of Projects**
We can't ignore risk.

■ **What Leads to Positive *NPVs*?**
What to watch for in the capital budgeting process.

■ **Other Capital Investment Decisions**
We aren't finished yet!

Intel is the world's largest manufacturer of microprocessor chips—the silicon "brains" that make a computer work. The vast majority of personal computers sold contain Intel chips. Intel dominates the market with its 486 processor, and its successor, the Pentium. Yet, others are attempting to seize part of Intel's market share: Advanced Micro Devices (AMD) and Cyrix, both much smaller firms, make Intel-compatible chips. In addition, IBM and Apple Computer have joined up to develop an alternative microprocessor, the PowerPC. While the combination of IBM and Apple Computer seems formidable, the PowerPC is handicapped in a couple of ways. First, it will not run many of the current software packages, and software makers are reluctant to redesign their programs to run on the PowerPC. Second, Microsoft, the developer of the DOS and Windows operating software, says its new Windows version will not be compatible with the PowerPC.

To maintain its lead in supplying microprocessors to the computer industry, Intel must keep spending larger and larger sums to develop the next generation of chips. While the 486 is still here, the Pentium chip is the dominate chip in personal computers. And the successor to the Pentium, the P6, is already far along in development at Intel. To keep ahead of the competition, Intel continues with a high level of capital expenditures every year.

Investment decisions can have unforeseen consequences, and it is not easy to conduct a capital budgeting analysis in the face of a continuing stream of future investment opportunities. As an executive of a major firm recently stated, "You simply can't put a dollar sign on a technological future that may have a tremendous payoff." He noted that quantitative analysis is complicated by uncertainty. Which opportunities should be pursued, and which neglected? Which will prove successful, and which will fail? What is the probability of each potential outcome?

In Chapters 7 and 8 we ignored risk by assuming that all projects are equally risky. Now we examine how managers should make capital budgeting decisions in the face of uncertainty, and consider other facets of a successful capital budgeting process.

LEARNING GOALS

After studying this chapter you should be able to:

1. Discuss the impact of risk on the capital budgeting process, and list the risk factors to consider.
2. Determine the opportunity cost of capital for specific projects.
3. Determine the net present value when risk decreases over time.
4. Use sensitivity analysis and break-even analysis in capital budgeting decisions.
5. Understand what actions by firms lead to positive *NPVs* and why using market information is important.
6. Discuss the procedure employed when deciding to keep or abandon some equipment.
7. Discuss capital budgeting strategy for international investments.

RISK AND STRATEGIC DECISIONS

■ **LEARNING GOAL 1**

Discuss the impact of risk on the capital budgeting process, and list the risk factors to consider.

We know that risk and return are positively related. To improve expected return, investors must expose themselves to more risk. Exactly the same relationship holds for capital budgeting decisions: For a firm to increase its expected return, it must increase its exposure to risk. Let's see how this works in practice and, along the way, answer some of the questions its application raises.

Strategic Decisions

Much of this chapter builds on Key Idea 6—risk and return go hand-in-hand. However, throughout the chapter the other six key ideas also come into play.

All sources of risk are important for the capital budgeting process because of their effect on cash flows. But cash flows are not the only source of uncertainty; managers must also consider the firm's strategic position in its segment of the industry and market. Unfortunately, when considering strategic and risky decisions, firms may find reasons to ignore the capital budgeting techniques described in Chapters 7 and 8. One reason is the inherent complexity of some projects—especially when future investments may be an option that can be exercised in the future. Another reason is the difficulty, both in practice and in theory, of effectively identifying and quantifying which of the risks should be considered in analyzing prospective capital budgeting projects. Taking risk into account is one of the most difficult tasks in the capital budgeting process, but it cannot be ignored. To do so is simply to invite further problems.

Risk Can Be Beneficial

Risk can also be a positive factor in project selection. That idea may seem strange, but remember that higher expected returns are possible only from exposure to additional risk. "If you know everything there is to know about a new product," said an executive of a major firm, "it's not going to be good business. There have to be some major uncertainties to be resolved. This is the only way to get a product with a major profit opportunity." This manager has learned an important lesson: If the firm is to prosper, it must find new product areas that have the potential to increase the value of the firm significantly. That is, it must find positive net present value projects from which the firm can earn excess returns due to its competitive advantages. To find these areas, the firm may expose itself to risks above and beyond the average risks it faces. Is that additional risk exposure bad? No—not unless the firm does a poor job of evaluating and considering the risks.

Another agency conflict: Stockholders capture any gain from additional risk undertaken by the firm, but bondholders do not because their payments are limited. Thus stockholders tend to favor risky projects more than bondholders do.

Most significant, profitable investments and innovations have faced high risks. But higher expected returns accompanied those higher risks. Of course, not all high risk capital investments pan out. But managers must foster an environment within the firm that does two things: (1) encourages the development and consideration of high risk, high expected return projects, and (2) provides a proper format for adequately considering and evaluating these projects. Otherwise, the environment either will discourage risk taking or will lead to making high risk, complex capital investment decisions based on seat-of-the-pants analysis. Either result can have serious—and perhaps fatal—long-run consequences for the firm.

A Common Mistake

Using the same discount rate implicitly assumes that longer-term cash flows are more risky. Why? Because the risk premium in the discount rate is for 1 year; when we discount a cash flow that occurs further than 1 year from now, we compound the risk premium.

Many managers believe they must increase the opportunity cost of capital to account for the greater risk of the more distant cash flows. This is wrong. The use of any discount rate (above the risk-free rate) automatically recognizes that more distant cash flows are proportionally more risky. One way to think about the opportunity cost of capital for a project, or its required return, is to view it as a function of both the risk-free rate and a risk premium. That is:

$$\begin{array}{c} \text{opportunity cost of capital} \\ \text{(required return)} \end{array} = \begin{array}{c} \text{risk-free} \\ \text{rate} \end{array} + \begin{array}{c} \text{risk premium} \\ \text{based on project risk} \end{array} \quad (9.1)$$

If the risk-free rate is 6 percent and the risk premium for the project is 8 percent, for a total of 14 percent, both the 6 percent and the 8 percent compound over time. The compounding of the 6 percent adjusts solely for differences in the timing of the cash flows—in the absence of risk. The compounding of the 8 percent risk premium recognizes that more distant cash flows for the project are more risky. Thus, if cash flow distributions become more risky over time (as shown in Figure 9.1), then discounting implicitly takes account of some or all of this increase.

The use of a discount rate that embodies a built-in risk premium compensates for the *risk borne per period*. The more distant the cash flows, the greater the number of periods and, hence, the greater the adjustment for risk. The only question is how much more risky the more distant cash flows are. If they are highly risky, then a higher discount rate, embodying a higher risk premium, may be needed. The point to remember is this: *Some, and perhaps all, of the increase in riskiness of more distant cash flows is already accounted for simply by using the opportunity cost of capital.*

Factors to Consider When Estimating Risk

Risk relates to variability in returns, particularly returns that are less than those expected. Although the assessment of the risk associated with capital budgeting decisions is not easy, executives make such judgments every day. Some of the things they need to consider are fudge factors, cyclicality, operating leverage, and financial leverage.

FIGURE 9.1

Increasing Risk over Time

As the dispersion increases, risk increases. Using any rate above the risk-free rate in the discounting process implicitly compensates for some increases in risk.

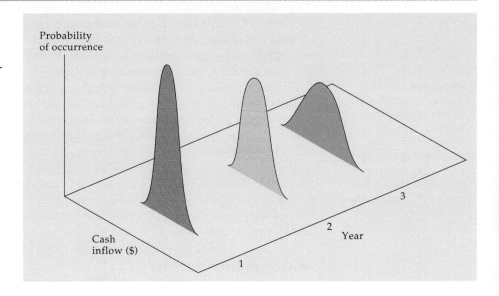

Fudge Factors, Instead of Making the Adjustments in Cash Flows

In working with firms, we have encountered situations in which the firm felt that some projects were more risky than the average risk of the firm. Their "solution" was to add a fudge factor to the opportunity cost of capital to compensate for the additional risk. Although that may be the correct procedure in some cases, too often the impact of potential bad outcomes is not fully reflected in the cash flows. Thus, mistakes in estimating cash flows are "compensated for" by adding a fudge factor to the discount rate.

Consider a project that requires a $5 million outflow and is expected to produce after-tax inflows of $2.25 million for each of 3 years. If the discount rate is 13 percent, the net present value of the project is:[1]

$$NPV = \frac{\$2,250,000}{(1.13)^1} + \frac{\$2,250,000}{(1.13)^2} + \frac{\$2,250,000}{(1.13)^3} - \$5,000,000$$

$$= \$1,991,150 + \$1,762,080 + \$1,559,363 - \$5,000,000$$
$$= \$5,312,593 - \$5,000,000 = \$312,593$$

It looks as if the project should be accepted. However, upon investigation you discover that due to problems getting government clearance, there is a strong possibility that no cash inflow will occur in the first year. If that happens, and assuming the $2.25 million in cash inflow will occur in each of years 2 through 4, the revised *NPV* is:[2]

$$NPV_{revised} = \frac{\$5,312,593}{(1.13)^1} - \$5,000,000 = \$4,701,410 - \$5,000,000$$

$$= -\$298,590$$

---

[1] *If present value tables are employed the NPV is $2,250,000(0.885) + $2,250,000(0.783) + $2,250,000(0.693) − $5,000,000 = $1,991,250 + $1,761,750 + $1,559,250 − $5,000,000 = $5,312,250 − $5,000,000 = $312,250.*
[2] *Using present value tables and the solution from footnote 1, the NPV is $5,312,250(0.885) − $5,000,000 = $4,701,341 − $5,000,000 = −$298,659.*

Clearly, this revised *NPV* greatly differs from the first *NPV*.

In this case, there is *some* discount rate that when applied to the original set of cash inflows of $2.25 million for years 1 through 3 will produce the revised *NPV* of −$298,590. That discount rate happens to be about 20.52 percent. But how do you know beforehand to add a fudge factor of 7.52% (i.e., 20.52% − 13.00%) to account for the probability that no cash flows will occur until year 2? The answer is you generally don't have any idea! Therefore, the preferable approach in *all* capital investment decisions is to position yourself so you can avoid such surprises: spend a lot of time, ask a lot of questions, and make sure that all possible assumptions and contingencies have been built into the cash flows. *Many of the problems in dealing with risk can be solved first and foremost by focusing on the cash flows.*

Cyclicality

The revenues and cash flows of some firms and projects are tied very closely to the state of the economy. Thus, firms and projects in high-tech industries, automobile firms, and retailers tend to be affected by the stage of the business cycle much more than firms in utilities or foods. Due to this greater risk, which typically cannot be diversified away, higher returns and discount rates are needed on investments whose performance is strongly tied to the stage of the business cycle.

Operating Leverage

OPERATING LEVERAGE
The commitment of the firm to incur fixed cash outflows for production and administration, no matter what the level of sales.

The concept of **operating leverage** refers to the commitment of the firm to incur fixed cash outflows for production and administration, no matter what the level of sales. Other things being equal, firms that have more operating leverage (that is, relatively more fixed cash outflows for operations) will see their cash flows fluctuate much more in response to a change in sales.

Consider two firms as follows:

	Low-Fixed-Cost Firm	High-Fixed-Cost Firm
Sales	$1,000,000	$1,000,000
Variable operating costs	600,000	200,000
Fixed operating costs	100,000	500,000
EBIT	$ 300,000	$ 300,000

Operating leverage can be determined by:

$$\text{operating leverage} = \frac{(\text{sales} - \text{variable costs})}{EBIT} \qquad (9.2)$$

where *EBIT* is the earnings before interest and taxes.[3] Using Equation 9.2, we find that the operating leverage for the low-fixed-cost firm is 1.33, whereas it is 2.67 for the high-fixed-cost firm. As sales fluctuate, the low-fixed-cost firm's *EBIT* will fluctuate 1.33 times as much. Thus, if sales go up by 20 percent, then due to the lower use of fixed operating costs, *EBIT* will go up by about 27 percent [i.e., (20%)(1.33) = 26.60% ≈ 27%]. For the high-fixed-cost firm, the higher operating leverage indicates

---

[3] *Operating leverage can also be measured by:*

$$\text{operating leverage} = \frac{\text{percentage change in EBIT}}{\text{percentage change in sales}}$$

that for a 20 percent increase in sales, *EBIT* will increase by about 53 percent [i.e., (20%)(2.67) = 53.40% ≈ 53%].

Firms or projects that have mostly high fixed operating costs have more operating leverage. Other things being equal, higher operating leverage means that the firm's or project's cash flows vary much more over the stage of the business cycle. These higher-risk projects require higher returns and discount rates.

Financial Leverage

Financial leverage refers to the presence or absence of fixed costs of financing. It is a concept that is similar to operating leverage, except that now the fixed costs relate to financing, not operations. Firms or projects that employ a lot of debt or other fixed-financing-cost sources of financing (such as leases or preferred stock) have more financial leverage. As *EBIT* fluctuates, high financial leverage means that more cash flows go to the fixed-cost providers of capital and less goes to the firm and its owners. The impact of financial leverage on the value of the firm is examined in Chapter 12.

Since many factors affect the riskiness of projects, estimating the specific amount of risk is not an easy task. By focusing first on the cash flows, financial managers can avoid many of the problems related to adjusting the opportunity cost of capital to reflect the project's riskiness. Then, the key is to focus on the major uncertainties facing the economy and how they will affect the proposed project, and to consider the action (and/or reaction) of competitors.

CONCEPT REVIEW QUESTIONS

- Why is consideration of a project's risk important for capital budgeting decisions?
- How can risk benefit the firm?
- Describe the factors that should be considered when estimating risk.
- What is the difference between operating leverage and financial leverage?

FINANCIAL MANAGEMENT TODAY

Strategic Decisions at Motorola

During the 1980s Motorola became a nimble giant committed to getting the most out of its employees in terms of new ideas and having the highest quality production and the lowest costs. Recognizing these accomplishments, the market bid up the price of Motorola's stock, which surged from the mid-teens in 1987 to the mid-50s in 1994. To foster innovation and even encourage dissent about ideas, every employee is entitled to file a "minority report" if he or she feels ideas are not being heard. And retribution for filing a minority report is rare; dissent and dispute at open meetings is encouraged. At the same time, Motorola has taken total quality management to levels almost unheard of by U.S. firms—it had to in order to compete with and beat Japanese firms. In the past 5 years Motorola claims to have reduced its defect rate in manufacturing by 99 percent, while generating cost savings estimated at $3.1 billion. Today, Motorola is the global market leader in cellular phones, two-way radios, and microprocessors used to control devices other than computers.

To illustrate how Motorola operates, consider how the firm reacted when managers discovered that a small Oregon firm, In Focus Systems, had developed a revolutionary type of video screen that Motorola badly needed. Within 3 months the two firms worked out a joint venture to manufacture the screens; 1 month later they launched the venture. The plant to produce the screens cost $70 million. Likewise, in 1985, a small group of engineers built a cellular phone that had 70 percent fewer components, was two-thirds smaller and lighter, and could be assembled by robots. The phones took one-tenth the time to assemble, and defects were reduced by 90 percent. When the phones were introduced in 1987, sales soared. Motorola's sales leapfrogged those of its Japanese competitors, even in Japan.

OPPORTUNITY COST OF CAPITAL FOR CAPITAL BUDGETING DECISIONS

Once we start considering risk adjustment, we need to distinguish between two different situations. The first is those situations in which *both initially and over time* the risks are above or below the average risk of the projects considered by the firm. The second involves projects for which *initially the risks are above the average risk of the firm, but after some initial period the risks decrease*. Because different approaches are needed to deal with these two cases, we examine them separately. In this section we first consider opportunity costs of capital for capital budgeting projects, and then we examine possible portfolio effects of such projects. Finally, we consider situations in which risk is expected to decrease after an initial start-up period.

Firm, Divisional, and Project-Specific Opportunity Costs

▤ LEARNING GOAL 2

Determine the opportunity cost of capital for specific projects.

In Chapters 7 and 8 we assumed, for simplicity, that risk was the same for all projects faced by the firm. We know, of course, that this cannot be true. Some projects are more risky, whereas others are considered very safe. In cases in which a project's risk differs significantly from the firm's overall level of risk, the use of a firmwide opportunity cost of capital results in the misallocation of resources.

Consider Figure 9.2, which depicts the effect of using a single firmwide opportunity cost of capital when risk is not uniform across projects. If the firm's opportunity cost is employed, project A will be rejected and project B will be accepted. However, if project A is less risky than the average project faced by the firm, then a lower discount rate (as given by the sloped project-specific opportunity cost of capital line) should be employed. All projects whose return and risk fall on the solid line whose

FIGURE 9.2

Firmwide and Project-Specific Opportunity Costs of Capital

Use of a firmwide cost of capital will overallocate funds to risky projects (like project B) and underallocate them to safe projects (project A).

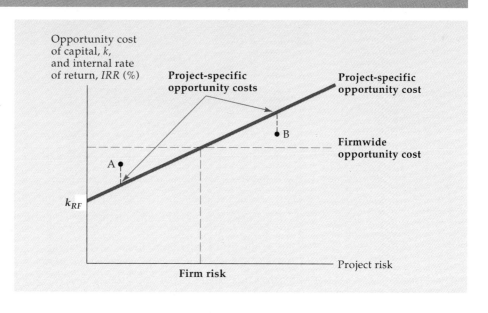

intercept is k_{RF} are zero *NPV* projects. Those above the line are positive *NPV* projects; those below the line are negative *NPV* projects. Because project A has an *IRR* greater than its appropriate opportunity cost of capital, it should be accepted. Project B is more risky; accordingly, an opportunity cost higher than the firm's overall opportunity cost of capital should be employed. Because the anticipated return on project B is less than its project-specific opportunity cost, it should be rejected. It is easy to see the effect of using a single rate for discounting all capital budgeting proposals: We overallocate resources to risky projects, while we underallocate resources to safer projects. The impact of such a mistake is to reduce the value of the firm.

As noted previously, the opportunity cost of capital appropriate for evaluating any capital budgeting project can be thought of as:

opportunity cost of capital = risk-free rate + risk premium based on project risk

There are, in fact, different approaches (as discussed in Chapter 6) to specifying what this opportunity cost should be. The first, based on the firm's weighted average cost of capital, provides a *single firmwide opportunity cost of capital*. This rate is appropriate for use when considering most replacement projects for a firm, or when the firm is homogeneous in terms of its projects and is not investing in any high- or low-risk projects.

The second approach is embodied in the form of *divisional opportunity costs of capital*. For example, an integrated oil company may have four divisions—domestic exploration, international exploration, refining, and marketing. Based on perceived risks in the different areas, the firm may establish divisional opportunity costs of capital as follows:

Domestic exploration	20%
International exploration	30
Refining	16
Marketing	12

These are the discount rates used in each division with net present value. The use of divisional rates may be thought of as a way station between the use of a single firmwide opportunity cost of capital and different opportunity costs of capital for each project. In practice many firms employ some type of divisional cost of capital for capital budgeting purposes.

Project-specific risk is greatest for projects unique to the firm or the industry, such as creating an entirely new product or developing new technology that will have only specific applications.

Finally, a *project-specific opportunity cost of capital* can be used, based on the risk associated with an individual project. Often the capital asset pricing model, CAPM, is employed to estimate these project-specific rates of return. Based on nondiversifiable risk, *for an all-equity-financed firm* a project's opportunity cost of capital using the CAPM would be

$$k_{\text{project}} = k_{RF} + \beta_{\text{project}}(k_M - k_{RF}) \tag{9.3}$$

where

k_{project} = the project's opportunity cost of capital

k_{RF} = the risk-free rate of interest

β_{project} = the project's nondiversifiable risk as measured by its beta coefficient

k_M = the expected rate of return on the market portfolio

Thus, if the firm is all equity financed, the project-specific discount rate based on the CAPM is given by the security market line, SML, introduced in Chapter 5. These approaches to estimating the opportunity cost of capital—firm, divisional, and project opportunity costs of capital—are depicted in Figure 9.3.

FIGURE 9.3

Alternative Opportunity Costs of Capital

Use of appropriate opportunity costs of capital, based on the risks and forgone opportunities, is essential for effective capital budgeting decision making.

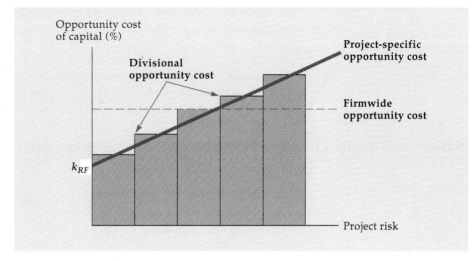

Two points should be emphasized about the use of alternative opportunity costs of capital to adjust for the risk of capital budgeting projects. First is the **stand-alone principle.** This principle says that a proposed project should be accepted or rejected by comparing it with the returns that could be secured based on investing in a similar-risk project. The forgone returns from the bypassed investment are captured by using the appropriate opportunity cost of the forgone alternative for the project. For example, if an equally risky investment involves investing in securities that would provide an expected return of 20 percent, then the proposed capital investment must return at least 20 percent. Otherwise the firm should reject the proposed capital project and invest in the securities. This stand-alone principle is important for all capital investment decisions made by the firm.

Second, estimation of the appropriate opportunity cost of capital in the face of risk is part science and part judgment. Although no method of dealing with risk is entirely precise, it is an important step that managers must take if they want to maximize the value of the firm. Failure to do so results in the same effect the ostrich achieves by burying its head in the ground—the world continues to spin and change while the ostrich (or firm) maintains its naive view that all is well.

STAND-ALONE PRINCIPLE
The principle that a capital budgeting project should be evaluated by comparing it with the return that could be secured by investing in a similar-risk project.

What About Portfolio Effects?

Should firms concern themselves about the possible interaction between the cash flows expected from a new project and those from existing projects? The answer to that question is generally "no," but it is more complicated than that. *First and foremost,* if a new project is expected to have any positive or negative effects on cash flows associated with existing projects, then (as noted in Chapter 8) these must be treated as opportunity costs or benefits and incorporated into the cash flows estimated for the new project.

The bigger question is this: Should the firm consider itself a portfolio and attempt to accept projects that reduce the risk (or standard deviation) of the portfolio returns? That is, are there risk-reducing benefits that arise when a firm undertakes a project whose returns are less than perfectly positively correlated with those of the firm? If financial markets are efficient, the answer is "no." The reason is that investors are able to diversify on

Investors can diversify most efficiently on their own. For a biotech company to add a telecommunications firm is folly. Investors who wanted such diversification could simply hold shares of each type of company.

their own; they do not receive any incremental benefits from having the firm diversify. In effect, the firm is performing a redundant service if it attempts to diversify.

In countries where financial markets are not completely efficient, there may be some risk reduction (in terms of the volatility of the firm's cash flows, probability of bankruptcy, and so forth) that can be achieved. It is very hard, however, to measure this benefit and very easy to overestimate its impact. For this reason, *projects should be considered on their individual merits*, without attempting to quantify any benefits from risk reduction. Then, if—and only if—it appears to be very important, possible portfolio effects can be introduced into the decision-making process.

When a Single Discount Rate Cannot Be Used

■ **LEARNING GOAL 3**

Determine the net present value when risk decreases over time.

Up to now we have considered how to deal with risk that is above or below the firm's risk over the entire economic life of the project. But what about the situation in which risk is high at first but then decreases?

To illustrate, consider the proposed development and marketing of "Clean-Ez," a portable electric car washer. In making its capital budgeting decision, the firm estimated that the preliminary phase, involving a small pilot plant and test marketing, would require a $7 million initial investment at time $t = 0$. If the preliminary phase is successful, a $40 million cash investment will be required to build the plant at time $t = 1$. Then for the next 9 years ($t = 2$ through $t = 10$), the after-tax cash inflows will be $12 million per year. Thus, the estimated cash flow stream is as follows:

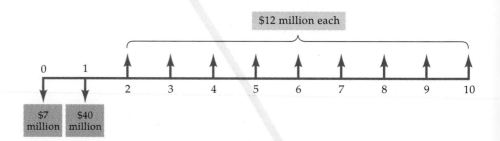

Because of the high risk of the project, the firm used a 20 percent return (versus the firm's opportunity cost of capital of 12 percent). Based on a 20 percent discount rate, the *NPV* was:[4]

$$NPV = \left(\sum_{t=2}^{10} \frac{\$12,000,000}{(1.20)^t} \right) \bigg/ (1.20)^1 - \frac{\$40,000,000}{(1.20)^1} - \$7,000,000$$

$$= \$40,309,665 - \$33,333,333 - \$7,000,000 = -\$23,668$$

Because the *NPV* is negative, the initial decision was to reject Clean-Ez.

[4]*If present value tables are employed, the answer is $12,000,000(4.031)(0.833) − $40,000,000(0.833) − $7,000,000 = $40,293,876 − $33,320,000 − $7,000,000 = − $26,124.*

However, Kay, a member of the finance staff, asked: "Have we accurately considered the riskiness of Clean-Ez? If risk decreases after the preliminary phase, then the use of a 20 percent discount rate over the entire life of Clean-Ez unnecessarily penalizes more distant cash flows." After some discussion, it was determined that there was only a 50–50 probability that the second investment (of $40 million) would be made at $t = 1$. If the test marketing in the preliminary phase was below expectations, then the additional funds would not be spent. On the other hand, if the preliminary phase was a success, then Clean-Ez would be of average risk, and a 12 percent discount rate would be appropriate over its remaining life.

SEQUENTIAL (decision tree) ANALYSIS
Method of representing alternative sequential decisions and the possible outcomes associated with the decisions.

Based on this additional information, Kay proceeded to analyze the project by looking at the risk and the opportunity cost at different points in the project. That is, she employed **sequential (decision tree) analysis**. First, she pointed out that there are two separate parts to the proposed project. The $7 million for the preliminary phase will be spent regardless. Depending on the results of that phase, there is a 50 percent chance that a $40 million cash investment will be made after 1 year for a project of average risk. Likewise, there is a 50 percent chance that no additional investment will be made. So:

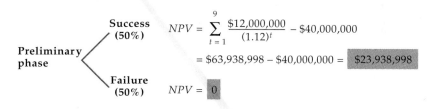

To find the net present value for the project's two phases, Kay needs to calculate the **expected _NPV_**, which is the average net present value obtained from the range of possible _NPVs_ for the project. For the Clean-Ez project, the expected _NPV_ in year 1 is simply $0.50(\$23,938,998) + 0.50(0) = \$11,969,499$. But this _NPV_ is for a project starting at $t = 1$, and we have not considered the $7 million initial investment. Looking at the _NPV_ of the total project from its inception, it is:[5]

EXPECTED _NPV_
The mean or average net present value obtained from a probability distribution of possible _NPVs_.

$$NPV = \frac{\$11,969,499}{(1.20)^1} - \$7,000,000 = \$9,974,582 - \$7,000,000 = \$2,974,582$$

Based on this analysis, Kay concluded—correctly—that the Clean-Ez project has a positive _NPV_ and should be funded.

One often hears executives or other critics of the present value approach say it unnecessarily penalizes long-term projects. As we have just seen, that does not have to be the case. By treating the decision as a sequential investment, we can handle the risk adjustment question. However, if we simply use a high discount rate, we _will_ be guilty of penalizing long-term projects if risk is not consistently at the higher level.

CONCEPT REVIEW QUESTIONS

■ What are the effects of using the firm's opportunity cost of capital when evaluating projects with different risks?

■ Describe how to adjust the decision-making process if you anticipate a decrease of risk in future years.

[5]Using present value tables the solution to the first phase is $\$12,000,000(5.328) - \$40,000,000 = \$63,936,000 - \$40,000,000 = \$23,936,000$. The expected NPV is $\$11,968,000$, so the NPV for the total project is $\$11,968,000(0.833) - \$7,000,000 = \$9,969,344 - \$7,000,000 = \$2,969,344$.

INFORMATION ABOUT THE RISKINESS OF PROJECTS

■ LEARNING GOAL 4

Discuss how to use sensitivity analysis and break-even analysis in capital budgeting decisions.

Up to now we have discussed risk in general as it relates to capital budgeting projects. We have considered how differences in risk can be dealt with through the use of different opportunity costs of capital. Before making capital budgeting decisions, it is important to examine the critical variables and assumptions that are expected to affect the project's success or failure. To do so we can employ sensitivity analysis or break-even analysis.

Sensitivity Analysis

SENSITIVITY ANALYSIS
An analysis of the effect of changing one of the input variables at a time to find out how much the result is affected.

Sensitivity analysis does not formally attempt to quantify risk. Rather, it focuses on determining how sensitive the net present value is to changes in any of the input variables. The method used in sensitivity analysis is to change one input variable at a time, to determine its effect on the result. To illustrate sensitivity analysis, let's consider the following example:

Year	CF
0	−$55,000
1	20,000
2	20,000
3	20,000
4	20,000
5	20,000

At a discount rate of 13 percent, the base-case *NPV* is:[6]

$$NPV = \sum_{t=1}^{5} \frac{\$20,000}{(1.13)^t} - \$55,000 = \$70,345 - \$55,000 = \$15,345$$

What if sales are less than anticipated? What if the competition introduces a new product? The purpose of sensitivity analysis is to see how sensitive the estimated NPV is to the underlying assumptions.

To conduct a sensitivity analysis, we need to change one of the input variables to determine how sensitive the *NPV* is to changes in that particular variable. The input data can be changed by a certain percentage, or by a given dollar amount.

To see how sensitive the *NPV* is to changes in the initial investment and number of years, we changed them each by 20 percent.[7] This results in an *NPV* of $4,345 for a 20 percent increase, or $26,345 for the same size decrease in the initial investment. Likewise, the *NPV* is $24,951 if the number of years increases by 20 percent (to 6 years), or $4,489 if it decreases by 20 percent (to 4 years).[8] In Figure 9.4, this information is plotted against the base-case *NPV*. The steeper the slope, the more sensitive the project's *NPV* is to a change in the input variable. We see that this project's *NPV* is slightly more sensitive to a 20 percent change in the initial investment than to a 20 percent change in its life. Thus, sensitivity analysis tells us which input variable has the greatest impact on the resulting net present value. Because of its ease of use and the information gained, sensitivity analysis is widely employed in practice. This is especially true with the increasing use of spreadsheet programs and on-line capital budgeting computer systems.

---

[6]*Using present value tables the NPV is $20,000(3.517) − $55,000 = $70,340 − $55,000 = $15,340.*
[7]*For simplicity we assume the per year depreciation remains constant, although the initial investment changes.*
[8]*Using present value tables the NPVs are $70,340 − $66,000 = $4,340, and $70,340 − $44,000 = $26,340 for the 20 percent increase or decrease in the initial investment. If the life is 6 years, the NPV using present value tables is $20,000(3.998) − $55,000 = $24,960, while if the life is 4 years, the NPV using present value tables is $20,000(2.974) − $55,000 = $4,480.*

Sensitivity Analysis of 20 Percent Change in Initial Investment and Years

The steeper the slope, the more sensitive the *NPV* is to a change in the input variable.

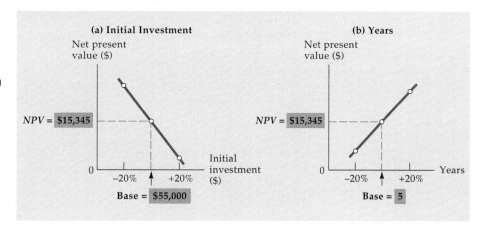

Break-Even Analysis

When undertaking a sensitivity analysis of a project, we are asking how serious it would be if some factor (e.g., cash inflows, life of the project, and so forth) turns out far worse than expected. Managers sometimes prefer to rephrase this question and ask how bad sales (and therefore, cash inflows) could get before the project loses money. This approach is known as **break-even analysis**.

BREAK-EVEN ANALYSIS
Analysis of the level of sales at which a project's *NPV* equals zero.

There are two approaches to conducting break-even analysis. The accounting approach relies on accounting-based revenues and costs, whereas the financial approach focuses on the discounted cash inflows and cash outflows. We shall see that the accounting approach, based on accounting costs and revenues, provides a biased estimate of the actual break-even point; it is too low. Hence, when firms break even in an accounting sense, they are losing money. The correct, financial-based break-even point occurs when the present value of the inflows equals the present value of the outflows, so that the net present value is zero.

Remember Key Idea 4— firms focus on cash flows and their incremental effects, not on accounting numbers.

To illustrate break-even analysis, assume that Whiz-Bang Motors is projecting net income and cash flows for its new product line as shown in Table 9.1. Under simplifying assumptions—where sales equal gross cash inflows, there are no accruals, and tax and GAAP depreciation are the same—Whiz-Bang estimates that when sales are $300, net income will be $54. To determine the accounting break-even point we need to find the dollar level of sales at which the net income is equal to zero. (To estimate an answer, we know that at sales of $300, net income is $54, so we know that the accounting-based break-even level of sales is less than $300.) The accounting-based break-even point is determined as follows:

$$zero\ sales = revenues - costs$$
$$0 = sales(1 - variable\ costs) - fixed\ costs - depreciation - taxes$$
$$0 = [sales(1 - variable\ costs) - fixed\ costs - depreciation](1 - tax\ rate)$$
$$0 = [sales(1 - 0.20) - \$50 - \$100](1 - 0.40)$$
$$0 = (0.80sales - \$150)(0.60)$$
$$0 = 0.48sales - \$90$$
$$0.48sales = \$90$$
$$sales = \$90/0.48 = \$187.50$$

TABLE 9.1

GAAP Net Income and Cash Flow for Whiz-Bang

For simplicity we assume the equipment costs $1,000 and is depreciated to zero over 10 years via straight-line for both accounting and tax purposes. Also, we assume that there are no accruals, and that sales and costs are all collected (or incurred) so they are equal to cash inflows and outflows.

	GAAP Income	Cash Flow
Sales	$300	$300
Variable costs (20% of sales)	60	60
Fixed costs	50	50
Depreciation	100	
Earnings before tax, *EBT*	90	
Taxes (40%)	36	36
Net income	$54	
Cash flow		$154

Thus, the accounting-based break-even level of sales occurs at $187.50. In Figure 9.5 we have plotted this relationship. The accounting-based break-even point indicates that the firm loses money up to a sales level of $187.50 and that it makes money (i.e., has revenue greater than costs) above a sales level of $187.50.

There are three differences between the accounting-based and the financial-based approaches to determining the break-even point. First, in finance we focus on cash flow, not on accounting-based revenues and costs. Second, we take account of the time value of money by discounting. Finally, in finance we consider the opportunity cost of the investment. Let's see the differences when the correct financial-based approach is employed. Going back to the sales level of $300 as discussed in Table 9.1, we see that based on an initial cash investment of $1,000, a 10-year life, and a discount rate of 15 percent, the per year cash flows after tax, CF_t, are $154. With cash flows of $154 per year for 10 years, the net present value of the proposed project for Whiz-Bang is:[9]

$$NPV = \sum_{t=1}^{10} \frac{\$154}{(1.15)^t} - \$1,000 = \$772.89 - \$1,000 = -\$227.11$$

At sales of $300 the accounting-based revenues and costs (from Table 9.1) indicate a profit of $54; but, we have just determined that the project has a negative net present value. Being financial experts by now, we know that if we accept negative *NPV* projects, we are lowering the value of the firm. How can the accounting-based analysis produce a profit, while we have just concluded that by accepting the project the value of the firm will decline? The crux of the problem is due to the accountants' lack of discounting and their treatment of the $1,000 initial investment, as we'll see.

[9]*Using present value tables the NPV is $154(5.019) − $1,000 = $772.93 − $1,000 = −$227.07.*

FIGURE 9.5

Break-Even Chart Based on GAAP Net Income

By ignoring the opportunity costs associated with capital investments, break-even analysis based on net income seriously understates the financial break-even point.

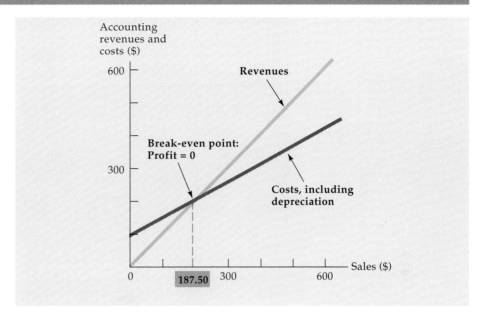

To continue our example, what happens taking the financial approach if (with all of the same assumptions) sales are zero or, alternatively, if they are $600? As shown in Table 9.2, when sales are zero the after-tax cash flows are $10 each year; with sales of $600 the after-tax cash flows are $298 each year. The net present value at zero sales is −$949.81, whereas the *NPV* when sales are $600 per year is $495.59.[10] To summarize, the accounting net income, cash flow, and net present value for the three levels of sales of zero, $300, and $600 are:

	Sales of $0 per Year	Sales of $300 per Year	Sales of $600 per Year
Net income	−$ 90	$ 54	$198
Cash flow per year, CF_t	10	154	298
NPV	−949.81	−227.11	495.59

We see that the *NPV* is highly negative when sales are zero, moderately negative when sales equal $300, and positive when sales equal $600 per year. Clearly, the zero *NPV* point occurs between $300 and $600 in sales.

To solve for the zero *NPV* level we proceed as follows:

zero *NPV* = *PV* of inflows − *PV* of outflows = 0

$$\sum_{t=1}^{10} \frac{CF_t}{(1.15)^t} - \$1{,}000 = 0$$

$$CF_t(5.0188) = \$1{,}000$$
$$CF_t = \$1{,}000/5.0188 = \$199.25$$

---

[10] *By financial calculator, when sales equal zero the NPV is $50.19 − $1,000 = −$949.81, whereas at sales of $600 the NPV is $1,495.59 − $1,000 = $495.59. Using present value tables the first NPV is $10(5.019) − $1,000 = $50.19 − $1,000 = − $949.81, and the second NPV is $298(5.019) − $1,000 = $1,495.66 − $1,000 = $495.66.*

> ### TABLE 9.2
>
> **Cash Flow for Whiz-Bang at Sales of Zero and $600**
>
> The same assumptions are maintained as in Table 9.1. With zero sales fixed cash outflows are still present, and assuming Whiz-Bang is profitable, the tax loss on this project can be recognized immediately.
>
> | | Zero Sales | $600 Sales |
> |---|---|---|
> | Sales | $ 00 | $ 600 |
> | Variable costs (20% of sales) | 00 | 120 |
> | Fixed costs | 50 | 50 |
> | Depreciation | 100 | 100 |
> | Earnings before tax, *EBT* | −150 | 330 |
> | Taxes (40%) | +60 | 132 |
> | Net income | $−90 | $ 198 |
>
> Cash flow $0 − 50 + 60 = $10 $600 − 120 − 50 − 132 = $298

The sales volume (before variable costs, fixed costs, and taxes) needed to generate after-tax cash inflows of $199.25 for each of 10 years is obtained as follows:

$$\text{sales} - (\text{variable} + \text{fixed costs}) - \text{taxes} = \$199.25$$
$$\text{sales} - (0.20\text{sales} + \$50) - (\text{sales} - 0.20\text{sales} - \$50 - \$100)(0.40) = \$199.25$$
$$\text{sales} - 0.20\text{sales} - \$50 - 0.40\text{sales} + 0.08\text{sales} + \$20 + \$40 = \$199.25$$
$$0.48\text{sales} + \$10 = \$199.25$$
$$\text{sales} = \$189.25/0.48 = \$394.27$$

This relationship is plotted in Figure 9.6. The present value of the cash inflows and the present value of the cash outflows cross at sales of $394.27. This is the point where the project has a zero *NPV*. As long as sales are greater than $394.27 per year, the project has a positive *NPV*.

What is the difference between the accounting and the financial approach to break-even analysis? First, the accounting approach, as shown in Figure 9.5, indicates Whiz-Bang breaks even at sales of $187.50. On the other hand, the financial approach (in Figure 9.6) indicates Whiz-Bang does not break even until sales are $394.27—a sales level over double that indicated by the accounting approach. What causes this vast difference? The difference in the two approaches hinges on the depreciation of $100 per year that is deducted for GAAP accounting purposes and the required rate of return of 15 percent for the project. *By treating break-even analysis in an accounting manner, managers are ignoring the opportunity cost of the $1,000 investment.* We must allow for the fact that the $1,000 could have been invested elsewhere to earn a return of 15 percent. Depreciation thus understates the true cost by ignoring the forgone opportunity to earn a return on the $1,000 initial investment. Companies that break even on an accounting basis are actually losing money—*they are losing the opportunity cost of their investment.* Whiz-Bang should not introduce the project unless sales are expected to be at least $394.27 per year. To do so will lower the value of the firm.

So far in this chapter we have identified a number of different ways of handling risk. Because risk comes from many sources, it is difficult to generalize about it. One thing is certain, however: Effective managers make a determined effort to probe for possible risks associated with capital budgeting projects. By proceeding in the manner described, *they are ensuring that the right questions about risk are asked at the right time and that reasonable methods of dealing with it are employed.*

FIGURE 9.6

Financial Break-Even Analysis

This is a form of sensitivity analysis, allowing sales (or the present value of the cash inflows) to change.

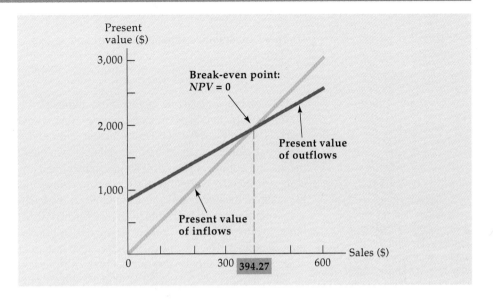

CONCEPT REVIEW QUESTIONS

■ What is the purpose of employing sensitivity analysis and break-even analysis?

■ What is wrong with using accounting revenues and costs to determine a break-even point? What factors does the financial approach to determining the break-even point consider that the accounting approach ignores?

WHAT LEADS TO POSITIVE *NPVS?*

■ **LEARNING GOAL 5**

Understand what actions by firms lead to positive NPVs and why using market information is important.

We have concluded that long-term investments having a positive net present value should be accepted. By doing so, the firm is maximizing its value. As discussed in Chapter 4, the value of the firm can be thought of as being equal to the present value of the assets in place (i.e., a nongrowing firm that is simply reinvesting enough to maintain its value) plus the present value of growth opportunities. There are still other facets of capital investment decision making; some of them are discussed in this section.[11] Let's start by considering the characteristics of projects with positive net present values.

Unique Attributes of the Firm or Projects

If product and labor markets are completely efficient, competition will quickly bid prices down or costs up to a level at which the *NPVs* are equal to zero. That is, competitors will continue to enter the market until prices allow no more than the minimum

---

[11]*One very important topic involves the use of options in order to assess the dynamic aspects of capital budgeting decision making. This is considered in Chapter 10 of* Financial Management.

acceptable return on capital, k. Hence, for a capital budgeting project to have a positive net present value, one of two situations must exist:

1. There are unique attributes of the firm or project.
2. We have estimated the data incorrectly—overstating the magnitude or timing of the cash inflows, understating the outflows, or employing too low a discount rate.

Let's examine these one by one. First, although we know that financial markets are reasonably efficient in developed countries, there is evidence that the labor and product markets are not as efficient. Less efficient labor and product markets may result from numerous causes—such as unique advantages in quality or cost (perhaps due in part to the special abilities of the firm's management and employees, or the use of nonunion employees) and legally imposed barriers to competition (such as patents). Other possible sources include consistent technological leadership, economies of scale that provide a continuing cost advantage, an established distribution and marketing system, or brand loyalty and trusted product warranties. All these barriers serve to accomplish one important goal: They delay the effective response of competitors and provide opportunities for firms to capture positive net present values before they erode. But unless there are legal or other effective barriers to entry, other firms will become aware of the excess returns (evidenced by positive *NPVs*) and devote the resources necessary to become effective competitors. Hence, *effective capital budgeting procedures must recognize the limited life potential of virtually all projects for producing positive* NPVs, and they should include an analysis of market imperfections, unique capabilities of the firm, and barriers to entry that form the keystone of positive *NPV* projects.

In less developed countries, simply producing and selling goods may provide unique advantages and the ability to earn excess returns. For example, within the last few years I spent some time in India. While there I visited with numerous executives about their capital budgeting decision-making process and the value-creating opportunities in India. A number of executives indicated that due to the tremendous demand for certain types of goods, simply having the goods available for sale, irrespective of their quality or price (within some limits), provided the opportunity to earn substantial returns. In an environment such as this, the combination of high demand and lack of effective competition means firms may enjoy the substantial returns that go along with positive *NPV* projects. In fact, it is not even necessary to do a very sophisticated capital budgeting analysis; back-of-the-envelope calculations may suffice. Over time, however, as the country's economy develops and competition enters, the ability to earn excess returns will be eroded away, just as in any other competitive market.

The second possible reason for positive *NPVs* is due to estimation problems. Several studies, along with discussions with numerous managers, suggest that in practice capital investment plans tend to be overly optimistic in their cash flow and risk estimates. Depending on the approach taken, this tendency can be traced to many different factors— the inherent optimism of managers, statistical problems, peer pressure, or ineffective performance and measurement systems. Whatever the cause, the result is that the input data used in the capital budgeting process may be deficient. The old data processing saying "garbage in, garbage out" clearly applies to the capital budgeting process as well. No matter how sophisticated the capital budgeting process, if the estimated cash flows or discount rate is incorrectly specified, the resulting net present value will also be incorrect.

Although there is no simple "cure" for measurement problems, there is one important ingredient of any successful capital investment program: a process and atmosphere that ensure that all assumptions are articulated and challenged and that the

By undertaking a project now, certain benefits not presently quantifiable may accrue to the firm. For example, expansion today may ensure a larger market share in the future; expanding today may discourage competition from entering the market.

unique strengths of the firm and project, and the potential reactions of competitors, are incorporated into the analysis. As I have told numerous firms, "If you don't quiz me too hard or look at the assumptions very closely, I can make the numbers in almost any investment project look good." But, that in no way ensures success for the project; poor analysis and making the numbers *look* good may be worse than seat-of-the-pants capital investment decision making by informed and demanding executives.

Relying on Market Values

The capital budgeting approach involves a detailed analysis of the magnitude, timing, and riskiness of expected cash flows associated with any project. Assuming a thorough analysis, the estimated *NPV* provides an indication of the potential outcome and wealth creation associated with the capital investment. But, the actual outcome may be more or less than the expected outcome due to unforeseen occurrences and/or forecasting errors. How should managers proceed in order to limit the potential for less-than-desired outcomes?

In many instances market value information can help assess the economic desirability of making the proposed investment. As an example, suppose a firm produces the "farmhelper," which promises to provide substantial time savings for most farmers. To ship the farmhelper to various retailers, the firm can employ either commercial trucking services or purchase its own trucks. The trucks require an initial investment of $3 million, whereas using the commercial trucking services requires after-tax cash outflows of $1.25 million per year. This market information, on the rates charged by commercial trucking services, is important. Alternatively, if the firm purchases the trucks, its after-tax cash outflows on the trucks will be $750,000 each year, and in 4 years the trucks will be replaced. Ignoring any subsequent replacement, the net present value problem faced by the firm if it purchases the trucks, as opposed to contracting with the commercial carriers at going market rates, is:

$$NPV = \sum_{t=1}^{4} \frac{(\$1,250,000 - \$750,000)}{(1 + k)^t} - \$3,000,000 + \frac{\text{resale value}}{(1 + k)^4}$$

$$+ \text{ extra gains from owning trucks}$$

Clearly, this net present value is negative unless the resale value is very large or there are substantial benefits associated with owning the trucks. Let's assume the after-tax resale value is $400,000 and the opportunity cost of capital is 14 percent. Then,[12]

$$NPV = \sum_{t=1}^{4} \frac{(\$500,000)}{(1.14)^t} - \$3,000,000 + \frac{\$400,000}{(1.14)^4} + \begin{array}{c}\text{extra gains from}\\ \text{owning trucks}\end{array}$$

$$= \$1,456,856 - \$3,000,000 + \$236,832 + \text{ extra gains from owning trucks}$$
$$= -\$1,306,312 + \text{ extra gains from owning trucks}$$

For the investment in the trucks to be beneficial, substantial extra gains must be associated with owning the trucks. What might those benefits be? Perhaps better and more reliable delivery times. Or, the firm might have additional uses for the trucks. The important point is that by using existing market values of what it would cost to contract with private shippers, the firm has an immediate idea of what the magnitude of the benefits have to be before investing in the trucks. Unless the benefits are substantial, the decision is straight-

---

[12]*Using present value tables the NPV is $500,000 (2.914) − $3,000,000 + $400,000 (0.592) = $1,457,000 − $3,000,000 + $236,000 = − $1,307,000 + extra gains from owning trucks.*

forward: Contract with commercial trucking firms for their services and concentrate the firm's attention on improvements in the farmhelper that will (1) increase its value, (2) keep it ahead of the competition, and/or (3) drive costs down and quality up.

Consider another example, in which MacroProducts has decided to acquire another firm through a merger. If the other firm is reasonably large, its stock will be traded and a market value already exists. How much will MacroProducts pay for the firm? Based on numerous studies and observations of ongoing mergers, we know that the typical premium paid is 30 to 50 percent above the going market value of the target firm. Say the target firm has a market value of $500 million, and MacroProducts pays a premium of 40 percent for a total of $700 million. Where is the value creation going to come from? The $500 million market value of the target firm reflects the investment community's best estimate of the fair (i.e., risk-adjusted) value of the firm's future cash flows. By paying 40 percent above the fair market value of the firm, MacroProducts has to achieve a lot of efficiencies just to recoup its investment. Will it be able to earn enough to more than cover the 40 percent premium paid? Many empirical studies indicate that, on average, mergers are zero *NPV* projects from the standpoint of the acquiring firm. The price paid is simply too great to allow them to earn any more than a normal return on their investment. Will such investments add value to the purchasing firm? Often the answer is emphatically "no!" Again, market values tell us much about what a group of assets is worth, and how much and where we have to look for value-enhancing benefits from the investment.

Although reliable market values aren't available for many assets, often they crop up in unexpected ways. For assets such as trucks, ships, real estate, crude oil and other minerals, some machine tools, and any financial assets such as stocks and bonds, reasonably competitive markets exist. When they exist, market values should always be employed either to serve as the starting point, to simplify the analysis, or to provide a straightforward direction concerning the general magnitude of the benefits needed and where they might come from. Although using existing market values does not solve all of the problems associated with capital budgeting, ignoring them results in valuable information being lost.

A key lesson to be learned from this discussion is that when market values exist, you need to ask yourself the question: *"Why are these assets worth more to me than their fair market value?" If a simple and direct answer to that question is not forthcoming, the acquisition of the assets is immediately suspect, no matter what a detailed capital investment analysis indicates.*

CONCEPT REVIEW QUESTIONS

■ What are the two situations that may exist in order for a capital budgeting project to have a positive net present value?

■ Why should effective capital budgeting procedures recognize the limited life potential of projects for producing positive net present values?

■ Why are market values important when evaluating capital budgeting projects?

OTHER CAPITAL INVESTMENT DECISIONS

Capital budgeting is a complex topic. While it may seem like we have covered every possible phase of it, we haven't. One area we haven't touched on is when to "cut and run," or abandon a project. A second area involves considering what factors, in addition to those presented so far, must be considered when capital budgeting decisions are made in a multinational environment. Finally, we summarize some guidelines that lead to more effective capital investment decisions.

Abandonment

■ **LEARNING GOAL 6**

Discuss the procedure employed when deciding to keep or abandon some equipment.

One of the most difficult problems in estimating cash flows is to make sure all the options are examined. Consider a manufacturing firm reevaluating an ongoing machine line. Assume the machine line has a 3-year life, and the expected after-tax cash inflows are as follows:

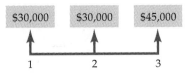

Looking at this cash flow stream, we might be tempted to conclude the machine line has a positive *NPV*. But what happens if you discover the machine line could be sold today for $85,000 after taxes? This $85,000 is an opportunity cost that must be considered. The choice is now between $85,000 today or the stream of expected after-tax cash flows, as follows:

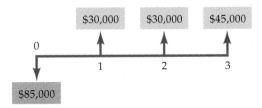

Assuming a discount rate of 14 percent, the *NPV* is:[13]

$$NPV = \frac{\$30,000}{(1.14)^1} + \frac{\$30,000}{(1.14)^2} + \frac{\$45,000}{(1.14)^3} - \$85,000$$
$$= \$26,316 + \$23,084 + \$30,374 - \$85,000 = -\$5,226$$

With this additional knowledge, the machine line has a negative *NPV*.

In the absence of any further information, the proper decision would be to abandon the project. This **abandonment decision** would maximize the value of the firm. Let's assume, however, the option to modernize the machine line exists, and the cash flows associated *solely* with the modernization are as follows:

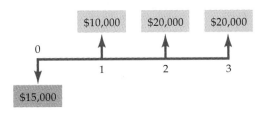

The relevant set of cash flows for decision making is now the combination of the existing and the new cash flows. Assuming the cash flows are additive (i.e., not

ABANDONMENT DECISION
Capital budgeting decision in which the net present value of continuing to operate a project is compared with the after-tax proceeds if the project is discontinued.

---

[13]*If present value tables are employed the NPV is $30,000(0.877) + $30,000(0.769) + $45,000(0.675) − $85,000 = $26,310 + $23,070 + $30,375 − $85,000 = − $5,245.*

complements or substitutes), the relevant cash flows for this abandon versus modernization decision are:

	t_0	t_1	t_2	t_3
Existing machine line	−$85,000	$30,000	$30,000	$45,000
Plus: Modernization	− 15,000	10,000	20,000	20,000
Relevant *CFs*	−$100,000	$40,000	$50,000	$65,000

At a discount rate of 14 percent, the *NPV* is:[14]

$$NPV = \frac{\$40,000}{(1.14)^1} + \frac{\$50,000}{(1.14)^2} + \frac{\$65,000}{(1.14)^3} - \$100,000$$

$$= \$35,088 + \$38,473 + \$43,873 - \$100,000 = \$17,434$$

Based on the relevant set of cash flows, the firm should keep and modernize the machine line. The second best alternative is to abandon the present line. The worst path is to continue operating the machine line as it is. By doing so, the firm passes up the opportunity of modernizing or abandoning—both of which are preferable.[15]

Capital Investments in an International Context

■ **LEARNING GOAL 7**

Discuss capital budgeting strategy for international investments.

Is Hardees a U.S. firm? Is HarperCollins (the publisher of this book)? Neither of the firms are U.S.-owned, but both conduct most of their business in the United States. The distinction between a U.S. firm and, say, a British firm, is increasingly meaningless in today's integrated economy.

We have examined how capital budgeting decisions are made for firms within a country. When investments are made outside the multinational firm's home country, the basic steps are the same; that is, we determine the opportunity cost of capital, identify the relevant incremental cash flows, and accept all projects with positive net present values. Although the steps are the same, there are some additional complications to consider. Two of these relate to what opportunity cost of capital to employ, and whether to conduct the analysis in the currency of the host country or to convert the forecasted cash flows into the domestic currency before evaluating the proposed investment. Generally, the analysis is conducted in the domestic currency after considering the impact of foreign and domestic taxes and expected exchange rates.[16]

Some additional issues have to be considered in international capital budgeting. If a firm has a foreign affiliate in Europe, the NPV of a project from the affiliate's perspective may be different from the NPV of the same project from the parent's perspective.

As discussed in Appendix 8B, an acquisition of part or all of another firm is simply a big capital investment decision. The general procedures to employ in evaluating proposed acquisitions outside of the bidder's home country follow those discussed in the appendix. One complicating factor when evaluating mergers outside of the home country revolves around the impact of exchange rates on the process. The approach favored by most firms is to make the analysis *in the currency of the proposed target*. Thus, if an acquisition is being contemplated in Mexico, the analysis would be done in terms of the Mexican peso. The one requirement of this approach is that there be a well developed capital market in the country of the proposed target so that a good estimate of the opportunity cost of capital can be obtained. Once the net present value is determined, it can be converted into units of the home country's currency at the present rate of exchange. If the capital market in the target's home country is not well developed, firms generally convert the incremental year-by-year cash flows back to the currency of the home country and then proceed as discussed previously for any other capital investment decision.

[14]*If present value tables are employed the NPV is $40,000(0.877) + $50,000(0.769) + $65,000(0.675) − $100,000 = $35,080 + $38,450 + $43,875 − $100,000 = −$17,405.*

[15]*Abandonment decisions are just another form of an option held by management. The divestiture of a firm's division is another type of abandonment decision. These topics are discussed in* Financial Management.

[16]*Multinational capital budgeting is discussed in detail in Chapter 27 of* Financial Management.

Increasingly, the world is being viewed as one big market by the most aggressive and successful firms, whatever their home country. These global firms must compete effectively in many parts of the world to cover their enormous fixed investment and/or research and development costs. The key is to develop the skills and corporate vision so that worldwide opportunities can be capitalized on while risks are dealt with effectively.

What does it take to develop an international capital budgeting strategy that will be effective in maximizing the value of the multinational firm? Some of the elements include:

International risk is increasingly pervasive. Even firms that do not buy or sell products in foreign markets are subject to international competition. With lower costs of transportation and communication, a firm's main competitor may be located anywhere in the world.

1. An ability to understand and capitalize on those factors that have led to successful *NPV* projects and strategies for a domestic firm. Then, these opportunities must be transferable to other countries while maintaining the competitive advantage that led to the firm's success in the first place. Advantages gained by patents that are about to run out or by trade restrictions, for instance, probably won't transfer into high *NPV* projects if implemented abroad.

2. A solid understanding of the best mechanisms for gaining successful and profitable entry into foreign countries. For example, must large capital investments for production facilities be made in the country, or can goods be imported effectively? What kinds of foreign ownership, licensing arrangements, and so forth are required? These and other related questions must be addressed, and investment and expansion decisions made.

3. The continual monitoring of the investment and its potential for the future. Given the rapidly changing world, assessing whether to increase the investment in a country, maintain it on a status quo level, or even reduce or abandon it is essential. Successful multinational firms take advantage of changes in the investment and political climates to shift production, research and development, and other components of a global strategy from country to country based on the economic opportunities presented.

4. A commitment to always consider the international dimension of all investment decisions. One way to provide this is to have an organizational structure that stresses local management while providing key executives with international experience. For example, at Dow Chemical the majority of top executives have extensive international experience.

The firm's primary objective remains the same in an international context as it is domestically—to maximize the value of the firm by undertaking positive *NPV* projects.

Some Guidelines for Structuring and Evaluating Capital Investments

The fact that there is a large body of capital budgeting theory, such as that covered in the last four chapters, does not mean that firms and managers can expect their capital expenditures to increase the value of the firm automatically. *Too often there are gaps between capital budgeting knowledge held by firms and managers and truly superior capital investment decision making.* Here we suggest some guidelines for improving the capital investment performance of the firm.

1. *Keep in Mind That the Discount Rate Is an Opportunity Cost.* It is vitally important to remember that the discount rate for any project is an opportunity cost. Thus, if you can earn 20 percent on a comparable-risk project, the opportunity cost of capital for that project has to be 20 percent; otherwise, the value of the firm will not be maximized.

2. *Don't Confuse Short-Run Profits or Cash Flows with Value Creation.* In visiting with managers we are always amazed at the overwhelming emphasis given to short-run goals and returns. Recently we visited a firm where if the capital investment couldn't pay for itself within *less than 1 year*, it was unacceptable. Clearly, for that firm short-run concerns are impeding the ability to make investments that create long-run value. Also, you need to recognize that some types of projects are necessarily much harder to quantify. Many firms that are emphasizing total quality management, TQM, have more difficulty relating cash flow figures to the hoped-for improved quality. But, remember, some studies have suggested that up to 50 percent of the effort in some businesses is spent in correcting something that was not done right the first time. Cash flow benefits often exist in a TQM environment; it's just that we have to work a lot harder to recognize and quantify them.

3. *Question the Cash Flows and Assumptions.* Remember, anyone with a good understanding of the capital budgeting process can "make the numbers look good" if not too many questions are asked about the sources or assumptions underlying the numbers. *A good capital investment process forces the right questions to be asked at the right time about the project, the unique strengths of the firm and project, and possible competitor action or reaction.*

4. *Recognize That Unique Ideas and Strengths Are Valuable and Have Limited Lives.* The cornerstone of value-enhancing *NPV* projects is the unique strengths and ideas that firms or projects possess. What are they? What type of steps can be taken to limit or impede the response of competitors from eroding the value-enhancing opportunities from the project? Attention to these areas must be incorporated into the capital budgeting process.

5. *Use Market Values.* When market values exist, it is foolish to begin the capital expenditure decision-making process by first doing a detailed cash flow analysis. Make use of the existing market data; if you can't convince yourself that the project has a positive *NPV* using the market value data, then it probably doesn't have one, no matter what a detailed cash flow analysis might indicate. Also, ask yourself why you think the asset is worth more to you than its going market value. What uniquely can the firm add that will result in the creation of a positive *NPV* project?

6. *Remember That Options Are Important.* Often we hear of major investment decisions that are negative *NPV* projects but are undertaken by firms because of "strategic considerations." The key missing ingredient is often a thorough assessment and valuation of the options embedded in the project. Numerous options exist—to abandon, expand on, defer, and so forth. Making capital investment decisions without explicitly considering these alternatives provides incomplete and potentially fatal information voids.

7. *Ask Why the Firm Should Continue with This Project (or Business).* Simply asking the question of what incremental value can be created by continuing with the project or business, versus putting the assets to alternative uses within the firm or selling then, is done all too infrequently by many firms. The implicit assumption is, "We are in this business, and to stay competitive we have to make this investment." But, that attitude often begs the real question: What is the most valuable usage that can be made of the assets and resources—physical, financial and human—of the firm?

8. *Provide Top Management with the Information It Needs.* This seems like a simple idea: Top management can make good decisions only if it has good information. But, individuals preparing capital expenditure proposals have vested interests in getting them accepted. Both personal pride and prestige are involved, along with financial remuneration and future promotions within the firm. Normally, when top management doesn't get the information it needs, there are informational, behavioral, or financial remuneration factors impeding the process.

9. *Tie the Measurement and Reward System to Long-Run Value Creation.* Increasingly, newspapers and magazines report the financial remuneration for top executives. Often, they are rewarded for short-term accounting profits or if the firm's stock price gets above a certain value and stays there for some minimum time, such as 30 days. But such actions are not in line with long-run value creation. Likewise, if the firm's compensation system rewards project initiators for short-run performance and/or accounting returns, the capital investment decisions that are made may maximize the wrong set of goals.

10. *Conduct Effective Postaudits.* It makes sense to conduct postaudits on some, but probably not all, of the capital investments the firm makes. The goal is simple—to learn from past mistakes so that future decisions are improved. Just having a postaudit program in place may accomplish this goal, but often the exercise is seen as unnecessary or is used to point the finger and assess blame. Effective postaudit plans avoid some or all of these tendencies.

We haven't covered all of the possible guidelines for improving the capital investment decision-making process. Others exist, and we encourage you to add to our list. *The key is to view the capital budgeting process, which is the primary source of value creation in firms, as a triggering and questioning form of structured decision making.* Merely doing things "by the numbers" and ignoring market values, options, managerial discretion, and the impact of the firm's decision-making process on the quality of the outcome invites disappointment and criticism of the entire capital budgeting process. It is not a panacea, but done properly, capital investment decision making forces the right questions to be asked at the right time. That is how an effective capital investment decision-making process and environment helps the firm create value and serve the needs of all of its interested parties.

CONCEPT REVIEW QUESTIONS

- Why is abandonment the reverse of the capital investment decision?
- What differences exist when firms invest internationally?
- Discuss the suggested guidelines for improving the capital investment performance of a firm.
- Why is it important to continue analyzing and questioning a firm's capital budgeting decisions?

Summary

- Risk may be beneficial; only by searching out its competitive advantages and accepting risks can firms expect to earn above-average returns.
- First and foremost, build all risk impacts into a project's cash flows if possible.
- Using any discount rate above the risk-free rate implicitly assumes that risk increases over time. The only questions are these: Is too much (too little) risk adjustment built into the discount rate employed? Does risk change over time more (or less) than accounted for by the discount rate employed?
- "High" cyclicality, operating leverage, and financial leverage can all lead to greater risk.
- Project-specific or divisional opportunity costs of capital should be employed for more- or less-risky projects.

■ The stand-alone principle is important: A project should be accepted or rejected by comparing it with the returns that could be secured based on investing in a similar-risk project.

■ Sequential analysis can be employed when risk changes over the economic life of a project. Sensitivity analysis is also widely used. Break-even analysis should be conducted based on discounted cash flows, not GAAP accounting numbers. Firms that break even on the basis of GAAP accounting numbers are losing money—they are losing the opportunity cost of their investment.

■ The capital budgeting process should focus first, and foremost, on the cash flows; it should ignore financing costs; it should consider abandonment decisions; and it should recognize the inherent differences when multinational projects are considered.

■ Effective capital budgeting procedures encourage decision makers to ask the right questions at the right time, as the firm strives to maximize its long-run value creation opportunities.

Questions

9.1 The divisional opportunity cost of capital approach to capital budgeting, employing categories of projects with different risks, might be graphed as follows:

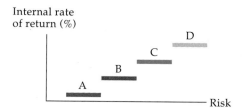

Explain how divisional opportunity costs capture many of the risk and return ideas of the capital asset pricing model. In what significant ways do the two differ?

9.2 Explain the importance of the stand-alone principle. Why are opportunity costs (or the forgone returns from bypassed investments) so important in making wealth-maximizing capital budgeting decisions?

9.3 Adam believes that sensitivity analysis is a viable way to deal with risk. Do you agree with him? Why or why not?

9.4 Why does break-even analysis, when conducted employing GAAP accounting numbers, result in understating the financial break-even point? Can you see any redeeming features of an accounting-based break-even analysis?

9.5 How are positive *NPVs*, the unique attributes of firms and projects, and good data related?

Concept Review Problems

See Appendix A for solutions.

CR9.1 Rodrigo Inc. is considering purchasing a coal mine in Wyoming. Cost of the coal mine is $8 million, and the opportunity cost is capital of 15 percent. Rodrigo's engineers believe (with 50 percent probability) there is enough coal to produce $2 million in after-tax cash flows for the next 5 years. On the other hand, there may be (with 50 percent probability) enough coal to produce $2 million in after-tax cash flows for 10 years. What is the expected net present value of the project?

CR9.2 Suzanne, owner of Belles Fleurs, is considering expanding into the silk floral market. She estimates the expansion will cost $60,000 and that she will sell approximately 600 different silk floral arrangements per year over the next 4 years, at an average price of $100 per arrangement. Her operating costs are estimated to be approximately 50 percent of revenue.

Note: For simplicity in (a), assume no depreciation will be taken on the $60,000 expenditure.

    a. If Belles Fleurs' tax rate is 28 percent and the opportunity cost of capital is 10 percent, what is the net present value of this project?

    b. Suzanne is concerned about the risk of the silk floral arrangement project. She is concerned that sales may not be 600 floral arrangements per year. Perform a sensitivity analysis on the number of silk floral arrangements sold per year in which the floral arrangements drop by 10 percent, 20 percent, or 30 percent, or increase by 10 percent, 20 percent, or 30 percent.

CR9.3 Using the information for Belles Fleurs given in CR9.2, what is the (accounting) break-even for the number of units of floral arrangements sold per year?

CR9.4 Suzanne is concerned about the effects of a fluctuating economy on the profitability of the silk flower expansion in CR9.3. If a downturn in the economy occurs, she will be able to sell only 500 units at $80 per unit. However, if the economy is better than anticipated, she will be able to sell 700 units at $120 per unit.

Note: In CR9.4, costs remain 50 percent of revenue.

    a. If the probabilities are 30 percent for a downturn in the economy, 40 percent for the base-case economy with 600 units sold at $100 per unit, and 30 percent for an improved economy, what is the expected net present value of the three scenarios?

    b. What is the standard deviation about the expected net present value?

CR9.5 Guy's Rentall is considering selling the company's supply of side-discharge lawnmowers. Because of the increased customer demand for mulching mowers, income from rental fees on the side-discharge mowers has declined. The mowers are expected to last 3 more years with an after-tax cash flow from the mowers of $5,000 for each year.

    a. Guy estimates the mowers could be sold for $10,000 after taxes, and the opportunity cost of capital is 15 percent. Should the side-discharge mowers be sold?

    b. Guy also has the option to increase the demand for his mowers by installing a conversion kit that easily allows the switch from a side-discharge mower to a mulching mower. Conversion kits cost $3,000 to purchase and install. Cash flows will increase to $7,000 per year for the next 3 years. Should Guy purchase the conversion kits?

Problems

See Appendix C for answers to selected problems.

CAPM

9.1 Lee-Sun Industries employs the capital asset pricing model to estimate project-specific costs of capital for capital budgeting decisions. The risk-free rate is 7 percent, the expected return on the market portfolio is 15 percent, and the project's beta is 1.50. The cash flow stream is as follows:

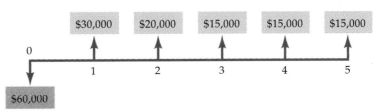

a. Should Lee-Sun undertake the proposed project?

b. Can you see any problems associated with using the capital asset pricing model to estimate project-specific costs of capital for capital budgeting decision making?

CAPM: Determining Beta

9.2 Millman is considering the investment in some new equipment. The *CFs* are as follows:

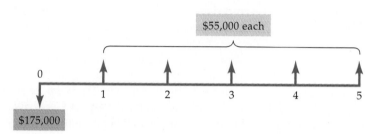

$55,000 each

0

1 2 3 4 5

$175,000

The CAPM approach will be used to estimate the appropriate project-specific opportunity cost of capital; $k_{RF} = 7$ percent, $\sigma_{project}$ (standard deviation of the project's returns)=32.20 percent, $Corr_{project,M} = +0.60$, and the distribution of the market's return is:

Probability, P_i	Market Return, k_{Mi}
0.20	30%
0.20	20
0.30	15
0.30	-5

Note: In (a), carry to two decimal places.

$\beta_{project} = \sigma_{project} Corr_{project,M}/\sigma_M.$

a. What is the project's beta?

b. Should Millman purchase the equipment?

Required Rate of Return

9.3 Your firm is considering two mutually exclusive projects with the following *CFs*:

	Project A		Project B	
Initial investment	$120,000		$150,000	
Probabilities of occurrence	0.30	$35,000	0.30	$60,000
and *CFs* for each of 6 years	0.40	30,000	0.40	40,000
	0.30	20,000	0.30	30,000

The following equation is employed to estimate the project-specific opportunity cost of capital:

Note: In (a) the coefficient of variation is standard deviation/mean. In (b) round the opportunity cost of capital to the nearest whole percent.

$$\text{opportunity cost of capital} = \text{risk-free rate} + 10\%(\text{coefficient of variation})$$
$$= 11\% + 10\%CV_{project}$$

a. Which project is riskier, based on its coefficient of variation?

b. Which, if either, of the projects should be selected?

Operating Leverage

9.4 Omar Industries produces various wood products. Their average selling price is $10 per unit. The variable cost is $6 per unit, and total fixed costs are $60,000.

a. What would the firm's *EBIT* be if the number of units sold were 20,000, 30,000, or 40,000?

b. Find the degree of operating leverage for each of the three production and sales levels given in (a).

c. What conclusion can we draw about the degree of operating leverage as the sales increase?

Expected *NPV*

9.5 Tolliver Enterprises is evaluating whether to build an exclusive resort on the island of St. Croix. The *CFs* are estimated to be $23 million for each of 15 years, the initial after-tax investment is $150 million, and the appropriate discount rate is 10 percent.

a. Should Tolliver proceed with the project?

b. Upon further investigation, it is decided that the *CFs* could be better characterized by the following probability distribution:

Condition	Probability	*CFs* per Year
Economy great	0.2	$30 million
Economy average	0.7	23 million
Hurricane: resort demolished	0.1	0

Does this new information affect the decision?

Sequential Analysis

9.6 Holmes has developed chocolate marbles. The product will be test marketed in the southeastern United States for 2 years, requires an initial investment of $2 million, and because of heavy promotional expenses is not expected to generate any positive *CFs* during the first 2 years. There is a 60 percent chance that demand for the chocolate marbles will be satisfactory; if that is so, an $8 million after-tax cash investment will be incurred at $t = 2$ to market the chocolate marbles in the eastern half of the United States. Subsequent *CFs* are as follows:

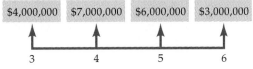

If the test-market results are unfavorable (a 40 percent chance), then the chocolate marbles will be withdrawn from the market. Once consumer preferences are known, Holmes considers chocolate marbles an average-risk project requiring a 14 percent return. During the test-marketing phase a 25 percent return is required. What decision should Holmes make?

Sequential Analysis

9.7 Flanigan Industries is considering investing in a capital budgeting project with the following *CFs*:

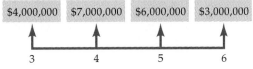

For the first 3 years, the appropriate opportunity cost of capital is 30 percent; after that, it drops to 10 percent. What decision should Flanigan make?

Sensitivity Analysis

9.8 Fresh 'N Clean Painters can purchase a mixing machine for an initial investment of $11,000. It would last 5 years and produce after-tax operating cash flows of $3,900 per year. The discount rate is 16 percent.

a. Decide whether the company should purchase the mixer under each of the following independent conditions. To which variable is the accept-reject decision most sensitive?

1. The estimates are correct.

2. The machine lasts only 4 years.

3. After-tax operating cash flows decrease by 10 percent, so they are ($3,900)(0.90) for each of years 1 through 5.

4. The discount rate is 3 percent too low.

b. Should the company invest in the mixer if all of the following conditions exist simultaneously?
1. Machine cost=$13,000.
2. Discount rate=15 percent.
3. Marginal tax rate=33 percent.
4. Terminal resale value (before tax)=$2,000.
5. Machine will last 10 years.
6. After-tax operating cash flows increase by 25 percent, so they are ($3,900)(1.25) for each of years 1 through 10.

Sensitivity Analysis

9.9 The board of directors of Island Industries has just received a proposal that requires an initial investment of $1 million and is expected to produce cash flows before tax, *CFBT,* of $300,000 for each year of its life. As presented, the project has a 7-year economic life, but the initial investment will be depreciated by straight-line over its 5-year normal recovery period. The discount rate is 15 percent, and the firm's tax rate is 35 percent.
  a. Should Island's board recommend acceptance of the project?
  b. After discussing the project, certain members of the board feel the economic life will be only **(1)** 5 years, or **(2)** 6 years, not 7. Does this new information change the previous decision?

Break-Even Analysis

9.10 Jacobi Hats is considering the extension of an existing product line. The incremental initial investment is $1.4 million, and the rest of the assumptions are as follows:
1. Depreciation for tax purposes to zero will occur over 7 years via straight-line; the economic life is also 7 years.
2. Variable costs are 30 percent of estimated sales.
3. Fixed costs are $100,000.
4. The tax rate is 40 percent and the discount rate is 20 percent.

What is the per year financial break-even level of sales?

Financial Versus Accounting Break-Even Analysis

9.11 Emanuel Products has developed a whole new concept for distributing "gee-whizzes." Excluding land costs, the new outlets require an initial investment of $4 million per location. The following conditions apply:
1. Depreciation for both GAAP accounting and for tax purposes will be to a value of zero over 10 years using straight-line.
2. Variable costs are 50 percent of sales.
3. Fixed costs are $300,000 per year.
4. The firm's marginal tax rate is 30 percent, and the discount rate is 18 percent.

Excluding land costs, what is the accounting break-even point per year? What is the financial break-even point (also excluding land costs)? Why does the accounting break-even point underestimate the volume of sales necessary to produce a zero *NPV* project?

Replacement Decision and Break-Even Initial Investment

Note: For the existing system, 5 years have already elapsed.

9.12 Costs have decreased, and Ventra Foods is considering replacing its existing refrigeration system. To help in negotiating the final purchase price, it has hired you as a consultant. The relevant facts are:

Existing System

Purchased 5 years ago for $800,000.

Being depreciated to zero employing straight-line over 10 years.

Will last 10 more years if retained.

Resale value if sold today is $150,000; resale value in 10 years is $20,000.

New System

Will be depreciated to zero employing straight-line over 10 years.

Will last 10 years.

Resale value in 10 years is $50,000.

Benefits are a before-tax reduction in operating cash outflows of $75,000 per year.

Note: *In (a) assume the firm is profitable, so it receives the tax benefit from selling the existing system at a loss.*

a. If the tax rate is 35 percent and the opportunity cost of capital is 15 percent, what is the initial purchase price on the new system so that the *NPV* equals zero?

b. Explain why the information calculated in (a) is important for effective decision making.

Keep Versus Abandon

9.13 Bavaro Corporation sells a number of specialized product lines. Due to increasing competition, the *CFs* for its Gamma product line are estimated as follows:

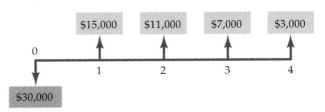

A competitor has approached Bavaro and offered $650,000, after taxes, for the product line. If Bavaro's opportunity cost for this product line is 17 percent, what should it do?

Keep, Abandon, or Modernize

9.14 Sivore Products is considering abandoning a product line. The line could be sold for $50,000 after taxes, or it could be kept and will produce after-tax cash flows of $17,500 for each of 4 years. In addition, the possibility of modernizing the line with after-tax cash flow consequences solely for the modernization is as follows:

$15,000 $11,000 $7,000 $3,000

0   1   2   3   4

$30,000

Should Sivore's abandon, keep, or modernize if the discount rate is 14 percent?

Risk and Capital Budgeting

9.15 **Mini Case** You were recently hired by Gannon Ltd. to head up its capital and strategic decisions group. Gannon has three major divisions: a farm implements division that continues to experience intense competition and weak demand, a high-tech metals and materials division, and a financial services division. The financial services division originally provided financing only to dealers and farmers, but over the last 15 years it has undergone tremendous changes. Now it provides many different financial services to firms worldwide. At present Gannon employs a firmwide opportunity cost of capital of 15 percent and does little to consider risk when making capital expenditure decisions.

a. One of your first jobs is to educate the board of directors and upper management on the basic ideas concerning the importance of risk taking when making capital budgeting decisions, and the negative impact that the reliance on a firmwide opportunity cost of capital may have on project selection. What should the firm be doing in terms of the opportunity costs of capital employed? How would you respond when one of the top executives challenges you by saying, "As long as we are discounting future cash flows we are considering risk, because future cash flows are treated as being inherently risky."

b. The metals and materials division is evaluating a new project. The division's projections for the after-tax cash flows associated with the proposed project are as follows:

Year	CF
0	− $2,500,000
1	− 3,000,000
2	− 4,000,000
3	5,000,000
4	6,000,000
5	6,000,000
6	3,000,000

(1) At the firm's opportunity cost of capital, what decision should be made?

(2) After listening to your presentation in (a), the board adopts a new divisional cost of capital structure. The new discount rate for the metals and materials division is 20 percent. Does this change the decision?

(3) After talking with individuals in the metals and materials division, you find that the proposed project is actually more complicated. Specifically, you find out that there are two phases to the proposed project. The preliminary phase requires the investments at times $t = 0$, $t = 1$, and $t = 2$. Depending on the outcome of the preliminary phase the following might happen:

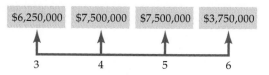

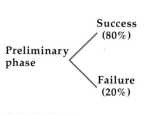

An additional $5,000,000 after-tax cash outlay will be required at $t = 2$ to shut the project down beyond the $4,000,000 already projected

The preliminary phase is viewed as being very risky; a 40 percent discount rate is appropriate. After the preliminary phase, the 20 percent discount rate is viable. Does this new information affect the decision to accept or reject the project?

c. Now the financial services division comes to you with a project that has cash flows as follows:

Year	Cash Inflow	Cash Outflow
0	$ 0	$80,000
1	30,000	5,000
2	30,000	5,000
3	50,000	10,000
4	50,000	10,000
5	50,000	10,000
6	40,000	25,000
7	40,000	25,000
8	40,000	25,000

Depreciation will be straight-line over 5 years, the appropriate tax rate is 30 percent, and the discount rate is 15 percent.

(1) What is the base-case *NPV*?

Note: In (2) each part is separate and distinct from the other parts.

(2) What is the *NPV* if each of the following occurs?

    (a) Cash inflows in time periods $t = 1$ through $t = 8$ decrease by 20 percent per year.

    (b) Cash outflows in time periods $t = 1$ through $t = 8$ increase by 20 percent per year.

    (c) The tax rate increases by 20 percent.

Note: In (2d) this also changes the per year depreciation.

    (d) The initial investment increases by 20 percent.

    (e) The discount rate increases by 20 percent.

    (f) The life of the project decreases to 6 years.

To which variable is the *NPV* most sensitive?

d. How is break-even analysis just another form of sensitivity analysis?

PART 4

LONG-TERM FINANCING DECISIONS

EXECUTIVE INTERVIEW WITH JAMES MACNAUGHTON

*Managing Director
Salomon Brothers,
New York, New York*

Salomon Brothers is one of the largest and best-known investment banking firms in the world. James H. MacNaughton, managing director at Salomon Brothers, co-heads the firm's investment banking business with financial institutions of all kinds. During his 15-year tenure at Salomon Brothers, he has run the Diversified Industrial Group in investment banking, the global insurance group, and also has worked with assorted companies in the Financial Institutions Department. Mr. MacNaughton earned his B.A. degree in history and an M.B.A. degree from Southern Methodist University. He is also a Certified Public Accountant in the state of Texas. We asked Mr. MacNaughton to discuss capital structure and dividend decisions in the financial institutions industry.

Developing a long-term financing strategy involves many interrelated factors. A financial manager must first understand the characteristics of the company's business and industry in order to develop an appropriate capital structure and financing strategy. Financing is not generic; companies in different industries and industry segments will have financing patterns and strategies that relate to the nature of their business. For example, the financing needs of a financial services company differ from those of a manufacturing firm.

The decision to go to the market for financing begins with the company's overall plan—including cost of capital, capital structure, and targeted debt and equity ratios. That decision is followed by consideration of more specific factors like the average maturity of existing long-term debt and the mix of floating versus fixed rate debt. The financing environment is also important: Financing trends, market conditions, and market demand for both your industry and the specific securities you wish to issue affect whether you can raise money efficiently and how much you pay for it.

Managing long-term financing involves more than obtaining debt and equity capital. Another critical aspect is working with lenders, to keep them well informed about the company's operations and to alert them to any potential problems. They don't like surprises. When a company gets into financial difficulties, it must work closely with its lenders to develop a financing strategy to work through the problems. This strategy may include obtaining waivers of financial covenants contained in loan agreements or renegotiating the loan.

Companies need long-term financing, both permanent and temporary capital, to support their business activities and growth. For example, a bank may wish to expand by acquiring another bank, while a manufacturing company may want to build a new plant. The only difference is the type of assets the financing supports: hard assets versus financial assets. The most permanent form of long-term financing is common stock, followed by preferred stock; long-term debt has varying maturities that can be matched to the use of funds. The types and proportion of a company's long-term funding comprise its capital structure.

Companies must determine an appropriate capital structure for several reasons. First, they must know the amount of permanent (long-term) versus temporary (short-term) capital required for operations and growth over a certain time horizon. Ideally, a firm should match the type of capital—the most permanent being common stock, relatively permanent being preferred stock or long-term debt—with its needs. Another important consideration is whether the company's capital structure is similar to other companies in its industry. Credit rating agencies look carefully at capital structure when assigning their ratings, and credit ratings are critical factors in determining what a company will pay for its capital. The amount of debt affects the firm's debt rating (credit quality), which affects the borrowing cost, which affects market value.

Many factors are involved in determining the types of capital financing companies use. One key consideration is the interest rate environment. When interest rates are low, as they were from 1992 to mid-1994, debt becomes more attractive. Also, companies are now more comfortable using leverage in their balance sheets than they were in the past.

A capital structure with all equity and no debt doesn't take advantage of leverage to improve return on equity. More debt and less equity may create more risk than desired. Finding the right balance is the key, and that also depends on your industry and competitors. Almost all companies today use leverage to raise return on equity and, therefore, maximize the total worth of the company.

Credit ratings are the lifeblood of financial institutions. Without adequate credit ratings, financial institutions can't compete. I can't overemphasize the importance of credit ratings for this industry. They determine borrowing cost and are also the imprimatur of a financial institution's safety. A company rated AA pays less for debt than one rated A. Dropping below an A rating from Standard & Poor's and Moody's signals that an institution has a financial, and maybe even an operating, disadvantage compared to its competitors.

Ratings are also a determinant of safety. Look at the recent crises in the thrift, commercial bank, and insurance industries. These were all large institutions who sold savings-type products to people who depended on the money being available when they needed it. Many of these firms were very highly leveraged or took on more risky loan assets than was prudent, increasing their risk. The failures of banks and insurance companies have scared the public, and rightly so. Now consumers are sensitive to credit ratings, too.

Dividend Policies

Along with the changes in capital structure of financial institutions that I've witnessed, dividend policies of financial institutions have also changed over time. The more mature public financial institutions typically allowed their dividends to increase at a small growth rate. In some cases the dividend growth rate kept edging higher; today, dividends at some financial institutions represent a high percentage of stock price. This is not necessarily good. Most financial institutions are capital-intensive, and dividends are counterproductive to a capital-intensive business, which should use the capital to grow its business rather than to pay dividends.

In my opinion, a company is better off retaining earnings than paying dividends. The additional equity helps the company grow faster, and investors benefit in the long run from a higher stock price. But many investors want a high dividend yield *plus* a high stock price appreciation. These two scenarios are in conflict in capital-intensive businesses like insurance and banking. Also, both the investment community and the general public are very concerned about credit quality, and a common stock dividend represents a high fixed charge that undercuts credit quality. Technically, of course, common stock dividends are discretionary. In practice, however, once a company starts paying dividends, they're *not* discretionary—unless you want to change the fundamental way that the market views the company.

I would advise companies to view their dividend policy in the same capital planning mode as other capital needs that support current operations and growth. Are dividends a good use of excess cash, or is there a better use? In recent years many companies have managed their capital using nominal or smaller dividends together with stock repurchase programs. That policy allows greater flexibility than common dividends to manage capital position. Buying back stock may be a better investment than an acquisition, another plant, or cash dividends. Basically, it's another capital investment decision for analysis: What is the best use of my capital given these different options?

Today, institutional investors have a dramatic effect on markets because they set values and can also dictate terms of bond and stock offerings as well as debt covenants. Big companies who borrow large amounts through bonds and sell large amounts of stock have to deal with institutions in the end. So they gear some of their capital structure and dividend policies to institutional investors' needs. For example, many recent initial public offerings have had nominal dividends. Why offer any dividend at all? Who cares about one-half of 1 percent, or even 1 percent? Pension funds do. The nominal dividend is necessary because some pension funds cannot buy a non-yielding stock. The small dividend is manageable, and the company broadens the market for its stock.

As high-tech communications have speeded market efficiency, the effects of capital structure and dividend decisions on a firm's market value are more pronounced than ever. Because the stakes are high, the financial professional must thoroughly understand various long-term financing options. Armed with such knowledge, he or she can provide the company with the capital it needs to expand through good times and bad.

Firms have two primary sources of funds: They can generate funds internally from continuing operations, or they can secure them externally from creditors or investors. It is these external, long-term sources we focus on now. Our attention in Chapters 10 and 11 will be primarily on the two main vehicles used by firms to raise external long-term capital—common stocks and bonds. In Chapter 12 we discuss capital structure, that is, the firm's ratio of debt to equity. Chapter 13 addresses the firm's policy toward paying dividends. In Chapter 14 we discuss leasing, options, and convertibles. These other forms of financing are also employed by firms in addition to common stock and debt.

CHAPTER 10

Raising Long-Term Funds

Sections in this chapter:

■ **Raising External Long-Term Funds**
Who to call when internal financing is not enough.

■ **Common Stock: Rights and Privileges**
The benefits attached to owning common stock.

■ **Features of Common Stock**
The types and characteristics of common stock.

■ **Common Stock Financing**
"How much money can we expect to raise from this issue?"

■ **Regulation of Public Issues**
Providing investors with accurate information.

■ **Venture Capital**
Sources of external financing for start-up firms.

ach year many firms go public—through an initial public offering, IPO. Some recent IPOs included Barrett Business Services, Casino Data Systems, Microchip Technology, Peoples Choice TV, and Physician Corp. of America. As firms become larger, they have an ever-growing need for additional capital. Growing firms generally do not pay cash dividends, preferring instead to "save" some funds for reinvestment in the firm. Yet they still find they need to acquire outside common equity capital. "Going public" generally involves the use of investment bankers, specialists in raising capital and advising firms on their financing needs and trends.

In addition to investment bankers, whose role is often short-term in nature, large institutional investors are increasingly becoming involved in monitoring the activities of firms. One of the leaders in this trend is the California Public Employees' Retirement System (CalPERS). This $80 billion fund has become a self-appointed advocate for activating shareholders wherever corporate directors are falling asleep at the wheel. They annually issue a list of the ten firms they judge to be providing the worst performance from the standpoint of a long-term investor. CalPERS has also initiated a campaign to determine how its 200 largest equity holdings measured up against 28 guidelines for boards of directors, issued in 1994 by General Motors. Another active institutional investor, Teachers Insurance & Annuity Associations' College Retirement Equities Fund (CREF), has also spoken out regarding the role and independence of a firm's board of directors. CREF recommends not only that boards of directors should consist of a majority of independent directors (not affiliated with the firm), but also that key committees of the board should have only unaffiliated outsiders. Recently there has also been increased attention to the importance and role of boards of directors in Great Britain and Germany.

The landscape of raising long-term funds, and the duties of firms, management, and boards of directors, are changing. With increased public ownership, both in the United States and around the world, firms must become more responsive to their owners and creditors. In this chapter we will look at how firms raise long-term funds and the role of common stock in that process.

LEARNING GOALS

After studying this chapter you should be able to:

1. Discuss the sources of external funds, and describe the process of investment banking.
2. Describe the rights and privileges of common stock ownership.
3. Describe the features of common stock, and explain why some firms issue more than one class of common stock.
4. Discuss how issuing stock affects the value of the firm.
5. Describe the key federal laws that regulate the securities markets.
6. Discuss the five phases of venture capital financing.

RAISING EXTERNAL LONG-TERM FUNDS

■ LEARNING GOAL 1

Discuss the sources of external funds, and describe the process of investment banking.

Firms raise long-term funds from two sources: (1) internally generated funds that are reinvested in the firm, and (2) external funds obtained by selling stock or debt. Table 10.1 indicates the funds raised by nonfarm, nonfinancial U.S. firms between 1984 and 1993 both from internally generated funds and from issuing stock and debt. As the data clearly indicate, over this time period firms raised over 80 percent of their total needs for funds from internally generated sources. Thus, *the primary source of financing is from retaining cash flows generated by the firm.* The data also show that, in total, *during the years 1984 through 1990 firms retired more stock than they issued.* That is, although some firms issued new common stock, the amount of stock retired was greater than the amount of newly issued common stock. This net retirement of stock was due to mergers and acquisitions, leveraged buyouts in which firms were taken private, debt-for-stock swaps, voluntary retirement of stock, and a "leveraging up" of firms in the United States. One other important point illustrated in Table 10.1 is the cyclical nature of new debt and equity financing.

Means of Raising External Funds

PUBLIC OFFERING
Sale of securities to the general public by a firm; can be either a cash offering or a rights offering.

Firms have a number of means of securing financing, as shown in Figure 10.1. Once the firm decides it has to raise funds externally,[1] it has three basic alternatives. First, it can use a **public offering,** either to investors at large (a cash offering) or to the firm's current stockholders (a rights offering). Second, large, creditworthy firms can take advantage of the *shelf registration* form of financing. Finally, if the securities are not of-

---

[1] This determination is made based on cash budgets or pro forma statements as discussed in Chapter 20.

TABLE 10.1

Internal and External Financing for Nonfarm, Nonfinancial U.S. Firms

In recent years firms have raised 80 percent and more of their funds from internally generated sources. The net use of equity financing dropped substantially in the 1980s, as more equity was retired than issued.

| | | Financing in Dollars (in billions) | | | | | Financing in Percentages | | | |
| | | External | | | | | External | | | |
Year	Internal	Net Equity	Net Debt	Total	Total Financing	Internal	Net Equity	Net Debt	Total
1984	321	−79	188	109	430	75	−18	43	25
1985	332	−85	161	76	408	81	−21	40	19
1986	311	−85	225	140	451	69	−19	50	31
1987	366	−76	141	65	431	85	−18	33	15
1988	412	−129	201	72	484	85	−27	42	15
1989	384	−124	186	62	446	86	−28	42	14
1990	380	−63	101	38	418	91	−15	24	9
1991	389	18	−11	7	396	98	−5	3	2
1992	429	27	42	69	498	86	6	8	14
1993	442	23	47	70	512	86	5	9	14

Source: Board of Governors of the Federal Reserve System, *Flow of Funds Accounts*, various issues.

fered to the general public, then a *private placement* is made. The securities are sold to one or more institutional investors such as insurance companies, banks, or pension funds. In this chapter we will look at the basic features of all three methods and at the role played by investment banking firms in helping firms secure external financing.

FIGURE 10.1

Methods of Securing Financing

Since its introduction, shelf registration has become important for most large firms.

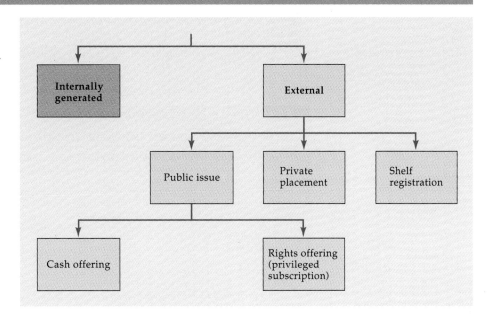

Cash Offerings

CASH OFFERING
Primary market transaction in which a firm sells securities to the general public for cash.

UNDERWRITTEN
The process whereby an investment banking firm purchases securities from an issuing firm and then immediately resells them.

FIRM COMMITMENT OFFERING
Procedure for selling a security issue in which the issue is underwritten by the investment banking firm, and the selling firm is guaranteed a fixed dollar amount.

BEST EFFORTS OFFERING
Procedure for selling a security issue in which an investment banking firm agrees to market the issue but does not underwrite the issue nor guarantee that the full amount of the issue will be sold.

Underwriting provides the issuing firm a floor below which the amount of new financing cannot fall; this floor has aspects of an option.

Firms can issue common stock, preferred stock, or long-term debt to the general public in exchange for cash; this transaction is a **cash offering.** Table 10.2 indicates the amount of funds raised by U.S. firms between 1988 and 1993. Note that the vast majority of funds raised involve long-term debt. This is not surprising, because firms can generate substantial equity capital internally but can secure debt financing only by going to the public markets or through private placements.

The Role of Investment Banking Firms

Most firms making a cash offering of securities use the services of an investment banking firm, which does the actual selling. Investment banking firms serve as an intermediary between the financial markets and firms needing capital. Firms generally prefer to have the new issue **underwritten:** The investment banking firm purchases the issue from the firm *at a fixed price* and then resells it. This transaction is generally called a **firm commitment offering**. When an issue is underwritten, the risk of it not selling is borne by the investment banking firm—that is, the selling firm is guaranteed a fixed dollar amount.

Another approach is for the investment banking firm to take the issue on a **best efforts basis:** The securities are sold for a fixed commission but any unsold securities are the responsibility of the selling firm, not the investment banking firm. This method is often used by large, well-known firms who feel the issue will sell easily or by very small firms when the risks and costs are too great for underwriting.

Investment banking firms, through the underwriting syndicate, provide marketing services, risk-bearing, certification, and monitoring of the firm's managers and its affairs. Marketing services include searching the primary market for buyers and compensating participants for their costs of providing funds. If the issue is underwritten on a firm commitment basis, the underwriters take the risk of the issue not selling. They have guaranteed the issuing firm a net amount from the issue; if the underwriters can't sell all of the issue at the offering price, they still must provide the issuing firm with the agreed net amount of cash for the issue. Certification involves bearing the liability imposed by the federal Securities Act of 1933 for the "fairness" of the offer price. That is, the underwriting firms implicitly certify that the offering price is fair to the purchasers. Finally, by engaging the services of well-known investment banking firms,

TABLE 10.2			
New Publicly Issued Long-Term Securities (in billions)			
Bonds typically have dominated the new-issue market.			
Year	Stock (Common and Preferred)	Debt	Total
1988	$ 57.8	$353.1	$410.9
1989	57.9	321.6	379.5
1990	40.2	299.3	339.5
1991	75.4	389.8	465.2
1992	88.3	471.5	559.8
1993	113.5	641.5	755.0

Source: Federal Reserve Bulletin, various issues.

the issuing firm is seeking additional monitoring in the hopes of adding value to the offering and firm.

The Underwriting Process

To understand the investment banking process, it is helpful to trace the steps required. Our focus is on the negotiated underwriting process and the role played by the lead investment banking firm or firms.

Preunderwriting Conference.   Members of the issuing firm and the investment banking firm hold preunderwriting conferences in which they discuss how much capital to raise, the type (or types) of security to employ, and the terms of the agreement. The investment banking firm then begins the underwriting investigation. In addition to its own investigation of the issuing firm, the investment banking firm calls in a public accounting firm to audit the firm's financial condition and to assist in preparing the registration statement submitted to the Securities and Exchange Commission, SEC. Lawyers are also required to rule on the legal aspects of the proposed issue.

After the investigation is completed, an underwriting agreement is drawn up. This agreement, which may be changed by subsequent approval of the parties, contains all the details of the issue except its price.

REGISTRATION STATEMENT
Statement filed with the SEC when a firm plans to issue securities to the public.

Registration and Pricing.   The **registration statement,** or *prospectus*, is then filed with the SEC. This statement presents all the pertinent facts concerning the firm and the proposed issue. During a waiting period, the SEC confirms the factual adequacy of the information. The SEC assesses only the accuracy of the information; *it does not judge the investment quality of the security*. The preliminary registration statement—often called a **red herring** because of the statement printed on it that the securities have not been approved or disapproved by the SEC—can, however, be distributed.

RED HERRING
Preliminary registration statement that can be distributed when a proposed security offering is being reviewed by the SEC.

Once the issue has cleared registration and an offering price has been determined, a "tombstone" advertisement listing the names of the underwriting firms from whom the prospectus may be obtained is often made. Figure 10.2 shows an example of a tombstone for a new issue—Beacon Properties common stock—that involved over 50 underwriters.

SYNDICATE
A group of investment banking firms that have agreed to cooperate in purchasing and then reselling an issue.

Underwriting Syndication and Selling.   The primary investment banking firm that the issuing firm has dealt with does not typically handle the purchase and distribution of an issue by itself. Instead, a **syndicate**—a group of investment banking firms—is formed for the purpose of underwriting (buying and then reselling) the issue. Syndicates often have between 10 and 60 underwriters in addition to the managing investment banking firm. The primary reasons for underwriting syndicates are to spread the risk and to ensure national or international marketing capability.

FLOTATION COST
The difference between what a security issue is sold to the public for and what the firm receives, including underwriting, accounting, and legal fees.

Costs.   The **flotation cost** to the issuing firm includes the underwriting fee and all the other expenses related to the offering. These other expenses include accounting and legal fees, an SEC registration fee, and printing costs. Total flotation costs are the difference between what the securities are sold to investors for (the gross proceeds) and what the issuing firm actually receives (the net proceeds). Thus, if a $50 million bond issue is sold to the public for $50.5 million and the issuing firm receives only $49.5 million, the flotation costs are $1 million, or slightly under 2 percent (i.e., $1 million/$50.50 million = 0.0198 = 1.98 percent). Flotation costs for large, creditworthy firms issuing debt average 0.5 to 0.6 percent of the value of the issue.

Remember Key Idea 6— risk and return (or in this case, cost) go hand-in-hand.

For common stock, flotation costs range from 3 to 10 percent for large, well-known firms, to over 20 percent for smaller firms. This high direct cost for small issues is a function both of the risks involved and of the higher actual distribution expenses,

FIGURE 10.2

Tombstone for Beacon Properties Corporation Common Stock Issue

Advertisements like this one appear in many financial sources, such as *The Wall Street Journal* and *Institutional Investor.*

This announcement is under no circumstances to be construed as an offer to sell or as a solicitation of an offer to buy any of these securities. The offering is made only by the Prospectus. The Attorney General of the State of New York has not passed on or endorsed the merits of this offering. Any representation to the contrary is unlawful.

New Issue

May 19, 1994

9,059,000 Shares

BEACON PROPERTIES CORPORATION

Common Stock

Price $17 Per Share

The New York Stock Exchange symbol is BCN

Copies of the Prospectus may be obtained in any State or jurisdiction in which this announcement is circulated from only such of the undersigned or other dealers or brokers as may lawfully offer these securities in such State or jurisdiction.

7,716,500 Shares

The above shares were underwritten by the following group of U.S. Underwriters.

Merrill Lynch & Co.

Kidder, Peabody & Co.
Incorporated

Lehman Brothers

Bear, Stearns & Co. Inc.	Alex. Brown & Sons Incorporated	Dean Witter Reynolds Inc.
Donaldson, Lufkin & Jenrette Securities Corporation	A.G. Edwards & Sons, Inc.	Goldman, Sachs & Co.
Oppenheimer & Co., Inc.	PaineWebber Incorporated	Prudential Securities Incorporated
Salomon Brothers Inc	Smith Barney Shearson Inc.	Wertheim Schroder & Co. Incorporated
Advest, Inc. J. C. Bradford & Co.	Cowen & Company Dain Bosworth Incorporated	Fahnestock & Co. Inc.
First Albany Corporation	Gruntal & Co., Incorporated	Interstate/Johnson Lane Corporation
Janney Montgomery Scott Inc.	Edward D. Jones & Co.	Kemper Securities, Inc.
Ladenburg, Thalmann & Co. Inc.	C. J. Lawrence/Deutsche Bank Securities Corporation	Legg Mason Wood Walker Incorporated
McDonald & Company Securities, Inc.	Morgan Keegan & Company, Inc.	Piper Jaffray Inc.
Principal Financial Securities, Inc.	Ragen MacKenzie Incorporated	Rauscher Pierce Refsnes, Inc.
Raymond James & Associates, Inc.	The Robinson-Humphrey Company, Inc.	Stifel, Nicolaus & Company Incorporated
Sutro & Co. Incorporated	Tucker Anthony Incorporated	Wheat First Butcher Singer
Adams, Harkness & Hill, Inc.	Dickinson & Co. Doft & Co., Inc.	Dominick & Dominick Incorporated
Fechtor, Detwiler & Co., Inc. Josephthal Lyon & Ross Incorporated	C. L. King & Associates, Inc.	Moors & Cabot, Inc.
Steiner Diamond & Co. Incorporated	Utendahl Capital Partners, L.P.	H. C. Wainwright & Co., Inc.

1,342,500 Shares

The above shares were underwritten by the following group of International Underwriters.

Merrill Lynch International Limited

Kidder, Peabody
International plc

Lehman Brothers

BNP Capital Markets Limited   Commerzbank Aktiengesellschaft   Nikko Europe Plc

because more effort is required to sell small common stock issues. For bonds and preferred stocks, the costs to large issuers are often less than 2 percent. This lower cost is due to the lower degree of risk involved compared to common stocks. The lower flotation costs for bonds and preferred stock are also a function of who buys the offering: Bonds and preferred stock are usually sold in large blocks to institutional investors, whereas thousands of investors may purchase common stock. Selling to fewer buyers lowers administrative costs related to the sale.

Shelf Registration

In 1982 the Securities and Exchange Commission modified its registration procedure for some types of offerings by adopting Rule 415, or what is called **shelf registration.** To register under this rule, a firm must file a relatively short form describing its financing needs and the securities it intends to issue over the next 2 years. In effect, the firm gets "pre-approval" for its securities during the time period. When it thinks market conditions are favorable, the firm can take part of the issue "off the shelf" in a matter of minutes, without any further disclosure, and offer the securities to investors.

The increased flexibility provided by shelf registration has been welcomed by chief financial officers at large corporations. In recent years, about half of all securities registered with the SEC were marketed through the shelf registration method. The rapid acceptance of shelf registration is due to its reduced cost and increased convenience— both of which are important when firms raise external capital. The reduced costs associated with shelf registrations primarily benefit firms that are considered less risky, as opposed to firms with more risk.

In 1992 the Securities and Exchange Commission liberalized the rules, allowing more firms to qualify for shelf registrations. In another move, this time designed to assist smaller firms, the SEC also increased to $1 million the amount of securities that could be issued in a year without any SEC registration.

Private Placements and Rule 144a

The private placement of securities has always been a means of financing. In recent years it has accounted for as much as 35 percent of total corporate financing in the United States. But even that is not as much as it may be in the future. In early 1990, the Securities and Exchange Commission approved Rule 144a, which is transforming the way many firms, both domestic and foreign, raise capital.

Rule 144a created a new private placement secondary market in which large investors can trade among themselves without going back to the registration and disclosure process. To limit the market to sophisticated investors who should be able to do their own homework about the merits of the securities, the SEC allows institutions that own $100 million or more in securities to participate as buyers in the new private placement secondary market. In addition, stocks or bonds that are traded on any public exchange, such as the NYSE, will not be allowed in the 144a market.

Before Rule 144a, buyers of private placement securities could not easily resell them without registering them with the SEC or holding them for at least 2 years. This regulation reduced the liquidity of the investments, and in turn sent many U.S. companies overseas to raise capital. In addition, many foreign firms could not easily enter the U.S. capital markets, even via private placement, without disclosing much more information than they were required to reveal in their home countries.

The SEC disclosure requirements, which provide for full and complete disclosure and therefore promote market efficiency in our public secondary markets, are relaxed in the 144a market. The trade-off is full disclosure versus helping both domestic and foreign firms raise capital in the cheapest, most effective manner. In designing Rule 144a, the SEC attempted to balance its role of providing for full disclosure for investors against helping firms with their financing needs.

Underwriters and the Cost of Financing

Investment banking firms assist in raising debt and equity capital both in the United States and around the world. In 1993 they helped bring a record $1.5 trillion in new

TABLE 10.3

Top Underwriting Investment Banking Firms, 1993 (in millions)

Though many firms, both in the United States and in other countries, provide investment banking services, U.S.-based firms dominate the global market.

Top Underwriters of U.S. Debt and Equity			Top Underwriters of Non-U.S. Debt and Equity		
Firm	Amount	Market Share	Firm	Amount	Market Share
Merrill Lynch	$173,784	16.4%	Goldman Sachs	$ 23,875	5.9%
Goldman Sachs	127,265	12.0	Deutsche Bank	23,526	5.8
Lehman Brothers	115,996	10.9	Morgan Stanley	21,217	5.2
Kidder Peabody	94,471	8.9	First Boston CS	20,152	5.0
Salomon Brothers	91,177	8.6	Merrill Lynch	19,000	4.7
First Boston	90,374	8.5	Nomura Securities	16,687	4.1
Morgan Stanley	67,717	6.4	Lehman Brothers	14,115	3.5
Bear Sterns	56,237	5.3	Banque Paribas	14,040	3.5
Donaldson Lufkin	36,911	3.5	Salomon Brothers	13,658	3.4
Paine Webber	29,890	2.8	J. P. Morgan	13,064	3.2
Total for top 10	$883,822	83.2%		$179,334	44.3%
Industry total	$1,062,871	100.0%		$404,925	100.0%

Source: Table, "Top Underwriting Investment Banking Firms, 1993 (in millions)," *The Wall Street Journal*, January 3, 1994, p. 32. Reprinted by permission of The Wall Street Journal, © 1994 Dow Jones & Company, Inc. All Rights Reserved Worldwide.

debt and equity to the market. This was an increase of over 36 percent from 1992, and triple the amount of capital raised as recently as 1990. Nearly three-quarters of 1993's volume was in U.S. stocks and bonds. Table 10.3 indicates the top investment banking firms for 1993 in terms of the dollars of underwritten financing secured for their clients. In the United States, Merrill Lynch was far and away the biggest underwriter, followed by Goldman Sachs, Lehman Brothers, and Kidder Peabody. In the rest of the world, Goldman Sachs was the leader, followed by Deutsche Bank, Morgan Stanley, and First Boston. In both markets the largest underwritings were dominated by U.S.-based firms.

The fees earned by investment bankers represent the cost to the issuing firm or government for the underwriting and marketing assistance received. New offerings of stock by firms that had no publicly issued stock before (called *initial public offerings, IPOs*) generated for investment banking firms fees of about 7.2 percent of the proceeds raised in 1993. Secondary offerings of common stock, where stock was already outstanding but a firm or individual wanted to sell a large block of stock, generated investment banking fees of about 5.5 percent. Preferred stock offerings resulted in investment banking fees of 2 percent in 1993. Turning to long-term debt financing, investment-grade debt (as discussed in Chapter 11, this is debt in the top four bond ratings) resulted in fees of about 0.05 percent of the total proceeds. More risky bonds provided investment bankers with fees of about 2.4 percent of the issue, and convertible bonds (i.e., bonds that can be converted into common stock) provided investment banking firms with fees about 2.9 percent of the proceeds raised in 1993. The differences in fees are a function of competition, the risk incurred by the investment banking firm, and how difficult it was to market the issue.

Investment Bankers and Financial Ethics

Rarely are investment bankers accused of unethical or illegal activities. The reason is obvious—their continued business and profitability are tied directly to their reputation. Any word of unethical or illegal activity can have serious short- and long-run consequences. However, exceptions do occur.

When auctioning Treasury bonds, the U.S. Treasury awards them first to the highest bidder and then moves to the next highest bidder. If the Treasury receives more than one bid at the price that exhausts the issue, it allocates the remaining bonds in proportion to the size of the bid. In 1990 Paul Mozer, the head of Salomon Brothers government-bond trading desk, submitted bids for more than 100 percent of the 4-year notes to be auctioned. He later followed this up with other similar bids, including a bid in December 1990 for a customer of Salomon Brothers, without the customer's consent. Mozer repeated this tactic in the spring of 1991, thereby attracting the attention of the Securities and Exchange Commission and the Justice Department. Finally, in August 1991 the Treasury Department announced it had barred Salomon Brothers from bidding in government securities auctions for customer accounts. On August 19, 1991, *The Wall Street Journal* carried seven different articles about this event. Within days of the news release, Moody's Investors Service put Salomon on its credit "watch list," and subsequently downgraded its bond and commercial paper ratings.

The damage to Salomon's reputation not only impaired its ability to sell new securities but actually raised concerns about whether the firm would survive. In response to these actions, Paul Mozer and other employees implicated in the scandal were removed, while Salomon's chairman, president, vice-chairman, and general counsel were all asked to resign by the firm's board of directors. Warren Buffett, of Berkshire Hathaway Corporation, was appointed interim chairman; a new chief operating officer was appointed; the firm liquidated some assets to pay off bank loans and other borrowings, and to forestall potentially serious liquidity problems; and it beefed up its internal controls.

Nine months later, on May 20, 1992, Salomon settled the suit with the government. The firm paid $122 million to the Treasury Department to settle charges that it violated securities laws, and another $68 million to the Justice Department. It also established a $100 million restitution fund for payments of private damage claims that might arise from the 50 or so civil lawsuits it was facing. Though it has suffered both direct and indirectly from this scandal, since that time Salomon has reestablished itself as one of the leading investment banking firms in the United States and the world.

In another example of the trouble that occasionally plagues investment banking firms, in the spring of 1994 Kidder Peabody reported that a scam had resulted in $350 million of fictitious profits from trading in the government bonds market. Joseph Jett, the chief government bond trader, was sacked by the firm. However, the issue is more complex than that. Jett maintains that he was only following orders from higher ups at Kidder. And to make the issue even more complex, Kidder is owned by General Electric, and there is some speculation that Kidder was engaged in these activities in order to reduce its bloated balance sheet to comply with limits set by General Electric. The case is progressing, though the final outcome has not been resolved.

Private markets, like the markets in which investment bankers trade, provide strong incentives for ethical behavior—by imposing substantial costs on the institutions and individuals who depart from it. Although private markets don't eliminate all ethical concerns, in general, ethical behavior is profitable. That is, firms that practice ethical behavior tend to get business, while those that practice unethical behavior suffer both direct out-of-pocket costs and indirect costs due to lost opportunities. However, whereas vigorous private markets may contribute to ethical behavior, they cannot guarantee it.

CONCEPT REVIEW QUESTIONS

- What is the primary source of financing for nonfarm, nonfinancial U.S. firms?
- What are the three basic alternatives available to firms to raise external funds?

■ Describe the process firms employ for raising external funds. What role do investment banking firms play?

■ How has the SEC's Rule 144a affected private placements?

■ How do private markets relate to ethical behavior?

COMMON STOCK: RIGHTS AND PRIVILEGES

■ LEARNING GOAL 2

Describe the rights and privileges of common stock ownership.

Now that we understand some of the issues and mechanics related to raising external funds, let's turn our attention to one of the sources of funds for firms—common stock. The common stockholders are both the owners of the firm and one of its suppliers of long-term capital. This capital is supplied in two ways: It may be in the form of funds invested in the firm directly in exchange for new shares of common stock. Or, it may occur through the action of the firm's board of directors by retaining funds rather than authorizing them to be paid out in the form of cash dividends.

Income

Common stockholders have a *residual right* to the income of the firm; that is, the claims of creditors, lessors, the government, and preferred stockholders must be met before common stockholders receive cash dividends. Assuming that cash flows are sufficient, firms typically pay out some proportion of their earnings in the form of cash dividends. They are not obligated to do so, and some firms, such as Genentech, Microsoft, and Toys 'R' Us, do not currently pay dividends.

The risk and potential returns are greater for common stock investors than for others with financial interests in the firm. To see why, consider a firm with interest payments of $50,000, a tax rate of 35 percent, and earnings before interest and taxes of either $50,000, $200,000, or $600,000, as follows:

EBIT	$50,000	$200,000	$600,000
Interest	50,000	50,000	50,000
EBT	0	150,000	550,000
Taxes (35%)	0	52,500	192,500
EAT	$ 0	$97,500	$357,500

With earnings before interest and taxes, *EBIT*, of $50,000, and interest payments of $50,000, earnings after taxes are zero and no funds are left for distribution to common stockholders. If *EBIT* is $200,000, then earnings after taxes, *EAT*, are $97,500. On the other hand, if *EBIT* increases to $600,000, *EAT* is $357,500 and larger cash dividends may be paid out. Any cash not paid out to common stockholders can be reinvested in the firm.

Control

MAJORITY VOTING
A system of electing the board of directors, whereby stockholders are permitted one vote per director for each share of stock; a simple majority is required to elect each director.

The firm's stockholders are granted voting rights (as specified by the firm's bylaws) on certain issues that affect the firm. One of those rights is to elect the members of the board of directors each year. Typically, each share of stock has one vote. Depending on the corporate charter or the law of the state in which the firm is incorporated, the board of directors is selected under a majority voting or a cumulative voting system. Under the **majority voting** system, each stockholder has one vote *per director* for each share of stock owned. Directors are elected if they secure one more vote than 50 percent of the votes cast. Instead of majority voting, the firm's charter or the state of incorporation may require **cumulative voting,** which permits multiple votes for a single director. Each share is entitled to the same number of votes as the number of directors being elected. Thus, a stockholder who owns 100 shares, voting in an election in which three directors are to be elected, would have 300 votes, which could be cast for any director or directors. The purpose of cumulative voting is to allow minority groups representation on the board of directors.

Sometimes an outside or dissident group may challenge management by proposing its own slate of directors. These challenges, or **proxy fights,** represent one of the more effective means of attempting to turn around the fortunes of a firm. In the past, they have been rare; however, recently, more proxy fights have been initiated, including some involving major firms. Obviously, it is only in firms that are providing lackluster performance (in terms of market price, dividends, and/or earnings) where successful proxy fights are possible.

In addition to voting on the board of directors, stockholders are frequently asked to approve the selection of the firm's accounting auditor for the next year and to vote on issues such as authorizing additional shares of common stock, approval of a merger financed by common stock, antitakeover amendments, and various other corporate governance issues.

Claim on Assets

As in the case of income, common stockholders have a residual claim with regard to the firm's assets in case of liquidation. In liquidation, creditors, bondholders, and preferred stockholders all have a prior claim on assets and will be paid something before common stockholders receive anything. This residual claim increases the risk to common stockholders.

Limited Liability

Remember Key Idea 7— options are valuable.

Under our legal system stockholders have limited liability. Because corporations are distinct entities under the law, stockholders are not personally responsible for the firm's debts. The impact of limited versus unlimited liability on stockholders is illustrated in Figure 10.3. Say a firm has $1,000 in debt. With limited liability, if the value of the firm's assets falls below $1,000, stockholders can default and walk away from the firm. But if unlimited liability existed, when the value of the firm's assets fell below $1,000, stockholders would have to use their personal resources to pay off the bondholders.

With either limited or unlimited liability, stockholders may be disappointed if a firm's operating performance is poor. But the right to default and walk away from the firm is a valuable privilege that exists due to limited liability.

Preemptive Right

The **preemptive right** is a provision that grants stockholders the right to purchase new shares of common stock in the same proportion as their current ownership. This right may exist in the corporate charter or may be required by state statute. The raising of funds through use of a preemptive right is called a **rights offering.** Although this provision used to be widespread, it is less so now because *many firms have amended their charters to eliminate the preemptive right*. One of the primary reasons for doing away with it is to provide the firm with more freedom to use common stock for mergers and acquisitions, or other corporate purposes.

FIGURE 10.3

Effect of Limited Versus Unlimited Liability on Stockholders

For a firm with $1,000 in debt, if the value of the firm at the maturity of the debt is below $1,000, with limited liability, as in (a), the stockholders default and bond-holders own the firm. But with un-limited liability, as in (b), stockhold-ers must reach into their own pockets to pay off the bondholders.

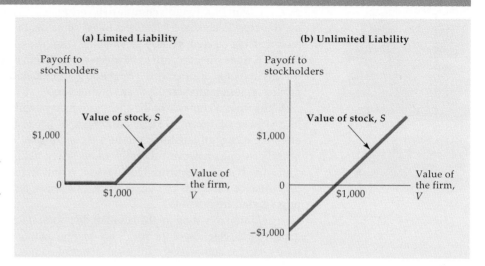

Rights, like any option, are valuable. They should be exercised (by purchasing more shares) or sold. The rights have value and should not be discarded.

When the preemptive right exists, current stockholders have first claim on any new shares to be issued.[2] For example, if a firm had 100,000 shares of stock outstanding and decided to issue 25,000 new shares, a stockholder owning 1,000 shares would have the opportunity to purchase 250 new shares. By doing so, the stockholder would maintain his or her current percentage ownership of 1 percent of the firm's outstanding shares. However, many firms have asked their stockholders to give up their preemptive right—and the stockholders have agreed. The rationale is fairly simple—firms often need to issue more shares of stock to finance mergers. The presence of a preemptive right makes it almost impossible for firms to issue stock to finance a merger. Obviously, the shareholders who voted to give up the preemptive right thought they would be better off providing the firm the flexibility to issue additional shares.

Right of Transfer

Common stockholders generally have the right to transfer ownership to another investor. All that is required is for an investor to sell the stock to another person and sign the stock over to the buyer (by endorsing it on the back of the stock certificate). If the stock is traded publicly, the stockholder may use the services of a securities broker to sell the stock. The purchaser of the stock (or the broker) sends the stock certificate to a *transfer agent* representing the firm. The transfer agent then issues a new certificate under the purchaser's name and records the transaction in the firm's records. At this point, the new owner is entitled to receive cash dividends and has any other rights or privileges associated with owning the common stock.

CONCEPT REVIEW QUESTIONS

■ Briefly describe the rights and privileges of owning common stock. Do you think it makes a difference whether the firm is large, or a small family owned one?
■ Describe the difference between majority voting and cumulative voting when electing a firm's board of directors.

---

[2] *In effect, the rights are simply a call option, as discussed briefly in Chapter 1 and in more detail in Chapter 14.*

FEATURES OF COMMON STOCK

Authorized, Outstanding, and Treasury Shares

■ **LEARNING GOAL 3**

Describe the features of common stock, and explain why some firms issue more than one class of common stock.

AUTHORIZED SHARES
The maximum number of shares of stock that can be issued by a firm without amending its charter.

OUTSTANDING SHARES
The shares of stock currently held by the public.

TREASURY STOCK
The shares of stock that have been reacquired by the firm and are being held in treasury for later reissue.

The firm's charter specifies the number of **authorized shares**—that is, the maximum number of shares that can be issued without amending the charter. Additional shares can be authorized by a vote of the common stockholders. For convenience, most firms have more shares authorized than they currently have issued. For example, in Table 10.4, EMC Corporation, as of December 1994, is shown to have 330 million shares authorized, but "only" 201.738 million have been issued. The **outstanding shares** are those issued to and held by the public. The firm can buy back issued stock and hold it for later reissue; such reacquired shares are called **treasury stock** (because it is held in the firm's treasury). The number of shares outstanding for EMC is 201,738,042 − 2,627,467 = 199,110,575. When calculating any per share figures, such as earnings per share, dividends per share, or book value per share, the number of shares of common stock outstanding are employed.

TABLE 10.4

Common Stockholders' Accounts and Related Information for EMC Corporation, as of December 31, 1994 (in thousands)

Additional paid-in capital is the difference between the selling price and par; it is recorded when firms sell stock. Retained earnings is the sum of all net income (and losses) less cash dividends. EMC has never paid any cash dividends.

Common stock, $0.01 par; 330,000,000 shares authorized; 201,738,042 shares issued	$ 2,017
Additional paid-in capital	281,625
Deferred compensation	(2,607)
Retained earnings	443,713
Currency translation adjustment	3,716
Less: Treasury stock (2,627,467)	(823)
Total common equity	$727,641

Earnings per share   = net income − dividends on preferred stock/shares of stock outstanding

= ($250,668 − 0)/(201,738 − 2,627) = $1.26

Book value per share   = total stockholders' equity − book value of preferred stock/shares outstanding

= ($727,641 − 0)/(201,738 − 2,627) = $3.65

Market price per share (range for the year) = $24 to $12.63

Source: 1994 Annual Report, EMC Corporation.

Par and Book Value

PAR VALUE
An arbitrary value used for accounting purposes; has economic significance only in rare circumstances.

RETAINED EARNINGS
An equity account on the balance sheet that reflects the sum of the firm's net income (or loss) over its life, less all cash dividends paid.

Retained earnings is not cash in the bank: a firm cannot pay its bills out of retained earnings.

BOOK VALUE PER SHARE
Common stockholders' equity divided by the number of shares of common stock outstanding.

Common stock can be issued with or without a par value. The **par value** of a share of common stock is stated in the firm's charter but is of no financial significance. Firms with a specific par value for their common stock try to issue new stock at prices higher than par, because the stockholders are liable as creditors for the difference between the issuance price, if below par, and the par value of the stock. For this reason, most par values are very low. EMC, for example, has a par value of $0.01 per share of common stock.

From Table 10.4 we can see that EMC has **retained earnings** of $444 million. Retained earnings represent the total residual amount that has been transferred from the firm's income statements over the years. In recent years firms have also had to report the impact of foreign currency translation adjustments in their stockholders' equity accounts; EMC has a foreign currency adjustment of almost $4 million.

The total of the common stock, preferred stock (if any), additional paid-in capital, retained earnings, and currency translation adjustment, less the treasury stock, is equal to total stockholders' equity. For EMC, this is $728 million.

Book value per share of common stock reflects the "accounting-recorded" worth of the firm. It is calculated by dividing the common stockholders' equity (i.e., total stockholders equity minus book value of preferred stock equity, or, equivalently, total assets minus total liabilities minus the book value of preferred stock) by the number of shares of common stock outstanding. EMC had a book value of $3.65 per share at the end of 1994, but its stock traded between $24 and $12.63 during that year. For many firms there is little or no relationship between book value per share and the actual market price of the stock.

Classes of Common Stock

Most firms have only one class of common stock, but some have more than one class. Where two classes exist, one is often sold to the general public and the other is retained by the founders, with all or part of the voting rights reserved for the founder's group. Three examples will help to illustrate the use of different classes of stock.

Ford has two classes of stock, both of which have voting privileges. As of December 31, 1994, the issued shares (in millions) were as follows:

	Shares Issued
Common	1,021
Class B	71
	1,092

Class B stock is owned by members of the Ford family and constitutes 40 percent of the voting power of the firm.[3] The common stock is held by the general public and has 60 percent of the total voting power. Each share of common stock is entitled to one vote. To maintain their 40 percent voting power, owners of class B shares have more than one vote per share. As of the end of 1994, each class B share had:

$$\left(\frac{1,021}{71}\right)\left(\frac{0.40}{0.60}\right) = 9.59 \text{ votes}$$

---

[3]*If the number of class B shares is below 60.7 million but equal to or greater than 33.7 million, then the voting power drops to 30 percent.*

Although each share of both classes participates equally in cash dividends or in liquidation if it were to occur, each class B share has more voting power than a similar share of common stock.

A second example is that of Adolph Coors Company. Coors has two classes of stock: class A, which is held by the founders and has voting power, and class B, which is held by the general public and, except for certain situations, has no voting power. Shares of both classes participate equally in dividends or liquidation.

A third, and somewhat different, example of stock classes occurs when a firm ties different classes of stock to distinct parts of its total business. For example, General Motors, GM, has three different classes of stock: General Motors common, GM class H, and GM class E. The class H shares are pegged to the automaker's Hughes Aircraft Company, and the class E shares are tied to its Electronic Data Systems business. As another example, recently USX separated its operations into three parts; all three— USX-Delhi, USX-Marathon, and USX-U.S. Steel—are listed on the New York Stock Exchange.

CONCEPT REVIEW QUESTIONS

■ Why is the par value of most firms significantly less than the market value of common stock?
■ Explain why some companies have several classes of common stock.

COMMON STOCK FINANCING

■ LEARNING GOAL 4

Discuss how issuing stock affects the value of the firm.

Although not the major external source of financing (internally generated funds that are reinvested in the firm and debt financing are more important), common stock is often employed to raise external capital, especially for smaller, growing firms. So it is important to understand more about the use of common stock as a means of raising long-term capital.

Issuing Equity and the Value of the Firm

In recent years a number of studies have examined the market impact of common stock issuance. The results, at first glance, have been surprising: When firms sell common stock publicly, their stock price declines. For industrial firms in the United States the decline amounts to an average of 2 to 3 percent. Although that may not sound overwhelming, the fall in the market value represents a dollar amount equal to 10 to 20 percent of the money raised by the issue. Thus, the net increase in the value of the firm, ΔS, due to issuing new common stock for cash is equal to the net proceeds from the issue *minus* the decrease in the value of the outstanding stock. Stated another way, the cost of issuing common stock includes the direct flotation costs plus the indirect costs captured by the loss in value of the firm's outstanding stock.

How can we account for the decline in the stock price? In an efficient market, investor expectations are built into the share price. These expectations may change as the firm issues new common stock. Consider two reasons why the price of the firm's stock may fall:

This explanation relies on Key Idea 3—individuals act in their own self-interest.

1. *Information Asymmetry.* Management always has some information about the firm that is not available to shareholders. What if this information allows management

to determine when the firm is overvalued in the marketplace and when it is undervalued? Management will then attempt to issue new shares only when the firm is overvalued. This move benefits existing stockholders, but potential new stockholders are not stupid. They will anticipate this situation and discount it by offering to pay less for the stock at the new issue date.

2. *Investment Prospects.* Investment demands exist for most firms, sometimes due to growth options with high *NPVs* and at other times for not-so-great projects. What if informed investors interpret the issuance of new common stock as a negative signal about the firm's investment projects? After all, if the new projects are really great, why should the firm let new stockholders in on them? In that case it could simply issue debt and let existing stockholders capture all the gain. Again, new investors are not stupid and will offer a lower price for the common stock on the new issue date.

Although we don't know which, if either, of these explanations accounts for the decline in stock prices when common stock is sold, we do know the decline occurs.

Instead of a public offering of stock, what about the private placement of common stock? Studies have shown that when firms sell stock through a private placement they actually experience *an increase* in the value of the firm. How can these findings of an increase in value be explained? Firms that engage in private equity issues are typically smaller and sell a larger percentage of ownership (relative to the already outstanding shares) than firms that sell stock through a public offering. Two possible explanations are that by securing private financing these firms (1) may be resolving a lot of uncertainty about the projects to be financed, or (2) they may have undervalued assets, and were encouraged to seek private financing.

When firms issue common stock publicly, they suffer a loss in value; when done privately, they have a gain in value. What occurs when they issue debt? Stock prices decline little, if at all, when the firm issues new debt. Thus, the type of financing employed—common stock sold publicly, common stock sold privately, and debt—impacts the value of the firm. Effective managers must keep these findings in mind when contemplating how to raise long-term financing.

IPOs and Underpricing

INITIAL PUBLIC OFFERING, IPO
The original sale of a firm's securities to the public; a primary market transaction.

UNDERPRICING
The issuance of securities below their fair market value.

Underpricing may be reduced by choosing an investment banker with a reputation for selling ability. But highly risky firms may not have this option; the major investment bankers appear to underwrite only higher quality issues.

When a firm first goes public with its common stock, the offering is referred to as an **initial public offering, IPO.** A number of studies have examined initial public offerings. By calculating the difference between the offering price and the price shortly after offering, these studies have examined the issue of **underpricing,** which is the issuance of securities below their fair market value. Underpricing is a real, but hidden, cost incurred by any firm when it first goes public. These studies have estimated that the magnitude of underpricing with IPOs is high—as much as 10 to 20 percent. As such, the cost of underpricing and the direct cash costs of financing (which includes underwriting fees, legal and accounting fees, and other related expenses) must both be considered when raising equity capital. The total costs, including underpricing, have been estimated to be about 25 percent of the value of the gross financing. Thus, issuance costs are significant.

Why does underpricing occur? Probably for at least two reasons: The first is that both the investment banking firm and the issuing firm have some vested interest in seeing that the issue is fully sold. One way—but an expensive one—to ensure that the issue is sold is to underprice it. The second is that determining the market worth of a firm that has never been traded is more an art than a science.

Pricing a New Issue

When a firm already has stock outstanding and is issuing additional shares, they are typically priced a few dollars below the closing price the day before the stock is sold. If the stock was priced at the going market price, no incentive exists for investors to purchase the new stock; accordingly, this is why the issue is priced below the existing market price. If the firm is making an initial public offering, however, the pricing decision is much more difficult.

One way to go about establishing the initial selling price is to determine what the total value of the firm should be after the issue, and then divide this value by the number of shares of common stock to be issued. For example, if we assume that United Transport is estimated to be worth $3.5 million and 350,000 shares of common stock will be issued, the estimated selling price is $3,500,000/350,000, or $10 per share. Note that we are interested in the total number of shares to be issued, including any privately held or founder's shares not issued to the public. If United Transport decides to sell 150,000 shares, the offering would consist of 150,000 shares priced at $10 each, for gross proceeds (before flotation costs and other direct issuance expenses) of $1,500,000. To use this approach, however, we must answer the following question: How do we determine the firm's total value—in this case, $3,500,000?

One way to determine a firm's value is to use the valuation approach described in Chapter 4. For the constant dividend growth situation, the value of the total firm can be estimated by[4]

$$S = \frac{D_1}{k_s - g} \tag{10.1}$$

where

S = the value of an all-equity firm

D_1 = total cash dividends expected to be paid to stockholders next year (at $t = 1$)

k_s = the equity investors' required return

g = the expected (compound) growth rate in cash dividends

Suppose that United expects earnings after taxes of $700,000 and plans to pay 50 percent out in the form of cash dividends, so that $D_1 = \$350,000$. Also, the firm expects its earnings and dividends to grow at approximately 7 percent per year for the foreseeable future. We have estimated D_1 and g in Equation 10.1; all that is needed now is an estimate of k_s.

Estimating the equity investors' required return, k_s, however, is not easy, especially for a firm that has never been traded publicly. United's investment banking firm could supply an estimate of k_s; we could use the k_s for some comparable publicly traded firm; or we could employ some approach like adding a risk premium to the expected interest rate on long-term corporate bonds. If the rate on long-term bonds is expected to be 9 percent and the risk premium is determined to be 8 percent, then our estimate of k_s is 17 percent. With this we can estimate the value of United Transport to be:

$$S = \frac{\$350,000}{0.17 - 0.07} = \frac{\$350,000}{0.10} = \$3,500,000$$

[4]*It is assumed no debt exists.*

In practice, an ad hoc approach based on comparative price/earnings ratios is often employed. The price/earnings, *P/E,* ratio is calculated by dividing the market price for a share of common stock by the earnings per share. To use this approach, United's investment banker might examine *P/E* ratios for publicly traded firms in the same industry, as well as the *P/E* ratios of firms that have recently gone public. Other pertinent information—such as United's financial condition and amount of debt, research and development, growth prospects, quality and stability of management, and size—is also compared. Once a *P/E* ratio for the firm is estimated, the total market value is determined by

$$S = \text{(net income)(estimated } P/E \text{ of stock)} \tag{10.2}$$

Continuing with our example, let's assume that United's investment banking firm determines the stock's estimated *P/E* ratio is 5. The total value of United would be ($700,000)(5) = $3,500,000. Once the total value of the firm is determined, the pricing of the new shares to be issued proceeds as described previously. With either the dividend valuation or comparative *P/E* approach, the pricing of new issues is an imperfect and subjective process.

Recording a Stock Issue

Once stock is issued, it must be recorded on the firm's balance sheet. To see how this occurs, let's continue with United Transport. It currently has 200,000 shares of $2 par value common stock outstanding. The value recorded in United's common stock ac-

FINANCIAL MANAGEMENT TODAY

Valuing a Closely Held Firm

Valuing a closely held firm, often a small business, is both difficult and subjective. Three approaches that are often used are the net asset valuation approach, the discounted cash flow approach, and the earnings-multiple approach.

The *net asset valuation approach* simply takes the appraised (or sometimes book) value of the firm's assets minus the claims in terms of liabilities and preferred stock. This may be useful if most of the assets are relatively liquid and their market value can be easily determined. A variation of this approach is a liquidation value approach, wherein the estimated liquidation value of the assets, net of any costs associated with the liquidation, is employed.

The *discounted cash flow approach* is very similar to the dividend valuation model discussed in Chapters 4 and 10. Cash flows are projected for a series of periods along with some estimated residual value of the firm; they are then discounted at an appropriate required rate of return. The senior claims are then subtracted to determine the estimated value of the firm's equity.

The third approach is the *earnings-multiple approach,* in which adjusted after-tax earnings (net of any extraordinary gains or losses) are multiplied by some appropriate estimated price/earnings ratio, or multiple. This multiple is often determined by looking at similar types of firms. A variation of the earnings-multiple approach is simply the capitalized earnings method; the adjusted after-tax earnings are divided by (or capitalized at) an appropriate required return.

Although each of these three methods has strengths and weaknesses, the results may differ substantially depending on who's doing the estimation and what approach is used. In one case, 15 experts were given the same data for a firm. The average firm value given by the 15 was about $11 million, but the high was $17.5 million while the low was $6 million. Obviously, there's a lot of judgment involved, no matter what method is used in valuing closely held firms.

count is $400,000 [i.e., (200,000 shares)($2 per share)]. United now sells 150,000 additional shares of common stock and receives $10 per share (ignoring flotation and other issuance costs). The entries are an increase in the common stock account of $300,000 [i.e., (150,000 new shares)($2 per share par value)] an increase in the additional paid-in capital account of $1,200,000 (150,000 shares times the difference between the issuance price of $10 per share and the par value of $2 per share); and an offsetting entry indicating that the cash account has increased by $1,500,000. The "before" and "after" balance sheets for United Transport are presented in Table 10.5.

Listing the Stock

In addition to selling stock to raise additional capital, publicly held firms must also decide whether the stock should be listed on an organized stock exchange. Small firms are typically traded in the over-the-counter market because there is simply not enough activity to justify the costs of listing. As a firm grows, it may be listed on one of the regional stock exchanges. A West Coast firm might be listed on the Pacific Coast Stock Exchange; one located in Milwaukee might be listed on the Midwest Stock Exchange. With continued growth, the firm may decide to apply for listing on the American Stock Exchange, or if it is one of the nation's largest firms, it may apply to the "Big Board"—the New York Stock Exchange.

To apply for listing on an organized exchange, the firm must meet certain conditions and file a listing application with both the exchange and the SEC. The minimum characteristics a firm must possess if it wants a listing on the NYSE are presented in

---

TABLE 10.5

Balance Sheet of United Transport Before and After Stock Issue

The $1,500,000 is split between the common stock and additional paid-in capital accounts on the basis of the par value and the issuance price. An offsetting entry is made indicating that the firm's cash account has increased by $1,500,000.

	Before the Issue	After the Issue
Assets		
Cash	$ 200,000	$1,700,000
Other	1,800,000	1,800,000
Total assets	$2,000,000	$3,500,000
Liabilities and Stockholders' Equity		
Liabilities	$1,000,000	$1,000,000
Stockholders' equity:		
Common stock ($2 par)	400,000	700,000*
Additional paid-in capital	200,000	1,400,000
Retained earnings	400,000	400,000
Total liabilities and stockholders' equity	$2,000,000	$3,500,000

* 350,000 shares at $2 par.

TABLE 10.6

New York Stock Exchange Listing Requirements for Common Stock

Other considerations include the degree of national interest in the firm, position in the industry, and prospects for both the firm and the industry.

Profitability

Earnings before taxes, *EBT*, for the most recent year must be at least $2.5 million. For the 2 preceding years, *EBT* must have been at least $2 million.

Assets

Net tangible assets of at least $16 million, but greater emphasis is placed on the aggregate market value.

Market Value

The market value of the publicly held stock must be at least $16 million.*

Public Ownership

At least 1 million shares must be publicly held, and there must be at least 2,000 stockholders, each of whom owns at least 100 shares.

Source: "Excerpts from *New York Stock Exchange Fact Book,* 1994." Reprinted by permission of The New York Stock Exchange, Inc.

* This requirement might conceivably be as low as $8 million, depending on the level of the NYSE Index of Common Stock prices.

Table 10.6. After a firm is listed, it must meet certain exchange requirements in order to continue its listing. The SEC also requires that both quarterly and annual financial reports be published by listed firms.

Off-board trading of NYSE-listed stocks has grown. In recent years the NYSE handled only about 65 percent of the trades in its listed stocks. More and more NYSE stocks are being traded on regional exchanges such as the Midwest Stock Exchange; on overseas exchanges, such as the London exchange, where disclosure and trading rules are looser; and in U.S. "third" or "fourth" markets of private dealers and electronic systems. Although many reasons exist for off-board trading of NYSE stocks, a primary reason relates to the NYSE's inability to execute trades of big blocks of stocks for institutional investors without moving prices sharply. Critics of the NYSE argue that its auction-based system, relying on specialists, simply doesn't provide the necessary infrastructure to deal with very large buy and sell orders. With the movements toward global equity markets and 24-hour trading, some question whether the NYSE will retain its status as one of the world's dominant secondary markets.

CONCEPT REVIEW QUESTIONS

■ Why does a company's stock price decline with a public common stock offering but increase with a private common stock offering?
■ Explain how an investment banking firm can estimate the stock price of a company that has never been traded publicly.

REGULATING PUBLIC ISSUES

■ **LEARNING GOAL 5**

Describe the key federal laws that regulate the securities markets.

Until 1933, regulation of the securities markets was done entirely by the individual states. One of the earliest state security laws was enacted by Kansas in 1911. A member of the Kansas legislature remarked that the new law would prevent sellers from promising the "blue sky" to unsophisticated investors; hence, state regulations are referred to as **blue sky laws.** But state regulation was spotty, and when the security markets collapsed in 1929, it became evident that many securities had been misrepresented. Today, state laws continue to exist, but the primary laws governing the securities markets have been enacted at the federal level.

BLUE SKY LAWS
State laws pertaining to security market regulation.

Primary Market Regulation

The primary market, where new issues are sold, is governed by the Securities Act of 1933. The basic objective of this act is to provide *full disclosure* of all pertinent information. To accomplish this objective, the act includes the following provisions:

1. All interstate offerings to the public are covered by the act, except for very small issues ($1 million to $5 million, depending on the circumstances), short-term issues (maturing in 270 days or less), and those regulated by other federal agencies (such as railroads, banks, and public utilities).
2. Securities must be registered for a minimum number of days before a public offering. The registration statement supplies financial, technical, and legal information about the issue and the firm. Any misleading or incomplete information may cause a delay in the registration.
3. After the registration has become effective, the securities can be offered for public sale if accompanied by the prospectus.
4. Under shelf registration, a firm may register all securities needed over a 2-year period and then issue them as desired during that period.

Be aware that the Securities and Exchange Commission, SEC, does not rule on whether or not an issue is a good buy—only on whether disclosure is adequate.

Note that the act does not attempt to prevent a firm from issuing highly questionable or risky securities.

Secondary Market Regulation

Once securities have been issued, they are traded between investors in the secondary market. This market is regulated by the Securities Exchange Act of 1934. The primary provisions of this legislation are as follows:

1. The act created the Securities and Exchange Commission, SEC. (For 1 year, the Federal Trade Commission administered the Securities Act of 1933.)
2. Major securities exchanges, such as the New York Stock Exchange and the American Stock Exchange, must register with the SEC. In addition, firms whose securities are listed on these exchanges must file periodic reports with both the exchange and the SEC.

3. Corporate insiders who are officers, directors, or major stockholders must file monthly reports. Any short-term profits from holding the firm's stock less than 6 months are payable to the firm.
4. Manipulative practices are prohibited.
5. Margin requirements are set, and may be changed as desired, by the Federal Reserve System.[5]

The SEC oversees all secondary security markets (except futures) and broker activities. For instance, the SEC, together with the exchanges and NASDAQ, uncover and prosecute violations of the insider trading statutes. The NYSE's StockWatch searches for abnormal stock trading patterns prior to important company announcements. If suspicious trades are found, computer networks can be used to trace the trades and uncover links between the trader and present and former company employees.

Regulation of the securities market has important consequences for financial managers. Because they are regulated, both the primary and the secondary markets are viewed as being both orderly and efficient. Firms can issue securities with full confidence that the issue will be sold in a manner that secures the needed capital and provides investors a ready market for resale. Without the development of an extensive investment banking community and efficient and orderly security markets, the costs and risks involved in issuing long-term securities would rise, increasing the firm's opportunity cost of capital and, through the capital budgeting process, influencing its investment decisions.

CONCEPT REVIEW QUESTIONS

- Explain the goal and the requirements of the Securities Act of 1933.
- What are the primary provisions of the Securities and Exchange Act of 1934?

VENTURE CAPITAL

■ LEARNING GOAL 6

Discuss the five phases of venture capital financing.

VENTURE CAPITAL
New, high-risk capital for start-up firms.

In the discussion so far in this chapter we have implicitly assumed the firm was big enough to be able to secure financing from the public markets or through "traditional" private placements. However, for very small firms this is not the case. For small businesses, finding **venture capital**—that is, new high-risk capital—is one of the major problems it faces.

One way to look at the initial financing stages is to break them into phases, as follows:

1. *Seed-Money Financing.* A small amount of financing needed to prove a concept or develop a product.
2. *Start-Up and First-Level Financing.* Financing for firms that need money for research and development, initial production, marketing, and the like.
3. *Second-Level Financing.* Financing for firms that are producing and selling a product but are not breaking even yet.

---

[5]*Instead of paying the full amount initially, an investor can buy on margin and borrow the remainder from a securities dealer.*

4. *Third-Level, or Mezzanine, Financing.* Financing for a firm that is producing a product, breaking even, and considering an expansion.
5. *Fourth-Level, or Bridge, Financing.* Financing provided for firms that are likely to go public within the next year.

Seed money almost always comes from personal savings or loans and from investments by family and friends. Start-up and first-level financing is needed to get the firm "off and running" and to help it meet production quality and quantity standards so that it may begin to break even. Although some firms provide start-up and first-level financing, many venture capital firms avoid this type of financing. Second-level financing is designed to help firms reach an economic break-even point. Third-level, or mezzanine, financing is often provided by venture capital firms. Some large industrial or financial firms (such as Citicorp Venture Capital) have venture capital operations, but most of this type of financing is provided by smaller firms specializing in providing venture capital. Some of these same firms also provide fourth-level, or bridge, financing.[6] Other venture capital financing is provided by pension funds, foreign investors, insurance companies, individual investors and families, and endowments and foundations.

For every ten first-level venture capital investments, only two or three may make it beyond a few years. In fact, some estimates are that 15 percent of new firms don't survive beyond the first year and 50 percent don't survive beyond the fifth year. Because of the very high risk in first- and second-level financing, and the long time before the firm is successful (if it ever is), we see why venture capital firms are reluctant to invest in these stages. They believe, probably rightly so, that the risk/reward prospects are better for later-level investments.

Remember Key Idea 6— risk and return go hand-in-hand.

CONCEPT REVIEW QUESTION

■ What are the five phases of initial financing a small firm typically experiences?

Summary

■ Internally generated funds supply the vast majority of long-term financing needed by firms. However, about 20 percent is provided by new long-term issues, of which bonds play the largest part.
■ Investment banking firms provide marketing services, risk-bearing, certification, and monitoring to issuing firms.
■ Shelf registration lowers the cost to the firm and increases the speed and flexibility of obtaining long-term financing. Rule 144a has provided benefits to both U.S. and non-U.S. firms who use the private placement market.
■ Stockholders can (in general) lose only the amount of their investment in the firm. Due to limited liability, stock is like a call option on the firm.
■ Outstanding shares equal issued shares minus treasury shares. Par value, book value, and market value are all quoted on a per share basis for common stock. Only market value has any financial meaning.
■ Firms issue new common stock only infrequently; studies indicate they suffer a loss in market value when they do issue common stock publicly. Cash expenses average 15 percent and total costs average 25 percent of the total value of new public common stock issues.

[6]*For more on venture capital, see Pratt's* Guide to Venture Capital *or the* Journal of Business Venturing.

■ The function of regulation of the securities market is to provide complete and accurate information and to protect against fraudulent practices.

■ Venture capital involves a number of different stages; for a fee (often substantial) risky firms can obtain start-up financing.

Questions

10.1 Because large firms often have extensive and well-trained finance staffs, they appear to be incurring extra costs by employing the services of investment banking firms. What reasons can you give for engaging the services of investment bankers?

10.2 The primary purpose of the preemptive right is to allow stockholders to maintain their proportionate ownership and control of a firm. How important do you believe this right is for the following:

a. The average stockholder of a firm listed on the New York Stock Exchange?

b. An institutional investor such as a mutual fund or a pension fund?

c. The stockholders of a closely held firm? Explain.

10.3 Differentiate among par value, book value, and market value per share. Why is market value generally the only important figure? Under what limited circumstances may par value or book value be of some importance? Explain.

10.4 The market price of a firm's common stock falls by 2 to 3 percent when it issues additional shares of common stock through a public offering. What possible reasons can we advance for this rather surprising finding? What happens when firms have a private placement of common stock? What possible reasons exist for this effect?

10.5 For underwritten common stock issues of about $5 million in size, issuance costs average about 20 percent. Does this mean the cost of external common equity is roughly 20 percent higher than the cost of internally generated funds for these firms?

Concept Review Problems

See Appendix A for solutions.

CR10.1 Orlando Publications is raising $500,000 in new equity. If direct flotation costs are estimated to be 15 percent of gross proceeds, how large does the offering need to be? How much will Orlando Publications pay in flotation costs?

CR10.2 Virgil Corporation has a current stock price of $35 per share and needs to raise $10 million. The investment banking firm underwriting Virgil's common stock offering stated the offering price will have to be $32 per share because of indirect costs such as investors' concerns about information asymmetry and the firm's investment prospects. Direct flotation costs charged by the investment banking firm are 5 percent of the issue price. How many shares must the firm sell to net $10 million after indirect and direct flotation costs?

CR10.3 SEK is going public and would like to issue 700,000 shares of common stock. Earnings for the year just ended were $700,000.

a. Assume SEK has a growth rate of 8 percent; a required return on equity, k_s, of 12 percent; and it plans to have a dividend payout ratio of 70 percent. What should be SEK's initial offering price?

b. Other firms similar to SEK have a P/E ratio of 18. If we apply this P/E ratio to SEK, what should be SEK's initial offering price?

CR10.4 Finch Corp. has the following balance sheet:

Cash	$ 50,000	Liabilities	$400,000
Other	750,000	Common stock ($1 par)	50,000
Total assets	$800,000	Additional paid-in capital	200,000
		Retained earnings	150,000
		Total liabilities and stockholders' equity	$800,000

Assume Finch sells 10,000 additional shares of stock at $20 per share. What is Finch's balance sheet after the stock issue?

Problems

See Appendix C for answers to selected problems.

Underwriting Costs

10.1 Webster Products recently sold a $30 million bond issue at par. The underwriting fees were 1.2 percent, and additional issuance costs were $125,000.
a. How many dollars did Webster net from the sale?
b. What were the fees (including both underwriting and other issuance costs) as a percentage of the gross proceeds of the bond issue?

Selling Costs

10.2 In an $80 million bond issue by Frontier Power, the bonds were purchased by the underwriting group at 99.125 percent of par and sold to the public at par, which was $1,000 per bond.
a. What was the total amount Frontier Power received from the issue?
b. What were the total underwriting costs? What were the underwriting costs as a percentage of the gross proceeds? What were the underwriting costs per $1,000 bond?
c. If an underwriting firm was also the seller, it received all the commission. Otherwise, other security dealers (not in the underwriting group) could buy the bonds and sell them for a commission of $2.50 per bond. If a dealer bought 50 bonds, how much in total did the dealer make, and how much did the dealer pay to the underwriter for the bonds?

Underwritten Versus Best Efforts

10.3 Slate Electronics, a new and rather speculative firm, wishes to raise additional capital by selling stock and going public. The firm's investment banker has suggested two alternatives. Plan I is a firm commitment offering of 1 million shares at $7.50 per share, with an underwriting fee of 8 percent of the gross proceeds. Plan II is a best efforts offering at $7.75 per share, subject to an underwriting commission of 3 percent of the expected gross proceeds sold, plus a $150,000 fee. The "best guess" is that 95 percent of the issue would be sold under plan II.
a. Based on the net proceeds to the firm, which plan should Slate choose?
b. Does your answer change if only 90 percent of the issue can be sold under the best efforts plan?
c. All things considered, which plan would you recommend? Why?

Private Placement

10.4 Hastings, Ltd. is planning a private placement of 60,000 new shares to an institutional investor at a 10 percent discount from the present market price of $40. There are presently 300,000 shares outstanding. If the current book value of the stockholders' equity is $6,000,000, calculate (a) book value per share both before and after the private placement, and (b) the market price per share after the private placement. Are existing stockholders better or worse off after the new shares are sold? Defend your answer, given your calculations.

Pricing a New Issue

10.5 J. Beasley is a new firm that needs to raise $16,560,000 to begin operations. No debt will be used. Beasley's common stock is expected to pay a $4 cash dividend next year, and dividends and earnings are expected to grow at 9 percent per year for the foreseeable future. If k_s is 19 percent and the cost of issuing the stock is 8 percent of the gross proceeds from the sale, how many shares must be issued and sold?

Pricing a New Issue

10.6 Jameson Enterprises is planning its first public offering of common stock. The CFO estimates that the equity investors' required return is between 11 and 14 percent. Earnings and cash dividends are expected to grow at 6 to 9 percent per year for the foreseeable future, and cash dividends to be paid next year, D_1, are $800,000.

a. What is the range of possible total current market values for the stock of Jameson Enterprises?

b. If 500,000 shares of stock are authorized and outstanding, but 300,000 will be held by the founders, what are the maximum and minimum selling prices per share and the maximum and minimum total proceeds from the issue?

Percent of Issue Sold

Note: Any unsold shares will be distributed among the firm's owners, so a total of 1 million shares will be outstanding.

10.7 Grant Resources is a new firm that needs to raise $6,412,500 through the issuance of 1 million shares of stock. No debt will be employed. Next year's cash dividends are expected to be $0.60 per share, and cash dividends and earnings are expected to grow at 8 percent per year for the foreseeable future. If k_s is 16 percent and the cost of issuing the stock is 10 percent of the gross proceeds, what percentage of the issue must be sold in order for Grant to obtain the net amount of $6,412,500?

Alternative Approaches to Pricing a New Issue

Note: Ignore any flotation or issuance costs.

10.8 Apollo Energy is planning its first public offering. Its past growth in cash dividends and earnings has averaged 10 percent per year. Based on the number of shares Apollo is planning to issue, cash dividends and earnings per share for next year ($t = 1$) are expected to be $0.90 and $2, respectively. The firm's investment banking firm, Best Associates, has recommended that the stock be issued at a price of $15 per share.

a. What is the P/E ratio implied by the recommended market price?

b. Two firms similar to Apollo Energy have the following characteristics:

	Firm Y	Firm Z
Expected *EPS*	$ 1.50	$ 3.00
Expected *DPS*	0.80	1.25
Expected growth rate per year	7%	9%
Market price	$15.00	$45.00

For firm Y and firm Z, determine (**1**) their P/E ratios and (**2**) their implied k_s. Then calculate an estimated market price for Apollo Energy using first the separate P/E's and k_s's, and then an average of them. Based on these comparable firms, what range of prices is implied for Apollo?

c. What required return, or cost of equity capital, k_s, is implied by the price of $15 if investors' expectations of the future are consistent with the past?

d. You believe the rate calculated in (c) is high; it should be between 11.5 and 13 percent. The expected growth rate of 10 percent is okay. What issue price is implied, given these estimates?

e. Based on your analysis in (a) through (d), how would you respond to Best Associates' proposal?

Recording a Stock Issue

10.9 Allen Printing is planning to issue 500,000 additional shares of common stock at an offering price of $12 each. Show the net effect of the transaction on the firm's balance sheet.

	Assets		Liabilities and Stockholders' Equity	
Cash	$ 3,000,000		Liabilities	$25,000,000
Other	62,000,000		Common stock ($2 par)	4,000,000
Total	$65,000,000		Additional paid-in capital	10,000,000
			Retained earnings	26,000,000
			Total	$65,000,000

Note: Ignore any underwriting or other issuance expenses.

Common Equity

10.10 Sayer Stores has 200,000 shares of common stock authorized. Its common equity shown on the firm's balance sheet is as follows:

Common stock ($2 par)	$300,000
Additional paid-in capital	95,000
Retained earnings	600,000
	995,000
Less: Treasury stock (3,000 shares)	25,000
Common stockholders' equity	$970,000

a. How many shares are issued?
b. How many are outstanding? Explain the difference between (a) and (b).
c. How many additional shares can be issued without the approval of Sayer's stockholders?
d. If the firm issues 5,000 more shares at $15 each, prepare the new common stockholders' equity accounts.

Securing Common Stock Financing

10.11 **Mini Case** Trident Software is a fast-growing privately held firm. In order to continue expanding into new markets, it needs additional common stock financing.

a. What different methods are available for selling common stock? What are the advantages and disadvantages of each?
b. If Trident decides to have the issue underwritten through a firm commitment offering, what sequence of events will occur?
c. If the current owners are concerned about giving up too much control of the firm in terms of voting rights, how might they proceed?
d. To determine the selling price of the new issue, Trident has made the following estimates. The firm does not presently pay cash dividends, nor are there any plans to start paying them in the near future. Based on internal projections, the rate of growth is expected to be 40 percent per year for each of the next 5 years, after which it will be 10 percent per year to infinity. Because no dividends are paid, a variation of the dividend valuation model will be employed as one way to estimate the total value of Trident Software. Under this approach the firm's free cash flow available after necessary expenses will be projected into the future, discounted at the opportunity cost of equity capital of 18 percent, and then the firm's liabilities will be subtracted. The free cash flow at time $t = 0$ is $3,000,000, and the liabilities are $25,000,000.
    The second way that will be used to estimate the value of the firm is based on comparable P/E ratios. The firm's current earnings are $2,500,000 and due to its high growth, a P/E ratio of 35 times earnings is believed to be appropriate.
    (1) Estimate Trident's total equity value, S, using both the discounted cash flow approach and the comparable P/E approach.
    (2) Then average them together to determine the estimated equity value of Trident Software.
e. Trident Software has 5,000,000 shares of common stock authorized. It will sell 2,000,000 to the public (with 3,000,000 being retained by the original owners), and the cash expenses of the sale will be 7 percent of the issue price.

(1) For what market price per share will the stock sell? How much per share will Trident receive after expenses? How much in total will it receive?

(2) Why are issuance expenses higher with common stock, especially for a smaller firm, than for bonds?

f. In what market will Trident Software stock trade? What are the advantages if in the future it decides to have its stock listed on one of the stock exchanges? What are the disadvantages?

Long-Term Liability Management

Sections in this chapter:

■ **Long-Term Debt**
The types and characteristics of bonds.
■ **Financing with Long-Term and Medium-Term Debt**
Debt and the value of the firm.
■ **Financing in the 1990s**
Selling zeros, junk, and more.
■ **Managing Long-Term Debt**
Alternatives to just sitting back and waiting for debt to mature.
■ **Preferred Stock**
Somewhere between debt and equity.
■ **Long-Term Financing and Financial Distress**
Conflicts of interest between bondholders and stockholders.

Virtually every day firms turn to the bond markets to raise large amounts of new capital. A glance at *The Wall Street Journal* shows the following: Rexene Corp. was raising $175 million with senior notes due in 2004; CIT Group Holdings sold $200 million in two-year notes; and Wheeling Pittsburgh Steel and Geneva Steel raised $50 million and $45 million, respectively, through the use of senior secured credit facilities. And commercial banks, among others, have turned to new kinds of securities in recent years, including adjustable-rate preferred stock. What a mere 15 or so years ago was the dull, conservative field of debt and preferred stock financing has changed dramatically. Now firms rely on liability management—the aggressive manipulation of fixed and variable rate long-term financing.

Look at how firms now take advantage of differences in worldwide interest rates. Thanks to heavy overseas demand, U.S. corporations have occasionally been able to issue securities in the Eurobond market at favorable interest rates—one-half to 1 percent lower than in the United States. And, around the world, more and more firms are turning to bond financing. Take firms in South Korea, Malaysia, and Thailand, for instance. Traditionally, bond markets have been very small in these countries, and the major source of debt financing was through banks. However, that is rapidly changing, and the expectation is that bond financing will explode in the coming years in the Far East. Likewise, firms from Venezuela, Brazil, and Mexico are increasingly turning to bonds to raise funds.

Likewise, new innovations continue to pop up as investment bankers create new securities. One recent security was the monthly income preferred stock, MIPS. By financing offshore (in the Turks and Caicos Islands), firms were trying to create preferred stock that appeared to enable the "dividends" to be treated like interest by the issuing firms and thus deducted as a business expense. There's only one problem—the Internal Revenue Service, IRS, typically takes a very dim view of such tax-driven securities.

Many developments continue to occur as firms and governments around the world need to raise increasingly larger amounts of debt financing. Changes have occurred, and continue to occur, in the area of liability management. Let's examine this fast changing area.

LEARNING GOALS

After studying this chapter you should be able to:

1. Understand what bonds are and various common bond provisions, including security and seniority, call provisions, and convertibility.
2. Discuss bond pricing and ratings, and compare long-term (bonds) and medium-term (notes and loans) financing.
3. Describe new forms of debt financing, including zero-coupon bonds, junk bonds, variable-rate loans, and asset-backed securities, and discuss the international bond market.
4. Discuss key techniques of managing long-term debt—refunding and alternatives to refunding, and interest rate swaps.
5. Compare preferred stock to debt and equity, and discuss the advantages and disadvantages of this form of financing.
6. Explain the conflicting interests of stock- and bondholders, and discuss the long-term financing alternatives for a firm in distress.

LONG-TERM DEBT

■ LEARNING GOAL 1

Understand what bonds are and various common bond provisions, including security and seniority, call provisions, and convertibility.

Long-term debt obligates the firm to pay an annual return (interest on debt and cash dividends on preferred stock). To secure funds, managers choose from among the various kinds of long-term securities depending on world markets, what investors are currently interested in, and the firm's financial position. This chapter focuses primarily on the two main types of long-term securities—bonds and preferred stock.

Bond Terms

INDENTURE
Legal agreement between the issuing firm and the bondholders; provides the specific terms of the bond.

When a firm borrows with bonds, it issues a long-term promissory note to a lender. The contract between the firm and the lender is called a bond **indenture.** For cash offerings a copy of the indenture is included in the registration statement filed with the Securities and Exchange Commission. It is a legal document specifying all the provisions attached to the bond. One specific provision states that the lenders will receive regular interest payments, generally semi-annually, during the term of the bond, and will receive the par or maturity value of the bond upon maturity. For example, if IBM issues a 20-year, $100 million bond with a coupon rate of 10.3 percent, it will pay $10.3 million per year in interest each year until maturity. The interest will be paid in two semi-annual installments of $5.15 million each. On the maturity date in 20 years, IBM would then repay the $100 million. While financially strong firms may issue bonds with a 20- to 30-year maturity, other firms are finding that they can sell bonds with even longer terms. For example, in 1992 and 1993 Boeing, Consolidated Rail (Conrail), Ford Motor, and Texaco all issued bonds with a 50-year maturity; Walt Disney and Coca-Cola both issued 100-year bonds.

Trustee

Bonds are not only long-term in nature, they are typically substantial in size. Issues of $50 to $500 million are not uncommon, and some are even larger. To ease communication between the issuing firm and the lenders, a trustee is appointed for all public issues of long-term debt. The primary responsibilities of the trustee (typically a bank) are as follows:

1. To see that all the legal requirements for drawing up the bond indenture are met before issuance.
2. To monitor the actions of the issuing firm to see that its performance is in agreement with the conditions specified by the indenture.
3. To take appropriate action on behalf of bondholders if the firm defaults on interest or principal payments.

Security and Seniority

Bonds come with many types of provisions. As Figure 11.1 shows, one primary distinction is between secured and unsecured bonds. We will discuss the provisions in order.

FIGURE 11.1

Types of Bonds

Many other variations exist, but the ones shown here represent the primary types. Note that other features, such as adjustable rates or zero-coupons, can be incorporated with any of these bonds.

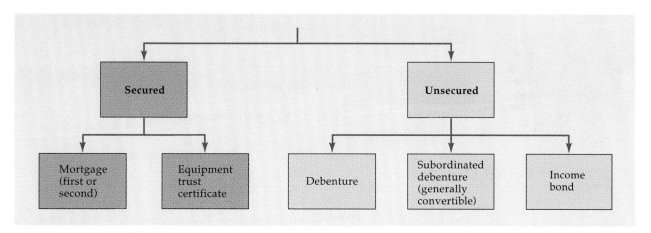

MORGAGE BOND
Bond secured by a lien on
real property of a firm.

**EQUIPMENT TRUST
CERTIFICATE**
Form of security in which a
trustee holds title to the assets until the security is
paid off in full by the firm
employing the financing.

*Firms are reluctant to ac-
cept restrictions on how
they invest in real assets,
such as plant and equip-
ment; they feel this is
management's value-
added component.*

DEBENTURE
Unsecured long-term bor-
rowing by a firm, backed
only by its full faith and
credit.

**SUBORDINATED
DEBENTURE**
Unsecured long-term bor-
rowing of the firm that has
a lower claim than other
unsecured claims.

INCOME BOND
Bond that will pay interest
only to the extent it has the
earnings to do so.

CUMULATIVE
Provisions in many pre-
ferred stocks and income
bonds that require full payment of all past cash dividends or interest before
any additional dividend or
interest is paid.

Forms of Secured Debt

Secured debt is backed ("secured") by specific assets. The vast majority of secured debt consists of **mortgage bonds,** which may be *first mortgage bonds* if they have a primary claim on assets in the event of default, or *second mortgage bonds*, whose claim is subordinate to that of the first mortgage bondholders. Bonds come with many different types of restrictions, or protective covenants. Some mortgage bonds have a "closed-end provision" that prohibits the firm from issuing additional debt with equal priority against the pledged assets. To strengthen the position of the bondholder, the indenture may also contain an "after-acquired property" clause. This provision speci-fies that any property acquired by the firm in the future will also serve as collateral for the bonds.

A second form of secured debt is the **equipment trust certificate.** These are fre-quently used to finance railroad cars and airplanes. Here, the trustee acquires formal ownership of the asset in question. The issuing firm arranges to purchase the equip-ment and provides a down payment of 10 to 25 percent; the remainder is provided by the purchasers of the equipment trust certificates. The certificates are issued with vary-ing maturities, often ranging from 1 to 15 years. After the entire issue is paid off, title to the equipment passes to the firm. Because the trustee holds title to the pledged equipment, equipment trust certificates provide good security to their purchasers.

Unsecured Debt

Unsecured bonds, called **debentures,** have no specific assets pledged as collateral. Instead, they are backed by the full faith and credit of the issuing corporation. Large firms with excellent credit ratings, such as Procter & Gamble, Exxon, and Shell, use debentures almost exclusively. Most debentures have a claim on assets in the event of default that comes after that held by bank loans, short-term debt, the government, and any mortgage bonds.

Although asset security is sometimes important, in the final analysis it is the firm's cash flow that determines the attractiveness of a bond issue. Debentures frequently contain a *negative pledge clause,* which prohibits issuing new debt with a priority over the debentures' claim on assets. This provision generally applies to assets that may be acquired in the future as well as to those already owned by the issuing firm.

Subordinated debentures, which have a claim on assets inferior to that of other debentures in the case of liquidation, are widely used in raising long-term debt capital. Subordinated debt allows the issuing firm to increase its borrowing without jeopardiz-ing the security position of its other long-term debt.

One last form of unsecured bond is the **income bond,** which requires interest to be paid only to the extent that it is earned by the firm. Income bonds typically arise out of reorganizations. They are somewhat like preferred stock in that the firm is not re-quired to pay interest if it is not earned. Income bonds have the advantage that any in-terest, if paid, is a tax-deductible expense to the firm, whereas cash dividends paid on preferred stock are not. The provisions attached to income bonds vary, but many are **cumulative;** that is, if interest is not paid in a given period, it must be paid in the fu-ture if it is earned.

Additional Bond Provisions

Many different types of provisions and protective covenants occur in bonds. There are three provisions that warrant additional consideration: these are the call provision, sinking funds, and convertibility.

Call Provision

A **call provision** gives the issuing firm the option to call the bond for redemption before it matures. This provision states that if it calls the bond, the firm must pay an amount *greater than* the par or maturity value of the bond; the additional amount is the **call premium.** For most long-term bonds, the call premium starts out close to the coupon rate on the bond. Thus, if the firm wants to call the bonds soon after issuance, it pays a penalty of about 1 year's additional interest. This rate declines over time.

The call provision, which is simply a call option held by the issuing firm, has value to the firm but is potentially detrimental to investors. The problem for investors is that the call provision enables the issuing firm to substitute bonds with a lower coupon rate for bonds with a higher rate, or bonds with less protective covenants for ones with more stringent covenants.[1] To make them more attractive investments, many bonds now carry a 5- to 10-year "nonrefundable provision" if the coupon rate on the new bonds will be below the current coupon rate on the bond to be refunded. With such a provision, bonds may be retired for some purposes, but not refunded for (or replaced by) another bond.

Sinking Fund

A **sinking fund** provision requires the firm to retire a given number of bonds over a specified time period. The logic behind sinking funds is to encourage firms to adopt a systematic pattern for retiring the largest portion of the debt before the maturity date. Generally bonds are redeemed for the sinking fund at par. Although it is called a sinking fund, we should emphasize that a separate fund is *not* set up and accumulated over the life of the bonds. Rather, a given number of bonds *are actually retired each year.*

In most cases, the firm can decide how to meet the sinking fund provision. If market interest rates have increased, causing the price of the bonds to fall below the par or sinking fund price, the firm can buy sufficient bonds on the open market to meet the requirement. But if market interest rates are low (and therefore bond prices are high), the firm will call the bonds by lottery at par. This flexibility obviously benefits the issuing firm.

In some cases firms use **serial bonds,** which are a package of bonds that mature in different years. Serial bonds are similar to a bond with a sinking fund provision, because both provide for the periodic repayment of the firm's debt. But the serial bond does not give the issuing firm an alternative—the bonds must be redeemed at par.

Convertibility

Some bonds, and an even smaller percentage of preferred stock, contain another feature—convertibility. **Convertible securities** are convertible bonds or convertible preferred stock, originally issued as debt or preferred stock, that can be exchanged for common stock of the issuing firm at the discretion of the investor. By combining elements of both debt and equity, convertible bonds assist in minimizing agency problems and conflicts between bondholders and stockholders. Convertibles are considered in Chapter 14.

CONCEPT REVIEW QUESTIONS

- What is the purpose of appointing a trustee for all long-term issuances?
- Give some examples of secured debentures and unsecured debentures.
- How do a callable bond and a convertible bond differ?

[1]*Refunding a bond issue involves calling one issue and replacing it with another. Refunding is considered later in the chapter.*

FINANCING WITH LONG-TERM AND MEDIUM-TERM DEBT

■ LEARNING GOAL 2

Discuss bond pricing and ratings, and compare long-term (bonds) and medium-term (notes and loans) financing.

The frequency with which firms issue long-term debt varies considerably. At one extreme are large public utility firms, which may issue debt every few years. Other firms issue long-term debt only infrequently. But, however often they employ it, managers must be aware of special considerations when they use long-term debt.

Pricing and Selling the Bond Issue

FULLY REGISTERED FORM
Form of bond in which ownership is recorded with a registration agent, who mails interest checks to bondholders.

BEARER FORM
Bonds that are not registered by the firm or an agent; whoever holds the bond is the owner.

Many large bond issues are underwritten through a firm commitment offering, although an increasing number are being offered through shelf registration and private placement. The coupon interest rate for the issue is determined shortly before the bonds come to market, so that they may be sold at a price close to par. Most bonds are issued in denominations of $1,000 in **fully registered form.** This means that the registration agent for the issuing firm (often a bank) will record the ownership of each bond, so that both interest and principal are paid directly to the owner of the bond. Until the last few decades, most bonds were issued in **bearer form,** in which the certificate is the primary evidence of ownership. The owner must send coupons in for payment of interest, and the bond itself must be returned upon maturity for repayment of principal. Because of the risk of loss and the time and inconvenience involved in "clipping" coupons (and also because of a change in the law passed by the U.S. Congress in 1982), most bonds are now issued in fully registered form.

The price of a bond is expressed as a percentage of its par value. Thus, a price of 99.5 means 99.5 percent of its $1,000 par value, or $995. When a bond is sold, the price is quoted net of accrued interest. This means the purchaser pays not only the purchase price, but also *any interest that may have accrued between interest payment dates.* Finally, the major secondary market for bonds is the over-the-counter, OTC, market.

Bond Ratings

BOND RATING
Professional judgment as to the probability of repayment of principal and interest on a bond.

Bonds ranked by increasing level of risk are U.S. Treasury bonds, corporate mortgage bonds, equipment trust certificates, debentures, subordinated debentures, and income bonds.

The most widely employed method for examining the relative quality of bonds is **bond ratings,** which reflect the probability of payment of both interest and principal. The two major rating agencies are Moody's Investors Service and Standard & Poor's Corporation. Their ratings are described in Table 11.1. In general, two bonds with similar ratings and the same maturity have approximately the same yield to maturity.[2]

The AAA/Aaa and AA/Aa bonds are of high quality; A and BBB/Baa bonds are also viewed as being of "investment grade." Bonds with these four top grades may be held by banks and other institutional investors. BB/Ba and B bonds are more speculative with respect to payment of interest and principal; bonds rated below B are either in default or have other characteristics that make them highly speculative. Bonds rated be-

---

[2]*Exceptions occur when we compare bonds issued by industrial firms and those issued by public utilities. Because of different provisions and demand, the yields on utilities are typically higher than those of similarly rated corporate bonds.*

TABLE 11.1

Bond Rating Classifications

Generally, both Moody's and Standard & Poor's rate a bond similarly, although differences in ratings can and do exist. Bonds in the top four classifications (AAA–BBB or Aaa–Baa, respectively) are considered "investment grade." All of the rest, in contrast, are non-investment grade, or "junk" bonds.

Standard & Poor's		Moody's	
AAA	Highest rating	Aaa	Best quality, "gilt edge"
AA	Very strong	Aa	High quality
A	Strong	A	Upper medium grade
BBB	Adequate	Baa	Medium grade
BB	Least speculative of the BB to CCC bonds	Ba	Have speculative elements
B	More speculative	B	Lack characteristics of a desirable investment
CCC	Possible default	Caa	Poor standing; may be in default
CC	Still more speculative	Ca	High degree of speculation; often in default
C	Often in bankruptcy	C	Extremely poor prospect of ever attaining any real investment standing
D	In default		

Source: Standard & Poor's Creditweek and *Moody's Bond Record.*
Note: AA to BB bonds may be modified by the addition of a plus or minus sign to show their relative standing, while Aa to B bonds carry a 1, 2, or 3 to designate the top, middle, and bottom range of the rating.

low BBB/Baa are collectively referred to as junk, or high-yield, bonds (because they must pay high interest to offset their risk and attract buyers).

Many factors influence bond ratings. Some of the most important are these:

1. Accounting ratios such as the debt/equity ratio, times interest earned, and various profitability ratios (as discussed in Chapter 19). These ratios provide some evidence of the strength and riskiness of the firm.
2. The current status of the firm in terms of its competitiveness and management. In addition, the industry or industries in which the firm is engaged is often a factor.
3. The attitude of the appropriate regulatory authorities, if the firm is in a regulated industry, such as public utilities.
4. Specific provisions or characteristics of the bonds. For example, first mortgage bonds generally carry a rating one level higher than debentures for the same firm, and debentures are often rated one level higher than subordinated debentures. In 1994 Associates Corp. of North America, Bankers Trust, Coastal Corp., and Ohio Power, among others, had bonds outstanding with different rankings.

Key Idea 6 is that risk and return go hand-in-hand; lower-rated bonds are more risky, and hence, cost the firm more. Certain features, such as subordination, also increase a bond's risk.

During World War II yields on Treasury bonds were less than 1%, to help control borrowing costs to pay for the war. Alternatively, in May 1981 yields on T-bills reached over 16% and yields on long-term T-bonds were close to 14%.

When originally issued, most bonds are awarded a rating of B or above, with the highest-quality bonds carrying an AAA/Aaa rating. Triple-A bonds are viewed by the rating agencies as having the lowest probability of default, so the issuing firms have to pay the least for debt financing. Table 11.2 indicates that between 1985 and 1994, the yield to maturity on Aaa-rated bonds was about 1.0 percent below that for Baa bonds. The differences in yields to maturity, although for bonds already outstanding, illustrate the differences in coupon rates attached to bonds in different rating groups.

Notice in Table 11.2 that all bonds, even the long-term Treasury bonds, carry a risk premium above that of short-term U.S. Treasury bills. Thus, we see that the average risk premium for long-term government bonds over this time period was 2.40 percent. As we move from long-term government bonds to corporate bonds, the yield to maturity increases, due to default risk. Yield spreads (that is, the difference in yields between different types of bonds) also vary over time. In 1986, for example, long-term U.S. Treasury bonds had a yield to maturity of 8.14 percent, whereas corporate Baa bonds were yielding 10.39 percent, for a difference—a yield spread—of 2.25 percent. However, in 1992 the difference in yields between the same two bond categories was 1.46 percent (8.98 − 7.52). For firms entering the bond market, the going interest rate on outstanding issues of similar maturity and quality provides a good point of reference for estimating the coupon interest rate (and hence the before-tax cost) for a new bond issue.

What about the actual rate of default on bonds? Do lower-quality bonds, with higher yields, actually have higher default rates? Table 11.3 presents cumulative default rates (for 1 year, 3 years, 5 years, 7 years, and 9 years after original issuance) for

TABLE 11.2

Yield to Maturity on Long-Term U.S. Treasury and Corporate Bonds

The differences in yields approximate the differences in coupon rates required from the issuing firm. Hence, other things being equal, firms strive for as high a rating as possible in order to reduce their interest costs.

Year	U.S. Treasury Bonds	Corporate Bonds			
		Aaa	Aa	A	Baa
1985	10.75%	11.37%	11.82%	12.28%	12.72%
1986	8.14	9.02	9.47	9.95	10.39
1987	8.64	9.38	9.68	9.99	10.58
1988	8.98	9.71	9.94	10.24	10.83
1989	8.58	9.26	9.46	9.74	10.18
1990	8.74	9.32	9.56	9.82	10.36
1991	8.16	8.77	9.05	9.30	9.80
1992	7.52	8.14	8.46	8.62	8.98
1993	6.45	7.22	7.40	7.58	7.93
1994	7.01	7.97	8.15	8.28	8.63
Average yield	8.30	9.02	9.30	9.58	10.22
Average risk premium (yield − Treasury bill yield)	2.40	3.12	3.40	3.68	4.32

Source: Federal Reserve Bulletin, various issues.

TABLE 11.3

Mortality Rates by Original Bond Rating, 1971–1991

The default rates indicate the cumulative percentage of bonds that have defaulted 1, 3, 5, 7, and 9 years after they were originally issued.

	Years After Original Issuance				
Original Rating	1	3	5	7	9
AAA	0.00%	0.00%	0.00%	0.17%	0.17%
AA	0.00	1.09	1.52	1.71	1.79
A	0.00	0.45	0.93	1.08	1.49
BBB	0.10	1.51	2.72	3.96	4.09
BB	0.00	4.53	8.97	14.02	14.02
B	1.72	14.90	25.00	30.09	35.54
C	1.55	26.01	35.40	38.85	na

Source: Adapted from Exhibit 10 in Edward I. Altman, "Revisiting the High-Yield Bond Market," *Financial Management* 21 (Summer 1992), pp.78–92.

Even during the Great Depression very few triple A bonds defaulted. Why? Because most of the triple A-rated bonds that eventually defaulted were speedily downrated prior to default.

bonds issued during the 1971–1991 period. As the table indicates, for bonds in the top three categories (the A's), default after 9 years of issuance was 0.17 percent for AAA bonds, 1.79 percent for AA bonds, and 1.49 percent for A-rated bonds. The default experience has been low for these bonds. The default rate of BBB bonds is 4.09 percent after 9 years. Moving to the non-investment-grade bonds of BB, B, or C, we find that default rates for bonds issued in the 1971–1991 time period are fairly high—from 14 percent after 9 years for BB-rated bonds, to over 35 percent for B-rated bonds. Finally, for C-rated bonds, we see that over 35 percent of them defaulted within 5 years and almost 40 percent defaulted within 7 years from the date they were issued. Based on this information, we see that bond ratings at the time of original issue do a good job of differentiating low-risk from high-risk bonds.

Medium-Term Note Financing

In recent years, due primarily to the shelf registration procedure implemented in 1982, firms have turned to using medium-term notes as another source of financing. *Medium-term notes* have a maturity of 1 to 10 years and traditionally are noncallable, senior, unsecured, fixed-rate instruments. As of the end of a recent year, U.S. corporate securities outstanding were as follows (in billions of dollars):

Security	Amount	Percentage of Total
Long-term bonds and notes	$ 791.1	37.4%
International bonds	131.1	6.2
Medium-term notes	97.6	4.6
Bank loans to nonfinancial firms	546.0	25.8
Asset-backed securities	68.1	3.2
Commercial paper	482.5	22.8
Total	$2,116.4	100.0%

The commercial paper is entirely short-term in nature (with a maturity of 270 days or less), as are some of the bank loans and asset-backed securities. Once these short-term securities are excluded, the amount of financing provided by medium-term notes was over 6 percent of total debt financing. Only firms that are of investment grade (with bond ratings of BBB/Baa or above) have been able to secure financing using medium-term notes. Although the effective cost of medium-term notes has been slightly more than that for comparable maturity bonds, medium-term notes are more flexible and can be tailored to meet any maturity needs of the issuing firm. They can also be quickly and easily issued.

Term Loans

TERM LOANS
Bank borrowings whose principal and interest are paid off on some predetermined schedule, typically from 5 to 10 years; also called amortized loans.

As an alternative to a bond issue or medium-term notes, firms—especially smaller ones—also rely on bank borrowings. The mechanics of these borrowings often take the form of **term loans** (also called amortized loans). The purpose of the amortization is to see that principal and interest are paid off on some predetermined schedule. Firms that borrow from banks may be smaller than firms that raise funds through a public bond issue, and the maturity (length) of financing is typically 5 to 10 years.

To illustrate, suppose Clark's Products borrowed $55,000 on a 3-year loan to be repaid in three equal annual installments. The nominal rate of interest is 12 percent on the declining principal balance of the loan. The annual payments, which include both principal and interest, are just an annuity. Thus, the size of each payment is:[3]

$$PMT = \frac{PV_0}{\sum_{t=1}^{n} \frac{1}{(1+k)^t}} = \frac{\$55,000}{\sum_{t=1}^{3} \frac{1}{(1.12)^t}}$$

AMORTIZATION SCHEDULE
Schedule that breaks down the payments between principal and interest over the life of a loan; an increasing portion of the payment goes to pay back the principal as the years go by.

Hence, Clark's makes three equal annual payments of approximately $22,899 to repay the loan.[4] The **amortization schedule,** which breaks down the payments between principal and interest, is presented in Table 11.4. Note that an increasing portion of the payment goes to pay back the principal as the years go by. Also, the last payment, as shown in Table 11.4, is often slightly different from the earlier payments. Home mortgage or car loans typically employ exactly the same approach

Key Idea 4 is that firms (and individuals) focus on cash flows, while 5 is that a dollar today is worth more than a dollar tomorrow. These cash flow and present value concepts are used to determine an amortization schedule.

TABLE 11.4

Principal and Interest Amortized over Three Annual Installments at 12 Percent

Typical of many term (or installment) loans, the last payment differs from the earlier ones.

Year	Payment	Interest[*]	Principal Repayment	Remaining Balance
1	$22,899.00	$6,600.00	$16,299.00	$38,701.00
2	22,899.00	4,644.12	18,254.88	20,446.12
3	20,899.65†	2,453.53	20,446.12	0

*First-year interest is (0.12)($55,000); for year 2 it is (0.12)($38,701.00); and for year 3 it is (0.12)($20,446.12).
†This last payment is the sum of the remaining balance of $20,446.12 and the interest of $2,453.53.

[3]*If present value tables are used PV$_0$ = $55,000/PVA$_{12\%,3}$ = $55,000/2.402 = $22,898.*
[4]*Most loans of this type are actually payable monthly or quarterly.*

Debt Financing and the Value of the Firm

Key Idea 2 is that financial markets are efficient. Looking at market reactions tells us something about the impact of different financing on the value of the firm.

In Chapter 10 we saw that firms issuing new equity experience a decrease in the value of their outstanding common stock. Does this same pattern hold for firms that issue bonds or take out bank loans? Issuing straight (i.e., nonconvertible) debt has little if any negative impact on the value of the firm. Taking out a new bank loan has no impact on the value of the firm. But, if a firm and a bank are revising a bank loan agreement, the impact on the value of the firm can be either positive (if the revision has favorable elements for the firm) or negative (if the bank appears to be tightening up on the firm). Thus, through their review process, banks appear to provide access to information about the firm that is not otherwise available to the capital markets.

CONCEPT REVIEW QUESTIONS

- Are most bonds currently issued in bearer form or in fully registered form? Why?
- What are some factors that influence a bond's rating?
- Describe the effects on a firm's stock price of issuing debt, and taking out or revising a bank loan.

FINANCIAL MANAGEMENT TODAY

The Changing Nature of Banking

Under the Glass-Steagall Act of 1933, investment banking and commercial banking were separated for U.S. banks. Other federal laws also erected a wall between the commercial banking industry and the insurance industry, and prevented banks from branching across state borders.

Other financial service firms are not so restricted. For example, General Electric Credit Corporation has aggressively moved into many areas occupied by commercial banks. They are the United States' largest issuer of commercial paper, the largest supplier of private-label credit cards for department stores, and the largest private insurer of home loans. They also lease cars, containers, aircraft, and railway cars, and provide commercial loans to firms. Others, like, Prudential, the United States' largest insurer, own a vast securities and investment firm, a bank, and a property company. Merrill Lynch, in addition to its very large investment banking operations, owns a bank, provides credit card and corporate lending, and sells home loans and life insurance. On the international scene, banks in Great Britain, Germany, and Japan are allowed to enter into both commercial and investment banking activities.

However, the restrictions faced by U.S. banks are being relentlessly washed away. In 1983 the Federal Reserve ruled that a bank could own and operate a discount brokerage firm. A year later the Federal Reserve allowed several big banks to underwrite commercial paper and mortgage-backed and other securities. Seventeen states now permit banks to sell insurance. Over the last 15 years the prohibition on interstate banking has slowly crumbled. In the mid-1970s two capital-hungry states, Alaska and Maine, opened their borders to bank holding companies from other states. In the early 1980s more states began to open their doors to allow out-of-state banks into their territory. The savings and loan crises of the 1980s also provided the opportunity for banks to expand across state lines, as troubled S&Ls were sold to banks that were expressly allowed to move into new territories. While interstate banking is already a reality, different states have created a hodgepodge of laws and regulations that have added significantly to the banks' cost of doing business.

At the end of World War II, banks controlled more than one-half of the U.S. financial services industry. Now their share is down to about one-quarter, and it continues to decline as consumers choose to put more of their wealth into other places. Corporate lending—once the dominant domain of commercial banks—is now a low-profit, high-competition business. Will banks go out of style in the United States? No, but we will continue to see consolidations and changes, as banks strive to compete in the vastly different world for financial services that exists today.

FINANCING IN THE 1990S

■ **LEARNING GOAL 3**

Describe new forms of debt financing, including zero-coupon bonds, junk bonds, variable rate loans, and asset-backed securities, and discuss the international bond market.

The degree of sophistication required for raising long-term capital has increased greatly in recent years. This change has been the result of several dramatic shifts in inflation over time, innovations in the financial markets, and the development of worldwide capital markets. As we'll see, firms now use many different forms of debt financing.

Zero-Coupon Bonds

ZERO-COUPON BOND
Long-term bond issued at a discount from its par value, for which interest is the difference between the original price and the maturity value.

Beginning in the 1980s, many firms issued **zero-coupon bonds.** These bonds, like Treasury bills, are issued at a discount; that is, the interest is the difference between their original issue price and the maturity value. Why would any firm issue zero-coupon bonds? The answer is that these bonds have a yield (or cost) to maturity of approximately 1 percent less than similar-quality coupon bonds sold at par. The cost to the firm is lower primarily because these bonds are callable only at a substantial premium. From the purchaser's standpoint there are two advantages to a zero-coupon bond: First, because there are no periodic interest payments to be received, there is no reinvestment rate risk. That is, the purchaser can lock in the expected compound return irrespective of what happens to interest rates over the life of the bond. Second, purchasers are more confident of not having the bond called by the issuing firm. Because of these characteristics, purchasers are willing to accept a lower return than on a coupon-paying bond.

The valuation of zero-coupon bonds is a straightforward application of Key Idea 5—a dollar today is worth more than a dollar tomorrow.

Zero-coupon bonds have some unusual characteristics that differentiate them from the coupon-bearing bonds we valued in Chapter 4. To illustrate, assume that Anderson Products is planning a $100 million par value, 10-year, 12 percent zero-coupon issue. Assuming (for simplicity) that interest is compounded annually, the net proceeds, B_0, from the bond (ignoring flotation costs) are equal to:[5]

$$B_0 \text{ (zero-coupon)} = \frac{\text{par}}{(1 + k_b)^n} \qquad (11.1)$$

$$B_0 \text{ (zero-coupon)} = \frac{\$100,000,000}{(1.12)^{10}} = \$32,197,324$$

Anderson will receive approximately $32 million from the bond issue, and in 10 years it will repay $100 million to the purchasers of the bonds. Although annual cash interest payments are not made, the Internal Revenue Service has ruled that *both the firm issuing the bonds and investors purchasing them* must impute and report interest (for tax purposes) just as if cash had changed hands. The actual amount of interest declared, as shown in Table 11.5, increases each year due to the compounding involved. Notice in the table that the total amount of interest (per $1,000 par value bond) of

[5] *With present value tables* $B_0 = \$100,000,000(PV_{12\%,10}) = \$100,000,000(0.322) = \$32,200,000.$

TABLE 11.5

Present Value and Interest per Year for a 12 Percent, $1,000 Par, Zero-Coupon Bond

The interest on zero-coupon bonds is determined using the present value techniques discussed in Chapter 3.

Year	Present Value (12%) at End of Year (1)	Present Value (12%) at Beginning of Year (2)	Interest $[(1) - (2)]$ (3)
1	$ 360.61†	$321.97††	$ 38.64
2	403.88	360.61	43.27
3	452.35	403.88	48.47
4	506.63	452.35	54.28
5	567.43	506.63	60.80
6	635.52	567.43	68.09
7	711.78	635.52	76.26
8	797.19	711.78	85.41
9	892.86	797.19	95.67
10	1,000.00	892.86	107.14
			$678.03

†For year 1, $321.97(1.12) = $360.61; for year 2, $360.61(1.12) = $403.88. The rest were computed in a similar manner.
††The original selling price is simply the present value of $1,000 discounted at 12 percent for 10 years.

$678.03 is just equal to the difference between the par (or maturity) value of the bond and its original price of $321.97 per $1,000 bond. If market interest rates remain constant over the entire 10-year period, the values given in column 1 of Table 11.5 show the market value at times $t = 1$, $t = 2$, and so forth.

So far, so good. Zero-coupon bonds seem simple and straightforward. Now let's compare them with a similar coupon (or interest-bearing) bond. We will see that when market interest rates change, the *percentage* price change on a zero-coupon bond is greater than that on a coupon bond. This makes perfect sense: With the zero-coupon bond nothing is received (or paid) until maturity, whereas with a coupon bond the current market value is a function of both the periodic coupon interest payments and the bond's par value.

Consider Figure 11.2, which shows the percentage change from the original price for the Anderson Products 12 percent zero-coupon bond and a similar 12 percent interest-bearing bond. If the market interest rate on the 10-year bonds is 12 percent, then the coupon bond will sell at its par value of $1,000 (par bond), while the zero-coupon bond will sell at $322 per bond. Assume you are an investor who has an equal dollar amount to invest in either bond. For simplicity, assume this amount is $322,000. With that you can buy 1,000 (i.e., $322,000/$322) zero-coupon bonds or 322 (i.e., $322,000/$1,000) interest-bearing bonds. If market interest rates increase from 12 to 16 percent, which choice exposes you to more interest rate risk? To see, let's calculate the new market price for both bonds.

FIGURE 11.2

Percentage Price Fluctuations for Zero-Coupon Versus Coupon Bonds

This figure is based on 10-year, 12 percent bonds selling at their original price. However, the general relationships hold for all similar zero-coupon and coupon interest-bearing bonds.

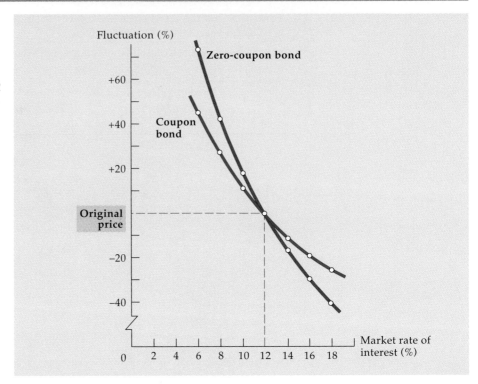

For the 322 12 percent coupon bonds, each with a par value of $1,000, the total interest to be received each year is $322,000(0.12) = $38,640, so their total value is:[6]

$$B_0 = \sum_{t=1}^{10} \frac{\$38,640}{(1.16)^t} + \frac{\$322,000}{(1.16)^t} = \$186,756 + \$72,992 = \$259,748$$

The 4 percent increase in interest rates led to a decrease in value of $62,252 (i.e., $322,000 − $259,748), or a decrease of about 19.33 percent.

From Equation 11.1, for the 1,000 zero-coupon bonds with a total par value in 10 years of $1,000,000, we have:[7]

$$B_0 \text{ (zero-coupon)} = \frac{\$1,000,000}{(1.16)^{10}} = \$226,684$$

Now the same 4 percent rise in interest rates leads to a decrease in value of $95,316 (i.e., $322,000 − $226,684), or a 29.60 percent decrease. These figures, when calculated for a number of other market interest rates and plotted (as in Figure 11.2), demonstrate the *increased price volatility or interest rate risk that investors experience with zero-coupon as opposed to coupon bonds*. By buying zero-coupon bonds, investors expose themselves to greater price fluctuations as market interest rates change.

So far we have considered a zero-coupon bond with 10 years to maturity. What happens to the interest rate risk (as evidenced by its price volatility) as the maturity is shortened? As Figure 11.3 shows, the shorter the maturity, the lower the interest rate

[6]With present value tables $B_0 = \$38,640(PVA_{16\%,10}) + \$322,000(PV_{16\%,10}) = \$38,640(4.833) + \$322,000(0.227) = \$186,747 + \$73,094 = \$259,841.$
[7]With present value tables $B_0 = \$1,000,000(PV_{16\%,10}) = \$1,000,000(0.227) = \$227,000.$

FIGURE 11.3

Relationship of a Zero-Coupon Bond's Price Fluctuation, the Current Market Rate of Interest, and Bond Maturity

This relationship for zero-coupon bonds is exactly the same as that discussed for coupon (interest-bearing) bonds in Chapter 4.

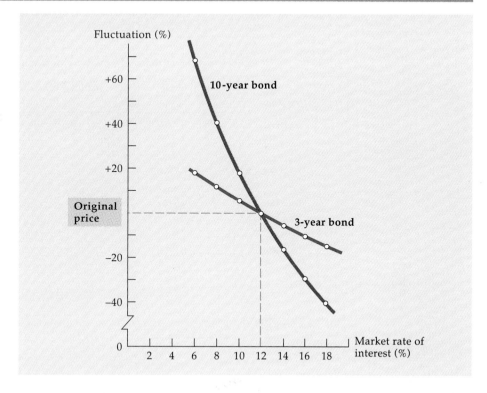

risk. This is due to the reduced impact of discounting with short- versus long-maturity bonds. From the issuing firm's standpoint, the primary attraction of "zeros" is their reduced cost vis-a-vis similar coupon bonds. For investors, their primary advantage when compared to coupon-bearing bonds is that they lock in the return.

Junk Bonds

JUNK BOND
Bond rated BB/Ba or below, which must pay a high yield to offset its high risk.

In line with Key Idea 6—risk and return go hand-in-hand—we should expect more risky debt to cost a firm more, which it does.

Junk bonds, or high-yield bonds, are those rated BB/Ba and below. During the 1980s, Michael Milken, then of the investment banking firm of Drexel Burnham Lambert, helped create a massive new bond market centered around these bonds. Table 11.6 shows that over the 1982–1991 time period, junk bonds accounted for 15.5 percent of the total financing secured from publicly issued bonds. Because of their lower priority relative to other debt in the event of financial distress, junk bonds have elements of both debt and equity securities.

Junk bonds are issued by firms with low credit ratings that are willing to pay anywhere from $1\frac{1}{2}$ to 3 or 4 percent more than a triple A-rated firm to raise long-term debt. These are often growing firms that would rather borrow from the public than from banks or other financial institutions. Toward the middle and latter parts of the 1980s, junk bonds became widely used to finance mergers and in leveraged buyouts. The high levels of borrowing forced firms to be more competitive. But in late 1988, the "father of the junk bond" Michael Milken was forced to leave Drexel Burnham after he was indicted for securities fraud. Without Milken, confidence in the junk bond market fell. More importantly, some firms that had issued junk bonds, such as Integrated Resources, Hillsborough Holdings, and Campeau, ran into financial difficulties.

TABLE 11.6

Total Publicly Issued Bonds and Junk (or High-Yield) Bonds, 1982–1991 (in millions)

Junk bond financing increased significantly in the 1980s before falling off. In 1991 and beyond the amount of junk bond financing again increased.

Year	Total Straight Debt (1)	Total Junk Bonds (2)	Junk to Total [(2)/(1)] (3)
1982	$ 47,798	$ 2,798	5.8%
1983	46,903	7,417	15.8
1984	99,416	14,952	15.0
1985	101,098	14,670	14.5
1986	155,672	34,177	22.0
1987	126,541	30,680	24.2
1988	113,840	26,380	23.2
1989	152,145	27,661	18.2
1990	92,105	1,297	1.4
1991	156,663	9,901	6.3
Total	$1,092,181	$169,933	15.6

Source: Adapted from Exhibit 1 in Edward I. Altman, "Revisiting the High-Yield Bond Market," *Financial Management* 21 (Summer 1992), pp.78–92.

Finally, by February 1990 Drexel itself was in such severe financial difficulty that it filed for bankruptcy. An era had come to an end.

However, the junk bond market has since stabilized and in fact is expanding rapidly. In 1993 some $68 billion ($54 billion in public issues and $14 billion in private placements) in below-investment-grade financing was secured. This was nearly twice the amount raised in 1992 and is equal to the *total amount* raised from 1982 through 1986. Most of this activity came from firms refinancing other debt to (1) reduce their interest outlay, and (2) get away from the strict principal payback requirements imposed by banks. Interestingly, the junk bond market is increasingly dominated by private, medium-size companies that once turned to insurance companies or banks for their financing through private placements. Among the underwriters, Merrill Lynch and Donaldson Lufkin were the top two in 1993. Some firms that issued junk bonds in 1994 include Genesis Health Ventures, Dan River Mills, AST Research, and Color Tile, Inc. Junk bonds will continue to fill an important, but more traditional, role as a source of financing in the future.

Variable Rates

PRIME RATE
The interest rate a bank's best customers are supposedly charged; most customers will pay more than prime, such as "prime plus 2 percent."

The majority of loans made by commercial banks are now *variable rate* loans. That is, the interest rate may vary over the 5- to 10-year life of the loan. Often the rate is expressed as some fixed percentage over the prime interest rate.[8] For example, the loan agreement may specify that the rate will be "2 percentage points over prime." This means that if the current **prime rate** charged by the bank to its best customers is 8.5 percent, the interest rate on the loan will be 10.5 percent. Because interest is typically changed every time the prime rate changes, the bank in effect varies the total payment

[8] As noted in Chapter 18, prime is an artificial (or administered) rate.

required each period to pay the principal and interest on the loan. In addition to bank loans that carry adjustable rates, there are also floating rate (or adjustable rate) notes that are issued directly by firms via cash offerings to the public or through private placements.

Hybrids, Asset-Backed Securities, and Other Innovations

Many of these new securities have options incorporated into them—evidence of Key Idea 7 that options are valuable.

During the last 15 years the types of securities available for corporate use have expanded dramatically. Many of the new securities combine elements of debt, equity, options, variable interest rates, and the like into new securities. Although we have examined a few of the innovations, like medium-term notes, zero-coupon bonds, and variable rate loans and securities, many other innovations have been added. Some of the more successful new securities are the following:

1. *Dual-Currency Bonds.* These bonds pay interest in U.S. dollars, but the repayment of principal is in a currency other than the dollar.
2. *Extendable Notes.* An extendable note has an interest rate that adjusts every 2 or 3 years; the noteholder has the right at that time to "put" the notes back to the issuing firm.
 3. *Puttable Bonds.* These bonds can be redeemed at the option of the bondholder, or if some "event" (as specified in the bond indenture) occurs.
4. *Standard & Poor's Index Notes.* These are zero-coupon notes whose principal repayment is linked to the value of the S&P Index, providing that the index is above a certain value.
5. *Liquid-Yield Option Notes.* These are a zero-coupon convertible debt issue.
6. *Puttable Convertible Bonds.* These are convertible bonds that can be redeemed prior to maturity at the option of the bondholder, on certain specified dates or at prespecified prices.

During this same period there has been another innovation—the increased use of asset-backed securities; this process is often referred to as **securitization**. Mortgage-backed securities, including *collateralized mortgage obligations, CMOs,* have been around for some time. But recently firms have also turned to other assets as collateral for financing. Thus, Citibank recently offered a $2.2 billion floating rate note backed by credit card receivables. Likewise, GPA Group, an aircraft leasing firm based in Ireland, sold a $521 million Eurobond that was securitized by aircraft lease receivables. While developments in the next 15 years may not be as rapid as in the past 15, innovative investment banking firms will continue to come up with new ways to help firms raise capital.

SECURITIZATION
The increased use of asset-backed securities, such as mortgage-backed securities.

International Debt Financing

Both U.S. firms and their foreign subsidiaries raise funds in various international markets. However, considerable differences exist in these markets compared to those in the United States. One of the biggest is the much broader role played by banks in the international market. Commercial banks in Europe, the Middle East, and Asia have more flexibility and often combine commercial banking, investment banking, and direct investment. As shown in Table 11.7, of the world's ten largest banks based on total assets, eight are Japanese, one is French, and the other is German. In fact, of the top 100 banks in the world in terms of total assets, only 5 (Citibank, Bank of America, Chemical Bank, Morgan Guaranty Trust, and Chase) are U.S. banks. The diminishing role played by U.S. commercial banks is due to the globalization of the banking industry and the ability of banks in most other countries to engage in all forms of financial activities,

TABLE 11.7

The World's Ten Largest Banks

Based on total assets, Japan's banks dominate the world banking scene.

Bank	Country	Assets (U.S. in billions)
Dai-Ichi Kangyo Bank	Japan	$472
Fuji Bank	Japan	468
Sumitomo Bank	Japan	464
Sanwa Bank	Japan	460
Sakura Bank	Japan	453
Mitsubishi Bank	Japan	440
Norinchukin Bank	Japan	384
Industrial Bank of Japan	Japan	348
Credit Lyonnais	France	338
Deutsche Bank	Germany	320

Source: Table, "The World's Ten Largest Banks." *The Wall Street Journal* (September 30, 1994), p. R27. Reprinted by permission of The Wall Street Journal, © 1994 Dow Jones & Company, Inc. All Rights Reserved Worldwide.

from investment banking to taking ownership positions in other firms, to being partially government owned.

The **Eurodollar** system that operates in the international capital markets was developed in the 1950s as banks located outside the United States began to accept interest-bearing deposits in U.S. dollars. Although most of the early activity was centered in Europe, the system (called the **Eurocurrency system**) is now worldwide and includes many different currencies. Eurodollar loans are typically in multiples of $1 million and have maturities lasting from a few days to 15 years or more. Generally these loans are unsecured, but they may contain certain restrictive provisions on the borrowing firms' activities. Large loans may be syndicated, with many banks participating; the lead bank coordinates the syndicate, structures the loan, and provides servicing when needed.

The model for such loans is the U.S. domestic multibank floating rate term loan. The interest rate is usually stated as some fixed percentage above the **London Interbank Offered Rate, LIBOR,** with adjustments at predetermined intervals. Since LIBOR reflects the rate on liquid funds that move among the developed nations' money markets, it dampens borrowing based on interest rate speculation. LIBOR is usually more volatile than the U.S. prime rate because of the sensitive nature of supply and demand for Eurodollar deposits. Accordingly, it may be more difficult to project the cost of a Eurodollar loan.

In addition to borrowing from banks, firms often issue bonds in the Eurobond market. A Eurobond is one underwritten by an international syndicate and sold primarily in countries other than the country in which the issue is denominated. Thus, a Eurobond could be denominated in the U.S. dollar, the German mark, or some other currency, but it would be sold mainly outside the country in which it was denominated. Some of the distinguishing features of the Eurobond market are:

1. Most bonds pay interest only once a year instead of semi-annually.
2. Because of investor desire for anonymity, virtually all bonds are issued in bearer form, as opposed to the registered form prevalent in the United States.

EURODOLLAR
U.S. dollars deposited in a U.S. branch bank located outside the United States or in a foreign bank.

EUROCURRENCY SYSTEM
The worldwide system in which one country's currency is on deposit in another country.

LONDON INTERBANK OFFERED RATE, LIBOR
Interest rate at which banks in different countries trade.

Most Eurobonds are issued in bearer form and pay interest only once a year.

3. Almost all Eurodollar issues are listed on one or more recognized securities exchanges—generally in London, Luxembourg, Frankfurt, or Switzerland.

CONCEPT REVIEW QUESTIONS

- Describe some different forms of debt financing firms have recently adopted.
- What are some advantages to a firm of issuing zero-coupon bonds?
- Why have junk bonds become a viable means of financing for some firms?
- How do international debt financing and the international bond market differ from domestic financing and the domestic bond market?

MANAGING LONG-TERM DEBT

■ LEARNING GOAL 4

Discuss key techniques of managing long-term debt—refunding and alternatives to refunding, and interest rate swaps.

Until recently, liability management consisted simply of deciding what securities to issue. Debt was left to mature, then was retired—perhaps with the proceeds from a new bond issue. High and volatile interest rates, the growth of international financial markets, and innovative investment banking firms have changed all that, and the management of long-term liabilities has taken a dramatic turn. Let's consider some of the techniques now available.

Refunding

REFUNDING
Process of replacing an old bond issue with a new one; often done if market interest rates have dropped so that the firm can save on interest costs.

When firms issue bonds that are callable, they have the option of retiring them early; thus, they hold a call option. Remember Key Idea 7—options are valuable.

A few years ago, when interest rates were high, many firms issued long-term debt. What happened when market rates fell? Astute managers saw the fall in rates as an opportunity to replace (or refund) the older, high interest rate bond with a similar bond offering a lower coupon rate. In a bond **refunding,** the firm calls all the old bonds at a fixed price and simultaneously issues new, lower coupon rate bonds. The bond holders have no choice; when a bond is called it must be surrendered, for the firm stops paying interest on it. The decision to refund depends on the net amount required to call the existing bond and the present value of the future incremental cash flows. It is thus just another use of the net present value, *NPV*, framework.[9]

However, two complications can arise. First, how does the firm decide on the best time to refund? The answer depends primarily on the relationship of current market interest rates to forecasted interest rates next month, in 3 months, and so forth. The firm may benefit from a refunding today, but it must also consider whether it would be better off waiting, in the hope that interest rates will fall further.

To protect investors, many bonds now carry a provision that prohibits them from being called for refunding for a period of 5 to 10 years. This brings us to the second complexity. What can the firm do if it wants to refund a bond issue but is prohibited by some provision in the bond indenture?

---

[9]*The details of refunding are covered in Appendix 16A of* Financial Management.

Alternatives to Refunding

Three alternatives are available when a firm is prohibited from refunding a bond issue.

TENDER OFFER
An offer by a firm or group directly to stock- or bond-holders to purchase their stock or bonds at a certain price.

PRIVATE MARKET PURCHASE
Purchase by a firm of its own bonds (or stock) directly from an institutional investor.

SIMULTANEOUS TENDER AND CALL
A refunding approach in which a firm offers to buy back its bonds (through a tender offer) at a slight premium to the call price while at the same time it threatens to call the bonds using a cash call.

1. One alternative is a public **tender offer.** This is an offer to the current bondholders to sell their bonds back to the firm at a predetermined price. This offer may not result in the retirement of the entire issue, but it can substantially reduce the size of the issue in question.
2. An alternative to the public tender offer is a **private market purchase.** Here the firm approaches one or several institutional investors that own a large amount of the firm's bonds and offers to buy them back. Another alternative sometimes employed is to swap debt for some of the firm's common stock.
3. The nonrefundable provision that has appeared in recent years appears to limit an issuing firm's flexibility to retire debt when interest rates fall. Recently, however, Wall Street has come up with a strategy that firms can use to circumvent the nonrefundable provision. Firms have always been able to call bonds through a *cash call* with money raised by selling additional equity, selling assets, or from internally generated funds. But if interest rates have fallen and the issuing firm wants to retire debt without using a cash call, it might employ a **simultaneous tender and call** approach. The essence of this approach is to offer to buy back the bonds (through a tender offer) at a slight premium to the call price; at the same time the firm (or its investment banker) threatens to call the bonds using a cash call. In late 1992 bondholders filed a lawsuit against May Department Stores and Morgan Stanley (its investment banking firm), alleging breach of contract, violation of the Trust Indenture Act, bad faith, and fraud after the simultaneous tender and call approach was employed on a $250 million May Department Store bond. Holders of the May bonds argue that the tender and call is coercive. The investment bankers disagree, believing "it's not coercive, it's a business proposition."

Interest Rate Swaps

INTEREST RATE SWAP
Agreement between two parties to swap interest, but not principal, payments.

Another innovation has been to separate the interest payments from the principal payments for long-term financing. This is done through use of a technique called **interest rate swaps,** which are increasingly used, especially with the widespread use of floating rate (or variable rate) financing. In an interest rate swap the firm raises funds wherever it can, as cheaply as possible—and then converts from floating to fixed rate, or vice versa, depending on the desires of the firm and expectations about the trend of future interest rates. This conversion is accomplished by agreeing to swap interest payments (but generally not the principal) with another party. For example, if the firm expects rates to go down, it will be able to reduce its interest charges if it is in a floating rate position. Why would the other party enter into the arrangement if interest rates are expected to decrease? The answer involves two items—first, the parties may have different ideas as to the future course of interest rates, and second, there are also other advantages of interest rate swaps that must be taken into consideration.[10]

CONCEPT REVIEW QUESTIONS

- Describe three alternatives to refunding a bond issue.
- What are interest rate swaps?

[10]*Interest rate swaps, and other techniques for hedging interest rate risk, are discussed in detail in Chapter 23 of* Financial Management.

PREFERRED STOCK

■ **LEARNING GOAL 5**

Compare preferred stock to debt and equity, and discuss the advantages and disadvantages of this form of financing.

Preferred stock is an intermediate form of financing between debt and equity. Like debt, preferred stock generally has a par value—typically $25, $50, or $100—and also pays a fixed return. But preferred stock is legally a form of ownership; cash dividends paid on preferred stock are similar to cash dividends on common stock in that they are not a tax-deductible expense for the issuing firm.

When preferred stock is issued, the selling price is set close to par. When a $100 par value, 13 percent preferred stock is issued, it will sell close to par and pay cash dividends of $13 [i.e., ($100)(0.13)] per year. The market price on preferred stock fluctuates: If the market yield (where yield = dividend per share/market price per share) on preferred stocks goes up, the market price of outstanding preferred stocks goes down. Because preferred stock is viewed by investors as being similar to bonds, the market yield on preferred stocks tends to move in much the same manner as the yield to maturity on bonds. As market interest rates on bonds rise, the market yield on preferred stocks also rises, due to the declining price of the latter.

If the firm does not have sufficient cash flow to pay dividends on its preferred stock, it can omit the payment. Unpaid dividends on preferred stock are called **arrearages.** Most preferred dividends are *cumulative:* All past or present dividends must be paid before any further cash dividends are paid on the firm's common stock. Managers view dividends on preferred stock like any other fixed obligation, and they fully intend to pay the preferred dividends on time. However, preferred stock does provide a safety valve if the firm needs it.

Like common stock, preferred stock does not have any fixed maturity date. However, many recent issues of preferred stock make a provision for periodic repayment via a sinking fund. Virtually all preferred stock is callable at the option of the issuing firm. If a firm goes out of business, the claim of preferred stockholders is junior to that of any creditors, but senior to that of common stockholders.

The use of preferred stock, like the issuance of long-term debt, may result in additional restrictions being placed on the firm. Examples of such restrictions are limitations on the payment of cash dividends for common stock, maintenance of a minimum level of common equity, and a minimum requirement for the ratio of net working capital to the total debt and preferred stock of the firm. The primary function of these restrictions is to ensure that the firm can make cash dividend payments to its preferred stockholders. Although many preferred stocks have only limited voting rights, the tendency in recent years has been toward fuller voting rights.

From the firm's standpoint, preferred stock has certain advantages:

1. Because the returns to preferred stockholders are limited, financial leverage is possible, because any extraordinary cash flows accrue only to common stockholders.
2. Nonpayment of cash dividends on preferreds does not throw the firm into default.
3. Control of the firm generally remains with the common stockholders.

The primary disadvantage of preferred stock from the firm's standpoint is that cash dividends paid to service the preferred stock are not an allowable deduction for tax purposes. Unlike debt, which preferred stock approximates in many respects, dividends on preferred stock must be paid out of after-tax earnings. This treatment makes the cost of most preferred stock much higher than the cost of debt.

ARREARAGES
Cash dividends on cumulative preferred stock that have not been paid.

Preferred stock is used on a widespread basis in only two industries—banking and public utilities. Banks have issued preferred stock in recent years in order to increase their capital base. They found that issuing preferred stock was preferable to issuing additional common stock in order to meet requirements for additional capital. Public utility firms, on the other hand, have used preferred stock for a long time. Due to their regulated nature, they can often pass the higher costs of preferred stock on to consumers through their customer rate base. Firms that have more than one issue of preferred stock outstanding include BankAmerica, Boston Edison, Georgia Power, Illinois Power, Royal Bank of Scotland, and Wells Fargo.

CONCEPT REVIEW QUESTIONS

■ Describe the similarities of preferred stock to both debt and common equity.
■ What are the advantages and disadvantages of preferred stock?

LONG-TERM FINANCING AND FINANCIAL DISTRESS

■ LEARNING GOAL 6

Explain the conflicting interests of stock- and bondholders, and discuss the long-term financing alternatives for a firm in distress.

Remember Key Idea 3—individuals act in their own self-interest. And, common stock is like a call option on the value of the firm—hence, Key Idea 7 comes into play again.

Differences and conflicts always exist between stockholders and bondholders. Stockholders want to maximize their return; as we know, higher returns and higher risks go hand-in-hand, so stockholders tend to favor higher risk. Bondholders, however, think they purchased a security safer than stock; they become upset when the firm engages in activities that cause this safety to erode.

If the firm prospers, the common stockholders exercise their option to pay off the bondholders (by retiring the bonds, either at maturity or sooner) and then claim everything else for themselves. Alternatively, if the firm fails, the stockholders (because of limited liability) walk away from the firm and turn it over to the bondholders. The stockholders may lose their initial investment, but at least they aren't liable for any further losses. We can summarize the effects as follows:

If the Firm Prospers	If the Firm Fails
Bondholders are paid off	Stockholders walk away
Stockholders claim the rest	Bondholders may receive something

Of course, there are many intermediate positions. We need to examine them briefly.

A firm facing financial distress has a number of alternatives open to it, depending on the severity of the situation. The fundamental decision is whether to modify the firm or to liquidate it. Within each alternative are out-of-court and in-court procedures.

Out-of-Court Alternatives

EXTENSION
Out-of-court agreement by which creditors grant a debtor additional time before paying the full amount of past-due obligations

The basic out-of-court alternatives for firms are as follows:

1. An **extension** involves nothing more than the creditor's agreeing to delay the payments due from the firm; that is, it extends the payment schedule. The creditor and the firm both hope that with a little more time, the firm can right itself and proceed on its way.

COMPOSITION
Out-of-court agreement between a firm and its creditors whereby the creditors receive less than the total amount due them in full settlement of their claims.

ASSIGNMENT
Out-of-court procedure by which a firm is voluntarily liquidated.

2. A **composition** is more serious. It gives creditors only a pro rata settlement on their claims. Generally, creditors will agree to composition only when it appears that they will receive more from accepting the settlement than from forcing the firm into bankruptcy, with its legal expenses and complications.

3. A "voluntary" liquidation is called an **assignment.** It is often more efficient, can be effected faster, and provides creditors with a higher settlement than an in-court liquidation. One problem, however, is getting all creditors to agree to the assignment.

In-Court Alternatives

LIQUIDATION
The process of dissolving the firm by selling its assets.

REORGANIZATION
An in-court procedure under Chapter 11 of the Bankruptcy Reform Act of 1978 during which the firm is revitalized.

Due to changes in the law, courts do not always follow a strict bankruptcy priority. Common shareholders, however, are still the residual claimants and usually receive little if anything.

The in-court alternatives are covered by the Bankruptcy Reform Act of 1978. The basic alternatives for firms are as follows:

1. In a **liquidation,** the assets of the firm are sold under the direction of the court, with the proceeds going to pay claimants in a general order of priority spelled out in the Act.

2. In a **reorganization,** the firm is actually put back on its feet, typically after extensive modifications both in terms of its businesses and in terms of the claims of creditors. Former stockholders usually end up with very little ownership in the reorganized firm.

Although somewhat different in detail, the liquidation versus reorganization decision is no different conceptually from keeping or divesting assets, or divisions, of a firm. The issue is whether the parties (primarily the creditors) are better off—that is, have a higher *NPV*—under liquidation or reorganization.

CONCEPT REVIEW QUESTIONS

■ Summarize the conflicting interests of stockholders and bondholders.

■ What are the out-of-court and in-court alternatives available to a firm experiencing financial distress?

Summary

■ Bonds and preferred stock take many different forms. These alternatives assist firms in raising long-term funds as cheaply as possible while providing features that appeal to investors.

■ AAA/Aaa-rated bonds have the lowest cost, or yield to maturity, of any long-term corporate bonds; they also have the lowest failure rate. As the bond rating decreases, the cost to the firm goes up, as does the probability of failure.

■ When firms issue straight debt or take out bank loans, the value of the firm is unaffected. However, when bank loan agreements are revised, common stockholders benefit if the revision is favorable, and they lose if it is unfavorable.

■ As interest rates fluctuate, zero-coupon bonds change in market price relatively more than similar coupon (or interest-bearing) bonds.

■ In the last 15 years numerous new securities have appeared in addition to medium-term notes, zero-coupon bonds, and variable rate securities. These new securities often incorporate elements of debt, equity, options, and the like.

■ Firms have increasingly begun to practice active liability management. Tactics include bond refundings (or buybacks) and interest rate swaps.

■ Preferred stock, while legally a form of equity, has many features that make it similar to debt.

Questions

11.1 As corporate treasurer, how would the following conditions influence your willingness to include a sinking fund provision and the need for a call feature in a new bond issue?

a. Market interest rates are expected to fall.

b. Your firm anticipates heavy cash outflows in relation to its cash needs in the next 5 to 10 years.

c. Market interest rates are expected to fluctuate substantially, both above and below the coupon rate on the new issue.

11.2 The percentage price fluctuation of zero-coupon bonds is greater than the percentage price fluctuation of similar coupon bonds as market interest rates fluctuate; it is also greater the longer the maturity of the bond. Explain.

11.3 In recent years, when interest rates were very high, a number of large firms issued medium-term notes. These notes paid interest periodically, and the principal was repaid when the notes matured. Why do you think firms issued these notes instead of obtaining similar-maturity term loans?

11.4 Preferred stock is often called a hybrid security. Why? It can be said that preferred stock combines the worst features of both common stock and bonds. Explain why this might be so.

11.5 If the corporate income tax were abolished, would we expect to see more, or less, debt? More, or less, preferred stock? Why?

Concept Review Problems

See Appendix A for solutions.

CR11.1 Fairchild Products has obtained a 5-year, $100,000 term loan with an interest rate of 15 percent. Interest is paid annually. Prepare a loan amortization schedule for Fairchild.

CR11.2 Assume Fairchild Products' term loan in CR11.1 required monthly payments. By developing an amortization schedule for the first 5 months of the loan, show how monthly payments will affect interest and principal repayments.

CR11.3 Tubman is considering issuing either a 5-year zero-coupon bond or a 5-year coupon-bearing bond with annual payments. Both bonds will pay a 10 percent interest rate. If Tubman needs $50 million from external debt financing, how many $1,000 maturity value zero-coupon bonds will have to be issued? How many $1,000 maturity value coupon-bearing bonds will have to be issued?

CR11.4 Emily recently purchased a $1,000 maturity value, 10 percent, 20-year, zero-coupon bond and a 10 percent, 20-year, coupon-bearing bond at par. If immediately after she purchased these bonds, overall bond rates increased by 2 percent, what was her percentage loss on each bond?

Problems

See Appendix C for answers to selected problems.

Restrictions on Additional Debt

11.1 Door County Corporation has no short-term debt, but it does have a $10 million, 10 percent coupon rate mortgage bond outstanding with a limited open-end provision. Additional 10 percent mortgage debt can be issued as long as all the following restrictions are met:

1. Ratio of debt to equity (i.e., total debt/total stockholders' equity) remains below 0.4.
2. Interest coverage (i.e., *EBIT*/interest) is at least 5.
3. The depreciated value of the mortgaged assets is at least 2.5 times the mortgage debt.

The firm has a depreciated value of mortgage assets of $60 million, equity of $80 million, and earnings before interest and taxes, *EBIT*, of $12 million. Assuming that half the new bond issue would be used to add assets to the base of mortgaged assets, how much additional debt can Door County Corporation issue?

Calling a Bond Issue

11.2 Sag Harbor Instruments has a $50 million bond issue outstanding, with a 12 percent coupon rate. The current market interest rate on comparable-quality bonds is 11 percent. The bonds have 25 years to maturity but can be called with a premium equal to 1 year's interest.
a. What is the market price of the bonds?
b. How much is the call price on the bonds?
c. Should Sag Harbor call these bonds or purchase them? In explaining your answer, remember to consider any other factors that might influence purchasing the bonds.

Sinking Fund

11.3 Lawson Cement has just issued $30 million of 10-year, 10 percent coupon rate bonds. A sinking fund provision requires equal payments to be made at the end of each of the next 10 years, in order to retire one-tenth of the bonds each year. Lawson's tax rate is 35 percent.

Note: In (b), remember: (1) Interest payments are tax-deductible, but sinking fund payments are not; and (2) no interest is paid on bonds once they are retired.

a. How large must the annual sinking fund payments be to retire the bond in 10 equal installments over the life of the bond? (The bonds will be retired at their par value.)
b. What is Lawson's *annual* after-tax cash outlay to meet the interest and sinking fund obligations each year? Note: The bonds will be retired at their par value.

Term Loan

Note: In (a), round all figures to the nearest dollar.

Note: In (c), round to the nearest dollar.

11.4 Hart Products is taking out an 8-year, $44,000 term loan, with an interest rate of 16 percent per year. Interest is paid annually, and the firm's marginal corporate tax rate is 40 percent.
a. What is the size of the yearly payment?
b. Determine the loan amortization schedule.
c. Determine the net cash outflow per year to service both principal and interest after taking into account the tax deductibility of interest for tax purposes.

Term Loan

Note: Round all figures to the nearest dollar.

11.5 A 4-year, 10 percent loan for $30,000 exists. Determine the amortization schedule if (a) annual discounting is employed, or (b) semi-annual discounting is used.

Bond Provisions and Financing Costs

11.6 Jarcho Manufacturing needs to raise approximately $10 million by issuing 20-year bonds. The following alternatives are available:
a. A public offering of $10 million of 8 percent coupon rate bonds at a price to net the firm $9,850,000.
b. A private placement of $10 million in bonds at par, with an 8.5 percent coupon rate and no flotation costs.
c. A public offering of a deep discount bond that will pay $400,000 in interest each year and have a maturity value of $25 million. The firm will net $9,800,000 from the bonds.
d. A private placement of zero-coupon bonds that will net the firm $9,900,000 and have a maturity value of $45 million.

Note: To solve, calculate the IRR for each of the four bonds.

Interest payments are annual and the principal will not be repaid until maturity. Which bond has the cheapest percentage cost to maturity?

Cash Flow to Service Debt

11.7 Gossage Corporation has two alternative $10 million bonds it can issue. If the bond carries a fixed coupon rate, the interest rate will be 11 percent. If a variable rate bond is used, the rate will be pegged 1.5 percent above prevailing rates on 1-year U.S. Treasury bills and adjusted annually. In both cases interest is paid annually. A sinking fund of $1 million per year will begin at the end of year 1 for either bond. The firm's marginal tax rate is 40 percent.

a. Determine the year-by-year after-tax cash flows Gossage will incur for each bond if 1-year U.S. Treasury bill rates turn out to be as follows:

Year	Prevailing 1-Year U.S. Treasury Bill Rate
1	10.0%
2	9.5
3	9.0
4	10.0
5	10.5
6	12.0
7	13.0
8	12.0
9	11.5
10	11.0

b. Without discounting the cash flows, does it appear that one bond would be preferable if Gossage knew what interest rates would be? Why?

Coupon-Bearing Versus Zero-Coupon Bonds

11.8 Keeley needs $100 million in new debt financing. If the firm uses a coupon-bearing bond, the interest rate is $9\frac{1}{2}$ percent and the bond will be issued at par. If it uses a zero-coupon bond, the interest rate is 9.2 percent. Assume that interest is paid annually and either bond will have a maturity of 10 years.

a. If the coupon-bearing bond is employed, (**1**) what is the per year interest, and (**2**) what is the cash outflow (ignoring any taxes) in the tenth year?

b. If the zero-coupon bond is employed:

(**1**) What is the par value of the zero-coupon bond in order to raise the $100 million needed?

(**2**) What is the imputed interest in year 1? In year 2?

(**3**) What is the cash outflow in the tenth year?

c. What can we say about the cash flow demands that the two securities will place on Keeley?

Zero-Coupon Bonds

11.9 Grier Industries is planning to issue $100 million par value of 15-year, zero-coupon bonds at a yield of 14 percent.

a. If interest is assumed to be paid annually, (**1**) what is the initial value, B_0, of the bonds, and (**2**) what is the imputed interest for year 2?

b. What happens to your answers for (a) if interest is assumed to be paid semi-annually? Why do your answers to (a) and (b) differ?

c. Recalculate (a) and (b) if the maturity of the bond issue is only 3 years. How does this change your answers to (a) and (b)? Graphically, which bond (the 15-year or the 3-year) would result in less percentage price fluctuation from the initial value as market interest rates change?

Issuing Preferred Stock

11.10 Carillo Products needs to raise $7.8 million through an issue of preferred stock. The preferred will have a $60 per share par value and pay an 8 percent dividend. Assume that there are no flotation costs, the preferred will be outstanding for a long time (so it can be treated as a perpetuity), and it will be sold to yield purchasers a 9.6 percent return.

a. What price will Carillo receive per share?

b. How many shares will Carillo have to issue?

c. Why might Carillo choose preferred stock instead of debt?

Preferred Stock Financing

11.11 MidWest Airlines needs to raise $9.5 million for capital improvements. One possibility is a new preferred stock issue. The 8 percent dividend, $100 par value stock would be sold to investors to yield 9 percent. Flotation costs for an issue of this size amount to 5 percent of the gross proceeds. These costs will be deducted from the gross proceeds in determining the net proceeds of $9.5 million. Assume that the preferred stock will be outstanding for a long time (so it can be valued as a perpetuity).

Note: In (a), carry to three decimal places.

a. At what price will the preferred be offered to investors?

b. How many shares must be issued to net $9.5 million?

Common Stock, Bonds, Preferred Stock, and *EPS*

11.12 Stemple Metals needs to raise $600,000. It has the following alternatives: (1) sell common stock at $50 per share; (2) sell 8 percent preferred stock at par ($100 par); or (3) sell 9 percent debentures at par ($1,000 par). Assume that there are no flotation costs. The firm expects *EBIT* to *increase* by 20 percent after the additional funds are secured and investments made. Partial balance and income statements are as follows:

Balance Sheet		Income Statement	
Current liabilities	$ 100,000	*EBIT*	$200,000
Common stock ($3 par)	300,000	Interest	20,000
Retained earnings	600,000	*EBT*	180,000
Total liabilities and		Taxes	63,000
stockholders' equity	$1,000,000	*EAT*	$117,000

a. What is the current *EPS before* the new financing is undertaken?

b. What is the estimated *EPS* under each of the financing plans, assuming that *EBIT* has increased?

Bonds, Preferred Stock, *EPS*, and Market Value

11.13 Cohen Industries is a fast-growing conglomerate operating in the mid-Atlantic states. Although it has used only short-term debt previously, Cohen is in the market for long-term financing. Based on its investment banking firm's recommendation, two plans are being considered, as follows:

Plan I	Plan II
$20 million of straight debt issued at par (ignore flotation costs)	$20 million preferred stock issued at par (ignore flotation costs)
Par is $1,000 per bond	Par is $80 per share
12% coupon rate	11.5% dividend rate
Expected common stock	Expected common stock
P/E = 12 times	*P/E* = 13 times

EBIT is estimated to be $14 million; short-term interest (under either plan) is $1 million; the tax rate is 30 percent; and there are 3 million shares of common stock outstanding.

a. For plans I and II, determine the expected *EPS*.

Long-Term Financing

b. If Cohen wants to maximize its market price per share, P_0, which plan should it choose?

11.14 Mini Case Rudolph Sports is in need of $25,000,000 of new long-term financing. Because it is inexperienced in seeking new financing, it has employed you to provide it with advice.

a. If Rudolph seeks long-term debt financing in the form of bonds or bank loans, what alternatives are available? What are the features of each?

b. If a bond issue is decided on, what type of features might be included in the bond indenture? What is the impact of these provisions?

c. If the term structure of interest rates is upward-sloping, is a long-term bond issue necessarily best? What if the term structure is downward-sloping?

d. Two different bond issues are being considered: a 25-year coupon bond that will pay interest semi-annually and carry a coupon interest rate of 12 percent, or a 25-year zero-coupon bond that has a yield to maturity of 11 percent (compounded semi-annually).

(1) From the firm's standpoint, what are the advantages and disadvantages of a zero-coupon bond versus a coupon bond? What are the tax consequences?

(2) Ignoring flotation costs, what is the size of the zero-coupon bond issue?

(3) Assume that after either bond is issued, interest rates jump 2 percent. What is the new price of the two bonds? Which has the bigger percentage change in its value? Why?

Note: In (d4), assume the firm is profitable, and its marginal tax rate is 35 percent.

(4) Independent of (3), assume it is now 10 years later. What are the cash flow consequences of the two different bonds on the firm? Compute year 10's net cash flows associated with the two bonds.

e. Instead of issuing debt, Rudolph could issue preferred stock. The preferred stock would carry a dividend of 11 percent.

(1) How is preferred stock similar to debt? To equity?

(2) What are the per year cash flows if everything is the same as in (d4) above?

CHAPTER 12

Capital Structure

Sections in this chapter:

■ **Capital Structure and the Value of the Firm**
What did Modigliani and Miller say?
■ **Looking Further for Capital Structure Impacts**
A whole lot of other factors may also matter.
■ **Debt/Equity Ratios in Practice**
We observe all different kinds of debt/equity ratios.
■ **Setting a Firm's Debt/Equity Ratio**
Think taxes, risk, and financial slack!

he Wall Street Journal reported that Philadelphia Electric was applying for an increase in the electric rates it is allowed to charge its customers. Philadelphia Electric, like other public utilities, is a regulated firm. It is permitted to charge rates designed to allow it to recover its operating costs and provide reasonable compensation for its providers of capital. Investors in stocks and bonds weigh their risk preferences and returns: The more the risk, the higher the required return. But a higher return to investors means higher costs to the firm. It's not surprising, then, that a major area of testimony—and controversy—in hearings before utility commissions is the cost to the firm of various sources of capital. Company witnesses argue that the firm's costs of capital are high, so higher rates are needed to compensate the providers of capital. Opponents, on the other hand, argue that the firm's capital costs are lower, and hence lower rate increases (or even rate decreases) are desirable; otherwise the firm's providers of capital will be overcompensated for the risks taken. Ultimately the regulatory authorities, by setting the allowable rates, determine the amount of revenue public utilities will have for operating expenses and returns to the providers of capital.

A nonregulated firm is not subject to the rate hearing process, but it too needs sufficient cash flows to cover the costs of operations and ensure a suitable return to investors. Although using capital efficiently may be commonplace to publicly traded U.S. firms, it is not necessarily so for firms in other countries. For example, Daimler-Benz is a German conglomerate that makes everything from luxury cars and trucks in North America and buses in South America, to aerospace equipment and white goods. In the past Daimler's main concern, shared with most other German firms, was to preserve the value of the capital invested. In the last few years, however, Daimler has decided that it is important to make new capital investments and to assess ongoing businesses based on two criteria: (1) the proportion of debt and equity it employs, and

(2) the returns demanded by investors. Knowing these two things—the reasonable proportion of debt and equity to use in raising funds, and the cost of capital—enables successful firms to make capital investments that provide adequate returns for the firm. If too low a cost estimate is employed, firms will make capital investments that provide inadequate returns, and the value of the firm will decline because the costs exceed the returns. Capital structure—that is, the proportions of debt and equity—is an important and hotly debated issue in finance. That's the issue we'll address in this chapter.

LEARNING GOALS

After studying this chapter you should be able to:

1. Explain the conclusion of the MM no-tax case.
2. Explain the effect of taxes on the firm's opportunity cost of capital and its capital structure.
3. Describe the effects of personal taxes and of non-debt tax shields on capital structure and the value of the firm.
4. Discuss how financial distress costs and agency costs affect capital structure and the value of the firm.
5. Discuss how a firm's capital structure can have a signaling effect on its market value.
6. Explain what the pecking order theory predicts about a firm's debt/equity ratio over time.
7. List some tools used to set a firm's debt/equity ratio, and discuss the three key variables that affect capital structure.

CAPITAL STRUCTURE AND THE VALUE OF THE FIRM

Until now we have not questioned the firm's debt/equity ratio, which signifies the amount of financial leverage being employed. We have taken it as a "given." For managers, however, it is not a given; it is one of the key decisions firms have to make. The issue can be visualized as follows, where we have two different ways of slicing up the pie between stockholders and bondholders:

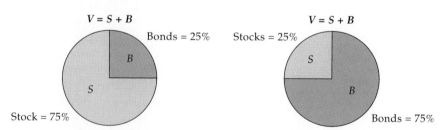

The question is this: Holding everything else constant, does how we slice the pie affect its size? *By holding everything else constant, we are assuming that the firm's investments remain the same, as well as its underlying cash flows and everything else.* If everything remains the same, then should the value of the firm be affected by how it is financed?

The answer to this simple question is not simple. In fact, a tremendous amount of controversy and discussion swirls around it. Determining a firm's financial structure means answering two basic questions: First, how should the firm's total sources of funds be divided among long-term and short-term financing? Second, what proportion of funds should be financed by debt and what proportion by equity? The first question, the maturity composition of the total sources of funds, requires focusing on the nature of the assets owned. We address short-term sources of funds in Chapter 15, where we see that the matching principle provides some guidance.

In this chapter, we focus our attention on the long-term sources of funds—debt, leases, preferred stock, internally generated funds, and common stock. The proportions of these long-term sources describe the capital structure of the firm. Our focus is therefore on the second of the two questions posed in the preceding paragraph: What do theory and practice say about the impact of the firm's capital structure on its value? For simplicity, we focus on the two main sources of capital—equity capital and debt capital.

In what follows, remember several Key Ideas: 1—the goal of the firm is to maximize its value; 4—firms focus on cash flows and their incremental effects; 5—a dollar today is worth more than a dollar tomorrow; and 6—risk and return go hand-in-hand.

The Assumptions of Capital Structure Theory

To highlight the issues involved, let's begin with a simplified example. The assumptions are as follows:

1. Only two types of securities are employed—long-term debt and common stock.
2. The firm is not expected to grow. Thus, the value of a share of stock can be determined by employing the basic no-growth dividend valuation approach (from Chapter 4), which capitalizes the perpetual cash dividend stream as follows:

$$P_0 = \frac{D_1}{k_s} \tag{12.1}$$

where

P_0 = the current stock price

D_1 = the expected constant amount of cash dividends in perpetuity

k_s = the equity investor's required rate of return, or oportunity cost of equity capital

3. All earnings are assumed to be paid out in the form of cash dividends, so dividends equal earnings in each future time period. Accordingly, Equation 12.1 can be rewritten as:

$$P_0 = \frac{EPS_1}{k_s} \tag{12.2}$$

or for the firm as a whole

$$S = \frac{E}{k_s} \tag{12.3}$$

where E is now the expected constant cash dividends (or earnings in perpetuity) and S is the total market value of the firm's stock.[1] Equation 12.3 is a straightforward statement of the present value of the assets the firm already has *in place* when

[1] As we will see in Chapter 13, the impact of cash dividends on the value of the firm's common stock is also a subject of debate. To avoid complicating this discussion, it is easier to assume that all earnings are paid out in the form of cash dividends.

no growth is expected. Thus, for an all-equity no-growth firm, and in the absence of corporate taxes, we can express this as

$$V \text{ (all-equity firm, no taxes)} = S = \frac{(EBIT - I)}{k_s} \tag{12.4}$$

4. There are no costs or penalties (such as legal fees or the disruption of operations resulting from default) if the firm does not pay interest on the debt, although the bondholders may take over the firm.

We are now in a position to investigate what impact, if any, the firm's capital structure can have on the value of the firm. We begin with the celebrated no-tax case presented by Modigliani and Miller (MM).

The MM No-Tax Case

■ **LEARNING GOAL 1**

Explain the conclusion of the MM no-tax case.

In its simplest situation, a firm has only common stock and debt financing. For the moment, we also assume that *there are no corporate taxes*. Under these conditions, how does the firm's financing decision affect the value of the firm? Franco Modigliani and Merton Miller, both recent Nobel prize winners in financial economics, answered this question in a very straightforward but what was at that time (and still is) controversial manner.[2] They said that the value of a firm is determined *solely by its investment, or capital budgeting, decisions* and, therefore, how the firm is financed is "irrelevant."

Their position can be described by examining Figure 12.1. Under the MM no-tax case, the value of the firm, V, and the firm's opportunity cost of capital are not affected by the use of more or less debt financing. In Figure 12.1(a), at the very left of the figure, the firm has zero debt; as the firm moves to the right it issues debt and retires equity—but the capital investments made by the firm stay the same, and according to

FIGURE 12.1

Value of the Firm and Opportunity Cost of Capital with No Taxes, According to Modigliani and Miller

As the firm moves to the right, it substitutes cheaper debt for more expensive equity capital. Because financial risk increases as you move to the right, the opportunity cost of equity capital increases, exactly offsetting any benefits from using more cheap debt financing.

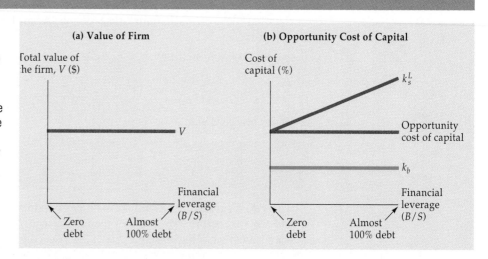

[2] *Franco Modigliani and Merton H. Miller, "The Cost of Capital, Corporation Finance, and the Theory of Investment," American Economic Review 48 (June 1958), pp. 261–297.*

Modigliani and Miller, the value of the firm is unchanged. From Chapter 6 we know that debt financing is cheaper than equity financing. By substituting debt for equity you might think that the firm's opportunity cost of capital decreases. But, as the firm adds debt financing, risk to the stockholders increases, just offsetting any benefits of cheaper debt financing. Accordingly, as shown in Figure 12.1(b), the opportunity cost of capital remains unchanged.

An example may help clarify the MM no-tax case. Assume a firm that has a market value of $100,000, is all-equity-financed, and its cost of equity capital is 10 percent. Thus, $k_s = 10\%$, and because there is no debt, the firm's opportunity cost of capital (using what we learned in Chapter 6) is:

$$\text{opportunity cost of capital} = k_b(1 - T)W_{\text{debt}} + k_sW_{\text{common equity}}$$

$$= k_b(1 - T)\left(\frac{B}{B + S}\right) + k_s\left(\frac{S}{B + S}\right) \qquad (12.5)$$

$$\text{opportunity cost of capital} = 0\%(1 - 0.00)\left(\frac{\$0}{\$100,000}\right) + 10.00\%\left(\frac{\$100,000}{\$100,000}\right)$$

$$= 0\% + 10.00\% = 10.00\%$$

What happens if the firm now issues $25,000 of debt, so that debt makes up 25 percent of the total market-value-based capital structure? Remember, when the firm issues debt it (1) simultaneously buys back stock—in this case $25,000 worth of common stock—and (2) the assets and capital investments of the firm remains the same. What if the debt, k_b, costs 6 percent? With debt financing, *equity risk has increased because the use of debt places a drain on the cash flow stream before anything goes to the common stockholders.* This risk is composed of (1) the possibility of not receiving any earnings or cash flow and (2) increased variability in earnings and cash flows due to the increased amount of debt employed. If the equity risk has increased, the required return on equity, k_s, also increases. Under the MM no-tax case, the overall opportunity cost of capital is constant; therefore, we can "back out" the new required return on equity after the debt is issued. The new cost of equity capital is:

$$\text{opportunity cost of capital} = k_b(1 - T)W_{\text{debt}} + k_sW_{\text{common equity}}$$

$$10\% = 6\%(1 - 0.00)\left(\frac{\$25,000}{\$100,000}\right) + k_s\left(\frac{\$75,000}{\$100,000}\right)$$

$$10\% = 1.50\% + 0.75k_s$$

$$k_s = (10\% - 1.50\%)/0.75 \approx 11.33\%$$

With a new cost of equity capital of 11.33 percent, the firm's opportunity cost of capital remains unchanged at 10 percent. Thus, MM conclude in the no-tax case that there is no advantage or disadvantage to financing with common stock. Any "savings" from debt financing are immediately offset by a higher return required by common stockholders (due to greater financial risk), leaving the firm and its stockholders in the same position as before.

Thus, according to MM, *the value of the firm does not change; rather, increased financial risk causes the stockholders' required rate of return to increase. Accordingly, the opportunity cost of equity capital increases so that any apparent gain from using cheaper debt financing is completely offset.* Both the value of the firm and its cost of capital are independent of financial leverage in the absence of taxes.

Importance of the MM No-Tax Case

The importance of the Modigliani and Miller no-tax model is that (1) it presents a theoretical, rigorous statement of the value of the firm, where none existed before, and (2) it tells us where to look to determine whether the firm's capital structure affects the value of the firm. In effect, the MM no-tax case says:

If there are no taxes,
if there are no transactions costs, and
if the investment (or capital budgeting) policies of the firm are fixed,

then capital structure does not affect a firm's value.

If there are no taxes, no transactions costs, and no impacts of financing on a firm's capital investments, then there is no optimal capital structure.

To determine whether capital structure affects firm value, we will look at the impact of taxes, both corporate and personal; the impact of transactions costs; and the capital investment policies of the firm. Along the way we will see that a tremendous amount of attention has been devoted to answering the simple question, "Does the firm's capital structure affect its value?"

The MM Tax Case

■ LEARNING GOAL 2

Explain the effect of taxes on the firm's opportunity cost of capital and its capital structure.

Almost immediately after Modigliani and Miller presented their no-tax case critics reminded them that corporate taxes are a fact of life for firms. Because of corporate taxes, and the fact that interest on debt is a tax-deductible expense, the after-tax cost of debt is less than the before-tax cost of debt. Thus, k_i, the after-tax cost of debt equals $k_b(1 - T)$, where k_b is the before-tax cost of debt and T is the firm's marginal tax rate. This is exactly in line with what we discussed previously in Chapter 6. The impact of interest on the amount of taxes actually paid by the firm is referred to as the **interest tax shield.** Other things being equal, the payment of interest by the firm shields (or reduces) the amount of corporate taxes paid by the firm.

INTEREST TAX SHIELD
The reduction of corporate taxes as a result of the interest paid on debt.

According to MM, *debt financing has value because on an after-tax basis it costs the firm less than equity.* Therefore, the value of the levered firm, V_L, once corporate taxes are introduced, is equal to the unlevered value of the firm, V_U, plus the present value of the interest tax shield. Assume a non-growing firm is using some amount of debt, represented by B, that has a cost (or interest rate) of k_b. The amount of interest per period is given by k_bB, and the interest tax shield is simply Tk_bB. Because debt is a perpetuity in the case being considered, the *present value of the interest tax shield* is given by capitalizing the interest tax shield at the appropriate discount rate, k_b, so that $Tk_bB/k_b = TB$. Thus, once corporate taxes are introduced, while everything else remains as before, MM conclude that the value of the levered firm is:

$$V_L = V_U + TB \tag{12.6}$$

Going to our previous example where the value of the firm in the absence of taxes was $100,000, its new value once corporate taxes are introduced, and assuming the firm's marginal tax rate is 40 percent, is:[3]

$$V_L = \$100,000 + (0.40)(\$25,000) = \$110,000$$

Because the total value of the firm, V_L, is also equal to the sum of its stock, S, and bonds, B, the value of the stock of the levered firm is $S = V_L - B$. Therefore, the new value of the stock for the levered firm is $S = \$110,000 - \$25,000 = \$85,000$.

Because the cost of equity capital, k_s, is the same with or without taxes, it is still 11.33 percent, as determined previously. Accordingly, the firm's opportunity cost of capital once corporate taxes are introduced is given by:

$$\text{opportunity cost of capital} = k_b(1 - T)\left(\frac{B}{B + S}\right) + k_s\left(\frac{S}{B + S}\right)$$

$$= 6\%(1 - 0.40)\left(\frac{\$25,000}{\$110,000}\right) + 11.33\%\left(\frac{\$85,000}{\$110,000}\right)$$

$$= 0.82\% + 8.75\% = 9.57\%$$

Figure 12.2 shows the MM results once corporate taxes are introduced. Note that *financial risk still remains and increases as debt is employed,* as signified by the rising cost of common stock, k_s. Even with this increase in the cost of equity, the presence of corporate taxes has the effect of *subsidizing the use of debt;* the result is that *increases in financial leverage lead to increases in the total value of the firm and decreases in the firm's overall opportunity cost of capital.* As long as firms are profitable, and the government provides an incentive for using debt through allowing

---

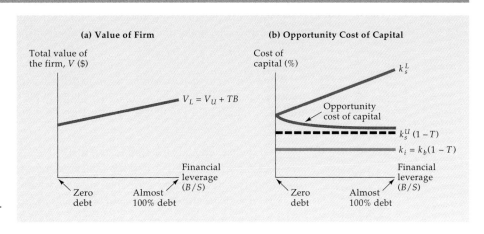

FIGURE 12.2

Value of the Firm and Opportunity Cost of Capital with Corporate Taxes, According to Modigliani and Miller

When corporate taxes are introduced, the government, in effect, supplies a subsidy for the use of debt as long as firms are profitable. This is so because interest is a tax-deductible expense. By using debt, the firm can increase its total value and decrease its opportunity cost of capital.

---

[3]*For simplicity we have left the value of the unlevered firm at $100,000. This ignores the fact that the introduction of taxes actually reduces a firm's after-tax earnings and cash flows. However, the conclusions remain the same with this simplification.*

interest to be tax-deductible, there is an advantage to using debt financing. This advantage leads to an *increase in the value of the firm,* providing that the investment decisions of the firm are unaffected.

Comparing the No-Tax Case and the Tax Case

Comparing the stock- versus the debt-financing plans for both the no-tax and the corporate tax case, Modigliani and Miller conclude that:

	No-Tax Case		Tax Case	
	All-Stock Financing	Combination Stock and Debt Financing	All-Stock Financing	Combination Stock and Debt Financing
Total stock value	$100,000	$75,000	$100,000	$85,000
Total debt value	0	$25,000	0	$25,000
Total value of firm	$100,000	$100,000	$100,000	$110,000
Cost of equity capital	10%	11.33%	10%	11.33%
After-tax cost of debt capital	0%	6%	0%	3.6%
Overall opportunity cost of capital	10%	10%	10%	9.58%

The overall conclusions from the MM no-tax and tax cases are:

1. With no corporate taxes, the capital structure decision is irrelevant.
2. Once corporate taxes are considered, firms maximize their value and lower their opportunity cost of capital by employing debt. In fact, the more debt used, the greater the value of the firm.

Before going any further, let's stop and summarize the important conclusions and equations presented by the MM no-tax and tax cases. Table 12.1 summarizes this information. In part I for the no-tax case, the value of the firm, that is, $V_L = S_L + B$, is shown to be independent of the amount of financial leverage employed. Once corporate taxes are introduced, the value of the firm can be found via either $V_L = S_L + B$, or $V_L = V_U + TB$, and the value increases as the firm replaces equity with debt in its capital structure. The opportunity cost of capital is constant in the MM no-tax case, while it decreases in the MM tax case.

When Modigliani and Miller presented their capital structure theory in the late 1950s and early 1960s, many individuals, both in the business and the academic communities, immediately took issue with them. The typical arguments, in simple form, were:

Of course, capital structure is important. That is why we see firms purposely select different capital structures—because they know it is important and, accordingly, select the one most appropriate for their firm.

If capital structure and the debt tax shield are important, why aren't all firms almost 100 percent debt-financed, because that is the point at which the value of their firm would be maximized? All we have to do is examine a few firms and see that they are not 100 percent, or even close to 100 percent, debt-financed. Therefore, MM, your theory is incorrect.

TABLE 12.1

Summary of the Fundamental Relationships for the MM No-Tax Case and the MM Corporate Tax Case

For simplicity, the tax-case equations should always be employed. If there are no corporate taxes, the tax-case equations collapse into the no-tax equations.

No-Tax Case	Tax Case

I. The Total Value of the Firm, V_L

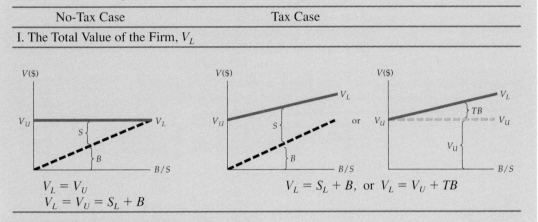

$$V_L = V_U$$
$$V_L = V_U = S_L + B$$

$$V_L = S_L + B, \text{ or } V_L = V_U + TB$$

II. Opportunity Cost of Capital, OCC

$$OCC = k_b(1 - T)W_{\text{debt}} + k_sW_{\text{common equity}} \qquad OCC = k_b(1 - T)W_{\text{debt}} + k_sW_{\text{common equity}}$$

Don't fall into the trap of rejecting MM as irrelevant without considering the full meaning of their position. In the simplest terms, *MM's argument was that the value of the firm is determined solely by the capital investments it makes.* Thus, the underlying message delivered by MM was simply to restate that the primary means of creating value is to focus on the left-hand side of the balance sheet (assets) and make "good" capital investment decisions. According to MM, any other decisions, such as the capital structure decision or the dividend decision (as we will see in Chapter 13), *are irrelevant as long as they don't affect taxes, transaction costs, or the capital investment decisions made by the firm.*

CONCEPT REVIEW QUESTIONS

■ Briefly explain Modigliani and Miller's no-tax capital structure model.
■ What three items have to exist for the MM no-tax case to hold?
■ What are the effects of corporate taxes on Modigliani and Miller's model?
■ Briefly summarize the difference in the conclusions of the MM no-tax case and the MM tax case.

LOOKING FURTHER FOR CAPITAL STRUCTURE IMPACTS

Many possible reasons for capital structure impacts on the value of the firm have been investigated in the last 35 years. First, we will examine the impact of personal taxes on the firm. Then we will consider other possible impacts on the firm's value.

Personal Taxes and the Value of the Firm

■ **LEARNING GOAL 3**

Describe the effects of personal taxes and of non-debt tax shields on capital structure and the value of the firm.

When MM developed their tax model, they included corporate taxes but not personal taxes on any income that investors receive from holding stocks or bonds. As a result, MM concluded, as shown in Equation 12.6, that the value of the levered firm is $V_L = V_U + TB$. Consequently, the gain from leverage, G_L, is simply the difference between the value of the levered and unlevered firms (which is the present value of the interest tax shield):

$$G_L = V_L - V_U = TB \tag{12.7}$$

This gain from leverage, and consequently the value of the levered firm, increases as a firm uses more debt. Thus, the optimal capital structure employs almost 100 percent debt.

What happens to the gain from leverage and the value of a firm that uses debt when both corporate and personal taxes exist? *With the inclusion of personal taxes in the model, the objective is to maximize income after all taxes, both corporate and personal.* Thus, the focus shifts. Rather than looking at the issue from the firm's viewpoint, we now look at it from that of investors: We now consider what they receive from investing in stocks and bonds after both corporate and personal taxes are paid. Years after the original MM article, Merton Miller introduced personal taxes into the model and developed the following equation:[4]

$$V_L = V_U + \left[1 - \frac{(1 - T)(1 - T_{ps})}{(1 - T_{pb})} \right] B \tag{12.8}$$

where

T = the corporate tax rate

T_{ps} = the personal tax rate on stock income (cash dividends and capital appreciation or loss)

T_{pb} = the personal tax rate on bond income (interest)

With this more complete and realistic tax structure, the gain from leverage is now:[5]

$$G_L = \left[1 - \frac{(1 - T)(1 - T_{ps})}{(1 - T_{pb})} \right] B \tag{12.9}$$

If the personal tax rates are zero ($T_{ps} = 0$ and $T_{pb} = 0$) or if they are equal to one another for both stock income and bond income ($T_{ps} = T_{pb}$), the gain from leverage re-

---

[4]Merton H. Miller, "Debt and Taxes," Journal of Finance *32 (May 1977), pp. 261–275.*
[5]*The marginal personal tax rate on stock income, and on bond income, is assumed to be the same for all investors in Miller's model.*

duces to *TB*. Thus, in either of these instances the benefits from the interest tax shield, once both corporate and personal taxes are considered, are the *same as those provided by the MM corporate tax model.*

What happens, however, if the rates are not equal? If the effective personal tax rate on stock income is less than the effective tax rate on bond income (if T_{ps} is less than T_{pb}), then, other things being equal, the before-tax return on bonds must be high enough to *compensate for the additional taxes* that must be paid on bond income. If this were not true, investors would never hold bonds. Although the firm receives a subsidy because of the tax-deductibility of the interest payment, this benefit may be offset because the interest payment has to be "grossed up" to compensate for the higher personal taxes that must be paid on the interest income. By grossing up, we mean that the interest paid by the firm is higher than it would be if personal taxes did not exist. Consequently, the gain from leverage diminishes and, in fact, will disappear completely if $(1 - T_{pb}) = (1 - T)(1 - T_{ps})$. If this happens, the results are the same as the MM model with no taxes: G_L will be zero, $V_U = V_L$, and, accordingly, the *amount of debt used by a firm will not have any effect on its value.* These relationships are illustrated in Figure 12.3.

Under the Budget Reconciliation Act of 1993 (the latest tax law as of the writing of this chapter), $T = 35$ percent, $T_{ps} = 39.6$ percent, and $T_{pb} = 39.6$ percent. If the *effective* personal tax rates on stock income and bond income are equal, then the gain from using debt is:

$$G_L = \left[1 - \frac{(1 - 0.35)(1 - 0.396)}{(1 - 0.396)} \right] B = 0.35B$$

which is the same as that given by the MM model with only corporate taxes. We would conclude, therefore, that there are substantial gains from using debt.

FIGURE 12.3

Gains from Financial Leverage: MM Models (With and Without Taxes) and Miller's Model

Depending on the effective rate of personal taxes on stock versus bond income, Miller's model may indicate an intermediate value for the firm.

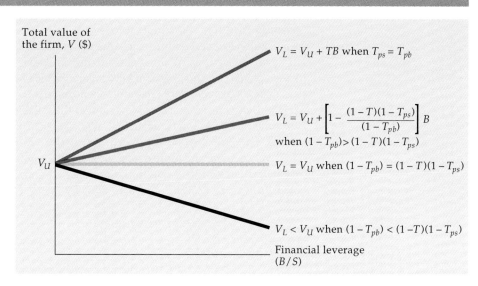

On the other hand, even with the stated marginal personal tax rate on stock income and bond income at 39.6 percent, there is one big tax advantage for investors who invest in stocks as opposed to bonds. It arises because about 60 percent of the return from investing in stock comes from capital gains, and an investor does not have to realize the capital gain (and pay taxes on it) immediately.[6] The *option to delay realizing capital gains* means the effective tax rate on stock income is probably less than that for bond income. What if the effective tax rate on stock income, T_{ps}, is 20 percent? Then the gain from using debt is:

Remember Key Idea 7—options are valuable.

$$G = \left[1 - \frac{(1 - 0.35)(1 - 0.20)}{(1 - 0.396)} \right] B = 0.139B$$

While still substantial, there is less subsidy than when the effective personal rates on stock and bond income are equal. Under the most likely scenario, the Miller model indicates that the value of the tax benefits to the firm is a compromise between the MM model with no taxes and the MM tax model. This effect is also illustrated in Figure 12.3.

Non-Debt Tax Shields

In the MM cases and in Miller's personal tax argument, *interest is the only relevant deduction for tax purposes.* However, firms also can—and do—shield themselves from paying taxes by using depreciation and depletion. DeAngelo and Masulis extended Miller's work by including the effects of tax shields other than interest.[7] They refer to the tax shields arising from depreciation and depletion as "non-debt tax shields." *The existence of non-debt tax shields serves to decrease a firm's taxable income, thus causing a decline in the probability of being able to use all of the interest tax shield.* Consequently, as more debt is used, the expected value of the interest tax shield declines. Thus, if a firm has "large" amounts of depreciation that are written off for tax purposes, it has less need for the interest tax shield that drives the Modigliani and Miller models.

The impact of non-debt tax shields reduces the incentive for the firm to use debt financing. Therefore, the firm is forced to balance the use of debt substitutes (such as depreciation and depletion) against the use of additional debt in order to be able to use all its tax deductions. Without considering any other factors, DeAngelo and Masulis demonstrated that this balancing procedure will lead to a capital structure that entails less than 100 percent debt (and more than zero debt).

With only corporate taxes we saw that the value of the firm should rise as firms substitute debt for equity financing. With personal taxes, firm value should still increase, but probably not as much, when debt is added to the capital structure. However, as more and more debt is added to the capital structure, the tax-deductibility of interest is less likely due to the presence of depreciation and depletion. Thus, as shown in Figure 12.4, tax considerations by themselves suggest that firms will issue

---

[6] *The tax rate on capital gains as of 1995 is 28 percent.*

[7] *Harry DeAngelo and Ronald W. Masulis, "Optimal Capital Structure Under Corporate and Personal Taxation,"* Journal of Financial Economics *8 (March 1980), pp. 3–30.*

FIGURE 12.4

Gains from Financial Leverage: MM and Miller Models and the Impact of Non-Debt Tax Shields

Once personal taxes and non-debt tax shields (such as depreciation and depletion) are considered, the gains from using financial leverage may be less than suggested by the MM tax case. An optimal capital structure, B^*/S, may exist at which the marginal benefits of additional debt are exactly offset by tax consequences of the additional debt.

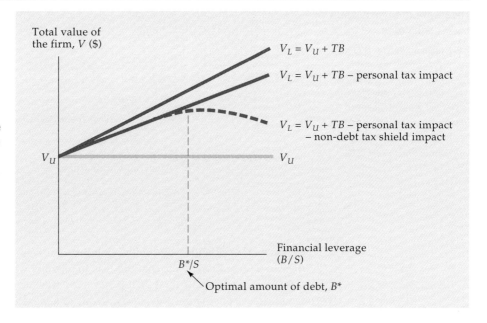

more than zero debt but will use less than 100 percent debt. The presence of taxes suggests there is some optimal level, or amount of debt, B^*, that leads to the maximization of the total market value of the firm.

Earlier we indicated three places to look in order to determine if a firm's capital structure affected its total market value: The first is taxes, the second is transactions costs, while the third is the impact on the firm's capital investment decisions. Let's now focus on transactions costs. The two primary transactions costs relate to financial distress and agency costs. In looking at the impact of transactions costs, we will ignore taxes, for the time being.

Financial Distress Costs

■ **LEARNING GOAL 4**

Discuss how financial distress costs and agency costs affect capital structure and the value of the firm.

FINANCIAL DISTRESS
Situation in which a firm is having difficulty meeting its financial obligations.

Not all firms succeed. Some experience periods of **financial distress,** when they do not have enough cash on hand or readily available to meet their current financial obligations; some may even fail. Think of the firm in terms of an option, as we discussed briefly in Chapter 1. The owners of the firm (or its stockholders) have a call option on the firm, as shown in Figure 12.5. If at the maturity of the firm's debt, the value of the firm's assets is greater than the value of the debt, the stockholders exercise the call option, pay off the bondholders, and claim the rest of the value of the firm for themselves. In the event of a *loss in value* of the firm's assets, the stockholders invoke

FIGURE 12.5

The Payoff to Stockholders and Bondholders

If the value of the firm is greater than the bondholders' claim, stockholders pay off the bonds when they mature and claim the rest of the value of the firm. Otherwise, they exercise their option and walk away, turning the firm over to the bondholders.

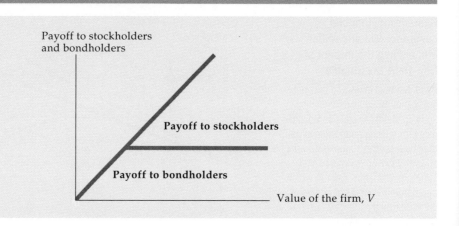

the protection provided by limited liability, and walk away from the firm, turning it over to the creditors. Note that the loss in value is what triggered exercising the option. Many individuals think that bankruptcy leads to a loss in value. In fact it is just the reverse: *The loss in value is what leads to bankruptcy.*

Bankruptcy Costs

BANKRUPTCY COSTS
Includes legal and other direct costs associated with bankruptcy or reorganization procedures.

If stockholders exercise their option and walk away from the firm, there are direct costs associated with the transaction. These **bankruptcy costs** include legal and other costs associated with the reorganization or bankruptcy proceedings. These costs are the "dead weight" of failing; only the accountants and lawyers benefit from them. How big are such costs? Studies of the direct costs of bankruptcy indicate they may be anywhere from less than 1 percent to a maximum of 4 or 5 percent of the firm's value. Although not trivial, bankruptcy costs are not large enough to make a material difference in the thrust of the Modigliani and Miller arguments.

In addition to the direct bankruptcy costs, other indirect costs are associated with financial difficulties. These include risk shifting, failing to invest, and operational and managerial inefficiencies.

Risk Shifting

Firms maximize their value by accepting positive net present value projects and rejecting negative net present value projects. But, faced with severe financial difficulties, firms may experience some perverse incentives. For example, consider Waste Masters, whose current market-value-based balance sheet is:

Cash	$100	Debt	$115
Other assets	25	Equity	10
Total	$125	Total	$125

The debt matures in 1 year at $200, but because of the high risk of Waste Masters, its current market value is only $115.

Two investment projects are available for Waste Masters—a low-risk project and a high-risk one:

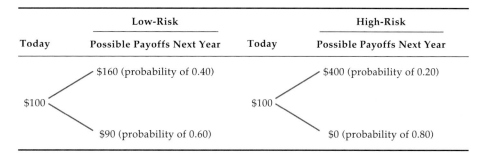

	Low-Risk			High-Risk	
Today	Possible Payoffs Next Year		Today	Possible Payoffs Next Year	
	$160 (probability of 0.40)			$400 (probability of 0.20)	
$100			$100		
	$90 (probability of 0.60)			$0 (probability of 0.80)	

At a discount rate of 10 percent, the net present value of the low-risk project is $7.27, while the *NPV* of the high-risk project is −$27.27. Clearly, any ordinary firm would accept the low-risk project and reject the high-risk project.

However, from the stockholders' standpoint there is no benefit from accepting the low-risk project because it would not even provide enough cash inflow to pay off the debt, let alone benefit the stockholders. The stockholders conclude that the low-risk project should be rejected and the high-risk project accepted. By accepting the high-risk project, if the project succeeds and produces the payoff of $400, the bondholders can be paid off and the stockholders walk away with the rest. Financial managers who act solely in the interest of the firm's stockholders—and therefore not in the interests of *all* of the firm's providers of capital—would favor the high-risk project. In fact, they may even invest in negative net present value projects. This type of problem is typically referred to as the **asset substitution problem.**

Failing to Invest

Conflicts of interest between stockholders and bondholders can also lead to firms' failing to raise additional equity capital. Say a firm has a "sure winner" that will produce a *NPV* of $25 in 1 year on a $50 investment. As in our Waste Masters example, assume the bondholders' claim is substantial, and bondholders do not want to invest any more in the firm. Unlike Waste Masters, this firm does not have enough cash on hand to fund the project; the only way to undertake this "sure winner" is to issue equity capital. Why would the stockholders (either the existing or new stockholders) make the investment? All, or virtually all, of the *NPV* will be claimed by the bondholders when the stockholders walk away from the firm in 1 year. The answer is, they won't make the investment.

The general point is this: Holding other things constant, any increase in the value of a firm making positive *NPV* investments is shared between stockholders and bondholders. When the debt claims are substantial relative to the equity claims, virtually all of the gains from making positive *NPV* investments are captured by the bondholders. Thus, it may not be in the stockholders' best interests to contribute additional capital even if "sure" *NPV* projects are forgone; this creates an **underinvestment problem.** In fact, faced with the previous situation, stockholders would favor distributing the assets of the firm to them in the form of a massive cash dividend. That way, they claim part of the assets. Of course, their gain comes at the expense of the bondholders.

Remember Key Idea 3—individuals act in their own self-interests. Differences in self-interest lead to agency problems.

ASSET SUBSTITUTION PROBLEM
Occurs when a firm invests in more risky assets than those expected by the firm's bondholders (or other creditors).

UNDERINVESTMENT PROBLEM
Occurs when a firm fails to take all growth opportunities (all positive *NPV* opportunities) because they primarily benefit the firm's bondholders (or other creditors) rather than the firm's stockholders.

Operational and Managerial Inefficiencies

There are other possible consequences of impending financial distress. There may be increased inefficiency caused by key employees leaving or having their attention diverted from managing the firm as an ongoing entity. Customers may cancel orders if they are worried about the ability of the firm to deliver the product or service. Or, the firm may tend to skimp on employee training, product quality, research and development, or even pay less attention to the safety of the work environment. Whatever form they take, increased inefficiencies do affect firms that are undergoing periods of high financial distress. In order to survive, the firm sacrifices some important activities that it normally undertakes, even though by doing so it may simply be buying only a little more time.

The sum of the direct and indirect costs associated with bankruptcy and financial difficulties is called **financial distress costs.** Financial distress costs can affect the firm directly and also lead to increased returns being demanded by both bondholders and stockholders. As bondholders perceive the probability of financial distress increasing, they may require a higher expected return. Likewise, stockholders face the same concerns; accordingly, they will also require a higher expected return before investing additional capital.

How high are the total direct and indirect costs of financial distress? Direct costs, as we mentioned earlier, are not very large. But when indirect costs are included, some estimates place the financial distress costs at 10 to 20 percent of a firm's value. At that level, they are large enough to have an impact on the value of the firm. Although analysis of the costs of financial distress does not tell us what the firm's capital structure should be, it does suggest that firms with a greater probability of experiencing financial distress will borrow less.

Other stakeholders are also affected when financial distress is present.

FINANCIAL DISTRESS COSTS
The sum of the direct and indirect costs associated with bankruptcy and financial difficulties.

Agency Costs

Other transactions costs, as discussed originally in Chapter 1, may arise because of the presence of stockholders, managers, and bondholders. First, consider stockholders and managers. As long as the firm is owned and operated by a single entrepreneur, no complications arise because management and the owner are the same person. As sole owner, the entrepreneur obtains part of his or her wealth through perquisites (or "perks") such as a company car, company jet, luxurious office, and so on. In this situation, the owner not only receives all of the benefits of these perks but also bears all of their costs. In this situation, the entrepreneur maximizes his or her wealth by balancing the combination of wages, perks, and the market value of the firm's common stock.

As the firm grows, however, the entrepreneur may meet financing needs by raising external funds, either by sharing ownership with others (issuing common stock) or by incurring debt financing. If the entrepreneur sells part ownership of the firm to outsiders while retaining the management capacity, he or she has an incentive to increase perks. Now the entrepreneur will receive all of the benefits of these perks but will pay only his or her ownership fraction of their costs. If the new co-owners realize this agency problem before they buy into the firm, they will not be willing to pay as much for each share. The difference between the price of the share without and with the agency problem represents an agency cost that serves to reduce the value of the firm. On the other hand, the entrepreneur and the new co-owners may enter into a monitoring agreement to ensure that the entrepreneur acts in the best interest of *all* stockholders. In either case agency costs are incurred. As the firm uses less equity and more debt, the agency costs of equity decrease.

Furthermore, as the firm grows the providers of new capital (the principals) delegate decision-making authority to a separate management group (the agent). This delegation of decision-making authority may result in an agency problem if a conflict of interest arises between the agent and principal, or among the principals, that affects the firm's operations. Such conflicts can be resolved only by incurring agency costs.

Another form of an agency problem occurs between stockholders and bondholders. The fact that the bondholders' claims on the firm's income are fixed in amount creates an incentive for stockholders to engage in riskier projects that transfer wealth from bondholders to stockholders, no matter what the possibility of financial distress. To prevent such expropriation of their wealth, bondholders will demand various types of restrictive covenants and monitoring devices. The cost of these instruments is another agency cost. As the use of debt increases, the agency costs of debt increase.

The impact of agency costs and their implication for the capital structure of the firm are shown in Figure 12.6. Note that the unlevered firm (one with no debt) has agency costs—these are the agency costs of equity. For example, if the value of a firm with no debt and *in the absence of any agency costs* would be $500, and equity agency costs are $100 when the firm is unlevered, then the observed value of the firm, V_U, is $500 − $100 = $400. As the firm adds debt, it reduces the agency costs of equity but increases the agency costs of debt. In the context of agency costs, the value of the firm is maximized at the point where *total agency costs are minimized.*

The analysis so far—which includes the tax subsidy associated with debt, personal taxes and other tax-related impacts, financial distress costs, and agency costs—is illustrated in Figure 12.7. In the MM tax model, once corporate taxes are considered, the value of the firm increases continuously as more debt is used. The value-maximizing firm would issue 100 percent debt. The introduction of personal taxes reduces the benefit of the interest tax shield somewhat, but firms still have an incentive to use more

---

FIGURE 12.6

Agency Costs and Financial Leverage

While the agency costs of equity decrease with increasing financial leverage, the agency costs of debt increase. The optimal capital structure, in the absence of other considerations, minimizes total agency costs.

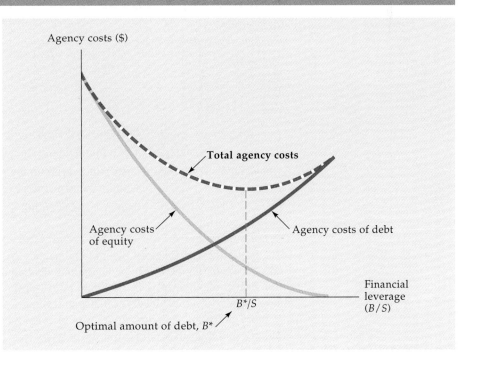

FIGURE 12.7

Gains from Leverage, Tax Aspects, and Transactions Costs

Part (a) indicates the gains from leverage considering taxes (as previously shown in Figure 12.4). Part (b) introduces the additional impact of transactions costs, in the form of financial distress and agency costs. Based on all of these factors, an optimal capital structure may exist.

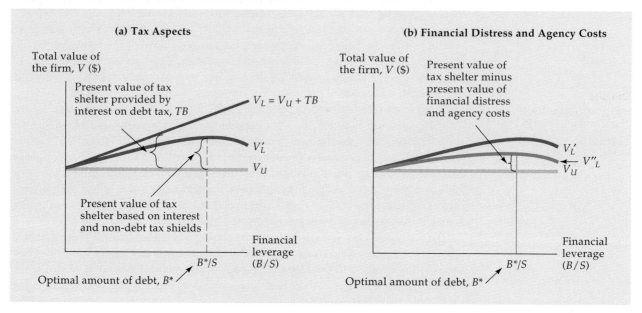

debt. However, when we include other tax-deductible items (such as depreciation and depletion), the costs of financial distress, and the agency costs, the total value of the firm becomes:

$$V_L' = V_U + \begin{matrix} \text{present value} \\ \text{of tax savings} \end{matrix} - \begin{matrix} \text{present value of} \\ \text{financial distress costs} \end{matrix} - \begin{matrix} \text{present value} \\ \text{of agency costs} \end{matrix} \quad (12.10)$$

where

$$V_U = \text{the unlevered value of the firm}$$
$$\text{tax savings} = TB - \text{non-debt tax shields}$$
$$\text{financial distress costs} = \text{costs that depend on the probability and costs associated with financial distress}$$
$$\text{agency costs} = \text{agency costs of equity} + \text{agency costs of debt}$$

The tax impacts are shown in Figure 12.7(a). The additional impact of transactions costs, in the form of financial distress and agency costs, is shown in Figure 12.7(b). Under this scenario there may be an optimal debt/equity ratio, B^*/S, where the value of the firm is maximized. This optimum ratio—or more likely a range of alternative, almost equally-desirable levels of financial leverage—would be such that substituting one more dollar of debt for equity would raise the costs more than the benefits. Similarly, cutting back would lower the costs by less than the benefits are reduced.

Impact on Capital Investment Decisions

■ LEARNING GOAL 5

Discuss how a firm's capital structure can have a signaling effect on its market value.

SIGNALING
Process of conveying information through a firm's actions.

The final place to look for impacts of capital structure on the value of the firm relates to the firm's capital investment decisions. In examining financial distress and agency issues in the preceding section, one topic that crept in was incentives either to overinvest or underinvest, which exist under certain conditions. Thus, it appears that a firm's capital structure decisions *do* impact the capital budgeting decisions made by the firm. A related argument on the interrelations between the capital structure and capital investment decisions arises when we consider a **signaling** approach to capital structure decisions. Under a signaling approach, the choice of a capital structure can convey information about the firm to investors and cause a change in the value of the firm.

Many models have been developed in this area. To illustrate one of them, think about the impact a capital investment decision may have on the value of a firm if the firm has to secure external financing in order to undertake a project. Suppose the equity of a firm is "undervalued" by the market and the firm has a "good" investment project, but can finance it only by securing outside financing. What if the firm issues equity when the equity is "undervalued"? The cost of the new equity financing may be so much that the new investors capture virtually all of the *NPV* of the new project, resulting in little or no gain to existing stockholders. In a case like this, the firm would probably bypass the "good" investment project, thereby not making a capital investment decision that assists in maximizing the value of the firm. This underinvestment can be avoided it the firm finances the project with debt or with internally generated funds, because the existing equityholders receive some of the benefits from the investment. The bottom line is that firms may signal to the markets that they consider the equity to be "undervalued" if they sell new equity to finance a capital investment project, while they may signal the stock is "overvalued" if they employ debt or internally generated funds to finance a new project.

While many different models and conclusions have been suggested, the important point to remember with regard to signaling is that *capital structure becomes more of a dynamic, ongoing, evolving decision.* There is not a single optimal level of debt, because managers continually have access to information before it is available to outside investors. Depending on the nature of the information, managers may choose to issue debt or equity in amounts that will at one time push the firm toward an optimal debt/equity ratio or range while at another time may push the firm away from an optimal debt/equity ratio or range.

CONCEPT REVIEW QUESTIONS

■ Briefly describe how personal taxes affect the MM tax case and the MM no-tax case.

■ How does the use of tax shields and long-term debt affect corporate capital structure?

■ Give some examples of bankruptcy and financial distress costs.

■ How is Miller and Modigliani's tax model affected by the presence of financial distress and agency costs?

■ What factors lead to capital structure impacting the market value of the firm?

DEBT/EQUITY RATIOS IN PRACTICE

■ **LEARNING GOAL 6**

Explain what the pecking order theory predicts about a firm's debt/equity ratio over time.

In practice we do not see firms financing with virtually 100 percent debt. Why not? Capital structure theory suggests a number of reasons. First, interest is not the only deduction that firms have for tax purposes; they also have non-debt tax shields in the form of depreciation and depletion. If firms are not likely to take full advantage of the interest tax subsidy, they are less likely to employ as much debt. In addition, other tax-related factors suggest that limits exist on the amount of debt employed. Second, the sum of the direct and indirect costs of financial distress appears to be substantial enough to encourage firms to use less than 100 percent debt. Third, agency costs ensure that management acts in the interests of stockholders, and bondholders protect themselves from having their wealth expropriated by imposing protective covenants and monitoring devices. These agency costs also indicate that firms will be less than 100 percent debt-financed. In addition, the firm's capital structure decision and its capital investment decisions are not always independent; in a dynamic context capital structure becomes an ongoing, evolving decision. All of these relationships are incorporated in the **pecking order theory.** The pecking order theory suggests that:

PECKING ORDER THEORY
Capital structure theory that suggests firms value the flexibility from financial slack; internally generated funds will be used first, then debt, and finally new common stock.

1. *Firms prefer internal (equity) financing first* because: (a) the total costs of obtaining new external financing are substantial and can be minimized by avoiding going to the financial markets more often than is absolutely necessary; and (b) by not going to the financial markets, specific attention is not drawn to the firm and its financial performance. (As discussed in Chapter 11, internal financing accounts for 75–80 percent of total financing for firms.) Poorly performing firms do not want to draw attention to themselves by having to sell a very expensive stock or bond issue, which substantiates the lack of performance and/or weakness of the firm.
2. *Firms prefer to pay cash dividends;* hence, some amount of cash flows out of the firm instead of funding capital investments. Under normal circumstances, reductions in the level of cash dividends are not viewed favorably by firms and their common stockholders. If fact, firms favor a "sticky" dividend policy: Firms increase cash dividends only when they think the higher level of dividends can be maintained but are reluctant to cut dividends when times get tough.
3. Given sticky cash dividend policies, uncertainty about future cash inflows from operations, and uncertainty concerning the cash outflow needs for capital investments, *firms want some financial flexibility in terms of a cash reserve*. When times are flush they will pay down debt, repurchase stock, or make acquisitions. When times aren't so good, firms reduce the level of cash.
4. *If they need external financing, firms issue debt first.* New equity financing is a last resort; both theoretical and empirical evidence indicates that by issuing equity the firm is signaling that its present and future prospects are not that strong.

The pecking order theory attempts to pull together what we know from financial theory and what we observe in practice. Firms appear to act much as described by the pecking order theory.

Firms also act as if they have a target capital structure; that is, there is some target debt/equity ratio or range they attempt to stay close to over time. We know it is the market value of the firm that is important in finance; therefore, the ratio of debt to the *market value* of equity is of primary interest. However, many firms and publications report the ratio of debt to the *book value* of equity. We examine both ratios.

Aggregate Debt/Equity Ratios

Figure 12.8 shows the two ratios—*debt/book value of equity* and *debt/market value of equity* for nonfarm, nonfinancial U.S. corporations for the 1960–1993 time period. Up to about 1972 the two ratios were about the same; after 1972 we see that the ratio of debt to market value of equity was greater than the ratio of debt to book value of equity. One important reason for the divergence between the ratio of debt/book value of equity and the ratio of debt/market value of equity is the decline in relative stock prices after the 1960s. Think of it this way: If the amount of debt remains constant, say at $4, but the market value of equity falls from $10 to $5, the ratio of debt/market value of equity increases from $4/$10 = 40 percent to $4/$5 = 80 percent.

One way to gauge the level of relative stock prices is to look at average price/earnings, *P/E*, ratios during various time periods. Using the Standard & Poor's 500 stock index, the average annual earnings and *P/E* ratios for three time periods selected to correspond with the time periods from Figure 12.8 are as follows:

Time Period	Earnings	Average *P/E* Ratio
1960–1972	$ 4.89	17.9 times
1973–1982	11.57	9.4
1983–1993	20.46	15.6

Although earnings rose over the 1960–1993 time period, we see that for the 1960–1972 time period the average price/earnings ratio of 17.9 was much higher than

FIGURE 12.8

Ratio of Total Debt to Book Value Equity and Market Value Equity for U.S. Nonfarm, Nonfinancial Corporations, 1960–1993

From 1972 to 1993 there was substantial divergence between debt/equity ratios using the book value of equity versus using the market value of equity.

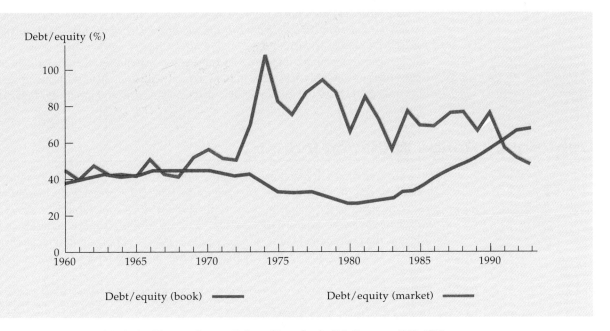

Source: Board of Governors of the Federal Reserve System, *Balance Sheets for the U.S. Economy, 1960–1993.*

that for the 1973–1982 period when it was 9.4 times earnings. Since 1983 the price/earnings ratio increased and averaged 15.6. Taking into account the decrease in relative stock prices, as reflected in lower P/E ratios during the 1973–1982 time period, we see that an important reason for the sharp increase in the ratio of debt/market value of equity (relative to debt/book value of equity) was lower relative stock prices.

What accounts for the convergence of the debt/market value of equity and debt/book value of equity ratios in the late 1980s and early 1990s? One factor is the increase in the relative price of stocks as reflected by the higher P/E ratios; other things being equal, higher stock prices result in a lower ratio of debt/market value of equity. A second factor is that during the 1980s U.S. firms issued substantial amounts of net new debt financing (both short- and long-term), while they actually *retired more stock than they issued*. Three factors contributed to the net retirement of stock: numerous mergers that were often financed in large part with debt; leveraged buyouts in which publicly traded firms were taken private and often ended up with debt/book value of equity ratios consisting of up to $9 of debt for every $1 of equity; and swaps or exchanges of debt for outstanding common stock. The net result of these activities was to rely more heavily on debt in the late 1980s and the 1990s (as shown in Figure 12.8 by the increase in the debt/book value of equity ratio). One of the important points to remember from Figure 12.8 is that over time the amount of debt relative to equity financing changes; that is, *firms do not always employ the same amount of financial leverage*.

Industry Debt/Equity Ratios

Although it is important to understand overall debt/equity ratios, it is also important to examine debt/equity ratios for different types of firms. For simplicity we group firms based on their dominant industry, and we look at industry groupings of firms.[8] Table 12.2 shows the 5-year (1989–1993) ratios of debt/book value of equity and debt/market value of equity for a number of different industries. An examination of this table indicates that: *(1) debt/book value of equity and debt/market value of equity figures are not the same, and (2) there are substantial differences in the use of debt among the industries examined (whether measured in book value or market value terms)*. For example, firms in metal mining, drugs and cosmetics, machinery, electronics, and instruments use substantially less debt in their capital structures than do firms in the construction, metal working, motor vehicle parts, and electric and gas utility industries.

Debt/Equity Ratios Within an Industry

It is also important to recognize that substantial differences in debt/equity ratios may exist between firms within the same industry. Table 12.3 presents debt/equity ratios for some firms in the chemical industry for 1989–1993. From Table 12.2 the average debt/book value of equity ratio for the 71 firms in the chemical industry is 0.74, whereas the debt/market value of equity ratio is 0.44. Looking at individual chemical firms in Table 12.3 (p. 362), we see that the following firms have less debt than the in-

---

[8]*Although any "industry" grouping is by necessity arbitrary, such groupings are employed in both practice and empirical research. We employ 2-digit SIC, Standard Industrial Classification, codes in Table 12.2; however, other sources, like* Value Line Investment Service, *use ad hoc groupings of firms.*

TABLE 12.2

Debt/Equity Ratios for Selected Industries, 1989–1993

The debt/equity ratios were computed from the Compustat data tapes based on firms that had a reasonable amount of equity and also had data available for all 5 years. Debt is defined as the total of short-term credit debt (i.e., bank loans, commercial paper, and the current portion of long-term debt) and long-term debt.

2-Digit SIC Code	Industry	Number of Observations	Mean (Debt/Book Equity)	Mean (Debt/Market Equity)
10	Metal mining	51	0.44	0.28
13	Petroleum exploration	129	0.53	0.41
15,16,17	Construction	33	0.99	0.98
20	Food	78	0.85	0.45
22	Textile mill products	25	0.95	0.81
23	Apparel	25	0.66	0.57
26	Paper	43	0.80	0.70
27	Publishing	61	0.61	0.45
28	Chemicals	71	0.74	0.44
2830 and 2840	Drugs and cosmetics	134	0.39	0.16
29	Petroleum refining	37	0.90	0.64
30	Rubber	47	0.64	0.53
33	Steel	47	0.59	0.58
34	Metal working	66	0.95	0.75
35	Machinery	246	0.56	0.50
36	Electronics	231	0.60	0.46
37	Motor vehicle parts	84	0.90	0.90
38	Instruments	217	0.52	0.35
49	Electric and gas utilities	222	1.21	0.83
53	Retail department stores	33	0.74	0.75

dustry: American Cyanamid, Ethyl, Great Lakes Chemical, Hercules, Monsanto, PPG Industries, and Rohm & Haas. At the other end of the spectrum, the following firms are using substantially more debt than the industry: American Vanguard, Cabot, W. R. Grace, Grow Group, ICN Biomedicals, ICM Fertilizer, Olin, Sterling Chemicals, and Union Carbide. Finally, Air Products & Chemicals, Dow Chemical, duPont, and Witco have capital structures fairly close to the industry averages given in Table 12.2. The important point from Table 12.3, and it is the same for other industries, is that *although firms in different industries employ more or less debt, there are also substantial differences within an industry.*

CONCEPT REVIEW QUESTIONS

■ What does the pecking order theory say about a firm's debt/equity ratio?
■ Give some examples of industries that make a substantial use of debt and some that use little debt.
■ Why might firms in the same industry use different amounts?

TABLE 12.3

Debt/Equity Ratios for Selected Firms in the Chemical Industry, 1989–1993

These firms were selected from the 71 observations that were in the chemical group from Table 12.2. Therefore, these debt/equity ratios are directly comparable to those presented in Table 12.2.

Firm	Debt/Book Equity	Debt/Market Equity
Air Products & Chemicals	0.59	0.32
American Cyanamid	0.39	0.16
American Vanguard	1.03	0.64
Cabot	1.13	0.71
Dow Chemical	0.83	0.46
duPont	0.68	0.31
Ethyl	0.68	0.25
W. R. Grace	1.16	0.69
Great Lakes Chemical	0.17	0.05
Grow Group	1.26	0.57
Hercules	0.38	0.32
ICN Biomedicals	1.91	0.54
IMC Fertilizer	1.07	0.76
Monsanto	0.56	0.27
Olin	0.95	0.71
PPG Industries	0.58	0.26
Rohm & Haas	0.57	0.24
Sterling Chemicals	1.96	0.71
Union Carbide	1.09	0.86
Witco	0.59	0.35

EXECUTIVE INTERVIEW WITH FONG WAN

Manager of Gas Services
Pacific Gas & Electric
Company
San Francisco, California

Wan began employment with Pacific Gas and Electric Company (PG&E) in 1988 as a financial analyst in the Financial Planning and Analysis Department. He was promoted to director in that department in 1991. Mr. Wan is currently manager of PG&E's Gas Services Department. His responsibilities include sales and services, product management, market planning, market relations, and business development.

Previously, Mr. Wan worked nearly three years as a business analyst for Exxon Corporation. He earned a Bachelor's of Science degree in Chemical Engineering from Columbia University and a Master's of Business Administration from the University of Michigan. We asked Mr. Wan to describe for us what is involved in managing the financial affairs of a public utility.

Financial management can be more challenging for utilities than for most corporations. Although every business must comply with some regulation, the regulatory environment is paramount for utilities. Each year, Pacific Gas and Electric, PG&E, files a Cost of Capital Testimony with the California Public Utility Commission. This filing represents the company's position for its capital structure and business environment. In addition, the filing also details the company's proposed cost of capital. The costs of debt and preferred equity are weighted averages of the existing and prospective issuances. The cost of common equity, on the other hand,

(continued)

involves extensive analyses of comparable utility studies and theoretical tools such as the capital asset pricing model (CAPM).

For 1995, PG&E has been authorized a capital structure of 48.00 percent common equity, 5.50 percent preferred equity, and 46.50 percent long-term debt. The authorized capital structure reflects, in part, purchased power contracts that limit PG&E's financial flexibility. Let me explain: Utilities that are in need of additional power but elect to purchase from other sources (other utilities or independent power generators) have to make long-term financial committmernts for that power. Such financial commitiments are viewed by credit rating agencies as debt equivalents, similar to a lease treatment. This debt equivalent is added onto the actual debt outstanding, thereby increasing the company's leverage from a debt-rating perspective.

PG&E targets a capital structure that supports a bond rating of either A or BBB in order to balance the objectives of (1) maintaining financial flexibility to withstand adverse business events and to take advantage of investment opportunities, (2) minimizing financial costs by taking advantage of the tax benefits of debt financing, while complying with regulatory guidelines.

We review our capital structure policy annually, and carefully evaluate each piece of our business during the review process. In addition to the utility business, PG&E also has investments in nonregulated industries. Our goal is to ensure that the creditworthiness of the company is not adversely affected by diversification. Therefore we look carefully at the risk profile of each of the nonregulated subsidiaries. If a subsidiary is large, we require it to be within one bond rating of the utility's. This will ensure that the utility will always be well-financed to provide reliable service to our customers for the long run.

SETTING A FIRM'S DEBT/EQUITY RATIO

■ LEARNING GOAL 7

List some tools used to set a firm's debt/equity ratio, and discuss the three key variables that affect capital structure.

It should be clear by now that there is no single answer to why we see different capital structures among industries and firms. We cannot make a blanket statement that firms should have a debt/equity ratio of 0.50 or 1.00, for example. But we can provide tools, guidelines, and some thoughts on planning ahead. The goal of the firm when determining its debt/equity ratio is to determine the firm's **debt capacity.** Knowing this will assist in maximizing the firm's value. By debt capacity, we mean the amount of debt, preferred stock, and leases a firm can effectively carry and service.

DEBT CAPACITY
The amount of debt or debt-type securities (like leases and preferred stock) a firm can service.

Tools for Digging

Some tools that can be employed to explore the capital structure issue include the following:

EPS-EBIT ANALYSIS
A technique used when examining the effect of alternative capital structures on a firm's earnings per share.

1. *EPS-EBIT Analysis.* To employ **EPS-EBIT analysis,** we begin with the firm's estimated *EBIT*. Consider the example of Seaboard Industries, which currently has $2 million of 10 percent debt outstanding and 1 million shares of common stock with

a market price of $20 each. Seaboard needs to raise $10 million in new capital and has two options. The first involves issuing 500,000 shares of additional common stock at $20 per share. The second would use debt financing to raise the $10 million. The debt would carry a coupon interest rate of 12 percent. After the new investment, Seaboard's *EBIT* is $6 million. As shown below, at the $6 million *EBIT*, Seaboard's *EPS* would be $2.32 with common stock financing or $2.76 with the debt financing.

	Common Stock Financing (in millions)	Debt Financing (in millions)
EBIT	$6.00	$6.00
Interest	0.20	1.40*
EBT	5.80	4.60
Taxes (40%)	2.32	1.84
EAT	$3.48	$2.76
Number of shares of common stock (millions of shares)	1.50	1.00
EPS	$2.32	$2.76

*$200,000 on existing debt plus $1,200,000 interest on new debt.

Instead of simply calculating *EPS*, it is generally helpful to consider what happens to *EPS* at various *EBIT* levels. We can also calculate the crossover *EBIT*, *EBIT**, which is the *EBIT* level that causes both financing alternatives to produce the same *EPS*, as follows:

$$\frac{(EBIT^* - I_1)(1 - T) - D_{ps1}}{N_1} = \frac{(EBIT^* - I_2)(1 - T) - D_{ps2}}{N_2} \qquad (12.11)$$

where

$EBIT^*$ = the unknown crossover point in *EBIT*

I_1, I_2 = the annual total interest charges under the two financing plans

T = the firm's marginal tax rate

N_1, N_2 = the number of shares of common stock outstanding under the two plans

D_{ps1}, D_{ps2} = the dollar amount of cash dividends on preferred stock under the two plans

EPS-EBIT analysis, although ignoring risk and the value of the firm, does provide some information on the impact of alternative financing plans on the firm's *EPS*.

2. *Coverage Ratios.* Most firms and analysts calculate various coverage ratios to ascertain how the firm's *EBIT* relates to the cash outflows resulting from the use of fixed-cost financing[9] These ratios range from the times interest earned and fixed charges coverage ratios (discussed in Chapter 19) to more complicated ratios that take into account principal repayments, sinking fund payments, and/or cash dividends on preferred stock. The basic intent of all these ratios is to ascertain how safe the firm is in terms of meeting its fixed-cost financing charges.

---

[9]*Although some long-term bonds and leases have floating or variable rates, they are still a fixed-cost type of financing, because there are periodic payments required and they have a prior but limited claim before common stockholders receive anything. In addition, adjustable rate preferred stock also exists; however, it still has the essential elements of a fixed-cost security.*

3. *Lender Standards*. Often a firm's lenders impose certain standards of financial performance. A bank loan or debt issue may contain financial performance standards that have to be met before assets can be sold, cash dividends paid, and so on. In addition, many larger firms tie their target capital structure decision to the bond rating the firm desires to maintain. For example, a firm may decide it always wants to be able to issue reasonable amounts of new debt with an A bond rating. (Bond ratings were considered in Chapter 11.) Accordingly, the capital structure and other financial affairs are maintained at a level that achieves this result.

4. *Cash Flow Analysis*. A final approach is to investigate what happens to the ability of the firm to survive a severe recession. This involves a scenario analysis, in which the firm focuses on the cash flow consequences under alternative, assumed future states of the economy.

All of these tools assist managers in determining the firm's appropriate, or target, capital structure.

Guidelines for Setting Debt/Equity Ratios

Although we have examined a wide variety of issues and factors related to a firm's capital structure decision, the primary results can be stated in a very straightforward way: *In making the capital structure decision, focus first and foremost on taxes, risk, and financial slack.*

1. *Taxes*. For firms in a taxpaying position, an increase in the amount of debt reduces the taxes paid by the firm. Of course, it's not just whether the firm is in a taxpaying position that is important; it's also whether it is expected to remain in a taxpaying position. Firms with less assurance of being able to benefit from the various tax shields will use less debt.

2. *Risk*. With or without bankruptcy, financial distress is costly. Although many factors affect risk, financial distress is most likely in firms that have high business risk. Business risk is often related to the type of assets employed. Where intangible assets play a major role, the value of the assets may erode quickly. Typically, firms that employ a lot of "brain power" or other intangible assets use less debt than do those whose assets have a ready secondary market. Also, competition and the nature of the industry often affect the firm's risk.

3. *Financial Slack*. In the long run, a firm's value depends first and foremost on the investment and operating decisions its managers make. These have the potential to add more value to the firm than its financing decisions. Therefore, firms want a certain amount of financial slack so they can react to new positive *NPV* opportunities. This is one of the reasons that high-growth firms tend to use less debt, because that posture provides greater financial slack.

Planning Ahead

The firm's capital structure decisions cannot be made in a vacuum. They have to be part of the firm's complete financial plan, which takes into account its investment opportunities, operating strategy, dividend policy, and so forth.

In Chapter 20 we will examine cash budgets and pro forma accounting statements. Although they don't tell you where to raise funds, they do provide insight into the anticipated amount and timing of the needs or surpluses. The use of sensitivity or scenario analysis is just as helpful when planning a firm's capital structure as it is for analyzing long-term investment decisions or the firm's cash budget. In addition, simulation is also useful because it allows the whole probability distribution of financial consequences to be examined. Remember that planning ahead, and having some financial slack, is important when considering how much debt the firm should have.

International Capital Structure Issues

At the foreign subsidiary level there are a number of important points that go into determining its capital structure. First and foremost, it is important to recognize that unless the parent is willing to let the subsidiary fail and default on its debt, there is *no independent risk for the subsidiary's debt*. Rather, its debt is explicitly or implicitly guaranteed by the multinational parent. Given this, it is really the parent's overall capital structure, not the subsidiary's, that is of primary concern.

Once this point is understood, then the objective is to acquire funds in the most cost effective manner at the subsidiary level. For example, a subsidiary that has low debt financing costs might have a capital structure of almost 100 percent debt. Yet another subsidiary, where the cost of debt was much higher, could have a capital structure with much less debt. The objective of the multinational parent is to raise capital as cheaply as possible on a worldwide basis and make suitable adjustments at the overall firm level to achieve its target worldwide capital structure.

Finally, multinational firms often call (and structure) their investment in a subsidiary as debt, rather than equity. They do so because of exchange controls and tax effects. From the standpoint of repatriating funds to the parent, a firm typically has wider latitude with interest and loan payments than with cash dividends or other reductions in equity. Also, by structuring the investment as debt, taxes are generally reduced.

Although some latitude exists, multinationals do not have complete freedom in choosing debt/equity ratios for foreign subsidiaries. If they have too little equity, they may run into restrictions placed on them by the host countries. But to the extent possible, the goal is to structure the foreign subsidiaries' capital structure to minimize capital costs subject to the requirement that the multinational parent be viewed as responsible by the host country. Then the multinational manages its capital structure on a global basis to maximize the value of the firm.

CONCEPT REVIEW QUESTIONS

■ Briefly describe some methods used to determine a firm's debt capacity.
■ What are three key variables that affect a firm's capital structure?
■ What factors impact the capital structure decision of a foreign subsidiary of a domestic firm?

Summary

■ In the absence of taxes and other financial market imperfections, the choice of a capital structure is "a mere detail." The value of the firm is a function of the investment decisions it makes, not its financing decisions.
■ There are three places to look when examining the possible impact of capital structure decisions on the value of the firm: taxes, transactions costs, and interrelationships between the firm's financing decisions and its capital investment decisions.
■ Once corporate taxes are introduced, the firm can increase its total value and reduce its opportunity cost of capital by replacing equity financing with debt financing.

- If the effective personal tax rate on stock income is less than the effective personal tax rate on bond income, there is less advantage to the firm from using debt financing than implied by the MM tax case.
- Because of taxes, transactions costs, and interactions between financing and investment decisions, firms choose capital structures that have more than zero debt and less than 100 percent debt.
- The pecking order theory and the observed behavior of firms suggest that the capital structure decision is a dynamic, evolving process.
- In practice, capital structures vary widely over time and among firms and industries.
- The key variables that affect the capital structure choice are the ability to take advantage of tax shields, risk differences related to the assets employed by the firm and its competition, and the need to maintain financial slack due to growth opportunities.
- Multinational firms raise capital as cheaply as possible from anywhere in the world, and they focus primarily in the parent firm's capital structure, not the subsidiaries' capital structure.

Questions

12.1 Assume the MM no-tax model holds. A firm exists that has 20 percent of its capital structure in the form of debt, which has a cost of 6 percent. Now the firm moves to 60 percent debt in its capital structure, again with a cost of 6 percent. What two effects occur as the firm moves from 20 percent debt to 60 percent debt? How do these effects counterbalance each other?

12.2 Compare the Modigliani and Miller no-tax case with the MM tax case. What similarities and differences are there between the two cases? What happens to the overall cost of capital under the no-tax case? Under the tax case? What limit does it approach in the tax case?

12.3 Explain Miller's personal tax model. Under what circumstances does it lead to the same conclusion as MM without corporate taxes? With corporate taxes?

12.4 The Modigliani and Miller no-tax model tells us that (1) if there are no taxes, (2) if there are no transactions costs, and (3) if the investment (or capital budgeting) policies of the firm are fixed, then capital structure does not affect a firm's value. Provide a complete discussion of the theoretical aspects of capital structure and its possible impact on the value of the firm.

12.5 Explain the pecking order theory. How does it relate to what we observe in practice and to the idea of a target capital structure? How would you go about explaining why we see so many different capital structures in practice, both between and within industries?

Concept Review Problems

See Appendix A for solutions.

CR12.1 Kennedy Equipment operates without debt, has *EBIT* of $4.5 million, and an opportunity cost of capital of 15 percent.
  a. If the firm's earnings have a zero growth rate and all the MM assumptions are met, including no corporate taxes, what is the market value of the firm?
  b. Now assume Kennedy issues $15 million in perpetual 10 percent bonds and uses the $15 million to retire equity in the firm. What is the new value of the firm, its opportunity cost of capital, and its cost of equity capital?

Note: In (a), with taxes, the value of an unleveraged firm is equal to $EBIT(1-T)/k_s$.

CR12.2 Megan is analyzing two firms—Unleveraged Partners and Leveraged Partners. Unleveraged Partners is totally financed with equity, whereas Leveraged Partners believe the value of the firm can be increased with the use of debt and has $60 million of 8 percent bonds outstanding. The cost of equity for Unleveraged Partners is 12 percent. Both firms have *EBIT* of $30 million and a corporate tax rate of 32 percent. The marginal personal tax rate for all individuals is 28 percent on debt income and 20 percent on equity income.

a. Employing Miller's model, what is the value of each firm? Is there a gain from leverage from the use of debt?

b. Now assume Congress passes a law instituting a flat tax rate of 30 percent for all corporate and individual income. What is the value of each firm? Is there a change in the gain from the use of debt?

CR12.3 High Rollers has had a long string of bad luck. All the firm's assets have been wiped out except for $100,000 in cash. On the liability side, the firm has debt of $150,000 due in 1 year. Two investment opportunities requiring an investment of $100,000 each and having a 1-year payoff are available. The first project has a 20 percent probability of having a $200,000 cash flow and an 80 percent probability of having an $80,000 cash flow in 1 year. The second project has a 50 percent chance of receiving $130,000 and a 50 percent chance of receiving $110,000 in 1 year. The opportunity cost of capital is 15 percent.

a. What are the expected cash flows and standard deviation of the cash flows for each project?

b. What is the *NPV* for each project?

c. If you were a stockholder, which project would you prefer? If you are a bond-holder, which project would you prefer?

CR12.4 Sullivan Music is an unlevered firm with a constant *EBIT* of $10 million per year. The corporate tax rate is 40 percent, and the cost of equity is 15 percent. Management is considering the use of debt that would cost the firm 10 percent regardless of the amount used. The firm's management asked a consulting firm to estimate the cost due to financial distress and the probability of these costs for each level of debt. The brokerage firm's analyst estimated the present value of future financial distress is $10 million and the probability of financial distress would increase with leverage as follows:

Value of Debt (in millions)	Probability of Distress
$ 0	0%
20	5
25	10
30	15
35	30
40	60
45	90

Using the pure MM model with corporate taxes, what is the optimal amount of debt for Sullivan (without and with financial distress)?

CR12.5 Safer Equipment currently has $10 million of 8 percent debt outstanding and 500,000 shares of common stock. The firm needs $1 million to finance an expansion project and can raise the funds by issuing debt at 8 percent or selling stock at $25 per share. The tax rate is 36 percent, and after the expansion *EBIT* will be $3,750,000.

a. What is the *EPS* under each financing option?

b. What is the crossover *EBIT* at which the decision to finance with debt or equity will not affect the firm's *EPS*?

CR12.6 Wells Associates has *EBIT* of $3 million, a zero growth rate, a tax rate of 40 percent, and $20 million of 9 percent debt outstanding. The firm has 288,000 shares of common stock outstanding and a *P/E* ratio of 15. Wells's opportunity cost of capital is 10 percent.

a. What is Wells Associates' stock price?

b. Recently management investigated an expansion project that would cost $6 million and would return $800,000 after-tax (in both cash flows and earnings) per year indefinitely. What is the *NPV* of the project?

c. If the firm issues debt to pay for the project, the cost of all debt becomes 10 percent, and the firm's *P/E* ratio drops to 14. What is the firm's stock price if it accepts the project from part (b)? Should the project be accepted?

Problems

See Appendix C for answers to selected problems.

Cost of Unlevered Equity

12.1 Richards Furnaces has $30,000 in debt and $20,000 in equity. The cost of debt, k_b, is 8 percent, and there are no taxes. Richards' cost of equity, k_s, given this use of debt is 17 percent. What would Richards' cost of equity be if there was no debt?

No-Tax Case

12.2 Singapore Power is an electric utility that operates in a taxless world. It has $200 million in 5 percent coupon rate bonds outstanding, and $400 million in stock outstanding. The cost of equity is 10 percent.

a. What is the firm's opportunity cost of capital?

b. Singapore Power has decided to issue $100 million in stock and use the proceeds to buy back $100 million in bonds. What is the firm's overall opportunity cost of capital? What must the new cost of equity capital be according to Modigliani and Miller?

Tax Case

Note: In (a) the value of the unlevered firm = S = EBIT(1 − T)/k_s.

12.3 Assume that the MM tax case holds. The market value of a firm that has $300,000 in debt is $1,200,000. The interest rate on debt is 12 percent, and the marginal corporate tax rate is 30 percent. If the firm was all-equity-financed, the required return (or cost of equity capital) would be 18 percent.

a. What is the firm's *EBIT*?

b. What would the market value be if the firm is all-equity-financed?

Debt Versus Equity: Tax Case

Note: In (a), S = EBIT(1 − T)/k_s.

12.4 Simpson International is an all-equity firm that generates earnings before interest and taxes, *EBIT*, of $3 million per year. The cost of equity capital, k_S^U, is 16 percent, and its marginal tax rate, *T*, is 35 percent.

a. What is the market value of Simpson International?

b. If Simpson now issues $4 million of debt, what is the market value of the firm? The market value of the firm's stock?

c. What assumptions are you making in order to come up with your answers in (b)?

Levered and Unlevered Firms

Note: In (a), the value of an unlevered firm, V, = S = EBIT (1 − T)/k_s.

12.5 Graphics Resources is an unlevered firm with an *EBIT* of $4 million. Its tax rate is 40 percent, and the opportunity cost of equity capital is 15 percent. Assume that the MM tax case holds and that Graphics is fairly valued.

a. What is the market value of Graphics?

b. Suppose that Graphics now issues $10 million of 8 percent bonds. What is the new market value of Graphics?

c. Assume there are two firms, Y and Z, that are identical in all respects to the unlevered Graphics and the levered Graphics, respectively. Explain what will happen if the current market value of Y is $14 million, while that of Z is $23 million.

Personal and Corporate Taxes

12.6 Debt-Free Co. is an unlevered firm that has an equilibrium market value of $7 million. The firm is contemplating issuing $4 million of 10 percent coupon bonds. The firm has a corporate tax rate of 30 percent and has estimated that the tax rates for its investors are 20 percent on stock income and 25 percent on bond income. Assume that Miller's personal tax case holds.

a. If only corporate taxes exist, what is the new total value of the firm and the gain from leverage?

b. With both corporate and personal taxes, what is the gain from leverage and the total value of the firm?

c. Why is the gain from leverage (or, alternatively, the total value of the firm) less in (b) than in (a)?

Personal and Corporate Taxes

12.7 A firm has long-term debt outstanding with a market value of $100,000. The corporate tax rate is 40 percent. Assume that Miller's personal tax case holds.

a. If there are no personal taxes, what is the value of the interest tax shield?

b. Now assume that personal taxes exist and the tax rate on bond income is twice the tax rate on stock income. At what personal tax rate on stock income does the advantage of debt financing vanish?

c. If the actual personal tax rate on stock income is 25 percent, and the relationship between personal taxes on stock and bond income from (b) still exists, what is the gain to leverage? What does this imply about the optimal level of debt for the firm?

Target Capital Structure

12.8 Carolina Enterprises currently has $100 million of 13 percent (coupon rate) debt outstanding, its *EBIT* is $80 million, and its cost of equity capital, k_s^L, is 12 percent. Due to a decrease in interest rates, Carolina has decided to call the bond issue. (The bonds will be called at par.) Because Carolina is not at its target capital structure, it will issue either $150 million or $200 million of new debt at par. In either case, $100 million will be used to refund the existing bond issue. The remainder will be used to buy back outstanding shares of Carolina's common stock. If the $150 million bond issue is employed, then the coupon interest rate will be 10 percent and k_s^L will increase to 12.5 percent. If the $200 million issue is employed, then the coupon interest rate is 11 percent and k_s^L will be 14 percent. The marginal corporate tax rate is 30 percent, and all earnings are paid out as cash dividends.

Note: In (a), EAT = EBIT − I − T; S = EAT/k_s. In (b), assume the market value of the bonds is equal to their par value.

a. If the bonds are selling at 115 percent of par, what is the current total value, V, of the firm (before any refinancing)?

b. What is the total value, V, of the firm if the $150 million bond issue is sold? If the $200 million issue is sold?

c. What action should Carolina take?

Minimize Opportunity Cost of Capital

12.9 Houser Metals is doing some capital structure planning. Its investment bankers have estimated after-tax costs of debt and equity at various levels of debt as follows:

Proportion of Debt	k_i	k_s
0.00	5.4%	12.0%
0.10	5.4	12.2
0.20	5.8	12.7
0.30	6.3	13.2
0.40	6.9	14.1
0.50	7.9	15.6
0.60	9.0	17.4

Based on this information, at what ratio of total debt to total equity is Houser's target capital structure?

EPS-EBIT Analysis

12.10 Thatcher Industries is considering raising $5 million by selling 200,000 shares of stock or by issuing 8 percent coupon rate bonds at par. There are presently 100,000 shares of common stock outstanding, the tax rate is 35 percent, and Thatcher already pays $100,000 in interest before any new financing.

Note: In (a), don't forget the existing interest.

   a. What is the crossover point where the *EPS* will be the same for either financing plan?

   b. If you are told there is a 50 percent chance *EBIT* will be $600,000, and a 50 percent chance it will be $1,000,000, which plan would you recommend? Why?

Crossover *EBIT*: Number of Shares

12.11 A firm is considering two different financing plans. Under plan I the interest is $8,000 and there are 1,000 shares of common stock outstanding. Under plan II the interest is $2,000. If the crossover *EBIT, EBIT**, is $20,000 and the marginal tax rate is 30 percent, how many shares of common stock are outstanding for plan II?

Preferred Stock, Common Stock, and Debt

12.12 JR Manufacturing currently has 100,000 shares of common stock outstanding with a market price of $60 per share. It also has $2 million (par value) in 6 percent coupon rate bonds outstanding. The firm is considering a $3 million expansion program that can be financed employing either (1) preferred stock sold at par with a 7 percent cash dividend, or (2) half common stock (sold at $60 per share) and half 8 percent coupon rate bonds (sold at par). The tax rate is 40 percent.

Note: In (a), don't forget the existing interest.

   a. What is the indifferent *EBIT* between the two plans?

   b. If *EBIT* is expected to be $1 million after the financing, what is the *EPS* under the two plans?

   c. If the marginal tax rate is 20 percent, what are your answers to (a) and (b)?

Impact of Investment and Financing Decisions on Value

12.13 Atlanta General is an all-equity firm. The firm has 200,000 shares of common stock outstanding, the *EPS* is $2, and all earnings are paid out to the stockholders as dividends. The current market value of the stock is $20 per share, and the opportunity cost of equity capital is 10 percent. Atlanta General is considering two alternative plans to raise $3 million for a new and highly promising investment project, as follows:

Plan A: Issue 150,000 more shares of common stock at $20 per share.
Plan B: Issue $3 million of 9 percent coupon rate bonds.

After the new investment, Atlanta General expects *EBIT* to be $1,400,000. The tax rate is 35 percent.

   a. Calculate the *EPS* (and dividends per share) under each plan after the expansion.

   b. If the opportunity cost of equity stays at 10 percent when common stock is employed, what is the new market price per share?

   c. If bonds are used, the opportunity cost of equity capital increases to 12 percent. What is the new market price per share under that plan?

   d. Explain why the market price calculated in (b) is higher than the beginning market price of $20. Then explain why the market price calculated in (c) is greater than that calculated in (b). How does this relate to the basic business of the firm, and the financing employed?

   e. Which financing plan do you recommend? Why?

Capital Structure Theory

12.14 Mini Case Broward Products is presently an all-equity firm. It needs to raise $2,500,000 in additional funds. After raising the funds it expects *EBIT* to be $600,000. The firm's unlevered cost of equity capital, k_s^U, is 12 percent, and its before-tax cost of debt, k_b, is 8 percent.

Note: In (a1) S = EBIT/k_s.

   a. (1) If there are no corporate taxes, under MM what is the value of Broward Products if it employs common stock to raise the needed funds?

(2) Alternatively, what happens to the value of the firm, the opportunity cost of capital, and k_s if it employs debt to raise the needed funds? **(3)** What is the fundamental determinant of the value of the firm in the MM no-tax case?

Note: In (b2), remember that the cost of equity remains the same in the after-tax case as in (a).

b. Now assume that the unlevered value of the all-equity-financed firm remains $5,000,000 as in (a), and the corporate tax rate is 35 percent. If the firm employs debt instead of equity to raise the $2,500,000, what is **(1)** the new value of the firm, and **(2)** its new opportunity cost of capital? **(3)** What if everything remains the same except that $4,000,000 in debt is employed?

c. So far the impact of personal tax has been ignored.
   (1) What is Miller's argument concerning the impact of personal taxes?
   (2) If everything is as in (b2), and the personal tax rates on debt and equity are both 40 percent, what is the value of Broward Products?
   (3) What if everything is as in (c2) except now the personal tax rate on stock is 20 percent?
   (4) Under what conditions, even after considering personal taxes, do we arrive at the same conclusion implied by the MM no-tax case? If T is 25 percent, and T_{pb} is 40 percent, what would the personal tax rate on stock, T_{ps}, have to be for the value of the firm to be independent of the firm's capital structure?

d. In addition to the MM and Miller arguments, a number of other factors have been cited as affecting the firm's capital structure decision. Discuss these factors. Then indicate how the pecking order theory may help explain what we observe in practice.

Dividend Policy

Sections in this chapter:

- **Dividends and Financing**
  How much should firms "give" to their stockholders?
- **Does Dividend Policy Matter? The Irrelevance Arguments**
  Why dividends may not matter.
- **Why *Do* Firms Pay Cash Dividends?**
  Reasons for paying dividends.
- **Is There an Optimal Dividend Policy?**
  Different preferences among firms and investors.
- **Dividend Policy in Practice**
  A smooth policy.
- **Dividend Payment Procedures**
  Who receives dividends, when, and how.
- **Stock Splits and Dividends**
  What it means when firms distribute additional stock.

A few years ago Chrysler was in the midst of operating losses and a very large cost-cutting campaign. It did not have enough in earnings to meet its cash dividend payments on common stock. The Chairman of Chrysler at that time, Lee Iacocca, said, ". . . all good companies go through some periods where they don't earn the dividend but continue to pay it." That is exactly what Chrysler did. Most firms treat cash dividends as important, yet there are vast differences in dividend policies. A few, such as TIE/Communications, Lotus Development, COMPAQ Computer, and Mack Trucks, have never paid cash dividends on their common stock. On the other hand, Citicorp has paid cash dividends since 1813, Manufacturers Hanover since 1852, General Motors since 1915, and Bassett Furniture since 1935.

Cash dividends have other consequences as well, since generally the more paid out in cash dividends, the less is available for reinvestment in the firm. In 1994 some political leaders in Great Britain argued that future Labour governments should seek to discourage the payment of high cash dividends. Their somewhat flawed logic was that restricting cash dividends would lead British companies, which traditionally have paid high dividends, to reinvest more into their businesses. The real issue was British macroeconomics, welfare, and fiscal policies, which have discouraged many British firms from making needed capital investments. Restricting firms from paying cash dividends would not solve some of the problems that have led British firms to minimize capital investments.

Other dividend-type decisions are also important. In the past few years many firms have started, or increased, stock repurchase plans. For example, recently Chase Manhattan bank indicated it planned to acquire about 4.5 percent of its outstanding common stock during the following 18 months. While technically not a dividend, we will see that repurchases of stock have some of the same effects as paying cash dividends. In this chapter we'll investigate cash dividends and these related issues.

LEARNING GOALS

After studying this chapter you should be able to:

1. Understand when, why, and how firms pay dividends, and describe the recent trend in dividend payments.
2. Explain the MM dividend irrelevance argument and the residual theory of dividends.
3. Discuss reasons for paying cash dividends, including capital gains and signaling.
4. Describe the clientele effect, and discuss factors firms consider in making the dividend decision.
5. Explain why most firms follow a smoothed residual dividend policy, and discuss dividend issues for international firms.
6. Explain dividend payment procedures and dates, and discuss dividend reinvestment plans and stock repurchases.
7. Explain the reasons for declaring stock splits and stock dividends.

DIVIDENDS AND FINANCING

■ LEARNING GOAL 1

Understand when, why, and how firms pay dividends, and describe the recent trend in dividend payments.

In order to maximize the value of the firm, the firm's financial managers also need to manage its cash dividend policy. The question is, does a policy of paying a high or a low cash dividend—or no dividend at all—maximize the value of the firm? Or should the firm simply repurchase shares of its common stock (which can be an alternative approach for distributing cash flows back to the owners)? We will see that the answers to these questions are somewhat messy. We are not even completely sure whether a firm's dividend policy *does* directly affect the value of the firm.

The first point to understand is that a decision to pay cash dividends is also a *decision not to reinvest this same cash in the firm*. To see this, consider the relationship between cash flow and possible uses, shown in Figure 13.1. A firm's available cash comes from two sources—internally generated financing and new external financing. Once cash is on hand, it has three general uses: First, ongoing operations must be maintained. These include paying salaries, the cost of materials, marketing expenses, taxes, financing charges and debt repayments, maintaining and updating equipment, and so forth. The remaining funds are then available for one of two other purposes: expansion (through new capital investments or the acquisition of other firms) or distribution to the firm's stockholders. Other things being equal, the more cash distributed to stockholders, the less internally generated equity capital is available (which affects the firm's capital structure) and the smaller the firm's capital budget. Thus, the firm's cash dividend decision may simultaneously affect its capital structure and capital budget-

FIGURE 13.1

Relationship Between Cash Flow and Potential Uses of Cash

The more cash distributed to stockholders, the less is available for maintaining ongoing operations and expansion, or the more new external financing that must be obtained.

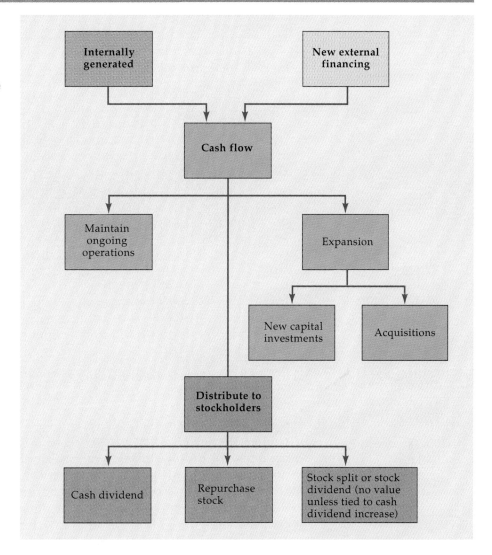

ing decisions. For analytical purposes we often separate the three decision areas—investment decisions, financing decisions, and dividend policy—but their interrelationships must be kept in mind.

Once the firm decides to make a distribution to investors, it has two primary means of doing so. These also appear in Figure 13.1. The first and most direct is through cash dividends. The second is through stock repurchases. Many firms also declare stock splits and stock dividends that they would like investors to consider valuable. As we shall see, however, other than signals about the financial health of the firms that some may read into these actions (i.e., their signaling effects), neither a stock split nor a stock dividend by itself alters the value of the firm.

Remember Key Idea 4—firms (and individuals) focus on cash flows and their incremental effects.

Before we discuss these topics, let's look at the magnitude of cash dividends. Table 13.1 shows total earnings, taxes, and cash dividends for firms during the 1984–1993 period. As we can see, taxes rose to over 45 percent of earnings before falling in recent years. The total amount of cash dividends increased every year until

TABLE 13.1

Total Earnings, Taxes, and Cash Dividends for Firms (in billions)

Dividend payout ratios have increased due to continued increases in total cash dividends being paid, coupled with slower growth in earnings.

		Taxes			Dividends	
Year	Taxes (1)	Earnings Before Taxes (2)	Taxes as a Percentage of Before-Tax Earnings [(1) / (2)] (3)	Cash Dividends Paid (4)	Earnings After Taxes (5)	Dividend Payout Ratio [(4) / (5)] (6)
1985	$ 96.4	$224.2	43.0 %	$ 83.2	$127.8	65.1 %
1986	106.6	236.3	45.1	88.2	129.8	68.0
1987	124.7	266.7	46.8	98.7	142.0	69.5
1988	137.9	306.8	44.9	110.4	168.9	65.4
1989	129.7	290.6	44.6	122.1	160.9	75.9
1990	136.7	355.4	38.5	149.3	218.7	68.3
1991	129.8	362.3	35.8	137.4	232.5	59.1
1992	139.7	395.9	35.3	171.1	256.2	66.8
1993	173.2	462.4	37.5	191.7	289.2	66.3
1994	202.5	524.5	38.6	205.5	322.0	63.8

Source: Federal Reserve Bulletin, various issues.

1991—from $83 billion in 1985 to $205 billion in 1994. Over this period the percentage increase in cash dividends was substantially in excess of the increase in earnings (before or after taxes); this was accomplished by increasing the dividend payout ratio (cash dividends divided by earnings after taxes).

Also, consider the following data, which show the percentage increase in both cash dividends and inflation:

Year	Total Cash Dividends (percent change)	Consumer Price Index (percent change)
1985	5.3	3.6
1986	6.0	1.9
1987	8.3	3.6
1988	11.9	4.1
1989	10.6	4.8
1990	22.3	6.1
1991	(8.0)	3.1
1992	24.5	2.9
1993	12.0	2.7
1994	7.2	2.7
Mean	10.0	3.6

Source: Federal Reserve Bulletin, various issues.

Many firms have expressly stated that one of their goals is to increase cash dividends at a rate at least equal to inflation. An examination of this data indicates that total cash dividends increased faster than inflation in all but 1 year—1991.

Although there are many differences among firms, in general they pay out a sizable portion of their cash flows in the form of cash dividends. This understanding is important given the many factors that influence dividend policy and the tremendous differences of opinion concerning the importance of dividend policy. We now turn to a discussion of these topics.

CONCEPT REVIEW QUESTIONS

■ What are two primary means a firm can use to distribute excess cash to its stockholders?
■ Briefly describe the general change in dividends paid over the period 1984–1993.

DOES DIVIDEND POLICY MATTER? THE IRRELEVANCE ARGUMENTS

■ **LEARNING GOAL 2**

Explain the MM dividend irrelevance argument and the residual theory of dividends.

Next to the firm's appropriate capital structure and capital budgeting techniques, the dividend decision has probably generated the most discussion in financial management. The controversy centers around this question: Does the firm's cash dividend policy influence the value of its common stock? To address this question, we begin by discussing the arguments of those who answer that question with a "no"—those who say that cash dividends don't matter.

Modigliani and Miller's Irrelevance Argument

DIVIDEND IRRELEVANCE ARGUMENT
Theory propounded by Modigliani and Miller that a firm's value is determined by its investment decisions, not its cash dividend policy.

As a corollary to their capital structure irrelevance argument, which we encountered in Chapter 12, Modigliani and Miller also concluded that the firm's cash dividend policy does not affect the value of the firm. To understand this position—called the **dividend irrelevance argument**—it is important to note three items: First, they assumed that capital markets are "perfect" in that no taxes, brokerage fees, or flotation costs exist. Second, the firm's capital structure is fixed so that we do not mix dividend policy with the firm's capital structure policy. Third, the firm's investment policy is fixed in that the firm follows a value-maximizing policy of accepting all positive *NPV* projects.

To understand the reasoning behind the Modigliani and Miller argument, let's look at an example—AMT Turbines. Its current market-value-based balance sheet is as follows:

Cash	$ 5,000	Debt	$ 20,000
Long-term assets	45,000	Equity	30,000 + *NPV*
Investment opportunity ($5,000 investment required)	*NPV*		
	$ 50,000 + *NPV*		$ 50,000 + *NPV*

Remember Key Ideas 1—firms act to maximize their market value—and 5—a dollar today is worth more than a dollar tomorrow, which is often captured by net present value.

The firm has $5,000 in cash that can be paid out to the firm's shareholders in the form of cash dividends or be invested in the new positive *NPV* investment opportunity. It seems that the firm has a dilemma: It can pay the cash dividend and return some of the firm to its owners, or it can take the investment opportunity and maximize its value. But, it also has the ability to do both—that is, to pay the dividends and also make the wealth-maximizing investment. All it has to do is to raise more funds so that it has $5,000 to make the investment. The firm can't issue debt, because that would change the capital structure proportions, so the firm sells more stock. How much does it need to sell? That's easy; it needs to sell $5,000 worth of stock to replace the $5,000 paid out in dividends.

What happens to the value of the original shareholders' stock during the process of paying the cash dividend, selling more stock, and making the investment? Shareholders' original claim on the firm was $30,000 + *NPV*. Because the investment and capital structure policies of AMT Turbines are unaffected, the total equity value of $30,000 + *NPV* must be unchanged. The value of the stock held by the original shareholders is now:

$$\begin{aligned}\text{value of new original} \atop \text{shareholders' shares} &= \text{equity value of firm} - \text{value of new shares}\\ &= (\$30{,}000 + NPV) - \$5{,}000\\ &= \$25{,}000 + NPV \end{aligned}$$

But, the original shareholders have also received a cash dividend of $5,000. Hence, their value is unaffected, and we can conclude that dividend policy does not matter to the original shareholders, nor does it affect the value of the firm.

Providing that AMT takes all positive *NPV* investment opportunities, the value of the firm is maximized. All that has happened is that cash is being recycled. AMT Turbines pays it out with one hand to the original shareholders, while with the other hand it sells new stock to raise additional cash.[1]

While the MM argument ignores taxes, flotation costs, and some other complications that exist in practice, it provides *the* frame of reference for considering what factors might cause cash dividends to affect the value of the firm. Before considering these issues, let's consider another version of the irrelevance argument.

The Residual Theory of Dividends

RESIDUAL THEORY OF DIVIDENDS
Theory that firms should obtain financing for all capital budgeting projects and then pay out any remaining internally generated funds as cash dividends.

The basis of the **residual theory of dividends** is that investors are as well or better off if the firm retains and reinvests internally generated funds as if it pays them out, *provided* the investment opportunities facing the firm are at least as good as those facing investors. Under the residual theory, the firm's dividend policy would be the following:

1. Establish the optimum capital budget—that is, accept all projects with positive net present values.
2. Determine the amount of common equity needed to finance the new investments while maintaining the firm's target capital structure.
3. Use internally generated funds to supply this equity whenever possible.
4. Pay cash dividends only to the extent that internally generated funds remain after taking all appropriate capital investment opportunities.

The residual theory of dividends is concerned with the "leftover"—*residual*—internally generated funds. Under this theory, cash dividends should be paid *only if* there is cash left over after making the investment decision.

---

[1]*Note that the original shareholders get the benefit of the positive NPV investment opportunity. All that the new shareholders receive is a fair return on their investment, provided that markets are efficient and the stock was sold at a fair price.*

Consider Pacific Industries, which finances 40 percent of its investments via debt and the remaining 60 percent with common equity. The firm's internally generated funds are $12 million which, in part or total, can be distributed to the stockholders or reinvested in the firm. The investment opportunities facing Pacific are as follows:[2]

Project	Initial Investment (in millions)	IRR
A	$5	25%
B	3	21
C	6	18
D	6	16
E	4	13
F	5	10

These opportunities are graphed in Figure 13.2, along with the opportunity cost of capital of 14 percent. As indicated, projects A, B, C, and D, requiring an initial investment of $20 million, should be undertaken. Out of this $20 million, $12 million [i.e., ($20 million)(0.60)] in equity financing would be used. Because the $12 million needed is exactly equal to the internally generated funds, Pacific would use these funds for capital investment and thus pay no cash dividends. The other $8 million required to finance the capital investments would be secured via debt financing.

If, on the other hand, Pacific's opportunity cost of capital had been higher, so that only projects A, B, and C could be undertaken, a total of $14 million would be needed for capital investment. Sixty percent of this, or $8.4 million [i.e., ($14 million)(0.60)], would be provided via internally generated funds. The remainder, $12 million minus $8.4 million, or $3.6 million, would be distributed to the firm's common stockholders as a cash dividend.

FIGURE 13.2

Investment Opportunities and Opportunity Cost of Capital Schedules for Pacific Industries

Pacific would accept all projects providing a return equal to or greater than its opportunity cost of capital of 14 percent. Thus, A, B, C, and D would be accepted, and E and F rejected.

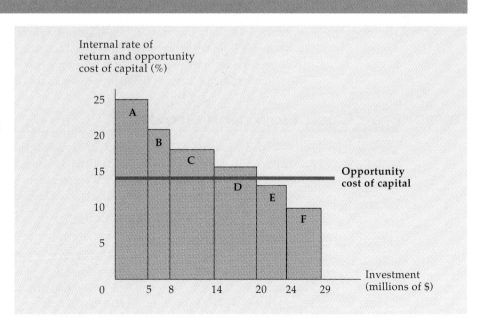

[2]For simplicity the internal rate of return criterion is employed to measure project desirability, and it is assumed that the ranking of project desirability is the same with internal rate of return as with net present value.

Under the residual dividend theory, cash dividends are paid only if funds are left over after accepting all profitable capital budgeting projects. *The value of the firm is a function of its investment decisions. Thus, like the MM dividend irrelevance argument, the residual theory suggests that dividend policy is a passive variable and has no influence on the value of the firm.*

We should pause here and clarify one point before going on. In Chapter 4, we said that cash dividends are the foundation for the valuation of common stock. That is, the market value of a share of stock is equal to the present value of all future cash dividends. While this remains true, the *timing* of the dividends can vary. When proponents of dividend irrelevance say that dividend policy does not matter, they are simply saying that the present value of the future cash dividends remains unchanged even though dividend policy may influence their timing. Dividends can still be paid, but it is a matter of indifference when they are paid, as long as their present value remains unchanged.

CONCEPT REVIEW QUESTIONS

- Briefly describe the MM dividend irrelevance argument.
- What is the firm's dividend payout policy under the residual theory of dividends?

WHY *DO* FIRMS PAY CASH DIVIDENDS?

■ LEARNING GOAL 3

Discuss reasons for paying cash dividends, including capital gains and signaling.

According to the irrelevance arguments, dividend policy does not affect the value of the firm. However, that is not all of the story. As we saw in Table 13.1, firms pay out about 60 percent of total earnings in the form of cash dividends. In addition, firms appear to value some stability in terms of their dividend payout. To understand dividend policy better, we will first examine taxes, cash flow, and growth options. Second, we will look at some signaling arguments related to the firm's cash dividend policy. Finally, we will consider some other factors potentially related to the dividend decision.

Taxes, Free Cash Flow, and Growth

As we have discussed previously, taxes affect many financial decisions. Not surprisingly, then, they also come into play in the dividend decision. Under the Budget Reconciliation Act of 1993 the top marginal tax rate for corporations is 35 percent. For individuals the ordinary marginal tax rates for 1995 are as follows based on taxable income:[3]

Single Individual	Married Couple Filing Joint Return	Marginal Tax Rate
Up to $23,350	Up to $39,000	15%
23,351 to 56,550	39,001 to 94,250	28
56,551 to 117,950	94,251 to 143,600	31
117,951 to 256,500	143,601 to 256,500	36
Over 256,500	Over 256,500	39.6

[3] *Taxable income = adjusted gross income − (exemptions and itemized deductions, or the standard deduction).*

On assets like common stock held for investment purposes and then sold, the capital gains tax (if the stock is held for 1 year or longer) is 28 percent; if it is held for less than 1 year, the ordinary marginal tax rate applies.

There are tax aspects for both corporations and individuals who *receive* cash dividends. First let's look at firms that own shares of common stock in another firm. For corporations, 70 percent of the cash dividends received from the investment in another firm are excluded from the firm's income.[4] For a firm in the 35 percent marginal tax bracket, the tax rate on cash dividend income is only 10.5 percent [i.e., $(1 - 0.70)(0.35)$]. This is lower than the effective tax rate of 35 percent that the same firm would pay on any gain realized from selling the stock. Thus, there is a minor tax issue for corporations receiving cash dividends. However, the major tax issue relates to individuals.

Prior to 1986, capital gains were taxed at a substantially lower rate than ordinary income—one half of the ordinary income tax rate. If an individual was in a 30 percent marginal tax bracket, the tax rate on capital gains was only 15 percent. The argument was often made that because of different tax rates on ordinary income versus capital gains, individuals would benefit from firms *not* paying cash dividends.

As we know from Key Idea 4, individuals focus on cash flows—just as firms do. Also, in line with Key Idea 7 (options are valuable), investors value the option of when to pay taxes (with capital gains).

To illustrate, assume a firm has a positive *NPV* project that requires an investment of $100. The firm also has free cash flow of $100. To make the investment, the firm has two alternatives. The first is to pay no cash dividends and simply take the $100 in free cash flow to make the investment. The value of the firm will increase by $100, so stockholders obtain the full benefit of the $100. If investors decide to sell $100 of the stock, their after-tax proceeds (given the 15 percent capital gains tax in the example) will be $85. The second alternative is to pay a cash dividend of $100, of which the investors only net $70 after paying taxes on ordinary income at a rate of 30 percent. The firm then turns around and sells $100 of new common equity to fund the positive *NPV* project. Considering the differential impact of taxes (i.e., 30 versus 15 percent in the example) and the fact that investors have an option of when they will pay the taxes if the return is in the form of capital gains, there was a tax-deferral advantage to not paying cash dividends.

Under the Budget Reconciliation Act of 1993 the top marginal tax rate for individuals is 39.6 percent, while the capital gains tax is 28 percent. While this differential is not as large as it sometimes has been, high-tax bracket investors may still have a modest preference for gains in the form of capital appreciation as opposed to cash dividends. On the other hand, low- or zero-tax bracket investors may have a preference for cash dividends since they will have the funds "in hand" with a cash dividend.[5] These differential tax impacts may provide a rationale for why firms pay cash dividends and, at the same time, continue to issue additional equity to replace the equity drained out through the dividend process. On both the theoretical and empirical level many studies have examined whether taxes directly impact dividend policy; the results are mixed and the answer is unclear.

Firms are generally reluctant to decrease cash dividends per share, and generally raise them only when they are confident the higher per share level can be maintained. Thus, dividends are "sticky," especially on the down side.

The free cash flow theory suggests there are some interrelationships between a firm's investment decision and its dividend decision. The greater the amount of new investment undertaken by the firm, the smaller the cash dividend that can be paid, or the more new equity that must be issued. The important point is that firms that have more growth options are expected to pay lower cash dividends. From a free cash flow standpoint, we see that a firm's growth options and its dividend policy are linked together.

---

[4] *If the firm owns 20 percent or more of the firm, it may exclude 80 percent of the dividends.*
[5] *Cash dividends received on stock held in an IRA (Individual Retirement Account), a Keogh account, a company pension account, and the like, are not subject to taxes at the time the cash dividend is received. Rather, taxes are deferred, and must be paid when funds are received (i.e., withdrawn) from retirement accounts.*

Signaling

Management does not want to be in the position of "crying wolf." Management may be penalized for sending a "false" signal if it increases a dividend that cannot be backed up by results.

Another way to examine the cash dividend decision is from a *signaling* perspective. The underlying thrust of this argument is that in a risky world with heterogeneous expectations and less-than-perfect markets, the cash dividend policy communicates information—*provides a signal*—about the firm's future cash flows over and above any other existing information. An increase in the payout ratio would be seen to indicate an increase in the future cash flows of the firm, and the market price of the firm's common stock would increase simply as a result of the increased cash dividends.

This viewpoint has been strengthened in recent years by empirical evidence. Initiating payment of a cash dividend or unexpectedly increasing cash dividends leads to an increase in the value of the firm's stock. Additionally, dividend initiations may also be associated with future increases in the firm's earnings (and hence, its cash flow). This line of theory and empirical support suggest that dividends may signal unique information about the future prospects of the firm.

Some Further Arguments for the Influence of Dividend Policy

In addition to the factors discussed above, other less theoretical arguments have been made that either a high or a low dividend payout ratio may affect the value of the firm. Some of these arguments are as follows.

Resolution of Uncertainty

One argument presented in favor of a price effect is that by paying dividends, the firm resolves investor uncertainty. Because the retention of funds and promise of future dividends is uncertain, investors may prefer higher current dividends. Accordingly, they would bid up the market price for firms with higher payout ratios. Although the risk and return of the firm is not influenced, it is argued that investor perception of riskiness may decrease, thereby causing the market price to increase.

The basic dividend valuation framework from Chapter 4 is $P_0 = D_1/(k_s - g)$, where P_0 is the current market price, D_1 is the cash dividend expected at time $t = 1$, k_s is the equity investors' required return, and g is the expected growth rate in cash dividends. If the investors' perception of risk decreases, their required return, k_s, will decrease. If the cash dividend, D_1, is $3, k_s is 16 percent, and g is 8 percent, the initial price is:

Key Idea 6 is that risk and return go hand-in-hand.

$$\text{price with no uncertainty resolution} = P_0 = \frac{\$3.00}{0.16 - 0.08} = \$37.50$$

If a higher payout ratio resolves investor uncertainty, and everything else remains the same, the required return might decrease to 15 percent. In that case, the market price would be[6]

$$\text{price with uncertainty resolution} = P_0 = \frac{\$3.00}{0.15 - 0.08} = \$42.86$$

Thus, if a high payout ratio reduces investor uncertainty, the market price of the firm's common stock increases.

---

[6] In reality, a higher payout ratio would increase the dividend above $3.00; that increase would further increase the price. For example, if the dividend increases to $3.50, the new price is $3.50/(0.15 − 0.08) = $50.

Desire for Current Income

Remember Key Idea 5—a dollar today is worth more than a dollar tomorrow.

Another factor might be investor preferences for current income. In Chapter 2 (Figure 2.6), we examined the total returns on common stock investment between 1960 and 1994. Cash dividends provided 35 to 40 percent of the total returns from investing in common stock during this period. In addition, there is much less risk associated with cash dividends than with capital appreciation or loss, as evidenced by the much lower variability for the dividends. Investors with a preference for current income would favor a high-payout firm and thus might bid up its price.

Flotation Costs

As we discussed in Chapter 6, the presence of flotation costs makes the cost of internally generated common equity cheaper than the cost of issuing new common stock. If a firm's cost of internal common equity is 16 percent, then its cost of issuing new common stock may be 18 or 19 percent. This is due to the transaction costs and underpricing that occur when additional common stock is sold. Flotation costs may cause firms to favor retaining more funds, via a low dividend payout policy, because doing so reduces their cost of equity capital.

Brokerage Costs

In the absence of brokerage costs, investors could always buy or sell securities to create their own cash "dividend" stream if they did not like the policy followed by the firm. The presence of brokerage costs, however, means that investors receive less than 100 percent on the dollar when they buy or sell securities. Investors preferring high current income cannot sell stock without incurring additional costs. Likewise, those preferring a low level of current income also incur additional costs on reinvesting the cash dividends. The net effect may cut both ways: Brokerage costs may create a preference for either a high or a low level of cash dividends.

CONCEPT REVIEW QUESTIONS

■ Why might investors prefer a return in the form of capital gains rather than cash dividends?
■ How are a firm's growth options and its dividend policy related?
■ Describe how the dividend policy can "signal" a firm's financial position.

IS THERE AN OPTIMAL DIVIDEND POLICY?

■ **LEARNING GOAL 4**

Describe the clientele effect, and discuss factors firms consider in making the dividend decision.

We see that firms and individuals may have a preference for different kinds of dividend policies due to various factors and considerations. From the firm's standpoint, firms with substantial growth options may prefer a low payout policy. From an investor's standpoint, we see that certain investors might have a preference for high- or low-payout firms. Investors with low incomes and high current needs might favor high-payout firms, whereas investors in high income brackets might favor low-payout firms. This preference has been called the **clientele effect.** That is, the cash dividend policy that a firm establishes attracts a certain clientele of investors. Once that clientele is established, the firm's dividend policy may not directly influence the value of the firm's stock. A significant shift in the dividend policy, however, would disrupt the firm's clientele, causing price effects until a new investor clientele owned the firm's common stock.

Although there has been both extensive debate and substantial empirical testing, there is no consensus on the primary issue: whether or not the firm's cash dividend policy *by itself* influences the value of the common stock. Some empirical studies have concluded that higher dividend yields are associated with higher expected returns; this would imply that dividend policy does affect the value of the firm. However, other researchers have serious questions about these empirical studies. The best that can be said right now is that the firm's cash dividend policy *may* influence the market value of the firm's stock—but then again it may not. Our personal view is that the dividend irrelevance arguments are essentially correct: A firm's cash dividend policy does not affect the value of the firm, *providing* that the policy does not affect its investment decisions. Therefore, most managers look at a number of other factors when they make the cash dividend decision.

Other Factors in the Dividend Decision

In addition to taxes, growth options, and possible price effects, other factors appear to influence dividend policy in practice. These include liquidity and profitability, earnings stability, access to equity markets, and control.

Liquidity and Profitability

The cash position of the firm can influence its decision on cash dividends. Firms with a shortage of cash often restrict or discontinue cash dividends. Highly profitable firms with substantial cash positions often increase their cash dividends (or repurchase some of their outstanding common stock). One reason cash-rich firms pay more dividends is to provide greater protection against a possible takeover by another firm. By paying higher dividends, the cash-rich firm accomplishes two things: It makes its current stockholders happy, and it reduces its cash position, thus becoming a less tempting takeover target.

Earnings Stability

Another factor often considered in practice is the stability of the firm's earnings. Other things being equal, more stable firms are often in a better position to pay larger cash dividends than are less stable firms. They plan for the future knowing they will be able to pay steady, or increasing, cash dividends. Public utility firms, for example, pay high cash dividends. They can do this, in part, because of their relatively stable operating environment.

Access to Equity Markets

Smaller firms generally have much more difficulty or incur substantially higher costs when they attempt to raise external equity capital than do larger firms. Because their access to equity markets is limited, small firms tend to hold cash in order to fund investment projects, and therefore they tend to pay lower cash dividends.

Control

For many small- and medium-sized firms, ownership control is an important issue. They may be reluctant to sell more common stock, opening ownership to "outsiders." They will also prefer to retain more internally generated funds to provide the equity capital needed for growth. By using internally generated common equity plus any borrowing required, they may be able simultaneously to maintain control *and* to meet the firm's capital needs.

Constraints on Dividends

Finally, certain constraints may inhibit the firm's ability to pay cash dividends. These involve contractual restrictions, legal restrictions, and taxes on improperly accumulated earnings.

Contractual Restrictions

Remember Key Idea 3— individuals act in their own self-interest. One way to control agency costs resulting from self-interest is by restrictions of this type.

Bond indentures, term loan agreements, and even preferred stock provisions may often impose restrictions on the payment of cash dividends. For example, a firm may be required to maintain a certain level of working capital or a minimum current or times interest earned ratio. Another common restriction states that common stockholders may not be paid cash dividends until the preferred stockholders have received their dividends. Although these (and similar) restrictions typically do not inhibit the firm's ability to pay dividends, they may do so when a firm is experiencing financial difficulties. From the creditors' or preferred stockholders' points of view, that is exactly what restrictions of this type are intended to do.

Legal Restrictions

Most state laws governing the incorporation of a firm provide statutory restrictions prohibiting the firm from paying cash dividends under certain conditions. These vary from state to state, but they usually include a restriction on the firm's dividend-paying ability when the firm's liabilities exceed its assets, when the anticipated dividend exceeds the retained earnings, or when the dividend would be paid from the firm's invested capital.

Taxes on Improperly Accumulated Earnings

Firms do not have to pay cash dividends as long as the funds are used to purchase productive assets. But if the firm does not pay cash dividends and instead elects to keep increasing its level of cash and marketable securities, problems may arise. If the Internal Revenue Service finds the level of cash and marketable securities to be beyond that deemed reasonable to meet liquidity needs, a special surtax is imposed on the improper accumulation. Although infrequently used, this requirement is designed to ensure that smaller firms do not avoid paying taxes through an excessive accumulation of cash.

CONCEPT REVIEW QUESTION

■ Briefly describe other factors that may impact a firm's cash dividend policy.

DIVIDEND POLICY IN PRACTICE

■ **LEARNING GOAL 5**

Explain why most firms follow a smoothed residual dividend policy, and discuss dividend issues for international firms.

Neither theory nor empirical testing provides a complete answer to the question of whether dividend policy influences the market value of the firm's common stock. But, in practice, firms (and their boards of directors) act as though dividend policy *is* an important decision. They view it as being important both in and of itself, and because of its signaling content. Stability of dividends is perceived as being important; firms prefer to maintain a steady and increasing level of cash dividends per share over time. Equally important, there is an extreme reluctance to reduce cash dividends.

SMOOTHED RESIDUAL DIVIDEND POLICY
Cash dividend policy whereby the firm sets a long-run target dividend payout ratio and ties it to a specific dividend per share.

Most firms in practice follow a **smoothed residual dividend policy.** This means that after taking into account many of the items discussed previously, they set the cash dividend policy based on the following considerations:

1. The dividend is set at a constant dollar amount per share.
2. A target dividend payout ratio, which the firm plans to maintain over time, is established.
3. Dividends will be increased when and if it appears the increased dollar amount per share can be maintained.
4. The dollar amount of cash dividends paid per share will be decreased only with great reluctance.
5. In the long run, the firm attempts to finance capital expenditures with internally generated funds and debt (supplemented only occasionally, if at all, by new common stock), while fluctuating around its target capital structure.

This smoothed residual dividend policy is consistent with some early findings by Lintner.[7] In addition, it is consistent with the pecking order theory (as discussed in Chapter 12). A firm's dividend policy is determined simultaneously with its investment and financing decisions.

Interfirm Differences

To assess dividend policy in practice, let's look at what some firms actually have done. The earnings per share, dividends per share, and dividend payout ratios are presented in Table 13.2 for Alcan Aluminum, Baltimore Gas & Electric, and Union Pacific. Alcan Aluminum has had widely fluctuating dividends and payout ratios as its earnings fluctuated dramatically over the 1985–1994 period. Baltimore Gas & Electric has had a very stable dividend policy: Up to 1990 the utility paid out 50 to 70 percent of earnings in the form of cash dividends; since 1990 lower earnings, along with roughly the same cash dividends per share, resulted in a higher dividend payout ratio. Union Pacific has had stable and increasing cash dividends in line with its increasing earnings per share.

---

[7]*John Lintner, "Distribution of Incomes of Corporations Among Dividends, Retained Earnings, and Taxes."* American Economic Review *46 (May 1956): 97–113.*

TABLE 13.2

Dividend Payouts of Three Firms

Alcan Aluminum's cash dividends and dividend payout ratio have fluctuated widely due to wide swings in earnings. Both Baltimore Gas & Electric and Union Pacific have had more consistent payout ratios.

	Alcan Aluminum Limited			Baltimore Gas & Electric Company			Union Pacific Corporation		
Year	Dividends Per Share	EPS	Dividend Payout	Dividends per Share	EPS	Dividend Payout	Dividends per Share	EPS	Dividend Payout
1985	$0.49	$(0.81)	*%	$1.10	$1.87	59%	$0.90	$2.09	43%
1986	0.35	0.97	36	1.17	2.10	56	0.90	2.28	39
1987	0.39	1.68	23	1.23	2.31	53	1.00	2.45	41
1988	0.59	3.85	15	1.30	2.31	56	1.02	2.45	42
1989	1.12	3.58	31	1.37	2.03	67	1.10	2.81	39
1990	1.12	2.33	48	1.40	1.40	100	1.16	3.09	38
1991	0.86	(0.25)	*	1.40	1.52	92	1.28	0.31	*
1992	0.45	(0.60)	*	1.42	1.63	87	1.39	3.57	39
1993	0.30	(0.54)	*	1.46	1.85	79	1.51	3.43	44
1994	0.30	0.30	100	1.52	1.93	79	1.66	4.66	36

* Not a meaningful figure.
Source: Annual reports for each of the firms cited.

(The lone exception was in 1991, when an extraordinary charge lowered earnings dramatically.) The cash dividend and earning patterns of these three firms are typical of some of the interfirm differences in cash dividends.

Industry Differences

Dividend payout policies also vary to some extent by the primary industry in which the firm is involved. This variation results from different amounts of risk, profitability, growth opportunities, and regulation among industries. In the following list, we see a wide range of dividend payout ratios:

Industry	Payout Ratio
Chemical	40%
Computer	50
Drug	48
Electric utility	77
Food processing	42
Machinery	22
Medical services	10
Newspaper	37
Restaurant	15
Steel	28

The machinery, medical services, restaurant, and steel industries paid out less than 35 percent of earnings in the form of cash dividends. On the other hand, the electric utilities industries paid out over 75 percent or more of their earnings in the form of cash dividends.

Not only do dividend payout ratios vary considerably among industries, they also vary among firms within a single industry. Consider the following data, which show the dividend payout ratios for firms in the machine tool industry:

Firm	Dividends per Share	Payout Ratio
Acme-Cleveland	$0.44	90%
Cincinnati Milacron	0.36	33
Giddings & Lewis	0.12	12
Gleason	0.40	48
Monarch Machine Tool	0.20	*
Snap-on-Tools	1.08	47
Stanley Works	1.38	49

* Not a meaningful figure.

We see that Monarch Machine Tool paid cash dividends even though it suffered losses, and Giddings & Lewis paid out only 12 percent of its earnings in the form of cash dividends. On the other hand, Gleason, Snap-on-Tools, and Stanley Works all paid out almost 50 percent of earnings in the form of cash dividends. These vastly different policies within an industry reflect the substantial differences among firms. Thus, although there do appear to be industry differences that influence cash dividend policies, we must not let these differences obscure the sizable interfirm differences that exist as well.

Dividend Changes

We can also examine the actions taken by firms with respect to increasing or decreasing cash dividends. Table 13.3 presents the number of firms increasing, resuming, decreasing, or omitting cash dividends for the 1985–1994 period. In the 1990–1992 period we see that the number of firms increasing their cash dividends has fallen compared to earlier years. This is the result of slowness in parts of the economy, with the attendant impact on earnings and internally generated funds. However, with the better economic climate in recent years the table indicates that many firms increased or resumed dividends. Also, the extreme reluctance of firms to decrease or eliminate cash dividends is highlighted by the relatively small number of decreases or omissions of cash dividends.

One other aspect of Table 13.3 deserves attention—the "Extra" column. Many firms follow the practice of paying a regular cash dividend and then in good years declaring a **dividend extra.** This practice allows the firm to have a stated amount of cash dividends per share that can be supplemented, if desired, without raising the stated rate to a new higher level. In this way, the basic per share rate will not have to be cut in bad years.

DIVIDEND EXTRA
Practice of paying an extra or special cash dividend in addition to the regular dividend.

International Dividend Policy

When investments are made on an international basis, they are often accomplished through the use of subsidiaries set up in various countries. In these situations dividend issues become more complex because of the numerous subsidiaries and the multiplicity of different laws, tax considerations, and government regulations. But the primary point to remember is that the *multinational firm's worldwide dividend*

TABLE 13.3

Number of Firms Taking Action on Cash Dividends

These data are based on over 10,000 publicly traded stocks. Note the increases relative to decreases, and the number of extras.

Year	Action				
	Increased	Resumed	Decreased	Omitted	Extra
1985	1,898	88	104	231	627
1986	1,685	93	148	257	462
1987	1,822	114	84	186	533
1988	1,858	62	83	175	579
1989	1,869	65	89	218	627
1990	1,433	52	195	328	491
1991	1,129	44	205	387	388
1992	1,364	73	133	294	399
1993	1,717	128	142	255	531
1994	1,844	71	95	449	499

Source: Moody's Annual Dividend Record.

policy should not be just the residual of the decisions made in individual country-based subsidiaries. Rather, worldwide issues need to be considered in order to maximize the value of the firm.

For firms with foreign subsidiaries, cash dividends are the most important means of transferring funds to the parent firm. Dividends often account for over 50 percent of such remittances. In setting the dividend policy for subsidiaries, two important considerations are exchange controls and financing requirements.

Multinational firms often set the dividend requirements for subsidiaries at or above the dividend payout ratio of the parent. Thus, if the parent firm has a 50 percent dividend payout ratio, then the foreign subsidiary is expected to contribute 50 percent of its earnings to the parent. By setting a dividend requirement, multinationals attempt to establish a worldwide cash dividend policy for their subsidiaries. This has two benefits: First, the subsidiaries are contributing their appropriate part to the parent's cash dividend policy. Second, and often more important, this worldwide policy provides the multinational firm with a rationale for dealing with the exchange or currency controls of different nations. Because many nations limit dividend remittances, either in absolute terms or as a percentage of either earnings or capital, multinational parents find it is important for subsidiaries to establish and meet a constant dividend requirement. Dividends are then paid each year to demonstrate a continuing policy to the local government where the subsidiary is located.

In addition to the need to remit funds in the form of dividends, subsidiaries have continuing financing needs. In high-growth situations, multinationals may need to reinvest more funds in the subsidiaries, whereas in low-growth areas the need for funds is lower. This difference in demand, other things being equal, suggests differing cash dividend policies between subsidiaries located in different countries. One way some multinationals deal with differing needs, while still establishing a stable dividend remittance policy, is to have high-need subsidiaries declare the dividend even though it isn't remitted. By doing so, they establish the principle that dividends are a necessary cash flow associated with doing business. With a constant policy of paying (or at least declaring) dividends, multinational firms attempt to partially meet financing needs while maintaining the requirement for dividends to be remitted to the parent.

CONCEPT REVIEW QUESTIONS

- How is a firm's dividend policy established?
- Do dividend payout ratios vary among industries, among firms within an industry, or both?
- What are the points multinational firms must consider when establishing their dividend policy?

DIVIDEND PAYMENT PROCEDURES

■ LEARNING GOAL 6

Explain dividend payment procedures and dates, and discuss dividend reinvestment plans and stock repurchases.

Cash dividends are normally paid quarterly. Assume that a firm has decided to pay a cash dividend of 75 cents each quarter. The relevant dates that stockholders would be concerned about if they owned or contemplated purchase of the stock might be as follows:

Amount	Declaration Date	Ex-Dividend Date	Record Date	Date Payable
$0.75	January 21	February 11	February 14	March 12
0.75	April 15	May 7	May 9	June 11
0.75	July 15	August 7	August 12	September 9
0.75	October 14	November 7	November 9	December 10

The ex-dividend date is determined by rules adopted by the securities industry. In 1995 the rules changed, leading to a 3-day settlement period.

1. *Declaration (or Announcement) Date.* The declaration date is the date the board of directors meets and issues a statement declaring the next quarter's cash dividends. For our example, the declaration date is January 21 in the first quarter, April 15 in the second quarter, and so on. Once the dividends are declared, they become a legal liability of the firm. The declaration would specify the amount and date of the dividend payment.

2. *Record Date.* The **record date** (fourth column in the table) is the date the stockholder books are closed to determine who the current stockholders are.

3. *Ex-Dividend Date.* The **ex-dividend date** (third column in the table) is an arbitrary date established for the convenience of the securities industry. It is the second business day (i.e., Monday through Friday) preceding the record date as fixed by the firm.

RECORD DATE
The date determined by a firm when the stockholder books are closed to determine who the current stockholders are.

EX-DIVIDEND DATE
The date set by the securities industry to determine who is entitled to receive a dividend; calculated as 2 business days before the record date.

Establishing this date enables the firm (or its *registrar,* which is usually a bank) to obtain an accurate determination of all stockholders by the record date. All shares owned *before* the ex-dividend date receive the cash dividend. Owners of stock purchased *on or after* the "ex day" will not be entitled to the next cash dividend, because they will not be listed as owners of record on the record date.

For the firm in our example, the first quarter's record date was February 14; accordingly, the ex day is February 11.[8] If you purchased the stock on or before

---

[8]*Note that in many cases a weekend will be involved, so the ex-dividend day is typically 2 to 4 calendar days preceding the record date.*

February 10, you would receive the dividend of 75 cents per share when it was paid on March 12. If you bought the stock on February 11, or any time thereafter, the former owner is entitled to the cash dividend paid on March 12.

4. *Payment Date.* The **payment date** is the date when the firm actually mails the dividend checks to its common stockholders.

Although the record date is important, the ex-dividend date is actually more important in terms of deciding who is the owner of the stock for dividend purposes. Because of its importance for determining who is entitled to the next cash dividend, we would expect to see an adjustment in the firm's common stock market price on the ex-dividend date. If you owned the stock in our example on the day before the ex date, you would receive 75 cents on the next pay date. Because you will be 75 cents better off and the firm will be 75 cents worse off, what should happen to the market price of the firm's common stock on the ex day? Other things being equal, it should decrease by an amount approximately equal to the value of the cash dividend to be received.

Dividend Reinvestment Plans

DIVIDEND REINVESTMENT PLAN
Plan in which stockholders can choose to have their cash dividends reinvested toward the purchase of additional shares of common stock.

In recent years many firms have instituted **dividend reinvestment plans.** Under these plans, stockholders can reinvest their cash dividends in additional shares of common stock. The stock can be existing or newly issued shares. Under one type of plan, a bank acting as trustee accumulates funds from all stockholders electing this option and then purchases shares in the open market. Costs are borne on a pro rata basis but are generally small because of the volume of purchases.

In a second type of plan the cash dividends go to buy newly issued shares of stock. In this plan, there may be a 3 to 5 percent reduction in the purchase price from the stock's current market price. Often no other fees are charged to the stockholders. A new-issue dividend reinvestment plan enables firms gradually to raise substantial amounts of new common stock capital. Over 500 firms listed on the New York and American Stock Exchanges had dividend reinvestment plans. It has been estimated that about 25 percent of all new common stock issued in recent years has been through dividend reinvestment plans. Due to their advantages, these plans have continued to grow in popularity.

By purchasing one share of stock investors can enroll in dividend reinvestment plans. Most plans allow voluntary cash contributions toward the purchase of additional shares.

Despite their growth in popularity, dividend reinvestment plans have one drawback from the stockholders' standpoint: Stockholders must pay taxes on the cash dividends each year, even though they never receive any cash. This factor, more than any other, has probably prevented more investors from signing up for dividend reinvestment plans.

Repurchasing Stock

In recent years many firms have entered into programs to repurchase some of their outstanding stock.

In addition to paying cash dividends, firms sometimes repurchase their stock and hold it as treasury stock. Repurchasing may be accomplished by a tender offer to all the firm's stockholders, by purchasing stock in the secondary market, or by agreeing with one or a small group of the firm's major investors to buy their shares. Many repurchases are small in amount; others are very large. With fewer shares outstanding after a repurchase, other things being equal, the earnings per share of the remaining shares will increase. This increase should result in a higher per share market price. For example, recently Philip Morris announced a substantial stock repurchase—and the market price of Philip Morris common stock immediately increased by about $3 per share.

To see how a stock repurchase works, let's consider Northern Airlines, which has earnings after taxes of $10 million. The firm plans to use 40 percent ($4 million) of its earnings after taxes for cash dividends or for repurchasing some of the firm's common stock. (Remember that neither usage affects the firm's reported net income nor the total market value of the firm.) There are 4 million shares outstanding, and the market price of the stock is $15 per share. Northern can use the $4 million to repurchase 250,000 shares of common stock at $16 per share, or it can pay a cash dividend of $1 per share.[9] The net effect of the repurchase would be as follows:

$$\text{current } EPS = \frac{\text{total earnings}}{\text{number of shares outstanding}} = \frac{\$10 \text{ million}}{4 \text{ million}} = \$2.50 \text{ per share}$$

$$\text{current } P/E = \frac{\text{market price per share}}{\text{earnings per share}} = \frac{\$15}{\$2.50} = 6 \text{ times}$$

$$EPS \text{ after repurchasing 250,000 shares} = \frac{\$10 \text{ million}}{3.75 \text{ million}} = \$2.667 \text{ per share}$$

$$\begin{array}{l}\text{expected market} \\ \text{price after repurchasing}\end{array} = (P/E)\,(EPS) = (6)\,(\$2.667) = \$16 \text{ per share}$$

From this example, we see that investors receive a $1 benefit either way. If cash dividends are paid, they receive the dollar directly; with the repurchase, the market price of the common stock increases by $1 to $16 per share. This occurs because we assumed that the shares would be repurchased at exactly $16 per share, and the *P/E* ratio remained constant. *If the firm pays less than $16, the remaining (or nonselling) investors are better off; if it pays more than $16, the remaining investors are worse off.*

Although this is a purely mechanical exercise so far, it serves to highlight some aspects of repurchasing. In fact, firms that repurchase their common stock *almost always repurchase shares while maintaining their current cash dividend policy.* With this background, it is now possible to consider some of the advantages and disadvantages of repurchasing.

Advantages of Stock Repurchases

From the firm's standpoint, there are a number of possible advantages to stock repurchases:

1. If a firm had a temporary excess of cash being generated but did not want to adjust its stated cash dividend policy, it might decide to repurchase some of its stock. This repurchase provides nonselling stockholders with an alternative form of a dividend.

---

[9] The $16 figure is chosen because it is the price at which nonselling investors are neither better nor worse off than selling investors.

2. By repurchasing, a firm may reduce its future cash dividend requirements or, alternatively, may raise the dividends per share paid to its remaining stockholders without increasing the total cash flow drain on the firm.

3. Repurchases can be used to effect an immediate and often large-scale change in the firm's capital structure. For example, if a firm previously had no debt and decided its target capital structure should include 20 percent debt, it could issue a bond and use the proceeds to repurchase common stock, thereby effecting the capital structure realignment.

4. Repurchasing can also be used to signal information about the firm's future cash flows. Only firms that expect substantial cash flows can confidently announce they will repurchase their stock.

Disadvantages of Stock Repurchases

From the firm's standpoint, some disadvantages may result from repurchasing its own shares:

1. In the past, firms that repurchased substantial amounts of stock often had poorer growth and investment opportunities than firms that did not. Announcing a repurchase program might signal to investors that good investment opportunities did not exist. This negative impact appears to have lessened in recent years as different

---

FINANCIAL MANAGEMENT TODAY

Stock Repurchase Programs

Stock repurchase, or buyback, agreements by U.S. firms are running at a record pace. In these agreements, most firms buy their shares on the open market, instead of through deals with specific investors. Rules set by the Securities and Exchange Commission restrict the times when firms can repurchase shares, and limit the volume of shares that can be repurchased on any day. Hence, there is little or no likelihood firms can use share repurchases to manipulate the price of their common stock.

However, in many countries, including Germany, such stock repurchases by firms are illegal. In Japan, the laws changed in 1995 to make the repurchase of shares legal. In the United States the repurchased shares are held as treasury stock, and sometimes used in the future to meet corporate needs for additional shares of stock for management or employee stock option programs or stock purchase plans. In Japan, however, the repurchased shares will have to be either canceled or sold to employees.

Recently some U.S. firms, including Intel and WMX Technologies, have added a new twist to their repurchase programs. They are using put options (discussed in Chapter 14), sold to investment bankers in conjunction with repurchase programs, to reduce the effective cost of the repurchases—providing the stock price stays steady or increases. If the stock price drops during the time the put option is out—a period of 3 months—the cost of the repurchases increases.

Since 1990 Intel has raked in $183 million extra from using put options in conjunction with buybacks. Both tax and accounting rules prohibit firms from treating premiums from stock-related transactions as earnings. Therefore, firms that use put options in conjunction with buybacks can record the transaction as a tax-free credit to both the cash and equity accounts on the firm's balance sheet. This technique is not for all firms, however. The key ingredient, aside from the predisposition of the firm and its management, is a volatile stock price. Volatility creates value for any option; therefore, only firms whose stock price tends to be volatile can benefit from the use of put options in conjunction with stock repurchases.

types of firms started viewing repurchases as an alternative to increasing their dividend payout ratio.

2. From a legal standpoint, the SEC may raise some questions for smaller or family-held firms if it appears the firm is using the repurchases to manipulate the price of its common stock. The Internal Revenue Service also may become interested, if it appears the repurchases are primarily for the avoidance of taxes on cash dividends. If this occurs, the IRS can impose penalties, because the firm's activities would fall under Section 531 of the tax code, which deals with improper accumulation of earnings.

On net, it appears that firms will continue to repurchase shares of their common stock. This is particularly true because repurchasing has gained favor as a means of attempting to fend off unwanted corporate suitors and as a means of "leveraging up" the firm's capital structure. Note, however, that by reducing the proportion of cash or marketable securities in a firm's asset structure, the firm may increase its risk composition. This increased risk, if it occurs, must be balanced against the benefits expected to be derived from the repurchase.

CONCEPT REVIEW QUESTIONS

■ Describe the dividend payment procedures of a firm.
■ Explain what a dividend reinvestment plan is.
■ What are some advantages and disadvantages of a stock repurchase?

STOCK SPLITS AND DIVIDENDS

Stock splits and dividends are more likely to occur after a firm's stock price has increased substantially. Thus, we see more stock splits and dividends during bull (upward) markets than during bear markets.

■ LEARNING GOAL 7

Explain the reasons for declaring stock splits and stock dividends.

In addition to paying cash dividends, and sometimes repurchasing their own outstanding common stock, firms often issue more shares via a stock split or a stock dividend. Stock splits and stock dividends have exactly the same effect from a financial standpoint. For accounting purposes, however, there are differences between a stock split and a stock dividend.

Stock Split

STOCK SPLIT
An action to increase the number of shares of common stock outstanding and simultaneously reduce their par value.

A **stock split** increases the number of shares of common stock and at the same time reduces their par value. The stockholders must approve increasing the number of shares of common stock. Then the accounting treatment for a stock split is straightforward: For a 2-for-1 split, for example, the number of shares of common stock is doubled and the par value is halved. For example, as shown in Table 13.4, Wilbur Industries had 1 million shares at a par value of $2 per share before the split. After the split, Wilbur had 2 million shares at a par of $1 per share.

Stock Dividend

By declaring a **stock dividend,** a company issues additional shares of common stock to its existing stockholders. With a stock dividend, the par value is not reduced, but an accounting entry is made to transfer capital from the retained earnings account to the common stock and additional paid-in capital accounts. The amount to be transferred is

TABLE 13.4

Effect of Stock Split or Stock Dividend on Wilbur Industries' Stockholders' Equity Accounts

In both cases, the total remains $7,000,000. However, a stock dividend involves capitalizing some of the firm's retained earnings by a transfer to the common stock and additional paid-in capital accounts.

Before Stock Split or Stock Dividend	
Common stock (1 million shares outstanding, $2 par)	$2,000,000
Additional paid-in capital	550,000
Retained earnings	4,450,000
Total stockholders' equity	$7,000,000

After 2-for-1 Stock Split	
Common stock (2 million shares outstanding, $1 par)	$2,000,000
Additional paid-in capital	550,000
Retained earnings	4,450,000
Total stockholders' equity	$7,000,000

After 10 Percent Stock Dividend	
Common stock (1.1 million shares outstanding, $2 par)*†	$2,200,000
Additional paid-in capital†	1,350,000
Retained earnings†	3,450,000
Total stockholders' equity	$7,000,000

* 100,000 shares are issued.
† Based on a market price of $10, ($2)(100,000 shares) = $200,000, which is added to the common stock. Likewise, ($10 − $2)(100,000 shares) = $800,000, which is added to the additional paid-in capital account. Retained earnings is reduced by $1,000,000 (i.e., $200,000 + $800,000).

STOCK DIVIDEND
The issuance of additional shares of common stock to existing stockholders; par value is not reduced, but an accounting entry transfers capital from the retained earnings to the common stock and paid-in capital accounts.

determined by the size of the stock dividend and the current market price of the firm's common stock. In our example, if Wilbur declared a 10 percent stock dividend, it would issue 100,000 (10 percent of 1,000,000 shares) more shares of stock. With a current market price of $10 per share, the transfer out of retained earnings would be $1,000,000. Finally, as also shown in Table 13.4, the common stock account would be increased by $200,000 [i.e., ($2 par)(100,000 shares)], and the remaining $800,000 would be added to the additional paid-in capital account. Note that for both a stock split and a stock dividend, Wilbur's total stockholders' equity would be $7 million both before and after the transaction.

Beware of False Gifts!

In the absence of any other simultaneous occurrence, the effects of a stock split or dividend can be summarized as follows:

1. There is no change in the firm's *total* assets, liabilities, stockholders' equity, earnings, cash dividends, or market value.

2. There is a drop in the *per share* earnings, cash dividends, and common stock market price, and a corresponding increase in the number of shares of common stock outstanding.

The consequence of a stock split or stock dividend is to increase the number of shares held by each investor. But each share is worth less, because nothing of value has been created. *The net effect would seem neither to increase nor to decrease* the total market value of the firm. To see this, consider the example of Wilbur Industries again. In Table 13.5 we see that before the split Wilbur had total earnings of $1,150,000, total

---

TABLE 13.5

Effect of 2-for-1 Stock Split on Both Wilbur Industries and an Individual Investor

There can be no benefit from a stock split unless it causes the total market value of the firm to increase. Stock dividends are similar.

Wilbur Industries	Investor

Before Stock Split

Total earnings $1,150,000	Owns 10,000 shares, which is
Total cash dividends $460,000	equal to 1 percent of total
Total shares outstanding 1,000,000	shares outstanding

$$EPS = \frac{\$1,150,000}{1,000,000} = \$1.15$$

$$DPS = \frac{\$460,000}{1,000,000} = \$0.46$$

Cash dividends received
= (10,000 shares)($0.46) = $4,600

$$\text{Dividend payout ratio} = \frac{\$0.46}{\$1.15} = 40\%$$

Market price per share = $10

Market value of stock
= (10,000 shares)($10) = $100,000

$$\text{Total market value, } S = (\$10)(1,000,000)$$
$$= \$10 \text{ million}$$

After Stock Split

Total earnings $1,150,000	Owns 20,000 shares, which is
Total cash dividends $460,000	equal to 1 percent of total
Total shares outstanding 2,000,000	shares outstanding

$$EPS = \frac{\$1,150,000}{2,000,000} = \$0.575$$

$$DPS = \frac{\$460,000}{2,000,000} = \$0.23$$

Cash dividends received
= (20,000 shares)($0.23) = $4,600

$$\text{Dividend payout ratio} = \frac{\$0.23}{\$0.575} = 40\%$$

Market price per share = $5

Market value of stock
= (20,000 shares)($5) = $100,000

$$\text{Total market value, } S = (\$5)(2,000,000)$$
$$= \$10 \text{ million}$$

cash dividends of $460,000, and with a stock price of $10 per share, a total market value of $10,000,000. After the 2-for-1 split, Wilbur still has earnings of $1,150,000, cash dividends of $460,000, and a total market value of $10,000,000. Likewise, as shown in Table 13.5, an investor owning 1 percent of Wilbur stock does not benefit directly from the stock split.[10]

Why Declare a Stock Split or Stock Dividend?

REVERSE SPLIT
An action to decrease the number of shares of common stock outstanding and simultaneously increase their par value.

In the absence of any value-creating activities, it would seem that not many companies would want to declare stock splits or stock dividends. As Table 13.6 shows, however, in all but 2 of the years from 1985 until 1994 over 1,000 companies every year declared one or the other. In addition to stock splits and stock dividends, firms sometimes announce reverse splits. A **reverse split** is just the opposite of a stock split. If a firm had 10,000 shares of stock outstanding selling at $5 per share, a 1-for-5 reverse split would reduce the number of shares to 2,000 and increase the market price to $25 per share.

There are a number of possible explanations as to why firms have stock splits and stock dividends. Some of these are:

1. Some firms declare a stock split or stock dividend at the same time as a cash dividend. They view this action as an extension of the firm's cash dividend policy. If the firm actually increases its total cash dividend payout, then stockholders are receiving more total cash dividends. Note, however, that the firm's dividend payout ratio could be increased without simultaneously declaring a stock split or stock dividend.

TABLE 13.6

Stock Splits, Reverse Splits, and Stock Dividends

These data are based on over 10,000 firms. Except for 1991 and 1992, 10 to 15 percent of the firms were involved in a stock split or stock dividend each year. A reverse split decreases the number of shares of common stock outstanding.

Year	Stock Splits	Reverse Stock Splits	Stock Dividends	Total
1985	516	84	763	1,363
1986	736	84	854	1,674
1987	602	128	791	1,521
1988	295	114	627	1,036
1989	408	182	610	1,200
1990	315	242	470	1,027
1991	285	267	344	896
1992	148	243	244	635
1993	528	333	482	1,343
1994	453	321	488	1,262

Source: Moody's Annual Dividend Record, various years.

---

[10] *If a stockholder is entitled to a fractional share, then the firm will pay cash in lieu of the fractional share. For example, if an investor holds 25 shares and a 10 percent stock dividend is declared, the stockholder would be entitled to 2.5 shares. If the market price of the stock is $30 per share, the stockholder would receive 2 full shares and $15 cash in lieu of the fractional share.*

2. Many firms apparently believe their stock has an optimal trading range. Perhaps this is between $20 and $50 per share. If the market price of the firm's common stock increases to, say, $70, the firm may declare a 2-for-1 split to drive down the price to about $35 per share. Implicit in this idea is that the total value of the firm will be more when it is in its "trading range" than when it is outside it.

3. A third possible reason for declaring stock splits or stock dividends involves the signaling idea discussed when we considered cash dividend policies. The essence of the argument is that firms declaring stock splits or dividends communicate, or signal, positive information about the firm's future cash flows over and above any existing information. Theoretical and empirical evidence lends support to this idea because the market value of a firm's stock tends, other things being equal, to increase when the firm has a stock split.

4. A final possible reason sometimes given is "to conserve the firm's cash." Firms in financial difficulty fairly frequently say they will declare the dividend in the form of stock *rather than* cash. By doing so the firms conserve cash, but stockholders are worse off. Stockholders suffer the loss of the cash dividend, and because the market value of each share of stock decreases proportionately as more shares are issued, the stockholders' total market value remains, at best, unchanged.

So why do firms continue to declare both stock dividends and stock splits? The answer appears to involve some elements of all the above. Although issuing additional shares of stock is much more expensive than issuing cash dividends, firms often use both stock splits and stock dividends to supplement their cash dividend policy and to signal positive information about the future cash flows of the firm.

CONCEPT REVIEW QUESTIONS

■ Describe the differences in accounting procedures between a stock split and a stock dividend.

■ Why do firms declare stock splits or stock dividends?

Summary

■ Firms pay out over 60 percent of earnings as cash dividends. The rate of increase in cash dividend payout exceeds the rate of inflation.

■ Under both the MM and residual dividend theories, the value of the firm is independent of the firm's cash dividend policy.

■ Tax impacts, in terms of differential tax rates on ordinary income versus capital gains, and the deferral option available with capital gains, may have only a small impact on a firm's dividend policy.

■ Firms with substantial growth options appear to adopt lower dividend payout ratios. Also, firms appear to signal future cash flows via their dividend policy.

■ In practice, firms act as if cash dividends are important. Most adopt a smoothed residual dividend policy. This policy includes maintaining a target payout ratio and a target capital structure.

■ Other things being equal, stock repurchases increase the earnings per share and market price of the remaining shares. It is an alternative way for the firm to pay "dividends" to its investors.

■ Neither stock splits nor stock dividends by themselves benefit stockholders. However, firms may signal future cash flow prospects with stock splits and stock dividends similar to signals given by cash dividends and stock repurchases.

Questions

Note: In 13.2, for some, the direction may not be clear.

13.1 Explain the trade-off between paying cash dividends and retaining internally generated funds.

13.2 How do you think the following conditions would affect dividend payout ratios, in general? Explain your answer.
   a. Interest rates fall.
   b. A reduction in the corporate tax rate is coupled with increased depreciation allowances for tax purposes.
   c. Taxes decrease for individuals.
   d. The firm is in a mature industry and faces intense foreign competition. It decides to meet the competition head on.
   e. The firm is repositioning itself into a new, young, growing industry.

13.3 Discuss the relationship among the dividend declaration date, the ex-dividend date, the record date, and the payment date. What should the market price do on the ex-dividend date? Why?

13.4 When a firm repurchases shares of stock to hold as treasury stock, the shares are not viewed as an asset, because they never show up on the left-hand (or asset) side of the firm's balance sheet. Why do firms pay money for them if they are not an asset? Are nonselling stockholders better or worse off after the firm repurchases shares? Explain.

13.5 Theoretically, investors should not benefit directly from a stock split or stock dividend.
   a. Explain fully why this is so.
   b. How would you react if an investor said her investment had a price of $50 before a 2-for-1 split, and a price of $28 after the split? Is the market still efficient?

Concept Review Problems

See Appendix A for solutions.

CR13.1 Westley Company has *EBT* of $50 million, a tax rate of 35 percent, and a debt/ total value ratio of 60 percent. The firm is interested in investing $25 million in profitable projects. If the firm wants to maintain its existing debt ratio, how large should Westley's dividend payout ratio be if its dividend policy is based on the residual dividend policy?

CR13.2 The accounts of Amwar Corporation are as follows:

Common stock ($1 par value)	$ 1,000
Additional paid-in capital	30,000
Retained earnings	50,000
Total equity	$81,000

   a. If Amwar's common stock is currently selling for $30 per share, what effect would a 10 percent stock dividend have on the firm's capital accounts?
   b. If the board of directors of Amwar declares a 4-for-1 stock split, what would happen to Amwar's capital accounts?

CR13.3 Voorhees Holdings has the following market-value-based balance sheet (in millions):

Current assets	$ 25		
Long-term assets	75		
Total assets	$100	Equity	$100

The company has 5 million shares of common stock outstanding, an *EPS* of $4, and it has declared a cash dividend of $1 per share. What are the firm's stock price and *P/E* ratio before the ex-dividend date? What are the stock price, *P/E* ratio, and total market value of equity after the ex-dividend date?

CR13.4 Assume Voorhees Holdings, in CR13.3, decides to repurchase $5 million of common stock (at $20 per share) rather than pay the $1 per share dividend. What would be the effect of the repurchase on the firm's market value of equity, stock price, and *P/E* ratio?

Problems

See Appendix C for answers to selected problems.

Residual Dividend Policy

13.1 Paolo Industries follows a residual cash dividend policy. For the next year, the firm expects to have internally generated funds of $1 million, profitable investment opportunities are $2 million, and the firm's target capital structure is 40 percent equity and 60 percent debt.

a. How much should Paolo pay out to its stockholders in cash dividends?

b. What if profitable investment opportunities are $3 million? If they are $1.5 million?

Residual Dividend Policy

13.2 Sarrazin International is considering seven average-risk capital expenditures as follows:

Capital Investment	CF_0	Internal Rate of Return
A	$200	25%
B	300	22
C	150	17
D	450	16
E	350	14
F	250	12
G	100	9

The firm's target capital structure is 30 percent debt and 70 percent equity. Sarrazin's opportunity cost of capital is 15 percent, and there is $1,200 available in internally generated funds that can be reinvested in the firm or paid out in the form of cash dividends.

a. Which capital budgeting projects should be accepted? If the firm follows a residual dividend policy, how much is available to be paid out in the form of cash dividends?

b. How does your answer change if Sarrazin's cost of capital is only 11 percent?

Dividend Preference

13.3 Ilyich just invested the same amount of money in two stocks, A and B, which have returns as follows:

	Dividends Expected, D_1	Dividends Expected, D_2	Capital Gain Expected When Sold at End of Year 2 (after receiving any cash dividend)
Stock A	$100	$100	$400
Stock B	0	0	600

Ilyich's required return is 10 percent, and he is in the 28 percent tax bracket for ordinary income.

a. Calculate the present value of his expected returns. Which stock provides higher returns? Why?

b. How much more would Ilyich have to receive from stock B to be indifferent between the two stocks?

Flotation Costs and Value

13.4 Medwick Steel has a current stock market value of $4 million. It has 1 million shares of stock outstanding and currently pays no cash dividends. Two dividend policies are under consideration: Plan I is to continue paying no cash dividends. Plan II involves selling $500,000 of new stock (with no flotation costs) and immediately paying the $500,000 to the existing (but not the new) stockholders. Because there are presently 1 million shares of common stock outstanding, every current stockholder would receive 50 cents per share in cash dividends. The new stock would have to be sold at $3.50 per share (the current market value of $4 million divided by the current 1 million shares, less the dividend of 50 cents).

Note: Ignore taxes.

a. How many shares will have to be issued to raise the $500,000? Compare the per share value of the current stockholders' holdings, taking into account both market price and dividends under Plan I versus Plan II.

b. Now assume that Medwick also has to incur flotation costs of 20 cents per share, so the new stock will sell at $3.30 per share. How many shares will now have to be issued to raise the $500,000? Compare the total per share value of the current stockholders' holdings for both plans now.

c. Comparing your answers to (a) and (b), what can you say about the impact of flotation costs on the dividend (and valuation) decision?

Dividend Extra

13.5 A firm has adopted a smoothed residual dividend policy. This is supplemented by declaring a dividend extra as follows:

a. Regular dividends paid out are presently 30 percent of earnings. The firm wants to keep its regular dividend payout at 30 percent and will increase the regular payout only when net income increases for 2 consecutive years.

Note: For the data given, this means that the regular cash dividend will not increase until time t = 4.

b. Once the regular dividend is increased, it remains at that level until it can be raised again (based on 2 consecutive years' increases in net income).

c. Each year the firm pays out a total of 40 percent of earnings by declaring an extra dividend. The size of the extra dividend is then the difference between the 30 percent payout policy and the 40 percent payout policy.

If the firm has earnings as follows, what are its regular and extra dividends per year?

$t = 1$	$t = 2$	$t = 3$	$t = 4$	$t = 5$	$t = 6$	$t = 7$	$t = 8$
$100	$100	$110	$140	$120	$160	$180	$220

Ex-Dividend Date

13.6 On March 1 (a Thursday), the board of directors of Selmore Enterprises met and declared a cash dividend of 50 cents per share, payable April 18 (a Wednesday) to stockholders of record March 22 (a Thursday).

a. If you were going to purchase some stock in Selmore and wanted to receive this cash dividend, by what date would the purchase have to be made?

b. Approximately how much should the market price of Selmore drop on the ex-dividend day?

c. What happens to the cash dividend if you already own the stock and the firm declares bankruptcy on March 12?

Stock Repurchase Price

13.7 A firm has 1,000,000 shares of common stock outstanding, selling at $90 per share. Its earnings after tax, *EAT*, is $6,000,000. Because it has excess cash, the firm has decided to buy back 200,000 shares of its common stock. However, because the excess cash has been invested in short-term marketable securities, the

EAT will decrease to $5,000,000 once the repurchase is completed. If we assume the *P/E* ratio remains the same after the repurchase as it is now, what is the price per share that should be offered so that both selling and nonselling stockholders are indifferent to the repurchase?

Repurchase of Common Stock

13.8 Meehan Drug has 50,000 shares of stock outstanding, total earnings of $600,000, and a market price per share of $96. It pays a cash dividend of $4 per share.

a. Determine the (1) total market value, (2) *EPS*, (3) *P/E* ratio, and (4) dividend payout ratio.

b. Patrick, who owns 2,000 shares, has expressed great displeasure with the management policies of Meehan Drug. Management has approached him with the idea of buying back his shares.

(1) If the firm offers Patrick $100 per share instead of paying a cash dividend of $4 per share, are the remaining stockholders better off, worse off, or the same? Assume that the *P/E* ratio remains the same.

(2) If after the repurchase the firm elects to pay the same *total* dollar amount out in the form of cash dividends, what happens to the dividends per share? What, if anything, happens to the dividend payout ratio?

Note: In (b3), assume that the firm spends more than $200,000, so it purchases all of Patrick's shares.

(3) Discuss, but do not work out, what the general effect would be on the remaining stockholders if Meehan Drug had to pay $125 per share to repurchase the shares from Patrick.

Accounting Treatment of Stock Split or Dividend

13.9 Silverspoon Industries lists the following on its annual report (dollars in thousands):

Common stock, $2.50 par; authorized, 6,000,000 shares; issued and outstanding, 3,589,970 shares	$ 8,975
Additional paid-in capital	2,239
Retained earnings	49,496
Total	$60,710

Note: In (a), assume that the authorized shares double to 12,000,000

a. What changes would occur if Silverspoon declared a 2-for-1 stock split?.

b. Independent of (a), what if Silverspoon declared a 20 percent stock dividend and the market price was $25 per share?

Stock Split: Effect on Firm and Investors

13.10 Willow Enterprises has 600,000 shares of common stock outstanding, and its *EPS* is $6. The firm has a dividend payout ratio of 20 percent and a current market price of $90 per share.

a. Before the split, what are Willow's (1) total earnings; (2) total cash dividends; (3) cash dividends per share; (4) total market value; and (5) *P/E* ratio?

b. Sam owns 50 shares of Willow. What are his (1) total cash dividends and (2) total market value?

Note: Assume that there are no signaling effects in (c) or (d).

c. Willow declares a 3-for-1 stock split. What are the new (1) total earnings; (2) *EPS*; (3) total cash dividends; (4) dividends per share; (5) dividend payout ratio; (6) *P/E* ratio; and (7) total market value?

d. After the split, what are Sam's total cash dividends and total market value?

e. Under what circumstances (if any) might an investor be better off after a stock split?

Stock Dividend

13.11 Rocha Distributors had a market price of $60 per share on September 1. On September 5, the firm announced a 20 percent stock dividend, payable October 20 to stockholders of record on September 30. You own 90 shares of Rocha.

a. What is the ex-dividend date?

b. If you sold your stock on September 20, what price would you receive? (Assume other things are equal and no brokerage costs.)

c. After the stock dividend, how many shares will you own?

d. What should be the market price per share, other things being equal, on September 28 if there are no signaling effects?

e. What is the total market value of your holdings both before and after the 20 percent stock dividend?

Dividend Policy

13.12 **Mini Case** SeniorCare is a 6-year-old firm that serves the fast-growing need for quality health care for those older than 50. Its target debt to total value ratio is 33 1/3 percent [i.e., for every $1 of debt the firm employs $2 of equity, so the debt/total value ratio is $1/($1 + $2)]. Up to this point in time, no cash dividends have been paid out. However, SeniorCare "went public" 3 years ago and now some investors are asking when the company will start paying cash dividends. There are 1 million shares of common stock outstanding.

a. What factors argue for the irrelevance of dividend policy? What factors argue for the relevance of dividend policy? That is, explain why you believe cash dividends do or do not affect the market price for the firm's common stock.

b. SeniorCare estimates that free cash flow available to be paid out in the form of cash dividends, to pay down debt, or to fund new capital investments is $2,000,000. It has the following set of independent capital investment opportunities available:

Project	Initial Investment	IRR
A	$ 200,000	50%
B	500,000	30
C	300,000	17
D	800,000	16
E	600,000	18
F	1,400,000	25
G	700,000	14
H	400,000	21

(1) If the firm's opportunity cost of capital is 20 percent and it follows a residual dividend policy, what should the firm do?

(2) What happens if everything is as in (1) except that SeniorCare initiates a policy of paying a cash dividend of $1.00 per share per year?

(3) What if in addition to the requirement in (2) the firm has a policy of not issuing any more debt?

Note: In (b1), with a target capital structure of 33 1/3 percent debt, to fund any new investment project the firm uses 1/3 debt and 2/3 equity financing. The $2,000,000 in free cash flow can, therefore, support $3,000,000 in new capital projects.

c. Assume now that the situation is as in (b2), except that the opportunity cost of capital is 15 percent and wealth-maximizing capital investments can be carried forward 1 year to time $t = 1$. If the free cash flow at $t = 1$ is estimated to be $2,400,000, the cash dividends are still $1.00 per share (and will be paid in each year), and the following additional capital projects exist (in addition to those carried forward), what decisions should be made?

Note: In (b2), assume SeniorCare still takes all wealth-maximizing projects and that it will not increase its debt/total value ratio. Also, the capital investment projects are not divisible; that is, partial projects may not be undertaken. Finally, any remaining funds can be invested at 10 percent.

Project	Initial Investment	IRR
I	$ 500,000	18%
J	300,000	35
K	1,000,000	22
L	800,000	12

d. If SeniorCare proceeds to start paying cash dividends, what sequence of events occurs? If investors are buying or selling the stock, how do they know whether they are entitled to receive a cash dividend or not?

e. What is a dividend reinvestment plan? What are the benefits to the firm? To shareholders? What tax consequences exist for shareholders?

f. One of the members of SeniorCare's board of directors recommends that the firm repurchase stock instead of paying cash dividends. Does this proposal make sense? Why or why not?

g. The same board member then suggests that instead of paying cash dividends, the firm pay the dividend in the form of additional shares of stock. Does this proposal make sense? Why or why not?

Leasing, Options, and Convertibles

Sections in this chapter:

■ **To Lease or Not to Lease?**
A question Hamlet might have asked if he had been in business.

■ **The Basics of Options**
Having an opportunity but not an obligation.

■ **What Determines the Value of an Option?**
You need to know what to look for to determine value.

■ **Warrants and Convertibles**
Financial products with option-like features.

BankAmerica sold its world headquarters complex in San Francisco and simultaneously leased back 60 percent of the space. The tower and two adjoining buildings had 1.8 million square feet and a depreciated book value of $80 million, but BankAmerica obtained a premium selling price—$660 million. Some real estate experts speculated that BankAmerica received that price by agreeing to pay inflated rents under the leaseback agreement. Leasing has become one of the primary sources of financing in the United States in recent years. While not all the decisions are as big or complex as BankAmerica's, it is estimated that more than 25 percent of the investment in new assets during the next 5 years will be financed with leases.

At the same time, the corporate use of derivatives has exploded in recent years. Derivatives get their name from the fact that their value is derived from some underlying asset, like a stock, a bond, oil, or the like. Derivatives are increasingly being employed to hedge risks and sometimes for speculation leading to profits or losses for firms. Although many firms are extremely satisfied with the results, disasters can happen. In 1994 Procter & Gamble reported it lost $102 million on two derivative transactions called interest rate swaps; Ashland Oil reported a $60 million loss from using similar derivative products. That same year the Japanese firm Kashima Oil reported $1.5 billion of unrealized losses in some forward-future-exchange contracts. And a German firm, Metallgellschaft, lost $1.4 billion on oil derivatives.

Other securities also exist, called convertible securities, that have elements of derivatives. Because of the stories about losses from derivatives, and the increasing risk derivatives create for investment bankers and commercial banks, some are calling for increased supervision of such securities. Whether they need additional supervision or not, most in the financial community believe that the benefits of derivatives far outweigh the costs.

There are many other forms of financing employed by firms. In this chapter we begin by examining how firms make the decision to lease rather than purchase assets. Then we consider options and how they are valued. Based on the ideas developed from options we then consider two other forms of financing employed by firms—warrants and convertible securities.

LEARNING GOALS

After studying this chapter you should be able to:

1. Determine the net present value of a leased asset, and discuss international leasing.
2. Understand basic option terminology, and determine the value of a call option at expiration.
3. Describe the factors that affect the value of an option, and determine the value of an option before expiration.
4. Discuss the option-like features of warrants and convertibles, why firms issue these securities, and how the value of a convertible is determined.

TO LEASE OR NOT TO LEASE?

■ **LEARNING GOAL 1**

Determine the net present value of a leased asset, and discuss international leasing.

LEASE
A rental agreement whereby the lessee obtains the use of an asset in exchange for fixed payments to the lessor.

It has been estimated that 20 to 25 percent of the assets employed by firms are rented via a **lease.** In fact, in recent years the amount of leasing has increased. What caused this increase? Rapidly changing economic conditions, deregulation, and growing international competition are factors. In addition, many lessors are increasingly providing shorter-term leases with greater flexibility and offering full leasing packages that include maintenance, insurance, and perhaps even personnel. The lessors are becoming asset managers, not just financiers.

Consider Ryder Truck, which is the largest full-service truck lessor in the world. They see a clear trend toward providing the entire distribution system for firms. To meet this need they provide a dedicated contract carriage, which includes drivers, labor management, and a distribution system as well as the trucks. In cases such as this, Ryder estimates that the equipment represents only 25 percent of the total dollars involved. Thus, Ryder's philosophy can be summarized as follows: "We're going to help companies assess their overall logistical needs and offer our resources to help them meet those needs in whatever way is most cost effective."

LESSOR
The owner of an asset that is leased to someone else.

LESSEE
The user of a leased asset.

The owner of the property, such as Ryder Truck in the above example, is the **lessor,** who leases it to the user, or the **lessee.** Virtually anything that is needed by the firm—machinery, buildings, warehouses, airplanes, computers, ships, and so forth—can be leased. The reasons for leasing are varied: tax deductibility, flexibility and convenience, and (depending on the lease agreement) the option to cancel the lease when the asset is no longer needed. In addition, when lessors, such as Ryder Truck, provide value-added services such as maintenance, insurance, and so forth, lessees are able to focus their primary attention on their businesses, not the maintenance of assets. Our focus in studying leases is from the standpoint of the lessee, or the user of the asset.

Remember Key Idea 1—the goal of the firm is to maximize its market value.

When a firm makes a capital budgeting decision concerning the possible acquisition of an asset (as discussed in Chapters 7–9), it calculates the net present value of the proposed project. If the capital budgeting *NPV* is positive, then the asset should be acquired because it assists in maximizing the value of the firm. *Capital budgeting im-*

NET PRESENT VALUE OF LEASED ASSET, NPV_{lease}
The cost of an asset minus the present value of after-tax lease payments and forgone depreciation tax shield.

plicitly assumes that assets to be acquired will be purchased. If leasing is a strong possibility, however, then the basic capital budgeting decision must be supplemented by further analysis to determine whether the asset should be leased or purchased. To make this supplemental financing decision the **net present value of leasing, NPV_{lease},** is calculated.[1] If the net present value from leasing is positive, then the asset should be acquired by leasing; otherwise, it should be purchased.[2] It should be stressed that, as throughout the book, our perspective is that of making a *financial decision*; we are not concerned about how accountants decide whether a lease should be capitalized and recorded on the firm's balance sheet.

Evaluation of Leases

Remember Key Ideas 4 and 5—firms focus on cash flows and their incremental effects, and a dollar today is worth more than a dollar tomorrow.

To evaluate whether leasing is preferred to purchasing, it is necessary to make an assumption about the mode of financing that would be employed if the asset were purchased. Leasing imposes the same kind of financial commitment on the firm that borrowing does. Thus, the relevant standard of comparison to use when evaluating leasing is to compare it with purchasing the asset and financing the capital needs via borrowing. We are interested in neutralizing the risk between the two alternatives. The way to accomplish this is by establishing an equivalent borrowing amount that, in terms of the after-tax cash flows in each future period, is exactly the same as the after-tax lease cash flows. Risk neutralization is accomplished by employing the after-tax cost of debt capital, or the borrowing rate, of the lessee as the discount rate in the NPV_{lease}. The lessee's after-tax cost of debt capital, k_i, is equal to $k_b(1 - T)$, where k_b is the lessee's before-tax borrowing rate and T is the firm's marginal tax rate.

A lease is evaluated in terms of the after-tax cash flows and opportunity costs incurred by leasing rather than purchasing the asset. The major elements of the decision are these:

1. The lease payments, L, made periodically by the lessee on an after-tax basis. *In line with industry practice, we assume the first payment occurs at the time the lease is signed, time $t = 0$.*
2. The depreciation tax shield, calculated by multiplying the annual IRS depreciation by the lessee's marginal tax rate. By entering into a lease, the firm incurs an opportunity cost equal to the forgone depreciation tax shield.
3. The cost of the leased asset, CLA_0.

Employing these variables in an incremental framework, the net present value of leasing is calculated as follows:

$$NPV_{lease} = \begin{matrix} \text{cost of} \\ \text{leased asset} \end{matrix} - \left(\begin{matrix} \text{present value of} \\ \text{the lease payments} \end{matrix} + \begin{matrix} \text{present value of the forgone} \\ \text{depreciation tax shield} \end{matrix} \right)$$

$$NPV_{lease} = CLA_0 - \left\{ \left[\sum_{t=1}^{n} \frac{L_t(1-T)}{(1+k_i)^t} \right](1+k_i) + \sum_{t=1}^{n} \frac{Dep_t(T)}{(1+k_i)^t} \right\} \qquad (14.1)$$

Because the lease payments, L, are an annuity due, the term $(1 + k_i)$ converts them from an ordinary annuity to an annuity due. The NPV_{lease} simply finds the cost of

---

[1] *The net present value from leasing versus purchasing is sometimes called the net advantage of leasing,* NAL. *The internal rate of return,* IRR, *could also be employed to make the lease-versus-purchase decision.*
[2] *More extensive treatment of leasing is provided in Chapter 18 of* Financial Management.

leasing the asset (the part of Equation 14.1 in braces, which includes both explicit and opportunity costs) versus the cost of the asset (represented by CLA_0). As long as the cost of leasing is less than the cost of the asset, Equation 14.1 will be positive and the asset should be leased.

To illustrate lease evaluation, look at SolarSound, which is considering whether to lease or purchase some specialized equipment. Because the capital budgeting analysis indicating the equipment should be secured has already been completed, the question is whether to lease or purchase the equipment. The equipment has a 5-year economic and tax life, and straight-line depreciation will be employed for tax purposes.[3] (The half-year convention is ignored in determining the per year depreciation.) The equipment's resale value is zero, the marginal tax rate is 40 percent, and the firm's before-tax cost of borrowing is 12 percent. The equipment costs $40,000 if purchased, or it can be leased for 5 years at $10,000 per year. The first lease payment is payable in advance.

To determine how to finance the equipment, the first step SolarSound undertakes is to calculate its after-tax cost of debt, k_i, which is the discount rate employed in Equation 14.1. Because k_b is 11.67 percent and the marginal tax rate is 40 percent, $k_i = k_b(1 - T) = 11.67\%(1 - 0.40) \approx 7.00$ percent. This is the discount rate that neutralizes the risk in terms of the after-tax cash flows under the two financing methods, and it should be used in the NPV_{lease} analysis as follows:

$$NPV_{\text{lease}} = CLA_0 - \left\{ \left[\sum_{t=1}^{n} \frac{L_t(1-T)}{(1+k_i)^t} \right](1+k_i) + \sum_{t=1}^{n} \frac{Dep_t(T)}{(1+k_i)^t} \right\}$$

$$= \$40,000 - \left\{ \left[\sum_{t=1}^{5} \frac{\$10,000(1-0.40)}{(1.07)^t} \right](1.07) + \sum_{t=1}^{5} \frac{\$8,000(0.40)}{(1.07)^t} \right\}$$

$$= \$40,000 - (\$26,323 + \$13,121) = \$556$$

Because the net present value of leasing versus purchasing is positive, SolarSound should lease the assets.[4]

Some Complications

Using the NPV_{lease} approach the leasing decision is straightforward. In addition, it is practical to employ and theoretically correct, because it focuses on which means of financing is most consistent with the firm's goal. Complications often encountered in practice can be readily incorporated into the analysis. Two primary complications often occur in making the comparison of leasing versus purchasing—incremental operating costs, O_t, and the estimated resale value, RV_n, if the asset is purchased. With these complications the NPV_{lease} equation becomes:

$$NPV_{\text{lease}} = CLA_0 - \left\{ \left[\sum_{t=1}^{n} \frac{L_t(1-T)}{(1+k_i)^t} \right](1+k_i) + \sum_{t=1}^{n} \frac{Dep_t(T)}{(1+k_i)^t} \right.$$

$$\left. - \sum_{t=1}^{n} \frac{O_t(1-T)}{(1+k)^t} + \frac{RV_n(1-T)}{(1+k)^n} \right\} \tag{14.2}$$

---

[3] *Remember that for tax purposes all assets are depreciated to zero over their normal recovery period.*
[4] *If present value tables are employed the* NPV_{lease} *is* $\$40,000 - [(\$10,000)(0.60)(4.100)(1.07) + (\$8,000)(0.40)(4.100)] = \$40,000 - (\$26,322 + \$13,120) = \$558.$

FINANCIAL MANAGEMENT TODAY

Automobile Financing Incentives

From time to time automobile firms offer incentives to spur sales. The current one provided by General Motors, which would apply to a $12,000 loan you, the buyer, are considering, provides for 2.9 percent financing with a 36-month loan. Alternatively, a rebate of $1,000 is available. If you take the rebate you would have to finance the remaining $11,000 (i.e., $12,000 − $1,000) at an interest rate of 10 percent for 36 months. Which incentive is worth more to you?

If you take the 2.9 percent financing, your loan payment for each of the 36 months would be:

$$PV_0 = PMT \sum_{t=1}^{n} \frac{1}{(1+k)^t}$$

$$\$12,000 = PMT \sum_{t=1}^{36} \frac{1}{[1+(0.029/12)]^t}$$

Rearranging and solving for the *PMT* using a financial calculator results in a payment of $348.45 per month.

With the rebate, your loan payment per month would be:

$$\$11,000 = PMT \sum_{t=1}^{36} \frac{1}{[1+(0.10/12)]^t}$$

which, via a financial calculator, is $354.94 per month. You would be better off by $6.49 (i.e., $354.94 − $348.45) each month with the 2.9 percent financing.

The appropriate opportunity cost of capital for the asset in question, k, is employed for discounting the incremental operating expenses and resale value, because risk neutralization does not extend to these items. If the assets' risk is equal to the average firm risk, then k is the firm's opportunity cost of capital.[5]

Leasing in an International Context

Leasing can be employed internationally to gain flexibility, defer or avoid taxes, and safeguard assets. For these reasons, leasing is an important part of the financing strategy for many multinational firms. For example, consider what happened in the airline industry a few years ago. With deregulation and greater opportunities for carriers to operate in many countries, airlines needed more planes suited to their specific requirements. But new aircraft were back-ordered up to 7 years in some cases. To have the flexibility to take advantage of opportunities, many airlines leased planes through operating leases. Lessors had taken the standard lease and adopted it to the commercial airline industry. Demand for leases was brisk because it provided airlines the flexibility to commit to new routes or increased service within a much shorter time frame than if they had to wait for delivery of new planes.

Leasing in the international arena also may have a substantial tax advantage through "double dipping." With a lease that is set up to double dip, the different leasing rules of the lessor's and lessee's countries let *both parties* be treated as the owner

---

[5] *These topics are examined in Problems 14.4 and 14.5.*

of the asset. Thus, both the lessor and the lessee are entitled to the depreciation tax benefits. This type of leasing results in higher returns for lessors and lower effective lease rates for lessees.

Double dipping is often achieved when the lessees are based in countries that examine the *economic reality* of the arrangement (such as Germany, Japan, and the United States) and the lessors are located in countries that simply look at the *legal ownership* of the lease (such as France, Great Britain, or Switzerland). The key is what is considered an operating lease versus what is considered a finance lease. By structuring the lease to take advantage of intercountry differences, savings result that benefit both the lessor and the lessee.

Leasing can also be used to limit the ownership of assets by subsidiaries in unstable countries. In the event of nationalization, the multinational parent often has more chance of recovering or receiving some compensation for assets taken over if they are not owned by the local subsidiary. Also, lease payments are sometimes treated differently from dividends, interest, or royalty payments. In these cases leasing is also beneficial to deal with the exchange controls that would make other means of bringing funds out of the host country unsatisfactory.

In addition to leasing many of their assets, some firms employ other types of financing not discussed previously. A few firms issue warrants, while substantially more employ convertible securities. Before considering warrants and convertible securities, we need to examine some of the underlying ideas of options, because they will help us understand warrants and convertibles.

CONCEPT REVIEW QUESTIONS

- What decision are we considering when leases are evaluated?
- Explain why the after-tax cost of debt is employed as the discount rate in determining NPV_{lease}.

THE BASICS OF OPTIONS

■ LEARNING GOAL 2

Understand basic option terminology, and determine the value of a call option at expiration.

Option trading is a specialized business and its participants speak a language all their own. Why, then, should we be interested in options? The answer is that financial managers routinely come in contact with decisions or securities that have options embedded in them. Our objective in this section is to develop an understanding of what options are all about, in order to see that owning equity in a firm is just like owning a call option on the assets of the firm.[6]

Remember Key Idea 7— options are valuable.

An *option* provides its owner with the right, but not the obligation, to buy or sell a particular good for a limited time at a specified price. The most familiar options are stock options—options to buy or sell shares of common stock. The development of options has been a major financial success story. Since they were first developed and traded on the Chicago Board Options Exchange, CBOE, in 1973, options have grown

---

[6] *Options and their valuation are discussed in more detail in Chapter 5 of* Financial Management.

to become one of the biggest financial markets in the world. Option trading now takes place on a number of exchanges, both in the United States and around the world. In addition to options on common stock, there are also options on stock indices, bonds, commodities, futures, and foreign exchange rates.

Some of the major U.S. options exchanges and the options traded on them are the following:

Chicago Board Options Exchange
 Individual stocks
 General stock market indices
 Treasury bonds
American Exchange
 Individual stocks
 General stock market indices
 Oil and gas index
 Transportation index
 Treasury bills
 Treasury notes
Philadelphia Exchange
 Individual stocks
 Foreign currencies
 Gold and silver indices

New options are introduced over time, and some options change as the market for them changes. When options on stocks were first introduced, for example, they were relatively short-term in nature; the longest maturity was less than 6 months. That market still exists, but in the last few years longer-term options, with maturities of up to 3 years, have begun being traded on major option exchanges.[7]

In order to discuss options we need to understand certain basic terms. These include:

1. *Call Option Versus Put Option.* A **call option** provides the owner of the option with the right, but not the obligation, to buy the underlying asset. Conversely, a **put option** provides the owner with the right, but not the obligation, to sell the asset. Since this is a financial management text, not an investments or options text, our primary focus is restricted to call options.
2. *Exercise Price (or Strike Price).* The fixed price stated in the option contract at which the underlying asset may be purchased or sold is the **exercise** (or **strike**) **price.**
3. *Expiration Date or Maturity.* The maturity date is when the option expires. After this date the option is worthless.
4. *Exercising an Option.* The act of buying or selling the underlying asset via an option contract is called exercising the option.
5. *American Option Versus European Option.* An **American option** may be exercised at any time up to and including the expiration date. On the other hand, a **European option** can be exercised only at the expiration date. Our discussion will be restricted to European options.

CALL OPTION
The right, but not the obligation, to buy an asset at a stated price within a specified time period.

PUT OPTION
The right, but not the obligation, to sell an asset at a stated price within a specified time period.

EXERCISE (STRIKE) PRICE
Price at which the owner of an option can buy or sell the underlying asset.

AMERICAN OPTION
A call or put option that can be exercised at any time up to its expiration date.

EUROPEAN OPTION
A call or put option that can be exercised only at its expiration date.

---

[7] *These long-term options are referred to as "leaps" in* The Wall Street Journal.

A Look at Options on Stocks

LONG POSITION
Owning an option contract or other financial asset.

SHORT POSITION
Selling an option contract or promising to deliver a financial asset at some time in the future.

IN-THE-MONEY
Option that is worth converting at the asset's current market price: A call option for which the market price is greater than the exercise price, or a put option for which the market price is less than the exercise price.

OUT-OF-THE-MONEY
Option that is not worth converting at the asset's current market price: A call option for which the market price is less than the exercise price, or a put option for which the market price is greater than the exercise price.

If you picked up *The Wall Street Journal* and looked at the listed options quotations, you would see information like that shown in Table 14.1. Let's examine what information is provided for options on the common stock of AT&T—American Telephone & Telegraph Company. The first column lists the firm, AT&T, followed by the *closing market price* (or last price of the day) for a share of AT&T common stock. The closing price for AT&T common stock was $49 1/8 per share. The second column lists the *exercise (or strike) prices* available. These exercise prices are set fairly close to the prevailing market price of the stock. For volatile stocks, more exercise prices will be available. Likewise, as the stock price changes, new exercise prices are opened for trading, at $5 intervals. Each contract is written for 100 shares, but the option prices are quoted per share. Upon purchase of an option, an investor would have the right, but not the obligation, to purchase (a call option) or sell (a put option) 100 shares of AT&T at the exercise (or strike) price.

The third column indicates the month the option expires. The fourth and fifth columns indicate the *volume* (or number of options traded) and the *last* (or closing) price for various call options on AT&T. Finally, the sixth and seventh columns indicate the *volume* and *last* price for put options. If you purchased the July call option on AT&T with a strike price of $45, you would pay (100 shares)($6) = $600, plus any commission fee. Once you own the call option, you can exercise it by paying (100 shares)($45) = $4,500. The writer of the option is obligated to sell you 100 shares at $45 per share, providing you exercise the option on the expiration date.

Before proceeding it is helpful to consider a few other terms often employed when options are being discussed. The buyer of an option contract has purchased the option and has a **long position,** or holds the contract long. On the other hand, the seller, or writer, of an option contract has a **short position,** or has sold the option. It should be noted that investors "create," or write, stock options. Thus, the options on AT&T common stock were created by investors, not by AT&T.

One often hears that an option is **in-the-money.** An option is in-the-money if by exercising the option it would produce a gain. A call option is in-the-money if the market price of the stock, P_0, is *greater* than the exercise price, X. Conversely, a put option is in-the-money if the market price of the stock, P_0, is *less* than the exercise price, X. On the other hand, an option can be **out-of-the-money.** An option is out-of-the-money if by exercising the option it would produce a loss. A call option is out-of-the-money if the market price of the stock, P_0, is less than the exercise price, X, while a put option is out-of-the-money if P_0 is greater than X.

Value of a Call Option at Expiration

The right to buy AT&T common stock at a specific exercise price as indicated in the call option is valuable. How valuable the option is depends on five specific factors, which we will discuss shortly. Before moving on, let's examine the value of a call option at one specific point in time—*at the date of expiration.*

For simplicity, we will restrict our discussion to European options—that is, options that can be exercised only at their maturity date. The value of a call option on the expiration date can be summarized as follows:

Condition	Value of Call Option
If market price of stock is greater than the exercise price	= market price − exercise price of the stock
If market price is less than the exercise price	= 0

TABLE 14.1

Information on Options from *The Wall Street Journal*

The closing market price of the underlying common stock is listed under the firm's name. This is followed by the strike (or exercise) price, the expiration date, and then the volume (or number of 100-share units traded) and last (or closing) price for both call and put options.

LISTED OPTIONS QUOTATIONS

Wednesday, November 30, 1994

Composite volume and close for actively traded equity and LEAPS, or long-term options, with results for the corresponding put or call contract. Volume figures are unofficial. Open interest is total outstanding for all exchanges and reflects previous trading day. Close when possible is shown for the underlying stock on primary market. **CB**-Chicago Board Options Exchange. **AM**-American Stock Exchange. **PB**-Philadelphia Stock Exchange. **PC**-Pacific Stock Exchange. **NY**-New York Stock Exchange. **XC**-Composite. **p**-Put.

MOST ACTIVE CONTRACTS

Option/Strike				Vol	Exch	Last		Net Chg	a-Close	Open Int
Intel	Dec	65	p	9,506	AM	2 13/16	+	1 5/8	63 1/8	6,525
TelMex	Dec	55		8,422	XC	3/4	−	7/16	53	20,957
I B M	Dec	70		4,147	CB	2	+	1/16	70 3/4	9,205
MicrTc	Dec	40	p	3,641	XC	15/16	+	1/16	41 1/2	3,238
TelMex	Jan	55		3,413	XC	1 13/16	−	3/4	53	44,411
ColHsp	Jan	40		3,371	XC	11/16	+	1/16	37 7/8	54
I B M	Dec	70	p	3,327	CB	1 1/8	+	1/16	70 3/4	8,858
Lotus	Dec	45		3,311	AM	2	+	1	44 3/4	1,512
Intel	Dec	65		3,021	AM	3/4	−	1 1/8	63 1/8	10,197
Signet	Jan	25		3,000	XC	5 3/8		...	29 7/8	...
MicrTc	Dec	45		2,978	XC	5/8		...	41 1/2	4,891
TelMex	Jan	60		2,971	XC	9/16	−	1/4	53	37,319
TelMex	Dec	50	p	2,932	XC	7/16	+	1/16	53	14,358
Compaq	Dec	40	p	2,854	PC	1 5/8	+	9/16	39 1/8	9,129
US Bio	Dec	7 1/2	p	2,811	AM	13/16	−	1/16	8 1/8	3,777
TelMex	Dec	55	p	2,665	XC	2 3/4	+	13/16	53	7,520
Ph Mor	Dec	60		2,652	AM	3/4	−	1/2	59 3/4	17,610
Amgen	Dec	60		2,648	AM	1	+	5/16	58 3/8	4,353
TelMex	Dec	50		2,587	XC	3 3/8	−	1	53	6,441
ArmWl	Jan	35		2,500	PB	5 3/8		...	40	...
TelMex	Dec	60		2,393	XC	1/16	−	1/16	53	18,546
Oracle	Dec	45		2,298	CB	1/4	−	1/4	41 1/4	9,068
Novell	Dec	20		2,270	AM	3/4	−	1/4	19 7/8	10,128
Lilly	Dec	70		2,260	AM	5/8	+	3/16	62 5/8	6,113
Marion	Dec	25		2,248	PC	1/2	−	7/16	22 1/2	21,673
Lotus	Dec	40		2,237	AM	5 1/4	+	2 1/4	44 3/4	2,549
Compaq	Dec	45		2,230	PC	1/16	−	1/16	39 1/8	4,560
Compaq	Dec	40		2,165	PC	15/16	−	7/16	39 1/8	11,439
Intel	Dec	60	p	2,130	AM	5/8	+	3/8	63 1/8	5,711
Chryslr	Dec	45		2,092	CB	3 3/4	+	7/8	48 3/8	1,522
Marion	Dec	30		2,078	PC	1/16	−	1/8	22 1/2	15,776
MicrTc	Jan	45		1,966	XC	1 1/2	−	1/4	41 1/2	5,942
Lilly	Dec	65		1,957	AM	1 7/16	+	7/16	62 5/8	7,161
Amgen	Dec	55		1,931	AM	3 7/8	+	1/2	58 3/8	4,501
AplMat	Dec	50		1,905	PC	1	−	2 3/4	47 7/8	5,838
Chryslr	Dec	50		1,904	CB	3/4	+	1/4	48 3/8	11,557
Motrla	Dec	60		1,835	AM	7/16	−	1/16	56 3/8	16,618
ABrrck	Jan	22 1/2		1,775	AM	9/16	−	1/4	20 7/8	5,069
Lilly	Jan	65		1,712	AM	2 11/16	+	9/16	62 5/8	5,165
Merck	Jan	40		1,707	CB	7/16		...	37 1/4	36,658

Option/Strike		Exp.	Call Vol.	Call Last	Put Vol.	Put Last
ADC Tel	45	Dec	52	13/16	3	3 1/2
AFLAC	35	Feb	30	1 3/16	...	...
33 7/8	40	Feb	30	5/16	...	...
A M R	50	Dec	60	1 1/2	...	...
50 3/4	50	May	...	...	23	3
50 3/4	55	Dec	40	3/16	...	...
50 3/4	60	May	130	1 3/8	...	...
A S A	40	Dec	...	...	30	1/8
43 5/8	45	Dec	154	7/16	30	1 11/16
43 5/8	45	Jan	35	1 3/16	62	2 1/8
43 5/8	45	Feb	92	1 5/8	39	2 3/4
43 5/8	50	Jan	20	5/16	23	6 1/4
43 5/8	50	Feb	111	5/16	9	6 5/8
43 5/8	50	May	64	1 3/16	...	...
43 5/8	55	Jan	109	1/16	...	...
43 5/8	55	Feb	49	3/16	...	...
AST Rs	12 1/2	Dec	31	2 1/2	...	...
15 1/8	12 1/2	Feb	4	3	75	1/2
15 1/8	15	Dec	305	11/16	...	...
15 1/8	15	Jan	135	1 1/16	...	...
15 1/8	15	Feb	25	1 1/2	70	1 1/8
15 1/8	15	May	136	2 3/8	10	1 13/16
15 1/8	17 1/2	Feb	120	1/2	30	3 1/4
AT&T	45	Jan	25	4 5/8	2	7/16
49 1/8	45	Apr	12	5 3/4	60	3/4
49 1/8	45	Jul	10	6	49	1 1/8
49 1/8	50	Dec	333	3/4	100	1
49 1/8	50	Jan	578	1 1/4	130	1 7/8
49 1/8	50	Apr	483	2 3/8	86	2 1/2
49 1/8	50	Jul	22	3 3/8	50	2 3/4
49 1/8	55	Jan	858	3/16	54	6
49 1/8	55	Apr	254	3/4	5	6
49 1/8	55	Jul	113	1 5/16	...	...
AbbeyH	15	Dec	125	8 3/4	...	...
23 1/2	25	May	600	2 1/8	...	...
Abbt L	30	Dec	70	2 1/4	155	3/16
31 7/8	30	Jan	71	2 7/8	650	1/2
31 7/8	35	May	412	1	...	...
Aclaim	15	Jan	495	1 1/2	68	15/16
15 5/8	17 1/2	Dec	40	3/16	10	1 15/16
15 5/8	17 1/2	Jan	130	5/8	10	2 11/16
15 5/8	17 1/2	Apr	46	1 1/4	...	...
15 5/8	20	Jan	24	5/16	...	...
A M D	10	Jan	40	15 1/2	...	...
25 1/4	20	Jan	100	5 3/8	...	...
25 1/4	25	Dec	285	1	10	3/4
25 1/4	25	Jan	360	1 7/8	55	1 1/4
25 1/4	30	Jan	55	5/16	32	4 3/4
25 1/4	30	Apr	49	1 1/8	10	5 3/8
BanySy	20	Jan	23	1	...	...
BarNbl	30	Jan	30	9/16	...	...
Barnet	40	Dec	...	...	50	1 3/16
39 3/8	40	Jan	...	...	60	1 3/4
BattlM	10	Dec	30	1/8	...	...
9 1/2	10	Jan	30	7/16	32	3/4
9 1/2	10	Apr	76	7/8	...	...
9 1/2	10	Jul	35	1 1/8	33	1 3/16
9 1/2	12 1/2	Jan	118	1/8	9	3
9 1/2	12 1/2	Apr	66	3/8	5	3
BausLm	35	Jan	110	7/8	110	2
Baxter	25	May	5	2 3/16	30	1 1/2
BayNtw	20	Jan	100	6 1/4	3	1/4
25 3/4	20	Mar	21	6 3/4	500	11/16
25 3/4	22 1/2	Mar	560	5 1/4	...	...
25 3/4	25	Dec	526	1 3/8	22	5/8
25 3/4	25	Jan	109	2 3/8	114	1 1/2
25 3/4	25	Mar	180	3 5/8	15	2 1/2
25 3/4	30	Dec	82	3/16	...	...
25 3/4	30	Jan	241	9/16	...	...
BedBth	25	Feb	...	...	50	7/8
BergBr	20	Dec	42	5/16	...	...
BestBuy	25	Dec	391	20	...	...
44 1/8	25	Mar	401	20 1/2	...	...
44 1/8	30	Dec	24	14 1/8	...	...
44 1/8	32 1/2	Jan	...	...	115	1/4
44 1/8	35	Dec	125	9 1/8	200	1/16
44 1/8	35	Jan	21	9 3/4	145	1/2
44 1/8	40	Dec	483	4 3/4	866	9/16
44 1/8	40	Jan	330	6	380	1 5/8
44 1/8	40	Mar	30	7 5/8	23	2 1/4
44 1/8	45	Dec	1660	1 3/8	355	2 1/4
44 1/8	45	Jan	201	2 7/8	104	3 1/2
44 1/8	45	Mar	83	4 3/8	12	4 1/2
44 1/8	45	Jun	32	6 1/2	...	...
44 1/8	50	Dec	140	1/4	28	6
44 1/8	50	Jan	221	1 5/16	37	6 3/8
Beth S	17 1/2	Jan	10	1	25	1
17 3/4	20	Jan	17	1/4	25	2 3/4
17 3/4	20	Apr	...	...	125	2 3/4
Bevrly	15	Jun	50	1 1/2	...	...
Biogen	35	Dec	285	4 1/4	262	3/8
38 3/4	35	Jan	70	5 7/8	31	1 1/4
38 3/4	35	Apr	50	7 5/8	10	2 5/16
38 3/4	40	Dec	628	1 1/8	158	2 1/8
38 3/4	40	Jan	408	2 3/8	30	3
38 3/4	40	Jul	60	6 3/8	...	...
38 3/4	45	Jan	26	1 1/8	...	...
38 3/4	45	Apr	74	2 7/8	...	...
77 1/4	70	Dec	287	7 1/4	630	3/8
77 1/4	70	Jan	25	8	463	6 1/2
77 1/4	70	Apr	42	9 7/8	5	13 5/8
77 1/4	75	Dec	39	3 1/4	125	3/4
77 1/4	75	Jan	437	4	...	...
77 1/4	75	Apr	452	5 1/8	16	18
77 1/4	80	Dec	1168	5/8	20	3 1/4
77 1/4	80	Jan	509	1 5/8	14	12
77 1/4	80	Apr	527	2 1/8	...	...
77 1/4	80	Jul	47	4	...	...
77 1/4	85	Dec	157	3/16	...	...
77 1/4	85	Jan	1005	3/4	180	15 1/2
77 1/4	85	Apr	670	1 1/8	101	27 5/8
77 1/4	90	Apr	35	5/8	53	32 3/4
Chryslr	40	Jan	232	8 7/8	13	3/16
48 3/8	45	Dec	2092	3 3/4	35	5/16
48 3/8	45	Jan	138	4 1/2	1432	1
48 3/8	45	Apr	42	5 5/8	173	2
48 3/8	50	Dec	1904	3/4	387	2 5/8
48 3/8	50	Jan	830	1 5/8	365	3 1/4
48 3/8	50	Apr	626	3 1/4	1	4 3/8
48 3/8	50	Jul	40	4 3/4	100	4 3/4
48 3/8	55	Jan	119	5/8	5	7
48 3/8	55	Apr	146	1 9/16	...	...
Chubb	70	Jan	...	...	30	1 3/4
CircaPh	12 1/2	Dec	30	4 3/4	...	...
17 1/8	15	Jan	42	2 5/8	11	3/8
17 1/8	17 1/2	Jan	124	1 1/8	...	...
CirCty	25	Dec	110	3/4	10	11/16
24 5/8	25	Jan	25	1 11/16	17	1 1/2
Circus	20	Jan	8	2	228	5/8
21	22 1/2	Jan	34	3/4	...	...
21	22 1/2	Mar	48	1 9/16	...	...
21	25	Mar	42	5/8	...	...
Cirrus	25	Dec	73	1 1/8	653	3/4
25 1/4	25	Jan	30	2	145	1 9/16
25 1/4	25	Mar	35	3 1/4	...	...
25 1/4	30	Dec	200	1/8	...	...
25 1/4	30	Jun	31	2 7/16	...	...
25 1/4	35	Dec	250	1/8	...	...
Cisco	25	Dec	32	7 7/8	...	...
32 1/4	25	Jan	35	8 1/2	18	3/16
32 1/4	30	Dec	261	2 5/8	30	1/4
32 1/4	30	Jan	193	3 1/2	111	3/4
32 1/4	30	Apr	91	5 5/8	60	2
32 1/4	35	Dec	540	1/4	6	2 1/8
32 1/4	35	Jan	354	1 1/16	34	3 5/8
32 1/4	35	Apr	199	2 9/16	9	4 1/8
32 1/4	35	Jul	23	3 5/8	20	4 3/4

Source: The Wall Street Journal (December 1, 1994), p. C14. Reprinted by permission of The Wall Street Journal,

*The day before the expira-
tion date is the last day an
option can be exercised.
The actual expiration date is
the Saturday following the
third Thursday of the month;
hence, Friday is the last day
to exercise the option.*

This relationship is shown in Figure 14.1. We see that as long as the market price of the common stock is greater than the exercise price, the value of the call option is equal to $P_0 - X$. But, if the market price of the stock *at the expiration date* is below the exercise price, the call option is worthless. The red line in Figure 14.1 indicates the lower limit on the call option's value. The value of a call option at expiration is often written as

value of call option at expiration, $V_c = \text{Max}(P_0 - X, 0)$

*Buying a call option is really
the same as buying the
stock today and borrowing
part of the purchase price,
with the loan repayment
due at the time the option
expires.*

For example, assume you paid $600 [i.e., (100 shares)($6)] to purchase the July call option on 100 shares of AT&T with an exercise price of $45 and the expiration date has now arrived. If the market price of AT&T common stock has increased and is now $60, while the exercise price is $45, you can exercise the option—purchase 100 shares at $45 per share—and immediately sell the shares at $60. The value of the option is (100 shares)($60 − $45) = $1,500. Your profit is equal to the value of the option of $1,500, less what you paid for the option of $600. Ignoring any commissions and taxes, your profit is $1,500 − $600 = $900. Alternatively, if the market price of AT&T common stock at the expiration date is at or below $51 per share, you will throw the option away and incur a loss of $600.[8] The value of the call option on AT&T common stock, V_c, at expiration is:

$$100(P_0 - X) \qquad \text{if } P_0 \text{ is greater than } X$$
$$0 \qquad \text{if } P_0 \text{ is less than } X$$

Thus, we see that the relationship of the stock price to the exercise price determines whether an option has any value *at the expiration date of the option.*

FIGURE 14.1

Value of a Call Option at Expiration

If the market price of the stock, P_0, is greater than the exercise price, X, then at expiration the value of the option (as given by the 45° line) is $P_0 - X$. Otherwise, the call option at expiration is worthless.

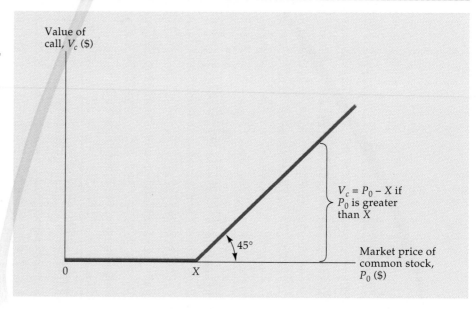

The Buyer's Position Versus the Seller's Position

Remember, individuals write or sell options; the firm the option is on is not involved in creating the option.

So far we have said that you can purchase an option, or alternatively, you can write, or sell, an option. There is a minor addition that needs to be made to what we said previously: We need to formally recognize the option premium. While the potential benefit to the purchaser of a call option may be evident, why would anyone want to write, or sell, a call option? The answer is that *on net* the seller expects to earn a profit. In the AT&T example above, the purchaser profits if at expiration the market price of AT&T is sufficiently above the exercise price to more than cover the cost, or premium paid, of the option. This position is shown graphically in Figure 14.2(a), where the price (or premium) paid per share for the option is $6.

How about the seller's position? For simplicity, assume the original writer, or seller, of the call option on AT&T common stock sold it for its current secondary market price of $6 per share. In this case the per share profit to the seller is shown in Figure 14.2(b). The writer of the call option receives the premium and realizes a gain as long as the value of the stock at the expiration date is less than the exercise price plus the premium. Thus, the expiration date gain or loss to the buyer and to the writer are mirror images of each other. *It is a zero-sum game where one can gain only at the*

FIGURE 14.2

Profit Opportunities for a Buyer and a Seller of an AT&T Call Option

With a premium of $6, the buyer profits if at expiration the price of AT&T common stock is above $51; otherwise, the seller profits.

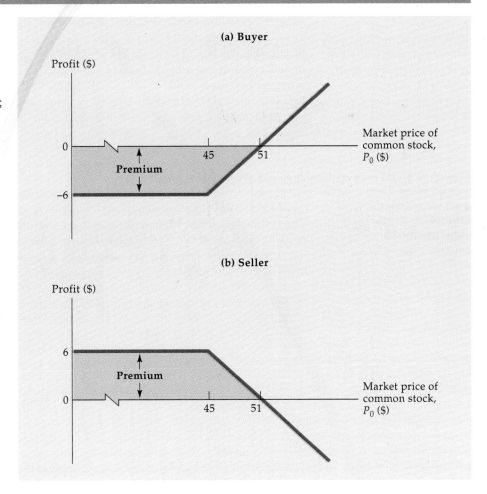

expense of the other. Because only 10 to 15 percent of all stock options written end up being in-the-money at expiration, there are sufficient incentives for some individuals or investment banking firms to write options, while those odds are enough to encourage others to buy the options.

CONCEPT REVIEW QUESTIONS

- What is an option? How does a call option differ from a put option?
- What is meant by saying an option is "in-the-money" versus saying the option is "out-of-the-money"?

WHAT DETERMINES THE VALUE OF AN OPTION?

■ LEARNING GOAL 3

Describe the factors that affect the value of an option, and determine the value of an option before expiration.

In the preceding section we discussed the value of the option on the expiration date. Now we discuss the factors that influence the value of an option at times other than the expiration date. At these times the value of the option will be greater than the lower limit of their value. (The lower limit is represented by $P_0 - X$, if P_0 is greater than X, or by 0, if P_0 is less than X, as shown previously in Figure 14.1.) This occurs because there is risk: We don't know whether *at expiration* the value, or stock price in the case of options on stocks, will be above or below the exercise price. The probability of expiring in-the-money is one of the primary forces that keeps the price of the option before expiration above the lower limit of its value. Thus, the actual value of a call option *prior to the expiration date* will lie above the lower limit. This is illustrated in Figure 14.3.

Basic Determinants of Option Values

A call option gives the holder the right to buy stock at a fixed price. The more the underlying stock is worth, the more the right to pay a fixed price is worth.

The factors that determine an option's value can be broken down into two basic sets. The first are those that relate to the option contract itself; the second relate to the underlying asset (or stock). Three factors related to the option contract affect the option's value: the exercise price, the expiration date, and the level of interest rates, as indicated by the risk-free rate.

1. *Exercise Price.* Other things being equal, the higher the exercise price, the lower will be the value of a call option. This makes sense because the higher the exercise price, the less likely it is that the market price of the underlying asset will be above the exercise price at the expiration date. As long as there is some probability that the price of the underlying asset will exceed the exercise price, however, the call option will have value.
2. *Expiration Date.* The longer the time until expiration, the higher the value of the call option. Thus, other things being equal, if you hold a 6-month option, and also a 1-year option, the 1-year option is more valuable because there is more time for the market price of the underlying asset to fluctuate. This increase in time provides greater opportunity for the price of the underlying asset to move, and hence increases the value of the option.

FIGURE 14.3

The Value of a Call Option Before Expiration

The lower bound on the value is given by the solid colored line. But, other things being equal, (a) the higher the price of the asset, P_0, (b) the longer the time to expiration, t, (c) the higher the risk-free rate, k_{RF}, or (d) the greater the variability, σ, the higher will be the value of the option, V_c, as indicated by the dashed line.

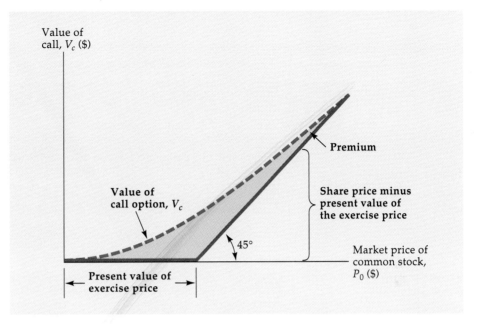

3. *Risk-Free Rate*. The level of interest rates also affects the value of call options. The reason is that the market price of the asset, P_0, is in today's dollars, while the exercise price is in future dollars. The two rates must be stated at the same time, which is today, at time $t = 0$. Based on the time value of money, the present value of the exercise price is less when the risk-free rate is high, and the present value of the exercise price is more when the risk-free rate is low. Because the value of the call option is equal to at least the stock price, P_0, minus the *present value of the exercise price*, a call option is more valuable the higher the risk-free rate. Thus, the value of a call option is positively related to the level of interest rates as measured by the risk-free rate.

In addition, two other factors related to the underlying asset also affect the value of call options. These are the price of the underlying asset and the variability (or riskiness) of the underlying asset.

1. *Asset Price*. Other things being equal, the higher the price of the underlying asset, the more valuable the call option. This occurs because at maturity the owner of the option will reap a larger return the more the asset price is above the exercise price.
2. *Variability of the Asset Price*. Finally, the greater the variability of the underlying asset, the more valuable a call option will be. To see this it is important to remember that a call option is valuable only when the market price of the underlying asset is greater than the exercise price. Call options on assets with greater price volatility will therefore be worth more, other things being equal. For example, consider two 6-month call options, both with an exercise price, X, of $60, and a current market price, P_0, of $55. Let's assume the volatility of asset A is more than that of asset B. The call option on asset A will be more valuable, because with more volatility, there is more likelihood that the value of the underlying asset may be above the exercise price than for asset B. As a consequence, *no matter what the degree of risk*

aversion of an individual investor, we find high variability in the underlying asset desirable.

To summarize, the value of a call option is a function of five variables:

1. Price of the underlying asset, P_0
2. Exercise price, X
3. Time to expiration, t
4. Risk-free rate, k_{RF}
5. Variability of the underlying asset, σ

Thus, the value of a call option, V_c, on a nondividend paying stock, or asset, is:

$$\text{value of call option, } V_c = f(P_0, X, t, k_{RF}, \sigma) \qquad (14.3)$$

where the plus (minus) sign by the variable indicates the effect of an increase in that variable on the price of the call option:

Variable	Effect of an Increase of Each Factor on V_c
Asset price, P_0	+
Exercise price, X	−
Time to expiration, t	+
Risk-free rate, k_{RF}	+
Variability of asset's return, σ	+

As long as it is before the expiration date, an increase in the price of the asset, the time to expiration, the risk-free rate, or the variability of the underlying asset will cause the value of the call option to go up. Thus, increases in any of these four variables will cause the actual option value to be farther above the lower limit, as shown previously in Figure 14.3.

Likewise, decreases in the price of the underlying asset, the time to expiration, the risk-free rate, or the variability of the asset's return cause the dashed option value line in Figure 14.3 to snuggle closer to the solid lower limit value line. For example, if a 1-year option and a 3-month option exist on the same asset and both have the same exercise price, their general relationship is shown in Figure 14.4.[9]

Stock Is Just a Call Option

In Chapter 4 we considered how to value both bonds and stock based on the present value of their future cash flows. Though this approach is widely used, it has one major shortcoming—it fails to consider simultaneously the interaction between the value of a firm's stock and its bonds. In a very informal way in Chapter 1 we employed option concepts to depict the value of the claims of both stockholders and bondholders on the firm. This representation is repeated in Figure 14.5 (p. 420). The claim, or payoff, for the stockholders at the maturity of the debt is simply a call option as shown in Figure

---

[9] *The intercept of the diagonal 45° line in Figures 14.3 and 14.4 is equal to the present value of the exercise price. While not shown in either of these figures, as time elapses and the option moves closer to its maturity, or expiration, date, the present value of the exercise price increases. Therefore, the diagonal 45° line actually shifts slightly to the right (while keeping its same slope).*

FIGURE 14.4

The Value of a Call Option as the Time to Maturity Decreases

As the maturity date of the option draws nearer, the value of the option, other things being equal, snuggles closer and closer to the lower bound given by the solid colored line.

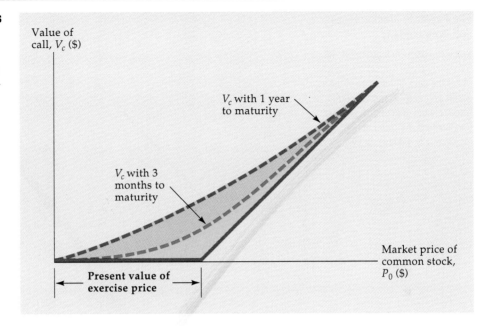

14.5(a). The bondholders, on the other hand, provide long-term debt financing for the firm. Suppose the bondholders lend the firm money that *at its maturity date* is worth X amount of dollars. As shown in Figure 14.5(b), the bondholders have a fixed, but limited, claim on the assets and value of the firm. If the value of the firm, V, is greater than the bondholders' claim when the debt matures, the debt will be paid off and the stockholders gain control of the remaining assets of the firm. The dual claims of both stockholders and bondholders on the firm are shown in Figure 14.5(c). The total value of the firm, V, is simply the sum of stockholders' and bondholders' claims, or:

$$\text{total value of firm} = \text{stockholders' claims} + \text{bondholders' claims}$$

$$V = S + B \qquad (14.4)$$

When valuing the claims of both stockholders and bondholders, the stockholders' claim, S, is simply a call option on the value of the firm, V, so that:

stockholders' claim, S = call option on firm value

= total value of firm − bondholders' claim

= $V - B$

Remember Key Idea 3— individuals act in their own self-interest. Stockholders and bondholders do not always have the same interests.

So far this is just a restatement of Equation 14.4. However, in an option pricing context, two separate items exist in place of the single risky claim of the bondholders, B. The first is equivalent to the risk-free present value of the exercise price, which is what the bondholders' claim is worth *if* there were no risk that the stockholders might default and turn the firm over to the bondholders. The second is the default option held by the stockholders. Due to limited liability, if the firm gets into serious financial

FIGURE 14.5

The Payoff to Stockholders and Bondholders

Stockholders have a call option on the assets of the firm. At the maturity of the debt, if the value of the assets is greater than the bondholder claims, they will pay off the bondholders and claim the remaining assets, or value, of the firm.

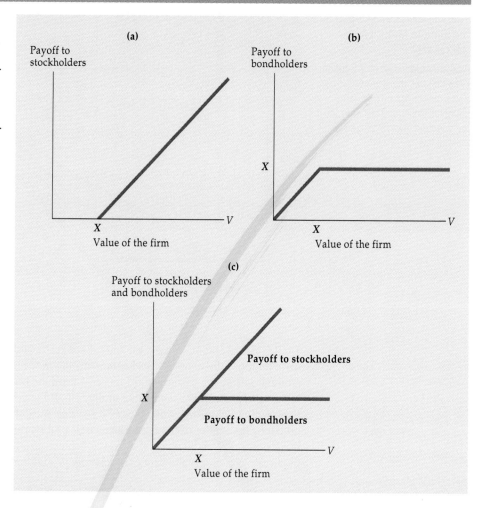

difficulties, the stockholders have the option to walk away from the firm and turn it and all of its remaining assets and liabilities over to the creditors. Thus, the stockholders have the option of "putting" the assets and liabilities to the bondholders. The bondholders' risky claim, B, is equal to their riskless claim minus the default option, which lowers the value of their riskless bonds so that:

$$\text{bondholders' risky claim, } B = \text{bondholders' riskless claim} - \text{default option}$$
$$B = B(\text{riskless}) - \text{default option} \qquad (14.5)$$

Putting this all together, we see that the stockholders' claim is simply:

$$\text{stockholders' claim, } S = V - B(\text{riskless}) + \text{default option} \qquad (14.6)$$

In effect, the stockholders have bought the firm's assets, borrowed the present value of the bondholders' riskless claims on the firm, and bought a default (or put) option that allows them to walk away from the firm and give it to the bondholders. The default option can be thought of as a loan guarantee that eliminates default risk for the stockholders.

Similarly, the market value of the risky bondholders' claim on the firm, B, may be determined by using either Equation 14.5:

bondholders' risky claim, $B = V - S$

or Equation 14.6:

bondholders' risky claim, $B = B(\text{riskless}) - \text{default option}$

From the bondholders' standpoint, the value of the default (put) option can be thought of as a *default risk discount* that bondholders apply to the current market value of the firm's riskless debt.

Viewing the stock and bonds issued by firms in an option context helps to see the differences between them and highlights the importance of limited liability for stockholders. It is limited liability that allows stockholders to walk away if severe financial difficulty occurs and turn the firm over to the bondholders. Option ideas and concepts are also present in many other activities that financial managers face in practice. Thus, the opportunity to make a capital investment, or to abandon an ongoing venture, are both options that management can exercise or not. Likewise, the opportunity to issue debt or equity at various points in time is, in fact, an option that can be exercised or not.

Option ideas also help us understand two additional means of financing available to firms—warrants and convertible securities—as we'll see in the next section.

CONCEPT REVIEW QUESTIONS

- Describe the three factors related to the option contract and the two factors related to the underlying asset that affect the value of an option.
- How is the stock of a firm like a call option? What about the bonds of a firm?

WARRANTS AND CONVERTIBLES

■ LEARNING GOAL 4

Discuss the option-like features of warrants and convertibles, why firms issue these securities, and how the value of a convertible is determined .

In Chapters 10 and 11 we considered the two external sources of long-term financing for the firm—common stock and long-term debt. Now we examine two other securities employed by firms to raise long-term financing. These are warrants and convertible, of which the most important are convertible bonds. Both of these securities have option-like characteristics.

Difference Between Warrants and Call Options

Warrants are simply a long-term call option that allows the purchaser or holder to buy shares of stock in a firm at a specific price.[10] A significant amount of privately

---

[10] *There are a few warrants outstanding that allow the purchase of the stock of another firm or the purchase of bonds. The valuation of warrants and convertibles is considered in more detail in Chapter 17 of* Financial Management.

WARRANT
A long-lived call option to purchase a fixed number of shares of common stock at a specified price during a specified time period.

Warrants are often issued with debt securities to lure investors. Everything else equal, the issuing firm can pay a slightly lower rate of interest by giving bondholders warrants with the bonds.

Warrants may also be used to mitigate concerns about agency costs. If bondholders are worried about wealth transfers from them to stockholders, issuing warrants provides the bondholders a claim on the firm's equity.

placed debt, and a far smaller percentage of public offerings, occurs in packages where warrants are issued along with debt. Warrants may also be given to investment bankers as compensation for underwriting services. Thus, a warrant is a long-term option that provides the investor with the right, but not the obligation, to buy a specific number of shares of common stock at a predetermined price for a certain time period. Warrants are almost always *detachable,* which means that shortly after the package of securities is issued, the bonds and the warrants can be sold separately. Table 14.2 shows the characteristics of some warrants. The original life for most of these warrants was 5 to 8 years. While some of the warrants have a low value, if the price of the common stock into which they are convertible rises, so will the value of the warrant.

As you can tell from the preceding discussion, warrants are like call options. In fact, from the investor's standpoint, a warrant is almost exactly the same as a call option on the common stock of the issuing firm. One key difference is that options are created by investors themselves (i.e., the firm on which the option is written is *not* involved in creating options), whereas warrants are created by the firm. Hence, the firm is directly involved in determining the number of warrants issued, the term (or expiration date) of the warrants, and the exercise price at which the firm's common stock can be purchased. Because the firm creates the warrant, when warrants are exercised the number of shares of common stock outstanding increases.[11] In contrast, when a call option is exercised, the writer of the call is responsible for having the required shares, and the number of shares of stock that the firm has outstanding does not change.

TABLE 14.2

Warrant Characteristics for Selected Firms

Most warrants can be exchanged for one share of common stock. Also, as the numbers indicate, some of the publicly traded warrants have a low price, as does the common stock for which the warrants can be exchanged.

Firm	Expiration Date	Warrant Exercise Price per Share	Number of Shares per Warrant	Common Stock Price per Share	Lower Limit of Warrant Value*	Actual Warrant Price	Premium over Lower Limit†
Koger Equity	6/30/99	8.00	1	8 1/8	0.125	3.4375	3.3125
Laser Technology	1/11/98	6.00	1	4 7/8	0	1.125	1.125
NVR Inc.	9/30/96	8.80	1	10 1/2	1.70	5.125	3.425
Magma Copper	11/11/95	8.50	1	13 1/2	5.00	5.875	0.875
Manville	1/6/96	9.40	1	8 3/4	0	1.875	1.875
Wheeling-Pittsburgh	3/3/96	6.3583	1	16 7/8	10.52	10.75	0.23

*Maximum of (market price of common stock − exercise price)(number of shares purchased with one warrant) or zero.
† Actual warrant price − lower limit of warrant price.
Source: Various financial publications as of January 6, 1994.

---

[11] *From an accounting standpoint, using the current number of shares of common stock outstanding to calculate earnings per share, EPS, produces simple EPS. Taking account of all the shares of common stock that will be outstanding after the warrants are exercised results in fully diluted EPS. The same accounting treatment exists for shares that may be issued when convertible securities are employed. See Chapter 19.*

Convertibles

CONVERSION PRICE
The effective price paid for common stock by converting a convertible security into common stock.

CONVERSION RATIO
The number of shares of common stock received for converting a convertible security; equals the par value of the convertible divided by the conversion price.

CONVERSION VALUE
The value of a convertible security in terms of the common stock into which it can be converted; equals the conversion ratio times the market price per share of common stock.

Some bonds, and an even smaller percentage of preferred stock, contain another feature—convertibility. *Convertible securities* are bonds or preferred stock that contain a provision that allows them to be exchanged for common stock of the issuing firm at the discretion of the investor.[12] There is no charge for making this exchange, and the exchange can be made whenever the investor wishes. Thus, investors who own convertibles have an option-like security. Consider a $1,000 par convertible bond that has a stated **conversion** (or exercise) **price** of $50. The number of shares the bond can be converted into, called the **conversion ratio,** is the par value of the convertible security divided by the conversion price, or $1,000/$50 = 20 shares.

A few other characteristics of convertible bonds are as follows: First, convertible bonds are typically debentures, and they are generally subordinated. Thus, *most convertible bonds are convertible subordinated debentures.*[13] Second, when convertible bonds are designed and issued, their stated coupon interest rate is less than that required on nonconvertible bonds of similar quality and maturity, and their conversion price is set above the current market price of the firm's common stock. The reason for the lower coupon interest rate is that the convertible contains an added feature that straight (non-convertible) debt doesn't—the option to convert the bond into common stock.

Table 14.3 presents some characteristics of convertible bonds for selected firms. The **conversion value** is simply the amount the bond is worth if it is immediately converted into common stock. The *dollar premium* is the difference between the actual price of the convertible bond and its conversion value. In examining Table 14.3, we see that the conversion value of all but a couple of the bonds is less than their par value of $1,000.

TABLE 14.3

Convertible Debt Characteristics for Selected Firms

Convertible bonds come in many shapes and sizes. While not shown, most convertible bonds are callable and are also subordinated.

| Firm | Bond or Note | | | Common Price per Share | Current Conversion Value* | Actual Convertible Price | Premium over Conversion Value† |
	Coupon Interest Rate	Maturity	Conversion Ratio				
Alaskan Airways	6.875	2014	29.76	14.625	435.24	835.00	399.76
Bank of New York	7.500	2001	25.58	57.250	1,464.46	1,580.00	115.54
General Instruments	5.000	2000	21.05	57.875	1,218.27	1,350.00	131.73
Potomac Electric Power	7.000	2018	37.04	25.625	949.15	1,035.00	85.85
Sun Company	6.750	2012	24.50	31.000	759.50	998.75	239.25
Western Digital	9.000	2014	69.20	10.000	692.00	980.00	288.00
Zenith	6.250	2011	32.00	7.375	236.00	697.50	461.50

* (Market price of common stock)(conversion ratio).
† Actual convertible price − current conversion value.
Source: Various financial publications as of January 6, 1994.

[12] There are a few convertibles outstanding that allow for the purchase of another firm's stock, or the purchase of bonds.
[13] Generally convertible subordinated debentures carry a bond rating that is one grade lower than the other long-term debt issued by the firm. Thus, if the firm's other bonds carry a rating of BBB, its convertible subordinated debentures would carry a bond rating of BB.

Valuing Convertibles

The owner of a convertible in essence owns a bond *and* a long-term call option on the firm's stock. This is very similar to owning a bond and a warrant. However, there is an important difference: To exercise the warrant, the investor keeps the bond and has to pay cash to the firm as determined by the exercise price in the warrant. To claim the shares with a convertible bond, the investor has to *surrender the bond* in order to exercise the call option.

In valuing convertibles there are three components that need to be considered: the straight bond value, the conversion value, and the call option value.

Remember Key Ideas 5 and 7—a dollar today is worth more than a dollar tomorrow, and options are valuable. Both concepts come into play in valuing convertibles.

Straight Bond Value. The straight bond value, or price, is what the security would sell for if it were not convertible into common stock. This is nothing more than our familiar bond valuation model which, as first considered in Chapter 4, is

$$B_0 = \sum_{t=1}^{n} \frac{I}{(1 + k_b)^t} + \frac{M}{(1 + k_b)^n}$$

where B_0 is the current price, I is the interest per period, M is the maturity value of the bond, and k_b *is the market rate of interest on comparable quality and maturity non-convertible bonds.*

When firms issue convertible bonds they pay less in terms of the coupon interest rate than if the bond were not convertible. This makes sense, because the firm is also providing the investor with an option that has value. Suppose that Shaws Discount Stores is issuing some $1,000 par value, 7 percent coupon rate convertible bonds; the market interest rate that Shaws would pay if the bond was not convertible is 11 percent; and the maturity of the convertible is 10 years. Assuming that interest is paid annually, the straight bond value (employing 11 percent as the discount rate) when the convertible is originally issued is:[14]

$$B_0 = \text{straight bond value} = \sum_{t=1}^{10} \frac{\$70}{(1.11)^t} + \frac{\$1,000}{(1.11)^{10}}$$

$$= \$412 + \$352 = \$764$$

The straight bond value is a minimum value, or floor, below which the value of the convertible bond will not trade. Although the convertible bond is issued at a discount from its par, or maturity, value, *when it matures* its value solely as a bond will be $1,000 per bond. This bond floor at the maturity of the bond is illustrated in Figure 14.6(a). As long as the value of the firm at the maturity of the bond is sufficient, bondholders are protected by the straight bond value floor; otherwise the firm defaults on the bond, and the bondholders claim the firm's assets.

Conversion Value. There is another floor that also limits the downward fluctuation in the market value of any convertible; this time it is provided by how much the convertible is worth solely in terms of its common stock value. Assume the conversion price for the Shaws Discount convertible bond is $50, and the market price of Shaws common stock when the convertible is first issued is $30 per share. The

---

[14] If present value tables are employed the straight bond value is ($70)(5.889) + ($1,000)(0.352) = $412 + $352 = $764.

FIGURE 14.6

Value of a Convertible Bond at Maturity

In (a) the conversion value is shown along with the straight bond value. If the value of the firm is low, the firm defaults on the bond; otherwise, its straight bond value is the maturity value of the bond. In (b) the value of the convertible at maturity is shown to depend on the maximum of the curves in (a).

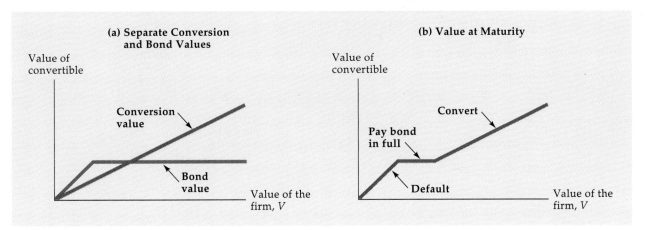

conversion ratio is $1,000/$50 = 20$ shares of stock, and the original conversion value is:[15]

$$\text{conversion value} = (\text{conversion ratio})(\text{common stock market price}) \qquad (14.7)$$

$$\text{conversion value} = (20)(\$30) = \$600$$

At the instant in time when the Shaws convertible bond is sold, its conversion value—that is, how much the stock it can be converted into is worth—is $600. As the market price of the firm's stock increases or decreases, the conversion value of the convertible security will fluctuate accordingly. As also shown in Figure 14.6(a), the conversion, or common stock, value is a straight upward-sloping line. At maturity, the value of a convertible is determined by the state of the firm and the value of its common stock. As shown in Figure 14.6(b), at maturity the value of the convertible will depend on whether the firm is solvent or insolvent, and whether the conversion value is above or below the straight bond value (which at maturity is the bond's par value of $1,000 per bond).

Value Before Maturity. So far we have considered the value of a convertible security at maturity. Before maturity the straight bond value of the convertible will be less than at maturity; that is, it will be discounted. This is because all convertibles have a coupon interest rate that is lower than the market rate of interest on comparable quality and maturity nonconvertible bonds when they are issued. Therefore, the

---

[15] *To be entirely correct, the price per share should be that which would exist if all available shares covered by warrants and convertible securities were already issued. Providing that the number of additional shares of common stock potentially to be issued is not too large, the error caused by employing the current stock market price is minimal.*

FIGURE 14.7

Value of a Convertible Bond Before Maturity

In (a) the conversion value is shown along with the bond value. As the value of the firm increases the bond value first increases rapidly; then as the firm value increases further the bond value approaches the maturity value of the bond. In (b) the higher of the bond or conversion value [from (a)] determines the lower limit on the value of the convertible. Due to the straight bond floor and the option to convert, the market value of the convertible is at a premium over the lower limit on the value of the convertible.

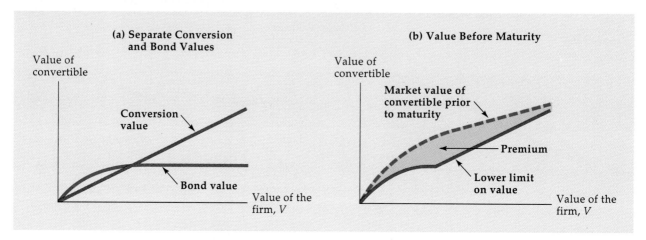

straight bond value will be less than the par, or maturity, value. This is shown as a curved line in Figure 14.7(a).

This straight bond value floor is not as solid as it looks; it will change as market interest rates fluctuate. Thus, if market interest rates go up, the straight bond value declines, and vice versa. Likewise, if the firm's financial condition deteriorates, the floor will also fall. The conversion value, which is the same as it is at maturity, is also shown in Figure 14.7(a).

There is a third element that also needs to be taken into consideration when valuing convertible securities before maturity—the value of the option that exists. Before maturity investors have the protection of the higher of the straight bond value floor or the conversion value floor, and they have also have an option to convert the bond into common stock. Because this option is valuable, *the value of the convertible security before maturity will always be greater than the lower limit on its value.*

For example, assume the value of the option to convert is worth $15 per share of Shaws stock. The convertible debenture can be exchanged for 20 shares of Shaws common stock, and with the option on each share of stock worth $15, the conversion option is worth ($15)(20) = $300. Adding the option value to the straight bond value of $764, we see that the value of the convertible before maturity is $300 + $764 = $1,064. The behavior of the convertible security's price before maturity is shown in Figure 14.7(b). The difference between the market price of the convertible and its lower limit is the premium, or value of the call option incorporated in the convertible bond. To determine the worth of a convertible before maturity, the most straightforward approach is to value the straight bond and then value the call option.

Forcing Conversion

Most convertibles contain a clause that allows the firm to call the security at a specific price. If the firm calls the convertible the investor has a brief period, generally 30 days or less, to either convert the security or accept the call price. From the investors' standpoint the choice is obvious: If the conversion value is greater than the call price, convert; otherwise, accept the call price. Many firms call a convertible security only when the conversion value is greater than the call price; this is often referred to as a **forced conversion.** If the conversion value is less than the call price, the firm cannot force conversion; if the firm calls the issue, rational investors will accept the call price. This situation is often referred to as an **overhanging issue.**

From the firm's standpoint there are two straightforward reasons for calling a convertible. To understand these reasons, you need to know that the value of the firm, or size of the pie, is not affected when the convertible is called. However, *the relative position of stockholders and bondholders is affected by the timing of the call.*

The first reason for calling a convertible focuses on the relationship of the call price and the market value of the convertible. Consider what happens if the firm calls the security when the convertible's market value is below the call price. In that case the firm pays more for the bond than it is worth, thereby transferring wealth from stockholders to bondholders. Likewise, if the bond is not called when the conversion value is above the convertible's market value, bondholders are allowed to hold a valuable asset at the expense of stockholders. The optimal policy for the firm to follow based on the relationship of the call price and the market value of the convertible is to call the bonds *when their market value equals their call price.* Empirical evidence suggests that most firms do not follow this policy; they typically wait until the bond's market value is substantially above the call price.

Why do they do this? Because of the second reason for calling convertibles, which involves the cash outflows to the firm. As long as the firm does not call the convertible, the after-tax cash outflow to service the convertible is a function of the interest rate on the convertible, the percent of the convertible outstanding, and the firm's effective tax rate. By forcing conversion, the new ongoing cash outflow to the firm equals the number of shares that will be issued by forcing conversion times the per share cash dividend rate, assuming the firm pays cash dividends. While interest is tax-deductible, the payment of cash dividends has to come out of after-tax cash flows. Thus, the firm's cash outflow generally increases after a conversion. From a cash flow standpoint, why should the firm force conversion if its after-tax cash outflow increases?

How and When Firms Employ Convertibles

One often hears the comment that convertibles are used on the one hand to provide cheap debt financing or, on the other hand, to allow the firm to sell common stock at a higher than market rate. The cheap debt financing argument rests on the premise that the coupon interest rate required with a convertible is less than the coupon rate that would have been required had the firm issued straight debt. However, you should be able to see that the logic behind this argument is faulty because the investor purchases *both* a bond and an option. The cheap debt financing argument ignores the option entirely.

Likewise, the argument that the firm can sell common stock at an above-market price rests on the assumption that the exercise price contained in the convertible is greater than the market price of the firm's common stock. The cheap equity argument, however, ignores both the bond and the option, and simply looks at the conversion value of the convertible versus the market price of the convertible. Given the nature of convertible securities, it is not surprising that the expected return required by investors falls between that required on straight bonds and on common stock.

If investors require an expected return that falls between that of bonds and stocks, what does that mean the cost to the firm has to be? You know enough finance not to be

FORCED CONVERSION
Situation in which a firm forces investors to convert their convertible securities by calling them when the conversion value is greater than the call price.

OVERHANGING ISSUE
Convertible security whose conversion value is less than its call price, so that conversion cannot be forced.

fooled by improper comparisons such as those incorporated in either the cheap debt or cheap equity financing arguments. Convertibles provide neither cheap debt nor cheap equity financing. Rather, they provide financing whose after-tax cost to the firm is between the costs of straight debt and common equity.

Firms employ convertibles when they provide benefits that are not generally available from other forms of financing. Let's briefly consider the factors that would make it beneficial for the firm to use convertibles and warrants:

Remember Key Idea 3—individuals act in their own self-interest.

1. *Risky Situations*. Convertibles and bond/warrant combinations tend to be issued by smaller or more speculative firms, or sometimes by larger firms that have a high degree of risk. Suppose you are approached by a small firm that wants some debt financing to develop and manufacture the next generation of optical scanners. You know that if the project goes well you will get your money back. However, if the project does not do well, you will receive nothing. While some information on the project exists, you know that the next generation of optical scanners rests on yet-to-be-proven advances on which the firm is still working. Even if this project does prove successful, the firm may be preempted by other firms that are also racing to develop the next generation of optical scanners. One way to compensate for the additional hard-to-evaluate risk is to require that you be given a "piece of the action." The firm can easily accomplish this by granting investors an option that can be exercised if the project is successful.

2. *Agency Cost*. Holders of the firm's straight debt are interested in the payment of principal and interest on the debt. To be more assured of receiving these payments, they favor low-risk investment projects. Stockholders, on the other hand, own a call option whose value increases when the firm undertakes high risk–high return projects. Therefore, stockholders want firms to issue debt as though it were going to be employed to finance low-risk projects and then switch and undertake high risk projects, thereby transferring wealth from bondholders to stockholders. To protect themselves from this possible expropriation of wealth, bondholders can require higher interest rates and more stringent bond covenants and restrictions. These actions are costly, however, and also restrict the flexibility of the firm. Using convertibles or warrants is a way of reducing these agency costs.

3. *Asymmetric Information and Adverse Financing Costs*. When firms issue new equity they suffer negative price reactions. Therefore, firms will issue equity only when the investment projects under consideration are not very good. Why share really good projects, and the expected increase in the value of the firm, with new equityholders? One possibility is that firms may issue convertible bonds to bridge the gap between the negative price consequences associated with an equity issue and the potential for costly financial distress associated with a debt issue. When coupled with a call provision that enables early forced conversion, convertibles provide an indirect way to issue equity that entails less adverse price impact than offering common stock.

4. *International Exposure*. Often when firms invest in international capital investment projects, or have substantial international exposure, they are exposed to additional risks. These include possible adverse actions by foreign host governments and exposure to fluctuating exchange rates. In such cases convertibles may tend to limit some of the firm's risk exposure due to the unusual risks faced by the firm, because they are debt instead of equity. While a country might be tempted to simply expropriate an equity investment, a debt claim may have more likelihood of being paid off—in part or full.

5. *Tax Consequences.* When a firm issues debt that is convertible, or a debt/warrant package, the coupon interest rate is lower than the coupon interest rate if straight debt had been issued. Hence, the tax shield provided by the financing is reduced. This is a disadvantage if the firm is in a high taxpaying situation. Therefore, firms that have less use for the tax shields associated with interest tend to issue convertibles or bonds with warrants. Such firms generally have lower effective marginal tax rates.

In this chapter we have examined some of the different methods and types of securities that firms use to assist in raising funds and financing their ongoing activities. In practice, these and many other financing arrangements and types of securities are employed.

CONCEPT REVIEW QUESTIONS

- How are warrants and call options different?
- Identify the characteristics of convertible bonds. What factors determine their value?
- Why do firms issue convertible securities?

Summary

- Leasing places a financial obligation on the firm similar to debt. Leases are evaluated based on the net present value of leasing versus purchasing the assets, using the after-tax cost of debt capital as the discount rate.
- Incremental operating expenses if purchased make leasing more attractive, while purchasing becomes more attractive if assets are expected to have some resale value at the end of the lease. A higher discount rate, which reflects the risk of the asset, should be employed when evaluating the effects of incremental operating expenses or estimated resale values.
- Options provide the right, but not the obligation, to buy (a call option) or sell (a put option) a particular asset for a limited time at a specified price.
- An in-the-money option has value if exercised, while an out-of-the-money option has no value if exercised.
- The value of an option on a nondividend paying stock, or asset, is a function of (a) the price of the underlying asset, (b) the exercise price, (c) the time to expiration, (d) the risk-free rate, and (e) the variability of the underlying asset. Risk preferences are not important in valuing options.
- Warrants are simply long-term call options.
- A convertible bond in essence is composed of a bond and a long-term option. The higher of the straight bond value and the conversion value of the security provides the floor, or minimum value, of the convertible. Due to the warrant, or long-term option part of the convertible, before maturity the convertible will trade at a premium to its minimum value.
- Convertibles *do not provide* either cheap debt or cheap equity financing. Their cost to the firm, and the return required by investors, is between that of straight debt and common equity.
- Due to the call option contained in convertibles, the firm can force conversion if the market value of the convertible is greater than the call value.

■ Warrants and convertibles are generally employed when the firm's risk is high, to reduce agency costs, to deal with asymmetric information and adverse financing costs, to deal with international risks, and when the firm has less use for the tax shields associated with interest.

Questions

14.1 Explain why it is important to neutralize risk in terms of the cash flow obligations of the firm when conducting a lease or buy analysis. How does the after-tax cost of debt, k_i, relate to this issue?

14.2 The NPV_{lease} equation is

$$NPV_{\text{lease}} = CLA_0 - \left\{ \left[\sum_{t=1}^{n} \frac{L_t(1-T)}{(1+k_i)^t} \right] (1+k_i) + \sum_{t=1}^{n} \frac{Dep_t(T)}{(1+k_i)^t} \right\}$$

Explain what each of the terms represents.

14.3 What incentives are there for buyers to purchase options and writers to sell options? How does the premium enter into their decision process?

14.4 Consider three securities—common stock, straight bonds, and convertible bonds. In each case indicate how the securities' value is affected. Which securities have their value affected the most (least) by the following?
a. The price of the firms' common stock increases.
b. Interest rates decline.
c. The firm embarks on a risky new project.
d. The firm increases its cash dividends on common stock.

14.5 It has been argued that convertibles have substantial advantages to firms as a means of financing. When compared to straight debt, firms get cheap debt financing because they pay less than the going market interest rate for the debt. When compared with selling common stock directly, firms are able to sell common stock at a price above the current market price of the firms' common stock. Thus, firms are in a "heads I win, tails you lose" situation. Evaluate this argument.

Concept Review Problems

See Appendix A for solutions.

CR14.1 Employee Temp is considering purchasing or leasing laptop computers and portable printers for its employees. The computers and printers cost $50,000, have an economic life of 5 years, will be depreciated using straight-line depreciation, and have zero resale value. The firm's cost of debt is 12 percent, and its tax rate is 35 percent. If the lease payments are $11,000 per year in advance, what is the net present value of leasing the equipment?

Note: Ignore the half-year convention when calculating depreciation.

CR14.2 BCI needs a crane that costs $100,000. The firm could borrow funds to purchase the crane at a before-tax cost of 14 percent or could rent the crane for $25,000 per year with the first payment made at $t = 0$. The crane has an economic life of 5 years with a resale value of $40,000 at $t = 5$, and it will be depreciated using a straight line depreciation. If the crane is purchased, annual property taxes of $4,000 will be assessed to BCI. The firm's opportunity cost of capital is 18 percent, and its tax rate is 30 percent. Should BCI lease the crane?

Note: Ignore the half-year convention when calculating depreciation.

CR14.3 Attempting to make a quick profit, Jana paid $300 for a call option on 100 shares of Texas stock with an exercise price of $55; she also paid $200 for a put option on 100 shares of ABM stock with an exercise price of $60 per share. What is Jana's total dollar profit if at the expiration date Texas stock closed at $54 per share and ABM stock closed at $49 per share?

CR14.4 Mappa Stores recently issued 20-year, 12 percent, semi-annual interest-paying convertible debentures with a conversion price of $25 per share. Mappa's common stock is trading at $10 per share.
  a. What is the straight bond value if other 20-year bonds of similar quality currently pay 14 percent semi-annually?
  b. What is the conversion ratio and the conversion value of the bond?
  c. What is the value of the convertible before maturity if the value of an option on each share of stock the convertible can be exchanged for is $4.48?

Problems

See Appendix C for answers to selected problems.

Lease Evaluation

Note: Ignore the half-year convention when calculating depreciation.

14.1 Mercer Industries needs three trucks that cost $100,000 in total. Miles Leasing has offered to lease the trucks to Mercer for a total of $25,000 per year for each of 5 years, with the lease payments payable in advance. Mercer will depreciate the trucks via straight-line depreciation over their 5-year normal recovery period, the firm's marginal tax rate is 30 percent, and Mercer's before-tax cost of debt is 10 percent. Should Mercer lease or purchase the trucks? (Assume that the capital budgeting decision has already been made and the acquisition of the trucks is desirable.)

Leasing Under Alternative Arrangements

Note: Ignore the half-year convention when calculating depreciation.

Note: In (a), the payments occur at t = 0, t = 1, and t = 2. In (b), the payments occur at t = 1, t = 2, and t = 3.

14.2 Southern Regional Bank has just completed a capital budgeting analysis on some automatic teller units. The conclusion was that the bank should acquire the units. They cost $250,000 and have a 3-year economic and tax life, and straight-line depreciation will be employed if they are purchased. Southern Regional Bank has a 35 percent marginal tax rate, and its before-tax borrowing cost is 13.85 percent. Consider whether Southern Regional Bank should purchase or lease the automatic tellers in each case below:
  a. The lease payment is $100,000 for each of 3 years, payable in advance.
  b. The lease payment is $100,000 for each of 3 years, payable at the end of each year.
  c. The lease rate is $90,000 for each of 3 years, payable at the beginning of each year (t = 0 through t = 2).

Annual Versus Semi-annual Lease Payments

Note: Ignore the half-year convention when calculating depreciation.

Note: In (b), continue to use annual depreciation.

14.3 Merion Mutual is thinking about buying or leasing a piece of used equipment. It is still in good shape and can be used for another 5 years. The equipment will be depreciated over its 5-year normal recovery period via straight-line depreciation, the firm's tax rate is 30 percent, and the before-tax cost of borrowing is 14.30 percent. The equipment will cost $2 million, but it can be leased for $540,000 per year, payable at the beginning of each of the 5 years.
  a. If the capital budgeting NPV is positive, should Merion Mutual lease or purchase the equipment?
  b. Rework (a) if 10 semi-annual lease payments of $270,000 each (payable at the beginning of each 6-month period) are made.

Alternative Lease Situations

Note: Ignore the half-year convention when calculating depreciation.

14.4 Schure Benefit is evaluating leasing or purchasing an asset that has a positive capital budgeting NPV. The following basic conditions exist: CLA_0 is $210,000, n is 3, depreciation is straight-line, T is 35 percent, L is $82,000, k_i is 11 percent, lease payments are made annually in advance, and k is 15 percent.
  a. Determine the base case NPV_{lease}.
  b. Determine the effect of the following conditions on the lease versus purchase decision for Schure Benefit.

Note: Each part is independent of the other parts.

Note: In (c), ignore the half-year convention when calculating depreciation.

(1) If the asset is purchased, Schure will incur incremental operating costs of $5,000 (before taxes) per year.

(2) If the asset is purchased, Schure estimates the before-tax resale value will be $40,000.

c. Now suppose that CLA_0 is $325,000, L is $90,000, n is 5, depreciation is straight-line, k_i is 13 percent, and k is 16 percent. If the asset is purchased, Schure will incur incremental operating costs of $10,000 (before taxes) per year. Finally, Schure estimates the before-tax resale value will be $75,000. Should Schure now lease or purchase the asset?

Maximum Lease Payment

Note: Ignore the half-year convention when calculating depreciation.

14.5 RunyanMarsh is considering a lease arrangement as a means of acquiring the use of some new equipment. The equipment costs $150,000, has a 3-year normal recovery period, and straight-line depreciation will be employed. If purchased, the *after-tax* resale value will be $10,000. The marginal tax rate is 30 percent, the appropriate opportunity cost of capital, k, is 14 percent, and the before-tax cost of debt is 11.43 percent. If the three lease payments are made in advance, what is the maximum lease payment RunyanMarsh can make and still lease the asset? Assume the capital budgeting NPV is positive.

Option Prices

14.6 Prices for Circus Circus's options appeared as follows in *The Wall Street Journal*:

Circus	35	Jan	68	$3\frac{5}{8}$	91	$\frac{1}{4}$
$38\frac{1}{2}$	35	Mar	22	$4\frac{1}{2}$	58	$1\frac{1}{8}$
$38\frac{1}{2}$	40	Jan	160	$\frac{9}{16}$	2	2
$38\frac{1}{2}$	40	Feb	68	$1\frac{3}{8}$	1	$3\frac{1}{8}$
$38\frac{1}{2}$	40	Jun	10	$3\frac{1}{2}$	100	$4\frac{1}{2}$
$38\frac{1}{2}$	50	Jun	103	1	...	...

a. For January calls, explain why the call price decreases as the exercise price increases. Would you expect the price of the put option to increase or decrease as the exercise price increases? Why?

b. For both calls and puts, explain why the option price increases as the maturity increases.

c. What other factors influence option values? In what direction?

Stockholders Versus Bondholders

14.7 Your firm is considering two new product lines. Product 1 is fairly certain and may result in a market value of the firm's assets as high as $80 million or as low as $60 million in 2 years. Product 2 is much more risky and may result in a market value for the firm of either $200 million or $0. Assume the outcomes for each product are equally likely and the firm's $40 million zero-coupon bonds mature in 2 years.

a. What are the possible outcomes for the stockholders from the two products?

b. What are the possible outcomes for the bondholders?

c. Which product would the stockholders favor? The bondholders? Explain.

Convertible Bond

14.8 Murdock Corporation pays cash dividends of $3 per share, has a dividend payout ratio of 75 percent, and a P/E ratio of 10. To raise additional funds, Murdock has decided to issue a $20,000,000 25-year convertible debenture ($1,000 par) with a coupon rate of 11 percent and a conversion price of $50. Interest is paid yearly.

a. What is Murdock's current EPS?

b. What is the market price per share of Murdock's common stock?

c. What is the conversion value per bond?

d. If 60 percent of the convertible debentures are ultimately converted, how many additional shares of common stock will be issued?

e. If comparable quality nonconvertible bonds are yielding 12 percent, what is the initial straight bond value (per bond) of the convertible? Its straight bond value in 10 years (assuming market interest rates remain constant)?

Value of Convertible

14.9 Ten years ago The Stayton Group issued 20-year, 11 percent, semi-annual interest-paying convertible debentures with a call provision of 10 percent above par allowed 10 years after issuance. The conversion price of the debentures is $50, and the current market price of Stayton common is $65.

a. What is the conversion value of the convertible debentures?

b. Straight debentures of similar risk and maturity to Stayton's convertible debentures have a semi-annual return of 8 percent. If the value of an option on each share of stock the convertible can be exchanged for is $38.11, what is the value of the convertible before conversion?

c. Now assume Stayton calls the debentures at 10 percent above par. Is there a transfer of wealth? If so, from whom to whom?

Conversion from an Investor's Standpoint

14.10 Martin owns one convertible bond ($1,000 par) issued by Allison Corp. He has gathered the following information:

Market price of the convertible bond	$1,280
Conversion price	20
Market price per share of common stock	25
Call price of the convertible bond	1,100

a. If Martin converts right now, what is the value of the common stock received? Should he voluntarily convert?

b. Assume Allison calls the convertible. At what common stock market price would Martin be indifferent between converting and receiving the call price?

Alternatives for New Financing

14.11 Micronic Instruments needs to raise $35,000,000 in new financing. Due to its fast growth the firm's investment banker thinks subordinated debt is the best bet. Two alternative plans have been proposed:

Plan I	Plan II
Straight subordinated debt issued at par (ignore flotation costs)	Straight subordinated debt with warrants issued at par (ignore flotation costs)
20-year maturity	30 warrants per $1,000 par bond;
10% coupon rate	each warrant can be used to purchase one
Expected common stock $P/E = 8$	share of stock; the exercise price is $20
	20-year maturity
	9% coupon rate
	Expected common stock $P/E = 8$

The firm anticipates *EBIT* will be $16,000,000, other interest charges are $2,000,000, the tax rate is 35 percent, and there are 2,000,000 shares of common stock outstanding.

a. Determine the straight bond value of the 9 percent subordinated debt issued in Plan II. What is the implied value of the warrants?

b. Calculate the *EPS* and market value of the common stock for both plans. Which plan should be employed? Why?

Note: In (b), in calculating EPS do not worry about the common stock that would be issued if the warrants are exercised.

c. Determine the *EPS* for Plan II as in (b), but now assume that the warrants are exercised. If the *P/E* increases to 9 times after the warrants are exercised, which plan should the firm choose? Does this agree with your conclusion in (b)? How much new cash will the firm receive when the warrants are exercised?

14.12 Wilmot Industries needs $10,000,000 for expansion. The company expects *EBIT* of $8,000,000 after the expansion, there is no other interest, the tax rate is 35 percent, and a common stock *P/E* of 9 times is estimated. There are currently 1,000,000 shares of common stock outstanding. Two financing plans being considered are as follows:

Plan I	Plan II
Straight debt at par (ignore flotation costs) with warrants	Convertible debt at par (ignore flotation costs)
20 warrants per $1,000 par bond; each for one share of common stock	Conversion price = $20
	10% coupon rate
	20-year maturity
12% coupon rate	Expected common stock *P/E* = 9 times
20-year maturity	
Expected common stock *P/E* = 9 times	

a. Determine the anticipated *EPS* under each plan and the market price per share. Which plan should Wilmot take? Why?

In (b), for Plan II assume no interest is paid in the fourth year.

b. To further analyze the effects of the two plans, Wilmot estimates that in 4 years *EBIT* will be $13 million, and that (1) the warrants will all be exercised, because they expire in 4 years; or (2) it will have forced all the convertibles to be converted. Assuming full warrant exercise or full conversion, and a *P/E* of 10 under Plan I and 11 under Plan II, what is the new *EPS* and common stock market price? Which plan should be chosen?

c. Why does the result in (b) conflict with your conclusion in (a)? Is it better to maximize value now (at time $t = 0$) or in four years? Considering your answers to both (a) and (b), which plan do you recommend?

14.13 **Mini Case** Espada Systems is a medium-sized firm that specializes in energy and cost-effective waste management systems. It has traditionally purchased equipment employing equity financing, but is now considering leasing and/or the use of debt financing. Your job is to inform and advise Espada Systems on how to proceed.

a. When a leasing decision is made, why must an alternative form of financing be specified? Why is leasing compared with purchasing and borrowing? What factors impact a firm's decision to lease or to purchase?

Note: Ignore the half-year convention when calculating depreciation.

b. The following information has been estimated for a new piece of equipment: The initial investment will be $1,400,000, the normal recovery period is 7 years, and straight-line depreciation will be employed. The firm's marginal tax rate is 35 percent, the before-tax cost of borrowing is 18.46 percent, and the equipment can be leased for $315,000 per year payable in advance. Should Espada lease or purchase the equipment?

c. Assume everything is the same as in (b) except now you find out there is a resale value at the end of the life of the equipment of $100,000, and additional maintenance charges of $30,000 per year before taxes will be required if the equipment is purchased. If the appropriate opportunity cost of capital is 17 percent, should the equipment be leased or purchased?

d. Espada management has decided they need to understand options, and how they apply to financial management. They want you to conduct a seminar on options. Explain what options are. Be sure to differentiate between call and put options, and between in-the-money and out-of-the-money.

e. Discuss the factors that determine the value of any call option. What specific effect do they have on the value of a call option?

f. Explain what is meant by the statement, "Stock is just a call option." What role does limited liability play? What is the value of the debt of a firm?

g. Summarize when a bond/warrant package or convertibles are desirable. Can they help Espada and at the same time provide benefits to investors?

h. You are evaluating two different financing packages. Comparable quality and maturity debt costs 12 percent. The two plans are as follows:

Plan I	Plan II
Straight debt at par with warrants (ignore flotation costs)	Convertible debt at par (ignore flotation costs)
3 warrants per $1,000 par bond; each for one share of common stock; 3-year expiration	Conversion price = $125
Exercise price = $90	8% coupon rate
11% coupon rate	8-year maturity
20-year bond maturity	

(1) Calculate the straight bond value of the bonds contained in the two plans.

(2) Assume that the value of each warrant in Plan I is $28.72, while the value of an option to convert each share of stock the convertible can be exchanged for in Plan II is $32.67. What is the total value of each financing Plan? What conclusion do you arrive at about the value of the two different plans? Does one appear to be superior in terms of the value to Espada?

SHORT-TERM FINANCIAL MANAGEMENT

EXECUTIVE INTERVIEW WITH WILLIAM J. SINKULA

*Executive Vice President
and Chief Financial
Officer
The Kroger Co.,
Cincinnati, Ohio*

The Kroger Co., the largest U.S. grocery chain in terms of sales volume, owns grocery and convenience stores as well as manufacturing plants that produce private-label goods for its stores. During his 15 years at Kroger, William J. Sinkula has moved from vice president of finance to his current position as executive vice president and chief financial officer. Prior positions included vice president of administration for Western Auto Supply Company, vice president of financial relations for F.W. Woolworth, and vice president and treasurer of Montgomery Ward Company. Mr. Sinkula co-founded Hydro-Conduit Corporation and served as treasurer and executive vice president before Ward's acquisition of Hydro-Conduit. He earned his B.S.B.A. from the University of Nebraska and his M.B.A. from the University of Denver, and is a Certified Public Accountant. We asked Mr. Sinkula to tell us how working capital is managed in the food merchandising industry.

Short-term, or working, capital management differs from company to company. For some, receivables management is the key; for others, it's inventory management. In food merchandising, managing cash and accounts payable are the most important aspects of working capital management.

The Kroger Co.'s working capital management changed considerably after 1988, when both Kohlberg, Kravis, and Roberts (KKR) and the Dart Group tried to take us over. As a takeover defense, we borrowed $4 billion and paid it out as a dividend to our shareholders. This action served as a successful defense against the raiders but made us a very highly leveraged company.

As a result, working capital management became more important to us. Before 1988, we managed the company from the income statement; we were pretty passive about working capital management. Since then, we manage from the balance sheet and cash flow statement, and debt ratios and working capital management now have a higher profile in the company.

Working Capital Policies at Kroger

For both our merchandising and manufacturing operations, the emphasis is the same—to operate with a minimum amount of net working capital. We focus first on accounts payable; cash ranks second; accounts receivable is third. Kroger has good purchasing power and can generally get favorable credit terms. Although we prefer a cash discount to extended payment terms, we analyze our options and choose the better alternative from a cash flow standpoint.

In our industry, managing inventories involves not just reducing the dollar investment but also allocating shelf space to products customers want. The customer is the driving force governing inventory levels. We use a technique called forward-buying to prepurchase inventory. Manufacturers that sell to our industry run frequent price promotions, at well below list price. We have invested as much as $150 million in forward-buy inventories. The key is to buy enough product to last until the next promotion. Although we have to store the inventory, quite often in outside facilities at extra cost, promotion prices are so deep that we can still earn a very good return.

The practice of forward-buying is now becoming less prevalent in favor of an industry practice called efficient consumer response, ECR. The intent of this practice is to remove the inefficiencies in the food supply chain, reduce excess inventories, level production, and pass on the benefits to consumers in the form of lower retail prices.

Cash Management

It's extremely important for us to manage our cash efficiently; our cash position can change by $70 million to $100 million in a couple of days. When weekends or holidays tie up cash in the stores, we have incredible swings in cash levels. So we have a working capital agreement with more than 40 major domestic and international banks to cover any shortfalls until we can clear the receipts. Then we transfer those funds from a bank in the same geographic area as the store to the main collection account at our primary bank.

In terms of managing float, we focus on collection float, because we receive large numbers of checks. To speed the clearing process we now encode checks right in the stores. We no longer use a disbursing bank in a remote location to increase float, but we have four different disbursement banks. The check-clearing pattern on each of those banks is fairly predictable, which allows us to know what's going to clear on a particular day and to plan for short-term financing if required. Knowing the level of expected shortfalls and surpluses is critical. As a highly leveraged company, we don't want to borrow money and then find out we have excess funds to invest overnight at a low rate like 2 1/2 percent.

Because we are in a cash-oriented business, accounts receivable are not a dominant factor for Kroger. Most of our receivables are due from the same people to whom we owe money—our suppliers—for promotional allowances and vendor coupons. We collect billions of vendor coupons in our stores, send them to be counted, and then get the money back. To reduce our receivables, we use accounts receivable and payable software that offsets the receivables against the payables.

Short-Term Financing and Banking Relationships

Our primary short- and long-term financing arrangement is a 7-year, $1.75 billion bank revolving credit facility from a syndicate of banks. All of our assets are pledged on our bank credit agreement.

We negotiated three special features into the working capital portion. First, we can issue unrated commercial paper, up to the whole $1.75 billion. Instead of borrowing from the banks under the interest rate formula, we can borrow at commercial paper rates and typically save a few basis points. The unrated commercial paper markets tend to be very short-term, primarily overnight, but we have been able to get 60- and 90-day maturities when necessary. We also negotiated a competitive bid agreement with our bank syndicate. Banks have the option of bidding the rate at which they would lend us money for 1 to 30 days. We accept bids up to the highest rate we're willing to pay. All banks receive the highest rate we accept (much like the auction process for Treasury bills). This year we have up to $600 million outstanding under the competitive bid agreement, in addition to our commercial paper borrowings.

Another feature that's been a marvelous help is the step-down provision: As our coverage of interest payments improves, our spread over the Eurodollar rate (LIBOR) decreases. For example, when our interest coverage ratio is 3.00:1 or greater, the margin over LIBOR is 5/8 of 1 percent. Right now we're paying 3/4 of 1 percent over LIBOR.

As a company, we work very hard to keep our banks informed. We invite our bankers to an annual meeting, host a dinner for them, have a full informational meeting, and take them to visit stores. Sometimes we talk about finance, other times, about operations. The better the bankers understand our business, the more responsive they'll be to our needs.

Decisions in three crucial areas directly affect the value of the firm—its investment decisions, its financing decisions, and its short-term (or day-to-day) financial management decisions. In Chapter 15 we examine the primary factors that are at play when a firm determines its short-term financial management policy. Then in Chapter 16 we look at cash and marketable securities, followed by accounts receivable and inventory in Chapter 17. Chapter 18 then shifts to the sources of short-term financing.

Short-Term Financial Management Policy

Sections in this chapter:

- **Managing Short-Term Assets and Liabilities**
  The importance of thinking short.
- **Liquidity and the Cash Cycle**
  Liquidity keeps the firm out of financial hot water.
- **Strategy for Managing Current Assets and Current Liabilities**
  A choice between aggressive or conservative strategies.
- **Putting It All Together**
  The whole enchilada.
- **The Changing Nature of Financial Management and Risk Management**
  It will never be the same again.

A few years ago Toyota had a problem many firms would like to face—how to manage record cash flows. Toyota was reaping the benefits of heavy investment in model redesign, automation of its production facilities, and increases in car prices, especially in the United States. But managing large amounts of cash effectively requires careful planning, and Toyota is one of the most financially conservative companies in the world. As one of Toyota's executives stated: "We like to remain independent," referring to independence from both Japan's powerful banks and the ups and downs of the economy.

With its cash, Toyota chose to repay all its long-term debt and to invest in automobile production facilities in other countries, particularly in the United States. In the area of working capital Toyota emphasizes liquidity, short-term investments with stable returns, and minimal exposure to risk from fluctuating foreign exchange rates. Its aim is to avoid any investments that smack of speculation. This approach earns Toyota less on its short-term investments than other Japanese firms earn. Even though some changes may come as the financial climate changes, Toyota's approach remains focused: "We don't really see ourselves in the business of making money from money. It takes away the focus from our main business, which is making cars," explained a company spokesperson.

This is a very conservative policy; other firms are far more aggressive. At the same time, there are tremendous changes occurring in the approach firms are taking toward risk management—that is, how to identify and hedge (if desired) some of the firm's risk exposure to changes in interest rates, foreign exchange rates, and prices of raw materials.

Short-term financial management is the lifeblood of the firm. In this chapter we'll examine some of the aspects of managing the day-to-day operations of the firm.

LEARNING GOALS

After studying this chapter you should be able to:

1. Explain the importance to the firm of working capital management.
2. Understand various measures of ongoing liquidity, and determine the firm's cash conversion cycle.
3. Contrast aggressive and conservative strategies for managing current assets and current liabilities.
4. Define the matching principle, and discuss strategies for dealing with liquidity problems.
5. Discuss risk management and changes occurring in the day-to-day financial operations of firms.

MANAGING SHORT-TERM ASSETS AND LIABILITIES

■ LEARNING GOAL 1

Explain the importance to the firm of working capital management.

WORKING CAPITAL
The firm's current assets and current liabilities.

A firm's assets are normally classified as either current or long-term. Current assets are those expected to be converted into cash within 1 year. They are cash and marketable securities, accounts receivable, inventory, and other current assets such as prepaid expenses. Liabilities also are split between current and long-term, with current liabilities those expected to be paid within 1 year. Current liabilities include short-term debt, accounts payable, and other current liabilities such as accruals and the current portion of long-term debt. Sometimes the term **working capital** is used to refer to both current assets and current liabilities. Thus, short-term financial management, or working capital management, focuses on the coordinated control of the firm's current assets and current liabilities.

Short-Term Financial Management Decisions

Firms are continuously managing the inflow and outflow of cash.

To gain some understanding of the types of decisions required in short-term financial management, consider Figure 15.1, which depicts the flow of cash through a firm. On the right-hand side of the figure are long-term financial management areas, which include capital investments, raising capital, and the related areas of determining the firm's opportunity cost of capital, capital structure, and dividend policy. The left-hand side of the figure focuses on the short-term, day-to-day activities of the firm's financial management. In Chapters 15, 16, 17, and 18 our focus is primarily on the upper left-hand portion of Figure 15.1—that is, on the flow of cash through the firm due to purchases, inventory, sales, and receivables. In Chapter 18 we also consider the firm's short-term financing. The basic short-term financial management decisions facing a firm include the following:

A firm's net cash flow from operations should be its primary source of cash inflow.

1. *Collections and Disbursements.* One of the primary responsibilities of a firm is to manage the collection of funds from customers and to pay suppliers, employees, marketing costs, taxes, and so forth. This frequently includes the implementation of some type of cash and check collection system and the development of various systems for cost effectively making cash disbursements.
2. *Cash Concentration.* Managers also have the responsibility for designing and implementing a system to gather funds from many banks so they can be concentrated for effective management and investment purposes.

FIGURE 15.1

Flow of Cash Through a Firm

Both short-term and long-term financial management are important for achieving the goal of maximizing the value of the firm. Short-term financial management is more operationally focused and less theoretical than long-term financial management.

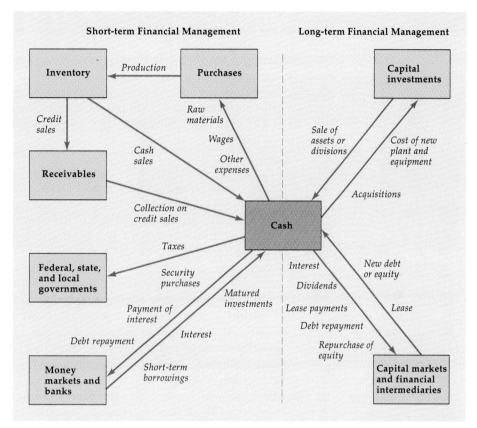

3. *Liquidity Management.* The firm's liquidity—both on the asset side and the liability side—must also be managed. Liquidity management includes decisions regarding the timing of cash inflows and outflows, and determination of the expected surpluses or deficits of cash (via cash budgets as discussed in Chapter 20). Liquidity management also includes managing the firm's portfolio of short-term marketable securities and choosing the type and maturity structure of the firm's short-term borrowings.

4. *Bank Relations.* Another responsibility is designing the firm's banking network and managing its banking relationships. This category includes determining which banks to deal with and the services that will be secured from each.

5. *Receivables.* Management of the firm's credit policy and the resulting collection procedures is also important. Although basic credit terms and customers must be determined in conjunction with marketing personnel, the ultimate responsibility for implementing and maintaining receivables policy falls in the short-term financial management area.

6. *Inventory.* Inventory is the responsibility of many individuals within the firm. The major activities we are concerned with include determining how much investment in inventory is needed and how to finance it.

We will examine each of these areas in Chapters 15 to 18. Before doing so, it is important to understand more about short-term financial management in general, why it is needed, and how firms can proceed with estimating how much they need in the way of current assets and current liabilities.

Why Do Firms Have Short-Term Assets and Liabilities?

In a world of perfect markets there are no transactions costs; no time delays in the production, marketing, and check-clearing system; and no financial distress costs. In such a world, the value of the firm would be independent of its current asset and current liability decisions—and there would be no need to study short-term financial management.

But markets are not perfect. Imperfect markets, and the resulting delays and costs, are what create the need for a firm to concern itself with short-term financial management. Let's briefly consider some of the reasons why firms need current assets and current liabilities.

LIQUIDITY
The ability to be quickly and cheaply available as cash in order to meet short-term needs.

1. *Transaction Costs*. Transaction costs consist of (1) the service fees for buying and selling securities, and (2) the potential loss in value when a sale must be quickly made at a price below what could be received if more time were available. Because of transactions costs, firms hold cash or marketable securities with a major emphasis on **liquidity**—that is, the ability to be quickly and cheaply available as cash in order to meet short-term needs.
2. *Time Delays*. Time delays arise in the production, marketing, and cash collection aspects of a firm's business. Because transactions do not happen instantaneously, many activities affect current asset and liability needs. These include (1) maintaining inventory (raw materials, work in process, or finished goods), (2) offering credit policies to help sell the product, (3) providing cash discounts for early payment, and (4) promptly collecting funds when customers pay their bills. All these steps involve some costs that must be weighed against the benefits involved.
3. *Financial Distress Costs*. Financial distress costs include legal and other direct and indirect costs such as managerial time associated with reorganization, bankruptcy, or fending off financial difficulties. Because of the high cost most managers equate with financial distress, they tend to keep significant liquid balances, even though they generally earn less on these funds than on the firm's long-term asset investments. Alternatively, firms may incur costs to have access to credit markets, although they do not anticipate actually having to take advantage of this additional borrowing capacity.

Key Idea 1—the goal of the firm is to maximize its market value—applies just as much to short-term financial management as to other areas of finance.

The point should be clear: In theory, short-term assets and liabilities are not needed; in practice, they become one of the most important topics with which managers must deal. In this and the next three chapters, we'll see the importance of effective short-term financial management decisions in maximizing the value of the firm.

The Importance of Short-Term Assets and Liabilities

Short-term assets and liabilities typically comprise a large part of a firm's total assets and liabilities. Consider the percentage breakdown of current assets and current liabilities (both compared to total assets) for manufacturing firms in 1992, 1993, and 1994:[1]

---

[1]*Bureau of the Census*, Quarterly Financial Report for Manufacturing, Mining and Trade Corporations, *Second Quarter 1992, 1993, and 1994.*

The structure of a firm's assets influences its liabilities. For example, short-term assets at Federal Express are 31% of total assets while short-term liabilities are 27%; for Coca-Cola they are 44% and 49%, respectively.

	1992	1993	1994
Current Assets			
Cash and marketable securities	4.8%	4.9%	5.1%
Accounts receivable	13.7	13.2	13.3
Inventory	13.7	13.1	12.8
Other	3.3	3.8	4.1
Total current assets	35.5%	35.0%	35.3%
Current Liabilities			
Short-term debt	4.3%	4.4%	4.1%
Accounts payable	7.5	7.3	7.6
Income tax payable	0.7	0.9	1.0
Current portion of long-term debt	2.1	1.7	1.5
Other	10.5	10.5	10.6
Total current liabilities	25.1%	24.8%	24.8%

For manufacturing firms current assets account for about 35 percent of the total assets, whereas current liabilities comprise about 25 percent. Among current assets, the largest investments are in inventory and receivables. For current liabilities, the largest percentages are in the "other" category (which includes accruals) and in accounts payable. Comparing the 3 years, we see that investment in current assets decreased slightly, while the amount of current liabilities also decreased slightly.

Some of the key reasons why short-term financial management is important are as follows:

Depending on conditions, the working capital components can either conserve or generate cash.

1. The size and volatility of current assets and current liabilities make them a major managerial concern. Managers spend much of their time on the day-to-day activities that revolve around short-term financial management.
2. The relationship between sales growth, or growth opportunities, and short-term assets and liabilities is both close and direct. As sales increase, firms must increase inventory and accounts payable. Increased sales generate a higher level of accounts receivable. So current assets and liabilities must be managed as firms increase or decrease their scale of operations and sales. At the same time, some of the current liabilities—especially accounts payable—tend to increase and decrease as inventory and accounts receivable increase and decrease. This **spontaneous short-term financing** (due to the use of trade credit as discussed in Chapter 16) must be kept in mind as we consider both the current assets and their financing.
3. Financial problems show up first in a firm's current asset and liability accounts, especially its level of accounts receivable, inventory, and the flow of cash into and out of the firm. Firms that are doing well maintain control of their accounts receivable and inventory, and ensure the continual flow of cash.
4. Current assets and liabilities are especially important for smaller firms, because these firms often carry a higher percentage of both than do larger firms. Their survival depends much more on effective short-term financial management than does that of larger firms.

SPONTANEOUS SHORT-TERM FINANCING
Short-term financing that tends to expand (contract) as the firm's current assets expand (contract).

CONCEPT REVIEW QUESTIONS

- Explain the terms *current assets*, *current liabilities*, and *working capital*.
- Why is short-term financial management important and necessary?
- Give some examples of short-term financial management decisions a firm must make.

LIQUIDITY AND THE CASH CYCLE

Remember Key Idea 4—firms focus on cash flows and their incremental effects.

ONGOING LIQUIDITY
The liquidity that results from the expected inflows and outflows of cash through the firm over time.

CASH CYCLE
The flow of cash through the firm in order to purchase, produce, sell, and collect on sales.

CASH CONVERSION CYCLE
The net time interval in days between actual cash expenditure by the firm on its productive resources and the ultimate recovery of cash.

DAYS INVENTORY
The average number of days it takes to produce and sell a firm's product.

DAYS SALES OUTSTANDING
The average number of days it takes to collect credit sales.

OPERATING CYCLE
The total number of days from purchase to when cash is received.

DAYS PAYABLE
The average number of days that the firm defers its accounts payable.

■ **LEARNING GOAL 2**

Understand various measures of ongoing liquidity, and determine the firm's cash conversion cycle.

Liquidity is an important factor in determining a firm's short-term financial management policies. It is a function of the level and composition of current assets and current liabilities, and the ability to raise cash when needed. The variability in current asset and current liability levels is also important; however, for many firms the ongoing level of current assets and liabilities is fairly steady. Accordingly, we focus our primary attention on the level, not the variability, of the firm's current assets and current liabilities. *Marketable securities,* which are short-term investments in which to place excess cash, are highly liquid. *Accounts receivable,* which arise from the sale of the firm's goods or services, are less liquid than marketable securities. *Inventory* is also considered a current asset but is often less liquid than accounts receivable.

Liquidity has two major aspects—ongoing liquidity and financial slack (sometimes called financial flexibility). **Ongoing liquidity** refers to the inflows and outflows of cash through the firm as the product acquisition, production, sales, payment, and collection process takes place over time. *Financial slack*, as discussed in Chapter 12, refers to the ability to adjust rapidly to unforeseen cash demands and to have backup means available to raise cash. We begin by addressing ongoing liquidity and defer a discussion of financial slack until later in the chapter.

The firm's ongoing liquidity is a function of its **cash cycle,** that is, the general flow of cash through the firm in order to purchase, produce, sell and collect on sales. As raw materials are purchased, the firm's current liabilities increase through accounts payable. Subsequently, the firm pays for these purchases. During the same time, the raw materials are converted into finished goods through the production process. After reaching the finished goods inventory, they can be sold—for cash or on credit. In the latter case, accounts receivable are created. Finally, the accounts receivable are collected, resulting in cash. (The cash cycle—involving purchases, inventory, receivables, and collections—is shown in the upper left-hand side of Figure 15.1.) Ongoing liquidity is influenced by all aspects of the cash cycle, because increases in purchases, inventory, or receivables will decrease liquidity. A decrease in any of the three, other things being equal, will increase ongoing liquidity.

A helpful way to look at the cash flow for the firm is to analyze the firm's cash conversion cycle. A **cash conversion cycle** reflects the net time interval in days between actual cash expenditures of the firm on productive resources and the ultimate recovery of cash. As shown in Figure 15.2, it consists of several measures: Once the purchase of the raw materials is made, the **days inventory** determines the average number of days it takes to produce and sell the product. The **days sales outstanding** determines the average number of days it takes to collect credit sales. The **operating cycle,** which is:

$$\text{operating cycle} = \text{days inventory} + \text{days sales outstanding} \qquad (15.1)$$

measures the total number of days from purchase of raw materials by the firm to the time when cash is received from the firm's ultimate customers. Because the raw materials typically are not paid for immediately, we must also determine how long the firm defers its payments. The difference between the operating cycle and the **days payable** is the cash conversion cycle:

$$\text{cash conversion cycle} = \text{operating cycle} - \text{days payable} \qquad (15.2)$$

FIGURE 15.2

Cash Conversion Cycle for a Typical Firm

By integrating both current assets and current liabilities, the cash conversion cycle emphasizes the firm's ongoing liquidity.

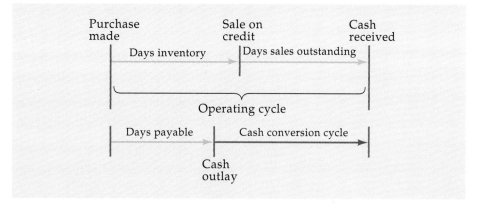

As the cash conversion cycle lengthens, the firm's ongoing liquidity worsens; as the cycle is shortened, the firm's ongoing liquidity improves.

To determine a cash conversion cycle, we employ the following steps:

RECEIVABLES TURNOVER
The number of times per year the firm collects its receivables.

STEP 1. Calculate the **receivables turnover,** which is the ratio of sales to accounts receivable, that is, the average number of times per year the firm collects its receivables:

$$\text{receivable turnover} = \frac{\text{sales}}{\text{accounts receivable}} \qquad (15.3)$$

INVENTORY TURNOVER
The number of times per year the firm turns over its inventory.

STEP 2. Calculate the **inventory turnover,** which measures how quickly inventory moves through the firm and is turned into sales—that is, the inventory's liquidity. It is calculated as:

$$\text{inventory turnover} = \frac{\text{cost of goods sold}}{\text{inventory}} \qquad (15.4)$$

PAYABLES TURNOVER
The number of times per year the firm receives financing from others who sell goods and services to the firm.

STEP 3. Determine the **payables turnover,** which is the average number of times per year the firm receives financing from others who sell goods, services, and materials to the firm on account (instead of for cash):

$$\text{payables turnover} = \frac{\text{cost of goods sold} + \text{general, selling, and administrative expenses}}{\text{accounts payable} + \text{salaries, benefits, and payroll taxes payable}} \qquad (15.5)$$

STEP 4. Divide the three turnover ratios into 365 days to calculate the days sales outstanding, days inventory, and days payable, respectively:

$$\text{days sales outstanding} = 365/\text{receivables turnover} \qquad (15.6)$$

$$\text{days inventory} = 365/\text{inventory turnover} \qquad (15.7)$$

$$\text{days payable} = 365/\text{payables turnover} \qquad (15.8)$$

STEP 5. Using Equations 15.1 and 15.2, and the values determined in Step 4 above, calculate the cash conversion cycle.

The cash conversion cycle is a measure of both operating efficiency and liquidity. A short conversion cycle usually means a low current ratio.

These steps are shown in Table 15.1 for Anacomp Inc., for 1992, 1993, and 1994. An examination of various liquidity measures (current ratio, quick ratio, and net working capital) in Table 15.1 indicates that the firm's liquidity appears to have deteriorated over this period. By calculating the cash conversion cycle, however, we see that its ongoing liquidity improved in 1993 before deteriorating in 1994. The cash conversion cycle is a quick and convenient way to analyze the ongoing liquidity of the firm over time. Although it does not show how risky the cash flows are, it does focus on our main concern—cash flows.

From a management standpoint, the cash conversion cycle points to action that can be taken to speed the inflow of cash or to slow the outflow. Anacomp's cash conversion cycle is 78. This has primarily occurred due to slow sales, along with increased receivables and inventory. If Anacomp wants to reduce the cash conversion cycle it can (1) control or reduce the cost of goods sold and general, selling, and administrative expenses while obtaining more spontaneous short-term financing, (2) increase sales at a faster rate than it increases receivables, or (3) reduce inventory relative to the cost of goods sold. Hence, the cash conversion cycle provides action guidelines that assist the firm in effectively dealing with the cash flow through the firm.

TABLE 15.1

Cash Conversion Cycle for Anacomp Inc.

Although traditional liquidity measures indicate Anacomp's liquidity has deteriorated somewhat, its cash conversion cycle has actually improved during this time period.

	1992	1993	1994
Liquidity Measures			
Current ratio (current assets/ current liabilities)	1.21	1.17	1.03
Quick ratio [(current assets − inventory)/ current liabilities)]	0.86	0.80	0.72
Net working capital (current assets − current liabilities; in millions of dollars)	$42.34	$30.93	$5.62
Turnover Ratios			
Receivables turnover	5.30	5.40	4.72
Inventory turnover	6.09	5.85	5.09
Payables turnover	6.08	5.27	5.14
Cash Conversion Cycle			
Days sales outstanding	68.87 days	67.59 days	77.33 days
Days inventory	59.93	62.39	71.71
Operating cycle	128.80	129.98	149.04
Less: Days payable	60.03	69.26	71.01
Cash conversion Cycle	68.77 days	60.72 days	78.03 days

CONCEPT REVIEW QUESTIONS

■ How is *ongoing liquidity* different from *financial slack (protective liquidity)*?
■ Explain how to calculate a firm's cash conversion cycle.

STRATEGY FOR MANAGING CURRENT ASSETS AND CURRENT LIABILITIES

■ **LEARNING GOAL 3**

Contrast aggressive and conservative strategies for managing current assets and current liabilities.

Essential elements that must be considered in establishing a firm's short-term financial management policies are cash flows, liquidity, risk, and the level of returns that are necessary to compensate for the risk. We begin by analyzing first the strategy for current asset management and then the strategy for current liabilities. Thus, the first important short-term financial management decision is to determine the size and composition of the firm's working capital. Then we consider the second important short-term financial management decision—how to finance the working capital.

Current Assets

The major current assets are cash, marketable securities, accounts receivable, and inventory. We will examine these assets in some detail in Chapters 16 and 17. Here, it is helpful to consider the factors that influence a firm's investment in current assets.

Current Asset Levels

Many factors influence the general level of current assets; four of the most important are:

1. *Nature of the Firm's Business.* The specific activities pursued by the firm often have an important influence on the level of the firm's current assets. Retail firms have much larger inventories than manufacturing firms, leading to a larger percentage of current assets. On the other hand, fast-food chains, such as McDonald's and Wendy's, always have more current liabilities than current assets. Due to the nature of the business, they operate—very successfully, we might add—with very few current assets.
2. *Size of the Firm.* As shown below, smaller firms have a much higher percentage of current assets (and current liabilities) relative to total assets than larger firms.[2]

	Manufacturing Firms	
	All Firms	Assets Under $25 Million
Assets		
Cash and marketable securities	5.1%	10.3%
Accounts receivable	13.4	27.2
Inventory	12.9	24.1
Other	4.0	3.3
Total	35.4%	64.9%

[2]*Bureau of the Census*, Quarterly Financial Report for Manufacturing, Mining, and Trade Corporations, *Third Quarter 1994.*

	Manufacturing Firms	
	All Firms	Assets Under $25 Million
Current Liabilities		
Short-term debt	4.0%	7.9%
Accounts payable	7.7	13.6
Income tax payable	1.0	0.6
Current portion of long-term debt	1.5	3.4
Other	10.8	7.3
Total	25.0%	32.7%

The primary reasons for the differences between current asset levels of small and large firms are that larger firms (a) can devote the resources and attention necessary to manage their current assets, (b) may have more predictable cash flows, (c) may have some economies of scale in current asset or current liability management, (d) have more access to the capital market than smaller firms, and (e) become more capital intensive. By *capital intensive* we mean they tend to use more machines and equipment in the production and distribution process.

3. *Rate of Increase (or Decrease) in Sales.* As sales increase, generally both accounts receivable and inventory also increase, along with a spontaneous increase in accounts payable. Consider Crown Products, which has been analyzing its current assets and liabilities in relation to sales, as shown in Table 15.2. Current assets have averaged about 30 percent of sales, and current liabilities have been about 8 percent of sales. Note that as sales have increased, current assets have increased by roughly the same proportion. Likewise, current liabilities have tended to increase due to the spontaneous change in accounts payable as inventory expands.

4. *Stability of the Firm's Sales.* The more stable the sales, the greater is the firm's ability to predict sales and cash flows which, therefore, leads to less current assets. On the other hand, firms with highly volatile sales must have more current assets, particularly cash and inventory.

Aggressive Versus Conservative Management

In examining the firm's current asset policies, we will concentrate on the composition of the firm's balance sheet. We will examine the effect that changes in the firm's poli-

---

TABLE 15.2

Working Capital for Crown Products (dollars in thousands)

Although there have been year-to-year fluctuations, the relationships among working capital components are stable enough for planning purposes.

Year	Current Assets	Current Liabilities	Net Working Capital	Sales	Current Assets/Sales	Current Liabilities/Sales	New Working Capital/Sales
1	$ 74	$20	$54	$250	29.6%	8.0%	21.6%
2	77	21	56	284	27.1	7.4	19.7
3	90	26	64	275	32.7	9.5	23.3
4	92	25	67	298	30.9	8.4	22.5
5	98	23	75	315	31.1	7.3	23.8
6	110	30	80	375	29.3	8.0	21.3
Average					30.1%	8.1%	22.0%

cies have on its asset composition, and thus on its cash conversion cycle, on expense levels, and on risk and the returns required by the firm. For the time being, we are not concerned with how the firm finances its current assets; *our concern is solely with the composition of these assets.*

Because current assets never drop to zero, we can think of the firm as having a need for some **permanent current assets** on an ongoing basis. At the same time, virtually all firms have a need for **seasonal (temporary) current assets** that fluctuate over the year (or business cycle). The size of both the permanent and temporary current assets is determined, in part, by how aggressive a firm is toward the level of current assets it maintains.

A firm can manage its current assets aggressively or conservatively. *Aggressive asset management* occurs when the firm actively controls and manages its current assets with the goal of minimizing them, or making sure they are currently needed. Under an active policy current assets are kept only when they are needed, and they will expand only when they are needed to facilitate the operation of the firm. *Conservative asset management*, on the other hand, can be thought of as a passive approach, which allows current assets to grow in size in order to have enough cash, inventory, and other current assets on hand to weather any situation. To see this, consider Figure 15.3, which illustrates both aggressive (with lower current asset levels) and conservative (with higher current asset levels) approaches for a firm at a specific point in time. Other things being equal, an aggressive asset management policy leads to lower current

PERMANENT CURRENT ASSETS
The minimum current assets the firm always needs to have on hand to maintain its operations.

SEASONAL (TEMPORARY) CURRENT ASSETS
The difference between the firm's need for current assets at its busiest period and the firm's permanent current assets.

Aggressive asset and liability management is closely related to a firm's competitive position in its industry, and its bargaining power with its customers and suppliers.

FIGURE 15.3

Aggressive Versus Conservative Asset Management for Crown Products

Aggressive management leads to higher risk and higher required returns; conservative management provides lower risk exposure and lower returns.

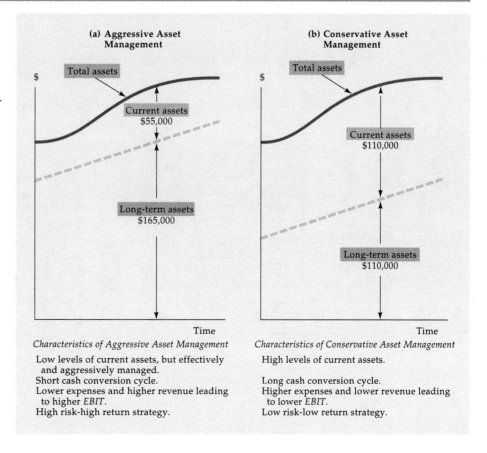

(a) Aggressive Asset Management

Total assets
Current assets $55,000
Long-term assets $165,000
Time

Characteristics of Aggressive Asset Management
Low levels of current assets, but effectively and aggressively managed.
Short cash conversion cycle.
Lower expenses and higher revenue leading to higher *EBIT.*
High risk-high return strategy.

(b) Conservative Asset Management

Total assets
Current assets $110,000
Long-term assets $110,000
Time

Characteristics of Conservative Asset Management
High levels of current assets.
Long cash conversion cycle.
Higher expenses and lower revenue leading to lower *EBIT.*
Low risk-low return strategy.

assets, a shorter cash conversion cycle, lower expenses, and higher returns in line with the higher risk. Conservative asset management practices have just the opposite effects. Let's look at each of these characteristics in turn.

The Level of Current Assets.   Aggressive asset management generally means lower levels of all current assets. The firm keeps only a minimal level of cash and marketable securities on hand and relies on effective management and the possibility of short-term borrowing to meet any unexpected cash needs. Likewise, aggressive accounts receivable and inventory management will generally lead to lower levels of both.[3]

A firm loses flexibility by financing short-term assets with long-term funds. During periods when funding is not needed, the long-term debt may be hard to retire unless the firm pays a penalty or incurs a capital loss.

Cash Conversion Cycle.   More aggressive management of current assets shortens the cash conversion cycle. Remember from Equation 15.1 that the operating cycle is determined by adding the days inventory to the days sales outstanding. Aggressive asset management increases turnover by lowering the average level of both receivables and inventory. So, an aggressive policy shortens the firm's operating cycle, which leads to a shorter cash conversion cycle. This shorter cash conversion cycle increases a firm's ongoing liquidity, because it does not have as large a proportion of its assets tied up in accounts receivable and inventory.

Expense and Revenue Levels.   Aggressive current asset management will have the effect of reducing expenses. Fewer accounts receivable will be carried, so there will be lower carrying costs. In addition, fewer receivables will have to be written off as uncollectible. Likewise, by keeping inventory to a minimum, the firm avoids the carrying cost associated with inventory, as well as the possibility for loss due to obsolescence, theft, and so forth. This, in turn, leads to higher earnings before interest and taxes, *EBIT*, and ultimately to higher cash flows, as compared with the results of a conservative asset management policy.

A further effect of aggressive asset management may be to increase expected revenues, which could also lead to a higher *EBIT* level. This can occur in two ways: First, if returns from investing in long-term assets are higher than on short-term assets, which they typically are, then total cash inflows should increase. Second, the firm could attempt to increase total cash inflows by tailoring its credit-granting policy to encourage sales. These more lenient credit terms, however, would be granted only if they were expected to lead to a higher level of *EBIT* than without them.[4]

Key Idea 6—risk and return go hand-in-hand—is also important in short-term financial management.

Risk and Return.   Finally, let's consider what happens to the risk and returns required by the firm. In Chapter 5 we developed the idea of the capital asset pricing model, CAPM, and nondiversifiable risk, beta, as a means of quantifying risk. Some of these ideas can be employed here, but it is easier to think of risk in terms of the variability in currents assets, a scarcity of cash, or other adverse consequences. We can still maintain the conceptual framework that the higher the risk, the higher the return, and vice versa.

The risks associated with an aggressive asset position include the possibility of running out of cash or inventory, or being otherwise so strapped for funds that effective management of the firm is impeded. Likewise, the firm might keep inventory so low that sales are lost when stockouts occur. The risk associated with an aggressive accounts receivable policy could also result in lost sales if too low a level is kept.

---

[3] *In some circumstances, an aggressive accounts receivable or inventory policy could result in a high level of one or both. This is an exception to the general idea that the more aggressive the current asset policy, the lower their level. As noted in Chapter 17, a net present value approach is employed to determine the proper level of accounts receivable and inventory to maintain.*
[4] *Based on accepting positive NPV projects, the tendency would be for higher, rather than lower, accounts receivable. They would still be aggressively and effectively managed, however, so that they do not get out of control.*

To see the effect of aggressive versus conservative asset management policies, while holding other risks constant, consider Crown Products. It can adopt an aggressive or a conservative asset management position, with anticipated effects as follows:[5]

	Aggressive	Conservative
Sales	$375,000	$375,000
All expenses	325,000	335,000
EBIT	$ 50,000	$ 40,000

As shown previously in Figure 15.3, the aggressive approach has only $55,000 in current assets, whereas the more conservative approach has $110,000. The impact of fewer current assets and therefore lower expenses shows up in an anticipated *EBIT* of $50,000 for the aggressive plan, as opposed to only $40,000 with the conservative plan. Thus, by employing a more active aggressive approach that exposes the firm to more risk (of running out of cash, inventory, and so forth), the firm has increased its anticipated *EBIT*, and ultimately its cash inflows.

Current Liabilities

Now that we have considered current assets, let's consider the financing needed to support these assets. There are two fundamental decisions the firm must make with regard to financing: First, how much will it secure from short-term versus long-term debt (or liability) sources? Second, how much should the firm borrow in relation to what is put up by its owners? The first of these, the short-term versus the long-term question, is considered here. As we will see, the matching principle is widely employed to address this question. The second part, how much debt relative to equity should be employed, is discussed in Chapter 12. Here, we ignore this aspect of the problem and confine our attention to short-term financing.

Current Liability Levels

Retail firms carry more current assets than do manufacturing firms. This is primarily because retail firms have to carry more inventory. Since most merchandise for inventory is bought on credit, what would you expect the level of a typical retail firm's accounts payable to be, compared to that of a typical manufacturing firm? It will be larger, simply because larger inventories lead spontaneously to larger accounts payable. So, a major factor influencing the firm's level of current liabilities is its level of inventory and other current assets. Other things being equal, businesses that require high levels of current assets will have a tendency for fairly high levels of current liabilities.

A second element influencing the level of current liabilities is the amount of financial flexibility desired by the firm. With a low level of current liabilities a firm has flexibility, because short-term borrowing can generally be easily obtained. Also, accounts payable can be built up in an emergency without endangering the firm. However, if the firm already has a high level of current liabilities, then little financial flexibility is left. The more flexibility the firm wants, the less it will finance with current liabilities.

Aggressive Versus Conservative Management

Other things being equal, the lower the current liabilities, the more conservative the firm's liability management policies, and the more financial flexibility the firm has.

[5]For simplicity, we assume total assets and revenues are constant.

Figure 15.4 illustrates the liability management alternatives available to a firm at a point in time. As shown in the figure, the higher the level of current liabilities, the more aggressive the policy. This is exactly opposite the effects of an aggressive versus a conservative asset policy. An aggressive liability management policy results in higher current liabilities, a shorter cash conversion cycle, lower interest costs (if short-term rates are less than long-term rates), and higher risk and higher returns required. Conservative policies have just the opposite effect. In the material that follows in this section, *we focus on the liabilities, holding assets constant.* Then, in the next section, we will consider assets and liabilities together.

The Level of Current Liabilities.   Current liabilities consist of accounts payable, short-term loans or notes payable, various accrued expenses, and the current principal portion of long-term debt due.[6] An aggressive management approach increases the firm's reliance on short-term liabilities. Accounts payable will be used to the greatest extent possible—and payments on them will be made as late as possible without incurring a bad credit reputation. Short-term borrowing will also be used extensively.

Cash Conversion Cycle.   By employing more accounts payable and accruals, aggressive liability management shortens the cash conversion cycle. Larger payables and accruals lead to a shorter payables turnover, which leads to a longer days payable

---

FIGURE 15.4

Aggressive Versus Conservative Liability Management for Crown Products

Aggressive liability management is a high risk–high return strategy, whereas a conservative approach produces lower risks and lower returns.

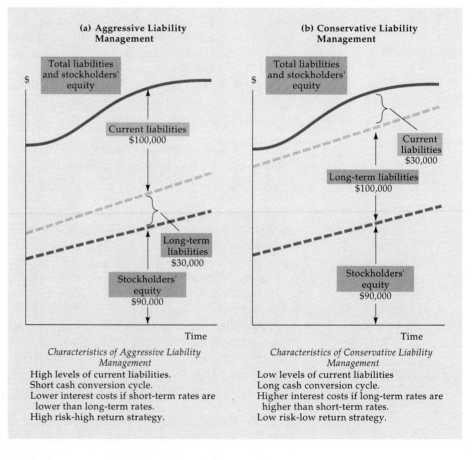

Characteristics of Aggressive Liability Management
High levels of current liabilities.
Short cash conversion cycle.
Lower interest costs if short-term rates are lower than long-term rates.
High risk-high return strategy.

Characteristics of Conservative Liability Management
Low levels of current liabilities
Long cash conversion cycle.
Higher interest costs if long-term rates are higher than short-term rates.
Low risk-low return strategy.

---

[6]*The management of current liabilities is discussed in Chapter 18.*

and a shorter cash conversion cycle. Aggressive liability management tends to increase the ongoing liquidity of the firm by shortening the cash conversion cycle—but it also provides less future flexibility.

Interest Costs.   To understand fully the impact of aggressive versus conservative liability management on a firm's interest costs, we need to consider the term structure of interest rates discussed in Chapter 2. The yield curve plots the term to maturity versus the yield to maturity for borrowings that are equally risky but that differ in terms of length to maturity. Yield curves are generally upward-sloping—which means that long-term debt financing is more expensive than short-term debt financing. An expected benefit of an aggressive liability management program is the ability to borrow funds at a cheaper rate, meaning less cash outflows, than the firm would pay for long-term debt financing.

To see the expected benefits of an aggressive versus a conservative policy, consider again the example of Crown Products. Figure 15.4 presented two different liability strategies. The aggressive strategy employs $100,000 in current liabilities and only $30,000 in long-term liabilities. The conservative strategy employs $30,000 in current liabilities and $100,000 in long-term liabilities. If short-term interest rates are 10 percent and long-term rates are 14 percent, then the total before-tax interest cash outflow is $14,200 [i.e., (0.10)($100,000) + (0.14)($30,000)] for the aggressive policy, versus $17,000 [i.e., (0.10)($30,000) + (0.14)($100,000)] for the conservative one. As long as long-term rates are higher than short-term rates, cash outflows associated with interest are reduced, leading to higher cash flows and earnings for the firm.

Risk and Return.   The main risk of an aggressive liability policy comes from general economic conditions and the continual need to refinance current liabilities. This is especially true if a firm is using extensive short-term financing through borrowing. Although the firm may be able to secure the financing, it is exposed to interest cost fluctuations. These fluctuating interest costs, and the continual need to refinance, increase the firm's risk exposure. An additional risk arises from reduced flexibility when the current liability level is high. Other things being equal, there are substantial risks associated with an aggressive liability policy that relies on large amounts of short-term debt. Greater returns are expected, however, by (1) reducing the cash conversion cycle, and (2) financing at interest rates that are generally (but not always) lower than long-term rates.

CONCEPT REVIEW QUESTIONS

- What factors affect a firm's level of current assets?
- Contrast an aggressive current asset management policy with a conservative current asset management policy.
- What are the effects on a firm of an aggressive current liability management policy and a conservative current liability management policy?

PUTTING IT ALL TOGETHER

■ LEARNING GOAL 4

Define the matching principle, and discuss strategies for dealing with liquidity problems.

We have considered separately both current assets and current liabilities. Now it is time to put them together and discuss the management of the firm's working capital in

FIGURE 15.5

Alternative Short-Term Financial Management Policies

By altering both its asset and its liability structure, the firm can vary its short-term financial management policies considerably.

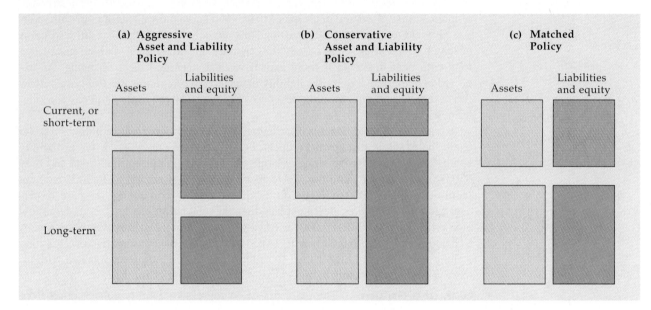

total. The three basic strategies a firm could follow, as illustrated in Figure 15.5, are aggressive, conservative, or matched. A firm could adopt an aggressive, or active, asset and liability management strategy by employing fewer current assets and more current liabilities. Alternatively, by having a larger level of current assets and a lower level of current liabilities, a firm could adopt a very conservative, or passive, asset and liability strategy. Although either of these options is available, many firms employ a matching strategy, which is often cited as a guideline employed for short-term financial management. The matching strategy is embodied in the matching principle, or the idea of self-liquidating debt.

The Matching Principle

MATCHING PRINCIPLE
Working capital guideline that holds that temporary short-term assets should be financed by short-term financing, and permanent current assets and long-term assets should be financed by long-term sources of financing.

The **matching principle** can be stated as follows: Permanent investments in assets (both long-term and current) should be financed with permanent sources of financing, and temporary assets should be financed with temporary financing sources. The idea behind the matching principle is to match, or counterbalance, the cash-flow-generating characteristics of the assets with the maturity of the financing. A temporary buildup in current assets should be financed with current liabilities, which can be liquidated as the investment in current assets is reduced. A buildup in permanent current and long-term assets will take longer to convert to cash; thus, long-term financing will be needed.[7]

---

[7] *Matching can be accomplished by matching on the basis of maturity, cash flows, or duration. Duration matching is discussed in Chapter 23 of* Financial Management.

Using short-term funds to acquire long-term assets is risky: Short-term loans must be rolled over many times during the life of the long-term asset, and long-term assets are not usually very marketable.

Based on the matching principle the following guidelines apply:

1. If a firm has an aggressive current asset position (with a low level of current assets), then it should counterbalance its risks by employing a conservative liability position (with a low level of current liabilities).
2. If a firm has a conservative current asset position (employing a high level of current assets), then it should counterbalance its risks by employing an aggressive liability position (with a low level of current liabilities).
3. If a firm has a moderate current asset position, then it should counterbalance its risks by employing a moderate liability position.

Using long-term funds to acquire short-term assets is a high-cost strategy because long-term funds usually cost more than short-term funds.

The implication of the matching principle is that the firm should establish some *target* for its net short-term financial management position that takes into account risks, the returns required, and the appropriate current asset and current liability positions.

To see this, let's reconsider Crown Products. With an aggressive asset approach it employs fewer current assets, so expenses are reduced and anticipated *EBIT* and cash inflows increase, compared to a conservative approach. Likewise, an aggressive liability approach employs more current liabilities and results in lower total cash outflows for interest than a more conservative liability policy. As shown in Table 15.3, the following combinations exist for Crown Products: (1) a high risk–high return policy employing both aggressive asset and aggressive liability strategies; (2) two intermediate matching strategies employing either an aggressive asset–conservative liability or a conservative asset–aggressive liability strategy; and (3) a low risk–low return policy employing both conservative asset and conservative liability policies.[8] Note that

TABLE 15.3

Impact of Alternative Current Asset and Liability Strategies on the Earnings of Crown Products

A high risk strategy employs low current assets and high current liabilities, whereas a low risk strategy is just the opposite. The matching principle, which attempts to match temporary current assets and current liabilities, results in a trade-off between risk and return.

	Asset and Liability Management Strategy				
	Aggressive Asset– Aggressive Liability	Aggressive Asset– Conversative Liability	Conservative Asset– Aggressive Liability	Conservative Asset– Conservative Liability	
Sales	$375,000	$375,000	$375,000	$375,000	
Expenses	325,000	325,000	335,000	335,000	◄——— Impact of asset strategy
EBIT	50,000	50,000	40,000	40,000	
Interest	14,200	17,000	14,200	17,000	◄——— Impact of liability strategy
EBT	35,800	33,000	25,800	23,000	
Taxes (35%)	12,530	11,550	9,030	8,050	
EAT	$ 23,270	$ 21,450	$ 16,770	$ 14,950	
	High risk– high return strategy	Intermediate positions more in line with matching principle		Low risk– low return strategy	

[8]*An alternative matching strategy would be a more moderate position in both current assets and current liabilities.*

the two intermediate strategies embody the matching principle. In line with the risks involved, the aggressive strategy has anticipated earnings of $23,270, whereas the conservative strategy has anticipated earnings of only $14,950.

Which working capital strategy should Crown select? As we know, it is not earnings that are important; it is the cash flows and market value of the firm. Assume that Crown Products has 10,000 shares of stock outstanding. The anticipated earnings per share for the four strategies will be as follows:

	Anticipated EAT	÷	Number of Shares	=	Anticipated EPS
Aggressive asset–aggressive liability	$23,270		10,000		$2.327
Aggressive asset–conservative liability	21,450		10,000		2.145
Conservative asset–aggressive liability	16,770		10,000		1.677
Conservative asset–conservative liability	14,950		10,000		1.495

Remember Key Idea 1—the goal of the firm is to maximize its market value.

To determine the per share market value, we know that $P_0 = (EPS)(P/E)$, where P/E is the firm's price/earnings ratio. Because aggressive asset or liability policies are viewed as being more risky by stockholders, other things being equal, they should have a lower P/E ratio than more conservative policies. Crown Products needs to estimate the potential impact of the various current asset and current liability strategies on its expected market value. One way is to forecast P/E's for various risk-return strategies. For our example, assume these estimates are as follows:

	Anticipated EPS	×	Anticipated P/E	=	Anticipated P_0
Aggressive asset–aggressive liability	$2.327		9		$20.94
Aggressive asset–conservative liability	2.145		10		21.45
Conservative asset–aggressive liability	1.677		11		18.45
Conservative asset–conservative liability	1.495		12		17.94

Based on these expected market values, Crown should implement one of the matching strategies (aggressive asset–conservative liability), because it results in the highest anticipated market value.

Recognizing and Dealing with Liquidity Problems

The firm's short-term financial management policies should consider many factors. No matter how much planning is done, however, the firm must be able to recognize signs of declining liquidity and know how to deal with the situation. Some of the most important signs of deteriorating liquidity are these:

1. An unexpected buildup in inventory (an increase in the days inventory).
2. An increase in the firm's level of outstanding accounts receivable (an increase in the days sales outstanding).
3. A decline in the firm's daily or weekly cash inflows.
4. Increased costs that the firm is unable to pass on to its customers.
5. A decline in the firm's net working capital, or an increase in its debt ratio.

Net operating cash flow is the best source of liquidity. Other primary sources are cash and marketable securities, and the ability to borrow short-term, to extend credit with suppliers, or to reduce receivables or inventory.

These and similar occurrences indicate the firm has (or will have) a liquidity problem.

There are many different approaches for dealing with liquidity problems, depending on the source of the problem, its severity, and its expected length. Managers often take some of the following steps to deal with liquidity problems:

1. Control and reduce investment in inventory.
2. Reexamine and tighten up on credit and reduce the firm's level of accounts receivable.

FINANCIAL MANAGEMENT TODAY

Within A Hair's-Breadth of Bankruptcy

Firms in financial difficulty need help. Such was the case of a large Los Angeles industrial distributor and service company that suffered due to its own mistakes and the worst local economic conditions in many years. Its bank of over 20 years, which had its own economic troubles, could not extend more credit; in fact, the bank refused to honor the existing line of credit. In order to survive, the firm decided it had to convince all of the stakeholders involved that it was in the stakeholders' best interests to help the firm survive the storm. The following major stakeholders were involved:

1. *Creditors.* After extensive negotiations, the creditors agreed to accept a smaller amount paid over a longer time period. That arrangement was better than what they could expect if the firm declared bankruptcy.
2. *Customers.* By working with customers the firm reduced receivables from 60 to 40 days, thereby increasing the speed of the flow of cash into the firm.
3. *Suppliers.* Why should suppliers extend even more credit to the firm? The argument made was that by extending more credit they were protecting their outstanding receivables and future business. Many suppliers agreed.

4. *Unions.* Wage concessions were needed, if the firm was to continue in operation; the alternative was no jobs at all. Equally important, it was agreed that employee salaries could be paid twice monthly, instead of weekly. This produced a one-time increase in working capital of $700,000 and provided a continuing reduction in payroll expenses.
5. *Government.* Sales taxes are paid monthly in California, and the Franchise Tax Board is responsible for seeing that all businesses pay on schedule. The firm was already behind and didn't have the cash to pay the taxes. However, the firm approached the tax board with this argument: Due to the seasonal nature of the firm's business, if granted an extension, the firm would have enough cash from projected sales and cash flows to be able to pay the back taxes and penalties due. Finally—and ever so reluctantly—the tax authorities agreed to the late payment schedule.

What are the results? Revenues fell, from $120 million to $80 million, and the work force shrunk from 500 to 350. But revenues have now stabilized, and the firm is once again in the black. With no more deterioration in the California economy, the company should make it. Credit for the recovery goes primarily to the firm's major stakeholders who determined it was in their best interests to work with the firm, instead of forcing it into bankruptcy.

Source: Bruce W. Ballenger, "Within a Hair's-Breadth of Bankruptcy," *The Wall Street Journal* (October 24, 1994), A14.

3. Increase short-term or long-term debt, or issue equity.
4. Control overhead and increase awareness of the need for effective asset management.
5. Reduce planned long-term (capital) expenditures.
6. Lay off employees.
7. Reduce or eliminate cash dividends.

If these measures are not sufficient, more drastic steps will be necessary. The important point is that firms must plan for meeting ongoing liquidity problems as part of their short-term financial management policies.

Financial Slack

Until now we have been talking about the firm's ongoing liquidity. There is, however, another aspect of liquidity, sometimes called *financial slack*, or financial flexibility, which is the ability to have liquid resources to meet unexpected cash demands. These demands may arise when, due to unforeseen circumstances, larger cash outflows (or smaller cash inflows) than expected occur. In some cases cash is needed to take advantage of unexpected opportunities. As we discussed earlier in Chapter 12, firms with high growth opportunities, or growth options, have more desire for financial slack than those with a low level of growth opportunities.

LINE OF CREDIT
Agreement between a firm and a bank whereby the firm can borrow up to a maximum amount for short-term needs.

The firm cannot plan its short-term financial management policies and liquidity needs without some uncertainty about future financial performance. A portion of this uncertainty can be eliminated by effective cash budgeting (discussed in Chapter 20), but some uncertainty still remains. Effective managers, whether they follow a conservative, aggressive, or matched short-term financial management policy, always maintain some financial slack. This may be in the form of one or more **lines of credit,** which are short-term borrowing agreements the firm has negotiated with a bank. At the firm's discretion, it may borrow or pay back on the line of credit.

Another strategy is to maintain a fairly large marketable securities portfolio or to have a bond or stock issue ready. Other firms establish bank relations and keep the bank regularly informed about possible borrowing needs. An alternative approach, to be discussed in Chapter 18, is to factor (or sell) the firm's accounts receivable.

Effective short-term financial management involves a continual trade-off between risk and return. To deal with the risk of running short on cash at a crucial point in time, firms establish various means of ensuring financial slack as they formulate their short-term financial management policies.

CONCEPT REVIEW QUESTIONS

- Explain the matching principle.
- What are some important signs of deteriorating liquidity?
- Describe some strategies of financial slack management.

THE CHANGING NATURE OF FINANCIAL MANAGEMENT AND RISK MANAGEMENT

■ LEARNING GOAL 5

Discuss risk management and changes occurring in the day-to-day financial operations of firms.

As discussed in Chapter 1, the person ultimately responsible for financial activities at most large firms is the chief financial officer, CFO. Although arrangements differ among companies, often there are treasury and finance departments reporting to the CFO. Traditionally the corporate treasurer's job was to see that there was enough money to pay the bills, but that view has changed in recent years. Increasingly, treasury departments have been viewed as *profit centers*. That is, the job of the department is seen not only as providing funding for the firm's operations, but also as making a profit. A recent survey indicated that 20 percent of the firms surveyed viewed the treasury department as a profit center. As such, treasury departments have to produce positive cash flows that add value to the firm. One way of doing that is to use derivatives for profits, not just for hedging.

At the same time, many firms have embarked on programs of risk management.[9] These firms are assessing how sensitive their profits and cash flows are to changes in interest rates, currency exchange rates, and even the price of some of the firm's major raw material resources. And, often the treasury department is responsible for hedging some of the risks involved using interest rate swaps, forwards, futures, and options. The essence of risk management is to take an offsetting position so if, for example, in-

---

[9]*Risk management is discussed in Chapters 23 and 28 of* Financial Management.

terest rates increase and the firm has to pay more interest on borrowings, it produces an offsetting gain from the hedge.

Take, for example, Merck & Co., the pharmaceutical firm. Merck has one of the more sophisticated risk management programs. Their 500-person unit engages in such activities as whether to buy insurance against such perils as environmental liabilities or to self-insure. It oversees a wide range of risk management, especially related to fluctuations in foreign exchange rates. However, that is only part of the activities with which Merck's risk managers get involved. One item that sets Merck apart is that the firm seeks to assess the risk of the firm's business activities. Based on the premise that risk management should enhance shareholder value, Merck assesses the risks and rewards of all kinds of business activities, from acquisitions and joint ventures, to research and development expenditures for new drugs.

Other firms have not carried risk management as far, but they still do much more than was true even 10 years ago. For example, Mobil Oil Corp. protects itself against swings in interest rates and foreign exchange rates, but not against changes in petroleum prices. Their rationale is that investors expect risk relative to the price of petroleum when they invest in or loan to Mobil. FMC Corp., a Chicago-based conglomerate, has to deal with 21 different business units and 35 currencies. At FMC the individual business units identify the risk exposure, and then turn to the Chicago headquarters for advice on hedging, cost-effective borrowing, and related matters. For example, one FMC unit is working to finance a new chemical plant in the People's Republic of China. The unit wants to finance the project in the local currency, but there's no easy way to borrow or hedge it. The solution is to borrow from another multinational in the People's Republic of China that has currency available, and then buy insurance in case the People's Republic of China devalues its currency or seizes FMC's assets.

Many firms have very successful risk management and hedging operations. Some of them include Coca-Cola, Colgate-Palmolive, FMC, Ford, Lexmark, McDonald's, Merck, Mobil, 3M, and Union Carbide. However, other firms have gotten into trouble and suffered losses. For example, Gibson Greeting Cards recently lost about $20 million, Procter & Gamble lost $102 million, and Dell Computer lost $32 million—all on derivatives transactions. Due to occurrences such as these, many firms are starting to rethink (1) whether treasury departments should be viewed as profit centers, if making them profit centers leads to speculating rather than hedging, and (2) how to establish adequate controls and the right environment for effective risk management.

Some companies are beginning to adopt the risk control model proposed in the 1992 report by the Committee of Sponsoring Organizations, COSO, a group of leading accounting and auditing associations. Unlike traditional risk-control programs, which typically include risk identification and measurement, written policies and procedures, and monitoring, this report also calls for the CEO and the board of directors to set the ethical tone for the company by establishing a control philosophy. As one of the coauthors of the COSO said, "The biggest risk you have is someone screwing up the reputation of the company."

Gone are the days when the corporate treasurer's job was simply to make sure there was enough money to pay the bills. Increasingly risk management, often on a very broad scale, is becoming a part of day-to-day financial management.

CONCEPT REVIEW QUESTIONS

■ How do Merck and Mobil Oil deal with risk management?
■ How is the role of a firm's treasury department changing?

Summary

- The goal of short-term financial management is to assist in maximizing the value of the firm. Short-term financial management focuses on the magnitude and timing of the cash flows and on the risks and returns involved. Although more operational in nature and based less on theory than is long-term financial management, effective short-term financial management is of vital importance to firms.
- The cash conversion cycle, by taking account of the turnover of receivables, inventory, and payables, provides information about ongoing liquidity.
- Both current assets and current liabilities may be managed conservatively or aggressively. A coordinated short-term financial management policy focuses on both asset and liability management.
- To finance current assets, many firms follow the matching principle: Temporary assets are financed with temporary funds, permanent assets with long-term sources of funds.
- Firms are also concerned about financial slack as they formulate their short-term financial management policies.
- Risk management is increasingly practiced, to deal with risks arising from fluctuating interest rates, foreign exchange rates, and material prices.

Questions

15.1 In a world of perfect markets, firms should not have current assets and current liabilities. What accounts for the sizable levels of current assets and current liabilities we observe in practice?

15.2 Determine the impact of the following actions on a firm's cash conversion cycle:
  a. The firm loosens its credit terms, leading to increased sales and accounts receivable. Sales increase more than receivables, on a percentage basis.
  b. Payments on accounts owed are stretched from a 20-day average to a 35-day average.
  c. The firm borrows on a short-term note instead of stretching payables, as in (b).
  d. By introducing new control procedures, the firm reduces its inventory.

15.3 At certain times the term structure of interest rates may be such that short-term rates are higher than long-term rates. Does it follow that the firm should finance entirely with long-term debt during such periods? Explain.

15.4 The firm faces two primary decisions with respect to its financing: the percentage of short- or long-term financing to employ, and the amount of borrowing to use relative to the owners' contribution. Discuss both decisions and how they might affect each other.

15.5 What is the matching principle? How does its use relate to the firm's cash conversion cycle, and its risk and returns?

Concept Review Problems

See Appendix A for solutions.

CR15.1 Joshua Corp. has a receivables turnover of 6.75, an inventory turnover of 9.54, and a payables turnover of 9.13.
  a. What is Joshua's operating cycle?
  b. Its cash conversion cycle?

CR15.2   Two companies—MaxIncome and SafetyFirst—producing similar products have completely different short-term financial management policies. Income statements and balance sheets for each of the companies are:

Balance Sheet

	MaxIncome	SafetyFirst
Cash and marketable securities	$ 6,598	$ 17,855
Accounts receivable	15,125	25,632
Inventory	18,365	46,123
Net long-term assets	48,306	48,306
Total assets	$88,394	$137,916
Short-term bank loans	$18,232	$ 5,362
Accounts payable	18,185	11,565
Long-term debt	4,930	77,816
Common stock	33,562	33,562
Retained earnings	13,485	9,611
Total liabilities and stockholders' equity	$88,394	$137,916

Income Statement

	MaxIncome	SafetyFirst
Sales	$265,233	$302,555
Cost of goods sold	162,900	177,930
General, selling, and administrative expenses	87,716	118,617
Taxes	5,847	2,403
Net income, *EAT*	$ 8,770	$ 3,605

What are the current ratio (current assets/current liabilities), quick ratio [(current assets − inventory)/current liabilities], net working capital (current assets − current liabilities), and cash conversion cycle for each firm?

CR15.3   Jamie, controller of Greensleeves Golf, is investigating different working capital policies. Two different pro forma (or projected) balance sheets have been developed as follows:

	Aggressive	Conservative
Cash and marketable securities	$ 6,873	$ 8,856
Accounts receivable	18,462	29,357
Inventory	22,300	46,659
Net long-term assets	16,180	16,180
Total assets	$63,815	$101,052
Short-term bank loans	$ 8,000	$ 3,000
Accounts payable	15,543	5,000
Long-term debt	0	57,440
Common stock	23,269	23,269
Retained earnings	17,003	12,343
Total liabilities and stockholders' equity	$63,815	$101,052

Note: These figures do not include interest expenses for Greensleeves Golf.

Jamie also estimated that sales under an aggressive policy will be $166,658, with cost of goods sold of $86,534 and general, selling, and administrative expenses of $57,689. A conservative policy would result in sales of $185,732, cost of goods sold of $92,344, and general, selling, and administrative expenses of $75,554.

a.   If the interest rate is 10 percent on long-term debt, it is 6 percent on short-term debt, and the tax rate is 40 percent, what are Greensleeves Golf's current ratio (current assets/current liabilities), cash conversion cycle, net profit margin (net income/sales), and return on equity (net income/stockholders' equity) under each policy?

b. Assume Greensleeves Golf has 5,000 shares of common stock outstanding. If the aggressive policy results in a *P/E* ratio of 8, while the conservative policy results in a *P/E* ratio of 12, what is the stock price under the two policies?

CR15.4 MoreSun Travel is considering adopting one of three short-term financial management policies: an aggressive policy, a matched policy, or a conservative policy. Ruth, the CFO, projects sales for each policy under three different economic scenarios: a robust economy, a standard economy, and a poor economy.

Sales	Aggressive	Matched	Conservative
Robust	$900	$1,200	$1,400
Standard	800	1,000	1,200
Poor	500	700	900

In each case all expenses *except interest* are expected to be 50 percent of sales.

a. Ruth estimates interest costs will be $36 for the aggressive policy, $50 for the matched policy, and $66 for a conservative policy, no matter what the economic condition. If the firm's tax rate is 40 percent, the number of shares of common stock is 100, and there is an equal probability for each economic state, what are the expected earnings per share and the standard deviation of earnings per share for each policy?

b. If investors assign a *P/E* ratio of 10 for the aggressive policy, 11 for the matched policy, and 12 for the conservative policy, which policy should MoreSun Travel adopt?

Problems

See Appendix C for answers to selected problems.

Additional Net Working Capital

15.1 Malek Distributors is planning to make a $10 million investment in long-term assets and is attempting to estimate how much additional net working capital will be needed to support this expansion. The long-term asset turnover ratio (sales/long-term assets) on the new investment is estimated to be 2. From past experience, Malek estimates its total asset turnover ratio (sales/total assets) is 1. Also, for every dollar increase in current assets the firm experiences, about 60 percent of the increase can be financed through spontaneous increases in current liabilities. Determine the increase in net working capital (current assets − current liabilities) that should accompany the anticipated increase in long-term assets.

Cash Conversion Cycle

15.2 Smith Enterprises has the following turnover ratios: receivables turnover, 6.0; inventory turnover, 4.0; payables turnover, 3.75.

a. Find Smith's cash conversion cycle.

b. Now find its cash conversion cycle if receivables turnover improves to 7.0 and inventory turnover increases to 5.5.

c. Now assume the inventory conversion period is as determined in (b) and the payables turnover increases to 5.3. If the firm then wants a cash conversion cycle of no more than 35 days, what must the receivables turnover be?

Cash Conversion Cycle

15.3 Pilgrim Systems specializes in the design, manufacture, and marketing of products for the transmission and control of power. For 2 recent years, information is as follows:

	Year −1	Year 0
Sales	$2,524	$2,711
Cost of goods sold	2,106	2,224
Cost of goods sold plus general, selling, and administrative expenses	2,353	2,497
Accounts receivable	377	382
Inventory	619	602
Accounts payable plus accrued wages and employee benefits	223	245

Freedom Paper produces and markets a variety of paper products through its five divisions. Information for the same 2 years is as follows:

	Year −1	Year 0
Sales	$1,233	$1,403
Cost of goods sold	1,021	1,173
Cost of goods sold plus general, selling, and administrative expenses	1,123	1,286
Accounts receivable	138	136
Inventory	138	153
Accounts payable plus accrued wages and employee benefits	78	82

a. Calculate the cash conversion cycle for both firms for both years.
b. What trends, if any, are evident between year −1 and year 0?
c. Do you think part of these differences are caused by the industries they operate in? Why or why not?

Current Asset Management

15.4 Wheeler Management Group is attempting to determine its optimal level of current assets. It is considering three alternative policies, as follows:

	Aggressive	Average	Conservative
Current assets	$500	$700	$900
Long-term assets	1,000	800	600
Total	$1,500	$1,500	$1,500

In any case, the firm will employ the following financing: current liabilities of $700, long-term debt of $200, and common equity of $600. Sales are expected to be $2,500. Because of lower costs with the more aggressive policies, the anticipated ratio of *EBIT* to sales is 13 percent with the aggressive policy, whereas it is 12 percent with the average risk policy and 11 percent with the conservative policy. Interest is $65, and the tax rate is 30 percent.
a. Determine anticipated net income under the three different plans.
b. In this problem, we assumed that both total assets and sales are the same with any of the policies. Are these typically valid assumptions?
c. How, specifically, does the risk vary under the three plans? As part of your analysis, calculate the current ratio (current assets/current liabilities) and net working capital (current assets − current liabilities).

Reducing Inventory

15.5 Warren Software keeps a large inventory, in order not to lose sales. Its new vice president for finance has recommended that the firm's inventory be cut. Doing so would reduce the inventory level by $150,000 and allow the firm to forgo renewing a $150,000 note payable with a 12 percent interest rate that matures soon. An abbreviated income statement for Warren is as follows:

EBIT	$1,000,000
Interest	140,000
EBT	860,000
Taxes (35%)	301,000
Net income, EAT	$ 559,000

With 100,000 shares of stock outstanding and a *P/E* ratio of 10 times earnings, Warren's current stock price is $55.90.

Note: Carry to three decimal places for EPS.

a. *Scenario 1*: If the anticipated *EBIT* and *P/E* ratio are unaffected by the reduction in inventory and notes payable, what would the new market price be?

b. *Scenario 2*: The marketing manager for Warren believes the inventory reduction will result in lower sales, and thus *EBIT* may decrease to $950,000. What would the anticipated market price be if this happens?

c. If there is a 60 percent chance that *EBIT* will stay at $1,000,000, and a 40 percent chance it will drop to $950,000, what action should Warren Software take?

d. What are your answers to (a) through (c) if the marginal tax rate is only 20 percent?

Working Capital Management

15.6 Three companies—Aggressive, Moderate, and Conservative—follow different working capital policies, as their names imply:

	Aggressive	Average	Conservative
Current assets	$ 300	$ 400	$ 600
Long-term assets	700	600	400
Total	$1,000	$1,000	$1,000
Current liabilities	$ 500	$ 350	$ 200
Long-term debt	100	250	400
Common equity	400	400	400
Total	$1,000	$1,000	$1,000

Selected income and balance sheet data are as follows:

	Aggressive	Average	Conservative
Sales	$1,800	$1,800	$1,800
Cost of goods sold	1,260	1,280	1,300
Cost of goods sold plus general, selling, and administrative expenses	1,560	1,580	1,600
Accounts receivable	120	160	240
Inventory	150	200	300
Accruals and accounts payable	250	200	100
Short-term borrowing	200	150	100

The interest rate on short-term debt is 10 percent, and on long-term debt it is 12 percent. The tax rate is 30 percent.

a. Determine the net income for each firm.

b. Calculate the cash conversion cycle for each firm.

c. What is the current ratio (current assets/current liabilities) and the net working capital (current assets − current liabilities) for each firm?

d. Are there other factors that would have to be taken into account in practice? What are the major ones?

Alternative Working Capital Policies

15.7 Morgan & Reese is considering whether to adopt Plan I or Plan II for its current assets and liabilities. Adopting one plan versus the other is expected to affect sales, expenses, and interest. As a result, taxes and anticipated earnings after tax, *EAT*, will also vary. Based on a 50 percent probability of a good or bad year, Morgan & Reese's finance department has made the following projections:

	Plan I		Plan II	
	Good Year	Bad Year	Good Year	Bad Year
Probability	0.50	0.50	0.50	0.50
Sales	$900,000	$800,000	$850,000	$760,000
All expenses except interest and taxes	750,000	710,000	730,000	680,000
EBIT	150,000	90,000	120,000	80,000
Interest	20,000	17,000	18,000	15,000
EBT	130,000	73,000	102,000	65,000
Taxes (40%)	52,000	29,200	40,800	26,000
EAT	$ 78,000	$ 43,800	$ 61,200	$ 39,000

Morgan & Reese has 10,000 shares of common stock outstanding. Risk will be measured by the coefficient of variation of earnings per share.

a. Calculate the mean *EPS*, standard deviation of *EPS*, and coefficient of variation of *EPS* for both plans.

b. If Plan I carries an anticipated *P/E* ratio of 10 times earnings and Plan II has an anticipated *P/E* of 11 times, which plan should Morgan & Reese choose?

Liquidity, New Debt, and Market Price

15.8 Gentry Resources has the following balance sheet and income statement:

Balance Sheet		Income Statement	
Cash and marketable securities	$ 50	Sales	$1,800
Accounts receivable	100	Cost of goods sold (70% of sales)	1,260
Inventory	100	General, selling, and	
Long-term assets	600	administrative expenses	190
Total assets	$850	*EBIT*	325
		Interest	25
Short-term debt	$ 50	*EBT*	350
Accounts payable	70	Taxes (36%)	117
Salaries, benefits, and payroll		Net income, *EAT*	$ 208
taxes payable	40		
Other current liabilities	40		
Long-term debt	150		
Stockholders' equity (100 shares)	500		
Total liabilities and stockholders' equity	$850		

a. Determine Gentry's current liquidity position by calculating its current ratio (current assets/current liabilities), net working capital (current assets—current liabilities), ratio of current assets to total assets, ratio of current liabilities to total assets, and cash conversion cycle.

b. If its current *P/E* ratio is 8 times earnings, what is Gentry's present market price per share?

c. The marketing vice president believes significant sales are being lost because of not offering enough credit to customers and lack of inventory. Working with the chief financial officer, she has prepared the following plan:

$250 will be raised: $100 will be additional short-term debt with a 12 percent interest rate, and the other $150 will be additional long-term debt with a 14 percent interest rate.

Note: Current assets increase by $30 more than the $250, due to the $30 of spontaneous short-term financing provided by the increase in accounts payable.

Cash will increase by a total of $50 (this includes the additional cash raised with the new financing), accounts receivable by $115, and inventory by $115. Because of the increase in inventory, accounts payable will increase $30.

Sales are expected to be $2,200, cost of goods sold will remain 70 percent of sales, and general, selling, and administrative expenses will increase by $30.

All other accounts remain the same.

Because investors are expected to view the new plan as being more risky, the new P/E ratio is estimated to be 7 times earnings.

(1) Calculating the same information as in (a), what is Gentry's new liquidity position?

(2) Calculate the new income statement. What is the new anticipated market price per share?

(3) Should Gentry proceed with the plan?

Liquidity, New Common Stock, and Market Price

15.9 Dashell Manufacturing has the following balance sheet and income statement:

Balance Sheet		Income Statement	
Cash	$ 25,000	Sales	$900,000
Accounts receivable	60,000	Cost of goods sold	400,000
Inventory	65,000	General, selling, and	
Long-term assets	350,000	administrative expenses	100,000
Total assets	$500,000	All other expenses	250,000
		Net income, *EAT*	$150,000
Accounts payable plus salaries, benefits, and payroll taxes payable	$ 80,000		
Other current liabilities	20,000		
Long-term debt	100,000		
Stockholders' equity (50,000 shares)	300,000		
Total liabilities and stockholders' equity	$500,000		

a. Determine Dashell's liquidity situation by calculating the current ratio (current assets/current liabilities), net working capital (current assets − current liabilities), the ratio of current assets to total assets, the ratio of current liabilities to total assets, and the cash conversion cycle.

b. What is the current market price per share of Dashell's stock if its P/E ratio is 8 times earnings?

c. Peter, Dashell's chief financial officer, is very conservative and believes that the current ratio needs to be raised to 2.0. To accomplish this, he proposes to sell 2,500 shares of common stock to net the firm $20 per share. The proceeds will be added to the firm's cash account. Assuming that everything else remains the same, determine the following:

(1) Dashell's new liquidity position, as in (a).

(2) Its new anticipated market price per share.

(3) Whether or not Dashell should issue the stock.

Matching Principle

15.10 Memphis Products is preparing a 2-year plan for its asset investments, as given in the following schedule. (For simplicity, long-term assets are assumed to be constant at $40 million, as is stockholders' equity. Thus, you have to concern yourself only with current assets, current liabilities, and long-term debt.)

Date		Total Current Assets per Period (in millions)
Year 1	3/31	$30
	6/30	36
	9/30	42
	12/31	39
Year 2	3/31	33
	6/30	39
	9/30	45
	12/31	42

a. Current liabilities tend to equal one-third of Memphis's current assets. If Memphis has a total of $15 million in long-term debt every quarter, determine the amount of short-term borrowing required per quarter to complete the financing of the firm's current assets.

b. Instead of (a), assume that no long-term debt exists. How much short-term debt will be needed per quarter to match, or counterbalance, current assets?

c. If short-term interest rates are 9 percent and long-term rates are 11 percent, how much interest does Memphis save over the 2 years by matching its current assets?

Working Capital

15.11 Mini Case REH Fashions is an aggressive, young firm that has grown dramatically during the last few years. Until now it has fared well, but lately it has been experiencing continuing working capital problems. You have been called in to evaluate REH's operations and suggest changes in funding in order to meet the continuing working capital problems.

a. What do we mean by the term "short-term financial management"? What are the primary short-term financial management decisions faced by firms? How are they related to each other?

b. REH Fashions' balance sheet and income statement are as follows:

Balance Sheet			Income Statement	
Cash and marketable securities	$ 125		Sales	$7,000
Accounts receivable	750		Cost of goods sold	3,150
Inventory	300		General, selling, and	
Long-term assets	1,625		administrative expenses	3,500
Total assets	$2,800		*EBIT*	350
			Interest	115
Short-term debt	$ 800		*EBT*	350
Accounts payable	800		Taxes (40%)	94
Salaries, benefits, and payroll			Net income, *EAT*	$ 141
taxes payable	400			
Other current liabilities	300			
Long term debt	100			
Stockholders' equity	400			
Total liabilities and				
stockholders' equity	$2,800			

Determine REH's current liability position by calculating its current ratio (current assets/current liabilities), ratio of current assets to total assets, ratio of current liabilities to total assets, and cash conversion cycle. In assessing REH's liquidity position, focus on the figures calculated above and other information that can be gleaned from the balance sheet and income statement. What conclusions do you reach?

c. In order to improve its liquidity ratios, one alternative open to REH is to increase the short-term debt by $1,000 and add the same amount to the cash position. While this is just a cosmetic change, it does affect the figures calculated in (b). What are the new figures if everything else remains as in (b)?

d. Explain in detail what an aggressive versus a conservative liquidity management system entails. In addition to the levels of current assets and current liabilities, are there other factors that should be considered?

e. Does REH have a liquidity problem? If so, what are the causes of the problem?

Cash and Marketable Securities

Sections in this chapter:

In 1985 E.F. Hutton, then the nation's fifth largest brokerage firm, pleaded guilty to 2,000 counts of bilking banks through an elaborate check overdraft scheme. It agreed to pay a fine of $2 million and prosecution costs of $750,000. In addition, Hutton agreed to pay back banks that may have been defrauded; it reserved some $8 million for that purpose. As a result of this case, the Justice Department attempted to draw some legal limits around many cash management practices where none existed before. In so doing, it sought to clarify the thin line between aggressive cash management—a tactic practiced by more and more firms—and outright fraud.

In the last decade cash management has become an increasingly important financial function. Higher interest rates in the 1980s were only one factor magnifying the impact of successful cash management on bottom-line profits. Firms have been beefing up their cash management staffs, and technological advances have given cash managers ready access to information on cash inflows, outflows, and idle balances. Cash managers are becoming part of the firm's overall planning function.

These developments have created a dynamic area, one that will continue to undergo rapid change. Advances are being made by banks and many firms as part of the continuing technological revolution that is occurring with the development of the information superhighway. National Westminster, a British clearing bank, has even developed a prototype of an electronic alternative to cash. With electronic cash, via the National Westminster model or some other model, businesses and individuals may be able to safely and securely pay for items electronically via Internet, where computers and computer networks talk to one another via telecommunication links using common data protocols. All of these developments herald vast changes for businesses and individuals. In this chapter we'll look at how firms deal with cash and marketable securities management.

LEARNING GOALS

After studying this chapter you should be able to:

1. Explain why firms hold cash, and discuss the risk-return tradeoff for liquid assets.
2. Explain the concept of float in controlling cash inflows, and discuss techniques for controlling disbursements.
3. Discuss the advantages of electronic funds transfer.
4. Explain how a firm calculates its optimal daily cash balance.
5. Discuss the risk, liquidity, maturity, and yield aspects of alternative marketable security investments.

THE CASH MANAGEMENT FUNCTION

■ **LEARNING GOAL 1**

Explain why firms hold cash, and discuss the risk-return tradeoff for liquid assets.

CASH
Currency on hand plus the demand deposits held in checking accounts.

MARKETABLE SECURITIES
Short-term investments that can be quickly converted into cash with little or no loss of principal.

LIQUID ASSETS
A firm's cash and marketable securities.

Remember Key Idea 1—the goal of the firm is to maximize its market value.

Cash refers to currency on hand plus the demand deposits held in checking accounts at various commercial banks. **Marketable securities** are the short-term investments the firm may temporarily hold which can be quickly converted into cash. Together, cash and marketable securities form the **liquid assets** of the firm. Three main questions relate to liquid asset management:

1. How should the firm design its cash-gathering and cash-disbursing systems?
2. How should the investment in liquid assets be split between cash and marketable securities?
3. How should the marketable securities portfolio be managed?

In this chapter we'll answer each of these questions. First, though, we need to consider some general aspects of the cash management function. Because liquid assets generally provide lower returns than long-term assets, we need to understand why firms choose to hold liquid assets. Then we will discuss the general risk-return aspects of liquid assets. Throughout, the goal of the firm is to design a cash management system that assists in maximizing the value of the firm.

The effective management of cash is an important function, often practiced by successful firms but neglected by others. Although the management of cash is important for all firms, it is especially important for smaller firms. There, the focus may be on "getting the firm's business accomplished," with cash management left as a "to-be-done-later" activity. However, signs of financial distress show up first and foremost in a firm's cash account. In larger firms a separate cash management department is common. In fact, in recent years a certification program has been developed for those working in cash management—the Certified Cash Manager. This certification, started in 1984 by the National Corporate Cash Management Association, NCCMA, is particularly important for those who have cash management responsibilities either in firms or in banks.

Reasons for Holding Cash

Firms hold cash for four basic reasons:

1. *Transactions Purposes.* In the everyday course of business, firms need a certain minimum amount of cash on hand to meet cash outflow requirements. These include routine items such as paying the monthly bills, making payments to suppliers, and the like. In addition, cash is needed for major items such as tax payments, dividends, salaries, and paying interest and/or principal related to debt.

2. *Hedge Against Uncertainty.* A second reason for holding liquid assets is as a hedge against uncertain future events. Funds for this purpose often are held in the form of marketable securities. An alternative to holding liquid assets to hedge against uncertainty is to obtain a line of credit. With a line of credit from a bank, the firm can borrow up to a specified maximum amount over some time period. Lines of credit generally require a commitment fee, whether they are used or not. Thus, financial slack is the second reason for holding cash.

3. *Flexibility.* Many firms hold substantial amounts of liquid assets in anticipation of unforeseen opportunities and in order to have the capability of funding growth options, or opportunities, quickly and easily. Likewise, during periods of economic downturn, firms postpone capital expenditures and attempt to hoard liquid assets to "weather the storm." Thus, they desire financial slack.

4. *Compensating Balance Requirement.* Banks perform many services for firms, such as collecting and disbursing funds, handling interbank transfers, providing lines of credit, and making loans. The compensation received by the bank comes from two sources—direct fees and *compensating balances.* A compensating balance is a specified amount the firm agrees to leave on deposit in its checking account. Typically this amount is set at some level related to the size of the loan or the amount of services provided.

Risk and Return

Remember Key Ideas 4, 6, and 7—firms focus on cash flows and their incremental effects, risk and return go hand-in-hand, and options are valuable.

Determining the right level of cash to hold is a matter of balancing risk and return. The fundamental risk involved in holding too little cash relates to an inability to operate in the normal manner. If cash inflow is a problem, paying bills may have to be deferred, capital expenditures curtailed, short-term financing obtained, and assets sold. Growth options, or opportunities, that present themselves will have to be bypassed. In an extreme case, the firm may have to file for protection under the bankruptcy code or be forced into liquidation. The risk-return tradeoff for liquid assets involves the following:

1. Having enough cash and liquid reserves (or financial slack), in the form of marketable securities and/or lines of credit, to meet all the firm's obligations and take advantage of growth opportunities.

2. Not holding excess liquid reserves, because investment in long-term assets generally provides higher returns than short-term investments.

3. Maintaining a minimum cash balance while actively managing the firm's portfolio of marketable securities to ensure as high a return as possible commensurate with the risk involved.

These tradeoffs will guide our discussion as firms make liquid asset decisions consistent with maximizing the value of the firm.

CONCEPT REVIEW QUESTIONS

- ◼ Why do firms hold cash?
- ◼ What are some of the risks of holding too much cash? Of holding too little cash?

CASH MANAGEMENT TECHNIQUES

◼ LEARNING GOAL 2

Explain the concept of float in controlling cash inflows, and discuss techniques for controlling disbursements.

The flow of cash into and out of the firm is continual. Although the level of cash at any point in time is a function of many factors, certain cash management ideas are fundamental to any firm, whatever its size, industry, or the state of the economy. Two major aspects of cash management involve *speeding the inflows* through a cash-gathering system and *controlling the outflows* via a cash-disbursing system. Before discussing these goals of cash management, however, we need to understand payment systems.

Paper-Based Versus Electronic Payment Systems

GIRO SYSTEM
Electronic payment system used in many countries (often run through the postal system) that provides direct transfer from the payor to the payee.

In the United States, Canada, and a relatively few other countries, the major means of making non-cash payments is through checks. Although electronic payment is becoming more widespread in the United States, particularly for larger transactions between firms, we will start our discussion assuming a paper-based system.

A paper-based system is in contrast to **giro systems**, which are employed in most European and many other countries for smaller transactions. Giro systems, often run by the postal service, operate on the basis of direct debits and credits. In these systems, a seller sends an invoice to the buyer. The invoice includes a giro payment stub (called a giro acceptance) encoded with the seller's bank and account number. The buyer signs the stub, takes it to the local post office, transmits the information through the girobank, and the buyer's account is debited and the seller's account is credited for the amount.

We will discuss large transaction electronic payment systems shortly; however, first we will consider cash-gathering and cash-disbursing in a paper-based system.

Speeding the Inflows

FLOAT
The length of time between the writing of a check and its receipt by the recipient.

AVERAGE COLLECTION FLOAT
The average time it takes to convert a payment into cash, or "good funds."

The complexity of the cash-gathering system depends on the size of the firm and the scope of its operations. Small local firms have very simple systems; large national or multinational firms have quite extensive systems. In the cash-gathering system, the concept of float is vital.

Float

Float is the length of time between the writing of a check and receipt of the funds so that the recipient can draw upon them (i.e., when it has "good funds"). The **average collection float** is found by multiplying the number of days of float times the average

MAIL FLOAT
The time between when a customer puts a check in the mail and its receipt.

PROCESSING FLOAT
The length of time it takes a firm to process and deposit a check.

TRANSIT FLOAT
The time it takes for a check to clear the banking system so the recipient can draw upon the funds.

DIRECT SEND
Sending a check to another bank or clearing system, bypassing the local Federal Reserve bank.

daily dollar amount that is in the collection system. The sources of cash-gathering float, as shown in Figure 16.1, are:

1. *Mail Float.* The time that elapses between when a customer places the check in the mail and when the selling firm receives it and begins to process it is the **mail float**.
2. *Processing Float.* The time it takes the selling firm to deposit the check in its bank after receiving the check is the **processing float**.
3. *Transit Float.* The time required for the check to clear through the banking system until the recipient can draw upon it (i.e., has "good funds") is the **transit float.**

There are three primary ways that checks can be cleared between banks. The first is when banks located near one another meet on a daily basis, either individually or through a local clearing house, to physically swap checks drawn on each other. The second way is based on the Federal Reserve check-clearing system. The Fed maintains 12 district banks, 25 branches, and 47 regional check processing centers that facilitate the physical and recording aspects of the check-clearing process. The third way is through a **direct send.** The process with a direct send is somewhat like that employed with a local clearing house, except the banks are not located geographically close to one another.

FIGURE 16.1

Typical Payment System and Resulting Float

All three types of float are important and should be minimized as the firm strives to shorten its cash collection cycle.

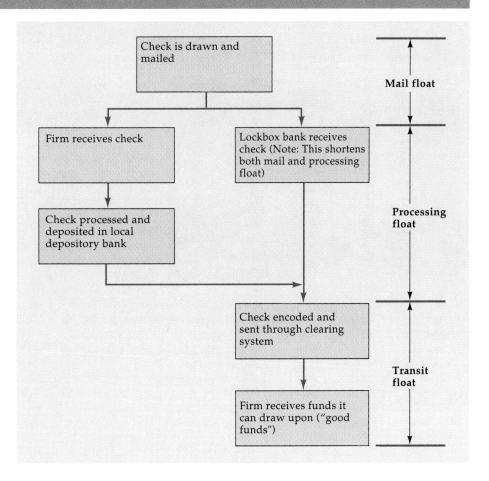

The Expedited Funds Availability Act of 1987 established rules on the maximum amount of time before banks grant consumers availability of funds (before they have "good funds"). The maximum number of business days after deposit by which the funds must be available are as follows:

Category	Available Date
Cash or electronic payment	Next day
Government check	Next day
Local checks	Two days
Nonlocal checks	Five days

Modern cash management practices have nearly eliminated most of the float in the U.S. banking system.

The float within the banking system has declined steadily due to requirements imposed on the Federal Reserve System by both the Depository Institutions Deregulation and Monetary Control Act of 1980, and the use of more sophisticated clearing mechanisms.

In managing receipt of cash payments, a firm should focus first on the processing float. That is, the firm must establish an efficient *internal system* to minimize the delay between receipt of the customer's check (if it comes directly to the firm) and when it is deposited in the bank. After this has been accomplished, other techniques for reducing float can be considered.

FINANCIAL MANAGEMENT TODAY

Clearing Checks—the Old Fashioned Way

Three helicopters land in rapid succession at the Burbank, California, airport. Workers scramble to unload 1,200 pounds of bundled checks, hurl them into carts, and run them out to the waiting Learjet. At 10:35 p.m., 5 minutes later than scheduled, the plane takes off with $600 million in checks that must get to banks in 46 cities by 8 a.m., or payment will be delayed by a day. At 5:10 a.m. the plane arrives at the airport in Columbus, Ohio. Waiting are 15 jets and 6 propeller planes already loaded with more than 25,000 pounds of checks, totaling about $20 billion. After the checks are quickly transferred, the fleet of planes takes off, rushing to 46 different cities, where couriers will meet them and deliver satchels of checks to 150 banks by the 8 a.m. deadline.

Things don't always work as planned. Weather can play havoc with the tight schedule, and other unforseen events occur. One time a bundle of checks slipped out of a helicopter on its way to Wall Street banks. Another time a batch was found in a dumpster behind the Doggie Diner in San Francisco. Sometimes the events are even more drastic. In early 1994 a plane carrying checks and credit-card receipts deposited at BankAmerica went down in the Pacific Ocean near San Diego. BankAmerica fished one bag of checks out of the water and dried them, one by one, with a hair dryer. Over 25,000 customers finally received credit for the deposits, but they lost the use of their funds for several days.

Although electronic funds transfer has been talked about for over 30 years in the United States, only now is significant progress being made. The biggest strides toward eliminating checks are being made by the largest firms. Gerald Milano, head of the California Bank Clearing House, expects the largest 1,000 firms to eliminate checks in the next 5 to 10 years. Some of these firms are becoming very aggressive in dealing with suppliers, encouraging them to move to electronic payment. However, at the consumer level the trend will be much slower. Until it becomes cost effective and/or more convenient, many consumers still like the float that occurs when payments are made by check.

Decentralized Collections

Mail float can be minimized by having decentralized collection points located in parts of the country where the firm has many customers. Two basic devices used for this purpose are local offices and lockboxes.

Local Offices.   If the firm has local offices in the major regions in which it operates, it can have collections directed to these offices. Once the checks are received, they can be deposited in a local depository bank, which is tied into the firm's overall banking network. Depending on the firm and the efficiency of its offices, a local office system may be efficient or very inefficient.

Lockboxes.   If the firm does not have local offices, or if it wants to keep collections out of the local offices—perhaps to boost the efficiency of the cash-gathering system, a widely used alternative is to establish lockboxes. With a **lockbox,** the customer is directed to send the payment to a post office box in a specified city.[1] A bank picks up the mail several times a day and begins the clearing process while notifying the firm, via electronic means, that the checks have been received. At the conclusion of the day, all check photocopies, invoices, deposit slips, and related materials are sent to the firm. To determine where to set up lockboxes, the firm can engage the services of banks or other cash management consulting services. Typically, a national firm will establish lockboxes in various parts of the country depending on its customer base and the regional efficiency of the postal service.

The purpose of both local office and lockbox collection points is to minimize mail float. Lockboxes also reduce the processing float. The benefits gained from the reduced float, however, must be compared to the cost involved. With a local office arrangement, the costs involve personnel, equipment, and space. With a lockbox arrangement, the cost is the fee charged by the bank either directly or through a compensating balance requirement.

Banking Network

Large firms employ more than one bank for their gathering and disbursing systems. A typical "tiered" banking arrangement suitable for a large national firm is shown in Figure 16.2. Using a local office system, customers mail their checks to local offices that process and then forward them to local depository banks. The deposits are transferred to regional *concentration banks* and finally to the firm's main account at its central concentration bank. The rationale for a tiered system is that the greatest check-clearing efficiency is often obtained by organizing the cash-gathering system in this manner.

If lockboxes are employed, they are generally set up at the regional concentration banks, and the local depository banks are bypassed. The regional concentration bank maintains the lockbox, forwards the funds to the firm's central concentration bank, and sends the supporting documents to the firm. Concentration banks typically are located in a Federal Reserve city, in order to speed up the clearing process. In addition, the lockbox should be close to the customers to be served so that mail float is kept to a minimum.

Once the funds are at the firm's central concentration bank, they can be used to meet the cash outflows of the firm, and any extra funds can be quickly invested in marketable securities. If the firm is short of cash, it can draw on its lines of credit. (The

LOCKBOX
An arrangement whereby a firm has its customers make payments to a post office box, from which a local bank collects the checks and forwards the funds to the firm's central bank.

---

[1]*Lockboxes are often classified in two categories: wholesale lockboxes, which are designed for low-volume but high-dollar value per item transactions, and retail lockboxes, which provide for efficient processing of high-volume, low-dollar value checks.*

FIGURE 16.2

Typical Banking and Cash Movement System for a Large Firm

If the firm uses lockboxes, most of the deposits go directly to the regional concentration banks, speeding up the cash-gathering system.

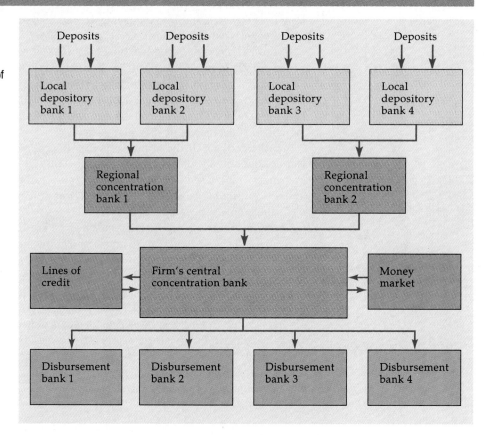

typical firm's banking network will also include various disbursement accounts at one or more banks.)

Other Approaches

Some other approaches that can be employed to improve the efficiency of the collection process include the following:

1. *Special Handling*. To provide special handling of large amounts, a courier might be dispatched to collect a check directly, in order to reduce mail and/or transit time.
2. *Preauthorized checks*. A **preauthorized check** system might be created when the firm receives a large volume of payments in fixed amounts from the same customers. With the preauthorized procedure, the customer authorizes the firm to draw checks directly on the customer's demand deposit account. This method reduces mail and processing float, and increases the regularity and certainty of cash inflows to the firm.
3. *Receipt of Payment Required*. A third alternative is for the firm to demand that the payment be received—not just mailed—by a certain date. This system can be used if a customer is going to take advantage of a cash discount. The receipt-of-payment approach eliminates mail float.
4. *Payment by Wire Transfer*. A fourth alternative would be for the firm to demand payment by a *wire transfer*. This also eliminates float.

PREAUTHORIZED CHECK
A check that does not require the signature of the person on whose account it is drawn.

Because all these approaches have costs and benefits related to reducing the float, they must be considered when determining the most effective means of structuring the firm's cash-gathering system.

Analysis of Cash-Gathering Techniques

A basic model that can be employed to assess the cost effectiveness of various cash-gathering techniques compares the incremental costs with the incremental benefits:

$$\Delta C = \text{after-tax costs}$$
$$\Delta B = \text{after-tax benefits} = (\Delta t)(TS)(I)(1 - T) \qquad (16.1)$$

where

ΔC = the incremental after-tax costs of a new method compared to an existing method

ΔB = the incremental after-tax benefits associated with a new method compared to an existing method

Δt = the time (in days) that float is changed

TS = the size of the transaction

I = yearly interest rate/365

T = the firm's marginal tax rate

With this method, the following decisions will be made:

1. If ΔC is greater than ΔB, stay with the present method.
2. If ΔC is less than ΔB, switch to the proposed method.
3. If ΔC is equal to ΔB, you are indifferent.

Note that $\Delta B - \Delta C$ is simply the net present value, *NPV*. The only difference from other *NPVs* is that discounting is not employed, due to the short time periods involved.

This approach is extremely flexible. It can be conducted on a per unit or total basis, and on a daily or yearly basis. To illustrate its use, we first consider a lockbox example and then alternative transfer mechanisms.

Lockbox Example.   Suppose that your firm now has all collections sent to the home office. To increase efficiency and reduce float, the firm is considering a lockbox operation. You estimate that the reduction in float (both mail and processing) will be 3 days, the average check size is $440, the yearly rate of interest is 10 percent, and the firm's marginal tax rate is 30 percent. Employing Equation 16.1, we can find the approximate *per unit* benefits of the lockbox, as follows:

$$\Delta B = (\Delta t)(TS)(I)(1 - T) = (3)(\$440)(0.10/365 \text{ days})(0.70) = \$0.253$$

On a per unit basis, the benefits are $0.253 per check processed. If the after-tax costs charged for the lockbox are less than this amount, the lockbox operation should be established, because the incremental benefits will be greater than the incremental costs. In addition, any employee time freed would be another benefit that also should be taken into account.

Exactly the same accept/reject decisions are made if the calculations are made per unit, per day, or per year. For consistency in the problems, however, they all state what basis is being employed.

Instead of determining the benefits on a per unit basis, we could calculate them on a daily basis. If there are 300 checks per day, then the average daily volume of checks processed through the lockbox is $132,000 [i.e., (300)($440)]. The incremental benefits *per day* are then:

$$\Delta B = (3)(\$132,000)(0.10/365 \text{ days})(0.70) = \$75.95$$

Thus, if the bank charged less than $75.95 per day after tax (on a 365-day year), then the firm should implement the lockbox arrangement.

Finally, we can also use Equation 16.1 to determine the incremental benefits *per year*. To do this, *either the daily volume, TS, must be converted to a yearly basis, or the daily interest rate, I/365, must be converted to a yearly interest rate.* The incremental after-tax benefits per year from the lockboxes are thus:

$$\Delta B = (3)[(365 \text{ days})(\$132,000)](0.10/365 \text{ days})(0.70) = \$27,720$$

or:

$$\Delta B = (3)(\$132,000)(0.10)(0.70) = \$27,720$$

Again, we would make our decision by comparing the incremental costs versus the incremental benefits. This time, however, we do it on a yearly basis, instead of on the per unit or per day basis determined previously.

Transfer Mechanism Example.   In the preceding example, we did not know the costs. We can also start out, however, by knowing what the incremental costs, ΔC, are, and then determine what the reduction in the float time, Δt, the average size, TS, or the interest rate, I, would have to be for us to be indifferent between the two methods. Suppose that your firm is in the 40 percent tax bracket and is investigating whether one of two methods should be employed to move funds between two banks. The first method costs $5 per unit, and the alternative costs $1, so that $\Delta C = (\$5 - \$1)(1 - 0.40) = \$2.40$. The reduction in float time, Δt, is 2 days, and the yearly interest rate, I, is 10 percent. Setting ΔC equal to ΔB, we have:

$$\Delta C = \Delta B$$

$$\$2.40 = (2)(TS)(0.10/365 \text{ days})(1 - 0.40)$$

$$TS = \frac{\$2.40}{(2)(0.10/365)(0.60)} = \$7,300 \text{ on a per unit basis}$$

If the average size of the checks transferred between the two banks is at least $7,300, it pays to use the first method. If the reduction in float time were only 1 day, the size of the average transfer would have to be $14,600 for the first method to be justified.

In practice, the models become more complex, because there are additional considerations, such as numerous locations and the service credits earned by having compensating balances at the banks. Nevertheless, the basic analytical concept of comparing the incremental benefits versus the incremental costs remains the same.

Controlling the Outflows

We've seen what can be done to speed the inflow of cash. The other side of the cash management "coin" is controlling the outflows. In the design of the firm's cash-disbursing system, the emphasis is on slowing down the outflow of cash as long as possible *without incurring the ill will of the firm's suppliers or damaging the firm's credit rating*. Note that just like individuals do not normally pay their bills before they are due, firms should not either. In addition, within limits there is nothing unethical about slowing down the outflow of cash. The place to begin is with payment procedures. They should be designed so the firm pays *just before* the due date. Paying earlier simply reduces the time that cash is available to the firm for investment.

Controlled Disbursing

Transit float is a function of the processing inefficiencies of various banks, their location, and the Federal Reserve System. To take advantage of transit float, firms may establish a **controlled disbursing** system. The idea is to locate the firm's disbursing banks so that payments to the firm's suppliers will remain outstanding as long as possible. The specific location of the controlled disbursing banks depends on the location and amount of billings by the firm, delays in transit time, and the costs involved. Generally the bank is located in a small- or medium-size city, and receives only one delivery of checks from the Fed per day.

CONTROLLED DISBURSING
System in which the firm maximizes transit float by using banks in distant small- or medium-size cities.

The cost analysis of alternative cash-disbursing systems is similar to that employed for cash-gathering systems. Suppose that a New Jersey-based firm in the 35 percent tax bracket is considering the establishment of two disbursing banks, one in northern California and the other in South Dakota. It expects that transit float will be increased by 2 days, the size of the average check is $5,000, and the yearly interest rate is 8 percent. Using Equation 16.1, we find that the incremental benefits are:

$$\Delta B = (2)(\$5,000)(0.08/365 \text{ days})(1 - 0.35) = \$1.425$$

As long as the two banks charge less than $1.425 per check, the firm should go ahead. For example, if the firm writes 800 checks per month, it can afford to pay up to $1,140 [i.e., (800)($1.425)] after-tax per month to establish the controlled disbursing system. By maximizing transit float, the firm can increase its cash level and employ the excess cash in other ways. The system does mean, however, that suppliers will be without payment for an additional number of days. The ill will created among suppliers must be taken into account when a controlled disbursing system is being established.

Zero-Balance Accounts

When a large firm is organized on a divisional basis, invoices from suppliers often go to divisional finance offices for payment. If each division has its own disbursing bank, excess cash balances may build up, reducing the efficiency of the firm's cash-disbursing system. To prevent this buildup, the firm may instead establish a system of **zero-balance accounts** at its central concentration bank (see Figure 16.3). Each division continues to write its own checks, which are all drawn on individual disbursing accounts at the concentration bank. Although these accounts are like individual demand deposit accounts, they contain no funds. Thus their name—"zero-balance."

ZERO-BALANCE ACCOUNTS
A demand deposit account that contains no funds at the start of each business day; amounts presented for payment are totaled and the negative balance paid off by a credit from the firm's master account at the end of each day.

Each day the checks written on the individual disbursing accounts presented for payment are paid by the concentration bank. As they are paid, a negative balance builds up in the individual accounts. At the end of the day, the negative balances are restored to zero by means of a credit from the firm's master account at the central concentration bank. Each day, the firm receives a report summarizing the activity of the various accounts, so that marketable securities can be bought or sold as needed, depending on the balance in the firm's master account. Zero-balance accounts allow

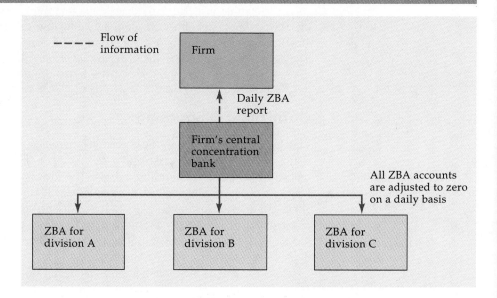

FIGURE 16.3

Zero-Balance Account System

Instead of divisional accounts, separate zero-balance accounts could be kept for payroll, suppliers, cash dividends, and so forth.

much more control, while maintaining divisional autonomy for payments. They are often an effective means of controlling the cash-disbursing system.

Other Approaches

Various other approaches for controlling cash disbursements include the following:

1. *Centralized Payables.* When a firm has many divisions, it could have the invoices received and verified at the divisional level but actually paid at the firm's headquarters. In this instance, all invoices must be forwarded to the central office for payment. Control can be maintained, and the disbursement cycle may be slowed by this procedure.

2. *Timing Check Issuances.* By issuing checks at certain times during the week, the firm may increase its float. Thus, if average mail float is 1.5 days, by issuing checks on Wednesday or Thursday the firm may gain an extra 2 days of float over the weekend. Likewise, issuing a payroll on Friday also means that not all the checks can clear the banking system before Monday or Tuesday of the next week.

The benefits and costs of all the cash-disbursing techniques must be analyzed. The basic framework to employ is the same as that presented earlier. In the disbursing situation, the benefit arises from the additional length of time the firm will have the funds available. This benefit has to be weighed against the additional costs incurred to gain better control of the disbursement of cash.

Interactions

Until now we have examined a number of techniques that could be used to improve the efficiency of the firm's cash-gathering system or to control the cash-disbursing system. In medium- to large-size firms, with various plants and offices, gathering and disbursing problems quickly become complex. In addition, there are obvious interactions between the two that must be taken into account. If the firm decides to employ lockboxes and/or have collections made by local offices, numerous banks will be involved. Using controlled disbursing also will lead to creating accounts at still other banks. In the end, the two decisions—gathering and disbursing—cannot be made in isolation. Rather, their joint effects, costs, and benefits must be considered in order to create an efficient cash management system that balances the risks and returns involved.

International Cash Management

Multinational firms pay particular attention to the effective management of their international cash flows. One important difference for international firms relates to the structure of the banking system in various countries. In many countries banks operate on a nationwide basis. This change from the still somewhat segmented banking structure in the United States has immediate implications. Instead of having to deal with a host of banks, as is generally the case in the United States, multinationals often need to deal with no more than one or two banks in other countries, even if they have substantial operations and sales in that country.

A second difference is the payment system in many countries. Although the payment system in the United States is largely check-driven, that is often not the case elsewhere. In many countries giro systems or other direct debit and credit mechanisms exist and are much more widely used than checks.

Some of the major issues in international money movement are as follows:

1. *Concentration Banking.* To control the flow of funds internationally, multinational firms concentrate their cash at a single bank within a country or on a regional level. Often European-wide systems are established at a bank in London or Amsterdam, and Asian systems are located in Tokyo or Singapore. Once cash is concentrated, funds can be controlled and invested, and a zero-balance type procedure can be implemented.
2. *Debit Transfer.* For disbursements, most European banks charge the customer's account immediately, so the bank, not the firm, gains the advantage of float. Also, on international transactions European banks generally take funds out of a customer's account 2 days *before* the foreign funds are made available.
3. *International Lockbox.* This technique involves establishing one or more lockboxes in a country so that payments can be settled in the country in which the currency is legal tender. With this system, cross-border check clearing is avoided, thus increasing the efficiency of the multinational firm's cash system.
4. *Intracompany Netting.* Many multinational firms have large sums of money tied up in intracompany transactions. With these transactions, one subsidiary's payables are another subsidiary's receivables. To avoid the physical transfer of funds, many multinational firms "net" the funds flowing between subsidiaries once a month.

CONCEPT REVIEW QUESTIONS

- Describe several approaches firms employ to decrease the cost of float.
- What are some ways a firm can employ to increase its transit float?
- Describe how a zero-balance account system can be used to control the cash-disbursing system of a firm.
- How is international cash management similar to or different from domestic cash management?

ADVANCES IN PAYMENT AND INFORMATION SYSTEMS

■ **LEARNING GOAL 3**

Discuss the advantages of electronic funds transfer.

Up to this point we have concentrated primarily on a paper-based check system. During the last 20 years or so there have been extensive discussions and projections about moving to a checkless and paperless society. Substantial progress toward that goal has been made in that period of time.

Electronic Payment Systems

ELECTRONIC FUNDS TRANSFER, EFT
Payment made electronically instead of using a paper-based system.

AUTOMATED CLEARING HOUSE, ACH
System that moves funds electronically between financial institutions using batch processing of information.

WIRE TRANSFER
Means of moving funds between banks through use of the wire system of the Federal Reserve or of a commercial bank.

FEDWIRE
A bank-to-bank payment system operated by the Federal Reserve System.

CLEARING HOUSE INTERBANK PAYMENT SYSTEM, CHIPS
A payment settlement system operated by the New York Clearing House Association, used to settle most international transactions.

Although checks are still widely employed in the United States, there has been slow but steady movement toward the use of electronic payment systems, often referred to as **electronic funds transfer, EFT**. Electronic funds transfer involves the replacement of paper checks with an electronic payment system. The electronic systems fall into two basic groups: The first is *automated clearing houses, ACHs*, whose primary task is to serve consumers and handle smaller payments. The second is various *wire transfer systems*.

To implement the movement of funds electronically between financial institutions, the **automated clearing house, ACH**, system was developed.[2] Today, there are 42 ACH associations; most are owned by groups of banks and other financial institutions. Over 20,000 financial institutions participate in the ACH network. The ACH system is a batch process, store-and-forward system, by which funds are moved electronically. To reduce costs, many items are sent at once. The majority of the ACHs are operated by the Federal Reserve System under contract with the ACH. In recent years, many changes have occurred in the ACH system, and the Federal Reserve System has initiated procedures for reducing risks associated with ACH transactions.

Some common uses of the ACH system by firms include (1) direct deposit of payroll, (2) payment of cash dividends to shareholders, (3) payment of taxes, insurance premiums, and the like, and (4) payment of suppliers. Among the largest users of the ACH system are the federal and state governments.

The second form of electronic payment is via **wire transfer**. This system is used by firms for large dollar transfers between banks. With wire transfer, the funds are transferred on a same-day basis, and transit float is eliminated. Wire transfers cost a good bit more, however, than using the ACH system. The **Fedwire** is a bank-to-bank payment system operated by the Federal Reserve System. Firms can initiate transfers by calling their bank or using a terminal hooked up to the bank's network. The **Clearing House Interbank Payment System, CHIPS**, is a payment settlement system operated by the New York Clearing House Association. CHIPS is used to settle most international transactions.[3] Recently it was estimated that approximately $1.3 trillion changes hands daily via wire transfers. Of this total, about half was via Fedwire, and the other half occurred via CHIPS. The average transfer on Fedwire was about $3 million; on CHIPS it approached $5 million per transaction.

---

[2] *Formally, depository transfer checks, DTCs, were widely used to move funds between banks via the mail. These are being replaced with electronic DTCs. Once the electronic DTC is initiated, it is actually processed as an ACH transfer.*

[3] *The equivalent of CHIPS in the United Kingdom is CHAPS. S.W.I.F.T., the Society for Worldwide Interbank Financial Communication, should also be mentioned. Although not a payment system, S.W.I.F.T. provides for the exchange of information between banks. The settlement of the financial transactions then takes place through CHIPS, CHAPS, or some other mechanism.*

Electronic Data Interchange

ELECTRONIC DATA INTER-CHANGE, EDI
Electronic transmission of virtually all of a firm's business correspondence.

At the same time that electronic payment systems have been growing, other advances in automation are affecting the whole ordering and payment system employed by firms. Increasingly firms are using **electronic data interchange, EDI**, which affects everything from the ordering and manufacturing cycle, to the flow of documents related to shipment and payment. Electronic data interchange refers to the exchange of all transaction-related information between two firms in computer-readable form. Thus, its implications are important in all aspects of a firm—both financial and nonfinancial. Interfacing EDI with electronic funds transfer enables firms to move from a paper-based system to a paperless system. Although there are obvious benefits to such a move, there are also costs. That is one of the reasons that moving to an integrated EDI/EFT system has been much slower than anticipated. At the same time there is increasing evidence that progress has and is still being made in implementing effective, cost efficient EDI/EFT systems.

The EDI Experience at Newell

Newell is a manufacturer of hardware, housewares, and office products that serves firms such as Kmart, Wal-Mart, Target, Ace Hardware, and Canadian Tire. To streamline their whole operations, manage inventory, and reduce stockouts at their customers' sites, Newell has designed the following program:

EDI is one of the fastest-growing systems to improve operating performance.

1. A retail store, such as Kmart, captures sales data at the point of sale when the UPC, universal price code, bars are scanned by laser at the check-out counter.
2. Sales data from various stores and warehouses are consolidated at the customer's headquarters daily and transmitted electronically to Newell.
3. When inventory falls to a predetermined level, a replenishment order is generated, and shipping documents are transmitted electronically to the appropriate Newell division.
4. Once an order has been shipped, the shipping data are transmitted electronically from the division to Newell headquarters.
5. An advance shipping notice and invoice are transmitted electronically to the customer's headquarters. The advanced shipping data are then retransmitted to individual stores by the customer's headquarters.
6. Newell is linked electronically to most of its common carriers, allowing it to monitor carrier performance and order progress from the time it is shipped until it arrives at the customer's warehouse or retail outlet.

Through EDI, Newell transmits the following items: point of sale data, forecasts, inventory data, purchase orders, advance shipping notices, invoices, electronic funds transfer, and information about shipping status. Although checks are still used by many businesses, more and more firms like Newell are turning to EDI/EFT.

CONCEPT REVIEW QUESTIONS

■ Describe how automatic clearing can benefit a firm.
■ How does the system at Newell work?

DETERMINING THE DAILY CASH BALANCE

Some fairly simple, but effective, methods can be employed to forecast routine cash inflows (such as payments on invoices) and outflows (such as payroll checks).

■ **LEARNING GOAL 4**

Explain how a firm calculates its optimal daily cash balance.

Now that we have examined cash gathering and disbursing, the second question raised at the beginning of the chapter can be addressed: How should the investment in liquid assets be split between cash and marketable securities? The approach we examine is based on the idea that firms will attempt to keep as little cash in demand deposits as possible. We assume that the firm has a marketable securities portfolio of a sufficient size that funds can be transferred from it to the demand deposit account as needed. Because marketable securities typically earn higher returns than demand deposits held by firms (which typically earn no interest), there is an incentive to leave excess funds in the marketable securities portfolio.

The following five-step procedure can be employed to determine the firm's daily cash balance. It involves estimating the major inflows and outflows and then modeling the routine cash flows.

STEP 1. Prepare cash budgets on a monthly basis. Updates will be made, often weekly, as needed.[4]

STEP 2. Break major cash inflows and outflows out of the cash budget. Major items would include such items as taxes, dividends, lease payments, debt service obligations, wages, and the like.

STEP 3. Identify the timing of the major inflows and outflows expected to occur during the month. From this information, we can estimate approximate times when daily transfers into or out of the marketable securities portfolio may be needed.

STEP 4. Model the remaining, or routine, cash inflows and outflows to determine when (based on historical patterns) we would expect their inflow and outflow to occur during the month.[5] In this process it is important to consider seasonal influences, day-of-the-month effects, day-of-the-week effects, vacations, and the like. The output of this modeling process provides an estimate of the net daily inflow or outflow from routine items. Based on this information, and the timing of the major inflows and outflows from Step 3, the planned times for adding to or selling marketable securities can be estimated. This step specifies the firm's estimated daily cash balance for each day of the month.

STEP 5. As the month progresses, compare the actual routine cash inflows and outflows with the projected ones. Also, the exact timing of major cash inflows and outflows is known, or can be more accurately estimated. Other developments can be added as they occur. The actual dates and amounts of marketable security purchases and sales will be adjusted from those estimated in Step 4 as the month progresses.

This approach to estimating the intramonth (or daily) cash balance is shown in Figure 16.4. The goal is to maintain the actual cash balance at some predetermined level. Obviously, this level depends on the charges or credits the bank passes on to the

---

[4] *Cash budgets are discussed in Chapter 20.*
[5] *See, for example, Rinne Heikki, Robert A. Wood, and Ned C. Hill, "Reducing Cash Concentration Costs by Anticipatory Forecasting,"* Journal of Cash Management *6 (March–April 1986), pp. 44–50; and Bernell K. Stone and Tom W. Miller, "Daily Cash Forecasting and Seasonal Resolution: Alternative Models and Techniques for Using the Distribution Approach,"* Journal of Financial and Quantitative Analysis *20 (September 1985), pp. 335–351.*

FIGURE 16.4

Model for Estimating and Controlling the Firm's Cash Balance

In practice, other factors need to be addressed. These will cause the model to increase in complexity, but the basic concepts remain the same.

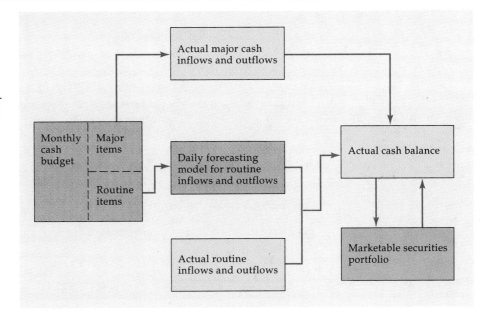

firm. However, by breaking out the major items and then modeling the routine ones, the firm's monthly cash budget can easily be broken down into a day-by-day estimate of the necessary cash balance.

Transfers to and from the marketable securities portfolio use the same balancing of incremental costs and benefits discussed earlier.[6] Therefore, it may not be profitable to switch funds to and from the marketable securities portfolio every day. For example, if it costs $50 to move funds in or out of the marketable securities portfolio, the incremental interest, ΔI, from having funds in marketable securities is 4 percent, and the marginal tax rate is 40 percent, we would calculate the minimum transaction size for moving funds into or out of marketable securities as follows:

$$\Delta C = \Delta B$$

$$\Delta C = (\Delta t)(TS)(\Delta I)(1 - T)$$

$$\$50(1 - 0.40) = (1)(TS)(0.04/365 \text{ days})(1 - 0.40)$$

where Δt is specified as one day's gain in interest. Solving for TS, the amount of cash transferred, we have:

$$TS = \frac{\$50(0.60)}{(0.04/365)(0.60)} = \$456,250$$

Therefore, there should be at least $456,250 that can be left in marketable securities for at least 1 day before the transfer is made. If we estimate, based on our daily cash

[6]Other approaches for determining the amount to transfer to and from marketable securities are discussed in Chapter 20 of Financial Management.

balance model, that funds can be transferred from cash to marketable securities and left for 5 days, then:

$$\$30 = (5)(TS)(0.04/365 \text{ days})(0.60)$$

$$TS = \frac{\$30}{5(0.04/365)(0.60)} = \$91,250$$

In this case the transfer should be made if there is a minimum of at least $91,250 in excess funds in the firm's cash account. Similar calculations can be made if the differential interest rates change, or if the cost of the transaction increases or decreases. The point, however, is that the same basic benefit-cost framework can be used to determine when to transfer funds into and out of the marketable securities portfolio.

CONCEPT REVIEW QUESTIONS

■ Detail the five-step procedure employed to determine the firm's daily cash balance.

MANAGEMENT OF THE MARKETABLE SECURITIES PORTFOLIO

■ LEARNING GOAL 5

Discuss the risk, liquidity, maturity, and yield aspects of alternative marketable security investments.

Once we have identified what amount can be considered excess cash, we need to make some decisions about what to do with that excess. *Because of the need for liquidity and stability of principal, long-term bonds or common stock generally are not appropriate investments for temporary excess cash, unless some type of hedge is employed to counteract any potential loss of principal.* Therefore, excess cash above what is needed to meet the firm's cash balance requirement will be invested in *marketable securities.*

Investment Alternatives

Marketable securities provide immediate liquidity. They are low-risk and low-return investments, where preservation of principal is paramount.

DUTCH AUCTION PRE-FERRED STOCK
Marketable security that is resold every 49 days by firms bidding on the lowest return they are willing to accept for the security.

Managers have a choice of many different marketable securities for short-term investments. These are shown in Table 16.1. (You should take the time to study the table and the individual securities listed in it; some of these securities will be discussed in more detail in this or other chapters of the text; some that are beyond the scope of this course will not be discussed further, but you should at least be aware of the existence of those securities and their general characteristics.) *Treasury bills* are direct obligations of the government. They are typically considered the safest marketable security. The yield on Treasury bills is often used as a proxy for the risk-free rate, k_{RF}. All other marketable securities are viewed as being more risky, because they are not issued or backed directly by the government. *Money market mutual funds* are a pool of short-term marketable securities managed by an investment adviser. **Dutch auction preferred stock** may also be employed. This is a short-term security that is resold every 49 days. The advantage is that the dividends received on a Dutch auction preferred stock are, like any other cash dividends received by one firm from another, partially exempt from corporate income taxes.

TABLE 16.1

Characteristics of Marketable Securities

Given the wide variety of securities, maturities, and denominations, firms can tailor a marketable securities portfolio to meet their needs.

Instrument	Description	Maturity	Interest Basis	Marketability	Denomination
Treasury bills	Direct obligation of the U.S. government; exempt from state and local income tax	91 days to 1 year	Discount	Excellent secondary market	$10,000 and up
Federal agency issues	Notes issued by agencies created by the U.S. government; not explicitly backed by the government	5 days to several years; over half less than 1 year	Typically interest-bearing, but may be discount	Good to excellent secondary market	$5,000 and up
Repurchase agreements (repos or buy-backs)	Sale of government securities by a bank or securities dealer with a simultaneous agreement to repurchase	1 day to 3 months	Repayment price set higher than selling price, paid at maturity	Limited	$500,000
Short-term tax exempts	Notes issued by states, municipalities, local housing agencies, and urban renewal agencies; exempt from federal income tax	2 months to 1 year	Interest-bearing paid at maturity, or discount	Good secondary market	$1,000
Finance paper	Unsecured notes issued by large finance companies or bank holding companies	3 to 270 days	Either discount or interest-bearing, paid at maturity	Limited secondary market, but firm will usually redeem early	$100,000
Commercial paper	Unsecured notes issued by smaller finance companies or industrial firms; increasingly used by non-U.S.-based firms	30 to 270 days	Discount	Limited secondary market, but dealer may arrange buy-back	$100,000
Negotiable certificates of deposit, CDs	Receipts for time deposits at commercial banks; very active market for overseas branches of U.S.-based banks	30 to 91 days or longer	Interest-bearing, paid at maturity	Good secondary market	$1,000,000
Banker's acceptances	Time draft (or order to pay) issued by a business firm (usually an importer) and accepted by a bank	30 to 180 days	Discount	Good secondary market	$100,000
Eurodollars	Dollar-denominated time deposits at overseas banks	1 day to 1 year	Interest-bearing, paid at maturity	Limited secondary market	$1,000,000
Money market mutual funds	Pool of short-term money market instruments	Shares may be sold any time	Credited to account monthly	Good; provided by fund itself	$500
Dutch auction preferred stock	Specially designed preferred stock	Resold every 7 weeks	Dividend-paying, at maturity	Limited secondary market	$100,000

In addition, in recent years numerous other investment alternatives have become available. Many firms that pay the full amount of corporate taxes find that investing in tax-exempt securities provides higher after-tax returns.[7] Short-term mortgage-backed and other asset-backed securities have also become more popular. Other firms have invested heavily in Eurodollar or LIBOR-denominated investments. Still others have bought long-term bonds and then entered into interest rate swaps to achieve a variable LIBOR rate return on their investment. Although these and many other innovations have occurred, we will focus on the basics of managing the marketable securities portfolio.[8]

Selection Criteria

To select among marketable securities, financial managers look at the risk, liquidity, maturity, and yield aspects of the alternative investments.

Risk

Remember Key Idea 6—risk and return go hand-in-hand.

As general economic conditions change from boom to recession, market rates of interest change. In addition, monetary and fiscal policies can also influence market interest rates. Remember as you read the following discussion of selection criteria that as market interest rates go up, the market price of outstanding debt instruments goes down. As market interest rates go down, the market price of outstanding debt goes up.

Figuring the Yield on Treasury Bills. To examine the risks as economic conditions change, let's consider one specific money market security—Treasury bills. Treasury bills are non-interest-bearing discount securities that are sold through regular weekly and monthly auctions; 91- and 182-day maturity bills are sold weekly, and 365-day maturity bills are sold monthly. Because they are redeemed at full face value at maturity, the interest earned is the difference between the face value (if held to maturity) and the discounted price. Two interest rates are quoted for Treasury bills—the bank discount yield, k_{BD}, and the bond equivalent yield, k_{BE}.

BANK DISCOUNT YIELD
The investor's expected return on a Treasury bill, expressed as a percent of the face value of the security.

The **bank discount yield** expresses the investor's expected return on a Treasury bill as a percent of the face value of the security, so that:

$$k_{BD} = \left(\frac{P_M - P_0}{P_M} \right) \left(\frac{360 \text{ days}}{n} \right) \tag{16.2}$$

where

k_{BD} = the bank discount yield

P_M = the maturity value of the Treasury bill

P_0 = the discounted price

n = the number of days until maturity

Note that the bank discount yield is based on 360 days.[9]

---

[7] Firms that purchase tax-exempt securities limit their purchases to no more than 2 percent of their assets. An IRS provision limits the amount of interest corporations can deduct if they invest more than 2 percent of their assets in tax-exempt securities.
[8] Interest rate swaps, and other techniques for managing interest rate risk, are discussed in Chapter 23 of Financial Management.
[9] Neither the bank discount nor the bond equivalent yield is calculated employing compound interest. Our presentation is in line with their use in practice.

To illustrate, suppose that you purchase a 182-day Treasury bill with a face value of $10,000 at a price of $9,500. What is your bank discount yield? Employing Equation 16.2, we have:

$$k_{BD} = \left(\frac{\$10,000 - \$9,500}{\$10,000} \right)\left(\frac{360}{182} \right) = \frac{\$180,000}{\$1,820,000} = 9.89\%$$

Alternatively, if you were told that the bank discount yield on a 182-day $10,000 Treasury bill was 9.89 percent and you wanted to find out how much you would pay for the security, we could rearrange Equation 16.2 and solve for P_0 as follows:

$$P_0 = P_M \left[1 - \frac{(k_{BD})(n)}{360 \text{ days}} \right] \tag{16.3}$$

$$P_0 = \$10,000\left[1 - \frac{(0.0989)(182)}{360} \right] = \$10,000(1 - 0.05) = \$9,500$$

BOND EQUIVALENT YIELD
Yield that converts the bank discount yield on Treasury bills to an approximate 365-day annualized yield.

Because the bank discount yield is based on 360 days, and most interest rates are for 365 days, the bond equivalent yield for a Treasury bill is generally calculated. It is as follows:[10]

$$k_{BE} = \frac{(365 \text{ days})(k_{BD})}{360 \text{ days} - (k_{BD})(n)} \tag{16.4}$$

For our example, the bond equivalent yield is:

$$k_{BE} = \frac{(365)(0.0989)}{360 - (0.0989)(182)} \approx 10.56\%$$

Because of the difference between the 360- and 365-day years, *the bond equivalent yield is always higher than the bank discount yield.*

To illustrate the risk that may exist with Treasury bills, let's continue with our example. If we buy the 182-day Treasury bill for $9,500 and hold it until maturity, then our bond equivalent yield is 10.56 percent. But what happens if we have to sell before it matures and interest rates on Treasury bills have increased from the time we purchased the Treasury bill? Suppose that we were forced to sell in 60 days, and the bank discount yield at that time was 11.00 percent.

To see the effect of having to sell when interest rates have moved higher, we first determine the price of the Treasury bill with 122 (i.e., 182 − 60) days to maturity as follows using Equation 16.3:

$$P_0 \text{ selling price} = \$10,000\left[1 - \frac{(0.11)(122)}{360} \right]$$

$$= \$10,000(1 - 0.037278) = \$9,627.22$$

---

[10]*This formula applies only to Treasury bills with 182 days or less to maturity; another formula is used for longer-maturity bills. For simplicity, we employ Equation 16.4 even when the maturity exceeds 182 days. It should be noted that the bond equivalent yield is not an effective annual interest rate based on compound interest, only an approximation.*

Then the actual bond equivalent yield over the 60 days the Treasury bill was owned can be determined using Equation 16.5:

$$k_{BE} = \frac{(\text{selling price} - \text{purchase price})(365)}{(\text{purchase price})(\text{days owned})} \qquad (16.5)$$

$$k_{BE} = \frac{(\$9,627.22 - \$9,500)(365)}{(\$9,500)(60)} \approx 8.15\%$$

Because of changes in market rates of interest, which adversely affected the price of the Treasury bill when we sold prematurely, our actual return was only 8.15 percent instead of our anticipated return of 10.56 percent.

Treasury bills are issued and backed by the government. Many other marketable securities are issued by individual firms or banks. **Commercial paper,** which is simply short-term unsecured borrowing, is issued by consumer finance companies or by industrial, retail, or even public utility firms. Likewise, many different banks issue negotiable **certificates of deposit, CDs,** which are short-term unsecured borrowings. The specific firm or issuer of the marketable security in these cases is responsible for payment. Managers must consider the ability of the firm issuing the marketable security to pay interest and principal on time.

COMMERCIAL PAPER
Short-term nonsecured promissory note issued by commercial finance and industrial firms.

CERTIFICATE OF DEPOSIT, CD
A short-term deposit issued by a bank.

Liquidity

Liquidity refers to the ability to convert the marketable security to cash quickly without taking a significant price discount to facilitate the sale. Most marketable securities have excellent or good secondary markets. For commercial paper, however, it may be necessary to see if the issuing firm will redeem the security early if needed. Likewise, there is a limited secondary market for Eurodollars and **repurchase agreements** (sale of government securities with a simultaneous agreement to repurchase them within a certain time period at a specified price). Because firms use their marketable securities portfolio as a source of ready cash, the liquidity aspect of the investment also requires careful consideration.

REPURCHASE AGREEMENT
Sale of government securities by a bank or dealer with a simultaneous agreement to repurchase them in a certain period of time at a specified price.

Maturity

The maturity of the marketable securities is also of prime importance. The shorter the maturity of the marketable securities the more they provide liquidity for the firm. Most large firms keep some cash invested overnight in repurchase agreements and other shorter-maturity securities. Then they follow a layered approach of matching longer cash availability with investments in longer term marketable securities.

Yield

The final selection criterion is the yield on the marketable securities. Table 16.2 presents the yields on various securities during the 1988–1994 period. We see that yields fell dramatically between 1990 and 1994. Thus, the yield on U.S. Treasury bills was 8.11 percent in 1989, while it was only 3.00 percent by 1993. Also notice that Eurodollar deposits always provide more returns than any other marketable security, whereas Treasury bills, being the least risky, provide the lowest returns.

TABLE 16.2

Yields on 3-Month Money Market Instruments

Treasury bills, being the least risky, provide the lowest returns. Eurodollars, being more risky and less liquid, provide the highest returns.

Instrument	Year						
	1988	1989	1990	1991	1992	1993	1994
Treasury Bills	6.67%	8.11%	7.51%	5.38%	3.43%	3.00%	4.27%
Finance paper—directly placed	7.38	8.72	7.87	5.71	3.65	3.16	4.53
Commercial paper	7.66	8.99	8.06	5.87	3.75	3.22	4.66
Certificates of deposit	7.73	9.09	8.15	5.83	3.68	3.17	4.63
Banker's acceptances	7.56	8.87	7.93	5.70	3.62	3.13	4.56
Eurodollars	7.85	9.16	8.16	5.86	3.70	3.18	4.63

Source: Federal Reserve Bulletin, various issues.

The Marketable Securities Portfolio

The basic considerations for designing the firm's marketable securities portfolio can be depicted as follows:

Considerations	Influence	Depends on	Decision
Risk Liquidity Maturity	→ Returns	→ Firm's risk-return position	→ Marketable securities portfolio mix

The interaction of risk, liquidity, and maturity determines the returns. The firm's risk-return posture then determines the specific composition of the marketable securities portfolio. Very risk-averse firms might have a marketable securities portfolio composed almost entirely of Treasury bills. More aggressive firms will opt for a large portion in higher-yielding Eurodollars or certificates of deposit issued by overseas branches of U.S.-based banks. The impact of the returns on a big marketable securities portfolio, particularly when short-term interest rates are high, can be significant.

CONCEPT REVIEW QUESTIONS

■ What are some marketable securities used by firms for short-term investments?
■ How do risk, liquidity, maturity, and yield affect the composition of a firm's marketable securities portfolio?

Summary

■ Management of the firm's liquid assets focuses on cash inflows and outflows, the trade-off between holding cash versus investing in marketable securities, and how to structure the marketable securities portfolio.
■ Because of float, firms attempt to speed the cash-gathering process while controlling (or slowing) disbursements. The primary means for speeding collections are

lockboxes and an efficient banking arrangement. Disbursements are managed by using controlled disbursing, zero-balance accounts, and similar arrangements.

■ When comparing cash management alternatives, the incremental costs and benefits are analyzed in a *NPV* framework.

■ Determining the amount to hold in a firm's demand deposit account versus the amount to invest in marketable securities depends on forecasting and the incremental interest to be earned in marketable securities.

■ Risk, liquidity, maturity, and return concerns determine how the firm's marketable securities portfolio is structured.

Questions

16.1 The objective of the firm is to maximize the value of the firm. Because the return on real assets typically exceeds the return on marketable securities, explain why firms generally keep 5 to 10 percent of their assets in cash and marketable securities.

16.2 Explain the different types of float and how they affect the firm's cash-gathering system. Do these same types of float apply to the firm's cash-disbursing system?

16.3 What impact would the following have on the firm's average cash balance?
  a. Interest rates on marketable securities decrease.
  b. Cost of trading marketable securities increases.
  c. The firm's concentration bank raises its compensating balance requirement.
  d. A zero-balance account procedure is implemented.
  e. New billing procedures allow a better correspondence between cash inflows and cash outflows.

16.4 Treasury bills are widely employed by firms as an investment for temporary excess cash. Because they have the lowest yield of any marketable security, why are Treasury bills chosen?

16.5 During the last 25 years or so, many retail firms and others that issue credit cards have shifted from billing all customers on the last day of the month to "cycle billing." With cycle billing, customers are billed (often in alphabetical order) throughout the month. From the standpoint of the credit card issuer, what effect does cycle billing have on cash flows and average cash balances? Does it also have an impact on accounts receivable? Explain.

Concept Review Problems

See Appendix A for solutions.

CR16.1 It takes Reynaud Company 6 days to receive and deposit checks from customers. Management of Reynaud is considering a lockbox system to decrease float time to 4 days. Average daily collections are $20,000 and the cost of funds is 6 percent.
  a. What will be the reduction in outstanding cash balances as a result of implementing the lockbox system?
  b. If the firm's tax rate is 36 percent, what is the maximum daily charge that Reynaud can afford to pay for the lockbox system?

Note: Assume a 365-day year.

CR16.2 Fifth Corporation disperses $500,000,000 in checks per year and they take an average of 2.84 days to clear. Fifth estimates it could increase the float to 4.15 days by opening a checking account in a small Kentucky bank. If $T = 40$ percent and $I = 8.7$ percent, what are the annual benefits from opening a checking account in Kentucky?

CR16.3 Cassie, assistant controller of CS Gear, is analyzing the firm's management of cash and marketable securities. Brokerage fees are $100 per transfer, the firm's tax rate is 40 percent, and incremental interest from having funds in marketable securities is 5 percent. If fund transfers occur every 7 days, what is the minimum amount that should be transferred?

CR16.4 Ken, cash manager for TMP Inc., is considering the purchase of a Treasury bill for $9,900 that will mature in 50 days.
  a. What is the bank discount yield on the Treasury bill?
  b. What is the bond equivalent yield on the Treasury bill?
  c. After 10 days, the bank discount yield on 40-day Treasury bills increased to 7.5%, and at that time Ken was forced to sell the Treasury bill and move funds into the firm's cash account. What was the bond equivalent return on the Treasury bill?

Problems

See Appendix C for answers to selected problems.

Float

16.1 Bolton Brothers projects its sales will be $120 million next year. All sales are for credit, but the credit policies are in good shape because there are very few bad debts and payments are mailed on time. Bolton is concerned, however, about the cost of float time. Its marginal tax rate is 30 percent.
  a. If funds could be invested to earn 7 percent, what is the incremental daily benefit of a 1-day reduction in float time using a 365-day year?
  b. What is the daily benefit of a 1.5-day reduction in float if the funds could earn 8 percent?

Float

16.2 Hampshire Healthcare currently has all incoming checks sent directly to its headquarters. The average mail time is 4 days, processing time is 2 days, and transit time is 1.5 days. The average cash inflow is $2 million per calendar day.
  a. What is the average collection float in dollars?

Note: Don't forget the 1.5 days of transit time.

  b. Although internal processing time is 2 days, Hampshire is actually able to record the incoming checks for accounting purposes on its accounting records in 1 day. How much in dollars does Hampshire have recorded on its accounting records that are not actually "good funds" in its bank account?

Note: In (c), solve for the yearly ΔB - ΔC.

  c. By modifying its system, Hampshire Healthcare can reduce total float time *by* 2.25 days. The proposed system will cost $350,000 before taxes per year to operate, the interest rate is 12 percent, a 365-day year is assumed, and the marginal tax rate is 40 percent. Should Hampshire implement the modified cash collection system?

Lockbox

16.3 Mead-Raleigh currently has a centralized cash-receiving system located in Raleigh, North Carolina. Its average float time on collections is 5.7 days. A Florida bank has approached Mead-Raleigh, offering to establish a lockbox system that should reduce the float time to 2.9 days. (So the net reduction is 5.7 − 2.9, or 2.8 days.) Mead's daily collections are $600,000, and excess funds can be invested at 10 percent. If there are 800 checks per day, how much is the maximum Mead-Raleigh can afford to pay *per check* for the lockbox operation? Assume a 365-day year and a tax rate of 30 percent.

Lockbox and Compensating Balance

16.4 Land Transport presently uses a two-lockbox system that has a total average daily transaction balance of $1 million (based on a 365-day year). The banks do not charge a direct fee, but they require Land to keep a total of $2 million in compensating balances on which no interest is paid.

Dave, a recent graduate, has recommended that Land switch to a new lockbox system. The savings in float time would be 1.2 days, the average check size is

Note: Don't forget that interest can be earned on the freed compensating balances.

$500, the interest rate is 9 percent, and the firm's marginal tax rate is 34 percent. As compensation to the banks, Land would have its compensating balance requirement reduced to $1.8 million (still no interest paid), pay $0.05 per check processed, and pay additional fixed fees of $50,000 to the banks each year. Based on the yearly incremental costs and benefits, should Land make the switch recommended by Dave?

Eliminating a Lockbox

16.5 Presently, Sampson Lighting is using a lockbox arrangement. Sampson believes, however, that it can save money by eliminating the lockbox system and handling the process internally. The lockbox costs $5 per day and $0.50 per check processed. Currently, 400 checks per day are being processed. If Sampson eliminates the lockbox, total costs will be $40,000 per year, and float time will increase by 2 days. Assume the average transaction size is $500 per check, the yearly interest rate is 11 percent, a 365-day year is employed, the tax rate is 40 percent, and all costs are on a before-tax basis.

Note: Compute the yearly incremental after-tax costs and benefits.

a. Should Sampson eliminate the lockbox system?

b. At what incremental float time would Sampson be indifferent between the two approaches?

Transfer Mechanisms

16.6 Fort Worth Industries receives a periodic deposit of $20,000 at its San Juan, Puerto Rico, office. A mail process that costs $1 and takes 3 days is presently used to transfer the funds to its concentration bank in Fort Worth. Alternatively, a wire transfer system costing $9 that makes the funds immediately available could be employed. Assume a 365-day year and a tax rate of 35 percent.

a. If Fort Worth earns 12 percent on excess funds once they reach the concentration bank, which transfer method should be employed?

b. What is the lowest dollar amount that should be transferred via wire transfer?

Lockbox and Concentration Banking

16.7 TurboSystems has been growing so fast it has not examined its cash-gathering system. Presently, all cash comes into its corporate office. A downturn in the economy, however, has affected both sales and profitability. Now appears to be an appropriate time to review the cash-gathering system. A consulting firm, for a fee of $100,000, has just presented the following information to TurboSystems:

Present	Proposed
Home office collection system costing $75,000 per year.	Five lockboxes; the cost per check processed is $0.30.
Average daily volume is $900,000, with an average check size of $1,500, based on receipts for 270 days per year.	Twice-daily transfer of funds from *each* lockbox via wire transfer at a cost of $8 each. Reduction in float time, 2.6 days. Home office expenses of $50,000 per year.

Note: When calculating ΔC, assume that checks are processed only 270 days a year. When calculating ΔB, assume the $900,000 is available for all 365 days.

a. If TurboSystems can earn 9 percent on the excess funds and it is in the 40 percent marginal tax bracket, what are the yearly incremental after-tax costs and benefits of moving to the new system (ignoring the consultant's one-time fee of $100,000)? Should the switch be made?

b. Was the consultant's report worthwhile?

Controlled Disbursing

16.8 Ellen of Allegheny Valley Tire needs to know how much money would be saved by a controlled disbursing system. The average daily payables are $200,000, the controlled disbursing will add 1.5 days to the float, and the excess funds can be invested at 13 percent. Based on a 365-day year and a marginal tax rate of 30 percent, what are the yearly incremental benefits associated with the controlled disbursing system?

Controlled Disbursing

16.9 Caribe Marine Supplies has set up a controlled disbursing system with two out-of-town banks. The net benefit ($\Delta B - \Delta C$) of the system to Caribe is $28,700 per year. If Caribe writes 200 checks per day with an average amount of $400, how many days of additional float will Caribe obtain if the interest rate is 7 percent and the banks charge $0.10 per check cleared? Assume a 365-day year and that Caribe is operating at a loss so that taxes are not relevant.

Zero-Balance Accounts and Compensating Balance

16.10 Brookes International maintains a number of checking accounts in various banks to allow its divisions to pay suppliers. The total average daily cash balance (over all the banks) is $480,000, on which no interest is earned. To control disbursements better, Brookes is investigating whether to set up a series of zero-balance accounts at the Second National Bank. The bank will provide the service for a direct fee of $10,000 a year before taxes, plus a daily average compensating balance of $400,000. By implementing the new arrangement, Brookes would free up $80,000 per day. No interest is earned on funds left with the bank in the $400,000 compensating balance arrangement.

Brookes expects the float time to increase by 0.75 days with the zero-balance account system. The average daily payables are $300,000, the excess funds can be invested at 12 percent, a 365-day year is assumed, and the marginal tax rate is 40 percent.

a. What is the yearly (before-tax) interest earned on the $80,000 freed?

b. What are the total yearly after-tax incremental costs and benefits of the zero-balance accounts?

Treasury Bill

16.11 A 91-day Treasury bill with a $10,000 maturity value was purchased at 97.40 (as a percent of its maturity value).

a. What is the bank discount yield on the Treasury bill?

b. What is its bond equivalent yield?

c. Why is the bond equivalent yield always higher than the bank discount yield?

Interest on Treasury Bill

Note: Round all answers to the nearest dollar.

16.12 World Communications had excess cash that it used to purchase a $1 million (maturity value) 182-day Treasury bill when the bank discount yield was 7.9 percent.

a. What market price (ignoring transactions costs) did World pay?

b. After 80 days, World had to sell the Treasury bill. Due to heavy government financing, the bank discount rate had climbed to 8.40 percent when World sold the bill. What was the actual bond equivalent yield on the Treasury bill?

c. If World sells the Treasury bill after 120 days, how does the answer in (b) change?

Marketable Securities Portfolio

16.13 Monroe Equipment has the following schedule of excess cash available and cash needs over the next 6 months:

Time	Cash Availability/Needs
Now	$2 million excess cash
In 2 months	An additional $2 million excess cash
In 4 months	$2 million cash needed
In 6 months	An additional $2 million cash needed

The structure of short-term interest rates is as follows:

Now		Expected in 2 Months	
Maturity Period	Yield (annual)	Maturity Period	Yield (annual)
2 months	7.3%	2 months	8.0%
4 months	7.4	4 months	8.1
6 months	7.5		

Hint: Remember the yields are on an annual basis. To convert to monthly, just divide the yearly figure by 12. For simplicity, (1) do not compound your results, and (2) take the transactions costs at the end of the time period.

Assume that once marketable securities are purchased, they are held to maturity. If it costs $100 every time marketable securities are purchased, which securities should be purchased to maximize the before-tax income from the added investment?

Cash and Marketable Securities

16.14 **Mini Case** You have just been hired by Allard Industries as their cash manager. On your first day on the job you find that the cash management system is in disarray. Consequently, it must be overhauled, and in the process you must educate your employees and the firm's management.

a. As a first step you find that the three basic issues relating to cash (or liquid asset) management are not clearly understood. Explain these issues.

b. There has been a lot of confusion concerning the issue of float. Explain what float is, how it exists for both cash inflows and cash outflows, what parts can be controlled (and how), and how the issue of "good funds" relates to float. The firm's accounting manager has typically provided estimates of "good funds" by examining the firm's day-by-day cash account as recorded by the firm's accounting system. Is this a good policy? Explain.

c. Three alternatives to the present cash flow system have been presented to you. What decisions should be made in each case?

Note: Assume a 365-day year throughout, and calculate the daily benefits and costs.

   (1) *Lockbox.* Average collection float is presently 6.3 days. By going to a lockbox system, the firm can reduce the float to 2.8 days. The daily collections are $1,500,000, excess funds can be invested at an incremental rate of 8 percent, and there are 2,500 checks per day. The bank will charge $200 per day plus 20 cents per check processed. Allard's effective tax rate is 40 percent.

   (2) *Controlled Disbursing.* The firm's average daily payables are $800,000, consisting of 1,000 checks, and the present payable float is 1.5 days. The new payables float will be 3.4 days. The bank will charge $400 per day plus 8 cents per check. The tax rate is still 40 percent, and the interest rate is 8 percent.

   (3) *Wire Transfer.* Allard currently employs ACH transactions to move funds between various banks and its concentration bank. Switching to wire transfers would reduce float by 1 day. The ACH transactions cost $1.78 per transfer, whereas wire transfers cost $4.45 per transfer. The number of transfers per day is 30, and the average size is $2,000. The tax rate is 40 percent, and the interest rate is 8 percent.

d. Excess funds will be invested in marketable securities. Summarize the different types of marketable securities available. Also, indicate what risks must be considered when constructing the firm's marketable securities portfolio.

e. Two different Treasury bills exist as follows:

   $10,000 maturity value, 90-day bill with P_0 of $9,780
   $10,000 maturity value, 245-day bill with P_0 of $9,390

   (1) Which Treasury bill has the higher bond equivalent yield?
   (2) Now assume that the Treasury bill has to be sold by Allard in 70 days. The bank discount yield on the shorter-maturity bill is 8.70 percent, whereas it is 8.90 percent on the longer-maturity bill. What would the actual yield on the two Treasury bills be over this time period?

Accounts Receivable and Inventory

Sections in this chapter:

■ **Receivables, Inventory, and the Firm**
Yet another tradeoff between risk and return.

■ **Credit and Collection Management**
Another use of NPVs.

■ **Inventory Management**
"You have how *many years' supply in the warehouse?"*

B ecause of the beliefs of its founder, James Cash Penney, J.C. Penney for years and years never sold on credit—it was strictly a cash-and-carry operation. That policy has changed dramatically; in addition to its own credit card, Penney now also accepts Visa, MasterCard, Discover, and American Express. Credit card operations are so important to J.C. Penney that it now has credit card service units and processing centers, all equipped with state-of-the-art technology.

In addition to credit policy, inventory decisions also have a dramatic effect on a firm. During the last 10 years many firms have switched to a just-in-time inventory system. Under this approach, inventory is kept to a minimum and suppliers in close proximity stand ready to supply needed material in short order. To gain the advantages of a just-in-time inventory system, firms must pay special attention to quality control and to streamlined production. With a just-in-time system, poor-quality work or an inefficient production system can shut down the production process and cause major inventory problems.

As the economy expanded in the last couple of years, many firms using just-in-time found that they had to adjust their systems. Some found they had to carry more inventory than previously, due to increasing demand for their final product. As one expert commented, "Tight capacity utilization is having a domino effect on supply chains." Others found they had to adjust their production processes, to expand their capacity to produce the goods when needed. And large companies are increasingly using computers to track retail sales, in order to obtain more accurate information on inventory levels. Does all of this mean the just-in-time inventory system will become less important? No, it simply means that adjustments in the whole production process continue to be made, as businesses learn to live, and flourish, with more efficient, leaner operations.

Whether it's a large retail firm or an auto parts store, the effective management of accounts receivable and inventory is essential to financial well-being. In this chapter we explore how these decisions are made.

LEARNING GOALS

After studying this chapter you should be able to:

1. Discuss why the level of receivables and inventory matter to the firm.
2. Understand credit terms and conditions for both domestic and international sales.
3. Describe credit scoring, and explain how to use net present value to make credit decisions.
4. Describe techniques for monitoring receivables, and explain how net present value is used to evaluate changes in collection policy.
5. Discuss the costs and benefits of holding inventory, and describe four inventory management approaches.

RECEIVABLES, INVENTORY, AND THE FIRM

TRADE CREDIT
Credit that arises when one firm sells to another through a credit sale; appears as an account receivable on the seller's books and as an account payable on the buyer's books.

RECEIVABLES
Credit sales that have not been collected.

BAD DEBT
Trade receivable not expected to be collected.

Remember Key Ideas 1, 4, and 5—the goal of the firm is to maximize its market value, firms focus on cash flows and their incremental effects, and a dollar today is worth more than a dollar tomorrow.

■ **LEARNING GOAL 1**

Discuss why the level of receivables and inventory matter to the firm.

To complete our analysis of the firm's current assets, we turn our attention to accounts receivable and inventory. Firms typically sell goods and services on both a cash and a credit basis. In the former, cash is received immediately; in the latter, **trade credit** extended to customers leads to the establishment of accounts receivable. **Receivables** represent credit sales that have not been collected. Over time, as the customers pay these accounts, the firm receives the cash associated with the original sale. If the customer does not pay an account, a **bad debt** loss is incurred. To make sales, most firms also carry various types of inventory. Choosing the right level of inventory ensures a smooth production cycle, assists in the marketing effort, and reduces costs associated with holding excess inventory or suffering loss due to spoilage or theft. Without both receivables and inventory, most firms would cease to operate or would be much less efficient.

The investment in accounts receivable and inventory is similar to the long-term, or capital budgeting, decision discussed in Chapters 6–9. Therefore, many of the techniques used in this chapter are similar to those used in making capital budgeting decisions. Throughout, the emphasis is on the magnitude, timing, and riskiness of the cash flows, and the opportunity costs associated with a firm's investment in receivables and inventory. In managing these the goal remains to maximize the overall value, V, of the firm.

Importance of Receivables and Inventory

Receivables and inventory management directly relate to other activities of the firm.

The financial goals of the firm must be coordinated with its marketing and production efforts. There is always a trade-off between risk and return, and different departments often want different policies. Nowhere is this more evident than in determining and maintaining proper levels of receivables and inventory. The marketing department may want lenient credit terms and collection policies in order to increase sales; the marketing effort also benefits from high inventory levels. With high inventory levels, the firm can promise immediate delivery, knowing that it will not lose sales because of stock outages. Higher inventory levels help the production department as well, enabling it to purchase in larger quantities, use longer production runs, and suffer less down time or unanticipated adjustments in the production schedule.

The desires of the marketing and production department often conflict, however, with the objectives of the chief financial officer. Other things being equal, the CFO wants to minimize the firm's accounts receivable and inventory levels. Lower levels have two important financial benefits: First, less financing has to be secured, because the firm has less investment in receivables and inventory. Second, profits should be higher relative to sales or assets, because long-term investments are expected to generate higher returns than short-term assets.

Key Idea 6—that risk and return go hand-in-hand— also applies to the firm's receivables and inventory policies.

The result must be a trade-off between risk and return. On the one hand, there is the risk of not granting enough credit or having enough inventory, thereby suffering sales losses. On the other hand, too high a level of receivables and inventory has a cost that may offset any sales or production benefits. A coordinated effort, involving marketing, production, and finance, is required to balance the risks and the returns. Most firms have substantial investments in receivables and inventory. Large manufacturing firms may have "only" 30 percent of total assets invested in receivables and inventory. But over 50 percent of the total assets of most retail and smaller manufacturing firms is invested in receivables and inventory, and that figure increases to over 60 percent for wholesale firms.

The investment in both receivables and inventory is influenced by many factors. One primary determinant is the industry in which the firm operates. The industry effect is caused by competition, the characteristics of the product, the production process, and so forth. Recent surveys of credit policies have indicated that the actions of competitors are the major factor governing the credit terms granted. At the same time, trade credit is more likely to be extended if the seller has a cost advantage over competing suppliers or lenders or has (or can achieve) greater market power. Likewise, a firm's investment in inventory is largely influenced by production processes and the requirements imposed by competition. The importance of the industry effect cannot be minimized when examining a firm's investment in both receivables and inventory. We'll examine various inventory management techniques later in the chapter. For now, let's concentrate on receivables.

Size of Accounts Receivable

The size of the investment in accounts receivable is influenced by factors in addition to industry effect, cost advantage, and market power effect. First, as shown in Figure 17.1, is total sales. Certain credit policies, such as liberal payment periods, encourage more sales. The state of the economy, the aggressiveness of the firm's marketing efforts, and other like factors also influence sales. As total sales increase, the level of credit sales and the investment in receivables usually increases. Second, the firm's credit and collection policies also influence the size of the investment in receivables. These policies can be broken down into four distinct aspects:

Credit terms are closely related to the bargaining power that exists between suppliers (sellers) and customers (buyers).

1. Terms and conditions of credit sales.
2. Credit analysis.
3. Credit decision.
4. Collection policy.

The decisions in these areas largely determine the length of time between the granting of credit and the receipt of cash. As the length of time before collection increases, the firm's investment in receivables increases. Shortening the *days sales outstanding*— the average number of days it takes to collect receivables—reduces the firm's investment in receivables. The level of investment in accounts receivable is a function of the firm's industry, its total sales, and its credit and collection policies.

FIGURE 17.1

Factors Affecting the Investment in Accounts Receivable

The level of sales, percentage of credit sales, and credit and collection policies determine the level of the firm's accounts receivable. Likewise, the credit management operation directly influences the flow of funds to the firm's cash account.

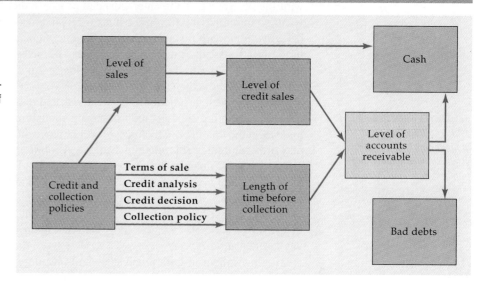

CONCEPT REVIEW QUESTIONS

■ What are the benefits and the risks of minimizing the firm's accounts receivable and inventory levels?

■ Describe factors that affect the size of a firm's accounts receivable.

CREDIT AND COLLECTION MANAGEMENT

In this section, we will explore in more detail the four main aspects of credit and collection policies. In doing so, we want to see how they are established and the effect they can have on the value of the firm.

Terms and Conditions of Sale

■ LEARNING GOAL 2

Understand credit terms and conditions for both domestic and international sales.

CASH ON DELIVERY, COD
Term of sale whereby payment is required at the time the goods are delivered to the buyer.

SEASONAL DATING
Payment of receivables timed to coincide with the buyer's anticipated cash inflows.

Although most firms and industries grant trade credit, there are substantial variations. If the goods are produced to the customer's specifications, the selling firm may ask for cash before delivery. If the deliveries are irregular or if some risk is involved, the seller may require **cash on delivery, COD.** If ordinary trade credit is granted, goods are on an open account, with payment due in some prespecified length of time, such as 30 or 60 days. In some industries **seasonal dating** is employed, with payment being timed to coincide with the buyer's anticipated cash inflows.

As an inducement to encourage early payment, firms often offer a cash discount. If a firm sells on a 2/10, net 30 basis, customers who pay within 10 days receive a 2 percent discount; in any case, full payment is due within 30 days. In an open-account agreement, the seller delivers the goods and provides an invoice, which constitutes the customer's bill and contains the terms of the arrangement.

If the goods are large in size, or if the seller is unsure about the payment ability of the customer, other devices may be employed. The most common is the use of a *draft*, which is simply a written order to pay a specified amount of money at a specified point in time to a given person (or to the bearer). The selling firm might agree to sell the goods only if the sale is made through a draft. If a **sight draft** is employed, before receiving title to the goods, the customer would have to pay when the draft is presented. Alternatively, the draft could be a **time draft,** which states that payment will be made a certain number of days after presentation to the customer. A time draft can be accepted by the customer or the customer's bank. If the customer accepts the draft, he or she acknowledges acceptance in writing on the back of the draft. This then becomes a **trade acceptance.** If the draft is accepted by the customer's bank, it becomes a **banker's acceptance.** The bank substitutes its creditworthiness for the customer's. As noted in Chapter 16, banker's acceptances are a major short-term marketable security; most of them arise from international trade.

The wide variety of terms and conditions have some logic to them, but tradition within an industry also plays a part. Sellers will demand early payment if the customers are in a high-risk class, if the accounts are small, or if the goods are perishable.

SIGHT DRAFT
An order to pay on sight.

TIME DRAFT
An order to pay at a stated future time.

TRADE ACCEPTANCE
Time draft drawn upon and accepted by a firm.

BANKER'S ACCEPTANCE
A draft drawn on a specific bank by a seller to obtain payment for goods shipped (sold) to a customer; by accepting, the bank assumes the obligation of payment.

International Purchases and Sales

Although most domestic trade is on an open-account basis, this is not the case for firms involved in international purchases or sales. Due to lack of credit knowledge, communications difficulties, and the like, the process becomes more complex. Many international transactions require three main documents: (1) an order to pay, or draft, (2) a bill of lading, and (3) a letter of credit. A draft, as discussed previously, is simply an order to pay on demand or at a specific point in time. Now let's briefly consider the use of bills of lading and letters of credit.

A **bill of lading** is a shipping document that has a number of functions. Primary among these are to serve as a contract to order the shipment of goods from one party (the seller) to another (the customer) and to provide title to the goods. The bill of lading and the draft proceed together. Their use is recognized in international law, and banks or other financial institutions in virtually all countries handle these documents. By using the draft and bill of lading, a seller can sell the goods and still obtain protection, because title is not released until the draft has been accepted.

The letter of credit is the third document. A **letter of credit** is a written statement made by the customer's bank that it will pay out money (honor a draft drawn on it), provided the bill of lading and other details are in order. Before the seller ships the goods, a letter of credit must be supplied. This letter is often irrevocable and confirmed by a bank in the seller's country. By obtaining the letter of credit, the seller ascertains before shipping the goods the creditworthiness and certainty of payment from the customer. Once the goods are shipped, they are covered by the bill of lading and accompanied by a draft (typically a time draft) that must be accepted by the customer's bank. The general sequence of events is illustrated in Figure 17.2. This process may seem complicated, but it is routine in international trade.

BILL OF LADING
Shipping document that authorizes the shipment of goods from one party (the seller) to another (the customer).

LETTER OF CREDIT
Agreement sent by one party (generally a bank) to another, concerning funds that will be made available.

FIGURE 17.2

Letter of Credit Transaction

The general sequence of transactions, in simplified form, is illustrated with those labeled (1) occurring before those labeled (2). Finally, as indicated by (3), payment is made and title to the goods passes to the buyer.

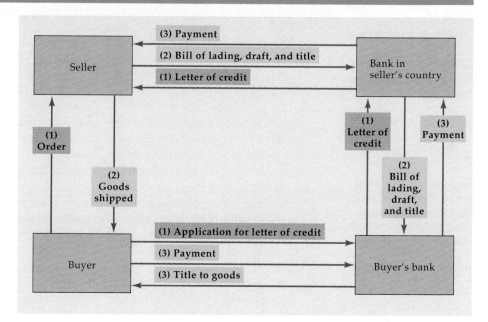

Credit Analysis

■ LEARNING GOAL 3

Describe credit scoring, and explain how to use net present value to make credit decisions.

Before offering a customer trade credit, it is wise to evaluate the likelihood that the customer will make its payments. This is done by conducting a credit analysis. For a credit analysis, information is needed on the customer's creditworthiness and paying potential. Numerous sources exist for securing this information, including:

1. *Accounting Statements.* The accounting statements provided by the potential customer enable a credit-granting firm to judge the firm's stability and cash-generating ability.
2. *Credit Ratings and Reports.* Several credit-rating agencies report on the creditworthiness of businesses. Dun & Bradstreet is probably the best known and most comprehensive credit agency. Its regular *Reference Book* provides credit ratings on about 2 million firms, both domestic and foreign. In addition, the National Association of Credit Management has enlisted TRW, Inc., to develop a computer-based credit retrieval system.

   A typical credit report includes the following information:

   a. Summary of recent accounting statements.
   b. Key ratios and trends over time.
   c. Information from the firm's suppliers indicating the firm's payment pattern.
   d. Description of the firm's physical condition and unusual circumstances related to the firm or its owners.
   e. A credit rating indicating the agency's assessment of the creditworthiness of the potential customer.

EXECUTIVE INTERVIEW WITH KATHERINE GREENBERG

*Chief Financial Officer
Ace Medical Company, Los
Angeles, California*

*Katherine Greenberg joined Ace Medical Company as
vice president and chief financial officer in 1987. Her
prior work experience included 3 years as a CPA at
Deloitte & Touche, New York, and 7 years in sales and
corporate communications at Norton Company,
Worcester, Massachusetts. She received her B.A. from
Mount Holyoke College and an M.B.A. from Columbia
University School of Business. We asked Ms.
Greenberg to discuss the importance of accounts receivable and inventory in the medical
equipment industry.*

Accounts receivable and inventory comprise 90 percent of total assets for Ace Medical
Company, a privately held manufacturer of titanium orthopedic implants for fracture repair.
When two assets account for such a large portion of the balance sheet, managing them efficiently is critical to the company's financial health. Also, bankers and other financial analysts
evaluate how well the company manages its working capital and cash flow by comparing the
firm's results (in terms of asset management ratios) to industry benchmarks.

Ace and its competitors set accounts receivable terms in line with practices in the health care
industry. Hospital buying groups, health care conglomerates, and government health institutions
contract for products at set terms. Typically we have little room to negotiate. Most hospital revenues come from third-party payers (insurance companies, Medicare, Medicaid), who pay very
slowly. Until the hospitals collect their receivables, they can't pay us. Our industry uses several
strategies to improve receivables collection: cash discounts for early payment, interest charges
on customers' accounts, and different pricing strategies. Cash discounts are not very effective for
us and are time-consuming to manage; interest charges seem to work better in our industry.

Our receivables terms for international customers (about 50 percent of sales) must be in line
with practices in the countries to which we sell. For example, some European and Latin
American countries have receivables terms of up to 180 days. We can't sell to distributors on
net 30-day terms if they won't collect from their customers for 180 days or more. Also, we set
terms in line with the company's goals. Building export sales requires more flexible receivables
terms. It's a tradeoff: Increasing market share calls for aggressive credit and pricing terms, but
it also carries greater risk.

Setting receivables policies requires cooperation between marketing and sales and finance.
These departments can be at cross purposes—although everyone should have the same end
goal, to make money and increase the firm's value. We promote good interdepartmental communication and work together to understand the other's viewpoint—for example, there may be
a cost in order to gain market share—and we develop a practical compromise.

Inventory management in the medical equipment industry is rather unique. We hold higher
levels of inventory than we would by choice, and it moves slowly. There is little tolerance of
stockouts in the industry; if we don't have the product when the doctor needs it, we lose the customer. With the rising cost of health care, hospitals now require manufacturers to carry their inventory and deliver it when needed; they don't pay until they use it. This helps the hospital's cash
flow but is a two-edged sword for them: We hold the inventory for them, but they pay a higher
price for the privilege. We really don't have an option if we want to compete in this market.

3. *Banks.* Most banks maintain credit departments and may provide credit information about firms for their customers who are considering extending credit to the
   firms.
4. *Trade Associations.* Many trade associations provide reliable means of obtaining
   credit information about their business members.
5. *Company's Own Experiences.* Past experience may have led the firm to establish
   some formal guidelines for gathering credit information and "sizing up" the

creditworthiness of a potential customer. For example, based on the size of the firm wanting credit, personal knowledge of the firm's CEO, or knowledge of the bank the firm does business with, firms may make informed judgments about the creditworthiness of the applicant firm.

Credit Decision

Once the information about a potential customer is collected, a credit decision must be made. That is, should credit be granted, and if so under what terms of sale? To make this decision, many firms classify potential customers into risk classes. With such a system, a firm might form a number of risk classes, as follows:

Risk Class	Estimated Percentage of Uncollectible Sales	Percentage of Customers in this Class
1	0–1%	35%
2	1–2½	30
3	2½–4	20
4	4–6	10
5	More than 6	5

Customers in class 1 might be extended credit automatically and their status reviewed only once a year. Those in class 2 might receive credit within specific limits, with their status checked semi-annually. Similar decisions could be made on the other categories. To protect against the possibility of loss, customers in class 5 might have to accept goods on a COD basis. This requirement for group 5 is perfectly legal, because it is the terms of the sale, *not* the sale price or cash discount (if any), that are affected. Some objective basis must exist, however, for placing a customer in one risk class as opposed to another.

CREDIT SCORING MODEL
Point-based system used to determine creditworthiness based on key financial and credit characteristics.

To make the risk class judgment, many firms use **credit scoring models.** A typical model might be as follows:

Variable	Weight	Credit Score*	Risk Class
Fixed charges coverage	4	Greater than 47	1
Quick ratio	11	40–47	2
Years in business (maximum of 15)	1	32–39	3
		24–31	4
		Less than 24	5

*Credit score = 4 (fixed charges coverage) + 11(quick ratio) + 1(years in business).

The success of credit scoring models is closely related to selecting the most important credit risk measures and determining the correct weights for each variable.

Based on either statistical or some other method of analysis, firms determine the relevant variables that are reliable indicators of their customers' creditworthiness. In this example three variables and their weights have been determined. The three variables are fixed charges coverage [($EBIT$ + lease expenses)/(interest + lease expenses)]; quick ratio [(current assets − inventory)/current liabilities]; and years in business. Suppose that a new customer with the following conditions applies for credit:

Fixed charges coverage	3.5
Quick ratio	0.8
Years in business	11

The customer's credit score would be 4(3.5) + 11(0.8) + 1(11) = 33.8, and it would be placed in risk category 3.

To limit risk exposure to credit losses, this traditional approach to credit scoring is being supplemented in larger firms by computer-based information systems. Smaller firms often employ time-sharing computer facilities to achieve many of the same benefits. For example, through Dun & Bradstreet a firm could designate a set of accounts to be monitored periodically for significant changes in the information in the D&B database. If and when changes occur, that information can be electronically transmitted to the firm granting trade credit so that it can take action by reducing or eliminating credit to the firm in question.

Let's start out with the basics of making credit decisions; complexities can be introduced later. To make the decision, firms compare the costs of granting credit with the benefits to be derived from granting credit, taking into account risk and the magnitude and timing of the cash flows.

The Basic Model

To make the credit decision, the firm needs the following information:

cash inflows   = the cash benefits expected to arise from the sale of goods on credit
cash outflows = the cash outflows associated with the goods to be sold. (Note that any fixed costs are not relevant, because they will be incurred by the firm whether or not credit is granted.)
T = the firm's marginal tax rate

In Chapter 8 the operating cash flows for a capital budgeting decision were determined to be (from Equation 8.1):

$$\text{operating } CF_t = (\text{cash inflows}_t - \text{cash outflows}_t) - \text{taxes}_t$$
$$= CFBT_t - \text{taxes}_t$$

where $CFBT_t$ is the cash flow before tax, $CFBT$. We concluded (Equation 8.3) that since taxes$_t$ are equal to $(CFBT_t - Dep_t) T$, the operating cash flows for capital budgeting purposes were equal to:

$$\text{operating } CF_t = CFBT_t - (CFBT_t - Dep_t)T$$
$$= CFBT_t - CFBT_t(T) + Dep_t(T)$$
$$= CFBT_t(1 - T) + Dep_t(T)$$

The same approach is employed to determine the after-tax cash flow for making accounts receivable decisions, except there (normally) is no investment in equipment required, so there is no depreciation tax shield. The operating cash flows for making the receivables decision are:

$$CF_t = (CFBT_t)(1 - T) \tag{17.1}$$

where $CFBT_t$ (cash flow before taxes) equals cash inflows minus cash outflows in time period t.

To determine whether to grant credit, we employ the same approach employed in making any capital expenditure decision by comparing the present value of the benefits with the cost of the investment, given the risks involved. The net present value, *NPV*, for the credit-granting decision[1] is:

$$NPV = \frac{CF_t}{k} - CF_0 \qquad (17.2)$$

where[1]

CF_t = the after-tax cash flows in each time period

k = the after-tax opportunity cost of capital reflecting the risk class of the potential customer

CF_0 = the investment the firm makes in its accounts receivable

The decision rule for the net present value when making the credit-granting decision is as follows:

1. If *NPV* is greater than zero, grant credit.
2. If *NPV* is less than zero, do not grant credit.
3. If *NPV* is equal to zero, you are indifferent.

Making the Credit Decision

To use Equation 17.2, the granting firm's *investment* in accounts receivable, CF_0, must be determined. The investment in receivables (at cost) is determined by calculating the variable cost of the credit sales outstanding as follows:

$$CF_0 = (VC)(S)(DSO/365 \text{ days}) \qquad (17.3)$$

where

VC = the variable cash outflow of producing and selling the goods as a percentage of cash inflows

S = the cash inflows (sales) expected each period

DSO = days sales outstanding

The after-tax cash inflows from granting additional credit, CF_t, are then determined by calculating the profit on the credit sales, less any bad debts and collection department expenses, and taking taxes into account, as follows:[2]

$$CF_t = [S(1 - VC) - S(BD) - CD](1 - T) \qquad (17.4)$$

where

BD = bad debts as a percentage of cash inflows from sales

CD = the dollar amount of additional credit department cash outflow for administering or collecting the accounts receivable

T = the firm's marginal tax rate

---

[1]*Equation 17.2 is the perpetuity form for the net present value. If the benefits are not expected to continue until infinity, then NPV techniques for limited-life projects should be employed.*
[2]*For simplicity, we ignore cash discounts in Equation 17.4.*

To illustrate this approach to the credit-granting decision, consider Empire Electronics, which groups firms into risk categories. Two of these risk classes, X and Y, are shown below:

Risk Class	Opportunity Cost of Capital k	Days Sales Outstanding DSO	Sales S	Bad Debt as a Percentage of Sales, BD	Additional Collection Department Cash Outflows, CD
X	18%	55 days	$200,000	9%	$10,000
Y	22	60	250,000	11	13,000

At present, Empire does not grant credit to firms in either class. The question is, should Empire modify its terms and now extend credit to firms in either or both risk classes? In addition to the data given above, Empire's variable cash outflows are 82 percent of sales, and its tax rate is 35 percent.

To make the decision, let's first consider class X. We can find the additional initial investment (at cost) in accounts receivable using Equation 17.3, as follows:

$$CF_0 = (VC)(S)(DSO/365 \text{ days})$$
$$= (0.82)(\$200,000)(55/365) = \$24,712$$

The additional expected cash inflows, CF_t, are found using Equation 17.4, as follows:

$$CF_t = [S(1 - VC) - S(BD) - CD](1 - T)$$
$$= [\$200,000(1 - 0.82) - \$200,000(0.09) - \$10,000](1 - 0.35)$$
$$= (\$36,000 - \$18,000 - \$10,000)(0.65) = (\$8,000)(0.65) = \$5,200$$

Thus, if Empire grants credit to firms in risk class X, it benefits by receiving incremental expected after-tax cash inflows of $5,200 per period. To obtain these additional CFs, Empire must make an additional investment of $24,712 in accounts receivable. Employing a time line, the cash flows are as follows:

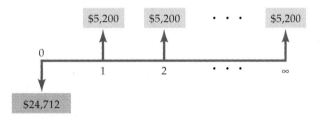

The net present value, which is the benefit to the firm from granting credit to firms in risk class X, employing Equation 17.2, is:

$$NPV = \frac{CF_t}{k} - CF_0 = \frac{\$5,200}{0.18} - \$24,712 = \$28,889 - \$24,712 = \$4,177$$

Because the net present value is positive, Empire should grant credit to potential customers in risk class X. By doing so, it is making a decision that increases the value of the firm.[3]

---

[3] Be careful using the perpetual form of the net present value approach. Because no growth is assumed, the NPV may be biased low. On the other hand, by assuming cash flows go on to infinity, the NPV may be biased high.

The same calculations can be carried out for firms in risk class Y:

$$CF_0 = (0.82)(\$250{,}000)(60/365) = \$33{,}699$$

and:

$$CF_t = [\$250{,}000(1 - 0.82) - \$250{,}000(0.11) - \$13{,}000](1 - 0.35)$$

$$= (\$45{,}000 - \$27{,}500 - \$13{,}000)(0.65) = (\$4{,}500)(0.65) = \$2{,}925$$

The net present value is then

$$NPV = \frac{\$2{,}925}{0.22} - \$33{,}699 = \$13{,}295 - \$33{,}699 = -\$20{,}404$$

Because the net present value is negative, Empire would not grant credit to firms in risk class Y.

In the first case, the additional investment in accounts receivable was less than the present value of the expected cash inflows arising from granting credit.[4] In the second case, the investment was greater. Thus, credit should be granted to customers in risk class X, but not to those in risk class Y.

Collection Policy

■ LEARNING GOAL 4

Describe techniques for monitoring receivables, and explain how net present value is used to evaluate changes in collection policy.

Once the granting decision has been made, we cannot ignore the final step—namely, following up to ensure the collection of these receivables. The rate at which receivables are converted into cash measures the efficiency of the collection policy. To ensure collections, the firm establishes a collections department that is responsible for monitoring and following up on receivables. We first consider some techniques for monitoring accounts receivable; then we consider how to analyze changes in collection policies.

Managing Collections

Two basic techniques for monitoring the receivables investment are the days sales outstanding and the receivables pattern approach.

Days Sales Outstanding. The days sales outstanding is calculated by dividing the firm's accounts receivable by average daily sales:

$$\text{days sales outstanding} = \frac{\text{accounts receivable}}{\text{sales}/365 \text{ days}} \tag{17.5}$$

If a firm's receivables are $1,800,000 and its sales for the year are $14,600,000, its days sales outstanding, *DSO*, is:

$$DSO = \frac{\$1{,}800{,}000}{\$14{,}600{,}000/365} = \frac{\$1{,}800{,}000}{\$40{,}000} = 45 \text{ days}$$

---

[4] In addition to the standard credit decision just discussed, the same basic approach can be employed to analyze the size of the cash discount offered or the terms of sale. Although these are also important issues, both the cash discount offered and the terms of sale are influenced by competition and are subject to infrequent change.

DSO is a popular measure, but it depends on sales performance. If sales are unstable because of seasonality or cyclical behavior, DSO results are seriously biased.

The *DSO* is easy to calculate, but it is not very effective for internal use in monitoring a firm's collections. It is an aggregate measure and tends to hide many individual differences among customers in terms of payments. In addition, the *DSO* is influenced by changes in the level of receivables or changes in the level of sales outside of the month the sales are made. For example, if receivables increase to $2,000,000, the days sales outstanding goes to 50 days in our example [i.e., $2,000,000 ÷ ($14,600,000/365) = 50]. If receivables stay at the original level of $1,800,000, the *DSO* can also increase to 50 days if sales drop to $13,140,000 [i.e., $1,800,000 ÷ ($13,140,000/365) = 50]. From a control standpoint, the increase in the level of receivables to $2,000,000 might require different actions by the collection department from those needed if sales decreased to $13,140,000.

RECEIVABLES PATTERN
Method for analyzing a firm's receivables, calculated by determining the percentage of credit sales outstanding in the month of the sale and in subsequent months.

A Receivables Pattern Approach.   Instead of using the days sales outstanding or some other aggregate measure of accounts receivable, it is usually better to take a management-by-exception approach. This approach uses data on the firm's receivables to highlight deviations from the pattern. The **receivables pattern** is that percentage of credit sales remaining unpaid in the month of the sale and in subsequent months. The key to understanding receivables patterns is to remember that *each* month's credit sales are kept separate, as well as the collections received on those credit sales.

To understand this approach, consider a firm that has credit sales of $100,000 in January. Collections on the $100,000 are as follows:

Month	Collections from January Sales	Payment Pattern	Receivables from January Sales Outstanding at End of Month	Receivables Pattern
January	$10,000	10%	$90,000	90%
February	30,000	30	60,000	60
March	30,000	30	30,000	30
April	30,000	30	0	0

The accuracy of cash inflow forecasts is closely related to the accuracy of the receivable payment patterns.

In January, 10 percent of the credit sales are paid, followed by 30 percent each in February, March, and April.[5] The receivables pattern, which is simply 100 percent minus the cumulative percentage payments, declines from 90 percent in January to zero in April. This information is graphed in Figure 17.3.

FIGURE 17.3

Graph of Payment and Receivables Pattern for January Credit Sales

The receivables pattern in (b) is derived from the payment pattern in (a). By focusing on the receivables pattern, the firm can easily determine whether payments are being made in the manner expected.

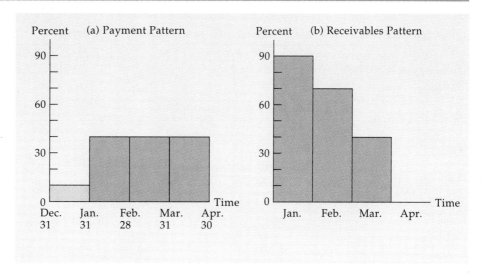

[5] *For simplicity, we ignore bad debts.*

A key is to compare receivables and sales growth. If receivables growth = sales growth, the change in receivables is a sales effect. If receivables growth > sales growth, the incremental difference can be attributed to collection or credit term effects.

Payment patterns are measured by product line. Monitoring payment pattern performance is a valuable early warning system of forecasting errors.

AGING SCHEDULE
List of customers and amounts unpaid.

Because the receivables pattern approach relates uncollected accounts receivable to the months in which they arise, it has two significant advantages from a management standpoint: First, it disaggregates the receivables into their collection pattern relative to the month in which they occur. Second, because accounts receivable are related to sales in the month of origin, they are sales-dependent *only* in the month of origin. No matter what the sales pattern, any changes in payment behavior can be recognized immediately.

To see how we might exercise collection control, consider Table 17.1, which provides both budgeted and actual receivables patterns over a 6-month period. Note that the budgeted receivables pattern was 91, 61, and 20 percent for January sales, whereas the actual receivables are 90, 65, and 30, respectively. In both the first and second months after the credit sales, the collections came in slower than expected. Further examination of Table 17.1 indicates this same pattern has been occurring since November. By focusing on the exceptions, or the deviations of the actual from the projected pattern, management is in a good position to change the collection policy or modify the classes of customers who are eligible to receive credit.

In addition to the collection pattern, firms often prepare an **aging schedule**, which is a list of customer accounts grouped by how long they are overdue. Thus, a simple aging schedule might appear as follows:

				Past Days Due		
Customer	Receivables	Current	1–30	31–60	61–90	Over 90
A	$ 58,000	$ 18,000	$10,000	0	$10,000	0
B	174,000	0	0	$50,000	65,000	$59,000
C	125,000	100,000	25,000	0	0	0

An examination of the aging schedule reveals that customer A is a little slow in paying its account; but, a far bigger problem exists with customer B, which has some of its account a minimum of 31 days overdue, with even more 61 or more days overdue. Additional credit would not be granted to customer B. On the other hand, customer C appears to be essentially current on paying its bill.

TABLE 17.1

Budgeted Versus Actual Accounts Receivable Patterns

Looking across the bottom two rows, we see that since November the actual receivables still outstanding both 1 and 2 months after the sales are greater than the budgeted receivables. The slow collection is not unique to January credit sales.

	October	November	December	January	February	March
Budgeted						
Percent of same month sales	90%	91%	93%	91%	91%	90%
Percent of 1 month before	65	64	62	61	61	62
Percent of 2 months before	36	26	24	22	20	20
Actual						
Percent of same month sales	91%	93%	96%	90%	88%	89%
Percent of 1 month before	70	68	69	66	65	65
Percent of 2 months before	34	32	30	30	28	30

Analysis of Changes in Collection Policy

Now that we have some idea of how to analyze and control collections, we can address other important questions. Should the firm change its existing credit-granting or collection policies? To evaluate changing policies and, possibly, curtailing credit previously granted, we simply employ the *NPV* approach discussed previously. A second decision is to tighten or loosen collection procedures related to existing customers. Consider the following, which shows the existing collection experience and proposed effects of improving the firm's collection procedures:

Situation	Opportunity Cost of Capital, k	Days Sales Outstanding, DSO	Sales, S	Bad Debts as a Percentage of Sales, BD	Department Cash Outflows, CD
Old	15%	60 days	$1,000,000	10%	$50,000
New	15	55	1,000,000	7	90,000

Under the existing procedures, the days sales outstanding is 60 days, sales are $1,000,000, bad debts are 10 percent of sales, and collection department cash outflows are $50,000. By expanding the collections department, the firm would be able to reduce the days sales outstanding to 55 days, and bad debts would drop to only 7 percent. Collection department cash outflows, however, would increase from $50,000 to $90,000. The question is this: Will the firm benefit from increasing its collection efforts?

To answer, we begin by calculating the incremental initial investment and incremental cash flows after taxes that are associated with the revised procedures. Then we can employ Equation 17.2 to determine whether the change adds to the profitability of the firm. The incremental investment at cost in the additional receivables, ΔCF_0, is determined by comparing the proposed investment in receivables with the existing investment so that

$$\text{incremental investment} = \text{investment, new } (N) - \text{investment, old } (O)$$
$$\Delta CF_0 = (VC_N)(S_N)(DSO_N/365) - (VC_O)(S_O)(DSO_O/365) \quad (17.6)$$

If the variable cash outflows are 80 percent of sales in either case, then using the data given above, the incremental investment is:

$$\Delta CF_0 = (0.80)(\$1,000,000)(55/365) - (0.80)(\$1,000,000)(60/365)$$

$$= \$120,548 - \$131,507 = -\$10,959$$

By reducing the days sales outstanding from 60 to 55 days, the new collection plan frees $10,959 that can be used elsewhere in the firm.

The incremental cash flow after-tax, ΔCF_t, due to the change in the collection policy is determined by comparing the after-tax cash flows under the proposed policy with the after-tax cash flows under the present policy as follows:

$$\text{incremental after-tax cash flow} = \text{after-tax cash flow, new } (N) - \text{after-tax cash flow, old } (O)$$
$$\Delta CF_t = [S_N(1 - VC_N) - S_N(BD_N) - CD_N](1 - T)$$
$$- [S_O(1 - VC_O) - S_O(BD_O) - CD_O](1 - T) \quad (17.7)$$

If the tax rate is 40 percent, then the incremental after-tax cash flow due to implementing the new collection policy is:

$$CF_t = [\$1,000,000(1 - 0.80) - \$1,000,000(0.07) - \$90,000](1 - 0.40)$$

$$-[\$1,000,000(1 - 0.80) - \$1,000,000(0.10) - \$50,000](1 - 0.40)$$

$$= (\$200,000 - \$70,000 - \$90,000)(0.60) - (\$200,000 - \$100,000$$

$$-\$50,000)(0.60)$$

$$= (\$40,000)(0.60) - (\$50,000)(0.60) = \$24,000 - \$30,000 = -\$6,000$$

Implementing the tighter policy reduces cash inflows by $6,000 per period. To determine if the firm should implement the proposed change, we calculate the NPV as follows:

$$\text{net present value} = \frac{-\$6,000}{0.15} - (-\$10,959)$$

$$= -\$40,000 + \$10,959 = -\$29,041$$

Because the net present value is negative, the firm is worse off with the new policy.

To carry this idea a little further, consider what would happen if everything were the same as in the preceding example, except that the days sales outstanding decreases to 40 days if we undertake the new collection policy. The incremental after-tax cash flows are still −$6,000 as before, but the firm is able to reduce its investment in receivables even more than before. With a 40-day average DSO, the incremental investment using Equation 17.6 is:

$$\Delta CF_0 = (0.80)(\$1,000,000)(40/365) - (0.80)(\$1,000,000)(60/365)$$

$$= \$87,671 - \$131,507 = -\$43,836$$

If the days sales outstanding drops to 40 days the NPV is:

$$NPV = \frac{-\$6,000}{0.15} - (-\$43,836) = -\$40,000 + \$43,836 = \$3,836$$

Because the NPV is positive, the firm would now proceed to implement the proposed change in collection policy.

Still other things might happen if the firm implements a new collection policy. One possibility is for the tighter collection policy to reduce sales. Any changes of this type can be investigated employing the approach just described. By focusing on the cash flows, risks, and opportunity costs, we can determine whether a change in the firm's credit-granting or collection policies will benefit the firm (those with positive NPVs) or not (those with negative NPVs). By making credit and collection management decisions that increase the value of the firm, we can assist in achieving our goal of maximizing the value of the firm. Policies should be based on maximizing net cash inflows, spending time on large or risky accounts, and looking beyond the immediate future. Then, the maximum benefits can be secured at the least possible cost.

International Collection Alternatives

Practically all countries provide *export credit insurance* for their exporters. This insurance protects exporters against the risk of nonpayment by the purchasers. In the United States export credit insurance is administered by the Foreign Credit Insurance Association, FCIA, which is a cooperative effort of the Export-Import Bank and a group of approximately 50 insurance companies. The insurance companies provide protection from commercial risks, while the Export-Import Bank covers political risks. Instead of selling insurance on a case-by-case basis, the FCIA approves limits for each exporter within which they are provided coverage.

Suppose you have just obtained your first overseas contract. The question is, "How do you get the cash in your hands?" There are four primary approaches:

1. *Banks*. Although larger banks often get involved in providing financing and letters of credit, increasingly they are finding that the returns don't justify their costs.
2. *Forfait Financing*. Forfait companies, such as London Forfaiting, started out financing international capital investments. Now they also will accept foreign receivables—the money you are owed by foreign firms—when it is backed by a government guarantee, such as that provided by the Export-Import Bank. They often convert the money to commercial paper, which is negotiable. You get your cash quickly, minus the forfaiter's fee.
3. *Factoring*. Factoring companies, such as Factor One Funding Resources, started out servicing the retail trade industry. They will accept a foreign receivable, and often will give you up to 85 percent of the money you are due, before they receive payment from the customer. This tends to work best for 30-, 60-, and 90-day transactions.
4. *Export Trading Companies*. Export trading companies will actually take title to your goods and complete the transaction. They will handle the shipment, and due to their specialized nature, they often have the expertise to do deals in even the most remote countries. The cost is slightly higher than other forms of collection.

While there is no easy approach to dealing in the international marketplace, given the rapid globalization of trade and finance it's relatively easy to find support for handling the collection of receivables from international customers. Firms dealing with international sales often find that collection involves expenses of 2 to 3 percent of the receivables.

CONCEPT REVIEW QUESTIONS

- What does a typical credit report contain?
- Describe how a credit scoring model can help a firm assign customers to risk classes.
- Describe two basic techniques for monitoring a firm's account receivables.
- Describe alternative approaches for collecting international receivables.

INVENTORY MANAGEMENT

■ LEARNING GOAL 5

Discuss the costs and benefits of holding inventory, and describe four inventory management approaches.

Inventory, like receivables, represents a sizable investment and must therefore be managed effectively. Although the formal responsibility for the control of inventory lies with operating divisions, financial managers are also concerned about inventory management. The more efficiently the firm manages its inventory, the lower the investment required—which, other things being equal, will increase the value of the firm.

Types of Inventory

Firms have different types of inventories. The three most common are raw materials, work-in-process, and finished goods. *Raw materials* consist of goods that are used to manufacture a product. *Work-in-process inventory* consists of partially completed goods requiring additional work before they become finished goods. *Finished goods* are those goods on which production has been completed and that are ready for sale. Manufacturing firms hold all three types of inventory. Wholesale and retail firms typically hold only a finished goods inventory. Service firms may have no inventory except for a few supplies related to their activities.

For manufacturing firms, the purpose of holding inventory is to uncouple various operations of the firm—acquisition of the goods, the stages of production, and selling activities. Without inventory, particularly work-in-process inventory, each stage of production would depend on completion of the preceding stage. As a result, there would be delays and considerable idle time at certain stages of production. Likewise, the raw materials and finished goods inventory uncouple the purchasing and selling functions from the production function.

Benefits from Inventory Investment

In addition to uncoupling the firm's operations, a number of other benefits may be associated with the investment a firm makes in its inventory:

1. *Taking Advantage of Quantity Discounts*. Often suppliers will offer customers quantity discounts if they purchase a certain number of items at the same time. To take advantage of such discounts, firms need to hold inventory.
2. *Avoiding Stock Outages*. If a firm runs out of inventory—has a stock outage—in the production process, it may disrupt the production cycle and even cause it to stop. If finished goods are not on hand, sales may be lost and the firm's reliability as a supplier comes into question.
3. *Marketing Benefits*. Often there are distinct marketing benefits in terms of increased sales associated with having a full and complete line of merchandise. Also, developing the reputation for always being able to supply the needed items may be part of the firm's marketing strategy.
4. *Inventory Speculation*. In times of inflation, or if other factors are causing prices to increase, firms can benefit by increasing inventory. Other things being equal, this stockpiling of inventory at current prices will increase the profitability of the firm.

Costs of Inventory Investment

The cost of a firm's investment in inventory consists of three main elements—ordering costs, carrying costs, and costs of running short.

1. *Ordering Costs.* The primary costs associated with ordering inventory include the clerical costs of placing the order, plus transportation and shipping costs.
2. *Carrying Costs.* Carrying costs include the direct investment the firm has in its inventory, including storage, insurance, property tax, and spoilage and deterioration. In addition, there is an opportunity cost associated with having funds tied up in nonproductive or excess inventory. Thus, if it keeps $5 million in inventory when only $2 million is needed, the firm has $3 million tied up that could be used or invested elsewhere.
3. *Costs of Running Short.* The main costs associated with running short (stock outages) include lost sales, loss of customer goodwill, and disruption of the firm's production process.

To avoid these costs, firms attempt to control their inventory levels.

Alternative Approaches for Managing Inventory

Many different approaches exist for managing inventory. Four important ones are the ABC method, the economic order quantity approach, material requirements planning, and the just-in-time method.

The ABC Method

ABC METHOD
Inventory control method in which items are grouped in categories by their value and need of control.

One relatively simple inventory management approach is the **ABC method.** To illustrate, consider a firm that has thousands of inventory items, ranging from very expensive to very inexpensive. With the ABC method, the firm categorizes inventory items based on cost: The A items require a high investment, B items a medium investment, and C items the lowest investment. For example, A items might account for 10 percent of the items and 50 percent of the dollar inventory investment. Category B items might constitute 30 percent of the items and 35 percent of the dollar value, while the C items contribute 60 percent of the items but only 15 percent of the dollar investment. Graphically, the ABC method is depicted in Figure 17.4

By separating the inventory into different groups, firms can concentrate their attention on items for which effective inventory control is most important. A formal system involving extensive and frequent monitoring is likely for category A items. Items in group B will be reviewed and adjusted less frequently—perhaps quarterly; C items may be reviewed only annually. The ABC method has two advantages: It focuses attention where it will do the most good, and it makes the financial management of inventory paramount. That is, other considerations (marketing, production, purchasing) are met, and then financial considerations are employed to control the firm's inventory investment.

The EOQ Model

ECONOMIC ORDER QUANTITY, EOQ
The optimal inventory order size that minimizes total cost (ordering cost + carrying cost).

A slightly more complex model for managing inventory is the **economic order quantity, EOQ, model.** The primary purpose of the economic order quantity model is to determine how often and what quantity to order, and the average inventory to have on hand. The EOQ model considers both ordering and carrying costs of inventory, in order to calculate the order quantity that minimizes total inventory cost. The basic EOQ model assumes constant demand, constant carrying costs, and constant ordering costs. However, modifications can be made to the basic model to make the model more realistic.

FIGURE 17.4

ABC Inventory Method

The ABC method provides a conceptual framework that suggests different control systems should be used for high- versus low-value items.

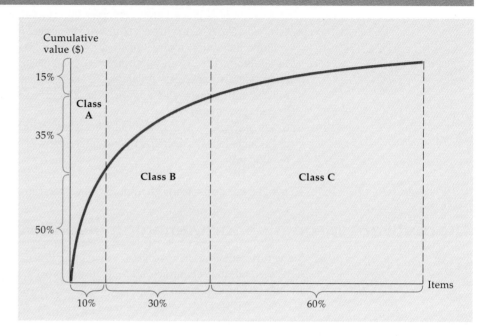

MRP and Just-in-Time Methods

MATERIAL REQUIRE-MENTS PLANNING
Centralized, demand-driven system to coordinate orders and inventory with production needs.

Under **material requirements planning, MRP,** the expected demand for the end product is used to project demands for raw materials and for the various components and subcomponents of the final product. This demand is then combined with knowledge of the existing inventory to determine when and how much additional inventory is needed to meet the demand. MRP is a top-down, or "pull," system that starts with an annual sales forecast, and the anticipated and current demand.

JUST-IN-TIME METHOD
Inventory and production system in which inventory is minimized by contracting with suppliers so that deliveries are made just as needed for production.

An inventory management system that has grown in popularity is the **just-in-time method**. With this system the firm contracts with suppliers for both the goods *and* the time when they will be received. Because the firm wants to maintain almost zero inventory, the suppliers must be located nearby in order to make delivery on a daily or even hourly basis. From the firm's standpoint, the method requires a totally different approach to the production and management process. That is why it often takes new or completely redesigned plants and labor contracts to achieve the anticipated benefits of the just-in-time approach to controlling investment in inventory.

Effective management of the firm's inventory involves a balancing of the costs and benefits associated with the investment in inventory. Investment in inventory is really just like any other investment a firm makes. So the *NPV* framework can also be employed to assist in deciding whether to increase or decrease inventory investment.

Analysis of Investment in Inventory

Often when a firm is considering an investment in some new long-term assets, such as building a new plant, streamlining storage facilities, and the like, part of that problem involves investment in current assets. As we saw in Chapter 8, any changes in net working capital (current assets minus current liabilities) must be analyzed as part of this larger problem.

However, some investments in inventory may not relate to the acquisition of long-term assets by the firm. Consider, for example, Thrifty Stores. After an extensive study by its marketing and finance departments, the firm concluded that sales could be increased significantly if the firm increased its level of inventory. The increased sales would result from carrying a more complete line, resulting in multiple sales and increased customer traffic. In support of this plan, it has data from a pilot study of its Birmingham store. The firm's inventory would have to be increased by $4 million, and the increased after-tax cash flows, CF_t, are estimated to be $600,000 per year. Assuming the cash flows are expected to last for a long time, the time line for the cash flows is as follows:

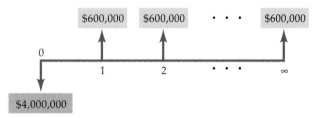

The question is this: Should the additional investment in the inventory be made?

After evaluation, the firm has concluded that a 12 percent discount rate is appropriate. Employing Equation 17.2, we find that the net present value of this inventory buildup is:

$$NPV = \frac{\$600,000}{0.12} - \$4,000,000 = \$5,000,000 - \$4,000,000 = \$1,000,000$$

Because the net present value is positive, the increased inventory investment should be made.

What happens, however, if Thrifty estimates that there will be increased expenses (storage, losses, and so forth) resulting from the increased inventory level? These expenses are expected to reduce cash inflows by $70,000 per year. In addition, the senior vice-president believes that $80,000 of the estimated cash flows are extremely unlikely to come in. The additional investment is still $4 million, but the expected cash inflows are now $450,000 (i.e., $600,000 − $70,000 − $80,000) per year, which produces the following projected cash flow stream:

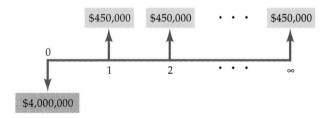

The net present value is now:

$$NPV = \frac{\$450,000}{0.12} - \$4,000,000 = \$3,750,000 - \$4,000,000 = -\$250,000$$

Obviously, based on this set of expected cash flows and the 12 percent opportunity cost of capital, Thrifty should not increase its inventory investment.

Three items must be stressed about making inventory decisions: First, the emphasis has to be on cash flows. Second, because various types of inventory are held by firms, close attention should be devoted to the most important items. A management-by-exception framework can be used to control investment in all other inventory items. Finally, the risks and returns must be considered. For many firms, inventory is the most important single investment; hence, effective management of inventory has direct implications for the firm. Carrying too much, or obsolete, inventory is one sure way to lower the value of the firm.

Interaction of Accounts Receivable and Inventory Decisions

Until now we have considered separately the management of receivables and the management of inventory. In practice, there are interactions between the firm's accounts receivable and its inventory. This interaction is often hard to see or to achieve, however, because the functions of inventory management and receivables management are typically separate areas of responsibility within the firm. However, to the extent possible, inventory and receivables policies should be developed and evaluated on a joint basis, because there are trade-offs between them. The investment includes those cash outflows required for the incremental investment in receivables given by Equation 17.3 plus the incremental investment in inventory. Likewise, the benefits are the incremental cash inflows from the joint receivables/inventory decision. Combinations of tighter inventory control with relaxed credit, looser inventory policy and tighter credit, and varying mixes between these two can be evaluated in terms of the cash flow consequences to the firm. By viewing the investment in these two current assets in an integrated manner, the firm is in a better position to maximize its value.

CONCEPT REVIEW QUESTIONS

■ Describe the costs and benefits of holding inventory.
■ Describe different approaches a firm may employ to manage its inventory.
■ How does the material requirements planning method differ from the just-in-time approach?

Summary

■ Accounts receivable and inventory represent a significant investment. Funds tied up in these uses are as costly as those employed elsewhere in the firm.
■ Management of account receivables involves the following areas: terms and conditions of credit sales, credit analysis, credit decision, and the collection policy.
■ Decisions on granting credit, changing credit or collection policies, and the investment in inventory involve an analysis of the magnitude and timing of the cash flows, risks, returns, and opportunity costs. This analysis is accomplished by calculating the net present value, *NPV*, of the proposed change in the firm's credit, collection, or inventory policies. For simplicity, the perpetuity form of the net present value decision criteria is employed.
■ Days sales outstanding is always influenced by changes in the level of sales; however, the receivables pattern approach is only affected by changes in sales in the month of origin.
■ The primary costs to consider in making inventory decisions are carrying costs, ordering costs, and the costs of running short.

Questions

17.1 Explain how the four parts of the firm's credit and collection policies interact.

17.2 What would be the effect of changes in the following on the level of accounts receivable?

    a. The economy improves, and interest rates decline.

    b. The credit manager tightens up on past due accounts.

    c. The credit terms are changed from 3/10, net 30, to 2/10, net 30.

    d. The firm's selling and production expenses decline relative to other firms.

17.3 Gail, the credit manager, is being criticized for the deterioration in her performance because the days sales outstanding has increased, as have bad debts. Under what circumstances is this criticism unjustified?

17.4 Why is the receivables pattern approach superior to the days sales outstanding in monitoring collections?

17.5 What would be the effect of the following on the level of inventory held by the firm?

    a. Inflation increases.

    b. The firm's suppliers switch from truck to air freight delivery.

    c. Competition increases in the firm's sales market.

    d. The firm's production cycle becomes shorter.

Concept Review Problems

See Appendix A for solutions.

CR17.1 Marconi & Sons uses the following model to determine customer trade credit: credit score = 5(current ratio) + 7(times interest earned) − 9(debt to tangible net worth). Three of Marconi's customers have the following ratios:

	A	B	C
Current ratio	2.2	2	2.5
Times interest earned	6	5	4
Debt to tangible net worth	2	4	3

What is each customer's credit score?

CR17.2 In addition to the credit scores from CR17.1, Marconi has determined that the following apply to each risk class:

Note: Use a 365-day year.

	Credit Score		
	Greater than 25	10–25	Less than 10
Risk class	1	2	3
Opportunity cost of capital	12%	14%	17%
Days sales outstanding	35	55	85
Sales	$300,000	$400,000	$200,000
Bad debts as a percentage of sales	4%	10%	15%
Additional collection department cash outflows	$8,000	$18,000	$16,000

Marconi's variable cash outflows are 75 percent of sales, and the tax rate is 40 percent. Should trade credit be offered to any of the firms?

CR17.3 Mathers & Associates has the following sales and receivables patterns:

Month	Sales	Collections from Current Month	Receivables from 1-Month Prior Sales	Receivables from 2-Month Prior Sales
August	$30,000	$2,700	$24,000	$12,000
September	20,000	1,600	15,000	12,000
October	10,000	700	8,000	12,300
November	20,000	1,400	3,000	10,400
December	30,000	2,100	5,000	6,300

Using the receivables pattern approach for months August, September, and October, comment on Mathers' collection of accounts receivable.

CR17.4 Kewal is unhappy with his firm's collection of accounts. The firm currently has annual sales of $20 million, 15 percent bad debt, and days sales outstanding of 65. Kewal wants to decrease both the percentage of bad debts and the days sales outstanding by doubling the size of the firm's collection department budget from $250,000 to $500,000. It is estimated that bad debts would decline to 12 percent and days sales outstanding would decrease to 55. However, Helen, the marketing director, pointed out that sales would also decrease, to an estimated $17 million. If variable costs are 70 percent of sales, the tax rate is 35 percent, and the opportunity cost of capital is 14 percent, should the collection department budget be increased?

CR17.5 Spencer Instruments believes the firm's after-tax cash flows could be increased by $200,000 per year if it increased its inventory by $1.5 million. If the firm's opportunity cost of capital is 15 percent, what is the net present value of increasing the firm's inventory?

Problems

See Appendix C for answers to selected problems.

Day Sales Outstanding and Sales

Note: Carry to five decimal places.

17.1 Landis Industries offers credit terms of 3/10, net 45. Twenty percent of its customers pay on the discount date, 40 percent pay on the net date, and the other 40 percent pay in 60 days. If Landis's average investment in accounts receivables is $500,000 and variable costs are 80 percent of sales, what is Landis's annual sales? Assume a 365-day year.

Credit Analysis

Note: Assume the number of bikes will decrease if the credit information is obtained. Also, do not worry about taxes.

17.2 BigSky Sports has decided to offer credit during its fall bicycle sale. Sales are expected to be 500 units at $450 each, and BigSky's cost is $315 per bike. The firm estimates that 94 percent of the customers will make their payments, and the others will have to be written off as bad debts. To eliminate the bad debts, NeverFail Credit will supply customer credit reports for a one-time fee of $1,500, plus $7.50 per report. Should BigSky obtain the credit information?

Credit Standards

17.3 Atlier Metal Works is in the process of evaluating its credit standards. Two potential classes of new customers exist, as follows:

Risk Class	Opportunity Cost of Capital, k	Days Sales Outstanding, DSO	Sales, S	Bad Debts as a Percentage of Sales, BD	Collection Department Cash Outflows, CD
4	16%	45 days	$511,999	8%	$15,000
5	20	55	438,000	12	25,000

The variable cash outflows as a percentage of sales are 80 percent, and the tax rate is 30 percent. Should Atlier extend credit to potential customers in risk class 4? In risk class 5? (Assume a 365-day year.)

Review of Credit Standards

17.4 Baines Industries makes all sales on a credit basis. It is evaluating the creditworthiness of its customers. The results of the analysis are as follows:

Risk Class	Opportunity Cost of Capital, k	Days Sales Outstanding, DSO	Sales, S	Bad Debts as a Percentage of Sales, BD	Collection Department Cash Outflows, CD
A	12%	20 days	$3 million	3%	$50,000
B	14	40	4	5	50,000
C	16	60	6	10	60,000
D	18	80	8	15	80,000

Variable cash outflows are 81 percent of sales, and taxes are 40 percent.

a. Analyze each of the present classes of customers. Should Baines continue to grant credit to all four risk classes? (Assume a 365-day year.)

b. What happens to the level of sales if Baines follows your recommendation in (a)? How would you proceed to convince Baines to follow your recommendation?

Marginal Tax Rate

17.5 Harris Products is evaluating whether to grant credit to a risky class of potential customers. Variable cash outflows are 82 percent of sales, the days sales outstanding is 65 days, sales per year (based on a 365-day year) are $10,950,000, bad debts are 12 percent of sales, additional collection department cash outflows are $300,000 per year, and the opportunity cost of capital is 12 percent. At what marginal tax rate is Harris indifferent between granting and not granting credit to this new class of customers?

Payment and Receivables Pattern

17.6 Blocker Products is a new firm. All sales are on credit, and the sales and payments for the first 6 months are as follows:

	March	April	May	June	July	August
Credit sales	$1,500	$2,000	$2,400	$2,800	$3,700	$4,900
Payments—same month	200	400	500	600	700	800
Payments—1 month later		600	800	1,000	1,250	1,500
Payments—2 months later			500	700	800	850

After 2 months the uncollected sales are written off as bad debts. Calculate the receivables pattern for Blocker. Is it becoming more or less effective? What is happening to its bad debts? Are there any indications of change occurring in July and August?

Monitoring Collections

17.7 Riggins Systems employs the days sales outstanding (based on a 365-day year) to monitor its receivables. The sales and receivables pattern for the 4 months of February through May are as follows:

	February	March	April	May	June	July
Credit sales	$150,000	$200,000	$300,000	$300,000		
Receivables—same month sales	120,000	160,000	237,000	234,000		
Receivables—1 month before		60,000	80,000	114,000	108,000	
Receivables—2 months before			0	0	0	0

Total sales for the year are $2,555,000.

a. Calculate the days sales outstanding (using the total yearly sales) for each of 3 months—March, April, and May.

b. What do your results from (a) suggest about the effectiveness of Riggins' collection policies?

c. Now calculate the receivables pattern for Riggins. Is its collection policy less effective in May than in March or April?

d. Explain why you got conflicting results from the days sales outstanding versus the receivables pattern approach.

Easing the Collections Effort

17.8 Percy Refrigeration has annual credit sales of $1.6 million. Current collection department cash outflows are $35,000, bad debts are 1.5 percent of sales, and the days sales outstanding is 30 days. Percy is considering easing its collection efforts so that collection department outflows will be reduced to $22,000 per year. The change is expected to increase bad debts to 2.5 percent of sales and to increase the days sales outstanding to 45 days. In addition, sales are expected to increase to $1.75 million. If the discount rate is 16 percent, variable cash outflows are 75 percent of sales, and the marginal tax rate is 35 percent, should Percy make the change?

Tightening the Credit Policy

17.9 RedRock Industries believes its collection policy may be out of hand. Currently, the firm has sales of $6 million and days sales outstanding of 55 days, bad debts are 6 percent of sales, and yearly collection department cash outflows are $100,000. Its existing variable cash outflows are 80 percent of sales. If it tightens the collection policy significantly, it anticipates sales will drop to $5 million, the days sales outstanding will become 25 days, bad debts will be 3 percent of sales, and collection department cash outflows will be $75,000 per year. At this level of sales, variable cash outflows will be 83 percent of sales. Assume the corporate tax rate is 30 percent and use a 365-day year.

a. If the opportunity cost of capital is 14 percent, should it tighten the collection policy?

b. What if the opportunity cost is 20 percent?

Collecting Overdue Receivables

17.10 Neufeld Products has $500,000 in overdue receivables that it is considering writing off as worthless. It has been approached by a collection agency. The agency will charge $75,000 plus 50 percent of the first $200,000 collected by the agency and 25 percent of the rest collected. Neufeld estimates there is a 60 percent probability that a total of $150,000 will be collected, a 30 percent probability that a total of $300,000 will be collected, and a 10 percent probability that a total of $450,000 will be collected.

a. Should Neufeld employ the collection agency?

b. If the collection agency's fixed charge is $125,000, instead of $75,000, should Neufeld employ the agency?

Inventory Management

17.11 MainStreet Stores is considering three different mutually exclusive proposals for increasing its inventory level. The initial investments and after-tax cash flows are as follows:

Inventory Level	Initial Investment, CF_0	Opportunity Cost of Capital, k	After-Tax Cash Flow, CF_t
A	$300,000	12%	$ 50,000
B	600,000	15	110,000
C	900,000	18	175,000

Which, if any, of the new inventory levels should MainStreet Stores adopt?

Reduction in Inventory

17.12   The Gupta Group presently carries an average inventory valued at $5 million. New management has proposed to reduce the inventory to $3.5 million. The expected loss in after-tax cash flows due to increased stock outages will be $200,000 per year if inventory is reduced, but losses due to theft and spoilage should decrease by $20,000 (after taxes). If the opportunity cost of capital is 16 percent, should the inventory be reduced?

Interrelated Receivables and Inventory

17.13   Gonzales Showrooms sells to its customers on a credit basis. It is considering loosening its credit-granting standards to two additional risk classes, P and Q.

Risk Class	Opportunity Cost of Capital k	Days Sales Outstanding DSO	Collection Bad Debts as a Sales S	Department Percentage of Sales BD	Cash Outflows CD
P	15%	50 days	$ 800,000	6%	$200,000
Q	20	60	1,300,000	10	60,000

Variable costs are 75 percent of sales, a 365-day year is used, and Gonzales's tax rate is 40 percent. In addition, granting credit to customers in risk class P would require an investment of an additional $60,000 in inventory. Extending credit to risk class Q would require an additional $150,000 investment in inventory beyond that required for class P.

a. Should Gonzales grant credit to customers in risk class P?

b. Assuming Gonzales has already decided to grant credit to class P, should it also grant credit to customers in risk class Q?

Seasonal Dating

17.14   Wetherall is considering changing to a seasonal dating policy under which it will produce and ship goods now but bill for the goods at a later date. The firm anticipates that this will increase sales by $800,000, the days sales outstanding will be 120 days, and the variable costs will be 0.85 of sales. Inventory will be reduced by $50,000, bad debts will be 8 percent, and additional collection department expenses will be $20,000. Wetherall's tax rate is 35 percent (assume a 365-day year).

a. If the opportunity cost of capital is 16 percent, should Wetherall change to seasonal dating?

b. If everything remains as in (a), how much more reduction in inventory would have to occur before Wetherall can profitably switch to seasonal dating?

Receivables and Inventory

17.15   **Mini Case** Nicholson Industries has grown so rapidly it has not had time to examine carefully its accounts receivable and inventory policies. Now, during the present slowdown in economic activity, the decision has been made to undertake a careful analysis of these important functions. As the senior analyst in the finance department, you have been assigned the responsibility for undertaking this analysis and ensuring Nicholson's policies are appropriate.

a. Your boss keeps saying that the investment in receivables and inventory is just as important as the investment in long-term assets, and that the analysis of this investment must take the same approach as any other investment made by the firm. Why is this so?

Note: In (c), interest coverage = EBIT / interest; current ratio = current assets / current liabilities; and quick ratio = (current assets − inventory) / current liabilites.

b. Explain, in some detail, what the major credit and collections policies are.

c. Nicholson is investigating changing its credit scoring model in order to tighten up its credit-granting policy. The present model is 5(interest coverage) + 6(current ratio) + 0.9(years in business). The proposed model is 4(interest coverage) + 4(quick ratio) + 1.5(years in business). Two firms have data as follows:

	Firm A	Firm B
EBIT	$600,000	$800,000
Interest	100,000	90,000
Total current assets	100,000	80,000
Inventory	30,000	45,000
Current liabilities	50,000	60,000
Years in business	8	12

Note: In (d), calculate the NPV for risk class 1 under the existing policy, and then under the proposed policy. Then take the difference in the two NPVs to determine whether to stay with the existing policy (i.e., if NPV$_{old}$ is greater than NPV$_{new}$) or switch to the new policy (i.e., if NPV$_{new}$ is greater than NPV$_{old}$). Do the same for risk class 2.

What are the credit scores under the existing and the proposed models?

d. Instead of changing the credit scoring model, Nicholson believes the opportunity cost of capital employed may be too low and that it also needs to increase its collection department expenditures to enable it to follow up more promptly. The existing and proposed policies for two classes of customers are as follows:

Risk Class	Opportunity Cost of Capital, k	Days Sales Outstanding, *DSO*	Sales, *S*	Bad Debts as a Percentage of Sales, *BD*	Collection Department Cash Outflows, *CD*
Existing					
1	14%	40 days	$15,000,000	4%	$250,000
2	16	60	30,000,000	8	600,000
Proposed					
1	16%	30 days	$13,000,000	1%	$300,000
2	17	35	25,000,000	2	700,000

Variable costs remain at 70 percent of sales in either case, and the firm's marginal tax rate is 35 percent. For which risk class, if either, should the proposed change be made?

e. Nicholson uses days sales outstanding to measure the performance of its collections manager. Is this appropriate? Why or why not?

f. Briefly explain the interrelationship between a firm's receivables and inventory decisions.

Short-Term Financing

Sections in this chapter:

■ **Sources and Importance of Short-Term Financing**
Why it's important to read the fine print, with a calculator near at hand.

■ **Accounts Payable, or Trade Credit**
The surprising value of purchasing on credit.

■ **Unsecured Loans**
How much is the cost of that bank loan?

■ **Secured Loans**
When lenders want more than just a promise to pay.

■ **Choosing Among Short-Term Financing Sources**
Considerations when making the short-term financing decision.

Gelco Corp., a billion-dollar Minnesota-based transportation firm, took a full year to put together a $90 million commercial paper issue. The firm maintains it was worth every day of the lengthy wait. That's because Gelco was pioneering an ingenious new credit-enhancement technique to reduce short-term financing costs. It set up a separate legal entity that held title to certain Gelco leases, making sure that even if Gelco failed, the leases in the separate entity would not be affected. Then Gelco had the separate entity issue commercial paper (backed by the leases) on its behalf. The net result was to raise the rating on Gelco's commercial paper offering from double-B to A-minus, thereby providing substantially cheaper financing.

Savings and loan associations employ a similar tactic: They use Treasury bills or Treasury notes they hold to provide collateral for commercial paper. Other lenders are turning to insurance firms—chiefly Aetna, INA, and Travelers—to guarantee their borrowings. These and other forms of credit enhancement are helping many firms significantly lower short-term borrowing costs.

In other industries, firms that have receivables due sell (factor) them to a firm that specializes in that business. Concerns about payment can have quick consequences. Early in 1994 Woolworth Corp. announced it was investigating some internal accounting irregularities. Woolworth sells through numerous divisions, including Northern Reflections, Champs Sports, and Foot Locker. The merchandise sold by these divisions is purchased from suppliers around the world. Factoring firms, which guarantee that suppliers will be paid by Woolworth, became nervous—and told some suppliers to hold further shipments until the situation cleared. When it did clear, the factoring firms told the suppliers to resume shipments to Woolworth, and no major shortages occurred. But the message was clear: Factoring firms play an important role in certain industries, and their actions can produce swift results.

In this chapter we focus on short-term financing. In doing so our attention again focuses on risks, required returns, and cash flows as we seek to maximize the value of the firm.

LEARNING GOALS

After studying this chapter you should be able to:

1. List some sources of short-term financing, and discuss key determinants of the cost of short-term financing.
2. Explain what spontaneous financing is and why it is offered, and calculate the cost of trade credit.
3. Discuss types of bank loans, and calculate their cost.
4. Explain the use of commercial paper, and calculate its cost.
5. Differentiate between pledging and factoring receivables, and discuss the methods of financing with inventory.
6. Discuss four factors in choosing short-term financing.

SOURCES AND IMPORTANCE OF SHORT-TERM FINANCING

■ LEARNING GOAL 1

List some sources of short-term financing, and discuss key determinants of the cost of short-term financing.

Among numerous sources of short-term financing are trade credit and short-term borrowing by the firm. As we saw in Chapter 17, trade credit arises when one firm purchases goods from another firm and does not pay cash immediately. This creates an account payable for the purchasing firm. Trade credit is often called *spontaneous short-term financing* because it tends to expand automatically ("spontaneously") as firms purchase more goods and build up inventory. Also, the firm may secure **negotiated short-term financing** by negotiating with commercial banks, finance companies, and the like for short-term borrowed funds.

> **NEGOTIATED SHORT-TERM FINANCING**
> Short-term financing such as bank loans or loans secured by accounts receivable that are negotiated and have a specific length.

Recall from Chapter 15 that the matching principle states that permanent investments in assets should be financed with permanent sources of financing, and that temporary assets should be financed by temporary financing sources. Besides following the matching principle, firms use short-term financing for two other reasons: The first is to meet seasonal needs. As firms enter into that part of the year where accounts receivable and inventory expand, they employ short-term financing. Later, when cash inflows increase, they pay down the short-term financing. The second reason for short-term financing is to "roll" it into longer-term financing. Many firms use short-term financing until the total amount of financing needed becomes large enough to justify long-term debt (or equity) financing.

> *Trade credit terms with suppliers are closely related to the bargaining power between suppliers and customers vis-a-vis the firm's competitive environment.*

Size of Short-Term Financing

To see the importance of short-term financing, consider that retail firms, wholesale firms, and small manufacturing firms (with assets of less than $25 million) usually have current liabilities that are 35 percent or more of total assets. For larger manufacturing

Short-term debt can be either "temporary," or continuing in nature, and therefore, be considered "permanent." If permanent, it should be viewed as a long-term loan.

firms, the current liabilities drop to about 25 percent. The large size of current liabilities for retail firms, wholesale firms, and small manufacturing firms is due to the fact that these firms have large amounts of current assets. Under the matching principle, we expect such firms to have large amounts of current liabilities, which they do. The majority of these current liabilities are in the form of accounts payable and short-term borrowings—the focus of this chapter. The other short-term liabilities include various accrued items, such as wages and taxes, and current maturities of long-term debt or lease obligations. The amount of current liabilities varies both among industries and among firms in the same industry.

Comparing the rate of growth of payables to the rate of growth of purchases reflects the firm's payment performance. If the growth of payables > the growth of purchases, the incremental difference is related to the firm's payment patterns.

Short-term financing is more important than ever because of a firm's size, the varying nature of a firm's needs over the course of the year, changes in business conditions and interest rates, and changes in the money market and financing alternatives. Securing funds at the most cost-effective rate is vitally important. At the same time, the firm must ensure the availability of funds, no matter what the time of year or economic conditions. In this chapter we focus on the nature of short-term financing available, how to determine its effective annual interest cost, and the typical conditions surrounding alternative sources of short-term financing.

Cost of Short-Term Financing

In determining the cost of alternative sources of short-term financing, three important ideas must be kept in mind:

Remember Key Ideas 4 and 5—firms focus on cash flows and their incremental effects, and a dollar today is worth more than a dollar tomorrow.

1. For the purpose of comparison, we must express the costs in the same units over the same period of time. If one source costs $800 for a month's financing, and another charges a monthly rate of interest of 1.5 percent for the same amount of funds, it is not immediately obvious which is more expensive. To deal with this difference, all costs are expressed in the same units over the same time period. Because of simplicity and tradition, we convert all costs to an effective annual rate (or cost) stated in percentage terms.
2. The ultimate cost to the firm is influenced by the tax rate of the firm. The after-tax cost to the firm is:

> after-tax cost = (before-tax cost)(1 − the tax rate)
>
> $$k_i = k_b(1 - T) \tag{18.1}$$

where

k_i = the after-tax cost

k_b = the before-tax annual cost

T = the firm's marginal tax rate

Although a firm can employ either the before- or after-tax cost for decision-making purposes, its ultimate cost is the after-tax cost given by Equation 18.1.

3. The basic equation to calculate the before-tax effective annual interest rate, or k_b, for any short-term financing is:

> $$k_b = \left(1 + \frac{\text{costs} - \text{benefits}}{\text{net amount of financing}}\right)^m - 1 \tag{18.2}$$

where m is the number of compounding periods per year. It is important to stress that *Equation 18.2 is employed throughout the chapter, but the calculation of the costs and benefits may change.*

To see these ideas in practice, consider the cost of a $100,000 loan on which the bank will charge interest of $3,500, which will be paid in 90 days when the loan is repaid. The before-tax annual effective cost of this loan, employing Equation 18.2 and a 365-day year, is:

$$k_b = \left(1 + \frac{\$3,500}{\$100,000}\right)^{365/90} - 1 = \left(1 + \frac{\$3,500}{\$100,000}\right)^{4.055556} - 1$$
$$= 1.1497 - 1 = 14.97\%$$

The after-tax cost, if the firm is in the 35 percent marginal tax bracket, is:

$$k_i = (14.97\%)(1 - 0.35) = 9.73\%$$

Thus, the firm's after-tax annual cost is 9.73 percent.

Consider what would happen to the same firm if its tax bracket were different. With a 20 percent tax bracket, the after-tax cost is:

$$k_i \text{ with 20 percent tax bracket} = (14.97\%)(1 - 0.20) = 11.98\%$$

If the firm's tax bracket is zero, then the after-tax cost is the same as the before-tax cost, so:

$$k_i \text{ with zero tax bracket} = (14.97\%)(1 - 0) = 14.97\%$$

This example shows the importance of the firm's tax bracket for the cost of borrowing. *As the tax bracket increases, other things being equal, the firm's after-tax cost of borrowing decreases.*[1]

While we will employ Equation 18.2 and assume either a 365-day year (or occasionally 12 equal months) throughout most of this chapter, there are two other complications that arise when determining the effective annual rate. The first involves nominal versus effective annual rates; the second is the number of days assumed in a year. Before we examine how to determine the effective interest rate for a number of different types of short-term financing, let's pause and examine these two issues.

Effective Annual Versus Nominal Interest Rate

The annual rate at which many loans and financial instruments are quoted is the *stated* or *nominal interest rate.*[2] Thus, you may make an investment that pays interest at a nominal annual rate of 8 percent. The *effective annual rate* adjusts the nominal rate

---

[1] *If compounding is not employed, the simple interest cost is given by:*

$$k_b = \left(\frac{costs - benefits}{net\ amount\ of\ financing}\right)\left(\frac{365\ days}{total\ number\ of\ days\ funds\ borrowed}\right)$$
$$= \left(\frac{\$3,500}{\$100,000}\right)\left(\frac{365}{90}\right) = 14.19\%$$

Simple interest always understates the annual effective interest rate.

[2] *Nominal and effective annual interest rates are discussed in Chapter 3. That chapter also contains a discussion of the annual percentage rate, APR, and annual percentage yield, APY. In 1968 the Truth-in-Lending Act specified the annual percentage rate, APR. Although many might think the APR is the effective annual rate stated in percent terms, the way it is employed is as a nominal annual rate per year, but compounded monthly. Thus, it is not an effective annual rate.*

based on the frequency of compounding employed and the number of days assumed in a year. When a nominal rate is given, the effective annual rate can be determined as follows:

$$k_b = \left(1 + \frac{k_{\text{nom}}}{m}\right)^m - 1 \tag{18.3}$$

where

k_b = the effective annual rate of interest

k_{nom} = the nominal annual rate of interest

m = the number of compounding intervals per year

As long as there is only one compounding interval per year ($m = 1$), the effective annual rate is equal to the nominal rate. But *as the compounding interval decreases, the effective annual rate increases*. To see this relationship, consider the impact of the compounding period on a 12 percent annual nominal rate:[3]

Compounding Interval	Effective Annual Rate, $k_b = \left(1 + \dfrac{0.12}{m}\right)^m = 1$
Annually ($m = 1$)	12.000%
Semi-annually ($m = 2$)	12.360
Quarterly ($m = 4$)	12.551
Monthly ($m = 12$)	12.683
Daily ($m = 365$)	12.747
Continuously	12.750

Often, the interest rates that banks and other lenders quote are effective annual rates. But for most other instruments—including bonds, mortgage loans, and commercial loans—only the nominal rate may be stated.

Assume, for example, that your firm wants to borrow money for a period of one year. Essex National Bank quotes a nominal annual rate of 12.5 percent compounded quarterly. Southern Bank quotes a nominal annual rate of 12.2 percent compounded daily. Which way is your firm better off in terms of the lower before-tax cost?

Employing Equation 18.3, we find that the effective annual cost from Essex National Bank is:

$$k_b = \left(1 + \frac{0.125}{4}\right)^4 - 1 = 13.098\%$$

From Southern, the effective annual cost is:

$$k_b = \left(1 + \frac{0.122}{365}\right)^{365} - 1 = 12.973\%$$

After adjusting for the difference in the compounding intervals, we see that the before-tax cost of the loan from Southern Bank is 12.97 percent, whereas it is 13.10 percent from Essex National. Other things being equal, the firm wants the cheapest

[3]*For the continuous case, the effective annual rate is:*
   $k_b = e^{k_{\text{nom}}} - 1 = e^{0.12} - 1 = 12.750\%$

financing available. Therefore, you would recommend that the loan be obtained from Southern National Bank.

Number of Days Assumed in a Year

In the preceding example, we saw that the compounding interval had an important impact on the effective cost or yield. It was assumed that the nominal interest was earned, or charged, over 365 days. Another approach used by many banks and for some money market instruments is to base their calculations on a 360-day year. *This assumption increases the cost to a borrower, or the yield to a saver.*

Consider a 1-year, $1,000 loan at a nominal annual interest rate of 11 percent. Using a 365-day year, the borrower pays interest of $110 after 365 days. Under the 360-day method, the borrower pays interest of $110 after just 360 days. To borrow for the extra 5 days (6 days in a leap year) at 11 percent costs the borrower additional interest of ($1,000)(0.11)(5/360) = $1.53. Thus, the total interest paid over the 365 days is actually $111.53. The cost of the 360-day method is higher than that of the 365-day method.

When calculating an effective annual rate or cost, two steps are required: First the 360-day nominal rate must be converted to a 365-day nominal rate. Second, the 365-day nominal rate is converted to an annual effective rate. The following equation can be used to adjust to a 365-day nominal rate, where $k_{360 \, nom}$ is a 360-day nominal interest rate:

$$k_{nom} = k_{360 \, nom}(365 \text{ days}/360 \text{ days}) \tag{18.4}$$

In this example, an 11 percent nominal rate with a 360-day year produces a 365-day nominal rate of $0.11(365/360) = 11.153$ percent. To determine the effective annual rate, we use Equation 18.3 again. Assuming daily compounding, k_b, the effective annual rate, is:

$$k_b = \left(1 + \frac{0.11153}{365}\right)^{365} - 1 = 11.797\%$$

From the standpoint of a borrower, the use of a 360-day year raises the effective cost of a loan.

CONCEPT REVIEW QUESTIONS

- Describe some alternative sources of short-term financing.
- What important ideas must be considered when determining the effective annual cost of alternative sources of short-term financing?

ACCOUNTS PAYABLE, OR TRADE CREDIT

■ LEARNING GOAL 2

Explain what spontaneous financing is and why it is offered, and calculate the cost of trade credit.

Most firms make purchases from other firms on credit. Such transactions show up on the purchaser's accounting records as an account payable. Trade credit is a spontaneous source of financing. Consider an example: If a firm typically makes purchases of $3,000 per day and pays its bills in 30 days, then the average accounts payable outstanding are $90,000. What happens, however, if as the busy season of the year draws near, purchases increase to $5,000 per day? Though the firm still pays in 30 days, the accounts payable have increased to $150,000. This difference of $60,000 (i.e., $150,000 − $90,000) in accounts payable occurred spontaneously as the firm geared up for its busy season. The firm generated $60,000 in additional financing just by increasing its purchases and taking advantage of the trade credit offered by its suppliers. It should be noted that the use of trade credit is especially important for small businesses; they generally do not have many other ways of raising short-term funds.

Cost of Trade Credit

CASH DISCOUNT
A provision included in credit terms that offers the customer a reduction in the purchase price for payment within a stated discount period.

Instead of being concerned about granting credit, as in Chapter 17, let's assume that you are now the *recipient* of trade credit. Trade credit terms typically are expressed as, for example, 1/10, net 30, which means that a 1 percent **cash discount** applies if the account is paid within 10 days. If not, the account should be paid in full within 30 days. If the firm takes advantage of the 1 percent discount, there is no cost associated with the trade credit. That is, 10 days of credit is available at no cost to the purchaser. If the firm does not take the cash discount, there is a direct cost to the firm. This annual cost is:

$$k_b = \left(1 + \frac{\text{discount percent}}{100\% - \text{discount percent}}\right)^{365/(\text{date paid} - \text{discount rate})} - 1 \qquad (18.5)$$

The direct before-tax annual cost of not taking a 1 percent discount by paying in 10 days is

$$k_b = \left(1 + \frac{1}{100 - 1}\right)^{365/(30 - 10)} - 1 = 20.13\%$$

Note in Equation 18.5 that the discount not taken is related to the number of additional days for which credit is obtained. With terms of 1/10, net 30, the 1 percent cash discount is the interest cost for an additional 20 days of credit. This assumes the purchaser pays on the 30th day if the cash discount is not taken. Often firms "stretch" their payables by not paying on the net date. What happens to the direct annual cost if the firm stretches its payables by paying them later—say, 50 days after the invoice date? The cost is

$$k_b = \left(1 + \frac{1}{100 - 1}\right)^{365/(50 - 10)} - 1 = 9.60\%$$

STRETCHING PAYABLES
The practice of not paying an account by its due date.

This is lower than before, because 40 (instead of 20) days of credit were obtained. As shown below, the effect of **stretching payables** is to reduce the direct cost of trade credit:

Credit Terms	If Paid on Net Date	If Paid 10 Days Past Net Date	If Paid 20 Days Past Net Date	If Paid 30 Days Past Net Date
$^1\!/_2$/10, net 30	9.58%	6.39%	4.68%	3.73%
1/10, net 30	20.13	13.01	9.60	7.61
2/10, net 30	44.59	27.86	20.24	15.89
2/10, net 60	15.89	13.08	11.11	9.66
3/10, net 60	24.90	20.36	17.21	14.91
4/10, net 60	34.72	28.19	23.72	20.47

Firms that pass up cash discounts can reduce the direct cost by stretching their payables. The effect of this practice, however, is to incur an opportunity cost. This is the loss of supplier goodwill, resulting in possible curtailment of trade credit. Equally important, a firm that continually stretches its payables will suffer lower credit ratings, thereby raising the future cost of funds. Firms should always take advantage of the free credit period (10 days in our example). Nevertheless, in assessing the desirability of stretching payables (if the cash discount is not taken), both direct and opportunity costs must be considered.

Advantages of Trade Credit

Trade credit has a number of advantages as a source of short-term financing. First, it is readily available and can be conveniently obtained as a normal part of the firm's everyday activities. Second, it is free (and actually results in a reduction in the purchase price) if the discount is taken. Third, it is flexible and can expand or contract as purchases expand or contract. Finally, there are no restrictive terms (or formal agreements). For these reasons, all efficiently managed firms take advantage of trade credit. Not to do so would increase the financial burden on the firm, resulting in lower returns.

CONCEPT REVIEW QUESTIONS

■ Explain what a spontaneous source of financing is and give an example of such a source.
■ What are the advantages and costs to a firm receiving trade credit?

UNSECURED LOANS

Unsecured loans[4] occur in two forms—bank loans and commercial paper. Bank loans are short-term borrowings obtained from banks or finance companies; commercial paper is a short-term security sold in the money market to investors. Firms must take an active role in obtaining short-term financing by these routes: They must negotiate a bank loan or issue commercial paper—as opposed to obtaining trade credit, which occurs spontaneously.

Bank Loans

■ LEARNING GOAL 3

Discuss types of bank loans, and calculate their cost.

Most bank loans have maturities of 1 year or less and often have a *variable interest rate*—that is, a rate that fluctuates over the life of the loan as interest rates change. The basic interest rate charged by banks is called the *prime rate*. It is defined as the rate at which their best customers can borrow.[5] Each bank sets its own prime rate, but competi-

---

[4]Some of these loans and even commercial paper may actually be backed by specific assets of the firm. This type of credit enhancement has gained popularity in recent years, as firms have moved to provide collateral to reduce the cost of financing. For simplicity we refer to all loans in this section as unsecured loans.

[5]Although prime is the rate banks supposedly charge their best customers, they also loan below prime to very important and financially strong firms. These firms have the option of issuing commercial paper that typically has a yield below the prime rate. Because of this competitive factor, banks may occasionally "split the difference" between the prime rate and the commercial paper rate for loans to very sound major firms. From the firm's standpoint bank loans may provide more flexibility than issuing commercial paper. Also, with relationship banking, firms may occasionally pay a little more interest simply to maintain and strengthen relationships with their (main) bank.

FINANCIAL MANAGEMENT TODAY

Small Businesses Pay More

Ouch! Bank deregulation, which was supposed to help small business, appears to have actually driven up the cost of borrowing money. A recent survey conducted by the National Federation of Independent Businesses shows that the following relationships hold between firm size (measured by sales) and the percent of firms in each group paying more than the prime rate of interest.

Borrowers' Annual Sales (thousands of dollars)	Percent Paying 2 or More Points Above Prime
Under 150	72%
150 – 299	64
300 – 449	73
450 – 749	48
750 – 1,499	50
1,500 – 2,999	40
3,000 or more	31

As these data indicate, other things being equal, smaller firms tend to pay more when borrowing from banks than do larger firms. While smallness is a virtue in many things, it is not a virtue when it comes to borrowing money.

TRANSACTION LOAN
Bank loan made for a specific purpose for a predetermined length of time.

LINE OF CREDIT
Bank loan agreement that enables a firm to borrow up to a maximum amount over a specified period of time.

tion forces them to be similar. Generally, the major banks set prime a certain number of percentage points (typically 1 to 2 percent) above the rate on negotiable certificates of deposit issued by banks. Other banks typically follow suit; however, prime may vary slightly, depending on the size and location of the bank. Some banks also use other rates, such as the Treasury bill rate or the London Interbank Offered Rate, LIBOR, in addition to prime. Rates on loans are generally tied to prime, so the borrower will be quoted a rate as prime plus half a percent, prime plus 1 percent, and so on. With a prime rate loan, as the bank's prime rate changes, so will the interest rate charged the borrowing firm.

Types of Bank Loans

A bank loan may be a single loan (called a transaction loan) or a line of credit. A **transaction loan** is made by the bank for a specific purpose. To obtain a transaction loan, the parties sign a promissory note. The note specifies the amount borrowed, the interest rate on the loan, the maturity date and repayment schedule, collateral (if any) involved, and any other conditions agreed upon by the two parties. When the note is signed, the borrower receives the funds.

A **line of credit** is another type of agreement between a bank and a firm. A line of credit agreement means the firm can borrow up to some maximum amount over a specified time period. For example, the agreement may be that the firm can borrow, or "draw down," a $500,000 line of credit over the next year. This amount, or any portion of it, may be borrowed during this time period. Repayment can be made as desired, but by the end of the agreement all borrowings must be paid off.[6] Although lines of credit can be informal agreements in which the lender has no legal obligation to make the loan, often they are formal agreements for which the firm pays a **commitment fee** to the bank, whether or not it draws on the line of credit.[7]

COMMITMENT FEE
A fee charged by a lender on a line of credit, generally on the unused portion of the line.

[6]Many lines of credit have a provision that sometime during the time the line is in effect, perhaps for a minimum 30-day period, the firm has to have zero borrowings from the line.
[7]The commitment fee may be 1/4 to 3/4 of 1 percent per year. Thus, on a $5 million line of credit, the commitment fee could be $12,500 to $37,500 annually, whether or not the line was used.

The Monitoring Role of Banks

Firms can obtain funds from the money and capital markets or from banks (and other financial institutions). Because of their role as an "inside" provider of funds, banks have access to information about the firm and its actions that is not available to the public. Thus, there is less information asymmetry between the firm and the provider of funds when the firm borrows from a bank instead of going directly to the money or capital markets.

The direct benefits to the firm of borrowing from a bank are twofold: First, the increased monitoring of the firm by the bank improves the likelihood of the firm fulfilling its payment obligation to the bank, and therefore reduces the cost of financial distress. Second, the increased monitoring by the bank may also reduce the direct cost to the firm of obtaining financing. The unique role played by banks has received substantial attention in recent years.

Cost of Bank Loans

The financial manager must be able to calculate the cost of bank loans in order to compare them to other sources of short-term financing. The cost of bank loans depends on the conditions attached to the agreement. We illustrate three different types—regular interest, discount interest, and installment interest. The effects of variable interest rates, compensating balance requirements, and interest for lines of credit are also considered.

Regular Interest. The cost of a loan with regular interest can be solved using Equation 18.2. Assume that there is a $10,000 loan, the bank will charge prime plus 1 percent, prime is 9 percent per year, and the loan is for 73 days. The two-step process to solve for the annual before-tax cost is as follows:

STEP 1. Determine the interest paid:

$$\text{interest paid} = \begin{pmatrix} \text{amount} \\ \text{borrowed} \end{pmatrix} \begin{pmatrix} \text{annual} \\ \text{interest rate} \end{pmatrix} \begin{pmatrix} \text{portion of year} \\ \text{borrowed for} \end{pmatrix}$$
$$= (\$10,000)(0.10)(73/365) = \$200$$

STEP 2. Employing Equation 18.2, determine k_b, which is:

$$k_b = \left(1 + \frac{\$200}{\$10,000}\right)^{365/73} - 1 = 10.41\%$$

Note that even though the stated rate is 10 percent, the annual effective rate is 10.41 percent.

Discount Interest. Under **discount interest** the bank deducts the interest at the beginning of the loan. In such a case, the borrower in our example receives $9,800 ($10,000 − $200). From Step 1 above, the interest is still $200. In Step 2, $9,800 (the amount actually secured) replaces the $10,000 previously employed. The effective annual cost of a discounted loan employing Equation 18.2 is:

$$k_b = \left(1 + \frac{\$200}{\$9,800}\right)^{365/73} - 1 = 10.63\%$$

Because the bank does not lend the full amount, the cost of a discounted loan is higher than a loan with regular interest.

Installment Interest. Instead of paying the loan off in a lump sum, banks and many other financial institutions charge **installment interest,** with payments to be made monthly. In this case the total amount of interest is calculated and added to the original face value of the note. Then the monthly installment represents a payment of both principal and interest. Let's assume that we borrow $10,000 for 1 year, that we agree to pay interest at a 13 percent annual stated rate, and that 12 monthly payments will be made. The note will be for the principal of $10,000 plus the interest of $1,300 [i.e., ($10,000)(0.13)] for a total of $11,300. The monthly payment is $941.67 (i.e., $11,300/12).

To solve for the cost of an installment loan, we employ present value techniques for an annuity. Thus:

$$PV_0 = PMT \sum_{t=1}^{n} \frac{1}{(1 + k_b)^t}$$

where PV is the present value, PMT is the per period payment, k_b is the effective before-tax cost per period, and n is the number of periods. Thus:

$$\$10,000 = \$941.67 \sum_{t=1}^{12} \frac{1}{(1+ k_b)^t}$$

Using a financial calculator, k_b is 1.9323 percent per month, or between 23 and 24 percent per year. The cost of an installment loan is always slightly less than twice the stated nominal rate.

Variable Rate Loans. Now that we know how interest is calculated, we can consider some additional complications. The first is a **variable rate loan**. Let's assume that a firm needs to borrow $10,000 for 150 days and is going to pay prime plus 1 percent. Interest will be figured employing the regular method. If prime was 12 percent annually for the first 73 days, $13\frac{3}{4}$ percent for the next 30 days, and $14\frac{1}{2}$ percent for the remaining 47 days, what is the cost of the loan to the firm? To solve this problem, the two-step procedure described above can be used:[8]

STEP 1. Determine the interest paid:

Prime Rate	Prime Plus 1 Percent	Number of Days	Interest Cost in Dollars	
12%	13%	73	($10,000)(0.13)(73/365)	= $260.00
$13\frac{3}{4}$	$14\frac{3}{4}$	30	(10,000)(0.1475)(30/365)	= 121.23
$14\frac{1}{2}$	$15\frac{1}{2}$	47	(10,000)(0.1550)(47/365)	= 199.59
			Total interest	= $580.82

STEP 2. Employing Equation 18.2, determine the before-tax effective annual cost, which is:

$$k_b = \left(1 + \frac{\$580.82}{\$10,000}\right)^{365/150} - 1 = 14.73\%$$

Compensating Balance. A **compensating balance** is an amount banks may require corporate customers to maintain in their demand deposit account if a loan is taken out. The compensating balance may be an average over some period, such as a month, or a minimum figure below which the account cannot drop. Average compensating balances are typical for firms. Two situations can be identified: The first is one

VARIABLE RATE LOAN
Loan on which the interest rate fluctuates based on the prime or some other specified rate.

COMPENSATING BALANCE
Amount that a bank requires be maintained on account if a loan is taken out or other services rendered.

---

[8]*Because the interest rate may change at any point in time with a variable rate loan, it may be impossible to determine the effective cost before the fact. Variable rate loans often have a cap, or maximum interest rate, and floor, or lower interest rate. In these cases a range of possible effective annual costs can be determined before the fact.*

in which the compensating balance requirement is less than the amount the firm typically keeps in the bank; in this case, the requirement does not change the cost to the firm. The second case is one in which the compensating balance requirement is above the amount the firm keeps in its demand deposit account. To illustrate this, let's use the same $10,000, 10 percent loan for 73 days that we used when computing the cost of both regular and discount interest.

Assume that the bank imposes a $2,000 compensating balance requirement, when the firm typically does not keep any money on deposit at the bank. The effect of the requirement is to reduce the proceeds of the loan by $2,000. If the loan is not discounted, the before-tax cost is:

$$k_b = \left(1 + \frac{\$200}{\$10,000 - \$2,000}\right)^{365/73} - 1 = 13.14\%$$

If the loan is discounted and a $2,000 compensating balance is required, then the before-tax effective annual cost becomes:

$$k_b = \left(1 + \frac{\$200}{\$10,000 - \$2,000 - \$200}\right)^{365/73} - 1 = 13.50\%$$

Line of Credit.   Finally, let's consider a more complicated situation, in which a line of credit is involved. Suppose a firm negotiates a 91-day, $1,000,000 bank line of credit that has a one-half of 1 percent annual commitment fee on the unused portion of the line, and an interest rate of prime plus 1 percent. Assume, for simplicity, that there is no compensating balance requirement and that during the entire 91-day period the prime rate is 10 percent. For the first 30 days the firm borrows $100,000 on the line of credit. For the remaining 61 days, an additional $300,000 is borrowed, so that $400,000 in total short-term financing is obtained. What is the cost of the loan? To answer this, we can still use our two-step procedure. There are, however, a few other complications.

STEP 1.   Determine the commitment fee and interest per period:

commitment fee = (unused portion)(annual commitment fee)(portion of year)

Using this equation, we obtain:

First 30 days	($1,000,000 − $100,000)(0.005)(30/365) = $369.86
Next 61 days	($1,000,000 − $400,000)(0.005)(61/365) = 501.37

Then we determine the interest as follows:

First 30 days	($100,000)(0.11)(30/365) = $ 904.11
Next 61 days	($400,000)(0.11)(61/365) = 7,353.42

STEP 2.   Employing a modification of Equation 18.2, we can determine the effective annual cost of the line of credit. This modification is necessary because the total costs and the average amount borrowed must be calculated and then annualized as follows:

$$k_b = \left(1 + \frac{\text{total commitment fee} + \text{interest}}{\text{average net amount of financing}}\right)^{365/\text{total number of days}} - 1 \qquad (18.6)$$

The total of the commitment fees and interest is $369.86 + $501.37 + $904.11 + $7,353.42 = $9,128.76. The average net amount of financing is determined as follows:

$$\text{average net amount of financing} = (\$100,000)\left(\frac{30}{91}\right) + (\$400,000)\left(\frac{61}{91}\right)$$
$$= \$32,967.03 + \$268,131.87 = \$301,098.90$$

The before-tax percentage cost of the credit line is:

$$k_b = \left(1 + \frac{\$9,128.76}{\$301,098.90}\right)^{365/91} - 1 = 12.73\%$$

If the bank imposes a 5 percent compensating balance on the total line of credit, the calculations will have to be redone if this change reduces the net amount of financing obtained. Suppose that the firm presently keeps no compensating balance in the bank. The effect of the 5 percent requirement is to reduce the net funds obtained by $50,000 [i.e., ($1,000,000)(0.05)]. Therefore, with the compensating balance requirement, the before-tax cost increases as follows:

$$k_b = \left(1 + \frac{\$9,128.76}{\$301,098.90 - \$50,000}\right)^{365/91} - 1 = 15.40\%$$

Eurodollar Loans

Another kind of loan that is becoming increasingly popular is the Eurodollar loan. *Eurodollars* are dollars deposited in banks outside the United States. These banks may be chartered in the specific country in question, or they may be branches of U.S.-based banks. Obtaining a Eurodollar loan is similar to obtaining a loan in the United States. The one major difference is that the rate is not tied to the U.S. prime rate but to the London Interbank Offered Rate, LIBOR. This rate fluctuates daily and reflects the strength of the world economy and foreign currency exchange rates. Rates on Eurodollar loans typically are comparable to those in the United States, although sometimes U.S. firms have been able to obtain cheaper financing overseas.

Commercial Paper

■ LEARNING GOAL 4

Explain the use of commercial paper, and calculate its cost.

Another important source of short-term borrowing is from *commercial paper*, a short-term promissory note sold by large firms to obtain financing. In recent years the market for commercial paper has grown rapidly. Because it is an alternative to short-term bank loans, the presence of a large commercial paper market tends to exert a downward pressure on borrowing costs for larger firms.

Nature and Use of Commercial Paper

The principal issuers of commercial paper include large industrial firms, finance companies, and bank holding companies. The issue size is commonly in multiples of $100,000. All commercial paper has a maturity of 270 days or less.[9] The paper is sold

---

[9]*The reason for the maximum is that if the maturity exceeds 270 days, then the issue will have to be registered with the Securities and Exchange Commission.*

through dealers or via direct placement. Dealers, who generally charge one-eighth of 1 percent commission, typically are used by firms that infrequently issue commercial paper. Larger firms, such as consumer finance companies, which obtain part of their permanent financing from commercial paper, generally market commercial paper directly.

Commercial paper is rated as to its quality. These ratings are as follows:[10]

Moody's		Standard & Poor's	
P-1	Superior capacity for repayment	A-1	Greatest capacity for timely repayment
P-2	Strong capacity	A-2	Strong capacity
P-3	Acceptable capacity	A-3	Satisfactory capacity
NP	Not prime	B	Adequate capacity
		C	Doubtful capacity
		D	In default or expected to be in default

The purpose of the ratings is to provide to the commercial paper buyer some indication of the riskiness of the investment. From the issuing firm's standpoint, ratings are important because they influence the cost of financing. Other things being equal, the higher the rating, the lower the cost to the firm.

Cost of Commercial Paper

The rate (or yield) on commercial paper tends to be 1 to 2 percentage points below the prime rate. This differential fluctuates as both general economic conditions and the level of interest rates change. Like Treasury bills, commercial paper is sold at a discount from its par value. At maturity, the difference between the selling price and the par value is the interest earned by the investor. Consider a $100,000, 180-day issue of commercial paper sold at $95,000. When it matures in 180 days, the firm will pay the holder $100,000. Employing Equation 18.2, we find that the before-tax annual cost to the firm is:

$$k_b = \left(1 + \frac{\$5,000}{\$100,000 - \$5,000}\right)^{365/180} - 1 = 10.96\%$$

This rate will typically be lower than the cost of a bank loan, due to the lower yield on commercial paper than the prime rate charged by banks.

Other costs also enter into the picture. In most cases, issuers must back their commercial paper 100 percent with lines of credit from commercial banks. This line of credit may cost the firm from one-fourth to three-fourths of 1 percent annual interest. Another common procedure is for the commercial paper issuer to have a compensating balance at a bank. In addition, there is a relatively small fee ($10,000 to $25,000) to have the commercial paper rated. Because of these additional costs, the savings from issuing commercial paper may not be as great as a firm originally thought. Suppose that the commercial paper issue just analyzed was backed by a line of credit that had a commitment fee of one-half of 1 percent a year. The total fee would be:

($100,000)(0.005)(180/365) = $246.58

---

[10]*From* Moody's Bond Record *and* Standard & Poor's Creditweek.

Adding this fee to the interest of $5,000 results in a total cost of $5,246.58. Employing Equation 18.2, we find that the before-tax effective annual cost of the commercial paper is now:[11]

$$k_b = \left(1 + \frac{\$5,246.58}{\$95,000}\right)^{365/180} - 1 = 11.52\%$$

Although commercial paper may be an attractive form of short-term financing, it is available only to relatively large firms. Also, the commercial paper market may dry up occasionally, forcing firms to use bank loans. Firms that make extensive use of commercial paper also keep their lines of communication open with banks and typically borrow from banks in addition to using the commercial paper market.

Euro- and Universal Commercial Paper

Euro-commercial paper is a short-term note usually denominated in dollars and issued by firms outside the United States. Typically, Euro-commercial paper has a longer maturity than commercial paper issued in the United States, and an active secondary market for it exists.

Universal commercial paper also exists to help U.S. firms raise short-term funds. *Universal commercial paper* is issued by U.S. firms but denominated and paid in specified foreign currencies. Although it sells in the United States, universal commercial paper provides a short-term liquid security whose interest rates are tied to various foreign markets. This proves beneficial when firms have dealings in currencies other than the U.S. dollar.

CONCEPT REVIEW QUESTIONS

- Describe different types of short-term bank loans.
- What is a compensating balance?
- If commercial paper is typically a cheaper source of financing than borrowing from financial institutions, explain why all firms do not finance their short-term borrowings using commercial paper.

SECURED LOANS

■ LEARNING GOAL 5

Differentiate between pledging and factoring receivables, and discuss the methods of financing with inventory.

Because the lender requires it, or to obtain cheaper financing, firms often use receivables or inventory to obtain short-term financing. Every state except Louisiana

---

[11]*Note that the commitment fee is not deducted from the financing received in the denominator. This approach treats the commitment fee as an ongoing cost that is paid over time and not a lump-sum deduction at the outset. If the commitment fee is deducted at the outset, the net proceeds are $94,753.42 (i.e., $95,000 − $246.68), and the before-tax cost is:*

$$k_b = \left(1 + \frac{\$5,246.58}{\$94,753.42}\right)^{365/180} - 1 = 11.55\%$$

This same approach is employed for the processing costs, factoring commissions, and warehousing fees discussed subsequently.

operates under the Uniform Commercial Code. Under the code, a security agreement or standardized document is provided to list the assets pledged as collateral. Procedures for short-term financing are described below.

Financing with Accounts Receivable

Financing with accounts receivable involves pledging receivables or factoring them. The *pledging* of receivables involves the specific use of receivables as collateral for the loan. If the borrower defaults on the loan, the funds provided when the receivables are collected will go to repay the loan. *Factoring* involves the sale of accounts receivable. The factoring firm is responsible both for credit checking and for collection of the receivables. Many banks engage in making accounts receivable loans or in purchasing receivables. Commercial finance companies and other specialized factoring firms also provide accounts receivable financing to firms. In addition, in recent years many firms have issued securities in the money or capital markets that are secured with accounts receivables. Such securities range from short-term receivables to longer-term receivables such as home mortgages and automobile loans.

Pledging Accounts Receivable

PLEDGING
Short-term borrowing in which the loan is secured by the borrower's accounts receivable.

Under a **pledging** agreement, the borrower uses the accounts receivable as collateral for the loan. The specific agreement between the borrower and the lending institution spells out the details of the transaction. The amount of the loan is stated as a percentage of the receivables pledged. In addition, the borrower typically pays a processing fee, which often is 1 percent of the total receivables pledged. This processing fee compensates the lending institution for the time involved in reviewing the pledged receivables.

If the loan agreement is based on all the firm's receivables, then the lender has no control over the quality of the receivables pledged. An alternative procedure is for the lender to review specific invoices to decide which ones it will lend against. This method is somewhat more expensive to the lender, because the lender must review each invoice and the creditworthiness of the customer, before deciding whether to lend against it. If the lender accepts all receivables, it may be willing to grant a loan for only 60 to 70 percent of the face value of the receivables. When it "screens" invoices, the loan agreement typically increases to 85 to 90 percent of the face value of the receivables.

The securitization of accounts receivable—using receivables as security on borrowing—is a new trend in American corporate finance.

The cost of accounts receivable financing is a function of both the processing fee and the annual interest rate charged. Because of the basic creditworthiness of the borrower, loans secured by receivables often have a stated interest rate of 2 to 4 percent above prime. To illustrate the cost, consider Hammond Associates, which sells merchandise on a net 45 days basis. Its average credit sales are $9,000 per day, and the days sales outstanding is 60 days, resulting in accounts receivable averaging $540,000. All the receivables are pledged to the bank, which will lend 75 percent of the amount pledged at 2.5 percent over prime. The loan will be for $405,000 [i.e., ($540,000)(0.75)] for 60 days. There also is a three-quarters of 1 percent processing fee on all receivables pledged. If prime currently is 7.8 percent per year, the cost of this loan can be found by employing the same two-step approach described earlier.

STEP 1.   Determine the interest paid and other costs:

$$\begin{aligned}
\text{Processing fee} &= (0.0075)(\$9,000)(60 \text{ days}) &&= \$\ 4,050 \\
\text{Interest} &= (0.103)(\$405,000)(60/365) &&= \underline{6,857} \\
\text{Total processing fee and interest} & &&= \$10,907
\end{aligned}$$

STEP 2. Employing Equation 18.2, we find that the effective annual before-tax cost is:

$$k_b = \left(1 + \frac{\$10{,}907}{\$405{,}000}\right)^{365/60} - 1 = 17.55\%$$

The processing fee increases the cost of the loan substantially above the nominal interest charge of 10.3 percent the bank levies for the loan.

Factoring Accounts Receivable

Instead of pledging its receivables, an alternative procedure employed in industries such as finished apparel, textiles, and home furnishings is to sell—or factor—them. Through **factoring**, a firm sells its accounts receivable to a bank or other firm engaged in factoring. The receivables may be sold *without recourse*; in such a case the factor makes the credit-granting decision and incurs any losses from nonpayment by the firm's customers. Alternatively, recourse factoring can be employed. Under *recourse* factoring, the granting firm typically makes the credit-granting decision and, therefore, bears the consequences of any nonpayment by the customers.

Factoring operates in two basic ways. The first is **maturity factoring**, in which the factor purchases all receivables and once a month pays the seller for the receivables. The typical maturity factoring procedure is shown in Figure 18.1. Firms that employ maturity factoring are primarily interested in the regularity of the cash flow and in avoiding credit analysis and collection expenses. The charge for maturity factoring is the commission, which is between three-fourths of 1 percent and 2 percent of the total receivables factored.

To illustrate this type of factoring, consider Gandy Wholesale. To avoid setting up a credit and collection department, it factors all its receivables. At the end of the month, the factor provides full payment on the average due date of the receivables. If the average month has $200,000 in receivables and the factoring commission is 1.5 percent per month, then Gandy pays $3,000 per month [i.e., ($200,000)(0.015)], or $36,000 per year [i.e., ($3,000)(12)], to the factor. For this amount, the factor assumes all bookkeeping and collection expenses. If this procedure allows Gandy to reduce

FACTORING
The sale of a firm's accounts receivable as a means of speeding up the inflow of funds or of obtaining a loan.

MATURITY FACTORING
Short-term financing in which the factor purchases all of a firm's receivables and pays for them once a month as they are collected.

FIGURE 18.1

Maturity Factoring Procedure

Under maturity factoring, the firm turns almost all of its credit and receivables management functions over to the factor.

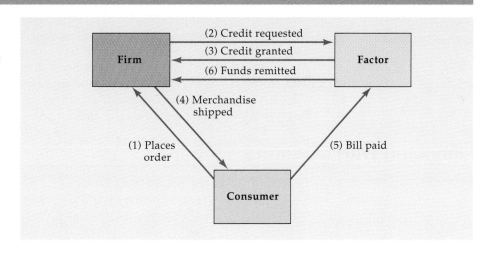

these expenses by $1,400 per month, then the net additional cost is $1,600 per month. The effective annual cost is then:

$$k_b = \left(1 + \frac{\$1,600}{\$200,000}\right)^{12/1} - 1 = 10.03\%$$

ADVANCE FACTORING
Short-term financing in which the factor provides a loan against receivables before they are collected.

The second factoring method is **advance factoring**, in which the factor provides a loan against the receivables. Thus, on the first of the month, a firm could borrow against the receivables it is selling. If the average due date is the 20th of the month, the factor will charge interest from the 1st to the 20th. This interest typically is 2 to 4 percent more than the annual prime rate. In addition, the factor still charges a factoring commission.

With advance factoring, the cost consists of both the factoring commission and the interest. To illustrate, Gandy Wholesale is now considering advance instead of maturity factoring. The receivables to be sold total $400,000, and they have an average due date of 1 month. The factoring commission is one-half of 1 percent, the annual prime rate is 9 percent, and the loan is for 1 month at 2 percent over prime. The factor will loan an amount equal to 70 percent of the face value of the receivables, or $280,000 [i.e., ($400,000)(0.70)], and the savings to Gandy will be $1,000 per month. Employing the two-step procedure, we proceed as follows:

STEP 1. Determine the interest paid and all other costs:

Factoring commission = (0.005)($400,000)	= $2,000
Interest = (0.11)($280,000)(1/12)	= 2,567
Total commission and interest	= 4,567
Less: Reduced cash outflows	= 1,000
	$3,567

STEP 2. Using Equation 18.2, we find that the before-tax annual cost is

$$k_b = \left(1 + \frac{\$3,567}{\$280,000}\right)^{12/1} - 1 = 16.41\%$$

As we saw with selling receivables, the cost increases when a fee is charged in addition to the basic interest rate.

The advantages of factoring from the firm's standpoint can be fourfold: First, the entire credit and collection operation can be shifted to the factor. This can result in a sizable savings to the selling firm. Second, more effective and timely cash management can be obtained. Third, if advance factoring is employed, then firms may also secure accelerated short-term financing from the factoring procedures. Finally, factors will often be willing to borrow money from the firm during periods when the firm has excess cash. For these reasons, factoring is continuing to become more common as an ongoing part of many firms' short-term financing strategy. Factoring is often a continuous process. Once the cycle is established, the firm automatically sends the receivables to the factor. Under continuous factoring, accounts receivable financing becomes a spontaneous source of short-term financing.

Financing with Inventory

A firm's inventory provides a second source of security for short-term loans. Because of the large size of the inventory for many firms and the associated carrying costs, firms often use part or all of their inventory to obtain short-term financing. The procedures are much like those discussed for receivables. That is, the bank determines the percentage of the inventory value for which it will provide a loan. There are alternative methods, however, by which inventory can be secured.

Under the Uniform Commercial Code, the borrower can pledge all of its inventory under a blanket lien. This is simple, but the bank has little protection because the borrower is free to sell the inventory. Because of this weakness, some types of inventory are secured through the use of a **trust receipt**. This type of lending agreement, also known as *floor planning*, is used by automobile dealers, equipment dealers, and others who deal in "large ticket" items. With a trust receipt, an automobile dealer might reach an agreement with a bank to finance its inventory of vehicles. When cars are shipped to the dealer, they are paid for in large part with funds borrowed from the bank. The trust receipt specifies that the goods are held in trust for the lender. When the cars are sold, the dealer obtains a release from the bank and then applies the proceeds to pay the loan. Under a trust receipt agreement, the bank periodically inspects the automobile dealer's inventory of cars to ensure that the pledged security is still on hand.

Another method is **warehouse financing**. Under a public (or terminal) warehouse agreement, the inventory is stored on the premises of a third party. The third party releases the inventory to the borrower only when authorized to do so by the lender. The lender can then maintain strict control over the collateral. Sometimes the warehouse is set up as a *field warehouse*. This is accomplished by establishing a separate building or area directly on the borrower's premises. To provide inventory control, the bank employs a third party to run the field warehouse. A warehouse receipt is issued by the warehouse company when it receives additional inventory. This receipt goes to the bank, and inventory cannot be released without the bank's permission.

The basic cost of inventory loans typically consists of two parts: The first is the processing fee if a blanket lien is employed, or the cost of storing the inventory if a public or field warehouse agreement is employed. Second, there is the interest cost, which is typically 2 to 4 percentage points above the prime rate.

Consider a firm that employs a field warehouse agreement. The inventory loan is for 90 days, the amount of the inventory is $500,000, and the bank will lend 70 percent of the value of the collateral. The amount of the loan is $350,000 [i.e., ($500,000)(0.70)]. The field warehouse fee is $40 per day, the interest rate is 2 percent over prime, and prime is 11 percent. The annual before-tax cost is computed as follows:

STEP 1. Determine the interest paid and all other costs:

Field warehousing fee = ($40)(90)	=	$ 3,600
Interest = (0.13)($350,000)(90/365)	=	11,219
Total warehousing fee and interest	=	$14,819

STEP 2. The effective annual before-tax cost is determined using Equation 18.2, so that:

$$k_b = \left(1 + \frac{\$14,819}{\$350,000}\right)^{365/90} - 1 = 18.31\%$$

Firms often enter into continuous agreements to finance their inventory through the use of field or terminal warehouse procedures. Like the use of factoring with accounts receivable, the continual use of these forms of inventory financing creates a spontaneous form of short-term financing.

TRUST RECEIPT
Lending agreement that specifies that the inventory used to secure the loan is held in trust for the lender; also known as *floor planning*.

WAREHOUSE FINANCING
Lending agreement under which the inventory used to secure the loan is stored on the premises of a third party, who releases the inventory to the borrower only when authorized to do so by the lender.

CONCEPT REVIEW QUESTIONS

■ Describe the difference between pledging receivables and factoring receivables when securing short-term financing.

■ What are the advantages of factoring accounts receivables?

■ Differentiate between a *blanket lien*, a *trust receipt*, and *warehouse financing*.

CHOOSING AMONG SHORT-TERM FINANCING SOURCES

■ LEARNING GOAL 6

Discuss four factors in choosing short-term financing.

In this chapter we have stressed the cost of alternative sources of short-term financing. Some of these sources, such as trade credit and factoring or field warehouse loans, are spontaneous. That is, they tend to expand or contract automatically as the firm's accounts receivable and inventory expand or contract. Other sources of short-term financing are negotiated between the borrower and the lender.

To determine what sources of short-term financing to employ, firms should consider four specific items: matching, cost, availability, and flexibility. By *matching*, we mean the firm must decide how much risk it is willing to incur in financing temporary assets with temporary liabilities. As discussed in Chapter 15, a more aggressive posture will require the firm to employ more sources and amounts of short-term financing than a conservative posture.

The second important item that influences the short-term financing selection is its *cost*. Employing the concepts developed in this chapter, we can determine the direct cost of alternative short-term financing sources. This is an important consideration, but there is more than the direct cost of the sources: *Opportunity costs* must also be considered. If firms anticipate the continued need to borrow from banks, good banking relations need to be maintained even if the bank charges a higher direct cost than some other source. Trade credit, if stretched, may be less costly than an inventory loan, but the firm may suffer from reduced credit ratings in the future if stretching occurs continually. Thus, opportunity costs must be considered along with the direct costs when considering the total cost of alternative sources of short-term financing.

The *availability of credit* is the third item to be considered when evaluating financing sources. If a firm cannot borrow through an unsecured loan or commercial paper offering, then some type of secured means will have to be employed. Also, over the course of the business cycle, certain sources of funds may be more or less available. Availability refers to both the amount and the conditions attached to the short-term financing. Only by examining both features will managers be in a position to consider the firm's short-term financing sources over time.

Finally, there is the issue of *flexibility*. Flexibility refers to the ability of the firm to pay off a loan and still retain the ability to renew or increase it. With factoring, bank loans, and lines of credit, the firm can pay off the loan when it has surplus funds. Flexibility also refers to how easily the firm can secure or increase the financing on short notice. A line of credit can be increased quickly and easily, but a negotiated short-term loan may take longer to secure. Trade credit, factoring of receivables, and field warehousing provide spontaneous sources of short-term financing that increase the firm's flexibility.

All of these items must be considered when a firm looks at its sources of short-term financing. Although the direct cost is a key element, it does not always provide the final answer. This arises because of opportunity costs relating to matching, availability, and flexibility. Because of the difficulty of quantifying opportunity costs, a practical approach is to rank sources according to their direct costs, and then consider these other factors. If the opportunity costs are significant, the ranking of the desirability of one source of short-term financing compared with another will change. Finally, because the firm's financing needs change over time, multiple sources of short-term financing must be considered, even if some of them are not being employed presently.

CONCEPT REVIEW QUESTION

■ What are four specific items that should be considered when determining the sources of short-term financing?

Summary

■ In order to compare the cost of alternative short-term financing arrangements, an effective annual rate, or cost, is determined. The procedure involves finding the nominal yearly cost and then converting it to an effective yearly rate of interest.
■ The effective annual interest rate provides the before-tax cost of alternative financing sources. Other dollar costs in addition to interest (or sometimes benefits) often need to be considered in order to find the cost of financing.
■ Trade credit, continuous factoring of accounts receivable, and field warehousing provide spontaneous short-term financing. Bank loans and commercial paper are negotiated short-term financing sources.
■ Although some short-term financing is unsecured, in recent years credit enhancement had become very popular. Thus, secured short-term financing has become more common. Accounts receivable may be used to secure bank loans or to obtain direct financing from the money and capital markets; an alternative is to factor accounts receivable. Inventory financing is also widely employed.
■ The specific short-term financing a firm employs depends on matching considerations, cost, availability, and flexibility.

Questions

18.1 The equation for calculating the before-tax effective annual interest rate, or cost of short-term financing, is:

$$k_b = \left(1 + \frac{\text{costs} - \text{benefits}}{\text{net amount of financing}}\right)^m - 1$$

Discuss why this approach must be employed.

18.2 The effective annual rate is a function of the compounding interval and the number of days assumed in the year. Explain how both influence the effective rate.

18.3 Other things being equal, how would changes in the following conditions affect a firm's after-tax cost of funds?
  a. The prime rate increases.
  b. The bank changes from discount interest to regular interest.
  c. The bank's compensating balance requirement decreases.
  d. Tax rates increase (assume the firm is profitable).

18.4 With discount interest, the interest is deducted at the beginning of the loan, thereby reducing the net amount of financing obtained.
  a. Discuss the effect of discount interest on the effective annual cost of the loan.

     b. What if a compensating balance requirement exists? Or what if commitment fees or loan processing (origination) fees are deducted at the start of the loan? Is the effect on the cost of the loan the same as with discount interest?

18.5 For many of the short-term financing sources, the direct cost is made up of the interest plus some other charge (or requirement). Explain this other charge for the following:

    a. Line of credit.

    b. Discount interest.

    c. Installment interest.

    d. Compensating balance.

    e. Commercial paper.

    f. Pledging accounts receivable.

    g. Advance factoring.

    h. Inventory loans.

Concept Review Problems

See Appendix A for solutions.

CR18.1 Aerovac Corporation wants to borrow money for a period of 365 days. First National Bank quotes a nominal annual rate of 10 percent compounded monthly, based on a 360-day year. Commerce National Bank quotes a 10.2 percent nominal annual rate compounded semi-annually, based on a 360-day year. What is the effective annual cost to Aerovac?

Note: For First Bank, assume 12 equal-length months.

CR18.2 Lucille's TV & Appliance is evaluating the cost of trade credit with terms of 1/15, net 30.

Note: Use a 365-day year.

    a. What is the effective annual cost of the trade credit?

    b. What is the cost if Lucille's can stretch its payables from 30 days to 60 days?

CR18.3 Production Associates needs a short-term loan of $500,000 for 275 days. Lincoln Bank & Trust has offered three different types of loans: a regular-interest loan with a stated rate of 12 percent, an 8 percent discount loan, and a 7 percent installment loan with 9 equal monthly payments. What is the effective annual cost for each type of loan?

Note: Use a 365-day year.

CR18.4 West Bay Resources borrowed $20,000 for a 60-day period to finance the increased sales and activities around the December holidays. The rate on the bank loan remained at 10 percent for 20 days, then increased to 12 percent for 20 days, and then dropped to 8 percent for the remainder of the lending period. What was the effective annual cost to West Bay?

Note: Use a 365-day year.

CR18.5 Frontier Industries has obtained a line of credit of $500,000 for the next 180 days with a commitment fee of 1 percent on the unused portion and an interest rate of 15 percent. In the first 60 days the firm borrowed $200,000 on the line of credit, then increased the borrowing to $400,000 for another 100 days. The firm then paid off the line of credit and maintained a balance of zero for the remaining 20 days. Based on a 365-day year, what was the effective annual cost of the line of credit?

CR18.6 South Beach Industries is issuing $1 million in commercial paper with a maturity of 60 days. A line of credit for 100 percent of the face value of the commercial paper was established with a financial institution; the commitment fee is 1/2 of 1 percent of the line of credit and the financial institution requires a compensating balance of 1 percent of the line of credit. Assume South Beach does not presently keep any funds at the financial institution, and use a 365-day year. What is the effective annual cost of the commercial paper if it is sold to investors for $985,000?

CR18.7 Mukherjee Industries has decided to borrow against its receivables, which average $80,000 per month. The firm's bank will lend against 80 percent of the receivables at 12 percent with a 1/2 of 1 percent processing fee of the amount borrowed. The receivables can also be factored: The factor will accept 80 percent of the monthly receivables for a factoring fee of 2 percent per month. If factoring is selected, collection expenses will decrease by $200 per month. What is the effective annual cost of each financing option (assuming 12 equal months)?

CR18.8 A third option available to Mukherjee Industries in CR18.7 is advance factoring. Terms of the advance factoring agreement are a monthly factor fee of 1 percent, a loan cost of 12 percent, with a loan amount equal to 80 percent of the receivables. Mukherjee Industries would experience reduced cash outflows of $300 per month. What is the effective annual cost of advance factoring?

CR18.9 Drake Motors has obtained a blanket lien for its inventory of automobiles. The average time an auto sits in inventory is 80 days. Drake has an average inventory of $800,000. Drake's bank charges a processing fee of 1 percent, will loan up to 60 percent of the face value of the inventory, and charges 15 percent interest rate for the inventory loan. Based on a 365-day year, what is the effective annual cost of the loan?

Problems

See Appendix C for answers to selected problems.

Effective Interest Rates

18.1 Washington Bank offers a nominal rate of 10 percent per year, compounds interest daily, and uses a 360-day year. Syed Bank offers a nominal rate of 10.25 percent per year, compounds interest monthly, and uses a 365-day year. By calculating the effective annual rate of interest for both banks, determine where you should place your money.

Compounding Frequencies

Continuous Compounding

18.2 What is the effective annual rate on an account paying 7 percent compounded continuously? What if it is compounded quarterly? Yearly?

18.3 A financial institution uses continuous compounding and claims that a dollar deposited today will be worth $2.7183 after 20 years. What is the nominal rate of interest?

Finding Interest Rates

Note: In (a), determine the net amount received by the bank, PV_0, the total amount (including interest) you will receive in half a year, FV_1, and then employ $FV_n = PV_0(1 + k/m)^{nm}$ to determine the cost to the bank.

18.4 United Wisconsin Bank has decided to offer a $10 gift certificate to any depositor who puts at least $400 into a new or existing savings account.
   a. Suppose you open a 7 percent savings account with a deposit of $500 and immediately cash the $10 gift certificate so that the bank receives a net amount of $490 from your deposit. If interest is compounded daily based on a 365-day year and the funds stay in the bank for exactly half a year, what is the effective annual cost of the funds to the bank?
   b. To entice even larger depositors, the bank offers a $30 certificate for deposits of $1,000 or more. What would the new effective annual cost of the funds to the bank be if you deposited $1,000, instead of $500?

18.5 A firm receives trade credit terms of 2/15, net 45. Based on a 365-day year, what is the before-tax effective annual cost if payment is made (**a**) by the 15th day, (**b**) on the 45th day, (**c**) by stretching to 60 days past the invoice date, (**d**) 90 days past the invoice date? What other costs or considerations should be considered in addition to this direct cost?

Cost of Trade Credit

Cost of Alternative Bank Loans

18.6 Stateside has four choices for a $50,000, 1-year loan from a bank. Which one of the following has the lowest before-tax effective annual interest rate?
   a. A 14 percent annual interest rate with no compensating balance requirement. Interest is paid at the end of the year.

b. A 13 percent annual interest rate discounted, with no compensating balance requirement.

c. A 9 percent annual stated interest rate with installment interest, paid in 12 equal installments.

d. An 11 percent annual interest rate discounted, with a 10 percent compensating balance requirement. Stateside does not typically keep any funds in this bank.

Discount Interest and Partial Compensating Balance

18.7 Omni Computers has just received a *net* amount (after interest and any compensating balance requirement) of financing of $450,000 for 146 days. Its bank loaned the money at a 15 percent annual rate, employing discount interest. The loan requires a $50,000 compensating balance, and Omni keeps an average of $30,000 on deposit in the bank. If the tax rate is 40 percent, what is the after-tax effective annual interest rate on the loan? Assume a 365-day year.

Line of Credit

18.8 Mattox Industries negotiated a line of credit as follows: 120-day, $2,000,000 line that has a 0.60 of 1 percent annual rate commitment fee on the unused portion of the line and an interest rate of prime plus 2 percent. Mattox anticipates borrowing $750,000 during the first 75 days, and an additional $900,000 (for a total of $1,650,000) over the last 45 days.

a. If prime is expected to be 11 percent, what is the expected before-tax annual interest rate, or cost, to Mattox? (Assume a 365-day year.)

b. What is the expected before-tax interest rate if Mattox borrows the maximum each of the 120 days?

c. How do you explain the difference in the answers between (a) and (b)?

Line of Credit

18.9 Border Manufacturing has a 6-month, $1 million line of credit agreement with the Free State Bank. There is a one-half of 1 percent per year commitment fee charged on the unused portion of the line. The prime rate is 14 percent per year, and the interest rate on the line of credit is 1 percent over prime. Over the next 6 months, Border anticipates drawing on the line of credit as follows:

Month	Additional Borrowed (Repaid) per Month	Total Borrowed per Month
April	$100,000	$ 100,000
May	300,000	400,000
June	400,000	800,000
July	200,000	1,000,000
August	−300,000	700,000
September	−400,000	300,000

By October 1, the line is paid off in full.

Note: In 18.9, do not worry about a 365-day year; simply treat each month as one-twelfth of the total.

a. What is the expected before-tax effective annual interest rate to Border Manufacturing?

b. If Border decides to borrow its full line of credit every month ($1,000,000 per month), what would its expected before-tax annual interest rate be? What if Border borrows nothing during the 6 months?

c. Now suppose that the prime rate decreased to 12 percent. What is the expected before-tax effective annual interest rate if the borrowing is as in (a)?

Commercial Paper

18.10 Data Resources is planning a $2 million issue of 270-day commercial paper. The interest rate is 11 ½ percent per year, and Data will incur $15,000 in other issue-related expenses. Interest is to be discounted, and a 365-day year is to be used.

a. What is the before-tax effective annual interest rate for the commercial paper issue?

b. What is the after-tax cost if Data Resource's marginal tax rate is 35 percent? If it is 25 percent?

c. What are some other factors Data Resources would need to consider in addition to the direct cost?

Commercial Paper

Note: Assume a 365-day year.

18.11 Hanley Distributors is going to issue $1,000,000 of commercial paper at a price of $940,822. If the issue is for 180 days and Hanley's marginal tax rate is 30 percent, what is the effective annual after-tax interest rate of the commercial paper?

Advance Factoring

18.12 Big Bend Products presently uses maturity factoring at a before-tax effective annual cost of 18 percent. Under advance factoring, which is being considered, Big Bend would sell $1,200,000 of receivables with an average due date of 20 days. The factoring commission is one-fourth of 1 percent, the prime rate is 8 percent, and the factor will make the loan for 20 days at 3 percent over prime. The factor will loan 50 percent of the face value of the receivables. (Assume a 365-day year.)

a. By calculating the before-tax effective annual interest rate, determine if Big Bend should switch to advance factoring.

b. What decision would be made if everything is the same as in (a) except the loan is at 2 percent over prime and the factor will loan (or advance) $1,000,000?

Pledging Versus Factoring Receivables

18.13 Barnes Industries has employed factoring for a number of years. Its sales average $1 million dollars every 30 days, with 80 percent being credit sales. The days sales outstanding, *DSO*, is 30 days, so the length of the loan is 30 days. The factor charges a 1 percent factoring commission on the total receivables. In addition, any loan, which may be up to 75 percent of credit sales, carries an interest rate of 11 percent per year. The factor employs a 365-day year. Barnes Industries estimates that the factoring agreement results in two savings: (1) a $1,000 reduction in credit and collection expenses for every 30-day period, and (2) a reduction in bad debts equal to one-half of 1 percent of the credit sales.

Recently, a finance company approached Barnes about a loan involving the pledging of receivables. The loan could be up to 75 percent of receivables. The costs would be interest at 9 percent per year plus a three-fourths of 1 percent processing fee on the size of the loan. [So, the total processing fee on the receivables loan is (0.0075)($600,000) = $4,500.]

a. By computing the effective annual interest rate, determine which plan is preferable.

b. If Barnes Industries borrows only $200,000 per 30 days on average, which plan is preferable? (*Note:* If Barnes factors the receivables, it still receives the $1,000 reduction in credit and collection expenses, plus the benefit of the one-half of 1 percent reduction in bad debts on the total receivables of $800,000, because it continues selling all the remaining receivables to the factor on a maturity factor basis.)

Inventory Loan

Note: Use 12 months, not 365 days.

18.14 Michaels Corporation has to build up its inventory for a 4-month period each year to meet future sales demands. It is considering a bank loan with a field warehouse security agreement. The inventory during this 4-month period averages $500,000 per month. The bank will loan a maximum of 70 percent of the average inventory at prime plus 1 percent. Prime is 9 percent per year. The field warehousing agreement costs $2,400 per month.

a. If Michaels borrows $250,000, what is the before-tax effective annual interest rate on the loan?

**Alternative
Inventory Loans**

b. If Michaels borrows the maximum, what is the rate on the loan?

18.15 Seattle Coffee Importers has experienced a severe cash squeeze and needs $300,000 for the next 75 days. The most likely source is to borrow against its inventory. Determine the better financing alternative of the two that are available. Use a 365-day year and calculate the before-tax effective annual interest rate.

a. Bay Area Bank will lend the $300,000 at a rate of 12 percent per year. It requires, however, that a field warehouse security agreement be employed. The field warehousing costs are $30 per day. Finally, Seattle Coffee believes that because of lower efficiency, before-tax cash flows will be reduced by $2,500 during this 75-day time period.

b. Verity Finance will loan Seattle Coffee the $300,000 at a rate of 18 percent per year under a blanket lien agreement. There are no other charges associated with this loan.

**Alternative
Inventory Loans**

18.16 Midden's Wholesalers presently uses a 90-day public warehouse agreement to finance most of its inventory. The average amount of inventory is $2,000,000, the bank lends Midden's 75 percent of the value of the inventory, and the public warehousing fee is $200 per day. Total transportation costs for the 90-day period make up 1 percent of the average value of the inventory [that is, $(0.01)(\$2,000,000)$], the prime rate is 8 percent, and the bank will loan at 2 percent over prime. Midden's is considering establishing a field warehouse on its premises, which would eliminate transportation costs but would cost $450 per day. The interest rate is 1 percent over prime, and the loan amount remains the same.

Note: Assume a 365-day year.

a. What is the before-tax effective annual interest rate for the public warehouse financing agreement?

b. Does the effective annual rate on the loan increase or decrease under the field warehousing agreement? By how much?

**Alternative
Short-Term
Sources**

18.17 Harlow Corporation has a need for $300,000 in short-term financing for the next 30 days. Based on the following four options, which source should Harlow select to minimize its costs?

Note: Use 12 months, not 365 days. Calculate the before-tax effective annual interest rate.

a. A 91-day line of credit with a bank in the amount of $500,000. There is a 1 percent per year commitment fee on the unused portion, and the rate of interest on borrowed funds is 14 percent per year.

b. Forgo cash discounts on $300,000 of payables. The terms are 2/10, net 40.

c. Issue commercial paper with a 30-day maturity. To borrow the entire $300,000, the maturity value of the issue will be $305,000. The firm incurs $1,000 additional expenses.

d. Obtain a 30-day loan against $400,000 worth of receivables. The factor will loan an amount equal to 75 percent of the receivables. The factoring commission is one-half of 1 percent, and the interest rate is 15 percent per year.

**Short-Term
Financing**

18.18 **Mini Case** Rieke Products, a New Jersey-based firm, manufactures and distributes legal and financial services and products directly to consumers. The firm has grown rapidly, causing a need for short-term financing. Part of its sales are for cash, but a majority are for credit. The credit sales are financed with short-term borrowings. As the CFO you have decided the whole short-term financing strategy needs to be reevaluated.

a. What is the difference between spontaneous and negotiated short-term financing? Would you expect Rieke to be more likely to use spontaneous or negotiated short-term financing?

b. How does the size of the firm, in general, influence its use of short-term financing? Its industry? Its aggressiveness versus conservatism?

c. Previously, the firm has not costed out various short-term financing alternatives. Explain how, by using the effective annual interest rate, the firm can capture the relevant costs and benefits of alternative financing alternatives.

d. Rieke can borrow from two banks as follows: Bank A will lend at a nominal rate of 16.85 percent with interest compounded monthly, and bank B will lend at a nominal rate of 16.60 percent compounded daily based on a 360-day year. If all else is equal, with which one is Rieke better off?

Note: In (e) use a 365-day year for the line of credit.

e. Presently Rieke has two bank loans. The first is a 6-month loan for $1,000,000 based on discount interest that carries an interest rate of 16 percent. The loan has a compensating balance requirement of $100,000; typically Rieke would have only $15,000 in the bank. The second is a 180-day, $2,500,000 line of credit that has an annual commitment fee of 2 percent on the unused portion of the line. Over the last 180 days the interest rates and usage have been as follows:

	First 75 Days	Second 75 Days	Last 30 Days
Interest rate	14.50%	15.75%	16%
Total borrowing	$1,250,000	$1,000,000	$1,900,000

What is the effective annual interest rate on both?

f. Rieke presently pays all of its accounts payable as soon as they are received. Why is this a good (or bad) policy? What about adopting a policy of paying all accounts 30 days past the due date?

g. Instead of the bank loans, Rieke is investigating pledging and/or factoring its receivables. Two alternatives are as follows:

Pledging Receivables	Factoring Receivables
Loan is for 6 months	The agreement is for 6 months
Total receivables are $3,000,000; of which the loan is for 70 percent	The loan is for 70 percent of the receivables, which are $3,000,000
The processing fee is 1 percent of the receivables pledged every 6 months	The factoring commission is 0.80 of 1 percent of the total receivables, per every 6 months
The interest rate is 15 percent	The interest rate is 16 percent

What is the effective annual interest rate, or cost, for both? Should either of these be employed instead of the present bank loan and/or line of credit?

h. What other factors need to be considered in deciding between alternative short-term sources of financing?

ANALYSIS AND PLANNING

EXECUTIVE INTERVIEW WITH **JAMES G. DUFF**

*Chairman and Chief
Executive Officer
USL Capital,
San Francisco, CA*

*In 1990 James G. Duff became chairman and chief executive officer of
USL Capital, one of the country's largest commercial financing organizations. Founded in 1952 and now part of Ford Motor Company's Financial
Services Group, USL Capital finances computers, industrial equipment,
railcars, aircraft, power plants, real estate, and the like, as well as provides financing to municipalities and corporations. An employee of Ford
for 33 years, Mr. Duff has served the firm as director of finance with Ford
of Europe and controller of the Ford and Lincoln Mercury Divisions' and
Ford's Car Product Development Group. He was executive vice president,
Diversified Operations, at Ford Motor Credit before moving to USL Capital.
A native midwesterner, Mr. Duff holds bachelor's and master's degrees in finance from the University
of Kansas. We asked Mr. Duff to describe financial management, planning, and analysis as he's seen
them in practice.*

What constitutes corporate financial management is, in essence, in the eye of the beholder. In other
words, what may be considered financial management at one organization may be far different at
another. There is no right or wrong organizational definition of financial management. At Ford, we
have a very broad view of what financial management encompasses. In my view, financial management has several essential components, which can be grouped and combined in various ways:

ACCOUNTING AND CONTROL You must start with a set of books that provides you with accurate results, using sound accounting practices. You also must have sound internal controls and
business practices. And, you need to support the operation of the business with cost-effective,
reliable, and customer-oriented accounts payable, accounts receivable, and tax functions.

TREASURY You must raise the capital necessary to support the business, and you must ensure its availability at the right time and the right price. You also must effectively collect and manage the cash generated by operations.

SYSTEMS You must have computer systems that provide the data necessary for planning and for decision making. Operating systems also must support the day-to-day goal of turning out high-quality products and services.

FINANCIAL PLANNING AND ANALYSIS Financial analysis is planning how the business should be run, monitoring the performance once a plan has been set, and participating in the decision making process required to execute the plans. Strategic planning can be separate or included, but business planning—the operating plans that outline where the business is going and how it will get there—is a must, from my perspective.

Equally important is the participation in the execution of the plan—reviewing the proposals for new products or facilities, allocating scarce capital among those wanting more resources, divesting the firm of businesses no longer needed, acquiring new businesses, and establishing the objectives for return to stockholders.

Financial Analysis Is Essential

Although accounting, treasury, and systems are essential to all businesses, you can live without world-class capabilities—at least for a while. The entrepreneurial startup operation with a one-person decision making process can survive for a while. It can't survive, however, when it grows, when decisions get more complex, and when a single individual's intuition is no longer adequate. Financial analysis is essential in order for a business to be well run over the long term.

At Ford, financial analysis encompasses looking at all aspects of the business in terms of achieving long-term strategic and operating objectives as well as short-term profit and return commitments. In this process we quantify business plans and budgets and the expected impacts of all decisions in financial terms before the fact, so the results can be reviewed before any action is taken. We also compare performance with expectations, so that corrective actions can be taken when things don't turn out as expected. To me, financial analysis is the backbone of progressive financial management. It's where finance becomes involved in the planning and execution of the decisions that are made to run the business.

Perspectives Differ

The perspectives of accounting and financial management differ. Accountants are happy when the books "foot" and are in accordance with generally accepted accounting principles, when the audit report is unqualified, when the SEC is happy, and so on. They're also happy when they can explain how the data compare to data from previous periods. But the explanation that makes accountants happy is where financial analysts begin. Accountants explain changes in accounting terms—higher revenues, higher costs, changes in cost levels, and so on. Financial analysts want to *know the reasons* for the changes.

Let's assume you receive the following "good news" from the accounting department: Revenues are up 20 percent, costs are up only 12.5 percent, and profits are up 50 percent. This seems to be a good story for the CEO to present to security analysts and to stockholders.

Looking at these numbers, however, the financial analyst discovers that the high revenue reflects strong industry sales and somewhat higher pricing, offset by a decline in the company's share of the market. That's not as good a story. And, the financial analyst may point out that the cost side doesn't look so good, either. Lower material and interest costs are more than offset by increased personnel expenses, at a time when the business world at large is downsizing. The financial analyst would conclude that a strong industry is making profits look good—and that management performance leaves something to be desired.

To be successful, financial analysis must be from a top-management perspective. It's of no value to have a finance-only view. The final view must take into consideration sales, manufacturing, product development, marketing personnel, customers, suppliers, and all other expected impacts—and it must incorporate these into the quantification or analysis. Otherwise, it's just another set of independent facts that someone else must put together—or worse, the decision must be made intuitively, based on an array of conflicting facts. As a CEO, I shudder when I hear, "From a finance perspective, I recommend . . ." As a CEO, I want to hear, "Based on all of the relevant factors, I recommend . . ." To be a good financial analyst, you must be able to make the right decision based on the right facts.

Finance Charts a Path to the Top

In the corporate world, financial analysis is a great place to be. If it's being done right, you get into everything—pricing, capital budgeting (you even get to use cost of capital, internal rate of return, net present value—the very things you've learned in this book), cost analysis, new product decisions, long-range planning, assessing operating performance, buying and selling businesses, and so on. It's all "real business"—and if your perspective is broad enough, it's looking at the various decisions as the CEO does. Remember, the good financial analyst never looks at it from a finance standpoint. He or she considers all of the factors involved and then recommends the course of action to be taken.

Although it is important to understand accounting ideas, we must be careful not to confuse maximizing accounting numbers with maximizing the market value of the firm. Chapter 19 focuses on accounting-based ideas, and Chapter 20 emphasizes the primary importance that cash flow, not net income, plays in financial forecasting and planning.

Analyzing Accounting Statements

Sections in this chapter:

■ **Different Statements for Different Purposes**
Narrowing in on GAAP statements.
■ **The Basic Accounting Statements**
Hitting the highlights of the income statement and balance sheet.
■ **Analysis of Accounting Statements**
What's cooking at General Mills.
■ **International Accounting Issues**
It's a different world.

A ll publicly owned firms regularly announce their profit or loss for the last year or quarter. Analysts for brokerage and advisory firms make recommendations to institutional investors to buy or sell stocks and bonds based on these reports. Individual investors analyze the reports for clues to a firm's progress, react to recommendations provided by investment advisors, or make decisions based on articles in *The Wall Street Journal*, *Forbes*, *Business Week*, *USA Today*, or other publications.

Financial data are reported based on a set of generally accepted accounting principles determined by the Financial Accounting Standards Board, FASB, a private standards-setting body. The FASB, in effect, sets the standard for thousands of U.S. corporations. By adopting a position (or not acting at all), the FASB can have a major impact on items such as reported profits, the amount of inventory or other assets shown on balance sheets, or the amount of long-term debt or other liabilities reported. Not surprisingly, many parties are concerned about the FASB and its role. A recent article commented that many accountants believe that the FASB moves too slowly—and often produces little of substance when it finally does act. Additionally, the FASB has found it difficult to please its various constituencies: Security analysts complain that the FASB has avoided accounting changes that would improve financial disclosures by public companies, whereas businesspeople say that accounting rules are unnecessarily complex and costly.

The FASB's job keeps getting tougher—new issues keep arising that need to be reported, but how they are best reported is open to a lot of question. And, increasingly, accounting firms are being sued due to their work or, depending on the perspective of the individuals bringing suit, lack of work in their auditing role. In a recent year the Big Six accounting firms (Arthur Andersen, Coopers & Lybrand, Deloitte Touche Tohmatsu, Ernst & Young, KPMG Peat Marwick, and Price Waterhouse) suffered litigation costs that were 13 percent of total income from audit fees. Liability suits are not limited to the United States; increasingly they are spreading across continental Europe.

Accounting statements are the primary source of historical information about the firm for managers, employees, creditors, and investors. Our interest in this chapter lies in using this information to gauge past performance and to make projections about the future.

LEARNING GOALS

After studying this chapter you should be able to:

1. Discuss the key purposes of the income statement and balance sheet, including three kinds of earnings per share.
2. Explain the bases on which the common-size income statement and common-size balance sheet are calculated.
3. Calculate key financial ratios.
4. Explain the focus of the du Pont system of financial analysis.
5. Discuss the limitations of ratio analysis.
6. Discuss international accounting considerations.

DIFFERENT STATEMENTS FOR DIFFERENT PURPOSES

Different types of accounting statements focus on different financial activities of the firm. The three types of statements used by most firms are:

1. *Financial accounting statements prepared according to generally accepted accounting principles, GAAP.* These data are presented in various publications and reported to the firm's stockholders in the **annual report.**
2. *Tax reporting statements.* Because of differences between what is allowed for tax reporting (Internal Revenue Service regulations) and what is required for GAAP purposes, separate tax statements are prepared. Tax consequences are of vital concern because the payment of taxes is a direct cash outflow for the firm.
3. *Reports for internal management.* Firms often develop their own internal reporting requirements, which are based on divisions, cost centers, or some other unit. Included are such items as direct costing, contribution margin analysis, standard costs and variances, and transfer pricing.

ANNUAL REPORT
Report issued to a firm's stockholders that contains basic accounting statements as well as management's opinion of the year's operations and prospects for the future.

Our interest in this chapter is in analyzing accounting statements, but we must specify *which* statements. The statements we focus on are those in category 1—the financial accounting statements prepared for external use and based on generally accepted accounting principles, GAAP. (For purposes of our discussion, we'll call them simply accounting statements, although more specifically they are *financial* accounting statements.) The objective of the generally accepted accounting principles on which accounting statements are based is to provide a consistent and objective account of the firm's status based on historical costs, where revenues and expenses are matched over the appropriate time periods. There are two reasons for focusing on GAAP statements: First, because they are prepared for the public, it is by analyzing GAAP statements that investors, creditors, and others gauge the performance of the firm. Second, unless we are employed by the firm, the GAAP statements are all we have; neither tax nor internal management statements are made public.

CONCEPT REVIEW QUESTIONS

■ Describe the different types of accounting statements prepared by a firm.

THE BASIC ACCOUNTING STATEMENTS

■ LEARNING GOAL 1

Discuss the key purposes of the income statement and balance sheet, including three kinds of earnings per share.

The annual report that a firm issues to stockholders contains important information. The primary accounting statements it contains are the income statement and the balance sheet. The *income statement* records the flow of revenue and related expenses through the firm over some period of time, typically a year. The *balance sheet* is a snapshot of the firm's assets, liabilities, and owner's claims as of a specific point in time—the end of its fiscal year. These two statements, along with the statement of cash flows (discussed in the next chapter) and the footnotes and discussion accompanying the statements, provide an accounting picture of the firm. Typically, an annual report provides statements for 2 or 3 years, along with summary information for several more years.

Remember Key Ideas 1 and 6—the goal of the firm is to maximize its market value, and risk and return go hand-in-hand.

Accounting statements report what happened to the firm in terms of sales, assets, liabilities, earnings, dividends, and so forth over time. This information is one of the inputs investors and the general investment community use to form expectations about the required returns and riskiness of the firm. As investors form or revise their expectations about the magnitude, timing, or riskiness of the firm's returns, the market value of the firm will be affected. Understanding accounting statements is therefore important for investors, creditors, and the firm's management.

The analysis we will make here is based on General Mills, a major consumer food firm.[1] Its primary operations consist of processed dairy products, dry grocery products, and cereals.

Income Statement

GROSS MARGIN
A measure of what a firm sells goods for in relation to the cost of the goods; computed as net sales minus cost of goods sold.

OPERATING PROFIT
The earnings of the firm after all expenses, except interest and taxes, and before any adjustments.

The income statement presents a summary of revenues and expenses for the firm during the last year. Table 19.1 presents the last 3 years' income statements for General Mills. Here are some highlights of the income statement:

1. Sales minus cost of goods sold equals **gross margin.** The gross margin indicates the amount that the firm sells goods for in relation to the cost of the goods.
2. **Operating profit** measures the earnings of the firm after all expenses, except interest and taxes, and before any adjustments.
3. Adjustments for General Mills include interest income, income from its subsidiaries, and nonrecurring items.

[1] *The information on General Mills came from its 1994 annual report. Some minor adjustments have been made to simplify the presentation and to improve consistency. In addition to the annual report, information can be obtained from the firm's 10-K report, which must be filed annually with the Securities and Exchange Commission. Annual reports and 10-Ks can be obtained by writing to most companies; many libraries also have them—often online or on microfilm or microfiche.*

TABLE 19.1

Income Statement for General Mills (in millions)

The format of this statement differs from that reported in the General Mills annual report, primarily due to breaking out interest as a separate item. General Mills' fiscal year ends on the last Sunday in May.

	For Fiscal Year		
	1992	1993	1994
Sales	$7,778	$8,135	$8,517
Cost of goods sold*	4,371	4,572	4,762
Gross margin	3,407	3,563	3,755
Selling, general, and administrative expenses	2,504	2,645	2,755
Operating profit	903	918	1,000
Other expenses ( ) or income	+14	(15)	(147)
Earnings before interest and taxes, *EBIT*	917	903	853
Interest	89	100	99
Earnings before taxes, *EBT*	828	803	754
Income taxes	332	297	284
Net income	$ 496	$ 506	$ 470

* Includes $304, $274, and $247 in GAAP depreciation expense in 1994, 1993, and 1992, respectively; and $70, $68, and $60 in lease expense, respectively.

4. The net operating income, or earnings before interest and taxes, *EBIT*, reflects the firm's earnings before the costs of financing and income taxes.[2]
5. Subtracting interest expenses results in earnings before taxes, *EBT*. By then subtracting income taxes, we arrive at net income, or earnings after tax, *EAT*. Note that if the firm has preferred stock outstanding, cash dividends on it have to be subtracted from net income to arrive at the **earnings available for common stockholders, *EAC*.**

EARNINGS AVAILABLE FOR COMMON STOCK-HOLDERS, *EAC*
Net income minus cash dividends on preferred stock.

6. Because GAAP statements are prepared on an accrual, not a cash, basis, the $470 million in net income in 1994 does not mean that General Mills earned $470 million in cash. In Table 19.1, we see that General Mills' net sales increased over these 3 years, while net income fluctuated.

One item of interest is the *earnings per share, EPS*, figure. By putting earnings on a per share basis, the effects of changes in the number of shares of common stock outstanding can be held constant. Earnings per share is calculated as follows:

$$EPS = \frac{\text{earnings available for common stockholders}}{\text{number of shares of common stock outstanding}} = \frac{\text{net income} - \text{cash dividends on preferred stock (if any)}}{\text{number of shares of common stock outstanding}} \quad (19.1)$$

[2]*For our purposes, it is important to present the income statement in a slightly different manner than that used by accountants. Because interest is a cost of financing and we are concerned about various financing alternatives, interest is broken out separately.*

For General Mills in 1994, *EPS* was $470/158.5 = $2.97.[3] During 1993 it was $3.15, and in 1992 it was $3.00. After adjusting for differences in the number of shares of common stock outstanding, General Mills' earnings per share fluctuated over the 3-year period.

There are actually three *EPS* figures that could be reported, depending on whether any complex securities, such as convertible securities, warrants, or stock options, are employed by a firm:

  1. *Simple* EPS. The first is simple *EPS* as calculated using Equation 19.1.
  2. *Primary* EPS. Another is primary *EPS*, in which the earnings available for common stockholders are divided by the number of shares that would have been outstanding if all "likely to be converted" securities were converted.
  3. *Fully Diluted* EPS. Finally, there is fully diluted *EPS*, in which the earnings available for common shareholders are divided by the total number of shares of common stock that would be outstanding after total conversion of the issue.

FINANCIAL MANAGEMENT TODAY

The Management of Earnings

General Electric is the third largest public company in the world in terms of its market value. It has eight different industrial businesses, and twenty-four financial service units. Both segments outperform their market peers. One of the hallmarks of General Electric, GE, is its consistent growth in earnings. During the past decade GE's earnings have risen every year.

How does General Electric accomplish such growth? While there is no doubt that the firm has selected and managed its divergent businesses very well, another part of the picture is General Electric's aggressive practice of managing earnings. To smooth out fluctuations, GE frequently offsets one-time gains from large asset sales with various restructuring charges, thereby keeping earnings from increasing so high they can't be topped the next year. Another tactic is to time sales of equity stakes in various businesses, or acquisitions, in order to boost profits when needed.

With such a large and complex firm, there are many ways to manage earnings. A major tactic is illustrated with a restructuring charge made recently. When General Electric realized a $1.43 billion pretax profit on the sale of its aerospace business, it also took a $1.01 billion charge to cover costs of "closing and downsizing and streamlining of certain production,

service and administrative facilities world-wide." After taxes, the gain and the charge matched up exactly at $678 million! By taking the restructuring charge, General Electric also helped its operating profits in subsequent years.

Another tactic practiced by General Electric is to purchase revenue and earnings growth through acquisitions. In the ever-growing financial services unit, which is one of the largest (if not the largest) in the world, acquisitions of other firms or parts of firms have been a way of life. By throwing off more income than General Electric's cost of financing, such acquisitions add immediate profitability to General Electric. Recently, General Electric financial services units acquired assets totaling $16.9 billion.

While some might question General Electric's accounting procedures, three points should be made. First, it is a very successful and well-managed firm. Second, any earnings management G.E. does is completely permissible within generally accepted accounting principles. Finally, the earnings management is also consistent with the stress that General Electric's CEO, Jack Welch, places on the importance of earnings growth. As he says, investors prize GE's ability "to deliver strong, consistent earnings growth in a myriad of global economic conditions."

[3] *There were 158.5 million shares of stock outstanding at the end of 1994, 160.5 million at the end of 1993, and 165.0 million at the end of 1992. Some of the figures in the analysis differ slightly from those reported by General Mills.*

Because our interest is in financial management, not accounting, we focus primarily on "simple *EPS*," or just *EPS*.

Balance Sheet

The balance sheet provides a record of the firm—its assets, liabilities, and resulting stockholders' equity—as of the end of its fiscal year. In looking at a balance sheet (Table 19.2), we need to recognize that the figures are presented in terms of *historical costs;* they do not reflect market values, the effects of inflation, or other current information. A balance sheet thus provides, at best, only a very rough idea of the value of the firm.[4] Some key aspects of the balance sheet are:

1. The assets are divided into two sections: current assets (less than or equal to 1 year) and long-term assets (longer than 1 year). Note that property and equipment is presented on both a gross basis and a net basis. The *net basis* reflects accumulated GAAP depreciation charged over the years as an expense in order to match expenses with associated revenues.
2. For simplicity, we have included "other" as long-term assets. Sometimes it is preferable to use another category for intangible assets.
3. Liabilities are also divided into current and long-term. Although not shown directly on the balance sheet, lease obligations for General Mills are recorded as part of its long-term debt. The present value of long-term capital lease commitments is recorded as a long-term liability, and a corresponding dollar amount is included in the property and equipment account to show the use of assets acquired by long-term capital leases. **Deferred taxes** represent the difference in the taxes actually paid to the Internal Revenue Service (discussed in Chapter 8) and those reported for GAAP purposes.
4. General Mills has only common stock outstanding; this is shown in the stockholders' equity section. General Mills also has, as part of its retirement plan, an *employee stock ownership plan, ESOP,* which is essentially an employee trust fund. Note that General Mills, like most firms that are worldwide in nature, also has an equity account that reflects foreign currency adjustments.
5. Retained earnings is an account that reflects the sum of the firm's net income over its life, less all cash dividends paid and any other adjustments. In a sense, it is a balancing account that (a) ties together the income statement and the balance sheet, and (b) allows assets to equal liabilities and stockholders' equity. It is important to recognize that *retained earnings is a claim on assets,* not an asset account. The retained earnings account *does not contain any cash;* the only cash is in the current asset account entitled "cash and marketable securities."

Table 19.2 shows that General Mills kept its current assets relatively constant but increased its long-term assets over the 3-year period. On the other side, the current liabilities increased, as did long-term liabilities and stockholder's equity.

Although it is not reported directly on its accounting statements, General Mills paid total cash dividends on its common stock of $299.4 million in 1994. Using the total cash dividend figure and knowing the number of shares of common stock outstanding, we can calculate the dividends per share—the dollar amount of cash dividends paid to investors during the year:

DEFERRED TAXES
The difference between the taxes actually paid to the IRS and those reported for GAAP purposes; a liability account on the balance sheet.

---

[4]*A figure often reported is book value per share, which is calculated as*

$$book\ value\ per\ share = \frac{stockholders'\ equity}{number\ of\ shares\ of\ common\ stock\ outstanding}.$$

For General Mills in 1994, this was $1,273/158.5 = $8.03. In 1993, it was $7.60; in 1992, it was $8.29. However, book value per share is not necessarily a meaningful figure because it does not represent the market value, the replacement value, or the liquidating value of the firm.

$$\text{dividend per share } = \frac{\text{total cash dividends paid to common stockholders}}{\text{number of shares of common stock outstanding}} \quad (19.2)$$

TABLE 19.2

Balance Sheet for General Mills (in millions)

The balance sheet lists assets, liabilities, and resulting stockholders' equity, or net worth, of the firm at a specific point in time. Because it is based on historical cost, it does not indicate the market value of the firm.

	1992	1993	1994
Assets			
Current assets			
Cash and marketable securities	$ 1	$ 100	$ 0
Accounts receivable	292	288	310
Inventory	487	439	488
Other expenses	255	250	331
Total current assets	1,035	1,077	1,129
Long-term assets			
Net property and equipment	2,648	2,860	3,093
Other	622	714	976
Total long-term assets	3,270	3,574	4,069
Total assets	$4,305	$4,651	$5,198
Liabilities and Stockholders' Equity			
Current liabilities			
Accounts payable	$ 632	$ 617	$ 650
Short-term debt*	202	404	549
Accruals and other	537	538	633
Total current liabilities	1,371	1,559	1,832
Long-term liabilities			
Long-term debt and leases	921	1,268	1,417
Deferred taxes	434	458	487
Other	207	147	189
Total long-term liabilities	1,562	1,873	2,093
Stockholders' equity			
Common stock: 204.2 shares issued	344	359	373
Less: Treasury stock	− 803	− 1,196	− 1,334
Retained earnings	2,049	2,285	2,457
Less: Unearned ESOP and restricted stock compensation	− 172	− 168	− 160
Less: Cumulative foreign currency adjustment	− 46	− 61	− 63
Total stockholders' equity	1,372	1,219	1,273
Total liabilities and stockholders' equity	$4,305	$4,651	$5,198

*Includes current maturities of long-term debt.

For 1994, the dividend per share figure was $299.4/158.5 = $1.89 per share. This compares with $1.71 in 1993 and $1.48 in 1992. General Mills thus substantially increased its cash dividends over this time period.

CONCEPT REVIEW QUESTIONS

■ Describe the items that are presented in an income statement.
■ What are the three kinds of earnings per share?
■ Describe the key aspects of the balance sheet.

ANALYSIS OF ACCOUNTING STATEMENTS

We've seen that a firm's balance sheet reports its assets, liabilities, and stockholders' equity at a point in time; the income statement reports operations over the period of a year. Careful analysis of these statements can provide some clues about future cash flows. The point of this analysis is to help diagnose trends that indicate the magnitude, timing, or riskiness of the firm's future cash flows.

When conducting an analysis, we need to keep five ideas in mind:

Before comparing a firm's ratios to the industry averages, find out how the industry averages are computed, to be sure you are using similar computations.

1. It is necessary to look at trends; generally 3 to 5 years' worth of data are necessary to ascertain how the firm's performance is changing over time.
2. It is helpful to compare the firm's performance to that of the industry (or industries) in which it operates.[5] Although industry averages may not indicate where a firm wants to be, because of different markets, management philosophy, or whatever, the comparison is helpful in analyzing trends.
3. *The importance of carefully reading and analyzing the annual report—including the discussion and footnotes accompanying the statements—cannot be overemphasized.* Often these will point to other factors—such as contractual obligations, past and future financing policies, plans for further expansion or restructuring, or the sale of part of the firm's assets—that significantly affect the entire analysis.
4. The "quality" of the earnings are also important. For instance, if the revenues are mostly in the form of cash sales, the quality of the earnings may be far higher than if the sales are due to longer-term credit sales or to sales that are impacted directly by some unusual accounting treatment.
5. The analysis may raise further questions for which additional information is needed. The important point is not to view the analysis as an end in itself.

Common-Size Statements

■ **LEARNING GOAL 2**

Explain the bases on which the common-size income statement and common-size balance sheet are calculated.

COMMON-SIZE STATEMENT
Accounting statement expressed in percentage terms.

Income Statement

One of the simplest and most direct ways to analyze changes over time is to calculate a **common-size statement.** A common-size income statement is constructed by divid-

[5]*It is often difficult to find comparable industry data. If good industry data are unavailable, it is generally best to use one or more similar firms for comparison. We used Quaker Oats and Heinz to generate "industry" data.*

ing the various components of the income statement by *net sales*. Thus, net sales equals 100 percent, and everything else is presented as a percentage of net sales. General Mills' common-size income statement is presented in Table 19.3. Note that two ratios, the gross profit margin and the net profit margin, are listed as items (a) and (b) in the table. The **gross profit margin** measures the sales relative to the cost of goods sold, while the **net profit margin** indicates how net income (after all expenses) relates to sales. Comparing General Mills and the consumer foods industry, we see that General Mills has about the same relative cost of goods sold and expenses; the consequence is that net income has fluctuated close to that of the industry, except in 1994 when it underperformed the industry.

Balance Sheet

A common-size balance sheet can be calculated in the same manner, except that all the statement components are divided by *total assets* to put them on a common percentage basis. General Mills' common-size balance sheet is presented in Table 19.4. An analysis of this statement indicates that General Mills' current assets have declined over this 3-year period. Compared to others in the consumer foods industry, General Mills carries substantially less cash, accounts receivable, and inventory. Examining the investment in long-term assets, we see that General Mills is well above the industry in property and equipment but has less in "other" assets.

An analysis of the liabilities indicates that General Mills has more accounts payable and more short-term debt than the industry. General Mills has increased its reliance on long-term debt in recent years and employs more long-term debt than the

TABLE 19.3
Common-Size Income Statement for General Mills and the Consumer Foods Industry

A common-size income statement is calculated by dividing the various components by net sales; thus, net sales equals 100 percent.

	General Mills			Industry		
	1992	1993	1994	1992	1993	1994
Net sales	100.0%	100.0%	100.0%	100.0%	100.0%	100.0%
Cost of goods sold	56.2	56.2	55.9	56.4	56.9	54.3
(a) Gross margin (gross profit margin)	43.8	43.8	44.1	43.6	43.1	45.7
Selling, general, and administrative expenses and adjustments	32.0	32.7	34.1	30.6	34.4	33.8
Earnings before interest and taxes, *EBIT*	11.8	11.1	10.0	13.0	8.7	11.9
Interest	1.2	1.2	1.2	1.8	1.6	1.9
Earnings before tax, *EBT*	10.6	9.9	8.8	11.2	7.1	10.0
Income tax	4.3	3.7	3.3	4.1	2.8	3.6
(b) Net income (net profit margin)	6.3%	6.2%	5.5%	7.1%	4.3%	6.4%

industry. The total of deferred taxes and other liabilities is slightly higher for General Mills than for the consumer foods industry. Overall, General Mills exhibits some substantial differences from the industry in terms of the composition of its assets, liabilities, and stockholders' equity. The biggest differences are its lower level of cash accounts receivable, and inventory, its higher levels of long-term assets, and its greater reliance on long-term debt.

In Chapter 15 we discussed aggressive versus conservative management policies. Note that by using less current assets than the consumer foods industry, General Mills is employing a more aggressive asset management policy. At the same time, it is also employing more long-term debt and less equity than the consumer foods industry. Thus, in line with the discussion in Chapter 12, it is employing more creditor funds, and, hence, is employing more financial leverage. Compared to the consumer goods industry, General Mills is more aggressive in terms of its asset management and is also more aggressive in terms of its financial leverage, as evidenced by the heavier reliance on long-term debt and lower reliance on equity financing.

TABLE 19.4

Common-Size Balance Sheet for General Mills and the Consumer Foods Industry

All assets, liabilities, and stockholders' equity accounts are expressed as a percentage of total assets. The use of a common-size statement highlights relative percentages in accounts receivable, inventory, long-term assets, and short-term liabilities.

	General Mills			Industry		
Assets	1992	1993	1994	1992	1993	1994
Current						
Cash and marketable securities	0.0%	2.2%	0.0%	3.8%	2.7%	2.5%
Accounts receivable	6.8	6.2	6.0	16.4	15.6	14.0
Inventory	11.3	9.4	9.4	15.9	15.0	16.3
Other	5.9	5.4	6.3	3.7	4.9	4.4
Total current	24.0	23.2	21.7	39.8	38.2	37.2
Long-term						
Property and equipment	61.5	61.5	59.5	37.1	37.6	35.9
Other	14.5	15.3	18.8	23.1	24.2	26.9
Total assets	100 %	100 %	100 %	100 %	100 %	100 %
Liabilities and Stockholders' Equity						
Current						
Accounts payable	14.7%	13.2%	12.5%	11.2%	10.9%	10.4%
Short-term debt	4.7	8.7	10.5	16.6	14.9	3.8
Accruals and other	12.5	11.6	12.2	13.5	14.8	12.5
Total current	31.9	33.5	35.2	41.3	40.6	26.7
Long-term						
Long-term debt and leases	21.4	27.3	27.3	12.9	18.7	24.3
Deferred taxes and other	14.9	13.0	13.0	11.9	12.2	16.7
Stockholders' equity	31.8	26.2	24.5	33.9	28.5	32.3
Total liability and stockholders' equity	100 %	100 %	100 %	100 %	100 %	100 %

Ratio Analysis

■ LEARNING GOAL 3

Calculate key financial ratios.

Another useful approach in analyzing a firm's financial performance is to compute ratios. These ratios compare accounting variables and draw from both the income statement and the balance sheet. Although many different ratios can be calculated, we will focus on a basic set. The ratios are grouped into five categories, as follows:[6]

1. *Liquidity Ratios.* Indicate the firm's ability to meet its short-run obligations.
2. *Asset Management Ratios.* Indicate how efficiently the firm is using its assets.
3. *Debt Management Ratios.* Deal with the amount of debt in the firm's capital structure and its ability to service (or meet) its legal obligations.
4. *Profitability Ratios.* Relate net income to sales, assets, or stockholders' equity.
5. *Market Ratios.* Indicate what is happening to the firm's relative market price, earnings, and cash dividends.

Liquidity Ratios

Liquidity ratios measure the firm's ability to fulfill its short-term commitments out of current or liquid assets. These ratios focus on current assets and liabilities, and are often of lesser importance than other ratios when considering the long-run viability and profitability of the firm. The two primary liquidity ratios are the current ratio and the quick ratio.

CURRENT RATIO
Indicates the ability of the firm to meet current obligations; current assets divided by current liabilities.

The **current ratio** measures the ability of the firm to meet obligations due within 1 year with short-term assets in the form of cash, marketable securities, accounts receivable, and inventory. It is calculated as follows:

$$\text{current ratio} = \frac{\text{current assets}}{\text{current liabilities}} = \frac{\$1,129}{\$1,832} = 0.6 \qquad (19.3)$$

The current ratio is usually inversely related to receivables, inventory, or payables turnover.

The current ratio assumes a regular cash flow and that both accounts receivable and inventory can be readily converted into cash.

A current ratio of 2.0 is sometimes employed as a standard of comparison. Current ratios of 1.0 and less are sometimes considered low and indicative of financial difficulties. Very high ratios suggest excess current assets that probably are having an adverse effect on the long-run profitability of the firm.[7]

QUICK RATIO
Indicates the firm's ability to meet current obligations without using inventory; current assets minus inventory divided by current liabilities.

By subtracting out inventory, which is often not highly liquid, we can calculate the **quick ratio,** which measures the firm's ability to meet its short-term obligations with cash, marketable securities, and accounts receivable:

$$\text{quick ratio} = \frac{\text{current assets} - \text{inventory}}{\text{current liabilities}} = \frac{\$1,129 - \$488}{\$1,832} = 0.3 \qquad (19.4)$$

---

[6] *These five groups are convenience groupings, which indicate that analysts might use them in combination to examine some aspect of the firm's operations. The ratios presented are general-purpose ratios applicable to most manufacturing and retail firms. However, some are not very useful or relevant in the financial, public utility, transportation, and service industries.*

[7] *Any interpretation of ratios is relative—either to the firm itself over time, or to the industry in which the firm operates. Also, knowledge of management's intent may be necessary. Consequently, what is "high" or "low," or "satisfactory" or "unsatisfactory," can be determined only in the context of a specific detailed analysis. Notice that too high a ratio may be just as indicative of a problem as too low a ratio. However, the action required is often far different.*

Also called the *acid-test ratio*, this ratio measures the near-term ability of the firm to meet its current liabilities without using its inventory.

Quick ratios of less than 1.0 are not alarming in and of themselves. Very high quick ratios suggest excess cash, a credit policy that needs revamping, or a change needed in the composition of current versus long-term assets.

Asset Management Ratios

Asset management ratios are sometimes called *activity ratios*. By looking at the amount of various types of assets, they attempt to determine if they are too high or too low with regard to current operating levels. If too many funds are tied up in certain types of assets that could be more productively employed elsewhere, the firm is not as profitable as it should be. Four basic asset management ratios are the days sales outstanding, inventory turnover, long-term asset turnover, and total asset turnover.[8]

As discussed in Chapters 15 and 17, the *days sales outstanding* ratio estimates how many days it takes on average to collect the sales of the firm. By dividing sales (in the denominator) by 365, we determine average sales per day.[9] Then, when receivables are divided by average sales, we can determine how many days it will take to collect the receivables:

The higher the days sales outstanding, the higher the cash conversion cycle.

$$\frac{\text{days sales}}{\text{outstanding}} = \frac{\text{accounts receivable}}{\text{sales}/65} = \frac{\$310}{\$8,517/365} = 13.3 \text{ days} \qquad (19.5)$$

This ratio provides an indication of how effective the credit-granting and management activities of the firm are. It can also be calculated using average accounts receivable for the year. If credit sales are available, then it would be preferable to employ that figure rather than total sales.

A very high days sales outstanding probably indicates many uncollectible receivables. A low ratio may indicate that credit-granting policies are overly restrictive, thus hurting sales.

The second asset management ratio is the *inventory turnover* ratio, which measures the number of times a year the firm turns over its inventory:

The lower the inventory turnover, the higher the cash conversion cycle.

$$\text{inventory turnover} = \frac{\text{cost of goods sold}}{\text{inventory}} = \frac{\$4,762}{\$488} = 9.8 \qquad (19.6)$$

This ratio can also be calculated using an average of the year's beginning and ending inventories.

The higher the inventory turnover ratio, the more times a year the firm is "moving," or turning over, its inventory. Other things being equal, and assuming that sales are progressing smoothly, a higher inventory turnover ratio suggests efficient inventory management. Low inventory turnover figures often indicate obsolete inventory or lack of effective inventory management.

LONG-TERM ASSET TURNOVER
Indicates the firm's ability to generate sales in relation to its long-term asset base; sales divided by fixed assets.

The **long-term asset turnover** ratio provides an indication of the firm's ability to generate sales based on its long-term asset base. For some industries, this figure is im-

---

[8]*Days sales outstanding is sometimes called the average collection period.*
[9]*Sometimes receivables turnover is employed. Receivables turnover = sales/accounts receivable, and days sales outstanding = 365/receivables turnover.*

portant; in others, like banking and many service industries, it is of questionable value. It is calculated as follows:

$$\text{long-term asset turnover} = \frac{\text{sales}}{\text{long-term assets}} = \frac{\$8,517}{\$4,069} = 2.1 \qquad (19.7)$$

By comparing long-term assets (primarily property and equipment) to sales, this ratio provides an indication of how effective the firm is in using these assets.

The higher the ratio, other things being equal, the more effective the utilization. A low ratio may indicate that the firm's marketing effort or basic area of business requires attention.

Total asset turnover provides an indication of the firm's ability to generate sales in relation to its total asset base. For General Mills it is:

$$\text{total asset turnover} = \frac{\text{sales}}{\text{total assets}} = \frac{\$8,517}{\$5,198} = 1.6 \qquad (19.8)$$

A high total asset turnover normally reflects good management, whereas a low ratio suggests the need to reassess the firm's overall strategy, marketing effort, and capital expenditure program.

Debt Management Ratios

Debt management ratios focus on the liabilities and stockholders' equity from the balance sheet and on the income statement.[10] Three primary ratios in this category are total debt to total assets, times interest earned, and fixed charges coverage.

The **total debt to total assets** ratio is calculated as follows:

$$\text{total debt to total assets} = \frac{\text{total debt}}{\text{total assets}} = \frac{\$1,832 + \$2,093}{\$5,198} = 0.76 \qquad (19.9)$$

This ratio attempts to measure how much of the total funds are being supplied by creditors. Total debt includes all current debt plus long-term debt, lease obligations, and so forth.

A high ratio indicates the use of financial leverage to magnify earnings, whereas a low ratio indicates relatively low use of creditor funds. General Mills has 74 percent of its *book-value-based* capital structure in debt-type instruments. This highlights the extensive use of debt, or financial leverage, by General Mills.

The second debt management ratio, **times interest earned,** is:

$$\text{times interest earned} = \frac{\text{earnings before interest and taxes, } EBIT}{\text{interest}} \qquad (19.10)$$

$$\text{times interest earned} = \frac{\$853}{\$99} = 8.6$$

TOTAL ASSET TURNOVER
Indicates the firm's ability to generate sales in relation to its total asset base; sales divided by total assets.

TOTAL DEBT TO TOTAL ASSETS
Indicates how much of the firm's funds are being supplied by creditors; total debt divided by total assets.

Normally, there is an inverse relationship between the ratios of total debt/total assets and times interest earned.

TIMES INTEREST EARNED
Indicates the firm's ability to meet its interest requirements; *EBIT* divided by interest charges.

DAYS PURCHASES OUTSTANDING
Indicates how prompt the firm is in paying its bills; accounts payable divided by credit purchases per day.

[10]An important ratio for creditors is **days purchases outstanding:**

$$\text{days purchases outstanding} = \frac{\text{accounts payable}}{\text{credit purchases}/365}$$

which provides an idea of how promptly the firm pays its bills. Accounts payable can be obtained for virtually all firms. (For General Mills, it was necessary to refer to the discussion in the annual report to separate accounts payable from accruals, which General Mills reported together.) The problem comes with credit purchases, which are virtually never reported in accounting statements. If total purchases are available, they are often used instead. Otherwise, some annual reports provide sufficient information so that a percentage of the cost of goods sold, such as 60 percent, may be employed as an estimate of purchases. For General Mills, a thorough analysis of its annual report fails to provide any information on purchases—credit or otherwise.

The ability of the firm to meet its interest payments (on both short- and long-term debt) is measured by this ratio. It shows how far *EBIT* can decline before the firm probably will have trouble servicing its interest obligations.

A high ratio indicates a "safe situation," but that perhaps not enough financial leverage is being used. A low ratio may call for immediate action.

The **fixed charges coverage** ratio provides a more comprehensive picture of the firm's ability to meet its legal financing requirements. While variations of this ratio exist, the one we calculate is:

FIXED CHARGES COVERAGE
Indicates the firm's ability to meet its legal financing obligations, including leases; *EBIT* plus lease expenses, divided by interest charges plus lease expenses.

$$\frac{\text{fixed charges}}{\text{coverage}} = \frac{EBIT + \text{lease expenses}}{\text{interest} + \text{lease expenses}} = \frac{\$853 + \$70}{\$99 + \$70} = 5.5 \qquad (19.11)$$

This is a more comprehensive ratio than times interest earned and includes lease expenses, which are also a fixed legal obligation.[11] Leasing is essentially like debt in that it results in a fixed cost to the firm and uses up some of the firm's debt capacity.[12] By debt capacity, we mean the amount of fixed-cost financing the firm can effectively employ in order to maximize its value. To be even more complete, the denominator may also include sinking fund payments on long-term debt, and/or preferred dividends multiplied by $[1/(1 - \text{tax rate})]$.

A high fixed charges ratio is more desirable than a low one, other things being equal. However, the question of financial leverage still needs to be considered.

Profitability Ratios

Three profitability ratios, which focus on the profit-generating ability of the firm, are net profit margin, return on total assets, and return on equity.

The *net profit margin*, as discussed when we calculated a common-size income statement, is:

$$\text{net profit margin} = \frac{\text{net income}}{\text{sales}} = \frac{\$470}{\$8,517} = 5.5\% \qquad (19.12)$$

A low net profit margin indicates that (1) the firm is not generating enough sales relative to its expenses, (2) expenses are out of control, or (3) both. It is a widely used ratio of the efficiency of management. Net profit margins vary considerably by industry, with, for example, jewelry stores having much higher profit margins than grocery stores.

RETURN ON TOTAL ASSETS
Indicates the ability of the firm to earn a satisfactory return on assets; net income divided by total assets.

The second profitability ratio, **return on total assets,** indicates the ability of the firm to earn a satisfactory return on all the assets it employs. It is calculated as follows:

$$\text{return on total assets} = \frac{\text{net income}}{\text{total assets}} = \frac{\$470}{\$5,198} = 9.0\% \qquad (19.13)$$

[11] Lease expenses is an income statement account that is often found only in the discussion accompanying a firm's accounting statements. Do not confuse it with "lease obligations" or "capitalized lease obligations" accounts that are reported either on the balance sheet or in the discussion accompanying the accounting statements.

[12] Many leases have a required payment and then a contingent payment based on sales. In addition, much of the debt being issued by firms is not strictly fixed but may "float" as general interest rates change. However, both of these are still fixed-cost types of financing because they have a legal claim on income and do not share in the final distribution of earnings, as do common stockholders.

Also known as *return on investment, ROI*, this ratio tells us how effective the firm is in terms of generating income, given its asset base. It is an important measure of the efficiency of management. The higher the ratio the better, because this provides some indication of future growth prospects.

The last profitability ratio is **return on equity, *ROE,*** which is:

$$\text{return on equity} = \frac{\text{net income}}{\text{stockholders' equity}} = \frac{\$470}{\$1{,}273} = 36.9\% \qquad (19.14)$$

This ratio provides an accounting-based indication of the effectiveness of the firm and its management. It is directly affected by the return on total assets and the amount of financial leverage employed. However, this ratio, although helpful, does not focus on the actual returns to the firms' owners in terms of cash dividends and/or market appreciation. For this reason, *return on equity is not a reliable measure of returns.*

Market Ratios

The last set of ratios is somewhat different, because they focus more on the investors' viewpoint. They are included here, though, because they are influenced by a firm's accounting statements, and because they are needed in any compete analysis of a firm's accounting statements. These ratios are the price/earnings ratio, dividend yield, and dividend payout.

The price/earnings, *P/E*, ratio indicates how much investors are willing to pay for the firm's current earnings. It is:[13]

$$\text{price/earnings} = \frac{\text{market price per share}}{\text{earnings per share}} = \frac{\$68.06}{\$2.97} = 22.9 \text{ times} \qquad (19.15)$$

In Chapter 4 we discussed two possible causes of high *P/E* ratios—little or no earnings or high expected growth. For General Mills it looks as if we can rule out the possibility of little or no expected earnings. Thus, the *P/E* ratio indicates how investors view the future prospects of General Mills. Because *P/E* ratios fluctuate over time, it is helpful to look at trends for both the company and the stock market in general.

The second market ratio is the *dividend yield*, which indicates the percentage amount of cash dividends paid by the firm relative to the market price of its common stock. Thus, its part of the total return an investor receives from investing in common stock. For General Mills it is:

$$\text{dividend yield} = \frac{\text{dividends per share}}{\text{market price per share}} = \frac{\$1.89}{\$68.06} = 2.8\% \qquad (19.16)$$

Because returns from investing in stocks come from cash dividends and from appreciation or loss in market price, the dividend yield is part of the total return expected by investors. Generally, firms with high growth prospects (or growth options) have relatively low cash dividends and a relatively high market price, meaning they have a low dividend yield. Conversely, firms with low growth prospects and options typically have higher dividend yields.

---

[13] *The market price can be an average of prices over some period of time, or the price as of the end of the firm's financial year. We employed an average of the high and low stock prices for the year.*

Finally, the *dividend payout ratio* provides an indication of how the firm is splitting its earnings between returning them to common stockholders and reinvesting them in the firm. It is calculated as follows:

$$\text{dividend payout} = \frac{\text{dividends per share}}{\text{earnings per share}} = \frac{\$1.89}{\$2.97} = 63.6\% \tag{19.17}$$

High-growth firms (i.e., those with substantial growth options) typically reinvest most of their earnings instead of paying them out, resulting in low payout ratios. Slow-growth

TABLE 19.5

Ratios for General Mills and the Consumer Foods Industry

By comparing General Mills with the industry over time, we can spot trends that may not be evident when only a single year is examined.

Ratio	Calculation	General Mills			Industry		
		1992	1993	1994	1992	1993	1994
Liquidity							
Current	$\dfrac{\text{current assets}}{\text{current liabilities}}$	0.8	0.7	0.6	1.0	0.9	1.4
Quick	$\dfrac{\text{current assets} - \text{inventory}}{\text{current liabilities}}$	0.4	0.4	0.3	0.6	0.6	0.8
Asset Management							
Days sales outstanding	$\dfrac{\text{accounts receivable}}{\text{sales}/365}$	13.7 days	12.9 days	13.3 days	41.8 days	40.0 days	37.1 days
Inventory turnover	$\dfrac{\text{costs of goods sold}}{\text{inventory}}$	9.0	10.4	9.8	5.2	5.9	4.6
Long-term asset turnover	$\dfrac{\text{sales}}{\text{long-term assets}}$	2.4	2.3	2.1	2.5	2.5	2.2
Total asset turnover	$\dfrac{\text{sales}}{\text{total assets}}$	1.8	1.7	1.6	1.4	1.6	1.4
Debt Management							
Total debt to total assets	$\dfrac{\text{total debt}}{\text{total assets}}$	0.7	0.7	0.7	0.6	0.7	0.7
Times interest earned	$\dfrac{EBIT}{\text{interest}}$	10.3	9.0	8.6	7.4	5.7	6.5
Fixed charges coverage	$\dfrac{EBIT + \text{lease expenses}}{\text{interest} + \text{lease expenses}}$	6.6	6.0	5.5	5.1	4.5	5.0

(Continued)

TABLE 19.5 (CONTINUED)

Ratio	Calculation	General Mills			Industry		
		1992	1993	1994	1992	1993	1994
Profitability							
Net profit margin	$\dfrac{\text{net income}}{\text{sales}}$	6.3%	6.2%	5.5%	7.1%	4.3%	6.4%
Return on total assets	$\dfrac{\text{net income}}{\text{total assets}}$	11.5%	10.9%	9.0%	9.4%	5.9%	8.9%
Return on equity	$\dfrac{\text{net income}}{\text{stockholders' equity}}$	36.2%	41.5%	36.9%	28.0%	21.7%	27.4%
Market							
Price/earnings	$\dfrac{\text{market price per share}}{\text{earnings per share}}$	21.2 times	20.0 times	22.9 times	10.2 times	17.5 times	18.1 times
Dividend yield	$\dfrac{\text{dividends per share}}{\text{market price per share}}$	2.3%	2.7%	2.8%	2.9%	2.9%	2.8%
Dividend payout	$\dfrac{\text{dividends per share}}{\text{earnings per share}}$	49.3%	54.3%	63.6%	29.9%	50.1%	45.1%

firms in stable industries typically pay out a much higher percentage of their earnings. Dividend payout ratios are an important part of the cash dividend policy decision.[14]

The ratios for General Mills and for the consumer foods industry are presented in Table 19.5.

The du Pont System

■ LEARNING GOAL 4

Explain the focus of the du Pont system of financial analysis.

In an attempt to improve its financial analysis, du Pont introduced an information system that highlights relationships that might otherwise be missed. As Figure 19.1 shows, the **du Pont system** ties together three ratios—net profit margin, total asset turnover, and total debt to total assets. The return on total assets is thus seen to be:

DU PONT SYSTEM
Accounting-based system of analysis that focuses on profitability, asset utilization, and financial leverage.

$$\text{return on total assets} = (\text{net profit margin})(\text{total asset turnover}) \qquad (19.18)$$

$$\text{return on total assets} = (5.52\%)(1.64) = 9.05\% \approx 9\%$$

The importance of breaking out the net profit margin and total asset turnover as components of the return on total assets, instead of calculating return on total assets directly, is that it focuses attention on the separate ideas of profitability and asset

[14]Another ratio sometimes employed is the market-to-book ratio, which is equal to the market price per share of stock divided by the book value per share.

FIGURE 19.1

Determinants of Return on Equity for General Mills

The du Pont system of analysis provides a framework for seeing how the firm's activities interrelate to affect its performance. Anything that changes net profit margin, total asset turnover, or total debt to total assets will affect return on equity.

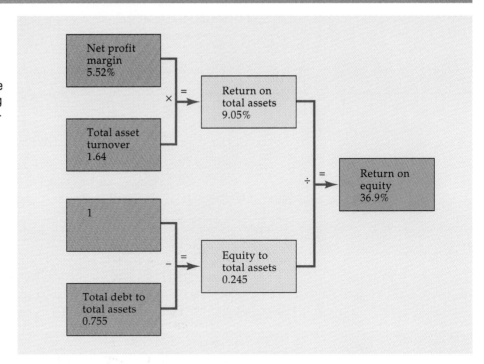

The du Pont system highlights the structural interrelationships among profitability, efficiency of asset management, and financial leverage.

utilization. General Mills' profitability as measured by net profit margin is in line with the consumer foods industry; its asset utilization is better than the consumer foods industry, leading to a higher return on total assets.

The bottom part of Figure 19.1 focuses on the capital structure, or financial leverage, employed by the firm. General Mills is using 75.5 percent debt (in book value terms) in its capital structure. Instead of calculating it directly, as we did earlier, return on equity can also be calculated as:

$$\text{return on equity} = \text{return on total assets}\bigg/\left(1 - \frac{\text{total debt}}{\text{total assets}}\right) \qquad (19.19)$$

$$\text{return on equity} = 9.05\%/(1 - 0.755) = 36.9\%$$

Using this approach, we see that return on equity is influenced by (1) net profit margin and total asset turnover, which jointly affect the return on total assets; and (2) the financial leverage employed. In order to *improve* return on equity, a firm has three choices: increase the profit margin, increase total asset turnover, or use more debt. Correspondingly, reductions in the net profit margin, total asset turnover, or using less debt will *lower* the firm's return on equity. In General Mills' case, the higher return on equity compared with the rest of the consumer foods industry is due primarily to its higher use of debt financing, or financial leverage. To a lesser extent, General Mills' higher return on equity is due to its ability to generate more sales from its assets, as evidenced by its higher total asset turnover ratio. The increased risk that General Mills has exposed itself to, in terms of a more aggressive asset management policy and its greater use of debt financing, has directly contributed to its higher return on equity.

Conclusions from the General Mills Analysis

Based on the common-size statements, the ratios, and the du Pont system, we can make the following observations:

1. General Mills' liquidity—in terms of cash and marketable securities—has declined in the last 3 years, and is lower than that of the industry as a whole.
2. Its receivables and inventory are far below the industry average, and have actually decreased in relative size over this 3-year period. By employing less current assets, General Mills has adopted a more aggressive asset management policy than the consumer goods industry.
3. General Mills' long-term and total asset turnovers have decreased in recent years. In comparison to the consumer foods industry, however, General Mills is generating slightly more sales from its total assets.
4. General Mills employs more debt than the consumer foods industry and less equity; they are more aggressive in terms of their use of financial leverage. Although General Mills' debt is higher than that of the industry, its coverage ratios are better than those of the consumer foods industry.
5. Comparing General Mills' net profit margin with that of the industry, we see that it was below the industry average in two of the three years. However, due to using more debt than the industry, its return on equity is higher than that of the industry.
6. Finally, General Mills' *P/E* ratio is higher th,an that of the industry, suggesting that the firm is regarded as having more growth prospects or growth options. At the same time General Mills is paying out a greater percentage of its earnings in the form of cash dividends.

Our analysis suggests that General Mills has a comparable profit margin, but a higher return on equity than the industry. The higher return on equity results from the fact that General Mills has a more aggressive asset management policy, a higher total asset turnover, and uses more debt. General Mills has lower cash, receivables, and inventory than the industry, is generating slightly higher revenue per dollar of assets, and appears very capable of servicing its higher level of debt.

Limitations

■ **LEARNING GOAL 5**

Discuss the limitations of ratio analysis.

Our in-depth analysis of General Mills provided many insights into the firm's financial condition. But any analysis of accounting statements is subject to the following limitations:

1. The basic data arise from the accounting process and are therefore based on *historical costs*. Because one of the main purposes of financial accounting is to match revenues and expenses in the appropriate period, there may be little or no *direct* relationship to the firm's cash flows, especially in the short run.
2. The accounting process allows for alternative treatment of numerous transactions. Thus, two identical firms may report substantially different accounting data by employing alternative GAAP treatments. This may affect both the assets and liabilities of the firm, and also the "quality" of the earnings reported by the firm.

3. "Window dressing" may appear in accounting statements. For example, by taking out a long-term loan before the end of its fiscal year and holding the proceeds as cash, a firm could significantly improve its current and quick ratios. Once the fiscal year has ended, the firm could turn around and pay back the loan—but the transaction has already served its purpose.

4. For the many firms that are multidivisional, sufficient data are generally not reported so that outsiders can examine the performance of the various divisions. Also, it is often difficult to find comparable industry data for multidivisional firms.

5. Inflation can have material effects on the firm that are not fully reflected in accounting statements. This is especially true for inventory and long-term assets, which may be seriously understated when inflation is present. The comparability of data within a firm over time, and also between firms, is therefore limited.

6. For firms with substantial international operations, other reporting problems exist in addition to those faced by domestic firms.

7. Industry averages are generally *not* where the successful firm wants to operate; rather, it wants to be at the top end of the performance ladder. Also, finding an appropriate industry for comparison is often not as simple as it sounds.

In addition to the data contained in accounting statements, many other sources of financial data exist. Some of these are listed in Table 19.6.

With the increasing use of derivatives (such as interest rate or foreign exchange swaps), firms are attempting to limit some of their risk exposure. However, the disclosure of these transactions is uneven from firm to firm, and, as one corporate treasurer stated: "The accounting for this stuff is still underdeveloped, to say the least." In an attempt to meet some of the needs for greater reporting the Financial Accounting Standards Board has issued a draft proposal that would increase the disclosure of derivatives employed by firms.

CONCEPT REVIEW QUESTIONS

- What five key ideas should be considered when conducting an analysis of the balance sheet and income statement?
- On what basis is a common-size income statement prepared? A common-size balance sheet?
- How is a firm's return on equity related to the firm's return on assets? To net profit margin? To total asset turnover?
- Describe some of the problems and limitations of any analysis using accounting statements.

INTERNATIONAL ACCOUNTING ISSUES

■ LEARNING GOAL 6

Discuss international accounting considerations.

When the results of foreign operations must be reported, the financial analysis of firms with international operations presents additional problems beyond those faced within the United States. Under FAS No. 52, U.S.-based firms must use the

TABLE 19.6

Sources of Financial Data

There are a great many sources of financial data. When in doubt about the availability of these or other sources, check with the reference librarian at your library.

Publication	Type of information
Annual reports of companies	Individual company data
Bank and Quotation Record	Prices and yields of securities
Barron's	Securities markets, individual securities, and analysis of individual companies
Business Week	General coverage, current and individual company trends
Cash Flow	General coverage of cash and working capital trends
Commercial and Financial Chronicle	Prices and yields of securities
Dun's Business Month	General coverage, current trends
Dun & Bradstreet's Key Business Ratios	Industry ratios
The Economist	General coverage of international developments
Federal Reserve Bulletin	Aggregate financial data
Forbes	General coverage, analysis of individual companies
Fortune	General coverage, size rankings of firms
Inc.	General coverage, especially of smaller firms
Institutional Investor	General coverage of financing trends and corporate security issues
Leo Troy's Almanac of Business and Industrial Financial Ratios	Industry ratios
Mergers & Acquisitions	General coverage of mergers, foreign involvement, and divestitures
Moody's Bank & Finance, Industrial, OTC Industrial, OTC Unlisted, International, and Transportation Manuals	Individual company data
Robert Morris Associates' *Annual Statement Studies*	Industry ratios
Standard & Poor's Corporation Records	Individual company data
Standard & Poor's Industry Surveys	Industry data
Statistical Bulletin of the Securities and Exchange Commission	Stock market activity and corporate security issues
Survey of Current Business	Aggregate financial data
Value Line Investment Survey	Individual company data
Various trade associations	Industry accounting data
The Wall Street Journal	General coverage, prices, and yields of securities

FUNCTIONAL CURRENCY
From an accounting standpoint, the primary currency in which a foreign subsidiary operates.

functional currency—that is, the primary currency in which a foreign subsidiary operates—as the basis for computing and translating adjustments.[15] All balance sheet items of the subsidiary are translated at the exchange rate prevailing on the final day of the parent's fiscal period. Any resulting gain or loss is reported both as an asset and in a special equity account on the parent's balance sheet.

To see the impact of this procedure, consider an example in which a German subsidiary of a U.S. firm purchases equipment for 100 marks (M) when 1M = $0.50. *If the functional currency is the mark,* the historical cost of the equipment is 100M. If the functional currency of the subsidiary is the U.S. dollar, the historical cost of the equipment is $50. Assume that at a later date the exchange rate is 1M = $0.80. If the functional currency is the mark, the historical cost is still 100M, but the translated amount is now $80. This $80 will be reported on the parent's balance sheet as an asset and in a special equity account recording the foreign currency translation adjustment. *If the dollar is the functional currency,* the historical cost is $50 regardless of any changes in the exchange ratio. Thus, only $50 would be reported on the parent's balance sheet.

From the standpoint of analysis, this reporting guideline affects the parent firm in several ways: (1) the U.S.-based firm's assets and equity change every year, depending on exchange rates; (2) firms facing similar situations may report different results, depending on the functional currency employed; and (3) firms are not required to provide information in the annual report concerning the functional currency employed. These and similar problems make the analysis of accounting statements for a multinational firm even more difficult and challenging than for a firm doing all its business within the United States.

In addition, accounting rules differ around the world. For example, in Germany the accounting standards and practices are such that firms can often hide their true profits from both the public and the taxing authority. This is accomplished because secret reserves can be established, and the value of inventories, pensions, and foreign-exchange transactions, for example, are dealt with in a different manner than required in the United States. To understand the impact of the different accounting standards, consider what occurred when the German manufacturer Daimler Benz applied to have its stock listed on the New York Stock Exchange. As part of the process the firm had to adopt U.S. accounting standards. Although Daimler reported a profit of 600 million marks in Germany, under U.S. accounting standards it reported a loss of 1.7 billion marks. Many German managers agree with the German accounting standards. They fear that greater exposure and less conservative accounting standards will expose them to increased pressure from disgruntled investors and other stakeholders.

For foreign affiliates of U.S. firms, the unit of account may be a foreign currency instead of the U.S. dollar, especially for analyzing local performance.

CONCEPT REVIEW QUESTIONS

■ What does "functional currency" mean? How does it relate to year-to-year impacts on a multinational firm's accounting statements?

Summary

■ It is very important not to become overly enamored with analyzing and/or maximizing accounting numbers. Accounting numbers are only a means to an end; the

---

[15]Statement of Financial Accounting Standard No. 52, *"Foreign Currency Translation,"* FASB, 1981 Stamford, Conn., 1981.

purpose of the firm is to produce and sell quality products or services and make financial decisions that lead to the maximization of the value of the firm.

■ An income statement is presented over a period of time (typically a year), whereas a balance sheet is presented as of an instant in time.

■ Ratios can be grouped into common-type categories; five common groupings are liquidity, asset management, debt management, profitability, and market.

■ Common-size accounting statements and ratios should be analyzed over time and compared to the industry. They should also form the basis for asking further questions about the firm.

■ Limitations of accounting statements include their use of historical cost basis, alternative generally accepted treatments available, window dressing at the end of the year, sometimes incomplete divisional data, lack of inflation adjustment, and difficulties in reflecting the financial consequences of international operations.

■ Additional complications arise in accounting for multinational operations.

Questions

19.1 Accounting statements may be prepared under generally accepted accounting principles, for tax purposes or for internal management purposes. Explain why we focus on those prepared under GAAP, and what the strengths and/or weaknesses of GAAP statements are.

19.2 If preferred stock is outstanding, the numerator of the earnings per share calculation is earnings available to common stockholders (net income − cash dividends on preferred stock), whereas it is simply net income if there is no preferred stock outstanding. Explain why this adjustment is necessary.

19.3 Explain in detail why:
a. Net income does not reflect cash.
b. Retained earnings do not include any cash.

19.4 Anna has been asked to conduct a complete analysis of the ability of Westbrook Enterprises to service its long-term financing obligations. In doing so, she determined that the firm has the following fixed charge obligations over the next few years:

1. Interest of $2 million per year for each of the next 3 years.
2. Sinking fund payments of $1 million per year for each of the next 3 years. (A sinking fund is a required obligation often present when bonds are issued in order to retire some of the bonds before maturity.)
3. Lease payments of $1.5 million per year for each of the next 3 years.
4. Cash dividends on preferred stock of $1 million per year for each of the next 3 years. (The tax rate is 30 percent.)

How would you advise Anna to proceed with the analysis? Should any new ratios be calculated?

19.5 Financial leverage arises from the use of financing sources that require a fixed-cost type of financing. By employing financial leverage, the firm may be able to magnify gains (and losses) to common stockholders. Which one of these situations has the most (least) financial leverage? Why?

	A	B	C	D	E	F
Short-term debt	$ 0	$ 0	$ 0	$ 20	$ 20	$ 0
Long-term debt	0	0	50	0	30	20
Leases	0	0	0	20	0	30
Preferred stock	0	50	0	10	0	0
Common stock	150	100	100	100	100	100

Concept Review Problems

See Appendix A for solutions.

CR19.1 Matthews Clothiers has operating profit, or *EBIT*, of $700,000. Interest expense for the year was $100,000, preferred dividends paid were $50,000, common dividends were $200,000, and taxes were $70,000. The firm has 30,000 shares of common stock outstanding and 10,000 warrants with a conversion privilege of one warrant for one share of stock. The probability of the warrants' conversion is 50 percent; therefore, there is likelihood of 5,000 warrants being converted.

    a. Calculate the simple earnings per share, the primary earnings per share, and the fully diluted earnings per share.

    b. What was the increase in retained earnings?

CR19.2 Buchman Inc. has a current stock price of $20 per share, with 50,000 shares outstanding. The firm recently paid a dividend of $1.00 per share. Use the accounting statements for Buchman to construct a common-size balance sheet and income statement, and then calculate the ratios found in the chapter.

Balance Sheet

Assets	
Cash	$ 70,000
Accounts receivable	200,000
Inventory	250,000
Long-term investments	30,000
Plant and equipment	700,000
Less: Accumulated depreciation	(280,000)
Total assets	$ 970,000

Liabilities and Stockholders' Equity	
Accounts payable	$ 100,000
Notes payable	150,000
Accrued taxes	20,000
Bond payable	300,000
Preferred stock, $50 par value, 8% dividend	50,000
Common stock, $1 par value	50,000
Capital paid in excess of par	100,000
Retained earnings	200,000
Total liabilities and stockholders' equity	$ 970,000

Income Statement

Sales (on credit)	$ 2,000,000
Cost of goods sold	1,500,000
Gross margin	500,000
Selling and administrative expense	200,000*
EBIT	300,000
Interest expense	50,000
EBT	250,000
Taxes	75,000
Net income	$ 175,000

*Includes $10,000 in lease payments

CR19.3   SVS has a net profit margin of 5 percent, total asset turnover of 2.5, and a total debt to total asset ratio of 0.40. What is the firm's return on equity?

CR19.4   The following information concerns two competitors, Johnson and Bartell.

Balance Sheet

Assets	Johnson	Bartell
Cash and marketable securities	$ 72,345	$138,722
Accounts receivable	41,343	73,848
Inventory	193,827	43,024
Net long-term assets	12,290	22,290
Total assets	$319,805	$277,884

Liabilities and Stockholders' Equity		
Short-term bank loans	$ 54,678	$ 20,400
Accounts payable	55,705	22,556
Accruals	35,480	18,776
Current liabilities	145,863	61,732
Long-term debt	22,116	43,555
Common stock	93,076	95,408
Retained earnings	58,750	77,189
Total liabilities and equity	$319,805	$277,884

Income Statement

	Johnson	Bartell
Sales	$701,092	$757,098
Cost of goods sold	564,504	622,020
Gross margin	136,588	135,078
Selling and administrative expense	51,160	61,380
Depreciation	6,376	6,632
Miscellaneous expenses	8,108	14,228
EBIT	70,944	52,838
Interest on short-term debt	5,468	2,040
Interest on long-term debt	2,677	4,016
EBT	62,799	46,782
Taxes	25,119	18,632
Net income	$ 37,680	$ 28,150

Calculate the accounting ratios for both firms.

a. To which firm would you as a credit manager or short-term lender be more likely to approve the extension of short-term trade credit or grant a short-term loan?

b. To which one would you as a banker be more likely to extend long-term credit?

c. In which firm would you as an investor be more likely to buy stock?

Problems

See Appendix C for answers to selected problems.

Preparing Statements

19.1 The COG Company is a diversified manufacturing and retailing firm. From the list of items that follows, prepare its balance sheet and income statement.

Accounts and notes payable	$ 65,377
Accounts receivable	63,836
Accumulated depreciation	69,467
Accrued expenses	81,797
Cash	17,542
Common stock	22,776
Cost of goods sold	875,727
Deferred taxes (long-term)	11,372
Interest expense	14,122
Inventory	156,230
Long-term debt and leases	108,962
Other current assets	13,675
Property, plant, and equipment (gross)	188,900
Retained earnings	?
Sales	1,093,611
Selling, general, and administrative expenses	170,505
Taxes	15,230

Balance Sheet

19.2 Complete the balance sheet, sales, and net income information below, given the following data:

Long-term asset turnover	4.0
Total asset turnover	2.4
Total debt to total assets	0.6
Current ratio	2.0
Quick ratio	1.0
Net profit margin	5.0%
Days sales outstanding (365-day year)	15.208

Cash	$_____	Current liabilities	$_____
Accounts receivable	_____	Long-term debt	_____
Inventory	_____	Common stock	100
Net plant and equipment	600	Retained earnings	_____
Total assets	$_____	Total liabilities and stockholders' equity	$_____
Sales	$_____	Net income	$_____

Current Assets

19.3 Lytel & Associates has the following data:

Long-term asset turnover   = 3.5
Total asset turnover   = 2.0

What percentage of total assets are current assets?

Changes in Current Assets

19.4 Phoebe Industries has a gross profit margin (gross margin/sales) of 25 percent on sales of $500,000 (all credit). Cash and marketable securities are $10,000, accounts receivable are $40,000, inventory is $50,000, and the current ratio is 2.0.

   a. What are Phoebe's days sales outstanding (use a 365-day year), inventory turnover, and quick ratio?

b. How much should inventory be if management wants the inventory turnover to increase to 10 times a year?

c. What would the accounts receivable be if management wants the days sales outstanding to be 21.9 days?

Financial Ratios

19.5 Walker Products is applying for a bank loan. It has given the bank the following data:

Balance Sheet

Cash	$ 40,000	Accounts payable	$ 5,000
Accounts receivable	40,000	Notes payable	20,000
Inventory	70,000	Long-term debt	75,000
Net plant and equipment	225,000	6% preferred stock	25,000
Total assets	$375,000	Common stock ($5 par)	150,000
		Retained earnings	100,000
		Total liabilities and stockholders' equity	$375,000

Sales	$390,000
Net income	$ 61,500
Dividends per share on common stock	$ 0.80
Market price per share of common stock	$ 60

As part of your analysis of the firm's request for a loan, you have decided to calculate the following items: (**1**) the number of shares of common stock outstanding, (**2**) earnings per share of common stock, (**3**) dividend payout, (**4**) return on total assets, (**5**) return on equity, (**6**) current ratio, and (**7**) quick ratio.

a. What are the calculated amounts for the seven items?

b. What can you conclude about the past profitability of Walker Products based on this data? Lacking any other information, would you recommend approving or disapproving the loan request?

Company Analysis

19.6 The following data are taken from the annual report of Khalin Drug Stores. In addition, relevant industry data are provided.

a. Compute the ratios for Khalin corresponding to the industry ratios.

b. What are its strengths (weaknesses) compared to the retail drug industry?

Khalin Drug Stores Balance Sheet as of January 31 (in thousands)

Cash	$ 8,143	Accounts payable	$ 54,449
Receivables	5,596	Notes payable	7,711
Inventory	148,554	Accrued expenses	28,823
Other current	11,608	Deferred income taxes	20,347
Net long-term assets	132,609	Long-term debt and leases	103,662
Total	$306,510	Stockholder's equity	91,518
		Total	$306,510

Khalin Drug Stores Income Statement for Year Ended January 31 (in thousands)

Sales		$761,734
Cost of goods sold		550,930
Gross profit		210,804
Selling, general, and administrative expenses	$156,070	
Depreciation	10,784	166,854

EBIT			43,950
Interest			15,245
EBT			28,705
Taxes			12,056
Net income			$ 16,649

Retail Drug Industry Ratios			
Current	2.00	Total asset turnover	3.20
Quick	0.50	Total debt to total assets	0.43
Days sales outstanding		Times interest earned	3.00
(365-day year)	12 days	Net profit margin	3.33%
Inventory turnover	4.00	Return on total assets	10.60%
Long-term asset		Return on equity	18.40%
turnover	8.00		

Liquidity Analysis

19.7 Rossiter Mills has applied to your firm for credit for future purchases it wants to make. As a first step, you calculated the following information:

	Year −1	Year 0
Current ratio	2.00	2.00
Quick ratio	1.25	1.34
Cash/total assets	10.00%	15.45%
Accounts receivable/total assets	15.00%	15.00%
Inventory/total assets	15.00%	15.00%

a. *Based on just this information,* do you believe credit should be granted to Rossiter Mills? Why or why not?

b. Upon further analysis, you gather the relevant data for the 2 years, which is:

	Year −1	Year 0
Cash	$ 100	$ 170
Accounts receivable	150	165
Inventory	150	165
Total assets	1,000	1,100
Accounts payable	100	200
Notes payable	100	50
Sales	3,000	2,000
Cost of goods sold	1,800	1,500
Credit purchases	1,300	1,200

Note: As given in footnote 10, days purchases outstanding equals accounts payable/(credit purchases/365).

Calculate the following: (**1**) days sales outstanding, (**2**) inventory turnover, and (**3**) days purchases outstanding. Based on this further analysis, what conclusion do you reach now?

Impact on Ratios

19.8 Indicate the impact of the following transactions on the current ratio, total debt to total assets, and return on total assets. Use a plus sign (+) to indicate an increase, a minus sign (−) to indicate a decrease, and a zero (0) to indicate either no effect or an indeterminant effect. Assume that the initial current ratio was greater than 1.0.

	Current Ratio	Total Debt to Total Assets	Return on Assets
a. Cash acquired through a short-term bank loan	_____	_____	_____

b. Accounts receivable
are collected _____ _____ _____
c. Payment made to creditors
for previous purchases _____ _____ _____
d. Cash acquired through issuance
of additional common stock _____ _____ _____
e. Cash dividend declared and paid
(the dividend has not been shown
as an accrual) _____ _____ _____

**Ratios and the
du Pont System**

19.9 The following are the balance sheet and income statement for Scallia Equipment:

Balance Sheet

Cash and marketable			
securities	$ 100,000	Accounts payable	$ 50,000
Accounts receivable	650,000	Notes payable	350,000
Inventory	1,050,000	Long-term debt	2,000,000
Property, plant, and		Common stock	1,000,000
equipment	6,000,000	Retained earnings	2,400,000
Less: Accumulated		Total liabilities	
depreciation	(2,000,000)	and stockholders'	
Total assets	$ 5,800,000	equity	$5,800,000

Income Statement

Sales	$16,000,000
Cost of goods sold	10,000,000
Gross margin	6,000,000
Other expenses	3,000,000
EBIT	3,000,000
Interest	300,000
EBT	2,700,000
Income taxes	1,080,000
Net income	$ 1,620,000

a. Calculate the following ratios: (**1**) current, (**2**) quick, (**3**) total debt to total assets, (**4**) net profit margin, and (**5**) total asset turnover.
b. Using the du Pont formula, calculate return on equity.
c. Now suppose that Scallia Equipment has decided to reduce its risk of running out of cash. To accomplish this, it will issue $1,000,000 in long-term debt and add the same amount to its cash and marketable securities account. This debt will be financed at a 10 percent yearly rate. What is the impact of this transaction on the ratios calculated in (a) and (b) above?

**Impact on
Return on Equity**

19.10 The following data apply to Downs Components:

Sales	$1,000,000
Cost of goods sold	800,000
Net income	50,000
Total debt	250,000
Preferred stock	100,000
Common stock	100,000
Retained earnings	50,000

Days sales outstanding (365-day year)	36.5 days
Inventory turnover	5

a. Determine (1) total asset turnover, (2) net profit margin, (3) return on total assets, and (4) return on equity.

b. If sales and cost of goods sold are constant and all the following events occur *simultaneously,* what are the new net income, total debt, and return on equity?

1. Inventory turnover increases to 10.
2. Days sales outstanding decreases to 18.25 days.
3. Return on assets increases to 15 percent.
4. There are no changes in long-term assets; any reduction in assets causes an equal dollar-for-dollar reduction in the firm's debt.

Market Data

19.11 An abbreviated balance sheet is shown below:

Total assets	$800
Current liabilities	$ 50
Long-term debt	150
Common stock ($1 par)	100
Retained earnings	500
Total liabilities and stockholders' equity	$800

a. If return on equity equals 10 percent, find net income and return on total assets.
b. What is the firm's earnings per share?
c. If it pays out one-quarter of its current earnings as cash dividends, what are the dividends per share?
d. If the market price of the firm's common stock is $9 per share, what is the price/earnings ratio and the dividend yield?

Investment and Financing Effects

19.12 Prewitt Industries has the following balance sheet and income statement:

Balance Sheet			
Total assets	$2,500,000	Total debt	$1,000,000
		Stockholders' equity	1,500,000
		Total liabilities and stockholders' equity	$2,500,000

Income Statement	
Sales	$5,000,000
Cost of goods sold	3,500,000
Gross margin	1,500,000
Operating expenses	900,000
EBIT	600,000
Interest	100,000
EBT	500,000
Income taxes (35%)	175,000
Net income	$ 325,000

a. If Prewitt has 50,000 shares of common stock outstanding, determine its present (1) total debt to total assets, (2) return on total assets, (3) return on equity, and (4) earnings per share.

b. Prewitt Industries is considering whether to renovate one of its existing plants by making an additional $1 million investment in total assets. The renovation will reduce the cost of goods sold by $300,000 per year, whichever plan is adopted. Two possible plans have been considered for financing the renovation. Plan I keeps the existing ratio of total debt to total assets, requires 20,000 additional shares of common stock to be issued, and the new level of *total* interest paid is $150,000 per year. Plan II employs all debt financing, no common stock is issued, and the new level of *total* interest is $225,000 per year.

(1) Determine total debt to total assets, return on total assets, return on equity, and earnings per share under plans I and II.

(2) Based on your analysis, do you think Prewitt should renovate the plant? If yes, should plan I or plan II be used?

Currency Translation and ROE

19.13 Hochmer Motors is based in the United States and has one plant in France. The firm has net income of $500, U.S. assets of $4,000, and U.S. equity of $1,000. The French subsidiary just started this year and bought equipment worth 10,000 francs when the exchange rate was 1 franc = $0.15. Thus, the cost of the purchase in U.S. dollars was $1,500 [i.e., (10,000)($0.15)]. At the end of the firm's fiscal year, the rate of exchange was 1 franc = $0.30. In reporting the results of its operations, Hochmer must report the subsidiary's assets along with its U.S. assets. These results appear both as assets and as a part of the firm's equity.

a. If the functional currency of the subsidiary is the dollar, what are Hochmer's total assets and its stockholders' equity? Its return on equity?

b. If the functional currency is the franc, what are Hochmer's total assets and its stockholders' equity? Its return on equity?

c. What will happen next year if the functional currency is the franc and everything remains the same except that the exchange rate changes?

Analyzing Accounting Statements

19.14 **Mini Case** Accounting information for Corning Inc. for 3 recent years is as follows:

Income Statement (in millions)

	For Fiscal Year		
	−2	−1	0
Sales	$2,301.5	$2,575.9	$3,049.6
Cost of goods sold	1,405.2	1,600.9	1,925.7
Selling, general, and administrative expenses	438.6	491.8	581.8
Research and development	95.2	109.6	124.5
Other expense (−) or income (+)	−7.6	+48.8	+64.5
Interest	41.0	44.5	54.0
Taxes	103.2	116.9	136.1
Net income	$ 210.7	$ 261.0	$ 292.0

Balance Sheet (in millions)

Assets	−2	−1	0
Current assets			
Cash and marketable securities	$ 156.5	$ 352.8	$ 133.0
Accounts receivable	397.5	452.4	527.2
Inventory	254.0	238.5	314.5
Other	121.8	125.6	123.2
Total current assets	929.8	1,169.3	1,097.9

Long-term assets			
Net property, plant, and equipment	991.5	1,160.6	1,351.8
Investment	818.3	826.0	804.5
Other	158.3	204.8	257.8
Total long-term assets	1,968.1	2,191.4	2,414.1
Total assets	$2,897.9	$3,360.7	$3,512.0

Liabilities and Stockholders' Equity

Current liabilities			
Accounts payable	$ 125.1	$ 158.6	$ 191.5
Short-term debt	18.5	40.4	52.8
Other	365.1	483.0	395.2
Total current liabilities	508.7	682.0	639.5
Long-term liabilities			
Long-term debt	499.0	624.5	611.2
Deferred taxes	71.0	53.1	72.8
Other	258.5	258.3	307.5
Total long-term liabilities	828.5	935.9	991.5
Stockholders' equity			
Convertible preferred stock	0	31.6	30.7
Common stock	233.8	255.5	139.6
Retained earnings	1,275.5	1,436.4	1,640.6
Currency translation adjustment	51.4	19.3	70.1
Total stockholders' equity	1,560.7	1,742.8	1,881.0
Total liabilities and stockholders' equity	$2,897.9	$3,360.7	$3,512.0
Other information:			
Shares of common stock (in millions)	88.86	94.22	91.85
Dividends paid on common stock (in millions)	86.0	99.7	85.3
Common stock price range	34⅞– 22½	49⅜– 32	51¾– 34⅞

Note: In (c), because lease expenses are not available, do not calculate fixed charges coverage. Also, for the market ratios, take an average of the high and low stock prices for the per share market price.

a. Accounting statements are prepared based on a set of generally accepted accounting principles, GAAP. What are some of the key ideas underlying GAAP that influence all accounting statements? What is the significance of these assumptions for an analyst examining a firm's accounting statements?

b. Prepare common-size income statements and balance sheets for Corning for the last 3 years.

c. Now calculate ratios for the firm.

d. What trends are evident from the analysis?

e. What additional information would be helpful in completing the analysis?

f. What limitations exist with any analysis of this type?

Financial Planning and Forecasting

Sections in this chapter:

■ **Cash Flow Analysis**
Cash is "the thing."

■ **Forecasting in Practice**
When things don't go as planned—taking variations into account.

■ **Pro Forma Accounting Statements**
A sample preparation of pro formas.

■ **Financial and Strategic Planning**
Tying short-term to long-term planning.

From the moment Walt Disney Co. began planning Euro Disneyland in the mid-1980s, doubters predicted a blase Europe would wipe the smile off Mickey Mouse's face. But Disney went right ahead; more than $4 billion ended up being spent on the theme park near Paris. Since its opening, Euro Disneyland has been plagued with problems—notably, high prices, lack of occupancy at the hotels around the park, and a startling lack of understanding of the customers the park would be serving. The result has been one financial setback after another. Now lenders are stretching out payments on the park's $3.4 billion debt, and Walt Disney Co.—which owns 49 percent of the park—is giving up its returns (which are partially in the form of licensing fees) for the time being. Though profits may rise in 1996, some predict that trouble will return after that, when interest payments and license payments kick in again.

Prediction of the future is never easy. Yet some firms do much better than others. In recent years a number of firms—such as Rockwell International, Deere, Chrysler, Hewlett-Packard, and Texas Instruments—have engineered turnarounds in their fortunes. Often this was accomplished by boosting productivity, changing operations, investing in plant and equipment, finding new markets, and focusing on strengths. By having a strategy, and being willing to undergo change, these companies have seen their market values increase dramatically. Market value is not only an indication of how well a firm is doing at any point in time, but also the ultimate arbiter of what the company is worth. It is a sensitive, impartial gauge of the firm's present value and future prospects.

Recently, a newspaper article noted that security analysts are now keeping a close eye on cash flows when advising investors. "Cash flows give a clear picture of company health," analysts say, and "get around some of the slick accounting that distorts earnings." In this chapter we show how both cash flows and accounting-based statements are used to plan for the future. Strategy and planning for the future are crucial elements of sound financial management that will lead to increases, not decreases, in the value of the firm.

LEARNING GOALS

After studying this chapter you should be able to:

1. Explain what the statement of cash flows shows, and discuss its pros and cons.
2. Discuss the six steps used to develop the cash budget.
3. Explain how scenario analysis is used in financial forecasting, and discuss how seasonal patterns and inflation affect sales forecasts.
4. Explain how pro forma statements are developed, including use of the percentage of sales method.
5. Explain the relationship between short- and long-term financial planning.

CASH FLOW ANALYSIS

Although accounting statements, as examined in Chapter 19, are prepared at least yearly for all firms, they don't directly tell us about the firm's past or expected cash flows, or about what actions should be taken to maximize the market value of the firm. Figure 20.1 shows that a firm's cash inflows arise from its operations (sales and collection of receivables), its investments in securities or subsidiaries, and its financing through bonds and stock or taking out loans. The firm's outflows, also shown in Figure 20.1, go to its operations (materials, wages and salaries, rent, taxes, and so forth), to its working capital and long-term investment needs, and to its financing needs through the payment of interest and dividends, and the repayment of loans and bonds.

Statement of Cash Flows

■ LEARNING GOAL 1

Explain what the statement of cash flows shows, and discuss its pros and cons.

STATEMENT OF CASH FLOWS
Accounting statement that reports the flow of cash into and out of the firm in terms of operating, investing, and financing activities.

In recognition of the importance of cash flows, the Financial Accounting Standards Board now requires that a **statement of cash flows** be reported along with a firm's balance sheet and income statement.[1] The cash flow statement replaces the former statement of changes in financial position. The statement of cash flows for General Mills is shown in Table 20.1(p. 591). Note two items: (1) the statement is broken into three basic categories—*operating* activities, *investing* activities, and *financing* activities; and (2) due to how most firms present their statement of cash flows, the specific accounts shown in Table 20.1 do not directly correspond to the inflows and outflows shown in Figure 20.1. We see that General Mills generated $831 million in cash from operations in 1994, used $783 million for investing activities, and used $148 million for financing activities. The net result was a $100 million decrease in the cash and marketable securities account.

---

[1] Statement of Financial Accounting Standards No. 95, *"Statement of Cash Flows" (Stamford, Conn.: FASB, 1987).*

FIGURE 20.1

Sources of Cash Inflows and Outflows

Inflows will not equal outflows over any period of time except by chance. The excess of inflows (outflows) over outflows (inflows) results in an increase (decrease) in the firm's cash account.

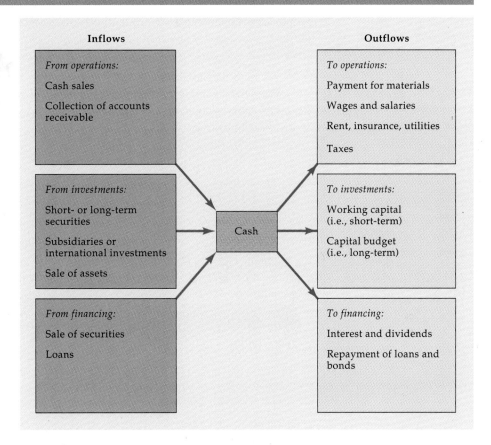

Advantages of the Statement of Cash Flows

The statement of cash flows is helpful for the following reasons:

1. The specific focus on the three separate activities of operations, investments, and financing is beneficial. This is especially so given that these are the three main functions of all firms.
2. The statement removes the effect of accruals, and it restates such items as collectibles or salaries to a cash basis.
3. The statement breaks out gross, as opposed to net, figures for such items as long-term debt transactions. This provides an analyst with an idea of the total long-term financing obtained, and what long-term financing was paid off.

Disadvantages of the Statement of Cash Flows

However, the statement does not fully convert all items to cash flows, and it introduces some additional confusion in other areas. The statement's main problems are:

1. The operating activities part of the statement of cash flows can be presented in one of two ways—the direct approach, or the indirect approach. Under the direct approach the operating activities portion of the statement might be presented as:

Operating activities

Collections from customers	$ 600,000
Payments to suppliers	(300,000)
Payments to employees for salaries	(180,000)
Payments to creditors for interest	(15,000)
Miscellaneous payments	(10,000)
Payments for taxes	(20,000)
Net cash flow provided by operating activities	$ 75,000

   The indirect approach starts from the firm's net income and then makes adjustments as needed. Comparing the direct approach (above) for determining the cash flow from operating activities with the indirect approach used by General Mills and shown in Table 20.1, we see that the direct approach provides much more useful information in terms of determining the source and use of cash from operations. Although *FAS No. 95* strongly recommends the direct method, most firms have adopted the indirect method. This choice reduces the usability of the statement of cash flows.

2. The statement of cash flows does not reconcile the differences between taxes as reported on the firm's income statement with what was actually paid. In the supplemental information for General Mills, the taxes actually paid in 1994 are recorded as $311 million. Comparing this amount with the firm's income statement (Table 19.1), we see the following figures (in millions) for taxes paid:

	1992	1993	1994
Per income statement	$332	$297	$284
Per supplemental data to cash flow statement	326	268	311

   For General Mills the taxes actually paid over these 3 years of $326 + $268 + $311 = $905 were almost the same as the taxes reported per the income statement of $332 + $297 + $284 = $913 million. For some firms the differences between the actual outflow for taxes and what is reported on the income statement may be substantial. This difference is primarily due to the differences in depreciation required by the Internal Revenue Service and the depreciation employed by firms under generally accepted accounting principles. Because our concern is the actual inflow and outflow of cash, the statement of cash flows would be more accurate and more helpful if it reported the actual cash outflow for taxes.

3. The statement permits but does not require separate disclosure of the cash flows associated with discontinued operations and extraordinary items. These cash flows may be substantial, and they are sometimes large enough to warrant consideration in terms of their cash flow consequences.

4. Non-cash investing and financing activities (such as capital leases, debt/equity swaps, and asset exchanges) are not included on the statement. They are simply reported in a supplemental statement or in narrative form. Again, since our concern in finance is the present and future inflow and outflow of cash, by omitting these items the statement fails to provide a complete picture of the flow of cash through the firm.

TABLE 20.1

Statement of Cash Flows for General Mills (in millions)

General Mills uses the indirect approach for estimating cash flows from operating activities. Many other firms also use this approach, even though the direct approach provides more useful cash flow information.

	For the Year		
	1992	1993	1994
Operating Activities			
Net income	$ 496	$ 506	$470
Deferred taxes	14	41	(28)
Depreciation and amortization	247	274	304
Nonrecurring items			
Change in cash from:			
Working capital	57	3	(72)
Other assets and liabilities	(42)	36	157
Net cash provided by operating activities	772	860	831
Investing Activities			
Capital expenditures	(695)	(624)	(560)
Proceeds from disposal of land, buildings, and equipment	8	5	7
Other investments (dispositions)	39	(165)	(230)
Net cash used by investing activities	(648)	(784)	(783)
Financing Activities			
Increase (decrease) in short-term debt	150	208	93
Issuance of long-term debt	189	423	274
Payment of long-term debt	(248)	(45)	(79)
Common stock issued (retired)	39	32	13
Purchases of common stock for treasury	(40)	(420)	(146)
Dividends paid	(245)	(275)	(299)
Other	(8)	(7)	(4)
Net cash provided (used) by financing activities	(163)	(84)	148
Reclassification of marketable security	—	108	—
Net increase (decrease) in cash and short-term investments	$ (39)	$ 100	$(100)

5. Interest or dividends received by the firm, as well as interest paid, are treated as operating activities; however, dividends paid by the firm are treated as a financing activity. This inconsistency in treatment is, at best, misleading.

The statement of cash flows is a step in the right direction. Even ignoring some of its deficiencies, however, it has one other disadvantage—it simply reports what has happened in the past. Although firms can simply react to whatever cash flows occur, most plan for the future by estimating inflows and outflows. To do this, firms use cash budgets and pro forma statements.

FINANCIAL MANAGEMENT TODAY

It's Just a Simulation Away!

Michael Parides, director of Compaq Computer Corporation's Desktop Division, got the firm to "bet the ship" on his new computer simulation models, and the results were spectacular: By holding off on producing more machines with the new Pentium chip and, instead, stocking up on 486-chip machines, the firm saw its fourth-quarter earnings increase by 61 percent.

Essentially a gigantic spreadsheet, the simulation developed by Compaq is far more detailed than most other simulations. As a result, it can simulate changes in the price of components, fluctuating demand for certain features or prices of computers, and the impact of the introduction of new models by rivals. Also, by modeling supplier and competitor behavior, the simulation allows managers to consider the risk of taking actions before they are actually taken.

The simulation is the main part of the new business strategy adopted by Compaq. It starts with customers in focus groups that allow Compaq to gauge consumer interest in and price sensitivity

to new computer features. The dealers are pooled on inventory levels and available cash, to gauge the timing of new-model introductions. Then comes logistics, where key purchases and production processes are acquired only after development hurdles are met. Finally, the system tracks production and develops alternative plans in the event forecasts are wrong.

Being wrong in the computer industry can have grave consequences. A model that is late, lacks the right features, or has the wrong price, quickly becomes slow-moving inventory or yields a pile of unusable components. In 1994, for example, IBM misjudged the computer market and saw its PC sales plunge 6 percent, for a $1 billion loss. And, before the use of the new simulation at Compaq, they too misjudged the market and lost at least $50 million in sales. The true test will be in the future, as Compaq uses and refines the models, in the ever-increasing effort to time the introduction of new models and price them competitively.

Cash Budgets

■ LEARNING GOAL 2

Discuss the six steps used to develop the cash budget.

CASH BUDGET
A detailed forecast of all expected cash inflows and outflows by the firm for some period of time.

Remember Key Idea 4— firms focus on cash flows and their incremental effects.

In order to plan for the future—instead of simply reporting the past inflow and outflow of cash via the statement of cash flows—firms forecast their expected cash flows. An important part of this forecasting process is the development of the firm's **cash budget,** which is simply a detailed statement of the firm's expected inflows and outflows. Cash budgets can be estimated for any period of time—often a month, a quarter, or a year. These budgets serve two purposes: First, they alert the firm to future cash needs or surpluses. Second, they provide a standard against which subsequent performance can be judged.

In preparing a cash budget, it is necessary to include all inflows and outflows expected by the firm. To do this, a detailed analysis of past cash flows is needed. *Although the future cannot be expected to be exactly like the past, a thorough examination of past cash flow trends is the first step in effective cash flow forecasting by means of cash budgets.*

The major items to be considered when estimating a cash budget are the following:

Cash Inflows	Cash Outflows
Cash sales	Cash purchases
Collection of accounts receivable	Payment of accounts payable
Income from investments	Wages and salaries
Income from subsidiaries	Rent, insurance, and utilities
Dividends from international ventures	Advertising, selling, and other related expenses
Sale of assets	Taxes (local, state, federal, and international)
Sale of securities	Capital investments
Loans	Interest and dividends
	Repayment of loans

A six-step procedure can be used to develop a cash budget:

1. Develop a scenario with an explicit set of assumptions.
2. Estimate sales.
3. Determine the cash inflows expected from operations.
4. Calculate the cash outflows expected to arise from operations.
5. Estimate any other expected cash inflows and outflows.
6. Determine the expected financing needed or surplus available.

The cash budget tells a manager if and when the firm will need to borrow money, how much to borrow, for how long, and when the loan can be repaid.

The steps necessary for developing a firm's cash budget are discussed in the next section.

Developing Different Scenarios

The first step in developing a cash budget is to determine the assumed conditions, or the scenario the cash budget is to cover. Because we are dealing with the future, which is uncertain, this is an important step. Assumptions concerning the state of the economy, competitor actions, conditions in the financial markets, and similar factors need to be spelled out in detail to set the stage for the rest of the analysis. Then the firm specifies various other sets of assumptions and reworks the analysis to see the impact of those assumptions on the firm's cash flow position. This process is called *scenario analysis*. Its purpose is to see how sensitive cash flows are to changes in the input data (or assumptions).

It is far better to allow for a range of outcomes rather than to rely on a single estimate. A firm that develops only a single estimate is likely to be caught short if there is a large deviation from the expected outcome. Likewise, managers can determine which estimates have the most impact on the firm's expected cash flows; then they can spend more time and money, if necessary, trying to improve these estimates. Finally, the longer the planning period, the more important the analysis of a number of sets of assumptions becomes. By doing these analyses, managers can gain an understanding of the possible consequences different events could have on the firm's cash inflows and outflows.

Forecasting Sales

The key element in developing an accurate cash budget is the *sales forecast*, which provides the basis for determining the size and timing of many of the forecasted cash inflows and outflows. The sales forecast can be based on an internal or an external analysis. The following are some forecasting techniques and their strengths and weaknesses:

Method	Time Period (Short, Medium, Long)	Accuracy	Reflects Changing Conditions
Internal			
Linear regression	S, M	Depends	No
Sales force composite	S, M	Depends	Yes
Time series	S, M, L	Often highly accurate	Yes, but often slow
External			
Market survey	M, L	Depends	Yes
Multivariate regression	S, M, L	Depends	Yes, if built in

Three popular *internal forecasting methods* are linear regression, sales force composite, and time series analysis. *Linear regression* takes past sales and projects them into the future without any adjustment. The *sales force composite method* bases expected sales on estimates provided by sales personnel and the firm's marketing department. Consistency of forecasts is a major concern when the sales force composite method is employed. The reason for concern about consistency is that the firm's sales forecast might be the sum of separate forecasts made by managers of many of the firm's units. Left to their own, these managers will make different assumptions about inflation, growth in the economy, growth in market share, and so forth. Therefore, some method of maintaining consistent assumptions is crucial for the accuracy of the sales force composite method. Finally, *time series analysis* models are available for forecasting expected sales based on past sales. These methods require more statistical expertise, but they are often best for generating accurate forecasts based on past data.

An *external sales forecast*, on the other hand, starts with factors outside the firm. This could be done by contracting with a firm to do a marketing research study or contacting firms like Data Resources or Chase Econometrics that specialize in preparing macroeconomic and industry forecasts. A statistical model that relates the firm's past sales to the projected level of gross national product, automobile sales, or whatever is most relevant might also be developed.

Most firms use a variety of methods for forecasting sales. Whatever method is used, firms often start the forecast on a divisional basis in order to obtain better accuracy. Once the divisional forecasts are made, they are combined into an overall forecast of expected sales. One common and simple approach is to begin by employing past data to forecast the future sales.

Linear Regression and Forecasting

Assume that in order to forecast sales we use linear regression plus information obtained from a sales force composite approach. Bartley Instruments, a robot components firm, begins with an analysis of its past sales (see Figure 20.2). Simple linear regression techniques can be used to forecast sales naively, simply by extrapolating the past trend in sales. Sales is the dependent variable (indicated by Y), and time is the independent variable (designated by X). The regression model to be estimated, ignoring the residual error term, is:

$$Y_t = \alpha + \beta X_t \tag{20.1}$$

where

Y_t = the forecasted sales in time period t

α = alpha, the intercept of the fitted regression equation

β = beta, the slope of the fitted regression equation

X_t = the time period

This method is easy to employ. Let's use the data from Figure 20.2 and forecast Bartley's 19X9 sales. The historical sales are as follows:

Year	Sales, Y_t (in millions)	Period, X_t
19X3	$2.10	1
19X4	1.85	2
19X5	3.00	3
19X6	2.90	4
19X7	4.05	5
19X8	4.15	6

The time periods are converted to 1 for the first year through 6 for 19X8. The exact procedure, the formulas employed, and the calculations are shown in Table 20.2. Based on this, the estimated regression equation is

$$Y_t = \$1.332 + \$0.479X_t$$

Because we want to forecast sales for 19X9, which is period 7, we substitute as follows:

$$19X9 \text{ forecasted sales} = \$1.332 + \$0.479(7)$$

$$= \$1.332 + \$3.353 = \$4.685 \text{ million}$$

If we wanted to forecast the subsequent year's sales, the same procedure would be employed, except the time period would be 8, resulting in forecasted sales of $5.164 million.

This approach is simple and inexpensive to implement. For a firm (or divisions of a firm) in a stable environment, it may provide a reasonable degree of accuracy. Because it ignores any factor *not* captured by a simple linear extrapolation of past sales, however, it can be misleading. Thus, influences caused by how the sales of the firm respond to changes in the business cycle are ignored. This is why other forecasting techniques and management expertise are needed when forecasting sales.

FIGURE 20.2

Projected Sales for Bartley Instruments

Bartley has experienced slow but reasonably steady growth since 19X4. The 19X9 projection assumes an "average" rate of growth—slightly higher than last year, but lower than the year before that.

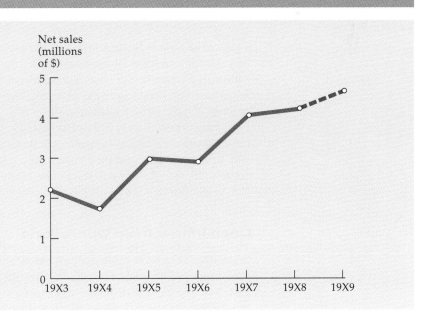

TABLE 20.2

Estimated Regression Equation to Forecast Sales of Bartley Instruments

Linear regression provides a simple means of projecting sales; however, because it is based solely on past sales, it ignores any other factors (such as the state of the economy) that may influence actual sales.

	Sales, Y_t	Period, X_t	Y_tX_t	X_t^2
	2.10	1	2.10	1
	1.85	2	3.70	4
	3.00	3	9.00	9
	2.90	4	11.60	16
	4.05	5	20.25	25
	4.15	6	24.90	36
Totals	18.05	21	71.55	91

Means

$\bar{Y} = \Sigma Y_t/n = 18.05/6 = 3.008$
$\bar{X} = \Sigma X_t/n = 21/6 = 3.50$

Calculation of β (slope)

$$\beta = \frac{\Sigma Y_tX_t - (n)(\bar{Y})(\bar{X})}{\Sigma X_t^2 - n(\bar{X}^2)}$$

$$= \frac{71.550 - (6)(3.008)(3.50)}{91 - (6)(3.50^2)} = \frac{71.550 - 63.168}{91 - 73.500} = 0.479$$

Calculation of α (intercept)

$\alpha = \bar{Y} - \beta\bar{X} = 3.008 - (0.479)(3.50) = 1.332$

Based on simple linear regression, Bartley's 19X9 estimated sales are $4.685 million. This information is supplemented by the sales force composite forecast, along with what Bartley knows about the actions of the competition and the estimated performance of the economy in the next year. Based on this analysis, Bartley arrives at an estimate of sales of $4.5 million.

Bartley is interested in both the expected level and the potential variability of sales. If the expected variability is small, then Bartley will have more confidence in its forecast. In that event, its operating plans can be relatively simple. If the sales forecasts are not so solid, then Bartley will want to build a lot of flexibility into its plans and should plan to monitor trends closely.

Cash Inflow from Operations

Once sales have been estimated, we can determine expected cash inflows. Because most firms sell on credit (at least in part), the pattern of collections must be examined. First, Bartley "distributes" its estimated sales over the months of the year. This may be done by using a historical percentage of the sales that occur each month. For example, assume that February has historically accounted for 4.4 percent of total yearly sales. The estimated February sales are then (0.044)($4.5 million) ≈ $200,000. The estimated monthly sales for February through August are shown in Table 20.3.

Bartley knows that 30 percent of its sales are cash sales, and the remaining are credit sales. The collection of sales made on credit is estimated to occur as follows: 42 percent of total sales are credit sales that will be collected in the month following the sale; the remaining 28 percent are credit sales that will be collected 2 months after the sales are made. For simplicity, we assume that there are no bad debts. In April, Bartley's sales are $430,000, of which $129,000 are for cash. In addition, Bartley expects to collect 28 percent of the sales made 2 months ago ($56,000), and 42 percent of last month's sales, for another $126,000. The operating cash inflows are estimated to be $311,000, which is substantially less than April's expected sales of $430,000. This difference is due to the delayed receipt of cash because of credit sales.

Cash Outflow from Operations

Next comes the forecast of expected cash outflows from operations. This begins with an estimate of the materials and related supplies needed in the production process. For Bartley, this figure is estimated to be 40 percent of expected sales, with the purchases made 2 months ahead of the anticipated sale. Of these purchases, Bartley pays cash for 20 percent, and the other 80 percent becomes an account payable. Bartley has a policy of paying all accounts payable in the month after they arise. In April, Bartley has total purchases of $176,000 [i.e., (0.40)(June's expected sales of $440,000)], of which $35,200 are for cash (see Table 20.4). In addition, $160,000 in accounts payable from the preceding month must be paid.

Bartley also has other cash outflows related to operations. For simplicity, these can be broken into three categories. The first is wages, rent, selling, and other cash outflows. The other two are interest and taxes. The reason for breaking out the last two separately is that they may vary from month to month. Income taxes are payable on

---

TABLE 20.3

Estimated Cash Inflows from Operations for Bartley Instruments (in thousands)

With a lag in the collection of accounts receivable, the cash inflow from sales ends up being less volatile than the sales pattern.

	February	March	April	May	June	July	August
1. Total sales	$200.00	$300.00	$430.00	$500.00	$440.00	$400.00	$300.00
2. Collections—1-month lag (42% of total sales)			84.00	126.00	180.60	210.00	184.80	168.00
3. Collections—2-month lag (28% of total sales)			56.00	84.00	120.40	140.00	123.20
4. Total collections (row 2 + row 3)			182.00	264.60	330.40	324.80	291.20
5. Cash sales (30% of total sales)			129.00	150.00	132.00	120.00	90.00
6. Total operating cash inflows			$311.00	$414.60	$462.40	$444.80	$381.20

Estimated Cash Outflows from Operations for Bartley Instruments (in thousands)

Many different classifications of cash outflows from operations can be employed. Which specific ones are most appropriate depends on the firm making the cash forecast.

	March	April	May	June	July	August
1. Total purchases(40% of expected sales; purchased 2 months ahead)	$200.00	$176.00	$160.00	$120.00	$100.00	$ 80.00
2. Credit purchases(80% of total purchases)	160.00	140.80	128.00	96.00	80.00	64.00
3. Payment of credit purchases (1-month lag)		160.00	140.80	128.00	96.00	80.00
4. Cash purchases (20% of current month's total purchases)		35.20	32.00	24.00	20.00	16.00
5. Wages, rent, selling, and other cash expenses*		146.30	186.00	188.80	168.00	145.50
6. Interest*		8.00	32.00	8.00	8.00	32.00
7. Taxes*		40.00	5.00	30.00	5.00	5.00
8. Total operating cash outflow (row 3 + row 4 + row 5 + row 6 + row 7)		$389.50	$395.80	$378.80	$297.00	$278.50

* As estimated by the firm based on past and expected trends.

the 15th of April, June, September, and December, whereas payroll and other taxes are payable monthly. Total expected cash outflows related to operations are $389,500 in April.

Other Cash Inflows or Outflows

Once all cash flows from operations are determined, we can turn our attention to other possible inflows or outflows. Bartley has two other expected inflows and three other expected outflows. The inflows are from the sale of assets and cash dividends received from a small foreign subsidiary. The outflows arise from the payment of cash dividends, repayment of a loan, and from capital investments. After all these other inflows and outflows are estimated, they are netted to produce the following monthly figures (in thousands):

	April	May	June	July	August
Net other inflow (+) or outflow (−)	−$45.00	−$98.00	−$55.00	−$95.00	$52.00

The Cash Budget

Once we know all anticipated cash inflows and outflows, we can determine the expected net cash inflow or outflow each month to see if additional financing will be needed. As shown in the top part of Table 20.5, Bartley is projecting that total cash outflows will exceed total cash inflows by $123,500 in April. The bottom part of the table shows that Bartley has $70,000 cash on hand on April 1 and a minimum cash balance of $20,000 that it needs to maintain. This results in an estimated final cash position of −$73,500 at the end of April.

In Table 20.5, we see that Bartley has a negative cumulative expected cash position for the months of April, May, June, and July. In August the expected cash position is positive. The worst month is May, when the cash position is estimated to be −$152,700. Obviously, Bartley must do something—cut production, reduce other expenses, increase collections, or secure short- or long-term financing—to cover the expected shortfall.

Armed with the information obtained from the cash budget, Bartley can plan for the future. If borrowing is planned, the lender can be notified and appropriate plans made. When excess cash is available, its investment can be planned. But the basis for borrowing or investment decisions is the firm's expected cash position as estimated by its cash budget.

CONCEPT REVIEW QUESTIONS

■ Explain why the statement of cash flows is broken down into three basic categories.
■ Discuss the procedures used to develop a firm's cash budget.
■ Describe and explain different methods a firm may employ to forecast sales.

FORECASTING IN PRACTICE

■ LEARNING GOAL 3

Explain how scenario analysis is used in financial forecasting, and discuss how seasonal patterns and inflation affect sales forecasts.

Scenario Analysis

Although forecasting techniques can be implemented by hand, most firms, large and small, are turning to computerized approaches, often employing spreadsheets like Lotus 1–2–3™ or Excel. The forecasting process, whether computerized or not, might involve the firm, and its divisions, preparing three different forecasts, or scenarios—a *best case*, a *most likely (normal) case*, and a *worst case*. Assuming that the forecast and cash budget for Bartley Instruments that we developed in the last two sections was for the normal case, we now need to develop best-case and worst-case scenarios.

In forecasting the best-case scenario, we need to be aware of the problems caused by high growth. As firms grow, their sales increase. Because most firms sell on credit, at least in part, the firm will need to finance a larger amount of accounts receivable. Likewise, larger inventory levels will be necessary. As growth continues, the firm will need to expand its plant and facilities, requiring additional investment in long-term assets. The funding for some of these increased needs can be provided by increased accounts payable, which will also grow with the firm. The rest, however, has to come

Table 20.5

Net Cash Flow and Financing Needed or Surplus Available for Bartley Instruments (in thousands)

Note that row 1 in the bottom part of the table, cash and marketable securities at the start of period, is carried over as the previous month's end-of-period cash figure from row 3.

	April	May	June	July	August
Calculating Net Cash Inflow or Outflow					
1. Total operating cash inflow	$311.00	$414.60	$462.40	$444.80	$381.20
2. Total operating cash outflow	−389.50	−395.80	−378.80	−297.00	−278.50
3. Other net inflow (+) or outflow (−)	−45.00	−98.00	−55.00	−95.00	+52.00
4. Net cash inflow (+) or outflow (−) (row 1 + row 2 + row 3)	−$123.50	−$79.20	$28.60	$52.80	$154.70
Calculating Short-Term Financing Needed					
1. Cash and marketable securities at start of period	$ 70.00	−$53.50	−$132.70	−$104.10	−$51.30
2. Change in cash balance (net cash inflow or outflow)	−123.50	−79.20	28.60	52.80	154.70
3. Cash at end of period (row 1 + row 2)	−53.50	−132.70	−104.10	−51.30	103.40
4. Minimum cash balance required	−20.00	−20.00	−20.00	−20.00	−20.00
5. Cumulative short-term financing needed (−) or surplus (+) (row 3 + row 4)	−$ 73.50	−152.70	−$124.10	−$71.30	$ 83.40

from two main sources—internally generated funds that are not paid out to the stockholders, and new external financing.

High rates of growth may put a firm in a cash bind. This occurs because it cannot finance the rapid cash needs with internally generated funds. Thus, most high-growth firms have low or zero cash dividend payouts. In addition, they build financial slack into the planning process. The ultimate solution to the cash needs of a growing firm is to acquire additional financing in the form of long-term debt, or additional common stock financing. However, many firms follow a "pecking order" approach to financing (see Chapters 12 and 13) and have a strong aversion to issuing additional common stock. In such a case, the growth of the firm may be constrained, or it may have to adopt a higher than desired debt/equity ratio. Thus, although growth is generally desirable, it places a strain on the cash needs of the firm; growth must therefore be planned carefully. Failure to do so is one of the primary shortcomings of many growing firms.

Likewise, problems may arise with the worst-case scenario. In the worst case both sales and cash inflows fall, but often cash outflows do not fall as fast. This is especially true if the firm has many fixed cash outflows (as opposed to variable cash outflows) that do not fall as sales and cash inflows fall. The net result may be that in the very short run problems are not too bad, but they get worse and worse unless the firm takes drastic actions to cut fixed cash outflows. Realistic forecasting of both the best- and worst-case scenarios may expose potential cash flow problems, but the causes and remedies are very different in the two cases.

Seasonality

One problem that often arises in practice is how to forecast for periods that are less than yearly intervals, during which the firm experiences seasonal patterns in its cash flows. Many firms experience distinct seasonal patterns. For example, many retail stores have higher levels of sales in the time between Thanksgiving and the December holidays than any other time of the year. For retail goods producers, the heaviest season occurs in the months leading up to Thanksgiving, so they can ship the goods in time for the retail stores to have inventory in stock. Likewise, the busiest time of the year for garden and farm equipment suppliers is in the spring and early summers months. By examining the historical pattern of sales over the past few years, firms often identify seasonal patterns that are of great assistance in forecasting sales *within the year*.

As an example, assume we have used quarterly data for the past 3 years (12 quarters of data) and used linear regression to forecast quarterly sales for the next 8 quarters as follows:[2]

Period	Forecasted Sales
13	$390
14	405
15	421
16	437
17	453
18	468
19	484
20	500

Plotting the data for these 12 quarters indicates there is a seasonal pattern to the sales. By employing standard techniques for dealing with seasonality,[3] we can determine that the necessary seasonal adjustments are as follows:

	Seasonal Adjustment Factor
Quarter 1	0.927
Quarter 2	1.038
Quarter 3	1.061
Quarter 4	0.974

---

[2] *For complete details of dealing with seasonality see Chapter 25 of* Financial Management.
[3] *As discussed in Chapter 25 of* Financial Management.

The forecasted sales pattern, adjusted for the seasonality in past sales, is then determined by multiplying the seasonal adjustment factor times the previously forecasted sales as follows:

Period	Previous Linear Forecast of Sales	Seasonal Adjustment Factor	Seasonally Adjusted Sales
13	$390	0.927	$362
14	405	1.038	420
15	421	1.061	447
16	437	0.974	426
17	453	0.927	420
18	468	1.038	486
19	484	1.061	514
20	500	0.974	487

Because sales are seasonally higher in the second and third quarters, seasonally adjusting the simple linear forecasts results in substantially higher forecasted sales in those quarters; lower sales are forecast in the first and fourth quarters. Both the unadjusted and seasonally adjusted forecasts are shown in Figure 20.3. Seasonal adjustment is very important in practice and improves many forecasts, provided there is some fairly consistent seasonal pattern to the firm's sales.[4]

Inflation

Inflation can have a profound impact on the cash flows of the firm. The whole forecasting process must be reexamined in times of rapid changes in the inflation rate.

FIGURE 20.3

Fitted Regression Equation and Forecasted Quarterly Sales, With and Without Seasonal Adjustment

Adjusting for seasonality can materially increase or decrease per quarter sales as compared to a forecast based on simple linear regression.

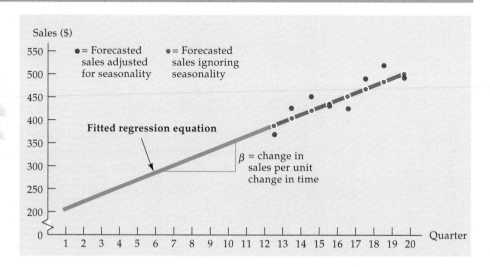

---

[4] The same basic procedures would be employed with monthly data, except 12-month moving averages are employed.

Very different strategies may be necessary during periods of rapid inflation, because the firm may not be able (or want) to pass on the effects of inflation to its customers. The presence of inflation also causes suppliers of funds to change strategies to protect themselves from its effect. They may provide only variable rate financing, in which the interest rate charged on a bond or loan is adjusted over time. Many banks lend primarily on a variable rate basis. All these factors, and many more, make the cash flow estimation process more difficult. The consequence is to reduce the reliability of the forecast, which makes close monitoring and evaluation of various scenarios even more important.

ROLLING FORECAST
Process in which cash budgets are updated periodically by dropping the most recent period and adding another period in the future.

Effective financial management is enhanced by the development of cash budgets, which help managers plan and control. Once the cash budget is determined, many firms employ a **rolling forecast** that is updated every week, month, or quarter by dropping the most recent period and adding another future period at the end of the forecast. But some care is in order. First, cash budgets were based on a set of specific assumptions—from the sales forecast on. Because events will differ in the future, the ability to do scenario analysis is essential. Second, cash needs may fluctuate *within* the budgeting period. Even though there may be plenty of cash on hand by the end of the period, different inflow and outflow patterns may leave the firm short of cash within the period.

CONCEPT REVIEW QUESTIONS

- What is the impact of inflation on a firm's forecasted sales?
- How can seasonal patterns impact a firm's forecasted sales?

PRO FORMA ACCOUNTING STATEMENTS

■ LEARNING GOAL 4

Explain how pro forma statements are developed, including use of the percentage of sales method.

PRO FORMA STATEMENTS
Forecasted accounting statements, typically an income statement and a balance sheet.

Pro forma statements project the firm's expected revenues, expenses, and position at the end of a forecast period.[5] Although less detailed than cash budgets, these forecasts are often required by current and prospective lenders. There are two basic approaches to developing pro forma statements:

PERCENTAGE OF SALES METHOD
Method of developing pro forma statements where historical percentages of items to sales or assets are used as projections.

1. One approach takes as its input the projections arising from the cash budget. These projections are then modified to account for differences between the firm's cash flows and its GAAP accounting data.
2. The second is the **percentage of sales method,** which starts with the historical relationship of sales to various income statement and balance sheet items. Pro forma statements and financing needs or surpluses are then estimated. This procedure may be naive if it assumes that all the firm's costs are variable and vary directly

---

[5] *Pro forma statements can also be constructed for some past time period. Comparison with actual past performance may best show the effect of some planned major event, such as a proposed merger or restructuring.*

with sales. In practice, some costs are fixed; therefore, judgment must be used when estimating how some expenses are expected to change.

In addition, some analysts start from industry averages in deriving historical relationships, and they make modifications based on information specific to the firm.

We use the percentage of sales method to estimate financing needs based on pro forma statements. Note that because pro forma statements start with accounting data, this method may not be as precise as a cash budgeting approach to projecting cash flows and financing needs. However, its simplicity and its focus on the impact on reported accounting statements may make it a supplement to the more elaborate cash budgeting process. Also, banks often require pro forma statements as part of a loan agreement.

Pro Forma Income Statement

We will use Smith Products, a manufacturer of specialty tools, to illustrate the use of pro forma statements. Smith begins by making its best estimate of next year's sales, which is $22 million. If sales are substantially higher or lower than the estimate, the pro forma statements will be off.

A good pro forma analysis should include a "base case" or "most likely scenario." It should also identify all the critical variables and how the pro forma will change if the critical variables deviate from their assumed values.

The next step is to estimate the historical relationship of expenses to sales for Smith. This is done by dividing Smith's income statement categories (cost of goods sold; selling, general, and administrative expenses; interest expenses; taxes; and cash dividends) by sales. If we use this information directly in a naive manner, Smith Products' estimated, or pro forma, income statement is as shown in Table 20.6. Based on this approach, Smith Products would expect net income to be $924,000; with projected cash dividends of $330,000, $594,000 would be shown as a transfer from the

TABLE 20.6
Present and Pro Forma Income Statement for Smith Products If Expenses Are Projected Naively Using a Strict Percentage of Sales Approach (in thousands)

This naive approach ignores fixed costs and often produces an estimate of net income that is biased low.

	Actual for Last Year	Basis of Projection	Pro Forma for Next Year
Sales	$20,000	Percentage of sales	$22,000
Cost of goods sold	13,500		14,850*
Gross margin	6,500		7,150
Selling, general, and administrative expenses	4,500	Percentage of sales	4,950
EBIT	2,000		2,200
Interest	600	Percentage of sales	660
EBT	1,400		1,540
Taxes (40%)	560	Historical tax rate	616
Net income	840		924
Cash dividends	300	Percentage of sales	330
Transferred to retained earnings	$ 540		$ 594

* $14,850 = ($22,000/$20,000)($13,500). The other percentage of sales estimates were calculated in the same manner.

TABLE 20.7

Revised Pro Forma Income Statement for Smith Products Based on a Modified Percentage of Sales Method and Judgment (in thousands)

By taking account of fixed costs, Smith Products obtains a more realistic estimate of its expected net income.

	Basis of Projection	Pro Forma for Next Year
Sales		$22,000
Cost of goods sold	Judgment: 66% of sales	14,520
Gross margin		7,480
Selling, general, and administrative expenses	Judgment: 23% of sales	5,060
EBIT		2,420
Interest	Percentage of sales	660
EBT		1,760
Taxes (40%)	Historical tax rate	704
Net income		1,056
Cash dividends	Management forecast	350
Transferred to retained earnings		$ 706

income statement to retained earnings on the firm's balance sheet.[6] The new retained earnings amount is equal to the previous years' retained earnings plus the amount transferred from the pro forma income statement.

Because the naive approach assumes that all costs are variable, it generally produces an estimate of net income that is *biased low*. This results from ignoring the presence of fixed operating costs that are spread over more sales dollars as sales increase. However, if sales are decreasing and fixed operating costs are actually present, then the naive percentage of sales method produces an estimate of net income that is too high.

After further analysis, Smith Products decides that all expenses and outflows will *not* vary directly with sales. Specifically, the firm estimates that the cost of goods sold will be 66 percent of sales; that selling, general, and administrative expenses will be 23 percent of sales; and that cash dividends will be $350,000. The same interest of $660,000 and 40 percent tax rate will be assumed. Smith Products' revised pro forma income statement is shown in Table 20.7. This analysis shows that net income is expected to be $1.056 million, and the estimated amount transferred to retained earnings will be $706,000. With these estimates, we can now proceed to estimate the balance sheet and obtain a rough approximation of the financing needed to support this expected increase in sales.

It is important to determine how each financial variable relates to past sales. For some variables past relationships will continue to hold; for others new policies will lead to changes, and the pro forma should reflect the new policies.

[6] Because the naive approach assumes that all costs are variable, it generally produces an estimate of net income that is biased low. This results from ignoring the presence of fixed operating costs that are spread over more sales dollars as sales increase. However, if sales are decreasing and fixed operating costs are actually present, then the naive percentage of sales method produces an estimate of net income that is too high.

Pro Forma Balance Sheet and Financing Needed

Smith's present balance sheet is given in Table 20.8, along with the projected asset and liability accounts, assuming most of them maintain their historical relationship to sales. Net long-term assets are projected based on the firm's current capital investment plan. Note that three items are not projected: Notes payable, long-term debt and lease obligations, and common stock are negotiated items that do not change as sales fluctuate. All other balance sheet items, except for net long-term assets and retained earnings, are assumed to change proportionally as sales change. Based on this procedure, Smith Products can obtain a rough estimate of its financing needs of $984,000. This is calculated as follows:

Total assets	$16,000,000
Less: Total liabilities and stockholders' equity	15,016,000
Additional financing needed (or surplus available)	$ 984,000

This figure, of course, assumes that the estimated increase in retained earnings is exactly equal to Smith's internally generated funds. In addition, it is based on maintaining the cash account at its forecasted level of $440,000.

TABLE 20.8

Forecast of Changes in Balance Sheet Items for Smith Products (in thousands)

In this example, judgment was used to estimate the long-term assets, and the naive percentage of sales method was used to forecast the other items.

Assets	Actual for Last Year	Basis of Projection	Pro Forma for Next Year
Cash	$ 400	Percentage of sales	$ 440*
Accounts receivable	2,100	Percentage of sales	2,310
Inventory	3,000	Percentage of sales	3,300
Total current	5,500		6,050
Net long-term assets	8,500	Judgment	9,950
Total assets	$14,000		$16,000
Liabilities and Stockholders' Equity			
Accounts payable	$ 1,300	Percentage of sales	$ 1,430
Notes payable	900	n.a.†	900
Accrued wages and taxes	1,200	Percentage of sales	1,320
Total current	3,400		3,650
Long-term debt and lease obligations	3,800	n.a.	3,800
Deferred taxes	600	Percentage of sales	660
Total long-term liabilities	4,400		4,460
Common stock and additional paid-in capital	3,000	n.a.	3,000
Retained earnings	3,200	Pro forma income statement	3,906‡
Total stockholders' equity	6,200		6,906
Total liabilities and stockholders' equity	$14,000	Total	15,016
		Additional needed	984
		Total to balance	$16,000

* $440 = ($400/$20,000)($22,000). The other percentage of sales estimates were calculated in the same manner.
† Not applicable.
‡ $3,200 from last year plus transfer to retained earnings of $706 from Table 20.7.

A slight modification can be made if a firm plans to draw down its cash account to meet part of its needs. To illustrate, assume that Smith plans to draw down its cash account by $240,000. In that case, the financing needed is:

After the pro forma is completed, a comparative ratio analysis and a statement of cash flows can be developed from the pro forma financial statements. This provides a good check on what the pro forma contains.

Total assets	$16,000,000
Less: Total liabilities and stockholders' equity	15,016,000
Additional financing needed	984,000
Less: Cash drawn down	240,000
External financing needed	$ 744,000

Now, of course, Smith Products must decide how to finance the needed expansion. To illustrate the basic elements, assume that Smith decides to finance the total $984,000 by issuing $1 million in additional long-term debt.[7] As shown in the revised balance sheet in Table 20.9, this new financing results in Smith's long-term debt and lease obligations account increasing by $1 million to $4.8 million. The difference between the $984,000 needed and the $1 million obtained (i.e., $16,000) is added to the firm's cash account.[8] Obviously, other plans and many factors have to be considered when firms plan for the future.

CONCEPT REVIEW QUESTIONS

- What are two basic approaches to developing pro forma statements?
- Describe how to develop a pro forma income statement and balance sheet using the percentage of sales method.

TABLE 20.9

Revised Pro Forma Balance Sheet for Smith Products (in thousands)

By increasing its ratio of total debt to total assets from 55.7 percent (Table 20.8) to 56.9 percent, Smith can meet the proposed increase without additional common equity financing.

Assets		Liabilities and Stockholders' Equity	
Cash	$ 456	Accounts payable	$ 1,430
Accounts receivable	2,310	Notes payable	900
Inventory	3,300	Accrued wages and taxes	1,320
Total current	6,066	Total current	3,650
Net long-term assets	9,950	Long-term debt and lease obligations	4,800
Total assets	$16,016	Deferred taxes	660
		Total long-term liabilities	5,460
		Common stock and additional paid-in capital	3,000
		Retained earnings	3,906
		Total stockholders' equity	6,906
		Total liabilities and stockholders' equity	$16,016

---

[7] It issues $1 million instead of $984,000 simply due to rounding the financing off to the nearest million dollars.

[8] Actually, the income statement should be reestimated to take into account additional interest above the existing $660,000 due to Smith's increasing its debt by $1 million. This would affect the size of the transfer to retained earnings. For simplicity, these secondary effects are ignored.

FINANCIAL AND STRATEGIC PLANNING

■ **LEARNING GOAL 5**

Explain the relationship between short- and long-term financial planning.

The essence of financial planning is to ensure that the firm is following a dynamic policy that emphasizes the creation of value and avoids options that destroy value. Financial and strategic planning processes and models come in many sizes and shapes. In any model, however, there is an important relationship between the short- and long-run aspects. Consider Figure 20.4, which shows the relationships between a firm's short- and long-term cash flows. The firm is experiencing cash inflows and outflows during the current period. At the end of this period, the net inflow or outflow, plus the beginning cash balance, determines how much cash is available at the start of period 1. To emphasize the longer term aspects, firms may start with short-term cash budgets (e.g., monthly or quarterly) and then move to yearly cash budgets.

Long-term planning, in a sense, is just a continuation of the ideas discussed earlier for short-term planning. But there are some differences in emphasis. Consider Figure 20.5, which depicts the firm's long-term needs. Note that the long-term requirements depend on the amount of spontaneous short-term financing secured, along with the amount of short-term borrowing employed. Firms that adopt an aggressive short-term financial management strategy (as discussed in Chapter 15) will, other things being equal, need less long-term financing. Also, in the long run the firm's strategic plan, its ability to forecast accurately, and the need for flexibility all become more important than in the short run, although the basic emphasis remains the same.

The long-term financial planning approach begins by continuing what was done in the short term. Obviously, the further in the future, the less detail in the cash budget. Likewise, the further in the future, the more uncertainty concerning the projected cash flows. The longer-term cash budgets should reflect any anticipated expansion, replacement, or restructuring of the firm's assets. Next the sources of financing need to be evaluated. During the planning process the firm should consider various alternative plans and their possible consequences. An important part of the planning process involves consideration of the various options (to expand, delay or defer, abandon, and so forth) faced by the firm. Whatever the final plan adopted, the important point to remember is that financial planning forces the firm to consider its goals and needs in advance. By doing so,

FIGURE 20.4

Relationship Between Short- and Long-Term Financial and Strategic Planning

In the short term, the emphasis is on quarterly cash flows. In the longer term, the emphasis is on the cumulative cash inflows or outflows and the financial and strategic aspects.

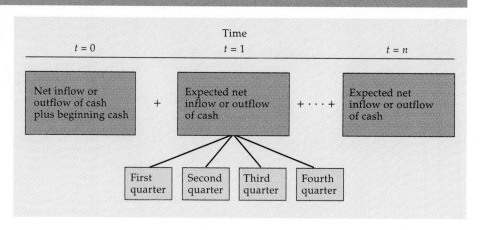

FIGURE 20.5

How Short- and Long-Term Financing Meet a Firm's Needs

Spontaneous short-term financing (through accounts payable, factoring of receivables, and continuous inventory loans) meets part of the firm's cumulative financing needs (as represented by the solid wavy line). The rest are met by short-term borrowings and long-term financing.

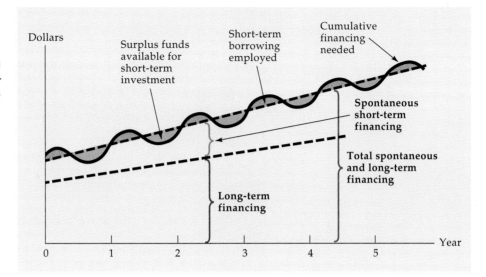

firms can consider all of the options available to them, ensure their flexibility, and keep attention focused on the goal of maximizing the market value of the firm.

CONCEPT REVIEW QUESTIONS

▓ How are short-term and long-term financial planning models related?
▓ What is the main goal of establishing a financial and strategic planning model?

Summary

▓ The statement of cash flows, which is required to be presented along with an income statement and balance sheet, records the firm's past flow of cash. Due to the use of the indirect approach to presenting the statement of cash flows, which is employed by most firms, the information is not as useful as it could be.

▓ Cash budgeting, perhaps supplemented by pro forma analysis, is the main method of forecasting cash flows and financing needs or excesses. Accurate forecasting of sales is most important when making any kind of financial projections.

▓ In practice, firms employ scenario analysis, find ways to deal with seasonality, and deal with inflation when making cash forecasts.

▓ Financial and strategic planning is a trial-and-error activity that does not attempt to minimize risk. Rather, it is the process of deciding which risks to take and which are not worth taking. Throughout the planning process all of the options available to the firm must be continually considered, or employed as the frame of reference, in order to make effective financial management decisions.

Questions

20.1 Explain both the advantages and disadvantages of the statement of cash flows in terms of providing useful cash flow information.

20.2 Explain the various components of a firm's cash budget. How can sales be estimated? Why may a cash budget not be sufficient for planning *within* a given period?

20.3 What are the strengths and weaknesses of and the differences between the cash budget and the percentage of sales method of forecasting future cash flows?

20.4 Gates Electronics is considering making the following policy changes. In each case, indicate whether *in the next period* the move will provide more cash inflows and/or reduce outflows (+), provide more outflows and/or reduce inflows (−), or have an indeterminate or no effect (0).

a. The firm becomes more socially responsible. _____

b. Increased competition is leading to price cutting and increased promotional expenses. _____

c. The firm decides to sell only for cash; previously some sales had been on credit. _____

d. By shifting to more debt, the firm expects its return on equity to increase. _____

e. The firm decides to change its inventory method from one GAAP method to another GAAP method. _____

f. The firm's dividend payout ratio is reduced. _____

g. Congress changes the tax laws, resulting in longer depreciation lives for tax purposes. _____

20.5 How would you go about distinguishing *after the fact* between good and bad financial and strategic planning versus good or bad luck?

Concept Review Problems

See Appendix A for solutions.

CR20.1 Marks Manufacturing is attempting to predict sales for the next 3 years using linear regression. What are the expected sales in the next 3 years?

Year	Sales, Y_t (in millions)
1	$10.0
2	10.0
3	10.5
4	11.5
5	13

CR20.2 Sand Corporation has sales for November and December of $165,000 and $175,000, respectively. Estimated sales are:

January	$220,000	May	$200,000
February	275,000	June	175,000
March	250,000	July	150,000
April	230,000	August	150,000

The firm makes 20 percent of its sales for cash, 50 percent are on credit and collected 1 month after the sale, and 30 percent are on credit and collected 2 months after the sale (assume there are no bad debts). Material costs are 20 percent of projected sales 2 months hence, and labor is 50 percent of next month's estimated sales. Sand typically pays for 25 percent of the materials 2 months prior to the sale and for 75 percent of the materials 1 month prior to the sale. The estimated administrative expenses are $25,000 per month. The firm anticipates paying $50,000 in taxes in both January and April. It will have a $150,000 cash outflow in May for new equipment. The minimum desired cash balance is $70,000; that is the beginning balance in January. Prepare a cash budget for the months of January through June and indicate the per month cumulative short-term financing needed (−) or surplus (+).

CR20.3 Tulsa Products has the following balance sheet and income statement. The firm estimates sales will increase by 10 percent next year. All income statement and balance sheet items are assumed to be a function of sales except long-term assets, short- and long-term debt, common stock, and dividends paid. These entries will remain constant, except for long-term assets, which will increase to $40, and taxes, which will be $8. Using the percent of sales method, develop a pro forma income statement and balance sheet for Tulsa Products. Will the firm need outside financing to support the 10 percent growth?

Balance Sheet (in millions)

Assets

Cash and marketable securities	$ 5
Accounts receivable	20
Inventory	18
Long-term assets	27
Total assets	$70

Liabilities and Stockholders' Equity

Short-term bank loan	$ 9
Accounts payable	11
Accruals	10
Long-term debt	15
Common stock	10
Retained earnings	15
Total liabilities and stockholders' equity	$70

Income Statement (in millions)

Net sales	$40
Cost of goods sold	10
Gross margin	30
Selling and administrative expenses	10
EBIT	20
Interest	2
EBT	18
Taxes	7
Net income	11
Cash dividends	3
Transferred to retained earnings	$ 8

Problems

See Appendix C for answers to selected problems.

Statement of Cash Flows

20.1 The statement of cash flows for Amoco Corp. for 3 recent years was as follows (in millions):

	−2	−1	0
Cash Flows from Operating Activities			
Net income	$1,953	$ 747	$1,360
Depreciation, depletion, amortization, and retirements and abandonments	2,059	2,418	2,295
Decrease (increase) in receivables	(73)	672	(197)
Decrease (increase) in inventories	17	75	(34)
Increase (decrease) in payables and accrued liabilities	159	(1,367)	331
Deferred taxes and other items	603	297	257
Net cash provided by operating activities	$4,718	$2,842	$4,012
Cash Flows from Investing Activities			
Capital expenditures	(3,881)	(2,256)	(2,332)
Proceeds from distribution of property	185	97	129
Distribution of cash of Cyprus Minerals Co.	(23)	—	—
New investments and advances	(42)	(192)	(42)
Proceeds from sale of investments	25	131	119
Other	(11)	(32)	141
Net cash used in investing activities	$(3,747)	$(2,252)	$(1,985)
Cash Flows from Financing Activities			
New long-term obligations	334	1,153	3
Repayment of long-term obligations	(375)	(979)	(259)
Cash dividends paid	(872)	(849)	(847)
Issuances of common stock	127	161	603
Acquisitions of common stock	(937)	(363)	(443)
Increase (decrease) in short-term obligations	324	(263)	(9)
Net cash used in financing activities	$(1,399)	$(1,140)	$ (952)
Increase (decrease) in cash and marketable securities	(428)	(550)	1,075
Cash and marketable securities— beginning of year	1,419	991	441
Cash and marketable securities— end of year	$ 991	$ 441	$1,516

Supplemental Cash Flow Information

The effect of foreign currency exchange fluctuations on total cash and marketable securities balances was not significant. Net cash provided by operating activities reflects cash payments for interest and income taxes as follows:

	−2	−1	0
Interest paid	$ 459	$408	$398
Income taxes paid	1,368	877	861

a. Analyze the firm's financial performance for the 3 years and comment on the primary sources of cash, the primary uses of cash, and any apparent trends. How else (in terms of a general approach) could the operating section of the statement be constructed?

b. What else would you like to know that is not reflected or apparent on Amoco's statement of cash flows?

Forecasting

20.2 Sales data for the last 7 years are as follows:

Year	Sales
1	$ 470
2	800
3	1,080
4	1,350
5	1,535
6	1,705
7	1,831

a. Calculate the slope, β, and intercept, α, and then predict sales for years 8, 9, and 10.

b. Plot (using graph paper) your estimated regression equation and the forecasted values for years 8, 9, and 10. Then plot the actual sales data for years 1 through 7. What conclusions can you draw about the growth in past sales and the estimated sales for years 8, 9, and 10?

Forecasting

20.3 J. C. Penney's revenue (in millions) for 5 recent years are shown below:

Year 1	$11,353	Year 4	$12,078
2	11,860	5	13,451
3	11,414		

a. Based on linear regression, forecast revenue for year 6.

b. How close is this to actual year 6 revenue of $14,146?

c. Based on actual revenue for years 1 through 6, plus actual revenue for years 7, 8, and 9 of $15,151, $15,747, and $15,296, respectively, forecast year 10 revenue.

d. How close is this to actual year 10 revenue of $16,405? What does this suggest about the use of linear regression for forecasting Penney's revenue for this time period?

Basic Cash Budget

20.4 Lansing Corporation has forecast its cash flows for the next 2 months as follows:

	First Month	Second Month
Total operating cash inflow	$210 million	$150 million
Total operating cash outflow	−140 million	−135 million
Other net inflow (+) or outflow (−)	−30 million	−90 million

Lansing's beginning cash balance is $15 million, and its minimum cash balance is $10 million. Determine Lansing's cumulative financing needed (−) or surplus (+) for both months.

Cash Budget

20.5 Perth Brothers is in the process of developing its cash budget for the months of January, February, March, and April. Twenty percent of sales are for cash; 50 percent of total sales are for credit and collected the next month. The remaining 30 percent are for credit and collected in 2 months. There are no bad debts.

Purchases of raw materials are made in the month prior to the expected sale and average 45 percent of expected sales. They are paid for in the month following their purchase. Wages, rent, and selling expenses are $300,000 in January and will increase by $50,000 per month. Interest of $25,000 is payable every month. Taxes of $75,000 are payable in January, and $150,000 is due in April. Cash dividends of $100,000 are payable in February. Finally, capital expenditures of $200,000 are forecast for January, and another $50,000 are expected in April.

Actual sales for November and December and forecasted sales for the next 5 months are as follows:

November	$1,000,000	March	$1,800,000
December	900,000	April	2,300,000
January	1,000,000	May	2,500,000
February	1,400,000		

Cash on hand on January 1 is $100,000, and a $50,000 minimum cash balance is required each month.

a. Prepare a cash budget for January, February, March, and April.
b. What is the maximum level of short-term financing required?
c. Suppose that sales receipts come in uniformly over the month, but all outflows are paid by the 10th of the month. Discuss the effect this would have on the cash budget. Would the cash budget just completed be valid? If not, what could be done to adjust the budget?
d. Now suppose Perth Brothers reestimates its forecasted sales as follows:

January	$ 800,000	April	$1,900,000
February	1,100,000	May	2,200,000
March	1,500,000		

What is the effect of this on Perth's cash budget in (a)? What is the maximum level of short-term financing now required?

Cash Budget

20.6 Hawkes Company is preparing plans for the next 6 months. The firm's special concern is a $2.5 million note that comes due in September. Sales (actual for May and June, and forecast for the rest) are as follows:

May	$3,400,000	October	$1,800,000
June	3,500,000	November	1,500,000
July	4,000,000	December	1,400,000
August	2,500,000	January	1,500,000
September	2,000,000		

Sales are 10 percent for cash, 75 percent credit collected in the next month, and 15 percent credit collected in 2 months. There are no bad debts. Purchases of raw materials are made as follows: 20 percent of sales 2 months ahead, paid in the month following the purchase; and 30 percent of sales expected 1 month ahead, paid in the month following the purchase. Wages, selling, and administrative expenses are estimated to be as follows:

July	$1,000,000	October	$700,000
August	900,000	November	700,000
September	800,000	December	700,000

In addition, there are lease payments of $100,000 per month. Interest payments on long-term borrowing of $300,000 in both August and November are required. Taxes of $325,000 are payable in September and December. Finally, there is the short-term note of $2,500,000 payable in September. There are no cash dividends or other inflows or outflows. Hawkes's beginning cash balance is $430,000 on July 1, and its required minimum balance is $400,000.

a. Prepare a monthly cash budget for the last 6 months of the year.
b. Will Hawkes be able to pay off the $2,500,000 note in full and on time?
c. Suppose that due to a recession sales fall off, but production does not decline as rapidly. Also, customers take longer to pay their bills. What effect might these changes have on Hawkes's ability to repay the note?

Short-term Cash Needs and Financing

20.7 Hallam Industries has forecast its cash flows for the next year as follows:

	First Quarter	Second Quarter	Third Quarter	Fourth Quarter
Total operating cash inflow	$175	$195	$220	$200
Total operating cash outflow	−140	−180	−120	−120
Other net inflow or outflow	−50	−90	−60	−30

a. Determine Hallam's net cash inflow or outflow per quarter and its cumulative short-term financing needs by quarter, if its beginning cash balance is $25 and its minimum cash balance is $15.
b. What is the maximum amount of short-term financing needed? In what quarter does it occur?
c. Ignoring any costs of short-term financing, is Hallam as well off at the end of the year as at the beginning?
d. The effective annual before-tax costs of alternative short-term financing sources are given below. Which one would be chosen? Is there any reason why the cheapest source might not be chosen?

Bank line of credit	16%	Accounts receivable loan	13%
Inventory loan	15	Factoring receivables	18
Stretching payables	20	Commercial paper (6 months)	12

Pro Forma Income Statement

20.8 J. M. Heider's condensed income statement as of December 31 is (in millions):

Sales	$4,841.4
Operating expenses	4,333.5
Income from operations	507.9
Other income	37.9
EBIT	545.8
Interest	180.7
EBT	365.1
Taxes	83.5
Net income	$ 281.6

a. If we had perfect foresight and knew next year's sales were going to be $5,432.2 million, estimate next year's income statement employing the percentage of sales method.

b. What differences exist between your pro forma income statement and Heider's actual income statement for the year, listed below (in million)?

Sales	$5,432.2
Operating expenses	4,823.7
Income from operations	608.5
+ Other income	70.0
EBIT	678.5
Interest	185.9
EBT	492.6
Taxes	124.9
Net income	$ 367.7

c. Do you believe some of these differences could be anticipated to obtain a more accurate pro forma income statement? Why or why not?

Pro Forma Balance Sheet and Financing Needed

20.9 Woolsey Inc.'s estimated sales for next year are $30 million. The percentage of sales for items that vary directly with sales for Woolsey is given below:

Cash	5%	Accounts payable	15%
Accounts receivable	25	Accruals	10
Inventory	30	Net profit margin	5

Its net long-term assets are $6 million, notes payable are $2 million, long-term debt is $2 million, and common stock is $5 million. Woolsey's present retained earnings are $5.1 million, and its dividend payout ratio is 40 percent.

a. Prepare a pro forma balance sheet and indicate the estimated amount of additional financing needed. Assume that long-term debt will be used to finance any shortfall.

b. What happens if Woolsey's sales are $40 million and its long-term assets increase to $8 million? If long-term debt is used, how does the ratio of total debt to total assets in (b) compare with the same ratio for (a)?

Financing Growth

20.10 Camden Corporation has decided to embark on a rapid expansion. Its most recent income statement and balance sheet are as follows:

Income Statement (in millions)

Sales	$30.0
Cost of goods sold	15.0
Selling, general, and administrative expenses	6.0
EBIT	9.0
Interest	1.0
EBT	8.0
Taxes (30%)	2.4
Net income	5.6
Cash dividends	3.0
Transferred to retained earnings	$ 2.6

Balance Sheet (in millions)

Current assets	$ 6.0	Accounts payable	$ 2.0
Long-term assets	14.0	Note payable	2.0
Total assets	$20.0	Long-term debt	6.0
		Common stock	3.0
		Retained earnings	7.0
		Total liabilities and stockholders' equity	$20.0

In attempting to determine its financial condition and needs, Camden believes the following will happen:

Sales	$40.0
Cost of goods sold	Same percent of sales as current year
Selling, general, and administrative expenses	$ 9.0
Interest	$ 1.0 (initially, before additional financing)
Taxes	Same percent of *EBT* as current year
Cash dividends	$ 3.0 (initially)
Current assets	$ 7.0
Long-term assets	$23.0
Accounts payable	$ 3.0
Notes payable	$ 2.0
Long-term debt	$ 6.0 (initially)
Common stock	$ 3.0

a. Based on these estimates, prepare a pro forma income statement and balance sheet for Camden. How much additional financing (regardless of where it comes from) do you estimate the firm needs?

b. What happens if Camden acquires sufficient additional long-term debt financing to keep its ratio of total debt to total assets at its original level? Assume interest expenses increase by $500,000.

c. By cutting its cash dividends in addition to the step taken in (b), can Camden finance all its cash needs? What do you think will happen to the market price of Camden's common stock if it cuts cash dividends? Do you see any alternative means of raising the needed funds?

Long-Term Needs

20.11 Nassau Metals is planning to meet its long-term needs. To arrive at its needs, it has come up with the following estimates:

	Year				
	1	2	3	4	5
Net cash inflow ($+$) or outflow ($-$) before short-term financing cash flows	$20	−$15	−$30	−$60	−$10
Short-term financing cash flows	− 3	− 4	− 4	− 6	− 2
Total cash inflow ($+$) or outflow ($-$)	$17	−$19	−$34	−$66	−$12

Nassau's beginning cash balance is $30. The minimum cash balance is $15 in years 1 and 2, $20 in year 3, and $25 in years 4 and 5. Prepare a year-by-year statement to show the maximum amount of long-term financing Nassau will need.

Capital Structure Proportions

20.12 Gardiner Systems is completing its long-run planning process. As a part of this, it has estimated the following needs for long-term funds and the amount it expects to provide out of internally generated equity funds:

	Year				
	1	2	3	4	5
Long-term financing needed per period	$5	$20	$15	$30	$43
To be provided by internally generated equity funds per period	− 6	− 7	− 7	− 8	− 10
To be raised externally ($+$) or surplus ($-$) per period	−$1	$13	$ 8	$22	$33

Note: It is okay if Gardiner raises too much long-term capital in any period; those funds are carried forward to the next year, but it cannot have a shortfall. That is, Gardiner cannot borrow on a short-term basis to cover any shortfall in long-term capital.

Gardiner's present capital structure contains $40 in debt and $60 in common equity. A primary goal when raising long-term capital is to remain as close as possible to this percentage target capital structure. Either long-term debt or common stock can be issued in amounts of $15 each.

a. Determine in which years Gardiner needs to secure additional long-term financing.

b. Indicate, by year, whether long-term debt or common stock should be issued. (Remember that the additional internally generated funds each year are added to the firm's equity base.)

c. What is the resulting capital structure at the end of year 5 and the ratio of total debt to total assets?

Financial Forecasting and Planning

20.13 **Mini Case** You have been on the job for a month as an analyst in the finance department of La Playa Enterprises. Every 3 months the firm plans for the next year and also assesses the firm's long-run financial strategy. The current planning process has been assigned to you to complete, after which it will be reviewed, and modified as needed, by the divisional vice-president and other senior management.

a. As a first step you have gathered the last 3 years' statements of cash flows. In brief, they are as follows:

	Year −2	Year −1	Year 0
Operating Activities			
Net income	$200	$245	$240
Depreciation	45	65	75
Other	(100)	50	180
	145	360	495
Investing Activities	(90)	(175)	(160)
Financing Activities			
Net change in debt	150	(200)	(50)
Dividends paid	(50)	(60)	(70)
	100	(260)	(120)
Net increase (decrease) in cash and marketable securities	155	(75)	215
Cash and marketable securities at beginning of the year	80	235	160
Cash and marketable securities at the end of the year	$235	$160	$375

What is the purpose of the statement of cash flows? In what format does La Playa Enterprises present its statement? What can we determine about La Playa from its statement of cash flows?

b. In order to develop a 4-quarter cash budget, you decide to estimate sales based on linear regression. Sales for the past 8 quarters are as follows:

Quarter	Sales
−7	$500
−6	525
−5	520

Quarter	Sales
−4	580
−3	580
−2	560
−1	590
0	610

Based on linear regression, what are estimated sales for the next 4 quarters? Are there other factors that need to be taken into consideration when forecasting sales? Also, without actually doing it, how would you adjust for seasonality?

c. In order to develop its cash budget, La Playa has made the following estimates: Forty percent of sales are for cash, 40 percent are credit and collected in the following quarter, and 20 percent are credit and collected in 2 quarters. There are no bad debts. Purchases are made in the quarter prior to the expected sales and average 35 percent of expected sales. They are paid in the quarter following their purchase. The other estimates have been made as follows:

	Year			
	1	2	3	4
Salaries	$100	$105	$105	$115
Selling, general, and administrative expenses	125	130	125	130
Interest	60	40	40	30
Taxes	20	20	20	20
Capital expenditures	50	130	80	70
Repay debt	100	—	100	20
Dividends	30	30	35	35

The present level of cash on hand should be taken from part (a) above, and past and projected sales are given in (b). The minimum cash balance is $80. Develop the firm's cash budget for the next 4 quarters. What does your analysis indicate?

d. In addition to the projected cash budget, you are considering preparing pro forma financial statements. What is the basic procedure employed in preparing pro forma statements? What are their strengths? Their weaknesses?

e. In preparing your report, what still remains?

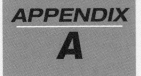

Solutions to
Concept Review Problems

(*Note:* For problems using present or future value concepts, the solution is given based on using a financial calculator; this is followed by the answer, in parenthesis, based on employing the financial tables in Appendix B. If no separate financial table answer is provided, the use of a financial calculator and financial tables provide the same answer.)

Chapter 1

CR1.1

Sales	$700,000
Cost of goods sold	100,000
Administrative expenses	300,000
Depreciation	50,000
Earnings before interest and taxes, *EBIT*	250,000
Interest	60,000
Earnings before taxes, *EBT*	190,000
Taxes (40%)	76,000
Earnings after tax, *EAT* (net income)	$114,000

CR1.2

Cash Inflows		Cash Outflows	
Sales for cash	$26,000	Cash expenses	$12,000
Cash on hand	500	Interest	6,000
Total	$26,500	Taxes	3,200
		Cash dividend	500
		Short-term debt	1,500
		Total	$23,200

Net cash flow = $3,330.

CR1.3 Their calculations were correct, and yes, it is possible to have a negative net income and a positive net cash flow.

Chapter 2

CR2.1 **a.** The term structure is humped, with 1-, 2-, and 5-year rates being higher than 6-month or 7-year rates. Inflation is expected to increase, and then fall in later years.

    b. 8.6%, 9.6%, 9.9%, 9.9%, 10.0%. Almost flat, due to the maturity premium.

CR2.2   **a.** $20,000(111.07) = ¥2,221,400
     b. M47,356(0.6335) = $30,000
     c. $15,000(0.6352) = £9,528

CR2.3   **a.** $E(S_{2/1}) = [5.3225(1.06)]/1.03 =$ FFr 5.4775

Chapter 3

CR3.1   **a.** $FV_{10} = \$6,000(1.10)^{10} = \$15,562\ (\$15,564)$
     b. $FV_5 = \$8,000(1.05)^5 = \$10,210\ (\$10,208)$
     c. $FV_7 = \$857$
     d. $FV_3 = \$11,910$

CR3.2   **a.** $PV_0 = \$6,000/(1.10)^{10} = \$2,313\ (\$2,316)$
     b. $PV_0 = \$8,000/(1.05)^5 = \$6,268\ (\$6,272)$
     c. $PV_0 = \$292$
     d. $PV_0 = \$8,396\ (\$8,400)$

CR3.3   **a.** $PV_0 = \$800$
     b. $PV_0 = \$80/(0.10 - 0.04) = \$1,333$

     c. $PV_0 = \left(\dfrac{\$80}{0.10}\right)\left[\dfrac{1}{(1.10)^3}\right] = \$601$

CR3.4

$$FV_3 = \$25,000\left(1 + \frac{0.08}{1}\right)^{3(1)} = \$31,493\ (\$31,500)$$

$$FV_7 = \$31,493\left(1 + \frac{0.10}{2}\right)^{4(2)} = \$46,530\ (\$46,526)$$

CR3.5   **a.** $PV_0 = \dfrac{\$5,000}{\left(1 + \frac{0.10}{12}\right)^{3(12)}} = \$3,709$

     b. $k_{\text{effective annual}} = 1 + \left(\dfrac{0.10}{1}\right)^{12} - 1 = 10.47\%$

CR3.6   **a.** $1,000,000/20 = $50,000$ per year

$$PV_0 = \sum_{t=1}^{20} \frac{\$50,000}{(1.08)^t} = \$490,907\ (\$490,900)$$

     b. $PV_0 = \$530,180$

CR3.7   **a.** $FV_5 = \$500\left[\dfrac{(1.10)^5 - 1}{0.10}\right] = \$3,053$

     b. $FV_5 = (\$3,053)(1.10) = \$3,358$

     c. $k_{\text{effective annual}} = \left(1 + \dfrac{0.08}{4}\right)^4 - 1 = 8.243\%$

$$FV_5 = \$500\left[\frac{(1.08243)^5 - 1}{0.08243}\right] = \$2,948$$

CR3.8 **a.** $NPV = \dfrac{\$140,000}{(1.12)^1} + \dfrac{\$200,000}{(1.12)^2} + \dfrac{\$250,000}{(1.12)^3} - \$500,000$

$$= -\$37,616\ (-\$37,580)$$

b. $\dfrac{\$140,000}{(1 + IRR)^1} + \dfrac{\$200,000}{(1 + IRR)^2} + \dfrac{\$250,000}{(1 + IRR)^3} - \$500,000 = 0$

$IRR = 7.96\%$

CR3.9 If the 2.9% financing is taken, the payment is

$$\$20,000 = PMT\left[\frac{1}{0.029/12} - \frac{1}{(0.029/12)[1 + (0.029/12)]^{2(12)}}\right]$$

$PMT = \$858.74$

If the rebate is taken and the remainder financed at 8 percent by the bank, the payment is

$$\$18,000 = PMT\left[\frac{1}{0.08/12} - \frac{1}{(0.08/12)[1 + (0.08/12)]^{2(12)}}\right]$$

The $PMT = \$814.09$; take the rebate.

Chapter 4

CR4.1 **a.** $B_0 = \$50\left[\dfrac{1}{0.04} - \dfrac{1}{0.04(1.04)^{30}}\right] + \dfrac{\$1,000}{(1.04)^{30}} = \$865 + \$308 = \$1,173$

b. $B_0 = \$1,149$

CR4.2 The interest per semi-annual period is $(0.06)(\$1,000)/2 = \$30$, and the number of periods is $(2)(20) = 40$.

$$\$945 = \sum_{t=1}^{40} \frac{\$30}{(1 + k_b)^t} + \frac{\$1,000}{(1 + k_b)^{40}}$$

The yield to maturity $= 3.25\%$ for half a year; annual $YTM = 6.50\%$.

CR4.3 **a.** $k_p = \dfrac{\$6.50}{\$70} = 9.29\%$

b. $P_0 = \dfrac{\$6.50}{0.10} = \$65$ per share

CR4.4

$$P_0 = \frac{\$1.65(1.06)}{0.14 - 0.06} = \frac{\$1.749}{0.08} = \$21.86$$

CR4.5

$$P_0 = \frac{\$1.980}{(1.14)^1} + \frac{\$2.376}{(1.14)^2} + \frac{\$2.851}{(1.14)^3} + \frac{\$3.421}{(1.14)^4} + \frac{\$45.328}{(1.14)^4}$$

$$= \$1.74 + \$1.83 + \$1.92 + \$2.03 + \$26.84 = \$34.36 \ (\$34.35)$$

CR4.6

$$P_0 = \frac{\$2.00(1 - 0.15)}{0.20 - (-0.15)} = \frac{\$1.70}{0.35} = \$4.86$$

Chapter 5

CR5.1

$$\bar{k}_{IBM} = 10\%, \bar{k}_{BC} = 9.6\%, \text{ and } \bar{k}_{market} = 9.4\%$$

CR5.2

$$\sigma_{IBM} = [0.2(-15 - 10)^2 + 0.6(10 - 10)^2 + 0.2(35 - 10)^2]^{0.5} = (250)^{0.5}$$

$$= 15.81\%; \sigma_{BC} = 22.96\%; \text{ and } \sigma_{market} = 10.46\%$$

CR5.3

$$\bar{K}_{p+IBM} = 0.8(9.4\%) + 0.2(10\%) = 9.52\%; \bar{K}_{p+BC} = 9.44\%$$

CR5.4

$$k_{Abraham} = 6.0\% + 0.55(11.0\% - 6.0\%) = 8.75\%; k_{Stoker} = 11.95\%$$

CR5.5

$$k_{Abraham} = 8.0\% + 0.55(13.0\% - 8.0\%) = 10.75\%; k_{Stoker} = 13.95\%$$

CR5.6 a. $$P_{0\,Abraham} = \frac{\$2.00(1.03)}{0.0875 - 0.03} = \$35.83; P_{0\,Stoker} = \$71.26$$

b. $P_{0\,Abraham} = \$26.58; P_{0\,Stoker} = \$53.33$

Chapter 6

CR6.1

$$\$1,198 = \sum_{t=1}^{40} \frac{\$50}{(1 + k_b/2)^t} + \frac{\$1,000}{(1 + k_b/2)^{40}}$$

$k_b = 4\%$ semi-annually, or 8 percent annually; $k_i = 5.20\%$

CR6.2 $k_{ps} = 9.14\%$

CR6.3

$$k_s(\text{dividend valuation approach}) = \frac{\$7.20(1 - 0.50)}{\$40} + 0.04 = 13\%$$

$k_s(\text{capital asset pricing model}) = 6\% + 1.5(14\% - 6\%) = 18\%$
$k_s(\text{bond yield} + \text{risk premium}) = 8\% + 6\% = 14\%$
The average cost of equity capital is 15%.

CR6.4 Opportunity cost of capital = 12.45%

CR6.5

Component		W
Short-term debt	$10,000,000	0.074
Long-term debt	38,280,000	0.283
Preferred stock	12,000,000	0.089
Equity	75,000,000	0.554
Total market value	$135,280,000	1.000

CR6.6 $k_{\text{short-term}} = 6\%(1 - 0.35) = 3.90\%$; $k_{\text{long-term}} = 9\%(1 - 0.35) = 5.85\%$; $k_{ps} = 10\%$; and the average $k_s = (16.67\% + 16.80\% + 15\%)/3 = 16.16\%$.

CR6.7 Opportunity cost of capital = 11.79%.

CR6.8 The new $k_s = 17.76\%$, so the opportunity cost of capital is 12.68%.

CR6.9

$$\beta_U = \frac{1.5}{1 + (1 - 0.40)(0.50)} = 1.15$$

$$\beta_{\text{levered division}} = (1.15)[1 + (1 - 0.35)(20\%/80\%)] = 1.34$$

$k_{\text{divisional}} = 18.06\%$, so the divisional opportunity cost of capital = 15.62%.

Chapter 7

CR7.1

$$\$500,000 = \frac{\$350,000}{(1 + IRR)^1} + \frac{\$250,000}{(1 + IRR)^2} + \frac{\$80,000}{(1 + IRR)^3}$$

$$IRR_A = 21.82\%$$

$$IRR_B = 16.96\%$$

CR7.2 $NPV_A = \$84,899$ ($84,730), while $NPV_B = \$101,052$ ($100,800).

CR7.3

$$\$500,000 = \frac{\$8,000,000}{(1 + IRR)^1} + \frac{\$8,000,000}{(1 + IRR)^2} + \frac{-\$20,000,000}{(1 + IRR)^3}$$

By trial-and-error, $IRR \approx 19\%$ and $\approx 1581\%$. The $NPV = -\$1,641,998$ (−$1,640,000). Do not accept C.

CR7.4 $FV_A = \$350,000(1.10)^2 + \$250,000(1.10)^1 + \$80,000 = \$778,500$. $MIRR_A = 15.90\%$ and $MIRR_B = 16.96\%$.

CR7.5 For Select Seed $NPV = \$985$, $IRR = 28.86\%$, and $MIRR = 20.53\%$. For Cheap Seed $NPV = \$524$, $IRR = 48.30\%$, and $MIRR = 31.63\%$. Plant the Select Seed.

CR7.6

$$NPV_{A \text{ over 3 years}} = \frac{\$25,000}{(1.15)^1} + \frac{\$25,000}{(1.15)^2} + \frac{\$25,000}{(1.15)^3} - \$40,000$$

$$= \$17,081 \ (\$17,075)$$

$$NPV_{A \text{ over 9 years}} = \$17,081 + \frac{\$17,081}{(1.15)^3} + \frac{\$17,081}{(1.15)^6} = \$35,697 \ (\$35,687)$$

$NPV_B = \$22,985 \ (\$22,990)$; accept A.

CR7.7

$$\text{Equivalent annual } NPV_A = \$17,081 \bigg/ \left[\frac{1}{0.15} - \frac{1}{0.15(1.15)^3} \right] = \$7,481 \ (\$7,479)$$

$$\text{Equivalent annual } NPV_B = \$22,985 \bigg/ \left[\frac{1}{0.15} - \frac{1}{0.15(1.15)^9} \right] = \$4,817 \ (\$4,818)$$

Accept A.

CR7.8

Project	NPV
A	$21 ($20)
B	41
C	0
D	27
E	36
F	18

Take A, D, E, and F, with a total *NPV* of $102 ($101).

Chapter 8

CR8.1   a. Depreciation is $3,600 per year.
b. The remaining undepreciated value is $7,200, and net cash proceeds are $8,460.
c. The net cash proceeds are $5,310.

CR8.2   The $500,000 is a sunk cost and should be ignored. $CF_0 = \$200,000 + \$100,000 + \$40,000 = \$340,000$.

CR8.3   The operating cash flows are $183,500 per year.

CR8.4

Estimated resale value	$10,000
Less: Tax on sale ($10,000)(0.35)	−3,500
Recovery of net working capital	40,000
Net terminal cash inflow	$46,500

CR8.5 $NPV = \$314,121 \ (\$314,089)$; expand.

CR8.6   The initial investment, depreciation tax shield, and terminal cash flows remain the same. The operating cash flows decrease by ($125,000)(1 − 0.35) = $81,250 per year. The new *NPV* is $35,183 ($35,158). Still expand.

CR8.7   The incremental initial cash flows are:

Cost of new ovens	$300,000
Tax on sale of old ovens	

($100,000 − $60,000)(0.40)	16,000
Less: Sale of old ovens	−100,000
Incremental initial investment	$216,000

$\Delta CFBT$:

Year	1	2	3
Δrevenues	$58,500	$67,240	$76,240
Δcosts	6,000	12,176	18,544
$\Delta CFBT$	52,500	55,064	57,696
ΔDep	80,000	80,000	80,000
ΔCF	63,500	65,038	66,618

The incremental terminal cash flows are:

After-tax proceeds of selling new ovens	
($50,000)(1 − 0.40)	$30,000
After-tax proceeds of selling old ovens	
($20,000)(1 − 0.40)	−12,000
Incremental terminal cash flow	$18,000

$NPV = -\$47,226\ (-\$47,211)$; do not replace.

Chapter 9

CR9.1 $NPV_{10\text{-year}} = \$2,037,537(\$2,038,000)$, while $NPV_{5\text{-year}} = -\$1,295,690$ ($-\$1,296,000$). The expected net present value $= \$370,924\ (\$371,000)$.

CR9.2   a. The after-tax operating cash flows $= \$21,600$ per year and $NPV = \$8,469$ ($\$8,472$).

b.

Percent Change	Arrangements Sold per Year	NPV
−30%	420	−$12,072 (−$12,070)
−20	480	−5,225 (−5,222)
−10	540	1,622 (1,625)
0	600	8,469 (8,472)
+10	660	15,316 (15,319)
+20	720	22,163 (22,166)
+30	780	29,010 (29,014)

CR9.3   The break-even point in dollars is $18,928; in units the break-even point is ≈ 526 units.

CR9.4   a. The *NPVs* are −$14,354 (−$14,352) for the downturn, $8,469 ($8,472) for the base case, and $35,857 ($35,861) for the improved economy.

b. The expected *NPV* is $9,838 ($9,841) and the standard deviation about the expected *NPV* is $19,479 ($19,480).

CR9.5   a. $NPV = \$1,416\ (\$1,415)$; keep the mowers.

b. $NPV = \sum_{t=1}^{3} \dfrac{(\$7,000)}{(1.15)^t} - (\$10,000 + \$3,000) = \$2,983\ (\$2,981)$

Purchase the conversion kits.

Chapter 10

CR10.1 The gross offering is = $500,000/(1 - 0.15) = $588,235$, so the flotation costs are $88,235.

CR10.2 Net proceeds per share = $32(1 - 0.05) = 30.40. Number of shares = $10,000,000/$30.40 = 328,947$.

CR10.3 a. $EPS = $700,000/700,000 = 1 per share. Dividend = ($1)(0.70) = 0.70.

$$P_0 = \frac{D_1}{k_s - g} = \frac{\$0.70(1.08)}{0.12 - 0.08} = \$18.90$$

b. $P_0 = (18)($1) = 18

CR10.4

Cash	$ 250,000	Liabilities	$ 400,000
Other	750,000	Common stock ($1 par)	60,000
Total assets	$1,000,000	Additional paid-in capital	390,000
		Retained earnings	150,000
		Total liabilities and stockholders' equity	$1,000,000

Chapter 11

CR11.1

Year	Payment	Interest	Principal Repayment	Remaining Balance
1	$29,832	$15,000	$14,832	$85,168
2	29,832	12,775	17,057	68,111
3	29,832	10,217	19,615	48,496
4	29,832	7,274	22,558	25,938
5	29,829	3,891	25,938	0

CR11.2

Month	Payment	Interest	Principal Repayment	Remaining Balance
1	$2,379	$1,250	$1,129	$98,871
2	2,379	1,236	1,143	97,728
3	2,379	1,222	1,157	96,571
4	2,379	1,207	1,172	95,399
5	2,379	1,192	1,187	94,212

CR11.3 $B_0(\text{zero-coupon}) = $1,000/(1.10)^5 = $620.92 ($621.00)$. Number of zero-coupon bonds = $50,000,000/$620.92 = 80,526 (80,515)$. Number of coupon-bearing bonds = $50,000,000/$1,000 = 50,000$.

CR11.4 The bond prices before the increase were zero-coupon bond = $1,000/(1.10)^{20} = $148.64 ($149.00)$, and coupon-bearing bond = $1,000$. After the increase B_0 (zero-coupon) = $1,000/(1.12)^{20} = $103.67 ($104.00)$ and B_0 (coupon-bearing) = $850.61 ($850.90)$. The percentage loss was ($103.67 - $148.64)/$148.64 = -30.25\% (-30.20\%)$ for the zero-coupon bond and ($850.61 - $1,000)/$1,000 = -14.94\% (-14.91\%)$ for the coupon-bearing bond.

Chapter 12

CR12.1 a.

$$V = \frac{\$4.5 \text{ million}}{0.15} = \$30 \text{ million}$$

b. V = \$30 million and opportunity cost of capital = 15%.

$$15\% = (10\%)(\$15/\$30) + (k_s)(\$15/\$30)$$
$$k_s = (15\% - 5\%)/0.50 = 20\%$$

CR12.2 a.

$$V_U = \frac{\$30 \text{ million}(1 - 0.32)}{0.12} = \$170 \text{ million}$$

$$V_L = \$170 \text{ million} + \left[1 - \frac{(1 - 0.32)(1 - 0.20)}{(1 - 0.28)}\right]\$60 \text{ million} = \$184.7 \text{ million}$$

The gain from leverage is \$14.7 million.

b.

$$V_U = \frac{\$30 \text{ million}(1 - 0.30)}{0.12} = \$175 \text{ million}$$

$$V_L = \$175 \text{ million} + \left[1 - \frac{(1 - 0.30)(1 - 0.30)}{(1 - 0.30)}\right]\$60 \text{ million} = \$193 \text{ million}$$

With the 30% tax rate and $T_{PS} = T_{PB}$, the gain to leverage is TB = \$18 million.

CR12.3 a. Project I:

expected CF = 0.20(\$200,000) + 0.80(\$80,000) = \$104,000
σ = $[0.2(\$200,000 - \$104,000)^2 + 0.8(\$80,000 - \$104,000)^2]^{0.5}$ = \$48,000
For Project II: \$120,000 and \$10,000.

b.

$$NPV_\text{I} = \frac{\$104,000}{1.15} - \$100,000 = -\$9,565$$

$$NPV_\text{II} = \frac{\$120,000}{1.15} - \$100,000 = \$4,348$$

c. A stockholder would prefer I, whereas a bondholder would prefer II.

CR12.4

$$V_U = \frac{\$10 \text{ million}(1 - 0.40)}{0.15} = \$40 \text{ million}$$

	Without Financial Distress	With Financial Distress Costs
Debt	$V_L = V_U + TB$	$V_L = V_U + TB -$ financial distress
\$ 0	\$40	\$40.0
20	48	47.5
25	50	49.0
30	52	50.5
35	54	51.0
40	56	50.0
45	58	49.0

With no financial distress, use \$45 million debt. When financial distress is considered, employ \$35 million of debt.

CR12.5 **a.** With equity financing, *EAT* is $1,880,000; shares of common stock are 540,000, and *EPS* is $3.50. With debt financing, *EAT* is $1,836,800, and *EPS* is $3.67.

b.

$$\frac{(EBIT^* - \$800,000)(1 - 0.36)}{540,000} = \frac{(EBIT^* - \$880,000)(1 - 0.36)}{500,000}$$

$$EBIT^* = \$1,880,000$$

CR12.6 **a.** *EPS* = $2.50 and P_0 = $37.50.
b. *NPV* = ($800,000/0.10) − $6,000,000 = $2,000,000
c. *EPS* = $3.61 and P_0 = $46.93; accept the project.

Chapter 13

CR13.1

Net income = $50,000,000(1 − 0.35) = $32,500,000; equity financing needed = $25,000,000(0.40) = $10,000,000; dividends = $32,500,000 − $10,000,000 = $22,500,000; so the dividend payout ratio = $22,500,000/$32,500,000 = 69.23%.

CR13.2 **a.**

Common stock ($1 par value)	$ 1,100
Additional paid-in capital	32,900
Retained earnings	47,000
Total equity	$81,000

b.

Common stock ($0.25 par value)	$ 1,000
Additional paid-in capital	30,000
Retained earnings	50,000
Total equity	$81,000

CR13.3 Before the ex-dividend date P_0 = $100,000,000/5,000,000 = $20 and *P/E* = $20/$4 = 5 times. The dividends are (5,000,000)($1) = $5,000,000, so after the ex-dividend date the market value of equity is $100,000,000 − $5,000,000 = $95,000,000, P_0 = $95,000,000/5,000,000 = $19 and *P/E* = $19/$4 = 4.75 times.

CR13.4 The shares repurchased = $5,000,000/$20 = 250,000; number of common shares outstanding = 5,000,000 − 250,000 = 4,750,000; market value of equity = $95,000,000, P_0 = $95,000,000/4,750,000 = $20, *EPS* is [($4)(5,000,000)]/4,750,000 = $4.21, and *P/E* = $20/$4.21 = 4.75 times.

Chapter 14

CR14.1

$$NPV_{\text{lease}} = \$50,000 - \left[\left(\sum_{t=1}^{5} \frac{\$11,000(1 - 0.35)}{(1.078)^t}\right)(1.078) + \sum_{t=1}^{5} \frac{(\$50,000/5)0.35}{(1.078)^t}\right]$$

$$= \$50,000 - (\$30,938 + \$14,048) = \$5,014$$

Only an approximate answer can be determined using present value tables (since 7.8% is not on the tables). Using 8 percent instead of 7.8 percent, the present value table answer is $5,191.

CR14.2

$$NPV_{\text{lease}} = \$100,000 - \left[\left(\sum_{t=1}^{5} \frac{\$25,000(1 - 0.30)}{(1.098)^t} \right)(1.098) \right.$$

$$\left. - \sum_{t=1}^{5} \frac{(\$100,000/5)0.30}{(1.098)^t} - \sum_{t=1}^{5} \frac{\$4,000(1 - 0.30)}{(1.18)^t} - \frac{\$40,000\,(1 - 0.30)}{(1.18)^5} \right]$$

$$= \$100,000 - (\$73,214 + \$22,861 - \$8,756 + \$12,239) = \$442.$$

Only an approximate answer can be determined using present value tables (since 9.8% is not on the tables). Using 10 percent throughout, the present value table answer is $797.

CR14.3 $V_c = \text{Max}(0, \$54 - \$55)(100) = \$0$; $V_p = \text{Max}(0, \$60 - \$49)(100) = \$1,100$; so the profit $= \$0 + \$1,100 - \$300 - \$200 = \$600$.

CR14.4 a.

$$B_0 = \sum_{t=1}^{2 \times 20} \frac{\$60}{(1.07)^t} + \frac{\$1,000}{(1.07)^{2 \times 20}} = \$867$$

b. Conversion ratio $= \$1,000/\$25 = 40$ and conversion value $= (40)(\$10) = \$400$.

c. Value of convertible $= \$867 + (40)(\$4.48) \approx \$1,046$

Chapter 15

CR15.1 a. Days sales outstanding $= 365/6.75 = 54.07$; days inventory $= 365/9.54 = 38.26$; and the operating cycle $= 54.07 + 38.26 = 92.33$.

b. Days payable $= 365/9.13 = 39.98$, and the cash conversion cycle $= 92.33 - 39.98 = 52.35$.

CR15.2

Ratio	MaxIncome	SafetyFirst
Current ratio	1.10	5.29
Quick ratio	0.60	2.57
Net working capital	$3,671	$72,683
Receivables turnover	17.54	11.80
Inventory turnover	8.87	3.86
Payables turnover	13.78	25.64
Cash conversion cycle	35.47	111.26

CR15.3 a.

	Aggressive	Conservative
Net income	$13,173	$7,146
Current ratio	2.02	10.61
Receivables turnover	9.03	6.33
Inventory turnover	3.88	1.98

Payables turnover	9.28	33.58
Cash conversion cycle	95.16	231.13
Net profit margin	7.90%	3.85%
Return on equity	32.71%	20.01%

b. $EPS_{aggressive} = \$13,173/5,000 = \$2.63$; $P_{0\ aggressive} = 8(\$2.63) = \$21.04$.
$EPS_{conservative} = \$7,146/5,000\ \$1.43$; $P_{0\ conservative} = 12(\$1.43) = \$17.16$.

CR15.4 a.

	Aggressive	Matched	Conservative
Earnings per share			
Robust economy	$3.98	$3.30	$2.30
Standard economy	3.38	2.70	2.00
Poor economy	2.48	1.80	1.25
Expected *EPS*	$3.28	$2.60	$1.85
Standard deviation	$0.62	$0.62	$0.44

b. $P_{0\ aggressive} = 10(\$3.28) = \$32.80$; $P_{0\ matched} = 11(\$2.60) = \$28.60$; $P_{0\ conservative} = 12(\$1.85) = \$22.20$. Adopt the aggressive policy.

Chapter 16

CR16.1 a. $(6 - 4)(\$20,000) = \$40,000$

b. $\Delta B = (\$40,000)(2)(0.06/365)(1 - 0.36) = \$8.42$

CR16.2 $\Delta B = (4.15 - 2.84)(\$500,000,000)(0.087/365)(1 - 0.40) = \$93,674$

CR16.3 $\$100(1 - 0.40) = (7)(TS)(0.05/365)(1 - 0.40)$; so $TS = \$104,286$.

CR16.4 a.

$$k_{BD} = \left(\frac{\$10,000 - \$9,900}{\$10,000}\right)\left(\frac{360}{50}\right) = 7.20\%$$

b.

$$k_{BE} = \frac{(365)(0.072)}{360 - (0.072)(50)} = 7.37\%$$

c.

$$P_0 = \$10,000\left[1 - \frac{(0.075)(40)}{360}\right] = \$9,917$$

$$k_{BE} = \frac{(\$9,917 - \$9,900)(365)}{(\$9,900)(10)} = 6.27\%$$

Chapter 17

CR17.1 Credit score$_A$ = 5(2.2) + 7(6) − 9(2) = 35; credit score$_B$ = 5(2) + 7(5) − 9(4) = 9; credit score$_C$ = 5(2.5) + 7(4) − 9(3) = 13.5.

CR17.2

$$NPV_A = \frac{\$33,000}{0.12} - \$21,575 = \$253,425; \; NPV_B = -\$20,814; \; \text{and} \; NPV_C$$

$$= \$134,795$$

CR17.3

	August	September	October	November	December
Percent of same month's sales	91%	92%	93%	93%	
Percent of 1 month before		41	52	63	68%
Percent of 2 months before			0	0	0

CR17.4

$$\Delta CF_0 = (0.70)(\$17,000,000)(55/365) - (0.70)(\$20,000,000)(65/365)$$
$$= -\$700,000$$
$$\Delta CF_t = [\$17,000,000(1 - 0.70) - \$17,000,000(0.12) - \$500,000](1 - 0.35)$$
$$- [\$20,000,000(1 - 0.70) - \$20,000,000(0.15) - \$250,000](1 - 0.35)$$
$$= -\$123,500$$

$$NPV = \frac{-\$123,500}{0.14} - (-\$700,000) = -\$182,143$$

CR17.5

$$NPV = \frac{\$200,000}{0.15} - \$1,500,000 = -\$166,667$$

Chapter 18

CR18.1 First National:
$$k_{\text{nom}} = 0.10(365/360) = 0.10139; \; k_b = 10.62\%$$

Commerce National Bank:
$$k_{\text{nom}} = 0.102(365/360) = 0.10342; \; k_b = 10.61\%$$

CR18.2 a.

$$k_b = \left(1 + \frac{0.01}{1 - 0.01}\right)^{365/(30-15)} - 1 = 27.71\%$$

b.

$$k_b = \left(1 + \frac{0.01}{1 - 0.01}\right)^{365/(60-15)} - 1 = 8.49\%$$

CR18.3 Interest with regular interest = (\$500,000)(0.12)(275/365) = \$45,205.

$$k_{b \text{ regular interest}} = \left(1 + \frac{\$45,205}{\$500,000}\right)^{365/275} - 1 = 12.17\%$$

Interest with discount interest = (\$500,000)(0.08)(275/365) = \$30,167.

$$k_{b \text{ discount loan}} = \left(1 + \frac{\$30,137}{\$469,863}\right)^{365/275} - 1 = 8.60\%$$

Interest with installment interest = ($500,000)(0.07)(275/365) = $26,370.

$$\text{monthly payment} = \frac{\$500,000 + \$26,370}{9} = \$58,486$$

$$\$500,000 = \sum_{t=1}^{9} \frac{\$58,486}{(1 + k_b)^t} = k_b = 1.0406\% \text{ per month, or } 12.49\% \text{ per year}$$

CR18.4   Interest = ($20,000)(0.10)(20/365) + ($20,000)(0.12)(20/365)
+ ($20,000)(0.08)(20/365) = $109.59 + $131.51 + $87.67 = $328.77.

$$k_b = \left(1 + \frac{\$328.77}{\$20,000}\right)^{365/60} - 1 = 10.43\%$$

CR18.5   Commitment fee = ($500,000 − $200,000)(0.01)(60/365) + ($500,000 −
− $400,000)(0.01)(100/365) + ($500,000 − 0)(0.01)(20/365)
= $493.15 + $273.97 + $273.97 = $1,041.09.
Interest = ($200,000)(0.15)(60/365) + ($400,000)(0.15)(100/365)
= $4,931.51 + $16,438.36 = $21,369.87.
Average financing = ($200,000)(60/180) + ($400,000)(100/180) = $288,888.89.

$$k_b = \left(1 + \frac{\$1,041.09 + \$21,369.87}{\$288,888.89}\right)^{365/180} - 1 = 16.36\%$$

CR18.6   Interest is $15,000, and commitment fee is ($1,000,000)(0.005)(60/365) =
$821.92.

$$k_b = \left(1 + \frac{\$15,000 + \$821.92}{\$985,000 - \$10,000}\right)^{365/60} - 1 = 10.29\%$$

CR18.7   The loan amount is ($80,000)(0.80) = $64,000 in either case. With the bank, processing fee is ($64,000)(0.005) = $320 and interest is ($64,000)(0.12)(1/12) = $640.

$$k_{b\ \text{bank}} = \left(1 + \frac{\$320 + \$640}{\$64,000}\right)^{12/1} - 1 = 19.56\%$$

The factoring fee is ($64,000)(0.02) = $1,280.

$$k_{b\ \text{factor}} = \left(1 + \frac{\$1,280 - \$200}{\$64,000}\right)^{12/1} - 1 = 22.24\%$$

CR18.8   The factoring fee is ($80,000)(0.01) = $800, and interest is
($64,000)(0.12)(1/12) = $640.

$$k_b = \left(1 + \frac{\$800 + \$640 - \$300}{\$64,000}\right)^{12/1} - 1 = 23.60\%$$

CR18.9   The loan amount is ($800,000)(0.60) = $480,000, processing fee is
($480,000)(0.01) = $4,800, and interest is ($480,000)(0.15)(80/365) =
$15,780.82.

$$k_b = \left(1 + \frac{\$4,800 + \$15,780.82}{\$480,000}\right)^{365/80} - 1 = 21.11\%$$

Chapter 19

CR19.1 **a.**

EBIT	$700,000
Interest	100,000
EBT	600,000
Taxes	70,000
EAT, or net income	530,000
Dividends on preferred stock	50,000
Earning available for common stockholders	$480,000

Simple *EPS* = $480,000/$30,000 = $16.00; primary *EPS* = $13.71; and fully diluted *EPS* = $12.00

b. $480,000 − $200,000 = $280,000

CR19.2

Cash	7.2%
Accounts receivable	20.6
Inventory	25.8
Long-term investment	3.1
Plant and equipment (net)	43.3
Total assets	100.0%

Accounts payable	10.3%
Notes payable	15.5
Accrued taxes	2.1
Bond payable	30.9
Preferred stock	5.2
Common stock	5.2
Capital paid in excess of par	10.3
Retained earnings	20.6
Total liabilities and stockholders' equity	≈ 100.0%

Sales	100.0%
Cost of goods sold	75.0
Gross margin	25.0
Selling and administrative expenses	10.0
EBIT	15.0
Interest expense	2.5
EBT	12.5
Taxes	3.8
Net income	8.7%

Current ratio = $520,000/$270,000 = 1.9
Quick ratio = $270,000/$270,000 = 1.0
Days sales outstanding = $200,000/($2,000,000/365) = 36.5 days
Inventory turnover = $1,500,000/$250,000 = 6.0
Long-term asset turnover = $2,000,000/$450,000 = 4.4
Total asset turnover = $2,000,000/$970,000 = 2.1
Total debt to total assets = $570,000/$970,000 = 58.8%
Times interest earned = $300,000/$50,000 = 6.0
Fixed charge coverage = $310,000/$60,000 = 5.2

Net profit margin = $175,000/$2,000,000 = 8.8%
Return on total assets = $175,000/$970,000 = 18.0%
Return on equity = $175,000/$400,000 = 43.8%
Earnings per share = ($175,000 − $4,000)/50,000 = $3.42
Price/earnings = $20/$3.42 = 5.8
Dividend yield = $1.00/$20 = 5.0%
Dividend payout = $1.00/$3.42 = 29.2%

CR19.3 Return on equity = 12.5%/(1 − 0.40) = 20.8%

CR19.4

	Johnson	Bartell
Current ratio	2.1	4.1
Quick ratio	0.8	3.4
Days sales outstanding	21.5	35.6
Inventory turnover	2.9	14.5
Long-term asset turnover	57.0	34.0
Total asset turnover	2.2	2.7
Total debt to total assets	0.5	0.4
Times interest earned	8.7	8.7
Net profit margin	5.4%	3.7%
Return on total assets	11.8%	10.1%
Return on equity	24.8%	16.3%

a. Both suppliers and short-term lenders are concerned with liquidity ratios; they would favor Bartell.

b. Johnson has more debt but the same times interest earned as Bartell. Johnson is more profitable; a slight nod to Johnson.

c. Stockholders are particularly concerned with profitability ratios; another slight nod to Johnson.

Chapter 20

CR20.1

	Sales (Y_t)	Period (X_t)	$Y_t X_t$	X_t^2
	10	1	10	1
	10	2	20	4
	10.5	3	31.5	9
	11.5	4	46	16
	13	5	65	25
Totals	55	15	172.5	55

$\overline{Y} = \sum Y_t/n = 55/5 = 11$

$\overline{X} = \sum X_t/n = 15/5 = 3$

$\beta = [172.5 − (5)(11)(3)]/[55 − 5(3^2)] = 0.75$
$\alpha = 11 − 0.75(3) = 8.75$
$Y_t = \$8.75 + \$0.75 X_t$

The predicted sales for the next 3 years are $13.25 million, $14.00 million, and $14.75 million.

CR20.2 Cumulative short-term financing needed ($-$) or surplus ($+$) per month is $-\$65{,}250$, $-\$46{,}750$, $-\$27{,}750$, $+\$32{,}250$, $-\$34{,}000$, and $-\$10{,}000$.

CR20.3 The transfer to retained earnings is $9.0 million, total assets are $87.3 million, and total liabilities and stockholders' equity is $81.1 million. The firm needs $6.2 million in outside financing.

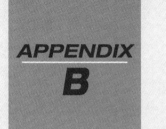

Financial Tables

TABLE B.1

Present Value Factors for $1 Discounted at k Percent for n Periods:

$$PV_{k,n} = \frac{1}{(1+k)^n}$$

Discount Rate, k

Period, n	1%	2%	3%	4%	5%	6%	7%	8%	9%	10%	11%	12%	13%	14%	15%	16%	17%	18%	19%	20%
1	0.990	0.980	0.971	0.962	0.952	0.943	0.935	0.926	0.917	0.909	0.901	0.893	0.885	0.877	0.870	0.862	0.855	0.847	0.840	0.833
2	0.980	0.961	0.943	0.925	0.907	0.890	0.873	0.857	0.842	0.826	0.812	0.797	0.783	0.769	0.756	0.743	0.731	0.718	0.706	0.694
3	0.971	0.942	0.915	0.889	0.864	0.840	0.816	0.794	0.772	0.751	0.731	0.712	0.693	0.675	0.658	0.641	0.624	0.609	0.593	0.579
4	0.961	0.924	0.888	0.855	0.823	0.792	0.763	0.735	0.708	0.683	0.659	0.636	0.613	0.592	0.572	0.552	0.534	0.516	0.499	0.482
5	0.951	0.906	0.863	0.822	0.784	0.747	0.713	0.681	0.650	0.621	0.593	0.567	0.543	0.519	0.497	0.476	0.456	0.437	0.410	0.402
6	0.942	0.888	0.837	0.790	0.746	0.705	0.666	0.630	0.596	0.564	0.535	0.507	0.480	0.456	0.432	0.410	0.390	0.370	0.352	0.335
7	0.933	0.871	0.813	0.760	0.711	0.665	0.623	0.583	0.547	0.513	0.482	0.452	0.425	0.400	0.376	0.354	0.333	0.314	0.296	0.279
8	0.923	0.853	0.789	0.731	0.677	0.627	0.582	0.540	0.502	0.467	0.434	0.404	0.376	0.351	0.327	0.305	0.285	0.266	0.249	0.233
9	0.914	0.837	0.766	0.703	0.645	0.592	0.544	0.500	0.460	0.424	0.391	0.361	0.333	0.308	0.284	0.263	0.243	0.225	0.209	0.194
10	0.905	0.820	0.744	0.676	0.614	0.558	0.508	0.463	0.422	0.386	0.352	0.322	0.295	0.270	0.247	0.227	0.208	0.191	0.176	0.162
11	0.896	0.804	0.722	0.650	0.585	0.527	0.475	0.429	0.388	0.350	0.317	0.287	0.261	0.237	0.215	0.195	0.178	0.162	0.148	0.135
12	0.887	0.788	0.701	0.625	0.557	0.497	0.444	0.397	0.356	0.319	0.286	0.256	0.231	0.208	0.187	0.168	0.152	0.137	0.124	0.112
13	0.879	0.773	0.681	0.601	0.530	0.469	0.415	0.368	0.326	0.290	0.258	0.229	0.204	0.182	0.163	0.145	0.130	0.116	0.104	0.093
14	0.870	0.758	0.661	0.577	0.505	0.442	0.388	0.340	0.299	0.263	0.232	0.205	0.181	0.160	0.141	0.125	0.111	0.099	0.088	0.078
15	0.861	0.743	0.642	0.555	0.481	0.417	0.362	0.315	0.275	0.239	0.209	0.183	0.160	0.140	0.123	0.108	0.095	0.084	0.074	0.065
16	0.853	0.728	0.623	0.534	0.458	0.394	0.339	0.292	0.252	0.218	0.188	0.163	0.141	0.123	0.107	0.093	0.081	0.071	0.062	0.054
17	0.844	0.714	0.605	0.513	0.436	0.371	0.317	0.270	0.231	0.198	0.170	0.146	0.125	0.108	0.093	0.080	0.069	0.060	0.052	0.045
18	0.836	0.700	0.587	0.494	0.416	0.350	0.296	0.250	0.212	0.180	0.153	0.130	0.111	0.095	0.081	0.069	0.059	0.051	0.044	0.038
19	0.828	0.686	0.570	0.475	0.396	0.331	0.277	0.232	0.194	0.165	0.138	0.116	0.098	0.083	0.070	0.060	0.051	0.043	0.037	0.031
20	0.820	0.673	0.554	0.456	0.377	0.312	0.258	0.215	0.178	0.149	0.124	0.104	0.087	0.073	0.061	0.051	0.043	0.037	0.031	0.026
21	0.811	0.660	0.538	0.439	0.359	0.294	0.242	0.199	0.164	0.135	0.112	0.093	0.077	0.064	0.053	0.044	0.037	0.031	0.026	0.022
22	0.803	0.647	0.522	0.422	0.342	0.278	0.226	0.184	0.150	0.123	0.101	0.083	0.068	0.056	0.046	0.038	0.032	0.026	0.022	0.018
23	0.795	0.634	0.507	0.406	0.326	0.262	0.211	0.170	0.138	0.112	0.091	0.074	0.060	0.049	0.040	0.033	0.027	0.022	0.018	0.015
24	0.788	0.622	0.492	0.390	0.310	0.247	0.197	0.158	0.126	0.102	0.082	0.066	0.053	0.043	0.035	0.028	0.023	0.019	0.015	0.013
25	0.780	0.610	0.478	0.375	0.295	0.233	0.184	0.146	0.116	0.092	0.071	0.059	0.047	0.038	0.030	0.024	0.020	0.016	0.013	0.010
26	0.772	0.598	0.464	0.361	0.281	0.220	0.172	0.135	0.106	0.084	0.066	0.053	0.042	0.033	0.026	0.021	0.017	0.014	0.011	0.009
27	0.764	0.586	0.450	0.347	0.268	0.207	0.161	0.125	0.098	0.076	0.060	0.047	0.037	0.029	0.023	0.018	0.014	0.011	0.009	0.007
28	0.757	0.574	0.437	0.333	0.255	0.196	0.150	0.116	0.090	0.069	0.054	0.042	0.033	0.026	0.020	0.016	0.012	0.010	0.008	0.006
29	0.749	0.563	0.424	0.321	0.243	0.185	0.141	0.107	0.082	0.063	0.048	0.037	0.029	0.022	0.017	0.014	0.011	0.008	0.006	0.005
30	0.742	0.552	0.412	0.308	0.231	0.174	0.131	0.099	0.075	0.057	0.044	0.033	0.026	0.020	0.015	0.012	0.009	0.007	0.005	0.004
35	0.706	0.500	0.355	0.253	0.181	0.130	0.094	0.068	0.049	0.036	0.026	0.019	0.014	0.010	0.008	0.006	0.004	0.003	0.002	0.002
40	0.672	0.453	0.307	0.208	0.142	0.097	0.067	0.046	0.032	0.022	0.015	0.011	0.008	0.005	0.004	0.003	0.002	0.001	0.001	0.001
45	0.639	0.410	0.264	0.171	0.111	0.073	0.048	0.031	0.021	0.014	0.009	0.006	0.004	0.003	0.002	0.001	0.001	0.001	*	*
50	0.608	0.372	0.228	0.141	0.087	0.054	0.023	0.021	0.013	0.009	0.005	0.003	0.002	0.001	0.001	0.001	*	*	*	*

TABLE B.1

$PV_{k,n}$ (Continued)

Period, n	Discount Rate, k																			
	21%	22%	23%	24%	25%	26%	27%	28%	29%	30%	31%	32%	33%	34%	35%	40%	45%	50%	55%	60%
1	0.826	0.820	0.813	0.806	0.800	0.794	0.787	0.781	0.775	0.769	0.763	0.758	0.752	0.746	0.741	0.714	0.690	0.667	0.645	0.625
2	0.683	0.672	0.661	0.650	0.640	0.630	0.620	0.610	0.601	0.592	0.583	0.574	0.565	0.557	0.549	0.510	0.476	0.444	0.416	0.391
3	0.564	0.551	0.537	0.524	0.512	0.500	0.488	0.477	0.466	0.455	0.445	0.435	0.425	0.416	0.406	0.364	0.328	0.296	0.269	0.244
4	0.467	0.451	0.437	0.423	0.410	0.397	0.384	0.373	0.361	0.350	0.340	0.329	0.320	0.310	0.301	0.260	0.226	0.198	0.173	0.153
5	0.386	0.370	0.355	0.341	0.328	0.315	0.303	0.291	0.280	0.269	0.259	0.250	0.240	0.231	0.223	0.186	0.156	0.132	0.112	0.095
6	0.319	0.303	0.289	0.275	0.262	0.250	0.238	0.227	0.217	0.207	0.198	0.189	0.181	0.173	0.165	0.133	0.108	0.088	0.072	0.060
7	0.263	0.249	0.235	0.222	0.210	0.198	0.188	0.178	0.168	0.159	0.151	0.143	0.136	0.129	0.122	0.095	0.074	0.059	0.047	0.037
8	0.218	0.204	0.191	0.179	0.168	0.157	0.148	0.139	0.130	0.123	0.115	0.108	0.102	0.096	0.091	0.068	0.051	0.039	0.030	0.023
9	0.180	0.167	0.155	0.144	0.134	0.125	0.116	0.108	0.101	0.094	0.088	0.082	0.077	0.072	0.067	0.048	0.035	0.026	0.019	0.015
10	0.149	0.137	0.126	0.116	0.107	0.099	0.092	0.085	0.078	0.073	0.067	0.062	0.058	0.054	0.050	0.035	0.024	0.017	0.012	0.009
11	0.123	0.112	0.103	0.094	0.086	0.079	0.072	0.066	0.061	0.056	0.051	0.047	0.043	0.040	0.037	0.025	0.017	0.012	0.008	0.006
12	0.102	0.092	0.083	0.076	0.069	0.062	0.057	0.052	0.047	0.043	0.039	0.036	0.033	0.030	0.027	0.018	0.012	0.008	0.005	0.004
13	0.084	0.075	0.068	0.061	0.055	0.050	0.045	0.040	0.037	0.033	0.030	0.027	0.025	0.022	0.020	0.013	0.008	0.005	0.003	0.002
14	0.069	0.062	0.055	0.049	0.044	0.039	0.035	0.032	0.028	0.025	0.023	0.021	0.018	0.017	0.015	0.009	0.006	0.003	0.002	0.001
15	0.057	0.051	0.045	0.040	0.035	0.031	0.028	0.025	0.022	0.020	0.017	0.016	0.014	0.012	0.011	0.006	0.004	0.002	0.001	0.001
16	0.047	0.042	0.036	0.032	0.028	0.025	0.022	0.019	0.017	0.015	0.013	0.012	0.010	0.009	0.008	0.005	0.003	0.002	0.001	0.001
17	0.039	0.034	0.030	0.026	0.023	0.020	0.017	0.015	0.013	0.012	0.010	0.009	0.008	0.007	0.006	0.003	0.002	0.001	0.001	*
18	0.032	0.028	0.024	0.021	0.018	0.016	0.014	0.012	0.010	0.009	0.008	0.007	0.006	0.005	0.005	0.002	0.001	0.001	*	*
19	0.027	0.023	0.020	0.017	0.014	0.012	0.011	0.009	0.008	0.007	0.006	0.005	0.004	0.004	0.003	0.002	0.001	*	*	*
20	0.022	0.019	0.016	0.014	0.012	0.010	0.008	0.007	0.006	0.005	0.005	0.004	0.003	0.003	0.002	0.001	0.001	*	*	*
21	0.018	0.015	0.013	0.011	0.009	0.008	0.007	0.006	0.005	0.004	0.003	0.003	0.003	0.002	0.002	0.001	*	*	*	*
22	0.015	0.013	0.011	0.009	0.007	0.006	0.005	0.004	0.004	0.003	0.003	0.002	0.002	0.002	0.001	0.001	*	*	*	*
23	0.012	0.010	0.009	0.007	0.006	0.005	0.004	0.003	0.003	0.002	0.002	0.002	0.001	0.001	0.001	*	*	*	*	*
24	0.010	0.008	0.007	0.006	0.005	0.004	0.003	0.003	0.002	0.002	0.002	0.001	0.001	0.001	0.001	*	*	*	*	*
25	0.009	0.007	0.006	0.005	0.004	0.003	0.003	0.002	0.002	0.001	0.001	0.001	0.001	0.001	0.001	*	*	*	*	*
26	0.007	0.006	0.005	0.004	0.003	0.002	0.002	0.002	0.001	0.001	0.001	0.001	0.001	*	*	*	*	*	*	*
27	0.006	0.005	0.004	0.003	0.002	0.002	0.002	0.001	0.001	0.001	0.001	0.001	*	*	*	*	*	*	*	*
28	0.005	0.004	0.003	0.002	0.002	0.001	0.001	0.001	0.001	0.001	0.001	*	*	*	*	*	*	*	*	*
29	0.004	0.003	0.002	0.002	0.002	0.001	0.001	0.001	0.001	*	*	*	*	*	*	*	*	*	*	*
30	0.003	0.003	0.002	0.002	0.001	0.001	0.001	0.001	*	*	*	*	*	*	*	*	*	*	*	*
35	0.001	0.001	0.001	0.001	*	*	*	*	*	*	*	*	*	*	*	*	*	*	*	*
40	*	*	*	*	*	*	*	*	*	*	*	*	*	*	*	*	*	*	*	*
45	*	*	*	*	*	*	*	*	*	*	*	*	*	*	*	*	*	*	*	*
50	*	*	*	*	*	*	*	*	*	*	*	*	*	*	*	*	*	*	*	*

*Value is zero to three decimal places.

TABLE B.2
Present Value Factors for an Annuity of $1 Discounted at k Percent for n Periods:

$$PVA_{k,n} = \sum_{t=1}^{n} \frac{1}{(1+k)^t} = \frac{1}{k} - \frac{1}{k(1+k)^n}$$

Period, n	1%	2%	3%	4%	5%	6%	7%	8%	9%	10%	11%	12%	13%	14%	15%	16%	17%	18%	19%	20%
1	0.990	0.980	0.971	0.962	0.952	0.943	0.935	0.926	0.917	0.909	0.901	0.893	0.885	0.877	0.870	0.862	0.855	0.847	0.840	0833
2	1.970	1.942	1.913	1.886	1.859	1.833	1.808	1.783	1.759	1.736	1.713	1.690	1.668	1.647	1.626	1.605	1.585	1.566	1.547	1.528
3	2.941	2.884	2.829	2.775	2.723	2.673	2.624	2.577	2.531	2.487	2.444	2.402	2.361	2.322	2.283	2.246	2.210	2.174	2.140	2.106
4	3.902	3.808	3.717	3.630	3.546	3.465	3.387	3.312	3.240	3.170	3.102	3.037	2.974	2.914	2.855	2.798	2.743	2.690	2.639	2.589
5	4.853	4.713	4.580	4.452	4.329	4.212	4.100	3.993	3.890	3.791	3.696	3.605	3.517	3.433	3.352	3.274	3.199	3.127	3.058	2.991
6	5.795	5.601	5.417	5.242	5.076	4.917	4.767	4.623	4.486	4.355	4.231	4.111	3.998	3.889	3.784	3.685	3.589	3.498	3.410	3.326
7	6.728	6.472	6.230	6.002	5.786	5.582	5.389	5.206	5.033	4.868	4.712	4.564	4.423	4.288	4.160	4.039	3.922	3.812	3.706	3.605
8	7.652	7.325	7.020	6.733	6.463	6.210	5.971	5.747	5.535	5.335	5.146	4.968	4.799	4.639	4.487	4.344	4.207	4.078	3.954	3.837
9	8.566	8.162	7.786	7.425	7.108	6.802	6.515	6.247	5.995	5.759	5.537	5.328	5.132	4.946	4.772	4.607	4.451	4.303	4.163	4.031
10	9.471	8.983	8.530	8.111	7.722	7.360	7.024	6.710	6.418	6.145	5.889	5.650	5.426	5.216	5.019	4.833	4.659	4.494	4.339	4.192
11	10.368	9.787	9.253	8.760	8.306	7.887	7.499	7.139	6.805	6.495	6.207	5.938	5.687	5.453	5.234	5.029	4.836	4.656	4.486	4.237
12	11.255	10.575	9.954	9.385	8.863	8.384	7.943	7.536	7.161	6.814	6.492	6.194	5.918	5.660	5.421	5.197	4.988	4.793	4.611	4.439
13	12.134	11.348	10.635	9.986	9.394	8.853	8.358	7.904	7.487	7.103	6.750	6.424	6.122	5.842	5.583	5.342	5.118	4.910	4.715	4.533
14	13.004	12.106	11.296	10.563	9.899	9.295	8.745	8.244	7.786	7.367	6.982	6.628	6.302	6.002	5.724	5.468	5.229	5.008	4.802	4.611
15	13.865	12.849	11.938	11.118	10.380	9.712	9.108	8.559	8.061	7.606	7.191	6.811	6.462	6.142	5.847	5.575	5.324	5.092	4.876	4.675
16	14.718	13.578	12.561	11.652	10.838	10.106	9.447	8.851	8.313	7.824	7.379	6.974	6.604	6.265	5.954	5.668	5.405	5.162	4.938	4.730
17	15.562	14.292	13.166	12.166	11.274	10.477	9.763	9.122	8.544	8.022	7.549	7.120	6.729	6.373	6.047	5.749	5.475	5.222	4.990	4.775
18	16.398	14.992	13.754	12.659	11.690	10.828	10.059	9.372	8.756	8.201	7.702	7.250	6.840	6.467	6.128	5.818	5.523	5.273	5.033	4.812
19	17.226	15.678	14.324	13.134	12.085	11.158	10.336	9.604	8.950	8.365	7.839	7.366	6.938	6.550	6.198	5.877	5.584	5.316	5.070	4.843
20	18.046	16.351	14.877	13.590	12.462	11.470	10.594	9.818	9.129	8.514	7.963	7.469	7.025	6.623	6.259	5.929	5.638	5.353	5.101	4.870
21	18.857	17.001	15.415	14.029	12.821	11.764	10.836	10.017	9.292	8.649	8.075	7.562	7.102	6.687	6.312	5.973	5.665	5.384	5.127	4.891
22	19.660	17.658	15.937	14.451	13.163	12.042	11.061	10.201	9.442	8.772	8.176	7.645	7.170	6.743	6.359	6.011	5.696	5.410	5.149	4.909
23	20.456	18.292	16.444	14.857	13.489	12.303	11.272	10.371	9.580	8.883	8.266	7.718	7.230	6.792	6.399	6.044	5.723	5.432	5.167	4.925
24	21.243	18.914	16.936	15.247	13.799	12.550	11.469	10.529	9.707	8.985	8.348	7.783	7.283	6.835	6.434	6.073	5.746	5.451	5.182	4.937
25	22.023	19.523	17.413	15.622	14.094	12.783	11.654	10.675	9.823	9.077	8.422	7.843	7.330	6.873	6.464	6.094	5.766	5.467	5.195	4.948
26	22.795	20.121	17.877	15.983	14.375	13.003	11.826	10.810	9.929	9.161	8.488	7.896	7.372	6.906	6.491	6.118	5.783	5.480	5.206	4.956
27	23.560	21.281	18.764	16.663	14.643	13.211	11.987	10.935	10.027	9.237	8.548	7.943	7.409	6.935	6.514	6.136	5.798	5.492	5.215	4.964
28	24.316	21.281	18.764	16.663	14.898	13.406	12.137	11.051	10.116	9.307	8.602	7.984	7.441	6.961	6.534	6.152	5.810	5.502	5.223	4.970
29	25.808	21.844	19.188	16.984	15.141	13.591	12.28	11.158	10.198	9.370	8.650	8.022	7.470	6.983	6.551	6.166	5.820	5.510	5.229	4.975
30	25.808	22.396	19.600	17.292	15.372	13.765	12.409	11.258	10.274	9.427	8.694	8.055	7.496	7.003	6.566	6.177	5.829	5.517	5.235	4.979
35	29.409	24.999	21.487	18.665	16.374	14.498	12.948	11.655	10.567	9.644	8.855	8.176	7.586	7.070	6.617	6.215	5.858	5.539	5.251	4.992
40	32.835	27.355	23.115	19.793	17.159	15.046	13.332	11.925	10.757	9.779	8.951	8.244	7.634	7.102	6.642	6.233	5.871	5.548	5.258	4.997
45	36.095	29.490	24.519	20.720	17.774	15.456	13.606	12.108	10.881	9.863	9.008	8.283	7.661	7.123	6.654	6.242	5.877	5.552	5.261	4.999
50	39.196	31.424	25.730	21.482	18.256	15.762	13.801	12.233	10.962	9.915	9.042	8.304	7.675	7.133	6.661	6.246	5.880	5.554	5.262	4.999

TABLE B.2

$PVA_{k,n}$ (Continued)

Period, n	21%	22%	23%	24%	25%	26%	27%	28%	29%	30%	31%	32%	33%	34%	35%	40%	45%	50%	55%	60%
1	0.826	0.820	0.813	0.806	0.800	0.794	0.787	0.781	0.775	0.769	0.763	0.758	0.752	0.746	0.741	0.714	0.690	0.667	0.645	0.625
2	1.509	1.492	1.474	1.457	1.440	1.424	1.407	1.392	1.376	1.361	1.346	1.331	1.317	1.303	1.289	1.224	1.165	1.111	1.061	1.016
3	2.074	2.042	2.011	1.981	1.952	1.923	1.896	1.868	1.842	1.816	1.791	1.766	1.742	1.719	1.696	1.589	1.493	1.407	1.330	1.260
4	2.540	2.494	2.448	2.404	2.362	2.320	2.280	2.241	2.203	2.166	2.130	2.096	2.062	2.029	1.997	1.849	1.720	1.605	1.503	1.412
5	2.926	2.864	2.803	2.745	2.689	2.635	2.583	2.532	2.483	2.436	2.390	2.345	2.302	2.260	2.220	2.035	1.876	1.737	1.615	1.508
6	3.245	3.167	3.092	3.020	2.951	2.885	2.821	2.759	2.700	2.643	2.588	2.534	2.483	2.433	2.385	2.168	1.983	1.824	1.687	1.567
7	3.508	3.416	3.327	3.242	3.161	3.083	3.009	2.937	2.868	2.802	2.739	2.677	2.610	2.562	2.508	2.263	2.057	1.883	1.734	1.605
8	3.726	3.619	3.518	3.421	3.329	3.241	3.156	3.076	2.999	2.925	2.854	2.786	2.721	2.658	2.598	2.331	2.109	1.922	1.764	1.628
9	3.905	3.786	3.673	3.566	3.463	3.366	3.273	3.184	3.100	3.019	2.942	2.868	2.798	2.730	2.665	2.379	2.144	1.948	1.783	1.642
10	4.054	3.923	3.799	3.682	3.571	3.465	3.364	3.269	3.178	3.092	3.009	2.930	2.855	2.784	2.715	2.414	2.168	1.965	1.795	1.652
11	4.177	4.035	3.902	3.776	3.656	3.543	3.437	3.335	3.239	3.147	3.060	2.978	2.899	2.824	2.752	2.438	2.185	1.977	1.804	1.657
12	4.278	4.127	3.985	3.851	3.725	3.606	3.493	3.387	3.286	3.190	3.100	3.013	2.931	2.853	2.779	2.456	2.196	1.985	1.809	1.661
13	4.362	4.203	4.053	3.912	3.780	3.656	3.538	3.427	3.322	3.223	3.129	3.040	2.956	2.876	2.799	2.469	2.204	1.990	1.812	1.663
14	4.432	4.265	4.108	3.962	3.824	3.695	3.573	3.459	3.351	3.249	3.152	3.061	2.974	2.892	2.814	2.478	2.210	1.993	1.814	1.664
15	4.489	4.315	4.153	4.001	3.859	3.726	3.601	3.483	3.373	3.268	3.170	3.076	2.988	2.905	2.825	2.484	2.214	1.995	1.816	1.665
16	4.536	4.357	4.189	4.033	3.887	3.751	3.623	3.503	3.390	3.283	3.183	3.088	3.000	2.914	2.834	2.489	2.216	1.997	1.817	1.666
17	4.576	4.391	4.219	4.059	3.901	3.771	3.640	3.518	3.403	3.295	3.193	3.097	3.007	2.921	2.840	2.492	2.218	1.998	1.817	1.666
18	4.608	4.419	4.243	4.080	3.928	3.786	3.654	3.529	3.413	3.304	3.201	3.104	3.012	2.926	2.844	2.494	2.219	1.999	1.818	1.666
19	4.635	4.442	4.263	4.097	3.942	3.799	3.664	3.539	3.421	3.311	3.207	3.109	3.017	2.930	2.848	2.496	2.220	1.999	1.818	1.666
20	4.657	4.460	4.279	4.110	3.954	3.808	3.673	3.546	3.427	3.316	3.211	3.113	3.020	2.933	2.850	2.497	2.221	1.999	1.818	1.667
21	4.675	4.476	4.292	4.121	3.963	3.816	3.679	3.551	3.432	3.320	3.215	3.116	3.023	2.935	2.852	2.498	2.221	2.000	1.818	1.667
22	4.690	4.488	4.302	4.130	3.970	3.822	3.684	3.556	3.436	3.323	3.217	3.118	3.025	2.936	2.853	2.498	2.222	2.000	1.818	1.667
23	4.703	4.499	4.311	4.137	3.976	3.827	3.689	3.559	3.438	3.325	3.219	3.120	3.026	2.938	2.854	2.499	2.222	2.000	1.818	1.667
24	4.713	4.507	4.318	4.143	3.981	3.831	3.692	3.562	3.441	3.327	3.221	3.121	3.027	2.939	2.855	2.499	2.222	2.000	1.818	1.667
25	4.721	4.514	4.323	4.147	3.985	3.834	3.694	3.564	3.442	3.329	3.222	3.122	3.028	2.939	2.856	2.499	2.222	2.000	1.818	1.667
26	4.728	4.520	4.328	4.151	3.988	3.837	3.696	3.566	3.444	3.330	3.223	3.123	3.028	2.940	2.856	2.500	2.222	2.000	1.818	1.667
27	4.734	4.524	4.332	4.154	3.990	3.839	3.698	3.567	3.445	3.331	3.224	3.123	3.029	2.940	2.856	2.500	2.222	2.000	1.818	1.667
28	4.739	4.528	4.335	4.157	3.992	3.840	3.699	3.568	3.446	3.331	3.224	3.124	3.029	2.941	2.857	2.500	2.222	2.000	1.818	1.667
29	4.743	4.531	4.337	4.159	3.994	3.841	3.700	3.569	3.446	3.332	3.225	3.124	3.030	2.941	2.857	2.500	2.222	2.000	1.818	1.667
30	4.746	4.534	4.339	4.160	3.995	3.842	3.701	3.569	3.447	3.332	3.225	3.124	3.030	2.941	2.857	2.500	2.222	2.000	1.818	1.667
35	4.756	4.541	4.345	4.164	3.998	3.845	3.703	3.571	3.448	3.333	3.226	3.125	3.030	2.941	2.857	2.500	2.222	2.000	1.818	1.667
40	4.760	4.544	4.347	4.166	3.999	3.846	3.703	3.571	3.448	3.333	3.226	3.125	3.030	2.941	2.857	2.500	2.222	2.000	1.818	1.667
45	4.761	4.545	4.347	4.166	4.000	3.846	3.704	3.571	3.448	3.333	3.226	3.125	3.030	2.941	2.857	2.500	2.222	2.000	1.818	1.667
50	4.762	4.545	4.348	4.167	4.000	3.846	3.704	3.571	3.448	3.333	3.226	3.125	3.030	2.941	2.857	2.500	2.222	2.000	1.818	1.667

TABLE B.3

Future Value Factors for $1 Compounded at *k* Percent for *n* Periods:

$$FV_{k,n} = (1+k)^n$$

Compound Rate, k

Period, n	1%	2%	3%	4%	5%	6%	7%	8%	9%	10%	11%	12%	13%	14%	15%	16%	17%	18%	19%	20%
1	1.010	1.020	1.030	1.040	1.050	1.060	1.070	1.080	1.090	1.100	1.110	1.120	1.130	1.140	1.150	1.160	1.170	1.180	1.190	1.200
2	1.020	1.040	1.061	1.082	1.102	1.124	1.145	1.166	1.188	1.210	1.232	1.254	1.277	1.300	1.323	1.346	1.369	1.392	1.416	1.440
3	1.030	1.061	1.093	1.125	1.158	1.191	1.225	1.260	1.295	1.331	1.368	1.405	1.443	1.482	1.521	1.561	1.602	1.643	1.685	1.728
4	1.041	1.082	1.126	1.170	1.216	1.262	1.311	1.360	1.412	1.464	1.518	1.574	1.630	1.689	1.749	1.811	1.874	1.939	2.005	2.074
5	1.051	1.104	1.159	1.217	1.276	1.338	1.403	1.469	1.539	1.611	1.685	1.762	1.842	1.925	2.011	2.100	2.192	2.288	2.386	2.488
6	1.062	1.126	1.194	1.265	1.340	1.419	1.501	1.587	1.677	1.772	1.870	1.974	2.082	2.195	2.313	2.436	2.565	2.700	2.840	2.986
7	1.072	1.149	1.230	1.316	1.407	1.504	1.606	1.714	1.828	1.949	2.076	2.211	2.353	2.502	2.660	2.826	3.001	3.185	3.379	3.583
8	1.083	1.172	1.267	1.369	1.477	1.594	1.718	1.851	1.993	2.144	2.305	2.476	2.658	2.853	3.059	3.278	3.511	3.759	4.021	4.300
9	1.094	1.195	1.305	1.423	1.551	1.689	1.838	1.999	2.172	2.358	2.558	2.773	3.004	3.252	3.518	3.803	4.108	4.435	4.785	5.160
10	1.105	1.219	1.344	1.480	1.629	1.791	1.967	2.159	2.367	2.594	2.839	3.106	3.395	3.707	4.046	4.411	4.807	5.234	5.695	6.192
11	1.116	1.243	1.384	1.539	1.710	1.898	2.105	2.332	2.580	2.853	3.152	3.479	3.836	4.226	4.652	5.117	5.642	6.176	6.777	7.430
12	1.127	1.268	1.426	1.601	1.796	2.012	2.252	2.518	2.813	3.138	3.498	3.896	4.335	4.818	5.350	5.936	6.580	7.288	8.064	8.916
13	1.138	1.294	1.469	1.665	1.886	2.133	2.410	2.720	3.066	3.452	3.883	4.363	4.898	5.492	6.153	6.886	7.699	8.599	9.596	10.699
14	1.149	1.319	1.513	1.732	1.980	2.261	2.579	2.937	3.342	3.797	4.310	4.887	5.555	6.261	7.076	7.988	9.007	10.147	11.420	12.839
15	1.161	1.346	1.558	1.801	2.079	2.397	2.759	3.172	3.642	4.177	4.785	5.474	6.254	7.138	8.137	9.266	10.539	11.974	13.590	15.407
16	1.173	1.373	1.605	1.873	2.183	2.540	2.952	3.426	3.970	4.595	5.311	6.130	7.067	8.137	9.358	10.748	12.330	14.129	16.172	18.488
17	1.184	1.400	1.653	1.948	2.292	2.693	3.159	3.700	4.328	5.054	5.895	6.866	7.986	9.276	10.761	12.468	14.426	16.672	19.244	22.186
18	1.196	1.428	1.702	2.026	2.407	2.854	3.380	3.996	4.717	5.560	6.544	7.690	9.024	10.575	12.375	14.463	16.879	19.673	22.901	26.623
19	1.208	1.457	1.754	2.107	2.527	3.026	3.617	4.316	5.142	6.116	7.263	8.613	10.197	12.056	14.232	16.777	19.748	23.214	27.252	31.948
20	1.220	1.486	1.806	2.191	2.653	3.207	3.870	4.661	5.604	6.727	8.062	9.646	11.523	13.743	16.367	19.461	23.106	27.393	32.429	38.338
21	1.232	1.516	1.860	2.279	2.786	3.400	4.141	5.034	6.109	7.400	8.949	10.804	13.021	15.668	18.822	22.574	27.034	32.324	38.591	46.005
22	1.245	1.546	1.916	2.370	2.925	3.604	4.430	5.437	6.659	8.140	9.934	12.100	14.714	17.861	21.645	26.186	31.629	38.142	45.923	55.206
23	1.257	1.577	1.974	2.465	3.072	3.820	4.741	5.871	7.258	8.954	11.026	13.552	16.627	20.362	24.871	30.376	37.006	45.008	54.649	66.247
24	1.270	1.608	2.033	2.563	3.225	4.049	5.072	6.341	7.922	9.850	12.239	15.179	18.788	23.212	28.625	35.236	43.297	53.109	65.032	79.497
25	1.282	1.641	2.094	2.666	3.386	4.292	5.427	6.848	8.623	10.835	13.585	17.000	21.231	26.462	32.919	40.874	50.658	62.669	77.388	95.396
26	1.295	1.673	2.157	2.772	3.556	4.549	5.807	7.396	9.399	11.918	15.080	19.040	23.991	30.167	37.857	47.414	59.270	73.949	92.092	114.48
27	1.308	1.707	2.221	2.883	3.733	4.822	6.214	7.988	10.245	13.110	16.739	21.325	27.109	34.390	43.535	55.000	69.345	87.260	109.59	137.37
28	1.321	1.741	2.288	2.999	3.920	5.112	6.649	8.627	11.167	14.421	18.580	23.884	30.633	39.204	50.066	63.800	81.134	102.97	130.41	164.84
29	1.335	1.776	2.357	3.119	4.116	5.418	7.114	9.317	12.172	15.863	20.624	26.750	34.616	44.693	57.575	75.009	94.927	121.50	155.19	197.81
30	1.348	1.811	2.427	3.243	4.322	5.743	7.612	10.063	13.268	17.449	22.892	29.960	39.116	50.950	66.212	85.850	111.06	143.37	184.68	237.38
35	1.417	2.000	2.814	3.946	5.516	7.686	10.677	14.785	20.414	28.102	38.575	52.800	72.068	98.100	133.18	180.31	243.50	328.00	440.70	590.67
40	1.489	2.208	3.262	4.801	7.040	10.286	14.974	21.725	31.409	45.259	65.001	93.051	132.78	188.88	267.86	378.72	533.87	750.38	1051.7	1469.8
45	1.565	2.438	3.782	5.841	8.985	13.765	21.002	31.920	48.327	72.890	109.53	163.99	244.64	363.68	538.77	795.44	1170.5	1716.7	2509.7	3657.3
50	1.645	2.692	4.384	7.107	11.467	18.420	29.457	46.902	74.358	117.39	184.56	289.00	450.74	700.23	1083.7	1670.7	2566.2	3927.4	5988.9	9100.4

TABLE B.3

FV (Continued)

$FV_{k,n}$

Period, n	Compound Rate, k																			
	21%	22%	23%	24%	25%	26%	27%	28%	29%	30%	31%	32%	33%	34%	35%	40%	45%	50%	55%	60%
1	1.210	1.220	1.230	1.240	1.250	1.260	1.270	1.280	1.290	1.300	1.310	1.320	1.330	1.340	1.350	1.400	1.450	1.500	1.550	1.600
2	1.464	1.488	1.513	1.538	1.563	1.588	1.613	1.638	1.664	1.690	1.716	1.742	1.769	1.796	1.823	1.960	2.103	2.250	2.403	2.560
3	1.772	1.816	1.861	1.907	1.953	2.000	2.048	2.097	2.147	2.197	2.248	2.300	2.353	2.406	2.460	2.744	3.049	3.375	3.724	4.096
4	2.144	2.215	2.289	2.364	2.441	2.520	2.601	2.684	2.769	2.856	2.945	3.036	3.129	3.224	3.322	3.842	4.421	5.063	5.772	6.554
5	2.594	2.703	2.815	2.932	3.052	3.176	3.304	3.436	3.572	3.713	3.858	4.007	4.162	4.320	4.484	5.378	6.410	7.594	8.947	10.486
6	3.138	3.297	3.463	3.635	3.815	4.002	4.196	4.398	4.608	4.827	5.054	5.290	5.535	5.789	6.053	7.530	9.294	11.391	13.867	16.777
7	3.797	4.023	4.259	4.508	4.768	5.042	5.329	5.629	5.945	6.275	6.621	6.983	7.361	7.758	8.172	10.541	13.476	17.086	21.494	26.844
8	4.595	4.908	5.239	5.590	5.960	6.353	6.768	7.206	7.669	8.157	8.673	9.217	9.791	10.395	11.032	14.758	19.541	25.629	33.316	42.950
9	5.560	5.987	6.444	6.931	7.451	8.005	8.595	9.223	9.893	10.604	11.362	12.166	13.022	13.930	14.894	20.661	28.334	38.443	51.640	68.719
10	6.728	7.305	7.926	8.594	9.313	10.086	10.915	11.806	12.761	13.786	14.884	16.060	17.319	18.666	20.107	28.925	41.085	57.665	80.042	109.95
11	8.140	8.912	9.749	10.657	11.642	12.708	13.862	15.112	16.462	17.922	19.498	21.199	23.034	25.012	27.144	40.496	59.573	86.498	124.06	175.92
12	9.850	10.872	11.991	13.215	14.552	16.012	17.605	19.343	21.236	23.298	25.542	27.983	30.635	33.516	36.644	56.694	86.381	129.75	192.30	281.47
13	11.918	13.264	14.749	16.386	18.190	20.175	22.359	24.759	27.395	30.288	33.460	36.937	40.745	44.912	49.470	79.371	125.25	194.62	298.07	450.36
14	14.421	16.182	18.141	20.319	22.737	25.421	28.396	31.691	35.339	39.374	43.833	48.757	54.190	60.182	66.784	111.12	181.62	291.93	462.00	720.58
15	17.449	19.742	22.314	25.196	28.422	32.030	36.062	40.565	45.587	51.186	57.421	64.359	72.073	80.644	90.158	155.57	263.34	437.89	716.10	1152.9
16	21.114	24.086	27.446	31.243	35.527	40.358	45.799	51.923	58.808	66.542	75.221	84.954	95.858	108.06	121.71	217.80	381.85	656.84	1110.0	1844.7
17	25.548	29.384	33.759	38.741	44.409	50.851	58.165	66.461	75.862	86.504	98.540	112.14	127.49	144.80	164.31	304.91	553.68	985.26	1720.4	2951.5
18	30.913	35.849	41.523	48.039	55.511	64.072	73.870	85.071	97.862	112.46	129.09	148.02	169.56	194.04	221.82	426.88	802.83	1477.9	2666.7	4722.4
19	37.404	43.736	51.074	59.568	69.389	80.731	93.815	108.89	126.24	146.19	169.10	195.39	225.52	260.01	299.46	597.63	1164.1	2216.8	4133.4	7555.8
20	45.259	53.358	62.821	72.864	86.736	101.72	119.14	139.38	162.85	190.05	221.53	257.92	299.94	348.41	404.27	836.68	1688.0	3325.3	6406.7	12098
21	54.764	65.096	77.269	91.592	108.42	128.17	151.31	178.41	210.08	247.06	290.20	340.45	398.92	466.88	545.77	1171.4	2447.5	4987.9	9930.4	19342
22	66.264	79.418	95.041	113.57	135.53	161.49	192.17	228.36	271.00	321.18	380.16	449.39	530.56	625.61	736.79	1639.9	3548.9	7481.8	15392	30948
23	80.180	96.889	116.90	140.83	169.41	203.48	244.05	292.30	349.59	417.54	498.01	593.20	705.67	838.32	994.66	2295.9	5145.9	11222	23857	49517
24	97.017	118.21	143.79	174.63	211.76	256.39	309.95	374.14	450.98	542.80	652.40	783.02	938.51	1123.4	1342.8	3214.2	7461.6	16834	36979	79228
25	117.39	144.21	176.86	216.54	264.70	323.05	393.63	478.90	581.76	705.64	854.64	1033.6	1248.2	1505.3	1812.8	4499.9	10819	25251	57318	126765
26	142.04	175.94	217.54	268.51	330.87	407.04	499.92	613.00	750.47	917.33	1119.6	1364.3	1660.1	2017.1	2447.2	6299.8	15688	37876	88843	202824
27	171.87	214.64	267.57	332.95	413.59	512.87	634.89	784.64	968.10	1192.5	1466.6	1800.9	2208.0	2702.9	3303.8	8819.8	22747	56815	137706	324518
28	207.97	261.86	329.11	412.86	516.99	646.21	806.31	1004.3	1248.9	1550.3	1921.3	2377.2	2936.6	3621.9	4460.1	12347	32984	85222	213445	519229
29	251.64	319.47	404.81	511.95	646.23	814.23	1024.0	1285.6	1611.0	2015.4	2516.9	3137.9	3905.7	4853.3	6021.1	17286	47826	127834	330840	830767
30	304.48	389.76	497.91	634.82	807.79	1025.9	1300.5	1645.5	2078.2	2620.0	3297.2	4142.1	5194.6	6503.5	8128.6	24201	69348	191751	512803	*
35	789.75	1053.4	1401.8	1861.1	2465.2	3258.1	4296.7	5653.9	7424.0	9727.9	12720	16599	21617	28097	36448	130161	444508	*	*	*
40	2048.4	2847.0	3946.4	5455.9	7523.2	10347	14195	19426	26520	36118	49074	66520	89963	121392	163437	700037	*	*	*	*
45	5313.0	7694.7	11110	15994	22958	32860	46899	66749	94740	134106	189325	266579	374389	524464	732857	*	*	*	*	*
50	13780	20796	31279	46890	70064	104358	154948	229349	338443	497929	730406	*	*	*	*	*	*	*	*	*

*Value is greater than 999999.

TABLE B.4

Future Value Factors for an Annuity of $1 Compounded at k Percent for n Periods:

$$FVA_{k,n} = \sum_{t=0}^{n-1}(1+k)^t = \frac{(1+k)^n - 1}{k}$$

Period, n	Compound Rate, k																			
	1%	2%	3%	4%	5%	6%	7%	8%	9%	10%	11%	12%	13%	14%	15%	16%	17%	18%	19%	20%
1	1.000	1.000	1.000	1.000	1.000	1.000	1.000	1.000	1.000	1.000	1.000	1.000	1.000	1.000	1.000	1.000	1.000	1.000	1.000	1.000
2	2.010	2.020	2.030	2.040	2.050	2.060	2.070	2.080	2.090	2.100	2.110	2.120	2.130	2.140	2.150	2.160	2.170	2.180	2.190	2.200
3	3.030	3.060	3.091	3.122	3.152	3.184	3.215	3.246	3.278	3.310	3.342	3.374	4.307	3.440	3.473	3.506	3.539	3.572	3.606	3.640
4	4.060	4.122	4.184	4.246	4.310	4.375	4.440	4.506	4.573	4.641	4.710	4.779	4.850	4.921	4.993	5.066	5.141	5.215	5.291	5.368
5	5.101	5.204	5.309	5.416	5.526	5.637	5.751	5.867	5.985	6.105	6.228	6.353	6.480	6.610	6.742	6.877	7.014	7.154	7.297	7.442
6	6.152	6.308	6.469	6.633	6.802	6.975	7.153	7.336	7.523	7.716	7.913	8.115	8.323	8.536	8.754	8.977	9.207	9.442	9.683	9.930
7	7.214	7.434	7.662	7.898	8.142	8.394	8.654	8.923	9.200	9.487	9.783	10.089	10.405	10.730	11.067	11.414	11.772	12.142	12.523	12.916
8	8.286	8.583	8.892	9.214	9.549	9.897	10.260	10.637	11.028	11.436	11.859	12.300	12.757	13.233	13.727	14.240	14.773	15.327	15.902	16.499
9	9.269	9.755	10.159	10.583	11.027	11.791	11.978	12.488	13.021	13.579	14.164	14.776	15.416	16.085	16.786	17.519	18.285	19.086	19.923	20.799
10	10.462	10.950	11.464	12.006	12.578	13.181	13.816	14.487	15.193	15.937	16.722	17.549	18.420	19.337	20.304	21.321	22.393	23.521	24.709	25.959
11	11.567	12.169	12.808	13.486	14.207	14.972	15.784	16.645	17.560	18.531	19.561	20.655	21.814	23.045	24.349	25.733	27.200	28.755	30.404	32.150
12	12.683	13.412	14.192	15.026	15.917	16.870	17.888	18.977	20.141	21.384	22.713	24.133	25.650	27.271	29.002	30.850	32.824	34.931	37.180	39.581
13	13.809	14.680	15.618	16.627	17.713	18.882	20.141	21.495	22.953	24.523	26.212	28.029	29.985	32.089	34.352	36.786	39.404	42.219	45.244	48.497
14	14.947	15.975	17.086	18.292	19.599	21.015	22.550	24.215	26.019	27.975	30.095	32.393	34.883	37.581	40.505	43.672	47.103	50.818	54.841	59.196
15	16.097	17.293	18.599	20.024	21.579	23.276	25.129	27.152	29.361	31.772	34.405	37.280	40.417	43.842	47.580	51.660	56.110	60.965	66.261	72.035
16	17.258	18.639	20.157	21.825	23.657	25.673	27.888	30.324	33.003	35.950	39.190	42.753	46.672	50.980	55.717	60.925	66.649	72.939	79.850	87.442
17	18.430	20.012	21.762	23.698	25.840	28.213	30.840	33.750	36.974	40.545	44.501	48.884	53.739	59.118	65.075	71.673	78.979	87.068	96.022	105.93
18	19.615	21.412	23.414	25.645	28.132	30.906	33.999	37.450	41.301	45.599	50.396	55.750	61.725	68.394	75.836	84.141	93.406	103.74	115.27	128.12
19	20.811	22.841	25.117	27.671	30.539	33.760	37.379	41.446	46.018	51.159	56.939	63.440	70.749	78.969	88.212	98.603	110.28	123.41	138.17	154.74
20	22.019	24.297	26.870	29.778	33.066	36.786	40.996	45.762	51.160	57.275	64.203	72.052	80.947	91.025	102.44	115.38	130.03	146.63	165.42	186.69
21	23.239	25.783	28.676	31.969	35.719	39.993	44.865	50.423	56.765	64.002	72.265	81.699	92.470	104.77	118.81	134.84	153.14	174.02	197.85	225.03
22	24.472	27.299	30.537	34.248	38.505	43.392	49.006	55.457	62.873	71.403	81.214	92.503	105.49	120.44	137.63	157.41	180.17	206.34	236.44	271.03
23	25.716	28.845	32.453	36.618	41.430	46.996	53.436	60.893	69.532	79.543	91.148	104.60	120.20	138.30	159.28	183.60	211.80	244.49	282.36	326.24
24	26.973	30.422	34.426	39.083	44.502	50.816	58.177	66.765	76.790	88.497	102.17	118.16	136.83	158.66	184.17	213.98	248.81	289.49	337.10	392.48
25	28.243	32.030	36.459	41.646	47.727	54.865	63.249	73.106	84.701	98.347	114.41	133.33	155.62	181.87	212.79	249.21	292.10	342.60	402.04	471.98
26	29.526	33.671	38.553	44.312	51.113	59.156	68.676	79.954	93.324	109.18	128.00	150.33	176.85	208.33	245.71	290.09	342.76	405.27	479.43	567.38
27	30.821	35.344	40.710	47.084	54.669	63.706	74.484	87.351	102.72	121.10	143.08	169.37	200.84	238.50	283.57	337.50	402.03	479.22	571.52	681.85
28	32.129	37.051	42.931	49.968	58.403	68.528	80.698	95.339	112.97	134.21	159.82	190.70	227.95	272.89	327.10	392.50	471.38	566.48	681.11	819.22
29	33.450	38.792	45.219	52.966	62.323	73.640	87.347	103.97	124.14	148.63	178.40	214.58	258.58	312.09	377.17	456.30	552.51	669.45	811.52	984.07
30	34.785	40.568	47.575	56.085	66.439	79.058	94.461	113.28	136.31	164.49	199.02	241.33	293.20	356.79	434.75	530.31	647.44	790.95	966.71	1181.9
35	41.660	49.994	60.462	73.652	90.320	111.43	138.24	172.32	215.71	271.02	341.59	431.66	546.68	693.57	881.17	1120.7	1426.5	1816.7	2314.2	2948.3
40	48.886	60.402	75.401	95.026	120.80	154.76	199.64	259.06	337.88	442.59	581.83	767.09	1013.7	1342.0	1779.1	2360.8	3134.5	4163.2	5529.8	7343.9
45	56.481	71.893	92.720	121.03	159.70	212.74	285.75	386.51	525.86	718.90	986.64	1358.2	1874.2	2590.6	3585.1	4967.3	6879.3	9531.6	13203	18281
50	64.463	84.579	112.80	152.67	209.35	290.34	406.53	573.77	815.08	1163.9	1668.8	2400.0	3459.5	4994.5	7217.7	10435	15089	21813	31515	45497

TABLE B.4 (Continued)

$FVA_{k,n}$

Compound Rate, k

Period, n	21%	22%	23%	24%	25%	26%	27%	28%	29%	30%	31%	32%	33%	34%	35%	40%	45%	50%	55%	60%
1	1.000	1.000	1.000	1.000	1.000	1.000	1.000	1.000	1.000	1.000	1.000	1.000	1.000	1.000	1.000	1.000	1.000	1.000	1.000	1.000
2	2.210	2.220	2.230	2.240	2.250	2.260	2.270	2.280	2.290	2.300	2.310	2.320	2.330	2.340	2.350	2.400	2.450	2.500	2.550	2.600
3	3.674	3.708	3.743	3.778	3.813	3.848	3.883	3.918	3.954	3.990	4.026	4.062	4.099	4.136	4.173	4.360	4.553	4.750	4.952	5.160
4	5.446	5.524	5.604	5.684	5.766	5.848	5.931	6.016	6.101	6.187	6.274	6.362	6.452	6.542	6.633	7.104	7.601	8.125	8.676	9.256
5	7.589	7.740	7.893	8.048	8.207	8.368	8.533	8.700	8.870	9.043	9.219	9.398	9.581	9.766	9.954	10.956	12.022	13.188	14.448	15.810
6	10.183	10.442	10.708	10.980	11.259	11.544	11.837	12.136	12.442	12.756	13.077	13.406	13.742	14.086	14.438	16.324	18.431	20.781	23.395	26.295
7	13.321	13.740	14.171	14.615	15.073	15.546	16.032	16.534	17.051	17.583	18.131	18.696	19.277	19.876	20.492	23.853	27.725	32.172	37.262	43.073
8	17.119	17.762	18.430	19.123	19.842	20.588	21.361	22.163	22.995	23.858	24.752	25.678	26.638	27.633	28.664	34.395	41.202	49.258	58.756	69.916
9	21.714	22.670	23.669	24.712	25.802	26.940	28.129	29.369	30.664	32.015	33.425	34.895	36.429	38.029	39.696	49.153	60.743	74.887	92.073	112.87
10	27.274	28.657	30.113	31.643	33.253	34.945	36.723	38.593	40.556	42.619	44.786	47.062	49.451	51.958	54.590	69.814	89.100	113.33	143.71	181.59
11	34.001	35.962	38.039	40.238	42.566	45.031	47.639	50.398	53.318	56.405	59.670	63.122	66.769	70.624	74.697	98.739	130.16	171.00	223.75	291.54
12	42.142	44.874	47.788	50.895	54.208	57.739	61.501	65.510	69.780	74.327	79.168	84.320	89.803	95.637	101.84	139.23	189.73	257.49	347.82	476.46
13	51.991	55.746	59.779	64.110	68.760	73.751	79.107	84.853	91.016	97.625	104.71	112.30	120.44	129.15	138.48	195.93	276.12	387.24	540.12	748.93
14	63.909	69.010	74.528	80.496	86.949	93.926	101.47	109.61	118.41	127.91	138.17	149.24	161.18	174.06	187.95	275.30	401.37	581.86	838.19	1199.3
15	78.330	85.192	92.669	100.82	109.69	119.35	129.86	141.30	153.75	167.29	182.00	198.00	215.37	234.25	254.74	386.42	582.98	873.79	1300.2	1919.9
16	95.780	104.93	114.98	126.01	138.11	151.38	165.92	181.87	199.34	218.47	239.42	262.36	287.45	314.89	344.90	541.99	846.32	1311.7	2016.3	3072.8
17	116.89	129.02	142.43	157.25	173.64	191.73	211.72	233.79	258.15	285.01	314.64	347.31	383.30	422.95	466.61	759.78	1228.2	1968.5	3126.2	4917.5
18	142.44	158.40	176.19	195.99	218.04	242.59	269.89	300.25	334.01	371.52	413.18	459.45	510.80	567.76	630.92	1064.7	1781.8	2953.8	4846.7	7868.9
19	173.35	194.25	217.71	244.03	273.56	306.66	343.76	385.32	431.87	483.97	542.27	607.47	680.36	761.80	852.75	1491.6	2584.7	4431.7	7513.4	12591
20	210.76	237.99	268.79	303.60	342.94	387.39	437.57	494.21	558.11	630.17	711.38	802.86	905.88	1021.8	1152.2	2089.2	3748.8	6648.5	11646	20147
21	256.02	291.35	331.61	377.46	429.69	489.11	556.72	633.59	720.96	820.22	932.90	1060.8	1205.8	1370.2	1556.5	2925.9	5436.7	9973.8	18053	32236
22	310.78	356.44	408.88	469.06	538.10	617.28	708.03	812.00	931.04	1067.3	1223.1	1401.2	1604.7	1837.1	2102.3	4097.2	7884.3	14961	27983	51579
23	377.05	435.86	503.92	582.63	673.63	778.77	900.20	1040.4	1202.0	1388.5	1603.3	1850.6	2135.3	2462.7	2839.0	5737.1	11433	22443	43375	82527
24	457.22	532.75	620.82	723.46	843.03	982.25	1144.3	1332.7	1551.6	1806.0	2101.3	2443.8	2840.9	3301.0	3833.7	8033.0	16579	33666	67233	132045
25	554.24	650.96	764.61	898.09	1054.8	1238.6	1454.2	1706.8	2002.6	2348.8	2753.7	3226.8	3779.5	4424.4	5176.5	11247	24040	50500	104213	211273
26	671.63	795.17	941.46	1114.6	1319.5	1561.7	1847.8	2185.7	2584.4	3054.4	3608.3	4260.4	5027.7	5929.7	6989.3	15747	34680	75751	161531	338038
27	813.68	971.10	1159.0	1383.1	1650.4	1968.7	2347.8	2798.7	3334.8	3971.8	4727.9	5624.8	6687.8	7946.8	9436.5	22046	50548	113628	250374	540862
28	985.55	1185.7	1426.6	1716.1	2064.0	2481.6	2982.6	3583.3	4302.9	5164.3	6194.5	7425.7	8895.8	10649	12740	30866	73295	170443	388081	865381
29	1193.5	1447.6	1755.7	2129.0	2580.9	3127.8	3789.0	4587.7	5551.8	6714.6	8115.8	9802.9	11832	14271	17200	43214	106279	255666	601527	*
30	1445.2	1767.1	2160.5	2640.9	3227.2	3942.0	4813.0	5873.2	7162.8	8730.0	10632	12940	15738	19124	23221	60501	154106	383500	932368	*
35	3755.9	4783.6	6090.3	7750.2	9856.8	12527	15909	20188	25596	32422	41029	51869	65504	82636	104136	325400	987794	*	*	*
40	9749.5	12936	17154	22728	30088	39792	52571	69377	91774	120392	158300	207874	272613	357033	466960	*	*	*	*	*
45	25295	34971	48301	66640	91831	126382	173697	238387	326688	447019	610723	833058	*	*	*	*	*	*	*	*
50	65617	94525	135992	195372	280255	401374	573877	819103	*	*	*	*	*	*	*	*	*	*	*	*

*Value is greater than 999999.

Answers to Selected Problems

(*Note:* For problems using present or future value concepts, the answer is given based on using a financial calculator; this is followed by the answer, in parenthesis, based on employing the financial tables in Appendix B. If no separate financial table answer is provided, the use of a financial calculator and financial tables provide the same answer.)

Chapter 1

1.1	$39 short.
1.2	$24,900.

Chapter 2

2.2	a.	7.00%, 9.25%, 10.50%, 10.75%, 11.00%.
2.5		3.256 marks per pound, or 0.307 pounds per mark.
2.7		$F_{\text{lira/\$}} = 1{,}298.544$.

Chapter 3

3.1	a.	$720 ($719).
	b.	$1,248.
	c.	$1,531.
	d.	$2,053 ($2,054).
3.3	a.	$13,806 ($13,805).
	b.	$12,783.
3.6		Company plan = $219,318; "do it yourself" = $228,827 ($228,820).
3.8	a.	$1,208,307 ($1,208,250).
	b.	$1,482,210 ($1,482,250).
	c.	$1,562,500.
3.12		24.01%.
3.13	a.	7.23%.
	b.	6.04%.
	c.	Approximately 10%.
	d.	Approximately 7.23%.
3.16	a.	12%, 15%, 11.05%.
3.19	a.	$928.18.
	b.	$29.11.
3.21	a.	10%.
	b.	10.25%, 10.38%, 10.47%, 10.52%.

Chapter 4

4.1	a.	(**1**) $1,147.20 ($1,146.80). (**2**) $1,148.78 ($1,149.08).
	b.	(**1**) $877.11 ($877.60). (**2**) $875.38 ($875.48).

4.3	a.	7.02%.
	b.	11.92%.
4.6	a.	$4,636.36.
	b.	$3,762.97 ($3,764.72).
4.9		$26.12.
4.10		$173,546.64 ($173,526.58).
4.11		$11.71 ($11.70).
4.14	a.	$66.67.
	b.	$72.89 ($72.82).
	c.	$60.20 ($60.13).
4.15	a.	**(1)** $6, $45.45. **(2)** $2.14, $41.95.

Chapter 5

5.1	a.	10%, 3%.
	b.	14.83%, 23.90%.
5.3	a.	12.5%.
	b.	**(1)** 9%. **(2)** 7.81%. **(3)** 4.58%.
5.6	a.	4.5%, 17%.
	b.	20.91%, 19.52%.
	c.	1.02.
5.8	a.	18%, 21%, 19.39%, 31.37%.
	b.	$Corr_{ZM} = +0.31$; $75.
5.9		13.49%.
5.12	a.	$22.50.
	b.	$26.25.
	c.	$35.00.
	d.	$40.00.
5.13	a.	10%, $50.
	b.	12%, $37.50.
	c.	14%, $30.
	d.	8%, $75.
5A.1	a.	2.0%, 4.10%, 8.0%, 10.84%.
	b.	2%, 4.10%; 3.5%, 3.18%; 5%, 4.97%; 6.5%, 7.78%; 8%, 10.84%.

Chapter 6

6.1	a.	5.92%.
	b.	6.94%.
	c.	8.10%.
	d.	7.80%.
6.2	a.	10.53%.
	b.	15.22%.
	c.	9.82%.
	d.	11%.
6.3	a.	14.25%.
	b.	17.02%.
	c.	12.86%.
	d.	15.93%.
6.5	a.	9%.

	b.	11.37%, 19%, 17%.
	d.	15.79%.
	e.	13.66%.
6.7	**a.**	14.18%.
	b.	16.58%.
6.10	**a.**	13.60%.
	b.	14.72%.
6.12		9.50%, 9.80%, 10.20%.

Chapter 7

7.1	**a.**	1.75, 3.14.
	b.	$98, $321 ($320).
7.3		15.69%.
7.4		$9,986 ($10,002), $13,525 ($13,500), 15.78%, 14.19%.
7.8	**a.**	$11,183 ($11,160), $13,287 ($13,254).
	b.	20.82%, 17.04%.
7.10		Equivalent annual *NPV:* $81.96 ($81.93), $71.15 ($71.12).
7.12	**a.**	23.38%, $436 ($435), 21.27%, $600 ($599).
	b.	Equivalent annual *NPV:* $201 ($200), $192. Replacement chain: $1,019 ($1,018), $977 (($974).
7.13	**a.**	$13,635 ($13,646), −$3,336 (−$3,322), $10,544 ($10,558), $4,325 ($4,320), $10,827 ($10,825), $7,217 ($7,225).
	b.	A, D, and E; $28,787 ($28,791).
	c.	$17,761 ($17,757).

Chapter 8

8.1	**a.**	$105,000.
	b.	$70,000.
8.3	**a.**	$19,200.
	b.	$22,560.
	c.	$40,000.
	d.	$17,440.
8.4		−$22,480 (−$22,305).
8.6		$1,230 ($1,228).
8.7	**a.**	$545 ($571).
	b.	−$104,973 (−$104,939).
8.11		$4,458 ($4,448).
8.12		$8,650 ($8,639).
8.15		$NPV_I = $31,686 ($31,640); $NPV_{Both} = $18,119 ($18,060).
8.16	**a.**	$2,112 ($2,110).
	b.	−$492 (−$493).

Chapter 9

9.1	**a.**	$2,000 ($1,983).
9.2	**a.**	1.5.
	b.	$5,086 ($5,070).
9.5	**a.**	$25 million.
	b.	$18 million.
9.6		$580,908 ($579,328).

9.9   **a.** $45,933 ($44,895).

      b.   −$111,679 (−$111,720); −$27,375 (−$27,480).

9.10 $877,126 ($877,024).

9.12   **a.** $476,893 ($476,830).

9.13   −$21,206 (−$21,000).

Chapter 10

10.1   **a.** $29,515,000.

      b.   1.62%.

10.4   Book value: before—$20; after—$22.67. Market value: before—$40; after—$39.33.

10.5   450,000.

10.7   95%.

10.8   **a.**   7.5.

      b.   (**1**) 10, 15. (**2**) 12.3%, 11.8%. Based on *P/E*: $20, $30. Based on implied k_s: $39.13, $50.

      c.   16%.

      d. $60, $30.

10.10 **a.**   150,000.

      b.   147,000.

      c.   50,000.

      d.

Common stock ($2 par value)	$ 310,000
Additional paid-in capital	160,000
Retained earnings	600,000
	1,070,000
Less: Treasury stock (3,000 shares)	25,000
Common stockholders' equity	$1,045,000

Chapter 11

11.1   Debt/equity—$22 million; interest coverage—$14 million; and mortgaged assets/mortgaged debt—$17.5 million.

11.2   **a.** $54.21 ($54.23) million.

      b. $56 million.

11.4   **a.** $10,130 ($10,129).

      b.   Interest per year: $7,040; $6,546; $5,972; $5,307; $4,535; $3,640; $2,602; and $1,397.

11.6   **a.**   8.15%.

      b.   8.5%.

      c.   7.62%.

      d.   7.86%.

11.8   **a.**   (**1**) $9,500,000. (**2**) $109,500,000.

      b.   (**1**)$241,116,196. (**2**) $9,200,000; $10,046,400 (**3**) $241,116,196.

11.11 **a.** $88.889.

      b.   112,500.

11.13 **a.** $2.47, $2.27.

      b. $29.46, $29.51.

Chapter 12

12.1		11.60%.
12.2	**a.**	8.334%.
	b.	9.005%.
12.4	**a.**	$12,187,500.
	b.	$13,587,500; $9,587,500.
12.5	**a.**	$16,000,000.
	b.	$20,000,000.
12.7	**a.**	$40,000.
	b.	28.57%.
	c.	$10,000.
12.10	**a.**	$700,000.
	b.	Common stock financing: expected *EPS* is $1.517; σ = $0.434; coefficient of variation = 0.29. Debt financing: $1.95; $1.30; and 0.67.
12.13	**a.**	$2.60 and $3.6725.
	b.	$26.
	c.	$30.60.

Chapter 13

13.1	**a.**	$200,000.
	b.	At $3 million—no cash dividends; at $1.5 million—$400,000.
13.3	**a.**	A—$362.6 ($362.9); B—$357.0 ($356.8).
	b.	$609.4 ($610.3).
13.4	**a.**	142,857; $4.00 for each.
	b.	151,515; $4.00, $3.97.
13.7		$93.75.
13.8	**a.**	(**1**) $4,800,000. (**2**) $12. (**3**) 8. (**4**) 33 1/3%.
	b.	(**1**) $100. (**2**) $4.167; 33 1/3%.
13.11	**a.**	September 28.
	b.	$60.
	c.	108.
	d.	$50.
	e.	$5,400 both before and after.

Chapter 14

14.1		−$1,377 (−$1,372).
14.2	**a.**	−$3,172 (−$3,143).
	b.	$11,636 ($11,663).
	c.	$14,762 ($14,789).
14.5		$53,685 ($53,688).
14.7	**a.**	$20, 0.
	b.	Project 1—$40; project 2—$40 or 0.
	c.	Stockholders—$30, $80; bondholders—$40, $20.
14.8	**a.**	$4.00.
	b.	$40.
	c.	$800.
	d.	240,000.
	e.	$921.57 ($921.73); $931.90 ($932.21).

14.11	a.	$914.86 ($915.26).
	b.	Plan I—$3.413, $27.30; plan II—$3.526, $28.21.
	c.	$2.312, $20.81.
14.12	a.	Plan I—$4.42, $39.78; plan II—$4.55, $40.95.
	b.	Plan I—$6.392, $63.92; plan II—$5.633, $61.96.

Chapter 15

15.1		$4 million.
15.2	a.	54.75.
	b.	21.17.
	c.	9.73.
15.4	a.	$182, $164.5, $147.
	c.	0.71, 1.00, 1.29, $-$200, 0, $200.
15.7	a.	Plan I—$6.09, $1.71, 0.28. Plan II—$5.01, $1.11, 0.22.
	b.	$60.90, $55.11.
15.8	a.	1.25, $50, 0.29, 0.24, 21.56.
	b.	$16.64.
	c.	(**1**) 1.61, $200, 0.47, 0.29, and 57.62. (**2**) $17.11.
15.10	a.	$5, $9, $13, $11, $7, $11, $15, $13.
	b.	$20, $24, $28, $26, $22, $26, $20, $28.
	c.	$600,000.

Chapter 16

16.1	a.	$44.14.
	b.	$75.66.
16.2	a.	$15,000,000.
	b.	$5,000,000.
	c.	$114,000.
16.4		$26,070.
16.6	a.	$7.62.
	b.	$8,111.
16.7		$99,240.
16.9		6.43.
16.12	a.	$960,061.
	b.	7.67%.
	c.	8.07%.

Chapter 17

17.1		$5,184,571.
17.4		$2,016,849, $1,830,646, $1,001,096, $-$620,274.
17.5		46.25%.
17.6		

	March	April	May	June	July	August
% of same month sales	86.7%	80.0%	79.2%	78.6%	81.1%	83.7%
% of 1 month before		46.7	40.0	37.5	33.9	40.5
% of 2 months before			13.3	5.0	4.2	3.6
Bad debts			13.3	5.0	4.2	3.6

17.9	a.	$-$135,959.
	b.	$36,541.

17.10	a.	Expected collections are $225,000; costs are $173,750.
	b.	Collections are $225,000; costs are $223,750.
17.12	$375,000.	
17.13	a.	$385,808.
	b.	$94,726.

Chapter 18

18.1	10.67%, 10.75%.	
18.2	7.25%, 7.19%, 7%.	
18.4	a.	11.04%.
	b.	13.10%.
18.6	a.	14%.
	b.	14.94%.
	c.	16.21%.
	d.	13.92%.
18.7	10.51%.	
18.9	a.	16.00%.
	b.	15.56%, fee of $2,500.
	c.	13.86%.
18.13	a.	18.49%, 19.71%.
	b.	33.51%, 19.71%.
18.14	a.	23.10%.
	b.	19.36%.
18.17	a.	19.63%.
	b.	27.86%.
	c.	27.24%
	d.	25.73%.

Chapter 19

19.1   Total assets, and total liabilities and stockholders' equity are $370,716; net income is $18,027.

19.2

Cash	$ 100	Current liabilities	$ 200
Accounts receivable	100	Long-term debt	400
Inventory	200	Common stock	100
Net plant and equipment	600	Retained earnings	300
Total assets	$1,000	Total liabilities and stockholders' equity	$1,000

Sales—$2,400; net income—$120.

19.3	42.9%.	
19.5	a.	(**1**) 30,000. (**2**) $2.00. (**3**) 40%. (**4**) 16.4%. (**5**) 22.4%. (**6**) 6.0. (**7**) 3.2.
19.7	b.	(**1**) Year −1—18.25; year 0—30.11. (**2**) 12.00; 9.09. (**3**) 28.07; 60.83.
19.10	a.	(**1**) 2.0. (**2**) 5.0%. (**3**) 10.0%. (**4**) 20.0%.
	b.	$55,500; $120,000; 22.2%.
19.11	a.	$60; 7.5%.
	b.	$0.60.
	c.	$0.15.

d. 15; 1.67%.

19.13 **a.** 20%.

b. 12.5%.

Chapter 20

20.2 **a.** 226.7; 346.2; $2,159.8; $2,386.5; $2,613.2.

20.4 $45 million; −$30 million.

20.5 **a.** −$50,000; −$105,000; $20,000; $90,000.

d. 0; −$80,000; −$90,000; −$160,000.

20.7 **a.** $15; −$20; −$40; $10.

20.9 **a.**

Cash	$ 1.5	Accounts payable	$ 4.5
Accounts receivable	7.5	Notes payable	2.0
Inventory	9.0	Accruals	3.0
Net long-term assets	6.0	Long-term debt	2.0
Total assets	$24.0	Common stock	5.0
		Retained earnings	6.0
		Total	22.5
		Additional needed	1.5
		Total to balance	$24.0

b. Debt/equity in (a.) = 54.2%; now 64.7%.

20.10 **a.** $5 million.

b. $1.35 million short.

20.11 $32; $13; −$26; −$97; −$109.

If the Last Is First

If you ask ten instructors what the sequence of chapters should be in *Essentials of Financial Management*, you'll probably get close to ten different answers! Everyone has his or her own style, and I have tried many different sequences myself. *Essentials of Financial Management* is designed so that after the first five chapters are covered, the order of the rest of the chapters can be changed as desired. However, some instructors like to cover short-term financial management (Chapters 15 through 18) before they cover Chapter 3 ("Time Value of Money"). This sequence may cause a minor problem because understanding a few basic concepts from Chapter 3 is required before Chapters 17 ("Accounts Receivable and Inventory") and 18 ("Short-Term Financing") are covered. The purpose of this appendix is to provide the minimum background needed by students, if instructors choose to cover Chapters 15–18 before covering Chapter 3.

Net Present Value

Key Idea 5 from Chapter 1 is "A dollar today is worth more than a dollar tomorrow." In discussing this idea we said that in order to assist in maximizing the value of the firm, we determine the *net present value* of proposed investments. The procedure is to discount the future cash inflows at a rate that reflects the opportunities bypassed and risks involved, and then subtract the initial investment. Thus, the net present value of any proposed investment is:

$$\text{net present value} = \frac{\text{future value of cash inflows}}{1 + \text{discount rate based on forgone opportunities}} - \text{initial investment} \qquad (D.1)$$

By maximizing net present value the firm is making the correct decision. In Chapters 16 and 17 we employ net present value ideas. In the first of these (Chapter 16) this procedure causes no problem because the time periods under consideration are short, and no discounting is employed. In Chapter 17 we assume, for simplicity, that the benefits from the cash inflows are constant for each period and go on for a long time, so they can be viewed as going on forever. In that case the net present value becomes:

$$\begin{aligned}\text{net present value} \\ \text{(constant long-} \\ \text{term benefits)}\end{aligned} = \frac{\text{future value of cash inflows}}{\text{discount rate based on forgone opportunities}} - \text{initial investment} \qquad (D.2)$$

This form of the net present value equation is employed in Chapter 17. Thus, if a constant cash inflow of $50 is expected forever, the discount rate is 8 percent, and the initial investment is $400, the net present value is $50/0.08 − $400 = $225.

A second issue is that Chapters 16 and 17 involve taxes, which must be taken into consideration when calculating the cash flows required for determining the net present value. The cash inflows from any proposed investment are determined on an after-tax basis; that is, firms, just like individuals, are concerned with their cash flows after they pay Uncle Sam (i.e., the Internal Revenue Service). The *cash flows before taxes* in any period are referred to as *CFBT*, and the tax rate is denoted by the uppercase letter *T*. One way to determine the *after-tax cash flow, CF*, per period, is:

$$CF = CFBT - CFBT(T) \tag{D.3}$$

where *CFBT(T)* determines the amount of taxes. An alternative, and equally correct, way to determine the after-tax cash flow is to multiply the before-tax cash flow by the quantity $(1 - T)$, so:

$$CF = CFBT(1 - T) \tag{D.4}$$

For example, if the cash flow before tax is $700, and the tax rate is 35 percent, using Equation D.3, we have:

$$CF = \$700 - \$700(0.35) = \$700 - \$245 = \$455$$

If we use Equation D.4, we have:

$$CF = \$700(1 - 0.35) = \$700(0.65) = \$455$$

We will use the approach embodied in Equation D.4 in Chapters 16, 17, and throughout the book.[1]

Effective Annual Interest Rates and the Present Value of an Annuity

Some basic elements of time value are also employed in Chapter 18 when considering the costs of alternative sources of short-term financing. First, it is important to be able to determine the *effective annual (or "true") cost* of various financing sources. What if one bank says it will loan you money at a nominal rate of 9 percent, with interest compounded semi-annually, whereas a second will loan you money at a nominal rate of 8.9 percent, with interest compounded daily? Which bank provides the cheaper financing? To determine this we convert each quoted, or nominal, interest rate to a true effective annual rate, where:

$$k_{\text{effective annual}} = \left(1 + \frac{k_{\text{nominal}}}{m}\right)^m - 1 \tag{D.5}$$

where *m* is the number of compounding periods per year. For the first bank we have:

$$k_{\text{effective annual (first bank)}} = \left(1 + \frac{0.09}{2}\right)^2 - 1 = 1.0920 = 9.20\%$$

---

[1] *When an investment in long-term assets is considered, a depreciation tax shield must also be taken into consideration in Equation D.4.*

For the second bank the effective annual cost is:

$$k_{\text{effective annual (second bank)}} = \left(1 + \frac{0.089}{365}\right)^{365} - 1 = 1.0931 = 9.31\%$$

Once we calculate the true cost of borrowing from each of the banks, we see that the first bank, even though the quoted nominal interest rate looks higher, offers the lower effective annual cost.

One other time value concept is needed—this time for determining the payments when you borrow money and make constant payments that cover both interest and repayment of principal, like on a car loan. In order to solve problems like this we need to understand how to find the present value (that is, the value today) of a constant sum that occurs, say, for each of 30 months. This constant sum is called an *annuity, PMT,* and to find the present value of it we can use the following equation (as discussed in Chapter 3):

$$\text{present value of an annuity, } PV_0 = PMT\left[\frac{1}{k} - \frac{1}{k(1+k)^n}\right] \tag{D.6}$$

where PV_0 is the present value today, PMT is the annuity, k is the interest rate, and n is the number of periods.

Let's say you want to borrow some money at a yearly rate of 10 percent, and you will repay the loan in 6 annual installments of $1,000 each, starting 1 year from now. How much can you borrow? To determine how much you can borrow we have:

$$PV_0 = \$1,000\left[\frac{1}{0.10} - \frac{1}{0.10(1.10)^6}\right] = \$1,000(4.35526\ldots) \approx \$4,355.26$$

Instead of using the complicated-looking Equation D.6, we can use a financial calculator.[2] Alternatively, financial tables are available for the bracketed portion in the equation; these are called *present value factors for an annuity, $PVA_{k,n}$.* Using the value from Table B.2 at the back of the book, the present value of this same annuity is:

$$PV_0 = PMT(PVA_{k,n}) \tag{D.7}$$

$$PV_0 = \$1,000(PVA_{10\%,6}) = \$1,000(4.355) = \$4,355$$

The difference between $4,355.26 (the answer arrived at using Equation D.6 or a financial calculator) and $4,355 (the answer from Equation D.7) is due to rounding in Table B.2.

---

[2] *Using a financial calculator the answer is also $4,355.26.*

INDEX

Note: Boldface page numbers indicate definitions. Page numbers followed by *n* indicate footnotes.

Standard deviation, σ:

$$\sigma = \left[\sum_{i=1}^{n} (k_i - \bar{k})^2 P_i \right]^{0.5}$$

Expected return on a portfolio of Z stocks, $\bar{K}p$:

$$\bar{K}_p = W_A\bar{k}_A + W_B\bar{k}_B + \cdots + W_Z\bar{k}_Z$$

where W = weight or proportion of the portfolio allocated to each stock, A, B, etc.

           $\bar{k}$ = expected return for each stock, A, B, etc.

Total risk for a portfolio consisting of assets A and B, σ_p:

$$\sigma_p = (W_A^2\sigma_A^2 + W_B^2\sigma_B^2 + 2W_AW_B\sigma_A\sigma_B Corr_{AB})^{0.5}$$

where σ_A^2, σ_B^2 = variances for assets A and B

           $Corr_{AB}$ = correlation between the returns on assets A and B

Nondiversifiable risk (beta), β, for asset j:

$$\beta_j = Cov_{jM}/\sigma_M^2$$

where Cov_{jM} = the comovement between the returns on asset j and the market return

Capital asset pricing model (*CAPM*):

$$k_s = k_{RF} + \beta_j(k_M - k_{RF})$$

where k_M = rate of return on the market portfolio

OPPORTUNITY COST OF CAPITAL (6)

After-tax cost of debt, k_i:

$$k_i = k_b(1 - T)$$

where T = the firm's marginal tax rate

Firm's opportunity cost of capital:

opportunity cost of capital = $k_i W_{debt} + k_s W_{common\ equity}$

where W = weights, or proportion, of the total, in this case, of the after-tax costs of debt

Cost of equity capital for a division of a firm:

$$k_{division} = k_{RF} + \beta_{division}(k_M - k_{RF})$$

CAPITAL BUDGETING (7–9)

After-tax operating cash flow, CF_t:

$$CF_t = CFBT_t - taxes_t = CFBT_t(1 - T) + Dep_t(T)$$

where $CFBT$ = cash flow before-tax in any period t

           Dep = depreciation in period t

Equivalent annual *NPV*:

$$\text{equivalent annual } NPV = \frac{NPV_n}{\sum_{t=1}^{n} \dfrac{1}{(1 + k)^n}}$$

DEBT FINANCING (11)

Payment under an amortized loan: